11. Format for Bank Reconciliation:

Cash balance according to bank statement		$xxx
Add: Additions by depositor not on bank statement	$xx	
Bank errors	xx	xx
		$xxx
Deduct: Deductions by depositor not on bank statement	$xx	
Bank errors	xx	xx
Adjusted balance		$xxx
Cash balance according to depositor's records		$xxx
Add: Additions by bank not recorded by depositor..	$xx	
Depositor errors...	xx	xx
		$xxx
Deduct: Deductions by bank not recorded by depositor	$xx	
Depositor errors.......................................	xx	xx
Adjusted balance..		$xxx

12. Inventory Costing Methods:

1. First-in, First-out (fifo)
2. Last-in, First-out (lifo)
3. Average Cost

13. Interest Computations:

$$\text{Interest} = \text{Face Amount (or Principal)} \times \text{Rate} \times \text{Time}$$

14. Methods of Determining Annual Depreciation:

STRAIGHT-LINE: $\dfrac{\text{Cost} - \text{Estimated Residual Value}}{\text{Estimated Life}}$

DECLINING-BALANCE: Rate* × Book Value at Beginning of Period

*Rate is commonly twice the straight-line rate (1 ÷ Estimated Life).

15. Cash Provided by Operations on Statement of Cash Flows (indirect method):

Net income, per income statement		$xx
Add: Depreciation of fixed assets	$xx	
Amortization of bond payable discount and intangible assets..................................	xx	
Decreases in current assets (receivables, inventories, prepaid expenses).................	xx	
Increases in current liabilities (accounts and notes payable, accrued liabilities)	xx	
Losses on disposal of assets and retirement of debt	xx	xx
Deduct: Amortization of bond payable premium......	$xx	
Increases in current assets (receivables, inventories, prepaid expenses).................	xx	
Decreases in current liabilities (accounts and notes payable, accrued liabilities)	xx	
Gains on disposal of assets and retirement of debt	xx	xx
Net cash flow from operating activities...................		$xx

16. Contribution Margin Ratio = $\dfrac{\text{Sales} - \text{Variable Costs}}{\text{Sales}}$

17. Break-Even Sales (Units) = $\dfrac{\text{Fixed Costs}}{\text{Unit Contribution Margin}}$

18. Sales (Units) = $\dfrac{\text{Fixed Costs} + \text{Target Profit}}{\text{Unit Contribution Margin}}$

19. Margin of Safety = $\dfrac{\text{Sales} - \text{Sales at Break-Even Point}}{\text{Sales}}$

20. Operating Leverage = $\dfrac{\text{Contribution Margin}}{\text{Operating Income}}$

21. Variances

$\dfrac{\text{Direct Materials}}{\text{Price Variance}} = \dfrac{\text{Actual Price per Unit} -}{\text{Standard Price}} \times \dfrac{\text{Actual Quantity}}{\text{Used}}$

$\dfrac{\text{Direct Materials}}{\text{Quantity Variance}} = \dfrac{\text{Actual Quantity Used} -}{\text{Standard Quantity}} \times \dfrac{\text{Standard Price}}{\text{per Unit}}$

$\dfrac{\text{Direct Labor}}{\text{Rate Variance}} = \dfrac{\text{Actual Rate per Hour} -}{\text{Standard Rate}} \times \dfrac{\text{Actual Hours}}{\text{Worked}}$

$\dfrac{\text{Direct Labor}}{\text{Time Variance}} = \dfrac{\text{Actual Hours Worked} -}{\text{Standard Hours}} \times \dfrac{\text{Standard Rate}}{\text{per Hour}}$

$\begin{matrix}\text{Variable Factory} \\ \text{Overhead Controllable} \\ \text{Variance}\end{matrix} = \begin{matrix}\text{Actual} \\ \text{Variable Factory} \\ \text{Overhead}\end{matrix} - \begin{matrix}\text{Budgeted Variable} \\ \text{Factory Overhead for} \\ \text{Actual Amount Produced}\end{matrix}$

$\begin{matrix}\text{Fixed Factory} \\ \text{Overhead Volume} \\ \text{Variance}\end{matrix} = \begin{matrix}\text{100\% of Normal} \\ \text{Capacity} - \text{Std. Capacity} \\ \text{for Amount Produced}\end{matrix} \times \begin{matrix}\text{Std. Fixed Factory} \\ \text{Overhead} \\ \text{Rate}\end{matrix}$

22. Rate of Return on Investment (ROI) = $\dfrac{\text{Income from Operations}}{\text{Invested Assets}}$

Alternative ROI Computation:

$\text{ROI} = \dfrac{\text{Income from Operations}}{\text{Sales}} \times \dfrac{\text{Sales}}{\text{Invested Assets}}$

23. Capital Investment Analysis Methods:

1. Methods That Ignore Present Values:
   A. Average Rate of Return Method
   B. Cash Payback Method
2. Methods That Use Present Values:
   A. Net Present Value Method
   B. Internal Rate of Return Method

24. Average Rate of Return = $\dfrac{\text{Estimated Average Annual Income}}{\text{Average Investment}}$

25. Present Value Index = $\dfrac{\text{Total Present Value of Net Cash Flow}}{\text{Amount to Be Invested}}$

26. Present Value Factor for an Annuity of $1 = $\dfrac{\text{Amount to Be Invested}}{\text{Equal Annual Net Cash Flows}}$

Warren
Reeve
Fess

Why Step Forward When You Can Leap?

innovation

motivation

results

Leadership:
The Product of Innovation

In a way, this book represents our most innovative response to the influences that shape the business world. **Why?** Because the book itself is just the tip of the iceberg. Besides its clear organization and comprehensive, tested content, *Financial & Managerial Accounting 7e* is also the gateway to a better way of teaching Accounting. But in spirit, its mission is unchanged – to break new ground and set new standards as the leading text in Accounting.

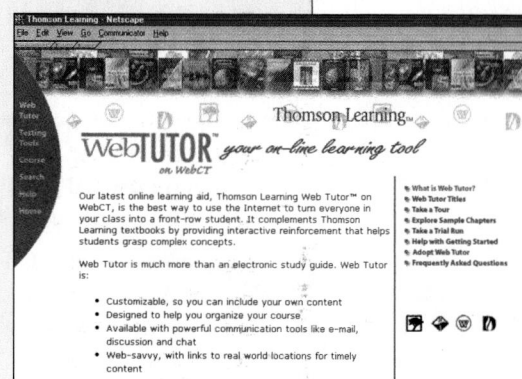

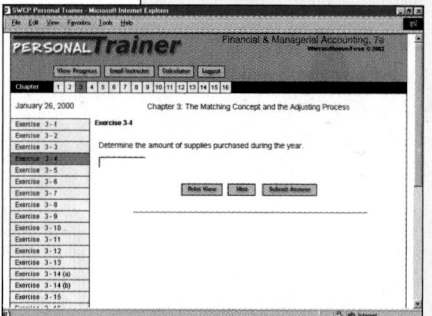

Interconnectivity and the classroom. On the cover you see a world pulsing with energy, each part connected to every other. That's how business runs today, and with *Financial & Managerial Accounting 7e* you can tap into that energy. This edition's Internet learning options aren't afterthoughts or add-ons – they're specially designed extensions of the classroom experience. So you can tailor them to suit the needs of any particular curriculum – or even a particular class. It's not just another text. It's a learning system – a system that helps bring accounting principles to life.

Inspiration to order. The instructor is the best judge of what technology supplements will best fit the class. So we make the selection as flexible as possible:

WebTutor® Advantage on WebCT® and **WebTutor Advantage on Blackboard** are platform-driven systems for complete Web-based course management and delivery. More than just an interactive study guide, WebTutor Advantage provides lecture replacement and concept review, in addition to reinforcement. Powerful instructor tools are also provided to assist communication and collaboration between students and faculty.

Personal WebTutor Advantage uses the Internet to complement *Financial & Managerial Accounting 7e* with interactive reinforcement – PowerPoint and review problems with audio – to help students grasp complex concepts.

Personal Trainer is an Internet-based product that gives students hints about the accuracy of their solutions to text exercises so that they can discover which concepts they're not grasping. Both you and your students can track scores, number of attempts, and the use of the hints.

WebTutor on WebCT and **WebTutor on Blackboard** are interactive, platform-driven study guides that turn everyone in your class into a front-row student. WebTutor complements this textbook by providing interactive reinforcement that helps students grasp complex concepts.

The Product Web Site has elements to help students learn and instructors teach principles of accounting, including downloadable instructors' supplements, quizzes, E-lectures, review problems and more.

General Ledger Software, now available on CD, is a self-grading system tailored to the text. With additional problems, including the Continuing Problem from Chapters F1-F4, it's easy to use for teaching accounting processes (journalizing and preparing financial statements).

PROFIT in the Classroom® is a commercial accounting software package that has been adapted for student use and tailored to specific assignments included in the textbook. With a complete instructor's package, you can easily integrate this software into your classroom activities and help students get a firm grasp of basic accounting principles.

11,000,000 successful results. This edition appears nearly 75 years after the first edition of the text from which it is derived, *Accounting,* was published in 1929. Yet this is the text that takes accounting into the 21st century – and not in spite of tradition, but *because* of it. For if *Financial & Managerial Accounting* and *Accounting* have a tradition, it can be summarized as innovation that produces results. Over 11 million students have been introduced to accounting via this family of texts. And that's a tradition you can build on.

Starting Fresh

Preparing a new edition of an innovative text takes an army of colleagues. A simple acknowledgments section alone is not enough – so we salute the people who continue to make this family of texts the most widely used textbooks for accounting principles.

Users of the 6th edition provided valuable classroom feedback. Focus groups and questionnaire respondents shared their personal insights. And dozens of reviewers kept us on track during the revision of this edition. We took these comments very seriously, and the text is stronger because of them.

But that's only part of the reason that this is the text of choice. The companies we profile have grown and changed over time, and so has *Financial & Managerial Accounting*. This evolution has been organized by a long list of distinguished authors, editors, and reviewers, all making unique and invaluable contributions whose echoes can still be heard today.

Looking Forward

Back in 1929, author James McKinsey could not have imagined the success and influence this family of texts has enjoyed, or that his original vision would remain intact. As the current authors, we appreciate the responsibility of protecting this vision, while continuing to shape it to meet the needs of students and instructors. We sincerely thank our many colleagues who have helped to make it happen.

> *"The teaching of accounting is no longer designed to train professional accountants only. With the growing complexity of business and the constantly increasing difficulty of the problems of management, it has become essential that everyone who aspires to a position of responsibility should have a knowledge of the fundamental principles of accounting."*
>
> – James O. McKinsey,
> author, first edition, 1929

The Business of Business is Accounting

Financial & ManagerialAccounting 7e focuses squarely on the business of business – how accounting contributes to effective management while emphasizing the most important accounting procedures. Why? Because it's a simple fact that 80% of accounting courses are filled with non-accounting majors. So we've designed *Financial & Managerial Accounting 7e* to speak to *anyone* who takes an introductory accounting course:

■ **Ch F1 Introduction to Accounting and Business.** This chapter begins with a section that defines business and describes common types of businesses, forms of organization, and the diverse interests of a business's stakeholders.

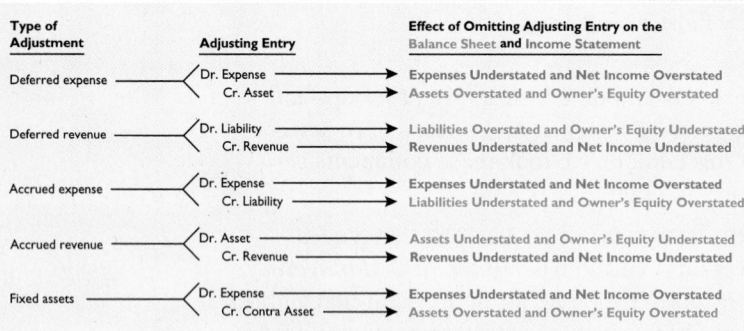

Type of Adjustment	Adjusting Entry	Effect of Omitting Adjusting Entry on the Balance Sheet and Income Statement
Deferred expense	Dr. Expense	Expenses Understated and Net Income Overstated
	Cr. Asset	Assets Overstated and Owner's Equity Overstated
Deferred revenue	Dr. Liability	Liabilities Overstated and Owner's Equity Understated
	Cr. Revenue	Revenues Understated and Net Income Understated
Accrued expense	Dr. Expense	Expenses Understated and Net Income Overstated
	Cr. Liability	Liabilities Understated and Owner's Equity Overstated
Accrued revenue	Dr. Asset	Assets Understated and Owner's Equity Understated
	Cr. Revenue	Revenues Understated and Net Income Understated
Fixed assets	Dr. Expense	Expenses Understated and Net Income Overstated
	Cr. Contra Asset	Assets Overstated and Owner's Equity Overstated

■ **Ch F3 The Matching Concept and the Adjusting Process.** A table summarizes each type of adjustment, adjusting entry, and the financial statement effect of omitting an adjusting entry. The discussion of adjustments ends with the adjusted trial balance.

■ **Ch F4 Completing the Accounting Cycle.** The work sheet is introduced in this chapter. Lines on the work sheet illustrations are numbered to assist you in your classroom presentation.

■ **Ch F5 Accounting Systems and Internal Controls.** An illustration of the revenue and collection cycle in a computerized accounting system, using QuickBooks®, is included.

■ **Ch F6 Accounting for Merchandising Businesses.** The discussion of perpetual inventory systems gives students a clear understanding of inventory accounting by drawing connections to buying groceries or fast food meals.

■ **Ch F8 Receivables.** The discussion of discounting notes receivable is in a chapter appendix.

■ **Ch F9 Inventories.** The concept of inventory cost flows is introduced without reference to the perpetual or periodic systems. The journal entries in a perpetual system are presented alongside the inventory subsidiary ledger to illustrate the FIFO and LIFO flow of costs.

■ **Ch F10 Fixed Assets and Intangible Assets.** Gains and losses on exchanges of fixed assets are discussed only from a GAAP viewpoint.

■ **Ch F13 Corporations: Income and Taxes, Stockholders' Equity, and Investments in Stocks.** A section on reporting stockholders' equity is included. A section covering short-term investments in stocks is included at the end of the chapter.

■ An **Appendix** contains the **Annual Report for Cisco Systems**.

Features That Speak to Students

The design is as colorful and dynamic as the text, which is broken into conceptual segments designed to help students make the connection between accounting and business:

Setting the Stage. The beginning of each chapter connects the student's own experiences to the chapter's topic. This tangible link is a great motivator.

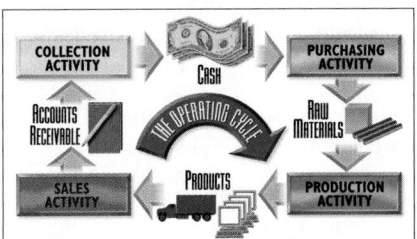

Business on Stage. This brief presentation of a business concept introduces accounting functions in a business context.

Encore. Did it work? Each chapter ends with a quick, fascinating story about a real business that succeeded or failed because it chose to observe or ignore the chapter's principle.

Other features that keep students on track and motivated:

Questions & Answers in the margin of the text help students check whether they understand what they've just read.

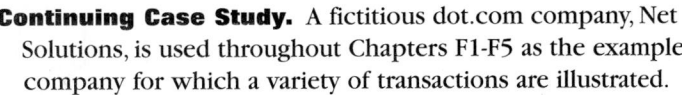 **Points of Interest.** These margin notes offer insight into subjects of special interest to students, such as careers and current events.

Summaries within each chapter bring special attention to important points.

Business Transactions. In Chapters F1 and F2, students are introduced to business transactions through non-business events that help them better understand the nature of transactions.

Continuing Case Study. A fictitious dot.com company, Net Solutions, is used throughout Chapters F1-F5 as the example company for which a variety of transactions are illustrated.

Real World Notes. J.C. Penney Co. and General Electric are just a couple of the familiar examples that provide a close-up look at how accounting operates in the marketplace. These examples are highlighted in the margin of the text: *AT&T*

Coca-Cola Enterprises Inc.

Ford Motor Co.

UPS

Financial Analysis and Interpretation. At the end of each chapter, a section describes an important element of financial analysis to help students understand the information in financial statements and how that information is used.

Taking Lessons Into Life

Procedures are important, but it takes much more to make a successful transition into the business world. This edition gives students the special tools they will need to thrive in the real world:

■ **Critical-Thinking and Decision-Making Activities.** Students need to develop analytical abilities, not just memorize rules. These activities focus on understanding and solving issues. Some are presented as dialogues – a conversation in which students can "observe" and "participate" when they respond to the issue being discussed.

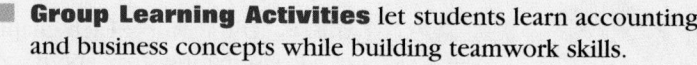

■ **Group Learning Activities** let students learn accounting and business concepts while building teamwork skills.

■ **Internet Activities** launch students into accounting-related areas of the Worldwide Web's ever-expanding universe.

■ **"What Do You Think?"** These exercises and activities let students speculate about the real-world effects of newly learned material.

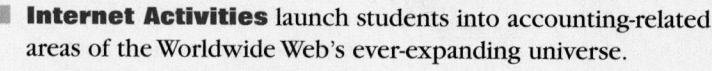

■ **"What's Wrong With This?"** These innovative exercises challenge students to analyze and discover what is wrong with a financial statement or a report.

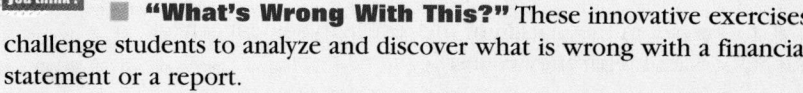

■ **Communications Items.** These activities help students develop communication skills that will be essential on the job, regardless of the fields they pursue.

Accounting must be practiced to be understood and retained. The quantity and quality of these end-of-chapter resources have always been distinguishing characteristics of *Financial & Managerial Accounting*:

■ **Continuing Problem in Chs. F1-F4.** Here's a great opportunity for students to practice what they've learned – and now they can use the General Ledger Software with this problem. As they study each step of the accounting cycle, students can follow a single company – *Dancin Music* – from its transactions to the effect of those transactions on its financial statements.

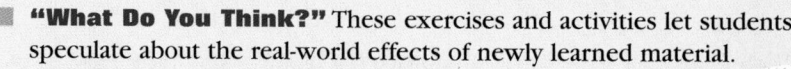

■ **Illustrative Problem and Solution.** A solved problem models one or more of a chapter's assignment problems, helping students make the most of the chapter and end-of-chapter materials.

■ **Self-Examination Questions** include a matching activity to help students review and retain terms and definitions.

■ **Exercises.** An average of 20 exercises at the end of each chapter – more than any other text on the market – can be assigned or used as examples in the classroom. Most of these exercises focus on only one specific chapter objective.

■ **Problems.** Each chapter includes two full sets of problems for use as classroom illustrations, for assignments, for alternate assignments, or for independent studying. This edition features shortened problems to provide better focus on key chapter topics.

■ **Comprehensive Problems.** At the end of Chs. F4, F6, F11, and F14, cumulative learning applications integrate and summarize the concepts of several chapters to test students' comprehension.

New Tools to Get the Job Done Right

We've designed our entire supplement package around the comments instructors have provided about their courses and teaching needs. These comments have made this supplement package the best in the business.

Available to Students – Because each student has different needs, *Financial & Managerial Accounting 7e* offers a broad range of supplements. Both print material and easy-to-use, affordable technologies help students succeed in the course and in the business world. Some of these supplements are:

■ **Working Papers.** The traditional Working Papers are available both with and without problem-specific forms for preparing solutions for all exercises and problems.

■ **Working Papers Plus**, prepared by John Wanlass of DeAnza College. This alternative to traditional working papers integrates the exercises and selected problems from the text with forms for preparing their solutions.

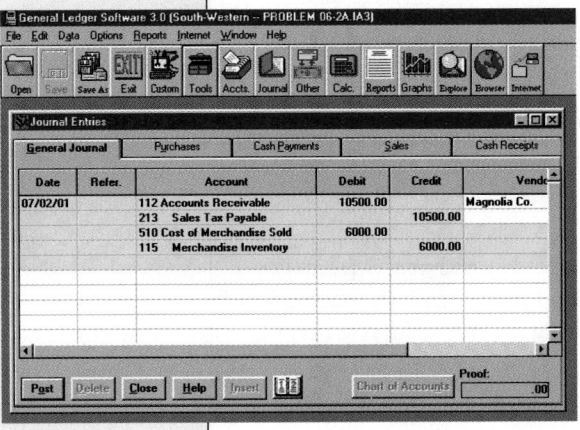

■ **General Ledger Software**, prepared by Dale Klooster and Warren Allen. This best-selling educational general ledger package is enhanced with a problem checker that enables students to determine if their entries are correct. Solving end-of-chapter problems, the continuing problem, and comprehensive problems as well as practice sets is as easy as clicking icons with a mouse.

■ **Spreadsheet Applications Software.** This completely revised software gives students the opportunity to solve dozens of problems by using Excel®.

■ **Study Guide**, prepared by Carl Warren and Jim Reeve. The Study Guide includes quiz and test tips, multiple choice, fill-in-the-blank, and true-false questions with solutions.

■ **PROFIT in the Classroom.** Using this award-winning software to solve specific problems in the textbook helps students get a firm grasp of debits and credits and the principles related to basic transactions for accounts receivable and payable, inventory, and payroll.

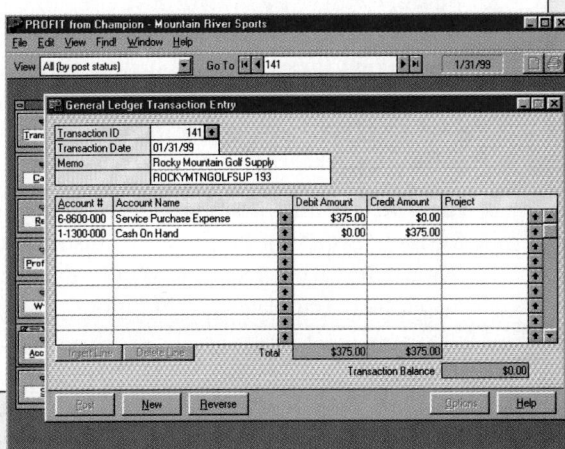

■ **WebTutor Advantage on WebCT** and **WebTutor Advantage on Blackboard** give students access to study resources and interactive experiences beyond the classroom. Special resources for instructors include powerful communication and other course management tools.

■ **Personal WebTutor Advantage.** This product includes a wealth of content, including PowerPoint, review problems with audio, automatically-scored quizzes, exercises, and terminology reinforcement.

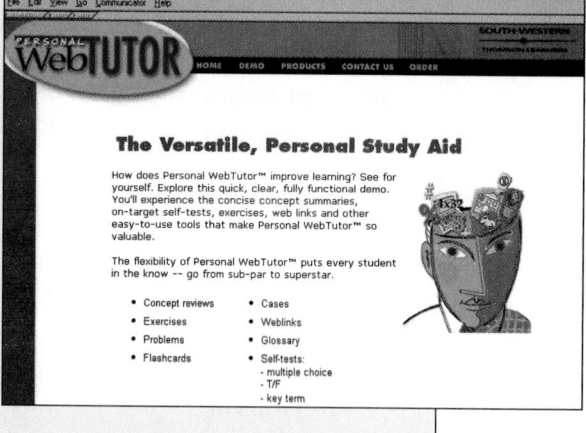

■ **Personal Trainer.** This innovative Internet-based tutorial gives students hints as they solve exercises from the text and allows them to track their progress.

■ **WebTutor on WebCT** and **WebTutor on Blackboard** provide interactive reinforcement to help students grasp complex concepts.

■ **Product Web Site.** At the text's Web site, students have free access to additional quizzes, drills, e-lectures, Excel application templates, review problems, and many other study resources.

Available to Instructors – South-Western Publishing continues to lead the field in supplements for instructors, from traditional printed materials to the latest integrated classroom technology. Among these support tools are:

■ **Product Support Site.** A variety of instructor resources are now available through South-Western's password-protected Web site. Text-specific and other related resources are organized by chapter and topic. Many of these resources are also available on CD-ROM.

■ **An Instructor's Guide to Making the Most of Online Resources** is an imaginative resource to help you connect your classroom with *Financial & Managerial Accounting 7e* and its dynamic spectrum of digital teaching and learning resources.

■ **Videos.** A complete video course is available for distance learning and to help complete a student's onsite classroom experience. A collection of brief **Business in Focus** videos highlight how accounting impacts people and processes in the business world.

■ **PowerPoint™ Presentation**, prepared by Doug Cloud of Pepperdine University. The PowerPoint Presentation enhances lectures and simplifies class preparation. You can also add your own custom slides, using this popular software package.

■ **Instructor's CD-ROM** is a convenient source for the PowerPoint Presentation, Instructor's Manual, Test Bank, ExamView®, and Excel Application Templates and Solutions.

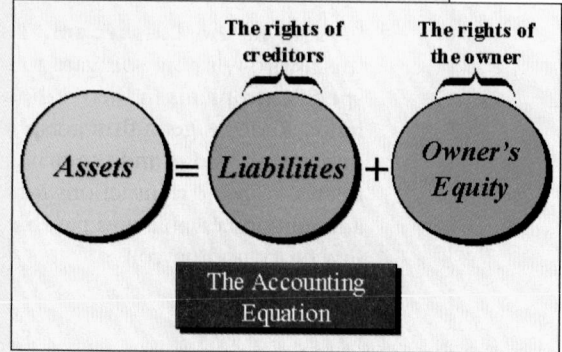

Warren
Reeve
Fess

■ **Traditional Ancillaries.** The Solutions Manual and Instructor's Manual are available on South-Western's password-protected Web site, on the instructor's CD-ROM, as well as in separate bound volumes. The Test Bank is also included in the ExamView® Pro Testing Software on the instructor's CD-ROM, as well as in separate bound volumes.

■ The **Instructor's Manual** contains a wide range of writing exercises, group learning activities, demonstration problems, and accounting scenarios.

■ The **Test Bank** includes more than 2,800 true/false questions, multiple choice questions, and problems, plus multi-chapter achievement tests.

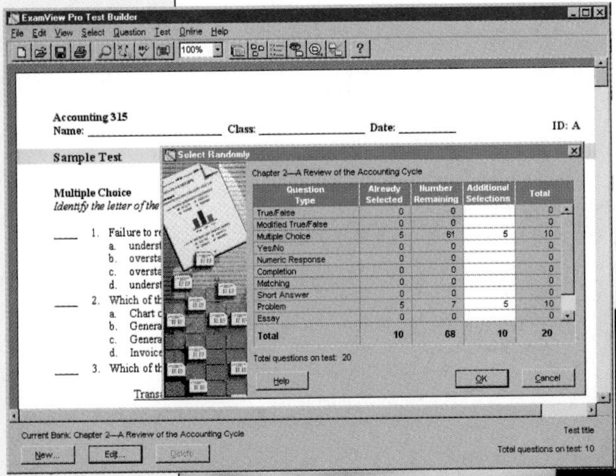

■ **ExamView Pro Testing Software** is easy-to-use software that allows you to customize exams, practice tests, and tutorials and deliver them over a network, on the Web, or in printed form.

Warren
Reeve
Fess

Acknowledging the Team of Leaders

A student's first impression of a course is the leader of the classroom – the instructor. Because the textbook plays an important supporting role in the teaching/learning environment, our collaboration with instructors is invaluable. We thank them for their contribution to making *Financial & Managerial Accounting 7e* a text unsurpassed in quality.

Sheila Ammons
Austin Community College

Tom Badley
Nick Kondyles
Bob Vandellan
Baker College

Pete Karsten
Baker College of Auburn Hills

Sheryl Alley
Ball State University

Richard Green
Baystate College

Ken Gustafson
Christopher Mayer
Florance McGovern
Bergen Community College

Laura Altomonte
Frank Paliotta
Berkeley College

Preston Wilks
Big Bend Community College

Bob Huzman
Blue River Community College

Stanley Chu
Stanley Solomon
*Borough of Manhattan
Community College*

Randy Glover
Brevard Community College

Clarice McCoy
Dave Weaver
Brookhaven College

Lois Slutsky
Broward Community College

Laurel Berry
Sam Lanzafame
Bryant & Stratton

Ann Rawl
Beverly Terry
Brad Zorn
*Central Piedmont
Community College*

Michael Farina
Cerritos College

Joan Ryan
Clackamas Community College

James Halstead
Clatsop Community College

Bonnie Goodwin
Corinthian Colleges

Jerry Holtke
Crafton Hills College

Larry Bender
James Burke
Alan Vogel
Vicki Vorell
Cuyahoga Community College

James Donovan
Deb Kiss
Davenport University

Patricia H. Holmes
Cindy Tomes
*Des Moines Area Community
College*

David Medved
Detroit College of Business

Karen Stewart
Devry - Addison

Richard Monbrod
Devry - Chicago

Joyce Barden
Devry - Phoenix

Kathy Perdue
DeVry Institute of Technology

Ron L. Hulstein
Dickinson State University

Terry Mullins
*Dyersburg State Community
College*

Aurora P. Delores
James L. Haydon
*East Los Angeles
Community College*

Donnie Krostof-Nelson
Edmonds Community College

Shirley Aoto
Phil Knypstra
El Camino College

Rose Garvey
*Elizabethtown
Community College*

W. T. Hall
Fayetteville Tech

Michael Procton
*Finger Lakes
Community College*

Lynn Clements
Florida Southern College

Alice Sineath
Forsyth Technical College

Joe Chandler
*Forsyth Technical
Community College*

Karen Brayden
*Front Range Community
College - Larimer Campus*

Allen Wash
Gaston College

Christy Kloeseman
Glendale Community College

Leo Chow
Gaspare Dilorenzo
Gloucester County College

Thomas Welsch
Harold Washington College

Robert Held
Harper College

Joni Onishi
Hawaii Community College

Bob Harden
Bill Harvey
*Henry Ford Community
College*

Irving Mason
*Herkimer County
Community College*

Tesfaye Bireda
Earl McMillen
Linda Overstreet
Margo Rock
Joe Teston
Allen Wright
*Hillsborough
Community College*

Audra Kimble
Holmes Community College

Eugene Cardamone
*Hudson Valley
Community College*

Todd Hansink
Imperial Valley College

John Klett
James Reap
*Indian River
Community College*

Dawn Humburg
*Iowa Central
Community College*

Gene Saatmann
*Iowa Western
Community College*

Robert Urell
Irvine Valley College

Vicki Greshik
Jamestown University

Kelly Cranford
*Jefferson State
Community College*

Jeanette Rogers
Jefferson State Junior College

David Moore
Kankakee Community College

Tim Holmeyer
Keller School of Business

Chuck Cunningham
Jim Crowther
Mary Tharp
Jack Zeller
Kirkwood Community College

Ronald L. Werley
Tom Grant
Kutztown University

Dick Ahrens
Al Partington
Terry Thomsen
L.A. Pierce College

Douglas Clouse
Janice Ivansek
Ted Latz
Lakeland Community College

Luke Waller
Lindenwood University

Jim Kahl
Lower Columbia College

Sam Dean
David Keys
Macon State College

Georgia Buckles
Patricia Cook
Alexandria Tommany
*Manchester
Community College*

Deborah Bowser
Marion Technical College

Gloria Worthy
*Memphis State Technical
Institute*

Joe Goodro
Robert Gronstol
David K. Ho
Peg Johnson
Ed Napravnik
Idalene Williams
Eileen Zuerlein
Metro Community College

Ana Cruz
Maria Mari
*Miami-Dade
Community College*

Ben Sadler
*Miami-Dade Community
College - Wolfson*

Cathy Larson
Middlesex Community College

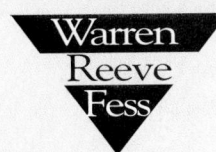

Eddie Evans
Jean Kiley
Janice Staudemire
Bruce Tallant
Barbara Wagers
Midlands Technical College

Rex Bruington
Elaine Evans
*Mississippi University
for Women*

Naomi Karolinski
Susan Murphy
Renee Rigoni
Jim Rolfe
Mike Ruff
Chris Sardone
Edward Vaneske
Monroe Community College

Gloria M. Halpren
William Johnstone
Richard Lenet
Robert Laycock
Hank Stupi
Montgomery College

Carl Essig
*Montgomery County
Community College*

Tom Barrett
Jim Lentz
*Moraine Valley
Community College*

Fran Haldar
*North Central
Technical College*

David Morris
*North Georgia College & State
University*

Stephen Carter
North Harris County College

Karen Russom
*North Harris County
Community College*

Joe Carthey
*Northeast Iowa
Community College*

Carol Shaver
Northeast Louisiana University

Linda Hischke
*Northeastern Wisconsin
Technical College*

Ellen Goldberg
Judy Grant
B. Kheradmand
Marsha Murphy
L. D. Pape
*Northern Virginia
Community College*

Dawn Stevens
*Northwest Mississippi
Community College*

Michael Milstein
Oakton Community College

Christopher Kwak
Carolyn Strickler
Oblone College

Myra Decker
Connie Nieser
*Oklahoma City
Community College*

Pat Garran
*Orlando College North
(FMU/Corinthian)*

Phil Reffitt
*Orlando College South
(FMU/Corinthian)*

Joan Holloway
Patrick McMahon
John Murphy
Joanne Nikides
Gracelyn Stuart
*Palm Beach
Community College*

Tom Joyce
Gary Woods
Pasadena City College

Richard Irvine
Carla Rich
Pensacola Junior College

Charles McCord
Portland Community College

Betty Habershon
*Prince Georges
Community College*

Dan Luna
*Raritan Valley
Community College*

Walt DeAguero
Saddleback College

Robert Dan
Hector Martinez
Cathy Sanders
San Antonio College

Janet Courts
San Bernardino Valley College

Randall Whitmore
San Jacinto College-Central

Bob Perkins
Dan Straut
San Jacinto College-North

Jeff Jackson
Roy Sanchez
San Jacinto College-South

Ken Couvillion
Richard Ghio
Nick Walker
J. Wiehler
San Joaquin Delta College

Susan Crosson
Santa Fe Community College

Pat Halliday
Teri Bernstein
Santa Monica College

Carol Chiarella
*Schenectady County
Community College*

Donna Chadwick
Mary Beth Govan
Bill Hoover
Jim Putoff
James Shimko
Sinclair Communtiy College

Dianne Bridges
South Plains College

Nap Lucchini
*South Puget Sound
Community College*

David Laurel
*South Texas
Community College*

John Davis
Southern Wesleyan University

Don Brunner
Bernie Hill
Jeff Waybright
*Spokane Falls
Community College*

Carlo Muzio
St. John's University

Carolyn Byrd
St. Petersburg Junior College

Steve Hester
Gloria Worthy
*State Technical
Institute at Memphis*

Charles Heck
Henri Leclerc
Thomas Lohmann
Alphonse Reggiero
Robert Rovegno
*Suffolk County
Community College*

Elliott Kamlet
SUNY - Binghamton

Bill Rose
*Tampa College-Brandon-
Tampa (FMU/Corinthian)*

Marilyn Fisher
*Tampa College-Lakeland
(FMU/Corinthian)*

Jon Baskins
*Tampa College-Pinellas
(FMU/Corinthian)*

Charles Zaruba
*Tampa College-Tampa
(FMU/Corinthian)*

Steve Fabian
Technical Careers Institute

Sherry Lenhart
Terra Technical College

Paul Cameron
Texas A & M - Corpus Christi

George Otto
Truman College

Susan Pope
University of Akron

Yvonne Brown
Jill Burnett
Constance Cooper
Tracey Hawkins
Sandy Kahn
University of Cincinnati

Barry Farber
University of Maine

Richard Campbell
University of Rio Grande

Ruby Brogan
James Poythress
Woody Wimmer
*Virginia Western
Community College*

Brenda Hester
*Volunteer State
Community College*

J. Thomas Love
*Walters State
Community College*

David R. Konrath
*Washington State
Community College*

Lana Bone
Randy Castello
Clo Hampton
West Valley College

Debbie Goorbin
*Westchester
Community College*

Jim Cassidy
Kurt Schindler
George Trent
*Wilbur Wright
Community College*

We also thank the following students who participated in focus groups:

Mark Dues
Adriana Goldenberg
Lise Pizza
Shinoosh Shafie
Roseann Tracy
Jason Wells
Sinclair Community College

Zach Michler
Corey Mills
Lucinda Nicklay
Sue Ellen Philpot
Nathan VanNatter
Ball State University

Brief Contents

SEVENTH EDITION 7

Financial & Managerial Accounting

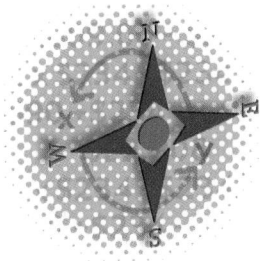

CARL S. WARREN
Professor of Accounting
University of Georgia, Athens

JAMES M. REEVE
Professor of Accounting
University of Tennessee, Knoxville

PHILIP E. FESS
Professor Emeritus of Accounting
University of Illinois, Champaign-Urbana

SOUTH-WESTERN
™
THOMSON LEARNING

Australia · Canada · Mexico · Singapore · Spain · United Kingdom · United States

FINANCIAL AND MANAGERIAL ACCOUNTING 7e,
by Warren, Reeve, and Fess

Team Director: David L. Shaut
Senior Acquisitions Editor: Sharon Oblinger
Senior Developmental Editor: Ken Martin
Senior Marketing Manager: Dan Silverburg
Production Editors: Mark Sears and Deanna Quinn
Editorial Assistant: Heather Mann
Manufacturing Coordinator: Doug Wilke and Michelle D. Allen
Internal Design: Lou Ann Thesing
Cover Design: Paul Neff Design
Cover Illustration: ©2000/Lou Beach
Photo Research: Feldman & Associates, Inc.
Photo Manager: Cary Benbow
Media Technology Editor: Diane Van Bakel
Media Developmental Editors: Christine Wittmer and Sally Nieman
Media Production Editor: Lora Craver
Production House: Litten Editing and Production, Inc.
Compositor: GGS Information Services, Inc.
Printer: Quebecor World

For more information contact South-Western, 5191 Natorp Boulevard, Mason, Ohio, 45040 or find us on the Internet at http://www.swcollege.com

For permission to use material from this text or product, contact us by
- **telephone: 1-800-730-2214**
- **fax: 1-800-730-2215**
- **web: http://www.thomsonrights.com**

Library of Congress Cataloging-in-Publication Data

Warren, Carl S.
    Financial & managerial accounting / Carl S. Warren, James M. Reeve, Philip E. Fess. — 7th ed.
        p. cm.
    Includes index.
    ISBN 0-324-02540-8 (alk. paper)
    1. Accounting.   2. Managerial accounting   I. Title: Financial and managerial accounting.
    II. Reeve, James M.   III. Fess, Philip E.   IV. Title.

    HF5635.W27   2001
    657—dc21   2001018400

ISBN: 0-324-02540-8

6 7 QWV 4

CARL S. WARREN

Dr. Carl S. Warren is the Arthur Andersen & Co. Alumni Professor of Accounting at the J.M. Tull School of Accounting at the University of Georgia, Athens. Professor Warren received his Ph.D. from Michigan State University in 1973. Dr. Warren's experience in listening to users of his texts sharpens his keen focus on helping students learn. When he is not teaching classes or writing text-books, Dr. Warren enjoys golf, racquetball, and fishing.

JAMES M. REEVE

Dr. James M. Reeve is Professor of Accounting at the University of Tennessee, Knoxville. He received his Ph.D. from Oklahoma State University in 1980. Dr. Reeve is founder of the Cost Management Institute and a member of the Institute for Productivity Through Quality faculty at the University of Tennessee. In addition to his teaching experience, Dr. Reeve brings to this text a wealth of experience consulting on managerial accounting issues with numerous companies, including Procter & Gamble, AMOCO, Rockwell International, Harris Corporation, and Freddie Mac. Dr. Reeve's interests outside the classroom and the business world include golf, skiing, reading, and travel.

PHILIP E. FESS

Dr. Philip E. Fess is the Arthur Andersen & Co. Alumni Professor of Account-ancy Emeritus at the University of Illinois, Champaign-Urbana. He received his Ph.D. from the University of Illinois. Dr. Fess has been involved in writing text-books for over twenty-five years, and his knowledge of how to make texts user-friendly is reflected on the pages of this edition. Dr. Fess plays golf and tennis, and he has represented the United States in international tennis competition.

Contents

Photo Credits

Introduction to Accounting and Business

F1

objectives

After studying this chapter, you should be able to:

1 Describe the nature of a business.

2 Describe the role of accounting in business.

3 Describe the importance of business ethics and the basic principles of proper ethical conduct.

4 Describe the profession of accounting.

5 Summarize the development of accounting principles and relate them to practice.

6 State the accounting equation and define each element of the equation.

7 Explain how business transactions can be stated in terms of the resulting changes in the basic elements of the accounting equation.

8 Describe the financial statements of a corporation and explain how they interrelate.

9 Use the ratio of liabilities to stockholders' equity to analyze the ability of a business to withstand poor business conditions.

D o you use accounting? Yes, we all use accounting information in one form or another. For example, when you think about buying a car, you use accounting-type information to determine whether you can afford it and whether to lease or buy. Similarly, when you decided to attend college, you considered the costs (the tuition, textbooks, and so on). Most likely, you also considered the benefits (the ability to obtain a higher-paying job or a more desirable job).

Is accounting important to you? Yes, accounting is important in your personal life as well as your career, even though you may not become an accountant. For example, assume that you are the owner/manager of a small Mexican restaurant and are considering opening another restaurant in a neighboring town. Accounting information about the restaurant will be a major factor in your deciding whether to open the new restaurant and the bank's deciding whether to finance the expansion.

Our primary objective in this text is to illustrate basic accounting concepts that will help you to make good personal and business decisions. We begin by discussing what a business is, how it operates, and the role that accounting plays.

Nature of a Business

objective 1

Describe the nature of a business.

You can probably list some examples of companies with which you have recently done business. Your examples might be large companies, such as **Coca-Cola**, **Dell Computer**, or **Amazon.com**. They might be local companies, such as gas stations or grocery stores, or perhaps employers. They might be restaurants, law firms, or medical offices. What do all these examples have in common that identify them as businesses?

In general, a **business** is an organization in which basic resources (inputs), such as materials and labor, are assembled and processed to provide goods or services (outputs) to customers.[1] Businesses come in all sizes, from a local coffee house to a **DaimlerChrysler**, which sells several billion dollars worth of cars and trucks each year. A business's customers are individuals or other businesses who purchase goods or services in exchange for money or other items of value. In contrast, a church is not a business because those who receive its services are not obligated to pay for them.

The objective of most businesses is to maximize profits. **Profit** is the difference between the amounts received from customers for goods or services provided and the amounts paid for the inputs used to provide the goods or services. Some businesses operate with an objective other than to maximize profits. The objective of such nonprofit businesses is to provide some benefit to society, such as medical research or conservation of natural resources. In other cases, governmental units such as cities operate water works or sewage treatment plants on a nonprofit basis. We will focus in this text on businesses operating to earn a profit. Keep in mind, though, that many of the same concepts and principles apply to nonprofit businesses as well.

Types of Businesses

There are three different types of businesses that are operated for profit: manufacturing, merchandising, and service businesses. Each type of business has unique characteristics.

---

[1] A complete glossary of terms appears at the end of the text.

Manufacturing businesses change basic inputs into products that are sold to individual customers. Examples of manufacturing businesses and some of their products are shown below.

Manufacturing Business	Product
General Motors	Cars, trucks, vans
Intel	Computer chips
Boeing	Jet aircraft
Nike	Athletic shoes and apparel
Coca-Cola	Beverages
Sony	Stereos and televisions

Merchandising businesses also sell products to customers. However, rather than making the products, they purchase them from other businesses (such as manufacturers). In this sense, merchandisers bring products and customers together. Examples of merchandising businesses and some of the products they sell are shown below.

Merchandising Business	Product
Wal-Mart	General merchandise
Toys "R" Us	Toys
Circuit City	Consumer electronics
Lands' End	Apparel
Amazon.com	Internet books, music, video retailer

Service businesses provide services rather than products to customers. Examples of service businesses and the types of services they offer are shown below.

Service Business	Service
Disney	Entertainment
Delta Air Lines	Transportation
Marriott Hotels	Hospitality and lodging
Merrill Lynch	Financial advice
Andersen Consulting	Management consulting

Roughly eight out of every ten workers in the United States are service providers. In the past twenty years, 90% of the new jobs created in the United States have been in service businesses.

Source: Walter Kiechel III, "How We Will Work in the Year 2000," *Fortune* (May 17, 1993), p. 46.

BUSINESS ON STAGE

The Factors of Production

Businesses convert basic inputs into goods and services for customers. These inputs are called *factors of production*. The factors of production common to all businesses are natural resources, labor, capital, and entrepreneurs. Natural resources are the basic raw materials, including farmland, forests, and mineral deposits. Labor is the employees who contribute their intellectual and physical efforts to a business. Capital represents the financial resources (money) invested in the business to purchase such items as machinery and buildings. Entrepreneurs are the people who combine natural resources, labor, and capital to produce goods and services.

Let's examine a small pizza restaurant as an example of a business. The pizza ingredients of dough, tomato sauce, sausage, pepperoni, and cheese represent the natural resources that are derived from farming the land. The employees (labor) are the servers, the delivery person, the cash register clerk, and the baker. The money required to purchase the land, building, and equipment is the capital. The owner/manager who began the business and operates it on a daily basis is the entrepreneur. ■

Types of Business Organizations

A business is normally organized as one of three different forms: proprietorship, partnership, or corporation. In the following paragraphs, we briefly describe each form and discuss its advantages and disadvantages.

A **proprietorship** is owned by one individual. More than 70% of the businesses in the United States are organized as proprietorships. The popularity of this form is due to the ease and the low cost of organizing. The primary disadvantage of proprietorships is that the financial resources available to the business are limited to the individual owner's resources. Small local businesses such as hardware stores, repair shops, laundries, restaurants, and maid services are often organized as proprietorships.

As a business grows and more financial and managerial resources are needed, it may become a partnership. A **partnership** is owned by two or more individuals. Like proprietorships, small local businesses such as automotive repair shops, music stores, beauty salons, and clothing stores may be organized as partnerships. Currently, about 10% of the businesses in the United States are organized as partnerships.

A **corporation** is organized under state or federal statutes as a separate legal entity. The ownership of a corporation is divided into shares of stock. A corporation issues the stock to individuals or other businesses, who then become owners or stockholders of the corporation.

A primary advantage of the corporate form is the ability to obtain large amounts of resources by issuing stock. For this reason, most companies that require large investments in equipment and facilities are organized as corporations. For example, **Toys "R" Us** has raised over $800 million by issuing shares of common stock to finance its operations. Other examples of corporations include **General Motors**, **Ford**, **International Business Machines (IBM)**, **Coca-Cola**, and **General Electric**.

About 20% of the businesses in the United States are organized as corporations. Given that most large companies are organized as corporations, over 90% of the total dollars of business receipts are received by corporations. Thus, corporations have a major influence on the economy.

> Manufacturing, merchandising, and service businesses are commonly organized as either proprietorships, partnerships, or corporations.

The three types of businesses we discussed earlier—manufacturing, merchandising, and service—may be either proprietorships, partnerships, or corporations. However, because of the large amount of resources required to operate a manufacturing business, most manufacturing businesses are corporations. Likewise, most large retailers such as **Wal-Mart**, **Sears**, and **JCPenney** are corporations.

Business Stakeholders

A **business stakeholder** is a person or entity having an interest in the economic performance of the business. These stakeholders normally include the owners, managers, employees, customers, creditors, and the government.

The **owners** who have invested resources in the business clearly have an interest in how well the business performs. Most owners want to get the most economic value for their investments. To the extent that the business is profitable, owners will expect to share in the business profits. Since owners may eventually decide to sell their businesses, they also have an interest in the total economic worth of the business. This economic worth may reflect results of past profits as well as prospects for future profits.

The **managers** are those individuals who the owners have authorized to operate the business. Managers are primarily evaluated on the economic performance of the business. The managers of poor-performing businesses are often fired by the owners. Thus, managers have an incentive to maximize the economic value of the business. Owners may offer managers salary contracts that are tied directly to how well the business performs. For example, a manager might receive a percent of the profits or a percent of the increase in profits. Such contracts are often referred to as profit-sharing plans.

The **employees** provide services to the business in exchange for a paycheck. The employees have an interest in the economic performance of the business because their jobs depend upon it. During business downturns, it is not unusual for a business to lay off workers for extended periods of time. Whenever a business fails, the employees lose their jobs permanently. Employee labor unions often use the good economic performance of a business to argue for wage increases. In contrast, businesses often cite poor economic performance as a reason for decreasing wages or denying raises.

The **customers** may also have an interest in the continued success of a business. For example, if **Apple Computer** were to fail, customers might not be able to get hardware and software for their computers. Likewise, customers who purchase advance tickets on **Southwest Airlines** have an interest in whether Southwest will continue in business. Frequent flyers on **Eastern Airlines** lost their accumulated frequent-flyer points when Eastern went out of business.

Like the owners, the **creditors** invest resources in the business by extending credit, such as a loan. They, too, have an interest in how well the business performs. In order for the creditors to recover their investment, the business must generate enough cash to pay them back. In addition, creditors view the business as their customer and thus have a stake in the continued success of the business.

Various **governments** have an interest in the economic performance of businesses. City, county, state, and federal governments collect taxes from businesses within their jurisdictions. The better a business does, the more taxes the government can collect. In addition, workers are taxed on their wages. In contrast, workers who are laid off and are unemployed can file claims for unemployment compensation, which results in a financial burden for the government. City and state governments often provide incentives for businesses to locate in their jurisdictions.

Real World The state of Alabama offered **Daimler-Chrysler** millions of dollars in incentives to locate a Mercedes plant in Alabama.

BUSINESS ON STAGE

Successful Entrepreneurs

What are the characteristics of entrepreneurs who successfully start and manage a new business?

It goes without saying that an entrepreneur must have a thorough technical knowledge of the business. For example, a successful computer consultant must have a thorough knowledge of computers. Entrepreneurs must also have basic management skills, such as the ability to organize and interact with others. Terms that are often used to describe entrepreneurs and examples of some well-known entrepreneurs and their companies are listed here.

Terms
Vision
Perseverance
Independent
Self-confident
Risk taker
High energy level
Motivated
Personal drive
Spirit of adventure
Need for achievement
Self-starter
Sense of commitment
Willingness to make personal sacrifices
Communication skills

Entrepreneur	Company
Jeffrey Yang	Yahoo!
Henry Ford	Ford Motor Company
George Eastman	Kodak
King C. Gillette	Gillette Company
Steven Jobs	Apple Computer
Bill Gates	Microsoft
Frederick Smith	Federal Express
Sam Walton	Wal-Mart

Examples of entrepreneurs also include the owners of many small businesses in your community, from local restaurants to video rental stores. ■

The Role of Accounting in Business

objective 2

Describe the role of accounting in business.

Accounting is an information system that provides reports to stakeholders about the economic activities and condition of a business.

What is the role of accounting in business? The simplest answer to this question is that accounting provides information for managers to use in operating the business. In addition, accounting provides information to other stakeholders to use in assessing the economic performance and condition of the business.

In a general sense, **accounting** can be defined as an information system that provides reports to stakeholders about the economic activities and condition of a business. As we indicated earlier in this chapter, we will focus our discussions on accounting and its role in business. However, many of the concepts in this text apply also to individuals, governments, and other types of organizations. For example, individuals must account for activities such as hours worked, checks written, and bills due. Stakeholders for individuals include creditors, dependents, and the government. A main interest of the government is making sure that individuals pay the proper taxes.

You may think of accounting as the "language of business." This is because accounting is the means by which business information is communicated to the stakeholders. For example, accounting reports summarizing the profitability of a new product help **Coca-Cola's** management decide whether to continue selling the product. Likewise, financial analysts use accounting reports in deciding whether to recommend the purchase of Coca-Cola's stock. Banks use accounting reports in determining the amount of credit to extend to Coca-Cola. Suppliers use accounting reports in deciding whether to offer credit for Coca-Cola's purchases of supplies and raw materials. State and federal governments use accounting reports as a basis for assessing taxes on Coca-Cola.

The process by which accounting provides information to business stakeholders is illustrated in Exhibit 1. A business must first identify its stakeholders. It must then

Exhibit 1 Accounting Information and the Stakeholders of a Business

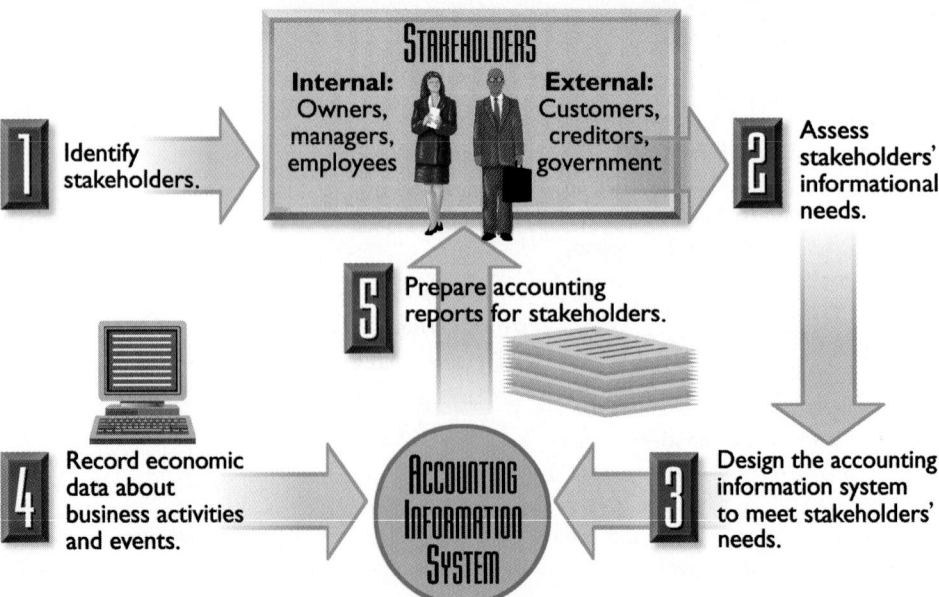

assess the various informational needs of those stakeholders and design its accounting system to meet those needs. Finally, the accounting system records the economic data about business activities and events, which the business reports to the stakeholders according to their informational needs.

Stakeholders use accounting reports as a primary source of information on which they base their decisions. They use other information as well. For example, in deciding whether to extend credit to an appliance store, a banker might use economic forecasts to assess the future demand for the store's products. During periods of economic downturn, the demand for consumer appliances normally declines. The banker might inquire about the ability and reputation of the managers of the business. For small corporations, bankers may require major stockholders to personally guarantee the loans of the business. Finally, bankers might consult industry publications that rank similar businesses as to their quality of products, customer satisfaction, and future prospects for growth.

Business Ethics

objective 3

Describe the importance of business ethics and the basic principles of proper ethical conduct.

Stanley James Cardiges, the former top U.S. sales representative for **American Honda**, admitted to receiving $2 million to $5 million in illegal kickbacks from dealers. After being sentenced to five years in prison, he admitted to "falling into a pattern [of unethical behavior] early in my career . . . and went along with the crowd."

Source: "Ex-Honda Executive Handed 5-Year Sentence," The Associated Press, *Knoxville News Sentinel*, August 26, 1995.

Individuals may have different views about what is "right" and "wrong" in a given situation. For example, you may believe it is wrong to copy another student's homework and hand it in as your own. Other students may feel that it is acceptable to copy homework if the instructor has no stated rule against it. Unfortunately, business managers sometimes find themselves in situations where they feel pressure to violate personal ethics. For example, managers of **Sears** automotive service departments were accused of recommending unnecessary repairs and overcharging customers for actual repairs in order to meet company goals and earn bonuses.

The moral principles that guide the conduct of individuals are called **ethics**. Regardless of differences among individuals, proper ethical conduct implies a behavior that considers the impact of one's actions on society and others. In other words, proper ethical conduct implies that you not only consider what's in your best interest, but also what's in the best interests of others.

Ethical conduct is good business. For example, an automobile manufacturer that fails to correct a safety defect to save costs may later lose sales due to lack of consumer confidence. Likewise, a business that pollutes the environment may find itself the target of lawsuits and customer boycotts.

Businesspeople should work within an ethical framework.[2] Although an ethical framework is based on individual experiences and training, there are a number of sound principles that form the foundation for ethical behavior:

1. *Avoid small ethical lapses.* Small ethical lapses may appear harmless in and of themselves. Unfortunately, such lapses can compromise your work. Small ethical lapses can build up and lead to larger consequences later.

Point of Interest
Most colleges and universities publish a Student Code of Conduct that sets forth the ethical conduct expected of students.

Real World
A survey of top managers by the accounting firm of **Deloitte & Touche** reported that "an enterprise actually strengthens its competitive position by maintaining high ethical standards." *Ethics in Business*, Deloitte & Touche (January 1988).

---

[2] An ethics discussion case is provided at the end of each chapter to focus attention on meaningful ethical situations that accountants often face in practice.

2. *Focus on your long-term reputation.* One characteristic of an ethical dilemma is that it places you under severe short-term pressure. The ethical dilemma is created by the stated or unstated threat that failure to "go along" may result in undesirable consequences. You should respond to ethical dilemmas by minimizing the short-term pressures and focusing on long-term reputation instead. Your reputation is very valuable. You will lose your effectiveness if your reputation becomes tarnished.

3. *Expect to suffer adverse personal consequences for holding to an ethical position.* In some unethical organizations, managers have endured career setbacks for not budging from their ethical positions. Some managers have resigned because they were unable to support management in what they perceived as unethical behavior. Thus, in the short term, ethical behavior can sometimes adversely affect your career.

Profession of Accounting

objective 4

Describe the profession of accounting.

Accountants engage in either private accounting or public accounting. Accountants employed by a business firm or a not-for-profit organization are said to be engaged in **private accounting**. Accountants and their staff who provide services on a fee basis are said to be employed in **public accounting**.

Because all functions within a business use accounting information, experience in private or public accounting provides a solid foundation for a career. Many positions in industry and in government agencies are held by individuals with accounting backgrounds. For example, in a Special Bonus Issue on "The Corporate Elite," *Business Week* reported the career paths for the chief executives of the 1,000 largest public corporations. These career paths are shown in Exhibit 2.

Exhibit 2 Career Paths of Corporate Executives

A career in accounting can be financially rewarding. Warren Jensen, a Certified Public Accountant, recently accepted a position with Amazon.com as its Chief Financial Officer (CFO). Mr. Jensen, the former CFO of Delta Air Lines, received stock options in Amazon.com that are potentially worth $745 million.

Source: Sara Nathan, *USA Today*, "Amazon Lured President with $1.3B in Options," March 17, 2000.

Private Accounting

The scope of activities and duties of private accountants varies widely. Private accountants are frequently called management accountants. If they are employed by a manufacturer, they may be referred to as *industrial* or *cost accountants*. The chief accountant in a business may be called the **controller**. Various state and federal agencies and other not-for-profit agencies also employ accountants.

The Institute of Certified Management Accountants, an affiliate of the Institute of Management Accountants (IMA), sponsors the **Certified Management Accountant (CMA)** program. The CMA certificate is evidence of competence in management accounting. Becoming a CMA requires a college degree, two years of experience, and successful completion of a two-day examination. Continuing professional education is required for renewal of the CMA certificate. In addition, members of the IMA must adhere to standards of ethical conduct.

The Institute of Internal Auditors sponsors a similar program for internal auditors. Internal auditors are accountants who review the accounting and operating procedures prescribed by their firms. Accountants who specialize in internal auditing may be granted the **Certified Internal Auditor (CIA)** certificate.

Public Accounting

In public accounting, an accountant may practice as an individual or as a member of a public accounting firm. Public accountants who have met a state's education, experience, and examination requirements may become **Certified Public Accountants (CPAs)**.

The requirements for obtaining a CPA certificate differ among the various states. All states require a college education in accounting, and most states require 150 semester hours of college credit. In addition, a candidate must pass a two-day examination prepared by the American Institute of Certified Public Accountants (AICPA).

Most states do not permit individuals to practice as CPAs until they have had from one to three years' experience in public accounting. Some states, however, accept similar employment in private accounting as equivalent experience. All states require continuing professional education and adherence to standards of ethical conduct.[3]

Specialized Accounting Fields

You may think that all accounting is the same. However, you will find several specialized fields of accounting in practice. The two most common are financial accounting and managerial accounting. Other fields include cost accounting, environmental accounting, tax accounting, accounting systems, international accounting, not-for-profit accounting, and social accounting.

Financial accounting is primarily concerned with the recording and reporting of economic data and activities for a business. Although such reports provide useful information for managers, they are the primary reports for owners, creditors, governmental agencies, and the public. For example, if you wanted to buy some stock in **PepsiCo**, **American Airlines**, or **McDonald's**, how would you know in which company to invest? One way is to review financial reports and compare the financial performance and condition of each company. The purpose of financial accounting is to provide such reports.

Managerial accounting, or **management accounting**, uses both financial accounting and estimated data to aid management in running day-to-day operations and in planning future operations. Management accountants gather and report information that is relevant and timely to the decision-making needs of management. For example, management might need information on alternative ways to finance

---

[3] The text of the *Code of Professional Conduct* of the American Institute of Certified Public Accountants is reproduced in Appendix B.

the construction of a new building. Alternatively, management might need information on whether to expand its operations into a new product line. Thus, reports to management can differ widely in form and content.

Generally Accepted Accounting Principles

 **Real World** The FASB is also developing a broad conceptual framework for financial accounting. Seven *Statements of Financial Accounting Concepts* have been published to date.

If the management of a company could record and report financial data as it saw fit, comparisons among companies would be difficult, if not impossible. Thus, financial accountants follow **generally accepted accounting principles (GAAP)** in preparing reports. These reports allow investors and other stakeholders to compare one company to another.

To illustrate the importance of generally accepted accounting principles, assume that each sports conference in college football used different rules for counting touchdowns. For example, assume that the Pacific Athletic Conference (PAC 10) counted a touchdown as six points and the Atlantic Coast Conference (ACC) counted a touchdown as two points. It would be difficult to evaluate the teams under such different scoring systems. A standard set of rules and a standard scoring system help fans compare teams across conferences. Likewise, a standard set of generally accepted accounting principles allows for the comparison of financial performance and condition across companies.

Accounting principles and concepts develop from research, accepted accounting practices, and pronouncements of authoritative bodies. Currently, the **Financial Accounting Standards Board (FASB)** is the authoritative body having the primary responsibility for developing accounting principles. The FASB publishes *Statements of Financial Accounting Standards* and *Interpretations* to these Standards.

Because generally accepted accounting principles impact how companies report and what they report, all stakeholders are interested in the setting of these principles. For example, the FASB proposed a standard on how to account for options granted employees and managers to purchase shares of ownership in the company. The proposal was opposed by managers because it would negatively impact the financial results of many companies. Managers and others, including the United States Senate, urged the FASB to revise or drop the proposal.[4] In response to these comments, the FASB significantly revised the proposed standard.

In this chapter and throughout this text, we emphasize accounting principles and concepts. It is through this emphasis on the "why" of accounting as well as the "how" that you will gain an understanding of the full significance of accounting. In the following paragraphs, we discuss the business entity concept and the cost concept.

Business Entity Concept

The individual business unit is the business entity for which economic data are needed. This entity could be an automobile dealer, a department store, or a grocery store. The business entity must be identified, so that the accountant can determine which economic data should be analyzed, recorded, and summarized in reports.

The **business entity concept** is important because it limits the economic data in the accounting system to data related directly to the activities of the business. In other words, the business is viewed as an entity separate from its owners, creditors, or other stakeholders. For example, the accountant for a business with one owner (a proprietorship) would record the activities of the business only, not the personal activities, property, or debts of the owner.

---

[4] Glenn Alan Cheney, "Senate Rips FASB on Stock Options," *Accounting Today* (May 23, 1994).

The Cost Concept

If a building is bought for $150,000, that amount should be entered into the buyer's accounting records. The seller may have been asking $170,000 for the building up to the time of the sale. The buyer may have initially offered $130,000 for the building. The building may have been assessed at $125,000 for property tax purposes. The buyer may have received an offer of $175,000 for the building the day after it was acquired. These latter amounts have no effect on the accounting records because they did not result in an exchange of the building from the seller to the buyer. The **cost concept** is the basis for entering the *exchange price, or cost, of $150,000* into the accounting records for the building.

Continuing the illustration, the $175,000 offer received by the buyer the day after the building was acquired indicates that it was a bargain purchase at $150,000. To use $175,000 in the accounting records, however, would record an illusory or unrealized profit. If, after buying the building, the buyer accepts the offer and sells the building for $175,000, a profit of $25,000 is then realized and recorded. The new owner would record $175,000 as the cost of the building.

Using the cost concept involves two other important accounting concepts—objectivity and the unit of measure. The **objectivity concept** requires that the accounting records and reports be based upon objective evidence. In exchanges between a buyer and a seller, both try to get the best price. Only the final agreed-upon amount is objective enough for accounting purposes. If the amounts at which properties were recorded were constantly being revised upward and downward based on offers, appraisals, and opinions, accounting reports would soon become unstable and unreliable.

The **unit of measure concept** requires that economic data be recorded in dollars. Money is a common unit of measurement for reporting uniform financial data and reports.

Assets, Liabilities, and Owner's Equity

objective 6

State the accounting equation and define each element of the equation.

The resources owned by a business are its **assets**. Examples of assets include cash, land, buildings, and equipment. The rights or claims to the properties are normally divided into two principal types: (1) the rights of creditors and (2) the rights of owners. The rights of creditors represent debts of the business and are called **liabilities**. The rights of the owners are called **owner's equity**. The relationship between the two may be stated in the form of an equation, as follows:

$$\textbf{Assets} = \textbf{Liabilities} + \textbf{Owner's Equity}$$

This equation is known as the **accounting equation**. It is usual to place liabilities before owner's equity in the accounting equation because creditors have first rights to the assets. The claim of the owners is sometimes given greater emphasis by transposing liabilities to the other side of the equation, which yields:

Assets − Liabilities = Owner's Equity

To illustrate, if the assets owned by a business amount to $100,000 and the liabilities amount to $30,000, the owner's equity is equal to $70,000, as shown below.

 *If a company's assets increase by $20,000 and its liabilities decrease by $5,000, how much did the owner's equity increase or decrease?*

Change in Assets	=	Change in Liabilities	+	Change in Owner's Equity
+$20,000	=	−$5,000	+	X
+$25,000	=			X

Assets	−	Liabilities	=	Owner's Equity
$100,000	−	$30,000	=	$70,000

Business Transactions and the Accounting Equation

Paying a monthly telephone bill of $168 affects a business's financial condition because it now has less cash on hand. Such an economic event or condition that directly changes an entity's financial condition or directly affects its results of operations is a **business transaction**. For example, purchasing land for $50,000 is a business transaction. In contrast, a change in a business's credit rating does not directly affect cash or any other element of its financial condition.

All business transactions can be stated in terms of changes in the elements of the accounting equation. You will see how business transactions affect the accounting equation by studying some typical transactions. As a basis for illustration, we will use a business organized by Chris Clark.

Assume that on November 1, 2002, Chris Clark organizes a corporation that will be known as NetSolutions. The first phase of Chris's business plan is to operate NetSolutions as a service business that provides assistance to individuals and small businesses in developing web pages and in configuring and installing application software. Chris expects this initial phase of the business to last one to two years. During this period, Chris will gather information on the software and hardware needs of customers. During the second phase of the business plan, Chris plans to expand NetSolutions into an Internet-based retailer of software and hardware for individuals and small businesses.

> **All business transactions can be stated in terms of changes in the elements of the accounting equation.**

Each transaction or group of similar transactions during NetSolutions' first month of operations is described in the following paragraphs. The effect of each transaction on the accounting equation is then shown.

 **NETSOLUTIONS**

Transaction a. Chris Clark deposits $25,000 in a bank account in the name of NetSolutions in return for shares of stock in the corporation. Stock issued to owners (stockholders), such as Chris Clark, is referred to as **capital stock**. The effect of this transaction is to increase the asset (cash), on the left side of the equation, by $25,000. To balance the equation, the owner's equity (capital stock), on the right side of the equation, is increased by the same amount. The effect of this transaction on NetSolutions' accounting equation is shown below.

Assets	=	**Owner's Equity**
Cash	=	Capital Stock
a. 25,000		25,000 Investment by stockholder

Note that the accounting equation shown above relates only to the business, NetSolutions. Under the business entity concept, Chris Clark's personal assets, such as a home or personal bank account, and personal liabilities are excluded from the equation.

Transaction b. If you purchased this textbook by paying cash, you entered into a transaction in which you exchanged one asset for another. That is, you exchanged cash for the textbook. Businesses often enter into similar transactions. NetSolutions, for example, exchanged $20,000 cash for land. The land is located in a new business park with convenient access to transportation facilities. Chris Clark plans to rent office space and equipment during the first phase of the business plan. During the second phase, Chris plans to build an office and warehouse on the land.

The purchase of the land changes the makeup of the assets but does not change the total assets. The items in the equation prior to this transaction and the effect of the transaction are shown next, as well as the new amounts, or *balances*, of the items.

If NetSolutions had purchased a van for $28,000, paying $8,000 cash and signing a loan agreement (note payable) for $20,000, how would the transaction be recorded using the accounting equation?

Cash	+	Van	=	Notes Payable
−8,000	+	28,000		+20,000

	Assets			=	Owner's Equity
	Cash	+	Land		Capital Stock
Bal.	25,000			=	25,000
b.	−20,000		+20,000		
Bal.	5,000		20,000		25,000

Transaction c. You have probably used a credit card at one time or another to buy clothing or other merchandise. In this type of transaction, you received clothing for a promise to pay your credit card bill in the future. That is, you received an asset and incurred a liability to pay a future bill. During the month, NetSolutions entered into a similar transaction, buying supplies for $1,350 and agreeing to pay the supplier in the near future. This type of transaction is called a purchase *on account*. The liability created is called an **account payable**. Items such as supplies that will be used in the business in the future are called **prepaid expenses**, which are assets. The effect of this transaction is to increase assets and liabilities by $1,350, as follows:

Other examples of common prepaid expenses include insurance and rent. Businesses usually report these assets together as a single item, prepaid expenses.

	Assets					=	Liabilities	+	Owner's Equity
							Accounts		Capital
	Cash	+	Supplies	+	Land		Payable	+	Stock
Bal.	5,000				20,000				25,000
c.			+1,350				+1,350		
Bal.	5,000		1,350		20,000		1,350		25,000

Transaction d. You may have earned money by painting houses. If so, you received money for rendering services to a customer. Likewise, a business earns money by selling goods or services to its customers. This amount is called **revenue**.

During its first month of operations, NetSolutions provided services to customers, earning fees of $7,500 and receiving the amount in cash. This transaction increased cash and the owner's equity by $7,500, as shown here.

	Assets					=	Liabilities +		Owner's Equity		
							Accounts		Capital		Retained
	Cash	+	Supplies	+	Land		Payable	+	Stock	+	Earnings
Bal.	5,000		1,350		20,000		1,350		25,000		
d.	+ 7,500										+ 7,500 Fees earned
Bal.	12,500		1,350		20,000		1,350		25,000		7,500

You should note that the increase in owner's equity from earning revenue is listed in the equation under "Retained Earnings." **Retained earnings** is the owner's equity created by the business operations (revenues less expenses). Transactions affecting earnings are kept separate from transactions related to owner's investments (capital stock). This is useful in preparing reports to owners and creditors and in satisfying legal requirements that we will discuss later in the text.

Special terms may be used to describe certain kinds of revenue, such as **sales** for the sale of merchandise. Revenue from providing services is called **fees earned**. For example, a physician would record fees earned for services to patients. Other examples include **rent revenue** (money received for rent) and **interest revenue** (money received for interest).

Instead of requiring the payment of cash at the time services are provided or goods are sold, a business may accept payment at a later date. Such revenues are called *fees on account* or *sales on account*. In such cases, the firm has an **account receivable**, which is a claim against the customer. An account receivable is an asset, and the revenue is earned as if cash had been received. When customers pay their accounts, there is an exchange of one asset for another. Cash increases, while accounts receivable decreases.

Transaction e. If you painted houses to earn money, you probably used your own ladders and brushes. NetSolutions also spent cash or used up other assets in earning revenue. The amounts used in this process of earning revenue are called **expenses**. Expenses include supplies used, wages of employees, and other assets and services used in operating the business.

For NetSolutions, the expenses paid during the month were as follows: wages, $2,125; rent, $800; utilities, $450; and miscellaneous, $275. Miscellaneous expenses include small amounts paid for such items as postage, coffee, and magazine subscriptions. The effect of this group of transactions is the opposite of the effect of revenues. These transactions reduce cash and owner's equity, as shown here.

	Assets			=	**Liabilities +**	**Owner's Equity**	
	Cash	+ Supplies	+ Land		Accounts Payable	+ Capital Stock	+ Retained Earnings
Bal.	12,500	1,350	20,000		1,350	25,000	7,500
e.	−3,650			=			−2,125 Wages expense
							− 800 Rent expense
							− 450 Utilities expense
							− 275 Misc. expense
	8,850	1,350	20,000		1,350	25,000	3,850

Businesses usually record each revenue and expense transaction separately as it occurs. However, to simplify this illustration, we have summarized NetSolutions' revenues and expenses for the month in transactions (d) and (e).

Transaction f. When you pay your monthly credit card bill, you decrease the cash in your checking account and also decrease the amount you owe to the credit card company. Likewise, when NetSolutions pays $950 to creditors during the month, it reduces both assets and liabilities, as shown below.

	Assets			=	**Liabilities**	+	**Owner's Equity**	
	Cash	+ Supplies	+ Land		Accounts Payable	+ Capital Stock	+	Retained Earnings
Bal.	8,850	1,350	20,000		1,350	25,000		3,850
f.	−950			=	−950			
Bal.	7,900	1,350	20,000		400	25,000		3,850

You should note that paying an amount on account is different from paying an amount for an expense. The payment of an expense reduces owner's equity, as illustrated in transaction (e). Paying an amount on account reduces the amount owed on a liability.

Transaction g. At the end of the month, the cost of the supplies on hand (not yet used) is $550. The remainder of the supplies ($1,350 − $550) was used in the operations of the business and is treated as an expense. This decrease of $800 in supplies and owner's equity is shown as follows:

If supplies of $2,500 were purchased during the month and supplies of $350 are on hand at the end of the month, how much is supplies expense for the month?

$2,150 ($2,500 supplies purchased − $350 on hand)

		Assets			=	Liabilities +	Owner's Equity	
						Accounts	Capital	Retained
	Cash	+ Supplies	+ Land		=	Payable	+ Stock	+ Earnings
Bal.	7,900	1,350	20,000			400	25,000	3,850
g.		−800						− 800 Supplies expense
Bal.	7,900	550	20,000			400	25,000	3,050

Transaction h. At the end of the month, NetSolutions pays $2,000 to stockholders (Chris Clark) as dividends. **Dividends** are distributions of earnings to stockholders. The payment of the dividends reduces both cash and owner's equity. The effect of this transaction is shown as follows:

		Assets			=	Liabilities +	Owner's Equity	
						Accounts	Capital	Retained
	Cash	+ Supplies	+ Land		=	Payable	+ Stock	+ Earnings
Bal.	7,900	550	20,000			400	25,000	3,050
h.	−2,000							−2,000 Dividends
Bal.	5,900	550	20,000			400	25,000	1,050

You should be careful not to confuse dividends with expenses. Dividends *do not* represent assets or services used in the process of earning revenues. The owner's equity decrease from dividends is listed in the equation under Retained Earnings. This is because dividends are considered a distribution of earnings to stockholders.

Summary. The transactions of NetSolutions are summarized as follows. They are identified by letter, and the balance of each item is shown after each transaction.

		Assets			=	Liabilities +	Owner's Equity	
						Accounts	Capital	Retained
	Cash	+ Supplies	+ Land		=	Payable	+ Stock	+ Earnings
a.	+25,000						25,000	Investment by stockholder
b.	−20,000		+20,000					
Bal.	5,000		20,000				25,000	
c.		+1,350				+1,350		
Bal.	5,000	1,350	20,000			1,350	25,000	
d.	+ 7,500							+7,500 Fees earned
Bal.	12,500	1,350	20,000			1,350	25,000	7,500
e.	− 3,650							−2,125 Wages expense
								− 800 Rent expense
								− 450 Utilities expense
								− 275 Misc. expense
Bal.	8,850	1,350	20,000			1,350	25,000	3,850
f.	− 950					− 950		
Bal.	7,900	1,350	20,000			400		3,850
g.		− 800						− 800 Supplies expense
Bal.	7,900	550	20,000			400	25,000	3,050
h.	− 2,000							−2,000 Dividends
Bal.	5,900	550	20,000			400	25,000	1,050

In reviewing the preceding summary, you should note the following, which apply to all types of businesses:

1. The effect of every transaction is *an increase or a decrease in one or more of the accounting equation elements.*
2. The two sides of the accounting equation are *always equal.*
3. The owner's equity is *increased by amounts invested by stockholders (capital stock)* and is *decreased by dividends to stockholders (retained earnings).* In addition, the owner's equity (retained earnings) is *increased by revenues* and is *decreased by expenses.* The effects of these four types of transactions on owner's equity are illustrated in Exhibit 3.

Exhibit 3 Effects of Transactions on Owner's Equity

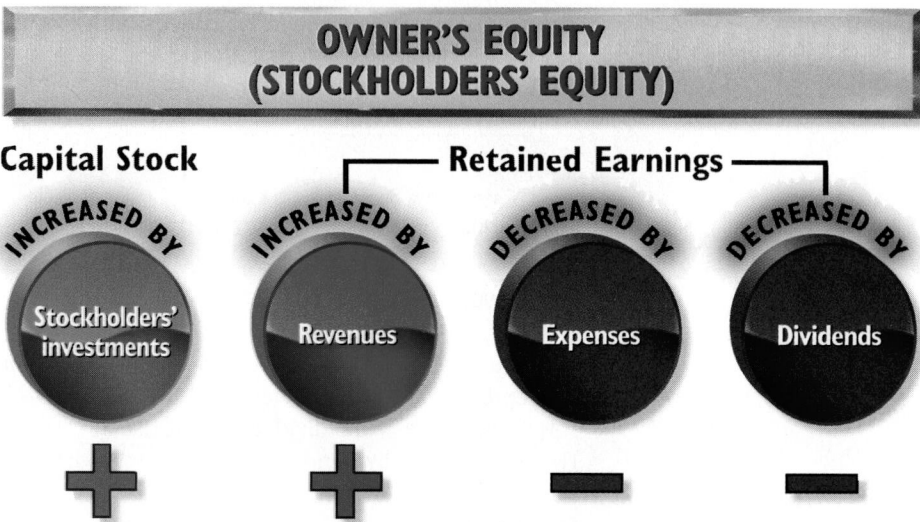

Financial Statements

objective 8

Describe the financial statements of a corporation and explain how they interrelate.

After transactions have been recorded and summarized, reports are prepared for users. The accounting reports that provide this information are called **financial statements**. The principal financial statements of a corporation are the income statement, the retained earnings statement, the balance sheet, and the statement of cash flows. The order in which the statements are normally prepared and the nature of the data presented in each statement are as follows:

• **Income statement**—A summary of the revenue and expenses *for a specific period of time,* such as a month or a year.
• **Retained earnings statement**—A summary of the changes in the earnings retained in the corporation for *a specific period of time,* such as a month or a year.
• **Balance sheet**—A list of the assets, liabilities, and owner's equity *as of a specific date,* usually at the close of the last day of a month or a year.
• **Statement of cash flows**—A summary of the cash receipts and cash payments *for a specific period of time,* such as a month or a year.

The basic features of the four statements and their interrelationships are illustrated in Exhibit 4. The data for the statements were taken from the summary of transactions of NetSolutions.

All financial statements should be identified by the name of the business, the title of the statement, and the *date* or *period of time.* The data presented in the income statement, the retained earnings statement, and the statement of cash flows are for a period of time. The data presented in the balance sheet are for a specific date.

Exhibit 4 Financial
Statements

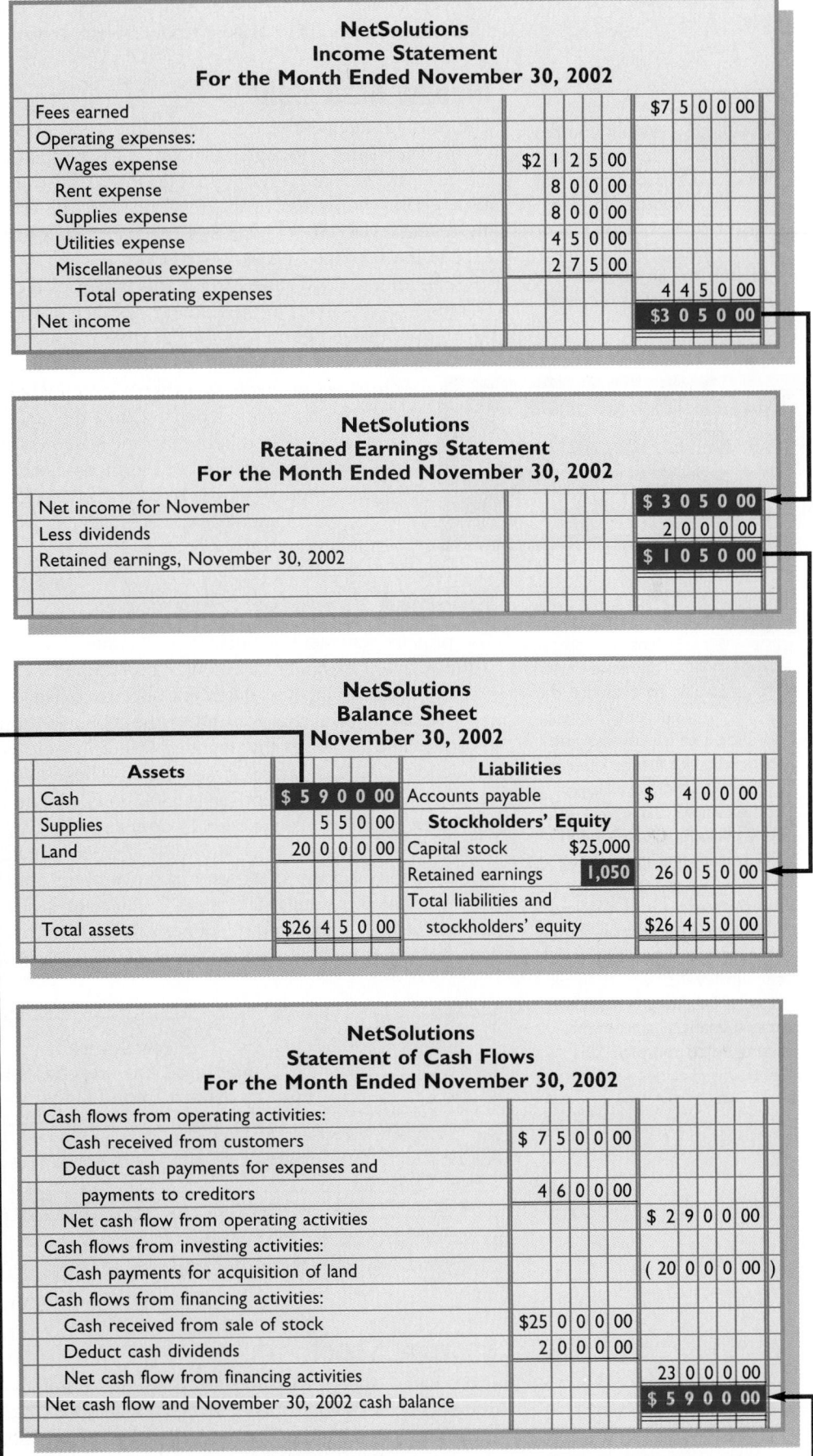

NetSolutions
Income Statement
For the Month Ended November 30, 2002

Fees earned				$7 5 0 0 00
Operating expenses:				
Wages expense	$2 1 2 5 00			
Rent expense	8 0 0 00			
Supplies expense	8 0 0 00			
Utilities expense	4 5 0 00			
Miscellaneous expense	2 7 5 00			
Total operating expenses			4 4 5 0 00	
Net income			$3 0 5 0 00	

NetSolutions
Retained Earnings Statement
For the Month Ended November 30, 2002

Net income for November		$ 3 0 5 0 00
Less dividends		2 0 0 0 00
Retained earnings, November 30, 2002		$ 1 0 5 0 00

NetSolutions
Balance Sheet
November 30, 2002

Assets		Liabilities	
Cash	$ 5 9 0 0 00	Accounts payable	$ 4 0 0 00
Supplies	5 5 0 00	**Stockholders' Equity**	
Land	20 0 0 0 00	Capital stock $25,000	
		Retained earnings 1,050	26 0 5 0 00
		Total liabilities and	
Total assets	$26 4 5 0 00	stockholders' equity	$26 4 5 0 00

NetSolutions
Statement of Cash Flows
For the Month Ended November 30, 2002

Cash flows from operating activities:		
Cash received from customers	$ 7 5 0 0 00	
Deduct cash payments for expenses and		
payments to creditors	4 6 0 0 00	
Net cash flow from operating activities		$ 2 9 0 0 00
Cash flows from investing activities:		
Cash payments for acquisition of land		(20 0 0 0 00)
Cash flows from financing activities:		
Cash received from sale of stock	$25 0 0 0 00	
Deduct cash dividends	2 0 0 0 00	
Net cash flow from financing activities		23 0 0 0 00
Net cash flow and November 30, 2002 cash balance		$ 5 9 0 0 00

You should note the use of indents, captions, dollar signs, and rulings in the financial statements. They aid the reader by emphasizing the sections of the statements.

Income Statement

When you buy something at a store, you may *match* the cash register total with the amount you paid the cashier and with the amount of change, if any, you received.

The income statement reports the revenues and expenses for a period of time, based on the **matching concept**. This concept is applied by *matching* the expenses with the revenue generated during a period by those expenses. The income statement also reports the excess of the revenue over the expenses incurred. This excess of the revenue over the expenses is called **net income** or **net profit**. If the expenses exceed the revenue, the excess is a **net loss**.

The effects of revenue earned and expenses incurred during the month for Net-Solutions were shown in the equation as increases and decreases in owner's equity (retained earnings). Net income for a period has the effect of increasing owner's equity (retained earnings) for the period, whereas a net loss has the effect of decreasing owner's equity (retained earnings) for the period.

> **Net income—the excess of revenue over expenses—increases owner's equity.**

The revenue, expenses, and the net income of $3,050 for NetSolutions are reported in the income statement in Exhibit 4. The order in which the expenses are listed in the income statement varies among businesses. One method is to list them in order of size, beginning with the larger items. Miscellaneous expense is usually shown as the last item, regardless of the amount.

Retained Earnings Statement

Financial statements are used to evaluate the current financial condition of a business and to predict its future operating results and cash flows. For example, bank loan officers use a business's financial statements in deciding whether to grant a loan to the business. Once the loan is granted, the borrower may be required to maintain a certain level of assets in excess of liabilities. The business's financial statements are used to monitor this level.

The primary statement for analyzing changes in the owner's equity of a corporation is the retained earnings statement. The retained earnings statement is a connecting link between the income statement and the balance sheet.

Two types of transactions affect the retained earnings during the month: (1) the revenues and expenses that resulted in net income of $3,050 for the month and (2) dividends of $2,000 paid to stockholders. These transactions are summarized in the retained earnings statement for NetSolutions shown in Exhibit 4.

Since NetSolutions has been in operation for only one month, it has no retained earnings at the beginning of November. For December, however, there is a beginning balance—the balance at the end of November. This balance of $1,050 is reported on the retained earnings statement. To illustrate, assume that NetSolutions earned net income of $4,155 and paid dividends of $2,000 during December. The retained earnings statement for NetSolutions for December is shown here.

NetSolutions Retained Earnings Statement For the Month Ended December 31, 2002			
Retained earnings, December 1, 2002			$1 0 5 0 00
Net income for the month	$4 1 5 5 00		
Less dividends	2 0 0 0 00		
Increase in retained earnings			2 1 5 5 00
Retained earnings, December 31, 2002			$3 2 0 5 00

Balance Sheet

The balance sheet in Exhibit 4 reports the amounts of NetSolutions' assets, liabilities, and owner's equity at the end of November. These amounts are taken from the last line of the summary of transactions presented earlier. The form of balance sheet shown in Exhibit 4 is called the **account form** because it resembles the basic format of the accounting equation, with assets on the left side and the liabilities and owner's equity sections on the right side. We illustrate an alternative form of balance sheet called the **report form** in a later chapter. It presents the liabilities and owner's equity sections below the assets section.

The assets section of the balance sheet normally presents assets in the order that they will be converted into cash or used in operations. Cash is presented first, followed by receivables, supplies, prepaid insurance, and other assets. The assets of a more permanent nature are shown next, such as land, buildings, and equipment.

In the liabilities section of the balance sheet in Exhibit 4, accounts payable is the only liability. When there are two or more categories of liabilities, each should be listed and the total amount of liabilities presented as follows.

Liabilities		
Accounts payable	$12,900	
Wages payable	2,570	
Total liabilities		$15,470

Statement of Cash Flows

The statement of cash flows consists of three sections, as we see in Exhibit 4: (1) operating activities, (2) investing activities, and (3) financing activities. Each of these sections is briefly described below.

Cash Flows from Operating Activities. This section reports a summary of cash receipts and cash payments from operations. The net cash flow from operating activities ($2,900 in Exhibit 4) will normally differ from the amount of net income for the period ($3,050 in Exhibit 4). This difference occurs because revenues and expenses may not be recorded at the same time that cash is received from customers or paid to creditors.

Cash Flows from Investing Activities. This section reports the cash transactions for the acquisition and sale of relatively permanent assets.

Cash Flows from Financing Activities. This section reports the cash transactions related to cash investments by the stockholders, borrowings, and cash dividends.

Preparing the statement of cash flows requires an understanding of concepts that we have not discussed in this chapter. Therefore, we will illustrate the preparation of the statement of cash flows in a later chapter.

FINANCIAL ANALYSIS AND INTERPRETATION

objective 9

Use the ratio of liabilities to stockholders' equity to analyze the ability of a business to withstand poor business conditions.

As we discussed earlier in this chapter, financial statements are useful to bankers, creditors, owners, and other stakeholders in analyzing and interpreting the financial performance and condition of a business. Throughout this text, we will discuss various tools that are often used in practice to analyze and interpret the financial performance and condition of a business. The first such tool we will introduce is especially useful in analyzing the ability of a business to pay its creditors.

The relationship between liabilities and owner's equity, expressed as a ratio, is calculated as follows:

$$\text{Ratio of liabilities to stockholders' equity} = \frac{\text{Total liabilities}}{\text{Total stockholders' equity}}$$

To illustrate, NetSolutions' ratio of liabilities to stockholders' equity at the end of November is 0.015, as calculated below.

$$\text{Ratio of liabilities to stockholders' equity} = \frac{\$400}{\$26,050} = 0.015$$

The rights of creditors to a business's assets take precedence over the rights of stockholders. Thus, the lower the ratio of liabilities to stockholders' equity, the better able the business is to withstand poor business conditions and still fully meet its obligations to creditors.

To illustrate, a ratio of 1 indicates that the liabilities and stockholders' equity are equal. In other words, if the business suffers a loss equal to the total liabilities, the amount of total assets available to creditors will not drop below their claims on the assets. If this were to happen, the creditors could collect their claims and the stockholders would be left with nothing.

ENCORE

Home Depot

Businesses begin in many ways. The beginning of Home Depot took place in the spring of 1978, with two words: "You're fired!"

At the time of their firing, Bernie Marcus was chief executive officer and Arthur Blank was chief financial officer of Handy Dan Stores, a subsidiary of Daylin Corporation. Under their leadership, Handy Dan had grown to 66 stores and almost $155 million in sales. Handy Dan was earning more ($7.8 million) than the corporation as a whole, which earned only $7 million. Bernie and Arthur's success, however, wasn't sufficient to shield them from the forces of corporate politics.

Bernie and Arthur used their firings to create a golden opportunity to develop their vision for a chain of home improvement stores that would challenge the industry's conventional wisdom. Unfortunately, not only were they out of work, but they had little

capital with which to start a new venture. Bernie and Arthur courted potential investors, including H. Ross Perot, who at that time was relatively unknown. If Perot would invest $2 million in the venture, he would receive 70 percent of the then unnamed company. The negotiations broke down, however, when Perot would not agree to let Bernie keep his used Cadillac as a company car. Instead, he suggested that Bernie purchase a new, more expensive Chevrolet. "My people don't drive Cadillacs," Perot insisted.

Though Bernie and Arthur had to plead with vendors, banks, and investors for financing and credit in the early years, they were able to scrape up enough financing to open three Home Depot stores in Atlanta in 1979 and a fourth in 1980.

In 1999, Home Depot celebrated its 20th anniversary, with over 800 stores throughout the United

States and South America. Sales have grown from $7 million in 1979 to over $30 billion today. Bernie and Arthur have become two of the richest men in America. As for Ross Perot, the investment that he backed out of would currently be worth approximately $60 billion!

Source: Adapted from *Built from Scratch*, by Bernie Marcus and Arthur Blank, with Bob Andelman (Times Business-Random House, 1999). ∎

KEY POINTS

1 Describe the nature of a business.

A business is an organization in which basic resources (inputs), such as materials and labor, are assembled and processed to provide goods or services (outputs) to customers. The objective of most businesses is to maximize profits.

There are three different types of businesses that are operated for profit: manufacturing, merchandising, and service businesses. A business is normally organized in one of three different forms: proprietorship, partnership, or corporation. A business stakeholder is a person or entity (such as an owner, manager,

employee, customer, creditor, or the government) who has an interest in the economic performance of the business.

2 Describe the role of accounting in business.

Accounting is an information system that provides reports to stakeholders about the economic activities and condition of a business. Accounting is the "language of business."

3 Describe the importance of business ethics and the basic principles of proper ethical conduct.

Ethics are moral principles that guide the conduct of individuals. Proper ethical conduct implies a behavior that considers the impact of one's actions on society and others. Sound ethical principles include (1) avoiding small ethical lapses, (2) focusing on your long-term reputation, and (3) being willing to suffer adverse personal consequences for holding to an ethical position.

4 Describe the profession of accounting.

Accountants are engaged in either private accounting or public accounting. The two most common specialized fields of accounting are financial accounting and managerial accounting. Other fields include cost accounting, environmental accounting, tax accounting, accounting systems, international accounting, not-for-profit accounting, and social accounting.

5 Summarize the development of accounting principles and relate them to practice.

Financial accountants follow generally accepted accounting principles (GAAP) in preparing reports so that stakeholders can compare one company to another. Accounting principles and concepts develop from research, accepted accounting practices, and pronouncements of authoritative bodies. Currently, the Financial Accounting Standards Board (FASB) is the authoritative body having the primary responsibility for developing accounting principles.

The business entity concept views the business as an entity separate from its owners, creditors, or other stakeholders. The business entity limits the economic data in the accounting system to that related directly to the activities of the business. The cost concept requires that properties and services bought by a business be recorded in terms of actual cost. The objectivity concept requires that the accounting records and reports be based upon objective evidence. The unit of measure concept requires that economic data be recorded in dollars.

6 State the accounting equation and define each element of the equation.

The resources owned by a business and the rights or claims to these resources may be stated in the form of an equation, as follows:

$$\text{Assets} = \text{Liabilities} + \text{Owner's Equity}$$

7 Explain how business transactions can be stated in terms of the resulting changes in the basic elements of the accounting equation.

All business transactions can be stated in terms of the change in one or more of the three elements of the accounting equation. That is, the effect of every transaction can be stated in terms of increases or decreases in one or more of these elements, while maintaining the equality between the two sides of the equation.

8 Describe the financial statements of a corporation and explain how they interrelate.

The principal financial statements of a corporation are the income statement, the retained earnings statement, the balance sheet, and the statement of cash flows. The income statement reports a period's net income or net loss, which also appears on the retained earnings statement. The ending retained earnings reported on the retained earnings statement is also reported on the balance sheet. The ending cash balance is reported on the balance sheet and the statement of cash flows.

9 Use the ratio of liabilities to stockholders' equity to analyze the ability of a business to withstand poor business conditions.

The ratio of liabilities to stockholders' equity is useful in analyzing the ability of a business to pay its creditors. The lower the ratio, the better able the business is to withstand poor business conditions and still fully meet its obligations to creditors.

ILLUSTRATIVE PROBLEM

Cecil Jameson, Attorney-at-Law, P.C., is organized as a professional corporation owned and operated by Cecil Jameson. On July 1 of the current year, Cecil Jameson, Attorney-at-Law, P.C., has the following assets, liabilities, and capital stock: cash, $1,000; accounts receivable, $3,200; supplies, $850; land, $10,000; accounts payable, $1,530; capital stock, $10,000. Office space and office equipment are currently being rented, pending the construction of an office complex on land purchased last year. Business transactions during July are summarized as follows:

a.   Received cash from clients for services, $3,928.
b.   Paid creditors on account, $1,055.

c. Received cash from Cecil Jameson as an additional investment and issued capital stock, $3,700.

d. Paid office rent for the month, $1,200.

e. Charged clients for legal services on account, $2,025.

f. Purchased office supplies on account, $245.

g. Received cash from clients on account, $3,000.

h. Received invoice for paralegal services from Legal Aid Inc. for July (to be paid on August 10), $1,635.

i. Paid the following: wages expense, $850; answering service expense, $250; utilities expense, $325; and miscellaneous expense, $75.

j. Determined that the cost of office supplies on hand was $980; therefore, the cost of supplies used during the month was $115.

k. Paid dividends of $1,000.

Instructions

1. Determine the amount of retained earnings as of July 1 of the current year.

2. State the assets, liabilities, and owner's equity as of July 1 in equation form similar to that shown in this chapter. In tabular form below the equation, indicate the increases and decreases resulting from each transaction and the new balances after each transaction. Explain the nature of each increase and decrease in owner's equity by an appropriate notation at the right of the amount.

3. Prepare an income statement for July, a retained earnings statement for July, and a balance sheet as of July 31.

Solution

1. Assets − Liabilities = Owner's Equity

$$\$15,050 - \$1,530 = \text{Capital Stock} + \text{Retained Earnings}$$
$$\$13,520 = \$10,000 + \text{Retained Earnings}$$
$$\$3,520 = \text{Retained Earnings}$$

2.

	Assets				= Liabilities +	Owner's Equity	
	Cash +	Accounts Receivable +	Supplies +	Land	= Payable	Capital + Stock +	Retained Earnings
Bal.	1,000	3,200	850	10,000	1,530	10,000	3,520
a.	+3,928						+3,928 Fees earned
Bal.	4,928	3,200	850	10,000	1,530	10,000	7,448
b.	−1,055				−1,055		
Bal.	3,873	3,200	850	10,000	475	10,000	7,448
c.	+3,700					+3,700	Investment
Bal.	7,573	3,200	850	10,000	475	13,700	7,448
d.	−1,200						−1,200 Rent expense
Bal.	6,373	3,200	850	10,000	475	13,700	6,248
e.		+2,025					+2,025 Fees earned
Bal.	6,373	5,225	850	10,000	475	13,700	8,273
f.			+ 245		+ 245		
Bal.	6,373	5,225	1,095	10,000	720	13,700	8,273
g.	+3,000	−3,000					
Bal.	9,373	2,225	1,095	10,000	720	13,700	8,273
h.					+1,635		−1,635 Paralegal exp.
Bal.	9,373	2,225	1,095	10,000	2,355	13,700	6,638
i.	−1,500						− 850 Wages exp.
							− 250 Answ. svc. exp.
							− 325 Utilities exp.
							− 75 Misc. exp.
Bal.	7,873	2,225	1,095	10,000	2,355	13,700	5,138
j.			− 115				− 115 Supplies exp.
Bal.	7,873	2,225	980	10,000	2,355	13,700	5,023
k.	−1,000						−1,000 Dividends
	6,873	2,225	980	10,000	2,355	13,700	4,023

3.

Cecil Jameson, Attorney-at-Law, P.C.
Income Statement
For the Month Ended July 31, 20—

Fees earned			$5 9 5 3 00
Operating expenses:			
Paralegal expense	$1 6 3 5 00		
Rent expense	1 2 0 0 00		
Wages expense	8 5 0 00		
Utilities expense	3 2 5 00		
Answering service expense	2 5 0 00		
Supplies expense	1 1 5 00		
Miscellaneous expense	7 5 00		
Total operating expenses			4 4 5 0 00
Net income			$1 5 0 3 00

Cecil Jameson, Attorney-at-Law, P.C.
Retained Earnings Statement
For the Month Ended July 31, 20—

Retained earnings, July 1, 20—			$3 5 2 0 00
Net income for the month	$1 5 0 3 00		
Less dividends	1 0 0 0 00		
Increase in retained earnings			5 0 3 00
Retained earnings, July 31, 20—			$4 0 2 3 00

Cecil Jameson, Attorney-at-Law, P.C.
Balance Sheet
July 31, 20—

Assets		Liabilities	
Cash	$ 6 8 7 3 00	Accounts payable	$ 2 3 5 5 00
Accounts receivable	2 2 2 5 00	**Stockholders' Equity**	
Supplies	9 8 0 00	Capital stock $13,700	
Land	10 0 0 0 00	Retained earnings 4,023	17 7 2 3 00
		Total liabilities and	
Total assets	$20 0 7 8 00	stockholders' equity	$20 0 7 8 00

SELF-EXAMINATION QUESTIONS   Answers at End of Chapter

Matching

Match each of the following statements with its proper term. Some terms may not be used.

A. Account form

B. Account payable

C. Account receivable

_____ 1. An organization in which basic resources (inputs), such as materials and labor, are assembled and processed to provide goods or services (outputs) to customers.

_____ 2. A type of business that changes basic inputs into products that are sold to individual customers.

D. **Accounting**

E. **Accounting equation**

F. **Assets**

G. **Balance sheet**

H. **Business**

I. **Business entity concept**

J. **Business stakeholder**

K. **Business transaction**

L. **Capital stock**

M. **Corporation**

N. **Cost concept**

O. **Dividends**

P. **Ethics**

Q. **Expenses**

R. **Financial accounting**

S. **Financial Accounting Standards Board (FASB)**

T. **Generally accepted accounting principles (GAAP)**

U. **Income statement**

V. **Liabilities**

W. **Managerial accounting**

X. **Managers**

Y. **Manufacturing**

Z. **Matching concept**

AA. **Merchandising**

BB. **Net income**

CC. **Net loss**

DD. **Objectivity concept**

EE. **Owner's equity**

FF. **Partnership**

GG. **Prepaid expenses**

HH. **Proprietorship**

II. **Report form**

JJ. **Retained earnings**

KK. **Retained earnings statement**

LL. **Revenue**

MM. **Service**

NN. **Statement of cash flows**

OO. **Unit of measure concept**

___ 3. A type of business that purchases products from other businesses and sells them to customers.

___ 4. A business owned by one individual.

___ 5. A business owned by two or more individuals.

___ 6. A business organized under state or federal statutes as a separate legal entity.

___ 7. A person or entity who has an interest in the economic performance of a business.

___ 8. Individuals authorized by the owners to operate the business.

___ 9. An information system that provides reports to stakeholders about the economic activities and condition of a business.

___ 10. Moral principles that guide the conduct of individuals.

___ 11. A specialized field of accounting concerned primarily with the recording and reporting of economic data and activities to stakeholders outside the business.

___ 12. A specialized field of accounting that uses estimated data to aid management in running day-to-day operations and in planning future operations.

___ 13. The authoritative body that has the primary responsibility for developing accounting principles.

___ 14. A concept of accounting that limits the economic data in the accounting system to data related directly to the activities of the business.

___ 15. A concept of accounting requiring that economic data be recorded in dollars.

___ 16. The resources owned by a business.

___ 17. The rights of creditors that represent debts of the business.

___ 18. The rights of the owners.

___ 19. Assets = Liabilities + Owner's Equity

___ 20. An economic event or condition that directly changes an entity's financial condition or directly affects its results of operations.

___ 21. The liability created by a purchase on account.

___ 22. Items such as supplies that will be used in the business in the future.

___ 23. A claim against the customer.

___ 24. The amounts used in the process of earning revenue.

___ 25. The amount a business earns by selling goods or services to its customers.

___ 26. A summary of the revenue and expenses *for a specific period of time*, such as a month or a year.

___ 27. A summary of the changes in the retained earnings in a corporation for *a specific period of time*, such as a month or a year.

___ 28. A list of the assets, liabilities, and owner's equity *as of a specific date*, usually at the close of the last day of a month or a year.

___ 29. A summary of the cash receipts and cash payments *for a specific period of time*, such as a month or a year.

___ 30. A concept of accounting in which expenses are matched with the revenue generated during a period by those expenses.

___ 31. The form of balance sheet that resembles the basic format of the accounting equation, with assets on the left side and the liabilities and owner's equity sections on the right side.

___ 32. Shares of ownership of a corporation.

___ 33. Distributions of earnings of a corporation to its owners (stockholders).

___ 34. Net income retained in a corporation.

Multiple Choice

1. A profit-making business operating as a separate legal entity and in which ownership is divided into shares of stock is known as a:
   A. proprietorship.
   C. partnership.
   B. service business.
   D. corporation.

2. The resources owned by a business are called:
   A. assets.
   B. liabilities.
   C. the accounting equation.
   D. owner's equity.

3. A listing of a business entity's assets, liabilities, and owner's equity as of a specific date is:
   A. a balance sheet.
   B. an income statement.
   C. a retained earnings statement.
   D. a statement of cash flows.

4. If total assets increased $20,000 during a period and total liabilities increased $12,000 during the same period, the amount and direction (increase or decrease) of the change in owner's equity for that period is:
   A. a $32,000 increase.
   C. an $8,000 increase.
   B. a $32,000 decrease.
   D. an $8,000 decrease.

5. If revenue was $45,000, expenses were $37,500, and dividends were $10,000, the amount of net income or net loss would be:
   A. $45,000 net income.
   C. $37,500 net loss.
   B. $7,500 net income.
   D. $2,500 net loss.

CLASS DISCUSSION QUESTIONS

1. What is the objective of most businesses?
2. Who are normally included as the stakeholders of a business?
3. What is the role of accounting in business?
4. What three sound principles form the foundation for ethical behavior?
5. Distinguish between private accounting and public accounting.
6. Identify what the abbreviation FASB stands for and describe how the FASB sets generally accepted accounting principles.
7. Lynda Lyons is the owner of Fast Delivery Service. Recently, Lynda paid interest of $3,500 on a personal loan of $60,000 that she used to begin the business. Should Fast Delivery Service record the interest payment? Explain.
8. On April 18, Neece Repair Service extended an offer of $95,000 for land that had been priced for sale at $100,000. On April 25, Neece Repair Service accepted the seller's counteroffer of $97,500. Describe how Neece Repair Service should record the land.
9. a. Land with an assessed value of $200,000 for property tax purposes is acquired by a business for $350,000. Seven years later, the plot of land has an assessed value of $240,000 and the business receives an offer of $400,000 for it. Should the monetary amount assigned to the land in the business records now be increased?
   b. Assuming that the land acquired in (a) was sold for $400,000, how would the various elements of the accounting equation be affected?
10. What are the two principal rights to the properties of a business?
11. Name the three elements of the accounting equation.
12. Describe the difference between an account receivable and an account payable.
13. A business had revenues of $130,000 and operating expenses of $145,000. Did the business (a) incur a net loss or (b) realize net income?
14. A business had revenues of $280,000 and operating expenses of $270,000. Did the business (a) incur a net loss or (b) realize net income?
15. What two types of transactions increase the owner's equity of a corporation?
16. Briefly describe the nature of the information provided by each of the following financial statements: the income statement, the retained earnings statement, the balance sheet, and the statement of cash flows.
17. Indicate whether each of the financial statements in Question 16 covers a period of time or is for a specific date.
18. What particular item of financial or operating data appears on both the income statement and the retained earnings statement? What item appears on both the balance sheet and the retained earnings statement?
19. What are the three types of activities reported in the statement of cash flows?

A TRADITION OF INNOVATION

Innovation. Motivation. Results.

Thank you for joining the thousands of other students who have achieved outstanding results using this innovative text. To help you even further, we have developed incredible resources to make learning accounting even easier. You can purchase these supplements by visiting

http://warren.swcollege.com.

Here are numerous resources to help you get the results you want:

Personal WebTutor Advantage
GO TO THIS URL TO PURCHASE THIS PRODUCT:
pwt.swcollege.com

- Automatic and immediate feedback from quizzes and exams.
- Interactive, multimedia rich explanation of concepts.
- Online exercises that reinforce what you've learned.
- Flashcards that include audio support.
- Greater interaction and involvement through online discussion forums.

General Ledger Software
0-324-05462-9
- This software package teaches you the basics of a computerized accounting system in an easy-to-use environment.
- You will get hints and tips completing end-of-chapter problems.
- You will get immediate feedback to determine if you have done the problems correctly.

Personal Trainer
FINANCIAL & MANAGERIAL ACCOUNTING
0-324-12384-1
CORPORATE FINANCIAL ACCOUNTING
0-324-12381-7
MANAGERIAL ACCOUNTING
0-324-12377-9
- This online tutorial will help you complete the end-of-chapter exercises from the textbook, with hints.
- You will get immediate feedback to determine if you have done the exercises correctly.
- This product will not only save you time on your homework but will help you learn the concepts.

Spreadsheet Applications Software
CORPORATE FINANCIAL 0-324-05464-5
MANAGERIAL 0-324-05465-3
- You will learn how Excel is used in accounting situations.

Study Guide
CORPORATE FINANCIAL 0-324-05460-2
MANAGERIAL 0-324-05461-0
- This guide will give you quiz and test hints.
- You can practice the concepts you learn through numerous multiple choice, fill-in-the-blank, true-false questions, and exercises, all with solutions.

Working Papers
CORPORATE FINANCIAL 0-324-05456-4
MANAGERIAL 0-324-05457-2
- This supplement contains forms that help you organize your solutions.

Working Papers Plus
CORPORATE FINANCIAL 0-324-05458-0
MANAGERIAL 0-324-05459-9
- This special edition of Working Papers integrates the Working Papers forms with exercises and selected problems from the text.

INTACCT
(Internet Accounting Tutor)
FINANCIAL 0-324-01592-5
MANAGERIAL 0-324-01613-1
rama.swcollege.com

- This product, designed to be used with any introductory accounting textbook, will give you reinforcement of key accounting concepts in an interactive format.
- You can see how to apply the concepts with practice problems and demonstration problems.
- You can email your INTACCT homework problems to your instructor to grade.

Save on these products by purchasing online at

http://warren.swcollege.com

EXERCISES

Exercise 1–1

Professional ethics

Objective 3

A fertilizer manufacturing company wants to relocate to Collier County. A 13-year-old report from a fired researcher at the company says the company's product is releasing toxic by-products. The company has suppressed that report. A second report commissioned by the company shows there is no problem with the fertilizer.

➤ Should the company's chief executive officer reveal the context of the unfavorable report in discussions with Collier County representatives? Discuss.

Source: "Business Leaders Ponder Ethical Questions," *Naples Daily News,* May 12, 1991, p. 1E.

Exercise 1–2

Business entity concept

Objective 5

Bag-One Sports sells hunting and fishing equipment and provides guided hunting and fishing trips. Bag-One Sports is owned and operated by Marc Trailer, a well-known sports enthusiast and hunter. Marc's wife, Robin, owns and operates Red Bird Boutique, a women's clothing store. Marc and Robin have established a trust fund to finance their children's college education. The trust fund is maintained by First Wyoming Bank in the name of the children, Sparrow and Trout.

For each of the following transactions, identify which of the entities listed should record the transaction in its records.

Entities

B   Bag-One Sports
F   First Wyoming Bank
R   Red Bird Boutique
X   None of the above

1. Marc received a cash advance from customers for a guided hunting trip.
2. Robin deposited a $5,000 personal check in the trust fund at First Wyoming Bank.
3. Robin purchased three dozen spring dresses from a Denver designer for a special spring sale.
4. Marc paid a local doctor for his annual physical, which was required by the workmen's compensation insurance policy carried by Bag-One Sports.
5. Marc paid for an advertisement in a hunters' magazine.
6. Robin purchased mutual fund shares as an investment for the children's trust.
7. Marc paid for dinner and a movie to celebrate their tenth wedding anniversary.
8. Robin donated several dresses from inventory for a local charity auction for the benefit of a women's abuse shelter.
9. Marc paid a breeder's fee for an English springer spaniel to be used as a hunting guide dog.
10. Robin paid her dues to the Optimist Club.

Exercise 1–3

Accounting equation

Objective 6

The total assets and total liabilities of **Coca-Cola** and **PepsiCo** at the end of their 1999 fiscal years are shown below.

	Coca-Cola (in millions)	PepsiCo (in millions)
Assets	$21,623	$17,551
Liabilities	12,110	10,670

Determine the stockholders' equity of each company.

Exercise 1–4

Accounting equation

Objective 6

✓ a. $51,500

Determine the missing amount for each of the following:

	Assets	=	Liabilities	+	Owner's Equity
a.	X	=	$20,000	+	$31,500
b.	$62,750	=	X	+	10,000
c.	57,000	=	38,000	+	X

Exercise 1–5
Accounting equation

Objectives 6, 8

✓ b. $230,000

Jason Seagle is the sole stockholder and operator of Go-For-It, a motivational consulting business. At the end of its accounting period, December 31, 2002, Go-For-It has assets of $325,000 and liabilities of $142,000. Using the accounting equation and considering each case independently, determine the following amounts:

a. Owner's equity, as of December 31, 2002.
b. Owner's equity, as of December 31, 2003, assuming that assets increased by $84,000 and liabilities increased by $37,000 during 2003.
c. Owner's equity, as of December 31, 2003, assuming that assets decreased by $8,000 and liabilities increased by $17,000 during 2003.
d. Owner's equity, as of December 31, 2003, assuming that assets increased by $75,000 and liabilities decreased by $17,500 during 2003.
e. Net income (or net loss) during 2003, assuming that as of December 31, 2003, assets were $425,000, liabilities were $105,000, and there were no additional investments or dividends.

Exercise 1–6
Asset, liability, owner's equity items

Objective 7

Indicate whether each of the following is identified with (1) an asset, (2) a liability, or (3) owner's equity:

a. fees earned
b. supplies
c. wages expense
d. land
e. accounts payable
f. cash

Exercise 1–7
Effect of transactions on accounting equation

Objective 7

Describe how the following business transactions affect the three elements of the accounting equation.

a. Issued capital stock for cash.
b. Received cash for services performed.
c. Purchased supplies for cash.
d. Paid for utilities used in the business.
e. Purchased supplies on account.

Exercise 1–8
Effect of transactions on accounting equation

Objective 7

✓ (a)(1) increase $50,000

a. A vacant lot acquired for $65,000 is sold for $115,000 in cash. What is the effect of the sale on the total amount of the seller's (1) assets, (2) liabilities, and (3) owner's equity?
b. Assume that the seller owes $28,000 on a loan for the land. After receiving the $115,000 cash in (a), the seller pays the $28,000 owed. What is the effect of the payment on the total amount of the seller's (1) assets, (2) liabilities, and (3) owner's equity?

Exercise 1–9
Effect of transactions on owner's equity

Objective 7

Indicate whether each of the following types of transactions will (a) increase owner's equity or (b) decrease owner's equity:

1. owner's investments
2. revenues
3. expenses
4. cash dividends

Exercise 1–10
Transactions

Objective 7

The following selected transactions were completed by Next Day Delivery Service during October:

1. Received cash for providing delivery services, $12,150.
2. Paid creditors on account, $2,500.
3. Received cash for capital stock, $75,000.
4. Paid advertising expense, $625.
5. Billed customers for delivery services on account, $6,900.
6. Purchased supplies for cash, $750.
7. Paid rent for October, $2,500.

8. Received cash from customers on account, $3,180.
9. Determined that the cost of supplies on hand was $180; therefore, $570 of supplies had been used during the month.
10. Paid cash dividends, $2,500.

Indicate the effect of each transaction on the accounting equation by listing the numbers identifying the transactions, (1) through (10), in a vertical column, and inserting at the right of each number the appropriate letter from the following list:

a. Increase in an asset, decrease in another asset.
b. Increase in an asset, increase in a liability.
c. Increase in an asset, increase in owner's equity.
d. Decrease in an asset, decrease in a liability.
e. Decrease in an asset, decrease in owner's equity.

Exercise 1–11

Nature of transactions

Objective 7

✓ d. $2,950

Joe Black operates his own catering service. Summary financial data for July are presented in equation form as follows. Each line designated by a number indicates the effect of a transaction on the equation. Each increase and decrease in owner's equity, except transaction (5), affects net income.

	Cash	+	Supplies	+	Land	=	Liabilities	+	Capital Stock	+	Retained Earnings
Bal.	6,000		750		30,000		7,500		5,000		24,250
1.	+15,000										+15,000
2.	− 2,000				+ 2,000						
3.	−11,250										−11,250
4.			+500				+ 500				
5.	− 1,500										− 1,500
6.	− 5,300						−5,300				
7.			−800								− 800
Bal.	950		450		32,000		2,700		5,000		25,700

a. Describe each transaction.
b. What is the amount of net decrease in cash during the month?
c. What is the amount of net increase in retained earnings during the month?
d. What is the amount of the net income for the month?
e. How much of the net income for the month was retained in the business?

Exercise 1–12

Net income and dividends

Objective 8

The income statement of a corporation for the month of January indicates a net income of $52,750. During the same period, $60,000 in cash dividends were paid.
    Would it be correct to say that the business incurred a net loss of $7,250 during the month? Discuss.

Exercise 1–13

Net income and owner's equity for four businesses

Objective 8

✓ Company Y: Net loss, ($25,000)

Four different corporations—W, X, Y, and Z—show the same balance sheet data at the beginning and end of a year. These data, exclusive of the amount of owner's equity, are summarized as follows:

	Total Assets	Total Liabilities
Beginning of the year	$375,000	$150,000
End of the year	$600,000	$325,000

On the basis of the above data and the following additional information for the year, determine the net income (or loss) of each company for the year. (*Hint:* First determine the amount of increase or decrease in owner's equity during the year.)

Company W: No additional capital stock was issued and no dividends were paid.

Company X: No additional capital stock was issued, but dividends of $30,000 were paid.
Company Y: Capital stock of $75,000 was issued, but no dividends were paid.
Company Z: Capital stock of $75,000 was issued, and dividends of $30,000 were paid.

Exercise 1–14
Balance sheet items
Objective 8

From the following list of selected items taken from the records of Kagy Appliance Service as of a specific date, identify those that would appear on the balance sheet:

1. Utilities Expense
2. Fees Earned
3. Supplies
4. Wages Expense
5. Accounts Payable
6. Cash
7. Supplies Expense
8. Land
9. Capital Stock
10. Wages Payable

Exercise 1–15
Income statement items
Objective 8

Based on the data presented in Exercise 1–14, identify those items that would appear on the income statement.

Exercise 1–16
Retained earnings statement
Objective 8

✓ Retained earnings June 30, 2003: $393,750

Financial information related to Douma Company for the month ended June 30, 2003, is as follows:

Net income for June	$ 91,250
Dividends during June	15,000
Retained earnings, June 1, 2003	317,500

Prepare a retained earnings statement for the month ended June 30, 2003.

Exercise 1–17
Income statement
Objective 8

✓ Net income: $63,800

Surgery Services was organized on April 1, 2003. A summary of the revenue and expense transactions for April follows:

Fees earned	$165,800
Wages expense	71,500
Miscellaneous expense	2,250
Rent expense	25,000
Supplies expense	3,250

Prepare an income statement for the month ended April 30.

Exercise 1–18
Missing amounts from balance sheet and income statement data
Objective 8

✓ (a) $130,250

One item is omitted in each of the following summaries of balance sheet and income statement data for four different corporations: I, II, III, and IV.

	I	II	III	IV
Beginning of the year:				
Assets	$600,000	$125,000	$100,000	(d)
Liabilities	360,000	65,000	76,000	$150,000
End of the year:				
Assets	745,000	175,000	90,000	310,000
Liabilities	325,000	55,000	80,000	170,000
During the year:				
Additional issue of capital stock	(a)	25,000	10,000	50,000
Dividends	40,000	8,000	(c)	75,000
Revenue	197,750	(b)	115,000	140,000
Expenses	108,000	32,000	122,500	160,000

Determine the missing amounts, identifying them by letter. (*Hint:* First determine the amount of increase or decrease in owner's equity during the year.)

Exercise 1–19
Balance sheets, net income

Objective 8

✓ b. $11,330

Financial information related to Revival Interiors for August and September of the current year is as follows:

	August 31, 20—	September 30, 20—
Accounts payable	$ 3,850	$ 4,150
Accounts receivable	8,500	9,780
Capital stock	10,000	10,000
Retained earnings	?	?
Cash	15,000	25,500
Supplies	750	600

a. Prepare balance sheets for Revival Interiors as of August 31 and as of September 30 of the current year.
b. Determine the amount of net income for September, assuming that no additional capital stock was issued and no dividends were paid.
c. Determine the amount of net income for September, assuming that no additional capital stock was issued but dividends of $7,500 were paid.

Exercise 1–20
Financial statements

Objective 8

Each of the following items is shown in the financial statements of **Exxon Mobil Corporation**. Identify the financial statement (balance sheet or income statement) in which each item would appear.

a. Operating expenses
b. Crude oil inventory
c. Income taxes payable
d. Sales
e. Investments
f. Marketable securities
g. Exploration expenses
h. Notes and loans payable

i. Cash equivalents
j. Long-term debt
k. Selling expenses
l. Notes receivable
m. Equipment
n. Accounts payable
o. Prepaid taxes

Exercise 1–21
Statement of cash flows

Objective 8

Indicate whether each of the following activities would be reported on the statement of cash flows as (a) an operating activity, (b) an investing activity, or (c) a financing activity:

1. Cash received as investment from stockholders
2. Cash paid for land
3. Cash received from fees earned
4. Cash paid for expenses

Exercise 1–22
Financial statements

Objective 8

✓ Correct Amount of Total Assets is $13,875

Aspen Realty, organized February 1, 2003, is owned and operated by Lynn Soby. How many errors can you find in the following financial statements for Aspen Realty, prepared after its second month of operations?

Aspen Realty
Income Statement
March 31, 2003

Sales commissions		$37,100
Operating expenses:		
Office salaries expense	$23,150	
Rent expense	7,800	
Automobile expense	1,750	
Miscellaneous expense	550	
Supplies expense	225	
Total operating expenses		33,475
Net income		$13,625

Lynn Soby
Retained Earnings Statement
March 31, 2002

Retained earnings, March 1, 2003	$ 2,450
Less dividends during March	1,000
	$ 1,450
Net income for the month	13,625
Retained earnings, March 31, 2003	$15,075

Balance Sheet
For the Month Ended March 31, 2003

Assets		Liabilities	
Cash	$2,350	Accounts receivable	$10,200
Accounts payable	2,300	Supplies	1,325
		Stockholders' Equity	
		Capital stock . . . . $ 6,500	
		Retained earnings 15,075	21,575
Total assets	$4,650	Total liabilities and stockholders' equity	$33,100

Exercise 1–23
Ratio of liabilities to stockholders' equity

Objective 9

The financial statements for **Cisco Systems, Inc.**, are presented in Appendix G at the end of the text.

Cisco Systems is the worldwide leader in networking for the Internet. Cisco Systems provides both hardware and software to enable its customers to create Internet solutions that provide seamless access to information. You can learn more about Cisco Systems by visiting its web site at **www.cisco.com**.

a. Determine the ratio of liabilities to stockholders' equity for Cisco Systems at the end of 2000 and 1999. Use only current liabilities in the numerator.
b. What conclusions regarding the margin of protection to the creditors can you draw from your analysis?

PROBLEMS SERIES A

Problem 1–1A
Transactions

Objective 7

✓ Cash Bal. at End of Feb.: $7,070

On February 1 of the current year, Linda Neece established a business to manage rental property. She completed the following transactions during February:

a. Opened a business bank account with a deposit of $10,000 in exchange for capital stock.
b. Purchased supplies (pens, file folders, and copy paper) on account, $1,150.
c. Received cash from fees earned for managing rental property, $4,500.
d. Paid rent on office and equipment for the month, $2,500.
e. Paid creditors on account, $675.
f. Billed customers for fees earned for managing rental property, $3,250.
g. Paid automobile expenses (including rental charges) for month, $980, and miscellaneous expenses, $775.
h. Paid office salaries, $1,500.
i. Determined that the cost of supplies on hand was $215; therefore, the cost of supplies used was $935.
j. Paid dividends, $1,000.

Instructions

1. Indicate the effect of each transaction and the balances after each transaction, using the following tabular headings:

Assets			=	Liabilities	+		Owner's Equity
Cash + Accounts Receivable + Supplies = Accounts Payable + Capital Stock + Retained Earnings							

Explain the nature of each increase and decrease in owner's equity by an appropriate notation at the right of the amount.

2. ▬▬► Briefly explain why the stockholders' investments and revenues increased owner's equity, while dividends and expenses decreased owner's equity.

Problem 1–2A

Financial statements

Objective 8

✓ 1. Net income: $40,865

Following are the amounts of the assets and liabilities of Fly Away Travel Agency at December 31, 2003, the end of the current year, and its revenue and expenses for the year. The retained earnings were $4,500 and the capital stock was $10,000 on January 1, 2003, the beginning of the current year. During the current year, dividends of $30,000 were paid.

Accounts payable	$ 3,200
Accounts receivable	19,500
Cash	7,200
Fees earned	117,480
Miscellaneous expense	1,750
Rent expense	27,000
Supplies	1,865
Supplies expense	2,125
Utilities expense	10,240
Wages expense	35,500

Instructions

1. Prepare an income statement for the current year ended December 31, 2003.
2. Prepare a retained earnings statement for the current year ended December 31, 2003.
3. Prepare a balance sheet as of December 31, 2003.

Problem 1–3A

Financial statements

Objective 8

✓ 1. Net income: $5,950

Loren Thurlow established Eagle Financial Services on January 1, 2003. Eagle Financial Services offers financial planning advice to its clients. The effect of each transaction and the balances after each transaction for January are as follows:

	Assets			=	Liabilities	+		Owner's Equity	
	Cash	+ Accounts Receivable	+ Supplies	=	Accounts Payable	+	Capital Stock	+ Retained Earnings	
a.	+12,500						+12,500		Investment
b.			+1,325		+1,325				
Bal.	12,500		1,325		1,325		12,500		
c.	− 900				− 900				
Bal.	11,600		1,325		425		12,500		
d.	+ 8,750							+8,750	Fees earned
Bal.	20,350		1,325		425		12,500	8,750	
e.	− 2,500							−2,500	Rent expense
Bal.	17,850		1,325		425		12,500	6,250	
f.	− 1,600							−1,250	Auto expense
								− 350	Misc. expense
Bal.	16,250		1,325		425		12,500	4,650	
g.	− 2,000							−2,000	Salaries expense
Bal.	14,250		1,325		425		12,500	2,650	
h.			−1,050					−1,050	Supplies expense
Bal.	14,250		275		425		12,500	1,600	
i.		+4,350						+4,350	Fees earned
Bal.	14,250	4,350	275		425		12,500	5,950	
j.	− 3,000							−3,000	Dividends
Bal.	11,250	4,350	275		425		12,500	2,950	

Instructions

1. Prepare an income statement for the month ended January 31, 2003.
2. Prepare a retained earnings statement for the month ended January 31, 2003.
3. Prepare a balance sheet as of January 31, 2003.

Problem 1–4A
Transactions; financial statements
Objectives 7, 8

✓ 2. Net income: $7,050

On March 1 of the current year, Dori French established Deal Realty. French completed the following transactions during the month of March:

a. Opened a business bank account with a deposit of $5,000 in exchange for capital stock.
b. Purchased supplies (pens, file folders, fax paper, etc.) on account, $1,250.
c. Paid creditor on account, $850.
d. Earned sales commissions, receiving cash, $16,200.
e. Paid rent on office and equipment for the month, $2,000.
f. Paid dividends, $4,500.
g. Paid automobile expenses (including rental charge) for month, $1,900, and miscellaneous expenses, $350.
h. Paid office salaries, $4,250.
i. Determined that the cost of supplies on hand was $600; therefore, the cost of supplies used was $650.

Instructions

1. Indicate the effect of each transaction and the balances after each transaction, using the following tabular headings:

Assets	=	Liabilities	+	Owner's Equity	
Cash + Supplies	=	Accounts Payable	+	Capital Stock + Retained Earnings	

   Explain the nature of each increase and decrease in owner's equity by an appropriate notation at the right of the amount.
2. Prepare an income statement for March, a retained earnings statement for March, and a balance sheet as of March 31.

Problem 1–5A
Transactions; financial statements
Objectives 7, 8

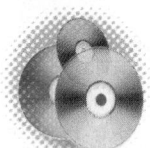

GENERAL LEDGER

✓ 3. Net income: $9,250

Persnickety Cleaners is owned and operated by Bea Cheever. A building and equipment are currently being rented, pending expansion to new facilities. The actual work of dry cleaning is done by another company at wholesale rates. The assets, liabilities, and capital stock of the business on July 1 of the current year are as follows: Cash, $6,250; Accounts Receivable, $18,100; Supplies, $2,200; Land, $40,000; Accounts Payable, $7,800; Capital Stock, $10,000. Business transactions during July are summarized as follows:

a. Received cash from cash customers for dry cleaning sales, $15,750.
b. Paid rent for the month, $2,500.
c. Purchased supplies on account, $1,650.
d. Paid creditors on account, $5,100.
e. Charged customers for dry cleaning sales on account, $8,920.
f. Received monthly invoice for dry cleaning expense for July (to be paid on August 10), $6,000.
g. Paid the following: wages expense, $2,400; truck expense, $1,580; utilities expense, $960; miscellaneous expense, $630.
h. Received cash from customers on account, $12,100.
i. Determined that the cost of supplies on hand was $2,500; therefore, the cost of supplies used during the month was $1,350.
j. Paid dividends, $7,500.

Instructions

1. Determine the amount of retained earnings as of July 1 of the current year.
2. State the assets, liabilities, and owner's equity as of July 1 in equation form similar to that shown in this chapter. In tabular form below the equation, indicate increases and decreases resulting from each transaction and the new balances after each transaction. Explain the nature of each increase and decrease in owner's equity by an appropriate notation at the right of the amount.
3. Prepare an income statement for July, a retained earnings statement for July, and a balance sheet as of July 31.

Problem 1–6A

Missing amount from financial statements

Objective 8

✓ i. $15,000

The financial statements at the end of Magic Realty's first month of operations are shown below.

Magic Realty
Income Statement
For the Month Ended April 30, 2003

Fees earned		$	(a)
Operating expenses:			
Wages expense	$4 2 5 0 00		
Rent expense	1 6 0 0 00		
Supplies expense	(b)		
Utilities expense	9 0 0 00		
Miscellaneous expense	5 5 0 00		
Total operating expenses		8 8 0 0 00	
Net income		$6 2 0 0 00	

Magic Realty
Retained Earnings Statement
For the Month Ended April 30, 2003

Net income for April		(c)
Less dividends	3 0 0 0 00	
Retained earnings, April 30, 2003		(d)

Magic Realty
Balance Sheet
April 30, 2003

Assets		Liabilities		
Cash	$ 2 9 0 0 00	Accounts payable	$ 8 0 0 00	
Supplies	1 1 0 0 00	**Stockholders' Equity**		
Land	20 0 0 0 00	Capital stock $20,000		
		Retained earnings (f)	$	(g)
		Total liabilities and		
Total assets	(e)	stockholders' equity		(h)

Magic Realty
Statement of Cash Flows
For the Month Ended April 30, 2003

Cash flows from operating activities:				
Cash received from customers	$	(i)		
Deduct cash payments for expenses and				
payments to creditors	9 1 0 0 00			
Net cash flow from operating activities			$	(j)
Cash flows from investing activities:				
Cash payments for acquisition of land				(k)
Cash flows from financing activities:				
Cash received from issuing capital stock		(l)		
Deduct dividends		(m)		
Net cash flow from financing activities				(n)
Net cash flow and April 30, 2003 cash balance				(o)

Instructions

By analyzing the interrelationships among the four financial statements, determine the proper amounts for (a) through (o).

PROBLEMS SERIES B

Problem 1–1B

Transactions

Objective 7

✓ Cash Bal. at End of March:
$14,695

Fran Cowles established an insurance agency on March 1 of the current year and completed the following transactions during March:

a. Opened a business bank account with a deposit of $15,000 in exchange for capital stock.
b. Purchased supplies on account, $750.
c. Paid creditors on account, $625.
d. Received cash from fees earned on insurance commissions, $5,250.
e. Paid rent on office and equipment for the month, $1,000.
f. Paid automobile expenses for month, $880, and miscellaneous expenses, $350.
g. Paid office salaries, $1,200.
h. Determined that the cost of supplies on hand was $175; therefore, the cost of supplies used was $575.
i. Billed insurance companies for sales commissions earned, $7,350.
j. Paid dividends, $1,500.

Instructions

1. Indicate the effect of each transaction and the balances after each transaction, using the following tabular headings:

Assets	=	Liabilities	+	Owner's Equity

Cash + Accounts Receivable + Supplies = Accounts Payable + Capital Stock + Retained Earnings

   Explain the nature of each increase and decrease in owner's equity by an appropriate notation at the right of the amount.
2. ➤ Briefly explain why the stockholders' investments and revenues increased owner's equity, while dividends and expenses decreased owner's equity.

Problem 1–2B

Financial statements

Objective 8

✓ 1. Net income: $27,775

Below are the amounts of the assets and liabilities of Hiawatha Travel Service at April 30, 2003, the end of the current year, and its revenue and expenses for the year. The retained earnings were $13,000 and the capital stock was $12,000 at May 1, 2002, the beginning of the current year. During the current year, dividends of $15,000 were paid.

Accounts payable	$ 6,100
Accounts receivable	15,675
Cash	26,525
Fees earned	131,600
Miscellaneous expense	1,475
Rent expense	18,900
Supplies	1,675
Supplies expense	3,550
Taxes expense	2,800
Utilities expense	11,250
Wages expense	65,850

Instructions

1. Prepare an income statement for the current year ended April 30, 2003.
2. Prepare a retained earnings statement for the current year ended April 30, 2003.
3. Prepare a balance sheet as of April 30, 2003.

Problem 1–3B
Financial statements

Objective 8

✓ 1. Net income: $2,970

Chester Hoche established Infinet Computer Services on October 1, 2003. The effect of each transaction and the balances after each transaction for October are as follows:

		Assets			=	Liabilities +	Owner's Equity		
	Cash	+ Accounts Receivable	+ Supplies	=		Accounts Payable	+ Capital Stock	+ Retained Earnings	
a.	+5,000						+5,000		Investment
b.			+720			+720			
Bal.	5,000		720			720	5,000		
c.	+4,500							+4,500	Fees earned
Bal.	9,500		720			720	5,000	4,500	
d.	−1,800							−1,800	Rent expense
Bal.	7,700		720			720	5,000	2,700	
e.	− 250					−250			
Bal.	7,450		720			470	5,000	2,700	
f.		+3,750						+3,750	Fees earned
Bal.	7,450	3,750	720			470	5,000	6,450	
g.	−1,155							− 780	Auto expense
								− 375	Misc. expense
Bal.	6,295	3,750	720			470	5,000	5,295	
h.	−2,000							−2,000	Salaries expense
Bal.	4,295	3,750	720			470	5,000	3,295	
i.			−325					− 325	Supplies expense
Bal.	4,295	3,750	395			470	5,000	2,970	
j.	−1,000							−1,000	Dividends
Bal.	3,295	3,750	395			470	5,000	1,970	

Instructions

1. Prepare an income statement for the month ended October 31, 2003.
2. Prepare a retained earnings statement for the month ended October 31, 2003.
3. Prepare a balance sheet as of Ocotber 31, 2003.

Problem 1–4B
Transactions; financial statements

Objectives 7, 8

✓ 2. Net income: $8,975

On August 1, 2003, of the current year, Angie Tate established Vogue Realty. Tate completed the following transactions during the month of August:

a. Opened a business bank account with a deposit of $10,000 in exchange for capital stock.
b. Paid rent on office and equipment for the month, $3,600.
c. Paid automobile expenses (including rental charge) for month, $900, and miscellaneous expenses, $550.
d. Purchased supplies (pens, file folders, and copy paper) on account, $1,325.
e. Earned sales commissions, receiving cash, $18,750.
f. Paid creditor on account, $690.
g. Paid office salaries, $4,000.
h. Paid dividends, $3,000.
i. Determined that the cost of supplies on hand was $600; therefore, the cost of supplies used was $725.

Instructions

1. Indicate the effect of each transaction and the balances after each transaction, using the following tabular headings:

Assets	=	Liabilities	+	Owner's Equity	
Cash + Supplies	=	Accounts Payable	+	Capital Stock + Retained Earnings	

(continued)

Explain the nature of each increase and decrease in owner's equity by an appropriate notation at the right of the amount.

2. Prepare an income statement for August, a retained earnings statement for August, and a balance sheet as of August 31.

Problem 1–5B
Transactions; financial statements

Objectives 7, 8

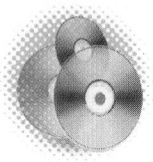
GENERAL LEDGER

✓ 3. Net income: $8,075

Swan Dry Cleaners is owned and operated by Merritt Paisley. A building and equipment are currently being rented, pending expansion to new facilities. The actual work of dry cleaning is done by another company at wholesale rates. The assets, liabilities, and capital stock of the business on November 1 of the current year are as follows: Cash, $7,400; Accounts Receivable, $13,750; Supplies, $1,560; Land, $25,000; Accounts Payable, $3,880; Capital Stock, $25,000. Business transactions during November are summarized as follows:

a. Paid rent for the month, $3,000.
b. Charged customers for dry cleaning sales on account, $6,150.
c. Paid creditors on account, $1,680.
d. Purchased supplies on account, $840.
e. Received cash from cash customers for dry cleaning sales, $14,600.
f. Received cash from customers on account, $11,750.
g. Received monthly invoice for dry cleaning expense for November (to be paid on December 10), $5,400.
h. Paid the following: wages expense, $1,800; truck expense, $725; utilities expense, $510; miscellaneous expense, $190.
i. Determined that the cost of supplies on hand was $1,350; therefore, the cost of supplies used during the month was $1,050.
j. Paid dividends, $5,000.

Instructions

1. Determine the amount of retained earnings as of November 1 of the current year.
2. State the assets, liabilities, and owner's equity as of November 1 in equation form similar to that shown in this chapter. In tabular form below the equation, indicate increases and decreases resulting from each transaction and the new balances after each transaction. Explain the nature of each increase and decrease in owner's equity by an appropriate notation at the right of the amount.
3. Prepare an income statement for November, a retained earnings statement for November, and a balance sheet as of November 30.

Problem 1–6B
Missing amount from financial statements

Objective 8

✓ j. $50,550

The financial statements at the end of Ruby River Realty's first month of operations are shown below.

Instructions

By analyzing the interrelationships among the four financial statements, determine the proper amounts for (a) through (o).

Ruby River Realty **Income Statement** **For the Month Ended June 30, 2003**		
Fees earned		$23 5 0 0 00
Operating expenses:		
Wages expense	$ (a)	
Rent expense	2 4 0 0 00	
Supplies expense	2 0 0 0 00	
Utilities expense	1 3 5 0 00	
Miscellaneous expense	8 2 5 00	
Total operating expenses		11 9 5 0 00
Net income		(b)

Ruby River Realty
Retained Earnings Statement
For the Month Ended June 30, 2003

Net income for June		(c)		
Less dividends		(d)		
Retained earnings, June 30, 2003				(e)

Ruby River Realty
Balance Sheet
June 30, 2003

Assets		Liabilities	
Cash	$14 7 5 0 00	Accounts payable	$ 1 2 0 0 00
Supplies	1 0 0 0 00	**Stockholders' Equity**	
Land	(f)	Capital stock $ (h)	
		Retained earnings (i)	(j)
		Total liabilities and	
Total assets	(g)	stockholders' equity	(k)

Ruby River Realty
Statement of Cash Flows
For the Month Ended June 30, 2003

Cash flows from operating activities:			
Cash received from customers	$	(l)	
Deduct cash payments for expenses and			
payments to creditors	$11 7 5 0 00		
Net cash flow from operating activities		$	(m)
Cash flows from investing activities:			
Cash payments for acquisition of land		(36 0 0 0 00)	
Cash flows from financing activities:			
Cash received from issuing capital stock	$45 0 0 0 00		
Deduct dividends	6 0 0 0 00		
Net cash flow from financing activities			(n)
Net cash flow and June 30, 2003 cash balance			(o)

CONTINUING PROBLEM

GENERAL
LEDGER

✓ 2. Net income: $265

Lynn Kwan enjoys listening to all types of music and owns countless CDs and tapes. Over the years, Lynn has gained a local reputation for knowledge of music from classical to rap and the ability to put together sets of recordings that appeal to all ages.

During the last several months, Lynn served as a guest disc jockey on a local radio station. In addition, Lynn has entertained at several friends' parties as the host deejay.

On November 1, 2002, Lynn established a corporation known as Dancin Music. Using an extensive collection of CDs and tapes, Lynn will serve as a disc jockey on a fee basis for weddings, college parties, and other events. During November, Lynn entered into the following transactions:

Nov. 1. Deposited $3,500 in a checking account in the name of Dancin Music in exchange for capital stock.

Nov. 2. Received $1,000 from a local radio station for serving as the guest disc jockey for November.

　2. Agreed to share office space with a local real estate agency, Golino Realty. Dancin Music will pay one-fourth of the rent. In addition, Dancin Music agreed to pay a portion of the salary of the receptionist and to pay one-fourth of the utilities. Paid $500 for the rent of the office.

　4. Purchased supplies (blank cassette tapes, poster board, extension cords, etc.) from Bruce Office Supply Co. for $175. Agreed to pay $50 within 10 days and the remainder by December 3, 2002.

　6. Paid $300 to a local radio station to advertise the services of Dancin Music twice daily for two weeks.

　8. Paid $325 to a local electronics store for rent on two CD players, two cassette players, and eight speakers.

　12. Paid $100 (music expense) to Dynamic Music for the use of its current demo CDs and tapes to make cassette tapes of various music sets.

　13. Paid Bruce Office Supply Co. $50 on account.

　16. Received $75 from a dentist for providing two music sets for the dentist to play for her patients.

　22. Served as disc jockey for a wedding party. The father of the bride agreed to pay $600 the 1st of December.

　25. Received $250 from a friend for serving as the disc jockey for a cancer charity ball hosted by the local hospital.

　29. Paid $120 (music expense) to Score Music for the use of its library of demo CDs and tapes.

　30. Received $450 for serving as disc jockey for a local club's monthly dance.

　30. Paid Golino Realty $200 for Dancin Music's share of the receptionist's salary for November.

　30. Paid Golino Realty $150 for Dancin Music's share of the utilities for November.

　30. Determined that the cost of supplies on hand is $85. Therefore, the cost of supplies used during the month was $90.

　30. Paid for miscellaneous expenses, $75.

　30. Paid $250 royalties (music expense) to Federated Clearing for use of various artists' music during the month.

　30. Paid dividends, $125.

Instructions

1. Indicate the effect of each transaction and the balances after each transaction, using the following tabular headings:

Assets	=	Liabilities	+	Owner's Equity

Cash + Accounts Receivable + Supplies = Accounts Payable + Capital Stock + Retained Earnings

Explain the nature of each increase and decrease in owner's equity by an appropriate notation at the right of the amount.

2. Prepare an income statement for Dancin Music for the month ended November 30, 2002.

3. Prepare a retained earnings statement for Dancin Music for the month ended November 30, 2002.

4. Prepare a balance sheet for Dancin Music as of November 30, 2002.

SPECIAL ACTIVITIES

Activity 1–1
Phinney Enterprises
Ethics and professional conduct in business

Joel Phinney, president of Phinney Enterprises, applied for a $150,000 loan from Bridger National Bank. The bank requested financial statements from Phinney Enterprises as a basis for granting the loan. Joel has told his accountant to provide the bank with a balance sheet. Joel has decided to omit the other financial statements because there was a net loss during the past year.

In groups of three or four, discuss the following questions:

1. Is Joel behaving in a professional manner by omitting some of the financial statements?
2. a. What types of information about their businesses would managers be willing to provide bankers? What types of information would managers not be willing to provide?
   b. What types of information about a business would bankers want before extending a loan?
   c. What common interests are shared by bankers and business managers?

Activity 1–2
Expert Opinion
Net income

On January 3, 2002, Dr. Brittany North established Expert Opinion, a medical practice organized as a professional corporation. The following conversation occurred next August between Dr. North and a former medical school classmate, Dr. Charles Ryder, at an American Medical Association convention in Bermuda.

Dr. Ryder: Brittany, good to see you again. Why didn't you call when you were in Las Vegas? We could have had dinner together.

Dr. North: Actually, I never made it to Las Vegas this year. My husband and kids went up to our Lake Tahoe condo twice, but I got stuck in New York. I opened a new consulting practice this January and haven't had any time for myself since.

Dr. Ryder: I heard about it . . . Expert . . . something . . . right?

Dr. North: Yes, Expert Opinion. My husband chose the name.

Dr. Ryder: I've thought about doing something like that. Are you making any money? I mean, is it worth your time?

Dr. North: You wouldn't believe it. I started by opening a bank account with $30,000, and my July bank statement has a balance of $180,000. Not bad for seven months—all pure profit.

Dr. Ryder: Maybe I'll try it in Las Vegas. Let's have breakfast together tomorrow and you can fill me in on the details.

Comment on Dr. North's statement that the difference between the opening bank balance ($30,000) and the July statement balance ($180,000) is pure profit.

Activity 1–3
Forty-Love
Transactions and financial statements

Yvonne Tobin, a junior in college, has been seeking ways to earn extra spending money. As an active sports enthusiast, Yvonne plays tennis regularly at the Racquet Club, where her family has a membership. The president of the club recently approached Yvonne with the proposal that she manage the club's tennis courts on weekends. Yvonne's primary duty would be to supervise the operation of the club's four indoor and six outdoor courts, including court reservations.

In return for her services, the club would pay Yvonne $75 per weekend, plus Yvonne could keep whatever she earned from lessons and the fees from the use of the ball machine. The club and Yvonne agreed to a one-month trial, after which both would consider an arrangement for the remaining two years of Yvonne's college career. On this basis, Yvonne organized Forty-Love. During September, Yvonne managed the tennis courts and entered into the following transactions:

a. Opened a business account by depositing $500.
b. Paid $160 for tennis supplies (practice tennis balls, etc.).
c. Paid $80 for the rental of videotape equipment to be used in offering lessons during September.
d. Arranged for the rental of two ball machines during September for $100. Paid $70 in advance, with the remaining $30 due October 1.
e. Received $800 for lessons given during September.
f. Received $150 in fees from the use of the ball machines during September.
g. Paid $300 for salaries of part-time employees who answered the telephone and took reservations while Yvonne was giving lessons.
h. Paid $75 for miscellaneous expenses.
i. Received $300 from the club for managing the tennis courts during September.
j. Determined that the cost of supplies on hand at the end of the month totaled $75; therefore, the cost of supplies used was $85.
k. Withdrew $400 for personal use on September 30.

As a friend and accounting student, you have been asked by Yvonne to aid her in assessing the venture.

1. Small businesses such as Forty-Love are often organized as proprietorships. The accounting for proprietorships is similar to that for a corporation, except for owner's equity. Instead of Capital Stock and Retained Earnings, an item entitled Yvonne Tobin, Capital, is used to indicate owner's equity in the accounting equation. Withdrawals for personal use are handled similarly to dividends. Indicate the effect of each transaction, using the following tabular headings:

Assets	=	Liabilities	+	Owner's Equity
Cash + Supplies	=	Accounts Payable	+	Yvonne Tobin, Capital

Explain the nature of each increase and decrease in owner's equity by an appropriate notation at the right of the amount.

2. Prepare an income statement for September.

3. a. Assume that Yvonne Tobin could earn $7 per hour working 20 hours each of the four weekends as a waitress. Evaluate which of the two alternatives, working as a waitress or operating Forty-Love, would provide Yvonne with the most income per month.

   b. Discuss any other factors that you believe Yvonne should consider before discussing a long-term arrangement with the Racquet Club.

Activity 1–4
Into the Real World
Certification requirements for accountants

By satisfying certain specific requirements, accountants may become certified as public accountants (CPAs), management accountants (CMAs), or internal auditors (CIAs). Find the certification requirements for one of these accounting groups by accessing the appropriate Internet site listed below.

Site	Description
www.ais-cpa.com	This site lists the address and/or Internet link for each state's board of accountancy. Find your state's requirements.
www.imanet.org	This site lists the requirements for becoming a CMA.
www.theiia.org	This site lists the requirements for becoming a CIA.

Activity 1–5
Amazon.com
Cash flows

Amazon.com, an Internet retailer, was incorporated in July 1994, and opened its virtual doors on the web in July 1995. On the statement of cash flows, would you expect Amazon.com's net cash flows from operating, investing, and financing activities to be positive or negative for each year, 1996, 1997, and 1998? Use the following format for your answers, and briefly explain your logic.

	1998	1997	1996
Net cash flows from operating activities	positive		
Net cash flows from investing activities			
Net cash flows from financing activities			

ANSWERS TO SELF-EXAMINATION QUESTIONS

Matching

1. H	6. M	11. R	16. F	21. B	26. U	31. A
2. Y	7. J	12. W	17. V	22. GG	27. KK	32. L
3. AA	8. X	13. S	18. EE	23. C	28. G	33. O
4. HH	9. D	14. I	19. E	24. Q	29. NN	34. JJ
5. FF	10. P	15. OO	20. K	25. LL	30. Z	

Multiple Choice

1. **D** A corporation, organized in accordance with state or federal statutes, is a separate legal entity in which ownership is divided into shares of stock (answer D). A proprietorship (answer A) is an unincorporated business owned by one individual. A service business (answer B) provides services to its customers. It can be organized as a proprietorship, partnership, or corporation. A partnership (answer C) is an unincorporated business owned by two or more individuals.

2. **A** The resources owned by a business are called assets (answer A). The debts of the business are called liabilities (answer B), and the equity of the owners is called owner's equity (answer D). The relationship between assets, liabilities, and owner's equity is expressed as the accounting equation (answer C).

3. **A** The balance sheet is a listing of the assets, liabilities, and owner's equity of a business at a specific date (answer A). The income statement (answer B) is a summary of the revenue and expenses of a business for a specific period of time. The retained earnings statement (answer C) summarizes the changes in retained earnings during a specific period of time. The statement of cash flows (answer D) summarizes the cash receipts and cash payments for a specific period of time.

4. **C** The accounting equation is:

Assets = Liabilities + Owner's Equity

Therefore, if assets increased by $20,000 and liabilities increased by $12,000, owner's equity must have increased by $8,000 (answer C), as indicated in the following computation:

Assets	=	Liabilities + Owner's Equity
+$20,000	=	+$12,000 + Owner's Equity
+$20,000 − $12,000	=	Owner's Equity
+$8,000	=	Owner's Equity

5. **B** Net income is the excess of revenue over expenses, or $7,500 (answer B). If expenses exceed revenue, the difference is a net loss. Dividends are the opposite of the stockholders investing in the business and do not affect the amount of net income or net loss.

Analyzing Transactions

objectives

After studying this chapter, you should be able to:

1 Explain why accounts are used to record and summarize the effects of transactions on financial statements.

2 Describe the characteristics of an account.

3 List the rules of debit and credit and the normal balances of accounts.

4 Analyze and summarize the financial statement effects of transactions.

5 Prepare a trial balance and explain how it can be used to discover errors.

6 Discover errors in recording transactions and correct them.

7 Use horizontal analysis to compare financial statements from different periods.

ssume that you have been hired by a pizza restaurant to deliver pizzas, using your own car. You will be paid $6.00 per hour plus $0.30 per mile plus tips. What is the best way for you to determine how many miles you have driven each day in delivering pizzas?

One method would be to record the odometer mileage before work and then at quitting time. The difference would be the miles driven. For example, if the odometer read 56,743 at the start of work and 56,889 at the end of work, you would have driven 146 miles. This method is subject to error, however, if you copy down the wrong reading or make a math error.

In the same way, business managers need information about the status of the business at different points in time. Such information is useful for analyzing the effects of transactions on the business and for making decisions. For example, the manager of your neighborhood dry cleaners needs to know how much cash is available, how much has been spent, and what services have been provided.

In Chapter 1, we analyzed and recorded this kind of information by using the accounting equation, Assets = Liabilities + Owner's Equity. Since such a format is not practical for most businesses, in Chapter 2 we will study more efficient methods of recording transactions. We will conclude this chapter by discussing how accounting errors may occur and how they may be detected by the accounting process.

Usefulness of an Account

objective 1

Explain why accounts are used to record and summarize the effects of transactions on financial statements.

Before making a major cash purchase, such as buying a CD player, you need to know the balance of your bank account. Likewise, managers need timely, useful information in order to make good decisions about their businesses.

How are accounting systems designed to provide this information? We illustrated a very simple design in Chapter 1, where transactions were recorded and summarized in the accounting equation format. However, this format is difficult to use when thousands of transactions must be recorded daily. Thus, accounting systems are designed to show the increases and decreases in each financial statement item in a separate record. This record is called an **account**. For example, since cash appears on the balance sheet, a separate record is kept of the increases and decreases in cash. Likewise, a separate record is kept of the increases and decreases for supplies, land, accounts payable, and the other balance sheet items. Similar records would be kept for income statement items, such as fees earned, wages expense, and rent expense.

The increases and decreases in each financial statement item are shown in an account.

A group of accounts for a business entity is called a **ledger**. A list of the accounts in the ledger is called a **chart of accounts**. The accounts are normally listed in the order in which they appear in the financial statements. The balance sheet accounts are usually listed first, in the order of assets, liabilities, and owner's equity. The income statement accounts are then listed in the order of revenues and expenses. Each of these major account classifications is briefly described below.

Assets are resources owned by the business entity. These resources can be physical items, such as cash and supplies, or intangibles that have value, such as patent rights. Some other examples of assets include accounts receivable, prepaid expenses (such as insurance), buildings, equipment, and land.

Liabilities are debts owed to outsiders (creditors). Liabilities are often identified on the balance sheet by titles that include the word *payable*. Examples of liabilities include accounts payable, notes payable, and wages payable. Cash received before services are delivered creates a liability to perform the services. These future service commitments are often called *unearned revenues*. Examples of unearned revenues are magazine subscriptions received by a publisher and tuition received by a college at the beginning of a term.

Owner's equity is the owner's right to the assets of the business. For a corporation, the owner's equity on the balance sheet is called **stockholders' equity** and is represented by the balance of the capital stock and retained earnings accounts. A **dividends** account represents distributions of earnings to stockholders.

Revenues are increases in owner's equity as a result of selling services or products to customers. Examples of revenues include fees earned, fares earned, commissions revenue, and rent revenue.

The using up of assets or consuming services in the process of generating revenues results in **expenses**. Examples of typical expenses include wages expense, rent expense, utilities expense, supplies expense, and miscellaneous expense.

A chart of accounts is designed to meet the information needs of a company's managers and other users of its financial statements. The accounts within the chart of accounts are numbered for use as references. A flexible numbering system is normally used, so that new accounts can be added without affecting other account numbers.

Exhibit 1 is NetSolutions' chart of accounts that we will be using in this chapter. Additional accounts will be introduced in later chapters. In Exhibit 1, each account number has two digits. The first digit indicates the major classification of the ledger in which the account is located. Accounts beginning with 1 represent assets; 2, liabilities; 3, owner's equity; 4, revenue; and 5, expenses. The second digit indicates the location of the account within its class.

Procter & Gamble's account numbers have over 30 digits to reflect P&G's many different operations and regions.

BUSINESS ON STAGE

The Telltale Chart of Accounts

What does a chart of accounts reveal about a business's operations? Look at the following revenue and expense accounts taken from the chart of accounts for a newspaper:

- Revenue accounts:
  - Circulation—carriers
  - Circulation—vending machines
  - Circulation—mail subscriptions
  - Advertising—commercial
  - Advertising—classified

- Expense accounts:
  - Newsprint
  - News ink
  - Wire services
  - Correspondent fees
  - Photography
  - Telephone
  - Postage
  - Delivery
  - Wages

These accounts reveal that the newspaper receives its primary revenues from circulation and advertising.

In addition, the accounts reflect some of the decision-making needs of management. For example, matching the revenues from commercial and classified advertising with the related expenses helps management determine whether these services are profitable. This might lead management to consider expanding the paper's advertising space to take advantage of this profitability. ■

Exhibit 1 Chart of Accounts for NetSolutions

Balance Sheet Accounts		Income Statement Accounts	
1. Assets		**4. Revenue**	
11	Cash	41	Fees Earned
12	Accounts Receivable		**5. Expenses**
14	Supplies	51	Wages Expense
15	Prepaid Insurance	52	Rent Expense
17	Land	54	Utilities Expense
18	Office Equipment	55	Supplies Expense
	2. Liabilities	59	Miscellaneous Expense
21	Accounts Payable		
23	Unearned Rent		
	3. Owner's Equity		
31	Capital Stock		
32	Retained Earnings		
33	Dividends		

Characteristics of an Account

objective 2

Describe the characteristics of an account.

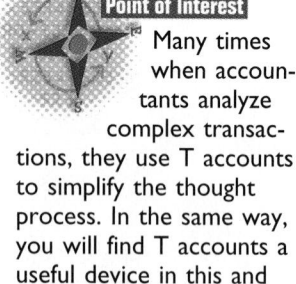

Point of Interest
Many times when accountants analyze complex transactions, they use T accounts to simplify the thought process. In the same way, you will find T accounts a useful device in this and later accounting courses.

An account, in its simplest form, has three parts. First, each account has a title, which is the name of the item recorded in the account. Second, each account has a space for recording increases in the amount of the item. Third, each account has a space for recording decreases in the amount of the item. The account form presented below is called a **T account** because it resembles the letter T. The left side of the account is called the *debit* side, and the right side is called the *credit* side.[1]

Title
Left side	Right side
debit	*credit*

Amounts entered on the left side of an account, regardless of the account title, are called **debits** to the account. When debits are entered in an account, the account is said to be *debited* (or charged). Amounts entered on the right side of an account are called **credits**, and the account is said to be *credited*. Debits and credits are sometimes abbreviated as *Dr.* and *Cr.*

In the cash account that follows, transactions involving receipts of cash are listed on the debit side of the account. The transactions involving cash payments are listed on the credit side. If at any time the total of the cash receipts is needed, the entries on the debit side of the account may be added and the total ($10,950) inserted below the last debit.[2] The total of the cash payments, $6,850 in the example, may be inserted on the credit side in a similar manner. Subtracting the smaller sum from the

> **Amounts entered on the left side of an account are debits, and amounts entered on the right side of an account are credits.**

[1] The terms *debit* and *credit* are derived from the Latin *debere* and *credere*.
[2] This amount, called a *memorandum balance*, should be written in small figures or identified in some other way to avoid mistaking the amount for an additional debit.

larger, \$10,950 − \$6,850, identifies the amount of cash on hand, \$4,100. This amount is called the **balance of the account**. It may be inserted in the account, next to the total of the debit column. In this way, the balance is identified as a **debit balance**. If a balance sheet were to be prepared at this time, cash of \$4,100 would be reported.

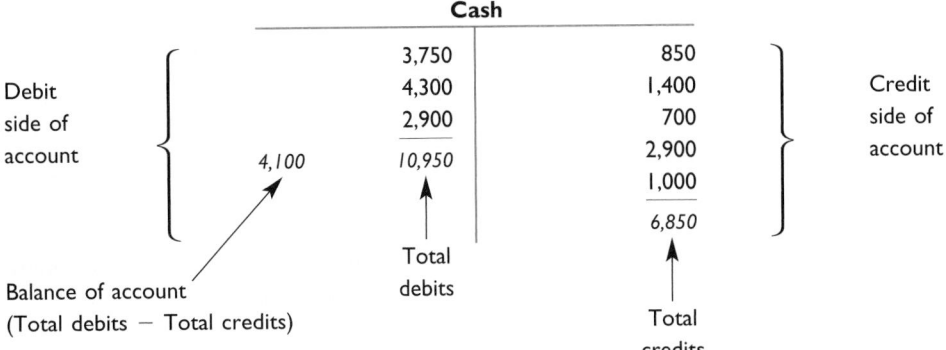

Analyzing and Summarizing Transactions in Accounts

Every business transaction affects at least two accounts. To illustrate how transactions are analyzed and summarized in accounts, we will use the NetSolutions transactions from Chapter 1, with dates added. First, we illustrate how transactions (a), (b), (c), and (f) are analyzed and summarized in balance sheet accounts (assets, liabilities, and owner's equity). Next, we illustrate how transactions (d), (e), and (g) are analyzed and summarized in income statement accounts (revenues and expenses). Finally, we illustrate how the payment of dividends, transaction (h), is analyzed and summarized in the accounts.

> **Every transaction affects at least two accounts.**

Transactions and Balance Sheet Accounts

Chris Clark's first transaction, (a), was to deposit \$25,000 in a bank account in the name of NetSolutions in exchange for capital stock. The effect of this November 1 transaction on the balance sheet is to increase cash and owner's equity, as shown below.

NetSolutions Balance Sheet November 1, 2002																			
Assets							**Owner's Equity**						
Cash		\$25	0	0	0	00	Capital Stock		\$25	0	0	0	00

Point of Interest

A journal can be thought of as being similar to an individual's diary.

This transaction is initially entered in a record called a **journal**. The title of the account to be debited is listed first, followed by the amount to be debited. The title of the account to be credited is listed below and to the right of the debit, followed by the amount to be credited. This process of recording a transaction in the journal is called **journalizing**. This form of recording a transaction is called a **journal entry**. The journal entry for transaction (a) is shown below.

Entry A

	Date		Description	Post. Ref.	Debit	Credit	
			JOURNAL			**Page 1**	
1	2002 Nov.	1	Cash		25 0 0 0 00		1
2			Capital Stock			25 0 0 0 00	2
3			Issued capital stock for cash.				3

The increase in the asset (Cash), which is reported on the left side of the balance sheet, is debited to the cash account. The increase in owner's equity (capital stock), which is reported on the right side of the balance sheet, is credited to the capital stock account. As other assets are acquired, the increases are also recorded as debits to asset accounts. Likewise, other increases in owner's equity will be recorded as credits to owner's equity accounts.

The effects of this transaction are shown in the accounts by transferring the amount and date of the journal entry to the left (debit) side of Cash and to the right (credit) side of Capital Stock, as follows:

Cash		Capital Stock	
Nov. 1 25,000			Nov. 1 25,000

On November 5 (transaction b), NetSolutions bought land for $20,000, paying cash. This transaction increases one asset account and decreases another. It is entered in the journal as a $20,000 increase (debit) to Land and a $20,000 decrease (credit) to Cash, as shown below.

Entry B

4							4
5		5	Land		20 0 0 0 00		5
6			Cash			20 0 0 0 00	6
7			Purchased land for building site.				7

The effect of this entry is shown in the accounts of NetSolutions as follows:

Cash		Land		Capital Stock	
Nov. 1 25,000	Nov. 5 20,000	Nov. 5 20,000			Nov. 1 25,000

On November 10 (transaction c), NetSolutions purchased supplies on account for $1,350. This transaction increases an asset account and increases a liability account. It is entered in the journal as a $1,350 increase (debit) to Supplies and a $1,350 increase (credit) to Accounts Payable, as shown below. To simplify the illustration, the effect of entry (c) and the remaining journal entries for NetSolutions will be shown in the accounts later.

Entry C

8							8
9		10	Supplies		1 3 5 0 00		9
10			Accounts Payable			1 3 5 0 00	10
11			Purchased supplies on account.				11

On November 30 (transaction f), NetSolutions paid creditors on account, $950. This transaction decreases a liability account and decreases an asset account. It is entered in the journal as a $950 decrease (debit) to Accounts Payable and a $950 decrease (credit) to Cash, as shown below.

Entry F

23					23
24	30	Accounts Payable		9 5 0 00	24
25		Cash			9 5 0 00	25
26		Paid creditors on account.			26

In the preceding examples, you should observe that the left side of asset accounts is used for recording increases and the right side is used for recording decreases. Also, the right side of liability and owner's equity accounts is used to record increases, and the left side of such accounts is used to record decreases. The left side of all accounts, whether asset, liability, or owner's equity, is the debit side, and the right side is the credit side. Thus, a debit may be either an increase or a decrease, depending on the account affected. Likewise, a credit may be either an increase or a decrease, depending on the account. The general rules of debit and credit for balance sheet accounts may be thus stated as follows:

> **The left side of all accounts is the debit side, and the right side is the credit side.**

	Debit	Credit
Asset accounts	Increase (+)	Decrease (−)
Liability accounts	Decrease (−)	Increase (+)
Owner's equity accounts	Decrease (−)	Increase (+)

The rules of debit and credit may also be stated in relationship to the accounting equation, as shown below.

Balance Sheet Accounts

ASSETS		LIABILITIES	
Asset Accounts		Liability Accounts	
Debit for increases (+)	Credit for decreases (−)	Debit for decreases (−)	Credit for increases (+)

		OWNER'S EQUITY	
		Owner's Equity Accounts	
		Debit for decreases (−)	Credit for increases (+)

Income Statement Accounts

The analysis of revenue and expense transactions focuses on how each transaction affects owner's equity. Transactions that increase revenue will increase owner's equity. Just as increases in owner's equity are recorded as credits, so, too, are increases in revenue accounts. Transactions that increase expense will decrease owner's equity. Just as decreases in owner's equity are recorded as debits, increases in expense accounts are recorded as debits.

We will use NetSolutions' transactions (d), (e), and (g) to illustrate the analysis of transactions and the rules of debit and credit for revenue and expense accounts. On November 18 (transaction d), NetSolutions received fees of $7,500 from customers for services provided. This transaction increases an asset account and increases a revenue account. It is entered in the journal as a $7,500 increase (debit) to Cash and a $7,500 increase (credit) to Fees Earned, as shown below.

Entry D

12						12
13		18	Cash	7 5 0 0 00		13
14			Fees Earned		7 5 0 0 00	14
15			Received fees from customers.			15

Throughout the month, NetSolutions incurred the following expenses: wages, $2,125; rent, $800; utilities, $450; and miscellaneous, $275. To simplify the illustration, the entry to journalize the payment of these expenses is recorded on November 30 (transaction e), as shown below. This transaction increases various expense accounts and decreases an asset account.

Entry E

17		30	Wages Expense	2 1 2 5 00		17
18			Rent Expense	8 0 0 00		18
19			Utilities Expense	4 5 0 00		19
20			Miscellaneous Expense	2 7 5 00		20
21			Cash		3 6 5 0 00	21
22			Paid expenses.			22

Regardless of the number of accounts, the sum of the debits is always equal to the sum of the credits in a journal entry. This equality of debits and credits for each transaction is built into the accounting equation: Assets = Liabilities + Owner's Equity. It is also because of this double equality that the system is known as **double-entry accounting**.

The sum of the debits must always equal the sum of the credits.

On November 30, NetSolutions recorded the amount of supplies used in the operations during the month (transaction g). This transaction increases an expense account and decreases an asset account. The journal entry for transaction (g) is shown below.

Entry G

28		30	Supplies Expense	8 0 0 00		28
29			Supplies		8 0 0 00	29
30			Recorded supplies used during			30
31			November.			31

The general rules of debit and credit for analyzing transactions affecting income statement accounts are stated as follows:

	Debit	Credit
Revenue accounts	Decrease (−)	Increase (+)
Expense accounts	Increase (+)	Decrease (−)

The rules of debit and credit for income statement accounts may also be summarized in relationship to the owner's equity in the accounting equation, as shown below.

Income Statement Accounts

Expense Accounts		Revenue Accounts	
Debit for increases (+)	Credit for decreases (−)	Debit for decreases (−)	Credit for increases (+)

Dividends

A corporation may from time to time distribute earnings from operations by paying dividends to its stockholders. The payment of dividends has the effect of decreasing owner's equity. Just as decreases in owner's equity are recorded as debits, dividends are recorded as debits. Debits to the dividends account are normally thought of as increasing dividends rather than as decreasing owner's equity.

On November 30 (transaction h), NetSolutions paid dividends of $2,000. This transaction increases the dividends account and decreases the cash account. The journal entry for transaction (h) is shown below.

Entry H

	2002					
1	Nov.	30	Dividends	2 0 0 0 00		1
2			Cash		2 0 0 0 00	2
3			Paid dividends to stockholders.			3

BUSINESS ON STAGE

Good Communication

Most managers would probably agree that they spend a majority of their time communicating with peers, employees, suppliers, stockholders, customers, and various others. To be successful in business, you must be a good communicator. Some helpful rules of good communication include the following:

- Have a clear idea of what you hope to accomplish from the communication and know what you want to say before you say it.
- Remember that oral communication is more than just words. Your tone of voice, facial expressions, and gestures can say more than your words.
- Keep your audience in mind by considering their needs and interests.
- Always follow up to see that your message was understood.
- Be a good listener by not interrupting, avoiding hasty judgments, asking questions, and paying attention. ■

Source: Adapted from *The World of Business* by L. Gitman and C. McDaniel (2d Edition), p. 262.

Normal Balances of Accounts

The sum of the increases recorded in an account is usually equal to or greater than the sum of the decreases recorded in the account. For this reason, the normal balances of all accounts are positive rather than negative. For example, the total debits (increases) in an asset account will ordinarily be greater than the total credits (decreases). Thus, asset accounts normally have debit balances.

The rules of debit and credit and the normal balances of the various types of accounts are summarized as follows:

	Increase (Normal Balance)	Decrease
Balance sheet accounts:		
Asset	Debit	Credit
Liability	Credit	Debit
Owner's (or Stockholders') Equity:		
Capital Stock	Credit	Debit
Retained Earnings	Credit	Debit
Dividends	Debit	Credit
Income statement accounts:		
Revenue	Credit	Debit
Expense	Debit	Credit

When an account normally having a debit balance actually has a credit balance, or vice versa, an error may have occurred or an unusual situation may exist. For example, a credit balance in the office equipment account could result only from an error. On the other hand, a debit balance in an accounts payable account could result from an overpayment.

A debit balance in which of the following accounts—Cash, Dividends, Wages Expense, Supplies, Fees Earned—would indicate that an error has occurred?

Fees Earned

Illustration of Analyzing and Summarizing Transactions

objective 4

Analyze and summarize the financial statement effects of transactions.

How does a transaction take place in a business? First, a manager or other employee authorizes the transaction. The transaction then takes place. The businesses involved in the transaction usually prepare documents that give details of the transaction. These documents then become the basis for analyzing and recording the transaction. For example, Chris Clark might authorize the purchase of supplies for NetSolutions by telling an employee to buy computer paper at the local office supply store. The employee purchases the supplies for cash and receives a sales slip from the office supply store listing the supplies bought. The employee then gives the sales slip to Chris Clark, who verifies and records the transaction.

Point of Interest

In computerized accounting systems, some transactions may be automatically authorized and recorded when certain events occur. For example, the salaries of managers may be paid automatically at the end of each pay period.

As we discussed in the preceding section, a transaction is first recorded in a journal. Thus, the journal is a history of transactions by date. Periodically, the journal entries are transferred to the accounts in the ledger. The ledger is a history of transactions by account. The process of transferring the debits and credits from the journal entries to the accounts is called **posting**. The flow of a transaction from its authorization to its posting in the accounts is shown in Exhibit 2.

Exhibit 2 Flow of Business
Transactions

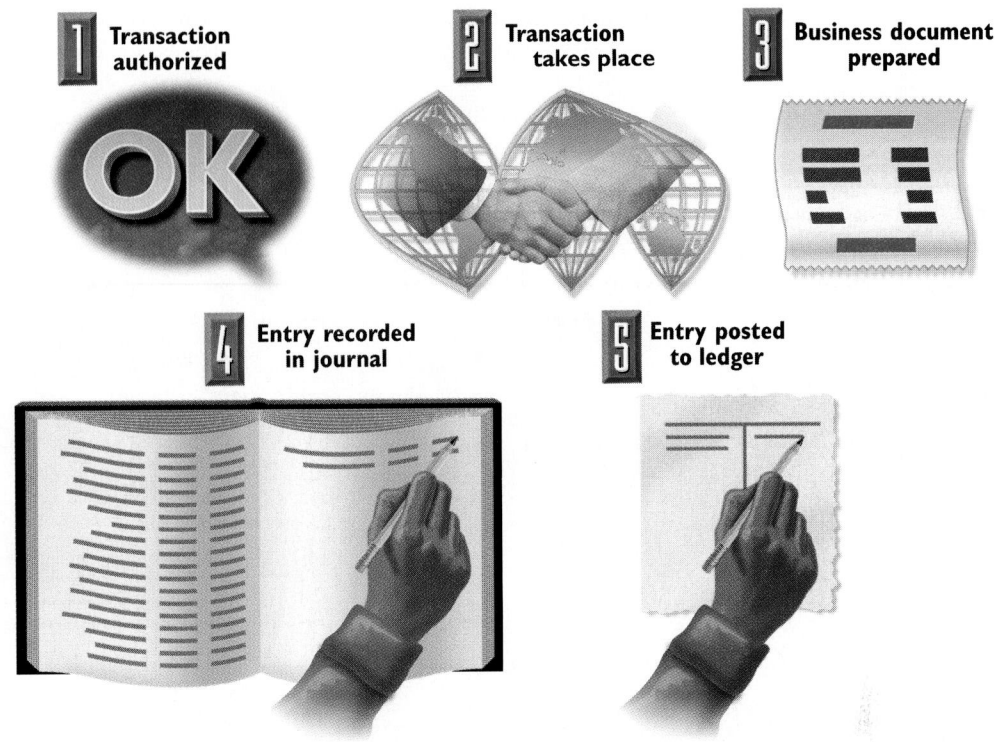

The double-entry accounting system is a very powerful tool in analyzing the effects of transactions. Using this system to analyze transactions is summarized as follows:

1. Determine whether an asset, a liability, owner's equity, revenue, or expense account is affected by the transaction.
2. For each account affected by the transaction, determine whether the account increases or decreases.
3. Determine whether each increase or decrease should be recorded as a debit or a credit.

In practice, businesses use a variety of formats for recording journal entries. A business may use one all-purpose journal, sometimes called a **two-column journal**, or it may use several journals. In the latter case, each journal is used to record different types of transactions, such as cash receipts or cash payments. The journals may be part of either a manual accounting system or a computerized accounting system.

To illustrate recording a transaction in an all-purpose journal and posting in a manual accounting system, we will use the December transactions of NetSolutions. The first transaction in December occurred on December 1.

Dec. 1. NetSolutions paid a premium of $2,400 for a comprehensive insurance policy covering liability, theft, and fire. The policy covers a two-year period.

Analysis: When you purchased insurance for your automobile, you may have been required to pay the insurance premium in advance. In this case, your transaction was similar to NetSolutions. Advance payments of expenses such as insurance are prepaid expenses, which are assets. For NetSolutions, the asset acquired for the cash payment is insurance protection for 24 months. The asset Prepaid Insurance increases and is debited for $2,400. The asset Cash decreases and is credited for $2,400.

The recording and posting of this transaction is shown in Exhibit 3.

Exhibit 3 Diagram of the Recording and Posting of a Debit and a Credit

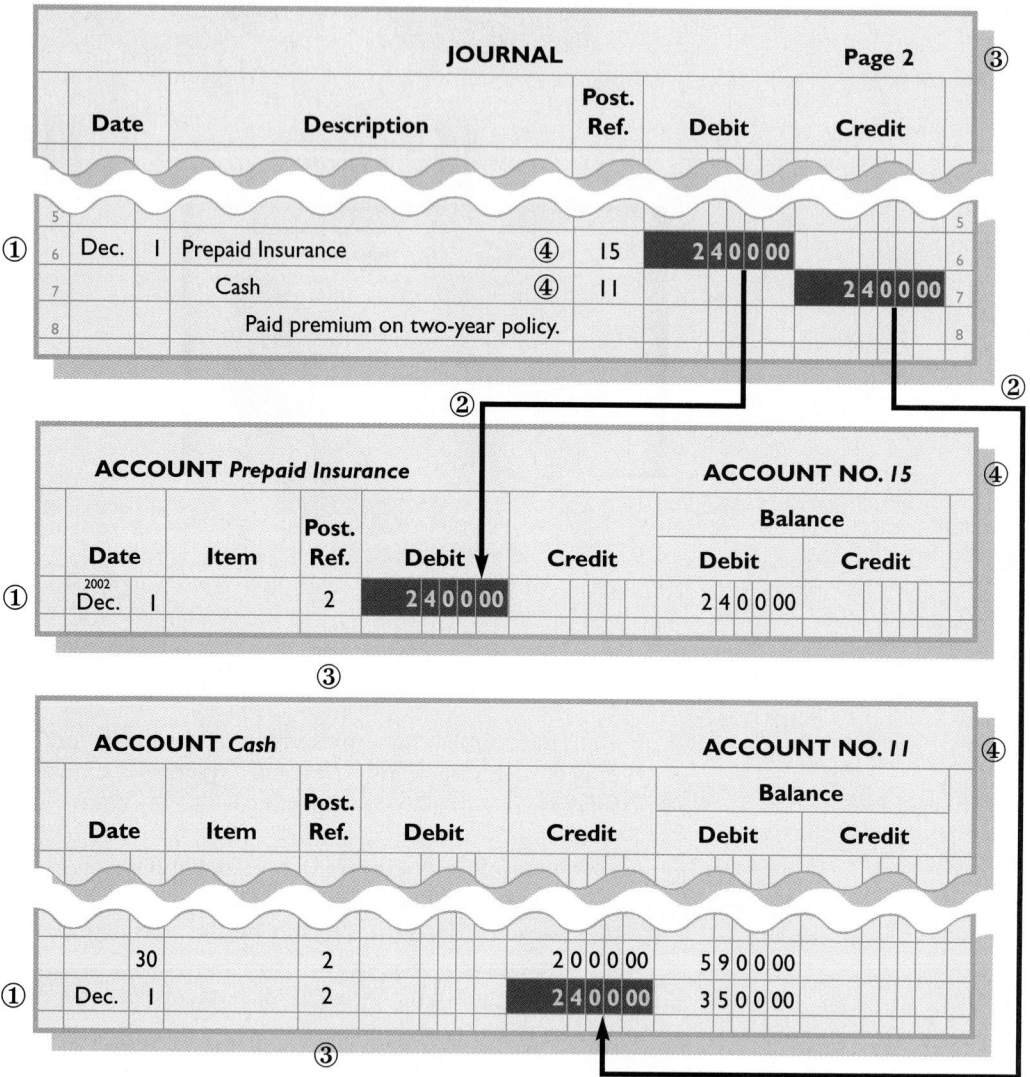

Note where the date of the transaction is recorded in the journal. Also note that the entry is explained as the payment of an insurance premium. Such explanations should be brief. For unusual and complex transactions, such as a long-term rental arrangement, the journal entry explanation may include a reference to the rental agreement or other business document.

You will note that the T account form is not used in this illustration. Although the T account clearly separates debit and credit entries, it is inefficient for summarizing a large quantity of transactions. In practice, the T account is usually replaced with the standard form shown in Exhibit 3.

The debits and credits for each journal entry are posted to the accounts in the order in which they occur in the journal. In posting to the standard account, (1) the date is entered, and (2) the amount of the entry is entered. For future reference, (3) the journal page number is inserted in the Posting Reference column of the account, and (4) the account number is inserted in the Posting Reference column of the journal.

The remaining December transactions for NetSolutions are analyzed in the following paragraphs. These transactions are posted to the ledger in Exhibit 4, shown later. To simplify and reduce repetition, some of the December transactions are stated in summary form. For example, cash received for services is normally recorded on a daily basis. In this example, however, only summary totals are recorded at the middle and end of the month. Likewise, all fees earned on account during December are recorded at the middle and end of the month. In practice, each fee earned is recorded separately.

Dec. 1. NetSolutions paid rent for December, $800. The company from which NetSolutions is renting its store space now requires the payment of rent on the 1st of each month, rather than at the end of the month.

Analysis: You may pay monthly rent on an apartment on the first of each month. Your rent transaction is similar to NetSolutions. The advance payment of rent is an asset, much like the advance payment of the insurance premium in the preceding transaction. However, unlike the insurance premium, this prepaid rent will expire in one month. When an asset that is purchased will be used up in a short period of time, such as a month, it is normal to debit an expense account initially. This avoids having to transfer the balance from an asset account (Prepaid Rent) to an expense account (Rent Expense) at the end of the month. Thus, when the rent for December is prepaid at the beginning of the month, Rent Expense is debited for $800 and Cash is credited for $800.

What would likely cause the cash account to have a credit balance?

An error or an overdrawn cash account.

10	1	Rent Expense	52	8 0 0 00	10
11		Cash	11		8 0 0 00	11
12		Paid rent for December.			12

Dec. 1. NetSolutions received an offer from a local retailer to rent the land purchased on November 5. The retailer plans to use the land as a parking lot for its employees and customers. NetSolutions agreed to rent the land to the retailer for three months, with the rent payable in advance. NetSolutions received $360 for three months' rent beginning December 1.

Analysis: By agreeing to rent the land and accepting the $360, NetSolutions has incurred an obligation (liability) to the retailer. This obligation is to make the land available for use for three months and not to interfere with its use. The liability created by receiving the cash in advance of providing the service is called **unearned revenue**. Thus, the $360 received is an increase in an asset and is debited to Cash. The liability account Unearned Rent increases and is credited for $360. As time passes, the unearned rent liability will decrease and will become revenue.

Magazines that receive subscriptions in advance must record the receipts as unearned revenues. Likewise, airlines that receive ticket payments in advance must record the receipts as unearned revenues until the passengers use the tickets.

14	1	Cash	11	3 6 0 00	14
15		Unearned Rent	23		3 6 0 00	15
16		Received advance payment for			16
17		three months' rent on land.			17

Dec. 4. NetSolutions purchased office equipment on account from Executive Supply Co. for $1,800.

Analysis: The asset account Office Equipment increases and is therefore debited for $1,800. The liability account Accounts Payable increases and is credited for $1,800.

19		4	Office Equipment	18	1 8 0 0 00		19
20			Accounts Payable	21		1 8 0 0 00	20
21			Purchased office equipment				21
22			on account.				22

Dec. 6. NetSolutions paid $180 for a newspaper advertisement.

Analysis: An expense increases and is debited for $180. The asset Cash decreases and is credited for $180. Expense items that are expected to be minor in amount are normally included as part of the miscellaneous expense. Thus, Miscellaneous Expense is debited for $180.

24		6	Miscellaneous Expense	59	1 8 0 00		24
25			Cash	11		1 8 0 00	25
26			Paid for newspaper ad.				26

Dec. 11. NetSolutions paid creditors $400.

Analysis: This payment decreases the liability account Accounts Payable, which is debited for $400. Cash also decreases and is credited for $400.

28		11	Accounts Payable	21	4 0 0 00		28
29			Cash	11		4 0 0 00	29
30			Paid creditors on account.				30

Dec. 13. NetSolutions paid a receptionist and a part-time assistant $950 for two weeks' wages.

Analysis: This transaction is similar to the December 6 transaction, where an expense account is increased and Cash is decreased. Thus, Wages Expense is debited for $950, and Cash is credited for $950.

	JOURNAL				Page 3	
	Date	**Description**	**Post. Ref.**	**Debit**	**Credit**	
1	2002 Dec. 13	Wages Expense	51	9 5 0 00		1
2		Cash	11		9 5 0 00	2
3		Paid two weeks' wages.				3

Dec. 16. NetSolutions received $3,100 from fees earned for the first half of December.

Analysis: Cash increases and is debited for $3,100. The revenue account Fees Earned increases and is credited for $3,100.

5		16	Cash		11		3	1	0	0	00				5
6			Fees Earned		41							3	1	0	0	00	6
7			Received fees from customers.													7

Dec. 16. Fees earned on account totaled $1,750 for the first half of December.

Analysis: Assume that you have agreed to take care of a neighbor's dog for a week for $100. At the end of the week, you agree to wait until the first of the next month to receive the $100. Like NetSolutions, you have provided services on account and thus have a right to receive the payment from your neighbor. When a business agrees that payment for services provided or goods sold can be accepted at a later date, the firm has an **account receivable**, which is a claim against the customer. The account receivable is an asset, and the revenue is earned even though no cash has been received. Thus, Accounts Receivable increases and is debited for $1,750. The revenue account Fees Earned increases and is credited for $1,750.

9		16	Accounts Receivable		12		1	7	5	0	00				9
10			Fees Earned		41							1	7	5	0	00	10
11			Recorded fees earned on account.													11

Dec. 20. NetSolutions paid $900 to Executive Supply Co. on the $1,800 debt owed from the December 4 transaction.

Analysis: This is similar to the transaction of December 11.

13		20	Accounts Payable		21			9	0	0	00				13
14			Cash		11								9	0	0	00	14
15			Paid part of amount owed to													15
16			Executive Supply Co.													16

Dec. 21. NetSolutions received $650 from customers in payment of their accounts.

Analysis: When customers pay amounts owed for services they have previously received, one asset increases and another asset decreases. Thus, Cash is debited for $650, and Accounts Receivable is credited for $650.

18		21	Cash		11			6	5	0	00				18
19			Accounts Receivable		12								6	5	0	00	19
20			Received cash from customers													20
21			on account.													21

Dec. 23. NetSolutions paid $1,450 for supplies.

Analysis: The asset account Supplies increases and is debited for $1,450. The asset account Cash decreases and is credited for $1,450.

23		23	Supplies	14	1 4 5 0 00		23
24			Cash	11		1 4 5 0 00	24
25			Purchased supplies.				25

Dec. 27. NetSolutions paid the receptionist and the part-time assistant $1,200 for two weeks' wages.

Analysis: This is similar to the transaction of December 13.

27		27	Wages Expense	51	1 2 0 0 00		27
28			Cash	11		1 2 0 0 00	28
29			Paid two weeks' wages.				29

Dec. 31. NetSolutions paid its $310 telephone bill for the month.

Analysis: You pay a telephone bill each month. Businesses, such as NetSolutions, also must pay monthly utility bills. Such transactions are similar to the transaction of December 6. The expense account Utilities Expense is debited for $310, and Cash is credited for $310.

31		31	Utilities Expense	54	3 1 0 00		31
32			Cash	11		3 1 0 00	32
33			Paid telephone bill.				33

Dec. 31. NetSolutions paid its $225 electric bill for the month.

Analysis: This is similar to the preceding transaction.

			JOURNAL			**Page 4**	
	Date		**Description**	**Post. Ref.**	**Debit**	**Credit**	
1	2002 Dec.	31	Utilities Expense	54	2 2 5 00		1
2			Cash	11		2 2 5 00	2
3			Paid electric bill.				3

Dec. 31. NetSolutions received $2,870 from fees earned for the second half of December.

Analysis: This is similar to the transaction of December 16.

5		31	Cash	11	2 8 7 0 00		5
6			Fees Earned	41		2 8 7 0 00	6
7			Received fees from customers.				7

Dec. 31. Fees earned on account totaled $1,120 for the second half of December.

Analysis: This is similar to the transaction of December 16.

9	31	Accounts Receivable	12	1 1 2 0 00		9
10		Fees Earned	41		1 1 2 0 00	10
11		Recorded fees earned on account.				11

Dec. 31. NetSolutions paid dividends of $2,000 to stockholders.

Analysis: This transaction resulted in an increase in the amount of dividends and is recorded by a $2,000 debit to Dividends. The decrease in business cash is recorded by a $2,000 credit to Cash.

13	31	Dividends	33	2 0 0 0 00		13
14		Cash	11		2 0 0 0 00	14
15		Paid dividends to stockholders.				15

The journal for NetSolutions since it was organized on November 1 is shown in Exhibit 4. Exhibit 4 also shows the ledger after the transactions for both November and December have been posted.

Exhibit 4 Journal and Ledger—NetSolutions

			JOURNAL			Page 1	
	Date		**Description**	**Post. Ref.**	**Debit**	**Credit**	
1	2002 Nov.	1	Cash	11	25 0 0 0 00		1
2			Capital Stock	31		25 0 0 0 00	2
3			Issued capital stock for cash.				3
4							4
5		5	Land	17	20 0 0 0 00		5
6			Cash	11		20 0 0 0 00	6
7			Purchased land for building site.				7
8							8
9		10	Supplies	14	1 3 5 0 00		9
10			Accounts Payable	21		1 3 5 0 00	10
11			Purchased supplies on account.				11
12							12
13		18	Cash	11	7 5 0 0 00		13
14			Fees Earned	41		7 5 0 0 00	14
15			Received fees from customers.				15
16							16
17		30	Wages Expense	51	2 1 2 5 00		17
18			Rent Expense	52	8 0 0 00		18
19			Utilities Expense	54	4 5 0 00		19
20			Miscellaneous Expense	59	2 7 5 00		20
21			Cash	11		3 6 5 0 00	21
22			Paid expenses.				22
23							23
24		30	Accounts Payable	21	9 5 0 00		24
25			Cash	11		9 5 0 00	25
26			Paid creditors on account.				26
27							27
28		30	Supplies Expense	55	8 0 0 00		28
29			Supplies	14		8 0 0 00	29
30			Supplies used during November.				30

Exhibit 4 (continued)

	Date		Description	Post. Ref.	Debit	Credit	
	2002 Nov.	30	Dividends	33	2 0 0 0 00		1
2			Cash	11		2 0 0 0 00	2
3			Paid dividends to stockholders.				3
4							4
5	Dec.	1	Prepaid Insurance	15	2 4 0 0 00		5
6			Cash	11		2 4 0 0 00	6
7			Paid premium on two-year policy.				7
8							8
9		1	Rent Expense	52	8 0 0 00		9
10			Cash	11		8 0 0 00	10
11			Paid rent for December.				11
12							12
13		1	Cash	11	3 6 0 00		13
14			Unearned Rent	23		3 6 0 00	14
15			Received advance payment for				15
16			three months' rent on land.				16
17							17
18		4	Office Equipment	18	1 8 0 0 00		18
19			Accounts Payable	21		1 8 0 0 00	19
20			Purchased office equipment				20
21			on account.				21
22							22
23		6	Miscellaneous Expense	59	1 8 0 00		23
24			Cash	11		1 8 0 00	24
25			Paid for newspaper ad.				25
26							26
27		11	Accounts Payable	21	4 0 0 00		27
28			Cash	11		4 0 0 00	28
29			Paid creditors on account.				29
30							30

JOURNAL — Page 2

	Date		Description	Post. Ref.	Debit	Credit	
1	2002 Dec.	13	Wages Expense	51	9 5 0 00		1
2			Cash	11		9 5 0 00	2
3			Paid two weeks' wages.				3
4							4
5		16	Cash	11	3 1 0 0 00		5
6			Fees Earned	41		3 1 0 0 00	6
7			Received fees from customers.				7
8							8
9		16	Accounts Receivable	12	1 7 5 0 00		9
10			Fees Earned	41		1 7 5 0 00	10
11			Recorded fees earned on account.				11

JOURNAL — Page 3

Exhibit 4 (continued)

	Date		Description	Post. Ref.	Debit	Credit	
13		20	Accounts Payable	21	9 0 0 00		13
14			Cash	11		9 0 0 00	14
15			Paid part of amount owed to				15
16			Executive Supply Co.				16
17							17
18		21	Cash	11	6 5 0 00		18
19			Accounts Receivable	12		6 5 0 00	19
20			Received cash from customers				20
21			on account.				21
22							22
23		23	Supplies	14	1 4 5 0 00		23
24			Cash	11		1 4 5 0 00	24
25			Purchased supplies.				25
26							26
27		27	Wages Expense	51	1 2 0 0 00		27
28			Cash	11		1 2 0 0 00	28
29			Paid two weeks' wages.				29
30							30
31		31	Utilities Expense	54	3 1 0 00		31
32			Cash	11		3 1 0 00	32
33			Paid telephone bill.				33

JOURNAL — Page 3

JOURNAL — Page 4

	Date		Description	Post. Ref.	Debit	Credit	
1	2002 Dec.	31	Utilities Expense	54	2 2 5 00		1
2			Cash	11		2 2 5 00	2
3			Paid electric bill.				3
4							4
5		31	Cash	11	2 8 7 0 00		5
6			Fees Earned	41		2 8 7 0 00	6
7			Received fees from customers.				7
8							8
9		31	Accounts Receivable	12	1 1 2 0 00		9
10			Fees Earned	41		1 1 2 0 00	10
11			Recorded fees earned on account.				11
12							12
13		31	Dividends	33	2 0 0 0 00		13
14			Cash	11		2 0 0 0 00	14
15			Paid dividends to stockholders.				15
16							16
17							17
18							18
19							19

Exhibit 4 (continued)

LEDGER

ACCOUNT Cash   ACCOUNT NO. 11

Date		Item	Post. Ref.	Debit	Credit	Balance Debit	Balance Credit
2002 Nov.	1		1	25 0 0 0 00		25 0 0 0 00	
	5		1		20 0 0 0 00	5 0 0 0 00	
	18		1	7 5 0 0 00		12 5 0 0 00	
	30		1		3 6 5 0 00	8 8 5 0 00	
	30		1		9 5 0 00	7 9 0 0 00	
	30		2		2 0 0 0 00	5 9 0 0 00	
Dec.	1		2		2 4 0 0 00	3 5 0 0 00	
	1		2		8 0 0 00	2 7 0 0 00	
	1		2	3 6 0 00		3 0 6 0 00	
	6		2		1 8 0 00	2 8 8 0 00	
	11		2		4 0 0 00	2 4 8 0 00	
	13		3		9 5 0 00	1 5 3 0 00	
	16		3	3 1 0 0 00		4 6 3 0 00	
	20		3		9 0 0 00	3 7 3 0 00	
	21		3	6 5 0 00		4 3 8 0 00	
	23		3		1 4 5 0 00	2 9 3 0 00	
	27		3		1 2 0 0 00	1 7 3 0 00	
	31		3		3 1 0 00	1 4 2 0 00	
	31		4		2 2 5 00	1 1 9 5 00	
	31		4	2 8 7 0 00		4 0 6 5 00	
	31		4		2 0 0 0 00	2 0 6 5 00	

ACCOUNT Accounts Receivable   ACCOUNT NO. 12

Date		Item	Post. Ref.	Debit	Credit	Balance Debit	Balance Credit
2002 Dec.	16		3	1 7 5 0 00		1 7 5 0 00	
	21		3		6 5 0 00	1 1 0 0 00	
	31		4	1 1 2 0 00		2 2 2 0 00	

ACCOUNT Supplies   ACCOUNT NO. 14

Date		Item	Post. Ref.	Debit	Credit	Balance Debit	Balance Credit
2002 Nov.	10		1	1 3 5 0 00		1 3 5 0 00	
	30		1		8 0 0 00	5 5 0 00	
Dec.	23		3	1 4 5 0 00		2 0 0 0 00	

Exhibit 4 *(continued)*

ACCOUNT *Prepaid Insurance*   **ACCOUNT NO. 15**

Date	Item	Post. Ref.	Debit	Credit	Balance Debit	Balance Credit
2002 Dec. 1		2	2 4 0 0 00		2 4 0 0 00	

ACCOUNT *Land*   **ACCOUNT NO. 17**

Date	Item	Post. Ref.	Debit	Credit	Balance Debit	Balance Credit
2002 Nov. 5		1	20 0 0 0 00		20 0 0 0 00	

ACCOUNT *Office Equipment*   **ACCOUNT NO. 18**

Date	Item	Post. Ref.	Debit	Credit	Balance Debit	Balance Credit
2002 Dec. 4		2	1 8 0 0 00		1 8 0 0 00	

ACCOUNT *Accounts Payable*   **ACCOUNT NO. 21**

Date	Item	Post. Ref.	Debit	Credit	Balance Debit	Balance Credit
2002 Nov. 10		1		1 3 5 0 00		1 3 5 0 00
30		1	9 5 0 00			4 0 0 00
Dec. 4		2		1 8 0 0 00		2 2 0 0 00
11		2	4 0 0 00			1 8 0 0 00
20		3	9 0 0 00			9 0 0 00

ACCOUNT *Unearned Rent*   **ACCOUNT NO. 23**

Date	Item	Post. Ref.	Debit	Credit	Balance Debit	Balance Credit
2002 Dec. 1		2		3 6 0 00		3 6 0 00

ACCOUNT *Capital Stock*   **ACCOUNT NO. 31**

Date	Item	Post. Ref.	Debit	Credit	Balance Debit	Balance Credit
2002 Nov. 1		1		25 0 0 0 00		25 0 0 0 00

Exhibit 4 (continued)

ACCOUNT *Dividends* **ACCOUNT NO. 33**

Date	Item	Post. Ref.	Debit	Credit	Balance Debit	Balance Credit
2002 Nov. 30		2	2 0 0 0 00		2 0 0 0 00	
Dec. 31		4	2 0 0 0 00		4 0 0 0 00	

ACCOUNT *Fees Earned* **ACCOUNT NO. 41**

Date	Item	Post. Ref.	Debit	Credit	Balance Debit	Balance Credit
2002 Nov. 18		1		7 5 0 0 00		7 5 0 0 00
Dec. 16		3		3 1 0 0 00		10 6 0 0 00
16		3		1 7 5 0 00		12 3 5 0 00
31		4		2 8 7 0 00		15 2 2 0 00
31		4		1 1 2 0 00		16 3 4 0 00

ACCOUNT *Wages Expense* **ACCOUNT NO. 51**

Date	Item	Post. Ref.	Debit	Credit	Balance Debit	Balance Credit
2002 Nov. 30		1	2 1 2 5 00		2 1 2 5 00	
Dec. 13		3	9 5 0 00		3 0 7 5 00	
27		3	1 2 0 0 00		4 2 7 5 00	

ACCOUNT *Rent Expense* **ACCOUNT NO. 52**

Date	Item	Post. Ref.	Debit	Credit	Balance Debit	Balance Credit
2002 Nov. 30		1	8 0 0 00		8 0 0 00	
Dec. 1		2	8 0 0 00		1 6 0 0 00	

ACCOUNT *Utilities Expense* **ACCOUNT NO. 54**

Date	Item	Post. Ref.	Debit	Credit	Balance Debit	Balance Credit
2002 Nov. 30		1	4 5 0 00		4 5 0 00	
Dec. 31		3	3 1 0 00		7 6 0 00	
31		4	2 2 5 00		9 8 5 00	

Exhibit 4 *(concluded)*

ACCOUNT ***Supplies Expense*** **ACCOUNT NO. 55**

Date		Item	Post. Ref.	Debit	Credit	Balance Debit	Balance Credit
2002 Nov.	30		1	800 00		800 00	

ACCOUNT ***Miscellaneous Expense*** **ACCOUNT NO. 59**

Date		Item	Post. Ref.	Debit	Credit	Balance Debit	Balance Credit
2002 Nov.	30		1	275 00		275 00	
Dec.	6		2	180 00		455 00	

Trial Balance

objective 5

Prepare a trial balance and explain how it can be used to discover errors.

How can you be sure that you have not made an error in posting the debits and credits to the ledger? One way is to determine the equality of the debits and credits in the ledger. This equality should be proved at the end of each accounting period, if not more often. Such a proof, called a **trial balance**, may be in the form of a computer printout or in the form shown in Exhibit 5.

Point of Interest

The proof of the equality of the debit and credit balances is called a trial balance because a "trial" is a process of proving or testing.

Exhibit 5 Trial Balance

NET SOLUTIONS

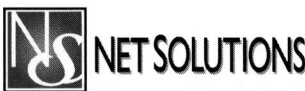

NetSolutions
Trial Balance
December 31, 2002

Cash	2,065 00	
Accounts Receivable	2,220 00	
Supplies	2,000 00	
Prepaid Insurance	2,400 00	
Land	20,000 00	
Office Equipment	1,800 00	
Accounts Payable		900 00
Unearned Rent		360 00
Capital Stock		25,000 00
Dividends	4,000 00	
Fees Earned		16,340 00
Wages Expense	4,275 00	
Rent Expense	1,600 00	
Utilities Expense	985 00	
Supplies Expense	800 00	
Miscellaneous Expense	455 00	
	42,600 00	42,600 00

The first step in preparing the trial balance is to determine the balance of each account in the ledger. When the standard account form is used, the balance of each account appears in the balance column on the same line as the last posting to the account.

The trial balance does not provide complete proof of the accuracy of the ledger. It indicates only that the debits and the credits are equal. This proof is of value, however, because errors often affect the equality of debits and credits. If the two totals of a trial balance are not equal, an error has occurred. In the remainder of this chapter, we will discuss procedures for discovering and correcting errors.

Discovery and Correction of Errors

objective 6

Discover errors in recording transactions and correct them.

Errors will sometimes occur in journalizing and posting transactions. In the following paragraphs, we describe and illustrate how errors may be discovered and corrected. In some cases, however, an error might not be significant enough to affect the decisions of management or others. In such cases, the **materiality concept** implies that the error may be treated in the easiest possible way. For example, an error of a few dollars in recording an asset as an expense for a business with millions of dollars in assets would be considered immaterial, and a correction would not be necessary. In the remaining paragraphs, we assume that errors discovered are material and should be corrected.

Many large corporations such as **Microsoft** and **Quaker Oats** round the figures in their financial statements to millions of dollars.

Discovery of Errors

As mentioned previously, preparing the trial balance is one of the primary ways to discover errors in the ledger. However, it indicates only that the debits and credits are equal. If the two totals of the trial balance are not equal, it is probably due to one or more of the errors described in Exhibit 6.

Among the types of errors that will *not* cause the trial balance totals to be unequal are the following:

1. Failure to record a transaction or to post a transaction.
2. Recording the same erroneous amount for both the debit and the credit parts of a transaction.
3. Recording the same transaction more than once.
4. Posting a part of a transaction correctly as a debit or credit but to the wrong account.

It is obvious that care should be used in recording transactions in the journal and in posting to the accounts. The need for accuracy in determining account balances and reporting them on the trial balance is also evident.

Errors in the accounts may be discovered in various ways: (1) through audit procedures, (2) by looking at the trial balance or (3) by chance. If the two trial balance totals are not equal, the amount of the difference between the totals should be determined before searching for the error.

The amount of the difference between the two totals of a trial balance sometimes gives a clue as to the nature of the error or where it occurred. For example, a difference of 10, 100, or 1,000 between two totals is often the result of an error in addition. A difference between totals can also be due to omitting a debit or a

Exhibit 6 Errors Causing
Unequal Trial Balance

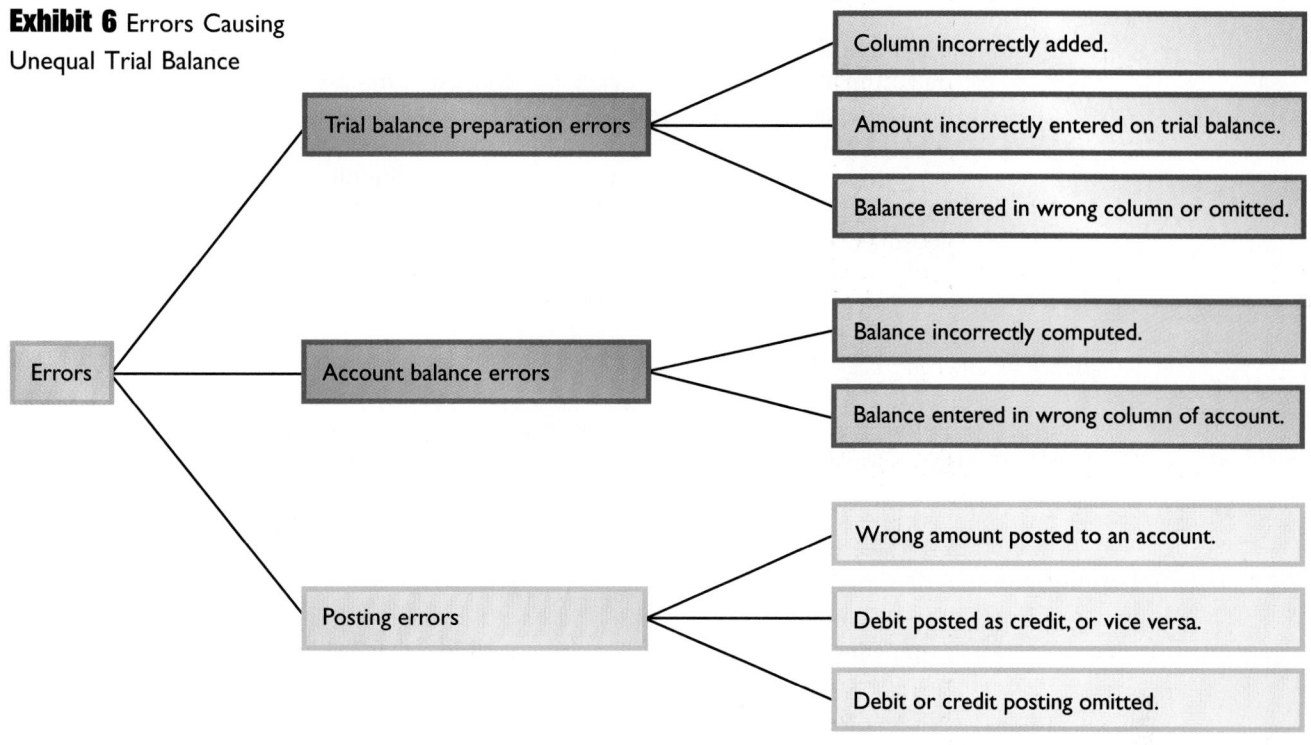

credit posting. If the difference can be evenly divided by 2, the error may be due to the posting of a debit as a credit, or vice versa. For example, if the debit total is $20,640 and the credit total is $20,236, the difference of $404 may indicate that a credit posting of $404 was omitted or that a credit of $202 was incorrectly posted as a debit.

Two other common types of errors are known as transpositions and slides. A **transposition** occurs when the order of the digits is changed mistakenly, such as writing $542 as $452 or $524. In a **slide**, the entire number is mistakenly moved one or more spaces to the right or the left, such as writing $542.00 as $54.20 or $5,420.00. If an error of either type has occurred and there are no other errors, the difference between the two trial balance totals can be evenly divided by 9.

If an error is not revealed by the trial balance, the steps in the accounting process must be retraced, beginning with the last step and working back to the entries in the journal. Usually, errors causing the trial balance totals to be unequal will be discovered before all of the steps are retraced.

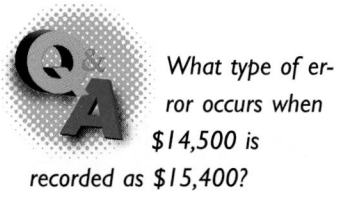

What type of error occurs when $14,500 is recorded as $15,400?

A transposition.

Correction of Errors

The procedures used to correct an error in journalizing or posting vary according to the nature of the error and when the error is discovered. These procedures are summarized in Exhibit 7.

Exhibit 7 Procedures for
Correcting Errors

Error	Correction Procedure
1. Journal entry is incorrect but not posted.	Draw a line through the error and insert correct title or amount.
2. Journal entry is correct but posted incorrectly.	Draw a line through the error and post correctly.
3. Journal entry is incorrect and posted.	Journalize and post a correcting entry.

Correcting the first two types of errors shown in Exhibit 7 involves simply drawing a line through the error and inserting the correct title or amount. Usually, the person making corrections initials the correction in case questions arise later.

Correcting the third type of error in Exhibit 7 is more complex. To illustrate, assume that on May 5 a $12,500 purchase of office equipment on account was incorrectly journalized and posted as a debit to Supplies and a credit to Accounts Payable for $12,500. This posting of the incorrect entry is shown in the following T accounts.

	Supplies		Accounts Payable	
Incorrect:	12,500			12,500

Before making a correcting entry, it is best to determine the debit(s) and credit(s) that should have been recorded. These are shown in the following T accounts.

	Office Equipment		Accounts Payable	
Correct:	12,500			12,500

Comparing the two sets of T accounts shows that the incorrect debit to Supplies may be corrected by debiting Office Equipment for $12,500 and crediting Supplies for $12,500. The following correcting entry is then journalized and posted:

Entry to Correct Error:

18	May	31	Office Equipment	18	12 5 0 0 00		18
19			Supplies	14		12 5 0 0 00	19
20			To correct erroneous debit				20
21			to Supplies on May 5. See invoice				21
22			from Bell Office Equipment Co.				22

FINANCIAL ANALYSIS AND INTERPRETATION

objective 7

Use horizontal analysis to compare financial statements from different periods.

A single item appearing in a financial statement is often useful in interpreting the financial results of a business. However, comparing this item in a current statement with the same item in prior statements often makes the financial information more useful. **Horizontal analysis** is the term used to describe such comparisons.

In horizontal analysis, the amount of each item on the current financial statements is compared with the same item on one or more earlier statements. The increase or decrease in the *amount* of the item is computed, together with the *percent* of increase or decrease. When two statements are being compared, the earlier statement is used as the base for computing the amount and the percent of change.

To illustrate, the horizontal analysis of two income statements for J. Holmes, Attorney-at-Law, organized as a professional corporation, is shown in Exhibit 8. Exhibit 8 indicates both favorable and unfavorable trends affecting the income statement of J. Holmes, Attorney-at-Law. The increase in fees earned is a favorable trend, as is the decrease in supplies expense. Unfavorable trends include the increase in wages expense, utilities expense, and miscellaneous expense. These expenses increased faster than the increase in revenues, with total operating expenses increasing by 30.6%. Overall, net income increased by $15,800, or 19.9%, a favorable trend.

The significance of the various increases and decreases in the revenue and expense items in Exhibit 8 should be investigated to see if operations could be further

Exhibit 8 Horizontal Analysis of Income Statement

J. Holmes, Attorney-at-Law, P.C.
Income Statement
For the Years Ended December 31, 2002 and 2003

	2003	2002	Increase (Decrease) Amount	Increase (Decrease) Percent
Fees earned	$187,500	$150,000	$37,500	25.0%
Operating expenses:				
Wages expense	$ 60,000	$ 45,000	$15,000	33.3%
Rent expense	15,000	12,000	3,000	25.0%
Utilities expense	12,500	9,000	3,500	38.9%
Supplies expense	2,700	3,000	(300)	(10.0)%
Miscellaneous expense	2,300	1,800	500	27.8%
Total operating expenses	$ 92,500	$ 70,800	$21,700	30.6%
Net income	$ 95,000	$ 79,200	$15,800	19.9%

improved. For example, the increase in utilities expense of 38.9% was the result of renting additional office space for use by a part-time law student in performing paralegal services. This explains the increase in rent expense of 25% and the increase in wages expense of 33.3%. The increase in revenues of 25% reflects the fees generated by the new paralegal.

The preceding example illustrates how horizontal analysis can be useful in interpreting and analyzing financial statements. Horizontal analyses similar to that shown in Exhibit 8 can also be performed for the balance sheet, the retained earnings statement, and the statement of cash flows.

The Hijacking Receivable

A company's chart of accounts should reflect the basic nature of its operations. Occasionally, however, transactions take place that give rise to unusual accounts. The following is a story of one such account.

During the early 1970s, before strict airport security was implemented across the United States, several airlines experienced hijacking incidents. One such incident occurred on November 10, 1972, when a Southern Airways DC-9 en route from Memphis to Miami was hijacked during a stopover in Birmingham, Alabama. The

three hijackers boarded the plane in Birmingham armed with handguns and hand grenades. At gunpoint, the hijackers took the plane, the plane's crew of four, and 27 passengers to nine American cities, Toronto, and eventually to Havana, Cuba.

During the long flight, the hijackers threatened to crash the plane into the Oak Ridge, Tennessee, nuclear facilities, insisted on talking with President Nixon, and demanded a ransom of $10 million. Southern Airways, however, was only able to come up with $2 million. Eventually, the pilot

talked the hijackers into settling for the $2 million when the plane landed in Chattanooga for refueling.

Upon landing in Havana, the Cuban authorities arrested the hijackers and, after a brief delay, sent the plane, passengers, and crew back to the United States. The hijackers and $2 million stayed in Cuba.

How did Southern Airways account for and report the hijacking payment in its subsequent financial statements? As you might have analyzed, the initial entry credited Cash for $2 million. The debit was to an account entitled "Hijacking Payment." This account was reported as a type of receivable under "other assets" on Southern's balance sheet. The company maintained that it would be able to collect the cash from the Cuban government and that, therefore, a receivable existed. In fact, in August 1975, Southern Airways was repaid $2 million by the Cuban government, which was, at that time, attempting to improve relations with the United States. ■

KEY POINTS

1 Explain why accounts are used to record and summarize the effects of transactions on financial statements.

The record used for recording individual transactions is an account. A group of accounts is called a ledger. The system of accounts that make up a ledger is called a chart of accounts. The accounts are numbered and listed in the order in which they appear in the balance sheet and the income statement.

2 Describe the characteristics of an account.

The simplest form of an account, a T account, has three parts: (1) a title, which is the name of the item recorded in the account; (2) a left side, called the debit side; (3) a right side, called the credit side. Amounts entered on the left side of an account, regardless of the account title, are called debits to the account. Amounts entered on the right side of an account are called credits. Periodically, the debits in an account are added, the credits in the account are added, and the balance of the account is determined.

3 List the rules of debit and credit and the normal balances of accounts.

General rules of debit and credit have been established for recording increases or decreases in asset, liability, owner's equity, revenue, expense, and dividends accounts. Each transaction is recorded so that the sum of the debits is always equal to the sum of the credits. Transactions are initially entered in a record called a journal.

The sum of the increases recorded in an account is usually equal to or greater than the sum of the decreases recorded in the account. For this reason, the normal balance of an account is indicated by the side of the account (debit or credit) that receives the increases.

The rules of debit and credit and normal account balances are summarized in the following table:

	Increase (Normal Balance)	Decrease
Balance sheet accounts:		
Asset	Debit	Credit
Liability	Credit	Debit
Owner's Equity:		
Capital Stock	Credit	Debit
Retained Earn.	Credit	Debit
Dividends	Debit	Credit
Income statement accounts:		
Revenue	Credit	Debit
Expense	Debit	Credit

4 Analyze and summarize the financial statement effects of transactions.

Transactions are analyzed by determining whether: (1) an asset, liability, owner's equity, revenue, or expense account is affected, (2) each account affected increases or decreases, and (3) each increase or decrease is recorded as a debit or a credit. A journal is used for recording the transaction initially. The journal entries are periodically posted to the accounts.

5 Prepare a trial balance and explain how it can be used to discover errors.

A trial balance is prepared by listing the accounts from the ledger and their balances. If the two totals of the trial balance are not equal, an error has occurred.

6 Discover errors in recording transactions and correct them.

Errors may be discovered (1) by audit procedures, (2) by looking at the trial balance or (3) by chance. The procedures for correcting errors are summarized in Exhibit 7.

7 Use horizontal analysis to compare financial statements from different periods.

In horizontal analysis, the amount of each item on the current financial statements is compared with the same item on one or more earlier statements. The increase or decrease in the *amount* of the item is computed, together with the *percent* of increase or decrease.

ILLUSTRATIVE PROBLEM

J. F. Outz, M.D., has been practicing as a cardiologist for three years in a professional corporation known as Hearts, P.C. During April, 2002, Hearts completed the following transactions:

April 1. Paid office rent for April, $800.
   3. Purchased equipment on account, $2,100.
   5. Received cash on account from patients, $3,150.
   8. Purchased X-ray film and other supplies on account, $245.
   9. One of the items of equipment purchased on April 3 was defective. It was returned with the permission of the supplier, who agreed to reduce the account for the amount charged for the item, $325.
   12. Paid cash to creditors on account, $1,250.
   17. Paid cash for renewal of a six-month property insurance policy, $370.
   20. Discovered that the balances of the cash account and the accounts payable account as of April 1 were overstated by $200. A payment of that amount to a creditor in March had not been recorded. Journalize the $200 payment as of April 20.
   24. Paid cash for laboratory analysis, $545.
   27. Paid cash dividends, $1,250.
   30. Recorded the cash received in payment of services (on a cash basis) to patients during April, $1,720.
   30. Paid salaries of receptionist and nurses, $1,725.
   30. Paid various utility expenses, $360.
   30. Recorded fees charged to patients on account for services performed in April, $5,145.
   30. Paid miscellaneous expenses, $132.

Hearts' account titles, numbers, and balances as of April 1 (all normal balances) are listed as follows: Cash, 11, $4,123; Accounts Receivable, 12, $6,725; Supplies, 13, $290; Prepaid Insurance, 14, $465; Equipment, 18, $19,745; Accounts Payable, 22, $765; Capital Stock, 31, $10,000; Retained Earnings, 32, $20,583; Dividends, 33; Professional Fees, 41; Salary Expense, 51; Rent Expense, 53; Laboratory Expense, 55; Utilities Expense, 56; Miscellaneous Expense, 59.

Instructions

1. Open a ledger of standard four-column accounts for Hearts as of April 1. Enter the balances in the appropriate balance columns and place a check mark (✓) in the posting reference column. (*Hint:* Verify the equality of the debit and credit balances in the ledger before proceeding with the next instruction.)
2. Journalize each transaction in a two-column journal.
3. Post the journal to the ledger, extending the month-end balances to the appropriate balance columns after each posting.
4. Prepare a trial balance as of April 30.

Solution

2. and **3.**

	Date		Description	Post. Ref.	Debit	Credit	
1	2002 April	1	Rent Expense	53	8 0 0 00		1
2			Cash	11		8 0 0 00	2
3			Paid office rent for April.				3
4							4
5		3	Equipment	18	2 1 0 0 00		5
6			Accounts Payable	22		2 1 0 0 00	6
7			Purchased equipment on account.				7

JOURNAL — Page 27

	Date	Description	Post. Ref.	Debit	Credit	
		JOURNAL			**Page 27**	
8						8
9	5	Cash	11	3 1 5 0 00		9
10		Accounts Receivable	12		3 1 5 0 00	10
11		Received cash on account.				11
12						12
13	8	Supplies	13	2 4 5 00		13
14		Accounts payable	22		2 4 5 00	14
15		Purchased supplies.				15
16						16
17	9	Accounts Payable	22	3 2 5 00		17
18		Equipment	18		3 2 5 00	18
19		Returned defective equipment.				19
20						20
21	12	Accounts Payable	22	1 2 5 0 00		21
22		Cash	11		1 2 5 0 00	22
23		Paid creditors on account.				23
24						24
25	17	Prepaid Insurance	14	3 7 0 00		25
26		Cash	11		3 7 0 00	26
27		Renewed 6-month property policy.				27
28						28
29	20	Accounts Payable	22	2 0 0 00		29
30		Cash	11		2 0 0 00	30
31		Recorded March payment				31
32		to creditor.				32

	Date	Description	Post. Ref.	Debit	Credit	
		JOURNAL			**Page 28**	
1	2002 April 24	Laboratory Expense	55	5 4 5 00		1
2		Cash	11		5 4 5 00	2
3		Paid for laboratory analysis.				3
4						4
5	27	Dividends	33	1 2 5 0 00		5
6		Cash	11		1 2 5 0 00	6
7		Paid dividends to stockholders.				7
8						8
9	30	Cash	11	1 7 2 0 00		9
10		Professional Fees	41		1 7 2 0 00	10
11		Received fees from patients.				11
12						12
13	30	Salary Expense	51	1 7 2 5 00		13
14		Cash	11		1 7 2 5 00	14
15		Paid salaries.				15
16						16

	JOURNAL			Page 28	
Date	Description	Post. Ref.	Debit	Credit	
17					17
18	30 Utilities Expense	56	3 6 0 00		18
19	Cash	11		3 6 0 00	19
20	Paid utilities.				20
21					21
22	30 Accounts Receivable	12	5 1 4 5 00		22
23	Professional Fees	41		5 1 4 5 00	23
24	Recorded fees earned on account.				24
25					25
26	30 Miscellaneous Expense	59	1 3 2 00		26
27	Cash	11		1 3 2 00	27
28	Paid expenses.				28

1. and **3.**

ACCOUNT *Cash* **ACCOUNT NO. 11**

Date	Item	Post. Ref.	Debit	Credit	Balance Debit	Balance Credit
2002 April 1	Balance	✓			4 1 2 3 00	
1		27		8 0 0 00	3 3 2 3 00	
5		27	3 1 5 0 00		6 4 7 3 00	
12		27		1 2 5 0 00	5 2 2 3 00	
17		27		3 7 0 00	4 8 5 3 00	
20		27		2 0 0 00	4 6 5 3 00	
24		28		5 4 5 00	4 1 0 8 00	
27		28		1 2 5 0 00	2 8 5 8 00	
30		28	1 7 2 0 00		4 5 7 8 00	
30		28		1 7 2 5 00	2 8 5 3 00	
30		28		3 6 0 00	2 4 9 3 00	
30		28		1 3 2 00	2 3 6 1 00	

ACCOUNT *Accounts Receivable* **ACCOUNT NO. 12**

Date	Item	Post. Ref.	Debit	Credit	Balance Debit	Balance Credit
2002 April 1	Balance	✓			6 7 2 5 00	
5		27		3 1 5 0 00	3 5 7 5 00	
30		28	5 1 4 5 00		8 7 2 0 00	

ACCOUNT *Supplies* **ACCOUNT NO. 13**

Date	Item	Post. Ref.	Debit	Credit	Balance Debit	Balance Credit
2002 April 1	Balance	✓			2 9 0 00	
8		27	2 4 5 00		5 3 5 00	

ACCOUNT Prepaid Insurance — ACCOUNT NO. 14

Date		Item	Post. Ref.	Debit	Credit	Balance Debit	Balance Credit
2002 April	1	Balance	✓			4 6 5 00	
	17		27	3 7 0 00		8 3 5 00	

ACCOUNT Equipment — ACCOUNT NO. 18

Date		Item	Post. Ref.	Debit	Credit	Balance Debit	Balance Credit
2002 April	1	Balance	✓			19 7 4 5 00	
	3		27	2 1 0 0 00		21 8 4 5 00	
	9		27		3 2 5 00	21 5 2 0 00	

ACCOUNT Accounts Payable — ACCOUNT NO. 22

Date		Item	Post. Ref.	Debit	Credit	Balance Debit	Balance Credit
2002 April	1	Balance	✓				7 6 5 00
	3		27		2 1 0 0 00		2 8 6 5 00
	8		27		2 4 5 00		3 1 1 0 00
	9		27	3 2 5 00			2 7 8 5 00
	12		27	1 2 5 0 00			1 5 3 5 00
	20		27	2 0 0 00			1 3 3 5 00

ACCOUNT Capital Stock — ACCOUNT NO. 31

Date		Item	Post. Ref.	Debit	Credit	Balance Debit	Balance Credit
2002 April	1	Balance	✓				10 0 0 0 00

ACCOUNT Retained Earnings — ACCOUNT NO. 32

Date		Item	Post. Ref.	Debit	Credit	Balance Debit	Balance Credit
2002 April	1	Balance	✓				20 5 8 3 00

ACCOUNT Dividends — ACCOUNT NO. 33

Date		Item	Post. Ref.	Debit	Credit	Balance Debit	Balance Credit
2002 April	27		28	1 2 5 0 00		1 2 5 0 00	

ACCOUNT *Professional Fees* **ACCOUNT NO. 41**

Date	Item	Post. Ref.	Debit	Credit	Balance Debit	Balance Credit
2002 April 30		28		1 7 2 0 00		1 7 2 0 00
30		28		5 1 4 5 00		6 8 6 5 00

ACCOUNT *Salary Expense* **ACCOUNT NO. 51**

Date	Item	Post. Ref.	Debit	Credit	Balance Debit	Balance Credit
2002 April 30		28	1 7 2 5 00		1 7 2 5 00	

ACCOUNT *Rent Expense* **ACCOUNT NO. 53**

Date	Item	Post. Ref.	Debit	Credit	Balance Debit	Balance Credit
2002 April 1		27	8 0 0 00		8 0 0 00	

ACCOUNT *Laboratory Expense* **ACCOUNT NO. 55**

Date	Item	Post. Ref.	Debit	Credit	Balance Debit	Balance Credit
2002 April 24		28	5 4 5 00		5 4 5 00	

ACCOUNT *Utilities Expense* **ACCOUNT NO. 56**

Date	Item	Post. Ref.	Debit	Credit	Balance Debit	Balance Credit
2002 April 30		28	3 6 0 00		3 6 0 00	

ACCOUNT *Miscellaneous Expense* **ACCOUNT NO. 59**

Date	Item	Post. Ref.	Debit	Credit	Balance Debit	Balance Credit
2002 April 30		28	1 3 2 00		1 3 2 00	

4.

Hearts, P. C.
Trial Balance
April 30, 2002

Cash			2	3	6	1	00								
Accounts Receivable			8	7	2	0	00								
Supplies				5	3	5	00								
Prepaid Insurance				8	3	5	00								
Equipment		21	5	2	0	00									
Accounts Payable										1	3	3	5	00	
Capital Stock									10	0	0	0	00	
Retained Earnings									20	5	8	3	00	
Dividends			1	2	5	0	00								
Professional Fees										6	8	6	5	00	
Salary Expense			1	7	2	5	00								
Rent Expense				8	0	0	00								
Laboratory Expense				5	4	5	00								
Utilities Expense				3	6	0	00								
Miscellaneous Expense				1	3	2	00								
		38	7	8	3	00			38	7	8	3	00		

SELF-EXAMINATION QUESTIONS   **Answers at End of Chapter**

Matching

Match each of the following statements with its proper term. Some terms may not be used.

A.	**account**
B.	**assets**
C.	**balance of the account**
D.	**chart of accounts**
E.	**credits**
F.	**debits**
G.	**dividends**
H.	**double-entry accounting**
I.	**expenses**
J.	**horizontal analysis**
K.	**journal**
L.	**journal entry**
M.	**journalizing**
N.	**ledger**
O.	**liabilities**
P.	**materiality concept**
Q.	**objectivity concept**
R.	**owner's equity**
S.	**posting**

____ 1. An accounting form that is used to record the increases and decreases in each financial statement item.

____ 2. A group of accounts for a business.

____ 3. A list of the accounts in the ledger.

____ 4. Resources that are owned by the business.

____ 5. Debts owed to outsiders (creditors).

____ 6. The owner's right to the assets of the business.

____ 7. Increases in owner's equity as a result of selling services or products to customers.

____ 8. Assets used up or services consumed in the process of generating revenues.

____ 9. The simplest form of an account.

____10. Amounts entered on the left side of an account.

____11. Amounts entered on the right side of an account.

____12. The amount of the difference between the debits and the credits that have been entered into an account.

____13. The initial record in which the effects of a transaction are recorded.

____14. The process of recording a transaction in the journal.

____15. The form of recording a transaction in a journal.

____16. A system of accounting for recording transactions, based on recording increases and decreases in accounts so that debits equal credits.

____17. The account used to record distributions of earnings to stockholders.

T.   revenues

U.   slide

V.   T account

W.   transposition

X.   trial balance

Y.   two-column journal

Z.   unearned revenue

AA. vertical analysis

____ 18. The process of transferring the debits and credits from the journal entries to the accounts.

____ 19. An all-purpose journal.

____ 20. The liability created by receiving revenue in advance.

____ 21. A summary listing of the titles and balances of accounts in the ledger.

____ 22. A concept of accounting that implies that an error may be treated in the easiest possible way.

____ 23. An error in which the order of the digits is changed, such as writing $542 as $452 or $524.

____ 24. An error in which the entire number is moved one or more spaces to the right or the left, such as writing $542.00 as $54.20 or $5,420.00.

____ 25. Financial analysis that compares an item in a current statement with the same item in prior statements.

Multiple Choice

1. A debit may signify:
   A. an increase in an asset account.
   B. a decrease in an asset account.
   C. an increase in a liability account.
   D. an increase in the capital stock account.

2. The type of account with a normal credit balance is:
   A. an asset.   C. a revenue.
   B. dividends.   D. an expense.

3. A debit balance in which of the following accounts would indicate a likely error?
   A. Accounts Receivable
   B. Cash
   C. Fees Earned
   D. Miscellaneous Expense

4. The receipt of cash from customers in payment of their accounts would be recorded by a:
   A. debit to Cash; credit to Accounts Receivable.
   B. debit to Accounts Receivable; credit to Cash.
   C. debit to Cash; credit to Accounts Payable.
   D. debit to Accounts Payable; credit to Cash.

5. The form listing the titles and balances of the accounts in the ledger on a given date is the:
   A. income statement.
   B. balance sheet.
   C. retained earnings statement.
   D. trial balance.

CLASS DISCUSSION QUESTIONS

1. What is the difference between an account and a ledger?
2. Describe in general terms the sequence of accounts in the ledger.
3. Do the terms *debit* and *credit* signify increase or decrease or can they signify either? Explain.
4. Explain why the rules of debit and credit are the same for liability accounts and owner's equity accounts.
5. What is the effect (increase or decrease) of a debit to an expense account (a) in terms of owner's equity and (b) in terms of expense?
6. What is the effect (increase or decrease) of a credit to a revenue account (a) in terms of owner's equity and (b) in terms of revenue?
7. Meadows Company adheres to a policy of depositing all cash receipts in a bank account and making all payments by check. The cash account as of July 31 has a credit balance of $900, and there is no undeposited cash on hand. (a) Assuming no errors occurred during journalizing or posting, what caused this unusual balance? (b) Is the $900 credit balance in the cash account an asset, a liability, owner's equity, a revenue, or an expense?
8. Rearrange the following in proper sequence: (a) entry is posted to ledger, (b) business transaction occurs, (c) entry is recorded in journal, (d) business document is prepared, (e) business transaction is authorized.
9. Describe the three procedures required to post the credit portion of the following journal entry (Fees Earned is account no. 41):

JOURNAL						Page 19	
Date		Description	Post. Ref.	Debit		Credit	
2003 Nov.	23	Accounts Receivable	12	3 0 2 0 00			1
		Fees Earned				3 0 2 0 00	2

10. In the journal, what indicates that an entry has been posted to the accounts?

11. Shaw Company performed services in October for a specific customer, for a fee of $4,230. Payment was received the following November. (a) Was the revenue earned in October or November? (b) What accounts should be debited and credited in (1) October and (2) November?

12. What proof is provided by a trial balance?

13. If the two totals of a trial balance are equal, does it mean that there are no errors in the accounting records? Explain.

14. Assume that a trial balance is prepared with an account balance of $21,750 listed as $21,570 and an account balance of $6,100 listed as $610. Identify the transposition and the slide.

15. Assume that when a purchase of supplies of $1,050 for cash was recorded, both the debit and the credit were journalized and posted as $1,500. (a) Would this error cause the trial balance to be out of balance? (b) Would the trial balance be out of balance if the $1,050 entry had been journalized correctly but the credit to Cash had been posted as $1,500?

16. How is a correction made when an error in an account title or amount in the journal is discovered before the entry is posted?

17. In journalizing and posting the entry to record the purchase of supplies on account, the accounts receivable account was credited in error. What is the preferred procedure to correct this error?

18. Banks rely heavily upon customers' deposits as a source of funds. Demand deposits normally pay interest to the customer, who is entitled to withdraw at any time without prior notice to the bank. Checking and NOW (negotiable order of withdrawal) accounts are the most common form of demand deposits for banks. Assume that ABC Storage has a checking account at American Savings Bank. What type of account (asset, liability, owner's equity, revenue, expense, dividends) does the account balance of $13,850 represent from the viewpoint of (a) ABC Storage and (b) American Savings Bank?

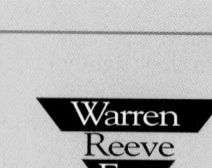

RESOURCES FOR YOUR SUCCESS ONLINE AT

http://warren.swcollege.com

Remember! If you need additional help, visit South-Western's Web site.
See page F26 for a description of the online and printed materials that are available.

EXERCISES

Exercise 2–1
Chart of accounts

Objective 1

The following accounts appeared in recent financial statements of **Continental Airlines**:

Accounts Payable	Flight Equipment
Aircraft Fuel Expense	Landing Fees
Air Traffic Liability	Passenger Revenue
Cargo and Mail Revenue	Purchase Deposits for Flight Equipment
Commissions	Spare Parts and Supplies

Identify each account as either a balance sheet account or an income statement account. For each balance sheet account, identify it as an asset, a liability, or owner's equity. For each income statement account, identify it as a revenue or an expense.

Exercise 2–2
Chart of accounts
Objective 1

Cameron Interiors is owned and operated by Kim Walks, an interior decorator. In the ledger of Cameron Interiors, the first digit of the account number indicates its major account classification (1—assets, 2—liabilities, 3—owner's equity, 4—revenues, 5—expenses). The second digit of the account number indicates the specific account within each of the preceding major account classifications.

Match each account number with its most likely account in the list below. The account numbers are 11, 12, 13, 21, 31, 32, 33, 41, 51, 52, and 53.

Accounts:

Accounts Payable	Land
Accounts Receivable	Miscellaneous Expense
Capital Stock	Retained Earnings
Cash	Supplies Expense
Dividends	Wages Expense
Fees Earned	

Exercise 2–3
Chart of accounts
Objective 1

The Charisma School is a newly organized business that teaches people how to inspire and influence others. The list of accounts to be opened in the general ledger is as follows:

Accounts Payable	Equipment	Retained Earnings
Accounts Receivable	Fees Earned	Supplies
Capital Stock	Miscellaneous Expense	Supplies Expense
Cash	Prepaid Insurance	Unearned Rent
Dividends	Rent Expense	Wages Expense

List the accounts in the order in which they should appear in the ledger of The Charisma School and assign account numbers. Each account number is to have two digits: the first digit is to indicate the major classification (*1* for assets, etc.), and the second digit is to identify the specific account within each major classification (*11* for Cash, etc.).

Exercise 2–4
Identifying transactions
Objectives 2, 3

World Co. is a travel agency. The nine transactions recorded by World during April, its first month of operations, are indicated in the following T accounts:

Cash			
(1) 30,000	(2) 1,500
(7) 9,500	(3) 10,000
	(4) 4,050
	(6) 7,500
	(8) 3,000

Equipment	
(3) 30,000	

Dividends	
(8) 3,000	

Accounts Receivable	
(5) 13,000	(7) 9,500

Accounts Payable	
(6) 7,500	(3) 20,000

Service Revenue	
	(5) 13,000

Supplies	
(2) 1,500	(9) 1,050

Capital Stock	
	(1) 30,000

Operating Expenses	
(4) 4,050	
(9) 1,050	

Indicate for each debit and each credit: (a) whether an asset, liability, owner's equity, dividends, revenue, or expense account was affected and (b) whether the account was increased (+) or decreased (−). Present your answers in the following form, with transaction (1) given as an example:

Transaction	Account Debited		Account Credited	
	Type	Effect	Type	Effect
(1)	asset	+	owner's equity	+

Exercise 2–5
Journal entries
Objectives 3, 4

Based upon the T accounts in Exercise 2–4, prepare the nine journal entries from which the postings were made. Journal entry explanations may be omitted.

Exercise 2–6
Trial balance
Objective 5

✓ Total Debit Column: $55,500

Based upon the data presented in Exercise 2–4, prepare a trial balance, listing the accounts in their proper order.

Exercise 2–7
Normal entries for accounts
Objective 3

During the month, Quark Labs Co. has a substantial number of transactions affecting each of the following accounts. State for each account whether it is likely to have (a) debit entries only, (b) credit entries only, or (c) both debit and credit entries.

1. Accounts Payable
2. Accounts Receivable
3. Cash
4. Fees Earned
5. Dividends
6. Miscellaneous Expense
7. Supplies Expense

Exercise 2–8
Normal balances of accounts
Objective 3

Identify each of the following accounts of Century Services Co. as asset, liability, owner's equity, revenue, or expense, and state in each case whether the normal balance is a debit or a credit.

a. Accounts Payable
b. Accounts Receivable
c. Cash
d. Capital Stock
e. Dividends
f. Equipment
g. Fees Earned
h. Rent Expense
i. Salary Expense
j. Supplies

Exercise 2–9
Rules of debit and credit
Objective 3

The following table summarizes the rules of debit and credit. For each of the items (a) through (n), indicate whether the proper answer is a debit or a credit.

	Increase	Decrease	Normal Balance
Balance sheet accounts:			
Asset	Debit	Credit	(a)
Liability	(b)	(c)	(d)
Owner's Equity:			
Capital Stock	(e)	(f)	Credit
Retained Earnings	Credit	(g)	(h)
Dividends	(i)	Credit	(j)
Income statement accounts:			
Revenue	(k)	Debit	(l)
Expense	(m)	Credit	(n)

Exercise 2–10
Capital account balance
Objectives 2, 3

As of January 1, Retained Earnings had a credit balance of $7,500. During the year, dividends totaled $5,000 and the business incurred a net loss of $6,000.

a. Calculate the balance of retained earnings as of the end of the year.
b. Assuming that there have been no recording errors, will the balance sheet prepared at December 31 balance? Explain.

Exercise 2–11
Cash account balance

Objectives 2, 3

During the month, Kapok Co. received $312,800 in cash and paid out $295,000 in cash.

a. Do the data indicate that Kapok Co. earned $17,800 during the month? Explain.
b. If the balance of the cash account is $26,300 at the end of the month, what was the cash balance at the beginning of the month?

Exercise 2–12
Account balances

Objectives 2, 3

✓ c. $13,800

a. On June 1, the cash account balance was $3,850. During June, cash receipts totaled $11,850 and the June 30 balance was $4,150. Determine the cash payments made during June.
b. On May 1, the accounts receivable account balance was $18,500. During May, $21,000 was collected from customers on account. Assuming the May 31 balance was $27,500, determine the fees billed to customers on account during May.
c. During January, $60,500 was paid to creditors on account and purchases on account were $77,700. Assuming the January 31 balance of Accounts Payable was $31,000, determine the account balance on January 1.

Exercise 2–13
Transactions

Objectives 3, 4

The Wildcat Co. has the following accounts in its ledger: Cash; Accounts Receivable; Supplies; Office Equipment; Accounts Payable; Capital Stock; Dividends; Fees Earned; Rent Expense; Advertising Expense; Utilities Expense; Miscellaneous Expense.

Journalize the following selected transactions in a two-column journal. Journal entry explanations may be omitted.

March 1. Paid rent for the month, $2,500.
       2. Paid advertising expense, $600.
       4. Paid cash for supplies, $1,050.
       6. Purchased office equipment on account, $4,500.
       8. Received cash from customers on account, $3,600.
      12. Paid creditor on account, $2,150.
      20. Paid dividends, $1,000.
      25. Paid cash for repairs to office equipment, $120.
      30. Paid telephone bill for the month, $195.
      31. Fees earned and billed to customers for the month, $11,150.
      31. Paid electricity bill for the month, $280.

Exercise 2–14
Journalizing and posting

Objectives 3, 4

On November 12, 2003, Trux Co. purchased $1,720 of supplies on account. In Trux Co.'s chart of accounts, the supplies account is No. 15 and the accounts payable account is No. 21.

a. Journalize the November 12, 2003 transaction on page 29 of Trux Co.'s two-column journal. Include an explanation of the entry.
b. Prepare a four-column account for Supplies. Enter a debit balance of $390 as of November 1, 2003. Place a check mark (✓) in the posting reference column.
c. Prepare a four-column account for Accounts Payable. Enter a credit balance of $9,681 as of November 1, 2003. Place a check mark (✓) in the posting reference column.
d. Post the November 12, 2003 transaction to the accounts.

Exercise 2–15
Transactions and T accounts

Objectives 2, 3, 4

SPREADSHEET

The following selected transactions were completed during September of the current year:

1. Billed customers for fees earned, $8,210.
2. Purchased supplies on account, $1,070.
3. Received cash from customers on account, $6,150.
4. Paid creditors on account, $750.

a. Journalize the above transactions in a two-column journal, using the appropriate number to identify the transactions. Journal entry explanations may be omitted.
b. Post the entries prepared in (a) to the following T accounts: Cash, Supplies, Accounts Receivable, Accounts Payable, Fees Earned. To the left of each amount posted in the accounts, place the appropriate number to identify the transactions.

Exercise 2–16
Trial balance

Objective 5

✓ Total Credit Column: $503,500

The accounts in the ledger of Bogart Park Co. as of August 31 of the current year are listed in alphabetical order as follows. All accounts have normal balances. The balance of the cash account has been intentionally omitted.

Accounts Payable	$ 13,710
Accounts Receivable	27,500
Capital Stock	75,000
Cash	?
Dividends	25,000
Fees Earned	333,500
Insurance Expense	5,000
Land	125,000
Miscellaneous Expense	9,900
Notes Payable	40,000
Prepaid Insurance	3,150
Rent Expense	58,000
Retained Earnings	35,290
Supplies	4,100
Supplies Expense	5,900
Unearned Rent	6,000
Utilities Expense	41,500
Wages Expense	175,000

Prepare a trial balance, listing the accounts in their proper order and inserting the missing figure for cash.

Exercise 2–17
Effect of errors on trial balance

Objective 5

Indicate which of the following errors, each considered individually, would cause the trial balance totals to be unequal:

a. Payment of dividends of $3,500 was journalized and posted as a debit of $5,300 to Salary Expense and a credit of $3,500 to Cash.
b. A payment of $6,100 for equipment purchased was posted as a debit of $1,600 to Equipment and a credit of $1,600 to Cash.
c. A fee of $1,850 earned and due from a client was not debited to Accounts Receivable or credited to a revenue account, because the cash had not been received.
d. A receipt of $325 from an account receivable was journalized and posted as a debit of $325 to Cash and a credit of $325 to Fees Earned.
e. A payment of $1,075 to a creditor was posted as a debit of $1,075 to Accounts Payable and a debit of $1,075 to Cash.

Exercise 2–18
Errors in trial balance

Objective 5

✓ Total of Credit Column: $167,255

The following preliminary trial balance of Entrée Co., a sports ticket agency, does not balance:

Entrée Co.
Trial Balance
December 31, 20—

Cash	75,350	
Accounts Receivable	23,600	
Prepaid Insurance		3,300
Equipment	86,000	
Accounts Payable		9,450
Unearned Rent		2,570
Capital Stock	30,000	
Retained Earnings	61,615	
Dividends	10,000	
Service Revenue		64,940
Wages Expense		33,400
Advertising Expense	5,200	
Miscellaneous Expense		1,380
	291,765	115,040

When the ledger and other records are reviewed, you discover the following: (1) the debits and credits in the cash account total $75,350 and $53,975, respectively; (2) a billing of $1,000 to a customer on account was not posted to the accounts receivable account; (3) a payment of $1,500 made to a creditor on account was not posted to the accounts payable account; (4) the balance of the unearned rent account is $2,750; (5) the correct balance of the equipment account is $68,000; and (6) each account has a normal balance.

Prepare a corrected trial balance.

Exercise 2–19
Effect of errors on trial balance
Objective 5

The following errors occurred in posting from a two-column journal:

1. A debit of $750 to Accounts Payable was posted as a credit.
2. A credit of $350 to Cash was posted as $530.
3. A debit of $800 to Cash was posted to Miscellaneous Expense.
4. A debit of $1,050 to Supplies was posted twice.
5. A debit of $1,575 to Wages Expense was posted as $5,175.
6. A credit of $3,175 to Accounts Payable was not posted.
7. An entry debiting Accounts Receivable and crediting Fees Earned for $4,500 was not posted.

Considering each case individually (i.e., assuming that no other errors had occurred), indicate: (a) by "yes" or "no" whether the trial balance would be out of balance; (b) if answer to (a) is "yes," the amount by which the trial balance totals would differ; and (c) whether the debit or credit column of the trial balance would have the larger total. Answers should be presented in the following form, with error (1) given as an example:

Error	(a) Out of Balance	(b) Difference	(c) Larger Total
1.	yes	$1,500	credit

Exercise 2–20
Errors in trial balance
Objective 5

What's Wrong
With This?

✓ Total of Credit Column: $120,900

How many errors can you find in the following trial balance? All accounts have normal balances.

Goulet Co.
Trial Balance
For the Month Ending January 31, 2003

Cash	8,010	
Accounts Receivable		16,400
Prepaid Insurance	2,400	
Equipment	52,000	
Accounts Payable	1,850	
Salaries Payable		750
Capital Stock		18,000
Retained Earnings		21,600
Dividends		5,000
Service Revenue		78,700
Salary Expense	28,400	
Advertising Expense		7,200
Miscellaneous Expense	1,490	
	94,150	94,150

Exercise 2–21
Entries to correct errors
Objective 6

The following errors took place in journalizing and posting transactions:

a. Dividends of $20,000 were recorded as a debit to Salary Expense and a credit to Cash.
b. Rent of $3,000 paid for the current month was recorded as a debit to Rent Expense and a credit to Accounts Payable.

Journalize the entries to correct the errors. Omit explanations.

Exercise 2–22
Entries to correct errors

Objective 6

The following errors took place in journalizing and posting transactions:

a. A $750 purchase of supplies on account was recorded as a debit to Miscellaneous Expense and a credit to Cash.
b. Cash of $2,700 received on account was recorded as a debit to Accounts Payable and a credit to Cash.

Journalize the entries to correct the errors. Omit explanations.

Exercise 2–23
Horizontal analysis of income statement

Objective 7

The financial statements for **Cisco Systems, Inc.**, are presented in Appendix G at the end of the text.

a. For Cisco Systems, comparing 2000 with 1999, determine the amount of change and the percent of change for
   1. net sales (revenues) and
   2. sales and marketing expenses.
b. ✏️➤　What conclusions can you draw from your analysis of the net sales and the selling, marketing, and administrative expenses?

PROBLEMS SERIES A

Problem 2–1A
Entries into T accounts and trial balance

Objectives 2, 3, 4, 5

✓ 3. Total of Debit Column: $33,925

Sherry Lundin, an architect, opened an office on March 1 of the current year. During the month, she completed the following transactions connected with her professional corporation, Lundin Designs, P.C.:

a. Transferred cash from a personal bank account to an account to be used for the business in exchange for capital stock, $15,000.
b. Paid March rent for office and workroom, $2,000.
c. Purchased used automobile for $11,500, paying $2,500 cash and giving a note payable for the remainder.
d. Purchased office and computer equipment on account, $5,500.
e. Paid cash for supplies, $750.
f. Paid cash for annual insurance policies, $1,050.
g. Received cash from client for plans delivered, $3,100.
h. Paid cash for miscellaneous expenses, $75.
i. Paid cash to creditors on account, $2,950.
j. Paid installment due on note payable, $400.
k. Received invoice for blueprint service, due in April, $525.
l. Recorded fee earned on plans delivered, payment to be received in April, $4,150.
m. Paid salary of assistant, $1,200.
n. Paid gas, oil, and repairs on automobile for March, $150.

Instructions

1. Record the foregoing transactions directly in the following T accounts, without journalizing: Cash; Accounts Receivable; Supplies; Prepaid Insurance; Automobiles; Equipment; Notes Payable; Accounts Payable; Capital Stock; Professional Fees; Rent Expense; Salary Expense; Automobile Expense; Blueprint Expense; Miscellaneous Expense. To the left of the amount entered in the accounts, place the appropriate letter to identify the transaction.
2. Determine the balances of the T accounts having two or more debits or credits. A memorandum balance should be inserted in accounts having both debits and credits, in the manner illustrated in the chapter. For accounts with entries on one side only (such as Professional Fees), there is no need to insert the memorandum balance in the item column. For accounts containing only a single debit and a single credit (such as Notes Payable), the memorandum balance should be inserted in the appropriate item column. Accounts containing a single entry only (such as Prepaid Insurance) do not need a memorandum balance.
3. Prepare a trial balance for Lundin Designs, P.C., as of March 31 of the current year.

Problem 2–2A
Journal entries and trial balance

Objectives 2, 3, 4, 5

GENERAL
LEDGER

✓ 4. c. $4,225

On May 1, 2003, Jim Lindley established Homestead Realty, which completed the following transactions during the month:

a. Jim Lindley transferred cash from a personal bank account to an account to be used for the business in exchange for capital stock, $7,500.
b. Paid rent on office and equipment for the month, $2,500.
c. Purchased supplies on account, $1,200.
d. Paid creditor on account, $900.
e. Earned sales commissions, receiving cash, $15,750.
f. Paid automobile expenses (including rental charge) for month, $2,400, and miscellaneous expenses, $1,250.
g. Paid office salaries, $4,500.
h. Determined that the cost of supplies used was $875.
i. Paid dividends, $2,500.

Instructions

1. Journalize entries for transactions (a) through (i), using the following account titles: Cash; Supplies; Accounts Payable; Capital Stock; Dividends; Sales Commissions; Office Salaries Expense; Rent Expense; Automobile Expense; Supplies Expense; Miscellaneous Expense. Explanations may be omitted.
2. Prepare T accounts, using the account titles in (1). Post the journal entries to these accounts, placing the appropriate letter to the left of each amount to identify the transactions. Determine the account balances, after all posting is complete, for all accounts having two or more debits or credits. A memorandum balance should also be inserted in accounts having both debits and credits, in the manner illustrated in the chapter. For accounts with entries on one side only, there is no need to insert a memorandum balance in the item column. For accounts containing only a single debit and a single credit, the memorandum balance should be inserted in the appropriate item column.
3. Prepare a trial balance as of May 31, 2003.
4. Determine the following:
    a. Amount of total revenue recorded in the ledger.
    b. Amount of total expenses recorded in the ledger.
    c. Amount of net income for May.

Problem 2–3A
Journal entries and trial balance

Objectives 2, 3, 4, 5

GENERAL
LEDGER

✓ 3. Total of Credit Column: $47,400

On April 5 of the current year, John Bike established an interior decorating business, Tucson Designs. During the remainder of the month, John completed the following transactions related to the business:

April 5. John transferred cash from a personal bank account to an account to be used for the business in exchange for capital stock, $18,000.
6. Paid rent for period of April 6 to end of month, $2,000.
7. Purchased office equipment on account, $10,500.
8. Purchased a used truck for $18,000, paying $10,000 cash and giving a note payable for the remainder.
10. Purchased supplies for cash, $1,315.
12. Received cash for job completed, $7,300.
20. Paid annual premiums on property and casualty insurance, $1,200.
23. Recorded jobs completed on account and sent invoices to customers, $4,950.
24. Received an invoice for truck expenses, to be paid in July, $450.
29. Paid utilities expense, $750.
29. Paid miscellaneous expenses, $210.
30. Received cash from customers on account, $2,200.
30. Paid wages of employees, $3,000.
30. Paid creditor a portion of the amount owed for equipment purchased on April 7, $1,800.
30. Paid dividends, $3,500.

Instructions

1. Journalize each transaction in a two-column journal, referring to the following chart of accounts in selecting the accounts to be debited and credited. (Do not insert the account numbers in the journal at this time.) Explanations may be omitted.

11	Cash	31	Capital Stock
12	Accounts Receivable	33	Dividends
13	Supplies	41	Fees Earned
14	Prepaid Insurance	51	Wages Expense
16	Equipment	53	Rent Expense
18	Truck	54	Utilities Expense
21	Notes Payable	55	Truck Expense
22	Accounts Payable	59	Miscellaneous Expense

2. Post the journal to a ledger of four-column accounts, inserting appropriate posting references as each item is posted. Extend the balances to the appropriate balance columns after each transaction is posted.
3. Prepare a trial balance for Tucson Designs as of April 30.

Problem 2–4A
Journal entries and trial balance

Objectives 2, 3, 4, 5

GENERAL LEDGER

✓ 4. Total of Debit Column:
$265,200

Eastside Realty acts as an agent in buying, selling, renting, and managing real estate. The account balances at the end of March of the current year are as follows:

11	Cash	18,150	
12	Accounts Receivable	48,750	
13	Prepaid Insurance	1,100	
14	Office Supplies	1,050	
16	Land	0	
21	Accounts Payable		11,510
22	Notes Payable		0
31	Capital Stock		10,000
32	Retained Earnings		24,340
33	Dividends	1,000	
41	Fees Earned		126,500
51	Salary and Commission Expense	74,100	
52	Rent Expense	15,000	
53	Advertising Expense	8,900	
54	Automobile Expense	2,750	
59	Miscellaneous Expense	1,550	
		172,350	172,350

The following business transactions were completed by Eastside Realty during April of the current year:

April 1. Paid rent on office for month, $5,000.
    2. Purchased office supplies on account, $1,375.
    5. Paid annual insurance premiums, $1,650.
    8. Received cash from clients on account, $20,200.
    15. Purchased land for a future building site for $75,000, paying $7,500 in cash and giving a note payable for the remainder.
    17. Paid creditors on account, $4,150.
    20. Returned a portion of the office supplies purchased on April 2, receiving full credit for their cost, $275.
    24. Paid advertising expense, $1,050.
    27. Discovered an error in computing a commission; received cash from the salesperson for the overpayment, $350.
    28. Paid automobile expense (including rental charges for an automobile), $715.
    29. Paid miscellaneous expenses, $215.
    30. Recorded revenue earned and billed to clients during the month, $28,400.
    30. Paid salaries and commissions for the month, $11,500.
    30. Paid dividends, $2,000.

Instructions

1. Record the April 1 balance of each account in the appropriate balance column of a four-column account, write *Balance* in the item section, and place a check mark (✓) in the posting reference column.

2. Journalize the transactions for April in a two-column journal. Journal entry explanations may be omitted.
3. Post to the ledger, extending the account balance to the appropriate balance column after each posting.
4. Prepare a trial balance of the ledger as of April 30.

If the working papers correlating with this textbook are not used, omit Problem 2–5A.

Problem 2–5A
Errors in trial balance

Objectives 5, 6

✓ 7. Total of Debit Column:

$33,338.10

The following records of Reliable TV Repair are presented in the working papers:

- Journal containing entries for the period March 1–31.
- Ledger to which the March entries have been posted.
- Preliminary trial balance as of March 31, which does not balance.

Locate the errors, supply the information requested, and prepare a corrected trial balance according to the following instructions. The balances recorded in the accounts as of March 1 and the entries in the journal are correctly stated. If it is necessary to correct any posted amounts in the ledger, a line should be drawn through the erroneous figure and the correct amount inserted above. Corrections or notations may be inserted on the preliminary trial balance in any manner desired. It is not necessary to complete all of the instructions if equal trial balance totals can be obtained earlier. However, the requirements of instructions (6) and (7) should be completed in any event.

Instructions

1. Verify the totals of the preliminary trial balance, inserting the correct amounts in the schedule provided in the working papers.
2. Compute the difference between the trial balance totals.
3. Compare the listings in the trial balance with the balances appearing in the ledger, and list the errors in the space provided in the working papers.
4. Verify the accuracy of the balance of each account in the ledger, and list the errors in the space provided in the working papers.
5. Trace the postings in the ledger back to the journal, using small check marks to identify items traced. Correct any amounts in the ledger that may be necessitated by errors in posting, and list the errors in the space provided in the working papers.
6. Journalize as of March 31 the payment of $100 for advertising expense. The bill had been paid on March 31 but was inadvertently omitted from the journal. Post to the ledger. (Revise any amounts necessitated by posting this entry.)
7. Prepare a new trial balance.

Problem 2–6A
Corrected trial balance

Objectives 5, 6

SPREADSHEET

✓ 1. Total of Debit Column: $90,000

Persian Carpet has the following trial balance as of March 31 of the current year:

Cash	7,315	
Accounts Receivable	5,545	
Supplies	1,010	
Prepaid Insurance	250	
Equipment	25,000	
Notes Payable		20,000
Accounts Payable		4,960
Capital Stock		6,000
Retained Earnings		12,800
Dividends	5,500	
Fees Earned		54,790
Wages Expense	31,100	
Rent Expense	7,455	
Advertising Expense	320	
Miscellaneous Expense	1,505	
	85,000	98,550

The debit and credit totals are not equal as a result of the following errors:

a. The balance of cash was understated by $900.
b. A cash receipt of $1,750 was posted as a debit to Cash of $7,150.

c. A debit of $2,500 for a dividend was posted as a credit to Retained Earnings.
d. The balance of $3,200 in Advertising Expense was entered as $320 in the trial balance.
e. A debit of $580 to Accounts Receivable was not posted.
f. A return of $125 of defective supplies was erroneously posted as a $215 credit to Supplies.
g. The balance of Notes Payable was overstated by $5,000.
h. An insurance policy acquired at a cost of $150 was posted as a credit to Prepaid Insurance.
i. Gas, Electricity, and Water Expense, with a balance of $3,150, was omitted from the trial balance.
j. A debit of $1,050 in Accounts Payable was overlooked when determining the balance of the account.

Instructions

1. Prepare a corrected trial balance as of March 31 of the current year.
2. ◖▬► Does the fact that the trial balance in (1) is balanced mean that there are no errors in the accounts? Explain.

PROBLEMS SERIES B

Problem 2–1B
Entries into T accounts and trial balance

Objectives 2, 3, 4, 5

✓ 3. Total of Debit Column: $48,175

James Bitnar, an architect, opened an office on September 1 of the current year. During the month, he completed the following transactions connected with his professional corporation, Bitnar Architecture, P.C.:

a. Transferred cash from a personal bank account to an account to be used for the business in exchange for capital stock, $25,000.
b. Purchased used automobile for $18,300, paying $6,000 cash and giving a note payable for the remainder.
c. Paid September rent for office and workroom, $2,500.
d. Paid cash for supplies, $300.
e. Purchased office and computer equipment on account, $6,200.
f. Paid cash for annual insurance policies on automobile and equipment, $1,200.
g. Received cash from a client for plans delivered, $3,725.
h. Paid cash to creditors on account, $2,100.
i. Paid cash for miscellaneous expenses, $120.
j. Received invoice for blueprint service, due in following month, $350.
k. Recorded fee earned on plans delivered, payment to be received in October, $3,500.
l. Paid salary of assistant, $1,500.
m. Paid cash for miscellaneous expenses, $105.
n. Paid installment due on note payable, $800.
o. Paid gas, oil, and repairs on automobile for September, $145.

Instructions

1. Record the foregoing transactions directly in the following T accounts, without journalizing: Cash; Accounts Receivable; Supplies; Prepaid Insurance; Automobiles; Equipment; Notes Payable; Accounts Payable; Capital Stock; Professional Fees; Rent Expense; Salary Expense; Blueprint Expense; Automobile Expense; Miscellaneous Expense. To the left of each amount entered in the accounts, place the appropriate letter to identify the transaction.
2. Determine the balances of the T accounts having two or more debits or credits. A memorandum balance should be inserted in accounts having both debits and credits, in the manner illustrated in the chapter. For accounts with entries on one side only (such as Professional Fees), there is no need to insert the memorandum balance in the item column. For accounts containing only a single debit and a single credit (such as Notes Payable), the memorandum balance should be inserted in the appropriate item column. Accounts containing a single entry only (such as Prepaid Insurance) do not need a memorandum balance.
3. Prepare a trial balance for Bitnar Architecture, P.C., as of September 30 of the current year.

Problem 2–2B
Journal entries and trial balance

Objectives 2, 3, 4, 5

GENERAL
LEDGER

✓ 4. c. $10,245

On December 1, 2003, Mary Jo Croy established Preferred Realty, which completed the following transactions during the month:

a. Mary Jo Croy transferred cash from a personal bank account to an account to be used for the business in exchange for capital stock, $10,000.
b. Purchased supplies on account, $1,900.
c. Earned sales commissions, receiving cash, $22,600.
d. Paid rent on office and equipment for the month, $4,500.
e. Paid creditor on account, $1,000.
f. Paid dividends, $3,000.
g. Paid automobile expenses (including rental charge) for month, $1,900, and miscellaneous expenses, $1,050.
h. Paid office salaries, $4,000.
i. Determined that the cost of supplies used was $905.

Instructions

1. Journalize entries for transactions (a) through (i), using the following account titles: Cash; Supplies; Accounts Payable; Capital Stock; Dividends; Sales Commissions; Rent Expense; Office Salaries Expense; Automobile Expense; Supplies Expense; Miscellaneous Expense. Journal entry explanations may be omitted.
2. Prepare T accounts, using the account titles in (1). Post the journal entries to these accounts, placing the appropriate letter to the left of each amount to identify the transactions. Determine the account balances, after all posting is complete, for all accounts having two or more debits or credits. A memorandum balance should be inserted in accounts having both debits and credits, in the manner illustrated in the chapter. For accounts with entries on one side only, there is no need to insert a memorandum balance in the item column. For accounts containing only a single debit and a single credit, the memorandum balance should be inserted in the appropriate item column.
3. Prepare a trial balance as of December 31, 2003.
4. Determine the following:
    a. Amount of total revenue recorded in the ledger.
    b. Amount of total expenses recorded in the ledger.
    c. Amount of net income for December.

Problem 2–3B
Journal entries and trial balance

Objectives 2, 3, 4, 5

GENERAL
LEDGER

✓ 3. Total of Credit Column: $33,480

On October 10 of the current year, Kirk Hurwitz established an interior decorating business, Marquis Designs. During the remainder of the month, Kirk Hurwitz completed the following transactions related to the business:

Oct. 10. Kirk transferred cash from a personal bank account to an account to be used for the business in exchange for capital stock, $15,000.
10. Paid rent for period of October 10 to end of month, $1,600.
11. Purchased a truck for $15,000, paying $5,000 cash and giving a note payable for the remainder.
13. Purchased equipment on account, $3,500.
14. Purchased supplies for cash, $1,050.
14. Paid annual premiums on property and casualty insurance, $750.
15. Received cash for job completed, $3,100.
21. Paid creditor for equipment purchased on October 13, $3,500.
24. Recorded jobs completed on account and sent invoices to customers, $5,100.
26. Received an invoice for truck expenses, to be paid in November, $280.
27. Paid utilities expense, $1,205.
27. Paid miscellaneous expenses, $180.
29. Received cash from customers on account, $2,420.
30. Paid wages of employees, $2,500.
31. Paid dividends, $1,000.

Instructions

1. Journalize each transaction in a two-column journal, referring to the following chart of accounts in selecting the accounts to be debited and credited. (Do not insert the account numbers in the journal at this time.) Journal entry explanations may be omitted.

11	Cash	31	Capital Stock
12	Accounts Receivable	33	Dividends
13	Supplies	41	Fees Earned
14	Prepaid Insurance	51	Wages Expense
16	Equipment	53	Rent Expense
18	Truck	54	Utilities Expense
21	Notes Payable	55	Truck Expense
22	Accounts Payable	59	Miscellaneous Expense

2. Post the journal to a ledger of four-column accounts, inserting appropriate posting references as each item is posted. Extend the balances to the appropriate balance columns after each transaction is posted.
3. Prepare a trial balance for Marquis Designs as of October 31.

Problem 2–4B

Journal entries and trial balance

Objectives 2, 3, 4, 5

GENERAL LEDGER

✓ 4. Total of Debit Column: $240,100

Gallatin Realty acts as an agent in buying, selling, renting, and managing real estate. The account balances at the end of November of the current year are as follows:

11	Cash	19,500	
12	Accounts Receivable	28,600	
13	Prepaid Insurance	1,750	
14	Office Supplies	625	
16	Land	0	
21	Accounts Payable		3,250
22	Notes Payable		0
31	Capital Stock		5,000
32	Retained Earnings		7,625
33	Dividends	10,000	
41	Fees Earned		158,725
51	Salary and Commission Expense	83,075	
52	Rent Expense	16,000	
53	Advertising Expense	10,500	
54	Automobile Expense	3,950	
59	Miscellaneous Expense	600	
		174,600	174,600

The following business transactions were completed by Gallatin Realty during December of the current year:

Dec. 1. Purchased office supplies on account, $1,100.
2. Paid rent on office for month, $1,600.
3. Received cash from clients on account, $24,200.
8. Paid annual insurance premiums, $1,925.
10. Returned a portion of the office supplies purchased on December 1, receiving full credit for their cost, $150.
14. Paid advertising expense, $2,150.
23. Paid creditors on account, $1,650.
29. Paid miscellaneous expenses, $215.
30. Paid automobile expense (including rental charges for an automobile), $850.
31. Discovered an error in computing a commission; received cash from the salesperson for the overpayment, $500.
31. Paid salaries and commissions for the month, $10,850.
31. Recorded revenue earned and billed to clients during the month, $26,200.
31. Purchased land for a future building site for $50,000, paying $10,000 in cash and giving a note payable for the remainder.
31. Paid dividends, $2,500.

Instructions

1. Record the December 1 balance of each account in the appropriate balance column of a four-column account, write *Balance* in the item section, and place a check mark (✓) in the posting reference column.

2. Journalize the transactions for December in a two-column journal. Journal entry explanations may be omitted.
3. Post to the ledger, extending the account balance to the appropriate balance column after each posting.
4. Prepare a trial balance of the ledger as of December 31.

If the working papers correlating with this textbook are not used, omit Problem 2–5B.

Problem 2–5B
Errors in trial balance

Objectives 5, 6

✓ 7. Total of Credit Column:
$33,338.10

The following records of Reliable TV Repair are presented in the working papers:

- Journal containing entries for the period March 1–31.
- Ledger to which the March entries have been posted.
- Preliminary trial balance as of March 31, which does not balance.

Locate the errors, supply the information requested, and prepare a corrected trial balance according to the following instructions. The balances recorded in the accounts as of March 1 and the entries in the journal are correctly stated. If it is necessary to correct any posted amounts in the ledger, a line should be drawn through the erroneous figure and the correct amount inserted above. Corrections or notations may be inserted on the preliminary trial balance in any manner desired. It is not necessary to complete all of the instructions if equal trial balance totals can be obtained earlier. However, the requirements of instructions (6) and (7) should be completed in any event.

Instructions

1. Verify the totals of the preliminary trial balance, inserting the correct amounts in the schedule provided in the working papers.
2. Compute the difference between the trial balance totals.
3. Compare the listings in the trial balance with the balances appearing in the ledger, and list the errors in the space provided in the working papers.
4. Verify the accuracy of the balance of each account in the ledger, and list the errors in the space provided in the working papers.
5. Trace the postings in the ledger back to the journal, using small check marks to identify items traced. Correct any amounts in the ledger that may be necessitated by errors in posting, and list the errors in the space provided in the working papers.
6. Journalize as of March 31 the payment of $163.40 for gas and electricity. The bill had been paid on March 31 but was inadvertently omitted from the journal. Post to the ledger. (Revise any amounts necessitated by posting this entry.)
7. Prepare a new trial balance.

Problem 2–6B
Corrected trial balance

Objectives 5, 6

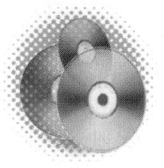

SPREADSHEET

✓ 1. Total of Debit Column:
$130,000

Patel Videography has the following trial balance as of December 31 of the current year:

Cash	1,865	
Accounts Receivable	7,250	
Supplies	1,232	
Prepaid Insurance	330	
Equipment	30,000	
Notes Payable		11,500
Accounts Payable		3,025
Capital Stock		8,000
Retained Earnings		13,000
Dividends	4,500	
Fees Earned		98,900
Wages Expense	56,730	
Rent Expense	11,585	
Advertising Expense	525	
Gas, Electricity, and Water Expense	3,150	
	117,167	134,425

The debit and credit totals are not equal as a result of the following errors:

a. The balance of cash was overstated by $2,500.
b. A cash receipt of $3,100 was posted as a credit to Cash of $1,300.

c. A debit of $1,250 to Accounts Receivable was not posted.

d. A return of $168 of defective supplies was erroneously posted as a $186 credit to Supplies.

e. An insurance policy acquired at a cost of $310 was posted as a credit to Prepaid Insurance.

f. The balance of Notes Payable was overstated by $1,500.

g. A credit of $75 in Accounts Payable was overlooked when the balance of the account was determined.

h. A debit of $3,000 for dividends was posted as a credit to Retained Earnings.

i. The balance of $5,250 in Advertising Expense was entered as $525 in the trial balance.

j. Miscellaneous Expense, with a balance of $1,320, was omitted from the trial balance.

Instructions

1. Prepare a corrected trial balance as of December 31 of the current year.

2. ✏️➤ Does the fact that the trial balance in (1) is balanced mean that there are no errors in the accounts? Explain.

CONTINUING PROBLEM

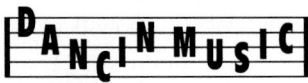

GENERAL LEDGER

✔ 4. Total of Debit Column: $15,880

The transactions completed by Dancin Music during November 2002 were described at the end of Chapter 1. The following transactions were completed during December, the second month of the business's operations:

Dec. 1. Lynn Kwan made an additional investment in Dancin Music by depositing $1,500 in Dancin Music's checking account, receiving capital stock in exchange.

1. Instead of continuing to share office space with a local real estate agency, Lynn decided to rent office space near a local music store. Paid rent for December, $800.

1. Paid a premium of $1,680 for a comprehensive insurance policy covering liability, theft, and fire. The policy covers a two-year period.

2. Received $600 on account.

3. On behalf of Dancin Music, Lynn signed a contract with a local radio station, KPRG, to provide guest spots for the next three months. The contract requires Dancin Music to provide a guest disc jockey for 80 hours per month for a monthly fee of $1,200. Any additional hours beyond 80 will be billed to KPRG at $20 per hour. In accordance with the contract, Lynn received $2,400 from KPRG as an advance payment for the first two months.

3. Paid $125 on account.

4. Paid an attorney $75 for reviewing the December 3rd contract with KPRG. (Record as Miscellaneous Expense.)

5. Purchased office equipment on account from One-Stop Office Mart, $2,500.

8. Paid for a newspaper advertisement, $100.

11. Received $300 for serving as a disc jockey for a college fraternity party.

13. Paid $250 to a local audio electronics store for rental of various equipment (speakers, CD players, etc.).

14. Paid wages of $600 to receptionist and part-time assistant.

16. Received $550 for serving as a disc jockey for a wedding reception.

18. Purchased supplies on account, $375.

21. Paid $120 to Dynamic Music for use of its current demo CDs and tapes in making cassettes of various music sets.

22. Paid $250 to a local radio station to advertise the services of Dancin Music twice daily for the remainder of December.

23. Served as disc jockey for an annual holiday party for $780. Received $200, with the remainder due January 6, 2003.

27. Paid electric bill, $280.

28. Paid wages of $600 to receptionist and part-time assistant.

29. Paid miscellaneous expenses, $85.

30. Served as a disc jockey for a pre-New Year's Eve charity ball for $600. Received $300, with the remainder due on January 10, 2003.

Dec. 31. Received $1,000 for serving as a disc jockey for a New Year's Eve party.
  31. Paid $300 royalties (music expense) to Federated Clearing for use of various artists' music during December.
  31. Paid dividends, $1,000.

Dancin Music's chart of accounts and the balance of accounts as of December 1, 2002 (all normal balances), are as follows:

11	Cash	$3,080
12	Accounts Receivable	600
14	Supplies	85
15	Prepaid Insurance	—
17	Office Equipment	—
21	Accounts Payable	125
23	Unearned Revenue	—
31	Capital Stock	3,500
33	Dividends	125
41	Fees Earned	2,375
50	Wages Expense	200
51	Office Rent Expense	500
52	Equipment Rent Expense	325
53	Utilities Expense	150
54	Music Expense	470
55	Advertising Expense	300
56	Supplies Expense	90
59	Miscellaneous Expense	75

Instructions

1. Enter the December 1, 2002 account balances in the appropriate balance column of a four-column account. Write *Balance* in the Item column, and place a check mark (✓) in the Posting Reference column. (*Hint:* Verify the equality of the debit and credit balances in the ledger before proceeding with the next instruction.)
2. Analyze and journalize each transaction in a two-column journal, omitting journal entry explanations.
3. Post the journal to the ledger, extending the account balance to the appropriate balance column after each posting.
4. Prepare a trial balance as of December 31, 2002.

SPECIAL ACTIVITIES

Activity 2–1
City Motors Co.
Ethics and professional conduct in business

At the end of the current month, Dana Fossum prepared a trial balance for City Motors Co. The credit side of the trial balance exceeds the debit side by a significant amount. Dana has decided to add the difference to the balance of the miscellaneous expense account in order to complete the preparation of the current month's financial statements by a 5 o'clock deadline. Dana will look for the difference next week when she has more time.

➤ Discuss whether Dana is behaving in a professional manner.

Activity 2–2
State College
Account for revenue

What do you think?

State College requires students to pay tuition each term before classes begin. Students who have not paid their tuition are not allowed to enroll or to attend classes.

What journal entry do you think State College would use to record the receipt of the students' tuition payments? Describe the nature of each account in the entry.

Activity 2–3
Landmark Data
Company
Record transactions

The following discussion took place between Marc Bolli, the office manager of Landmark Data Company, and a new accountant, Kelly Holt.

Kelly: I've been thinking about our method of recording entries. It seems that it's inefficient.
Marc: In what way?
Kelly: Well—correct me if I'm wrong—it seems like we have unnecessary steps in the process. We could easily develop a trial balance by posting our transactions directly into the ledger and bypassing the journal altogether. In this way we could combine the recording and posting process into one step and save ourselves a lot of time. What do you think?
Marc: We need to have a talk.

➤ What should Marc say to Kelly?

Activity 2–4
Lodge Construction Co.
Debits and credits

The following excerpt is from a conversation between Jill Rhyne, the president and chief operating officer of Lodge Construction Co., and her neighbor, Sean Resnik.

Sean: Jill, I'm taking a course in night school, "Intro to Accounting." I was wondering—could you answer a couple of questions for me?
Jill: Well, I will if I can.
Sean: Okay, our instructor says that it's critical we understand the basic concepts of accounting, or we'll never get beyond the first test. My problem is with those rules of debit and credit . . . you know, assets increase with debits, decrease with credits, etc.
Jill: Yes, pretty basic stuff. You just have to memorize the rules. It shouldn't be too difficult.
Sean: Sure, I can memorize the rules, but my problem is I want to be sure I understand the basic concepts behind the rules.

For example, why can't assets be increased with credits and decreased with debits like revenue? As long as everyone did it that way, why not? It would seem easier if we had the same rules for all increases and decreases in accounts.

Also, why is the left side of an account called the debit side? Why couldn't it be called something simple . . . like the "LE" for Left Entry. The right side could be called just "RE" for Right Entry.

Finally, why are there just two sides to an entry? Why can't there be three or four sides to an entry?

In a group of four or five, select one person to play the role of Jill and one person to play the role of Sean.

1. After listening to the conversation between Jill and Sean, help Jill answer Sean's questions.
2. What information (other than just debit and credit journal entries) could the accounting system gather that might be useful to Jill in managing Lodge Construction Co.?

Activity 2–5
Fairway Caddy Service
Transactions and income statement

Shelley Dolvin is planning to manage and operate Fairway Caddy Service at Livingston Golf and Country Club during June through August. Shelley will rent a small maintenance building from the country club for $200 per month and will offer caddy services, including cart rentals, to golfers. Shelley has had no formal training in record keeping.

Shelley keeps notes of all receipts and expenses in a shoe box. An examination of Shelley's shoe box records for June revealed the following:

June 1. Withdrew $1,500 from personal bank account to be used to operate the caddy service.
    1. Paid rent to Livingston Golf and Country Club, $200.
    2. Paid for golf supplies (practice balls, etc.), $150.
    3. Arranged for the rental of forty regular (pulling) golf carts and ten gasoline-driven carts for $1,000 per month. Paid $750 in advance, with the remaining $250 due June 20.
    7. Purchased supplies, including gasoline, for the golf carts on account, $180. Livingston Golf and Country Club has agreed to allow Shelley to store the gasoline in one of its fuel tanks at no cost.

June 15. Received cash for services from June 1–15, $1,120.
   17. Paid cash to creditors on account, $180.
   20. Paid remaining rental on golf carts, $250.
   22. Purchased supplies, including gasoline, on account, $170.
   25. Accepted IOUs from customers on account, $380.
   28. Paid miscellaneous expenses, $125.
   30. Received cash for services from June 16–30, $1,475.
   30. Paid telephone and electricity (utilities) expenses, $105.
   30. Paid wages of part-time employees, $260.
   30. Received cash in payment of IOUs on account, $175.
   30. Determined the amount of supplies on hand at the end of June, $98.

Shelley has asked you several questions concerning her financial affairs to date, and she has asked you to assist with her record keeping and reporting of financial data.

a. To assist Shelley with her record keeping, prepare a chart of accounts that would be appropriate for Fairway Caddy Service. Note: Small businesses such as Fairway Caddy Services are often organized as proprietorships. The accounting for proprietorships is similar to that for a corporation, except that the owner's equity accounts differ. Specifically, instead of the account for Capital Stock, a capital account entitled Shelley Dolvin, Capital is used to record investments in the business. In addition, instead of a dividends account, withdrawals from the business are debited to Shelley Dolvin, Drawing. A proprietorship has no retained earnings account.
b. Prepare an income statement for June in order to help Shelley assess the profitability of Fairway Caddy Service. For this purpose, the use of T accounts may be helpful in analyzing the effects of each June transaction.
c. Based on Shelley's records of receipts and payments, calculate the amount of cash on hand on June 30. For this purpose, a T account for cash may be useful.
d. ✎➤ A count of the cash on hand on June 30 totaled $2,120. Briefly discuss the possible causes of the difference between the amount of cash computed in (c) and the actual amount of cash on hand.

Activity 2–6
Into the Real World
Opportunities for accountants

The increasing complexity of the current business and regulatory environment has created an increased demand for accountants who can analyze business transactions and interpret their effects on the financial statements. In addition, a basic ability to analyze the effects of transactions is necessary to be successful in all fields of business as well as in other disciplines, such as law. To better understand the importance of accounting in today's environment, search the Internet or your local newspaper for job opportunities. One possible Internet site is **www.jobweb.com**. Then do one of the following:

1. Print a listing of at least two ads for accounting jobs. Alternatively, bring to class at least two newspaper ads for accounting jobs.
2. Print a listing of at least two ads for nonaccounting jobs for which some knowledge of accounting is preferred or necessary. Alternatively, bring to class at least two newspaper ads for such jobs.

ANSWERS TO SELF-EXAMINATION QUESTIONS

Matching

1. A	6. R	11. E	16. H	21. X
2. N	7. T	12. C	17. G	22. P
3. D	8. I	13. K	18. S	23. W
4. B	9. V	14. M	19. Y	24. U
5. O	10. F	15. L	20. Z	25. J

Multiple Choice

1. **A** A debit may signify an increase in an asset account (answer A) or a decrease in a liability or capital stock account. A credit may signify a decrease in an asset account (answer B) or an increase in a liability or capital stock account (answers C and D).

2. **C** Liability, capital stock, and revenue (answer C) accounts have normal credit balances. Asset (answer A), dividends (answer B), and expense (answer D) accounts have normal debit balances.

3. **C** Accounts Receivable (answer A), Cash (answer B), and Miscellaneous Expense (answer D) would all normally have debit balances. Fees Earned should normally have a credit balance. Hence, a debit balance in Fees Earned (answer C) would indicate a likely error in the recording process.

4. **A** The receipt of cash from customers on account increases the asset Cash and decreases the asset Accounts Receivable, as indicated by answer A. Answer B has the debit and credit reversed, and answers C and D involve transactions with creditors (accounts payable) and not customers (accounts receivable).

5. **D** The trial balance (answer D) is a listing of the balances and the titles of the accounts in the ledger on a given date, so that the equality of the debits and credits in the ledger can be verified. The income statement (answer A) is a summary of revenue and expenses for a period of time. The balance sheet (answer B) is a presentation of the assets, liabilities, and owner's equity on a given date. The retained earnings statement (answer C) is a summary of the changes in retained earnings for a period of time.

The Matching Concept and the Adjusting Process

F3

objectives

After studying this chapter, you should be able to:

1   Explain how the matching concept relates to the accrual basis of accounting.

2   Explain why adjustments are necessary and list the characteristics of adjusting entries.

3   Journalize entries for accounts requiring adjustment.

4   Summarize the adjustment process and prepare an adjusted trial balance.

5   Use vertical analysis to compare financial statement items with each other and with industry averages.

Assume that you rented an apartment last month and signed a nine-month lease. When you signed the lease agreement, you were required to pay the final month's rent of $500. This amount is not returnable to you.

You are now applying for a student loan at a local bank. The loan application requires a listing of all your assets. Should you list the $500 deposit as an asset?

The answer to this question is "yes." The deposit is an asset to you until you receive the use of the apartment in the ninth month.

A business faces similar accounting problems at the end of a period. A business must determine what assets, liabilities, and owner's equity should be reported on its balance sheet. It must also determine what revenues and expenses should be reported on its income statement.

As we illustrated in previous chapters, transactions are normally recorded as they take place. Periodically, financial statements are prepared, summarizing the effects of the transactions on the financial position and operations of the business.

At any one point in time, however, the accounting records may not reflect all transactions. For example, most businesses do not record the daily use of supplies. Likewise, revenue may have been earned from providing services to customers, yet the customers have not been billed by the time the accounting period ends. Thus, at the end of the period, the revenue and receivable accounts must be updated.

In this chapter, we describe and illustrate this updating process. We will focus on accounts that normally require updating and the journal entries that update them.

The Matching Concept

objective 1

Explain how the matching concept relates to the accrual basis of accounting.

American Airlines uses the accrual basis of accounting. Revenues are recognized when passengers take flights, not when the passenger makes the reservation or pays for the ticket.

When accountants prepare financial statements, they assume that the economic life of the business can be divided into time periods. Using this **accounting period concept**, accountants must determine in which period the revenues and expenses of the business should be reported. To determine the appropriate period, accountants will use either (1) the cash basis of accounting or (2) the accrual basis of accounting.

Under the **cash basis**, revenues and expenses are reported in the income statement in the period in which cash is received or paid. For example, fees are recorded when cash is received from clients, and wages are recorded when cash is paid to employees. The net income (or net loss) is the difference between the cash receipts (revenues) and the cash payments (expenses).

Under the **accrual basis**, revenues are reported in the income statement in the period in which they are earned. For example, revenue is reported when the services are provided to customers. Cash may or may not be received from customers during this period. The concept that supports this reporting of revenues is called the **revenue recognition concept**.

Under the accrual basis, expenses are reported in the same period as the revenues to which they relate. For example, employee wages are reported as an expense in the

A bank loan officer requires an individual, who normally keeps records on a cash basis, to list assets (automobiles, homes, investments, etc.) on an application for a loan or a line of credit. In addition, the application often asks for an estimate of the individual's liabilities, such as outstanding credit card amounts and automobile loan balances. In a sense, the loan application converts the individual's cash-basis accounting system to an estimated accrual basis. The loan officer uses this information to assess the individual's ability to repay the loan.

> **The matching concept supports reporting revenues and related expenses in the same period.**

period in which the employees provided services to customers, and not necessarily when the wages are paid.

The accounting concept that supports reporting revenues and related expenses in the same period is called the matching concept, or **matching principle**. Under this concept, an income statement will report the resulting income or loss for the period.

Generally accepted accounting principles require the use of the accrual basis. However, small service businesses may use the cash basis because they have few receivables and payables. For example, attorneys, physicians, and real estate agents often use the cash basis. For them, the cash basis will yield financial statements similar to those prepared under the accrual basis.

For most large businesses, the cash basis will not provide accurate financial statements for user needs. For this reason, we will emphasize the accrual basis in the remainder of this text. The accrual basis and its related matching concept require an analysis and updating of some accounts when financial statements are prepared. In the following paragraphs, we will describe and illustrate this process, called the adjusting process.

Nature of the Adjusting Process

objective 2

Explain why adjustments are necessary and list the characteristics of adjusting entries.

At the end of an accounting period, many of the balances of accounts in the ledger can be reported, without change, in the financial statements. For example, the balance of the cash account is normally the amount reported on the balance sheet.

Some accounts in the ledger, however, require updating. For example, the balances listed for prepaid expenses are normally overstated because the use of these assets is not recorded on a day-to-day basis. The balance of the supplies account usually represents the cost of supplies at the beginning of the period plus the cost of supplies acquired during the period. To record the daily use of supplies would require many entries with small amounts. In addition, the total amount of supplies is small relative to other assets, and managers usually do not require day-to-day information about supplies.

The journal entries that bring the accounts up to date at the end of the accounting period are called adjusting entries. All adjusting entries affect at least one income statement account and one balance sheet account. Thus, an adjusting entry will *always* involve a revenue or an expense account *and* an asset or a liability account.

> **All adjusting entries affect at least one income statement account and one balance sheet account.**

Is there an easy way to know when an adjusting entry is needed? Yes, four basic items require adjusting entries. The first two items are **deferrals**. Deferrals are created by recording a transaction in a way that *delays* or *defers* the recognition of an expense or a revenue, as described below.

- Deferred expenses, or **prepaid expenses**, are items that have been initially recorded as assets but are expected to become expenses over time or through the normal operations of the business. Supplies and prepaid insurance are two examples of prepaid expenses that may require adjustment at the end of an accounting period. Other examples include prepaid advertising and prepaid interest.
- Deferred revenues, or **unearned revenues**, are items that have been initially recorded as liabilities but are expected to become revenues over time or through the normal operations of the business. An example of deferred revenue is unearned rent. Other examples include tuition received in advance by a school, an annual retainer fee received by an attorney, premiums received in advance by an insurance company, and magazine subscriptions received in advance by a publisher.

The second two items that require adjusting entries are accruals. **Accruals** are created by an unrecorded expense that has been incurred or an unrecorded revenue that has been earned, as described below.

- Accrued expenses, or **accrued liabilities**, are expenses that have been incurred *but have not been recorded* in the accounts. An example of an accrued expense is accrued wages owed to employees at the end of a period. Other examples include accrued interest on notes payable and accrued taxes.
- Accrued revenues, or **accrued assets**, are revenues that have been earned *but have not been recorded* in the accounts. An example of an accrued revenue is fees for services that an attorney has provided but hasn't billed to the client at the end of the period. Other examples include unbilled commissions by a travel agent, accrued interest on notes receivable, and accrued rent on property rented to others.

How do you tell the difference between deferrals and accruals? Determine when cash is received or paid, as shown in Exhibit 1. If cash is received (for revenue) or paid (for expense) in the *current* period, but the revenue or expense relates to a future period, the revenue or expense is a deferred item. If cash will not be received or paid until a *future* period, but the revenue or expense relates to the current period, the revenue or expense is an accrued item.

Exhibit 1 Deferrals and Accruals

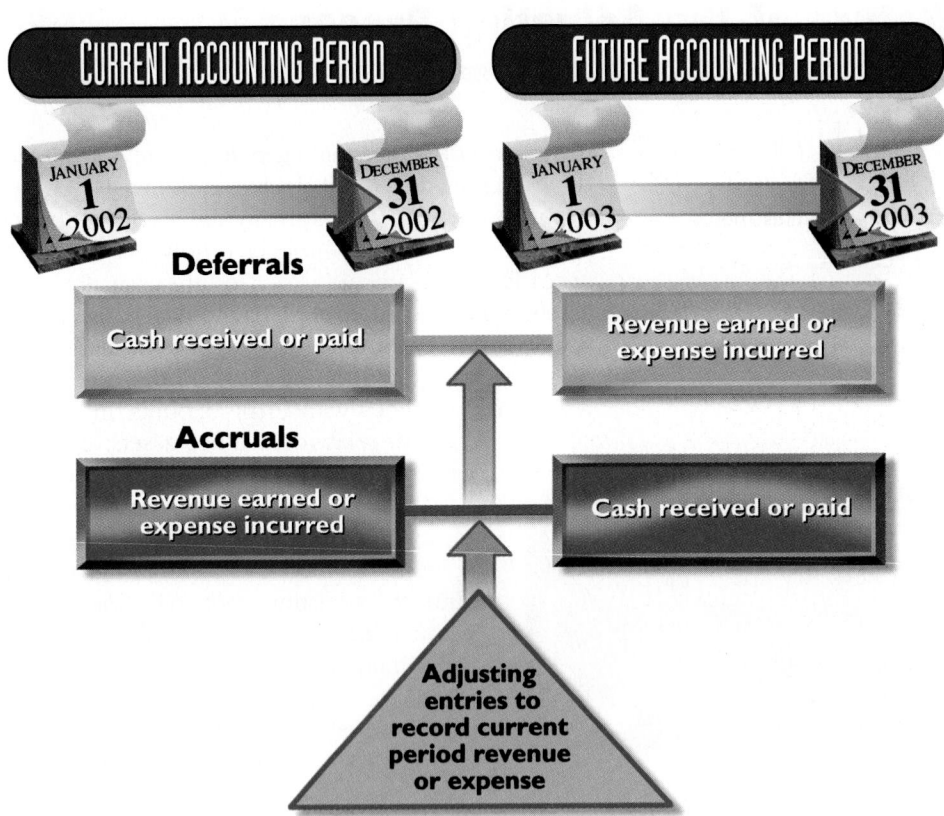

Recording Adjusting Entries

objective 3

Journalize entries for accounts requiring adjustment.

The examples of adjusting entries in the following paragraphs are based on the ledger of NetSolutions as reported in the December 31, 2002 trial balance in Exhibit 2. To simplify the examples, T accounts are used. The adjusting entries are shown in color in the accounts to separate them from other transactions.

Exhibit 2 Unadjusted Trial Balance for NetSolutions

 NET SOLUTIONS

NetSolutions Trial Balance December 31, 2002											
Cash	2	0	6	5	00						
Accounts Receivable	2	2	2	0	00						
Supplies	2	0	0	0	00						
Prepaid Insurance	2	4	0	0	00						
Land	20	0	0	0	00						
Office Equipment	1	8	0	0	00						
Accounts Payable							9	0	0	00	
Unearned Rent							3	6	0	00	
Capital Stock						25	0	0	0	00	
Dividends	4	0	0	0	00						
Fees Earned						16	3	4	0	00	
Wages Expense	4	2	7	5	00						
Rent Expense	1	6	0	0	00						
Utilities Expense		9	8	5	00						
Supplies Expense		8	0	0	00						
Miscellaneous Expense		4	5	5	00						
	42	6	0	0	00	42	6	0	0	00	

An expanded chart of accounts for NetSolutions is shown in Exhibit 3. The additional accounts that will be used in this chapter are shown in color.

Exhibit 3 Expanded Chart of Accounts for NetSolutions

Balance Sheet Accounts	Income Statement Accounts
1. Assets	**4. Revenue**
11 Cash	41 Fees Earned
12 Accounts Receivable	42 Rent Revenue
14 Supplies	**5. Expenses**
15 Prepaid Insurance	51 Wages Expense
17 Land	52 Rent Expense
18 Office Equipment	53 Depreciation Expense
19 Accumulated Depreciation	54 Utilities Expense
2. Liabilities	55 Supplies Expense
21 Accounts Payable	56 Insurance Expense
22 Wages Payable	59 Miscellaneous Expense
23 Unearned Rent	
3. Stockholders' Equity	
31 Capital Stock	
32 Retained Earnings	
33 Dividends	

Deferred Expenses (Prepaid Expenses)

The concept of adjusting the accounting records was introduced in Chapters 1 and 2 in the illustration for NetSolutions. In that illustration, supplies were purchased on November 10 (transaction c). The supplies used during November were recorded on November 30 (transaction g).

The balance in NetSolutions' **supplies** account on December 31 is $2,000. Some of these supplies (computer diskettes, paper, envelopes, etc.) were used during December, and some are still on hand (not used). If either amount is known, the other can be determined. It is normally easier to determine the cost of the supplies on hand at the end of the month than it is to keep a daily record of those used. Assuming that on December 31 the amount of supplies on hand is $760, the amount to be transferred from the asset account to the expense account is $1,240, computed as follows:

Supplies available during December (balance of account)	$2,000
Supplies on hand, December 31	760
Supplies used (amount of adjustment)	$1,240

As we discussed in Chapter 2, increases in expense accounts are recorded as debits and decreases in asset accounts are recorded as credits. Hence, at the end of December, the supplies expense account should be debited for $1,240, and the supplies account should be credited for $1,240 to record the supplies used during December. The adjusting journal entry and T accounts for Supplies and Supplies Expense are as follows:

2	2002 Dec. 31	Supplies Expense	55	1 2 4 0 00		2
3		Supplies	14		1 2 4 0 00	3

Supplies				**Supplies Expense**		
Bal.	2,000	Dec. 31	1,240	Bal.	800	
760				Dec. 31	1,240	
					2,040	

> **The balance of a prepaid (deferred) expense is an asset that will become an expense in a future period.**

After the adjustment has been recorded and posted, the supplies account has a debit balance of $760. This balance represents an asset that will become an expense in a future period.

The debit balance of $2,400 in NetSolutions' **prepaid insurance** account represents a December 1 prepayment of insurance for 24 months. At the end of December, the insurance expense account should be increased (debited), and the prepaid insurance account should be decreased (credited) by $100, the insurance for one month. The adjusting journal entry and T accounts for Prepaid Insurance and Insurance Expense are as follows:

5	31	Insurance Expense	56	1 0 0 00		5
6		Prepaid Insurance	15		1 0 0 00	6

Prepaid Insurance				**Insurance Expense**		
Bal.	2,400	Dec. 31	100	Dec. 31	100	
2,300						

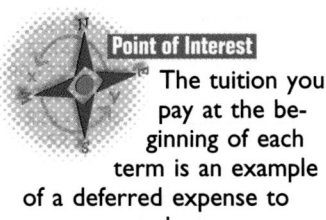

After the adjustment has been recorded and posted, the prepaid insurance account has a debit balance of $2,300. This balance represents an asset that will become an expense in future periods. The insurance expense account has a debit balance of $100, which is an expense of the current period.

What is the effect of omitting adjusting entries? If the preceding adjustments for supplies ($1,240) and insurance ($100) are not recorded, the financial statements prepared as of December 31 will be misstated. On the income statement, Supplies Expense and Insurance Expense will be understated by a total of $1,340, and net income will be overstated by $1,340. On the balance sheet, Supplies and Prepaid Insurance will be overstated by a total of $1,340. Since net income increases stockholders' equity (retained earnings), stockholders' equity will also be overstated by $1,340 on the balance sheet. The effects of omitting these adjusting entries on the income statement and balance sheet are shown below.

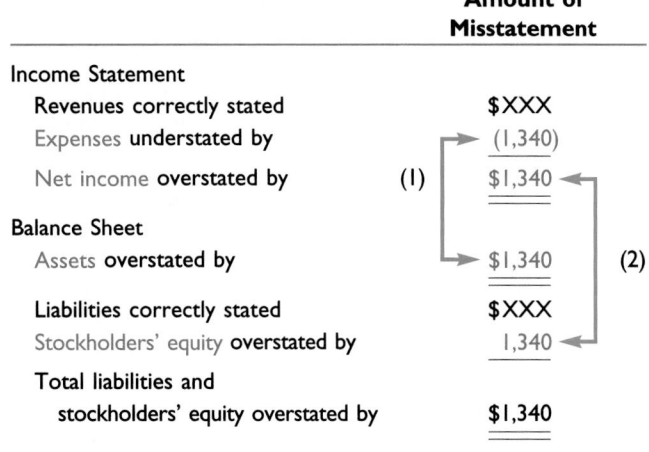

	Amount of Misstatement
Income Statement	
Revenues correctly stated	$XXX
Expenses understated by	(1,340)
Net income overstated by (1)	$1,340
Balance Sheet	
Assets overstated by	$1,340 (2)
Liabilities correctly stated	$XXX
Stockholders' equity overstated by	1,340
Total liabilities and stockholders' equity overstated by	$1,340

Arrow (1) indicates the effect of the understated expenses on assets. Arrow (2) indicates the effect of the overstated net income on stockholders' equity.

Prepayments of expenses are sometimes made at the beginning of the period in which they will be *entirely consumed.* On December 1, for example, NetSolutions paid rent of $800 for the month. On December 1, the rent payment represents the asset prepaid rent. The prepaid rent expires daily, and at the end of December, the entire amount has become an expense (rent expense). In cases such as this, the initial payment is recorded as an expense rather than as an asset. Thus, if the payment is recorded as a debit to Rent Expense, no adjusting entry is needed at the end of the period.[1]

Deferred Revenue (Unearned Revenue)

According to NetSolutions' trial balance on December 31, the balance in the **unearned rent** account is $360. This balance represents the receipt of three months' rent on December 1 for December, January, and February. At the end of December, the unearned rent account should be decreased (debited) by $120, and the rent revenue account should be increased (credited) by $120. The $120 represents the rental revenue for one month ($360/3). The adjusting journal entry and T accounts are shown below.

8	31	Unearned Rent	23	1 2 0 00		8
9		Rent Revenue	42		1 2 0 00	9

----

[1] This alternative treatment of recording the cost of supplies, rent, and other prepayments of expenses is discussed in Appendix C.

Unearned Rent				Rent Revenue		
Dec. 31	120	Bal.	360		Dec. 31	120
		240				

Sears sells extended warranty contracts with terms between 12 and 36 months. The receipts from sales of these contracts are reported as unearned revenue (deferred revenue) on Sears' balance sheet. Revenue is recorded as the contracts expire.

After the adjustment has been recorded and posted, the unearned rent account, which is a liability, has a credit balance of $240. This amount represents a deferral that will become revenue in a future period. The rent revenue account has a balance of $120, which is revenue of the current period.[2]

If the preceding adjustment of unearned rent and rent revenue is not recorded, the financial statements prepared on December 31 will be misstated. On the income statement, Rent Revenue and the net income will be understated by $120. On the balance sheet, Unearned Rent will be overstated by $120, and stockholders' equity (retained earnings) will be understated by $120. The effects of omitting this adjusting entry are shown below.

If NetSolutions had incorrectly adjusted unearned rent for $180 instead of $120, what would have been the effect on the financial statements?

Revenues would have been overstated by $60; net income would have been overstated by $60; liabilities would have been understated by $60; and stockholders' equity would have been overstated by $60.

	Amount of Misstatement
Income Statement	
Revenues understated by	$ (120)
Expenses correctly stated	XXX
Net income understated by	$ (120)
Balance Sheet	
Assets correctly stated	$ XXX
Liabilities overstated by	$ 120
Stockholders' equity understated by	(120)
Total liabilities and stockholders' equity correctly stated	$ XXX

[2] An alternative treatment of recording revenues received in advance of their being earned is discussed in Appendix C.

BUSINESS ON STAGE

Technology and Business

The business environment is a dynamic one in which there is constant change, with challenges and opportunities. The current technology revolution affects all businesses.

Computer and telecommunication technologies affect the production, storage, and use of information by businesses. Many businesses have developed web sites for use in marketing products and services and for communicating with stakeholders. New software applications range from

accounting software that provides updated accounting information to business simulation software capable of gauging the impact of alternative business decisions on operations.

The technological revolution challenges businesses to adapt quickly to software and hardware improvements. Such improvements offer opportunities for businesses to develop new products, reach more customers, develop new channels of product distribution, lower operating costs, im-

prove product quality, obtain immediate customer feedback, and react quickly to market changes. Businesses unable to adapt quickly to the technological revolution may find themselves at a competitive disadvantage.

Technology also provides you with new and exciting opportunities. To the extent that you develop your computer and technological skills and talents, you will improve your chances of finding a job and advancing rapidly in your career. ■

Callaway Golf Company, a manufacturer of such innovative golf clubs as the "Big Bertha" driver, reports accrued warranty expense on its balance sheet.

Accrued Expenses (Accrued Liabilities)

Some types of services, such as insurance, are normally paid for *before* they are used. These prepayments are deferrals. Other types of services are paid for *after* the service has been performed. For example, wages expense accumulates or *accrues* hour by hour and day by day, but payment may be made only weekly, biweekly, or monthly. The amount of such an accrued but unpaid item at the end of the accounting period is both an expense and a liability. In the case of wages expense, if the last day of a pay period is not the last day of the accounting period, the accrued wages expense and the related liability must be recorded in the accounts by an adjusting entry. This adjusting entry is necessary so that expenses are properly matched to the period in which they were incurred.

At the end of December, accrued wages for NetSolutions were $250. This amount is an additional expense of December and is debited to the **wages expense** account. It is also a liability as of December 31 and is credited to Wages Payable. The adjusting journal entry and T accounts are shown below.

11	31	Wages Expense	51	2 5 0 00		11
12		Wages Payable	22		2 5 0 00	12

Wages Expense		Wages Payable	
Bal.	4,275	Dec. 31	250
Dec. 31	250		
	4,525		

After the adjustment has been recorded and posted, the debit balance of the wages expense account is $4,525, which is the wages expense for the two months, November and December. The credit balance of $250 in Wages Payable is the amount of the liability for wages owed as of December 31.

The accrual of the wages expense for NetSolutions is summarized in Exhibit 4. Note that NetSolutions paid wages of $950 on December 13 and $1,200 on December 27. These payments covered the biweekly pay periods that ended on those days. The wages of $250 incurred for Monday and Tuesday, December 30 and 31, are accrued at December 31. The wages paid on January 10 totaled $1,275, which included the $250 accrued wages of December 31.

What would be the effect on the financial statements if the adjustment for wages ($250) is not recorded? On the income statement, Wages Expense will be understated by $250, and the net income will be overstated by $250. On the balance sheet, Wages Payable will be understated by $250, and stockholders' equity (retained earnings) will be overstated by $250. The effects of omitting this adjusting entry are shown below.

Q&A Assume that weekly wages of $1,500 are paid on Fridays. If wages are incurred evenly throughout the week, what is the accrued wages payable if the accounting period ends on a Tuesday?

$600 ($1,500/5 × 2 days)

	Amount of Misstatement
Income Statement	
Revenues correctly stated	$ XXX
Expenses **understated** by	(250)
Net income **overstated** by	$ 250
Balance Sheet	
Assets correctly stated	$ XXX
Liabilities **understated** by	$ (250)
Stockholders' equity **overstated** by	250
Total liabilities and stockholders' equity correctly stated	$ XXX

Exhibit 4 Accrued Wages

1. Wages are paid on the second and fourth Fridays for the two-week periods ending on those Fridays. The payments were $950 on December 13 and $1,200 on December 27.

2. The wages accrued for Monday and Tuesday, December 30 and 31, are $250.

3. Wages paid on Friday, January 10, total $1,275.

		December				
S	M	T	W	T	F	S
1	2	3	4	5	6	7
8	9	10	11	12	13	14
15	16	17	18	19	20	21
22	23	24	25	26	27	28
29	30	31				

Wages expense (paid), $950

Wages expense (paid), $1,200

Wages expense (accrued), $250

		January				
				1	2	3	4
5	6	7	8	9	10	11

Wages expense (paid), $1,275

Tandy Corporation and Subsidiaries is engaged in consumer electronics retailing and owns **Radio Shack** and **Incredible Universe**. Tandy accrues revenue (accrued receivables) for finance charges, late charges, and returned check fees related to its credit operations.

Accrued Revenues (Accrued Assets)

During an accounting period, some revenues are recorded only when cash is received. Thus, at the end of an accounting period, there may be items of revenue that have been earned *but have not been recorded*. In such cases, the amount of the revenue should be recorded by debiting an asset account and crediting a revenue account.

To illustrate, assume that NetSolutions signed an agreement with Dankner Co. on December 15. The agreement provides that NetSolutions will be on call to answer computer questions and render assistance to Dankner Co.'s employees. The services provided will be billed to Dankner Co. on the fifteenth of each month at a rate of $20 per hour. As of December 31, NetSolutions had provided 25 hours of assistance to Dankner Co. Although the revenue of $500 (25 hours × $20) will be billed and collected in January, NetSolutions earned the revenue in December. The adjusting journal entry and T accounts to record the claim against the customer (an account receivable) and the **fees earned** in December are shown below.

14	31	Accounts Receivable	12	5 0 0 00			14
15		Fees Earned	41		5 0 0 00		15

Accounts Receivable			Fees Earned	
Bal.	2,220		Bal.	16,340
Dec. 31	500		Dec. 31	500
	2,720			16,840

If the adjustment for the accrued asset ($500) is not recorded, Fees Earned and the net income will be understated by $500 on the income statement. On the balance sheet, Accounts Receivable and stockholders' equity (retained earnings) will be understated by $500. The effects of omitting this adjusting entry are shown below.

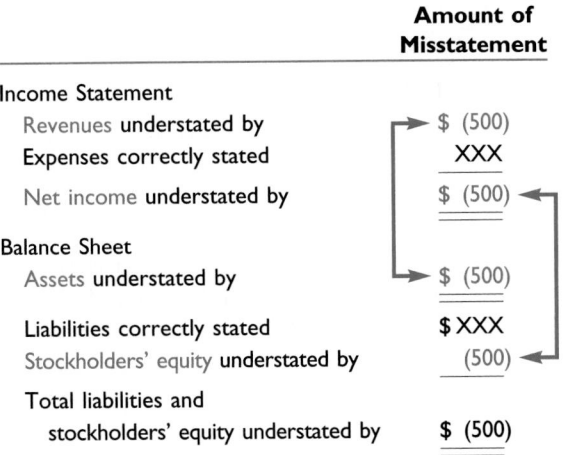

	Amount of Misstatement
Income Statement	
Revenues understated by	$ (500)
Expenses correctly stated	XXX
Net income understated by	$ (500)
Balance Sheet	
Assets understated by	$ (500)
Liabilities correctly stated	$ XXX
Stockholders' equity understated by	(500)
Total liabilities and stockholders' equity understated by	$ (500)

Fixed Assets

Physical resources that are owned and used by a business and are permanent or have a long life are called **fixed assets**, or **plant assets**. In a sense, fixed assets are a type of long-term deferred expense. However, because of their nature and long life, they are discussed separately from other deferred expenses, such as supplies and prepaid insurance.

NetSolutions' fixed assets include office equipment that is used much like supplies are used to generate revenue. Unlike supplies, however, there is no visible reduction in the quantity of the equipment. Instead, as time passes, the equipment loses its ability to provide useful services. This decrease in usefulness is called **depreciation**.

All fixed assets, except land, lose their usefulness. Decreases in the usefulness of assets that are used in generating revenue are recorded as expenses. However, such decreases for fixed assets are difficult to measure. For this reason, a portion of the cost of a fixed asset is recorded as an expense each year of its useful life. This periodic expense is called **depreciation expense**. Methods of computing depreciation expense are discussed and illustrated in a later chapter.

The adjusting entry to record depreciation is similar to the adjusting entry for supplies used. The account debited is a depreciation expense account. However, the asset account Office Equipment is not credited because both the original cost of a fixed asset and the amount of depreciation recorded since its purchase are normally reported on the balance sheet. The account credited is an **accumulated depreciation** account. Accumulated depreciation accounts are called **contra accounts**, or **contra asset accounts** because they are deducted from the related asset accounts on the balance sheet.

Normal titles for fixed asset accounts and their related contra asset accounts are as follows:

Lowe's Companies, Inc. and Subsidiaries reported land, buildings, and store equipment at a cost of over $2.3 billion and accumulated depreciation of over $460 million.

Fixed Asset	Contra Asset
Land	None—Land is not depreciated.
Buildings	Accumulated Depreciation—Buildings
Store Equipment	Accumulated Depreciation—Store Equipment
Office Equipment	Accumulated Depreciation—Office Equipment

The adjusting entry to record depreciation for December for NetSolutions is illustrated in the following journal entry and T accounts. The estimated amount of depreciation for the month is assumed to be $50.

	31	Depreciation Expense	53	5 0 00		
17						17
18		Accumulated Depreciation—				18
19		Office Equipment	19		5 0 00	19

Office Equipment		**Accumulated Depreciation**	
Bal.	1,800	Dec. 31	50

	Depreciation Expense	
Dec. 31	50	

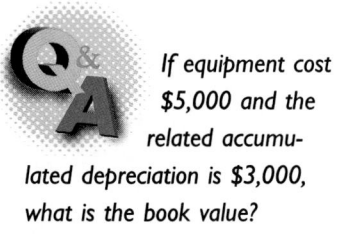

If equipment cost $5,000 and the related accumulated depreciation is $3,000, what is the book value?

$2,000 ($5,000 − $3,000)

The $50 increase in the accumulated depreciation account is subtracted from the $1,800 cost recorded in the related fixed asset account. The difference between the two balances is the $1,750 cost that has not yet been depreciated. This amount ($1,750) is called the **book value of the asset** (or **net value**), which may be presented on the balance sheet in the following manner:

Office equipment	$1,800	
Less accumulated depreciation	50	$1,750

You should note that the market value of a fixed asset usually differs from its book value. This is because depreciation is an *allocation* method, not a *valuation* method. That is, depreciation allocates the cost of a fixed asset to expense over its estimated life. Depreciation does not attempt to measure changes in market values, which may vary significantly from year to year.

If the previous adjustment for depreciation ($50) is not recorded, Depreciation Expense on the income statement will be understated by $50, and the net income will be overstated by $50. On the balance sheet, the book value of Office Equipment and stockholders' equity (retained earnings) will be overstated by $50. The effects of omitting the adjustment for depreciation are shown below.

	Amount of Misstatement
Income Statement	
Revenues correctly stated	$XX
Expenses understated by	(50)
Net income overstated by	$ 50
Balance Sheet	
Assets overstated by	$ 50
Liabilities correctly stated	$XX
Stockholders' equity overstated by	50
Total liabilities and stockholders' equity overstated by	$ 50

Summary of Adjustment Process

objective 4

Summarize the adjustment process and prepare an adjusted trial balance.

We have described and illustrated the basic types of adjusting entries in the preceding section. A summary of these basic adjustments, including the type of adjustment, the adjusting entry, and the effect of omitting an adjustment on the financial statements, is shown in Exhibit 5.

Exhibit 5 Summary of Basic Adjustments

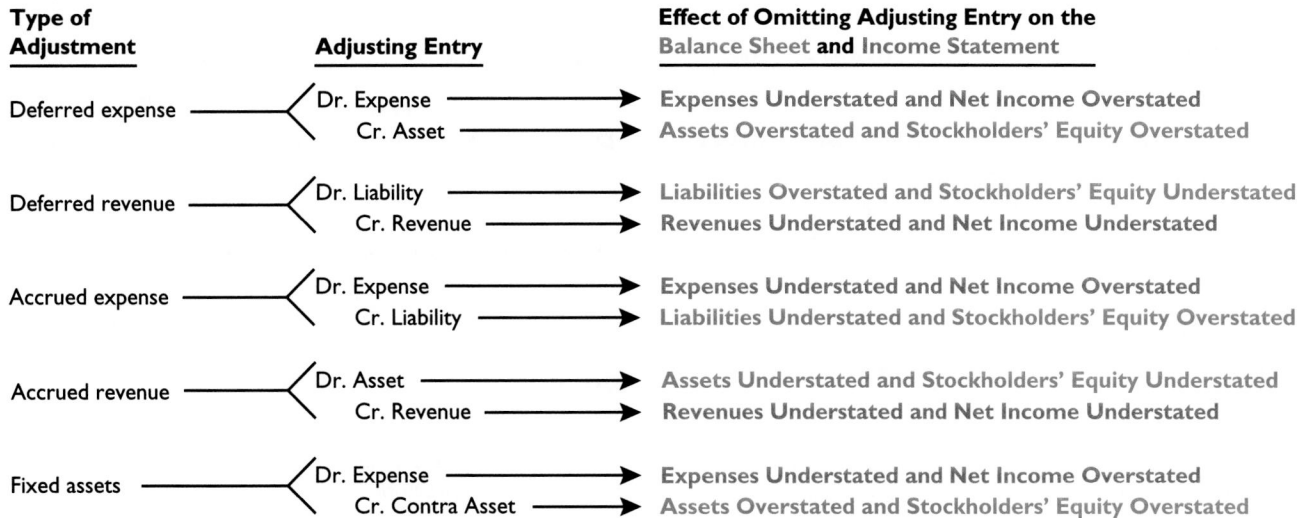

Type of Adjustment	Adjusting Entry	Effect of Omitting Adjusting Entry on the Balance Sheet **and Income Statement**
Deferred expense	Dr. Expense	Expenses Understated and Net Income Overstated
	Cr. Asset	Assets Overstated and Stockholders' Equity Overstated
Deferred revenue	Dr. Liability	Liabilities Overstated and Stockholders' Equity Understated
	Cr. Revenue	Revenues Understated and Net Income Understated
Accrued expense	Dr. Expense	Expenses Understated and Net Income Overstated
	Cr. Liability	Liabilities Understated and Stockholders' Equity Overstated
Accrued revenue	Dr. Asset	Assets Understated and Stockholders' Equity Understated
	Cr. Revenue	Revenues Understated and Net Income Understated
Fixed assets	Dr. Expense	Expenses Understated and Net Income Overstated
	Cr. Contra Asset	Assets Overstated and Stockholders' Equity Overstated

Q&A *Which of the accounts—Fees Earned, Miscellaneous Expense, Cash, Wages Expense, Supplies, Accounts Receivable, Dividends, Equipment, Accumulated Depreciation— would normally require an adjusting entry?*

Fees Earned; Wages Expense; Supplies; Accounts Receivable; Accumulated Depreciation.

The adjusting entries for NetSolutions that we illustrated in this chapter are shown in Exhibit 6. The adjusting entries are dated as of the last day of the period. However, because some time may be needed for collecting the adjustment information, the entries are usually recorded at a later date. Each entry may be supported by an explanation, but a caption above the first adjusting entry is acceptable.

These adjusting entries have been posted to the ledger for NetSolutions, and are shown in color in Exhibit 7. You should note that in the posting process the Post. Ref. column of the journal indicates the account number to which the entry was posted. The corresponding Post. Ref. column of the account indicates the journal page from which the entry was posted.

Exhibit 6 Adjusting Entries —NetSolutions

	Date		Description	Post. Ref.	Debit	Credit	
1			Adjusting Entries				1
2	2002 Dec.	31	Supplies Expense	55	1 2 4 0 00		2
3			Supplies	14		1 2 4 0 00	3
4							4
5		31	Insurance Expense	56	1 0 0 00		5
6			Prepaid Insurance	15		1 0 0 00	6
7							7
8		31	Unearned Rent	23	1 2 0 00		8
9			Rent Revenue	42		1 2 0 00	9
10							10
11		31	Wages Expense	51	2 5 0 00		11
12			Wages Payable	22		2 5 0 00	12
13							13
14		31	Accounts Receivable	12	5 0 0 00		14
15			Fees Earned	41		5 0 0 00	15
16							16
17		31	Depreciation Expense	53	5 0 00		17
18			Accumulated Depreciation—				18
19			Office Equipment	19		5 0 00	19

JOURNAL — PAGE 5

Exhibit 7 Ledger with Adjusting Entries—NetSolutions

ACCOUNT Cash   ACCOUNT NO. 11

Date	Item	Post. Ref.	Debit	Credit	Balance Debit	Balance Credit
2002 Nov. 1		1	25,000		25,000	
5		1		20,000	5,000	
18		1	7,500		12,500	
30		1		3,650	8,850	
30		1		950	7,900	
30		2		2,000	5,900	
Dec. 1		2		2,400	3,500	
1		2		800	2,700	
1		2	360		3,060	
6		2		180	2,880	
11		2		400	2,480	
13		3		950	1,530	
16		3	3,100		4,630	
20		3		900	3,730	
21		3	650		4,380	
23		3		1,450	2,930	
27		3		1,200	1,730	
31		3		310	1,420	
31		4		225	1,195	
31		4	2,870		4,065	
31		4		2,000	2,065	

ACCOUNT Accounts Receivable   ACCOUNT NO. 12

Date	Item	Post. Ref.	Debit	Credit	Balance Debit	Balance Credit
2002 Dec. 16		3	1,750		1,750	
21		3		650	1,100	
31		4	1,120		2,220	
31	Adjusting	5	500		2,720	

ACCOUNT Supplies   ACCOUNT NO. 14

Date	Item	Post. Ref.	Debit	Credit	Balance Debit	Balance Credit
2002 Nov. 10		1	1,350		1,350	
30		1		800	550	
Dec. 23		3	1,450		2,000	
31	Adjusting	5		1,240	760	

ACCOUNT Prepaid Insurance   ACCOUNT NO. 15

Date	Item	Post. Ref.	Debit	Credit	Balance Debit	Balance Credit
2002 Dec. 1		2	2,400		2,400	
31	Adjusting	5		100	2,300	

ACCOUNT Land   ACCOUNT NO. 17

Date	Item	Post. Ref.	Debit	Credit	Balance Debit	Balance Credit
2002 Nov. 5		1	20,000		20,000	

ACCOUNT Office Equipment   ACCOUNT NO. 18

Date	Item	Post. Ref.	Debit	Credit	Balance Debit	Balance Credit
2002 Dec. 4		2	1,800		1,800	

ACCOUNT Accumulated Depreciation   ACCOUNT NO. 19

Date	Item	Post. Ref.	Debit	Credit	Balance Debit	Balance Credit
2002 Dec. 31	Adjusting	5		50		50

ACCOUNT Accounts Payable   ACCOUNT NO. 21

Date	Item	Post. Ref.	Debit	Credit	Balance Debit	Balance Credit
2002 Nov. 10		1		1,350		1,350
30		1	950			400
Dec. 4		2		1,800		2,200
11		2	400			1,800
20		3	900			900

ACCOUNT Wages Payable   ACCOUNT NO. 22

Date	Item	Post. Ref.	Debit	Credit	Balance Debit	Balance Credit
2002 Dec. 31	Adjusting	5		250		250

ACCOUNT Unearned Rent   ACCOUNT NO. 23

Date	Item	Post. Ref.	Debit	Credit	Balance Debit	Balance Credit
2002 Dec. 1		2		360		360
31	Adjusting	5	120			240

ACCOUNT Capital Stock   ACCOUNT NO. 31

Date	Item	Post. Ref.	Debit	Credit	Balance Debit	Balance Credit
2002 Nov. 1		1		25,000		25,000

Exhibit 7 (concluded)

ACCOUNT *Dividends*   **ACCOUNT NO. 33**

Date	Item	Post. Ref.	Debit	Credit	Balance Debit	Balance Credit
2002 Nov. 30		2	2,000		2,000	
Dec. 31		4	2,000		4,000	

ACCOUNT *Fees Earned*   **ACCOUNT NO. 41**

Date	Item	Post. Ref.	Debit	Credit	Balance Debit	Balance Credit
2002 Nov. 18		1		7,500		7,500
Dec. 16		3		3,100		10,600
16		3		1,750		12,350
31		4		2,870		15,220
31		4		1,120		16,340
31	Adjusting	5		500		16,840

ACCOUNT *Rent Revenue*   **ACCOUNT NO. 42**

Date	Item	Post. Ref.	Debit	Credit	Balance Debit	Balance Credit
2002 Dec. 31	Adjusting	5		120		120

ACCOUNT *Wages Expense*   **ACCOUNT NO. 51**

Date	Item	Post. Ref.	Debit	Credit	Balance Debit	Balance Credit
2002 Nov. 30		1	2,125		2,125	
Dec. 13		3	950		3,075	
27		3	1,200		4,275	
31	Adjusting	5	250		4,525	

ACCOUNT *Rent Expense*   **ACCOUNT NO. 52**

Date	Item	Post. Ref.	Debit	Credit	Balance Debit	Balance Credit
2002 Nov. 30		1	800		800	
Dec. 1		2	800		1,600	

ACCOUNT *Depreciation Expense*   **ACCOUNT NO. 53**

Date	Item	Post. Ref.	Debit	Credit	Balance Debit	Balance Credit
2002 Dec. 31	Adjusting	5	50		50	

ACCOUNT *Utilities Expense*   **ACCOUNT NO. 54**

Date	Item	Post. Ref.	Debit	Credit	Balance Debit	Balance Credit
2002 Nov. 30		1	450		450	
Dec. 31		3	310		760	
31		4	225		985	

ACCOUNT *Supplies Expense*   **ACCOUNT NO. 55**

Date	Item	Post. Ref.	Debit	Credit	Balance Debit	Balance Credit
2002 Nov. 30		1	800		800	
Dec. 31	Adjusting	5	1,240		2,040	

ACCOUNT *Insurance Expense*   **ACCOUNT NO. 56**

Date	Item	Post. Ref.	Debit	Credit	Balance Debit	Balance Credit
2002 Dec. 31	Adjusting	5	100		100	

ACCOUNT *Miscellaneous Expense*   **ACCOUNT NO. 59**

Date	Item	Post. Ref.	Debit	Credit	Balance Debit	Balance Credit
2002 Nov. 30		1	275		275	
Dec. 6		2	180		455	

Point of Interest
One way for an accountant to check whether all adjustments have been made is to compare the current period's adjustments with those of the prior period.

After all the adjusting entries have been posted, another trial balance, called the **adjusted trial balance**, is prepared. The purpose of the adjusted trial balance is to verify the equality of the total debit balances and total credit balances before we prepare the financial statements. If the adjusted trial balance does not balance, an error has occurred. However, as we discussed in Chapter 2, errors may have occurred even though the adjusted trial balance totals agree. For example, the adjusted trial balance totals would agree if an adjusting entry has been omitted.

To highlight the effect of the adjustments on the accounts, Exhibit 8 shows the unadjusted trial balance, the accounts affected by the adjustments, and the adjusted

Exhibit 8 Trial Balances

	NetSolutions Unadjusted Trial Balance December 31, 2002				Effect of Adjusting Entry		NetSolutions Adjusted Trial Balance December 31, 2002			
1	Cash	2,065		1		1	Cash	2,065		1
2	Accounts Receivable	2,220		2	+ 500	2	Accounts Receivable	2,720		2
3	Supplies	2,000		3	−1,240	3	Supplies	760		3
4	Prepaid Insurance	2,400		4	− 100	4	Prepaid Insurance	2,300		4
5	Land	20,000		5		5	Land	20,000		5
6	Office Equipment	1,800		6		6	Office Equipment	1,800		6
7	Accumulated Depreciation			7	+ 50	7	Accumulated Depreciation		50	7
8	Accounts Payable		900	8		8	Accounts Payable		900	8
9	Wages Payable			9	+ 250	9	Wages Payable		250	9
10	Unearned Rent		360	10	− 120	10	Unearned Rent		240	10
11	Capital Stock		25,000	11		11	Capital Stock		25,000	11
12	Dividends	4,000		12		12	Dividends	4,000		12
13	Fees Earned		16,340	13	+ 500	13	Fees Earned		16,840	13
14	Rent Revenue			14	+ 120	14	Rent Revenue		120	14
15	Wages Expense	4,275		15	+ 250	15	Wages Expense	4,525		15
16	Rent Expense	1,600		16		16	Rent Expense	1,600		16
17	Depreciation Expense			17	+ 50	17	Depreciation Expense	50		17
18	Utilities Expense	985		18		18	Utilities Expense	985		18
19	Supplies Expense	800		19	+1,240	19	Supplies Expense	2,040		19
20	Insurance Expense			20	+ 100	20	Insurance Expense	100		20
21	Miscellaneous Expense	455		21		21	Miscellaneous Expense	455		21
22		42,600	42,600	22		22		43,400	43,400	22

trial balance. In Chapter 4, we discuss how financial statements, including a classified balance sheet, can be prepared from an adjusted trial balance. We also discuss the use of a work sheet as an aid to summarize the data for preparing adjusting entries and financial statements.

FINANCIAL ANALYSIS AND INTERPRETATION

objective 5

Use vertical analysis to compare financial statement items with each other and with industry averages.

Comparing each item in a current statement with a total amount within that same statement can be useful in highlighting significant relationships within a financial statement. **Vertical analysis** is the term used to describe such comparisons.

In vertical analysis of a balance sheet, each asset item is stated as a percent of the total assets. Each liability and stockholders' equity item is stated as a percent of the total liabilities and stockholders' equity. In vertical analysis of an income statement, each item is stated as a percent of revenues or fees earned.

Vertical analysis may also be prepared for several periods to highlight changes in relationships over time. Vertical analysis of two years of income statements for J. Holmes, Attorney-at-Law, is shown in Exhibit 9.

Exhibit 9 indicates both favorable and unfavorable trends affecting the income statement of J. Holmes, Attorney-at-Law, P.C. The increase in wages expense of 2% (32% − 30%) is an unfavorable trend, as is the increase in utilities expense of 0.7% (6.7% − 6.0%). A favorable trend is the decrease in supplies expense of 0.6% (2.0% − 1.4%). Rent expense and miscellaneous expense as a percent of fees earned were

Exhibit 9 Vertical Analysis of Income Statements

J. Holmes, Attorney-at-Law, P.C.
Income Statements
For the Years Ended December 31, 2002 and 2003

	2003		2002	
	Amount	Percent	Amount	Percent
Fees earned	$187,500	100.0%	$150,000	100.0%
Operating expenses:				
Wages expense	$60,000	32.0%	$45,000	30.0%
Rent expense	15,000	8.0%	12,000	8.0%
Utilities expense	12,500	6.7%	9,000	6.0%
Supplies expense	2,700	1.4%	3,000	2.0%
Miscellaneous expense	2,300	1.2%	1,800	1.2%
Total operating expenses	$92,500	49.3%	$70,800	47.2%
Net income	$95,000	50.7%	$79,200	52.8%

constant. The net result of these trends was that net income decreased as a percent of fees earned from 52.8% to 50.7%.

The analysis of the various percentages shown for J. Holmes, Attorney-at-Law, can be enhanced by comparisons with industry averages published by trade associations and financial information services. Any major differences between industry averages should be investigated.

ENCORE

"Intel Inside"

Intel Corporation develops and produces microprocessors for personal computers. Intel's earnings have grown from a $195 million loss in 1986 to over $7 billion of operating income in 1999. Intel's success has been driven by its ability to design, develop, and produce newer and faster microprocessors. This ability has been a result of a strong research and development effort in which spending has increased at an annual rate of 21% over the past ten years. Intel's current microprocessor is so tiny that it would take 500 of them placed end to end to be as large as a human hair!

Intel's microprocessors have become well-known, beginning with the 8086 processor and continuing with the 286, 386, and 486 processors. Rather than name its next generation of microprocessor the 586, Intel named its new chip the "Pentium" and registered it as a trademark. This prevented Intel's competitors from selling their products as "Pentiums," which they had been able to do with the numbers 386 and 486. In addition, Intel began a promotional campaign to identify its microprocessor as unique. Intel did this by entering into a cooperative program with computer manufacturers and distributors to label personal computers with the slogan "Intel Inside" or "Pentium Inside."

Intel has been highly successful. However, technology companies such as Intel are subject to significant risks

that their products will become outdated as technology changes. This is why Intel has invested so heavily in research and development over the years. In addition, Intel has the potential risk for faulty product designs or production of faulty processors due to poor quality control. For example, Intel discovered an error related to the divide function in the floating point unit of one of its Pentium micro-processors. This error required an adjusting entry for replacement processors and inventory write-downs, which cost Intel approximately $475 million. More recently, Intel has had to recall its Pentium III chip. ∎

KEY POINTS

1 Explain how the matching concept relates to the accrual basis of accounting.

The accrual basis of accounting requires the use of an adjusting process at the end of the accounting period to match revenues and expenses properly. Revenues are reported in the period in which they are earned, and expenses are matched with the revenues they generate.

2 Explain why adjustments are necessary and list the characteristics of adjusting entries.

At the end of an accounting period, some of the amounts listed on the trial balance are not necessarily current balances. For example, amounts listed for prepaid expenses are normally overstated because the use of these assets has not been recorded on a daily basis. A delay in recognizing an expense already paid or a revenue already received is called a deferral.

Some revenues and expenses related to a period may not be recorded at the end of the period, since these items are normally recorded only when cash has been received or paid. A revenue or expense that has not been paid or recorded is called an accrual.

The entries required at the end of an accounting period to bring accounts up to date and to ensure the proper matching of revenues and expenses are called adjusting entries. Adjusting entries require a debit or a credit to a revenue or an expense account and an offsetting debit or credit to an asset or a liability account.

Adjusting entries affect amounts reported in the income statement and the balance sheet. Thus, if an adjusting entry is not recorded, these financial statements will be incorrect (misstated).

3 Journalize entries for accounts requiring adjustment.

Adjusting entries illustrated in this chapter include deferred (prepaid) expenses, deferred (unearned) revenues, accrued expenses (accrued liabilities), and accrued revenues (accrued assets). In addition, the adjusting entry necessary to record depreciation on fixed assets was illustrated.

4 Summarize the adjustment process and prepare an adjusted trial balance.

A summary of adjustments, including the type of adjustment, the adjusting entry, and the effect of omitting an adjustment on the financial statements, is shown in Exhibit 5. After all the adjusting entries have been posted, the equality of the total debit balances and total credit balances is verified by an adjusted trial balance.

5 Use vertical analysis to compare financial statement items with each other and with industry averages.

Comparing each item in a current statement with a total amount within the same statement is called vertical analysis. In vertical analysis of a balance sheet, each asset item is stated as a percent of the total assets. Each liability and stockholders' equity item is stated as a percent of the total liabilities and stockholders' equity. In vertical analysis of an income statement, each item is stated as a percent of revenues or fees earned.

ILLUSTRATIVE PROBLEM

Three years ago, T. Roderick organized Harbor Realty Inc. At July 31, 2003, the end of the current year, the unadjusted trial balance of Harbor Realty appears as shown at the top of the following page. The data needed to determine year-end adjustments are as follows:

a.   Supplies on hand at July 31, 2003, $380.
b.   Insurance premiums expired during the year, $315.
c.   Depreciation of equipment during the year, $4,950.
d.   Wages accrued but not paid at July 31, 2003, $440.
e.   Accrued fees earned but not recorded at July 31, 2003, $1,000.
f.   Unearned fees on July 31, 2003, $750.

Harbor Realty Inc.
Trial Balance
July 31, 2003

	Debit	Credit
Cash	3 4 2 5 00	
Accounts Receivable	7 0 0 0 00	
Supplies	1 2 7 0 00	
Prepaid Insurance	6 2 0 00	
Office Equipment	51 6 5 0 00	
Accumulated Depreciation		9 7 0 0 00
Accounts Payable		9 2 5 00
Wages Payable		0 00
Unearned Fees		1 2 5 0 00
Capital Stock		5 0 0 0 00
Retained Earnings		24 0 0 0 00
Dividends	5 2 0 0 00	
Fees Earned		59 1 2 5 00
Wages Expense	22 4 1 5 00	
Depreciation Expense	0 00	
Rent Expense	4 2 0 0 00	
Utilities Expense	2 7 1 5 00	
Supplies Expense	0 00	
Insurance Expense	0 00	
Miscellaneous Expense	1 5 0 5 00	
	100 0 0 0 00	100 0 0 0 00

Instructions

1. Prepare the necessary adjusting journal entries.
2. Determine the balance of the accounts affected by the adjusting entries and prepare an adjusted trial balance.

Solution

1.

JOURNAL

	Date		Description	Post. Ref.	Debit	Credit	
1	2003 July	31	Supplies Expense		8 9 0 00		1
2			Supplies			8 9 0 00	2
3							3
4		31	Insurance Expense		3 1 5 00		4
5			Prepaid Insurance			3 1 5 00	5
6							6
7		31	Depreciation Expense		4 9 5 0 00		7
8			Accumulated Depreciation			4 9 5 0 00	8
9							9
10		31	Wages Expense		4 4 0 00		10
11			Wages Payable			4 4 0 00	11
12							12
13		31	Accounts Receivable		1 0 0 0 00		13
14			Fees Earned			1 0 0 0 00	14
15							15
16		31	Unearned Fees		5 0 0 00		16
17			Fees Earned			5 0 0 00	17

2.

Harbor Realty Inc. Adjusted Trial Balance July 31, 2003		
Cash	3 4 2 5 00	
Accounts Receivable	8 0 0 0 00	
Supplies	3 8 0 00	
Prepaid Insurance	3 0 5 00	
Office Equipment	51 6 5 0 00	
Accumulated Depreciation		14 6 5 0 00
Accounts Payable		9 2 5 00
Wages Payable		4 4 0 00
Unearned Fees		7 5 0 00
Capital Stock		5 0 0 0 00
Retained Earnings		24 0 0 0 00
Dividends	5 2 0 0 00	
Fees Earned		60 6 2 5 00
Wages Expense	22 8 5 5 00	
Depreciation Expense	4 9 5 0 00	
Rent Expense	4 2 0 0 00	
Utilities Expense	2 7 1 5 00	
Supplies Expense	8 9 0 00	
Insurance Expense	3 1 5 00	
Miscellaneous Expense	1 5 0 5 00	
	106 3 9 0 00	106 3 9 0 00

SELF-EXAMINATION QUESTIONS   Answers at End of Chapter

Matching

Match each of the following statements with its proper term. Some terms may not be used.

A. accounting period concept

B. accrual basis

C. accrued expenses

D. accrued revenues

E. accumulated depreciation

F. adjusted trial balance

G. adjusting entries

H. adjusting process

I. book value of the asset

J. cash basis

K. closing entries

L. contra account

M. deferred expenses

N. deferred revenues

O. depreciation

___ 1. The accounting concept that assumes that the economic life of the business can be divided into time periods.

___ 2. Under this basis of accounting, revenues and expenses are reported in the income statement in the period in which cash is received or paid.

___ 3. Under this basis of accounting, revenues are reported in the income statement in the period in which they are earned.

___ 4. The accounting concept that supports reporting revenues when the services are provided to customers.

___ 5. The accounting concept that supports reporting revenues and the related expenses in the same period.

___ 6. An analysis and updating of the accounts when financial statements are prepared.

___ 7. The journal entries that bring the accounts up to date at the end of the accounting period.

___ 8. Items that have been initially recorded as assets but are expected to become expenses over time or through the normal operations of the business.

___ 9. Items that have been initially recorded as liabilities but are expected to become revenues over time or through the normal operations of the business.

___10. Expenses that have been incurred *but not recorded* in the accounts.

___11. Revenues that have been earned *but not recorded* in the accounts.

P.   depreciation expense

Q.   final trial balance

R.   fixed assets

S.   horizontal analysis

T.   matching concept

U.   objectivity concept

V.   post-closing trial balance

W.   revenue recognition concept

X.   vertical analysis

____ 12. Physical resources that are owned and used by a business and are permanent or have a long life.

____ 13. The decrease in the ability of a fixed asset to provide useful services.

____ 14. The portion of the cost of a fixed asset that is recorded as an expense each year of its useful life.

____ 15. The asset account credited when recording the depreciation of a fixed asset.

____ 16. The difference between the cost of a fixed asset and its accumulated depreciation.

____ 17. The trial balance prepared after all the adjusting entries have been posted.

____ 18. An analysis that compares each item in a current statement with a total amount within the same statement.

____ 19. An account offset against another account.

Multiple Choice

1. Which of the following items represents a deferral?
    A. Prepaid insurance
    B. Wages payable
    C. Fees earned
    D. Accumulated depreciation

2. If the supplies account, before adjustment on May 31, indicated a balance of $2,250, and supplies on hand at May 31 totaled $950, the adjusting entry would be:
    A. debit Supplies, $950; credit Supplies Expense, $950.
    B. debit Supplies, $1,300; credit Supplies Expense, $1,300.
    C. debit Supplies Expense, $950; credit Supplies, $950.
    D. debit Supplies Expense, $1,300; credit Supplies, $1,300.

3. The balance in the unearned rent account for Jones Co. as of December 31 is $1,200. If Jones Co. failed to record the adjusting entry for $600 of rent earned during December, the effect on the balance sheet and income statement for December is:
    A. assets understated $600; net income overstated $600.

B. liabilities understated $600; net income understated $600.
C. liabilities overstated $600; net income understated $600.
D. liabilities overstated $600; net income overstated $600.

4. If the estimated amount of depreciation on equipment for a period is $2,000, the adjusting entry to record depreciation would be:
    A. debit Depreciation Expense, $2,000; credit Equipment, $2,000.
    B. debit Equipment, $2,000; credit Depreciation Expense, $2,000.
    C. debit Depreciation Expense, $2,000; credit Accumulated Depreciation, $2,000.
    D. debit Accumulated Depreciation, $2,000; credit Depreciation Expense, $2,000.

5. If the equipment account has a balance of $22,500 and its accumulated depreciation account has a balance of $14,000, the book value of the equipment is:
    A. $36,500.   C. $14,000.
    B. $22,500.   D. $8,500.

CLASS DISCUSSION QUESTIONS

1. How are revenues and expenses reported on the income statement under (a) the cash basis of accounting and (b) the accrual basis of accounting?
2. Fees for services provided are billed to a customer during 2002. The customer remits the amount owed in 2003. During which year would the revenues be reported on the income statement under (a) the cash basis? (b) the accrual basis?
3. Employees performed services in 2002, but the wages were not paid until 2003. During which year would the wages expense be reported on the income statement under (a) the cash basis? (b) the accrual basis?
4. Is the matching concept related to (a) the cash basis of accounting or (b) the accrual basis of accounting?
5. Is the balance listed for cash on the trial balance, before the accounts have been adjusted, the amount that should normally be reported on the balance sheet? Explain.
6. Is the balance listed for supplies on the trial balance, before the accounts have been adjusted, the amount that should normally be reported on the balance sheet? Explain.

7. Why are adjusting entries needed at the end of an accounting period?

8. Are adjusting entries in the journal dated as of the last day of the fiscal period or as of the day the entries are actually made? Explain.

9. What is the difference between *adjusting entries* and *correcting entries?*

10. Identify the five different categories of adjusting entries frequently required at the end of an accounting period.

11. If the effect of the credit portion of an adjusting entry is to increase the balance of a liability account, which of the following statements describes the effect of the debit portion of the entry?
    a. Increases the balance of a revenue account.
    b. Increases the balance of an expense account.
    c. Increases the balance of an asset account.

12. Does every adjusting entry have an effect on determining the amount of net income for a period? Explain.

13. What is the nature of the balance in the prepaid insurance account at the end of the accounting period (a) before adjustment? (b) after adjustment?

14. On November 1 of the current year, a business paid the November rent on the building that it occupies. (a) Do the rights acquired at November 1 represent an asset or an expense? (b) What is the justification for debiting Rent Expense at the time of payment?

15. In accounting for depreciation on equipment, what is the name of the contra asset account?

16. (a) Explain the purpose of the two accounts: Depreciation Expense and Accumulated Depreciation. (b) What is the normal balance of each account? (c) Is it customary for the balances of the two accounts to be equal in amount? (d) In what financial statements, if any, will each account appear?

RESOURCES FOR YOUR SUCCESS ONLINE AT

http://warren.swcollege.com

Remember! If you need additional help, visit South-Western's Web site.
See page F26 for a description of the online and printed materials that are available.

EXERCISES

Exercise 3–1
Classify accruals and deferrals

Objectives 2, 3

Classify the following items as (a) deferred expense (prepaid expense), (b) deferred revenue (unearned revenue), (c) accrued expense (accrued liability), or (d) accrued revenue (accrued asset).

1. Fees earned but not yet received.
2. Taxes owed but payable in the following period.
3. Salary owed but not yet paid.
4. Supplies on hand.
5. Fees received but not yet earned.
6. Utilities owed but not yet paid.
7. A two-year premium paid on a fire insurance policy.
8. Subscriptions received in advance by a magazine publisher.

Exercise 3–2
Classify adjusting entries

Objectives 2, 3

The following accounts were taken from the unadjusted trial balance of O'Neil Co., a congressional lobbying firm. Indicate whether or not each account would normally require an adjusting entry. If the account normally requires an adjusting entry, use the following notation to indicate the type of adjustment:

AE—Accrued Expense
AR—Accrued Revenue
DR—Deferred Revenue
DE—Deferred Expense

To illustrate, the answers for the first two accounts are shown below.

Account	Answer
Dividends	Does not normally require adjustment.
Accounts Receivable	Normally requires adjustment (AR).
Accumulated Depreciation	
Cash	
Interest Payable	
Interest Receivable	
Land	
Office Equipment	
Prepaid Insurance	
Supplies Expense	
Unearned Fees	
Wages Expense	

Exercise 3–3
Adjusting entry for supplies
Objective 3

The balance in the supplies account, before adjustment at the end of the year, is $1,475. Journalize the adjusting entry required if the amount of supplies on hand at the end of the year is $241.

Exercise 3–4
Determine supplies purchased
Objective 3

The supplies and supplies expense accounts at December 31, after adjusting entries have been posted at the end of the first year of operations, are shown in the following T accounts:

	Supplies			Supplies Expense	
Bal.	418		Bal.	1,943	

Determine the amount of supplies purchased during the year.

Exercise 3–5
Effect of omitting adjusting entry
Objective 3

At December 31, the end of the first month of operations, the usual adjusting entry transferring supplies used to an expense account is omitted. Which items will be incorrectly stated, because of the error, on (a) the income statement for December and (b) the balance sheet as of December 31? Also indicate whether the items in error will be overstated or understated.

Exercise 3–6
Adjusting entries for prepaid insurance
Objective 3

The balance in the prepaid insurance account, before adjustment at the end of the year, is $4,280. Journalize the adjusting entry required under each of the following *alternatives* for determining the amount of the adjustment: (a) the amount of insurance expired during the year is $1,020; (b) the amount of unexpired insurance applicable to future periods is $3,260.

Exercise 3–7
Adjusting entries for prepaid insurance
Objective 3

The prepaid insurance account had a balance of $3,600 at the beginning of the year. The account was debited for $1,200 for premiums on policies purchased during the year. Journalize the adjusting entry required at the end of the year for each of the following situations: (a) the amount of unexpired insurance applicable to future periods is $3,450; (b) the amount of insurance expired during the year is $1,875.

Exercise 3–8

Adjusting entries for unearned fees

Objective 3

✓ Amount of entry: $3,950

The balance in the unearned fees account, before adjustment at the end of the year, is $6,750. Journalize the adjusting entry required if the amount of unearned fees at the end of the year is $2,800.

Exercise 3–9

Effect of omitting adjusting entry

Objective 3

At the end of March, the first month of the business year, the usual adjusting entry transferring rent earned to a revenue account from the unearned rent account was omitted. Indicate which items will be incorrectly stated, because of the error, on (a) the income statement for March and (b) the balance sheet as of March 31. Also indicate whether the items in error will be overstated or understated.

Exercise 3–10

Adjusting entries for accrued salaries

Objective 3

✓ a. Amount of entry: $5,500

Taylor Fork Realty Co. pays weekly salaries of $13,750 on Friday for a five-day week ending on that day. Journalize the necessary adjusting entry at the end of the accounting period, assuming that the period ends (a) on Tuesday, (b) on Wednesday.

Exercise 3–11

Determine wages paid

Objective 3

The wages payable and wages expense accounts at December 31, after adjusting entries have been posted at the end of the first year of operations, are shown in the following T accounts:

Wages Payable		Wages Expense	
	Bal. 1,960	Bal. 87,430	

Determine the amount of wages paid during the year.

Exercise 3–12

Effect of omitting adjusting entry

Objective 3

Accrued salaries of $3,100 owed to employees for December 30 and 31 are not considered in preparing the financial statements for the year ended December 31. Indicate which items will be erroneously stated, because of the error, on (a) the income statement for the year and (b) the balance sheet as of December 31. Also indicate whether the items in error will be overstated or understated.

Exercise 3–13

Effect of omitting adjusting entry

Objective 3

Assume that the error in Exercise 3–12 was not corrected and that the $3,100 of accrued salaries was included in the first salary payment in January. Indicate which items will be erroneously stated, because of failure to correct the initial error, on (a) the income statement for the month of January and (b) the balance sheet as of January 31.

Exercise 3–14

Adjusting entries for prepaid and accrued taxes

Objective 3

✓ b. $10,975

Millennium Financial Services was organized on April 1 of the current year. On April 2, Millennium prepaid $1,020 to the city for taxes (license fees) for the *next* 12 months and debited the prepaid taxes account. Millennium is also required to pay in January an annual tax (on property) for the *previous* calendar year. The estimated amount of the property tax for the current year (April 1 to December 31) is $10,210. (a) Journalize the two adjusting entries required to bring the accounts affected by the two taxes up to date as of December 31, the end of the current year. (b) What is the amount of tax expense for the current year?

Exercise 3–15

Effects of errors on financial statements

Objective 3

For a recent period, **Circuit City Stores** reported accrued expenses and other current liabilities of $204,561,000. For the same period, Circuit City reported earnings of $528,758,000 before income taxes. If accrued expenses and other current liabilities had not been recorded, what would have been the earnings (loss) before income taxes?

Exercise 3–16
Effects of errors on financial statements

Objective 3

Real World

✓ b. 85.7%

The balance sheet for **The Quaker Oats Company** as of December 31, 1999, includes the following accrued expenses as liabilities:

Accrued payroll, benefits, and bonus	$139,100,000
Accrued advertising and merchandising	138,700,000
Other accrued liabilities	252,300,000

The income before taxes for The Quaker Oats Company for the year ended December 31, 1999, was $618,300,000. (a) If the accruals had not been recorded at December 31, 1999, by how much would income before taxes have been misstated for the fiscal year ended December 31, 1999? (b) What is the percentage of the misstatement in (a) to the reported income of $618,300,000?

Exercise 3–17
Effects of errors on financial statements

Objective 3

✓ 1. a. Revenue understated, $10,390

The accountant for Maxim Medical Co., a medical services consulting firm, mistakenly omitted adjusting entries for (a) unearned revenue ($10,390) and (b) accrued wages ($2,440). Indicate the effect of each error, considered individually, on the income statement for the current year ended December 31. Also indicate the effect of each error on the December 31 balance sheet. Set up a table similar to the following, and record your answers by inserting the dollar amount in the appropriate spaces. Insert a zero if the error does not affect the item.

	Error (a)		Error (b)	
	Over-stated	Under-stated	Over-stated	Under-stated
1. Revenue for the year would be	$	$	$	$
2. Expenses for the year would be	$	$	$	$
3. Net income for the year would be	$	$	$	$
4. Assets at December 31 would be	$	$	$	$
5. Liabilities at December 31 would be	$	$	$	$
6. Stockholders' equity at December 31 would be	$	$	$	$

Exercise 3–18
Effects of errors on financial statements

Objective 3

If the net income for the current year had been $437,720 in Exercise 3–17, what would be the correct net income if the proper adjusting entries had been made?

Exercise 3–19
Adjusting entry for accrued fees

Objective 3

At the end of the current year, $7,260 of fees have been earned but have not been billed to clients.

a. Journalize the adjusting entry to record the accrued fees.
b. If the cash basis rather than the accrual basis had been used, would an adjusting entry have been necessary? Explain.

Exercise 3–20
Adjusting entries for unearned and accrued fees

Objective 3

The balance in the unearned fees account, before adjustment at the end of the year, is $48,000. Of these fees, $16,000 have been earned. In addition, $7,500 of fees have been earned but have not been billed. Journalize the adjusting entries (a) to adjust the unearned fees account and (b) to record the accrued fees.

Exercise 3–21
Effect on financial statements of omitting adjusting entry

Objective 3

The adjusting entry for accrued fees was omitted at December 31, the end of the current year. Indicate which items will be in error, because of the omission, on (a) the income statement for the current year and (b) the balance sheet as of December 31. Also indicate whether the items in error will be overstated or understated.

Exercise 3–22
Adjustment for depreciation

Objective 3

The estimated amount of depreciation on equipment for the current year is $3,000. Journalize the adjusting entry to record the depreciation.

Exercise 3–23
Determine fixed asset's book value

Objective 3

The balance in the equipment account is $518,500, and the balance in the accumulated depreciation—equipment account is $120,750.

a.   What is the book value of the equipment?
b.   Does the balance in the accumulated depreciation account mean that the equipment's loss of value is $120,750? Explain.

Exercise 3–24
Book value of fixed assets

Objective 3

Microsoft Corporation reported *Property, Plant, and Equipment* of $3,321 million and *Accumulated Depreciation* of $1,418 million at June 30, 2000.

a.   What was the book value of the fixed assets at June 30, 2000?
b.   Would the book value of Microsoft Corporation's fixed assets normally approximate their fair market values?

Exercise 3–25
Adjusting entries for depreciation; effect of error

Objective 3

On December 31, a business estimates depreciation on equipment used during the first year of operations to be $8,500. (a) Journalize the adjusting entry required as of December 31. (b) If the adjusting entry in (a) were omitted, which items would be erroneously stated on (1) the income statement for the year and (2) the balance sheet as of December 31?

Exercise 3–26
Adjusting entries from trial balances

Objectives 3, 4

The unadjusted and adjusted trial balances for Medico Services Co. on December 31, 2003, are shown below.

Medico Services Co.
Trial Balance
December 31, 2003

	Unadjusted		Adjusted	
Cash	8		8	
Accounts Receivable	19		21	
Supplies	6		2	
Prepaid Insurance	10		6	
Land	13		13	
Equipment	20		20	
Accumulated Depreciation—Equipment		4		5
Accounts Payable		13		13
Wages Payable		0		1
Capital Stock		25		25
Retained Earnings		21		21
Dividends	4		4	
Fees Earned		37		39
Wages Expense	12		13	
Rent Expense	4		4	
Insurance Expense	0		4	
Utilities Expense	2		2	
Depreciation Expense	0		1	
Supplies Expense	0		4	
Miscellaneous Expense	2		2	
Totals	100	100	104	104

Journalize the five entries that adjusted the accounts at December 31, 2003. None of the accounts were affected by more than one adjusting entry.

Exercise 3–27
Adjusting entries from trial balances

Objectives 3, 4

✓ Corrected trial balance totals, $171,520

The accountant for St. Elmo Laundry prepared the following unadjusted and adjusted trial balances. Assume that all balances in the unadjusted trial balance and the amounts of the adjustments are correct. How many errors can you find in the accountant's adjusting entries?

St. Elmo Laundry
Trial Balance
October 31, 2003

	Unadjusted		Adjusted	
Cash	3,790		3,790	
Accounts Receivable	8,000		12,500	
Laundry Supplies	3,750		5,660	
Prepaid Insurance*	2,825		1,325	
Laundry Equipment	85,600		80,880	
Accumulated Depreciation		55,700		55,700
Accounts Payable		4,950		4,950
Wages Payable				850
Capital Stock		7,500		7,500
Retained Earnings		16,400		16,400
Dividends	8,000		8,000	
Laundry Revenue		76,900		76,900
Wages Expense	24,500		24,500	
Rent Expense	15,575		15,575	
Utilities Expense	8,500		8,500	
Depreciation Expense			4,720	
Laundry Supplies Expense			1,910	
Insurance Expense			500	
Miscellaneous Expense	910		910	
	161,450	161,450	168,770	162,300

*$1,500 of insurance expired during the year.

Exercise 3–28
Vertical analysis of income statement

Objective 5

The financial statements for **Cisco Systems, Inc.**, are presented in Appendix G at the end of the text.

a. Determine for Cisco Systems:
  1. The amount of the change and percent of change in net income for the year ended July 29, 2000.
  2. The percentage relationship between net income and net sales (net income divided by net sales) for the years ended July 29, 2000 and July 31, 1999.
b. What conclusions can you draw from your analysis?

PROBLEMS SERIES A

Problem 3–1A
Adjusting entries

Objective 3

On December 31, the end of the current year, the following data were accumulated to assist the accountant in preparing the adjusting entries for Epoch Realty:

a. The supplies account balance on December 31 is $1,750. The supplies on hand on December 31 are $245.
b. The unearned rent account balance on December 31 is $6,750, representing the receipt of an advance payment on December 1 of three months' rent from tenants.
c. Wages accrued but not paid at December 31 are $1,800.
d. Fees accrued but unbilled at December 31 are $10,600.
e. Depreciation of office equipment for the year is $3,100.

Instructions

1. Journalize the adjusting entries required at December 31.
2. Briefly explain the difference between adjusting entries and entries that would be made to correct errors.

Problem 3–2A
Adjusting entries
Objective 3

Selected account balances before adjustment for Gibraltar Realty at December 31, the end of the current year, are as follows:

	Debits	Credits		Debits	Credits
Accounts Receivable	$ 9,250		Unearned Fees		$ 7,000
Supplies	2,750		Fees Earned		97,950
Prepaid Rent	30,000		Wages Expense	$39,400	
Equipment	52,500		Rent Expense	—	
Accumulated Depreciation		$8,900	Depreciation Expense	—	
Wages Payable		—	Supplies Expense	—	

Data needed for year-end adjustments are as follows:

a. Unbilled fees at December 31, $3,150.
b. Supplies on hand at December 31, $555.
c. Rent expired during year, $18,000.
d. Depreciation of equipment during year, $1,575.
e. Unearned fees at December 31, $2,700.
f. Wages accrued but not paid at December 31, $875.

Instructions

Journalize the six adjusting entries required at December 31, based upon the data presented.

Problem 3–3A
Adjusting entries
Objective 3

**GENERAL
LEDGER**

Jupiter Company, an electronics repair store, prepared the following trial balance at the end of its first year of operations:

**Jupiter Company
Trial Balance
November 30, 2003**

Cash	1,150	
Accounts Receivable	7,500	
Supplies	1,800	
Equipment	37,900	
Accounts Payable		1,750
Unearned Fees		2,000
Capital Stock		7,500
Retained Earnings		18,500
Dividends	1,500	
Fees Earned		45,250
Wages Expense	10,500	
Rent Expense	8,000	
Utilities Expense	5,750	
Miscellaneous Expense	900	
	75,000	75,000

For preparing the adjusting entries, the following data were assembled:

a. Fees earned but unbilled on November 30 were $1,100.
b. Supplies on hand on November 30 were $380.
c. Depreciation of equipment was estimated to be $2,200 for the year.
d. The balance in unearned fees represented the November 1 receipt in advance for services to be provided. Only $800 of the services was provided between November 1 and November 30.
e. Unpaid wages accrued on November 30 were $400.

Instructions
Journalize the adjusting entries necessary on November 30.

Problem 3–4A
Adjusting entries

Objectives 3, 4

SPREADSHEET

GENERAL
LEDGER

Oriole Company specializes in the repair of music equipment and is owned and operated by Kaye Santora. On April 30, 2003, the end of the current year, the accountant for Oriole Company prepared the following trial balances:

Oriole Company
Trial Balance
April 30, 2003

	Unadjusted		Adjusted	
Cash	7,825		7,825	
Accounts Receivable	30,500		30,500	
Supplies	3,950		800	
Prepaid Insurance	3,750		1,500	
Equipment	92,150		92,150	
Accumulated Depreciation—Equipment		33,480		42,500
Automobiles	36,500		36,500	
Accumulated Depreciation—Automobiles		18,250		22,900
Accounts Payable		8,310		9,390
Salaries Payable		—		1,800
Unearned Service Fees		5,000		3,000
Capital Stock		15,000		15,000
Retained Earnings		54,470		54,470
Dividends	5,000		5,000	
Service Fees Earned		244,600		246,600
Salary Expense	172,300		174,100	
Rent Expense	18,000		18,000	
Supplies Expense	—		3,150	
Depreciation Expense—Equipment	—		9,020	
Depreciation Expense—Automobiles	—		4,650	
Utilities Expense	4,700		5,780	
Taxes Expense	2,725		2,725	
Insurance Expense	—		2,250	
Miscellaneous Expense	1,710		1,710	
	379,110	379,110	395,660	395,660

Instructions
Journalize the seven entries that adjusted the accounts at April 30. None of the accounts were affected by more than one adjusting entry.

Problem 3–5A
Adjusting entries and adjusted trial balances

Objectives 3, 4

SPREADSHEET

GENERAL
LEDGER

✓ 2. Total of Debit Column:
$538,320

Guantanamo Company is a small editorial services company owned and operated by Ronaldo Manuel. On December 31, 2003, the end of the current year, Guantanamo Company's accounting clerk prepared the trial balance shown at the top of the next page.

The data needed to determine year-end adjustments are as follows:

a. Unexpired insurance at December 31, $1,900.
b. Supplies on hand at December 31, $475.
c. Depreciation of building for the year, $1,620.
d. Depreciation of equipment for the year, $5,500.
e. Rent unearned at December 31, $1,500.
f. Accrued salaries and wages at December 31, $2,050.
g. Fees earned but unbilled on December 31, $4,150.

Instructions

1. Journalize the adjusting entries. Add additional accounts as needed.
2. Determine the balances of the accounts affected by the adjusting entries and prepare an adjusted trial balance.

Guantanamo Company
Trial Balance
December 31, 2003

Cash	5,700	
Accounts Receivable	21,900	
Prepaid Insurance	4,500	
Supplies	1,720	
Land	75,000	
Building	141,500	
Accumulated Depreciation—Building		91,700
Equipment	90,100	
Accumulated Depreciation—Equipment		65,300
Accounts Payable		8,100
Unearned Rent		7,500
Capital Stock		50,000
Retained Earnings		84,000
Dividends	10,000	
Fees Earned		218,400
Salaries and Wages Expense	110,580	
Utilities Expense	28,250	
Advertising Expense	20,200	
Repairs Expense	11,500	
Miscellaneous Expense	4,050	
	525,000	525,000

Problem 3–6A

Adjusting entries and errors

Objective 3

✓ Corrected Net Income:
$135,300

At the end of April, the first month of operations, the following selected data were taken from the financial statements of Jay Harriman, P.C., a professional services corporation owned and operated by Jay Harriman, an attorney:

Net income for April	$129,575
Total assets at April 30	275,600
Total liabilities at April 30	18,575
Total stockholders' equity at April 30	257,025

In preparing the financial statements, adjustments for the following data were overlooked:

a. Supplies used during April, $1,125.
b. Unbilled fees earned at April 30, $10,200.
c. Depreciation of equipment for April, $2,500.
d. Accrued wages at April 30, $850.

Instructions

1. Journalize the entries to record the omitted adjustments.
2. Determine the correct amount of net income for April and the total assets, liabilities, and stockholders' equity at April 30. In addition to indicating the corrected amounts, indicate the effect of each omitted adjustment by setting up and completing a columnar table similar to the following. Adjustment (a) is presented as an example.

	Net Income	Total Assets	Total Liabilities	Total Stockholders' Equity
Reported amounts	$129,575	$275,600	$18,575	$257,025
Corrections:				
Adjustment (a)	−1,125	−1,125	0	−1,125
Adjustment (b)				
Adjustment (c)				
Adjustment (d)				
Corrected amounts				

PROBLEMS SERIES B

Problem 3–1B
Adjusting entries

Objective 3

On December 31, the end of the current year, the following data were accumulated to assist the accountant in preparing the adjusting entries for Bravo Realty:

a. Fees accrued but unbilled at December 31 are $6,300.
b. The supplies account balance on December 31 is $2,100. The supplies on hand at December 31 are $310.
c. Wages accrued but not paid at December 31 are $1,500.
d. The unearned rent account balance at December 31 is $5,200, representing the receipt of an advance payment on December 1 of four months' rent from tenants.
e. Depreciation of office equipment for the year is $3,500.

Instructions

1. Journalize the adjusting entries required at December 31.
2. Briefly explain the difference between adjusting entries and entries that would be made to correct errors.

Problem 3–2B
Adjusting entries

Objective 3

Selected account balances before adjustment for Lambada Realty at July 31, the end of the current year, are as follows:

	Debits	Credits		Debits	Credits
Accounts Receivable	$10,250		Unearned Fees		$ 6,500
Supplies	1,970		Fees Earned		100,850
Prepaid Rent	18,000		Wages Expense	$39,750	
Equipment	70,500		Rent Expense	—	
Accumulated Depreciation		$26,900	Depreciation Expense	—	
Wages Payable		—	Supplies Expense	—	

Data needed for year-end adjustments are as follows:

a. Supplies on hand at July 31, $600.
b. Depreciation of equipment during year, $2,000.
c. Rent expired during year, $12,000.
d. Wages accrued but not paid at July 31, $1,060.
e. Unearned fees at July 31, $3,000.
f. Unbilled fees at July 31, $7,180.

Instructions

Journalize the six adjusting entries required at July 31, based upon the data presented.

Problem 3–3B
Adjusting entries

Objective 3

GENERAL LEDGER

Brown Trout Co., an outfitter store for fishing treks, prepared the following trial balance at the end of its first year of operations:

Brown Trout Co.
Trial Balance
June 30, 2003

Cash	1,150	
Accounts Receivable	8,500	
Supplies	1,300	
Equipment	19,900	
Accounts Payable		750
Unearned Fees		2,000
Capital Stock		2,500
Retained Earnings		24,500
Dividends	1,000	
Fees Earned		36,750
Wages Expense	20,150	
Rent Expense	9,850	
Utilities Expense	3,750	
Miscellaneous Expense	900	
	66,500	66,500

For preparing the adjusting entries, the following data were assembled:

a. Supplies on hand on June 30 were $280.
b. Fees earned but unbilled on June 30 were $2,750.
c. Depreciation of equipment was estimated to be $1,500 for the year.
d. Unpaid wages accrued on June 30 were $450.
e. The balance in unearned fees represented the June 1 receipt in advance for services to be provided. Only $900 of the services were provided between June 1 and June 30.

Instructions
Journalize the adjusting entries necessary on June 30.

Problem 3–4B
Adjusting entries

Objectives 3, 4

SPREADSHEET

GENERAL
LEDGER

Tinker Company specializes in the maintenance and repair of signs, such as billboards. On October 31, 2003, the accountant for Tinker Company prepared the following trial balances:

Tinker Company
Trial Balance
October 31, 2003

	Unadjusted		Adjusted	
Cash	6,750		6,750	
Accounts Receivable	18,400		18,400	
Supplies	5,880		1,030	
Prepaid Insurance	2,700		1,100	
Land	47,500		47,500	
Buildings	107,480		107,480	
Accumulated Depreciation—Buildings		79,600		85,100
Trucks	72,000		72,000	
Accumulated Depreciation—Trucks		22,800		31,900
Accounts Payable		8,920		9,595
Salaries Payable		—		960
Unearned Service Fees		7,500		3,500
Capital Stock		18,000		18,000
Retained Earnings		75,890		75,890
Dividends	5,000		5,000	
Service Fees Earned		152,680		156,680
Salary Expense	81,200		82,160	
Depreciation Expense—Trucks	—		9,100	
Rent Expense	9,600		9,600	
Supplies Expense	—		4,850	
Utilities Expense	6,200		6,875	
Depreciation Expense—Buildings	—		5,500	
Taxes Expense	1,720		1,720	
Insurance Expense	—		1,600	
Miscellaneous Expense	960		960	
	365,390	365,390	381,625	381,625

Instructions
Journalize the seven entries that adjusted the accounts at October 31. None of the accounts were affected by more than one adjusting entry.

Problem 3–5B
Adjusting entries and adjusted trial balances

Objectives 3, 4

Humvee Service Co., which specializes in appliance repair services, is owned and operated by Jon Grabowski. Humvee Service Co.'s accounting clerk prepared the following trial balance at December 31, 2003:

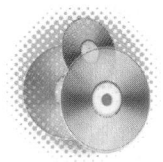

SPREADSHEET

GENERAL LEDGER

✓ 2. Total of Debit Column:

$535,620

Humvee Service Co.
Trial Balance
December 31, 2003

Cash	5,200	
Accounts Receivable	16,200	
Prepaid Insurance	4,000	
Supplies	2,450	
Land	100,000	
Building	141,500	
Accumulated Depreciation—Building		95,700
Equipment	90,100	
Accumulated Depreciation—Equipment		65,300
Accounts Payable		7,500
Unearned Rent		6,000
Capital Stock		60,000
Retained Earnings		67,100
Dividends	5,000	
Fees Earned		218,400
Salaries and Wages Expense	90,800	
Utilities Expense	28,200	
Advertising Expense	19,000	
Repairs Expense	13,500	
Miscellaneous Expense	4,050	
	520,000	520,000

The data needed to determine year-end adjustments are as follows:

a. Depreciation of building for the year, $2,100.
b. Depreciation of equipment for the year, $4,000.
c. Accrued salaries and wages at December 31, $3,170.
d. Unexpired insurance at December 31, $1,900.
e. Fees earned but unbilled on December 31, $6,350.
f. Supplies on hand at December 31, $675.
g. Rent unearned at December 31, $3,500.

Instructions

1. Journalize the adjusting entries. Add additional accounts as needed.
2. Determine the balances of the accounts affected by the adjusting entries and prepare an adjusted trial balance.

Problem 3–6B

Adjusting entries and errors

Objective 3

✓ Corrected Net Income:

$422,345

At the end of August, the first month of operations, the following selected data were taken from the financial statements of Toreka Bowen, P.C., a professional services corporation owned and operated by Toreka Bowen, an attorney:

Net income for August	$417,950
Total assets at August 31	771,500
Total liabilities at August 31	210,350
Total stockholders' equity at August 31	561,150

In preparing the financial statements, adjustments for the following data were overlooked:

a. Unbilled fees earned at August 31, $13,800.
b. Depreciation of equipment for August, $5,000.
c. Accrued wages at August 31, $1,300.
d. Supplies used during August, $3,105.

Instructions

1. Journalize the entries to record the omitted adjustments.

(continued)

2. Determine the correct amount of net income for August and the total assets, liabilities, and stockholders' equity at August 31. In addition to indicating the corrected amounts, indicate the effect of each omitted adjustment by setting up and completing a columnar table similar to the following. Adjustment (a) is presented as an example.

	Net Income	Total Assets	Total Liabilities	Total Stockholders' Equity
Reported amounts	$417,950	$771,500	$210,350	$561,150
Corrections:				
Adjustment (a)	+13,800	+13,800	0	+13,800
Adjustment (b)	_____	_____	_____	_____
Adjustment (c)	_____	_____	_____	_____
Adjustment (d)	_____	_____	_____	_____
Corrected amounts	_____	_____	_____	_____

CONTINUING PROBLEM

GENERAL LEDGER

✓ 3. Total of Debit Column:
$16,595

The trial balance that you prepared for Dancin Music at the end of Chapter 2 should appear as follows:

Dancin Music
Trial Balance
December 31, 2002

Cash	3,665	
Accounts Receivable	880	
Supplies	460	
Prepaid Insurance	1,680	
Office Equipment	2,500	
Accounts Payable		2,875
Unearned Revenue		2,400
Capital Stock		5,000
Dividends	1,125	
Fees Earned		5,605
Wages Expense	1,400	
Office Rent Expense	1,300	
Equipment Rent Expense	575	
Utilities Expense	430	
Music Expense	890	
Advertising Expense	650	
Supplies Expense	90	
Miscellaneous Expense	235	
	15,880	15,880

The data needed to determine adjustments for the two-month period ending December 31, 2002, are as follows:

a. During December, Dancin Music provided guest disc jockeys for KPRG for a total of 110 hours. For information on the amount of the accrued revenue to be billed to KPRG, see the contract described in the December 3, 2002 transaction at the end of Chapter 2.
b. Supplies on hand at December 31, $85.
c. The balance of the prepaid insurance account relates to the December 1, 2002 transaction at the end of Chapter 2.
d. Depreciation of the office equipment is $50.

e. The balance of the unearned revenue account relates to the contract between Dancin Music and KPRG, described in the December 3, 2002 transaction at the end of Chapter 2.

f. Accrued wages as of December 31, 2002, were $65.

Instructions

1. Prepare adjusting journal entries. You will need the following additional accounts:

   18 Accumulated Depreciation—Office Equipment
   22 Wages Payable
   57 Insurance Expense
   58 Depreciation Expense

2. Post the adjusting entries, inserting balances in the accounts affected.
3. Prepare an adjusted trial balance.

SPECIAL ACTIVITIES

Activity 3–1
Nadu Real Estate Co.
Ethics and professional conduct in business

Stacey Nairn opened Nadu Real Estate Co. on January 1, 2002. At the end of the first year, the business needed additional capital. On behalf of Nadu Real Estate, Stacey applied to American City Bank for a loan of $75,000. Based on Nadu Real Estate's financial statements, which had been prepared on a cash basis, the American City Bank loan officer rejected the loan as too risky.

After receiving the rejection notice, Stacey instructed her accountant to prepare the financial statements on an accrual basis. These statements included $31,500 in accounts receivable and $11,200 in accounts payable. Stacey then instructed her accountant to record an additional $18,000 of accounts receivable for commissions on property for which a contract had been signed on December 27, 2002, but which would not be formally "closed" and the title transferred until January 20, 2003.

Stacey then applied for a $75,000 loan from First National Bank, using the revised financial statements. On this application, Stacey indicated that she had not previously been rejected for credit.

Discuss the ethical and professional conduct of Stacey Nairn in applying for the loan from First National Bank.

Activity 3–2
Ford Motor Co.
Accrued expense

On December 30, 2003, you buy a Ford Expedition. It comes with a three-year, 36,000-mile warranty. On January 21, 2004, you return the Expedition to the dealership for some basic repairs covered under the warranty. The cost of the repairs to the dealership is $610. In what year, 2003 or 2004, should Ford Motor Co. recognize the cost of the warranty repairs as an expense?

Activity 3–3
United Airlines
Accrued revenue

The following is an excerpt from a conversation between Dawn Abrams and Kala Wiggins just before they boarded a flight to Paris on United Airlines. They are going to Paris to attend their company's annual sales conference.

Dawn: Kala, aren't you taking an introductory accounting course at State College?
Kala: Yes, I decided it's about time I learned something about accounting. You know, our annual bonuses are based upon the sales figures that come from the accounting department.
Dawn: I guess I never really thought about it.
Kala: You should think about it! Last year, I placed a $200,000 order on December 26. But when I got my bonus, the $200,000 sale wasn't included. They said it hadn't been shipped until January 6, so it would have to count in next year's bonus.
Dawn: A real bummer!

Kala: Right! I was counting on that bonus including the $200,000 sale.

Dawn: Did you complain?

Kala: Yes, but it didn't do any good. Ed, the head accountant, said something about matching revenues and expenses. Also, something about not recording revenues until the sale is final. I figure I'd take the accounting course and find out whether he's just jerking me around.

Dawn: I never really thought about it. When do you think United Airlines will record its revenues from this flight?

Kala: Mmm . . . I guess it could record the revenue when it sells the ticket . . . or . . . when the boarding passes are taken at the door . . . or . . . when we get off the plane . . . or when our company pays for the tickets . . . or . . . I don't know. I'll ask my accounting instructor.

Discuss when United Airlines should recognize the revenue from ticket sales to properly match revenues and expenses.

Activity 3–4
Eminent Television Repair
Adjustments and financial statements

Several years ago, your father opened Eminent Television Repair. He made a small initial investment and added money from his personal bank account as needed. He withdrew wages for living expenses at irregular intervals. As the business grew, he hired an assistant. He is now considering adding more employees, purchasing additional service trucks, and purchasing the building he now rents. To secure funds for the expansion, your father submitted a loan application to the bank and included the most recent financial statements (shown below) prepared from accounts maintained by a part-time bookkeeper.

Eminent Television Repair
Income Statement
For the Year Ended December 31, 2003

Service revenue		$51,750
Less: Rent paid	$18,000	
Wages paid	12,300	
Supplies paid	5,100	
Utilities paid	4,175	
Insurance paid	2,400	
Miscellaneous payments	2,150	44,125
Net income		$ 7,625

Eminent Television Repair
Balance Sheet
December 31, 2003

Assets

Cash	$ 8,600
Amounts due from customers	3,100
Truck	30,000
Total assets	$41,700

Equities

Stockholders' equity	$41,700

After reviewing the financial statements, the loan officer at the bank asked your father if he used the accrual basis of accounting for revenues and expenses. Your father responded that he did and that is why he included an account for "Amounts Due from Customers." The loan officer then asked whether or not the accounts were adjusted prior to the preparation of the statements. Your father answered that they had not been adjusted.

a. Why do you think the loan officer suspected that the accounts had not been adjusted prior to the preparation of the statements?

b. Indicate possible accounts that might need to be adjusted before an accurate set of financial statements could be prepared.

Activity 3–5
Into the Real World
Codes of ethics

Group Activity

Obtain a copy of your college or university's student code of conduct. In groups of three or four, answer the following questions.

1. Compare this code of conduct with the accountant's Codes of Professional Conduct in Appendix B at the end of this text. What are the similarities and differences between the two codes of conduct?
2. One of your classmates asks you for permission to copy your homework, which your instructor will be collecting and grading for part of your overall term grade. Although your instructor has not stated whether one student may or may not copy another student's homework, is it ethical for you to allow your classmate to copy your homework? Is it ethical for your classmate to copy your homework?

ANSWERS TO SELF-EXAMINATION QUESTIONS

Matching

1. A	5. T	9. N	13. O	17. F
2. J	6. H	10. C	14. P	18. X
3. B	7. G	11. D	15. E	19. L
4. W	8. M	12. R	16. I	

Multiple Choice

1. **A** A deferral is the delay in recording an expense already paid, such as prepaid insurance (answer A). Wages payable (answer B) is considered an accrued expense or accrued liability. Fees earned (answer C) is a revenue item. Accumulated depreciation (answer D) is a contra account to a fixed asset.

2. **D** The balance in the supplies account, before adjustment, represents the amount of supplies available. From this amount ($2,250) is subtracted the amount of supplies on hand ($950) to determine the supplies used ($1,300). Since increases in expense accounts are recorded by debits and decreases in asset accounts are recorded by credits, answer D is the correct entry.

3. **C** The failure to record the adjusting entry debiting unearned rent, $600, and crediting rent revenue, $600, would have the effect of overstating liabilities by $600 and understating net income by $600 (answer C).

4. **C** Since increases in expense accounts (such as depreciation expense) are recorded by debits and it is customary to record the decreases in usefulness of fixed assets as credits to accumulated depreciation accounts, answer C is the correct entry.

5. **D** The book value of a fixed asset is the difference between the balance in the asset account and the balance in the related accumulated depreciation account, or $22,500 − $14,000, as indicated by answer D ($8,500).

Completing the Accounting Cycle

F4

objectives

After studying this chapter, you should be able to:

1 Prepare a work sheet.

2 Prepare financial statements from a work sheet.

3 Prepare the adjusting and closing entries from a work sheet.

4 Review the seven basic steps of the accounting cycle.

5 Explain what is meant by the fiscal year and the natural business year.

6 Analyze and interpret the financial solvency of a business by computing working capital and the current ratio.

ost of us have had to file a personal tax return. At the beginning of the year, you estimate your upcoming income and decide whether you need to increase your payroll tax withholdings or perhaps pay estimated taxes. During the year, you earn income, make investments, and enter into other tax-related transactions, such as making charitable contributions. At the end of the year, your employer sends you a tax withholding information form (W-2 form), and you collect the tax records needed for completing your yearly tax forms. If any tax is owed, you pay it; if you overpaid your taxes, you file for a refund. As the next year begins, you start the cycle all over again.

Businesses also go through a cycle of activities. At the beginning of the cycle, management plans where it wants the business to go and begins the necessary actions to achieve its operating goals. Throughout the cycle, which is normally one year, the accountant records the operating activities (transactions) of the business. At the end of the cycle, the accountant prepares financial statements that summarize the operating activities for the year. The accountant then prepares the accounts for recording the operating activities in the next cycle.

As we saw in Chapter 1, the initial cycle for NetSolutions began with Chris Clark's investment in the business on November 1, 2002. The cycle continued with recording NetSolutions' transactions for November and December, as we discussed in Chapters 1 and 2. In Chapter 3, the cycle continued and we recorded the adjusting entries for the two months ending December 31, 2002. Now, in this chapter, we discuss the flow of the adjustment data into the accounts and into the financial statements. We show this process by using a work sheet. We conclude this chapter by discussing how the accounting records are prepared for the next period.

Work Sheet

objective 1

Prepare a work sheet.

> The work sheet is a useful device for understanding the flow of the accounting data from the unadjusted trial balance to the financial statements.

Accountants often use **working papers** for collecting and summarizing data they need for preparing various analyses and reports. Such working papers are useful tools, but they are not considered a part of the formal accounting records. This is in contrast to the chart of accounts, the journal, and the ledger, which are essential parts of the accounting system. Working papers are usually prepared by using a spreadsheet program on a computer.

Real World

Common spreadsheet programs used in business include Microsoft Excel® and Lotus 1-2-3®.

The work sheet is a working paper that accountants can use to summarize adjusting entries and the account balances for the financial statements. In small companies with few accounts and adjustments, a work sheet may not be necessary. For example, the financial statements for NetSolutions can be prepared directly from the adjusted trial balance illustrated in Chapter 3. In a computerized accounting system, a work sheet may not be necessary because the software program automatically posts entries to the accounts and prepares financial statements.

The work sheet (Exhibits 1 through 4) is a useful device for understanding the flow of the accounting data from the unadjusted trial balance to the financial statements (Exhibit 5). This flow of data is the same in either a manual or a computerized accounting system.

Unadjusted Trial Balance Columns

To begin the work sheet, list at the top the name of the business, the type of working paper (work sheet), and the period of time, as shown in Exhibit 1. Next, enter the unadjusted trial balance directly on the work sheet. The work sheet in Exhibit 1 shows the unadjusted trial balance for NetSolutions at December 31, 2002.

Adjustments Columns

The adjustments that we explained and illustrated for NetSolutions in Chapter 3 are entered in the Adjustments columns, as shown in Exhibit 2. Cross-referencing (by letters) the debit and credit of each adjustment is useful in reviewing the work sheet. It is also helpful for identifying the adjusting entries that need to be recorded in the journal.

The order in which the adjustments are entered on the work sheet is not important. Most accountants enter the adjustments in the order in which the data are assembled. If the titles of some of the accounts to be adjusted do not appear in the trial balance, they should be inserted in the Account Title column, below the trial balance totals, as needed.

To review, the entries in the Adjustments columns of the work sheet are:

(a) **Supplies.** The supplies account has a debit balance of $2,000. The cost of the supplies on hand at the end of the period is $760. Therefore, the supplies expense for December is the difference between the two amounts, or $1,240. Enter the adjustment by writing (1) $1,240 in the Adjustments Debit column on the same line as Supplies Expense and (2) $1,240 in the Adjustments Credit column on the same line as Supplies.

Exhibit 1 Work Sheet with Unadjusted Trial Balance Entered

NetSolutions
Work Sheet
For the Two Months Ended December 31, 2002

	Account Title	Trial Balance Dr.	Trial Balance Cr.	Adjustments Dr.	Adjustments Cr.	Adjusted Trial Balance Dr.	Adjusted Trial Balance Cr.	Income Statement Dr.	Income Statement Cr.	Balance Sheet Dr.	Balance Sheet Cr.	
1	Cash	2,065										1
2	Accounts Receivable	2,220										2
3	Supplies	2,000										3
4	Prepaid Insurance	2,400										4
5	Land	20,000										5
6	Office Equipment	1,800										6
7	Accounts Payable		900									7
8	Unearned Rent		360									8
9	Capital Stock		25,000									9
10	Dividends	4,000										10
11	Fees Earned		16,340									11
12	Wages Expense	4,275										12
13	Rent Expense	1,600										13
14	Utilities Expense	985										14
15	Supplies Expense	800										15
16	Miscellaneous Expense	455										16
17		42,600	42,600									17
18												18

> The work sheet is used for summarizing the effects of adjusting entries. It also aids in preparing financial statements.

Exhibit 2 Work Sheet with Unadjusted Trial Balance, Adjustments, and Adjusted Trial Balance Entered

NetSolutions
Work Sheet
For the Two Months Ended December 31, 2002

	Account Title	Trial Balance Dr.	Trial Balance Cr.	Adjustments Dr.	Adjustments Cr.	Adjusted Trial Balance Dr.	Adjusted Trial Balance Cr.	Income Statement Dr.	Income Statement Cr.	Balance Sheet Dr.	Balance Sheet Cr.	
1	Cash	2,065				2,065						1
2	Accounts Receivable	2,220		(e) 500		2,720						2
3	Supplies	2,000			(a)1,240	760						3
4	Prepaid Insurance	2,400			(b) 100	2,300						4
5	Land	20,000				20,000						5
6	Office Equipment	1,800				1,800						6
7	Accounts Payable		900				900					7
8	Unearned Rent		360	(c) 120			240					8
9	Capital Stock		25,000				25,000					9
10	Dividends	4,000				4,000						10
11	Fees Earned		16,340		(e) 500		16,840					11
12	Wages Expense	4,275		(d) 250		4,525						12
13	Rent Expense	1,600				1,600						13
14	Utilities Expense	985				985						14
15	Supplies Expense	800		(a)1,240		2,040						15
16	Miscellaneous Expense	455				455						16
17		42,600	42,600									17
18	Insurance Expense			(b) 100		100						18
19	Rent Revenue				(c) 120		120					19
20	Wages Payable				(d) 250		250					20
21	Depreciation Expense			(f) 50		50						21
22	Accumulated Depreciation				(f) 50		50					22
23				2,260	2,260	43,400	43,400					23
24												24
25												25

> The adjustments on the work sheet are used in preparing the adjusting journal entries.

> The adjusted trial balance amounts are determined by adding the adjustments to or subtracting the adjustments from the trial balance amounts. For example, the Wages Expense debit of $4,525 is the trial balance amount of $4,275 plus the $250 adjustment debit.

> Accounts are added, as needed, to complete the adjustments.

(b) **Prepaid Insurance.** The prepaid insurance account has a debit balance of $2,400, which represents the prepayment of insurance for 24 months beginning December 1. Thus, the insurance expense for December is $100 ($2,400/24). Enter the adjustment by writing (1) $100 in the Adjustments Debit column on the same line as Insurance Expense and (2) $100 in the Adjustments Credit column on the same line as Prepaid Insurance.

(c) **Unearned Rent.** The unearned rent account has a credit balance of $360, which represents the receipt of three months' rent, beginning with December. Thus, the rent revenue for December is $120. Enter the adjustment by writing (1) $120 in the Adjustments Debit column on the same line as Unearned Rent and (2) $120 in the Adjustments Credit column on the same line as Rent Revenue.

(d) **Wages.** Wages accrued but not paid at the end of December total $250. This amount is an increase in expenses and an increase in liabilities. Enter the adjustment by writing (1) $250 in the Adjustments Debit column on the same line as Wages Expense and (2) $250 in the Adjustments Credit column on the same line as Wages Payable.

(e) **Accrued Fees.** Fees accrued at the end of December but not recorded total $500. This amount is an increase in an asset and an increase in revenue. Enter the adjustment by writing (1) $500 in the Adjustments Debit column on the same line as Accounts Receivable and (2) $500 in the Adjustments Credit column on the same line as Fees Earned.

(f) **Depreciation.** Depreciation of the office equipment is $50 for December. Enter the adjustment by writing (1) $50 in the Adjustments Debit column on the same line as Depreciation Expense and (2) $50 in the Adjustments Credit column on the same line as Accumulated Depreciation.

Total the Adjustments columns to verify the mathematical accuracy of the adjustment data. The total of the Debit column must equal the total of the Credit column.

Adjusted Trial Balance Columns

The adjustment data are added to or subtracted from the amounts in the unadjusted Trial Balance columns. The adjusted amounts are then extended to (placed in) the Adjusted Trial Balance columns, as shown in Exhibit 2. For example, the cash amount of $2,065 is extended to the Adjusted Trial Balance Debit column, since no adjustments affected Cash. Accounts Receivable has an initial balance of $2,220 and a debit adjustment (increase) of $500. The amount to write in the Adjusted Trial Balance Debit column is the debit balance of $2,720. The same procedure continues until all account balances are extended to the Adjusted Trial Balance columns. Total the columns of the Adjusted Trial Balance to verify the equality of debits and credits.

Income Statement and Balance Sheet Columns

The work sheet is completed by extending the adjusted trial balance amounts to the Income Statement and Balance Sheet columns. The amounts for revenues and expenses are extended to the Income Statement columns. The amounts for assets, liabilities, capital stock, and dividends are extended to the Balance Sheet columns.[1]

In the NetSolutions work sheet, the first account listed is Cash, and the balance appearing in the Adjusted Trial Balance Debit column is $2,065. Cash is an asset, is listed on the balance sheet, and has a debit balance. Therefore, $2,065 is extended to the Balance Sheet Debit column. The Fees Earned balance of $16,840 is extended to the Income Statement Credit column. The same procedure continues until all account balances have been extended to the proper columns, as shown in Exhibit 3.

After all of the balances have been extended to the four statement columns, total each of these columns, as shown in Exhibit 4. The difference between the two Income Statement column totals is the amount of the net income or the net loss for the period. Likewise, the difference between the two Balance Sheet column totals is also the amount of the net income or net loss for the period.

If the Income Statement Credit column total (representing total revenue) is greater than the Income Statement Debit column total (representing total expenses), the difference is the net income. If the Income Statement Debit column total is greater than the Income Statement Credit column total, the difference is a net loss. For Net-Solutions, the computation of net income is as follows:

Total of Credit column (revenues)	$16,960
Total of Debit column (expenses)	9,755
Net income (excess of revenues over expenses)	$ 7,205

As shown in Exhibit 4, write the amount of the net income, $7,205, in the Income Statement Debit column and the Balance Sheet Credit column. Write the term

---

[1] The balances of the retained earnings and dividends accounts are also extended to the Balance Sheet columns because this work sheet does not provide for separate Retained Earnings Statement columns.

Exhibit 3 Work Sheet with Amounts Extended to Income Statement and Balance Sheet Columns

NetSolutions
Work Sheet
For the Two Months Ended December 31, 2002

	Account Title	Trial Balance Dr.	Trial Balance Cr.	Adjustments Dr.	Adjustments Cr.	Adjusted Trial Balance Dr.	Adjusted Trial Balance Cr.	Income Statement Dr.	Income Statement Cr.	Balance Sheet Dr.	Balance Sheet Cr.	
1	Cash	2,065				2,065				2,065		1
2	Accounts Receivable	2,220		(e) 500		2,720				2,720		2
3	Supplies	2,000			(a)1,240	760				760		3
4	Prepaid Insurance	2,400			(b) 100	2,300				2,300		4
5	Land	20,000				20,000				20,000		5
6	Office Equipment	1,800				1,800				1,800		6
7	Accounts Payable		900				900				900	7
8	Unearned Rent		360	(c) 120			240				240	8
9	Capital Stock		25,000				25,000				25,000	9
10	Dividends	4,000				4,000				4,000		10
11	Fees Earned		16,340		(e) 500		16,840		16,840			11
12	Wages Expense	4,275		(d) 250		4,525		4,525				12
13	Rent Expense	1,600				1,600		1,600				13
14	Utilities Expense	985				985		985				14
15	Supplies Expense	800		(a)1,240		2,040		2,040				15
16	Miscellaneous Expense	455				455		455				16
17		42,600	42,600									17
18	Insurance Expense			(b) 100		100		100				18
19	Rent Revenue				(c) 120		120		120			19
20	Wages Payable				(d) 250		250				250	20
21	Depreciation Expense			(f) 50		50		50				21
22	Accumulated Depreciation				(f) 50		50				50	22
23				2,260	2,260	43,400	43,400					23
24												24
25												25

The revenue and expense amounts are extended to (placed in) the Income Statement columns.

The asset, liability, capital stock, and dividends amounts are extended to (placed in) the Balance Sheet columns.

Net income in the Account Title column. If there was a net loss instead of net income, you would write the amount in the Income Statement Credit column and the Balance Sheet Debit column and the term *Net loss* in the Account Title column. Inserting the net income or net loss in the statement columns on the work sheet shows the effect of transferring the net balance of the revenue and expense accounts to the retained earnings account. Later in this chapter, we explain how to journalize this transfer.

After the net income or net loss has been entered on the work sheet, again total each of the four statement columns. The totals of the two Income Statement columns must now be equal. The totals of the two Balance Sheet columns must also be equal.

Exhibit 4 Completed Work Sheet with Net Income Shown

NetSolutions
Work Sheet
For the Two Months Ended December 31, 2002

	Account Title	Trial Balance Dr.	Trial Balance Cr.	Adjustments Dr.	Adjustments Cr.	Adjusted Trial Balance Dr.	Adjusted Trial Balance Cr.	Income Statement Dr.	Income Statement Cr.	Balance Sheet Dr.	Balance Sheet Cr.	
1	Cash	2,065				2,065				2,065		1
2	Accounts Receivable	2,220		(e) 500		2,720				2,720		2
3	Supplies	2,000			(a)1,240	760				760		3
4	Prepaid Insurance	2,400			(b) 100	2,300				2,300		4
5	Land	20,000				20,000				20,000		5
6	Office Equipment	1,800				1,800				1,800		6
7	Accounts Payable		900				900				900	7
8	Unearned Rent		360	(c) 120			240				240	8
9	Capital Stock		25,000				25,000				25,000	9
10	Dividends	4,000				4,000				4,000		10
11	Fees Earned		16,340		(e) 500		16,840		16,840			11
12	Wages Expense	4,275		(d) 250		4,525		4,525				12
13	Rent Expense	1,600				1,600		1,600				13
14	Utilities Expense	985				985		985				14
15	Supplies Expense	800		(a)1,240		2,040		2,040				15
16	Miscellaneous Expense	455				455		455				16
17		42,600	42,600									17
18	Insurance Expense			(b) 100		100		100				18
19	Rent Revenue				(c) 120		120		120			19
20	Wages Payable				(d) 250		250				250	20
21	Depreciation Expense			(f) 50		50		50				21
22	Accumulated Depreciation				(f) 50		50				50	22
23				2,260	2,260	43,400	43,400	9,755	16,960	33,645	26,440	23
24	Net income							7,205			7,205	24
25								16,960	16,960	33,645	33,645	25

> The difference between the Income Statement column totals is the net income (or net loss) for the period. The difference between the Balance Sheet column totals is also the net income (or net loss) for the period.

Financial Statements

objective 2

Prepare financial statements from a work sheet.

The work sheet is an aid in preparing the income statement, the retained earnings statement, and the balance sheet, which are presented in Exhibit 5. In the following paragraphs, we discuss these financial statements for NetSolutions, prepared from the completed work sheet in Exhibit 4. The statements are similar in form to those presented in Chapter 1.

 NETSOLUTIONS

Exhibit 5 Financial Statements Prepared from Work Sheet

NetSolutions
Income Statement
For the Two Months Ended December 31, 2002

Fees earned	$16 8 4 0 00	
Rent revenue	1 2 0 00	
Total revenues		$16 9 6 0 00
Expenses:		
Wages expense	$ 4 5 2 5 00	
Supplies expense	2 0 4 0 00	
Rent expense	1 6 0 0 00	
Utilities expense	9 8 5 00	
Insurance expense	1 0 0 00	
Depreciation expense	5 0 00	
Miscellaneous expense	4 5 5 00	
Total expenses		9 7 5 5 00
Net income		$ 7 2 0 5 00

NetSolutions
Retained Earnings Statement
For the Two Months Ended December 31, 2002

Net income for November and December		$ 7 2 0 5 00
Less dividends		4 0 0 0 00
Retained earnings, December 31, 2002		$ 3 2 0 5 00

NetSolutions
Balance Sheet
December 31, 2002

Assets			Liabilities		
Current assets:			Current liabilities:		
Cash	$ 2 0 6 5 00		Accounts payable	$ 9 0 0 00	
Accounts receivable	2 7 2 0 00		Wages payable	2 5 0 00	
Supplies	7 6 0 00		Unearned rent	2 4 0 00	
Prepaid insurance	2 3 0 0 00		Total liabilities		$ 1 3 9 0 00
Total current assets		$ 7 8 4 5 00			
Property, plant, and equipment:					
Land	$20 0 0 0 00				
Office equipment $1,800			**Stockholders' Equity**		
Less accum. depr. 50	1 7 5 0 00		Capital stock	$ 25 0 0 0 00	
Total property, plant,			Retained earnings	3 2 0 5 00	28 2 0 5 00
and equipment		21 7 5 0 00	Total liabilities and		
Total assets		$29 5 9 5 00	stockholders' equity		$29 5 9 5 00

Income Statement

The income statement is normally prepared directly from the work sheet. However, the order of the expenses may be changed. As we did in Chapter 1, we list the expenses in the income statement in Exhibit 5 in order of size, beginning with the larger items. Miscellaneous expense is the last item, regardless of its amount.

Retained Earnings Statement

The first item normally presented on the retained earnings statement is the balance of the retained earnings account at the beginning of the period. Since NetSolutions began operations on November 1, the retained earnings statement in Exhibit 5 begins with the net income for the two months ended December 31, 2002. The amount of dividends is then deducted to arrive at the retained earnings as of December 31, 2002.

For the following period, there would be a beginning balance of retained earnings for NetSolutions. As we noted, this beginning balance would be reported as the first amount on the retained earnings statement. For example, assume that during 2003, NetSolutions earned net income of $159,595 and paid dividends of $24,000. The retained earnings statement for the year ending December 31, 2003, for NetSolutions is as follows:

NetSolutions
Retained Earnings Statement
For the Year Ended December 31, 2003

Retained earnings, January 1, 2002		$ 3,205 00
Net income for the year	$159,595 00	
Less dividends	24,000 00	
Increase in retained earnings		135,595 00
Retained earnings, December 31, 2003		$138,800 00

For NetSolutions, the amount of dividends was less than the net income. If the dividends had exceeded the net income, the order of the net income and the dividends could have been reversed. The difference between the two items would then be deducted from the beginning Retained Earnings balance. Other factors, such as a net loss, may also require some change in the form of the retained earnings statement, as shown in the following example:

Retained earnings, January 1, 20—		$45,000
Net loss for the year	$5,600	
Dividends	9,500	
Decrease in retained earnings		15,100
Retained earnings, December 31, 20—		$29,900

Some accountants prefer to debit dividends directly to Retained Earnings. When you are preparing a retained earnings statement and there is no dividends account in the ledger, you will need to refer to the retained earnings account to determine the beginning balance of Retained Earnings and the amount of the dividends paid during the period.

Balance Sheet

The balance sheet in Exhibit 5 was expanded by adding subsections for current assets; property, plant, and equipment; and current liabilities. Such a balance sheet is a *classified* balance sheet. In the following paragraphs, we describe some of the sections and subsections that may be used in a balance sheet. We will introduce additional sections in later chapters.

Assets

Assets are commonly divided into classes for presentation on the balance sheet. Two of these classes are (1) current assets and (2) property, plant, and equipment.

Two common classes of assets are current assets and property, plant, and equipment.

Current Assets. Cash and other assets that are expected to be converted to cash or sold or used up usually within one year or less, through the normal operations of the business, are called **current assets**. In addition to cash, the current assets usually owned by a service business are notes receivable, accounts receivable, supplies, and other prepaid expenses.

Notes receivable are amounts customers owe. They are written promises to pay the amount of the note and possibly interest at an agreed-upon rate. Accounts receivable are also amounts customers owe, but they are less formal than notes and do not provide for interest. Accounts receivable normally result from providing services or selling merchandise on account. Notes receivable and accounts receivable are current assets because they will usually be converted to cash within one year or less.

Property, Plant, and Equipment. The property, plant, and equipment section may also be described as **fixed assets** or **plant assets**. These assets include equipment, machinery, buildings, and land. With the exception of land, as we discussed in Chapter 3, fixed assets depreciate over a period of time. The cost, accumulated depreciation, and book value of each major type of fixed asset is normally reported on the balance sheet or in accompanying notes.

BUSINESS ON STAGE

The Operating Cycle

The operations of a manufacturing business involve the purchase of raw materials (purchasing activity), the conversion of the raw materials into a product through the use of labor and machinery (production activity), the sale and distribution of the products to customers (sales activity), and the receipt of cash from customers (collection activity). This overall process is referred to as the *operating cycle*. Thus, the operating cycle begins with spending cash and it ends with receiving cash from customers. The operating cycle for a manufacturing business is shown below.

Operating cycles differ, depending upon the nature of the business and its operations. For example, the operating cycles for tobacco, distillery, and lumber industries are much longer than the operating cycles of the automobile, consumer electronics, and home furnishings industries. Likewise, the operating cycles for retailers are usually shorter than for manufacturers because retailers purchase goods in a form ready for sale to the customer. Of course, some retailers will have shorter operating cycles than others because of the nature of their products. For example, a jewelry store or an automobile dealer normally has a longer operating cycle than a consumer electronics store or a grocery store.

Businesses with longer operating cycles normally have higher profit margins on their products than businesses with shorter operating cycles. For example, it is not unusual for jewelry stores to price their jewelry at 30%–50% above cost. In contrast, grocery stores operate on very small profit margins, often below 5%. Grocery stores make up the difference by selling their products more quickly. ■

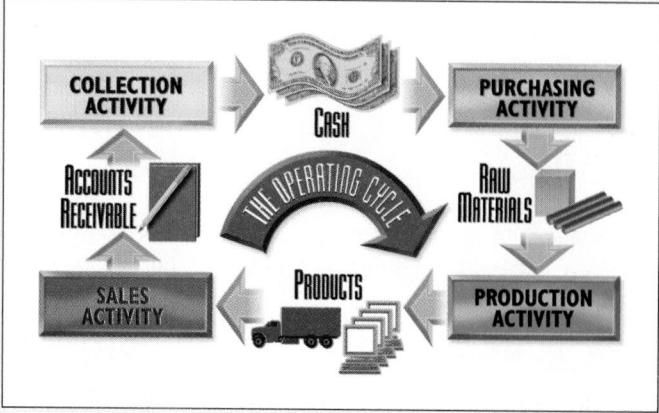

Two common classes of liabilities are current liabilities and long-term liabilities.

Liabilities

Liabilities are the amounts the business owes to creditors. The two most common classes of liabilities are (1) current liabilities and (2) long-term liabilities.

Current Liabilities. Liabilities that will be due within a short time (usually one year or less) and that are to be paid out of current assets are called current liabilities. The most common liabilities in this group are notes payable and accounts payable. Other current liability accounts commonly found in the ledger are Wages Payable, Interest Payable, Taxes Payable, and Unearned Fees.

Long-Term Liabilities. Liabilities that will not be due for a long time (usually more than one year) are called long-term liabilities. If NetSolutions had long-term liabilities, they would be reported below the current liabilities. As long-term liabilities come due and are to be paid within one year, they are classified as current liabilities. If they are to be renewed rather than paid, they would continue to be classified as long-term. When an asset is pledged as security for a liability, the obligation may be called a *mortgage note payable* or a *mortgage payable*.

Stockholders' Equity

The stockholders' right to the assets of the business is presented on the balance sheet below the liabilities section. The stockholders' equity is added to the total liabilities, and this total must be equal to the total assets.

Adjusting and Closing Entries

objective 3

Prepare the adjusting and closing entries from a work sheet.

As we discussed in Chapter 3, the adjusting entries are recorded in the journal at the end of the accounting period. If a work sheet has been prepared, the data for these entries are in the Adjustments columns. For NetSolutions, the adjusting entries prepared from the work sheet are shown in Exhibit 6.

After the adjusting entries have been posted to NetSolutions' ledger, shown in Exhibit 10, the ledger is in agreement with the data reported on the financial statements. The balances of the accounts reported on the balance sheet are carried forward from year to year. Because they are relatively permanent, these accounts are called real accounts. The balances of the accounts reported on the income statement are *not* carried forward from year to year. Likewise, the balance of the dividends account, which is reported on the retained earnings statement, is not carried forward. Because these accounts report amounts for only one period, they are called temporary accounts or **nominal accounts**.

To report amounts for only one period, temporary accounts should have zero balances at the beginning of a period. How are these balances converted to zero? The revenue and expense account balances are transferred to an account called Income Summary. The balance of Income Summary is then transferred to the retained earnings account. The balance of the dividends account is also transferred to the retained earnings account. The entries that transfer these balances are called closing entries. The transfer process is called the **closing process**. Exhibit 7 is a diagram of this process.

Closing entries transfer the balances of temporary accounts to the retained earnings account.

Exhibit 6 Adjusting Entries for NetSolutions

	Date		Description	Post. Ref.	Debit	Credit	
1			Adjusting Entries				1
2	2002 Dec.	31	Supplies Expense	55	1 2 4 0 00		2
3			Supplies	14		1 2 4 0 00	3
4							4
5		31	Insurance Expense	56	1 0 0 00		5
6			Prepaid Insurance	15		1 0 0 00	6
7							7
8		31	Unearned Rent	23	1 2 0 00		8
9			Rent Revenue	42		1 2 0 00	9
10							10
11		31	Wages Expense	51	2 5 0 00		11
12			Wages Payable	22		2 5 0 00	12
13							13
14		31	Accounts Receivable	12	5 0 0 00		14
15			Fees Earned	41		5 0 0 00	15
16							16
17		31	Depreciation Expense	53	5 0 00		17
18			Accumulated Depreciation—				18
19			Office Equipment	19		5 0 00	19

JOURNAL — PAGE 5

Exhibit 7 The Closing Process

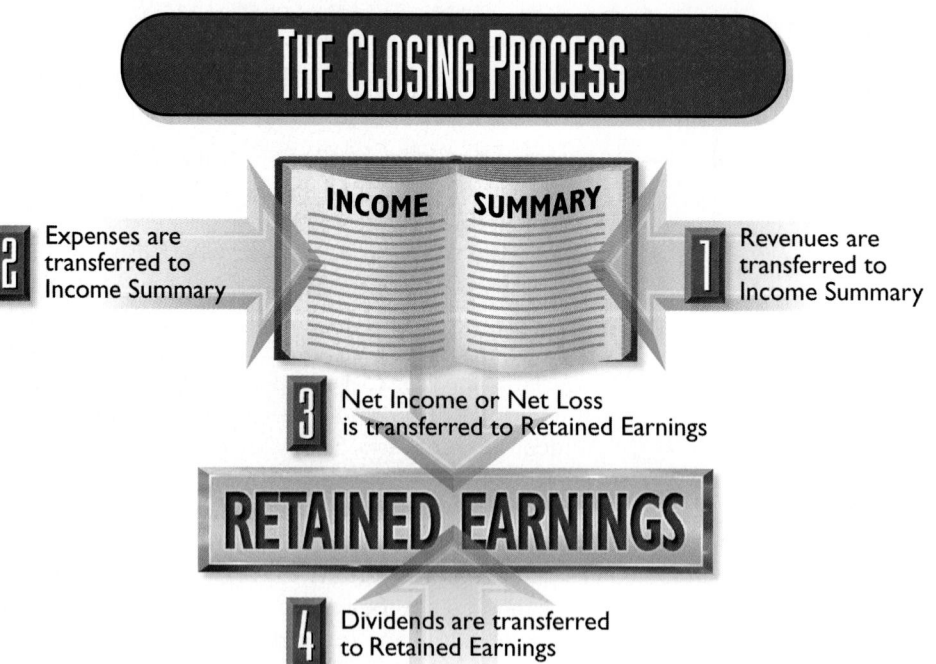

THE CLOSING PROCESS

INCOME SUMMARY

2 Expenses are transferred to Income Summary

1 Revenues are transferred to Income Summary

3 Net Income or Net Loss is transferred to Retained Earnings

RETAINED EARNINGS

4 Dividends are transferred to Retained Earnings

> The income summary account does **not** appear on the financial statements.

You should note that Income Summary is used only at the end of the period. At the beginning of the closing process, Income Summary has no balance. During the closing process, Income Summary will be debited and credited for various amounts. At the end of the closing process, Income Summary will again have no balance. Because Income Summary has the effect of clearing the revenue and expense accounts of their balances, it is sometimes called a **clearing account**. Other titles used for this account include Revenue and Expense Summary, Profit and Loss Summary, and Income and Expense Summary.

It is possible to close the temporary revenue and expense accounts without using a clearing account such as Income Summary. In this case, the balances of the revenue and expense accounts are closed directly to the retained earnings account. This process is automatic in a computerized accounting system. In a manual system, the use of an income summary account aids in detecting and correcting errors.

Journalizing and Posting Closing Entries

Four closing entries are required at the end of an accounting period, as outlined in Exhibit 7. The account titles and balances needed in preparing these entries may be obtained from the work sheet, the income statement and the retained earnings statement, or the ledger. If a work sheet is used, the data for the first two entries appear in the Income Statement columns. The amount for the third entry is the net income or net loss appearing at the bottom of the work sheet. The amount for the fourth entry is the dividends account balance that appears in the Balance Sheet Debit column of the work sheet.

A flowchart of the closing entries for NetSolutions is shown in Exhibit 8. The balances in the accounts are those shown in the Adjusted Trial Balance columns of the work sheet in Exhibit 2.

Exhibit 8 Flowchart of Closing Entries for NetSolutions

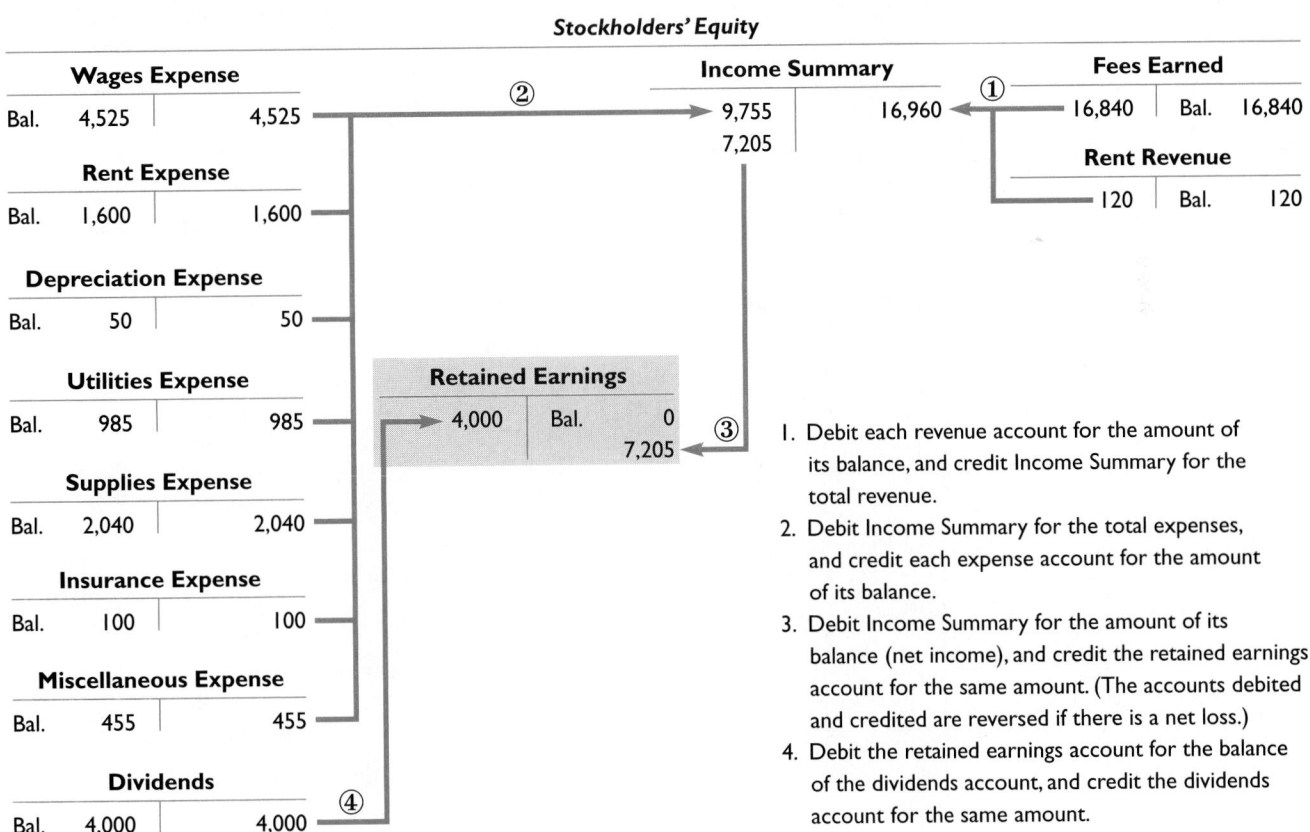

The closing entries for NetSolutions are shown in Exhibit 9. After the closing entries have been posted to the ledger, as shown in Exhibit 10, the balance in the retained earnings account will agree with the amount reported on the retained earnings statement and the balance sheet. In addition, the revenue, expense, and dividends accounts will have zero balances.

Exhibit 9 Closing Entries for NetSolutions

	Date		Description	Post. Ref.	Debit	Credit	
1			Closing Entries				1
2	2002 Dec.	31	Fees Earned	41	16 84 0 00		2
3			Rent Revenue	42	1 20 00		3
4			Income Summary	34		16 96 0 00	4
5							5
6		31	Income Summary	34	9 75 5 00		6
7			Wages Expense	51		4 52 5 00	7
8			Rent Expense	52		1 60 0 00	8
9			Depreciation Expense	53		50 00	9
10			Utilities Expense	54		98 5 00	10
11			Supplies Expense	55		2 04 0 00	11
12			Insurance Expense	56		1 00 00	12
13			Miscellaneous Expense	59		45 5 00	13
14							14
15		31	Income Summary	34	7 20 5 00		15
16			Retained Earnings	32		7 20 5 00	16
17							17
18		31	Retained Earnings	32	4 00 0 00		18
19			Dividends	33		4 00 0 00	19

JOURNAL — PAGE 6

Exhibit 10 Ledger for NetSolutions

LEDGER

ACCOUNT Cash — ACCOUNT NO. 11

Date		Item	Post. Ref.	Debit	Credit	Balance Debit	Balance Credit
2002 Nov.	1		1	25 0 0 0 00		25 0 0 0 00	
	5		1		20 0 0 0 00	5 0 0 0 00	
	18		1	7 5 0 0 00		12 5 0 0 00	
	30		1		3 6 5 0 00	8 8 5 0 00	
	30		1		9 5 0 00	7 9 0 0 00	
	30		2		2 0 0 0 00	5 9 0 0 00	
Dec.	1		2		2 4 0 0 00	3 5 0 0 00	
	1		2		8 0 0 00	2 7 0 0 00	
	1		2	3 6 0 00		3 0 6 0 00	
	6		2		1 8 0 00	2 8 8 0 00	
	11		2		4 0 0 00	2 4 8 0 00	
	13		3		9 5 0 00	1 5 3 0 00	
	16		3	3 1 0 0 00		4 6 3 0 00	
	20		3		9 0 0 00	3 7 3 0 00	
	21		3	6 5 0 00		4 3 8 0 00	
	23		3		1 4 5 0 00	2 9 3 0 00	
	27		3		1 2 0 0 00	1 7 3 0 00	
	31		3		3 1 0 00	1 4 2 0 00	
	31		4		2 2 5 00	1 1 9 5 00	
	31		4	2 8 7 0 00		4 0 6 5 00	
	31		4		2 0 0 0 00	2 0 6 5 00	

Exhibit 10 (continued)

ACCOUNT Accounts Receivable — ACCOUNT NO. 12

Date		Item	Post. Ref.	Debit	Credit	Balance Debit	Balance Credit
2002 Dec.	16		3	1 7 5 0 00		1 7 5 0 00	
	21		3		6 5 0 00	1 1 0 0 00	
	31		4	1 1 2 0 00		2 2 2 0 00	
	31	Adjusting	5	5 0 0 00		2 7 2 0 00	

ACCOUNT Supplies — ACCOUNT NO. 14

Date		Item	Post. Ref.	Debit	Credit	Balance Debit	Balance Credit
2002 Nov.	10		1	1 3 5 0 00		1 3 5 0 00	
	30		1		8 0 0 00	5 5 0 00	
Dec.	23		3	1 4 5 0 00		2 0 0 0 00	
	31	Adjusting	5		1 2 4 0 00	7 6 0 00	

ACCOUNT Prepaid Insurance — ACCOUNT NO. 15

Date		Item	Post. Ref.	Debit	Credit	Balance Debit	Balance Credit
2002 Dec.	1		2	2 4 0 0 00		2 4 0 0 00	
	31	Adjusting	5		1 0 0 00	2 3 0 0 00	

ACCOUNT Land — ACCOUNT NO. 17

Date		Item	Post. Ref.	Debit	Credit	Balance Debit	Balance Credit
2002 Nov.	5		1	20 0 0 0 00		20 0 0 0 00	

ACCOUNT Office Equipment — ACCOUNT NO. 18

Date		Item	Post. Ref.	Debit	Credit	Balance Debit	Balance Credit
2002 Dec.	4		2	1 8 0 0 00		1 8 0 0 00	

ACCOUNT Accumulated Depreciation — ACCOUNT NO. 19

Date		Item	Post. Ref.	Debit	Credit	Balance Debit	Balance Credit
2002 Dec.	31	Adjusting	5		5 0 00		5 0 00

Exhibit 10 (continued)

ACCOUNT Accounts Payable					ACCOUNT NO. 21	
Date	Item	Post. Ref.	Debit	Credit	Balance Debit	Balance Credit
2002 Nov. 10		1		1 3 5 0 00		1 3 5 0 00
30		1	9 5 0 00			4 0 0 00
Dec. 4		2		1 8 0 0 00		2 2 0 0 00
11		2	4 0 0 00			1 8 0 0 00
20		3	9 0 0 00			9 0 0 00

ACCOUNT Wages Payable					ACCOUNT NO. 22	
Date	Item	Post. Ref.	Debit	Credit	Balance Debit	Balance Credit
2002 Dec. 31	Adjusting	5		2 5 0 00		2 5 0 00

ACCOUNT Unearned Rent					ACCOUNT NO. 23	
Date	Item	Post. Ref.	Debit	Credit	Balance Debit	Balance Credit
2002 Dec. 1		2		3 6 0 00		3 6 0 00
31	Adjusting	5	1 2 0 00			2 4 0 00

ACCOUNT Capital Stock					ACCOUNT NO. 31	
Date	Item	Post. Ref.	Debit	Credit	Balance Debit	Balance Credit
2002 Nov. 1		1		25 0 0 0 00		25 0 0 0 00

ACCOUNT Retained Earnings					ACCOUNT NO. 32	
Date	Item	Post. Ref.	Debit	Credit	Balance Debit	Balance Credit
2002 Dec. 31	Closing	6		7 2 0 5 00		7 2 0 5 00
31	Closing	6	4 0 0 0 00			3 2 0 5 00

ACCOUNT Dividends					ACCOUNT NO. 33	
Date	Item	Post. Ref.	Debit	Credit	Balance Debit	Balance Credit
2002 Nov. 30		2	2 0 0 0 00		2 0 0 0 00	
Dec. 31		4	2 0 0 0 00		4 0 0 0 00	
31	Closing	6		4 0 0 0 00	—	—

Exhibit 10 (continued)

ACCOUNT Income Summary — ACCOUNT NO. 34

Date		Item	Post. Ref.	Debit	Credit	Balance Debit	Balance Credit
2002 Dec.	31	Closing	6		16 9 6 0 00		16 9 6 0 00
	31	Closing	6	9 7 5 5 00			7 2 0 5 00
	31	Closing	6	7 2 0 5 00		—	—

ACCOUNT Fees Earned — ACCOUNT NO. 41

Date		Item	Post. Ref.	Debit	Credit	Balance Debit	Balance Credit
2002 Nov.	18		1		7 5 0 0 00		7 5 0 0 00
Dec.	16		3		3 1 0 0 00		10 6 0 0 00
	16		3		1 7 5 0 00		12 3 5 0 00
	31		4		2 8 7 0 00		15 2 2 0 00
	31		4		1 1 2 0 00		16 3 4 0 00
	31	Adjusting	5		5 0 0 00		16 8 4 0 00
	31	Closing	6	16 8 4 0 00		—	—

ACCOUNT Rent Revenue — ACCOUNT NO. 42

Date		Item	Post. Ref.	Debit	Credit	Balance Debit	Balance Credit
2002 Dec.	31	Adjusting	5		1 2 0 00		1 2 0 00
	31	Closing	6	1 2 0 00		—	—

ACCOUNT Wages Expense — ACCOUNT NO. 51

Date		Item	Post. Ref.	Debit	Credit	Balance Debit	Balance Credit
2002 Nov.	30		1	2 1 2 5 00		2 1 2 5 00	
Dec.	13		3	9 5 0 00		3 0 7 5 00	
	27		3	1 2 0 0 00		4 2 7 5 00	
	31	Adjusting	5	2 5 0 00		4 5 2 5 00	
	31	Closing	6		4 5 2 5 00	—	—

ACCOUNT Rent Expense — ACCOUNT NO. 52

Date		Item	Post. Ref.	Debit	Credit	Balance Debit	Balance Credit
2002 Nov.	30		1	8 0 0 00		8 0 0 00	
Dec.	1		2	8 0 0 00		1 6 0 0 00	
	31	Closing	6		1 6 0 0 00	—	—

Exhibit 10 (concluded)

ACCOUNT Depreciation Expense					ACCOUNT NO. 53	
Date	Item	Post. Ref.	Debit	Credit	Balance Debit	Balance Credit
2002 Dec. 31	Adjusting	5	5 0 00		5 0 00	
31	Closing	6		5 0 00	—	—

ACCOUNT Utilities Expense					ACCOUNT NO. 54	
Date	Item	Post. Ref.	Debit	Credit	Balance Debit	Balance Credit
2002 Nov. 30		1	4 5 0 00		4 5 0 00	
Dec. 31		3	3 1 0 00		7 6 0 00	
31		4	2 2 5 00		9 8 5 00	
31	Closing	6		9 8 5 00	—	—

ACCOUNT Supplies Expense					ACCOUNT NO. 55	
Date	Item	Post. Ref.	Debit	Credit	Balance Debit	Balance Credit
2002 Nov. 30		1	8 0 0 00		8 0 0 00	
Dec. 31	Adjusting	5	1 2 4 0 00		2 0 4 0 00	
31	Closing	6		2 0 4 0 00	—	—

ACCOUNT Insurance Expense					ACCOUNT NO. 56	
Date	Item	Post. Ref.	Debit	Credit	Balance Debit	Balance Credit
2002 Dec. 31	Adjusting	5	1 0 0 00		1 0 0 00	
31	Closing	6		1 0 0 00	—	—

ACCOUNT Miscellaneous Expense					ACCOUNT NO. 59	
Date	Item	Post. Ref.	Debit	Credit	Balance Debit	Balance Credit
2002 Nov. 30		1	2 7 5 00		2 7 5 00	
Dec. 6		2	1 8 0 00		4 5 5 00	
31	Closing	6		4 5 5 00	—	—

Q&A If total revenues are $600,000, total expenses are $525,000, and dividends are $50,000, what is the balance of the income summary account that is closed to Retained Earnings?

$75,000 ($600,000 − $525,000). The dividends account balance is closed directly to Retained Earnings, rather than to Income Summary.

After the entry to close an account has been posted, a line should be inserted in both balance columns opposite the final entry. The next period's transactions for the revenue, expense, and dividends accounts will be posted directly below the closing entry.

Post-Closing Trial Balance

The last accounting procedure for a period is to prepare a trial balance after the closing entries have been posted. The purpose of the **post-closing** (after closing) **trial balance** is to make sure that the ledger is in balance at the beginning of the next period. The accounts and amounts should agree exactly with the accounts and amounts listed on the balance sheet at the end of the period. The post-closing trial balance for Net-Solutions is shown in Exhibit 11.

Exhibit 11 Post-Closing Trial Balance

NetSolutions Post-Closing Trial Balance December 31, 2002		
Cash	2 0 6 5 00	
Accounts Receivable	2 7 2 0 00	
Supplies	7 6 0 00	
Prepaid Insurance	2 3 0 0 00	
Land	20 0 0 0 00	
Office Equipment	1 8 0 0 00	
Accumulated Depreciation		5 0 00
Accounts Payable		9 0 0 00
Wages Payable		2 5 0 00
Unearned Rent		2 4 0 00
Capital Stock		25 0 0 0 00
Retained Earnings		3 2 0 5 00
	29 6 4 5 00	29 6 4 5 00

Instead of preparing a formal post-closing trial balance, it is possible to list the accounts directly from the ledger, using a computer. The computer printout, in effect, becomes the post-closing trial balance. Without such a printout, there is no efficient means of determining the cause of unequal trial balance totals.

Accounting Cycle

objective 4

Review the seven basic steps of the accounting cycle.

The process that begins with analyzing and journalizing transactions and ends with the post-closing trial balance is called the **accounting cycle**. The most important output of the accounting cycle is the financial statements.

Understanding the steps of the accounting cycle is essential for further study of accounting. The basic steps of the cycle are shown, by number, in the flowchart in Exhibit 12.

Real World

In a computerized accounting system, the software automatically records and posts transactions. The ledger and supporting records are maintained in computerized master files. In addition, a work sheet is normally not prepared.

Fiscal Year

objective 5

Explain what is meant by the fiscal year and the natural business year.

In the NetSolutions illustration, operations began on November 1 and the accounting period was for two months, November and December. Since Chris Clark, the sole stockholder, decided to adopt a calendar-year accounting period, NetSolutions' accounts were closed on December 31, 2002. In future years, the financial statements for NetSolutions will be prepared for twelve months, ending on December 31 of each year.

NET SOLUTIONS

Exhibit 12 Accounting Cycle

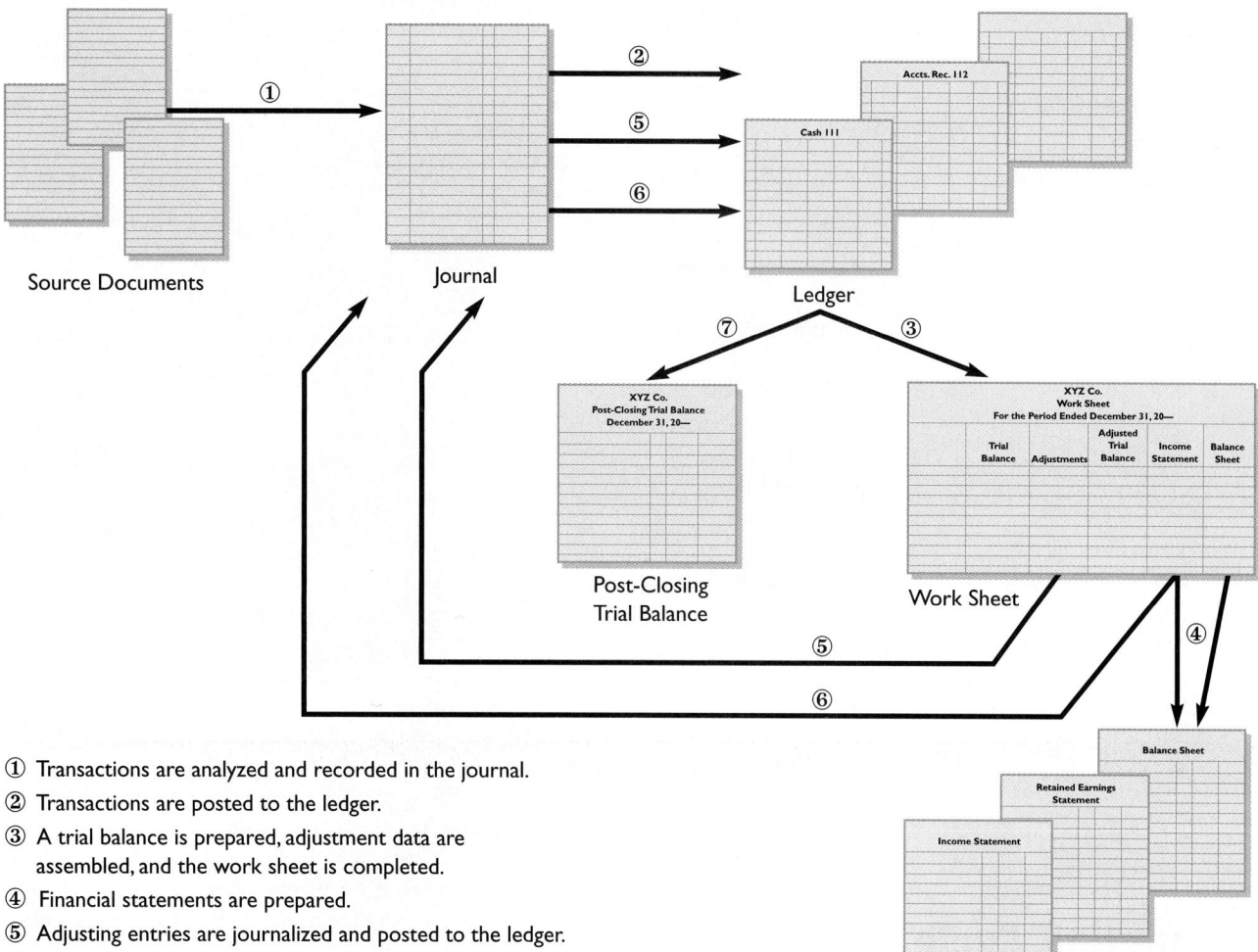

① Transactions are analyzed and recorded in the journal.

② Transactions are posted to the ledger.

③ A trial balance is prepared, adjustment data are assembled, and the work sheet is completed.

④ Financial statements are prepared.

⑤ Adjusting entries are journalized and posted to the ledger.

⑥ Closing entries are journalized and posted to the ledger.

⑦ A post-closing trial balance is prepared.

Percentage of Companies with Fiscal Years Ending in the Month of:

January	4%	July	1%
February	2	August	2
March	2	September	6
April	2	October	4
May	2	November	3
June	9	December	63

The annual accounting period adopted by a business is known as its **fiscal year**. Fiscal years begin with the first day of the month selected and end on the last day of the following twelfth month. The period most commonly used is the calendar year. Other periods are not unusual, especially for businesses organized as corporations. For example, a corporation may adopt a fiscal year that ends when business activities have reached the lowest point in its annual operating cycle. Such a fiscal year is called the **natural business year**. At the low point in its operating cycle, a business has more time to analyze the results of operations and to prepare financial statements.

Because companies with fiscal years often have highly seasonal operations, investors and others should be careful in interpreting partial-year reports for such companies. That is, you should expect the results of operations for these companies to vary significantly throughout the fiscal year.

The financial history of a business may be shown by a series of balance sheets and income statements for several fiscal years. If the life of a business is expressed by a line moving from left to right, the series of balance sheets and income statements may be graphed as follows:

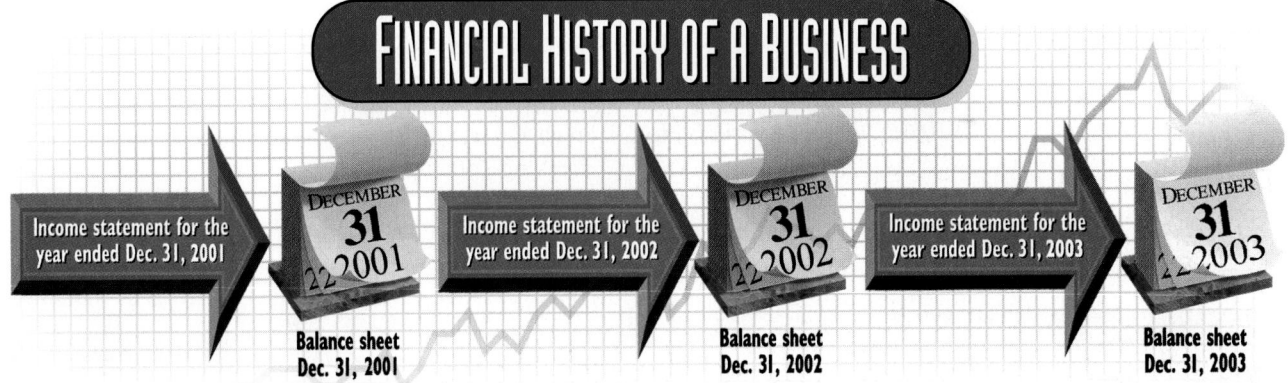

You may think of the income statements, balance sheets, and financial history of a business as similar to the record of a college football team. The final score of each football game is similar to the net income reported on the income statement of a business. The team's season record after each game is similar to the balance sheet. At the end of the season, the final record of the team measures its success or failure. Likewise, at the end of a life of a business, its final balance sheet is a measure of its financial success or failure.

FINANCIAL ANALYSIS AND INTERPRETATION

objective 6

Analyze and interpret the financial solvency of a business by computing working capital and the current ratio.

The ability of a business to pays its debts is called **solvency**. Two financial measures for evaluating a business's short-term solvency are working capital and the current ratio. **Working capital** is the excess of the current assets of a business over its current liabilities, as shown below.

Working capital = Current assets − Current liabilities

An excess of the current assets over the current liabilities implies that the business is able to pay its current liabilities. If the current liabilities are greater than the current assets, the business may not be able to pay its debts and continue in business.

To illustrate, NetSolutions' working capital at the end of 2002 is $6,455, as computed below. This amount of working capital implies that NetSolutions can pay its current liabilities.

Working capital = Current assets − Current liabilities
Working capital = $7,845 − $1,390
Working capital = $6,455

The **current ratio** is another means of expressing the relationship between current assets and current liabilities. The current ratio is computed by dividing current assets by current liabilities, as shown below.

Current ratio = Current assets/Current liabilities

To illustrate, the current ratio for NetSolutions at the end of 2002 is 5.6, computed as follows:

Current ratio = Current assets/Current liabilities
Current ratio = $7,845/$1,390 = 5.6

The current ratio is useful in making comparisons across companies and with industry averages. To illustrate, assume that as of December 31, 2002, the working capital of a company that competes with NetSolutions is much greater than $6,455, but its current ratio is only 1.3. Considering these facts alone, NetSolutions is in a more favorable position to obtain short-term credit, even though the competing company has a greater amount of working capital.

ENCORE

BMW

Financial statements prepared under accounting practices in other countries often differ from those prepared under generally accepted accounting principles found in the United States. This is to be expected, since cultures and market structures differ from country to country.

To illustrate, **BMW Group** prepares its financial statements under German law and German accounting principles. In doing so, BMW's balance sheet reports fixed assets first, followed by current assets. It also reports owner's equity before the liabilities. In contrast, balance sheets prepared under U.S. accounting principles report current assets followed by fixed assets and current liabilities followed by long-term liabilities and owner's equity. The U.S. form of balance sheet is organized to emphasize creditor interpretation and analysis. For example, current assets and current liabilities are presented first, so that working capital and the current ratio can be easily computed. Likewise, to emphasize their importance, liabilities are reported before owner's equity.

Regardless of these differences, the basic principles underlying the accounting equation and the double-entry accounting system are the same in Germany and the United States.

Even though differences in recording and reporting exist, the accounting equation holds true: the total assets still equal the total liabilities and owner's equity. ■

APPENDIX: REVERSING ENTRIES

Some of the adjusting entries recorded at the end of an accounting period have an important effect on otherwise routine transactions that occur in the following period. A typical example is accrued wages owed to employees at the end of a period. If there has been an adjusting entry for accrued wages expense, the first payment of wages in the following period will include the accrual. In the absence of some special provision, Wages Payable must be debited for the amount owed for the earlier period, and Wages Expense must be debited for the portion of the payroll that represents expense for the later period. However, an *optional* entry—the reversing entry—may be used to simplify the analysis and recording of this first payroll entry in a period. As the term implies, a **reversing entry** is the exact opposite of the adjusting entry to which it relates. The amounts and accounts are the same as the adjusting entry; the debits and credits are reversed.

We will illustrate the use of reversing entries by using the data for NetSolutions' accrued wages, which were presented in Chapter 3. These data are summarized in Exhibit 13.

Exhibit 13 Accrued Wages

1. Wages are paid on the second and fourth Fridays for the two-week periods ending on those Fridays.

2. The wages accrued for Monday and Tuesday, December 30 and 31, are $250.

3. Wages paid on Friday, January 10, total $1,275.

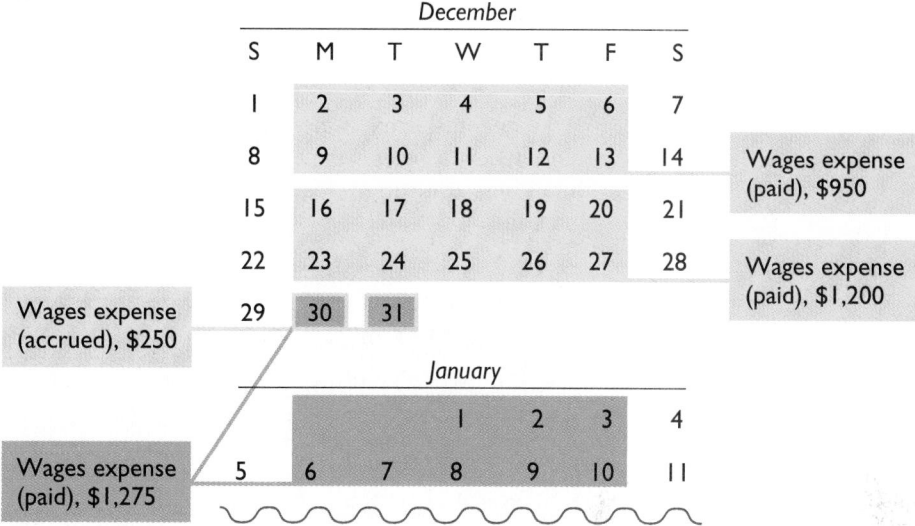

The adjusting entry for the accrued wages of December 30 and 31 is as follows:

Dec.	31	Wages Expense	51	2 5 0 00	
		Wages Payable	22		2 5 0 00

After the adjusting entry has been posted, Wages Expense will have a debit balance of $4,525 ($4,275 + $250), and Wages Payable will have a credit balance of $250. After the closing process is completed, Wages Expense will have a zero balance and will be ready for entries in the next period. Wages Payable, on the other hand, has a balance of $250. Without a reversing entry, it is necessary to record the $1,275 payroll on January 10 as follows:

2003 Jan.	10	Wages Payable	22	2 5 0 00	
		Wages Expense	51	1 0 2 5 00	
		Cash	11		1 2 7 5 00

The employee who records the January 10th entry must refer to the prior period's adjusting entry to determine the amount of the debits to Wages Payable and Wages Expense. Because the January 10th payroll is not recorded in the usual manner, there is a greater chance that an error may occur. This chance of error is reduced by recording a reversing entry as of the first day of the fiscal period. For example, the reversing entry for the accrued wages expense is as follows:

2003 Jan.	1	Wages Payable	22	2 5 0 00	
		Wages Expense	51		2 5 0 00

The reversing entry transfers the $250 liability from Wages Payable to the credit side of Wages Expense. The nature of the $250 is unchanged—it is still a liability. When the payroll is paid on January 10, the following entry is recorded:

				Debit	Credit
Jan.	10	Wages Expense	51	1 2 7 5 00	
		Cash	11		1 2 7 5 00

After this entry is posted, Wages Expense has a debit balance of $1,025. This amount is the wages expense for the period January 1–10. The sequence of entries, including adjusting, closing, and reversing entries, is illustrated in the following accounts:

ACCOUNT *Wages Payable*					**ACCOUNT NO. 22**	
		Post.			Balance	
Date	Item	Ref.	Debit	Credit	Debit	Credit
2002 Dec. 31	Adjusting	5		2 5 0 00		2 5 0 00
2003 Jan. 1	Reversing	7	2 5 0 00		—	—

ACCOUNT *Wages Expense*					**ACCOUNT NO. 51**	
		Post.			Balance	
Date	Item	Ref.	Debit	Credit	Debit	Credit
2002 Nov. 30		1	2 1 2 5 00		2 1 2 5 00	
Dec. 13		3	9 5 0 00		3 0 7 5 00	
27		3	1 2 0 0 00		4 2 7 5 00	
31	Adjusting	5	2 5 0 00		4 5 2 5 00	
31	Closing	6		4 5 2 5 00	—	—
2003 Jan. 1	Reversing	7		2 5 0 00		2 5 0 00
10		7	1 2 7 5 00		1 0 2 5 00	

In addition to accrued expenses (accrued liabilities), reversing entries may be journalized for accrued revenues (accrued assets). For example, the following reversing entry could be recorded for NetSolutions' accrued fees earned:

				Debit	Credit
Jan.	1	Fees Earned	41	5 0 0 00	
		Accounts Receivable	12		5 0 0 00

Reversing entries may also be journalized for prepaid expenses that are initially recorded as expenses and unearned revenues that are initially recorded as revenues. These situations are described and illustrated in Appendix C.

As we mentioned, the use of reversing entries is optional. However, with the increased use of computerized accounting systems, data entry personnel may be inputting routine accounting entries. In such an environment, reversing entries may be useful, since these individuals may not recognize the impact of adjusting entries on the related transactions in the following period.

KEY POINTS

1 Prepare a work sheet.

The work sheet is prepared by first entering a trial balance in the Trial Balance columns. The adjustments are then entered in the Adjustments Debit and Credit columns. The Trial Balance amounts plus or minus the adjustments are extended to the Adjusted Trial Balance columns. The work sheet is completed by extending the Adjusted Trial Balance amounts of assets, liabilities, capital stock, retained earnings, and dividends to the Balance Sheet columns. The Adjusted Trial Balance amounts of revenues and expenses are extended to the Income Statement columns. The net income (or net loss) for the period is entered on the work sheet in the Income Statement Debit (or Credit) column and the Balance Sheet Credit (or Debit) column. Each of the four statement columns is then totaled.

2 Prepare financial statements from a work sheet.

The income statement is normally prepared directly from the work sheet. On the income statement, the expenses are normally presented in the order of size, from largest to smallest.

The basic form of the retained earnings statement is prepared by listing the beginning balance of retained earnings, adding net income during the period, and deducting the dividends.

Various sections and subsections are often used in preparing a balance sheet. Two common classes of assets are current assets and fixed assets. Cash and other assets that are normally expected to be converted to cash or sold or used up within one year or less are called current assets. Property, plant, and equipment may also be called fixed assets or plant assets. The cost, accumulated depreciation, and book value of each major type of fixed asset are normally reported on the balance sheet.

Two common classes of liabilities are current liabilities and long-term liabilities. Liabilities that will be due within a short time (usually one year or less) and that are to be paid out of current assets are called current liabilities. Liabilities that will not be due for a long time (usually more than one year) are called long-term liabilities.

The stockholders' claim against the assets is presented below the liabilities section and added to the total liabilities. The total liabilities and total stockholders' equity must equal the total assets.

3 Prepare the adjusting and closing entries from a work sheet.

The data for journalizing the adjusting entries are in the Adjustments columns of the work sheet. The four entries required in closing the temporary accounts are:

1. Debit each revenue account for the amount of its balance, and credit Income Summary for the total revenue.
2. Debit Income Summary for the total expenses, and credit each expense account for the amount of its balance.
3. Debit Income Summary for the amount of its balance (net income), and credit the retained earnings account for the same amount. (Debit and credit are reversed if there is a net loss.)
4. Debit the retained earnings account for the balance of the dividends account, and credit the dividends account for the same amount.

After the closing entries have been posted to the ledger, the balance in the retained earnings account will agree with the amount reported on the retained earnings statement and balance sheet. In addition, the revenue, expense, and dividends accounts will have zero balances.

The last step of the accounting cycle is to prepare a post-closing trial balance. The purpose of the post-closing trial balance is to make sure that the ledger is in balance at the beginning of the next period.

4 Review the seven basic steps of the accounting cycle.

The basic steps of the accounting cycle are:

1. Transactions are analyzed and recorded in a journal.
2. Transactions are posted to the ledger.
3. A trial balance is prepared, adjustment data are assembled, and the work sheet is completed.
4. Financial statements are prepared.
5. Adjusting entries are journalized and posted to the ledger.
6. Closing entries are journalized and posted to the ledger.
7. A post-closing trial balance is prepared.

5 Explain what is meant by the fiscal year and the natural business year.

The annual accounting period adopted by a business is known as its fiscal year. A corporation may adopt a fiscal year that ends when business activities have reached the lowest point in its annual operating cycle. Such a fiscal year is called the natural business year.

6 Analyze and interpret the financial solvency of a business by computing working capital and the current ratio.

The ability of a business to pay its debts is called solvency. Two financial measures for evaluating a business's short-term solvency are working capital and the current ratio. Working capital is the excess of the current assets of a business over its current liabilities. The current ratio is computed by dividing current assets by current liabilities.

ILLUSTRATIVE PROBLEM

Three years ago, T. Roderick organized Harbor Realty Inc. At July 31, 2003, the end of the current fiscal year, the trial balance of Harbor Realty is as follows:

Harbor Realty Inc. Trial Balance July 31, 2003		
Cash	3 4 2 5 00	
Accounts Receivable	7 0 0 0 00	
Supplies	1 2 7 0 00	
Prepaid Insurance	6 2 0 00	
Office Equipment	51 6 5 0 00	
Accumulated Depreciation		9 7 0 0 00
Accounts Payable		9 2 5 00
Unearned Fees		1 2 5 0 00
Capital Stock		5 0 0 0 00
Retained Earnings		24 0 0 0 00
Dividends	5 2 0 0 00	
Fees Earned		59 1 2 5 00
Wages Expense	22 4 1 5 00	
Rent Expense	4 2 0 0 00	
Utilities Expense	2 7 1 5 00	
Miscellaneous Expense	1 5 0 5 00	
	100 0 0 0 00	100 0 0 0 00

The data needed to determine year-end adjustments are as follows:

a. Supplies on hand at July 31, 2003, are $380.
b. Insurance premiums expired during the year are $315.
c. Depreciation of equipment during the year is $4,950.
d. Wages accrued but not paid at July 31, 2003, are $440.
e. Accrued fees earned but not recorded at July 31, 2003, are $1,000.
f. Unearned fees on July 31, 2003, are $750.

Instructions

1. Enter the trial balance on a ten-column work sheet and complete the work sheet.
2. Prepare an income statement, a retained earnings statement, and a balance sheet.
3. On the basis of the data in the work sheet, journalize the closing entries.

Solution

1.

Harbor Realty Inc.
Work Sheet
For the Year Ended July 31, 2003

Account Title	Trial Balance Dr.	Trial Balance Cr.	Adjustments Dr.	Adjustments Cr.	Adjusted Trial Balance Dr.	Adjusted Trial Balance Cr.	Income Statement Dr.	Income Statement Cr.	Balance Sheet Dr.	Balance Sheet Cr.	
Cash	3 4 2 5				3 4 2 5				3 4 2 5		
Accounts Receivable	7 0 0 0		(e)1 0 0 0		8 0 0 0				8 0 0 0		1
Supplies	1 2 7 0			(a) 8 9 0	3 8 0				3 8 0		2
Prepaid Insurance	6 2 0			(b) 3 1 5	3 0 5				3 0 5		3
Office Equipment	51 6 5 0				51 6 5 0				51 6 5 0		4
Accum. Depreciation		9 7 0 0		(c)4 9 5 0		14 6 5 0				14 6 5 0	5
Accounts Payable		9 2 5				9 2 5				9 2 5	6
Unearned Fees		1 2 5 0	(f) 5 0 0			7 5 0				7 5 0	7
Capital Stock		5 0 0 0				5 0 0 0				5 0 0 0	8
Retained Earnings		24 0 0 0				24 0 0 0				24 0 0 0	9
Dividends	5 2 0 0				5 2 0 0				5 2 0 0		10
Fees Earned		59 1 2 5		(e)1 0 0 0		60 6 2 5		60 6 2 5			11
				(f) 5 0 0							12
Wages Expense	22 4 1 5		(d) 4 4 0		22 8 5 5		22 8 5 5				13
Rent Expense	4 2 0 0				4 2 0 0		4 2 0 0				14
Utilities Expense	2 7 1 5				2 7 1 5		2 7 1 5				15
Miscellaneous Expense	1 5 0 5				1 5 0 5		1 5 0 5				16
	100 0 0 0	100 0 0 0									17
Supplies Expense			(a) 8 9 0		8 9 0		8 9 0				18
Insurance Expense			(b) 3 1 5		3 1 5		3 1 5				19
Depreciation Expense			(c)4 9 5 0		4 9 5 0		4 9 5 0				20
Wages Payable				(d) 4 4 0		4 4 0				4 4 0	21
			8 0 9 5	8 0 9 5	106 3 9 0	106 3 9 0	37 4 3 0	60 6 2 5	68 9 6 0	45 7 6 5	22
Net Income							23 1 9 5			23 1 9 5	23
							60 6 2 5	60 6 2 5	68 9 6 0	68 9 6 0	24

2.

Harbor Realty Inc.
Income Statement
For the Year Ended July 31, 2003

Fees earned			$60 6 2 5 00
Operating expenses:			
Wages expense	$22 8 5 5 00		
Depreciation expense	4 9 5 0 00		
Rent expense	4 2 0 0 00		
Utilities expense	2 7 1 5 00		
Supplies expense	8 9 0 00		
Insurance expense	3 1 5 00		
Miscellaneous expense	1 5 0 5 00		
Total operating expenses		37 4 3 0 00	
Net income			$23 1 9 5 00

Harbor Realty Inc.
Retained Earnings Statement
For the Year Ended July 31, 2003

Retained earnings, August 1, 2002		$24 0 0 0 00
Net income for the year	$23 1 9 5 00	
Less dividends	5 2 0 0 00	
Increase in retained earnings		17 9 9 5 00
Retained earnings, July 31, 2003		$41 9 9 5 00

Harbor Realty Inc.
Balance Sheet
July 31, 2003

Assets			Liabilities		
Current assets:			Current liabilities:		
Cash	$ 3 4 2 5 00		Accounts payable	$ 9 2 5 00	
Accounts receivable	8 0 0 0 00		Unearned fees	7 5 0 00	
Supplies	3 8 0 00		Wages payable	4 4 0 00	
Prepaid insurance	3 0 5 00		Total liabilities		$ 2 1 1 5 00
Total current assets		$12 1 1 0 00			
Property, plant, and equipment:			**Stockholders' Equity**		
Office equipment	$51 6 5 0 00		Capital stock	$ 5 0 0 0 00	
Less accumulated depr.	14 6 5 0 00	37 0 0 0 00	Retained earnings	41 9 9 5 00	$46 9 9 5 00
Total assets		$49 1 1 0 00	Total liabilities and		
			stockholders' equity		$49 1 1 0 00

3.

	JOURNAL			PAGE	
Date	**Description**	**Post. Ref.**	**Debit**	**Credit**	
	Closing Entries				1
2003 July 31	Fees Earned		60 6 2 5 00		2
	Income Summary			60 6 2 5 00	3
					4
31	Income Summary		37 4 3 0 00		5
	Wages Expense			22 8 5 5 00	6
	Rent Expense			4 2 0 0 00	7
	Utilities Expense			2 7 1 5 00	8
	Miscellaneous Expense			1 5 0 5 00	9
	Supplies Expense			8 9 0 00	10
	Insurance Expense			3 1 5 00	11
	Depreciation Expense			4 9 5 0 00	12
					13
31	Income Summary		23 1 9 5 00		14
	Retained Earnings			23 1 9 5 00	15
					16
31	Retained Earnings		5 2 0 0 00		17
	Dividends			5 2 0 0 00	18

SELF-EXAMINATION QUESTIONS

Matching

Match each of the following statements with its proper term. Some terms may not be used.

A.	**accounting cycle**
B.	**adjusted trial balance**
C.	**adjusting entries**
D.	**closing entries**
E.	**current assets**
F.	**current liabilities**
G.	**current ratio**
H.	**fiscal year**
I.	**Income Summary**
J.	**long-term liabilities**
K.	**natural business year**
L.	**note receivable**
M.	**owner's equity**
N.	**permanent assets**
O.	**post-closing trial balance**
P.	**property, plant, and equipment**
Q.	**real accounts**
R.	**solvency**
S.	**temporary accounts**
T.	**work sheet**
U.	**working capital**

___ 1. A working paper that accountants may use to summarize adjusting entries and the account balances for the financial statements.

___ 2. Cash and other assets that are expected to be converted to cash or sold or used up, usually within one year or less, through the normal operations of the business.

___ 3. A customer's written promise to pay an amount and possibly interest at an agreed-upon rate.

___ 4. Liabilities that will be due within a short time (usually one year or less) and that are to be paid out of current assets.

___ 5. Liabilities that usually will not be due for more than one year.

___ 6. An account to which the revenue and expense account balances are transferred at the end of a period.

___ 7. The trial balance prepared after the closing entries have been posted.

___ 8. The annual accounting period adopted by a business.

___ 9. A fiscal year that ends when business activities have reached the lowest point in an annual operating cycle.

___ 10. The process that begins with analyzing and journalizing transactions and ends with the post-closing trial balance.

___ 11. The ability of a business to pays its debts.

___ 12. The excess of the current assets of a business over its current liabilities.

___ 13. A financial ratio that is computed by dividing current assets by current liabilities.

___ 14. The entries that transfer the balances of the revenue, expense, and dividends accounts to the retained earnings account.

___ 15. The section of the balance sheet that includes equipment, machinery, buildings, and land.

___ 16. Accounts that report amounts for only one period.

Multiple Choice

1. Which of the following accounts in the Adjusted Trial Balance columns of the work sheet would be extended to the Balance Sheet columns?
   A. Utilities Expense   C. Dividends
   B. Rent Revenue   D. Miscellaneous Expense

2. Which of the following accounts would be classified as a current asset on the balance sheet?
   A. Office Equipment
   B. Land
   C. Accumulated Depreciation
   D. Accounts Receivable

3. Which of the following entries closes the dividends account at the end of the period?
   A. Debit the dividends account, credit the income summary account.
   B. Debit the retained earnings account, credit the dividends account.

   C. Debit the income summary account, credit the dividends account.
   D. Debit the dividends account, credit the retained earnings account.

4. Which of the following accounts would not be closed to the income summary account at the end of a period?
   A. Fees Earned
   B. Wages Expense
   C. Rent Expense
   D. Accumulated Depreciation

5. Which of the following accounts would not be included in a post-closing trial balance?
   A. Cash
   B. Fees Earned
   C. Accumulated Depreciation
   D. Capital Stock

CLASS DISCUSSION QUESTIONS

1. Is the work sheet a substitute for the financial statements? Discuss.
2. In the Income Statement columns of the work sheet, the Debit column total is greater than the Credit column total before the amount for the net income or net loss has been included. Would the income statement report a net income or a net loss? Explain.
3. In the Balance Sheet columns of the work sheet for Teton Co. for the current year, the Debit column total is $68,500 greater than the Credit column total before the amount for net income or net loss has been included. Would the income statement report a net income or a net loss? Explain.
4. Describe the nature of the assets that compose the following sections of a balance sheet: (a) current assets, (b) property, plant, and equipment.
5. What is the difference between a current liability and a long-term liability?
6. What types of accounts are referred to as temporary accounts?
7. Why are closing entries required at the end of an accounting period?
8. What is the difference between adjusting entries and closing entries?
9. Describe the four entries that close the temporary accounts.
10. What type of accounts are closed by transferring their balances (a) as a debit to Income Summary, (b) as a credit to Income Summary?
11. To what account is the income summary account closed?
12. To what account is the dividends account closed?
13. What is the purpose of the post-closing trial balance?
14. What is the natural business year?
15. Why might a department store select a fiscal year ending January 31, rather than a fiscal year ending December 31?
16. The fiscal years for several well-known companies were as follows:

Company	Fiscal Year Ending
Kmart	January 30
JCPenney	January 26
Zayre Corp.	January 26
Toys "R" Us, Inc.	February 3
Federated Department Stores	February 3
The Limited, Inc.	February 2

What general characteristic shared by these companies explains why they do not have fiscal years ending December 31?

EXERCISES

Exercise 4–1
Place account balances in a work sheet

Objective 1

The balances for the accounts listed below appear in the Adjusted Trial Balance columns of the work sheet. Indicate whether each balance should be extended to (a) an Income Statement column or (b) a Balance Sheet column.

1. Accounts Payable	6. Supplies
2. Accounts Receivable	7. Unearned Fees
3. Fees Earned	8. Utilities Expense
4. Dividends	9. Wages Expense
5. Retained Earnings	10. Wages Payable

Exercise 4–2
Classify accounts

Objective 1

Balances for each of the following accounts appear in the Adjusted Trial Balance columns of the work sheet. Identify each as (a) asset, (b) liability, (c) revenue, or (d) expense.

1. Accounts Receivable	7. Rent Revenue
2. Fees Earned	8. Salary Expense
3. Insurance Expense	9. Salary Payable
4. Land	10. Supplies
5. Prepaid Advertising	11. Supplies Expense
6. Prepaid Insurance	12. Unearned Rent

Exercise 4–3
Steps in completing a work sheet

Objective 1

The steps performed in completing a work sheet are listed below in random order.

a. Enter the amount of net income or net loss for the period in the proper Income Statement column and Balance Sheet column.

b. Add the Debit and Credit columns of the Balance Sheet and Income Statement columns of the work sheet to verify that the totals are equal.

c. Enter the unadjusted account balances from the general ledger into the unadjusted Trial Balance columns of the work sheet.

d. Add the Debit and Credit columns of the Balance Sheet and Income Statement columns of the work sheet to determine the amount of net income or net loss for the period.

e. Extend the adjusted trial balance amounts to the Income Statement columns and the Balance Sheet columns.

f. Add the Debit and Credit columns of the Adjusted Trial Balance columns of the work sheet to verify that the totals are equal.

g. Add or deduct adjusting entry data to trial balance amounts and extend amounts to the Adjusted Trial Balance columns.

h. Add the Debit and Credit columns of the Adjustments columns of the work sheet to verify that the totals are equal.

i. Add the Debit and Credit columns of the unadjusted Trial Balance columns of the work sheet to verify that the totals are equal.

j. Enter the adjusting entries into the work sheet, based upon the adjustment data.

Indicate the order in which the preceding steps would be performed in preparing and completing a work sheet.

Exercise 4–4
Adjustment data on work sheet

Objective 1

SPREADSHEET

Francesca Services Co. offers cleaning services to business clients. The trial balance for Francesca Services Co. has been prepared on the work sheet for the year ended December 31, 2003, shown at the top of the following page.

The data for year-end adjustments are as follows:

a. Fees earned, but not yet billed, $3.

b. Supplies on hand, $1.

c. Insurance premiums expired, $5.

d. Depreciation expense, $2.

e. Wages accrued, but not paid, $1.

Enter the adjustment data, and place the balances in the Adjusted Trial Balance columns.

✓ Total debits of Adjustments column: $14

Francesca Services Co.
Work Sheet
For the Year Ended December 31, 2003

Account Title	Trial Balance		Adjustments		Adjusted Trial Balance	
	Dr.	Cr.	Dr.	Cr.	Dr.	Cr.
Cash	4					
Accounts Receivable	25					
Supplies	4					
Prepaid Insurance	6					
Land	25					
Equipment	16					
Accumulated Depr.—Equip.		1				
Accounts Payable		13				
Wages Payable		0				
Capital Stock		7				
Retained Earnings		49				
Dividends	4					
Fees Earned		30				
Wages Expense	8					
Rent Expense	4					
Insurance Expense	0					
Utilities Expense	2					
Depreciation Expense	0					
Supplies Expense	0					
Miscellaneous Expense	2					
Totals	100	100				

Exercise 4–5

Complete a work sheet

Objective 1

✓ Net income: $6

Francesca Services Co. offers cleaning services to business clients. Complete the following work sheet for Francesca Services Co.

Francesca Services Co.
Work Sheet
For the Year Ended December 31, 2003

Account Title	Adjusted Trial Balance		Income Statement		Balance Sheet	
	Dr.	Cr.	Dr.	Cr.	Dr.	Cr.
Cash	4					
Accounts Receivable	28					
Supplies	1					
Prepaid Insurance	1					
Land	25					
Equipment	16					
Accumulated Depr.—Equip.		3				
Accounts Payable		13				
Wages Payable		1				
Capital Stock		7				
Retained Earnings		49				
Dividends	4					
Fees Earned		33				
Wages Expense	9					
Rent Expense	4					
Insurance Expense	5					
Utilities Expense	2					
Depreciation Expense	2					
Supplies Expense	3					
Miscellaneous Expense	2					
Totals	106	106				
Net income (loss)						

Exercise 4–6
Financial statements
Objective 2

Based on the data in Exercise 4–5, prepare an income statement, retained earnings statement, and balance sheet for Francesca Services Co.

✓ Stockholders' equity, Dec. 31, 2003; $58

Exercise 4–7
Adjusting entries
Objective 3

Based on the data in Exercise 4–4, prepare the adjusting entries for Francesca Services Co.

Exercise 4–8
Closing entries
Objective 3

Based on the data in Exercise 4–5, prepare the closing entries for Francesca Services Co.

Exercise 4–9
Income statement
Objective 2

The following account balances were taken from the Adjusted Trial Balance columns of the work sheet for Speedy Messenger Service, a delivery service firm, for the current fiscal year ended April 30, 2003:

Fees Earned	$173,700
Salaries Expense	37,100
Rent Expense	12,500
Utilities Expense	7,500
Supplies Expense	2,750
Miscellaneous Expense	1,350
Insurance Expense	1,500
Depreciation Expense	4,200

Prepare an income statement.

Exercise 4–10
Income statement; net loss
Objective 2

The following revenue and expense account balances were taken from the ledger of Panda Services Co. after the accounts had been adjusted on January 31, 2003, the end of the current fiscal year:

Depreciation Expense	$ 7,500
Insurance Expense	3,500
Miscellaneous Expense	2,250
Rent Expense	31,270
Service Revenue	101,125
Supplies Expense	3,100
Utilities Expense	8,500
Wages Expense	46,800

Prepare an income statement.

Exercise 4–11
Income statement
Objective 2

✓ a. Net income: $631,263

FedEx Corporation had the following revenue and expense account balances (in thousands) at its fiscal year-end of May 31, 1999:

Rentals and Landing Fees	$ 1,396,694
Maintenance and Repairs	958,873
Purchased Transportation	1,537,785
Fuel	604,929
Salaries and Employee Benefits	7,087,728
Other Operating Expenses	2,989,257
Depreciation and Amortization	1,035,118
Interest Expense	98,191
Revenues	16,773,400
Provision for Income Taxes	429,731
Other Expenses	3,831

a. Prepare an income statement.
b. Compare your income statement with the 1999 income statement that is available at the FedEx Corporation web site, which is linked to the text's web site at **warren.swcollege.com**. What similarities and differences do you see?

Exercise 4–12
Statement of owner's equity
Objective 2

Greenhorn Services Co. offers its services to new arrivals in the Belgrade area. Selected accounts from the ledger of Greenhorn Services Co. for the current fiscal year ended July 31, 2003, are as follows:

Retained Earnings				Dividends			
July 31	11,000	Aug. 1	183,750	Oct. 30	2,000	July 31	11,000
		July 31	44,250	Jan. 31	2,000		
				Apr. 30	2,000		
				July 31	5,000		

Income Summary			
July 31	577,150	July 31	621,400
31	44,250		

Prepare a retained earnings statement for the year.

Exercise 4–13
Statement of owner's equity; net loss
Objective 2

✓ Retained earnings, Oct. 31, 2003; $256,150

Selected accounts from the ledger of Yankee Sports for the current fiscal year ended October 31, 2003, are as follows:

Retained Earnings				Dividends			
Oct. 31	6,000	Nov. 1	310,300	Jan. 31	2,000	Oct. 31	6,000
31	48,150			Apr. 30	2,000		
				July 31	1,000		
				Oct. 31	1,000		

Income Summary			
Oct. 31	523,400	Oct. 31	475,250
		31	48,150

Prepare a retained earnings statement for the year.

Exercise 4–14
Classify assets
Objective 2

Identify each of the following as (a) a current asset or (b) property, plant, and equipment:

1. Accounts receivable
2. Building
3. Cash
4. Equipment
5. Prepaid insurance
6. Supplies

Exercise 4–15
Balance sheet classification
Objective 2

At the balance sheet date, a business owes a mortgage note payable of $375,000, the terms of which provide for monthly payments of $12,500.
Explain how the liability should be classified on the balance sheet.

Exercise 4–16
Balance sheet
Objective 2

✓ Total assets: $96,550

Shoshone Co. offers personal weight reduction consulting services to individuals. After all the accounts have been closed on June 30, 2003, the end of the current fiscal year, the balances of selected accounts from the ledger of Shoshone Co. are as follows:

Accounts Payable	$ 8,750	Prepaid Insurance	$ 3,100
Accounts Receivable	18,725	Prepaid Rent	2,400
Accumulated Depreciation—Equipment	21,100	Retained Earnings	59,850
Capital Stock	25,000	Salaries Payable	1,750
Cash	2,150	Supplies	675
Equipment	90,600	Unearned Fees	1,200

Prepare a classified balance sheet.

Exercise 4–17
Balance sheet

Objective 2

✓ Corrected balance sheet, total assets: $158,660

List the errors you find in the following balance sheet. Prepare a corrected balance sheet.

ZigZag Services Co.
Balance Sheet
For the Year Ended March 31, 2003

Assets			Liabilities		
Current assets:			Current liabilities:		
Cash	$ 3,170		Accounts receivable	$ 8,390	
Accounts payable	4,390		Accum. depr.—building	23,000	
Supplies	750		Accum. depr.—equipment	16,000	
Prepaid insurance	1,600		Net loss	10,000	
Land	100,000		Total liabilities	$ 57,390	
Total current assets		$109,910			
Property, plant,			**Stockholders' Equity**		
and equipment:			Wages payable	$ 975	
Building	$ 55,500		Capital stock	40,000	
Equipment	28,250		Retained earnings	113,295	
Total property, plant,			Total stockholders' equity	$154,270	
and equipment		$101,750	Total liabilities and		
Total assets		$211,660	stockholders' equity	$211,660	

Exercise 4–18
Adjusting entries from work sheet

Objective 3

The Purification Co. is a consulting firm specializing in pollution control. The entries in the Adjustments columns of the work sheet for The Purification Co. are shown below.

	Adjustments	
	Dr.	**Cr.**
Accounts Receivable	5,100	
Supplies		1,225
Prepaid Insurance		1,000
Accumulated Depreciation—Equipment		1,800
Wages Payable		900
Unearned Rent	2,500	
Fees Earned		5,100
Wages Expense	900	
Supplies Expense	1,225	
Rent Revenue		2,500
Insurance Expense	1,000	
Depreciation Expense	1,800	

Prepare the adjusting journal entries.

Exercise 4–19
Identify accounts to be closed

Objective 3

From the following list, identify the accounts that should be closed to Income Summary at the end of the fiscal year:

a. Accounts Payable
b. Accumulated Depreciation—
   Buildings
c. Capital Stock
d. Depreciation Expense—Buildings
e. Dividends
f. Equipment

g. Fees Earned
h. Land
i. Salaries Expense
j. Salaries Payable
k. Supplies
l. Supplies Expense

Exercise 4–20
Closing entries

Objective 3

Prior to its closing, Income Summary had total debits of $631,335 and total credits of $812,575.

➤ Briefly explain the purpose served by the income summary account and the nature of the entries that resulted in the $631,335 and the $812,575.

Exercise 4–21
Closing entries
Objective 3

✓ b. $582,150

After all revenue and expense accounts have been closed at the end of the fiscal year, Income Summary has a debit of $512,900 and a credit of $729,350. At the same date, Retained Earnings has a credit balance of $405,700, and Dividends has a balance of $40,000. (a) Journalize the entries required to complete the closing of the accounts. (b) Determine the amount of Retained Earnings at the end of the period.

Exercise 4–22
Closing entries
Objective 3

Image Services Co. offers its services to individuals desiring to improve their personal images. After the accounts have been adjusted at January 31, the end of the fiscal year, the following balances were taken from the ledger of Image Services Co.

Retained Earnings	$325,750	Rent Expense	$74,000
Dividends	45,000	Supplies Expense	15,500
Fees Earned	380,700	Miscellaneous Expense	4,500
Wages Expense	205,300		

Journalize the four entries required to close the accounts.

Exercise 4–23
Identify permanent accounts
Objective 3

Which of the following accounts will usually appear in the post-closing trial balance?

a.   Accounts Receivable
b.   Accumulated Depreciation
c.   Cash
d.   Depreciation Expense
e.   Equipment
f.   Capital Stock

g.   Dividends
h.   Fees Earned
i.   Supplies
j.   Wages Expense
k.   Wages Payable

Exercise 4–24
Post-closing trial balance
Objective 3

✓ Correct column totals, $59,725

An accountant prepared the following post-closing trial balance:

Buchanan Repairs Co.
Post-Closing Trial Balance
July 31, 2003

Cash	5,125	
Accounts Receivable	18,500	
Supplies		1,100
Equipment		35,000
Accumulated Depreciation—Equipment	11,100	
Accounts Payable	6,250	
Salaries Payable		1,500
Unearned Rent	3,000	
Capital Stock	8,000	
Retained Earnings	29,875	
	81,850	37,600

Prepare a corrected post-closing trial balance. Assume that all accounts have normal balances and that the amounts shown are correct.

Exercise 4–25
Steps in the accounting cycle
Objective 4

Rearrange the following steps in the accounting cycle in proper sequence:

a.   Financial statements are prepared.
b.   Closing entries are journalized and posted to the ledger.
c.   Adjusting entries are journalized and posted to the ledger.
d.   A post-closing trial balance is prepared.
e.   Transactions are analyzed and recorded in the journal.
f.   Transactions are posted to the ledger.
g.   A trial balance is prepared, adjustment data are assembled, and the work sheet is completed.

Exercise 4–26
Working capital and current ratio

Objective 6

Real World

The financial statements for **Cisco Systems, Inc.,** are presented in Appendix G at the end of the text.

a. Determine the working capital and the current ratio for Cisco Systems as of July 29, 2000 and July 31, 1999.
b. ✏ What conclusions concerning the company's ability to meets its financial obligations can you draw from these data?

Appendix
Exercise 4–27
Adjusting and reversing entries

On the basis of the following data, (a) journalize the adjusting entries at December 31, 2003, the end of the current fiscal year, and (b) journalize the reversing entries on January 1, 2004, the first day of the following year.

1. Sales salaries are uniformly $13,500 for a five-day workweek, ending on Friday. The last payday of the year was Friday, December 28.
2. Accrued fees earned but not recorded at December 31, $8,175.

Appendix
Exercise 4–28
Entries posted to the wages expense account

Portions of the wages expense account of a business are as follows:

ACCOUNT	Wages Expense					ACCOUNT NO. 53	
			Post.			Balance	
Date	Item		Ref.	Dr.	Cr.	Dr.	Cr.
2003							
Dec. 26	(1)		81	25,000		1,275,000	
31	(2)		82	15,000		1,290,000	
31	(3)		83		1,290,000	—	—
2004							
Jan. 1	(4)		84		15,000		15,000
2	(5)		85	25,000		10,000	

a. Indicate the nature of the entry (payment, adjusting, closing, reversing) from which each numbered posting was made.
b. Journalize the complete entry from which each numbered posting was made.

PROBLEMS SERIES A

Problem 4–1A
Work sheet and related items

Objectives 1, 2, 3

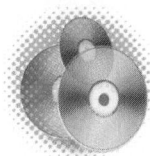
SPREADSHEET
GENERAL
LEDGER

✓ 2. Net income: $14,980

The trial balance of The Pickerel Laundromat at July 31, 2003, the end of the current fiscal year, is shown at the top of the following page. The data needed to determine year-end adjustments are as follows:

a. Laundry supplies on hand at July 31 are $1,140.
b. Insurance premiums expired during the year are $1,500.
c. Depreciation of equipment during the year is $6,000.
d. Wages accrued but not paid at July 31 are $1,100.

Instructions

1. Enter the trial balance on a ten-column work sheet and complete the work sheet. Add accounts as needed.
2. Prepare an income statement, a retained earnings statement, and a balance sheet.
3. On the basis of the adjustment data in the work sheet, journalize the adjusting entries.
4. On the basis of the data in the work sheet, journalize the closing entries.

The Pickerel Laundromat
Trial Balance
July 31, 2003

Cash	3,290	
Laundry Supplies	5,850	
Prepaid Insurance	3,000	
Laundry Equipment	109,750	
Accumulated Depreciation		52,700
Accounts Payable		4,950
Capital Stock		9,000
Retained Earnings		30,450
Dividends	3,500	
Laundry Revenue		77,900
Wages Expense	23,400	
Rent Expense	16,400	
Utilities Expense	8,500	
Miscellaneous Expense	1,310	
	175,000	175,000

Problem 4–2A

Adjusting and closing entries; retained earnings statement

Objectives 2, 3

SPREADSHEET

✓ 2. Retained earnings, April 30: $51,230

The Breakthrough Company is an investigative services firm that is owned and operated by Chandra Domir. On April 30, 2003, the end of the current fiscal year, the accountant for The Breakthrough Company prepared a work sheet, a part of which is shown here.

The Breakthrough Company
Work Sheet (Partial)
April 30, 2003

	Income Statement		Balance Sheet	
Cash			4,325	
Accounts Receivable			18,600	
Supplies			1,610	
Prepaid Insurance			1,350	
Equipment			80,750	
Accumulated Depreciation—Equipment				23,995
Accounts Payable				6,230
Salaries Payable				2,480
Taxes Payable				1,200
Unearned Rent				1,500
Capital Stock				20,000
Retained Earnings				44,715
Dividends			7,500	
Service Fees Earned		175,900		
Rent Revenue		3,000		
Salary Expense	129,865			
Rent Expense	16,000			
Supplies Expense	4,310			
Depreciation Expense—Equipment	3,500			
Utilities Expense	3,460			
Taxes Expense	3,115			
Insurance Expense	2,925			
Miscellaneous Expense	1,710			
	164,885	178,900	114,135	100,120
Net income	14,015			14,015
	178,900	178,900	114,135	114,135

Instructions

1. Journalize the entries that were required to close the accounts at April 30.
2. Prepare a retained earnings statement for the fiscal year ended April 30, 2003.
3. If Retained Earnings decreased $20,000 after the closing entries were posted, what was the amount of net income or net loss?

If the working papers correlating with this textbook are not used, omit Problem 4–3A.

Problem 4–3A
Ledger accounts, work sheet, and related items

Objectives 1, 2, 3

✓ 2. Net income: $18,703

The ledger and trial balance of Idiom.com as of January 31, 2003, the end of the first month of its current fiscal year, are presented in the working papers.

Instructions

1. Complete the ten-column work sheet. Data needed to determine the necessary adjusting entries are as follows:
   a. Service revenue accrued at January 31 is $1,750.
   b. Supplies on hand at January 31 are $350.
   c. Insurance premiums expired during January are $100.
   d. Depreciation of the building during January is $500.
   e. Depreciation of equipment during January is $150.
   f. Unearned rent at January 31 is $2,040.
   g. Wages accrued at January 31 are $400.
2. Prepare an income statement, a retained earnings statement, and a balance sheet.
3. Journalize and post the adjusting entries, inserting balances in the accounts affected.
4. Journalize and post the closing entries. Indicate closed accounts by inserting a line in both Balance columns opposite the closing entry.
5. Prepare a post-closing trial balance.

Problem 4–4A
Work sheet and financial statements

Objectives 1, 2, 3

GENERAL LEDGER

✓ 2. Net income: $58,270

Figure-Eight Company maintains and repairs warning lights, such as those found on radio towers and lighthouses. Figure-Eight Company prepared the following trial balance at October 31, 2003, the end of the current fiscal year:

Figure-Eight Company
Trial Balance
October 31, 2003

Cash	5,500	
Accounts Receivable	16,500	
Prepaid Insurance	3,000	
Supplies	1,950	
Land	70,000	
Building	100,500	
Accumulated Depreciation—Building		81,700
Equipment	72,400	
Accumulated Depreciation—Equipment		63,800
Accounts Payable		4,100
Unearned Rent		1,500
Capital Stock		18,000
Retained Earnings		39,700
Dividends	4,000	
Fees Revenue		171,200
Salaries and Wages Expense	60,200	
Advertising Expense	18,500	
Utilities Expense	15,100	
Repairs Expense	9,300	
Miscellaneous Expense	3,050	
	380,000	380,000

The data needed to determine year-end adjustments are as follows:

a. Fees revenue accrued at October 31 is $2,500.
b. Insurance expired during the year is $2,000.
c. Supplies on hand at October 31 are $450.
d. Depreciation of building for the year is $1,620.
e. Depreciation of equipment for the year is $3,160.
f. Accrued salaries and wages at October 31 are $2,000.
g. Unearned rent at October 31 is $500.

Instructions

1. Enter the trial balance on a ten-column work sheet and complete the work sheet. Add accounts as needed.
2. Prepare an income statement for the year ended October 31.
3. Prepare a retained earnings statement for the year ended October 31.
4. Prepare a balance sheet as of October 31.
5. Compute the percent of net income to total revenue for the year.

Problem 4–5A

Ledger accounts, work sheet, and related items

Objectives 1, 2, 3

GENERAL LEDGER

✓ 3. Net income: $33,655

The trial balance of Parachute Repairs at March 31, 2003, the end of the current year, and the data needed to determine year-end adjustments are as follows:

Parachute Repairs
Trial Balance
March 31, 2003

11	Cash	2,950	
13	Supplies	4,295	
14	Prepaid Insurance	2,735	
16	Equipment	40,650	
17	Accumulated Depreciation—Equipment		9,209
18	Trucks	36,300	
19	Accumulated Depreciation—Trucks		6,400
21	Accounts Payable		2,015
31	Capital Stock		5,000
32	Retained Earnings		21,426
33	Dividends	5,000	
41	Service Revenue		91,950
51	Wages Expense	23,925	
53	Rent Expense	10,600	
55	Truck Expense	7,350	
59	Miscellaneous Expense	2,195	
		136,000	136,000

a. Supplies on hand at March 31 are $750.
b. Insurance premiums expired during year are $2,000.
c. Depreciation of equipment during year is $3,380.
d. Depreciation of trucks during year is $4,400.
e. Wages accrued but not paid at March 31 are $900.

Instructions

1. For each account listed in the trial balance, enter the balance in the appropriate Balance column of a four-column account and place a check mark (✓) in the Posting Reference column.
2. Enter the trial balance on a ten-column work sheet and complete the work sheet. Add accounts as needed.
3. Prepare an income statement, a retained earnings statement, and a balance sheet.
4. Journalize and post the adjusting entries, inserting balances in the accounts affected. The following additional accounts from Parachute's chart of accounts should be used:

Wages Payable, 22; Supplies Expense, 52; Depreciation Expense—Equipment, 54; Depreciation Expense—Trucks, 56; Insurance Expense, 57.

5. Journalize and post the closing entries. (Income Summary is account #34 in the chart of accounts.) Indicate closed accounts by inserting a line in both Balance columns opposite the closing entry.
6. Prepare a post-closing trial balance.

PROBLEMS SERIES B

Problem 4–1B

Work sheet and related items

Objectives 1, 2, 3

SPREADSHEET
GENERAL LEDGER

✓ 2. Net income: $21,690

The trial balance of Ford's Laundry at October 31, 2003, the end of the current fiscal year, and the data needed to determine year-end adjustments are as follows:

Ford's Laundry
Trial Balance
October 31, 2003

Cash	3,100	
Laundry Supplies	6,560	
Prepaid Insurance	4,490	
Laundry Equipment	105,100	
Accumulated Depreciation		40,200
Accounts Payable		6,100
Capital Stock		6,000
Retained Earnings		31,800
Dividends	2,000	
Laundry Revenue		150,900
Wages Expense	61,400	
Rent Expense	36,000	
Utilities Expense	13,650	
Miscellaneous Expense	2,700	
	235,000	235,000

a. Wages accrued but not paid at October 31 are $1,150.
b. Depreciation of equipment during the year is $7,000.
c. Laundry supplies on hand at October 31 are $1,750.
d. Insurance premiums expired during the year are $2,500.

Instructions

1. Enter the trial balance on a ten-column work sheet and complete the work sheet. Add accounts as needed.
2. Prepare an income statement, a retained earnings statement, and a balance sheet.
3. On the basis of the adjustment data in the work sheet, journalize the adjusting entries.
4. On the basis of the data in the work sheet, journalize the closing entries.

Problem 4–2B

Adjusting and closing entries; statement of owner's equity

Objectives 2, 3

The Epitome Company is a financial planning services firm owned and operated by Kerri Latimer. As of December 31, 2003, the end of the current fiscal year, the accountant for The Epitome Company prepared a work sheet, part of which is shown on the following page.

Instructions

1. Journalize the entries that were required to close the accounts at December 31.
2. Prepare a retained earnings statement for the fiscal year ended December 31. There were no additional investments during the year.
3. If the balance of Retained Earnings decreased $18,000 after the closing entries were posted, what was the amount of net income or net loss?

SPREADSHEET

✓ 2. Retained earnings, Dec. 31: $130,080

The Epitome Company
Trial Balance
December 31, 2003

	Income Statement		Balance Sheet	
Cash			5,650	
Accounts Receivable			18,960	
Supplies			2,790	
Prepaid Insurance			2,500	
Land			55,000	
Buildings			120,000	
Accumulated Depreciation—Buildings				72,400
Equipment			82,000	
Accumulated Depreciation—Equipment				40,900
Accounts Payable				7,870
Salaries Payable				1,150
Taxes Payable				4,000
Unearned Rent				500
Capital Stock				30,000
Retained Earnings				81,750
Dividends			10,000	
Service Fees Earned		174,260		
Rent Revenue		1,500		
Salary Expense	72,650			
Depreciation Expense—Equipment	11,100			
Rent Expense	9,000			
Supplies Expense	7,970			
Utilities Expense	5,300			
Depreciation Expense—Buildings	5,200			
Taxes Expense	4,150			
Insurance Expense	1,000			
Miscellaneous Expense	1,060			
	117,430	175,760	296,900	238,570
Net income	58,330			58,330
	175,760	175,760	296,900	296,900

If the working papers correlating with this textbook are not used, omit Problem 4–3B.

Problem 4–3B
Ledger accounts and work sheet, and related items

Objectives 1, 2, 3

✓ 2. Net income: $19,448

The ledger and trial balance of Idiom.com as of January 31, 2003, the end of the first month of its current fiscal year, are presented in the working papers.

Instructions

1. Complete the ten-column work sheet. Data needed to determine the necessary adjusting entries are as follows:
   a. Service revenue accrued at January 31 is $2,750.
   b. Supplies on hand at January 31 are $500.
   c. Insurance premiums expired during January are $150.
   d. Depreciation of the building during January is $625.
   e. Depreciation of equipment during January is $200.
   f. Unearned rent at January 31 is $2,020.
   g. Wages accrued but not paid at January 31 are $600.
2. Prepare an income statement, a retained earnings statement, and a balance sheet.
3. Journalize and post the adjusting entries, inserting balances in the accounts affected.
4. Journalize and post the closing entries. Indicate closed accounts by inserting a line in both Balance columns opposite the closing entry. Insert the new balance of the capital account.
5. Prepare a post-closing trial balance.

Problem 4-4B
Work sheet and financial statements

Objectives 1, 2, 3

GENERAL LEDGER

✓ 2. Net loss: $9,470

Sanguine Company offers legal consulting advice to death-row inmates. Sanguine Company prepared the following trial balance at June 30, 2003, the end of the current fiscal year:

Sanguine Company
Trial Balance
June 30, 2003

Cash	2,200	
Accounts Receivable	7,500	
Prepaid Insurance	1,800	
Supplies	1,350	
Land	50,000	
Building	137,500	
Accumulated Depreciation—Building		51,700
Equipment	90,100	
Accumulated Depreciation—Equipment		35,300
Accounts Payable		3,500
Unearned Rent		3,000
Capital Stock		70,000
Retained Earnings		142,500
Dividends	10,000	
Fees Revenue		188,400
Salaries and Wages Expense	101,200	
Advertising Expense	58,200	
Utilities Expense	19,000	
Repairs Expense	11,500	
Miscellaneous Expense	4,050	
	494,400	494,400

The data needed to determine year-end adjustments are as follows:

a. Accrued fees revenue at June 30 are $1,750.
b. Insurance expired during the year is $800.
c. Supplies on hand at June 30 are $650.
d. Depreciation of building for the year is $1,620.
e. Depreciation of equipment for the year is $3,500.
f. Accrued salaries and wages at June 30 are $1,050.
g. Unearned rent at June 30 is $1,000.

Instructions

1. Enter the trial balance on a ten-column work sheet and complete the work sheet. Add accounts as needed.
2. Prepare an income statement for the year ended June 30.
3. Prepare a retained earnings statement for the year ended June 30.
4. Prepare a balance sheet as of June 30.
5. Compute the percent of total revenue to total assets for the year.

Problem 4-5B
Ledger accounts, work sheet, and related items

Objectives 1, 2, 3

The trial balance of Dagwood Repairs at December 31, 2003, the end of the current year, is shown at the top of the following page. The data needed to determine year-end adjustments are as follows:

a. Supplies on hand at December 31 are $800.
b. Insurance premiums expired during year are $1,500.
c. Depreciation of equipment during year is $6,080.
d. Depreciation of trucks during year is $5,500.
e. Wages accrued but not paid at December 31 are $500.

GENERAL
LEDGER

✓ 2. Net income: $18,695

Dagwood Repairs
Trial Balance
December 31, 2003

11	Cash	1,825	
13	Supplies	3,820	
14	Prepaid Insurance	2,500	
16	Equipment	44,200	
17	Accumulated Depreciation—Equipment		9,050
18	Trucks	45,000	
19	Accumulated Depreciation—Trucks		27,100
21	Accounts Payable		4,015
31	Capital Stock		4,000
32	Retained Earnings		20,885
33	Dividends	3,000	
41	Service Revenue		79,950
51	Wages Expense	22,010	
53	Rent Expense	10,100	
55	Truck Expense	9,350	
59	Miscellaneous Expense	3,195	
		145,000	145,000

Instructions

1. For each account listed in the trial balance, enter the balance in the appropriate Balance column of a four-column account and place a check mark (✔) in the Posting Reference column.
2. Enter the trial balance on a ten-column work sheet and complete the work sheet. Add accounts as needed.
3. Prepare an income statement, a retained earnings statement, and a balance sheet.
4. Journalize and post the adjusting entries, inserting balances in the accounts affected. The following additional accounts from Dagwood's chart of accounts should be used: Wages Payable, 22; Supplies Expense, 52; Depreciation Expense—Equipment, 54; Depreciation Expense—Trucks, 56; Insurance Expense, 57.
5. Journalize and post the closing entries. (Income Summary is account #34 in the chart of accounts.) Indicate closed accounts by inserting a line in both Balance columns opposite the closing entry.
6. Prepare a post-closing trial balance.

CONTINUING PROBLEM

GENERAL
LEDGER

✓ 2. Net income: $1,275

The unadjusted trial balance of Dancin Music as of December 31, 2002, along with the adjustment data for the two months ended December 31, 2002, are shown in Chapter F3.

Instructions

1. Prepare a ten-column work sheet.
2. Prepare an income statement, a retained earnings statement, and a balance sheet.
3. Add the retained earnings account (#32) and the income summary account (#34) to the ledger of Dancin Music. Journalize and post the closing entries. Indicate closed accounts by inserting a line in both Balance columns opposite the closing entry.
4. Prepare a post-closing trial balance.

COMPREHENSIVE PROBLEM 1

GENERAL LEDGER

✓ 4. Net income: $7,925

For the past several years, Dustin Larkin has operated a part-time consulting business from his home. As of June 1, 2003, Dustin decided to move to rented quarters and to operate the business, which was to be known as Quixote Consulting, on a full-time basis. Quixote Consulting entered into the following transactions during June:

June 1. The following assets were received from Dustin Larkin in exchange for capital stock: cash, $10,000; accounts receivable, $1,500; supplies, $1,250; and office equipment, $7,500. There were no liabilities received.

    1. Paid three months' rent on a lease rental contract, $4,500.

    2. Paid the premiums on property and casualty insurance policies, $1,800.

    4. Received cash from clients as an advance payment for services to be provided and recorded it as unearned fees, $3,000.

    5. Purchased additional office equipment on account from Crawford Company, $1,800.

    6. Received cash from clients on account, $800.

    10. Paid cash for a newspaper advertisement, $120.

    12. Paid Crawford Company for part of the debt incurred on June 5, $800.

    12. Recorded services provided on account for the period June 1–12, $2,250.

    14. Paid part-time receptionist for two weeks' salary, $400.

    17. Recorded cash from cash clients for fees earned during the period June 1–16, $3,175.

    18. Paid cash for supplies, $750.

    20. Recorded services provided on account for the period June 13–20, $1,100.

    24. Recorded cash from cash clients for fees earned for the period June 17–24, $1,850.

    26. Received cash from clients on account, $1,600.

    27. Paid part-time receptionist for two weeks' salary, $400.

    29. Paid telephone bill for June, $130.

    30. Paid electricity bill for June, $200.

    30. Recorded cash from cash clients for fees earned for the period June 25–30, $2,050.

    30. Recorded services provided on account for the remainder of June, $1,000.

    30. Paid dividends, $4,500.

Instructions

1. Journalize each transaction in a two-column journal, referring to the following chart of accounts in selecting the accounts to be debited and credited. (Do not insert the account numbers in the journal at this time.)

11	Cash	31	Capital Stock
12	Accounts Receivable	32	Retained Earnings
14	Supplies	33	Dividends
15	Prepaid Rent	41	Fees Earned
16	Prepaid Insurance	51	Salary Expense
18	Office Equipment	52	Rent Expense
19	Accumulated Depreciation	53	Supplies Expense
21	Accounts Payable	54	Depreciation Expense
22	Salaries Payable	55	Insurance Expense
23	Unearned Fees	59	Miscellaneous Expense

2. Post the journal to a ledger of four-column accounts.

3. Prepare a trial balance as of June 30, 2003, on a ten-column work sheet, listing all the accounts in the order given in the ledger. Complete the work sheet, using the following adjustment data:

    a. Insurance expired during June is $150.

    b. Supplies on hand on June 30 are $1,020.

    c. Depreciation of office equipment for June is $500.

    d. Accrued receptionist salary on June 30 is $120.

    e. Rent expired during June is $1,500.

    f. Unearned fees on June 30 are $2,000.

4. Prepare an income statement, a retained earnings statement, and a balance sheet.

5. Journalize and post the adjusting entries. *(continued)*

6. Journalize and post the closing entries. (Income Summary is account #34 in the chart of accounts.) Indicate closed accounts by inserting a line in both Balance columns opposite the closing entry.
7. Prepare a post-closing trial balance.

SPECIAL ACTIVITIES

Activity 4–1
Van Dyck Co.
Ethics and professional conduct in business

Van Dyck Co. is a graphics arts design consulting firm. Chadwick Joiner, its treasurer and vice president of finance, has prepared a classified balance sheet as of October 31, 2003, the end of its fiscal year. This balance sheet will be submitted with Van Dyck's loan application to Western Trust & Savings Bank.

In the Current Assets section of the balance sheet, Chadwick reported a $50,000 receivable from Christie Shariff, the president of Van Dyck, as a trade account receivable. Christie borrowed the money from Van Dyck in February 2002 for a down payment on a new home. She has orally assured Chadwick that she will pay off the account receivable within the next year. Chadwick reported the $50,000 in the same manner on the preceding year's balance sheet.

✎▶ Evaluate whether it is acceptable for Chadwick Joiner to prepare the October 31, 2003 balance sheet in the manner indicated above.

Activity 4–2
Flanders Supplies Co.
Financial statements

The following is an excerpt from a telephone conversation between Gail Richie, president of Flanders Supplies Co., and Gary Weir, owner of On-Time Employment Co.

Gail: Gary, you're going to have to do a better job of finding me a new computer programmer. That last guy was great at programming, but he didn't have any common sense.
Gary: What do you mean? The guy had a master's degree with straight A's.
Gail: Yes, well, last month he developed a new financial reporting system. He said we could do away with manually preparing a work sheet and financial statements. The computer would automatically generate our financial statements with "a push of a button."
Gary: So what's the big deal? Sounds to me like it would save you time and effort.
Gail: Right! The balance sheet showed a minus for supplies!
Gary: Minus supplies? How can that be?
Gail: That's what I asked.
Gary: So, what did he say?
Gail: Well, after he checked the program, he said that it must be right. The minuses were greater than the pluses . . .
Gary: Didn't he know that supplies can't have a credit balance—it must have a debit balance?
Gail: He asked me what a debit and credit were.
Gary: I see your point.

1. ✎▶ Comment on (a) the desirability of computerizing Flanders Supplies Co.'s financial reporting system, (b) the elimination of the work sheet in a computerized accounting system, and (c) the computer programmer's lack of accounting knowledge.
2. ✎▶ Explain to the programmer why supplies could not have a credit balance.

Activity 4–3
Megabit.com
Financial statements

Assume that you recently accepted a position with the Big Timber National Bank as an assistant loan officer. As one of your first duties, you have been assigned the responsibility of evaluating a loan request for $50,000 from Megabit.com, a small corporation. In support of the loan application, Erica Salley, the sole stockholder and manager, submitted a "Statement of Accounts" (trial balance) for the first year of operations ended December 31, 2003.

1. ✎▶ Explain to Erica Salley why a set of financial statements (income statement, retained earnings statement, and balance sheet) would be useful to you in evaluating the loan request.

2. In discussing the "Statement of Accounts" with Erica Salley, you discovered that the accounts had not been adjusted at December 31. Analyze the "Statement of Accounts" (shown below) and indicate possible adjusting entries that might be necessary before an accurate set of financial statements could be prepared.

Megabit.com
Statement of Accounts
December 31, 2003

Cash	3,120	
Billings Due from Others	10,150	
Supplies (chemicals, etc.)	14,950	
Trucks	32,750	
Equipment	26,150	
Amounts Owed to Others		6,700
Investment in Business		57,260
Service Revenue		117,300
Wages Expense	70,100	
Utilities Expense	16,900	
Rent Expense	4,800	
Insurance Expense	1,400	
Other Expenses	940	
	181,260	181,260

3.  Assuming that an accurate set of financial statements will be submitted by Erica Salley in a few days, what other considerations or information would you require before making a decision on the loan request?

Activity 4–4
Into the Real World
Compare balance sheets

In groups of three or four, compare the balance sheets of two different companies, and present to the class a summary of the similarities and differences of the two companies. You may obtain the balance sheets you need from one of the following sources:

1. Your school or local library.
2. The investor relations department of each company.
3. The company's web site on the Internet.
4. EDGAR (Electronic Data Gathering, Analysis, and Retrieval), the electronic archives of financial statements filed with the Securities and Exchange Commission.

SEC documents can be retrieved using the EdgarScan™ service from Pricewaterhouse-Coopers at **edgarscan.pwcglobal.com**. To obtain annual report information, key in a company name in the appropriate space. EdgarScan will list the reports available to you for the company you've selected. Select the most recent annual report filing, identified as a 10-K or 10-K405. EdgarScan provides an outline of the report, including the separate financial statements, which can also be selected in an Excel spreadsheet.

ANSWERS TO SELF-EXAMINATION QUESTIONS

Matching

1. T	3. L	5. J	7. O	9. K	11. R	13. G	15. P
2. E	4. F	6. I	8. H	10. A	12. U	14. D	16. S

Multiple Choice

1. **C** The dividends account (answer C), would be extended to the Balance Sheet columns of the work sheet. Utilities Expense (answer A), Rent Revenue (answer B), and Miscellaneous Expense (answer D) would all be extended to the Income Statement columns of the work sheet.

2. **D** Cash or other assets that are expected to be converted to cash or sold or used up within one year or less, through the normal operations of the business, are classified as current assets on the balance sheet. Accounts Receivable (answer D) is a current asset, since it will normally be converted to cash within one

year. Office Equipment (answer A), Land (answer B), and Accumulated Depreciation (answer C) are all reported in the property, plant, and equipment section of the balance sheet.

3. **B** The entry to close the dividends account is to debit the retained earnings account and credit the dividends account (answer B).

4. **D** Since all revenue and expense accounts are closed at the end of the period, Fees Earned (answer A), Wages Expense (answer B), and Rent Expense (answer C) would all be closed to Income Summary. Accumulated Depreciation (answer D) is a contra asset account that is not closed.

5. **B** Since the post-closing trial balance includes only balance sheet accounts (all of the revenue, expense, and dividends accounts are closed), Cash (answer A), Accumulated Depreciation (answer C), and Capital Stock (answer D) would appear on the post-closing trial balance. Fees Earned (answer B) is a temporary account that is closed prior to preparing the post-closing trial balance.

Accounting for Merchandising Businesses

objectives

After studying this chapter, you should be able to:

1 Distinguish the activities of a service business from those of a merchandising business.

2 Journalize the entries for merchandise transactions, including:
   a. Merchandise purchases
   b. Merchandise sales
   c. Merchandise transportation costs
   d. Transactions for both the buyer and the seller

3 Prepare a chart of accounts for a merchandising business.

4 Prepare an income statement for a merchandising business.

5 Describe the accounting cycle for a merchandising business.

6 Compute the ratio of net sales to assets as a measure of how effectively a business is using its assets.

A ssume that you bought groceries at a store and received the receipt shown here. This receipt indicates that you purchased three items totaling $5.28, the sales tax was $0.32 (6%), the total due was $5.60, you gave the clerk $10.00, and you received change of $4.40. The receipt also indicates that the sale was made by Store #426 of the Ingles chain, located in Athens, Georgia. The date and time of the sale and other data used internally by the store are also indicated.

When you buy groceries, textbooks, school supplies, or an automobile, you are doing business with a retail or merchandising business. The accounting for a merchandising business is more complex than for a service business. For example, the accounting system for a merchandiser must be designed to record the receipt of goods for resale, keep track of the goods available for sale, and record the sale and cost of the merchandise sold.

In this chapter, we will focus on the accounting principles and concepts for merchandising businesses. We begin our discussion by highlighting the basic differences between the activities of merchandise and service businesses. We then describe and illustrate purchases and sales transactions and financial statements for merchandising businesses.

```
INGLES #426
ATHENS GA

                                  10/02/02
GROCERY                              2.99L
GROCERY                              1.00L
FZ FOOD                              1.29L
SUBTOTAL                             5.28
TAX                                   .32
TOTAL                                5.60

CASH                                10.00

CHANGE                               4.40

# ITEMS      3


      THANK YOU C123 R03 T12:38
```

Nature of Merchandising Businesses

objective 1

Distinguish the activities of a service business from those of a merchandising business.

How do the activities of NetSolutions, an attorney, and an architect, which are service businesses, differ from those of **Wal-Mart** or **Kmart**, which are merchandising businesses? These differences are best illustrated by focusing on the revenues and expenses in the following condensed income statements:

Service Business		Merchandising Business	
Fees earned	$XXX	Sales	$XXX
Operating expenses	−XXX	Cost of merchandise sold	−XXX
Net income	$XXX	Gross profit	$XXX
		Operating expenses	−XXX
		Net income	$XXX

The revenue activities of a service business involve providing services to customers. On the income statement for a service business, the revenues from services are reported as *fees earned*. The operating expenses incurred in providing the services are subtracted from the fees earned to arrive at *net income*.

In contrast, the revenue activities of a merchandising business involve the buying and selling of merchandise. A merchandising business must first purchase merchandise to sell to its customers. When this merchandise is sold, the revenue is reported

as sales, and its cost is recognized as an expense called the **cost of merchandise sold**. The cost of merchandise sold is subtracted from sales to arrive at gross profit. This amount is called **gross profit** because it is the profit *before* deducting operating expenses.

For many merchandising businesses, the cost of merchandise sold is usually the largest expense. For example, the approximate percentage of cost of merchandise sold to sales is 70% for **JC Penney Company** and 72% for **The Home Depot**.

Merchandise on hand (not sold) at the end of an accounting period is called **merchandise inventory**. Merchandise inventory is reported as a current asset on the balance sheet.

In the remainder of this chapter, we illustrate transactions that affect the income statement (sales, cost of merchandise sold, and gross profit) and the balance sheet (merchandise inventory). We will assume that NetSolutions implemented the second phase of its business plan in January 2004. During the fall of 2003, NetSolutions notified its customers that it would terminate its consulting services on December 31, 2003. Beginning on January 1, 2004, NetSolutions began operations as an Internet-based retailer of software and hardware for individuals and small businesses.

Merchandise transactions are recorded in a journal and posted to the accounts, using the rules of debit and credit that we described and illustrated in earlier chapters. This simple manual system is often modified, however, to more efficiently record transactions. For example, as the number of suppliers increases, the ledger becomes unwieldy when a separate account for each supplier is included. Thus, individual accounts payable to suppliers may be placed in a separate ledger, called a **subsidiary ledger**. Similarly, individual accounts receivable from customers may be placed in a subsidiary ledger. Each subsidiary ledger is represented in the primary ledger (now called the **general ledger**) by a summarizing account, called a **controlling account**. The balance of this controlling account must equal the sum of the balances of the individual accounts in the subsidiary ledger. For example, the accounts payable controlling account must equal the sum of the balances of the accounts in the accounts payable subsidiary ledger.[1]

> Sales – Cost of Merchandise Sold = Gross Profit
>
> Gross Profit – Operating Expenses = Net Income

Accounting for Purchases

objective 2a

Journalize the entries for merchandise purchases.

There are two systems for accounting for merchandise: perpetual and periodic. In the **perpetual inventory system**, each purchase and sale of merchandise is recorded in an inventory account. As a result, the amount of merchandise available for sale and the amount sold are continuously (perpetually) disclosed in the inventory records. In the **periodic inventory system**, the inventory records do not show the amount available for sale or sold during the period. Instead, a detailed listing of the merchandise for sale (called a **physical inventory**) at the end of the accounting period is prepared. This physical inventory is used to determine the cost of the merchandise on hand at the end of the period and the cost of the merchandise sold during the period.

Large retailers and many small merchandising businesses use computerized perpetual inventory systems. Such systems

> **In a perpetual inventory system, each purchase and the cost of each sale are recorded in Merchandise Inventory.**

---

[1] Subsidiary ledgers are further described and illustrated in Appendix D.

normally use bar codes, such as the one on the back of this textbook. An optical scanner reads the bar code to record merchandise purchased and sold.

Because the perpetual inventory system is widely used, we illustrate it in this chapter. We describe and illustrate the periodic inventory system in a later chapter and in an appendix at the end of the text.

Under the perpetual inventory system, cash purchases of merchandise are recorded as follows:

Retailers, such as **Best Buy**, **Kmart**, **Sears**, and **Wal-Mart**, and grocery store chains, such as **Winn-Dixie** and **Kroger**, use bar codes and optical scanners as part of their computerized inventory systems.

	Date		Description	Post. Ref.	Debit	Credit	
	JOURNAL					**PAGE 24**	
1	20— Jan.	3	Merchandise Inventory		2 5 1 0 00		1
2			Cash			2 5 1 0 00	2
3			Purchased inventory from Bowen Co.				3

Purchases of merchandise on account are recorded as follows:

	Date		Description	Post. Ref.	Debit	Credit	
5	Jan.	4	Merchandise Inventory		9 2 5 0 00		5
6			Accounts Payable—Thomas Corporation			9 2 5 0 00	6
7			Purchased inventory on account.				7

Purchases Discounts

The terms of a purchase are normally indicated on the **invoice** or bill that the seller sends to the buyer. An example of such an invoice is shown in Exhibit 1.

Exhibit 1 Invoice

Omega Technologies
1000 Matrix Blvd.
San Jose, CA. 95116-1000

Made in U.S.A.

SOLD TO	CUSTOMER'S ORDER NO. & DATE
NetSolutions 5101 Washington Ave. Cincinnati, OH 45227-5101	412 Jan. 10, 2004
	REFER TO INVOICE NO. 106-8

DATE SHIPPED	HOW SHIPPED AND ROUTE	TERMS	INVOICE DATE
Jan. 12, 2004	US Express Trucking Co.	2/10, n/30	Jan. 12, 2004
FROM San Francisco	**F.O.B.** Cincinnati	**PREPAID OR COLLECT?** Prepaid	

QUANTITY	DESCRIPTION	UNIT PRICE	AMOUNT
10	3COM Megahertz 10/100 Lan PC Card	150.00	1,500.00

If an invoice dated August 13 has terms n/30, what is the due date of the invoice?

September 12 [30 days = 18 days in August (31 days − 13 days) + 12 days in September]

The terms for when payments for merchandise are to be made, agreed on by the buyer and the seller, are called the **credit terms**. If payment is required on delivery, the terms are *cash* or *net cash*. Otherwise, the buyer is allowed an amount of time, known as the **credit period**, in which to pay.

The credit period usually begins with the date of the sale as shown on the invoice. If payment is due within a stated number of days after the date of the invoice, such as 30 days, the terms are *net 30 days*. These terms may be written as *n/30*.[2] If payment is due by the end of the month in which the sale was made, the terms are written as *n/eom*.

As a means of encouraging the buyer to pay before the end of the credit period, the seller may offer a discount. For example, a seller may offer a 2% discount if the buyer pays within 10 days of the invoice date. If the buyer does not take the discount, the total amount is due within 30 days. These terms are expressed as *2/10, n/30* and are read as *2% discount if paid within 10 days, net amount due within 30 days*. The credit terms of 2/10, n/30 are summarized in Exhibit 2, using the information from the invoice in Exhibit 1.

Exhibit 2 Credit Terms

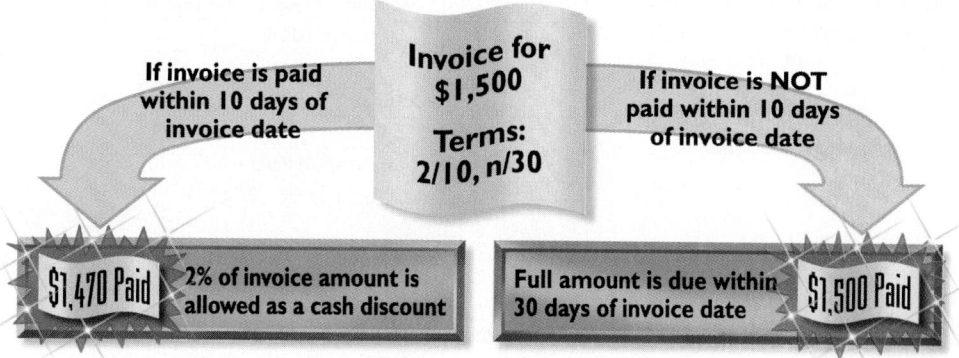

If an invoice dated November 22 has credit terms 2/10, n/30, what is (a) the last day the invoice may be paid within the discount period and (b) the last day of the credit period if the discount is not taken?

(a) December 2 [10 days = 8 days in November (30 days − 22 days) + 2 days in December];
(b) December 22 [30 days = 8 days in November (30 days − 22 days) + 22 days in December]

Discounts taken by the buyer for early payment of an invoice are called **purchases discounts**. These discounts reduce the cost of the merchandise purchased. Most businesses design their accounting systems so that all available discounts are taken. Even if the buyer has to borrow to make the payment within a discount period, it is normally to the buyer's advantage to do so. To illustrate, assume that NetSolutions borrows money to pay the invoice for $1,500, shown in Exhibit 1. The last day of the discount period in which the $30 discount can be taken is January 22, 2004. The money is borrowed for the remaining 20 days of the credit period. If we assume an annual interest rate of 12% and a 360-day year, the interest on the loan of $1,470 ($1,500 − $30) is $9.80 ($1,470 × 12% × 20/360). The net savings to NetSolutions is $20.20, computed as follows:

Discount of 2% on $1,500	$30.00
Interest for 20 days at rate of 12% on $1,470	− 9.80
Savings from borrowing	$20.20

The savings can also be seen by comparing the interest rate on the money saved by taking the discount and the interest rate on the money borrowed to take

---

[2] The word *net* as used here does not have the usual meaning of a number after deductions have been subtracted, as in *net income*.

the discount. For NetSolutions, the interest rate on the money saved in this example is estimated by converting 2% for 20 days to a yearly rate, as follows:

$$2\% \times \frac{360 \text{ days}}{20 \text{ days}} = 2\% \times 18 = 36\%$$

If NetSolutions borrows the money to take the discount, it *pays* interest of 12%. If NetSolutions does not take the discount, it *pays* estimated interest of 36% for using the $30 for an additional 20 days.

Under the perpetual inventory system, the buyer initially debits the merchandise inventory account for the amount of the invoice. When paying the invoice, the buyer credits the merchandise inventory account for the amount of the discount. In this way, the merchandise inventory shows the *net* cost to the buyer. For example, NetSolutions would record the invoice in Exhibit 1 and its payment at the end of the discount period as follows:

Jan.	12	Merchandise Inventory	1 5 0 0 00	
		Accounts Payable—Omega Technologies		1 5 0 0 00
		Invoice 106-8.		
	22	Accounts Payable—Omega Technologies	1 5 0 0 00	
		Cash		1 4 7 0 00
		Merchandise Inventory		3 0 00
		Paid Invoice 106-8.		

If NetSolutions does not take the discount because it does not pay Invoice 106-8 until February 11, it would record the payment as follows:

Feb.	11	Accounts Payable—Omega Technologies	1 5 0 0 00	
		Cash		1 5 0 0 00
		Paid Invoice 106-8 after discount		
		period.		

Purchases Returns and Allowances

When merchandise is returned (**purchases return**) or a price adjustment is requested (**purchases allowance**), the buyer (debtor) usually sends the seller a letter or a debit memorandum. A **debit memorandum**, shown in Exhibit 3, informs the seller of the amount the buyer proposes to *debit* to the account payable due the seller. It also states the reasons for the return or the request for a price reduction.

The buyer may use a copy of the debit memorandum as the basis for recording the return or allowance or wait for approval from the seller (creditor). In either case, the buyer must debit Accounts Payable and credit Merchandise Inventory. To illustrate, NetSolutions records the return of the merchandise indicated in the debit memo in Exhibit 3 as follows:

Mar.	7	Accounts Payable—Maxim Systems	9 0 0 00	
		Merchandise Inventory		9 0 0 00
		Debit Memo No. 18.		

Exhibit 3 Debit
Memorandum

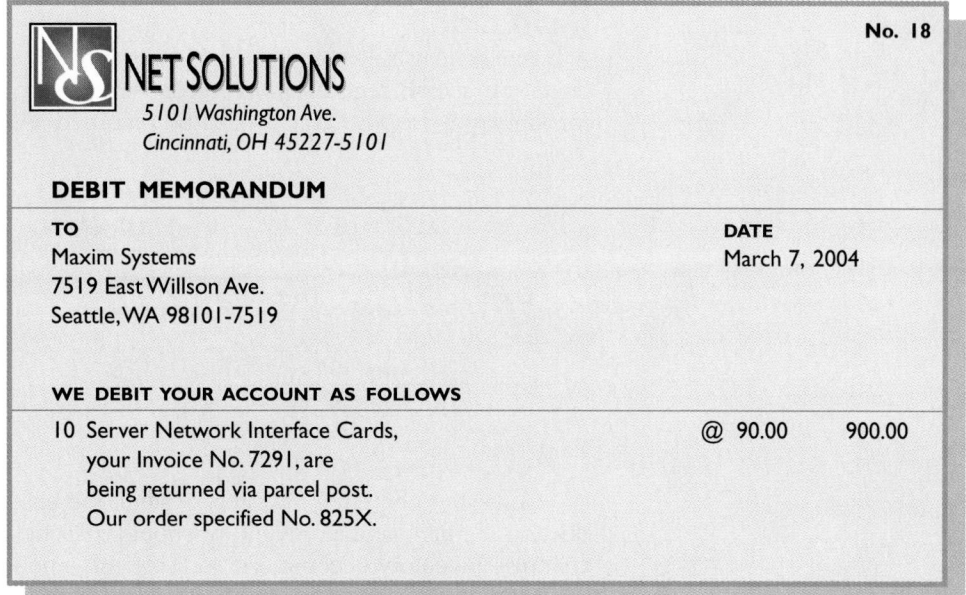

When a buyer returns merchandise or has been granted an allowance prior to paying the invoice, the amount of the debit memorandum is deducted from the invoice amount. The amount is deducted before the purchase discount is computed. For example, assume that on May 2, NetSolutions purchases $5,000 of merchandise from Alpha Data Link, subject to terms 2/10, n/30. On May 4, NetSolutions returns $3,000 of the merchandise, and on May 12, NetSolutions pays the original invoice less the return. NetSolutions would record these transactions as follows:

Ennis Co. purchases merchandise of $8,000 on terms 2/10, n/30. Ennis pays the original invoice, less a return of $2,500, within the discount period. How much did Ennis Co. pay?

$5,390 [($8,000 − $2,500) × 2% = $110 discount; $8,000 − $2,500 − $110 = $5,390]

May	2	Merchandise Inventory		5 0 0 0 00		
		Accounts Payable—Alpha Data Link			5 0 0 0 00	
		Purchased merchandise.				
	4	Accounts Payable—Alpha Data Link		3 0 0 0 00		
		Merchandise Inventory			3 0 0 0 00	
		Returned portion of merchandise				
		purchased.				
	12	Accounts Payable—Alpha Data Link		2 0 0 0 00		
		Cash			1 9 6 0 00	
		Merchandise Inventory			4 0 00	
		Paid invoice [($5,000 − $3,000) × 2%				
		= $40; $2,000 − $40 = $1,960].				

Accounting for Sales

objective 2b

Journalize the entries for merchandise sales.

Revenue from merchandise sales is usually identified in the ledger as *Sales*. Sometimes a business will use a more exact title, such as *Sales of Merchandise*.

Cash Sales

A business may sell merchandise for cash. Cash sales are normally rung up (entered) on a cash register and recorded in the accounts. To illustrate, if cash sales for January 3 are $1,800, they can be recorded as follows:

	Date		Description	Post. Ref.	Debit	Credit	
			JOURNAL			**PAGE 25**	
1	20— Jan.	3	Cash		1 8 0 0 00		1
2			Sales			1 8 0 0 00	2
3			To record cash sales.				3

Under the perpetual inventory system, the cost of merchandise sold and the reduction in merchandise inventory should also be recorded. In this way, the merchandise inventory account will indicate the amount of merchandise on hand (not sold). On the income statement at the end of the period, the balance of the cost of merchandise sold account is subtracted from the related sales for the period in order to determine the gross profit. To illustrate, assume that the cost of merchandise sold on January 3 was $1,200. The entry to record the cost of merchandise sold and the reduction in the merchandise inventory is as follows:

	Date		Description		Debit	Credit
	Jan.	3	Cost of Merchandise Sold		1 2 0 0 00	
			Merchandise Inventory			1 2 0 0 00
			To record the cost of merchandise			
			sold.			

How do retailers record sales made with the use of credit cards? Sales made to customers using credit cards issued by banks, such as **MasterCard** or **VISA**, are recorded as *cash sales*. The seller deposits the credit card receipts for these sales directly into its bank account.

Normally, banks charge service fees for handling credit card sales. The seller debits these service fees to an expense account. An entry at the end of a month to record the payment of service charges on bank credit card sales is shown below.

	Date		Description		Debit	Credit
	Jan.	31	Credit Card Expense		4 8 00	
			Cash			4 8 00
			To record service charges on credit			
			card sales for the month.			

Sales on Account

A business may sell merchandise on account. The seller records such sales as a debit to Accounts Receivable and a credit to Sales. An example of an entry for a sale on account of $510 follows. The cost of merchandise sold was $280.

	Date		Description		Debit	Credit
	Jan.	12	Accounts Receivable—Sims Co.		5 1 0 00	
			Sales			5 1 0 00
			Invoice No. 7172.			

Jan.	12	Cost of Merchandise Sold		2 8 0 00			
		Merchandise Inventory				2 8 0 00	
		Cost of merchandise sold on Invoice					
		No. 7172.					

A retailer may accept **MasterCard** or **VISA** but not **American Express**. Why? The service fees that credit card companies charge retailers are the primary reason that some businesses do not accept all credit cards. For example, American Express Co.'s service fees are normally higher than MasterCard's or VISA's. As a result, some retailers choose not to accept American Express cards. The disadvantage of this practice is that the retailer may lose customers to competitors who do accept American Express cards.

Sales may also be made to customers using nonbank credit cards. An example of a nonbank credit card is the **American Express** card. Nonbank credit card sales must first be reported to the card company before cash is received. Therefore, such sales create a *receivable* with the card company. Before the card company pays cash, it normally deducts a service fee. For example, assume that American Express card sales of $1,000 are made and reported to the card company on January 20. The cost of the merchandise sold was $550. On January 27, the card company deducts a service fee of $50 and sends $950 to the seller. These transactions are recorded by the seller as follows:

Jan.	20	Accounts Receivable—American Express		1 0 0 0 00			
		Sales				1 0 0 0 00	
		American Express (nonbank) credit card					
		sales.					
	20	Cost of Merchandise Sold		5 5 0 00			
		Merchandise Inventory				5 5 0 00	
		Cost of merchandise sold on American					
		Express credit card sales.					
	27	Cash		9 5 0 00			
		Credit Card Expense		5 0 00			
		Accounts Receivable—American Express				1 0 0 0 00	
		Received cash from American Express for					
		sales reported on January 20.					

Sales Discounts

As we mentioned in our discussion of purchase transactions, a seller may offer the buyer credit terms that include a discount for early payment. The seller refers to such discounts as **sales discounts**, which reduce sales revenue.

To reduce sales, the sales account could be debited. However, managers may want to know the amount of the sales discounts for a period in deciding whether to change credit terms. For this reason, the seller records the sales discounts in a separate account. The sales discounts account is a *contra* (or *offsetting*) account to Sales. To illustrate, assume that cash is received within the discount period (10 days) from the credit sale of $1,500, shown on the invoice in Exhibit 1. Omega Technologies would record the receipt of the cash as follows:

Jan.	22	Cash		1 4 7 0 00			
		Sales Discounts		3 0 00			
		Accounts Receivable—NetSolutions				1 5 0 0 00	
		Collection on Invoice No. 106-8, less					
		2% discount.					

Sales Returns and Allowances

Merchandise sold may be returned to the seller (**sales return**). In addition, because of defects or for other reasons, the seller may reduce the initial price at which the goods were sold (**sales allowance**). If the return or allowance is for a sale on account, the seller usually issues the buyer a **credit memorandum**. This memorandum shows the amount of and the reason for the seller's credit to an account receivable. A credit memorandum is illustrated in Exhibit 4.

Exhibit 4 Credit Memorandum

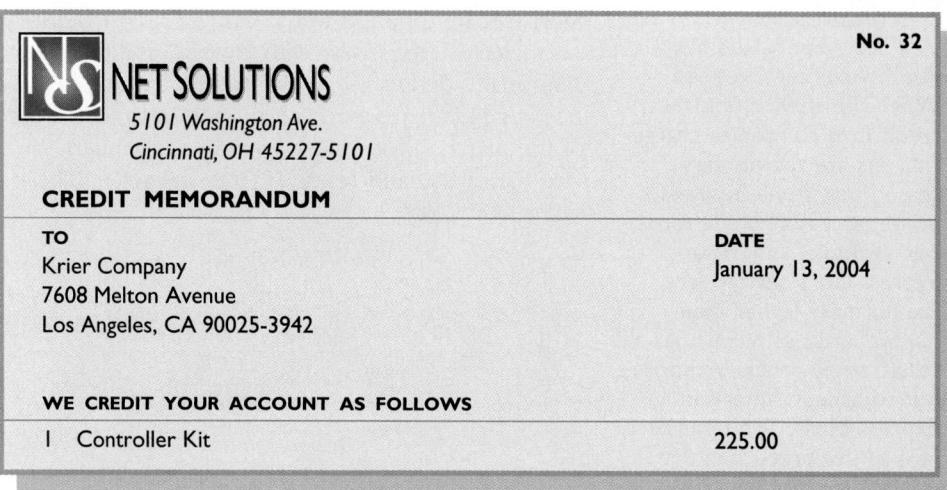

NET SOLUTIONS
5101 Washington Ave.
Cincinnati, OH 45227-5101

No. 32

CREDIT MEMORANDUM

TO	DATE
Krier Company	January 13, 2004
7608 Melton Avenue	
Los Angeles, CA 90025-3942	

WE CREDIT YOUR ACCOUNT AS FOLLOWS

| 1 | Controller Kit | 225.00 |

Like sales discounts, sales returns and allowances reduce sales revenue. They also result in additional shipping and other expenses. Since managers often want to know the amount of returns and allowances for a period, the seller records sales returns and allowances in a separate account. Sales Returns and Allowances is a *contra* (or *offsetting*) account to Sales.

The seller debits Sales Returns and Allowances for the amount of the return or allowance. If the original sale was on account, the seller credits Accounts Receivable. Since the merchandise inventory is kept up to date in a perpetual system, the seller adds the cost of the returned merchandise to the merchandise inventory account. The seller must also credit the cost of returned merchandise to the cost of merchandise sold account, since this account was debited when the original sale was recorded. To illustrate, assume that the cost of the merchandise returned in Exhibit 4 was $140. NetSolutions records the credit memo in Exhibit 4 as follows:

Jan.	13	Sales Returns and Allowances	2 2 5 00	
		Accounts Receivable—Krier Company		2 2 5 00
		Credit Memo No. 32.		
	13	Merchandise Inventory	1 4 0 00	
		Cost of Merchandise Sold		1 4 0 00
		Cost of merchandise returned, Credit		
		Memo No. 32.		

What if the buyer pays for the merchandise and the merchandise is later returned? In this case, the seller may issue a credit and apply it against other accounts receivable owed by the buyer, or the cash may be refunded. If the credit is applied against the buyer's other receivables, the seller records entries similar to those preceding. If cash is refunded for merchandise returned or for an allowance, the seller debits Sales Returns and Allowances and credits Cash.

Sales Taxes

The five states with the highest sales tax are Illinois, Minnesota, Nevada, Texas, and Washington. Some states have no sales tax, including Alaska, Delaware, Montana, New Hampshire, and Oregon.

Almost all states and many other taxing units levy a tax on sales of merchandise.[3] The liability for the sales tax is incurred when the sale is made.

At the time of a cash sale, the seller collects the sales tax. When a sale is made on account, the seller charges the tax to the buyer by debiting Accounts Receivable. The seller credits the sales account for the amount of the sale and credits the tax to Sales Tax Payable. For example, the seller would record a sale of $100 on account, subject to a tax of 6%, as follows:

Business collects sales tax from customers

Business remits sales tax to state

Aug.	12	Accounts Receivable—Lemon Co.		1 0 6 00		
		Sales			1 0 0 00	
		Sales Tax Payable			6 00	
		Invoice No. 339.				

Normally on a regular basis, the seller pays to the taxing unit the amount of the sales tax collected. The seller records such a payment as follows:

Sept.	15	Sales Tax Payable		2 9 0 0 00	
		Cash			2 9 0 0 00
		Payment for sales taxes collected			
		during August.			

Trade Discounts

Wholesalers are businesses that sell merchandise to other businesses rather than to the general public. Many wholesalers publish catalogs. Rather than updating their catalogs frequently, wholesalers often publish price updates, which may involve large discounts from the list prices in their catalogs. In addition, wholesalers may offer special discounts to certain classes of buyers, such as government agencies or businesses that order large quantities. Such discounts are called **trade discounts**.

Sellers and buyers do not normally record the list prices of merchandise and the related trade discounts in their accounts. For example, assume that an item has a list price of $1,000 and a 40% trade discount. The seller records the sale of the item at $600 [$1,000 less the trade discount of $400 ($1,000 × 40%)]. Likewise, the buyer records the purchase at $600.

A seller offered a 30% trade discount on an item listed in its catalog for $2,400. At what amount would the buyer record the purchase?

$1,680 [$2,400 − ($2,400 × 30%), or $2,400 × 70%]

----

[3] Businesses that purchase merchandise for resale to others are normally exempt from paying sales taxes on their purchases. Only final buyers of merchandise normally pay sales taxes.

Transportation Costs

objective 2c

Journalize the entries for merchandise transportation costs.

The terms of a sale should indicate when the ownership (title) of the merchandise passes to the buyer. This point determines which party, the buyer or the seller, must pay the transportation costs.[4]

The ownership of the merchandise may pass to the buyer when the seller delivers the merchandise to the transportation company or freight carrier. For example, **DaimlerChrysler** records the sale and the transfer of ownership of its vehicles to dealers when the vehicles are shipped. In this case, the terms are said to be **FOB (free on board) shipping point**. This term means that DaimlerChrysler is responsible for the transportation charges to the shipping point, which is where the shipment originates. The dealer then pays the transportation costs to the final destination. Such costs are part of the dealer's total cost of purchasing inventory and should be added to the cost of the inventory by debiting Merchandise Inventory.

> **The buyer bears the transportation costs if the shipping terms are FOB shipping point.**

To illustrate, assume that on June 10, NetSolutions buys merchandise from Magna Data on account, $900, terms FOB shipping point, and pays the transportation cost of $50. NetSolutions records these two transactions as follows:

Date		Description		Debit	Credit
June	10	Merchandise Inventory		900 00	
		Accounts Payable—Magna Data			900 00
		Purchased merchandise, terms FOB			
		shipping point.			
	10	Merchandise Inventory		50 00	
		Cash			50 00
		Paid shipping cost on merchandise			
		purchased.			

> **The seller bears the transportation costs if the shipping terms are FOB destination.**

The ownership of the merchandise may pass to the buyer when the buyer receives the merchandise. In this case, the terms are said to be **FOB (free on board) destination**. This term means that the seller delivers the merchandise to the buyer's final destination, free of transportation charges to the buyer. The seller thus pays the transportation costs to the final destination. The seller debits Transportation Out or Delivery Expense, which is reported on the seller's income statement as an expense.

To illustrate, assume that on June 15, NetSolutions sells merchandise to Kranz Company on account, $700, terms FOB destination. The cost of the merchandise sold is $480, and NetSolutions pays the transportation cost of $40. NetSolutions records the sale, the cost of the sale, and the transportation cost as follows:

---

[4] The passage of title also determines whether the buyer or seller must pay other costs, such as the cost of insurance, while the merchandise is in transit.

June	15	Accounts Receivable—Kranz Company	7 0 0 00	
		Sales		7 0 0 00
		Sold merchandise, terms FOB		
		destination.		
	15	Cost of Merchandise Sold	4 8 0 00	
		Merchandise Inventory		4 8 0 00
		Recorded cost of merchandise sold to		
		Kranz Company.		
	15	Transportation Out	4 0 00	
		Cash		4 0 00
		Paid shipping cost on merchandise sold.		

Sometimes FOB shipping point and FOB destination are expressed in terms of the location at which the title to the merchandise passes to the buyer. For example, if **Toyota Motor Co.'s** assembly plant in Osaka, Japan, sells automobiles to a dealer in Chicago, FOB shipping point could be expressed as FOB Osaka. Likewise, FOB destination could be expressed as FOB Chicago.

Shipping terms, the passage of title, and whether the buyer or seller is to pay the transportation costs are summarized in Exhibit 5.

Exhibit 5 Transportation Terms

TERMS: FOB SHIPPING POINT

Buyer pays freight costs and debits Merchandise Inventory

Seller's warehouse — Freight costs — Buyer's warehouse

SHIPPING POINT   DESTINATION

Title passes to buyer

TERMS: FOB DESTINATION

Seller pays freight costs and debits Transportation Out

Seller's warehouse — Freight costs — Buyer's warehouse

SHIPPING POINT   DESTINATION

Title passes to buyer

Q&A Martin Co. sells $4,000 of merchandise to Oblinger Co. on account on terms 2/10, n/30, FOB shipping point. As a convenience to Oblinger, Martin Co. pays transportation costs of $250 and adds those costs to the invoice. (a) How much will Martin Co. bill Oblinger? (b) If Oblinger Co. pays within the discount period, what amount will Oblinger pay Martin?

(a) $4,250 ($4,000 + $250); (b) $4,170 [$4,000 − ($4,000 × 2%) + $250]

As a convenience to the buyer, the seller may prepay the transportation costs, even though the terms are FOB shipping point. The seller will then add the transportation costs to the invoice. The buyer will debit Merchandise Inventory for the total amount of the invoice, including the transportation costs.

To illustrate, assume that on June 20, NetSolutions sells merchandise to Planter Company on account, $800, terms FOB shipping point. NetSolutions pays the transportation cost of $45 and adds it to the invoice.

The cost of the merchandise sold is $360. NetSolutions records these transactions as follows:

June	20	Accounts Receivable—Planter Company		8 0 0 00	
		Sales			8 0 0 00
		Sold merchandise, terms FOB shipping point.			
	20	Cost of Merchandise Sold		3 6 0 00	
		Merchandise Inventory			3 6 0 00
		Recorded cost of merchandise sold to Planter Company.			
	20	Accounts Receivable—Planter Company		4 5 00	
		Cash			4 5 00
		Prepaid shipping cost on merchandise sold.			

Illustration of Accounting for Merchandise Transactions

objective 2d

Journalize the entries for merchandise transactions for both the buyer and the seller.

Each merchandising transaction affects a buyer and a seller. In the following illustration, we show how the same transactions would be recorded by both the seller and the buyer. In this example, the seller is Scully Company and the buyer is Burton Co.

Transaction	Scully Company (Seller)			Burton Co. (Buyer)		
July 1. Scully Company sold merchandise on account to Burton Co., $7,500, terms FOB shipping point, n/45. The cost of the merchandise sold was $4,500.	Accounts Receivable—Burton Co.	7,500		Merchandise Inventory	7,500	
	Sales		7,500	Accounts Payable—Scully Co.		7,500
	Cost of Merchandise Sold	4,500				
	Merchandise Inventory		4,500			
July 2. Burton Co. paid transportation charges of $150 on July 1 purchase from Scully Company.	No entry.			Merchandise Inventory	150	
				Cash		150
July 5. Scully Company sold merchandise on account to Burton Co., $5,000, terms FOB destination, n/30. The cost of the merchandise sold was $3,500.	Accounts Receivable—Burton Co.	5,000		Merchandise Inventory	5,000	
	Sales		5,000	Accounts Payable—Scully Co.		5,000
	Cost of Merchandise Sold	3,500				
	Merchandise Inventory		3,500			

Transaction	Scully Company (Seller)			Burton Co. (Buyer)		
July 7. Scully Company paid transportation costs of $250 for delivery of merchandise sold to Burton Co. on July 5.	Transportation Out Cash	250	250	No entry.		
July 13. Scully Company issued Burton Co. a credit memorandum for merchandise returned, $1,000. The merchandise had been purchased by Burton Co. on account on July 5. The cost of the merchandise returned was $700.	Sales Returns & Allowances Accounts Receivable—Burton Co. Merchandise Inventory Cost of Merchandise Sold	1,000 700	1,000 700	Accounts Payable—Scully Co. Merchandise Inventory	1,000	1,000
July 15. Scully Company received payment from Burton Co. for purchase of July 5.	Cash Accounts Receivable—Burton Co.	4,000	4,000	Accounts Payable—Scully Co. Cash	4,000	4,000
July 18. Scully Company sold merchandise on account to Burton Co., $12,000, terms FOB shipping point, 2/10, n/eom. Scully Company prepaid transportation costs of $500, which were added to the invoice. The cost of the merchandise sold was $7,200.	Accounts Receivable—Burton Co. Sales Accounts Receivable—Burton Co. Cash Cost of Merchandise Sold Merchandise Inventory	12,000 500 7,200	12,000 500 7,200	Merchandise Inventory Accounts Payable—Scully Co.	12,500	12,500
July 28. Scully Company received payment from Burton Co. for purchase of July 18, less discount (2% × $12,000).	Cash Sales Discounts Accounts Receivable—Burton Co.	12,260 240	12,500	Accounts Payable—Scully Co. Merchandise Inventory Cash	12,500	240 12,260

Chart of Accounts for a Merchandising Business

The chart of accounts for a merchandising business should reflect the types of merchandising transactions we have described in this chapter. As a basis for illustration, we use NetSolutions.

On January 1, 2004, when NetSolutions began its operations as an Internet-based retailer of software and hardware, it stopped providing consulting services. As a result, NetSolutions' chart of accounts changed from that of a service business to that of a merchandiser. A new chart of accounts for NetSolutions is shown in Exhibit 6. The accounts related to merchandising transactions are shown in color.

NetSolutions is now using three-digit account numbers, which permits it to add new accounts as they are needed. The first digit indicates the major financial statement classification (1 for assets, 2 for liabilities, and so on). The second digit indicates the subclassification (e.g., 11 for current assets, 12 for noncurrent assets).

Exhibit 6 Chart of Accounts for NetSolutions, Merchandising Business

Balance Sheet Accounts		Income Statement Accounts	
	100 Assets		400 Revenues
110	Cash	410	Sales
111	Notes Receivable	411	Sales Returns and Allowances
112	Accounts Receivable	412	Sales Discounts
113	Interest Receivable		500 Costs and Expenses
115	Merchandise Inventory	510	Cost of Merchandise Sold
116	Office Supplies	520	Sales Salaries Expense
117	Prepaid Insurance	521	Advertising Expense
120	Land	522	Depreciation Expense—Store Equipment
123	Store Equipment		
124	Accumulated Depreciation— Store Equipment	523	Transportation Out
		529	Miscellaneous Selling Expense
125	Office Equipment	530	Office Salaries Expense
126	Accumulated Depreciation— Office Equipment	531	Rent Expense
		532	Depreciation Expense—Office Equipment
	200 Liabilities		
210	Accounts Payable	533	Insurance Expense
211	Salaries Payable	534	Office Supplies Expense
212	Unearned Rent	539	Misc. Administrative Expense
215	Notes Payable		600 Other Income
	300 Stockholders' Equity	610	Rent Revenue
310	Capital Stock	611	Interest Revenue
311	Retained Earnings		700 Other Expense
312	Dividends	710	Interest Expense
313	Income Summary		

The third digit identifies the specific account (e.g., 110 for Cash, 123 for Store Equipment).

NetSolutions is using a more complex numbering system because it has a greater variety of transactions. In addition, its growth creates a need for more detailed information for use in managing it. For example, a wages expense account was adequate for NetSolutions when it was a small service business with few employees. However, as a merchandising business, NetSolutions now uses two payroll accounts, one for Sales Salaries Expense and one for Office Salaries Expense.

Income Statement for a Merchandising Business

objective 4

Prepare an income statement for a merchandising business.

Although merchandising transactions affect the balance sheet in reporting inventory, they primarily affect the income statement. There are two widely used formats for preparing an income statement for a merchandising business: multiple step and single step.

Multiple-Step Form

The multiple-step income statement contains several sections, subsections, and subtotals. We use NetSolutions' income statement, shown in Exhibit 7, as a basis for illustrating this form of statement.

Exhibit 7 Multiple-Step Income Statement

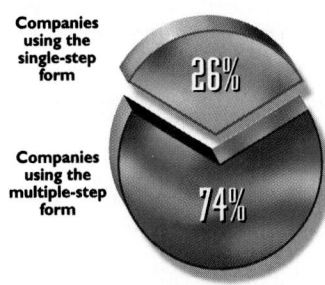

The multiple-step form is used more often than the single-step form, as shown here.

Companies using the single-step form **26%**

Companies using the multiple-step form **74%**

Source: 1999 edition of Accounting Trends & Techniques.

NetSolutions
Income Statement
For the Year Ended December 31, 2004

Revenue from sales:				
Sales			$720 1 8 5 00	
Less: Sales returns and allowances	$ 6 1 4 0 00			
Sales discounts	5 7 9 0 00		11 9 3 0 00	
Net sales				$708 2 5 5 00
Cost of merchandise sold				525 3 0 5 00
Gross profit				$182 9 5 0 00
Operating expenses:				
Selling expenses:				
Sales salaries expense	$60 0 3 0 00			
Advertising expense	10 8 6 0 00			
Depr. expense—store equipment	3 1 0 0 00			
Miscellaneous selling expense	6 3 0 00			
Total selling expense			$ 74 6 2 0 00	
Administrative expenses:				
Office salaries expense	$21 0 2 0 00			
Rent expense	8 1 0 0 00			
Depr. expense—office equipment	2 4 9 0 00			
Insurance expense	1 9 1 0 00			
Office supplies expense	6 1 0 00			
Misc. administrative expense	7 6 0 00			
Total administrative expenses			34 8 9 0 00	
Total operating expenses				109 5 1 0 00
Income from operations				$ 73 4 4 0 00
Other income:				
Interest revenue	$ 3 8 0 0 00			
Rent revenue	6 0 0 00			
Total other income			$ 4 4 0 0 00	
Other expense:				
Interest expense			2 4 4 0 00	1 9 6 0 00
Net income				$ 75 4 0 0 00

The amount of detail presented in the various sections varies from company to company. For example, instead of reporting gross sales, sales returns and allowances, and sales discounts, some companies just report net sales.

Revenue from Sales

The total amount charged customers for merchandise sold, for cash and on account, is reported in this section. Sales returns and allowances and sales discounts are deducted from this total to yield *net sales*.

Cost of Merchandise Sold

The cost of merchandise sold during the period may also be called the **cost of goods sold** or the **cost of sales**.

If net sales is $500,000 and gross profit is $180,000, what is the cost of merchandise sold?

$320,000

Gross Profit

The excess of net sales over the cost of merchandise sold is called the **gross profit**. It is sometimes called **gross profit on sales** or **gross margin**.

Operating Expenses

Most merchandising businesses classify operating expenses as either selling expenses or administrative expenses. Expenses that are incurred directly in the selling of merchandise are selling expenses. They include such expenses as salespersons' salaries, store supplies used, depreciation of store equipment, and advertising. Expenses incurred in the administration or general operations of the business are administrative expenses or **general expenses**. Examples of these expenses are office salaries, depreciation of office equipment, and office supplies used. Credit card expense is also normally classified as an administrative expense.

Expenses that are related to both selling and administration may be divided between the two classifications. In small businesses, however, such expenses as rent,

BUSINESS ON STAGE

Retailing

Retail operations can be classified as either (1) in-store retailing or (2) non-store retailing. There are ten general types of in-store retailing and four general types of nonstore retailing. Each type is briefly described below.

In-Store Retailing	Description	Examples
Department	Offers a variety of merchandise in many departments under one roof; each department is a separate buying and selling center	Sears, Rich's, JCPenney, Bloomingdale's
Specialty store	Offers a specific type of merchandise and carries a complete assortment	Toys R Us, Radio Shack, Zales Jewelers, Circuit City
Variety store	Offers a variety of inexpensive goods	Dollar General, Ben Franklin
Convenience store	Offers convenience goods, with long store hours	Circle K, 7 Eleven
Supermarket	Offers a wide variety of food, with self-service	Safeway, Kroger, Publix
Discount store	Offers low prices and high turnover of merchandise	Target, Kmart, Wal-Mart
Off-price retailer	Offers merchandise at prices 25% or more below normal prices, with low service	T.J. Maxx, Ross
Factory outlet store	Offers close-outs and factory seconds; usually owned by the manufacturer	Levi Strauss, Bass, Polo, Lenox
Wholesale club	Offers food and general merchandise at deeply discounted prices to members	Sam's, Costco
Catalog store	Offers merchandise in showrooms where customers order from catalogs	Sears, Cabela's

Nonstore Retailing	Description	Examples
Vending machine	Offers merchandise for sale from machines	Canteen
Direct selling	Salesperson sells merchandise in customer's home	Avon, Amway
Direct response marketing	Offers merchandise for sale through catalogs, direct mail, and advertising	Lands' End, J. Crew, L.L. Bean
Internet selling	Offers merchandise for sale through the Internet	Amazon.com CDNOW

insurance, and taxes are commonly reported as administrative expenses. Transactions for small, infrequent expenses are often reported as Miscellaneous Selling Expense or Miscellaneous Administrative Expense.

Income from Operations

The excess of gross profit over total operating expenses is called income from operations or operating income. The relationships of income from operations to total assets and to net sales are important factors in judging the efficiency and profitability of operations. If operating expenses are greater than the gross profit, the excess is called a loss from operations.

Other Income and Other Expense

Revenue from sources other than the primary operating activity of a business is classified as other income. In a merchandising business, these items include income from interest, rent, and gains resulting from the sale of fixed assets.

Expenses that cannot be traced directly to operations are identified as other expense. Interest expense that results from financing activities and losses incurred in the disposal of fixed assets are examples of these items.

Other income and other expense are offset against each other on the income statement. If the total of other income exceeds the total of other expense, the difference is added to income from operations. If the reverse is true, the difference is subtracted from income from operations.

Net Income

The final figure on the income statement is called **net income** (or **net loss**). It is the net increase (or net decrease) in the owner's equity as a result of the period's profit-making activities.

Single-Step Form

In the single-step income statement, the total of all expenses is deducted *in one step* from the total of all revenues. Such a statement is shown in Exhibit 8 for NetSolutions. The statement has been condensed to focus on its primary features.

The single-step form emphasizes total revenues and total expenses as the factors that determine net income. A criticism of the single-step form is that such amounts as gross profit and income from operations are not readily available for analysis.

Intel Corporation recently reported over $2 billion in other income from gains on the sale of investments in **Micron Technology Inc.** and other investment income.

Exhibit 8 Single-Step Income Statement

NetSolutions Income Statement For the Year Ended December 31, 2004		
Revenues:		
Net sales		$708 2 5 5 00
Interest revenue		3 8 0 0 00
Rent revenue		6 0 0 00
Total revenues		$712 6 5 5 00
Expenses:		
Cost of merchandise sold	$525 3 0 5 00	
Selling expenses	74 6 2 0 00	
Administrative expenses	34 8 9 0 00	
Interest expense	2 4 4 0 00	
Total expenses		637 2 5 5 00
Net income		$ 75 4 0 0 00

The Accounting Cycle for a Merchandising Business

objective 5

Describe the accounting cycle for a merchandising business.

Earlier in this chapter, we described and illustrated the chart of accounts and the analysis and recording of transactions for a merchandising business. We also illustrated the preparation of an income statement for a merchandiser, NetSolutions, at the end of an accounting cycle. In the remainder of this chapter, we describe the other elements of the accounting cycle for a merchandising business. In this discussion, we will focus primarily on the elements of this cycle that are likely to differ from those of a service business.

Merchandise Inventory Shrinkage

In 2000, retailers lost an estimated $28 billion to inventory shrinkage. The primary causes of the shrinkage were employee theft (44.2%), shoplifting (33.5%), and errors (17.2%).

"Crooked Workers Cost Stores," Renee DeGross, *The Atlanta Journal Constitution*, September 21, 2000.

Under the perpetual inventory system, a separate merchandise inventory account is maintained in the ledger. During the accounting period, this account shows the amount of merchandise for sale at any time. However, merchandising businesses may experience some loss of inventory due to shoplifting, employee theft, or errors in recording or counting inventory. As a result, the physical inventory taken at the end of the accounting period may differ from the amount of inventory shown in the inventory records. Normally, the amount of merchandise for sale, as indicated by the balance of the merchandise inventory account, is larger than the total amount of merchandise counted during the physical inventory. For this reason, the difference is often called **inventory shrinkage** or **inventory shortage**.

To illustrate, NetSolutions' inventory records indicate that $63,950 of merchandise should be available for sale on December 31, 2004. The physical inventory taken on December 31, 2004, however, indicates that only $62,150 of merchandise is actually available. Thus, the inventory shrinkage for the year ending December 31, 2004, is $1,800 ($63,950 − $62,150), as shown at the right. This amount is recorded by the following adjusting entry:

If the inventory account has a balance of $280,000 and the physical inventory indicates merchandise on hand of $265,000, what is the amount of inventory shrinkage?

$15,000 ($280,000 − $265,000)

		Adjusting Entry												
Dec.	31	Cost of Merchandise Sold	1	8	0	0	00							
		Merchandise Inventory						1	8	0	0	00		

After this entry has been recorded, the accounting records agree with the actual physical inventory at the end of the period. Since no system of procedures and safeguards can totally eliminate it, inventory shrinkage is often considered a normal cost of operations. If the amount of the shrinkage is abnormally large, it may be disclosed separately on the income statement. In such cases, the shrinkage may be recorded in a separate account, such as Loss from Merchandise Inventory Shrinkage.

Work Sheet

Merchandising businesses that use a perpetual inventory system are also likely to use a computerized accounting system. In a computerized system, the adjusting entries are recorded and financial statements prepared without using a work sheet. For this reason, we illustrate the work sheet and the adjusting entries for NetSolutions in the appendix at the end of this chapter.

Retained Earnings Statement

The retained earnings statement for NetSolutions is shown in Exhibit 9. This statement is prepared in the same manner that we described previously for a service business.

Exhibit 9 Retained Earnings Statement for Merchandising Business

NetSolutions Retained Earnings Statement For the Year Ended December 31, 2004		
Retained earnings, January 1, 2004		$128 8 0 0 00
Net income for year	$75 4 0 0 00	
Less dividends	18 0 0 0 00	
Increase in retained earnings		57 4 0 0 00
Retained earnings, December 31, 2004		$186 2 0 0 00

Balance Sheet

As we discussed and illustrated in previous chapters, the balance sheet may be presented with assets on the left-hand side and the liabilities and stockholders' equity on the right-hand side. This form of the balance sheet is called the **account form**. The balance sheet may also be presented in a downward sequence in three sections. This form of balance sheet is called the **report form**. The report form of balance sheet for NetSolutions is shown in Exhibit 10. In this balance sheet, note that merchandise inventory at the end of the period is reported as a current asset and that the current portion of the note payable is $5,000.

Closing Entries

The closing entries for a merchandising business are similar to those for a service business. The first entry closes the temporary accounts with credit balances, such as Sales, to the income summary account. The second entry closes the temporary accounts with debit balances, including Sales Returns and Allowances, Sales Discounts, and Cost of Merchandise Sold, to the income summary account. The third entry closes the balance of the income summary account to the retained earnings account. The fourth entry closes the dividends account to the retained earnings account.

In a computerized accounting system, the closing entries are prepared automatically. For this reason, we illustrate the closing entries for NetSolutions in the appendix at the end of this chapter.

Exhibit 10 Report Form of
Balance Sheet

NetSolutions Balance Sheet December 31, 2004				
Assets				
Current assets:				
Cash		$52 9 5 0 00		
Notes receivable		35 0 0 0 00		
Accounts receivable		55 8 8 0 00		
Interest receivable		2 0 0 00		
Merchandise inventory		62 1 5 0 00		
Office supplies		4 8 0 00		
Prepaid insurance		2 6 5 0 00		
Total current assets			$209 3 1 0 00	
Property, plant, and equipment:				
Land		$20 0 0 0 00		
Store equipment	$27 1 0 0 00			
Less accumulated depreciation	5 7 0 0 00	21 4 0 0 00		
Office equipment	$15 5 7 0 00			
Less accumulated depreciation	4 7 2 0 00	10 8 5 0 00		
Total property, plant, and equipment			52 2 5 0 00	
Total assets			$261 5 6 0 00	
Liabilities				
Current liabilities:				
Accounts payable		$22 4 2 0 00		
Note payable (current portion)		5 0 0 0 00		
Salaries payable		1 1 4 0 00		
Unearned rent		1 8 0 0 00		
Total current liabilities			$ 30 3 6 0 00	
Long-term liabilities:				
Note payable (final payment due 2014)			20 0 0 0 00	
Total liabilities			$ 50 3 6 0 00	
Stockholders' Equity				
Capital stock		$ 25 0 0 0 00		
Retained earnings		186 2 0 0 00	211 2 0 0 00	
Total liabilities and stockholders' equity			$261 5 6 0 00	

FINANCIAL ANALYSIS AND INTERPRETATION

objective 6

Compute the ratio of net sales to assets as a measure of how effectively a business is using its assets.

The ratio of net sales to assets measures how effectively a business is using its assets to generate sales. A high ratio indicates an effective use of assets. The assets used in computing the ratio may be the total assets at the end of the year, the average of the total assets at the beginning and end of the year, or the average of the monthly assets. For our purposes, we will use the average of the total assets at the beginning and end of the year. The ratio is computed as follows:

$$\text{Ratio of net sales to assets} = \frac{\textbf{Net sales}}{\textbf{Average total assets}}$$

To illustrate the use of this ratio, the following data are taken from annual reports of **Sears** and **JCPenney**:

	Sears	JCPenney
Net sales (in millions)	$41,071	$30,678
Total assets (in millions):		
Beginning of year	37,675	23,638
End of year	36,954	23,493

The ratio of net sales to assets for each company is as follows:

	Sears	JCPenney
Ratio of net sales to assets:	1.10*	1.30**

*$41,071/[($37,675 + $36,954)/2]
**$30,678/[($23,638 + $23,493)/2]

Based on these ratios, JCPenney appears better than Sears in utilizing its assets to generate sales. Comparing this ratio over time for both Sears and JCPenney, as well as comparing it with industry averages, would provide a better basis for interpreting the financial performance of each company.

ENCORE

Wal-Mart

As a young man just out of the Army, Sam Walton wanted to go into retailing and operate his own business. With $5,000 of his own money and a loan of $20,000 from his father-in-law, he opened his first store in Newport, Arkansas, on September 1, 1945. This first store was a Ben Franklin variety store. Within five years, this store was the No. 1 Ben Franklin store—for sales and profit—not only in Arkansas, but in a six-state region. Unfortunately, Sam forgot to include a renewal clause in the lease for his store building. His landlord decided not to renew Sam's lease, but instead offered to buy the business, including fixtures and inventory. The landlord wanted to purchase the profitable store for his son to own and operate. Without any other suitable location in town, Sam had to sell.

Unwilling to quit, Sam purchased a new store in Bentonville, Arkansas, and opened Walton's Five and Dime on August 1, 1951. By 1960, Sam had opened fifteen variety stores, with revenues of $1.4 million. Sam realized the potential of discounting when a regional discounter moved into Arkansas. So Sam opened his first Wal-Mart on July 2, 1962, choosing the name Wal-Mart because it didn't have many letters, which would make it cheaper to build and maintain the store signs. To avoid competing with Kmart, Sam initially expanded into small towns of less than 10,000 people.

The rest of the story is history. Wal-Mart grew from 32 stores and $31 million in sales in 1970 to 276 stores and $1.2 billion in sales in 1980.

Sam Walton

Today it has over 2,000 stores and $95 billion in sales. During that time, Wal-Mart issued stock, opened Sam's Clubs, and Sam Walton became one of the richest men in America. ■

APPENDIX: WORK SHEET AND ADJUSTING AND CLOSING ENTRIES FOR A MERCHANDISING BUSINESS

A merchandising business that does not use a computerized accounting system may use a work sheet in assembling the data for preparing financial statements and adjusting and closing entries. In this appendix, we illustrate such a work sheet, along with the adjusting and closing entries for a merchandising business.

The work sheet in Exhibit 11 is for NetSolutions on December 31, 2004, the end of its first year of operations as a merchandiser. In this work sheet, we list all of the accounts, including the accounts that have no balances, in the order that they appear in NetSolutions' ledger.

The data needed for adjusting the accounts of NetSolutions are as follows:

 NET SOLUTIONS

Interest accrued on notes receivable on December 31, 2004		$ 200
Physical merchandise inventory on December 31, 2004		62,150
Office supplies on hand on December 31, 2004		480
Insurance expired during 2004		1,910
Depreciation during 2004 on: Store equipment		3,100
Office equipment		2,490
Salaries accrued on December 31, 2004: Sales salaries	$780	
Office salaries	360	1,140
Rent earned during 2004		600

There is no specific order in which to analyze the accounts in the work sheet, assemble the adjustment data, and make the adjusting entries. However, you can normally save time by selecting the accounts in the order in which they appear on the trial balance. Using this approach, the adjustment for accrued interest is listed first {entry (a) on the work sheet}, followed by the adjustment for merchandise inventory shrinkage {entry (b) on the work sheet}, and so on.

After all the adjustments have been entered on the work sheet, the Adjustments columns are totaled to prove the equality of debits and credits. As we illustrated in previous chapters, the adjusted amounts of the balances in the Trial Balance columns are extended to the Adjusted Trial Balance columns.[5] The Adjusted Trial Balance columns are then totaled to prove the equality of debits and credits.

The balances, as adjusted, are then extended to the statement columns. The four statement columns are totaled, and the net income or net loss is determined. For NetSolutions, the difference between the credit and debit columns of the Income Statement section is $75,400, the amount of the net income. The difference between the debit and credit columns of the Balance Sheet section is also $75,400, which is the increase in retained earnings as a result of the net income. Agreement between the two balancing amounts is evidence of debit-credit equality and mathematical accuracy.

The income statement, retained earnings statement, and balance sheet are prepared from the work sheet in a manner similar to that of a service business. The Adjustments columns in the work sheet provide the data for journalizing the adjusting entries. NetSolutions' adjusting entries at the end of 2004 are shown on page F210.

---

[5] Some accountants prefer to eliminate the Adjusted Trial Balance columns and to extend the adjusted balances directly to the statement columns. Such a work sheet is often used if there are only a few adjustment items.

Exhibit 11 Work Sheet for Merchandising Business

NetSolutions
Work Sheet
For the Year Ended December 31, 2004

	Account Title	Trial Balance Dr.	Trial Balance Cr.	Adjustments Dr.	Adjustments Cr.	Adjusted Trial Balance Dr.	Adjusted Trial Balance Cr.	Income Statement Dr.	Income Statement Cr.	Balance Sheet Dr.	Balance Sheet Cr.	
1	Cash	52,950				52,950				52,950		1
2	Notes Receivable	35,000				35,000				35,000		2
3	Accounts Receivable	55,880				55,880				55,880		3
4	Interest Receivable			(a) 200		200				200		4
5	Merchandise Inventory	63,950			(b)1,800	62,150				62,150		5
6	Office Supplies	1,090			(c) 610	480				480		6
7	Prepaid Insurance	4,560			(d)1,910	2,650				2,650		7
8	Land	20,000				20,000				20,000		8
9	Store Equipment	27,100				27,100				27,100		9
10	Accum. Depr.—Store Equip.		2,600		(e)3,100		5,700				5,700	10
11	Office Equipment	15,570				15,570				15,570		11
12	Accum. Depr.—Office Equip.		2,230		(f) 2,490		4,720				4,720	12
13	Accounts Payable		22,420				22,420				22,420	13
14	Salaries Payable				(g)1,140		1,140				1,140	14
15	Unearned Rent		2,400	(h) 600			1,800				1,800	15
16	Notes Payable											16
17	(final payment due 2014)		25,000				25,000				25,000	17
18	Capital Stock		25,000				25,000				25,000	18
19	Retained Earnings		128,800				128,800				128,800	19
20	Dividends	18,000				18,000				18,000		20
21	Sales		720,185				720,185		720,185			21
22	Sales Returns and Allowances	6,140				6,140		6,140				22
23	Sales Discounts	5,790				5,790		5,790				23
24	Cost of Merchandise Sold	523,505		(b)1,800		525,305		525,305				24
25	Sales Salaries Expense	59,250		(g) 780		60,030		60,030				25
26	Advertising Expense	10,860				10,860		10,860				26
27	Depr. Exp.—Store Equip.			(e)3,100		3,100		3,100				27
28	Miscellaneous Selling Expense	630				630		630				28
29	Office Salaries Expense	20,660		(g) 360		21,020		21,020				29
30	Rent Expense	8,100				8,100		8,100				30
31	Depr. Exp.—Office Equip.			(f)2,490		2,490		2,490				31
32	Insurance Expense			(d)1,910		1,910		1,910				32
33	Office Supplies Expense			(c) 610		610		610				33
34	Misc. Administrative Expense	760				760		760				34
35	Rent Revenue				(h) 600		600		600			35
36	Interest Revenue		3,600		(a) 200		3,800		3,800			36
37	Interest Expense	2,440				2,440		2,440				37
38		932,235	932,235	11,850	11,850	939,165	939,165	649,185	724,585	289,980	214,580	38
39	Net income							75,400			75,400	39
40								724,585	724,585	289,980	289,980	40

(a) Interest earned but not received on notes receivable, $200.

(b) Merchandise inventory shrinkage for period, $1,800 ($63,950 − $62,150).

(c) Office supplies used, $610 ($1,090 − $480).

(d) Insurance expired, $1,910.

(e) Depreciation of store equipment, $3,100.

(f) Depreciation of office equipment, $2,490.

(g) Salaries accrued but not paid
   (sales salaries, $780; office salaries, $360), $1,140.

(h) Rent earned from amount received in advance, $600.

	Date		Description	Post. Ref.	Debit	Credit	
			JOURNAL			**PAGE 28**	
1	2004		Adjusting Entries				1
2	Dec.	31	Interest Receivable	113	2 0 0 00		2
3			Interest Revenue	611		2 0 0 00	3
4							4
5		31	Cost of Merchandise Sold	510	1 8 0 0 00		5
6			Merchandise Inventory	115		1 8 0 0 00	6
7							7
8		31	Office Supplies Expense	534	6 1 0 00		8
9			Office Supplies	116		6 1 0 00	9
10							10
11		31	Insurance Expense	533	1 9 1 0 00		11
12			Prepaid Insurance	117		1 9 1 0 00	12
13							13
14		31	Depreciation Expense—				14
15			Store Equipment	522	3 1 0 0 00		15
16			Accumulated Depreciation—				16
17			Store Equipment	124		3 1 0 0 00	17
18							18
19		31	Depreciation Expense—				19
20			Office Equipment	532	2 4 9 0 00		20
21			Accumulated Depreciation—				21
22			Office Equipment	126		2 4 9 0 00	22
23							23
24		31	Sales Salaries Expense	520	7 8 0 00		24
25			Office Salaries Expense	530	3 6 0 00		25
26			Salaries Payable	211		1 1 4 0 00	26
27							27
28		31	Unearned Rent	212	6 0 0 00		28
29			Rent Revenue	610		6 0 0 00	29

The Income Statement columns of the work sheet provide the data for preparing the closing entries. The closing entries for NetSolutions at the end of 2004 are as follows:

	Date		Description	Post. Ref.	Debit	Credit	
			JOURNAL			**PAGE 29**	
1	2004						1
2		31	Sales	410	720 1 8 5 00		2
3			Rent Revenue	610	6 0 0 00		3
4			Interest Revenue	611	3 8 0 00		4
5			Income Summary	313		724 5 8 5 00	5

	Date	Description	Post. Ref.	Debit	Credit	
7	31	Income Summary	313	649 1 8 5 00		7
8		Sales Returns and Allowances	411		6 1 4 0 00	8
9		Sales Discounts	412		5 7 9 0 00	9
10		Cost of Merchandise Sold	510		525 3 0 5 00	10
11		Sales Salaries Expense	520		60 0 3 0 00	11
12		Advertising Expense	521		10 8 6 0 00	12
13		Depr. Expense—Store Equipment	522		3 1 0 0 00	13
14		Miscellaneous Selling Expense	529		6 3 0 00	14
15		Office Salaries Expense	530		21 0 2 0 00	15
16		Rent Expense	531		8 1 0 0 00	16
17		Depr. Expense—Office Equipment	532		2 4 9 0 00	17
18		Insurance Expense	533		1 9 1 0 00	18
19		Office Supplies Expense	534		6 1 0 00	19
20		Misc. Administrative Expense	539		7 6 0 00	20
21		Interest Expense	710		2 4 4 0 00	21
22						22
23	31	Income Summary	313	75 4 0 0 00		23
24		Retained Earnings	311		75 4 0 0 00	24
25						25
26	31	Retained Earnings	311	18 0 0 0 00		26
27		Dividends	312		18 0 0 0 00	27

JOURNAL **PAGE 29**

The balance of Income Summary, after the first two closing entries have been posted, is the net income or net loss for the period. The third closing entry transfers this balance to the retained earnings account. NetSolutions' income summary account after the closing entries have been posted is as follows:

	Date	Item	Post. Ref.	Debit	Credit	Balance Debit	Balance Credit
	2004 Dec. 31	Revenues	29		724 5 8 5 00		724 5 8 5 00
	31	Expenses	29	649 1 8 5 00			75 4 0 0 00
	31	Net income	29	75 4 0 0 00		—	—

ACCOUNT *Income Summary* **ACCOUNT NO. 313**

After the closing entries have been prepared and posted to the accounts, a post-closing trial balance may be prepared to verify the debit-credit equality. The only accounts that should appear on the post-closing trial balance are the asset, contra asset, liability, and stockholders' equity accounts with balances. These are the same accounts that appear on the end-of-period balance sheet.

KEY POINTS

1 Distinguish the activities of a service business from those of a merchandising business.

The primary differences between a service business and a merchandising business relate to revenue activities. Merchandising businesses purchase merchandise for selling to customers.

On a merchandising business's income statement, revenue from selling merchandise is reported as sales. The cost of the merchandise sold is subtracted from sales to arrive at gross profit. The operating expenses are subtracted from gross profit to arrive at net income.

Merchandise inventory, which is merchandise not sold, is reported as a current asset on the balance sheet.

2a Journalize the entries for merchandise purchases.

Purchases of merchandise for cash or on account are recorded by debiting Merchandise Inventory. For purchases of merchandise on account, the credit terms may allow cash discounts for early payment. Such purchases discounts are viewed as a reduction in the cost of the merchandise purchased. When merchandise is returned or a price adjustment is granted, the buyer credits Merchandise Inventory.

2b Journalize the entries for merchandise sales.

Sales of merchandise for cash or on account are recorded by crediting Sales. The cost of merchandise sold and the reduction in merchandise inventory are also recorded for the sale.

For sales of merchandise on account, the credit terms may allow sales discounts for early payment. Such discounts are recorded by the seller as a debit to Sales Discounts. Sales

discounts are reported as a deduction from the amount initially recorded in Sales. Likewise, when merchandise is returned or a price adjustment is granted, the seller debits Sales Returns and Allowances. The liability for sales tax is incurred when the sale is made and is recorded by the seller as a credit to the sales tax payable account. When the amount of the sales tax is paid to the taxing unit, Sales Tax Payable is debited and Cash is credited.

Many wholesalers offer trade discounts, which are discounts off the list prices of merchandise. Normally, neither the seller or the buyer records the list price and the related trade discount in the accounts.

2c Journalize the entries for merchandise transportation costs.

When merchandise is shipped FOB shipping point, the buyer pays the transportation costs and debits Merchandise Inventory. When merchandise is shipped FOB destination, the seller pays the transportation costs and debits Transportation Out or Delivery Expense. If the seller prepays transportation costs as a convenience to the buyer, the seller debits Accounts Receivable for the costs.

2d Journalize the entries for merchandise transactions for both the buyer and the seller.

The illustration in this chapter summarizes the entries that the seller and the buyer of merchandise would record.

3 Prepare a chart of accounts for a merchandising business.

The chart of accounts for a merchandising business is more complex than that for a service business and normally includes accounts such as Sales, Sales Discounts, Sales Returns and Allowances, Cost of Merchandise Sold, and Merchandise Inventory.

4 Prepare an income statement for a merchandising business.

The income statement for a merchandising business reports sales, cost of merchandise sold, and gross profit. The income statement can be prepared in either the multiple-step form or the single-step form.

5 Describe the accounting cycle for a merchandising business.

The accounting cycle for a merchandising business is similar to that of a service business. However, a merchandiser is likely to experience inventory shrinkage, which must be recorded. The normal adjusting entry is to debit Cost of Merchandise Sold and credit Merchandise Inventory for the amount of the shrinkage.

The balance sheet may be prepared in either the account form or the report form. Merchandise inventory should be reported as a current asset.

6 Compute the ratio of net sales to assets as a measure of how effectively a business is using its assets.

The assets used in computing the ratio of net sales to assets may be total assets at the end of the year, the average of the total assets at the beginning and end of the year, or the average of the monthly assets. A high ratio of net sales to assets indicates an effective use of assets.

ILLUSTRATIVE PROBLEM

The following transactions were completed by Montrose Company during May of the current year. Montrose Company uses a perpetual inventory system.

May 3. Purchased merchandise on account from Floyd Co., $4,000, terms FOB shipping point, 2/10, n/30, with prepaid transportation costs of $120 added to the invoice.

5. Purchased merchandise on account from Kramer Co., $8,500, terms FOB destination, 1/10, n/30.

6. Sold merchandise on account to C. F. Howell Co., list price $4,000, trade discount 30%, terms 2/10, n/30. The cost of the merchandise sold was $1,125.

8. Purchased office supplies for cash, $150.

10. Returned merchandise purchased on May 5 from Kramer Co., $1,300.

13. Paid Floyd Co. on account for purchase of May 3, less discount.

14. Purchased merchandise for cash, $10,500.

15. Paid Kramer Co. on account for purchase of May 5, less return of May 10 and discount.

16. Received cash on account from sale of May 6 to C. F. Howell Co., less discount.

19. Sold merchandise on nonbank credit cards and reported accounts to the card company, American Express, $2,450. The cost of the merchandise sold was $980.

22. Sold merchandise on account to Comer Co., $3,480, terms 2/10, n/30. The cost of the merchandise sold was $1,400.

24. Sold merchandise for cash, $4,350. The cost of the merchandise sold was $1,750.

25. Received merchandise returned by Comer Co. from sale on May 22, $1,480. The cost of the returned merchandise was $600.

31. Received cash from card company for nonbank credit card sales of May 19, less $140 service fee.

Instructions

1. Journalize the preceding transactions.
2. Journalize the adjusting entry for merchandise inventory shrinkage, $3,750.

Solution

1.

May	3	Merchandise Inventory	4,120	
		Accounts Payable—Floyd Co.		4,120
	5	Merchandise Inventory	8,500	
		Accounts Payable—Kramer Co.		8,500
	6	Accounts Receivable—C. F. Howell Co.	2,800	
		Sales		2,800
		[$4,000 − (30% × $4,000)]		
	6	Cost of Merchandise Sold	1,125	
		Merchandise Inventory		1,125
	8	Office Supplies	150	
		Cash		150
	10	Accounts Payable—Kramer Co.	1,300	
		Merchandise Inventory		1,300
	13	Accounts Payable—Floyd Co.	4,120	
		Merchandise Inventory		80
		Cash		4,040
		[$4,000 − (2% × $4,000) + $120]		
	14	Merchandise Inventory	10,500	
		Cash		10,500

(continued)

May 15	Accounts Payable—Kramer Co.		7,200	
	Merchandise Inventory			72
	Cash			7,128
	[($8,500 − $1,300) × 1% = $72;			
	$8,500 − $1,300 − $72 = $7,128]			
16	Cash		2,744	
	Sales Discounts		56	
	Accounts Receivable—C. F. Howell Co.			2,800
19	Accounts Receivable—American Express		2,450	
	Sales			2,450
19	Cost of Merchandise Sold		980	
	Merchandise Inventory			980
22	Accounts Receivable—Comer Co.		3,480	
	Sales			3,480
22	Cost of Merchandise Sold		1,400	
	Merchandise Inventory			1,400
24	Cash		4,350	
	Sales			4,350
24	Cost of Merchandise Sold		1,750	
	Merchandise Inventory			1,750
25	Sales Returns and Allowances		1,480	
	Accounts Receivable—Comer Co.			1,480
25	Merchandise Inventory		600	
	Cost of Merchandise Sold			600
31	Cash		2,310	
	Credit Card Expense		140	
	Accounts Receivable—American Express			2,450

2.

May 31	Cost of Merchandise Sold		3,750	
	Merchandise Inventory			3,750

SELF-EXAMINATION QUESTIONS

Answers at End of Chapter

Matching

Match each of the following statements with its proper term. Some terms may not be used.

A. **account form**

B. **administrative expenses (general expenses)**

C. **controlling account**

D. **cost of merchandise sold**

E. **credit memorandum**

F. **debit memorandum**

G. **FOB (free on board) destination**

___ 1. The cost that is reported as an expense when merchandise is sold.

___ 2. Sales minus the cost of merchandise sold.

___ 3. Merchandise on hand (not sold) at the end of an accounting period.

___ 4. The account in the general ledger that summarizes the balances of the accounts in a subsidiary ledger.

___ 5. The primary ledger, when used in conjunction with subsidiary ledgers, that contains all of the balance sheet and income statement accounts.

___ 6. A ledger containing individual accounts with a common characteristic.

___ 7. The inventory system in which each purchase and sale of merchandise is recorded in an inventory account.

H.	**FOB (free on board) shipping point**
I.	**general ledger**
J.	**gross profit**
K.	**income from operations (operating income)**
L.	**inventory shrinkage**
M.	**invoice**
N.	**loss from operations**
O.	**merchandise inventory**
P.	**multiple-step income statement**
Q.	**other expense**
R.	**other income**
S.	**periodic inventory system**
T.	**perpetual inventory system**
U.	**physical inventory**
V.	**purchases return or allowance**
W.	**purchases discounts**
X.	**report form**
Y.	**sales discounts**
Z.	**sales return or allowance**
AA.	**selling expenses**
BB.	**single-step income statement**
CC.	**subsidiary ledger**
DD.	**trade discounts**

___ 8. The inventory system in which the inventory records do not show the amount available for sale or sold during the period.

___ 9. A detailed listing of the merchandise for sale at the end of an accounting period.

___ 10. The bill that the seller sends to the buyer.

___ 11. Discounts taken by the buyer for early payment of an invoice.

___ 12. From the buyer's perspective, returned merchandise or an adjustment for defective merchandise.

___ 13. A form used by a buyer to inform the seller of the amount the buyer proposes to debit to the account payable due the seller.

___ 14. From the seller's perspective, discounts that a seller may offer the buyer for early payment.

___ 15. From the seller's perspective, returned merchandise or an adjustment for defective merchandise.

___ 16. A form used by a seller to inform the buyer of the amount the seller proposes to credit to the account receivable due from the buyer.

___ 17. Discounts from the list prices in published catalogs or special discounts offered to certain classes of buyers.

___ 18. Freight terms in which the buyer pays the transportation costs from the shipping point to the final destination.

___ 19. Freight terms in which the seller pays the transportation costs from the shipping point to the final destination.

___ 20. A form of income statement that contains several sections, subsections, and subtotals.

___ 21. Expenses that are incurred directly in the selling of merchandise.

___ 22. Expenses incurred in the administration or general operations of the business.

___ 23. The excess of gross profit over total operating expenses.

___ 24. The excess of operating expenses over gross profit.

___ 25. Revenue from sources other than the primary operating activity of a business.

___ 26. Expenses that cannot be traced directly to operations.

___ 27. A form of income statement in which the total of all expenses is deducted from the total of all revenues.

___ 28. The amount by which the merchandise for sale, as indicated by the balance of the merchandise inventory account, is larger than the total amount of merchandise counted during the physical inventory.

___ 29. The form of balance sheet in which assets are reported on the left-hand side and the liabilities and stockholders' equity on the right-hand side.

___ 30. The form of balance sheet in which assets, liabilities, and stockholders' equity are reported in a downward sequence.

Multiple Choice

1. If merchandise purchased on account is returned, the buyer may inform the seller of the details by issuing:
   A. a debit memorandum
   B. a credit memorandum
   C. an invoice
   D. a bill

2. If merchandise is sold on account to a customer for $1,000, terms FOB shipping point, 1/10, n/30, and the seller prepays $50 in transportation costs, the amount of the discount for early payment would be:
   A. $0   C. $10.00
   B. $5.00   D. $10.50

3. The income statement in which the total of all expenses is deducted from the total of all revenues is termed:
   A. multiple-step form C. account form
   B. single-step form D. report form

4. On a multiple-step income statement, the excess of net sales over the cost of merchandise sold is called:
   A. operating income
   B. income from operations
   C. gross profit
   D. net income

5. Which of the following expenses would normally be classified as Other expense on a multiple-step income statement?
   A. Depreciation expense—office equipment
   B. Sales salaries expense
   C. Insurance expense
   D. Interest expense

CLASS DISCUSSION QUESTIONS

1. What distinguishes a merchandising business from a service business?
2. Can a business earn a gross profit but incur a net loss? Explain.
3. What is the name of the account in which purchases of merchandise are recorded in a perpetual inventory system?
4. What is the name of the account in which sales of merchandise are recorded?
5. How does the accounting for sales to customers using bank credit cards, such as MasterCard and VISA, differ from accounting for sales to customers using nonbank credit cards, such as American Express?
6. The credit period during which the buyer of merchandise is allowed to pay usually begins with what date?
7. What is the meaning of (a) 1/10, n/60; (b) n/30; (c) n/eom?
8. It is not unusual for a customer to drive into some Texaco, Chevron, or Conoco gasoline stations and discover that the cash price per gallon is 3 or 4 cents less than the credit price per gallon. As a result, many customers pay cash rather than use their credit cards. Why would a gasoline station owner establish such a policy?
9. What is the nature of (a) a credit memorandum issued by the seller of merchandise, (b) a debit memorandum issued by the buyer of merchandise?
10. Who bears the transportation costs when the terms of sale are (a) FOB shipping point, (b) FOB destination?
11. Name at least three accounts that would normally appear in the chart of accounts of a merchandising business but would not appear in the chart of accounts of a service business.
12. Differentiate between the multiple-step and the single-step forms of the income statement.
13. What are the major advantages and disadvantages of the single-step form of income statement compared to the multiple-step statement?
14. What type of revenue is reported in the Other income section of the multiple-step income statement?
15. The Hansen Office Equipment, which uses a perpetual inventory system, experienced a normal inventory shrinkage of $12,860. What accounts would be debited and credited to record the adjustment for the inventory shrinkage at the end of the accounting period?
16. Assume that Hansen Office Equipment in Question 15 experienced an abnormal inventory shrinkage of $210,500. Hansen Office Equipment has decided to record the abnormal inventory shrinkage so that it would be separately disclosed on the income statement. What account would be debited for the abnormal inventory shrinkage?

EXERCISES

Exercise 5–1
Determining gross profit
Objective 1

During the current year, merchandise is sold for $170,000 cash and for $620,000 on account. The cost of the merchandise sold is $474,000.

a. What is the amount of the gross profit?
b. Compute the gross profit percentage (gross profit divided by sales).
c. ✏️ Will the income statement necessarily report a net income? Explain.

Exercise 5–2
Determining cost of merchandise sold
Objective 1

In 1999, **Walgreen Co.** reported net sales of $17,838.8 million. Its gross profit was $4,860.2 million. What was the amount of Walgreen's cost of merchandise sold?

Exercise 5–3
Purchase-related transaction
Objective 2

Degas Company purchased merchandise on account from a supplier for $3,500, terms 2/10, n/30. Degas Company returned $750 of the merchandise and received full credit.

a. If Degas Company pays the invoice within the discount period, what is the amount of cash required for the payment?
b. Under a perpetual inventory system, what account is credited by Degas Company to record the return?

Exercise 5–4
Determining amounts to be paid on invoices
Objective 2

✓ a. $2,772

Determine the amount to be paid in full settlement of each of the following invoices, assuming that credit for returns and allowances was received prior to payment and that all invoices were paid within the discount period.

	Merchandise	Transportation Paid by Seller		Returns and Allowances
a.	$4,000	—	FOB shipping point, 1/10, n/30	$1,200
b.	1,500	$50	FOB shipping point, 2/10, n/30	700
c.	9,500	—	FOB destination, n/30	400
d.	2,500	75	FOB shipping point, 1/10, n/30	600
e.	5,000	—	FOB destination, 2/10, n/30	—

Exercise 5–5
Purchase-related transactions

Objective 2

✓ B: $5,049

A retailer is considering the purchase of ten units of a specific item from either of two suppliers. Their offers are as follows:

A: $500 a unit, total of $5,000, 2/10, n/30, plus transportation costs of $175.
B: $510 a unit, total of $5,100, 1/10, n/30, no charge for transportation.

Which of the two offers, A or B, yields the lower price?

Exercise 5–6
Purchase-related transactions

Objective 2

The debits and credits from four related transactions are presented in the following T accounts. Describe each transaction.

Cash		
(2)	75
(4)	3,920

Accounts Payable			
(3)	1,000	(1)	5,000
(4)	4,000		

Merchandise Inventory			
(1)	5,000	(3)	1,000
(2)	75	(4)	80

Exercise 5–7
Purchase-related transactions

Objective 2

✓ (c) Cash, cr. $8,330

Citron Co., a women's clothing store, purchased $12,000 of merchandise from a supplier on account, terms FOB destination, 2/10, n/30. Citron Co. returned $3,500 of the merchandise, receiving a credit memorandum, and then paid the amount due within the discount period. Journalize Citron Co.'s entries to record (a) the purchase, (b) the merchandise return, and (c) the payment.

Exercise 5–8
Purchase-related transactions

Objective 2

✓ (e) Cash, dr. $960

Journalize entries for the following related transactions of Aloha Company:

a. Purchased $9,000 of merchandise from Green Co. on account, terms 2/10, n/30.
b. Paid the amount owed on the invoice within the discount period.
c. Discovered that $2,000 of the merchandise was defective and returned items, receiving credit.
d. Purchased $1,000 of merchandise from Green Co. on account, terms n/30.
e. Received a check for the balance owed from the return in (c), after deducting for the purchase in (d).

Exercise 5–9
Sales-related transactions, including the use of credit cards

Objective 2

Journalize the entries for the following transactions:

a. Sold merchandise for cash, $15,000. The cost of the merchandise sold was $8,500.
b. Sold merchandise on account, $7,500. The cost of the merchandise sold was $4,000.
c. Sold merchandise to customers who used MasterCard and VISA, $7,750. The cost of the merchandise sold was $3,850.
d. Sold merchandise to customers who used American Express, $8,100. The cost of the merchandise sold was $5,860.
e. Paid an invoice from First National Bank for $350, representing a service fee for processing MasterCard and VISA sales.
f. Received $7,776 from American Express Company after a $324 collection fee had been deducted.

Exercise 5–10
Sales returns and allowances

Objective 2

During the year, sales returns and allowances totaled $112,150. The cost of the merchandise returned was $67,300. The accountant recorded all the returns and allowances by debiting the sales account and crediting Cost of Merchandise Sold for $112,150. Was the accountant's method of recording returns acceptable? Explain. In your explanation, include the advantages of using a sales returns and allowances account.

Exercise 5–11
Sales-related transactions

Objective 2

After the amount due on a sale of $5,500, terms 2/10, n/eom, is received from a customer within the discount period, the seller consents to the return of the entire shipment. The cost of the merchandise returned was $3,380. (a) What is the amount of the refund owed to the customer? (b) Journalize the entries made by the seller to record the return and the refund.

Exercise 5–12
Sales-related transactions

Objective 2

The debits and credits for three related transactions are presented in the following T accounts. Describe each transaction.

	Cash					Sales	
(5)	7,425					(1)	10,000

	Accounts Receivable					Sales Discounts	
(1)	10,000	(3)	2,500	(5)	75		
		(5)	7,500				

	Merchandise Inventory					Sales Returns and Allowances	
(4)	1,500	(2)	6,000	(3)	2,500		

	Cost of Merchandise Sold		
(2)	6,000	(4)	1,500

Exercise 5–13
Sales-related transactions

Objective 2

✓ d. $15,175

Merchandise is sold on account to a customer for $15,000, terms FOB shipping point, 3/10, n/30. The seller paid the transportation costs of $625. Determine the following: (a) amount of the sale, (b) amount debited to Accounts Receivable, (c) amount of the discount for early payment, and (d) amount due within the discount period.

Exercise 5–14
Sales tax

Objective 2

✓ c. $3,180

A sale of merchandise on account for $3,000 is subject to a 6% sales tax. (a) Should the sales tax be recorded at the time of sale or when payment is received? (b) What is the amount of the sale? (c) What is the amount debited to Accounts Receivable? (d) What is the title of the account to which the $180 is credited?

Exercise 5–15
Sales tax transactions

Objective 2

Journalize the entries to record the following selected transactions:

a. Sold $6,000 of merchandise on account, subject to a sales tax of 5%. The cost of the merchandise sold was $3,600.
b. Paid $4,380 to the state sales tax department for taxes collected.

Exercise 5–16
Sales-related transactions

Objective 2

Sterile Co., a furniture wholesaler, sells merchandise to Bawd Co. on account, $8,000, terms 2/15, n/30. The cost of the merchandise sold is $4,800. Sterile Co. issues a credit memorandum for $500 for merchandise returned and subsequently receives the amount due within the discount period. The cost of the merchandise returned is $300. Journalize Sterile Co.'s entries for (a) the sale, including the cost of the merchandise sold, (b) the credit memorandum, including the cost of the returned merchandise, and (c) the receipt of the check for the amount due from Bawd Co.

Exercise 5–17
Purchase-related transactions

Objective 2

Based on the data presented in Exercise 5–16, journalize Bawd Co.'s entries for (a) the purchase, (b) the return of the merchandise for credit, and (c) the payment of the invoice within the discount period.

Exercise 5–18
Normal balances of merchandise accounts
Objective 2

What is the normal balance of the following accounts: (a) Cost of Merchandise Sold, (b) Merchandise Inventory, (c) Sales, (d) Sales Discounts, (e) Sales Returns and Allowances, (f) Transportation Out?

Exercise 5–19
Chart of accounts
Objective 3

Chime Co. is a newly organized business with the following list of accounts, arranged in alphabetical order:

Accounts Payable	Miscellaneous Selling Expense
Accounts Receivable	Notes Payable (short-term)
Accumulated Depreciation—Office Equipment	Notes Receivable (short-term)
Accumulated Depreciation—Store Equipment	Office Equipment
Advertising Expense	Office Salaries Expense
Capital Stock	Office Supplies
Cash	Office Supplies Expense
Cost of Merchandise Sold	Prepaid Insurance
Depreciation Expense—Office Equipment	Rent Expense
Depreciation Expense—Store Equipment	Retained Earnings
Dividends	Salaries Payable
Income Summary	Sales
Insurance Expense	Sales Discounts
Interest Expense	Sales Returns and Allowances
Interest Receivable	Sales Salaries Expense
Interest Revenue	Store Equipment
Land	Store Supplies
Merchandise Inventory	Store Supplies Expense
Miscellaneous Administrative Expense	Transportation Out

Construct a chart of accounts, assigning account numbers and arranging the accounts in balance sheet and income statement order, as illustrated in Exhibit 6. Each account number is three digits: the first digit is to indicate the major classification ("1" for assets, and so on); the second digit is to indicate the subclassification ("11" for current assets, and so on); and the third digit is to identify the specific account ("110" for Cash, and so on).

Exercise 5–20
Income statement for merchandiser
Objective 4

For the fiscal year, sales were $7,230,000, sales discounts were $320,000, sales returns and allowances were $580,000, and the cost of merchandise sold was $4,338,000. What was the amount of net sales and gross profit?

Exercise 5–21
Income statement for merchandiser
Objective 4

The following expenses were incurred by a merchandising business during the year. In which expense section of the income statement should each be reported: (a) selling, (b) administrative, or (c) other?

1. Advertising expense.
2. Depreciation expense on office equipment.
3. Insurance expense on store equipment.
4. Interest expense on notes payable.
5. Office supplies used.
6. Rent expense on office building.
7. Salaries of office personnel.
8. Salary of sales manager.

Exercise 5–22
Single-step income statement
Objective 4

✓ Net income: $1,532,500

Summary operating data for The Lifeboat Company during the current year ended April 30, 2003, are as follows: cost of merchandise sold, $1,460,000; administrative expenses, $225,000; interest expense, $37,500; rent revenue, $30,000; net sales, $3,600,000; and selling expenses, $375,000. Prepare a single-step income statement.

Exercise 5–23
Determining amounts for items omitted from income statement

Objective 4

✓ a. $10,000
✓ h. $690,000

Two items are omitted in each of the following four lists of income statement data. Determine the amounts of the missing items, identifying them by letter.

Sales	$298,000	$500,000	$700,000	$ (g)
Sales returns and allowances	(a)	15,000	(e)	30,500
Sales discounts	8,000	8,000	10,000	37,000
Net sales	280,000	(c)	665,000	(h)
Cost of merchandise sold	(b)	285,000	(f)	540,000
Gross profit	130,000	(d)	200,000	150,000

Exercise 5–24
Multiple-step income statement

Objective 4

How many errors can you find in the following income statement?

The Functor Company
Income Statement
For the Year Ended July 31, 2003

Revenue from sales:			
Sales			$3,000,000
Add: Sales returns and allowances	$58,000		
Sales discounts	14,500	72,500	
Gross sales			$3,072,500
Cost of merchandise sold			1,495,000
Income from operations			$1,577,500
Operating expenses:			
Selling expenses		$ 145,000	
Transportation out		5,300	
Administrative expenses		87,200	
Total operating expenses			237,500
			$1,340,000
Other expense:			
Interest revenue			47,500
Gross profit			$1,292,500

Exercise 5–25
Multiple-step income statement

Objective 4

✓ Net income: $97,500

On August 31, 2003, the balances of the accounts appearing in the ledger of Noble Company, a furniture wholesaler, are as follows:

Administrative Expenses	$ 60,000	Office Supplies	$ 10,600
Building	512,500	Retained Earnings	558,580
Capital Stock	50,000	Salaries Payable	3,220
Cash	48,500	Sales	775,000
Cost of Merchandise Sold	450,000	Sales Discounts	20,000
Dividends	25,000	Sales Returns and Allowances	45,000
Interest Expense	7,500	Selling Expenses	95,000
Merchandise Inventory	130,000	Store Supplies	7,700
Notes Payable	25,000		

a. Prepare a multiple-step income statement for the year ended August 31, 2003.
b. Compare the major advantages and disadvantages of the multiple-step and single-step forms of income statements.

Exercise 5–26
Adjusting entry for merchandise inventory shrinkage

Objective 5

Nocturnal Inc.'s perpetual inventory records indicate that $417,200 of merchandise should be on hand on October 31, 2003. The physical inventory indicates that $400,680 of merchandise is actually on hand. Journalize the adjusting entry for the inventory shrinkage for Nocturnal Inc. for the year ended October 31, 2003.

Exercise 5–27
Closing the accounts of a merchandiser
Objective 5

From the following list, identify the accounts that should be closed to Income Summary at the end of the fiscal year: (a) Accounts Receivable, (b) Cost of Merchandise Sold, (c) Merchandise Inventory, (d) Sales, (e) Sales Discounts, (f) Sales Returns and Allowances, (g) Salaries Expense, (h) Salaries Payable, (i) Supplies, (j) Supplies Expense.

Exercise 5–28
Ratio of net sales to total assets
Objective 6

The financial statements for **Cisco Systems, Inc.**, are presented in Appendix G at the end of the text.

a. Determine the ratio of net sales to average total assets for Cisco Systems for the years ended July 29, 2000 and July 31, 1999.
b. What conclusions can be drawn from these ratios concerning the trend in the ability of Cisco Systems to effectively use its assets to generate sales?

Note: Cisco Systems' total assets on July 25, 1998 were $9,043,000,000.

Exercise 5–29
Ratio of net sales to total assets
Objective 6

Winn-Dixie Stores reported the following data in its financial statements for 1999:

Net sales and revenues	$14,136,503,000
Total assets at end of 1999	3,149,147,000
Total assets at end of 1998	3,068,714,000

a. Compute the ratio of net sales to assets for 1999. Round to two decimal places.
b. ✏️ Would you expect the ratio of net sales to assets for Winn-Dixie to be similar to or different from that of **Zales Jewelers**? Why?

Appendix
Exercise 5–30
Closing entries

Based on the data presented in exercise 5–25, journalize the closing entries.

Problem 5–1A
Purchase-related transactions
Objective 2

GENERAL
LEDGER

The following selected transactions were completed by Bushwhack Company during October of the current year:

Oct. 1. Purchased merchandise from Riverhill Co., $10,500, terms FOB destination, n/30.
   3. Purchased merchandise from Windsor Co., $8,000, terms FOB shipping point, 2/10, n/eom. Prepaid transportation costs of $150 were added to the invoice.
   4. Purchased merchandise from Picadilly Co., $7,500, terms FOB destination, 2/10, n/30.
   6. Issued debit memorandum to Picadilly Co. for $1,000 of merchandise returned from purchase on October 4.
   13. Paid Windsor Co. for invoice of October 3, less discount.
   15. Paid Picadilly Co. for invoice of October 4, less debit memorandum of October 6 and discount.
   19. Purchased merchandise from Ivy Co., $5,000, terms FOB shipping point, n/eom.
   19. Paid transportation charges of $120 on October 19 purchase from Ivy Co.
   20. Purchased merchandise from Hatcher Co., $8,000, terms FOB destination, 1/10, n/30.
   30. Paid Hatcher Co. for invoice of October 20, less discount.
   31. Paid Riverhill Co. for invoice of October 1.
   31. Paid Ivy Co. for invoice of October 19.

Instructions
Journalize the entries to record the transactions of Bushwhack Company for October.

Problem 5–2A
Sales-related transactions

Objective 2

SPREADSHEET

GENERAL LEDGER

The following selected transactions were completed by Fastball Supply Co., which sells office supplies primarily to wholesalers and occasionally to retail customers.

July 2. Sold merchandise on account to Magnolia Co., $10,500, terms FOB destination, 2/10, n/30. The cost of the merchandise sold was $6,000.

3. Sold merchandise for $2,000 plus 5% sales tax to cash customers. The cost of merchandise sold was $1,100.

4. Sold merchandise on account to McNutt Co., $2,800, terms FOB shipping point, n/eom. The cost of merchandise sold was $1,800.

5. Sold merchandise for $1,400 plus 5% sales tax to customers who used Master-Card. Deposited credit card receipts into the bank. The cost of merchandise sold was $750.

12. Received check for amount due from Magnolia Co. for sale on July 2.

14. Sold merchandise to customers who used American Express cards, $8,600. The cost of merchandise sold was $6,200.

16. Sold merchandise on account to Westpark Co., $12,000, terms FOB shipping point, 1/10, n/30. The cost of merchandise sold was $7,200.

18. Issued credit memorandum for $3,000 to Westpark Co. for merchandise returned from sale on July 16. The cost of the merchandise returned was $1,800.

19. Sold merchandise on account to Hempel Co., $7,500, terms FOB shipping point, 1/10, n/30. Added $85 to the invoice for transportation costs prepaid. The cost of merchandise sold was $4,500.

26. Received check for amount due from Westpark Co. for sale on July 16 less credit memorandum of July 18 and discount.

27. Received $9,410 from American Express for $10,000 of sales reported July 1–12.

28. Received check for amount due from Hempel Co. for sale of July 19.

31. Received check for amount due from McNutt Co. for sale of July 4.

31. Paid Fast Delivery Service $1,050 for merchandise delivered during July to customers under shipping terms of FOB destination.

Aug. 3. Paid First National Bank $690 for service fees for handling MasterCard sales during July.

15. Paid $3,100 to state sales tax division for taxes owed on July sales.

Instructions
Journalize the entries to record the transactions of Fastball Supply Co.

Problem 5–3A
Sales-related and purchase-related transactions

Objective 2

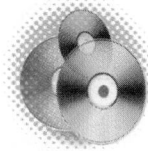

GENERAL LEDGER

The following were selected from among the transactions completed by The Knapsack Company during April of the current year:

Apr. 3. Purchased merchandise on account from Velcro Co., list price $30,000, trade discount 20%, terms FOB destination, 2/10, n/30.

4. Sold merchandise for cash, $5,100. The cost of the merchandise sold was $3,000.

5. Purchased merchandise on account from Summit Co., $7,500, terms FOB shipping point, 2/10, n/30, with prepaid transportation costs of $200 added to the invoice.

6. Returned $4,000 of merchandise purchased on April 3 from Velcro Co.

11. Sold merchandise on account to Bowles Co., list price $2,250, trade discount 20%, terms 1/10, n/30. The cost of the merchandise sold was $1,050.

13. Paid Velcro Co. on account for purchase of April 3, less return of April 6 and discount.

14. Sold merchandise on nonbank credit cards and reported accounts to the card company, American Express, $7,850. The cost of the merchandise sold was $3,900.

15. Paid Summit Co. on account for purchase of April 5, less discount.

21. Received cash on account from sale of April 11 to Bowles Co., less discount.

24. Sold merchandise on account to Hardigree Co., $4,200, terms 1/10, n/30. The cost of the merchandise sold was $1,850.

28. Received cash from American Express for nonbank credit card sales of April 14, less $314 service fee.

30. Received merchandise returned by Hardigree Co. from sale on April 24, $1,100. The cost of the returned merchandise was $600.

Instructions
Journalize the transactions.

Problem 5–4A
Sales-related and purchase-related transactions for seller and buyer

Objective 2

The following selected transactions were completed during July between Snap Company and Buckle Co.:

July 1. Snap Company sold merchandise on account to Buckle Co., $11,750, terms FOB destination, 2/15, n/eom. The cost of the merchandise sold was $7,000.

2. Snap Company paid transportation costs of $350 for delivery of merchandise sold to Buckle Co. on July 1.

5. Snap Company sold merchandise on account to Buckle Co., $17,500, terms FOB shipping point, n/eom. The cost of the merchandise sold was $10,000.

6. Buckle Co. returned $2,000 of merchandise purchased on account on July 1 from Snap Company. The cost of the merchandise returned was $1,200.

9. Buckle Co. paid transportation charges of $200 on July 5 purchase from Snap Company.

15. Snap Company sold merchandise on account to Buckle Co., $20,000, terms FOB shipping point, 1/10, n/30. Snap Company paid transportation costs of $1,750, which were added to the invoice. The cost of the merchandise sold was $12,000.

16. Buckle Co. paid Snap Company for purchase of July 1, less discount and less return of July 6.

25. Buckle Co. paid Snap Company on account for purchase of July 15, less discount.

31. Buckle Co. paid Snap Company on account for purchase of July 5.

Instructions
Journalize the July transactions for (1) Snap Company and (2) Buckle Co.

Problem 5–5A
Multiple-step income statement and report form of balance sheet

Objectives 4, 5

GENERAL
LEDGER

✓ 1. Net income: $100,000

The following selected accounts and their current balances appear in the ledger of Mandolin Co. for the fiscal year ended March 31, 2003:

Cash	$ 33,750	Sales	$1,275,000
Notes Receivable	120,000	Sales Returns and Allowances	23,100
Accounts Receivable	121,000	Sales Discounts	21,900
Merchandise Inventory	175,000	Cost of Merchandise Sold	775,000
Office Supplies	5,600	Sales Salaries Expense	173,200
Prepaid Insurance	3,400	Advertising Expense	43,800
Office Equipment	85,000	Depreciation Expense—	
Accumulated Depreciation—		Store Equipment	6,400
Office Equipment	12,800	Miscellaneous Selling Expense	1,600
Store Equipment	153,000	Office Salaries Expense	84,150
Accumulated Depreciation—		Rent Expense	31,350
Store Equipment	34,200	Depreciation Expense—	
Accounts Payable	55,600	Office Equipment	12,700
Salaries Payable	2,400	Insurance Expense	3,900
Note Payable		Office Supplies Expense	1,300
(final payment due 2013)	56,000	Miscellaneous Administrative	
Capital Stock	75,000	Expense	1,600
Retained Earnings	395,750	Interest Revenue	11,000
Dividends	35,000	Interest Expense	6,000

Instructions

1. Prepare a multiple-step income statement.
2. Prepare a retained earnings statement.
3. Prepare a report form of balance sheet, assuming that the current portion of the note payable is $7,500.
4. Briefly explain (a) how multiple-step and single-step income statements differ and (b) how report-form and account-form balance sheets differ.

Problem 5–6A
Single-step income statement and account form of balance sheet

Objectives 4, 5

SPREADSHEET

✓ 3. Total assets: $649,750

Selected accounts and related amounts for Mandolin Co. for the fiscal year ended March 31, 2003, are presented in Problem 5–5A.

Instructions

1. Prepare a single-step income statement in the format shown in Exhibit 8.
2. Prepare a retained earnings statement.
3. Prepare an account form of balance sheet, assuming that the current portion of the note payable is $7,500.

Appendix
Problem 5–7A
Work sheet, financial statements, and adjusting and closing entries

✓ 2. Net income: $126,750

The accounts and their balances in the ledger of Thorax Co. on December 31, 2003, are as follows:

Cash	$ 28,000	Accounts Payable	$ 66,700
Accounts Receivable	132,500	Salaries Payable	—
Merchandise Inventory	195,000	Unearned Rent	1,200
Prepaid Insurance	9,700	Note Payable	
Store Supplies	4,250	(final payment due 2013)	105,000
Office Supplies	2,100	Capital Stock	50,000
Store Equipment	157,000	Retained Earnings	174,600
Accumulated Depreciation—		Dividends	30,000
Store Equipment	40,300	Income Summary	—
Office Equipment	50,000	Sales	915,000
Accumulated Depreciation—		Sales Returns and Allowances	11,900
Office Equipment	17,200	Sales Discounts	7,100
Sales Salaries Expense	76,400	Cost of Merchandise Sold	576,200
Advertising Expense	25,000	Insurance Expense	—
Depreciation Expense—		Depreciation Expense—	
Store Equipment	—	Office Equipment	—
Store Supplies Expense	—	Office Supplies Expense	—
Miscellaneous Selling Expense	1,600	Miscellaneous Administrative	
Office Salaries Expense	34,000	Expense	1,650
Rent Expense	16,000	Rent Revenue	—
		Interest Expense	11,600

The data needed for year-end adjustments on December 31 are as follows:

Physical merchandise inventory on December 31		$189,000
Insurance expired during the year		5,000
Supplies on hand on December 31:		
Store supplies		1,300
Office supplies		750
Depreciation for the year:		
Store equipment		4,500
Office equipment		2,800
Salaries payable on December 31:		
Sales salaries	$3,850	
Office salaries	1,150	5,000
Unearned rent on December 31		400

Instructions

1. Prepare a work sheet for the fiscal year ended December 31, 2003. List all accounts in the order given.
2. Prepare a multiple-step income statement.
3. Prepare a retained earnings statement.
4. Prepare a report form of balance sheet, assuming that the current portion of the note payable is $20,000.
5. Journalize the adjusting entries.
6. Journalize the closing entries.

PROBLEMS SERIES B

Problem 5–1B
Purchase-related transactions

Objective 2

GENERAL LEDGER

The following selected transactions were completed by Beagley Co. during March of the current year:

Mar. 1. Purchased merchandise from Lumpkin Co., $9,000, terms FOB shipping point, 2/10, n/eom. Prepaid transportation costs of $350 were added to the invoice.

  5. Purchased merchandise from Guthrie Co., $9,200, terms FOB destination, n/30.

  10. Paid Lumpkin Co. for invoice of March 1, less discount.

  13. Purchased merchandise from Mickle Co., $7,500, terms FOB destination, 1/10, n/30.

  14. Issued debit memorandum to Mickle Co. for $2,500 of merchandise returned from purchase on March 13.

  18. Purchased merchandise from Aschor Company, $11,500, terms FOB shipping point, n/eom.

  18. Paid transportation charges of $200 on March 18 purchase from Aschor Company.

  19. Purchased merchandise from Hatcher Co., $7,500, terms FOB destination, 2/10, n/30.

  23. Paid Mickle Co. for invoice of March 13, less debit memorandum of March 14 and discount.

  29. Paid Hatcher Co. for invoice of March 19, less discount.

  31. Paid Aschor Company for invoice of March 18.

  31. Paid Guthrie Co. for invoice of March 5.

Instructions
Journalize the entries to record the transactions of Beagley Co. for March.

Problem 5–2B
Sales-related transactions

Objective 2

SPREADSHEET
GENERAL LEDGER

The following selected transactions were completed by Sprinkle Supplies Co., which sells irrigation supplies primarily to wholesalers and occasionally to retail customers.

May 1. Sold merchandise on account to Lynlex Co., $4,500, terms FOB shipping point, n/eom. The cost of merchandise sold was $2,300.

  2. Sold merchandise for $5,000 plus 6% sales tax to cash customers. The cost of merchandise sold was $3,750.

  5. Sold merchandise on account to Maple Company, $11,500, terms FOB destination, 1/10, n/30. The cost of merchandise sold was $7,000.

  8. Sold merchandise for $4,150 plus 6% sales tax to customers who used VISA cards. Deposited credit card receipts into the bank. The cost of merchandise sold was $2,800.

  13. Sold merchandise to customers who used American Express cards, $4,500. The cost of merchandise sold was $2,600.

  14. Sold merchandise on account to Blech Co., $7,500, terms FOB shipping point, 1/10, n/30. The cost of merchandise sold was $4,000.

  15. Received check for amount due from Maple Company for sale on May 5.

  16. Issued credit memorandum for $800 to Blech Co. for merchandise returned from sale on May 14. The cost of the merchandise returned was $360.

  18. Sold merchandise on account to Fortson Company, $6,850, terms FOB shipping point, 2/10, n/30. Paid $210 for transportation costs and added them to the invoice. The cost of merchandise sold was $4,100.

  24. Received check for amount due from Blech Co. for sale on May 14 less credit memorandum of May 16 and discount.

  27. Received $7,680 from American Express for $8,000 of sales reported during the week of May 1–12.

  28. Received check for amount due from Fortson Company for sale of May 18.

  31. Paid Anywhere Delivery Service $1,500 for merchandise delivered during May to customers under shipping terms of FOB destination.

  31. Received check for amount due from Lynlex Co. for sale of May 1.

June 3. Paid First National Bank $525 for service fees for handling MasterCard sales during May.

  10. Paid $1,100 to state sales tax division for taxes owed on May sales.

Instructions

Journalize the entries to record the transactions of Sprinkle Supplies Co.

Problem 5–3B

Sales-related and purchase-related transactions

Objective 2

GENERAL
LEDGER

The following were selected from among the transactions completed by Pelops Company during March of the current year:

Mar. 3. Purchased merchandise on account from Spruce Co., list price $18,000, trade discount 35%, terms FOB shipping point, 2/10, n/30, with prepaid transportation costs of $620 added to the invoice.

5. Purchased merchandise on account from Blake Co., $10,000, terms FOB destination, 1/10, n/30.

6. Sold merchandise on account to Howell Co., list price $7,500, trade discount 40%, terms 2/10, n/30. The cost of the merchandise sold was $1,850.

7. Returned $1,800 of merchandise purchased on March 5 from Blake Co.

13. Paid Spruce Co. on account for purchase of March 3, less discount.

15. Paid Blake Co. on account for purchase of March 5, less return of March 7 and discount.

16. Received cash on account from sale of March 6 to Howell Co., less discount.

19. Sold merchandise on nonbank credit cards and reported accounts to the card company, American Express, $4,450. The cost of the merchandise sold was $2,950.

22. Sold merchandise on account to Morton Co., $3,480, terms 2/10, n/30. The cost of the merchandise sold was $1,400.

23. Sold merchandise for cash, $7,350. The cost of the merchandise sold was $3,750.

25. Received merchandise returned by Morton Co. from sale on March 22, $1,480. The cost of the returned merchandise was $600.

31. Received cash from American Express for nonbank credit card sales of March 19, less $290 service fee.

Instructions

Journalize the transactions.

Problem 5–4B

Sales-related and purchase-related transactions for seller and buyer

Objective 2

The following selected transactions were completed during November between Subliminal Company and Bungee Company:

Nov. 2. Subliminal Company sold merchandise on account to Bungee Company, $12,000, terms FOB shipping point, 2/10, n/30. Subliminal Company paid transportation costs of $500, which were added to the invoice. The cost of the merchandise sold was $7,500.

8. Subliminal Company sold merchandise on account to Bungee Company, $13,500, terms FOB destination, 1/15, n/eom. The cost of the merchandise sold was $9,500.

8. Subliminal Company paid transportation costs of $750 for delivery of merchandise sold to Bungee Company on November 8.

12. Bungee Company returned $3,000 of merchandise purchased on account on November 8 from Subliminal Company. The cost of the merchandise returned was $1,600.

12. Bungee Company paid Subliminal Company for purchase of November 2, less discount.

23. Bungee Company paid Subliminal Company for purchase of November 8, less discount and less return of November 12.

24. Subliminal Company sold merchandise on account to Bungee Company, $9,000, terms FOB shipping point, n/eom. The cost of the merchandise sold was $5,400.

26. Bungee Company paid transportation charges of $250 on November 24 purchase from Subliminal Company.

30. Bungee Company paid Subliminal Company on account for purchase of November 24.

Instructions

Journalize the November transactions for (1) Subliminal Company and (2) Bungee Company.

Problem 5–5B

Multiple-step income statement and report form of balance sheet

Objectives 4, 5

GENERAL LEDGER

✓ 1. Net income: $68,000

The following selected accounts and their current balances appear in the ledger of Cypress Co. for the fiscal year ended June 30, 2003:

Cash	$ 26,500	Sales	$1,500,000
Notes Receivable	50,000	Sales Returns and Allowances	21,000
Accounts Receivable	62,000	Sales Discounts	11,000
Merchandise Inventory	100,000	Cost of Merchandise Sold	1,070,000
Office Supplies	2,600	Sales Salaries Expense	210,000
Prepaid Insurance	6,800	Advertising Expense	28,300
Office Equipment	64,000	Depreciation Expense—	
Accumulated Depreciation—		Store Equipment	4,600
Office Equipment	10,800	Miscellaneous Selling Expense	1,100
Store Equipment	117,500	Office Salaries Expense	41,000
Accumulated Depreciation—		Rent Expense	22,150
Store Equipment	48,600	Insurance Expense	12,750
Accounts Payable	27,000	Depreciation Expense—	
Salaries Payable	2,000	Office Equipment	9,000
Note Payable		Office Supplies Expense 900	
(final payment due 2013)	30,000	Miscellaneous Administrative	
Capital Stock	60,000	Expense	1,200
Retained Earnings	208,000	Interest Revenue	5,000
Dividends	25,000	Interest Expense	4,000

Instructions

1. Prepare a multiple-step income statement.
2. Prepare a retained earnings statement.
3. Prepare a report form of balance sheet, assuming that the current portion of the note payable is $2,500.
4. Briefly explain (a) how multiple-step and single-step income statements differ and (b) how report-form and account-form balance sheets differ.

Problem 5–6B

Single-step income statement and account form of balance sheet

Objectives 4, 5

SPREADSHEET

✓ 3. Total assets: $370,000

Selected accounts and related amounts for Cypress Co. for the fiscal year ended June 30, 2003, are presented in Problem 5–5B.

Instructions

1. Prepare a single-step income statement in the format shown in Exhibit 8.
2. Prepare a retained earnings statement.
3. Prepare an account form of balance sheet, assuming that the current portion of the note payable is $2,500.

Appendix
Problem 5–7B

Work sheet, financial statements, and adjusting and closing entries

✓ 2. Net income: $258,865

The accounts and their balances in the ledger of Zirconium Co. on December 31, 2003, are as follows:

Cash	$ 31,165	Accumulated Depreciation—	
Accounts Receivable	126,100	Office Equipment	$ 17,200
Merchandise Inventory	435,000	Accounts Payable	66,700
Prepaid Insurance	10,600	Salaries Payable	—
Store Supplies	3,750	Unearned Rent	1,200
Office Supplies	1,700	Note Payable	
Store Equipment	225,000	(final payment due 2013)	195,000
Accumulated Depreciation—		Capital Stock	75,000
Store Equipment	40,300	Retained Earnings	257,100
Office Equipment	72,000	Dividends	50,000
		Income Summary	—

Sales	$1,147,500	Office Salaries Expense	$60,000
Sales Returns and Allowances	15,500	Rent Expense	30,000
Sales Discounts	6,000	Insurance Expense	—
Cost of Merchandise Sold	601,200	Depreciation Expense— Office Equipment	—
Sales Salaries Expense	86,400		
Advertising Expense	29,450	Office Supplies Expense	—
Depreciation Expense— Store Equipment	—	Miscellaneous Administrative Expense	1,650
Store Supplies Expense	—	Rent Revenue	—
Miscellaneous Selling Expense	1,885	Interest Expense	12,600

The data needed for year-end adjustments on December 31 are as follows:

Physical merchandise inventory on December 31		$418,500
Insurance expired during the year		6,000
Supplies on hand on December 31:		
Store supplies		1,500
Office supplies		700
Depreciation for the year:		
Store equipment		8,500
Office equipment		4,500
Salaries payable on December 31:		
Sales salaries	$3,450	
Office salaries	2,550	6,000
Unearned rent on December 31		400

Instructions

1. Prepare a work sheet for the fiscal year ended December 31, 2003. List all accounts in the order given.
2. Prepare a multiple-step income statement.
3. Prepare a retained earnings statement.
4. Prepare a report form of balance sheet, assuming that the current portion of the note payable is $35,000.
5. Journalize the adjusting entries.
6. Journalize the closing entries.

COMPREHENSIVE PROBLEM 2

GENERAL LEDGER

✓ 5. Net income: $184,440

Fluorescent Co. is a merchandising business. The account balances for Fluorescent Co. as of May 1, 2003 (unless otherwise indicated), are as follows:

110	Cash	$ 19,160
111	Notes Receivable	5,000
112	Accounts Receivable	31,220
115	Merchandise Inventory	153,900
116	Prepaid Insurance	3,750
117	Store Supplies	2,550
123	Store Equipment	104,300
124	Accumulated Depreciation—Store Equipment	12,600
210	Accounts Payable	18,450
211	Salaries Payable	—

(continued)

310	Capital Stock	$ 25,000
311	Retained Earnings, June 1, 2002	88,280
312	Dividends	10,000
313	Income Summary	—
410	Sales	815,750
411	Sales Returns and Allowances	20,600
412	Sales Discounts	13,200
510	Cost of Merchandise Sold	460,500
520	Sales Salaries Expense	64,400
521	Advertising Expense	18,000
522	Depreciation Expense	—
523	Store Supplies Expense	—
529	Miscellaneous Selling Expense	2,800
530	Office Salaries Expense	30,500
531	Rent Expense	18,600
532	Insurance Expense	—
539	Miscellaneous Administrative Expense	1,650
611	Interest Revenue	50

During May, the last month of the fiscal year, the following transactions were completed:

May 1. Paid rent for May, $2,000.
  3. Purchased merchandise on account from Tredwell Co., terms 2/10, n/30, FOB shipping point, $10,000.
  4. Paid transportation charges on purchase of May 3, $375.
  6. Sold merchandise on account to Parish Co., terms 2/10, n/30, FOB shipping point, $8,500. The cost of the merchandise sold was $5,000.
  7. Received $6,500 cash from Oxford Co. on account, no discount.
  10. Sold merchandise for cash, $15,300. The cost of the merchandise sold was $9,000.
  13. Paid for merchandise purchased on May 3, less discount.
  14. Received merchandise returned on sale of May 6, $1,500. The cost of the merchandise returned was $900.
  15. Paid advertising expense for last half of May, $1,500.
  16. Received cash from sale of May 6, less return of May 14 and discount.
  19. Purchased merchandise for cash, $7,400.
  19. Paid $5,950 to Lipham Co. on account, no discount.
  20. Sold merchandise on account to Petroski Co., terms 1/10, n/30, FOB shipping point, $16,000. The cost of the merchandise sold was $9,600.
  21. For the convenience of the customer, paid shipping charges on sale of May 20, $600.
  21. Received $11,750 cash from Gant Co. on account, no discount.
  21. Purchased merchandise on account from Walden Co., terms 1/10, n/30, FOB destination, $15,000.
  24. Returned $3,500 of damaged merchandise purchased on May 21, receiving credit from the seller.
  26. Refunded cash on sales made for cash, $600. The cost of the merchandise returned was $360.
  28. Paid sales salaries of $2,750 and office salaries of $1,220.
  29. Purchased store supplies for cash, $350.
  30. Sold merchandise on account to Hartel Co., terms 2/10, n/30, FOB shipping point, $23,100. The cost of the merchandise sold was $13,200.
  30. Received cash from sale of May 20, less discount, plus transportation paid on May 21.
  31. Paid for purchase of May 21, less return of May 24 and discount.

Instructions
(*Note:* If the work sheet described in the appendix is used, follow the alternative instructions.)

1. Enter the balances of each of the accounts in the appropriate balance column of a four-column account. Write *Balance* in the item section, and place a check mark (✓) in the Posting Reference column.
2. Journalize the transactions for May.
3. Post the journal to the general ledger, extending the month-end balances to the appropriate balance columns after all posting is completed. In this problem, you are not required to update or post to the accounts receivable and accounts payable subsidiary ledgers.
4. Journalize and post the adjusting entries, using the following adjustment data:

a.	Merchandise inventory on May 31		$139,750
b.	Insurance expired during the year		1,250
c.	Store supplies on hand on May 31		1,050
d.	Depreciation for the current year		7,400
e.	Accrued salaries on May 31:		
	Sales salaries	$350	
	Office salaries	180	530

5. Prepare a multiple-step income statement, a retained earnings statement, and a report form of balance sheet.
6. Journalize and post the closing entries. Indicate closed accounts by inserting a line in both balance columns opposite the closing entry. Insert the new balance in the retained earnings account.
7. Prepare a post-closing trial balance.

Alternative Instructions

1. Enter the balances of each of the accounts in the appropriate balance column of a four-column account. Write *Balance* in the item section, and place a check mark (✓) in the Posting Reference column.
2. Journalize the transactions for May.
3. Post the journal to the general ledger, extending the month-end balances to the appropriate balance columns after all posting is completed. In this problem, you are not required to update or post to the accounts receivable and accounts payable subsidiary ledgers.
4. Prepare a trial balance as of May 31 on a ten-column work sheet, listing all accounts in the order given in the ledger. Complete the work sheet for the fiscal year ended May 31, using the following adjustment data:

a.	Merchandise inventory on May 31		$139,750
b.	Insurance expired during the year		1,250
c.	Store supplies on hand on May 31		1,050
d.	Depreciation for the current year		7,400
e.	Accrued salaries on May 31:		
	Sales salaries	$350	
	Office salaries	180	530

5. Prepare a multiple-step income statement, a retained earnings statement, and a report form of balance sheet.
6. Journalize and post the adjusting entries.
7. Journalize and post the closing entries. Indicate closed accounts by inserting a line in both balance columns opposite the closing entry. Insert the new balance in the retained earnings account.
8. Prepare a post-closing trial balance.

SPECIAL ACTIVITIES

Activity 5–1
Couperin Company
Ethics and professional conduct in business

On October 1, 2003, Couperin Company, a garden retailer, purchased $15,000 of corn seed, terms 2/10, n/30, from Kernel Co. Even though the discount period had expired, Bryant Harness subtracted the discount of $300 when he processed the documents for payment on October 15, 2003.

 Discuss whether Bryant Harness behaved in a professional manner by subtracting the discount, even though the discount period had expired.

Activity 5–2
The Movie Store Co.
Purchases discounts and accounts payable

The Movie Store Co. is owned and operated by Amy Lell. The following is an excerpt from a conversation between Amy Lell and Tammi Beach, the chief accountant for The Movie Store.

Amy: Tammi, I've got a question about this recent balance sheet.
Tammi: Sure, what's your question?
Amy: Well, as you know, I'm applying for a bank loan to finance our new store in Three Forks, and I noticed that the accounts payable are listed as $130,000.
Tammi: That's right. Approximately $100,000 of that represents amounts due our suppliers, and the remainder is miscellaneous payables to creditors for utilities, office equipment, supplies, etc.
Amy: That's what I thought. But as you know, we normally receive a 2% discount from our suppliers for earlier payment, and we always try to take the discount.
Tammi: That's right. I can't remember the last time we missed a discount.
Amy: Well, in that case, it seems to me the accounts payable should be listed minus the 2% discount. Let's list the accounts payable due suppliers as $98,000, rather than $100,000. Every little bit helps. You never know. It might make the difference between getting the loan and not.

 How would you respond to Amy Lell's request?

Activity 5–3
Mega Sound versus Decibel Electronics
Determining cost of purchase

The following is an excerpt from a conversation between Gina Bellamy and Kim Craft. Gina is debating whether to buy a stereo system from Mega Sound, a locally owned electronics store, or Decibel Electronics, a mail-order electronics company.

Gina: Kim, I don't know what to do about buying my new stereo.
Kim: What's the problem?
Gina: Well, I can buy it locally at Mega Sound for $495.00. However, Decibel Electronics has the same system listed for $499.99.
Kim: So what's the big deal? Buy it from Mega Sound.
Gina: It's not quite that simple. Decibel said something about not having to pay sales tax, since I was out-of-state.
Kim: Yes, that's a good point. If you buy it at Mega Sound, they'll charge you 5% sales tax.
Gina: But Decibel Electronics charges $12.50 for shipping and handling. If I have them send it next-day air, it'll cost $25 for shipping and handling.
Kim: I guess it is a little confusing.
Gina: That's not all. Mega Sound will give an additional 1% discount if I pay cash. Otherwise, they will let me use my MasterCard, or I can pay it off in three monthly installments.
Kim: Anything else???
Gina: Well . . . Decibel says I have to charge it on my MasterCard. They don't accept checks.
Kim: I am not surprised. Many mail-order houses don't accept checks.
Gina: I give up. What would you do?

1. Assuming that Decibel Electronics doesn't charge sales tax on the sale to Gina, which company is offering the best buy?
2.  What might be some considerations other than price that might influence Gina's decision on where to buy the stereo system?

Activity 5–4
Hercules Parts Company
Sales discounts

Your sister operates Hercules Parts Company, a mail-order boat parts distributorship that is in its third year of operation. The following income statement was recently prepared for the year ended July 31, 2003:

Hercules Parts Company
Income Statement
For the Year Ended July 31, 2003

Revenues:		
Net sales		$600,000
Interest revenue		5,000
Total revenues		$605,000
Expenses:		
Cost of merchandise sold	$420,000	
Selling expenses	66,000	
Administrative expenses	34,000	
Interest expense	10,000	
Total expenses		530,000
Net income		$ 75,000

Your sister is considering a proposal to increase net income by offering sales discounts of 2/15, n/30, and by shipping all merchandise FOB shipping point. Currently, no sales discounts are allowed and merchandise is shipped FOB destination. It is estimated that these credit terms will increase net sales by 10%. The ratio of the cost of merchandise sold to net sales is expected to be 70%. All selling and administrative expenses are expected to remain unchanged, except for store supplies, miscellaneous selling, office supplies, and miscellaneous administrative expenses, which are expected to increase proportionately with increased net sales. The amounts of these preceding items for the year ended July 31, 2003, were as follows:

Store supplies expense	$5,000
Miscellaneous selling expense	2,000
Office supplies expense	1,000
Miscellaneous administrative expense	1,800

The other income and other expense items will remain unchanged. The shipment of all merchandise FOB shipping point will eliminate all transportation-out expenses, which for the year ended July 31, 2003, were $20,150.

1. Prepare a projected single-step income statement for the year ending July 31, 2004, based on the proposal.
2. a. ▬▬▶ Based on the projected income statement in (1), would you recommend the implementation of the proposed changes?
   b. Describe any possible concerns you may have related to the proposed changes described in (1).

Activity 5–5
Into the Real World
Shopping for a television

Assume that you are planning to purchase a 50-inch Sony television. In groups of three or four, determine the lowest cost for the television, considering the available alternatives and the advantages and disadvantages of each alternative. For example, you could purchase locally, through mail order, or through an Internet shopping service. Consider such factors as delivery charges, interest-free financing, discounts, coupons, and availability of warranty services. Prepare a report for presentation to the class.

ANSWERS TO SELF-EXAMINATION QUESTIONS

Matching

1. D	6. CC	11. W	16. E	21. AA	26. Q		
2. J	7. T	12. V	17. DD	22. B	27. BB		
3. O	8. S	13. F	18. H	23. K	28. L		
4. C	9. U	14. Y	19. G	24. N	29. A		
5. I	10. M	15. Z	20. P	25. R	30. X		

Multiple Choice

1. **A** A debit memorandum (answer A), issued by the buyer, indicates the amount the buyer proposes to debit to the accounts payable account. A credit memorandum (answer B), issued by the seller, indicates the amount the seller proposes to credit to the accounts receivable account. An invoice (answer C) or a bill (answer D), issued by the seller, indicates the amount and terms of the sale.

2. **C** The amount of discount for early payment is $10 (answer C), or 1% of $1,000. Although the $50 of transportation costs paid by the seller is debited to the customer's account, the customer is not entitled to a discount on that amount.

3. **B** The single-step form of income statement (answer B) is so named because the total of all expenses is deducted in one step from the total of all revenues. The multiple-step form (answer A) includes numerous sections and subsections with several subtotals. The account form (answer C) and the report form (answer D) are two common forms of the balance sheet.

4. **C** Gross profit (answer C) is the excess of net sales over the cost of merchandise sold. Operating income (answer A) or income from operations (answer B) is the excess of gross profit over operating expenses. Net income (answer D) is the final figure on the income statement after all revenues and expenses have been reported.

5. **D** Expenses such as interest expense (answer D) that cannot be associated directly with operations are identified as *Other expense* or *Nonoperating expense*. Depreciation expense—office equipment (answer A) is an administrative expense. Sales salaries expense (answer B) is a selling expense. Insurance expense (answer C) is a mixed expense with elements of both selling expense and administrative expense. For small businesses, insurance expense is usually reported as an administrative expense.

Accounting Systems, Internal Controls, and Cash

objectives

After studying this chapter, you should be able to:

1. Define an accounting system and describe its implementation.

2. List the three objectives of internal control, and define and give examples of the five elements of internal control.

3. Describe the nature of cash and the importance of internal control over cash.

4. Summarize basic procedures for achieving internal control over cash receipts.

5. Summarize basic procedures for achieving internal control over cash payments, including the use of a voucher system.

6. Describe the nature of a bank account and its use in controlling cash.

7. Prepare a bank reconciliation and journalize any necessary entries.

8. Account for small cash transactions using a petty cash fund.

9. Summarize how cash is presented on the balance sheet.

10. Compute and interpret the ratio of cash to current liabilities.

ontrols are a part of your everyday life. At one extreme, laws are used to govern your behavior. For example, the speed limit is a control on your driving, designed for traffic safety. In addition, you are also affected by many nonlegal controls. For example, you can keep credit card receipts in order to compare your transactions to the monthly credit card statement. Comparing receipts to the monthly statement is a control designed to catch mistakes made by the credit card company. Likewise, recording checks in your checkbook is a control that you can use at the end of the month to verify the accuracy of your bank statement. In addition, banks give you a personal identification number (PIN) as a control against unauthorized access to your cash if you lose your automated teller machine (ATM) card. Dairies use freshness dating on their milk containers as a control to prevent the purchase or sale of soured milk. As you can see, you use and encounter controls every day.

Just as there are many examples of controls throughout society, businesses must also implement controls to help guide the behavior of their employees toward business objectives. For example, some businesses require you to punch a time card when you enter and leave the workplace. This is a control used to verify that you get paid for the actual hours you worked.

In the previous chapters, we discussed completing the accounting cycle and preparing financial statements for NetSolutions. In this chapter, we will discuss accounting systems, which are the source of the financial statements. We also discuss controls that can provide assurance that these statements are reliable. As a basis for illustration, we apply these concepts to the control of cash receipts and cash payments. We illustrate how businesses reconcile their monthly bank statements as a means of accounting for and controlling cash. You may want to use this illustration as a guide for reconciling your own bank statement to your checking account.

Basic Accounting Systems

objective 1

Define an accounting system and describe its implementation.

In the previous chapters, we developed an accounting system for NetSolutions. An **accounting system** is the methods and procedures for collecting, classsifying, summarizing, and reporting a business's financial and operating information. The accounting system for most businesses, however, is more complex than NetSolutions'. Accounting systems for large businesses must be able to collect, accumulate, and report many types of transactions. For example, **United Airlines'** accounting system collects and maintains information on ticket reservations, credit card collections, aircraft maintenance, employee hours, frequent-flier mileage balances, fuel consumption, and travel agent commissions, just to name a few. As you might expect, United Airlines' accounting system has evolved as the company has grown.

Accounting systems evolve through a three-step process as a business grows and changes. The first step in this process is **analysis**, which consists of (1) identifying the needs of those who use the business's financial information and (2) determining how the system should provide this information. For NetSolutions, we determined that Chris Clark would need financial statements for the new business. In the second step, the system is **designed** so that it will meet the users' needs. For NetSolutions, a very basic manual system was designed. This system included a chart of accounts, a two-column journal, and a general ledger. Finally, the system is **implemented** and used. For NetSolutions, the system was used to record transactions and prepare financial statements.

Hershey Foods learned the hard way about the importance of careful analysis and design prior to implementing a complex information system. Hershey implemented a $112 million computer system by using a "big-bang" start-up, rather than using a gradual implementation strategy. When the switch was thrown, the company ran into immediate problems shipping orders to customers. As a result, profits were cut by 20%, and product shipments during the all-important Halloween selling season were delayed.

An accounting system must be able to adapt to changing information needs. Thus, once a system has been implemented, **feedback**, or input, from the users of the information can be used to analyze and improve the system.

Internal controls and information processing methods are essential in an accounting system. **Internal controls** are the policies and procedures that protect assets from misuse, ensure that business information is accurate, and ensure that laws and regulations are being followed. **Processing methods** are the means by which the system collects, summarizes, and reports accounting information. These methods may be either *manual* or *computerized*.

In the preceding chapters, we described and illustrated manual accounting systems. In many cases, a modified manual accounting system may be adequate to meet the needs of a business.[1] Understanding manual systems helps you understand how computerized systems function. Computerized accounting systems use electronic technology and media to perform more rapidly the same processing functions as manual accounting systems.

Internal Control

Businesses use internal controls to guide their operations and prevent abuses of their systems. For example, assume that you own and manage a lawn care service. Your business uses several employee teams, and you provide each team with a vehicle and lawn equipment. What are some of the issues you would face as a manager in controlling the operations of this business? Below are some examples.

- Lawn care must be provided on time.
- The quality of lawn care services must meet customer expectations.
- Employees must provide work for the hours they are paid.
- Lawn care equipment should be used for business purposes only.
- Vehicles should be used for business purposes only.
- Customers must be billed and bills collected for services rendered.

> **Internal controls protect assets, ensure that business information is accurate, and ensure that regulations are being followed.**

How would you address these issues? You could, for example, develop a schedule at the beginning of each day and then inspect the work at the end of the day to verify that it was completed according to quality standards. You could have "surprise" inspections by arriving on site at random times to verify that the teams are working according to schedule. You could require employees to "clock in" at the beginning of the day and "clock out" at the end of the day to make sure that they are paid for hours worked. You could require the work teams to return the vehicles and equipment to a central location to prevent unauthorized use. You could keep a log of odometer readings at the end of each day to verify

---

[1] One means by which manual systems can be modified is to use special journals. In each special journal, selected kinds of transactions are recorded. The basic features of special journals are presented in Appendix D.

that the vehicle has not been used for "joy riding." You could bill customers after you have inspected the work and then monitor the collection of all receivables. All of these are examples of internal control.

Objectives of Internal Control

The objectives of internal control are to provide reasonable assurance that:

1. assets are safeguarded and used for business purposes.
2. business information is accurate.
3. employees comply with laws and regulations.

Internal control can safeguard assets by preventing theft, fraud, misuse, or misplacement. One of the most serious breaches of internal control is employee fraud. **Employee fraud** is the intentional act of deceiving an employer for personal gain. Such deception may range from purposely overstating expenses on a travel expense report in order to receive a higher reimbursement to embezzling millions of dollars through complex schemes.

Accurate business information is necessary for operating a business successfully. The safeguarding of assets and accurate information often go hand-in-hand. The reason is that employees attempting to defraud a business will also need to adjust the accounting records in order to hide the fraud.

Businesses must comply with applicable laws, regulations, and financial reporting standards. Examples of such standards and laws include environmental regulations, contract terms, safety regulations, and generally accepted accounting principles (GAAP).

Elements of Internal Control

How does management achieve its internal control objectives? Management is responsible for designing and applying five **elements of internal control** to meet the three internal control objectives. These elements are:[2]

1. the control environment
2. risk assessment
3. control procedures
4. monitoring
5. information and communication

The elements of internal control are illustrated in Exhibit 1. In this exhibit, the elements of internal control form an umbrella over the business to protect it from control threats. The business's control environment is represented by the size of the umbrella. Risk assessment, control procedures, and monitoring are the fabric that keeps the umbrella from leaking. Information and communication links the umbrella to management. In the following paragraphs, we discuss each of these elements.

Control Environment

A business's control environment is the overall attitude of management and employees about the importance of controls. One of the factors that influences the control environment is *management's philosophy and operating style*. A management that overemphasizes operating goals and deviates from control policies may indirectly encourage employees to ignore controls. For example, the pressure to achieve revenue targets may encourage employees to fraudulently record sham sales. On the other hand, a management that emphasizes the importance of controls and encourages adherence to control policies will create an effective control environment.

The business's *organizational structure*, which is the framework for planning and controlling operations, also influences the control environment. For example, a

---

[2] *Internal Control—Integrated Framework by the Committee of Sponsoring Organizations* of the Treadway Commission (COSO), pp. 12–14. This document provides a professionally sponsored framework for internal control.

Exhibit 1 Elements of
Internal Control

department store chain might organize each of its stores as separate business units. Each store manager has full authority over pricing and other operating activities. In such a structure, each store manager has the responsibility for establishing an effective control environment.

Personnel policies also affect the control environment. Personnel policies involve the hiring, training, evaluation, compensation, and promotion of employees. In addition, job descriptions, employee codes of ethics, and conflict-of-interest policies are part of the personnel policies. Such policies and procedures can enhance the internal control environment if they provide reasonable assurance that only competent, honest employees are hired and retained.

Risk Assessment

All organizations face risks. Examples of risk include changes in customer requirements, competitive threats, regulatory changes, changes in economic factors such as interest rates, and employee violations of company policies and procedures. Management should assess these risks and take necessary actions to control them, so that the objectives of internal control can be achieved.

Once risks are identified, they can be analyzed to estimate their significance, to assess their likelihood of occurring, and to determine actions that will minimize them. For example, the manager of a warehouse operation may analyze the risk of employee back injuries, which might give rise to lawsuits. If the manager determines that the risk is significant, the company may take action by purchasing back support braces for its warehouse employees and requiring them to wear the braces.

An accounting clerk for the Grant County (Washington) Alcoholism Program was in charge of collecting money, making deposits, and keeping the records. While the clerk was away on maternity leave, the replacement clerk discovered a fraud: $17,800 in fees had been collected but had been hidden for personal gain.

Control Procedures

Control procedures are established to provide reasonable assurance that business goals will be achieved, including the prevention of fraud. In the following paragraphs, we will briefly discuss control procedures that can be integrated throughout the accounting system. These procedures are listed in Exhibit 2.

Competent Personnel, Rotating Duties, and Mandatory Vacations.

The successful operation of an accounting system requires procedures to ensure that people are able to perform the duties to which they are assigned. Hence, it is necessary that all accounting employees be adequately trained and supervised in performing their jobs. It may also be advisable to rotate duties of clerical personnel and mandate vacations for nonclerical personnel. These policies encourage employees to adhere to prescribed procedures. In addition, existing errors or fraud may be detected.

Exhibit 2 Internal Control
Procedures

Separating Responsibilities for Related Operations. To decrease the possibility of inefficiency, errors, and fraud, the responsibility for related operations should be divided among two or more persons. For example, the responsibilities for purchasing, receiving, and paying for computer supplies should be divided among three persons or departments. If the same person orders supplies, verifies the receipt of the supplies, and pays the supplier, the following abuses are possible:

1. Orders may be placed on the basis of friendship with a supplier, rather than on price, quality, and other objective factors.
2. The quantity and quality of supplies received may not be verified, thus causing payment for supplies not received or poor-quality supplies.
3. Supplies may be stolen by the employee.
4. The validity and accuracy of invoices may be verified carelessly, thus causing the payment of false or inaccurate invoices.

The "checks and balances" provided by dividing responsibilities among various departments requires no duplication of effort. The business documents prepared by one department are designed to coordinate with and support those prepared by other departments.

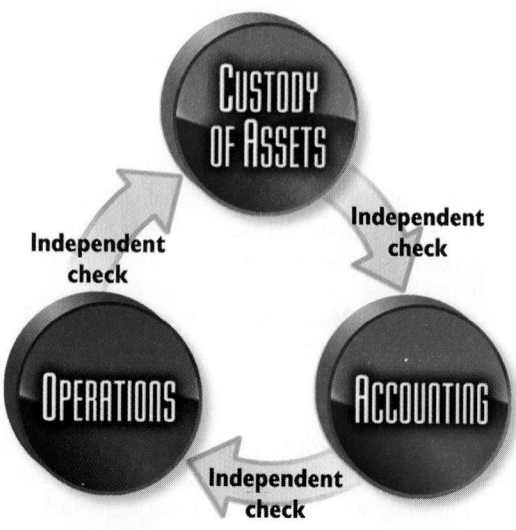

Separating Operations, Custody of Assets, and Accounting. Control policies should establish the responsibilities for various business activities. To reduce the possibility of errors and fraud, the responsibilities for operations, custody of assets, and accounting should be separated. The accounting records then serve as an independent check on the individuals who have custody of the assets and who engage in the business operations. For example, the employees entrusted with handling cash receipts from credit customers should not record cash receipts in the accounting records. To do so would allow employees to borrow or steal cash and hide the theft in the records. Likewise, if those engaged in operating activities also record the results of operations, they could distort the accounting reports to show favorable results. For example, a store manager whose year-end bonus is based upon operating profits might be tempted to record fictitious sales in order to receive a larger bonus.

 Over $700,000 of child support money disappeared over seven years due to the alleged falsification of checks by an accountant in Indiana's Family and Social Services Administration. The fraud could have been discovered, according to the State Examiner, if the agency reconciled its books, controlled access to blank checks, and used receipts.

 *Why is separation of duties considered a control procedure?*

Internal control is enhanced by separating the control of a transaction from the record-keeping function. Fraud is more easily committed when a single individual controls both the transaction and the accounting for the transaction.

Proofs and Security Measures. Proofs and security measures should be used to safeguard assets and ensure reliable accounting data. This control procedure applies to many different techniques, such as authorization, approval, and reconciliation procedures. For example, employees who travel on company business may be required to obtain a department manager's approval on a travel request form.

Other examples of control procedures include the use of bank accounts and other measures to ensure the safety of cash and valuable documents. A cash register that displays the amount recorded for each sale and provides the customer a printed receipt can be an effective part of the internal control structure. An all-night convenience store could use the following security measures to deter robberies:

1. Locate the cash register near the door, so that it is fully visible from outside the store; have two employees work late hours; employ a security guard.
2. Deposit cash in the bank daily, before 5 p.m.
3. Keep only small amounts of cash on hand after 5 p.m. by depositing excess cash in a store safe that can't be opened by employees on duty.
4. Install cameras and alarm systems.

Monitoring

Monitoring the internal control system locates weaknesses and improves control effectiveness. The internal control system can be monitored through either ongoing efforts by management or by separate evaluations. Ongoing monitoring efforts may include observing both employee behavior and warning signs from the accounting system. The indicators shown in Exhibit 3 may be clues to internal control problems.[3]

Exhibit 3 Indicators of Internal Control Problems

CLUES TO POTENTIAL PROBLEMS

Warning signs with regard to people

1. Abrupt change in lifestyle (without winning the lottery).
2. Close social relationships with suppliers.
3. Refusing to take a vacation.
4. Frequent borrowing from other employees.
5. Excessive use of alcohol or drugs.

Warning signs from the accounting system

1. Missing documents or gaps in transaction numbers (could mean documents are being used for fraudulent transactions).
2. An unusual increase in customer refunds (refunds may be phony).
3. Differences between daily cash receipts and bank deposits (could mean receipts are pocketed before being deposited).
4. Sudden increase in slow payments (employee may be pocketing the payment).
5. Backlog in recording transactions (possibly an attempt to delay detection of fraud).

---

[3] Edwin C. Bliss, "Employee Theft," *Boardroom Reports*, July 15, 1994, pp. 5–6.

Real World

In one of the largest frauds ever committed against a university, a former financial aid officer for **New York University** was charged with stealing $4.1 million from the state of New York. The aid officer allegedly falsified over a thousand tuition assistance checks to students who were not entitled to receive aid and who did not know about the checks. The aid officer deposited the bogus checks for personal use. The initial evidence of the fraud was the officer's spending of $785,000 on expensive jewelry.

Separate monitoring evaluations are generally performed when there are major changes in strategy, senior management, business structure, or operations. In large businesses, internal auditors who are independent of operations normally are responsible for monitoring the internal control system. Internal auditors can report issues and concerns to an audit committee of the board of directors, who are independent of management. In addition, external auditors also evaluate internal control as a normal part of their annual financial statement audit.

Information and Communication

Information and communication are essential elements of internal control. Information about the control environment, risk assessment, control procedures, and monitoring are needed by management to guide operations and ensure compliance with reporting, legal, and regulatory requirements.

Management can also use external information to assess events and conditions that impact decision making and external reporting. For example, management uses information from the Financial Accounting Standards Board (FASB) to assess the impact of possible changes in reporting standards.

Nature of Cash and the Importance of Controls Over Cash

objective 3

Describe the nature of cash and the importance of internal control over cash.

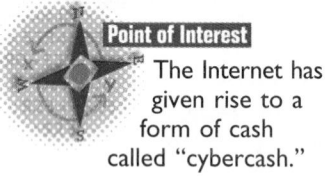

Point of Interest

The Internet has given rise to a form of cash called "cybercash."

Cash includes coins, currency (paper money), checks, money orders, and money on deposit that is available for unrestricted withdrawal from banks and other financial institutions. Normally, you can think of cash as anything that a bank would accept for deposit in your account. For example, a check made payable to you could normally be deposited in a bank and thus is considered cash.

We will assume in this chapter that a business maintains only *one* bank account, represented in the ledger as *Cash*. In practice, however, a business may have several bank accounts, such as one for general cash payments and another for payroll. For each of its bank accounts, the business will maintain a ledger account, one of which may be called *Cash in Bank—First Bank*, for example. It will also maintain separate ledger accounts for cash that it does not keep in the bank, such as cash for small payments, and cash used for special purposes, such as travel reimbursements. We will introduce some of these other cash accounts in the chapter.

Because of the ease with which money can be transferred, cash is the asset most likely to be diverted and used improperly by employees. In addition, many transactions either directly or indirectly affect the receipt or the payment of cash. Businesses must therefore design and use controls that safeguard cash and control the authorization of cash transactions. In the following paragraphs, we will discuss these controls.

Control of Cash Receipts

objective 4

Summarize basic procedures for achieving internal control over cash receipts.

To protect cash from theft and misuse, a business must control cash from the time it is received until it is deposited in a bank. Such procedures are called **preventive controls**. Procedures that are designed to detect theft or misuse of cash are called **detective controls**. In a sense, detective controls are also preventive in nature, since employees are less likely to steal or misuse cash if they know there is a good chance they will be discovered.

Retail businesses normally receive cash from two main sources: (1) cash receipts from customers and (2) mail receipts from customers making payments on account. These two sources of cash are shown in Exhibit 4.

Exhibit 4 Retailers' Sources of Cash

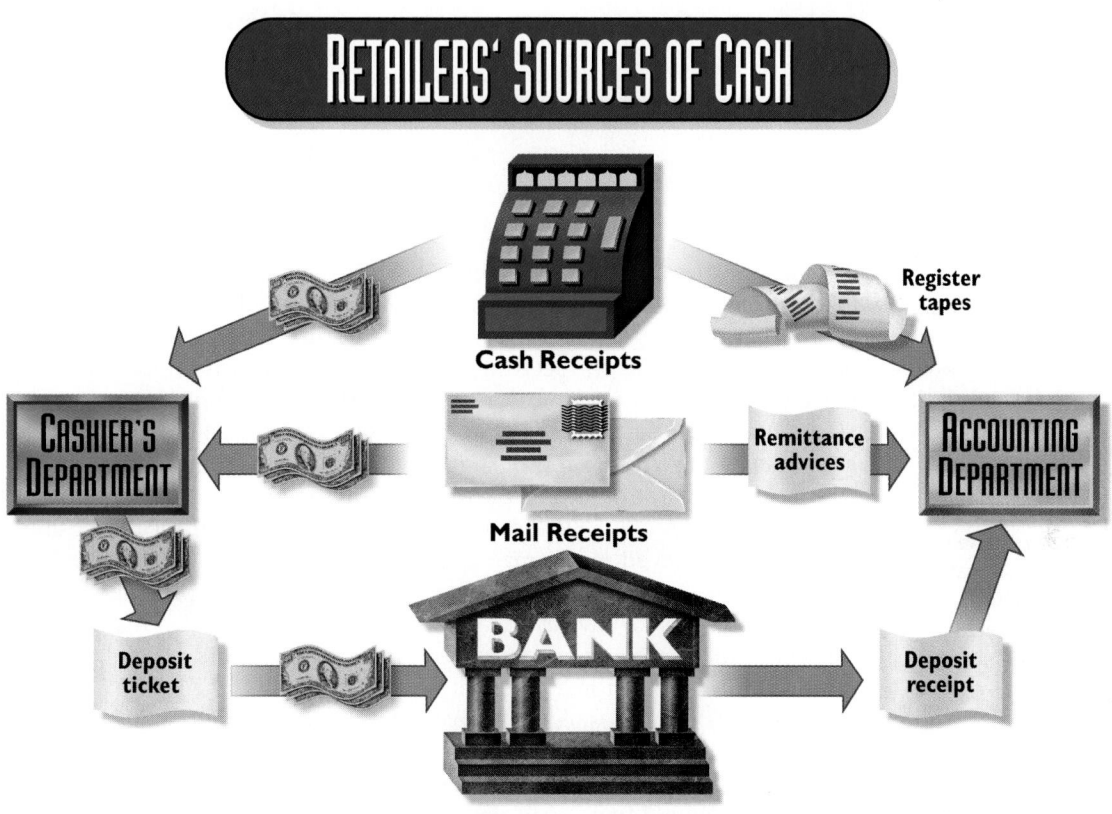

Controlling Cash Received from Cash Sales

 Fast-food restaurants, such as **McDonald's**, **Wendy's**, and **Burger King**, receive cash primarily from over-the-counter sales to customers. Mail-order and Internet retailers, such as **Lands' End, Orvis, L.L. Bean**, and **Amazon.com**, receive cash primarily through the mail and from credit card companies.

Regardless of the source of cash receipts, every business must properly safeguard and record its cash receipts. One of the most important controls to protect cash received in over-the-counter sales is a cash register. You may have noticed that when a clerk (cashier) enters the amount of a sale, the cash register normally displays the amount. This is a control to ensure that the clerk has charged you the correct amount. You also receive a receipt to verify the accuracy of the amount.

At the beginning of a work shift, each cash register clerk is given a cash drawer that contains a predetermined amount of cash for making change for customers. The amount in each drawer is sometimes called a **change fund**. At the end of the work shift, each clerk and the supervisor count the cash in the clerk's cash drawer. The amount of cash in each drawer should equal the beginning amount of cash plus the cash sales for the day. However, errors in recording cash sales or errors in making change cause the amount of actual cash on hand to differ from this amount. Such differences are recorded in a **cash short and over account**. For example, the following entry records a clerk's cash sales of $3,150 when the actual cash on hand is $3,142:

Cash		3 1 4 2 00	
Cash Short and Over		8 00	
Sales			3 1 5 0 00
To record cash sales and actual cash			
on hand.			

At the end of the accounting period, a debit balance in the cash short and over account is included in Miscellaneous Administrative Expense in the income statement. A credit balance is included in the Other Income section. If a clerk consistently has significant cash short and over amounts, the supervisor may require the clerk to take additional training.

After a cash register clerk's cash has been counted and recorded on a memorandum form, the cash is then placed in a store safe in the Cashier's Department until it can be deposited in the bank. The supervisor forwards the clerk's cash register tapes to the Accounting Department, where they become the basis for recording the transactions for the day.

Controlling Cash Received in the Mail

Some retail companies use debit card systems to transfer and record the receipt of cash. In a debit card system, a customer pays for goods at the time of purchase by presenting a plastic card. The card authorizes the electronic transfer of cash from the customer's checking account to the retailer's bank account at the time of the sale.

Cash is received in the mail when customers pay their bills. This cash is usually in the form of checks and money orders. Most companies' invoices are designed so that customers return a portion of the invoice, called a **remittance advice**, with their payment. The employee who opens the incoming mail should initially compare the amount of cash received with the amount shown on the remittance advice. If a customer does not return a remittance advice, an employee prepares one. Like the cash register, the remittance advice serves as a record of cash initially received. It also helps ensure that the posting to the customer's account is accurate. Finally, as a preventive control, the employee opening the mail normally also stamps checks and money orders "For Deposit Only" in the bank account of the business.

All cash received in the mail is sent to the Cashier's Department. An employee there combines it with the receipts from cash sales and prepares a bank deposit ticket. The remittance advices and their summary totals are delivered to the Accounting Department. An accounting clerk then prepares the records of the transactions and posts them to the customer accounts.

When cash is deposited in the bank, the bank normally stamps a duplicate copy of the deposit ticket with the amount received. This bank receipt is returned to the Accounting Department, where a clerk then compares the receipt with the total amount that should have been deposited. This control helps ensure that all the cash is deposited and that no cash is lost or stolen on the way to the bank. Any shortages are thus promptly detected.

The separation of the duties of the Cashier's Department, which handles cash, and the Accounting Department, which records cash, is a preventive control. If Accounting Department employees both handled and recorded cash, an employee could steal cash and change the accounting records to hide the theft.

Internal Control of Cash Payments

objective 5

Summarize basic procedures for achieving internal control over cash payments, including the use of a voucher system.

Internal control of cash payments should provide reasonable assurance that payments are made for only authorized transactions. In addition, controls should ensure that cash is used efficiently. For example, controls should ensure that all available discounts, such as purchase and trade discounts, are taken.

In a small business, an owner/manager may sign all checks, based upon personal knowledge of goods and services purchased. In a large business, however, checks are often prepared by employees who do not have such a complete knowledge of the transactions. In a large business, for example, the duties of purchasing goods, inspecting the goods received, and verifying the invoices are usually performed by different employees. These duties must be coordinated to ensure that checks for proper amounts are issued to creditors. One system used for this purpose is the voucher system.

Howard Schultz & Associates (HS&A) specializes in reviewing cash payments for its clients. HS&A searches for errors, such as duplicate payments, failures to take discounts, and inaccurate computations. The typical amount recovered for a client is about one-tenth of 1 percent (0.1%) of the total payments reviewed. This averages to about $300,000 per client. In one case, HS&A recovered over $4.5 million for a client.

Source: Thomas Buell, Jr., "Demand Grows for Auditor," *The Naples Daily News*, January 12, 1992, p. 14E.

Basic Features of the Voucher System

A **voucher system** is a set of procedures for authorizing and recording liabilities and cash payments. A voucher system normally uses (1) vouchers, (2) a file for unpaid vouchers, and (3) a file for paid vouchers. Generally, a voucher is any document that serves as proof of authority to pay cash. For example, an invoice properly approved for payment could be considered a voucher. In many businesses, however, a **voucher** is a special form for recording relevant data about a liability and the details of its payment. An example of such a form is shown in Exhibit 5.

Each voucher includes the creditor's invoice number and the amount and terms of the invoice. The accounts used in recording the purchase (or transaction) are listed in the *account distribution*.

A voucher is normally prepared in the Accounting Department, after all necessary supporting documents have been received. For example, when a voucher is prepared for the purchase of goods, the voucher should be supported by the supplier's invoice, a purchase order, and a receiving report. In preparing the voucher, an accounts payable clerk verifies the quantity, price, and mathematical accuracy of the supporting documents. This provides assurance that the payment is for goods that were properly ordered and received.

After a voucher is prepared, the voucher and its supporting documents are given to the proper official for approval. After it has been approved, the voucher is returned to the Accounting Department, where it is recorded in the accounts. It is

Exhibit 5 Voucher

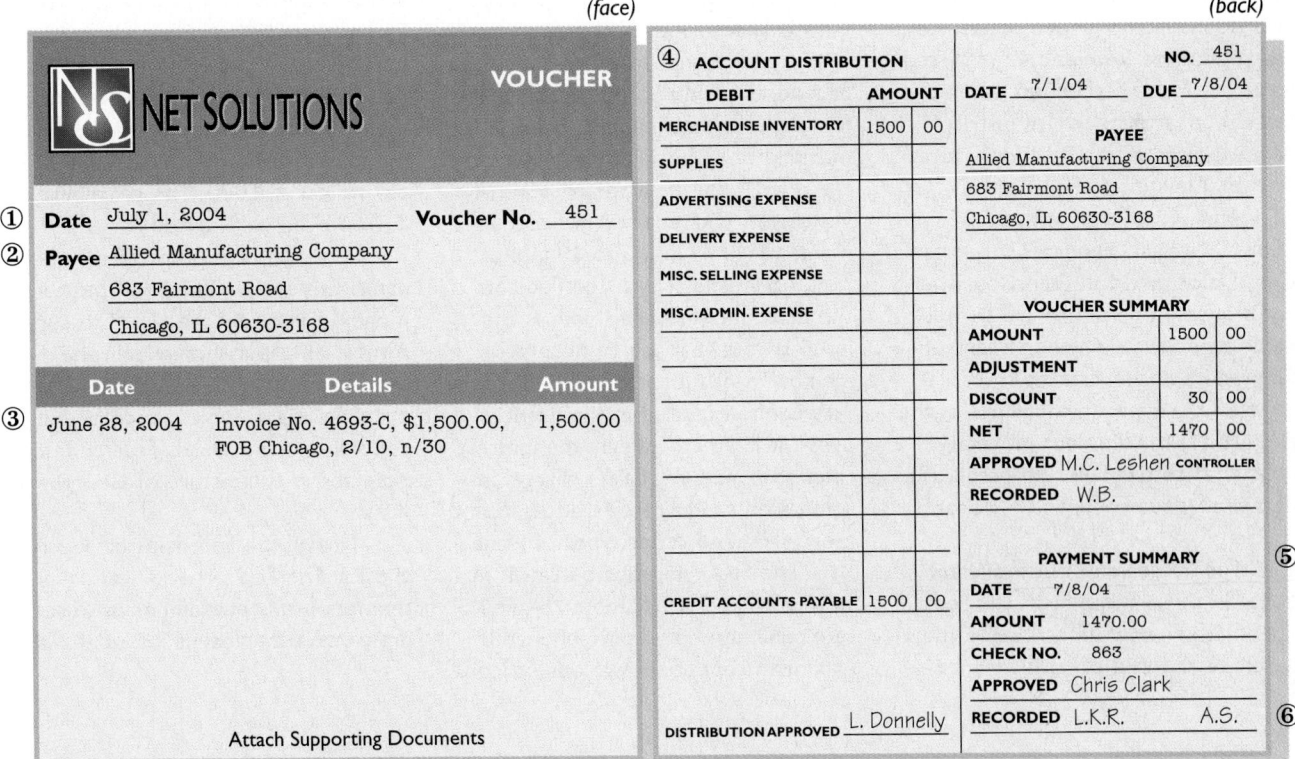

① Date the voucher was prepared

② Name and address of the creditor

③ Description of the supporting documents

④ Accounts used to record the purchase or transaction

⑤ Details of payment

⑥ Spaces for signature or initials of approving employees

then filed in an unpaid voucher file by its due date so that all available purchase discounts are taken.[4]

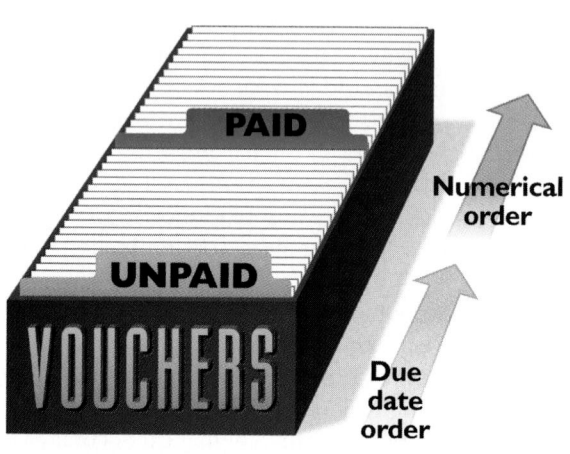

On its due date, the voucher is removed from the unpaid voucher file. The date, the number, and the amount of the check written in payment are listed on the back of the voucher. The payment of the voucher is recorded in the same manner as the payment of an account payable.

After payment, vouchers are marked "Paid" and are usually filed in numerical order in a paid voucher file. They are then readily available for examination by employees needing information about past payments.

A voucher system may be either manual or computerized. In a computerized system, properly approved supporting documents (such as purchase orders and receiving reports) would be entered directly into computer files. At the due date, the checks would be automatically generated and mailed to creditors. At that time, the voucher would be automatically transferred to a paid voucher file. In some cases, payments may be made electronically rather than by check.

BUSINESS ON STAGE

The Federal Reserve System

One of the most powerful financial institutions in the United States is the *Federal Reserve System*, often referred to as the *Fed*. The Federal Reserve System consists of twelve district banks located in the following cities: Boston, New York, Philadelphia, Cleveland, Charlotte, Atlanta, St. Louis, Chicago, Minneapolis, Kansas City, Dallas, and San Francisco. The Fed's overall operations are coordinated by a seven-member Board of Governors headquartered in Washington, D.C. Four key activities of the Fed are (1) carrying out monetary policy, (2) setting rules on credit, (3) distributing currency, and (4) clearing checks.

The Fed carries out monetary policy in three ways. First, the Fed's open-market operations involve the purchase and sale of government se-

curities. For example, when the Fed buys U.S. securities in the open market, it puts money into the economy. Second, the Fed sets the requirements for reserves that member banks must maintain on deposit. These reserves are unavailable for loans or other investments. Current reserve requirements range from 3% to 10% of a bank's deposits. Third, the Fed sets the discount rate. This rate is the interest rate that the Fed charges member banks for loans. The discount rate is often quoted in the financial press. It indirectly affects the interest rates that member banks charge customers on credit card balances, home mortgages, and other types of loans.

The Fed sets rules on credit in various ways. For example, the Fed sets minimum down payments and maximum repayment periods on con-

sumer loans of member banks. The Fed also sets margin requirements for purchasing securities such as stocks. For example, if the margin requirement is 40%, then an investor who purchases stocks worth $20,000 must pay at least $8,000. The remaining $12,000 can be financed.

The Fed distributes to member banks the coins minted and the paper money printed by the U.S. Treasury. Almost all paper money is in the form of Federal Reserve Notes. For example, if you look at a dollar bill, you will see the words *Federal Reserve Note* above the picture of George Washington.

Finally, the Fed helps banks clear checks. The Fed's check-clearing system lets banks quickly convert checks drawn on other banks into cash. ■

---

[4] Occasionally, a purchase discount is missed. Some companies record the amounts of missed discounts in an account titled *Discounts Lost*. Doing so allows managers to monitor the significance of discounts lost. Since most companies design controls to take all purchase discounts, we do not illustrate the use of a discounts lost account.

Electronic Funds Transfer

With rapidly changing technology, new systems are being devised to more efficiently record and transfer cash among companies. Such systems often use **electronic funds transfer (EFT)**. In an EFT system, computers rather than paper (money, checks, etc.) are used to effect cash transactions. For example, a business may pay its employees by means of EFT. Under such a system, employees may authorize the deposit of their payroll checks directly into checking accounts. Each pay period, the business electronically transfers the employees' net pay to their checking accounts through the use of computer systems and telephone lines. Likewise, many companies are using EFT systems to pay their suppliers and other vendors.

TeleCheck Services, Inc., the world's leading check acceptance company, is offering an online real-time check payment option for purchases made over the Internet. "It is apparent from the rapid growth of online sales that many consumers are as comfortable writing checks for Internet purchases as they are at their local brick-and-mortar store," explains Steve Shaper, chief executive officer of TeleCheck.

Bank Accounts: Their Nature and Use as a Control Over Cash

objective 6

Describe the nature of a bank account and its use in controlling cash.

Most of you are already familiar with bank accounts. You have a checking account at a local bank, credit union, savings and loan association, or other financial institution. In this section, we discuss the nature of a bank account used by a business. The features of such accounts will be similar to your own bank account. We then discuss the use of bank accounts as an additional control over cash.

Business Bank Accounts

A business often maintains several bank accounts. The forms used with each bank account are a signature card, deposit ticket, check, and record of checks drawn.

When you open a checking account, you sign a **signature card**. This card is used by the bank to verify the signature on checks that are submitted for payment. Also, when you open an account, the bank assigns an identifying number to the account.

The details of a deposit are listed by the depositor on a printed **deposit ticket** supplied by the bank. These forms are often prepared in duplicate. The bank teller stamps or initials a copy of the deposit ticket and gives it to the depositor as a receipt. Other types of receipts may also be used to give the depositor written proof of the date and the total amount of the deposit.

A **check** is a written document signed by the depositor, ordering the bank to pay a sum of money to an individual or entity. There are three parties to a check—the drawer, the drawee, and the payee. The **drawer** is the one who signs the check, ordering payment by the bank. The **drawee** is the bank on which the check is drawn. The **payee** is the party to whom payment is to be made.

The name and address of the depositor are usually printed on each check. In addition, checks are prenumbered, so that they can easily be kept track of by both the issuer and the bank. Banks encode their identification number and the depositor's account number in magnetic ink on each check. These numbers make it possible for the bank to sort and post checks automatically. When a check is presented for payment, the amount for which it is drawn is inserted, next to the account number, in magnetic ink.

A record of each check should be prepared at the time a check is written. A small booklet called a **transactions register** is often used by both businesses and individuals for this purpose.

The purpose of a check may be written in space provided on the check or on an attachment to the check. Normally, checks issued to a creditor on account are sent with a form that identifies the specific invoice that is being paid. The purpose of this **remittance advice** is to make sure that proper credit is recorded in the accounts of the creditor. In this way, mistakes are less likely to occur. A check and remittance advice is shown in Exhibit 6.

Exhibit 6 Check and Remittance Advice

POWER NETWORKING				363
1000 Belkin Los Angeles, CA 90014-1000			July 07 20 03	9-42/720

Pay to the Order of ___ Interface Data Systems ___ $ 921.20

Nine hundred twenty-one 20/100 --- Dollars

VALLEY NATIONAL BANK OF LOS ANGELES
LOS ANGELES, CA 90020-4283   (310) 851-5151   MEMBER FDIC

K.R. Simons   Treasurer
Earl M. Hartman   Vice President

⑆07 20004 23⑆   ⑆6 27042   363⑈

DETACH THIS PORTION BEFORE CASHING

Date	Description	Gross Amount	Deductions	Net Amount
07/07/03	Invoice No. 529482	940.00	18.80	921.20

POWER NETWORKING

Before depositing the check, the payee removes the remittance advice. The payee may then use the remittance advice as written proof of the details of the cash receipt.

Bank Statement

Banks usually maintain a record of all checking account transactions. A summary of all transactions, called a **statement of account**, is mailed to the depositor, usually each month. Like any account with a customer or a creditor, the bank statement shows the beginning balance, additions, deductions, and the balance at the end of the period. A typical bank statement is shown in Exhibit 7.

Exhibit 7 Bank Statement

```
                              MEMBER FDIC                          PAGE   1

VALLEY NATIONAL BANK                    ACCOUNT NUMBER   1627042
OF LOS ANGELES
                                        FROM  6/30/03   TO  7/31/03
LOS ANGELES, CA 90020-4253   (310)851-5151
                                        BALANCE          4,218.60

                                     22 DEPOSITS         13,749.75

         POWER NETWORKING            52 WITHDRAWALS      14,698.57
         1000 Belkin Street
         Los Angeles, CA 90014-1000   3 OTHER DEBITS
                                        AND CREDITS        90.00CR

                                        NEW BALANCE      3,359.78


* — — CHECKS AND OTHER DEBITS — — — * — — — DEPOSITS — — * — — DATE — — * — — BALANCE — — *

  819.40       122.54                   585.75        07/01      3,862.41
  369.50       732.26       20.15       421.53        07/02      3,162.03
  600.00       190.70       52.50       781.30        07/03      3,100.13
   25.93       160.00                   662.50        07/05      3,576.70
  921.20    NSF 300.00                  503.18        07/07      2,858.68
```
```
   32.26       535.09                   932.00        07/29      3,404.40
   21.10       126.20                   705.21        07/30      3,962.31
            SC  18.00                MS 408.00        07/30      4,352.31
   26.12     1,615.13                   648.72        07/31      3,359.78


         EC — ERROR CORRECTION              OD — OVERDRAFT
         MS — MISCELLANEOUS                 PS — PAYMENT STOPPED
         NSF — NOT SUFFICIENT FUNDS         SC — SERVICE CHARGE

     * * *                        * * *                      * * *

         THE RECONCILEMENT OF THIS STATEMENT WITH YOUR RECORDS IS ESSENTIAL.
            ANY ERROR OR EXCEPTION SHOULD BE REPORTED IMMEDIATELY.
```

The depositor's checks received by the bank during the period may accompany the bank statement, arranged in the order of payment. The paid checks are stamped "Paid," together with the date of payment. Other entries that the bank has made in the depositor's account may be described in debit or credit memorandums enclosed with the statement.

You should note that a depositor's checking account balance *in the bank's records* is a liability with a credit balance. Debit memorandums issued by the bank on a depositor's account therefore decrease the depositor's balance. Likewise, credit memorandums increase the depositor's balance. A bank issues a debit memorandum to charge (decrease) a depositor's account for service charges or for deposited checks returned because of insufficient funds. Likewise, a bank issues a credit memorandum when it increases the depositor's account for collecting a note receivable for the depositor, making a loan to the depositor, receiving a wire deposit, or adding interest to the depositor's account.[5]

---

[5] Although interest-bearing checking accounts are common for individuals, Federal Reserve Regulation Q prohibits the paying of interest on corporate checking accounts.

Bank Accounts as a Control Over Cash

A bank account is one of the primary tools a business uses to control cash. For example, businesses often require that all cash receipts be initially deposited in a bank account. Likewise, businesses usually use checks to make all cash payments, except for very small amounts. When such a system is used, there is a double record of cash transactions—one by the business and the other by the bank.

A business can use a bank statement to compare the cash transactions recorded in its accounting records to those recorded by the bank. The cash balance shown by a bank statement is usually different from the cash balance shown in the accounting records of the business, as shown in Exhibit 8.

> A bank account and a business's records provide a double record of cash transactions.

Exhibit 8 Power Networking's Records and Bank Statement

Bank Statement				Power Networking Records	
Beginning Balance		$ 4,218.60		Beginning Balance	$ 4,227.60
Additions:					
Deposits		13,749.75		Deposits	14,565.95
Miscellaneous		408.00			
Deductions:					
Checks		14,698.57		Checks	16,243.56
NSF Check	$300				
Service Charge	18	318.00			
Ending Balance		$ 3,359.78		Ending Balance	$ 2,549.99

Power Networking should determine the reason for the difference in these two amounts.

This difference may be the result of a delay by either party in recording transactions. For example, there is a time lag of one day or more between the date a check is written and the date that it is presented to the bank for payment. If the depositor mails deposits to the bank or uses the night depository, a time lag between the date of the deposit and the date that it is recorded by the bank is also probable. The bank may also debit or credit the depositor's account for transactions about which the depositor will not be informed until later.

The difference may be the result of errors made by either the business or the bank in recording transactions. For example, the business may incorrectly post to Cash a check written for $4,500 as $450. Likewise, a bank may incorrectly record the amount of a check, as we illustrated at the beginning of this chapter.

Bank Reconciliation

objective 7

Prepare a bank reconciliation and journalize any necessary entries.

For effective control, the reasons for the difference between the cash balance on the bank statement and the cash balance in the accounting records should be determined by preparing a bank reconciliation. A **bank reconciliation** is a listing of the items and amounts that cause the cash balance reported in the bank statement to differ from the balance of the cash account in the ledger.

A bank reconciliation is usually divided into two sections. The first section begins with the cash balance according to the bank statement and ends with the adjusted balance. The second section begins with the cash balance according to the depositor's records and ends with the adjusted balance. The two amounts designated as the adjusted balance must be equal. The content of the bank reconciliation is shown below.

Cash balance according to bank statement		$XXX		Cash balance according to depositor's records . .		$XXX
Add: Additions by depositor not on				Add: Additions by bank not recorded by		
bank statement	$XX			depositor	$XX	
Bank errors	XX	XX		Depositor errors	XX	XX
		$XXX				$XXX
Deduct: Deductions by depositor not on				Deduct: Deductions by bank not recorded		
bank statement	$XX			by depositor	$XX	
Bank errors	XX	XX		Depositor errors	XX	XX
Adjusted balance		$XXX		Adjusted balance		$XXX

must be equal

The following steps are useful in finding the reconciling items and determining the adjusted balance of Cash:

1. Compare each deposit listed on the bank statement with unrecorded deposits appearing in the preceding period's reconciliation and with deposit receipts or other records of deposits. *Add deposits not recorded by the bank to the balance according to the bank statement.*
2. Compare paid checks with outstanding checks appearing on the preceding period's reconciliation and with recorded checks. *Deduct checks outstanding that have not been paid by the bank from the balance according to the bank statement.*
3. Compare bank credit memorandums to entries in the journal. For example, a bank would issue a credit memorandum for a note receivable and interest that it collected for a depositor. *Add credit memorandums that have not been recorded to the balance according to the depositor's records.*
4. Compare bank debit memorandums to entries recording cash payments. For example, a bank normally issues debit memorandums for service charges and check printing charges. A bank also issues debit memorandums for not-sufficient-funds checks. A *not-sufficient-funds (NSF) check* is a customer's check that was recorded and deposited but was not paid when it was presented to the customer's bank for payment. NSF checks are normally charged back to the customer as an account receivable. *Deduct debit memorandums that have not been recorded from the balance according to the depositor's records.*
5. List any errors discovered during the preceding steps. For example, if an amount has been recorded incorrectly by the depositor, the amount of the error should be added to or deducted from the cash balance according to the depositor's records. Similarly, errors by the bank should be added to or deducted from the cash balance according to the bank statement.

To illustrate a bank reconciliation, we will use the bank statement for Power Networking in Exhibit 7. This bank statement shows a balance of $3,359.78 as of July 31. The cash balance in Power Networking's ledger as of the same date is $2,549.99. The following reconciling items are revealed by using the steps outlined above:

Deposit of July 31, not recorded on bank statement . . . . $ 816.20
Checks outstanding: No. 812, $1,061.00; No. 878, $435.39; No. 883, $48.60 . . . . . .   1,544.99
Note plus interest of $8 collected by bank (credit memorandum), not recorded
   in the journal 408.00
Check from customer (Thomas Ivey) returned by bank because of insufficient
   funds (NSF) 300.00
Bank service charges (debit memorandum), not recorded in the journal 18.00
Check No. 879 for $732.26 to Taylor Co. on account, recorded in the journal
   as $723.26 . . . .   9.00

The bank reconciliation based on the bank statement and the reconciling items is shown in Exhibit 9.

Exhibit 9 Bank Reconciliation for Power Networking

Power Networking
Bank Reconciliation
July 31, 2003

Cash balance according to				Cash balance according to		
bank statement		$3 3 5 9 78		depositor's records		$2 5 4 9 99
Add deposit of July 31, not				Add note and interest		
recorded by bank		8 1 6 20		collected by bank		4 0 8 00
		$4 1 7 5 98				$2 9 5 7 99
				Deduct: Check returned because		
Deduct outstanding checks:				of insufficient funds	$ 3 0 0 00	
No. 812	$1 0 6 1 00			Bank service charges	1 8 00	
No. 878	4 3 5 39			Error in recording		
No. 883	4 8 60	1 5 4 4 99		Check No. 879	9 00	3 2 7 00
Adjusted balance		$2 6 3 0 99	Adjusted balance			$2 6 3 0 99

> **Entries must be made in the depositor's accounts for any items that affect the business's record of cash.**

No entries are necessary on the depositor's records as a result of the information included in the first section of the bank reconciliation. This section begins with the cash balance according to the bank statement. However, the bank should be notified of any errors that need to be corrected on its records.

Any items in the second section of the bank reconciliation must be recorded in the depositor's accounts. This section begins with the cash balance according to the depositor's records. For example, journal entries should be made for any unrecorded bank memorandums and any depositor's errors.

The journal entries for Power Networking, based on the preceding bank reconciliation, are as follows:

1	July	31	Cash	4 0 8 00	
2			Notes Receivable		4 0 0 00
3			Interest Revenue		8 00
4			Note collected by bank.		

6	31	Accounts Receivable—Thomas Ivey	3	0	0	00						6
7		Miscellaneous Administrative Expense		1	8	00						7
8		Accounts Payable—Taylor Co.			9	00						8
9		Cash					3	2	7	00		9
10		NSF check, bank service charges, and error										10
11		in recording Check No. 879.										11

Assume that the bank recorded a deposit of $4,100 as $1,400. How would this bank error be shown on the bank reconciliation?

The error of $2,700 would be added to the cash balance according to the bank statement.

After these entries have been posted, the cash account will have a debit balance of $2,630.99. This balance agrees with the adjusted cash balance shown on the bank reconciliation. This is the amount of cash available as of July 31 and the amount that would be reported on Power Networking's July 31 balance sheet.

Although businesses may reconcile their bank accounts in a slightly different format from what we described above, the objective is the same: to control cash by reconciling the company's records to the records of an independent outside source, the bank. In doing so, any errors or misuse of cash may be detected.

For effective control, the bank reconciliation should be prepared by an employee who does not take part in or record cash transactions. When these duties are not properly separated, mistakes are likely to occur, and it is more likely that cash will be stolen or otherwise misapplied. For example, an employee who takes part in all of these duties could prepare and cash an unauthorized check, omit it from the accounts, and omit it from the reconciliation.

Point of Interest

If you reconcile your bank account each month, you first scan your bank statement for any bank entries that you have not yet recorded. Examples of such entries include service charges (a debit entry) and interest earned (a credit entry). You then enter these amounts in your checkbook (register) and determine the balance of your account. If you stop at this point, you are assuming that the bank hasn't made any errors.

If you fully reconcile your account, you should also scan your checkbook for items that the bank has not yet recorded: (1) deposits in transit and (2) outstanding checks. Deposits in transit should be added to the bank balance, and outstanding checks should be subtracted from the bank balance. The result is an adjusted bank balance, which should agree with the balance of your checkbook. If the two are not equal, either you or the bank has made an error.

Petty Cash

objective 8

Account for small cash transactions using a petty cash fund.

As in your own day-to-day life, it is usually not practical for a business to write checks to pay small amounts, such as postage. Yet, these small payments may occur often enough to add up to a significant total amount. Thus, it is desirable to control such payments. For this purpose, a special cash fund, called a **petty cash fund**, is used.

A petty cash fund is established by first estimating the amount of cash needed for payments from the fund during a period, such as a week or a month. After necessary approvals, a check is written and cashed for this amount. The money

Real World Businesses often use other cash funds to meet their special needs, such as travel expenses for salespersons. For example, each salesperson might be given $200 for travel-related expenses. Periodically, the salesperson submits a detailed expense report and the travel funds are replenished.

obtained from cashing the check is then given to an employee, called the petty cash custodian, who is authorized to disburse monies from the fund. For control purposes, the company may place restrictions on the maximum amount and the types of payments that can be made from the fund.

Each time monies are paid from petty cash, the custodian records the details of the payment on a petty cash receipt form. A typical petty cash receipt is illustrated in Exhibit 10.

Exhibit 10 Petty Cash Receipt

PETTY CASH RECEIPT		
No. _____ 121 _____	Date _____ August 1, 2003 _____	
Paid to _____ Metropolitan Times _____	**Amount**	
For _____ Daily newspaper _____	3	00
Charge to _____ Miscellaneous Administrative Expense _____		
Payment received:		
_____ S.O. Hall _____	Approved by _____ N.E.R. _____	

The petty cash fund is normally replenished at periodic intervals, or when it is depleted or reaches a minimum amount. When a petty cash fund is replenished, the accounts debited are determined by summarizing the petty cash receipts. A check is then written for this amount, payable to the petty cash custodian.

To illustrate normal petty cash fund entries, assume that a petty cash fund of $100 is established on August 1. The entry to record this transaction is as follows:

13	Aug.	1	Petty Cash	1 0 0 00		13
14			Cash		1 0 0 00	14
15			Established petty cash fund.			15

Q&A *If the petty cash account has a balance of $200, the cash in the fund totals $20, and the petty cash receipts total $180 at the end of a period, what account is credited and what is the amount of the credit in the entry to replenish the fund?*

Cash is credited for $180.

At the end of August, the petty cash receipts indicate expenditures for the following items: office supplies, $28; postage (office supplies), $22; store supplies, $35; and daily newspapers (miscellaneous administrative expense), $3. The entry to replenish the petty cash fund on August 31 is as follows:

17	Aug.	31	Office Supplies	5 0 00		17
18			Store Supplies	3 5 00		18
19			Miscellaneous Administrative Expense	3 00		19
20			Cash		8 8 00	20
21			Replenished petty cash fund.			21

Replenishing the petty cash fund restores it to its original amount of $100. You should note that there is no entry in Petty Cash when the fund is replenished. Petty Cash is debited only when the fund is initially set up or when the amount of the fund is increased at a later time. Petty Cash is credited if it is being decreased.

> **Petty Cash is debited only when the fund is set up or the amount of the fund is increased.**

Presentation of Cash on the Balance Sheet

objective 9

Summarize how cash is presented on the balance sheet.

Cash is the most liquid asset, and therefore it is listed as the first asset in the Current Assets section of the balance sheet. Most companies present only a single cash amount on the balance sheet by combining all their bank and cash fund accounts.

A company may have cash in excess of its operating needs. In such cases, the company normally invests in highly liquid investments in order to earn interest. These investments are called **cash equivalents**.[6] Examples of cash equivalents include U.S. Treasury Bills, notes issued by major corporations (referred to as commercial paper), and money market funds. Companies that have invested excess cash in cash equivalents usually report *Cash and cash equivalents* as one amount on the balance sheet.

Banks may require depositors to maintain minimum cash balances in their bank accounts. Such a balance is called a **compensating balance**. This requirement is often imposed by the bank as a part of a loan agreement or line of credit. A *line of credit* is a preapproved amount the bank is willing to lend to a customer upon request. Compensating balance requirements should be disclosed in notes to the financial statements.

Real World The following note discloses compensating balance requirements for **Kmart Corporation**: . . . *In support of lines of credit, it is expected that compensating balances will be maintained on deposit with the banks, which will average 10% of the line to the extent that it is not in use and an additional 10% on the portion in use. . . .*

FINANCIAL ANALYSIS AND INTERPRETATION

objective 10

Compute and interpret the ratio of cash to current liabilities.

In an earlier chapter, we discussed the use of working capital and the current ratio in evaluating a company's ability to pay its current liabilities (short-term solvency). Both of these measures assume that the noncash current assets will be converted to cash in time to pay the current liabilities. For most companies, these measures are useful for assessing short-term solvency. However, a company that is in financial distress may have difficulty converting its receivables, inventory, and prepaid assets to cash on a timely basis. In these cases, the ratio of cash to current liabilities may be useful in assessing the ability of creditors to collect what they are owed. Because this ratio is most relevant for companies in financial distress, it is

---

[6] To be classified as a cash equivalent, according to *FASB Statement 95*, the investment is expected to be converted to cash within 90 days.

called the **doomsday ratio**.[7] Its name comes from the worst case assumption that the business ceases to exist and only the cash on hand is available to meet creditor obligations.

In computing the ratio of cash to current liabilities, cash and cash equivalents are used in the numerator, as shown below.

$$\text{Doomsday ratio} = \frac{\textbf{Cash and cash equivalents}}{\textbf{Current liabilities}}$$

To illustrate, assume the following data for Laettner Co. and Oakley Co. for the current year:

	Laettner Co.	Oakley Co.
Cash and cash equivalents	$100,000	$ 120,000
Current liabilities	400,000	1,500,000

The doomsday ratio for each company is computed as follows. In this case, Oakley Co. is more risky to creditors than is Laettner.

	Doomsday Ratio	
Laettner Co.	0.25	($100,000/$400,000)
Oakley Co.	0.08	($120,000/$1,500,000)

Because most businesses maintain cash and cash equivalents at amounts substantially less than their current liabilities, the doomsday ratio is almost always less than one. For example, the doomsday ratio for **Tandy Corporation** is 0.18. For **La-Z-Boy Chair Company**, it is 0.25.

Differences among companies will occur because of differences in management philosophy and operating styles. Nevertheless, a comparison over time that indicates a decreasing ratio generally indicates more risk for creditors.

---

[7] This ratio is discussed more fully in *101 Business Ratios* by Sheldon Gates, McLane Publications, Scottsdale, Arizona, 1993.

The Theft at Perini Corporation

The financial vice-president of **Perini Corporation** received a disturbing call from one of the company's banks. The bank reported that Perini's bank account was substantially overdrawn. Perini, a large construction company based near Boston, had never overdrawn any of its bank accounts in over twenty-five years. Shortly thereafter, another of Perini's banks called and reported that its Perini account was also overdrawn. A review of the recent bank statements, which had been lying around unreconciled for two weeks, revealed canceled checks of more than $1.1 million that had not been recorded.

Perini kept its unused checks in an unlocked room. Perini also kept its supply of coffee cups in the same

room, where every clerk and secretary had access to them. A quick review revealed two missing boxes of checks.

Perini used a checkwriting machine that automatically signed the vice-president's name. Unfortunately, Perini didn't implement the controls suggested by its auditor. Instead, the machine-processed checks were placed in an unlocked box, there was no reconciliation of the counter on

the machine with the number of checks that should have been written, and the keys to lock the machine were not carefully safeguarded. The vice-president said that such controls were "too much trouble."

The rest of the story involves a possible suspect who is killed in a lovers' feud involving a neurosurgeon; a bizarre arson in Perini's financial offices; a hit-and-run accident involving

a boat; and a quiet accountant who purchased a new Continental, moved to Las Vegas, bought an expensive house, and began running sex shows in casinos. Even though the FBI assigned one of its best agents to the case, the money was never recovered and the perpetrator of the theft remains a mystery. ■

KEY POINTS

1 Define an accounting system and describe its implementation.

An accounting system is the methods and procedures for collecting, classifying, summarizing, and reporting a business's financial information. The three steps through which an accounting system evolves are (1) analysis of information needs, (2) design of the system, and (3) implementation of the systems design.

2 List the three objectives of internal control, and define and give examples of the five elements of internal control.

Internal control provides reasonable assurance that (1) assets are safeguarded and used for business purposes, (2) business information is accurate, and (3) laws and regulations are complied with. The five elements of internal control are the control environment, risk assessment, control procedures, monitoring, and information and communication.

3 Describe the nature of cash and the importance of internal control over cash.

Cash includes coins, currency (paper money), checks, money orders, and money on deposit

that is available for unrestricted withdrawal from banks and other financial institutions. Because of the ease with which money can be transferred, businesses should design and use controls that safeguard cash and authorize cash transactions.

4 Summarize basic procedures for achieving internal control over cash receipts.

One of the most important controls to protect cash received in over-the-counter sales is a cash register. A remittance advice is a preventive control for cash received through the mail. Separating the duties of handling cash and recording cash is also a preventive control.

5 Summarize basic procedures for achieving internal control over cash payments, including the use of a voucher system.

A voucher system is a set of procedures for authorizing and recording liabilities and cash payments. A voucher system uses vouchers, a file for unpaid vouchers, and a file for paid vouchers.

6 Describe the nature of a bank account and its use in controlling cash.

The forms used with bank accounts are a signature card, deposit ticket, check, and record of checks drawn. Each month, the bank usually sends a bank statement to the depositor, summarizing all of the transactions for the month. The bank statement allows a business to compare the cash transactions recorded in the accounting records to those recorded by the bank.

7 Prepare a bank reconciliation and journalize any necessary entries.

The first section of the bank reconciliation begins with the cash balance according to the bank statement. This balance is adjusted for the depositor's changes in cash that do not appear on the bank statement and for any bank errors. The second section begins with the cash balance according to the depositor's records. This balance is adjusted for the bank's changes in cash that do not appear on the depositor's records and for any depositor errors. The adjusted balances for the two sections must be equal.

No entries are necessary on the depositor's records as a result of the information included in the first section of the bank reconciliation. However, the items in the second section must be journalized on the depositor's records.

8 Account for small cash transactions using a petty cash fund.

A petty cash fund may be used by a business to make small payments that occur frequently. The money in a petty cash fund is placed in the custody of a specific employee, who authorizes payments from the fund. Periodically or when the amount of money in the fund is depleted or reduced to a minimum amount, the fund is replenished.

9 Summarize how cash is presented on the balance sheet.

Cash is listed as the first asset in the Current Assets section of the balance sheet. Companies that have invested excess cash in highly liquid investments usually report *Cash and cash equivalents* on the balance sheet.

10 Compute and interpret the ratio of cash to current liabilities.

A company that is in financial distress may have difficulty converting its receivables, inventory, and prepaid assets to cash on a timely basis. In these cases, the ratio of cash to current liabilities, called the doomsday ratio, may be useful in assessing the ability of creditors to collect what they are owed.

ILLUSTRATIVE PROBLEM

The bank statement for Urethane Company for June 30, 2003, indicates a balance of $9,143.11. All cash receipts are deposited each evening in a night depository, after banking hours. The accounting records indicate the following summary data for cash receipts and payments for June:

Cash balance as of June 1	$ 3,943.50
Total cash receipts for June	28,971.60
Total amount of checks issued in June	28,388.85

Comparing the bank statement and the accompanying canceled checks and memorandums with the records reveals the following reconciling items:

a. The bank had collected for Urethane Company $1,030 on a note left for collection. The face of the note was $1,000.
b. A deposit of $1,852.21, representing receipts of June 30, had been made too late to appear on the bank statement.
c. Checks outstanding totaled $5,265.27.
d. A check drawn for $139 had been incorrectly charged by the bank as $157.
e. A check for $30 returned with the statement had been recorded in the depositor's records as $240. The check was for the payment of an obligation to Avery Equipment Company for the purchase of office supplies on account.
f. Bank service charges for June amounted to $18.20.

Instructions

1. Prepare a bank reconciliation for June.
2. Journalize the entries that should be made by Urethane Company.

Solution

1.

Urethane Company
Bank Reconciliation
June 30, 2003

Cash balance according to bank statement		$ 9,143.11
Add: Deposit of June 30 not recorded by bank	$1,852.21	
Bank error in charging check as $157 instead of $139	18.00	1,870.21
		$11,013.32
Deduct: Outstanding checks		5,265.27
Adjusted balance		$ 5,748.05

Cash balance according to depositor's records		$ 4,526.25*
Add: Proceeds of note collected by bank, including $30 interest	$1,030.00	
Error in recording check	210.00	1,240.00
		$ 5,766.25
Deduct: Bank service charges		18.20
Adjusted balance		$ 5,748.05

*$3,943.50 + $28,971.60 − $28,388.85

2.

Cash	1,240.00	
Notes Receivable		1,000.00
Interest Revenue		30.00
Accounts Payable—Avery Equipment		210.00
Miscellaneous Administrative Expense	18.20	
Cash		18.20

SELF-EXAMINATION QUESTIONS

Answers at End of Chapter

Matching

Match each of the following statements with its proper term. Some terms may not be used.

A. accounting system	
B. bank reconciliation	
C. bank statement	
D. cash	
E. cash equivalents	
F. cash short and over	
G. doomsday ratio	
H. electronic funds transfer (EFT)	
I. elements of internal control	
J. employee fraud	
K. internal controls	
L. notes receivable	
M. petty cash fund	
N. voucher	
O. voucher system	
P. working capital ratio	

____ 1. Coins, currency (paper money), checks, money orders, and money on deposit that is available for unrestricted withdrawal from banks and other financial institutions.

____ 2. A set of procedures for authorizing and recording liabilities and cash payments.

____ 3. A special form for recording relevant data about a liability and the details of its payment.

____ 4. A system in which computers rather than paper (money, checks, etc.) are used to effect cash transactions.

____ 5. A special cash fund to pay relatively small amounts.

____ 6. The analysis that details the items responsible for the difference between the cash balance reported in the bank statement and the balance of the cash account in the ledger.

____ 7. Highly liquid investments that are usually reported with cash on the balance sheet.

____ 8. The ratio of cash and cash equivalents to current liabilities.

____ 9. The intentional act of deceiving an employer for personal gain.

____10. The methods and procedures used by a business to collect, classify, summarize, and report financial data for use by management and external users.

____11. The policies and procedures used to safeguard assets, ensure accurate business information, and ensure compliance with laws and regulations.

____12. The control environment, risk assessment, control activities, information and communication, and monitoring.

Multiple Choice

1. The initial step in the process of developing an accounting system is called:
   A. analysis   C. implementation
   B. design   D. feedback

2. The policies and procedures used by management to protect assets from misuse, ensure accurate business information, and ensure compliance with laws and regulations are called:
   A. internal controls   C. systems design
   B. systems analysis   D. systems implementation

3. In preparing a bank reconciliation, the amount of checks outstanding would be:
   A. added to the cash balance according to the bank statement.
   B. deducted from the cash balance according to the bank statement.
   C. added to the cash balance according to the depositor's records.
   D. deducted from the cash balance according to the depositor's records.

4. Journal entries based on the bank reconciliation are required for:
   A. additions to the cash balance according to the depositor's records.
   B. deductions from the cash balance according to the depositor's records.
   C. both A and B.
   D. neither A nor B.

5. A petty cash fund is:
   A. used to pay relatively small amounts.
   B. established by estimating the amount of cash needed for disbursements of relatively small amounts during a specified period.
   C. reimbursed when the amount of money in the fund is reduced to a predetermined minimum amount.
   D. all of the above.

CLASS DISCUSSION QUESTIONS

1. Why is the accounting system of a business an information system?
2. What is the three-step process of systems evolution?
3. What are the three objectives of internal control?
4. Name and describe the five elements of internal control.
5. How does a policy of rotating clerical employees from job to job aid in strengthening the control procedures within the control environment?
6. Why should the responsibility for a sequence of related operations be divided among different persons?
7. Why should the employee who handles cash receipts not have the responsibility for maintaining the accounts receivable records?
8. In an attempt to improve operating efficiency, one employee was made responsible for all purchasing, receiving, and storing of supplies. Is this organizational change wise from an internal control standpoint? Explain.
9. The ticket seller at a movie theater doubles as a ticket taker for a few minutes each day while the ticket taker is on a break. Which control procedure of a business's system of internal control is violated in this situation?
10. Why should the responsibility for maintaining the accounting records be separated from the responsibility for operations?
11. Why is cash the asset that often warrants the most attention in the design of an effective internal control structure?
12. The combined cash count of all cash registers at the close of business is $110 less than the cash sales indicated by the cash register tapes. (a) In what account is the cash shortage recorded? (b) Are cash shortages debited or credited to this account?
13. In which section of the income statement would a credit balance in Cash Short and Over be reported?
14. Before a voucher for the purchase of merchandise is approved for payment, supporting documents should be compared to verify the accuracy of the liability. Name an example of a supporting document for the purchase of merchandise.
15. When is a voucher recorded?
16. The accounting clerk pays all obligations by prenumbered checks. What are the strengths and weaknesses in the internal control over cash payments in this situation?
17. In what order are vouchers ordinarily filed (a) in the unpaid voucher file and (b) in the paid voucher file? Give reasons for the answers.

18. The balance of Cash is likely to differ from the bank statement balance. What two factors are likely to be responsible for the difference?
19. What is the purpose of preparing a bank reconciliation?
20. Do items reported on the bank statement as credits represent (a) additions made by the bank to the depositor's balance, or (b) deductions made by the bank from the depositor's balance?
21. What entry should be made if a check received from a customer and deposited is returned by the bank for lack of sufficient funds (an NSF check)?
22. Explain why some cash payments are made in coins and currency from a petty cash fund.
23. What account or accounts are debited when (a) establishing a petty cash fund and (b) replenishing a petty cash fund?
24. The petty cash account has a debit balance of $750. At the end of the accounting period, there is $112 in the petty cash fund, along with petty cash receipts totaling $638. Should the fund be replenished as of the last day of the period? Discuss.
25. How are cash equivalents reported in the financial statements?
26. How is a compensating balance reported in the financial statements?

RESOURCES FOR YOUR SUCCESS ONLINE AT

http://warren.swcollege.com

Remember! If you need additional help, visit South-Western's Web site.
See page F26 for a description of the online and printed materials that are available.

EXERCISES

Exercise 6–1
Internal controls

Objective 2

Connie Stevens has recently been hired as the manager of Big Apple Deli. Big Apple Deli is a national chain of franchised delicatessens. During her first month as store manager, Connie encountered the following internal control situations:

a. Big Apple Deli has one cash register. Prior to Connie's joining the deli, each employee working on a shift would take a customer order, accept payment, and then prepare the order. Connie made one employee on each shift responsible for taking orders and accepting the customer's payment. Other employees prepare the orders.
b. Since only one employee uses the cash register, that employee is responsible for counting the cash at the end of the shift and verifying that the cash in the drawer matches the amount of cash sales recorded by the cash register. Connie expects each cashier to balance the drawer to the penny *every* time—no exceptions.
c. Connie caught an employee putting a box of 100 single-serving bags of potato chips in his car. Not wanting to create a scene, Connie smiled and said, "I don't think you're putting those chips on the right shelf. Don't they belong inside the deli?" The employee returned the chips to the stockroom.

State whether you agree or disagree with Connie's method of handling each situation and explain your answer.

Exercise 6–2
Internal controls

Objective 2

Summer Breeze is a retail store specializing in women's clothing. The store has established a liberal return policy for the holiday season in order to encourage gift purchases. Any item purchased during November and December may be returned through January 31, with a receipt, for cash or exchange. If the customer does not have a receipt, cash will still be refunded for any item under $25. If the item is more than $25, a check is mailed to the customer.

Whenever an item is returned, a store clerk completes a return slip, which the customer signs. The return slip is placed in a special box. The store manager visits the return counter approximately once every two hours to authorize the return slips. Clerks are instructed to place the returned merchandise on the proper rack on the selling floor as soon as possible.

This year, returns at Summer Breeze have reached an all-time high. There are a large number of returns under $25 without receipts.

a. How can sales clerks employed at Summer Breeze use the store's return policy to steal money from the cash register?

b. 1. What internal control weaknesses do you see in the return policy that make cash thefts easier?

   2. Would issuing a store credit in place of a cash refund for all merchandise returned without a receipt reduce the possibility of theft? List some advantages and disadvantages of issuing a store credit in place of a cash refund.

   3. Assume that Summer Breeze is committed to the current policy of issuing cash refunds without a receipt. What changes could be made in the store's procedures regarding customer refunds in order to improve internal control?

Exercise 6–3
Internal controls for bank lending

Objective 2

United Savings Bank provides loans to businesses in the community through its Commercial Lending Department. Small loans (less than $100,000) may be approved by an individual loan officer, while larger loans (greater than $100,000) must be approved by a board of loan officers. Once a loan is approved, the funds are made available to the loan applicant under agreed-upon terms. The president of United Savings Bank has instituted a policy whereby she has the individual authority to approve loans up to $5,000,000. The president believes that this policy will allow flexibility to approve loans to valued clients much quicker than under the previous policy.

As an internal auditor of United Savings Bank, how would you respond to this change in policy?

Exercise 6–4
Internal controls

Objective 2

One of the largest fraud losses in history involved a securities trader for the Singapore office of **Barings Bank**, a British merchant bank. The trader established an unauthorized account number that was used to hide $1.4 billion in losses. Even after Barings' internal auditors noted that the trader both executed trades and recorded them, management did not take action. As a result, a lone individual in a remote office bankrupted an internationally recognized firm overnight.

What general weaknesses in Barings' internal controls contributed to the occurrence and size of the fraud?

Exercise 6–5
Internal controls

Objective 2

In the **Equity Funding** fraud, approximately $2 billion of insurance policies that were claimed to have been sold by the company were bogus. The bogus policies, which were supported by falsified policy applications, were listed along with real policies on Equity Funding's computer files (records). Equity Funding personnel, including the computer programmers, kept these files in a separate room where they were easily accessible. In addition, computer programmers and other company personnel had access to the computer.

What general weaknesses in Equity Funding's internal controls contributed to the occurrence and size of the fraud?

Exercise 6–6
Financial statement fraud

Objective 2

The former chairman, the CFO, and the controller of **Donnkenny**, an apparel company that makes sportswear for Pierre Cardin and Victoria Jones, pleaded guilty to financial statement fraud. These managers used false journal entries to record fictitious sales, hid inventory in public warehouses so that it could be recorded as "sold," and required sales orders to be backdated so that the sale could be moved back to an earlier period. The combined effect of these actions caused $25 million out of $40 million in quarterly sales to be phony.

a. Why might control procedures listed in this chapter be insufficient in stopping this type of fraud?

b. How could this type of fraud be stopped?

Exercise 6–7

Internal control of cash receipts

Objective 4

The procedures used for over-the-counter receipts are as follows. At the close of each day's business, the sales clerks count the cash in their respective cash drawers, after which they determine the amount recorded by the cash register and prepare the memorandum cash form, noting any discrepancies. An employee from the cashier's office counts the cash, compares the total with the memorandum, and takes the cash to the cashier's office.

a. ━━━➤ Indicate the weak link in internal control.

b. ━━━➤ How can the weakness be corrected?

Exercise 6–8

Internal control of cash receipts

Objective 4

Kathy Beal works at the drive-through window of Fletch's Burgers. Occasionally, when a drive-through customer orders, Kathy fills the order and pockets the customer's money. She does not ring up the order on the cash register.

━━━➤ Identify the internal control weaknesses that exist at Fletch's Burgers, and discuss what can be done to prevent this theft.

Exercise 6–9

Internal control of cash receipts

Objective 4

The mailroom employees send all remittances and remittance advices to the cashier. The cashier deposits the cash in the bank and forwards the remittance advices and duplicate deposit slips to the Accounting Department.

a. ━━━➤ Indicate the weak link in internal control in the handling of cash receipts.

b. ━━━➤ How can the weakness be corrected?

Exercise 6–10

Entry for cash sales; cash short

Objective 4

The actual cash received from cash sales was $18,153.79, and the amount indicated by the cash register total was $18,178.31. Journalize the entry to record the cash receipts and cash sales.

Exercise 6–11

Entry for cash sales; cash over

The actual cash received from cash sales was $9,357.69, and the amount indicated by the cash register total was $9,346.22. Journalize the entry to record the cash receipts and cash sales.

Exercise 6–12

Internal control of cash payments

Objective 5

Fiedler Co. is a medium-size merchandising company. An investigation revealed that in spite of a sufficient bank balance, a significant amount of available cash discounts had been lost because of failure to make timely payments. In addition, it was discovered that several purchases invoices had been paid twice.

━━━➤ Outline procedures for the payment of vendors' invoices, so that the possibilities of losing available cash discounts and of paying an invoice a second time will be minimized.

Exercise 6–13

Internal control of cash payments

Objective 5

Herringbone Company, a communications equipment manufacturer, recently fell victim to an embezzlement scheme masterminded by one of its employees. To understand the scheme, it is necessary to review Herringbone's procedures for the purchase of services.

The purchasing agent is responsible for ordering services (such as repairs to a photocopy machine or office cleaning) after receiving a service requisition from an authorized manager. However, since no tangible goods are delivered, a receiving report is not prepared. When the Accounting Department receives an invoice billing Herringbone for a service call, the accounts payable clerk calls the manager who requested the service in order to verify that it was performed.

The embezzlement scheme involves Kellie Barth, the manager of plant and facilities. Kellie arranged for her uncle's company, Barth Industrial Supply and Service, to be placed on Herringbone's approved vendor list. Kellie did not disclose the family relationship.

On several occasions, Kellie would submit a requisition for services to be provided by Barth Industrial Supply and Service. However, the service requested was really not needed, and it was never performed. Barth would bill Herringbone for the service and then split the cash payment with Kellie.

━━━➤ Explain what changes should be made to Herringbone's procedures for ordering and paying for services in order to prevent such occurrences in the future.

Exercise 6–14
Bank reconciliation

Objective 7

Identify each of the following reconciling items as: (a) an addition to the cash balance according to the bank statement, (b) a deduction from the cash balance according to the bank statement, (c) an addition to the cash balance according to the depositor's records, or (d) a deduction from the cash balance according to the depositor's records. (None of the transactions reported by bank debit and credit memorandums have been recorded by the depositor.)

1. Outstanding checks, $3,512.30.
2. Deposit in transit, $10,000.
3. Note collected by bank, $8,000.
4. Check for $89 incorrectly charged by bank as $98.
5. Check drawn by depositor for $200 but incorrectly recorded as $2,000.
6. Check of a customer returned by bank to depositor because of insufficient funds, $775.
7. Bank service charges, $25.

Exercise 6–15
Entries based on bank reconciliation

Objective 7

Which of the reconciling items listed in Exercise 6–14 require an entry in the depositor's accounts?

Exercise 6–16
Bank reconciliation

Objective 7

SPREADSHEET

✓ Adjusted balance: $8,961.45

The following data were accumulated for use in reconciling the bank account of Juno Co. for July:

a. Cash balance according to the depositor's records at July 31, $8,530.20.
b. Cash balance according to the bank statement at July 31, $3,457.25.
c. Checks outstanding, $1,276.20.
d. Deposit in transit, not recorded by bank, $6,780.40.
e. A check for $270 in payment of an account was erroneously recorded in the check register as $720.
f. Bank debit memorandum for service charges, $18.75.

Prepare a bank reconciliation, using the format shown in Exhibit 9.

Exercise 6–17
Entries for bank reconciliation

Objective 7

Using the data presented in Exercise 6–16, journalize the entry or entries that should be made by the depositor.

Exercise 6–18
Entries for note collected by bank

Objective 7

Accompanying a bank statement for Lyric Company is a credit memorandum for $12,500, representing the principal ($12,000) and interest ($500) on a note that had been collected by the bank. The depositor had been notified by the bank at the time of the collection but had made no entries. Journalize the entry that should be made by the depositor to bring the accounting records up to date.

Exercise 6–19
Bank reconciliation

Objective 7

✓ Adjusted balance: $13,445.00

An accounting clerk for Noxious Co. prepared the following bank reconciliation:

Noxious Co.
Bank Reconciliation
March 31, 2003

Cash balance according to depositor's records		$10,100.75
Add: Outstanding checks	$7,557.12	
Error by Noxious Co. in recording Check		
No. 1621 as $2,510 instead of $2,150	360.00	
Note for $2,500 collected by bank, including interest	3,000.00	10,917.12
		$21,017.87
Deduct: Deposit in transit on March 31	$6,150.00	
Bank service charges	15.75	6,165.75
Cash balance according to bank statement		$14,852.12

a. From the data in the above bank reconciliation, prepare a new bank reconciliation for Noxious Co., using the format shown in the illustrative problem.
b. If a balance sheet were prepared for Noxious Co. on March 31, 2003, what amount should be reported for cash?

Exercise 6–20
Bank reconciliation
Objective 7

What's Wrong With This?

✓ Corrected adjusted balance:
$9,998.02

How many errors can you find in the following bank reconciliation?

Protractor Co.
Bank Reconciliation
For the Month Ended November 30, 2003

Cash balance according to bank statement		$ 9,767.76
Add outstanding checks:		
No. 721	$ 545.95	
739	172.75	
743	459.60	
744	601.50	1,779.80
		$11,547.56
Deduct deposit of November 30, not recorded by bank		2,010.06
Adjusted balance		$10,537.50
Cash balance according to depositor's records		$ 4,363.62
Add: Proceeds of note collected by bank:		
Principal	$5,000.00	
Interest	750.00	$5,750.00
Service charges		20.00	5,770.00
		$10,133.62
Deduct: Check returned because of		
insufficient funds	$ 635.60	
Error in recording November 10		
deposit of $3,718 as $3,178	540.00	1,175.60
Adjusted balance		$ 8,958.02

Exercise 6–21
Using bank reconciliation to determine cash receipts stolen
Objective 7

Ovation Co. records all cash receipts on the basis of its cash register tapes. Ovation Co. discovered during November 2003 that one of its sales clerks had stolen an undetermined amount of cash receipts when he took the daily deposits to the bank. The following data have been gathered for November:

Cash in bank according to the general ledger	$11,573.22
Cash according to the November 30, 2003 bank statement	14,271.14
Outstanding checks as of November 30, 2003	2,901.38
Bank service charge for November	25.10
Note receivable, including interest collected by bank in November	3,060.00

No deposits were in transit on November 30, which fell on a Sunday.

a. Determine the amount of cash receipts stolen by the sales clerk.
b. What accounting controls would have prevented or detected this theft?

Exercise 6–22
Petty cash fund entries
Objective 8

Journalize the entries to record the following:

a. Check No. 3910 is issued to establish a petty cash fund of $600.
b. The amount of cash in the petty cash fund is now $69.98. Check No. 4183 is issued to replenish the fund, based on the following summary of petty cash receipts: office supplies, $315.83; miscellaneous selling expense, $112.60; miscellaneous administrative expense, $88.10. (Since the amount of the check to replenish the fund plus the balance in the fund do not equal $600, record the discrepancy in the cash short and over account.)

Exercise 6–23
Variation in cash balances

Objective 9

For a recent fiscal year, **Kmart's** quarterly balances of cash and cash equivalents were as follows:

End of January	$498 million
End of April	$733 million
End of July	$556 million
End of October	$350 million

What would you expect would be the cause of the variation in Kmart's balances of cash and cash equivalents?

Exercise 6–24
Doomsday ratio

Objective 10

The financial statements for **Cisco Systems, Inc.**, are presented in Appendix G at the end of the text.

a. Compute the doomsday ratio for Cisco Systems, Inc. for 2000 and 1999.
b. What conclusions can be drawn from comparing the ratios for 2000 and 1999?

PROBLEMS SERIES A

Problem 6–1A
Evaluating internal control of cash

Objectives 2, 3, 4, 5

The following procedures were recently installed by Gambrel Company:

a. Along with petty cash expense receipts for postage, office supplies, etc., several post-dated employee checks are in the petty cash fund.
b. The accounts payable clerk prepares a voucher for each disbursement. The voucher along with the supporting documentation is forwarded to the treasurer's office for approval.
c. At the end of each day, an accounting clerk compares the duplicate copy of the daily cash deposit slip with the deposit receipt obtained from the bank.
d. The bank reconciliation is prepared by the cashier, who works under the supervision of the treasurer.
e. At the end of the day, cash register clerks are required to use their own funds to make up any cash shortages in their registers.
f. All mail is opened by the mail clerk, who forwards all cash remittances to the cashier. The cashier prepares a listing of the cash receipts and forwards a copy of the list to the accounts receivable clerk for recording in the accounts.
g. After necessary approvals have been obtained for the payment of a voucher, the treasurer signs and mails the check. The treasurer then stamps the voucher and supporting documentation as paid and returns the voucher and supporting documentation to the accounts payable clerk for filing.
h. At the end of each day, any deposited cash receipts are placed in the bank's night depository.

Instructions

Indicate whether each of the procedures of internal control over cash represents (1) a strength or (2) a weakness. For each weakness, indicate why it exists.

Problem 6–2A
Transactions for petty cash; cash short and over

Objectives 4, 8

Towaway Company completed the following selected transactions during January of the current year:

Jan. 3. Established a petty cash fund of $750.
10. The cash sales for the day, according to the cash register tapes, totaled $5,970.60. The actual cash received from cash sales was $6,001.75.

Jan. 28. Petty cash on hand was $145.18. Replenished the petty cash fund for the following disbursements, each evidenced by a petty cash receipt:

Jan. 4. Store supplies, $181.50.

5. Express charges on merchandise sold, $80 (Transportation Out).

8. Office supplies, $12.75.

15. Office supplies, $39.30.

17. Postage stamps, $66 (Office Supplies).

20. Repair to office calculator, $37.50 (Miscellaneous Administrative Expense).

22. Postage due on special delivery letter, $15.00 (Miscellaneous Administrative Expense).

24. Express charges on merchandise sold, $125 (Transportation Out).

27. Office supplies, $41.15.

30. The cash sales for the day, according to the cash register tapes, totaled $5,055.50. The actual cash received from cash sales was $5,010.25.

31. Increased the petty cash fund by $50.

Instructions

Journalize the transactions.

Problem 6–3A

Bank reconciliation and entries

Objective 7

SPREADSHEET
GENERAL LEDGER

✓ 1. Adjusted balance: $20,395.95

The cash account for Wok Co. at November 30, 2003, indicated a balance of $16,190.95. The bank statement indicated a balance of $21,016.30 on November 30, 2003. Comparing the bank statement and the accompanying canceled checks and memorandums with the records revealed the following reconciling items:

a. Checks outstanding totaled $5,169.75.

b. A deposit of $4,189.40, representing receipts of November 30, had been made too late to appear on the bank statement.

c. The bank had collected $4,500 on a note left for collection. The face of the note was $4,000.

d. A check for $2,850 returned with the statement had been incorrectly recorded by Wok Co. as $2,580. The check was for the payment of an obligation to Kiser Co. for the purchase of office equipment on account.

e. A check drawn for $1,375 had been erroneously charged by the bank as $1,735.

f. Bank service charges for November amounted to $25.00.

Instructions

1. Prepare a bank reconciliation.

2. Journalize the necessary entries. The accounts have not been closed.

Problem 6–4A

Bank reconciliation and entries

Objective 7

GENERAL LEDGER

✓ 1. Adjusted balance: $3,599.87

The cash account for Magneto Co. at August 1 of the current year indicated a balance of $2,705.37. During August, the total cash deposited was $21,077.75, and checks written totaled $21,770.25. The bank statement indicated a balance of $3,465.50 on August 31. Comparing the bank statement, the canceled checks, and the accompanying memorandums with the records revealed the following reconciling items:

a. Checks outstanding totaled $2,003.84.

b. A deposit of $1,148.21, representing receipts of August 31, had been made too late to appear on the bank statement.

c. The bank had collected for Magneto Co. $1,620 on a note left for collection. The face of the note was $1,500.

d. A check for $110 returned with the statement had been incorrectly charged by the bank as $1,100.

e. A check for $86 returned with the statement had been recorded by Magneto Co. as $68. The check was for the payment of an obligation to Adgate Co. on account.

f. Bank service charges for August amounted to $15.

Instructions

1. Prepare a bank reconciliation as of August 31.

2. Journalize the necessary entries. The accounts have not been closed.

Problem 6–5A
Bank reconciliation and entries

Objective 7

✓ I. Adjusted balance: $10,622.02

Kudzu Company deposits all cash receipts each Wednesday and Friday in a night depository, after banking hours. The data required to reconcile the bank statement as of June 30 have been taken from various documents and records and are reproduced as follows. The sources of the data are printed in capital letters. All checks were written for payments on account.

CASH ACCOUNT:

Balance as of June 1 $7,317.40

CASH RECEIPTS FOR MONTH OF JUNE $8,451.58

DUPLICATE DEPOSIT TICKETS:

Date and amount of each deposit in June:

Date	Amount	Date	Amount	Date	Amount
June 1	$1,080.50	June 10	$ 896.61	June 22	$897.34
3	854.17	15	882.95	24	942.71
8	840.50	17	1,246.74	29	810.06

CHECKS WRITTEN:

Number and amount of each check issued in June:

Check No.	Amount	Check No.	Amount	Check No.	Amount
740	$237.50	747	Void	754	$249.75
741	495.15	748	$450.90	755	272.75
742	501.90	749	640.13	756	113.95
743	671.30	750	276.77	757	407.95
744	506.88	751	299.37	758	159.60
745	117.25	752	537.01	759	501.50
746	298.66	753	380.95	760	486.39

Total amount of checks issued in June $7,605.66

BANK RECONCILIATION FOR PRECEDING MONTH:

Kudzu Company
Bank Reconciliation
May 31, 20—

Cash balance according to bank statement		$7,447.20
Add deposit for May 31, not recorded by bank		690.25
		$8,137.45
Deduct outstanding checks:		
No. 731	$162.15	
736	345.95	
738	251.40	
739	60.55	820.05
Adjusted balance		$7,317.40
Cash balance according to depositor's records		$7,352.50
Deduct service charges		35.10
Adjusted balance		$7,317.40

JUNE BANK STATEMENT:

		MEMBER FDIC		PAGE 1
AB **AMERICAN NATIONAL BANK OF DETROIT** DETROIT, MI 48201-2500 (313)933-8547			ACCOUNT NUMBER	
			FROM 6/01/20–	TO 6/30/20–
			BALANCE	7,447.20
			9 DEPOSITS	8,691.77
			20 WITHDRAWALS	7,345.91
KUDZU COMPANY			4 OTHER DEBITS AND CREDITS	2,298.70CR
			NEW BALANCE	11,091.76

* – – – –CHECKS AND OTHER DEBITS – – – – – *				* – – DEPOSITS – – *	– DATE – *	– – BALANCE– – *
No.731	162.15	No.738	251.40	690.25	06/01	7,723.90
No.739	60.55	No.740	237.50	1,080.50	06/02	8,506.35
No.741	495.15	No.742	501.90	854.17	06/04	8,363.47
No.743	671.30	No.744	506.88	840.50	06/09	8,025.79
No.745	117.25	No.746	298.66	MS 2,500.00	06/09	10,109.88
No.748	450.90	No.749	640.13	MS 125.00	06/09	9,143.85
No.750	276.77	No.751	299.37	896.61	06/11	9,464.32
No.752	537.01	No.753	380.95	882.95	06/16	9,429.31
No.754	449.75	No.756	113.95	1,606.74	06/18	10,472.35
No.757	407.95	No.760	486.39	897.34	06/23	10,475.35
				942.71	06/25	11,418.06
		NSF	291.90		06/28	11,126.16
		SC	34.40		06/30	11,091.76

EC — ERROR CORRECTION	OD — OVERDRAFT
MS — MISCELLANEOUS	PS — PAYMENT STOPPED
NSF — NOT SUFFICIENT FUNDS	SC — SERVICE CHARGE

* * *   * * *   * * *

THE RECONCILEMENT OF THIS STATEMENT WITH YOUR RECORDS IS ESSENTIAL.
ANY ERROR OR EXCEPTION SHOULD BE REPORTED IMMEDIATELY.

Instructions

1. Prepare a bank reconciliation as of June 30. If errors in recording deposits or checks are discovered, assume that the errors were made by the company. Assume that all deposits are from cash sales. All checks are written to satisfy accounts payable.
2. Journalize the necessary entries. The accounts have not been closed.
3. What is the amount of Cash that should appear on the balance sheet as of June 30?
4. ✏️► If in preparing the bank reconciliation you note that a canceled check for $270 has been incorrectly recorded by the bank as $720, briefly explain how the error would be included in the bank reconciliation and how it should be corrected.

PROBLEMS SERIES B

Problem 6–1B

Evaluate internal control of cash

Objectives 2, 3, 4, 5

The following procedures were recently installed by The Recipe Company:

a. The bank reconciliation is prepared by the accountant.
b. Disbursements are made from the petty cash fund only after a petty cash receipt has been completed and signed by the payee.

c. Checks received through the mail are given daily to the accounts receivable clerk for recording collections on account and for depositing in the bank.

d. At the end of a shift, each cashier counts the cash in his or her cash register, unlocks the tape, and compares the amount of cash with the amount on the tape to determine cash shortages and overages.

e. Each cashier is assigned a separate cash register drawer to which no other cashier has access.

f. All sales are rung up on the cash register, and a receipt is given to the customer. All sales are recorded on a tape locked inside the cash register.

g. Vouchers and all supporting documents are perforated with a PAID designation after being paid by the treasurer.

Instructions

Indicate whether each of the procedures of internal control over cash represents (1) a strength or (2) a weakness. For each weakness, indicate why it exists.

Problem 6–2B

Transactions for petty cash, cash short and over

Objectives 4, 8

Spandex Company completed the following selected transactions during September of the current year:

Sept. 1. Established a petty cash fund of $800.

    8. The cash sales for the day, according to the cash register tapes, totaled $8,995.60. The actual cash received from cash sales was $9,008.15.

   29. Petty cash on hand was $100.50. Replenished the petty cash fund for the following disbursements, each evidenced by a petty cash receipt:

      Sept. 3. Store supplies, $110.75.

         7. Express charges on merchandise purchased, $180.75 (Merchandise Inventory).

        10. Office supplies, $74.30.

        11. Office supplies, $35.20.

        12. Postage stamps, $52.00 (Office Supplies).

        16. Repair to adding machine, $69.50 (Miscellaneous Administrative Expense).

        21. Repair to typewriter, $51.50 (Miscellaneous Administrative Expense).

        22. Postage due on special delivery letter, $10.00 (Miscellaneous Administrative Expense).

        27. Express charges on merchandise purchased, $105.60 (Merchandise Inventory).

   30. The cash sales for the day, according to the cash register tapes, totaled $10,009.50. The actual cash received from cash sales was $9,999.90.

   30. Decreased the petty cash fund by $200.

Instructions

Journalize the transactions.

Problem 6–3B

Bank reconciliation and entries

Objective 7

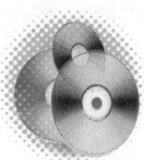

SPREADSHEET
GENERAL LEDGER

✓ 1. Adjusted balance: $21,506.10

The cash account for Viaduct Systems at March 31, 2003, indicated a balance of $17,474.35. The bank statement indicated a balance of $23,391.40 on March 31, 2003. Comparing the bank statement and the accompanying canceled checks and memorandums with the records reveals the following reconciling items:

a. Checks outstanding totaled $5,010.80.

b. A deposit of $3,215.50, representing receipts of March 31, had been made too late to appear on the bank statement.

c. The bank had collected $3,600 on a note left for collection. The face of the note was $3,000.

d. A check for $1,050 returned with the statement had been incorrectly recorded by Viaduct Systems as $1,500. The check was for the payment of an obligation to Bates Co. for the purchase of office supplies on account.

e. A check drawn for $878 had been incorrectly charged by the bank as $788.

f. Bank service charges for March amounted to $18.25.

Instructions

1. Prepare a bank reconciliation.

2. Journalize the necessary entries. The accounts have not been closed.

Problem 6–4B

Bank reconciliation and entries

Objective 7

GENERAL LEDGER

✓ 1. Adjusted balance: $12,001.88

The cash account for Actuator Co. on June 1, 2003, indicated a balance of $6,911.95. During June, the total cash deposited was $70,500.40, and checks written totaled $67,568.47. The bank statement indicated a balance of $13,880.45 on June 30, 2003. Comparing the bank statement, the canceled checks, and the accompanying memorandums with the records revealed the following reconciling items:

a. Checks outstanding totaled $6,180.27.
b. A deposit of $4,481.70, representing receipts of June 30, had been made too late to appear on the bank statement.
c. A check for $310 had been incorrectly charged by the bank as $130.
d. A check for $257.25 returned with the statement had been recorded by Actuator Co. as $527.25. The check was for the payment of an obligation to Sylvester & Son on account.
e. The bank had collected for Actuator Co. $1,908 on a note left for collection. The face of the note was $1,800.
f. Bank service charges for June amounted to $20.

Instructions

1. Prepare a bank reconciliation as of June 30.
2. Journalize the necessary entries. The accounts have not been closed.

Problem 6–5B

Bank reconciliation and entries

Objective 7

✓ 1. Adjusted balance: $14,219.09

Mademoiselle Interiors deposits all cash receipts each Wednesday and Friday in a night depository, after banking hours. The data required to reconcile the bank statement as of August 31 have been taken from various documents and records and are reproduced as follows. The sources of the data are printed in capital letters. All checks were written for payments on account.

CASH ACCOUNT:
Balance as of August 1 $10,578.00

CASH RECEIPTS FOR MONTH OF AUGUST   6,305.60

DUPLICATE DEPOSIT TICKETS:
Date and amount of each deposit in August:

Date	Amount	Date	Amount	Date	Amount
Aug. 2	$569.50	Aug. 12	$580.70	Aug. 23	$ 731.45
5	701.80	16	600.10	26	601.50
9	819.24	19	701.26	31	1,000.05

CHECKS WRITTEN:
Number and amount of each check issued in August:

Check No.	Amount	Check No.	Amount	Check No.	Amount
614	$243.50	621	$309.50	628	$ 737.70
615	350.10	622	Void	629	329.90
616	279.90	623	Void	630	882.80
617	395.50	624	770.01	631	1,081.56
618	435.40	625	158.63	632	62.40
619	320.10	626	550.03	633	310.08
620	238.87	627	318.73	634	103.30

Total amount of checks issued in August $7,878.01

AUGUST BANK STATEMENT:

			MEMBER FDIC		PAGE 1

AMERICAN NATIONAL BANK OF DETROIT
DETROIT, MI 48201-2500   (313)933-8547

ACCOUNT NUMBER

FROM 8/01/20–   TO 8/31/20–

BALANCE	10,422.80
9 DEPOSITS	6,086.35
20 WITHDRAWALS	7,514.11
4 OTHER DEBITS AND CREDITS	5,150.50CR
NEW BALANCE	14,145.54

MADEMOISELLE INTERIORS

------CHECKS AND OTHER DEBITS------				– DEPOSITS – *	– DATE – *	– BALANCE – *
No.580	310.10	No.612	92.50	780.80	08/01	10,801.00
No.613	137.50	No.614	243.50	569.50	08/03	10,989.50
No.615	350.10	No.616	279.90	701.80	08/06	11,061.30
No.617	395.50	No.618	435.40	819.24	08/11	11,049.64
No.619	320.10	No.620	238.87	580.70	08/13	11,071.37
No.621	309.50	No.624	707.01	MS 5,000.00	08/14	15,054.86
No.625	158.63	No.626	550.03	MS 400.00	08/14	14,746.20
No.627	318.73	No.629	329.90	600.10	08/17	14,697.67
No.630	882.80	No.631	1,081.56 NSF 225.40		08/20	12,507.91
No.632	62.40	No.633	310.08	701.26	08/21	12,836.69
				731.45	08/24	13,568.14
				601.50	08/28	14,169.64
		SC	24.10		08/31	14,145.54

EC — ERROR CORRECTION   OD — OVERDRAFT
MS — MISCELLANEOUS   PS — PAYMENT STOPPED
NSF — NOT SUFFICIENT FUNDS   SC — SERVICE CHARGE

* * *   * * *   * * *

THE RECONCILEMENT OF THIS STATEMENT WITH YOUR RECORDS IS ESSENTIAL.
ANY ERROR OR EXCEPTION SHOULD BE REPORTED IMMEDIATELY.

BANK RECONCILIATION FOR PRECEDING MONTH:

Mademoiselle Interiors
Bank Reconciliation
July 31, 20—

Cash balance according to bank statement		$10,422.80
Add deposit of July 31, not recorded by bank		780.80
		$11,203.60
Deduct outstanding checks:		
No. 580	$310.10	
No. 602	85.50	
No. 612	92.50	
No. 613	137.50	625.60
Adjusted balance		$10,578.00
Cash balance according to depositor's records		$10,605.70
Deduct service charges		27.70
Adjusted balance		$10,578.00

Instructions

1. Prepare a bank reconciliation as of August 31. If errors in recording deposits or checks are discovered, assume that the errors were made by the company. Assume that all deposits are from cash sales. All checks are written to satisfy accounts payable.
2. Journalize the necessary entries. The accounts have not been closed.
3. What is the amount of Cash that should appear on the balance sheet as of August 31?
4. ✏️ ➤ If in preparing the bank reconciliation you note that a canceled check for $275 has been incorrectly recorded by the bank as $725, briefly explain how the error would be included in the bank reconciliation and how it should be corrected.

SPECIAL ACTIVITIES

Activity 6–1
The Breadbasket Co.
Ethics and professional conduct in business

During the preparation of the bank reconciliation for The Breadbasket Co., Lee Roberts, the assistant controller, discovered that City National Bank incorrectly recorded a $718 check written by The Breadbasket Co. as $178. Lee has decided not to notify the bank but wait for the bank to detect the error. Lee plans to record the $540 error as Other Income if the bank fails to detect the error within the next three months.

✏️ ➤ Discuss whether Lee is behaving in a professional manner.

Activity 6–2
Zoom Electronics
Internal controls

The following is an excerpt from a conversation between two sales clerks, Karol Bolton and Bill Hall. Both Karol and Bill are employed by Zoom Electronics, a locally owned and operated computer retail store.

Karol: Did you hear the news?
Bill: What news?
Karol: Melanie and Richard were both arrested this morning.
Bill: What? Arrested? You're putting me on!
Karol: No, really! The police arrested them first thing this morning. Put them in handcuffs, read them their rights—the whole works. It was unreal!
Bill: What did they do?
Karol: Well, apparently they were filling out merchandise refund forms for fictitious customers and then taking the cash.
Bill: I guess I never thought of that. How did they catch them?
Karol: The store manager noticed that returns were twice that of last year and seemed to be increasing. When he confronted Melanie, she became flustered and admitted to taking the cash, apparently over $1,800 in just three months. They're going over the last six months' transactions to try to determine how much Richard stole. He apparently started stealing first.

✏️ ➤ Suggest appropriate control procedures that would have prevented or detected the theft of cash.

Activity 6–3
Ethnic Grocery Stores
Internal controls

The following is an excerpt from a conversation between the store manager of Ethnic Grocery Stores, Jill Allen, and Gary Malone, president of Ethnic Grocery Stores.

Gary: Jill, I'm concerned about this new scanning system.
Jill: What's the problem?
Gary: Well, how do we know the clerks are ringing up all the merchandise?
Jill: That's one of the strong points about the system. The scanner automatically rings up each item, based on its bar code. We update the prices daily, so we're sure that the sale is rung up for the right price.
Gary: That's not my concern. What keeps a clerk from pretending to scan items and then simply not charging his friends? If his friends were buying 10–15 items, it would be easy for the clerk to pass through several items with his finger over the bar code or just pass the merchandise through the scanner with the wrong side showing. It would look normal for anyone observing. In the old days, we at least could hear the cash register ringing up each sale.
Jill: I see your point.

Suggest ways that Ethnic Grocery Stores could prevent or detect the theft of merchandise as described.

Activity 6–4
Mammoth Markets
Ethics and professional conduct in business

Devon Payne and Meredith Sibley are both cash register clerks for Mammoth Markets. Kelley Russell is the store manager for Mammoth Markets. The following is an excerpt of a conversation between Devon and Meredith:

Devon: Meredith, how long have you been working for Mammoth Markets?
Meredith: Almost five years this October. You just started two weeks ago . . . right?
Devon: Yes. Do you mind if I ask you a question?
Meredith: No, go ahead.
Devon: What I want to know is, have they always had this rule that if your cash register is short at the end of the day, you have to make up the shortage out of your own pocket?
Meredith: Yes, as long as I've been working here.
Devon: Well, it's the pits. Last week I had to pay in almost $30.
Meredith: It's not that big a deal. I just make sure that I'm not short at the end of the day.
Devon: How do you do that?
Meredith: I just short-change a few customers early in the day. There are a few jerks that deserve it anyway. Most of the time, their attention is elsewhere and they don't think to check their change.
Devon: What happens if you're over at the end of the day?
Meredith: Kelley lets me keep it as long as it doesn't get to be too large. I've not been short in over a year. I usually clear about $10 to $20 extra per day.

Discuss this case from the viewpoint of proper controls and professional behavior.

Activity 6–5
Pegasus Company
Bank reconciliation and internal control

The records of Pegasus Company indicate a March 31 cash balance of $9,806.05, which includes undeposited receipts for March 30 and 31. The cash balance on the bank statement as of March 31 is $8,004.95. This balance includes a note of $2,500 plus $200 interest collected by the bank but not recorded in the journal. Checks outstanding on March 31 were as follows: No. 670, $481.20; No. 679, $510; No. 690, $616.50; No. 1996, $127.40; No. 1997, $520; and No. 1999, $851.50.

On March 3, the cashier resigned, effective at the end of the month. Before leaving on March 31, the cashier prepared the following bank reconciliation:

Cash balance per books, March 31		$ 9,806.05
Add outstanding checks:		
No. 1996	$127.40	
1997	520.00	
1999	851.50	1,198.90
		$11,004.95
Less undeposited receipts		3,000.00
Cash balance per bank, March 31		$ 8,004.95
Deduct unrecorded note with interest		2,700.00
True cash, March 31		$ 5,304.95

Calculator Tape of Outstanding Checks:
0.00 *
127.40 +
520.00 +
851.50 +
1,198.90 *

Subsequently, the manager of Pegasus Company discovered that the cashier had stolen all undeposited receipts in excess of the $3,000 on hand on March 31. The manager, a close family friend, has asked your help in determining the amount that the former cashier has stolen.

1. Determine the amount the cashier stole from Pegasus Company. Show your computations in good form.
2. How did the cashier attempt to conceal the theft?
3. a. Identify two major weaknesses in internal controls, which allowed the cashier to steal the undeposited cash receipts.
   b. ➤ Recommend improvements in internal controls, so that similar types of thefts of undeposited cash receipts can be prevented.

Activity 6–6
Into the Real World
Observe internal controls over cash

Select a business in your community and observe its internal controls over cash receipts and cash payments. The business could be a bank or a bookstore, restaurant, department store, or other retailer. In groups of three or four, identify and discuss the similarities and differences in each business's cash internal controls.

Activity 6–7
Cisco Systems, Inc.
Internal controls and the annual report

Corporations can take up to several weeks to close their books after an accounting period ends (often quarterly). During this time, adjusting entries are made, mistakes are corrected, and various journal entries are posted. As a result, management must wait until the books are closed before it can use the financial accounting information for decision making.
➤ What does the annual report for **Cisco Systems, Inc.**, in Appendix G (page G-4) indicate about how Cisco Systems closes its books, and how does this impact the decision-making ability of Cisco's management?

Activity 6–8
Into the Real World
Invest excess cash

You have $50,000 cash. Go to the Web site of (or visit) a local bank and collect information about the savings and checking options that are available. Identify the option that is best for you and why it is best.

ANSWERS TO SELF-EXAMINATION QUESTIONS

Matching

1. D	3. N	5. M	7. E	9. J	11. K
2. O	4. H	6. B	8. G	10. A	12. I

Multiple Choice

1. **A** Analysis (answer A) is the initial step of determining the informational needs and how the system provides this information. Design (answer B) is the step in which proposals for changes are developed.

Implementation (answer C) is the final step involving carrying out or implementing the proposals for changes. Feedback (answer D) is not a separate step but is considered part of the systems implementation.

2. **A** The policies and procedures that are established to safeguard assets, ensure accurate business information, and ensure compliance with laws and regulations are called internal controls (answer A). The three steps in setting up an accounting system are (1) analysis (answer B), (2) design (answer C), and (3) implementation (answer D).

3. **B** On any specific date, the cash account in a depositor's ledger may not agree with the account in the bank's ledger because of delays and/or errors by either party in recording transactions. The purpose of a bank reconciliation, therefore, is to determine the reasons for any differences between the two account balances. All errors should then be corrected by the depositor or the bank, as appropriate. In arriving at the adjusted (correct) cash balance according to the bank statement, outstanding checks must be deducted (answer B) to adjust for checks that have been written by the depositor but that have not yet been presented to the bank for payment.

4. **C** All reconciling items that are added to and deducted from the cash balance according to the depositor's records on the bank reconciliation (answer C) require that journal entries be made by the depositor to correct errors made in recording transactions or to bring the cash account up to date for delays in recording transactions.

5. **D** To avoid the delay, annoyance, and expense that is associated with paying all obligations by check, relatively small amounts (answer A) are paid from a petty cash fund. The fund is established by estimating the amount of cash needed to pay these small amounts during a specified period (answer B), and it is then reimbursed when the amount of money in the fund is reduced to a predetermined minimum amount (answer C).

Receivables

objectives

After studying this chapter, you should be able to:

1 List the common classifications of receivables.

2 Summarize and provide examples of internal control procedures that apply to receivables.

3 Describe the nature of and the accounting for uncollectible receivables.

4 Journalize the entries for the allowance method of accounting for uncollectibles, and estimate uncollectible receivables based on sales and on an analysis of receivables.

5 Journalize the entries for the direct write-off of uncollectible receivables.

6 Describe the nature and characteristics of promissory notes.

7 Journalize the entries for notes receivable transactions.

8 Prepare the Current Assets presentation of receivables on the balance sheet.

9 Compute and interpret the accounts receivable turnover and the number of days' sales in receivables.

A ssume that you have decided to sell your car to a neighbor for $7,500. Your neighbor agrees to pay you $1,500 immediately and the remaining $6,000 in a year. How much should you charge your neighbor for interest?

You could determine an appropriate interest rate by asking some financial institutions what they currently charge their customers. Using this information as a starting point, you could then negotiate with your neighbor and agree upon a rate. Assuming that the agreed-upon rate is 8%, you will receive interest totaling $480 for the one-year loan.

In this chapter, we will describe and illustrate how interest is computed. In addition, we will discuss the accounting for receivables, including uncollectible receivables. Most of these receivables result from a business rendering services or selling merchandise on account.

Classification of Receivables

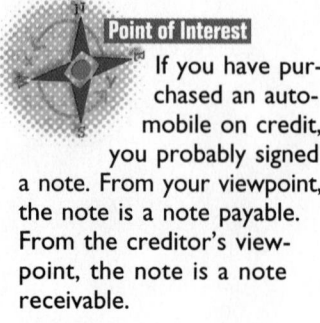

objective 1

List the common classifications of receivables.

Many companies sell on credit in order to sell more services or products. The receivables that result from such sales are normally classified as accounts receivable or notes receivable. The term **receivables** includes all money claims against other entities, including people, business firms, and other organizations. These receivables are usually a significant portion of the total current assets.

Real World An annual report of La-Z-Boy Chair Company reported that receivables made up over 60% of La-Z-Boy's current assets.

Accounts Receivable

The most common transaction creating a receivable is selling merchandise or services on credit. The receivable is recorded as a debit to the accounts receivable account. Such **accounts receivable** are normally expected to be collected within a relatively short period, such as 30 or 60 days. They are classified on the balance sheet as a current asset.

Notes Receivable

Notes receivable are amounts that customers owe, for which a formal, written instrument of credit has been issued. As long as notes receivable are expected to be collected within a year, they are normally classified on the balance sheet as a current asset.

Notes are often used for credit periods of more than sixty days. For example, a dealer in automobiles or furniture may require a down payment at the time of sale and accept a note or a series of notes for the remainder. Such arrangements usually provide for monthly payments.

Notes may be used to settle a customer's account receivable. Notes and accounts receivable that result from sales transactions are sometimes called **trade receivables**. Unless we indicate otherwise, we will assume that all notes and accounts receivable in this chapter are from sales transactions.

Point of Interest
If you have purchased an automobile on credit, you probably signed a note. From your viewpoint, the note is a note payable. From the creditor's viewpoint, the note is a note receivable.

Other Receivables

Other receivables are normally listed separately on the balance sheet. If they are expected to be collected within one year, they are classified as current assets. If collection is expected beyond one year, they are classified as noncurrent assets and reported under the caption *Investments*. **Other receivables** include interest receivable, taxes receivable, and receivables from officers or employees.

Internal Control of Receivables

objective 2

Summarize and provide examples of internal control procedures that apply to receivables.

The principles of internal control that we discussed in prior chapters can be used to establish controls to safeguard receivables. For example, the four functions of credit approval, sales, accounting, and collections should be separated, as shown in Exhibit 1.

The individuals responsible for sales should be separate from the individuals accounting for the receivables and approving credit. By doing so, the accounting and credit approval functions serve as independent checks on sales. The employee who handles the accounting for receivables should not be involved with collecting receivables. Separating these functions reduces the possibility of errors and misuse of funds.

Exhibit 1 Separating the Receivable Functions

SEPARATING THE RECEIVABLE FUNCTIONS

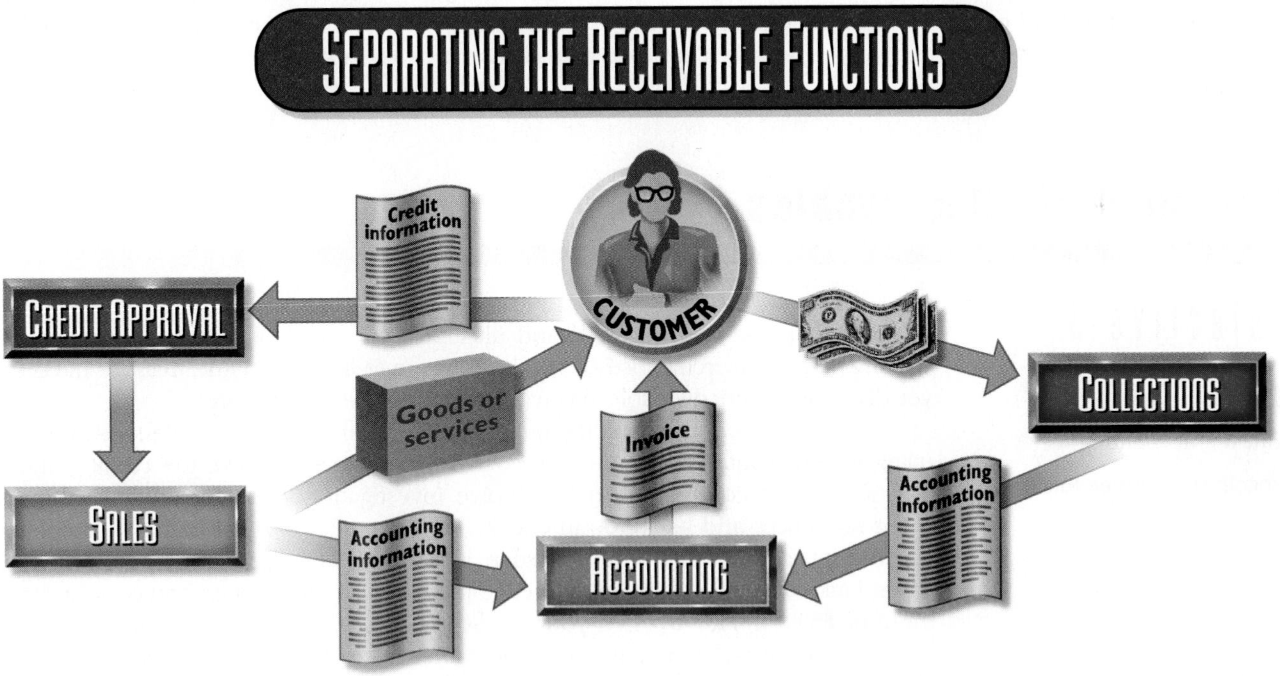

To illustrate the need to separate functions, assume that the accounts receivable billing clerk has access to cash receipts from customer collections. The clerk can steal a customer's cash payment and then alter the customer's monthly statement to indicate that the payment was received. The customer would not complain and the theft could go undetected.

To further illustrate the need for internal control of receivables, assume that salespersons have authority to approve credit. If the salespersons are paid commissions, say 10% of sales, they can increase their commissions by approving poor credit risks. Thus, the credit approval function is normally assigned to individuals outside the sales area.

BUSINESS ON STAGE

The Five "Cs"

Credit standards are used by businesses to decide which customers should receive credit and how much credit they should receive. Setting credit standards requires businesses to assess the customer's "creditworthiness" or credit "quality." Traditionally, assessing creditworthiness involves considering the five Cs of credit. Each of these five Cs is briefly described below.

1. *Character* refers to the probability that the customer will honor an obligation. Many credit managers insist that this is the most important of the Cs. It reflects on the honesty of the customer and the customer's feeling of moral responsibility to honor debts.

Credit managers often seek information on a customer's character by making inquiries within the business community. Such inquiries may be made with local bankers, attorneys, other creditors, and even competitors.

2. *Capacity* refers to a customer's ability to pay. Credit managers assess this factor by reviewing the customer's past payment history, a general knowledge of the customer's business, and perhaps even a physical observation of the customer's operations.

3. *Capital* refers to the general condition of the customer's business as assessed from the financial statements. Credit managers usually place special emphasis on

solvency and liquidity measures and ratios such as working capital and the current ratio.

4. *Collateral* refers to assets that the customer may be willing to pledge as security for the credit. Financial institutions usually require collateral for major loans to businesses. The collateral may take the form of any asset, such as land, buildings, or inventory.

5. *Conditions* refers to the national and regional economic trends that may affect a customer's ability to pay. For example, during economic downturns credit managers usually tighten credit standards, with the anticipation that more customers will not be able to pay. ■

Uncollectible Receivables

 In addition to their own credit departments, many businesses use external credit agencies, such as **Dun and Bradstreet**, to evaluate credit customers.

In prior chapters, we described and illustrated the accounting for transactions involving sales of merchandise or services on credit. A major issue that we have not yet discussed is uncollectible receivables from these transactions.

Businesses attempt to limit the number and amount of uncollectible receivables by using various controls. The primary controls in this area involve the credit-granting function. These controls normally involve investigating customer creditworthiness, using references and background checks. For example, most of us have completed credit application forms requiring such information. Companies may also impose credit limits on new customers. For example, you may have been limited to a maximum of $500 or $1,000 when your credit card was first issued to you.

Once a receivable is past due, companies should use procedures to maximize the collection of an account. After repeated attempts at collection, such procedures may include turning an account over to a collection agency.

Retail businesses often attempt to shift the risk of uncollectible receivables to other companies. For example, some retailers do not accept sales on account but will accept only cash or credit cards. Such policies effectively shift the risk to the credit card companies. Other retailers, however, such as **Macy's**, **Sears**, and **JCPenney's**, have issued their own credit cards.

Companies often sell their receivables to other companies. This transaction is called **factoring** the receivables, and the buyer of the receivables is called a **factor**. An advantage of factoring is that the company selling its receivables receives immediate cash for operating and other needs. In addition, depending upon the factoring agreement, some of the risk of uncollectible accounts may be shifted to the factor.[1]

Regardless of the care used in granting credit and the collection procedures used, a part of the credit sales will not be collectible. The operating expense incurred because of the failure to collect receivables is called **uncollectible accounts expense**, **bad debts expense**, or **doubtful accounts expense**.[2]

When does an account or a note become uncollectible? There is no general rule for determining when an account becomes uncollectible. The fact that a debtor fails to pay an account according to a sales contract or fails to pay a note on the due date does not necessarily mean that the account will be uncollectible. The debtor's bankruptcy is one of the most significant indications of partial or complete uncollectibility. Other indications include the closing of the customer's business and the failure of repeated attempts to collect.

There are two methods of accounting for receivables that appear to be uncollectible. The **allowance method** provides an expense for uncollectible receivables in advance of their write-off.[3] The other procedure, called the **direct write-off method**, recognizes the expense only when accounts are judged to be worthless. We will discuss each of these methods next.

Allowance Method of Accounting for Uncollectibles

objective 4

Journalize the entries for the allowance method of accounting for uncollectibles, and estimate uncollectible receivables based on sales and on an analysis of receivables.

Most large businesses use the allowance method to estimate the uncollectible portion of their trade receivables. To illustrate this method, we will use assumed data for Richards Company. This new business began in August and chose to use the calendar year as its fiscal year. The accounts receivable account has a balance of $105,000 at the end of December.

The customer accounts making up the $105,000 balance in Accounts Receivable include some that are past due. However, Richards doesn't know which specific accounts will be uncollectible at this time. It is likely that some accounts will be collected only in part and that others will become worthless. Based on a careful study, Richards estimates that a total of $4,000 will eventually be uncollectible. The following adjusting entry at the end of the fiscal period records this estimate:

		Adjusting Entry						
Dec.	31	Uncollectible Accounts Expense			4 0 0 0 00			
		Allowance for Doubtful Accounts					4 0 0 0 00	

Because the $4,000 reduction in accounts receivable is an estimate, it cannot be credited to specific customer accounts or to the accounts receivable controlling account. Instead, a **contra asset** account entitled *Allowance for Doubtful Accounts* is credited.

As with all periodic adjustments, the entry above serves two purposes. First, it reduces the value of the receivables to the amount of cash expected to be realized in the future. This amount, which is $101,000 ($105,000 − $4,000), is called the **net**

---

[1] The accounting for the factoring of accounts receivable is discussed in advanced accounting texts.
[2] If both notes and accounts are involved, both may be included in the expense account title, as in Uncollectible Notes and Accounts Expense, or Uncollectible Receivables Expense.
[3] The allowance method is not acceptable for determining the federal income tax of most taxpayers.

realizable value of the receivables. Second, the adjusting entry matches the $4,000 expense of uncollectible accounts with the related revenues of the period.

After the adjusting entry has been posted, as shown in the following T accounts, Accounts Receivable still has a debit balance of $105,000. This balance is the amount of the total claims against customers on account. The credit balance of $4,000 in Allowance for Doubtful Accounts is the amount to be deducted from Accounts Receivable to determine the net realizable value. The balance of the Uncollectible Accounts Expense is reported in the current period income statement, normally as an administrative expense. This classification is used because the credit-granting and collection duties are the responsibilities of departments within the administrative area.

> **The adjusting entry reduces receivables to their net realizable value and matches the uncollectible expense with revenues.**

Q&A

If the balance of accounts receivable is $380,000 and the balance of the allowance for doubtful accounts is $56,000, what is the net realizable value of the receivables?

- -

$324,000 ($380,000 − $56,000)

Accounts Receivable			
Aug. 31	20,000	Sept. 30	15,000
Sept. 30	25,000	Oct. 31	25,000
Oct. 31	40,000	Nov. 30	23,000
Nov. 30	38,000	Dec. 31	30,000
Dec. 31	75,000		93,000
Bal. 105,000	198,000		

Allowance for Doubtful Accounts	
	Dec. 31 Adj. 4,000

Uncollectible Accounts Expense	
Dec. 31 Adj. 4,000	

Write-Offs to the Allowance Account

When a customer's account is identified as uncollectible, it is written off against the allowance account as follows:

Jan.	21	Allowance for Doubtful Accounts		6 1 0 00	
		Accounts Receivable—John Parker			6 1 0 00
		To write off the uncollectible			
		account.			

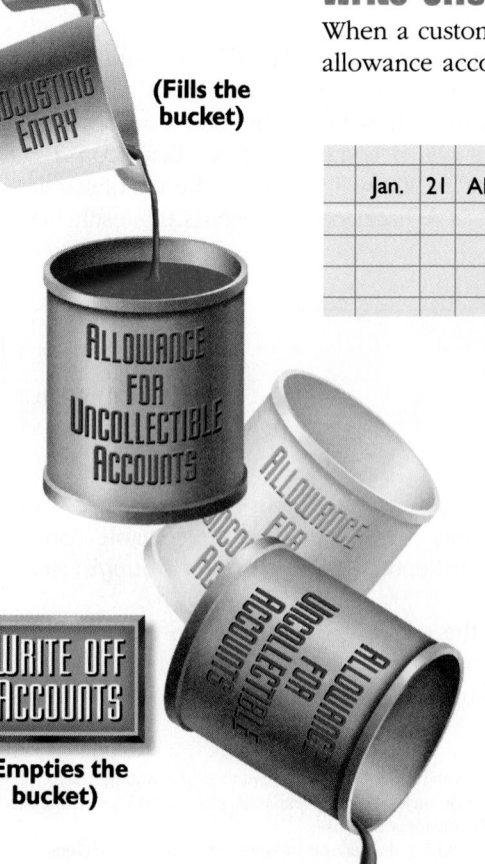

ADJUSTING ENTRY (Fills the bucket)

ALLOWANCE FOR UNCOLLECTIBLE ACCOUNTS

WRITE OFF ACCOUNTS (Empties the bucket)

The authorization to support this entry should come from a designated manager. It should normally be in writing.

The total amount written off against the allowance account during a period will rarely be equal to the amount in the account at the beginning of the period. The allowance account will have a credit balance at the end of the period if the write-offs during the period are less than the beginning balance. It will have a debit balance if the write-offs exceed the beginning balance. However, after the year-end adjusting entry is recorded, the allowance account should have a credit balance. The flow into and out of the allowance account can be shown as in the illustration at the left.

An account receivable that has been written off against the allowance account may later be collected. In such cases, the account should be reinstated by an entry that reverses the write-off entry. The cash received in payment should then be recorded as a receipt on account. For example, assume that the account of $610 written off in the preceding entry is later collected on June 10. The entry to reinstate the account and the entry to record its collection are as follows:

June	10	Accounts Receivable—John Parker		6 1 0 00	
		Allowance for Doubtful Accounts			6 1 0 00
		To reinstate account written off			
		earlier in the year.			
	10	Cash		6 1 0 00	
		Accounts Receivable—John Parker			6 1 0 00
		To record collection on account.			

The percentage of uncollectible accounts will vary across companies and industries. For example, in their annual reports, **JCPenney** reported 1.7% of its receivables as uncollectible, **Deere & Company** (manufacturer of John Deere tractors, etc.) reported only 1.0% of its dealer receivables as uncollectible, and **Columbia HCA Healthcare Corporation** reported 45.6% of its receivables as uncollectible.

The two preceding entries can be combined. However, recording two separate entries in the customer's account, with proper notation of the write-off and reinstatement, provides useful credit information.

Estimating Uncollectibles

How is the amount of uncollectible accounts estimated? The estimate of uncollectibles at the end of a fiscal period is based on past experience and forecasts of the future. When the general economy is doing well, the amount of uncollectible expense is normally less than it would be when the economy is doing poorly. The estimate of uncollectibles is usually based on either (1) the amount of sales, as shown on the income statement for the period, or (2) the amount of the receivables, as shown on the balance sheet at the end of the period, and the age of the receivable accounts.

Estimate Based on Sales

The estimate based on sales is _added_ to any balance in Allowance for Doubtful Accounts.

Accounts receivable are created by credit sales. The amount of credit sales during the period may therefore be used to estimate the amount of uncollectible accounts expense. The amount of this estimate is added to whatever balance exists in Allowance for Doubtful Accounts. For example, assume that the allowance account has a credit balance of $700 before adjustment. It is estimated from past experience that 1% of credit sales will be uncollectible. If credit sales for the period are $300,000, the adjusting entry for uncollectible accounts at the end of the period is as follows:

		Adjusting Entry			
Dec.	31	Uncollectible Accounts Expense		3 0 0 0 00	
		Allowance for Doubtful Accounts			3 0 0 0 00

Before the year-end adjustment, Allowance for Doubtful Accounts has a credit balance of $45,000. Uncollectible accounts are estimated as 2% of credit sales of $1,200,000. The accounts receivable balance before adjustment is $290,000. What are (1) the uncollectible expense for the period, (2) the balance of Allowance for Doubtful Accounts after adjustment, and (3) the net realizable value of the receivables after adjustment?

(1) $24,000 (2% × $1,200,000); (2) $69,000 ($24,000 + $45,000); and (3) $221,000 ($290,000 − $69,000)

After the adjusting entry has been posted, the balance of the allowance account is $3,700. If there had been a debit balance of $200 in the allowance account before the year-end adjustment, the amount of the adjustment would still have been $3,000. The balance in the allowance account would have been $2,800 ($3,000 − $200).

The estimate-based-on-sales method _emphasizes the matching of uncollectible accounts expense with the related sales of the period._ Thus, this method places more emphasis on the income statement than on the balance sheet.

The Commercial Collection Agency Section of the Commercial Law League of America reported the following collection rates by number of months past due:

COLLECTION RATES

100% 93.4%
90 84.6%
80 72.9%
70
60 57.0%
50 41.9%
40
30 25.4%
20
10 12.5%
0
① ② ③ ⑥ ⑨ ⑫ ㉔
Number of months past due

Estimate Based on Analysis of Receivables

The longer an account receivable remains outstanding, the less likely that it will be collected. Thus, we can base the estimate of uncollectible accounts on how long the accounts have been outstanding. For this purpose, we can use a process called **aging the receivables**.

In aging the receivables, an aging schedule is prepared by classifying each receivable by its due date. The number of days an account is past due is determined from the due date of the account to the date the aging schedule is prepared. To illustrate, assume that Rodriguez Company is preparing an aging schedule as of August 31. Its account receivable for Saxon Woods Company was due on May 29. As of August 31, Saxon's account is 94 days past due, as shown below.

Number of days past due in May	2 days (31–29)
Number of days past due in June	30 days
Number of days past due in July	31 days
Number of days past due in August	31 days
Total number of days past due	94 days

After the number of days past due has been determined for each account, an aging schedule is prepared similar to the one shown in Exhibit 2.

Exhibit 2 Aging of Accounts Receivable

Customer	Balance	Not Past Due	Days Past Due					
			1–30	31–60	61–90	91–180	181–365	over 365
Ashby & Co.	$ 150				$ 150			
B.T. Barr	610						$ 350	$260
Brock Co.	470	$ 470						
Saxon Woods Co.	160					160		
Total	$86,300	$75,000	$4,000	$3,100	$1,900	$1,200	$800	$300

The aging schedule is completed by adding the columns to determine the total amount of receivables in each age class. A sliding scale of percentages, based on industry or company experience, is used to estimate the amount of uncollectibles in each age class, as shown in Exhibit 3.

Based on Exhibit 3, the desired balance for the Allowance for Doubtful Accounts is estimated as $3,390. Comparing this estimate with the unadjusted balance of the allowance account determines the amount

The estimate based on receivables is compared to the balance in the allowance account to determine the amount of the adjusting entry.

Exhibit 3 Estimate of Uncollectible Accounts

Age Interval	Balance	Estimated Uncollectible Accounts	
		Percent	Amount
Not past due	$75,000	2%	$1,500
1–30 days past due	4,000	5	200
31–60 days past due	3,100	10	310
61–90 days past due	1,900	20	380
91–180 days past due	1,200	30	360
181–365 days past due	800	50	400
Over 365 days past due	300	80	240
Total	$86,300		$3,390

of the adjusting entry for Uncollectible Accounts Expense. For example, assume that the unadjusted balance of the allowance account is a credit balance of $510. The amount to be added to this balance is therefore $2,880 ($3,390 − $510). The adjusting entry is as follows:

		Adjusting Entry			
Aug.	31	Uncollectible Accounts Expense	2 8 8 0 00		
		Allowance for Doubtful Accounts		2 8 8 0 00	

Q&A

Before the year-end adjustment, Allowance for Doubtful Accounts has a debit balance of $3,000. Using the aging-of-receivables method, the desired balance of the allowance for doubtful accounts is estimated as $55,000. The accounts receivable balance before adjustment is $290,000. What are (1) the uncollectible expense for the period, (2) the balance of Allowance for Doubtful Accounts after adjustment, and (3) the net realizable value of the receivables after adjustment?

-----

(1) $58,000 ($3,000 + $55,000); (2) $55,000; and (3) $235,000 ($290,000 − $55,000)

After the adjusting entry has been posted, the credit balance in the allowance account is $3,390, the desired amount. The net realizable value of the receivables is $82,910 ($86,300 − $3,390). If the unadjusted balance of the allowance account had been a debit balance of $300, the amount of the adjustment would have been $3,690 ($3,390 + $300).

Estimates of the uncollectible accounts expense based on the analysis of receivables *emphasizes the current net realizable value of the receivables.* Thus, this method places more emphasis on the balance sheet than on the income statement.

Direct Write-Off Method of Accounting for Uncollectibles

objective 5

Journalize the entries for the direct write-off of uncollectible receivables.

The allowance method emphasizes reporting uncollectible accounts expense in the period in which the related sales occur. This emphasis on matching expenses with related revenue is the preferred method of accounting for uncollectible receivables.

There are situations, however, where it is impossible to estimate, with reasonable accuracy, the uncollectibles at the end of the period. Also, if a business sells most of its goods or services on a cash basis, the amount of its expense from uncollectible accounts is usually small. In such cases, the amount of receivables is also likely to represent a small part of the current assets. Examples of such a business are a restaurant, an attorney's office, and a small retail store such as a hardware store. In such cases, the direct write-off method of recording uncollectible expense may be used.

Under the direct write-off method, uncollectible accounts expense is not recorded until an account has been determined to be worthless. Thus, an allowance account and an adjusting entry are not needed at the end of the period. The entry to write off an account that has been determined to be uncollectible is as follows:

May	10	Uncollectible Accounts Expense		4 2 0 00	
		Accounts Receivable—D. L. Ross			4 2 0 00
		To write off uncollectible account.			

What if a customer later pays on an account that has been written off? If this happens, the account should be reinstated. The account is reinstated by reversing the earlier write-off entry. For example, assume that the account written off in the May 10 entry is collected in November of the same fiscal year.[4] The entry to reinstate the account is as follows:

Nov.	21	Accounts Receivable—D. L. Ross		4 2 0 00	
		Uncollectible Accounts Expense			4 2 0 00
		To reinstate account written off			
		earlier in the year.			

Cash received in payment of the reinstated amount is recorded in the usual manner. That is, Cash is debited and Accounts Receivable is credited for $420.

Characteristics of Notes Receivable

objective 6

Describe the nature and characteristics of promissory notes.

A claim supported by a note has some advantages over a claim in the form of an account receivable. By signing a note, the debtor recognizes the debt and agrees to pay it according to the terms listed. A note is therefore a stronger legal claim if there is a court action.

A **promissory note** is a written promise to pay a sum of money on demand or at a definite time. It is payable to the order of a person or firm or to the bearer or holder of the note. It is signed by the person or firm that makes the promise. The one to whose order the note is payable is called the **payee**, and the one making the promise is called the **maker**. In the example in Exhibit 4, Judson Company is the payee and Willard Company is the maker.

Notes have several characteristics that affect how they are recorded and reported in the financial statements. We describe these characteristics next.

---

[4] As a practical matter, the entries to record the collection on an account previously written off are the same, regardless of whether the collection occurs in the current period or in a later fiscal period.

Exhibit 4 Promissory Note

Due Date

The date a note is to be paid is called the **due date** or **maturity date**. The period of time between the issuance date and the due date of a short-term note may be stated in either days or months. When the term of a note is stated in days, the due date is the specified number of days after its issuance. To illustrate, the due date of the 90-day note in Exhibit 4 is determined as follows:

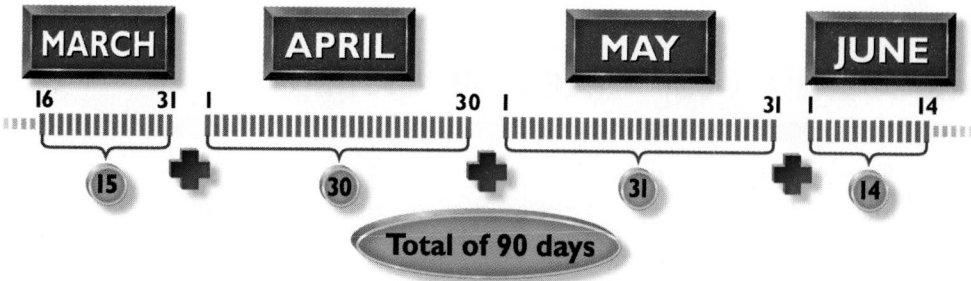

What is the due date of a 120-day note receivable dated September 9?

January 7 [21 days in September (30 days − 9 days) + 31 days in October + 30 days in November + 31 days in December + 7 days in January = 120 days]

The term of a note may be stated as a certain number of months after the issuance date. In such cases, the due date is determined by counting the number of months from the issuance date. For example, a three-month note dated June 5 would be due on September 5. A two-month note dated July 31 would be due on September 30.

Interest

A note normally specifies that interest be paid for the period between the issuance date and the due date.[5] Notes covering a period of time longer than one year normally provide that the interest be paid semiannually, quarterly, or at some other stated interval. When the term of the note is less than one year, the interest is usually payable at the time the note is paid.

----

[5] You may occasionally see references to non-interest-bearing notes receivable. Such notes, which are not widely used, normally include an implicit interest rate.

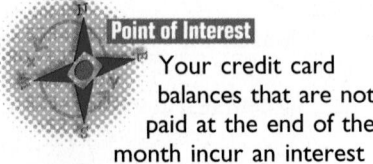

Point of Interest
Your credit card balances that are not paid at the end of the month incur an interest charge expressed as a percent per month. Interest charges of 1½% per month are common. Such charges approximate an annual interest rate of 18% per year (1½% × 12). Thus, if you can borrow money at less than 18%, you are better off borrowing the money to pay off the credit card balance.

What is the maturity value of a $15,000, 90-day, 12% note?

$15,450 [$15,000 + ($15,000 × 0.12 × 90/360)]

The interest rate on notes is normally stated in terms of a year, regardless of the actual period of time involved. Thus, the interest on $2,000 for one year at 12% is $240 (12% of $2,000). The interest on $2,000 for one-fourth of one year at 12% is $60 (1/4 of $240).

The basic formula for computing interest is as follows:

> **Face Amount (or Principal) × Rate × Time = Interest**

To illustrate the formula, the interest on the note in Exhibit 4 is computed as follows:

$$\$2,500 \times 0.10 \times \frac{90}{360} = \$62.50 \text{ interest}$$

In computing interest for a period of less than one year, agencies of the federal government and many financial institutions use the actual number of days in the year, 365. In the preceding computation, for example, the time would have been stated as 90/365 of one year. To simplify computations, however, we will use 360 days.

Maturity Value

The amount that is due at the maturity or due date is called the **maturity value**. The maturity value of a note is the sum of the face amount and the interest. In the note in Exhibit 4, the maturity value is $2,562.50 ($2,500 face amount plus $62.50 interest).

Accounting for Notes Receivable

objective 7

Journalize the entries for notes receivable transactions.

As we mentioned earlier, a note may be received from a customer to replace an account receivable. To illustrate, assume that a 30-day, 12% note dated November 21, 2003, is accepted in settlement of the account of W. A. Bunn Co., which is past due and has a balance of $6,000. The entry to record the transaction is as follows:

Nov.	21	Notes Receivable	6 0 0 0 00	
		Accounts Receivable—W. A. Bunn Co.		6 0 0 0 00
		Received 30-day, 12% note dated		
		November 21, 2003.		

When the note matures, the entry to record the receipt of $6,060 ($6,000 principal plus $60 interest) is as follows:

Dec.	21	Cash	6 0 6 0 00	
		Notes Receivable		6 0 0 0 00
		Interest Revenue		6 0 00
		Received principal and interest on		
		matured note.		

If the maker of a note fails to pay the debt on the due date, the note is a **dishonored note receivable**. When a note is dishonored, the face value of the note plus any interest due is transferred to the accounts receivable account. For example, assume that the $6,000, 30-day, 12% note received from W. A. Bunn Co. and recorded on November 21 is dishonored at maturity. The entry to transfer the note and the interest back to the customer's account is as follows:

Dec.	21	Accounts Receivable—W. A. Bunn Co.	6 0 6 0 00			
		Notes Receivable			6 0 0 0 00	
		Interest Revenue			6 0 00	
		To record dishonored note and				
		interest.				

The interest of $60 has been earned, even though the note has been dishonored. If the account receivable is uncollectible, the amount of $6,060 will be written off against the Allowance for Doubtful Accounts.

If a note matures in a later fiscal period, the interest accrued in the period in which the note is received must be recorded by an adjusting entry. For example, assume that a 90-day, 12% note dated December 1, 2003, is received from Crawford Company to settle its account, which has a balance of $4,000. Assuming that the accounting period ends on December 31, the entries to record the receipt of the note, accrued interest, and payment of the note at maturity are shown below.

2003 Dec.	1	Notes Receivable	4 0 0 0 00			
		Accounts Receivable—Crawford				
		Company			4 0 0 0 00	
		Received note in settlement of				
		account.				
	31	Interest Receivable	4 0 00			
		Interest Revenue			4 0 00	
		Adjusting entry for accrued				
		interest, $4,000 × 0.12 × 30/360.				

2004 Mar.	1	Cash	4 1 2 0 00			
		Notes Receivable			4 0 0 0 00	
		Interest Receivable			4 0 00	
		Interest Revenue			8 0 00	
		Received payment of note and				
		interest; maturity value, $4,000 +				
		($4,000 × 0.12 × 90/360).				

The interest revenue account is closed at the end of each accounting period. The amount of interest revenue is normally reported in the Other Income section of the income statement.

BUSINESS ON STAGE

Interest and the Length of a Year

Whenever a business borrows money or enters into a credit agreement that requires the payment of interest, it is important that the business understand how the interest will be computed. For example, the difference in 180 days' interest computed on the basis of a 365-day year versus a 360-day year is shown below for a loan of $40,000 at an interest rate of 12%.

$40,000 × 0.12 × 180/365
= $2,367.12

$40,000 × 0.12 × 180/360
= $2,400.00

The difference of $32.88 may seem small, but for a business that might enter into thousands of such transactions for millions of dollars, the difference between computing interest on a 360-day year versus a 365-day year can be significant. ■

Receivables on the Balance Sheet

objective 8

Prepare the Current Assets presentation of receivables on the balance sheet.

All receivables that are expected to be realized in cash within a year are presented in the Current Assets section of the balance sheet. It is normal to list the assets in the order of their liquidity. This is the order in which they are expected to be converted to cash during normal operations. An example of the presentation of receivables is shown in the partial balance sheet for Crabtree Co. in Exhibit 5.

The following credit risk disclosure appeared in the financial statements of **Deere & Company:**

Credit receivables have significant concentrations of credit risk in the agricultural, industrial, lawn and grounds care, and recreational (non-Deere equipment) business sectors. . . . The portion of credit receivables related to the agricultural equipment business was 60%; that related to the industrial equipment business was 12%; that related to the lawn and grounds care equipment business was 7%; and that related to the recreational equipment business was 21%. On a geographic basis, there is not a disproportionate concentration of credit risk in any area. . . .

Exhibit 5 Receivables on Balance Sheet

Crabtree Co. Balance Sheet December 31, 2003			
Assets			
Current assets:			
Cash			$119 5 0 0 00
Notes receivable			250 0 0 0 00
Accounts receivable	$445 0 0 0 00		
Less allowance for doubtful accounts	15 0 0 0 00	430 0 0 0 00	
Interest receivable		14 5 0 0 00	

The balance of Crabtree's notes receivable, accounts receivable, and interest receivable accounts are reported in Exhibit 5. The allowance for doubtful accounts is subtracted from the accounts receivable. Alternatively, the accounts receivable may be listed on the balance sheet at its net realizable value of $430,000, with a note showing the amount of the allowance. If the allowance account includes provisions for doubtful notes as well as accounts, it should be deducted from the total of Notes Receivable and Accounts Receivable.

Other disclosures related to receivables are presented either on the face of the financial statements or in the accompanying notes. Such disclosures include the market (fair) value of the receivables.[6] In addition, if unusual credit risks exist within the receivables, the nature of the risks should be disclosed. For example, if the majority of the receivables are due from one customer or are due from customers located in one area of the country or one industry, these facts should be disclosed.[7]

FINANCIAL ANALYSIS AND INTERPRETATION

objective 9

Compute and interpret the accounts receivable turnover and the number of days' sales in receivables.

Businesses that grant long credit terms tend to have relatively greater amounts tied up in accounts receivable than those granting short credit terms. In either case, it is desirable to collect receivables as promptly as possible. The cash collected from receivables improves solvency and lessens the risk of loss from uncollectible accounts. Two financial measures that are especially useful in evaluating the efficiency in collecting receivables are (1) the accounts receivable turnover and (2) the number of days' sales in receivables.

The **accounts receivable turnover** measures how frequently during the year the accounts receivable are being converted to cash. For example, with credit terms of 2/10, n/30 days, the accounts receivable should turn over more than twelve times per year. The accounts receivable turnover is computed as follows:

$$\text{Accounts receivable turnover} = \frac{\text{Net sales on account}}{\text{Average accounts receivable}}$$

The average accounts receivable can be determined by using monthly data or by simply adding the beginning and ending accounts receivable balances and dividing by two. For example, assume that Sidner Company offers credit terms of 2/10, n/30 and has net sales on account of $36,000,000 and beginning and ending accounts receivable balances of $1,080,000 and $1,220,000. The accounts receivable turnover is 31.3, as shown below.

$$\text{Accounts receivable turnover} = \frac{\text{Net sales on account}}{\text{Average accounts receivable}}$$

$$= \frac{\$36,000,000}{(\$1,080,000 + \$1,220,000)/2} = 31.3$$

The **number of days' sales in receivables** is an estimate of the length of time the accounts receivable have been outstanding. With credit terms of 2/10, n/30 days, the number of days' sales in receivables should be approximately 10 days. It is computed as follows:

$$\text{Number of days' sales in receivables} = \frac{\text{Accounts receivable, end of year}}{\text{Average daily sales on account}}$$

Average daily sales on account is determined by dividing net sales on account by 365 days. For example, using the preceding data for Sidner Company, the number of days' sales in receivables is 12.4, as shown on the following page.

---

[6] *Statement of Financial Accounting Standards, No. 107*, "Disclosures about Fair Value of Financial Instruments," Financial Accounting Standards Board, Norwalk, 1991, pars. 10 and 19.

[7] *Statement of Financial Accounting Standards, No. 105*, "Disclosure of Information about Financial Instruments with Off-Balance-Sheet Risk and Financial Instruments with Concentrations of Credit Risk," Financial Accounting Standards Board, Norwalk, 1990, par. 20, and *Statement of Financial Accounting Standards, No. 107, op.cit.*, par. 13.

$$\text{Number of days' sales in receivables} = \frac{\text{Accounts receivable, end of year}}{\text{Average daily sales on account}}$$

$$= \frac{\$1,220,000}{(\$36,000,000/365 \text{ days})} = 12.4$$

For these measures to be meaningful, a company should compare its current measures with those from prior periods and with industry figures. An improvement in the efficiency in collecting accounts receivable is indicated when the accounts receivable turnover increases and the number of days' sales in receivables decreases.

ENCORE

Need a Friendly Loan?

If you are approached by a stranger and offered a quick loan to help you out of a financial bind, you should probably think twice. A young police officer in Hong Kong wishes he had.

Sergeant Li Chi-lok went to a local casino on a Friday night to play pai kau (Chinese dominoes). By 4 a.m. Saturday, he had lost his $9,000 gambling stake. Tired and out of money, he watched other gamblers until a young man approached him. "Did you win or lose? If you need money, we have some," the loan shark said. Sergeant Li yielded to temptation and borrowed $10,000, but was only given $9,000—$1,000 was taken as a service charge. When he stopped gambling, he had borrowed $20,000 and owed $25,000.

The loan sharks took Sergeant Li to an apartment, where he was told to call relatives to pay off his debt. However, the interest accumulated

rapidly. By midday on Saturday, the amount owed had risen to $33,000. Twelve hours later, it rose to $44,000, and by lunchtime on Sunday it had risen to $60,000. Sergeant Li was allowed to go after his mother deposited $20,000 in a bank account and he signed an IOU for the remaining debt. During his ordeal, Sergeant Li was tied up and severely beaten. His injuries included a punctured lung and a broken leg, arm, and finger.

Loan sharks aren't confined to Hong Kong. In the United Kingdom, there are more than 27,000 legal moneylenders, who charge annual interest rates up to 500%. In the United States, most states have usury laws restricting the amount of interest that a creditor may charge. However, illegal loan sharking still exists. For example, a Boston loan shark and gambling bookie recently pleaded guilty to charging 100 customers

interest rates ranging from 100% to 500%. In New York, a restaurant owner testified that he had paid $60,000 on a $20,000 loan, but it was still not enough to satisfy a Buffalo loan shark. In another case, a woman embezzled more than $100,000 from a doctor she worked for in order to pay her husband's loan shark. She escaped prosecution by cooperating with the FBI's case against the loan shark. ■

APPENDIX: DISCOUNTING NOTES RECEIVABLE

Although it is not a common transaction, a company may endorse its notes receivable and transfer them to a bank. The bank transfers cash (the **proceeds**) to the company after deducting a **discount** (interest) that is computed on the maturity value of the note for the discount period. The discount period is the time that the bank must hold the note before it becomes due.

To illustrate, assume that a 90-day, 12%, $1,800 note receivable from Pryor & Co., dated April 8, is discounted at the payee's bank on May 3 at the rate of 14%. The data used in determining the effect of the transaction are as follows:

Face value of note dated April 8	$1,800.00
Interest on note (90 days at 12%)	54.00
Maturity value of note due July 7	$1,854.00
Discount on maturity value (65 days from May 3 to July 7, at 14%)	46.87
Proceeds	$1,807.13

The endorser records as interest revenue the excess of the proceeds from discounting the note, $1,807.13, over its face value, $1,800, as follows:

May	3	Cash	1 80713		
		Notes Receivable		1 80000	
		Interest Revenue			713
		Discounted $1,800, 90-day, 12% note at 14%.			

What if the proceeds from discounting a note receivable are less than the face value? When this situation occurs, the endorser records the excess of the face value over the proceeds as interest expense. The length of the discount period and the difference between the interest rate and the discount rate determine whether interest expense or interest revenue will result from discounting.

Without a statement limiting responsibility, the endorser of a note is committed to paying the note if the maker defaults. This potential liability is called a **contingent liability**. Thus, the endorser of a note that has been discounted has a contingent liability until the due date. If the maker pays the promised amount at maturity, the contingent liability is removed without any action on the part of the endorser. If, on the other hand, the maker dishonors the note and the endorser is notified according to legal requirements, the endorser's liability becomes an actual one.

When a discounted note receivable is dishonored, the bank notifies the endorser and asks for payment. In some cases, the bank may charge a **protest fee** for notifying the endorser that a note has been dishonored. The entire amount paid to the bank by the endorser, including the interest and protest fee, should be debited to the account receivable of the maker. For example, assume that the $1,800, 90-day, 12% note discounted on May 3 is dishonored at maturity by the maker, Pryor & Co. The bank charges a protest fee of $12. The endorser's entry to record the payment to the bank is as follows:

July	7	Accounts Receivable—Pryor & Co.	1 86600	
		Cash		1 86600
		Paid dishonored, discounted note (maturity value of $1,854 plus protest fee of $12).		

KEY POINTS

1 List the common classifications of receivables.

The term receivables includes all money claims against other entities, including people, business firms, and other organizations. They are normally classified as accounts receivable, notes receivable, or other receivables.

2 Summarize and provide examples of internal control procedures that apply to receivables.

The internal controls that apply to receivables include the separation of responsibilities for related functions. In this way, the work of one employee can serve as a check on the work of another employee.

3 Describe the nature of and the accounting for uncollectible receivables.

The two methods of accounting for uncollectible receivables are the allowance method and the direct write-off method. The allowance method provides in advance for uncollectible receivables. The direct write-off method recognizes the expense only when the account is judged to be uncollectible.

4 Journalize the entries for the allowance method of accounting for uncollectibles, and estimate uncollectible receivables based on sales and on an analysis of receivables.

A year-end adjusting entry provides for (1) the reduction of the value of the receivables to the amount of cash expected to be realized from them in the future and (2) the allocation to the current period of the expected expense resulting from such reduction. The adjusting entry debits Uncollectible Accounts

Expense and credits Allowance for Doubtful Accounts. When an account is believed to be uncollectible, it is written off against the allowance account.

When the estimate of uncollectibles is based on the amount of sales for the fiscal period, the adjusting entry is made without regard to the balance of the allowance account. When the estimate of uncollectibles is based on the amount and the age of the receivable accounts at the end of the period, the adjusting entry is recorded so that the balance of the allowance account will equal the estimated uncollectibles at the end of the period.

The allowance account, which will have a credit balance after the adjusting entry has been posted, is a contra asset account. The uncollectible accounts expense is generally reported on the income statement as an administrative expense.

5 Journalize the entries for the direct write-off of uncollectible receivables.

Under the direct write-off method, the entry to write off an account debits Uncollectible Accounts Expense and credits Accounts Receivable. Neither an allowance account nor an adjusting entry is needed at the end of the period.

6 Describe the nature and characteristics of promissory notes.

A note is a written promise to pay a sum of money on demand or at a definite time. Characteristics of notes that affect how they are recorded and reported include the due date, interest rate, and maturity value. The basic formula for computing interest on a note is: Principal × Rate × Time = Interest. The due date is the date a note is to be paid, and the period of time between the issuance date and the due date is

normally stated in either days or months. The maturity value of a note is the sum of the face amount and the interest.

7 Journalize the entries for notes receivable transactions.

A note received in settlement of an account receivable is recorded as a debit to Notes Receivable and a credit to Accounts Receivable. When a note matures, Cash is debited, Notes Receivable is credited, and Interest Revenue is credited. If the maker of a note fails to pay the debt on the due date, the note is said to be dishonored. When the holder of a dishonored note has been paid by the endorser, the amount of the endorser's claim against the maker of the note is debited to an accounts receivable account.

8 Prepare the Current Assets presentation of receivables on the balance sheet.

All receivables that are expected to be realized in cash within a year are presented in the Current Assets section of the balance sheet. It is normal to list the assets in the order of their liquidity, which is the order in which they can be converted to cash in normal operations.

9 Compute and interpret the accounts receivable turnover and the number of days' sales in receivables.

The accounts receivable turnover is net sales on account divided by average accounts receivable. It measures how frequently accounts receivable are being converted into cash. The number of days' sales in receivables is the end-of-year accounts receivable divided by the average daily sales on account. It measures the length of time the accounts receivable have been outstanding.

ILLUSTRATIVE PROBLEM

Ditzler Company, a construction supply company, uses the allowance method of accounting for uncollectible accounts receivable. Selected transactions completed by Ditzler Company are as follows:

Feb. 1. Sold merchandise on account to Ames Co., $8,000. The cost of the merchandise sold was $4,500.

Mar. 15. Accepted a 60-day, 12% note for $8,000 from Ames Co. on account.

Apr. 9. Wrote off a $2,500 account from Dorset Co. as uncollectible.

21. Loaned $7,500 cash to Jill Klein, receiving a 90-day, 14% note.

May 14. Received the interest due from Ames Co. and a new 90-day, 14% note as a renewal of the loan. (Record both the debit and the credit to the notes receivable account.)

June 13. Reinstated the account of Dorset Co., written off on April 9, and received $2,500 in full payment.

July 20. Jill Klein dishonored her note.

Aug. 12. Received from Ames Co. the amount due on its note of May 14.

19. Received from Jill Klein the amount owed on the dishonored note, plus interest for 30 days at 15%, computed on the maturity value of the note.

Dec. 16. Accepted a 60-day, 12% note for $12,000 from Global Company on account.

31. It is estimated that 3% of the credit sales of $1,375,000 for the year ended December 31 will be uncollectible.

Instructions

1. Journalize the transactions. Omit explanations.
2. Journalize the adjusting entry to record the accrued interest on December 31 on the Global Company note.

Solution

1.

Feb.	1	Accounts Receivable—Ames Co.	8 0 0 0 00	
		Sales		8 0 0 0 00
	1	Cost of Merchandise Sold	4 5 0 0 00	
		Merchandise Inventory		4 5 0 0 00
Mar.	15	Notes Receivable—Ames Co.	8 0 0 0 00	
		Accounts Receivable—Ames Co.		8 0 0 0 00
Apr.	9	Allowance for Doubtful Accounts	2 5 0 0 00	
		Accounts Receivable—Dorset Co.		2 5 0 0 00
	21	Notes Receivable—Jill Klein	7 5 0 0 00	
		Cash		7 5 0 0 00
May	14	Notes Receivable—Ames Co.	8 0 0 0 00	
		Cash	1 6 0 00	
		Notes Receivable—Ames Co.		8 0 0 0 00
		Interest Revenue		1 6 0 00
June	13	Accounts Receivable—Dorset Co.	2 5 0 0 00	
		Allowance for Doubtful Accounts		2 5 0 0 00
	13	Cash	2 5 0 0 00	
		Accounts Receivable—Dorset Co.		2 5 0 0 00

July	20	Accounts Receivable—Jill Klein	7 7 6 2 50			
		Notes Receivable—Jill Klein			7 5 0 0 00	
		Interest Revenue			2 6 2 50	
Aug.	12	Cash	8 2 8 0 00			
		Notes Receivable—Ames Co.			8 0 0 0 00	
		Interest Revenue			2 8 0 00	
	19	Cash	7 8 5 9 53			
		Accounts Receivable—Jill Klein			7 7 6 2 50	
		Interest Revenue			9 7 03	
		($7,762.50 × 15% × 30/360)				
Dec.	16	Notes Receivable—Global Company	12 0 0 0 00			
		Accounts Receivable—Global Company			12 0 0 0 00	
	31	Uncollectible Accounts Expense	41 2 5 0 00			
		Allowance for Doubtful Accounts			41 2 5 0 00	

2.

Dec.	31	Interest Receivable	6 0 00			
		Interest Revenue			6 0 00	
		($12,000 × 12% × 15/360)				

SELF-EXAMINATION QUESTIONS
Answers at End of Chapter

Matching
Match each of the following statements with its proper term. Some terms may not be used.

A.	accounts receivable
B.	accounts receivable turnover
C.	aging the receivables
D.	allowance method
E.	contra asset
F.	direct write-off method
G.	dishonored note receivable
H.	maturity value
I.	notes receivable
J.	number of days' sales in receivables
K.	promissory note
L.	receivables
M.	uncollectible accounts expense

___ 1. All money claims against other entities, including people, business firms, and other organizations.

___ 2. A receivable created by selling merchandise or services on credit.

___ 3. Amounts customers owe, for which a formal, written instrument of credit has been issued.

___ 4. The operating expense incurred because of the failure to collect receivables.

___ 5. The method of accounting for uncollectible accounts that provides an expense for uncollectible receivables in advance of their write-off.

___ 6. The method of accounting for uncollectible accounts that recognizes the expense only when accounts are judged to be worthless.

___ 7. The process of analyzing the accounts receivable and classifying them according to various age groupings, with the due date being the base point for determining age.

___ 8. The amount that is due at the maturity or due date of a note.

___ 9. A note that the maker fails to pay on the due date.

___ 10. An estimate of the length of time the accounts receivable have been outstanding.

___ 11. Measures how frequently during the year the accounts receivable are being converted to cash.

___ 12. A written promise to pay a sum of money on demand or at a definite time.

Multiple Choice

1. At the end of the fiscal year, before the accounts are adjusted, Accounts Receivable has a balance of $200,000 and Allowance for Doubtful Accounts has a credit balance of $2,500. If the estimate of uncollectible accounts determined by aging the receivables is $8,500, the amount of uncollectible accounts expense is:
   A. $2,500
   C. $8,500
   B. $6,000
   D. $11,000

2. At the end of the fiscal year, Accounts Receivable has a balance of $100,000 and Allowance for Doubtful Accounts has a balance of $7,000. The expected net realizable value of the accounts receivable is:
   A. $7,000
   C. $100,000
   B. $93,000
   D. $107,000

3. What is the maturity value of a 90-day, 12% note for $10,000?

   A. $8,800
   C. $10,300
   B. $10,000
   D. $11,200

4. What is the due date of a $12,000, 90-day, 8% note receivable dated August 5?
   A. October 31
   C. November 3
   B. November 2
   D. November 4

5. When a note receivable is dishonored, Accounts Receivable is debited for what amount?
   A. The face value of the note
   B. The maturity value of the note
   C. The maturity value of the note less accrued interest
   D. The maturity value of the note plus accrued interest

CLASS DISCUSSION QUESTIONS

1. What are the three classifications of receivables?
2. What types of transactions give rise to accounts receivable?
3. In what section of the balance sheet should a note receivable be listed if its term is (a) 120 days, (b) 6 years?
4. Give two examples of other receivables.
5. The accounts receivable clerk is also responsible for handling cash receipts. Which principle of internal control is violated in this situation?
6. Which of the two methods of accounting for uncollectible accounts provides for the recognition of the expense at the earlier date?
7. What kind of an account (asset, liability, etc.) is Allowance for Doubtful Accounts, and is its normal balance a debit or a credit?
8. After the accounts are adjusted and closed at the end of the fiscal year, Accounts Receivable has a balance of $783,150 and Allowance for Doubtful Accounts has a balance of $41,694. Describe how the accounts receivable and the allowance for doubtful accounts are reported on the balance sheet.
9. A firm has consistently adjusted its allowance account at the end of the fiscal year by adding a fixed percent of the period's net sales on account. After five years, the balance in Allowance for Doubtful Accounts has become very large in relationship to the balance in Accounts Receivable. Give two possible explanations.
10. Which of the two methods of estimating uncollectibles provides for the most accurate estimate of the current net realizable value of the receivables?
11. For a business, what are the advantages of a note receivable in comparison to an account receivable?
12. Fryer Company issued a promissory note to Corbett Company. (a) Who is the payee? (b) What is the title of the account used by Corbett Company in recording the note?
13. If a note provides for payment of principal of $75,000 and interest at the rate of 8%, will the interest amount to $6,000? Explain.
14. The maker of a $6,000, 10%, 120-day note receivable failed to pay the note on the due date of April 30. What accounts should be debited and credited by the payee to record the dishonored note receivable?
15. The note receivable dishonored in Question 14 is paid on May 30 by the maker, plus interest for 30 days, 9%. What entry should be made to record the receipt of the payment?
16. Under what caption should accounts receivable be reported on the balance sheet?

EXERCISES

Exercise 7–1
Internal control procedures

Objective 2

Lunar Company sells carpeting. Over 60% of all carpet sales are on credit. The following procedures are used by Lunar to process this large number of credit sales and the subsequent collections.

a. All credit sales to a first-time customer must be approved by the Credit Department. Salespersons will assist the customer in filling out a credit application, but an employee in the Credit Department is responsible for verifying employment and checking the customer's credit history before granting credit.

b. Lunar's standard credit period is 30 days. The Credit Department may approve an extension of this repayment period of up to one year. Whenever an extension is granted, the customer signs a promissory note. Up to 10% of the credit sales in any one year are for repayment periods exceeding 30 days.

c. A formal ledger is not maintained for customers who sign promissory notes. Lunar simply keeps a copy of each signed note in a file cabinet. These unpaid notes are filed by due date.

d. Lunar employs an accounts receivable clerk. The clerk is responsible for recording customer credit sales (based on sales tickets), receiving cash from customers, giving customers credit for their payments, and handling all customer billing complaints.

e. The general ledger control account for Accounts Receivable is maintained by the General Accounting Department at Lunar. This department records total credit sales, based on credit sale information from the store's electronic cash register, and total customer receipts, based on the bank deposit slip.

State whether each of these procedures is appropriate or inappropriate, considering the principles of internal control. If inappropriate, state which internal control procedure is violated.

Exercise 7–2
Nature of uncollectible accounts

Objective 3

✓ a. 4.3%

Hilton Hotels Corporation owns and operates casinos at several of its hotels, located primarily in Nevada. At the end of a recent fiscal year, the following accounts and notes receivable were reported (in thousands):

Hotel accounts and notes receivable	$75,796	
Less: Allowance for doubtful accounts	3,256	
		$72,540
Casino accounts receivable	$26,334	
Less: Allowance for doubtful accounts	6,654	
		19,680

a. Compute the percentage of allowance for doubtful accounts to the gross hotel accounts and notes receivable for the end of the fiscal year.

b. Compute the percentage of the allowance for doubtful accounts to the gross casino accounts receivable for the end of the fiscal year.

c. Discuss possible reasons for the difference in the two ratios computed in (a) and (b).

Exercise 7–3
Number of days past due

Objective 4

✓ The Body Shop, 58 days

Diamond Auto Supply distributes new and used automobile parts to local dealers throughout the Southeast. Diamond's credit terms are n/30. As of the end of business on July 31, the following accounts receivable were past due.

Account	Due Date	Amount
The Body Shop	June 3	$3,000
Custom Auto	July 1	2,500
Hometown Repair	March 22	500
Jake's Auto Repair	May 19	1,000
Like New	June 18	750
Sally's	April 12	1,800
Uptown Auto	May 8	500
Westside Repair & Tow	May 31	1,100

Determine the number of days each account is past due.

Exercise 7–4
Aging-of-receivables schedule

Objective 4

The accounts receivable clerk for Romance Mattress Company prepared the following partially completed aging-of-receivables schedule as of the end of business on November 30.

Customer	Balance	Not Past Due	Days Past Due 1–30	31–60	61–90	Over 90
Aaron Brothers Inc.	2,000	2,000				
Abell Company	1,500		1,500			
Zollo Company	5,000			5,000		
Subtotals	872,500	540,000	180,000	78,500	42,300	31,700

The following accounts were unintentionally omitted from the aging schedule.

Customer	Balance	Due Date
Tamika Industries	$25,000	August 24
Ruppert Company	8,500	September 3
Welborne Inc.	35,000	October 17
Kristi Company	6,500	November 5
Simrill Company	12,000	December 3

a. Determine the number of days past due for each of the preceding accounts.
b. Complete the aging-of-receivables schedule.

Exercise 7–5
Estimating allowance for doubtful accounts

Objective 4

✓ $62,690

Romance Mattress Company has a past history of uncollectible accounts, as shown below. Estimate the allowance for doubtful accounts, based on the aging-of-receivables schedule you completed in Exercise 7–4.

Age Class	Percentage Uncollectible
Not past due	2%
1–30 days past due	4
31–60 days past due	10
61–90 days past due	20
Over 90 days past due	40

Exercise 7–6
Adjustment for uncollectible accounts
Objective 4

Using the data in Exercise 7–5, assume that the allowance for doubtful accounts for Romance Mattress Company has a credit balance of $6,890 before adjustment on November 30. Journalize the adjusting entry for uncollectible accounts as of November 30.

Exercise 7–7
Estimating doubtful accounts
Objective 4

Phoenician Co. is a wholesaler of office supplies. An aging of the company's accounts receivable on December 31, 2003, and a historical analysis of the percentage of uncollectible accounts in each age category are as follows:

Age Interval	Balance	Percent Uncollectible
Not past due	$350,000	1%
1–30 days past due	90,000	3
31–60 days past due	17,000	6
61–90 days past due	13,000	10
91–180 days past due	9,400	60
Over 180 days past due	3,600	80
	$483,000	

Estimate what the proper balance of the allowance for doubtful accounts should be as of December 31, 2003.

Exercise 7–8
Entry for uncollectible accounts
Objective 4

Using the data in Exercise 7–7, assume that the allowance for doubtful accounts for Phoenician Co. had a debit balance of $1,891 as of December 31, 2003.
Journalize the adjusting entry for uncollectible accounts as of December 31, 2003.

Exercise 7–9
Providing for doubtful accounts
Objective 4

✓ a. $15,000
✓ b. $14,600

At the end of the current year, the accounts receivable account has a debit balance of $775,000, and net sales for the year total $6,000,000. Determine the amount of the adjusting entry to provide for doubtful accounts under each of the following assumptions:

a. The allowance account before adjustment has a credit balance of $4,750. Uncollectible accounts expense is estimated at 1/4 of 1% of net sales.
b. The allowance account before adjustment has a credit balance of $3,750. An aging of the accounts in the customer's ledger indicates estimated doubtful accounts of $18,350.
c. The allowance account before adjustment has a debit balance of $5,050. Uncollectible accounts expense is estimated at 1/2 of 1% of net sales.
d. The allowance account before adjustment has a debit balance of $5,050. An aging of the accounts in the customer's ledger indicates estimated doubtful accounts of $31,400.

Exercise 7–10
Entries to write off accounts receivable
Objectives 4, 5

 SPREADSHEET

Query.com, a computer consulting firm, has decided to write off the $4,800 balance of an account owed by a customer. Journalize the entry to record the write-off, (a) assuming that the allowance method is used, and (b) assuming that the direct write-off method is used.

Exercise 7–11
Entries for uncollectible receivables, using allowance method
Objective 4

Journalize the following transactions in the accounts of Rhino Company, a restaurant supply company that uses the allowance method of accounting for uncollectible receivables:

Jan. 13. Sold merchandise on account to Renee Hart, $8,100. The cost of the merchandise sold was $4,750.

Feb. 12. Received $2,000 from Renee Hart and wrote off the remainder owed on the sale of January 13 as uncollectible.

July 3. Reinstated the account of Renee Hart that had been written off on February 12 and received $6,100 cash in full payment.

Exercise 7–12
Entries for uncollectible accounts, using direct write-off method

Objective 5

Journalize the following transactions in the accounts of Menthol Co., a hospital supply company that uses the direct write-off method of accounting for uncollectible receivables:

Aug. 8. Sold merchandise on account to Dr. Beth Mears, $10,500. The cost of the merchandise sold was $6,175.

Sept. 7. Received $8,000 from Dr. Beth Mears and wrote off the remainder owed on the sale of August 8 as uncollectible.

Dec. 20. Reinstated the account of Dr. Beth Mears that had been written off on September 7 and received $2,500 cash in full payment.

Exercise 7–13
Effect of doubtful accounts on net income

Objectives 4, 5

✓ $104,600

During its first year of operations, Yarmouth Automotive Supply Co. had net sales of $3,050,000, wrote off $52,800 of accounts as uncollectible using the direct write-off method, and reported net income of $112,800. If the allowance method of accounting for uncollectibles had been used, 2% of net sales would have been estimated as uncollectible. Determine what the net income would have been if the allowance method had been used.

Exercise 7–14
Effect of doubtful accounts on net income

Objectives 4, 5

✓ a. $150,800
✓ b. $19,700

Using the data in Exercise 7–13, assume that during the second year of operations Yarmouth Automotive Supply Co. had net sales of $3,800,000, wrote off $64,500 of accounts as uncollectible using the direct write-off method, and reported net income of $162,300.

a. Determine what net income would have been in the second year if the allowance method (using 2% of net sales) had been used in both the first and second years.

b. Determine what the balance of the allowance for doubtful accounts would have been at the end of the second year if the allowance method had been used in both the first and second years.

Exercise 7–15
Determine due date and interest on notes

Objective 6

✓ a. May 5; $150

Determine the due date and the amount of interest due at maturity on the following notes:

	Date of Note	Face Amount	Term of Note	Interest Rate
a.	March 6	$10,000	60 days	9%
b.	May 20	6,000	60 days	10%
c.	June 2	7,500	90 days	12%
d.	August 30	15,000	120 days	10%
e.	October 1	12,500	60 days	12%

Exercise 7–16
Entries for notes receivable

Objectives 6, 7

✓ b. $15,300

Funchal Interior Decorators issued a 90-day, 8% note for $15,000, dated April 6, to Maderia Furniture Company on account.

a. Determine the due date of the note.
b. Determine the maturity value of the note.
c. Journalize the entries to record the following: (1) receipt of the note by the payee, and (2) receipt by the payee of payment of the note at maturity.

Exercise 7–17
Entries for notes receivable

Objective 7

The series of seven transactions recorded in the following T accounts were related to a sale to a customer on account and the receipt of the amount owed. Briefly describe each transaction.

Cash		Notes Receivable	
(7)	23,028	(5) 22,000	(6) 22,000

Accounts Receivable				Sales Returns and Allowances		
(1)	25,000	(3)	3,000	(3)	3,000	
(6)	22,725	(5)	22,000			
		(7)	22,725			

Merchandise Inventory				Cost of Merchandise Sold		
(4)	1,800	(2)	15,000	(2)	15,000	(4)	1,800

Sales				Interest Revenue		
		(1)	25,000			(6)	725
						(7)	303

Exercise 7–18

Entries for notes receivable, including year-end entries

Objective 7

The following selected transactions were completed by Lupine Co., a supplier of elastic bands for clothing:

2002
Dec. 13. Received from Stout Co., on account, a $30,000, 120-day, 9% note dated December 13.
     31. Recorded an adjusting entry for accrued interest on the note of December 13.
     31. Closed the interest revenue account. The only entry in this account originated from the December 31 adjustment.
2003
Apr. 12. Received payment of note and interest from Stout Co.

Journalize the transactions.

Exercise 7–19

Entries for receipt and dishonor of note receivable

Objective 7

Journalize the following transactions of Galaxy Theater Productions:

July 3. Received a $50,000, 90-day, 7% note dated July 3 from Hermes Company on account.
Oct. 1. The note is dishonored by Hermes Company.
     31. Received the amount due on the dishonored note plus interest for 30 days at 9% on the total amount charged to Hermes Company on October 1.

Exercise 7–20

Entries for receipt and dishonor of notes receivable

Objectives 4, 7

Journalize the following transactions in the accounts of Dimitrious Co., which operates a riverboat casino:

Apr. 1. Received a $10,000, 30-day, 6% note dated April 1 from Wilcox Co. on account.
     18. Received a $12,000, 30-day, 9% note dated April 18 from Aaron Co. on account.
May 1. The note dated April 1 from Wilcox Co. is dishonored, and the customer's account is charged for the note, including interest.
June 17. The note dated April 18 from Aaron Co. is dishonored, and the customer's account is charged for the note, including interest.
July 30. Cash is received for the amount due on the dishonored note dated April 1 plus interest for 90 days at 8% on the total amount debited to Wilcox Co. on May 1.
Sept. 3. Wrote off against the allowance account the amount charged to Aaron Co. on June 17 for the dishonored note dated April 18.

Exercise 7–21

Receivables in the balance sheet

Objective 8

List any errors you can find in the following partial balance sheet.

Dragonfly Company
Balance Sheet
December 31, 2003

Assets		
Current assets:		
Cash		$ 63,750
Notes receivable	$200,000	
Less interest receivable	12,000	188,000
Accounts receivable	$376,180	
Plus allowance for doubtful accounts	30,500	406,680

Exercise 7–22
*Accounts receivable
turnover; number of days'
sales in receivables*

Objective 9

Real World

The financial statements for **Cisco Systems, Inc.**, are presented in Appendix G at the end of the text. Assume that all sales are credit sales and that the accounts receivable were $1,303,000,000 at July 25, 1998.

a. Compute the accounts receivable turnover for 1999 and 2000.
b. Compute the number of days' sales in receivables at July 31, 1999 and July 29, 2000.
c. ✏️▶ What conclusions can be drawn from these analyses regarding Cisco Systems' efficiency in collecting receivables?

Appendix
Exercise 7–23
Discounting notes receivable

Dacca Co., a building construction company, holds a 90-day, 6% note for $40,000, dated May 15, which was received from a customer on account. On June 14, the note is discounted at the bank at the rate of 10%.

a. Determine the maturity value of the note.
b. Determine the number of days in the discount period.
c. Determine the amount of the discount. Round to the nearest dollar.
d. Determine the amount of the proceeds.
e. Journalize the entry to record the discounting of the note on June 14.

Appendix
Exercise 7–24
*Entries for receipt and
discounting of note
receivable and dishonored
notes*

Journalize the following transactions in the accounts of Shapiro Theater Productions:

April 1. Received a $75,000, 60-day, 8% note dated April 1 from Creswell Company on account.
May 1. Discounted the note at First City Bank at 9%.
       31. The note is dishonored by Creswell Company; paid the bank the amount due on the note, plus a protest fee of $500.
June 30. Received the amount due on the dishonored note plus interest for 30 days at 12% on the total amount charged to Creswell Company on May 31.

PROBLEMS SERIES A

Problem 7–1A
*Entries related to
uncollectible accounts*

Objective 4

GENERAL
LEDGER

✓ 3. $755,050

The following transactions, adjusting entries, and closing entries were completed by The AllStar Gallery during the current fiscal year ended December 31:

Feb. 21. Reinstated the account of Merryl Alber, which had been written off in the preceding year as uncollectible. Journalized the receipt of $2,025 cash in full payment of Alber's account.
Mar. 31. Wrote off the $5,500 balance owed by Amos Co., which is bankrupt.
July 7. Received 35% of the $8,000 balance owed by Morton Co., a bankrupt business, and wrote off the remainder as uncollectible.
Aug. 29. Reinstated the account of Louis Sabo, which had been written off two years earlier as uncollectible. Recorded the receipt of $1,200 cash in full payment.
Dec. 31. Wrote off the following accounts as uncollectible (compound entry): Dailey Co., $10,050; Sun Co., $7,260; Zheng Furniture, $3,775; Carey Wenzel, $2,820.
       31. Based on an analysis of the $787,550 of accounts receivable, it was estimated that $32,500 will be uncollectible. Journalized the adjusting entry.
       31. Journalized the entry to close the appropriate account to Income Summary.

Instructions

1. Record the January 1 credit balance of $30,000 in Allowance for Doubtful Accounts.
2. Journalize the transactions and the adjusting and closing entries. Post each entry that affects the following three selected accounts and determine the new balances:

    115 Allowance for Doubtful Accounts
    313 Income Summary
    718 Uncollectible Accounts Expense

(continued)

3. Determine the expected net realizable value of the accounts receivable as of December 31.
4. Assuming that instead of basing the provision for uncollectible accounts on an analysis of receivables, the adjusting entry on December 31 had been based on an estimated expense of 1/2 of 1% of the net sales of $7,400,000 for the year, determine the following:
   a. Uncollectible accounts expense for the year.
   b. Balance in the allowance account after the adjustment of December 31.
   c. Expected net realizable value of the accounts receivable as of December 31.

Problem 7–2A
*Aging of receivables;
estimating allowance for
doubtful accounts*

Objective 4

SPREADSHEET

✓ 3. $57,283

Lipshy Wigs Company supplies wigs and hair care products to beauty salons throughout California and the Pacific Northwest. The accounts receivable clerk for Lipshy Wigs prepared the following partially completed aging-of-receivables schedule as of the end of business on December 31, 2003:

Customer	Balance	Not Past Due	Days Past Due				
			1–30	31–60	61–90	91–120	Over 120
Austin Beauty	10,000	10,000					
Blount Wigs	5,500			5,500			
Zabka's	2,900		2,900				
Subtotals	780,000	398,600	197,250	98,750	33,300	29,950	22,150

The following accounts were unintentionally omitted from the aging schedule.

Customer	Due Date	Balance
Houseal Uniquely Yours	July 1, 2003	900
Country Designs	Aug. 2, 2003	4,000
Treat's	Sept. 9, 2003	1,200
Molina's Beauty Store	Sept. 29, 2003	1,100
Ginburg Supreme	Oct. 10, 2003	1,500
Steve's Hair Products	Oct. 17, 2003	600
Hairy's Hair Care	Oct. 31, 2003	2,000
VanDiver's Images	Nov. 18, 2003	700
Lopez's Blond Bombs	Nov. 28, 2003	1,800
Josset Ritz	Nov. 30, 2003	3,500
Cool Designs	Dec. 1, 2003	1,000
Buttram Images	Jan. 3, 2004	6,200

Lipshy Wigs has a past history of uncollectible accounts by age category, as follows:

Age Class	Percentage Uncollectible
Not past due	1%
1–30 days past due	4
31–60 days past due	8
61–90 days past due	15
91–120 days past due	30
Over 120 days past due	80

Instructions

1. Determine the number of days past due for each of the preceding accounts.
2. Complete the aging-of-receivables schedule.
3. Estimate the allowance for doubtful accounts, based on the aging-of-receivables schedule.
4. Assume that the allowance for doubtful accounts for Lipshy Wigs has a credit balance of $11,350 before adjustment on December 31, 2003. Illustrate the effect on the accounts and financial statements of the adjustment for uncollectible accounts.

Problem 7–3A

Compare two methods of accounting for uncollectible receivables

Objectives 4, 5

✓ 1. Year 4: Balance of allowance account, end of year, $6,750

Minaret Company, which operates a chain of 30 electronics supply stores, has just completed its fourth year of operations. The direct write-off method of recording uncollectible accounts expense has been used during the entire period. Because of substantial increases in sales volume and amount of uncollectible accounts, the firm is considering changing to the allowance method. Information is requested as to the effect that an annual provision of 1/2% of sales would have had on the amount of uncollectible accounts expense reported for each of the past four years. It is also considered desirable to know what the balance of Allowance for Doubtful Accounts would have been at the end of each year. The following data have been obtained from the accounts:

| | | Uncollectible Accounts Written | Year of Origin of Accounts Receivable Written Off as Uncollectible | | | |
Year	Sales	Off	1st	2nd	3rd	4th
1st	$ 750,000	$ 600	$ 600			
2nd	820,000	1,650	750	$ 900		
3rd	1,050,000	6,200	1,800	1,400	$3,000	
4th	2,250,000	9,150		1,900	2,950	$4,300

Instructions

1. Assemble the desired data, using the following column headings:

| | Uncollectible Accounts Expense | | | Balance of Allowance Account, End of Year |
Year	Expense Actually Reported	Expense Based on Estimate	Increase (Decrease) in Amount of Expense	

2. Experience during the first four years of operations indicated that the receivables were either collected within two years or had to be written off as uncollectible. Does the estimate of 1/2% of sales appear to be reasonably close to the actual experience with uncollectible accounts originating during the first two years? Explain.

Problem 7–4A

Details of notes receivable and related entries

Objectives 6, 7

SPREADSHEET

✓ 1. Note 2: Due date, Sept. 4; Interest due at maturity, $150

Diaz Co. produces advertising videos. During the last six months of the current fiscal year, Diaz Co. received the following notes.

	Date	Face Amount	Term	Interest Rate
1.	May 17	$12,000	45 days	8%
2.	July 6	10,000	60 days	9%
3.	Aug. 1	16,500	90 days	8%
4.	Sept. 1	20,000	90 days	7%
5.	Nov. 29	18,000	60 days	9%
6.	Dec. 18	36,000	60 days	12%

Instructions

1. Determine for each note (a) the due date and (b) the amount of interest due at maturity, identifying each note by number.
2. Journalize the entry to record the dishonor of Note (3) on its due date. *(continued)*

3. Journalize the adjusting entry to record the accrued interest on Notes (5) and (6) on December 31.
4. Journalize the entries to record the receipt of the amounts due on Notes (5) and (6) in January and February.

Problem 7–5A
Notes receivable entries

Objective 7

The following data relate to notes receivable and interest for Robbins Co., a financial services company. (All notes are dated as of the day they are received.)

Mar. 1. Received a $13,000, 9%, 60-day note on account.
     21. Received a $7,500, 8%, 90-day note on account.
Apr. 30. Received $13,195 on note of March 1.
May 16. Received a $40,000, 7%, 90-day note on account.
     31. Received a $6,000, 8%, 30-day note on account.
June 19. Received $7,650 on note of March 21.
     30. Received $6,040 on note of May 31.
July 1. Received a $5,000, 12%, 30-day note on account.
     31. Received $5,050 on note of July 1.
Aug. 14. Received $40,700 on note of May 16.

Instructions
Journalize the entries to record the transactions.

Problem 7–6A
Sales and notes receivable transactions

Objective 7

GENERAL
LEDGER

The following were selected from among the transactions completed during the current year by Sonora Co., an appliance wholesale company:

Jan. 7. Sold merchandise on account to Thi Co., $7,500. The cost of merchandise sold was $3,800.
Mar. 8. Accepted a 60-day, 8% note for $7,500 from Thi Co. on account.
May 7. Received from Thi Co. the amount due on the note of March 8.
June 1. Sold merchandise on account to Kohl's for $5,000. The cost of merchandise sold was $3,500.
     5. Loaned $11,000 cash to Michele Duncan, receiving a 30-day, 6% note.
    11. Received from Kohl's the amount due on the invoice of June 1, less 2% discount.
July 5. Received the interest due from Michele Duncan and a new 60-day, 9% note as a renewal of the loan of June 5. (Record both the debit and the credit to the notes receivable account.)
Sept. 3. Received from Michele Duncan the amount due on her note of July 5.
    4. Sold merchandise on account to Stover Co., $8,000. The cost of merchandise sold was $5,500.
Oct. 4. Accepted a 60-day, 6% note for $8,000 from Stover Co. on account.
Dec. 3. Stover Co. dishonored the note dated October 4.
    29. Received from Stover Co. the amount owed on the dishonored note, plus interest for 26 days at 6% computed on the maturity value of the note.

Instructions
Journalize the transactions. Round to the nearest dollar.

PROBLEMS SERIES B

Problem 7–1B
Entries related to uncollectible accounts

Objective 4

GENERAL
LEDGER

✓ 3. $623,050

The following transactions, adjusting entries, and closing entries were completed by Cascade Contractors Co. during the current fiscal year ended December 31:

Mar. 17. Received 80% of the $17,500 balance owed by Baxter Co., a bankrupt business, and wrote off the remainder as uncollectible.
Apr. 20. Reinstated the account of Susan Evans, which had been written off in the preceding year as uncollectible. Journalized the receipt of $3,782 cash in full payment of Evans' account.
July 29. Wrote off the $4,500 balance owed by Cofer Co., which has no assets.
Oct. 31. Reinstated the account of Mostafa Co., which had been written off in the preceding year as uncollectible. Journalized the receipt of $7,500 cash in full payment of the account.

Dec. 31. Wrote off the following accounts as uncollectible (compound entry): Grovner
Co., $1,950; Nance Co., $2,600; Powell Distributors, $3,500; J. J. Levi, $5,200.
31. Based on an analysis of the $635,750 of accounts receivable, it was estimated
that $12,700 will be uncollectible. Journalized the adjusting entry.
31. Journalized the entry to close the appropriate account to Income Summary.

Instructions

1. Record the January 1 credit balance of $10,050 in Allowance for Doubtful Accounts.
2. Journalize the transactions and the adjusting and closing entries. Post each entry that
affects the following three selected accounts and determine the new balances:

115 Allowance for Doubtful Accounts
313 Income Summary
718 Uncollectible Accounts Expense

3. Determine the expected net realizable value of the accounts receivable as of December 31.
4. Assuming that instead of basing the provision for uncollectible accounts on an analysis of receivables, the adjusting entry on December 31 had been based on an estimated expense of 1/4 of 1% of the net sales of $5,100,000 for the year, determine the following:
   a. Uncollectible accounts expense for the year.
   b. Balance in the allowance account after the adjustment of December 31.
   c. Expected net realizable value of the accounts receivable as of December 31.

Problem 7–2B
*Aging of receivables;
estimating allowance for
doubtful accounts*

Objective 4

SPREADSHEET

✓ 3. $69,810

Wickman Company supplies flies and fishing gear to sporting goods stores and outfitters throughout the western United States. The accounts receivable clerk for Wickman prepared the following partially completed aging-of-receivables schedule as of the end of business on December 31, 2003:

Customer	Balance	Not Past Due	1–30	31–60	61–90	91–120	Over 120
				Days Past Due			
Alexandra Fishery	15,000	15,000					
Cutthroat Sports	5,500			5,500			
Yellowstone Sports	2,900		2,900				
Subtotals	880,000	448,600	247,250	98,750	33,300	29,950	22,150

The following accounts were unintentionally omitted from the aging schedule.

Customer	Due Date	Balance
Adel Sports & Flies	June 21, 2003	1,500
Buzzer Sports	July 30, 2003	3,000
Marabou Flies	Sept. 9, 2003	2,500
Midge Co.	Sept. 30, 2003	1,100
Adventure Outfitters	Oct. 10, 2003	2,500
Pheasant Tail Sports	Oct. 17, 2003	600
Red Tag Sporting Goods	Oct. 30, 2003	2,000
Ross Sports	Nov. 18, 2003	500

Customer	Due Date	Balance
Sawyer's Pheasant Tail	Nov. 28, 2003	1,800
Tent Caddis Outfitters	Nov. 30, 2003	3,500
Wulff Company	Dec. 1, 2003	1,000
Zug Bug Sports	Jan. 6, 2004	6,200

Wickman Company has a past history of uncollectible accounts by age category, as follows:

Age Class	Percentage Uncollectible
Not past due	2%
1–30 days past due	4
31–60 days past due	8
61–90 days past due	20
91–120 days past due	40
Over 120 days past due	80

Instructions

1. Determine the number of days past due for each of the preceding accounts.
2. Complete the aging-of-receivables schedule.
3. Estimate the allowance for doubtful accounts, based on the aging-of-receivables schedule.
4. Assume that the allowance for doubtful accounts for Wickman Company has a debit balance of $1,800 before adjustment on December 31, 2003. Journalize the adjusting entry for uncollectible accounts.

Problem 7–3B
Compare two methods of accounting for uncollectible receivables

Objectives 4, 5

✓ 1. Year 4: Balance of allowance account, end of year, $12,250.

Interlink Company, a telephone service and supply company, has just completed its fourth year of operations. The direct write-off method of recording uncollectible accounts expense has been used during the entire period. Because of substantial increases in sales volume and amount of uncollectible accounts, the firm is considering changing to the allowance method. Information is requested as to the effect that an annual provision of 3/4% of sales would have had on the amount of uncollectible accounts expense reported for each of the past four years. It is also considered desirable to know what the balance of Allowance for Doubtful Accounts would have been at the end of each year. The following data have been obtained from the accounts:

Year	Sales	Uncollectible Accounts Written Off	Year of Origin of Accounts Receivable Written Off as Uncollectible			
			1st	2nd	3rd	4th
1st	$ 650,000	$2,500	$2,500			
2nd	760,000	2,950	1,900	$1,050		
3rd	950,000	5,700	700	4,000	$1,000	
4th	1,800,000	7,800		1,200	2,550	$4,050

Instructions

1. Assemble the desired data, using the following column headings:

	Uncollectible Accounts Expense			Balance of Allowance Account, End of Year
Year	Expense Actually Reported	Expense Based on Estimate	Increase (Decrease) in Amount of Expense	

2. ▬▶ Experience during the first four years of operations indicated that the receivables were either collected within two years or had to be written off as uncollectible. Does the estimate of 3/4% of sales appear to be reasonably close to the actual experience with uncollectible accounts originating during the first two years? Explain.

Problem 7–4B
Details of notes receivable and related entries

Objectives 6, 7

SPREADSHEET

✓ 1. Note 2: Due date, July 15; Interest due at maturity, $175.

Matrix Co. wholesales bathroom fixtures. During the current fiscal year, Matrix Co. received the following notes.

	Date	Face Amount	Term	Interest Rate
1.	March 3	$36,000	60 days	8%
2.	June 15	17,500	30 days	12%
3.	Aug. 20	9,200	120 days	6%
4.	Oct. 31	12,000	60 days	9%
5.	Nov. 23	15,000	60 days	6%
6.	Dec. 27	9,000	30 days	12%

Instructions

1. Determine for each note (a) the due date and (b) the amount of interest due at maturity, identifying each note by number.
2. Journalize the entry to record the dishonor of Note (3) on its due date.
3. Journalize the adjusting entry to record the accrued interest on Notes (5) and (6) on December 31.
4. Journalize the entries to record the receipt of the amounts due on Notes (5) and (6) in January.

Problem 7–5B
Notes receivable entries

Objective 7

The following data relate to notes receivable and interest for Teleport Optic Co., a cable manufacturer and supplier. (All notes are dated as of the day they are received.)

June 1. Received a $15,800, 9%, 60-day note on account.
July 16. Received a $30,000, 10%, 120-day note on account.
   31. Received $16,037 on note of June 1.
Sept. 1. Received a $24,000, 9%, 60-day note on account.
Oct. 31. Received $24,360 on note of September 1.
Nov. 8. Received a $24,000, 7%, 30-day note on account.
   13. Received $31,000 on note of July 16.
   30. Received a $15,000, 10%, 30-day note on account.
Dec. 8. Received $24,140 on note of November 8.
   30. Received $15,125 on note of November 30.

Instructions
Journalize entries to record the transactions.

Problem 7–6B
Sales and notes receivable transactions

Objective 7

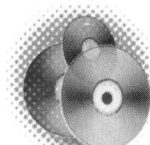

GENERAL LEDGER

The following were selected from among the transactions completed by Greco Co. during the current year. Greco Co. sells and installs home and business security systems.

Jan. 8. Loaned $6,000 cash to Mark Tift, receiving a 90-day, 8% note.
Feb. 3. Sold merchandise on account to Messina and Son, $18,000. The cost of the merchandise sold was $10,000.
Feb. 12. Sold merchandise on account to Gwyn Co., $25,000. The cost of merchandise sold was $15,000.
Mar. 5. Accepted a 60-day, 6% note for $18,000 from Messina and Son on account.
   14. Accepted a 60-day, 12% note for $25,000 from Gwyn Co. on account.
Apr. 8. Received the interest due from Mark Tift and a new 90-day, 9% note as a renewal of the loan of January 8. (Record both the debit and the credit to the notes receivable account.)
May 4. Received from Messina and Son the amount due on the note of March 5.
   13. Gwyn Co. dishonored its note dated March 14.
June 12. Received from Gwyn Co. the amount owed on the dishonored note, plus interest for 30 days at 12% computed on the maturity value of the note.
July 7. Received from Mark Tift the amount due on his note of April 8.
Aug. 23. Sold merchandise on account to MacKenzie Co., $8,000. The cost of the merchandise sold was $5,000.
Sept. 2. Received from MacKenzie Co. the amount of the invoice of August 23, less 1% discount.

Instructions

Journalize the transactions.

SPECIAL ACTIVITIES

Activity 7–1
Billings National Bank
Ethics and professional conduct in business

Tricia Fenton, vice-president of operations for Billings National Bank, has instructed the bank's computer programmer to use a 365-day year to compute interest on depository accounts (payables). Tricia also instructed the programmer to use a 360-day year to compute interest on loans (receivables).

➤ Discuss whether Tricia is behaving in a professional manner.

Activity 7–2
Jefferson Construction Supplies Co.
Collecting accounts receivable

The following is an excerpt from a conversation between the office manager, Jamie Luthi, and the president of Jefferson Construction Supplies Co., David King. Jefferson sells building supplies to local contractors.

Jamie: David, we're going to have to do something about these overdue accounts receivable. One-third of our accounts are over 60 days past due, and I've had accounts that have stayed open for almost a year!

David: I didn't realize it was that bad. Any ideas?

Jamie: Well, we could stop giving credit. Make everyone pay with cash or a credit card. We accept MasterCard and Visa already, but only the walk-in customers use them. Almost all of the contractors put purchases on their bills.

David: Yes, but we've been allowing credit for years. As far as I know, all of our competitors allow contractors credit. If we stopped giving credit, we'd lose many of our contractors. They'd just go elsewhere. You know, some of these guys run up bills as high as $40,000 or $60,000. There's no way they could put that kind of money on a credit card.

Jamie: That's a good point. But we've got to do something.

David: How many of the contractor accounts do you actually end up writing off as uncollectible?

Jamie: Not many. Almost all eventually pay. It's just that they take so long!

➤ Suggest one or more solutions to Jefferson Construction Supplies Co.'s problem concerning the collection of accounts receivable.

Activity 7–3
Retriever Wholesale Co.
Value of receivables

The following is an excerpt from a conversation between Kay Kinder, the president and owner of Retriever Wholesale Co., and Michele Stephens, Retriever's controller. The conversation took place on January 4, 2003, shortly after Michele began preparing the financial statements for the year ending December 31, 2002.

Michele: Kay, I've completed my analysis of the collectibility of our accounts receivable. My staff and I estimate that the allowance for doubtful accounts should be somewhere between $60,000 and $90,000. Right now, the balance of the allowance account is $18,000.

Kay: Oh, no! We are already below the estimated earnings projection I gave the bank last year. We used that as a basis for convincing the bank to loan us $100,000. They're going to be upset! Is there any way we can increase the allowance without the adjustment increasing expenses?

Michele: I'm afraid not. The allowance can only be increased by debiting the uncollectible accounts expense account.

Kay: Well, I guess we're stuck. The bank will just have to live with it. But let's increase the allowance by only $42,000. That gets us into our range of estimates with the minimum expense increase.

Michele: Kay, there is one more thing we need to discuss.

Kay: What now?

Michele: Jill, my staff accountant, noticed that you haven't made any payments on your receivable for over a year. Also, it has increased from $20,000 last year to $80,000. Jill thinks we ought to reclassify it as a noncurrent asset and report it as an "other receivable."

Kay: What's the problem? Didn't we just include it in accounts receivable last year?

Michele: Yes, but last year it was immaterial.

Kay: Look, I'll make a $60,000 payment next week. So let's report it as we did last year.

✏️➤ If you were Michele, how would you address Kay's suggestions?

Activity 7–4
Sheepshank Co.
Estimate uncollectible accounts

For several years, sales have been on a "cash only" basis. On January 1, 2000, however, Sheepshank Co. began offering credit on terms of n/30. The amount of the adjusting entry to record the estimated uncollectible receivables at the end of each year has been 1/4 of 1% of credit sales, which is the rate reported as the average for the industry. Credit sales and the year-end credit balances in Allowance for Doubtful Accounts for the past four years are as follows:

Year	Credit Sales	Allowance for Doubtful Accounts
2000	$7,800,000	$ 5,100
2001	8,000,000	11,100
2002	8,100,000	16,850
2003	9,250,000	25,375

Carisa Parker, president of Sheepshank Co., is concerned that the method used to account for and write off uncollectible receivables is unsatisfactory. She has asked for your advice in the analysis of past operations in this area and for recommendations for change.

1. Determine the amount of (a) the addition to Allowance for Doubtful Accounts and (b) the accounts written off for each of the four years.
2. a. ✏️➤ Advise Carisa Parker as to whether the estimate of 1/4 of 1% of credit sales appears reasonable.
   b. ✏️➤ Assume that after discussing (a) with Carisa Parker, she asked you what action might be taken to determine what the balance of Allowance for Doubtful Accounts should be at December 31, 2003, and what possible changes, if any, you might recommend in accounting for uncollectible receivables. How would you respond?

Activity 7–5
Into the Real World
Granting credit

In groups of three or four, determine how credit is typically granted to customers. Interview an individual responsible for granting credit for a bank, a department store, an automobile dealer, or other business in your community. You should ask such questions as the following:

1. What procedures are used to decide whether to grant credit to a customer?
2. What procedures are used to try to collect from customers who are delinquent in their payments?
3. Approximately what percentage of customers' accounts are written off as uncollectible in a year?

✏️➤ Summarize your findings in a report to the class.

Activity 7–6
Into the Real World
Collection of receivables

Go to the Web page of two department store chains, **Federated Department Stores Inc.** and **Dillard's Inc.** The Internet sites for these companies are:

www.federated-fds.com
www.dillards.com

Using the financial information provided at each site, calculate the most recent accounts receivable turnover for each company, and identify which company is collecting its receivables faster.

ANSWERS TO SELF-EXAMINATION QUESTIONS

Matching

1. L	3. I	5. D	7. C	9. G	11. B
2. A	4. M	6. F	8. H	10. J	12. K

Multiple Choice

1. **B** The estimate of uncollectible accounts, $8,500 (answer C), is the amount of the desired balance of Allowance for Doubtful Accounts after adjustment. The amount of the current provision to be made for uncollectible accounts expense is thus $6,000 (answer B), which is the amount that must be added to the Allowance for Doubtful Accounts credit balance of $2,500 (answer A) so that the account will have the desired balance of $8,500.

2. **B** The amount expected to be realized from accounts receivable is the balance of Accounts Receivable, $100,000, less the balance of Allowance for Doubtful Accounts, $7,000, or $93,000 (answer B).

3. **C** Maturity value is the amount that is due at the maturity or due date. The maturity value of $10,300 (answer C) is determined as follows:

Face amount of note	$10,000
Plus interest ($10,000 × 0.12 × 90/360)	300
Maturity value of note	$10,300

4. **C** November 3 is the due date of a $12,000, 90-day, 8% note receivable dated August 5 [26 days in August (31 days − 5 days) + 30 days in September + 31 days in October + 3 days in November].

5. **B** If a note is dishonored, Accounts Receivable is debited for the maturity value of the note (answer B). The maturity value of the note is its face value (answer A) plus the accrued interest. The maturity value of the note less accrued interest (answer C) is equal to the face value of the note. The maturity value of the note plus accrued interest (answer D) is incorrect, since the interest would be added twice.

Inventories

objectives

After studying this chapter, you should be able to:

1 Summarize and provide examples of internal control procedures that apply to inventories.

2 Describe the effect of inventory errors on the financial statements.

3 Describe three inventory cost flow assumptions and how they impact the income statement and balance sheet.

4 Compute the cost of inventory under the perpetual inventory system, using the following costing methods:

First-in, first-out
Last-in, first-out
Average cost

5 Compute the cost of inventory under the periodic inventory system, using the following costing methods:

First-in, first-out
Last-in, first-out
Average cost

6 Compare and contrast the use of the three inventory costing methods.

7 Compute the proper valuation of inventory at other than cost, using the lower-of-cost-or-market and net realizable value concepts.

8 Prepare a balance sheet presentation of merchandise inventory.

9 Estimate the cost of inventory, using the retail method and the gross profit method.

10 Compute and interpret the inventory turnover ratio and the number of days' sales in inventory. ■ ■ ■

Assume that you purchased a compact disc (CD)/receiver in June. You planned on attaching two pairs of speakers to the system. Initially, however, you could afford only one pair of speakers, which cost $160. In October, you purchased the second pair of speakers at a cost of $180.

Over the holidays, someone broke into your home and stole one pair of speakers. Luckily, your renters/homeowners insurance policy will cover the theft, but the insurance company needs to know the cost of the speakers that were stolen.

All of the speakers are identical. To respond to the insurance company, however, you will need to identify which pair of speakers was stolen. Was it the first pair, which cost $160? Or was it the second pair, which cost $180? Whichever assumption you make may determine the amount that you receive from the insurance company.

Merchandising businesses make similar assumptions when identical merchandise is purchased at different costs. At the end of a period, some of the merchandise will be in inventory and some will have been sold. But which costs relate to the sold merchandise and which costs relate to the merchandise in inventory? The company's assumption can involve large dollar amounts and thus can have a significant impact on the financial statements. For example, **The Home Depot, Inc.** has merchandise inventories that total almost $5.5 billion, while **Xerox Corporation's** inventories total almost $3 billion.

In this chapter, we will discuss such issues as how to determine the cost of merchandise in inventory and the cost of merchandise sold. However, we begin this chapter by discussing internal controls over merchandise inventory.

Internal Control of Inventories

objective 1

Summarize and provide examples of internal control procedures that apply to inventories.

The cost of inventory is a significant item in many businesses' financial statements. What do we mean by the term inventory? **Inventory** is used to indicate (1) merchandise held for sale in the normal course of business and (2) materials in the process of production or held for production. In this chapter, we focus primarily on inventory of merchandise purchased for resale.

What costs should be included in inventory? As we have illustrated in earlier chapters, the cost of merchandise is its purchase price, less any purchases discounts. These costs are usually the largest portion of the inventory cost. Merchandise inventory also includes other costs, such as transportation, import duties, and insurance against losses in transit.

> **Real World**
>
> Circuit City's inventory represents over 75% of its current assets and over 50% of its total assets. Circuit City's cost of merchandise sold represents over 70% of its net sales.

For companies such as **Circuit City**, good internal control over inventory must be maintained. Two primary objectives of internal control over inventory are safeguarding the inventory and properly reporting it in the financial statements. These internal controls can be either preventive or detective in nature. A preventive control is designed to prevent errors or misstatements from occurring. A detective control is designed to detect an error or misstatement after it has occurred.

Jewelry stores normally keep diamond rings, bracelets, and other items in a locked glass case. Is this a preventive or a detective control?

This is a preventive control to protect against theft (shoplifting).

Control over inventory should begin as soon as the inventory is received. Prenumbered receiving reports should be completed by the company's receiving department in order to establish the initial accountability for the inventory. To make sure the inventory received is what was ordered, each receiving report should agree with the company's original purchase order for the merchandise. Likewise, the price at which the inventory was ordered, as shown on the purchase order, should be compared to the price at which the vendor billed the company, as shown on the vendor's invoice. After the receiving report, purchase order, and vendor's invoice have been reconciled, the company should record the inventory and related account payable in the accounting records.

Controls for safeguarding inventory include developing and using security measures to prevent inventory damage or employee theft. For example, inventory should be stored in a warehouse or other area to which access is restricted to authorized employees. The removal of merchandise from the warehouse should be controlled by using requisition forms, which should be properly authorized. The storage area should also be climate controlled to prevent damage from heat or cold. Further, when the business is not operating or is not open, the storage area should be locked.

When shopping, you may have noticed how retail stores protect inventory from customer theft. Retail stores often use such devices as two-way mirrors, cameras, and security guards. High-priced items are often displayed in locked cabinets. Retail clothing stores often place plastic alarm tags on valuable items such as leather coats. Sensors at the exit doors set off alarms if the tags have not been removed by the clerk. These controls are designed to prevent customers from shoplifting.

Using a perpetual inventory system for merchandise also provides an effective means of control over inventory. The amount of each type of merchandise is always readily available in a subsidiary **inventory ledger**. In addition, the subsidiary ledger can be an aid in maintaining inventory quantities at proper levels. Frequently comparing balances with predetermined maximum and minimum levels allows for the timely reordering of merchandise and prevents the ordering of excess inventory.

To ensure the accuracy of the amount of inventory reported in the financial statements, a merchandising business should take a **physical inventory** (i.e., count the merchandise). In a perpetual inventory system, the physical inventory is compared to the recorded inventory in order to determine the amount of shrinkage or shortage. If the inventory shrinkage is unusually large, management can investigate further and take any necessary corrective action. Knowledge that a physical inventory will be taken also helps prevent employee thefts or misuses of inventory.

How does a business "take" a physical inventory? The first step in this process is to determine the quantity of each kind of merchandise owned by the business. A common practice is to use teams of two persons. One person determines the quantity, and the other lists the quantity and description on inventory count sheets. Quantities of high-cost items are usually verified by supervisors or a second count team.

What merchandise should be included in inventory? All the merchandise *owned* by the business on the inventory date should

Sam's Club and Wal-Mart stores use a greeter at the entry of each store to welcome customers. The greeter also serves as a preventive control by asking customers not to bring in packages or other bags, which could be used for shoplifting.

Most companies take their physical inventories when their inventory levels are the lowest. For example, most retailers take their physical inventory in late January or early February, which is after the holiday selling season but before restocking for spring.

All merchandise <u>owned</u> by a business should be included in the business's inventory.

be included. For merchandise in transit, the party (the seller or the buyer) who has title to the merchandise on the inventory date is the owner. To determine who has title, it may be necessary to examine purchases and sales invoices of the last few days of the current period and the first few days of the following period.

As we discussed in an earlier chapter, shipping terms determine when title passes. When goods are purchased or sold **FOB shipping point**, title passes to the buyer when the goods are shipped. When the terms are **FOB destination**, title passes to the buyer when the goods are delivered.

To illustrate, assume that Roper Co. orders $25,000 of merchandise on December 28, 2003. The merchandise is shipped FOB shipping point by the seller on December 30 and arrives at Roper Co.'s warehouse on January 4, 2004. As a result, the merchandise is not counted by the inventory crew on December 31, the end of Roper Co.'s fiscal year. However, the $25,000 of merchandise should be included in Roper's inventory because title has passed. Roper Co. should record the merchandise in transit on December 31, debiting Merchandise Inventory and crediting Accounts Payable for $25,000.

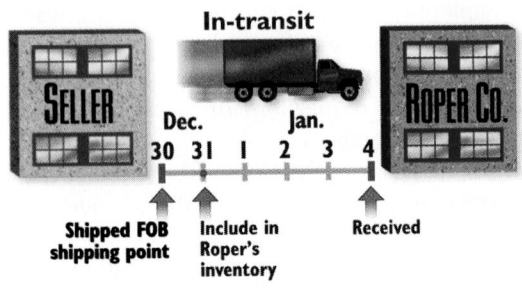

Manufacturers sometimes ship merchandise to retailers who act as the manufacturer's agent when selling the merchandise. The manufacturer retains title until the goods are sold. Such merchandise is said to be shipped *on consignment* to the retailers. The unsold merchandise is a part of the manufacturer's (consignor's) inventory, even though the merchandise is in the hands of the retailers. The consigned merchandise should not be included in the retailer's (consignee's) inventory.

Effect of Inventory Errors on Financial Statements

Any errors in the inventory count will affect both the balance sheet and the income statement. For example, an error in the physical inventory will misstate the ending inventory, current assets, and total assets on the balance sheet. This is because the physical inventory is the basis for recording the adjusting entry for inventory shrinkage. Also, an error in taking the physical inventory misstates the cost of goods sold, gross profit, and net income on the income statement. In addition, because net income is closed to retained earnings at the end of the period, total stockholders' equity will also be misstated on the balance sheet. This misstatement of stockholders' equity (retained earnings) will equal the misstatement of the ending inventory, current assets, and total assets.

To illustrate, assume that in taking the physical inventory on December 31, 2003, Sapra Company incorrectly recorded its physical inventory as $115,000 instead of the correct amount of $125,000. As a result, the merchandise inventory, current assets, and total assets reported on the December 31, 2003 balance sheet would be understated by $10,000 ($125,000 − $115,000). Because the ending physical inventory is understated, the inventory shrinkage and the cost of merchandise sold will be overstated by $10,000. Thus, the gross profit and the net income for the year will be understated by $10,000. Since the net income is closed to retained earnings at the end of the period, the total stockholders' equity on the December 31, 2003 balance sheet will also be understated by $10,000. The effects on Sapra Company's financial statements are summarized as follows:

One of the most famous inventory frauds was perpetrated by **Crazy Eddie Inc.**, which operated electronics stores. The company reported rapid gains in sales and earnings due to what the company said was store expansion, adept sales-floor techniques, and catchy commercials. However, Crazy Eddie had overstated inventory counts at one warehouse by $10 million, drafted phony inventory count sheets, and included in inventory $4 million of merchandise that, in fact, was being returned to suppliers. As a result, income was overstated. The apparent purpose of the scheme was to "artificially inflate the net worth of the company" and the value of stock owned by the store's founder, Eddie Antar, and others.

Source: Jeffrey A. Tannenbaum, "Filings by Crazy Eddie Suggest Founder Led Scheme to Inflate Company's Value," *The Wall Street Journal*, May 31, 1988, p. 28.

At the end of 2003, the physical ending inventory of Melchor Co. was overstated by $25,000. What is the effect of this error on the financial statements?

On the 2003 balance sheet, the merchandise inventory, current assets, total assets, and total stockholders' equity are overstated by $25,000. On the income statement, the cost of merchandise sold is understated by $25,000, and the gross profit and net income are overstated by $25,000.

	Amount of Misstatement
Balance Sheet:	
Merchandise inventory understated	$(10,000)
Current assets understated	(10,000)
Total assets understated	(10,000)
Total stockholders' equity understated	(10,000)
Income Statement:	
Cost of merchandise sold overstated	$ 10,000
Gross profit understated	(10,000)
Net income understated	(10,000)

Now assume that in the preceding example the physical inventory had been *overstated* on December 31, 2003, by $10,000. That is, Sapra Company erroneously recorded its inventory as $135,000. In this case, the effects on the balance sheet and income statement would be just the *opposite* of those indicated above.

Errors in the physical inventory are normally detected in the period after they occur. In such cases, the financial statements of the prior year must be corrected. We will discuss such corrections in a later chapter.

Inventory Cost Flow Assumptions

objective 3

Describe three inventory cost flow assumptions and how they impact the income statement and balance sheet.

A major accounting issue arises when identical units of merchandise are acquired at different unit costs during a period. In such cases, when an item is sold, it is necessary to determine its unit cost so that the proper accounting entry can be recorded. To illustrate, assume that three identical units of Item X are purchased during May, as shown below.

Item X		Units	Cost
May 10	Purchase	1	$ 9
18	Purchase	1	13
24	Purchase	1	14
Total		3	$36
Average cost per unit			$12

Assume that one unit is sold on May 30 for $20. If this unit can be identified with a specific purchase, the **specific identification method** can be used to determine the cost of the unit sold. For example, if the unit sold was purchased on May 18, the cost assigned to the unit is $13 and the gross profit is $7 ($20 − $13). If, however, the unit sold was purchased on May 10, the cost assigned to the unit is $9 and the gross profit is $11 ($20 − $9).

The specific identification method is not practical unless each unit can be identified accurately. An automobile dealer, for example, may be able to use this method, since each automobile has a unique serial number. For many businesses, however, identical units cannot be separately identified, and a cost flow must be assumed. That is, which units have been sold and which units are still in inventory must be assumed.

The specific identification method is normally used by automobile dealerships, jewelry stores, and art galleries.

There are three common cost flow assumptions used in business. Each of these assumptions is identified with an inventory costing method, as shown below.

Cost Flow Assumption	1. Cost flow is in the order in which the costs were incurred.	2. Cost flow is in the reverse order in which the costs were incurred.	3. Cost flow is an average of the costs.
Inventory Costing Method	First-in, first-out (fifo)	Last-in, first-out (lifo)	Average cost

When the **first-in, first-out (fifo) method** is used, the ending inventory is made up of the most recent costs. When the **last-in, first-out (lifo) method** is used, the ending inventory is made up of the earliest costs. When the **average cost method** is used, the cost of the units in inventory is an average of the purchase costs.

To illustrate, we use the preceding example to prepare the income statement for May and the balance sheet as of May 31 for each of the cost flow methods. These financial statements are shown in Exhibit 1.

As you can see, the selection of an inventory costing method can have a significant impact on the financial statements. For this reason, the selection has important implications for managers and others in analyzing and interpreting the financial statements. The chart in Exhibit 2 shows the frequency with which fifo, lifo, and the average methods are used in practice.

Inventory Costing Methods Under a Perpetual Inventory System

objective 4

Compute the cost of inventory under the perpetual inventory system, using the following costing methods:

First-in, first-out

Last-in, first-out

Average cost

In a perpetual inventory system, all merchandise increases and decreases are recorded in a manner similar to the recording of increases and decreases in cash. The merchandise inventory account at the beginning of an accounting period indicates the merchandise in stock on that date. Purchases are recorded by debiting *Merchandise Inventory* and crediting *Cash* or *Accounts Payable*. On the date of each sale, the cost of the merchandise sold is recorded by debiting *Cost of Merchandise Sold* and crediting *Merchandise Inventory*.

As we illustrated in the preceding section, when identical units of an item are purchased at different unit costs during a period, a cost flow must be assumed. In such cases, the fifo, lifo, or average cost method is used. We illustrate each of these methods, using the data for Item 127B, shown at the top of page F320.

Exhibit 1 Effect of Inventory Costing Methods on Financial Statements

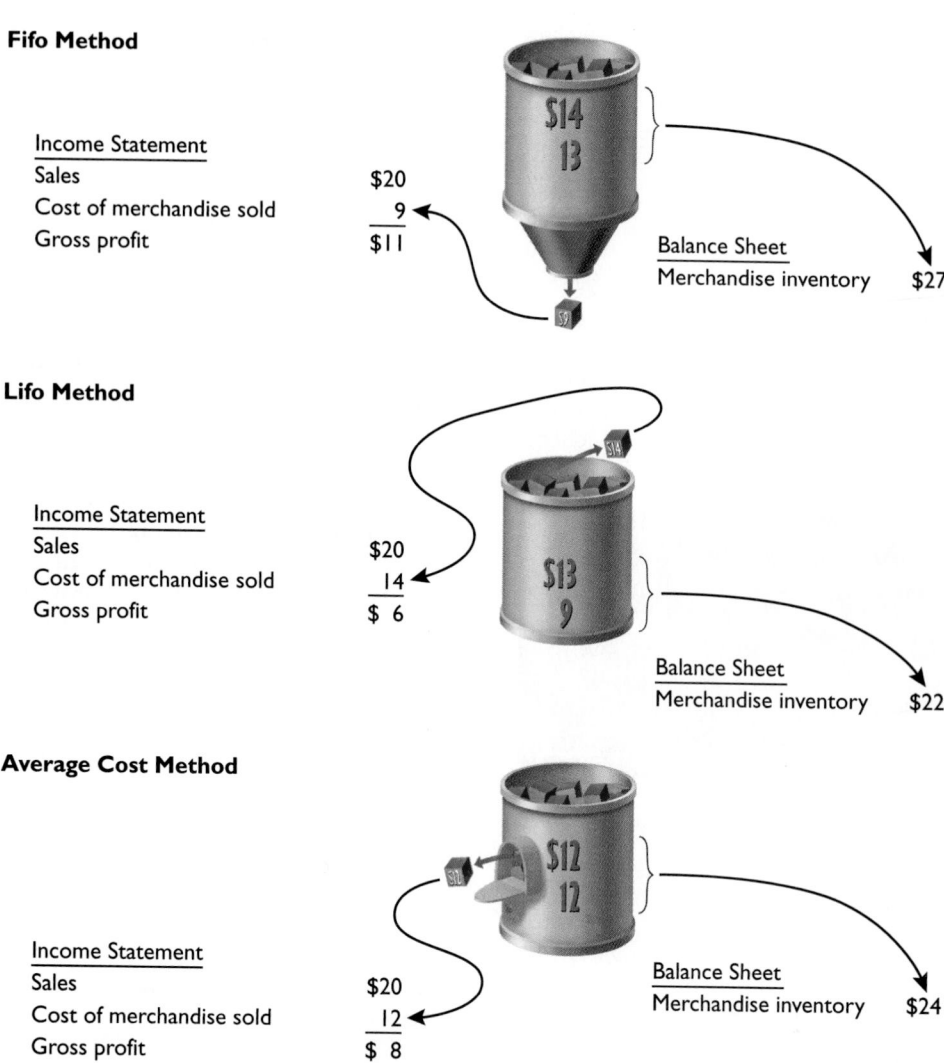

Fifo Method

Income Statement
Sales $20
Cost of merchandise sold   9
Gross profit $11

Balance Sheet
Merchandise inventory $27

Lifo Method

Income Statement
Sales $20
Cost of merchandise sold   14
Gross profit $ 6

Balance Sheet
Merchandise inventory $22

Average Cost Method

Income Statement
Sales $20
Cost of merchandise sold   12
Gross profit $ 8

Balance Sheet
Merchandise inventory $24

Exhibit 2 Inventory Costing Methods

Source: *Accounting Trends & Techniques*, 53rd ed., American Institute of Certified Public Accountants, New York, 1999.

Item 127B		Units	Cost
Jan. 1	Inventory	10	$20
4	Sale	7	
10	Purchase	8	21
22	Sale	4	
28	Sale	2	
30	Purchase	10	22

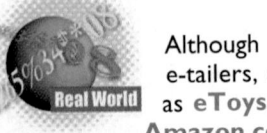

Although e-tailers, such as eToys, Amazon.com, and Furniture.com, don't have retail stores, they still take possession of inventory in warehouses. Thus, they must account for inventory as we are illustrating in this chapter.

Using fifo, costs are included in the merchandise sold in the order in which they were incurred.

First-In, First-Out Method

Most businesses dispose of goods in the order in which the goods are purchased. This would be especially true of perishables and goods whose styles or models often change. For example, grocery stores shelve their milk products by expiration dates. Likewise, men's and women's clothing stores display clothes by season. At the end of a season, they often have sales to clear their stores of off-season or out-of-style clothing. Thus, the fifo method is often consistent with the *physical flow* or movement of merchandise. To the extent that this is the case, the fifo method provides results that are about the same as those obtained by identifying the specific costs of each item sold and in inventory.

When the fifo method of costing inventory is used, costs are included in the cost of merchandise sold in the order in which they were incurred. To illustrate, Exhibit 3 shows the journal entries for purchases and sales and the inventory subsidiary ledger account for Item 127B. The number of units in inventory after each transaction, together with total costs and unit costs, are shown in the account. We assume that the units are sold for $30 each on account.

Exhibit 3 Entries and Perpetual Inventory Account (Fifo)

Jan. 4	Accounts Receivable	210	
	Sales		210
4	Cost of Merchandise Sold	140	
	Merchandise Inventory		140
10	Merchandise Inventory	168	
	Accounts Payable		168
22	Accounts Receivable	120	
	Sales		120
22	Cost of Merchandise Sold	81	
	Merchandise Inventory		81
28	Accounts Receivable	60	
	Sales		60
28	Cost of Merchandise Sold	42	
	Merchandise Inventory		42
30	Merchandise Inventory	220	
	Accounts Payable		220

Item 127B

	Purchases			Cost of Merchandise Sold			Inventory		
Date	Quantity	Unit Cost	Total Cost	Quantity	Unit Cost	Total Cost	Quantity	Unit Cost	Total Cost
Jan. 1							10	20	200
4				7	20	140	3	20	60
10	8	21	168				3	20	60
							8	21	168
22				3	20	60			
				1	21	21	7	21	147
28				2	21	42	5	21	105
30	10	22	220				5	21	105
							10	22	220

You should note that after the 7 units were sold on January 4, there was an inventory of 3 units at $20 each. The 8 units purchased on January 10 were acquired at a unit cost of $21, instead of $20. Therefore, the inventory after the January 10 purchase is reported on two lines, 3 units at $20 each and 8 units at $21 each. Next, note that the $81 cost of the 4 units sold on January 22 is made up of the remaining 3 units at $20 each and 1 unit at $21. At this point, 7 units are in inventory at a cost of $21 per unit. The remainder of the illustration is explained in a similar manner.

Last-In, First-Out Method

Using lifo, the cost of units sold is the cost of the most recent purchases.

When the lifo method is used in a perpetual inventory system, the cost of the units sold is the cost of the most recent purchases. To illustrate, Exhibit 4 shows the journal entries for purchases and sales and the subsidiary ledger account for Item 127B, prepared on a lifo basis.

Exhibit 4 Entries and Perpetual Inventory Account (Lifo)

Jan. 4	Accounts Receivable	210	
	Sales		210
4	Cost of Merchandise Sold	140	
	Merchandise Inventory		140
10	Merchandise Inventory	168	
	Accounts Payable		168
22	Accounts Receivable	120	
	Sales		120
22	Cost of Merchandise Sold	84	
	Merchandise Inventory		84
28	Accounts Receivable	60	
	Sales		60
28	Cost of Merchandise Sold	42	
	Merchandise Inventory		42
30	Merchandise Inventory	220	
	Accounts Payable		220

Item 127B

	Purchases			Cost of Merchandise Sold			Inventory		
Date	Quantity	Unit Cost	Total Cost	Quantity	Unit Cost	Total Cost	Quantity	Unit Cost	Total Cost
Jan. 1							10	20	200
4				7	20	140	3	20	60
10	8	21	168				3	20	60
							8	21	168
22				4	21	84	3	20	60
							4	21	84
28				2	21	42	3	20	60
							2	21	42
30	10	22	220				3	20	60
							2	21	42
							10	22	220

If you compare the ledger accounts for the fifo perpetual system and the lifo perpetual system, you should discover that the accounts are the same through the January 10 purchase. Using lifo, however, the cost of the 4 units sold on January 22 is the cost of the units from the January 10 purchase ($21 per unit). The cost of the 7 units in inventory after the sale on January 22 is the cost of the 3 units remaining from the beginning inventory and the cost of the 4 units remaining from the January 10 purchase. The remainder of the lifo illustration is explained in a similar manner.

When the lifo method is used, the inventory ledger is sometimes maintained in units only. The units are converted to dollars when the financial statements are prepared at the end of the period.

The use of the lifo method was originally limited to rare situations in which the units sold were taken from the most recently acquired goods. For tax reasons, which we will discuss later, its use has greatly increased during the past few decades. Lifo is now often used even when it does not represent the physical flow of goods.

Average Cost Method

When the average cost method is used in a perpetual inventory system, an average unit cost for each type of item is computed each time a purchase is made. This unit cost is then used to determine the cost of each sale until another purchase is made and a new average is computed. This averaging technique is called a *moving average*. Since the average cost method is rarely used in a perpetual inventory system, we do not illustrate it in this chapter.

Computerized Perpetual Inventory Systems

The records for a perpetual inventory system may be maintained manually. However, such a system is costly and time consuming for businesses with a large number of inventory items with many purchase and sales transactions. In most cases, the record keeping for perpetual inventory systems is computerized.

An example of using computers in maintaining perpetual inventory records for retail stores is described below.

1. The relevant details for each inventory item, such as a description, quantity, and unit size, are stored in an inventory record. The individual inventory records make up the computerized inventory file, the total of which agrees with the balance of the inventory ledger account.
2. Each time an item is purchased or returned by a customer, the inventory data are entered into the computer's inventory records and files.
3. Each time an item is sold, a salesclerk scans the item's bar code with an optical scanner. The scanner reads the magnetic code and rings up the sale on the cash register. The inventory records and files are then updated for the cost of goods sold.
4. After a physical inventory is taken, the inventory count data are entered into the computer. These data are compared with the current balances, and a listing of the overages and shortages is printed. The inventory balances are then adjusted to the quantities determined by the physical count.

Such systems can be extended to aid managers in controlling and managing inventory quantities. For example, items that are selling fast can be reordered before the stock is depleted. Past sales patterns can be analyzed to determine when to mark down merchandise for sales and when to restock seasonal merchandise. In addition, such systems can provide managers with data for developing and fine-tuning their marketing strategies. For example, such data can be used to evaluate the effectiveness of advertising campaigns and sales promotions.

 The fifo, lifo, and average cost flow assumptions also apply to other areas of business. For example, individuals and businesses often purchase marketable securities at different costs per share. When such investments are sold, the investor must either specifically identify which shares are sold or use the fifo cost flow assumption. To illustrate, assume that a business purchased 100 shares of **Microsoft Corporation** at $85 and 100 shares at $95. If the business later sells 100 shares for $90, which shares did it sell? The business must determine the cost of the shares sold so that it can report either a gain or loss on the sale for tax purposes. In addition, it must report the gain or loss on its income statement.

 **Wal-Mart, Kmart, Sears**, and other retailers use bar code scanners as part of their perpetual inventory systems.

Inventory Costing Methods Under a Periodic Inventory System

objective 5

Compute the cost of inventory under the periodic inventory system, using the following costing methods:

First-in, first-out

Last-in, first-out

Average cost

When the periodic inventory system is used, only revenue is recorded each time a sale is made. No entry is made at the time of the sale to record the cost of the merchandise sold. At the end of the accounting period, a physical inventory is taken to determine the cost of the inventory and the cost of the merchandise sold.

For merchandising businesses that use the periodic system, the cost of merchandise sold during a period is reported in a separate section in the income statement. To illustrate, assume that NetSolutions opened a merchandising outlet selling personal computers and software. During 2004, NetSolutions purchased $340,000 of merchandise. If the inventory at December 31, 2004, the end of the year, is $59,700, the cost of merchandise sold during 2004 would be reported as follows:

Cost of merchandise sold:

Purchases	$340,000	
Less merchandise inventory, December 31, 2004	59,700	
Cost of merchandise sold		$280,300

To continue the illustration, assume that during 2005 NetSolutions purchased additional merchandise of $521,980. It received credit for purchases returns and allowances of $9,100, took purchases discounts of $2,525, and paid transportation costs of $17,400. The purchases returns and allowances and the purchases discounts are deducted from the total purchases to yield the *net purchases.* The transportation costs are added to the net purchases to yield the *cost of merchandise purchased.* These amounts would be reported in the cost of merchandise sold section of Net-Solutions' income statement for 2005 as follows:

Purchases		$521,980	
Less: Purchases returns and allowances	$9,100		
Purchases discounts	2,525	11,625	
Net purchases		$510,355	
Add transportation in		17,400	
Cost of merchandise purchased			$527,755

The ending inventory of NetSolutions on December 31, 2004, $59,700, becomes the beginning inventory for 2005. In the cost of merchandise sold section of the income statement for 2005, this beginning inventory is added to the cost of merchandise purchased to yield the *merchandise available for sale.* The ending inventory, which is assumed to be $62,150, is then subtracted from the merchandise available for sale to yield the cost of merchandise sold. The cost of merchandise sold during 2005 would be reported as follows:

Cost of merchandise sold:			
Merchandise inventory, January 1, 2005			$ 59,700
Purchases		$521,980	
Less: Purchases returns and allowances	$9,100		
Purchases discounts	2,525	11,625	
Net purchases		$510,355	
Add transportation in		17,400	
Cost of merchandise purchased			527,755
Merchandise available for sale			$587,455
Less merchandise inventory, December 31, 2005			62,150
Cost of merchandise sold			$525,305

Like the perpetual inventory system, a cost flow assumption must be made when identical units are acquired at different unit costs during a period. In such cases, the fifo, lifo, or average cost method is used.

First-In, First-Out Method

To illustrate the use of the fifo method in a periodic inventory system, we assume the following data:

Jan. 1	Inventory:	200 units at	$ 9	$ 1,800
Mar. 10	Purchase:	300 units at	10	3,000
Sept. 21	Purchase:	400 units at	11	4,400
Nov. 18	Purchase:	100 units at	12	1,200
Available for sale during year		1,000		$10,400

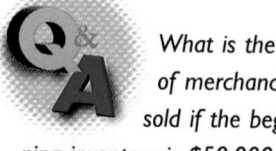

What is the cost of merchandise sold if the beginning inventory is $50,000, the ending inventory is $65,000, the net purchases are $400,000, and the transportation in is $12,000?

$397,000 ($50,000 + $400,000 + $12,000 − $65,000)

The physical count on December 31 shows that 300 units have not been sold. Using the fifo method, the cost of the 700 units sold is determined as follows:

Earliest costs, Jan. 1:	200 units at	$ 9	$1,800
Next earliest costs, Mar. 10:	300 units at	10	3,000
Next earliest costs, Sept. 21:	200 units at	11	2,200
Cost of merchandise sold:	700		$7,000

Deducting the cost of merchandise sold of $7,000 from the $10,400 of merchandise available for sale yields $3,400 as the cost of the inventory at December 31. The $3,400 inventory is made up of the most recent costs incurred for this item. Exhibit 5 shows the relationship of the cost of merchandise sold during the year and the inventory at December 31.

Exhibit 5 First-In, First-Out Flow of Costs

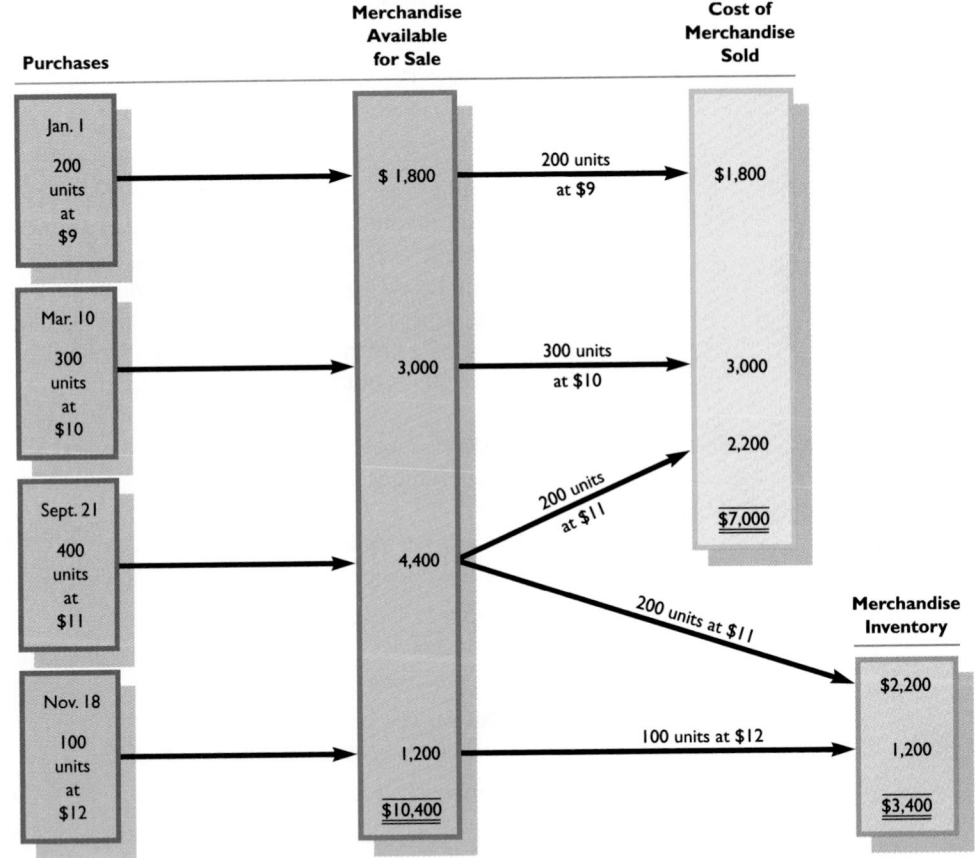

Last-In, First-Out Method

When the lifo method is used, the cost of merchandise sold is made up of the most recent costs. Based on the data in the fifo example, the cost of the 700 units of inventory is determined as follows:

Most recent costs, Nov. 18:	100 units at $12	$1,200
Next most recent costs, Sept. 21:	400 units at 11	4,400
Next most recent costs, Mar. 10:	200 units at 10	2,000
Cost of merchandise sold:	700	$7,600

Deducting the cost of merchandise sold of $7,600 from the $10,400 of merchandise available for sale yields $2,800 as the cost of the inventory at December 31. The $2,800 inventory is made up of the earliest costs incurred for this item. Exhibit 6 shows the relationship of the cost of merchandise sold during the year and the inventory at December 31.

Exhibit 6 Last-In, First-Out Flow of Costs

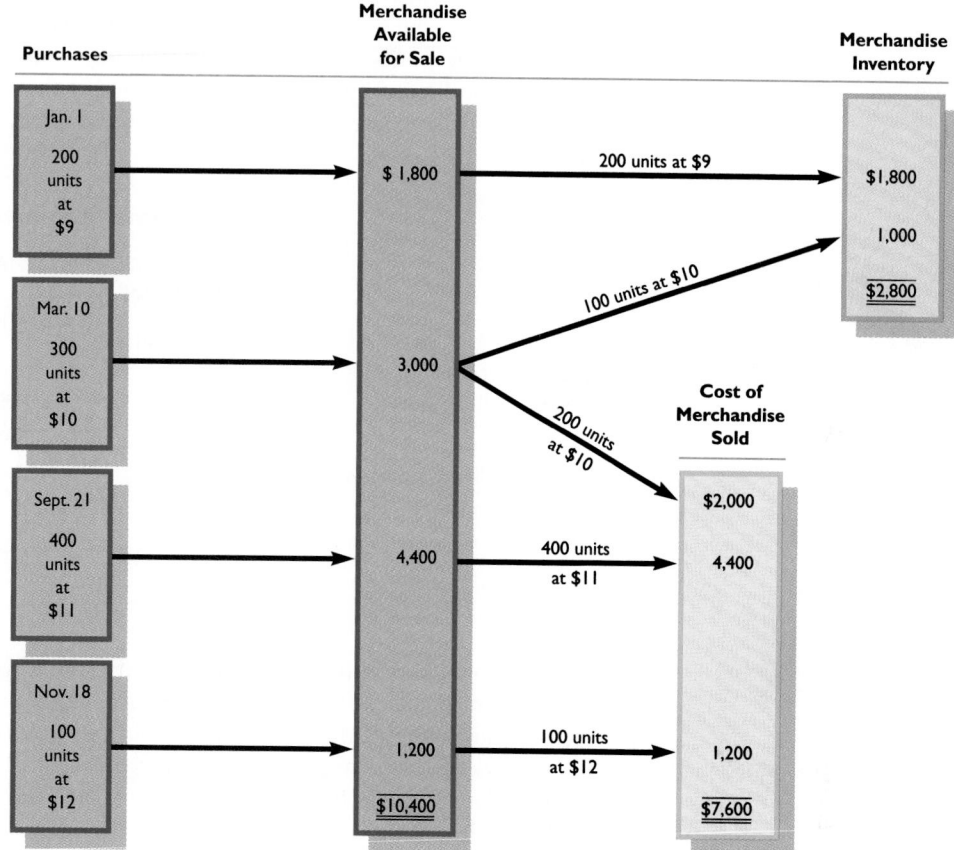

Average Cost Method

The average cost method is sometimes called the **weighted average method**. When this method is used, costs are matched against revenue according to an average of the unit costs of the goods sold. The same weighted average unit costs are used in determining the cost of the merchandise inventory at the end of the period. For businesses in which merchandise sales may be made up of various purchases of identical units, the average method approximates the physical flow of goods.

The weighted average unit cost is determined by dividing the total cost of the units of each item available for sale during the period by the related number of units of that item. Using the same cost data as in the fifo and lifo examples, the average cost of the 1,000 units, $10.40, and the cost of the 700 units, $7,280, are determined as follows:

Average unit cost: **$10,400/1,000 units = $10.40**
Cost of merchandise sold: **700 units at $10.40** = $7,280

Deducting the cost of merchandise sold of $7,280 from the $10,400 of merchandise available for sale yields $3,120 as the cost of the inventory at December 31.

Comparing Inventory Costing Methods

As we have illustrated, a different cost flow is assumed for each of the three alternative methods of costing inventories. You should note that if the cost of units had remained stable, all three methods would have yielded the same results. Since prices do change, however, the three methods will normally yield different amounts for (1) the cost of the merchandise sold for the period, (2) the gross profit (and net income) for the period, and (3) the ending inventory. Using the preceding examples for the periodic inventory system and assuming that net sales were $15,000, the following partial income statements indicate the effects of each method when prices are rising:[1]

Partial Income Statements

	First-In, First-Out		Average Cost		Last-In, First-Out	
Net sales		$15,000		$15,000		$15,000
Cost of merchandise sold:						
Beginning inventory	$ 1,800		$ 1,800		$ 1,800	
Purchases	8,600		8,600		8,600	
Merchandise available for sale	$10,400		$10,400		$10,400	
Less ending inventory	3,400		3,120		2,800	
Cost of merchandise sold		7,000		7,280		7,600
Gross profit		$ 8,000		$ 7,720		$ 7,400

As shown above, the fifo method yielded the lowest amount for the cost of merchandise sold and the highest amount for gross profit (and net income). It also yielded the highest amount for the ending inventory. On the other hand, the lifo method yielded the highest amount for the cost of merchandise sold, the lowest amount for gross profit (and net income), and the lowest amount for ending inventory. The average cost method yielded results that were between those of fifo and lifo.

Use of the First-In, First-Out Method

When the fifo method is used during a period of inflation or rising prices, the earlier unit costs are lower than the more recent unit costs, as shown in the preceding fifo example. Much of the benefit of the larger amount of gross profit is lost, however, because the inventory must be replaced at ever higher prices. In fact, the balance sheet will report the ending merchandise inventory at an amount that is about the same as its current replacement cost. When the rate of inflation reaches double digits, as it did during the 1970s, the larger gross profits that result from the fifo method are often called *inventory profits* or *illusory profits*. You should note that in a period of deflation or declining prices, the effect is just the opposite.

Use of the Last-In, First-Out Method

When the lifo method is used during a period of inflation or rising prices, the results are opposite those of the other two methods. As shown in the preceding example, the lifo method will yield a higher amount of cost of merchandise sold, a lower amount of gross profit, and a lower amount of inventory at the end of the

Daimler-Chrysler's **Real World** **reason for changing from the fifo method to the lifo method was stated in the following footnote that accompanied its financial statements:** *DaimlerChrysler changed its method of accounting from first-in, first-out (fifo) to last-in, first-out (lifo) for substantially all its domestic productive inventories. The change to lifo was made to more accurately match current costs with current revenues.*

---

[1] Similar results would also occur when comparing inventory costing methods under a perpetual inventory system.

In the following note, Sears, Roebuck and Co. reported the difference in its inventory if fifo had been used instead of lifo: *Inventories would have been $730 million higher if valued on the first-in, first-out, or FIFO, method.*

period than the other two methods. The reason for these effects is that the cost of the most recently acquired units is about the same as the cost of their replacement. In a period of inflation, the more recent unit costs are higher than the earlier unit costs. Thus, it can be argued that the lifo method more nearly matches current costs with current revenues.

During periods of rising prices, using lifo offers an income tax savings. The income tax savings results because lifo reports the lowest amount of net income of the three methods. During the double-digit inflationary period of the 1970s, many businesses changed from fifo to lifo for the tax savings. However, the ending inventory on the balance sheet may be quite different from its current replacement cost. In such cases, the financial statements normally include a note that states the estimated difference between the lifo inventory and the inventory if fifo had been used. Again, you should note that in a period of deflation or falling price levels, the effects are just the opposite.

Use of the Average Cost Method

As you might have already reasoned, the average cost method of inventory costing is, in a sense, a compromise between fifo and lifo. The effect of price trends is averaged in determining the cost of merchandise sold and the ending inventory. For a series of purchases, the average cost will be the same, regardless of the direction of price trends. For example, a complete reversal of the sequence of unit costs presented in the preceding illustration would not affect the reported cost of merchandise sold, gross profit, or ending inventory.

BUSINESS ON STAGE

What Does It Cost to Have an Inventory?

Inventories are essential for merchandising and manufacturing businesses. Inventories are necessary in order to generate sales, and sales are necessary in order to generate profits.

The primary benefit of carrying inventory is that it provides protection against unexpected events and disruptions in business operations. For example, an unexpected strike by a supplier's employees can halt production for a manufacturer or cause lost sales for a merchandiser. Businesses that rely upon foreign suppliers are particularly affected by disruptions caused by international crises and events. Carrying inventory also allows a business to meet unexpected increases in the demand for its product. Thus, you can think of inventories as a buffer or cushion against the unexpected.

Inventory is not free, however. The costs of carrying inventory are classified as (1) holding costs, (2) ordering costs, and (3) stockout costs.

Holding costs include the costs of handling, storage, insurance, property taxes, and depreciation. In addition, holding costs for a merchandising business include losses that occur when customer preferences and tastes change unexpectedly and inventory is marked down. Finally, holding costs include the cost of funds that could be used for other purposes if they were not tied up in inventory. For example, if a business must borrow $100,000 at 10% to finance its inventories, then the interest of $10,000 per year is part of the cost of holding inventory.

Ordering costs are the costs of placing and processing orders with

suppliers. Ordering costs also include the costs of investigating possible suppliers and negotiating contracts with suppliers.

Stockout costs include the costs of failing to meet customer demands—the cost of lost sales and lost profits, as well as lost customer goodwill. For a manufacturer, stockout costs include the costs of production delays and downtime, as well as the related costs of restarting production.

Inventory management involves the difficult task of balancing the benefits of carrying inventory against the related costs. In a merchandise business, inventory management is normally the responsibility of a merchandising manager or buyer. ■

Valuation of Inventory at Other than Cost

As we indicated earlier, cost is the primary basis for valuing inventories. In some cases, however, inventory is valued at other than cost. Two such cases arise when (1) the cost of replacing items in inventory is below the recorded cost and (2) the inventory is not salable at normal sales prices. This latter case may be due to imperfections, shop wear, style changes, or other causes.

Valuation at Lower of Cost or Market

If the cost of replacing an item in inventory is lower than the original purchase cost, the **lower-of-cost-or-market (LCM) method** is used to value the inventory. *Market*, as used in *lower of cost or market*, is the cost to replace the merchandise on the inventory date. This market value is based on quantities normally purchased from the usual source of supply. In businesses where inflation is the norm, market prices rarely decline. In businesses where technology changes rapidly (e.g., microcomputers and televisions), market declines are common. The primary advantage of the lower-of-cost-or-market method is that gross profit (and net income) is reduced in the period in which the market decline occurred.

Dell Computer Company recorded over $39.3 million of charges (expenses) in writing down its inventory of notebook computers. The remaining inventories of computers were then sold at significantly reduced prices.

In applying the lower-of-cost-or-market method, the cost and replacement cost can be determined in one of three ways. Cost and replacement cost can be determined for (1) each item in the inventory, (2) major classes or categories of inventory, or (3) the inventory as a whole. In practice, the cost and replacement cost of each item are usually determined.

To illustrate, assume that there are 400 identical units of Item A in inventory, acquired at a unit cost of $10.25 each. If at the inventory date the item would cost $10.50 to replace, the cost price of $10.25 would be multiplied by 400 to determine the inventory value. On the other hand, if the item could be replaced at $9.50 a unit, the replacement cost of $9.50 would be used for valuation purposes.

Exhibit 7 illustrates a method of organizing inventory data and applying the lower-of-cost-or-market method to each inventory item. The amount of the market decline, $450 ($15,520 − $15,070), may be reported as a separate item on the income statement or included in the cost of merchandise sold. Regardless, net income will be reduced by the amount of the market decline.

Q&A If the cost of an item is $410, its current replacement cost is $400, and its selling price is $525, at what amount should the item be included in the inventory according to the LCM method?

$400

Exhibit 7 Determining Inventory at Lower of Cost or Market

Commodity	Inventory Quantity	Unit Cost Price	Unit Market Price	Total Cost	Total Market	Total Lower of C or M
A	400	$10.25	$ 9.50	$ 4,100	$ 3,800	$ 3,800
B	120	22.50	24.10	2,700	2,892	2,700
C	600	8.00	7.75	4,800	4,650	4,650
D	280	14.00	14.75	3,920	4,130	3,920
Total				$15,520	$15,472	$15,070

Out-of-date merchandise is a major problem for many types of retailers. For example, you may have noticed the shelf-life dates of grocery products, such as milk, eggs, canned goods, and meat. Grocery stores often mark down the prices of products nearing the end of their shelf life to avoid having to dispose of the products as waste.

Valuation at Net Realizable Value

As you would expect, merchandise that is out of date, spoiled, or damaged or that can be sold only at prices below cost should be written down. Such merchandise should be valued at net realizable value. **Net realizable value** is the estimated selling price less any direct cost of disposal, such as sales commissions. For example, assume that damaged merchandise costing $1,000 can be sold for only $800, and direct selling expenses are estimated to be $150. This inventory should be valued at $650 ($800 − $150), which is its net realizable value.

Presentation of Merchandise Inventory on the Balance Sheet

objective 8

Prepare a balance sheet presentation of merchandise inventory.

Merchandise inventory is usually presented in the Current Assets section of the balance sheet, following receivables. Both the method of determining the cost of the inventory (fifo, lifo, or average) and the method of valuing the inventory (cost or the lower of cost or market) should be shown. It is not unusual for large businesses with varied activities to use different costing methods for different segments of their inventories. The details may be disclosed in parentheses on the balance sheet or in a footnote to the financial statements. Exhibit 8 shows how parentheses may be used.

General Motors Corporation uses the last-in, first-out (lifo) method to account for all U.S. inventories other than those of **Saturn Corporation** and **Hughes Electronics Corporation**. The cost of non-U.S., Saturn, and Hughes inventories is determined by using either first-in, first-out (fifo) or average cost.

Exhibit 8 Merchandise Inventory on the Balance Sheet

Afro-Arts Balance Sheet December 31, 2004			
Assets			
Current assets:			
Cash			$ 19 4 0 0 00
Accounts receivable	$80 0 0 0 00		
Less allowance for doubtful accounts	3 0 0 0 00		77 0 0 0 00
Merchandise inventory—at lower of cost (first-in,			
first-out method) or market			216 3 0 0 00

A company may change its inventory costing methods for a valid reason. In such cases, the effect of the change and the reason for the change should be disclosed in the financial statements for the period in which the change occurred.

Estimating Inventory Cost

It may be necessary for a business to know the amount of inventory when perpetual inventory records are not maintained and it is impractical to take a physical inventory. For example, a business that uses a periodic inventory system may need monthly income statements, but taking a physical inventory each month may be too costly. Moreover, when a disaster such as a fire has destroyed the inventory, the amount of the loss must be determined. In this case, taking a physical inventory is impossible, and even if perpetual inventory records have been kept, the accounting records may also have been destroyed. In such cases, the inventory cost can be estimated by using (1) the retail method or (2) the gross profit method.

Retail Method of Inventory Costing

The **retail inventory method** of estimating inventory cost is based on the relationship of the cost of merchandise available for sale to the retail price of the same merchandise. To use this method, the retail prices of all merchandise are maintained and totaled. Next, the inventory at retail is determined by deducting sales for the period from the retail price of the goods that were available for sale during the period. The estimated inventory cost is then computed by multiplying the inventory at retail by the ratio of cost to selling (retail) price for the merchandise available for sale, as illustrated in Exhibit 9.

Exhibit 9 Determining Inventory by the Retail Method

	Cost	Retail
Merchandise inventory, January 1	$ 19,400	$ 36,000
Purchases in January (net)	42,600	64,000
Merchandise available for sale	$ 62,000	$100,000
Ratio of cost to retail price: $\dfrac{\$\,62,000}{\$100,000} = 62\%$		
Sales for January (net)		70,000
Merchandise inventory, January 31, at retail		$ 30,000
Merchandise inventory, January 31, at estimated cost ($30,000 × 62%)		$ 18,600

When estimating the percent of cost to selling price, we assume that the mix of the items in the ending inventory is the same as the entire stock of merchandise available for sale. In Exhibit 9, for example, it is unlikely that the retail price of every item was made up of exactly 62% cost and 38% gross profit. We assume, however, that the weighted average of the cost percentages of the merchandise in the inventory ($30,000) is the same as in the merchandise available for sale ($100,000).

When the inventory is made up of different classes of merchandise with very different gross profit rates, the cost percentages and the inventory should be developed for each class of inventory.

One of the major advantages of the retail method is that it provides inventory figures for use in preparing monthly or quarterly statements when the periodic system is used. Department stores and similar merchandisers like to determine gross profit and operating income each month but may take a physical inventory only once a year. In addition, comparing the estimated ending inventory with the physical ending inventory, both at retail prices, will help identify inventory shortages resulting from shoplifting and other causes. Management can then take appropriate actions.

The retail method may also be used as an aid in taking a physical inventory. In this case, the items counted are recorded on the inventory sheets at their retail (selling) prices instead of their cost prices. The physical inventory at selling price is then converted to cost by applying the ratio of cost to selling (retail) price for the merchandise available for sale.

To illustrate, assume that the data in Exhibit 9 are for an entire fiscal year rather than for only January. If the physical inventory taken at the end of the year totaled $29,000, priced at retail, this amount rather than the $30,000 would be converted to cost. Thus, the inventory at cost would be $17,980 ($29,000 × 62%) instead of $18,600 ($30,000 × 62%). The $17,980 would be used for the year-end financial statements and for income tax purposes.

If the ratio of cost to retail is 70% and the ending inventory at retail is $100,000, what is the estimated ending inventory at cost?

- -

$70,000 (70% × $100,000)

Gross Profit Method of Estimating Inventories

The **gross profit method** uses the estimated gross profit for the period to estimate the inventory at the end of the period. The gross profit is usually estimated from the actual rate for the preceding year, adjusted for any changes made in the cost and sales prices during the current period. By using the gross profit rate, the dollar amount of sales for a period can be divided into its two components: (1) gross profit and (2) cost of merchandise sold. The latter amount may then be deducted from the cost of merchandise available for sale to yield the estimated cost of the inventory.

Exhibit 10 illustrates the gross profit method for estimating a company's inventory on January 31. In this example, the inventory on January 1 is assumed to be $57,000, the net purchases during the month are $180,000, and the net sales during the month are $250,000. In addition, the historical gross profit was 30% of net sales.

Exhibit 10 Estimating Inventory by Gross Profit Method

Merchandise inventory, January 1		$ 57,000
Purchases in January (net)		180,000
Merchandise available for sale		$237,000
Sales in January (net)	$250,000	
Less estimated gross profit ($250,000 × 30%)	75,000	
Estimated cost of merchandise sold		175,000
Estimated merchandise inventory, January 31		$ 62,000

What is the estimated cost of the ending inventory if the merchandise available for sale is $350,000, sales are $500,000, and the gross profit percentage is 40%?

- -

$50,000 [$350,000 − (60% × $500,000)]

The gross profit method is useful for estimating inventories for monthly or quarterly financial statements in a periodic inventory system. It is also useful in estimating the cost of merchandise destroyed by fire or other disasters.

FINANCIAL ANALYSIS AND INTERPRETATION

objective 10

Compute and interpret the inventory turnover ratio and the number of days' sales in inventory.

A merchandising business should keep enough inventory on hand to meet the needs of its customers. A failure to do so may result in lost sales. At the same time, too much inventory reduces solvency by tying up funds that could be better used to expand or improve operations. In addition, excess inventory increases expenses such as storage, insurance, and property taxes. Finally, excess inventory increases the risk of losses due to price declines, damage, or changes in customers' buying patterns.

As with many types of financial analyses, it is possible to use more than one measure to analyze the efficiency and effectiveness by which a business manages its inventory. Two such measures are the inventory turnover and the number of days' sales in inventory.

Inventory turnover measures the relationship between the volume of goods (merchandise) sold and the amount of inventory carried during the period. It is computed as follows:

$$\textbf{Inventory turnover} = \frac{\textbf{Cost of merchandise sold}}{\textbf{Average inventory}}$$

The average inventory can be computed using weekly, monthly, or yearly figures. To simplify, we determine the average inventory by dividing the sum of the inventories at the beginning and end of the year by 2. As long as the amount of inventory carried throughout the year remains stable, this average will be accurate enough for our analysis.

To illustrate, the following data have been taken from recent annual reports for SUPERVALU INC. and Zale Corporation:

	SUPERVALU	Zale
Cost of merchandise sold	$15,620,127,000	$737,188,000
Inventories:		
Beginning of year	$1,115,529,000	$478,467,000
End of year	$1,067,837,000	$571,669,000
Average	$1,091,683,000	$525,068,000
Inventory turnover	14.3	1.4

The inventory turnover is 14.3 for SUPERVALU and 1.4 for Zale. Generally, the larger the inventory turnover, the more efficient and effective the management of inventory. However, differences in companies and industries are too great to allow specific statements as to what is a good inventory turnover. For example, SUPERVALU is a leading food distributor and the tenth largest food retailer in the United States. Because SUPERVALU's inventory is perishable, we would expect it to have a high inventory turnover. In contrast, Zale Corporation is the largest speciality retailer of fine jewelry in the United States. Thus, we would expect Zale to have a lower inventory turnover than SUPERVALU. As with other financial measures we have discussed, a comparison of a company's inventory turnover over time and with industry averages will provide useful insights into the management of its inventory.

The **number of days' sales in inventory** is a rough measure of the length of time it takes to acquire, sell, and replace the inventory. It is computed as follows:

$$\textbf{Number of days' sales in inventory} = \frac{\textbf{Inventory, end of year}}{\textbf{Average daily cost of merchandise sold}}$$

The average daily cost of merchandise sold is determined by dividing the cost of merchandise sold by 365. The number of days' sales in inventory for SUPERVALU and Zale is computed as shown below.

	SUPERVALU	Zale
Average daily cost of merchandise sold:		
$15,620,127,000/365	$42,794,868	
$737,188,000/365		$2,019,693
Ending inventory	$1,067,837,000	$571,669,000
Number of days' sales in inventory	25 days	283 days

Generally, the lower the number of days' sales in inventory, the better. As with inventory turnover, we should expect differences among industries, such as those for SUPERVALU and Zale.

ENCORE

Unusual Inventories—The Strange but True

We usually think of inventory in terms of retail stores such as grocery stores, department stores, and convenience stores. In the following paragraphs, however, we describe what you might think of as unusual inventories.

- **Studio Props.** Theaters periodically have sales to clear out items from past shows. The Studio Theatre in Washington, D.C., included the following items in one of its sales: patio furniture from "Together, Teeth Apart"; restaurant equipment from the ultra-real diner in "The Wash"; "Goblin Market's" giant rocking horse, doll house, quilt, and toy chest; an evening gown from "Death and the Maiden"; and stuffed bunnies from "The Baltimore Waltz."
- **Movie Vehicles.** The mud-spattered 1930 Ford Model A pickup sat in a huge, heated garage. Although it looked like just an old truck, this Model A was a star of "The Untouchables." Pierre Laginess is the owner of Antique and Classic Rental Service, a Michigan-based business that provides used collector

cars, trucks, and bicycles to film studios. The business began in the early 1970s when Laginess provided a stately, but menacing, 1928 Buick sedan for the original "Godfather." Since then, the business has provided vehicles for "Billy Bathgate," "Hoffa," "Lost in Yonkers," and the television series, "The Young Indiana Jones Chronicles." The business sells many of the cars that have been used in films. Laginess says producers shy away from a vehicle that has had too much exposure. Eagle-eyed fans recognize them, he said. So they go on sale.

- **Real Used Jeans.** While some jeans makers prewash, "stonewash," or even shotgun their garments to achieve the popular used look, at Whiskey Dust in New York City, you can get the sweaty cowboy finish the old-fashioned way: with real cowboy scent. Whiskey Dust's customers, which include rock stars Jon Bon Jovi and Eric Clapton, pay $65 for Montana Broke jeans that the store says were worn by genuine cowboys. Each well-used

pair comes with a guarantee of authenticity and a "Montana Broke Tracking Guide," explaining the origin of each rip, splotch, and frayed hem. The store's customers enthusiastically embrace its unusual inventory. "It's wonderful value. You get a lot of history." Several thousand miles away, Judy McFarlane, a 55-year-old Montana homemaker and a used jeans supplier, has little problem getting her inventory. "I don't even bother to advertise. People call me all the time." The cowboys "think it's a riot," says Ms. McFarlane.

- **Unwanted Ashes.** The merger of two funeral homes has caused an unusual inventory problem:

the unwanted, unclaimed ashes of 1,500 people who were cremated. The remains are those of eastern Washington residents who died between 1917 and 1972. A lot of remains come from the Great

Depression era of the 1930s and include doctors, lawyers, and people from all walks of life. For various reasons, relatives didn't claim the ashes. The state law provides that a funeral home can

dispose of unclaimed remains after a two-year holding period. The funeral home plans to pack the urns into caskets and bury them at a local cemetery. ■

KEY POINTS

1 Summarize and provide examples of internal control procedures that apply to inventories.

Internal control procedures for inventories include those developed to protect the inventories from damage, employee theft, and customer theft. In addition, a physical inventory count should be taken periodically to detect shortages as well as to deter employee thefts.

2 Describe the effect of inventory errors on the financial statements.

Any errors in reporting inventory based upon the physical inventory will misstate the ending inventory, current assets, total assets, and stockholders' equity (retained earnings) on the balance sheet. In addition, the cost of goods sold, gross profit, and net income will be misstated on the income statement.

3 Describe three inventory cost flow assumptions and how they impact the income statement and balance sheet.

The three common cost flow assumptions used in business are the (1) first-in, first-out method, (2) last-in, first-out method, and (3) average cost method. Each method normally yields different amounts for the cost of merchandise sold and the ending merchandise inventory. Thus, the choice of a cost flow assumption directly affects the income statement and balance sheet.

4 Compute the cost of inventory under the perpetual inventory system, using the following costing methods:

First-in, first-out
Last-in, first-out
Average cost

In a perpetual inventory system, the number of units and the cost of each type of merchandise are recorded in a subsidiary inventory ledger, with a separate account for each type of merchandise. Inventory costs and the amounts charged against revenue are illustrated using the fifo and lifo methods.

5 Compute the cost of inventory under the periodic inventory system, using the following costing methods:

First-in, first-out
Last-in, first-out
Average cost

In a periodic inventory system, a physical inventory is taken to determine the cost of the inventory and the cost of merchandise sold. Inventory costs and the amounts charged against revenue are illustrated using fifo, lifo, and average cost methods.

6 Compare and contrast the use of the three inventory costing methods.

The three inventory costing methods will normally yield different amounts for (1) the ending inventory, (2) the cost of the

merchandise sold for the period, and (3) the gross profit (and net income) for the period. During periods of inflation, the fifo method yields the lowest amount for the cost of merchandise sold, the highest amount for gross profit (and net income), and the highest amount for the ending inventory. The lifo method yields the opposite results. During periods of deflation, the preceding effects are reversed. The average cost method yields results that are between those of fifo and lifo.

7 Compute the proper valuation of inventory at other than cost, using the lower-of-cost-or-market and net realizable value concepts.

If the market price of an item of inventory is lower than its cost, the lower market price is used to compute the value of the item. Market price is the cost to replace the merchandise on the inventory date. It is possible to apply the lower of cost or market to each item in the inventory, to major classes or categories, or to the inventory as a whole.

Merchandise that can be sold only at prices below cost should be valued at net realizable value, which is the estimated selling price less any direct cost of disposal.

8 Prepare a balance sheet presentation of merchandise inventory.

Merchandise inventory is usually presented in the Current Assets section of the balance sheet, following receivables. Both the method of determining the cost of the inventory (fifo, lifo, or average) and the method of valuing the inventory (cost or the lower of cost or market) should be shown.

9 Estimate the cost of inventory, using the retail method and the gross profit method.

In using the retail method to estimate inventory, the retail prices of all merchandise acquired are accumulated. The inventory at retail is determined by deducting sales for the period from the retail price of the goods that were available for sale during the period. The inventory at retail is then converted to cost on the basis of the ratio of cost to selling (retail) price for the merchandise available for sale.

In using the gross profit method to estimate inventory, the estimated gross profit is deducted from the sales to determine the estimated cost of merchandise sold. This amount is then deducted from the cost of merchandise available for sale to determine the estimated ending inventory.

10 Compute and interpret the inventory turnover ratio and the number of days' sales in inventory.

The inventory turnover ratio, computed as the cost of merchandise sold divided by the average inventory, measures the relationship between the volume of goods (merchandise) sold and the amount of inventory carried during the period. The number of days' sales in inventory, computed as the ending inventory divided by the average daily cost of merchandise sold, measures the length of time it takes to acquire, sell, and replace the inventory.

ILLUSTRATIVE PROBLEM

Stewart Co.'s beginning inventory and purchases during the year ended December 31, 2004, were as follows:

		Units	Unit Cost	Total Cost
January 1	Inventory	1,000	$50.00	$ 50,000
March 10	Purchase	1,200	52.50	63,000
June 25	Sold 800 units			
August 30	Purchase	800	55.00	44,000
October 5	Sold 1,500 units			
November 26	Purchase	2,000	56.00	112,000
December 31	Sold 1,000 units			
Total		5,000		$269,000

Instructions

1. Determine the cost of inventory on December 31, 2004, using the perpetual inventory system and each of the following inventory costing methods:
   a. first-in, first-out
   b. last-in, first-out
2. Determine the cost of inventory on December 31, 2004, using the periodic inventory system and each of the following inventory costing methods:
   a. first-in, first-out
   b. last-in, first-out
   c. average cost
3. Assume that during the fiscal year ended December 31, 2004, sales were $290,000 and the estimated gross profit rate was 40%. Estimate the ending inventory at December 31, 2004, using the gross profit method.

Solution

1. a. First-in, first-out method: $95,200

Date	Purchases Quantity	Unit Cost	Total Cost	Cost of Merchandise Sold Quantity	Unit Cost	Total Cost	Inventory Quantity	Unit Cost	Total Cost
2004 Jan. 1							1,000	50.00	50,000
Mar. 10	1,200	52.50	63,000				1,000	50.00	50,000
							1,200	52.50	63,000
June 25				800	50.00	40,000	200	50.00	10,000
							1,200	52.50	63,000
Aug. 30	800	55.00	44,000				200	50.00	10,000
							1,200	52.50	63,000
							800	55.00	44,000
Oct. 5				200	50.00	10,000	700	55.00	38,500
				1,200	52.50	63,000			
				100	55.00	5,500			
Nov. 26	2,000	56.00	112,000				700	55.00	38,500
							2,000	56.00	112,000
Dec. 31				700	55.00	38,500	1,700	56.00	95,200
				300	56.00	16,800			

b.   Last-in, first-out method: $91,000 ($35,000 + $56,000)

Date	Purchases Quantity	Unit Cost	Total Cost	Cost of Merchandise Sold Quantity	Unit Cost	Total Cost	Inventory Quantity	Unit Cost	Total Cost
2004 Jan. 1							1,000	50.00	50,000
Mar. 10	1,200	52.50	63,000				1,000	50.00	50,000
							1,200	52.50	63,000
June 25				800	52.50	42,000	1,000	50.00	50,000
							400	52.50	21,000
Aug. 30	800	55.00	44,000				1,000	50.00	50,000
							400	52.50	21,000
							800	55.00	44,000
Oct. 5				800	55.00	44,000	700	50.00	35,000
				400	52.50	21,000			
				300	50.00	15,000			
Nov. 26	2,000	56.00	112,000				700	50.00	35,000
							2,000	56.00	112,000
Dec. 31				1,000	56.00	56,000	700	50.00	35,000
							1,000	56.00	56,000

2. a.   First-in, first-out method:
1,700 units at $56 = $95,200

b.   Last-in, first-out method:

1,000 units at $50.00	$50,000
700 units at $52.50	36,750
1,700 units	$86,750

c.   Average cost method:

Average cost per unit: $269,000 ÷ 5,000 units = $53.80
Inventory, December 31, 2004:   1,700 units at $53.80 = $91,460

3. Merchandise inventory, January 1, 2004		$ 50,000
Purchases (net)		219,000
Merchandise available for sale		$269,000
Sales (net)	$290,000	
Less estimated gross profit ($290,000 × 40%)	116,000	
Estimated cost of merchandise sold		174,000
Estimated merchandise inventory, December 31, 2004		$ 95,000

SELF-EXAMINATION QUESTIONS   Answers at End of Chapter

Matching

Match each of the following statements with its proper term. Some terms may not be used.

A. average cost method	__ 1. A detailed listing of merchandise on hand.
B. first-in, first-out (fifo) method	__ 2. A method of inventory costing based on the assumption that the costs of merchandise sold should be charged against revenue in the order in which the costs were incurred.
C. gross profit method	__ 3. A method of inventory costing based on the assumption that the most recent merchandise inventory costs should be charged against revenue.
D. inventory turnover	
E. last-in, first-out (lifo) method	__ 4. The method of inventory costing that is based upon the assumption that costs should be charged against revenue by using the weighted average unit cost of the items sold.
F. lower-of-cost-or-market (LCM) method	__ 5. A method of valuing inventory that reports the inventory at the lower of its cost or current market value (replacement cost).
G. net realizable value	__ 6. The estimated selling price of an item of inventory less any direct costs of disposal, such as sales commissions.
H. number of days' sales in inventory	__ 7. A method of estimating inventory cost that is based on the relationship of the cost of merchandise available for sale to the retail price of the same merchandise.
I. physical inventory	
J. retail inventory method	__ 8. A method of estimating inventory cost that is based on the relationship of gross profit to sales.
	__ 9. A ratio that measures the relationship between the volume of goods (merchandise) sold and the amount of inventory carried during the period.
	__ 10. A measure of the length of time it takes to acquire, sell, and replace the inventory.

Multiple Choice

1. If the inventory shrinkage at the end of the year is overstated by $7,500, the error will cause an:
   A. understatement of cost of merchandise sold for the year by $7,500.
   B. overstatement of gross profit for the year by $7,500.
   C. overstatement of merchandise inventory for the year by $7,500.
   D. understatement of net income for the year by $7,500.

2. The inventory costing method that is based on the assumption that costs should be charged against revenue in the order in which they were incurred is:
   A. fifo   C. average cost
   B. lifo   D. perpetual inventory

3. The following units of a particular item were purchased and sold during the period:

Beginning inventory	40 units at $20
First purchase	50 units at $21
Second purchase	50 units at $22
First sale	110 units
Third purchase	50 units at $23
Second sale	45 units

   What is the cost of the 35 units on hand at the end of the period as determined under the perpetual inventory system by the lifo costing method?
   A. $715   C. $700
   B. $705   D. $805

4. The following units of a particular item were available for sale during the period:

Beginning inventory	40 units at $20
First purchase	50 units at $21
Second purchase	50 units at $22
Third purchase	50 units at $23

What is the unit cost of the 35 units on hand at the end of the period as determined under the periodic inventory system by the fifo costing method?

A. $20   C. $22
B. $21   D. $23

5. If merchandise inventory is being valued at cost and the price level is steadily rising, the method of costing that will yield the highest net income is:
A. lifo   C. average
B. fifo   D. periodic

CLASS DISCUSSION QUESTIONS

1. What security measures may be used by retailers to protect merchandise inventory from customer theft?

2. Which inventory system provides the more effective means of controlling inventories (perpetual or periodic)? Why?

3. Before inventory purchases are recorded, the receiving report should be reconciled to what documents?

4. What document should be presented by an employee requesting inventory items to be released from the company's warehouse?

5. Why is it important to periodically take a physical inventory if the perpetual system is used?

6. The inventory shrinkage at the end of the year was understated by $15,000. (a) Did the error cause an overstatement or an understatement of the gross profit for the year? (b) Which items on the balance sheet at the end of the year were overstated or understated as a result of the error?

7. Bray Co. sold merchandise to Mansfield Company on December 31, FOB shipping point. If the merchandise is in transit on December 31, the end of the fiscal year, which company would report it in its financial statements? Explain.

8. A manufacturer shipped merchandise to a retailer on a consignment basis. If the merchandise is unsold at the end of the period, in whose inventory should the merchandise be included?

9. Do the terms *fifo* and *lifo* refer to techniques used in determining quantities of the various classes of merchandise on hand? Explain.

10. Does the term *last-in* in the lifo method mean that the items in the inventory are assumed to be the most recent (last) acquisitions? Explain.

11. If merchandise inventory is being valued at cost and the price level is steadily rising, which of the three methods of costing—fifo, lifo, or average cost—will yield (a) the highest inventory cost, (b) the lowest inventory cost, (c) the highest gross profit, (d) the lowest gross profit?

12. Which of the three methods of inventory costing—fifo, lifo, or average cost—will in general yield an inventory cost most nearly approximating current replacement cost?

13. If inventory is being valued at cost and the price level is steadily rising, which of the three methods of costing—fifo, lifo, or average cost—will yield the lowest annual income tax expense? Explain.

14. Can a company change its method of costing inventory? Explain.

15. Because of imperfections, an item of merchandise cannot be sold at its normal selling price. How should this item be valued for financial statement purposes?

16. How is the method of determining the cost of the inventory and the method of valuing it disclosed in the financial statements?

17. What uses can be made of the estimate of the cost of inventory determined by the gross profit method?

EXERCISES

Exercise 8–1
Internal control of inventories
Objective 1

Langley Hardware Store currently uses a periodic inventory system. Kevin White, the owner, is considering the purchase of a computer system that would make it feasible to switch to a perpetual inventory system.

Kevin is unhappy with the periodic inventory system because it does not provide timely information on inventory levels. Kevin has noticed on several occasions that the store runs out of good-selling items, while too many poor-selling items are on hand.

Kevin is also concerned about lost sales while a physical inventory is being taken. Langley Hardware currently takes a physical inventory twice a year. To minimize distractions, the store is closed on the day inventory is taken. Kevin believes that closing the store is the only way to get an accurate inventory count.

Will switching to a perpetual inventory system strengthen Langley Hardware's control over inventory items? Will switching to a perpetual inventory system eliminate the need for a physical inventory count? Explain.

Exercise 8–2
Internal control of inventories
Objective 1

Flyer's Luggage Shop is a small retail establishment located in a large shopping mall. This shop has implemented the following procedures regarding inventory items:

a. Since the display area of the store is limited, only a sample of each piece of luggage is kept on the selling floor. Whenever a customer selects a piece of luggage, the salesclerk gets the appropriate piece from the store's stockroom. Since all salesclerks need access to the stockroom, it is not locked. The stockroom is adjacent to the break room used by all mall employees.
b. Since the shop carries mostly high-quality, designer luggage, all inventory items are tagged with a control device that activates an alarm if a tagged item is removed from the store.
c. Whenever Flyer's receives a shipment of new inventory, the items are taken directly to the stockroom. Flyer's accountant uses the vendor's invoice to record the amount of inventory received.

State whether each of these procedures is appropriate or inappropriate, considering the principles of internal control. If it is inappropriate, state which internal control procedure is violated.

Exercise 8–3
Identifying items to be included in inventory
Objective 1

Mainstreet Co., which is located in Mason City, Iowa, has identified the following items for possible inclusion in its December 31, 2002 year-end inventory.

a. Mainstreet has segregated $6,570 of merchandise ordered by one of its customers for shipment on January 3, 2003.
b. Mainstreet has in its warehouse $30,500 of merchandise on consignment from Mahogany Co.
c. Merchandise Mainstreet shipped FOB shipping point on December 31, 2002, was picked up by the freight company at 11:50 p.m.
d. Merchandise Mainstreet shipped to a customer FOB shipping point was picked up by the freight company on December 26, 2002, but had still not arrived at its destination as of December 31, 2002.

e.   Mainstreet has $15,750 of merchandise on hand, which was sold to customers earlier in the year, but which has been returned by customers to Mainstreet for various warranty repairs.

f.   Mainstreet has sent $48,000 of merchandise to various retailers on a consignment basis.

g.   On December 31, 2002, Mainstreet received $11,050 of merchandise that had been returned by customers because the wrong merchandise had been shipped. The replacement order is to be shipped overnight on January 3, 2003.

h.   On December 27, 2002, Mainstreet ordered $18,000 of merchandise from a supplier in Des Moines. The merchandise was shipped FOB Des Moines on December 30, 2002, but had not been received by December 31, 2002.

i.   On December 21, 2002, Mainstreet ordered $58,000 of merchandise, FOB Mason City. The merchandise was shipped from the supplier on December 28, 2002, but had not been received by December 31, 2002.

Indicate which items should be included (I) and which should be excluded (E) from the inventory.

Exercise 8–4
Effect of errors in physical inventory
Objective 2

Whitewater Co. sells canoes, kayaks, whitewater rafts, and other boating supplies. During the taking of its physical inventory on December 31, 2003, Whitewater incorrectly counted its inventory as $112,800 instead of the correct amount of $121,500.

a.   State the effect of the error on the December 31, 2003 balance sheet of Whitewater.

b.   State the effect of the error on the income statement of Whitewater for the year ended December 31, 2003.

Exercise 8–5
Effect of errors in physical inventory
Objective 2

Dean's Motorcycle Shop sells motorcycles, jet skis, and other related supplies and accessories. During the taking of its physical inventory on December 31, 2003, Dean's Motorcycle Shop incorrectly counted its inventory as $179,600 instead of the correct amount of $153,750.

a.   State the effect of the error on the December 31, 2003 balance sheet of Dean's Motorcycle Shop.

b.   State the effect of the error on the income statement of Dean's Motorcycle Shop for the year ended December 31, 2003.

Exercise 8–6
Error in inventory shrinkage
Objective 2

During 2003, the accountant discovered that the physical inventory at the end of 2002 had been understated by $20,500. Instead of correcting the error, however, the accountant assumed that a $20,500 overstatement of the physical inventory in 2003 would balance out the error.

➤ Are there any flaws in the accountant's assumption? Explain.

Exercise 8–7
Perpetual inventory using fifo
Objectives 3, 4

✓ Inventory balance, June 30, $806

Beginning inventory, purchases, and sales data for portable CD players are as follows:

June	1	Inventory	25 units at $41
	6	Sale	16 units
	13	Purchase	18 units at $42
	18	Sale	12 units
	22	Sale	4 units
	30	Purchase	8 units at $43

The business maintains a perpetual inventory system, costing by the first-in, first-out method. Determine the cost of the merchandise sold for each sale and the inventory balance after each sale, presenting the data in the form illustrated in Exhibit 3.

Exercise 8–8
Perpetual inventory using lifo

Objectives 3, 4

✓ Inventory balance, June 30, $797

Assume that the business in Exercise 8–7 maintains a perpetual inventory system, costing by the last-in, first-out method. Determine the cost of merchandise sold for each sale and the inventory balance after each sale, presenting the data in the form illustrated in Exhibit 4.

Exercise 8–9
Perpetual inventory using lifo

Objectives 3, 4

✓ Inventory balance, October 31, $1,680

Beginning inventory, purchases, and sales data for cell phones for October are as follows:

Inventory		Purchases		Sales	
Oct. 1	30 units at $110	Oct. 6	10 units at $120	Oct. 11	9 units
		21	15 units at $130	16	24 units
				31	8 units

Assuming that the perpetual inventory system is used, costing by the lifo method, determine the cost of the inventory balance at October 31, presenting data in the form illustrated in Exhibit 4.

Exercise 8–10
Perpetual inventory using fifo

Objectives 3, 4

✓ Inventory balance, October 31, $1,820

Assume that the business in Exercise 8–9 maintains a perpetual inventory system, costing by the first-in, first-out method. Determine the cost of the inventory balance at October 31, presenting the data in the form illustrated in Exhibit 3.

Exercise 8–11
Fifo, lifo costs under perpetual inventory system

Objectives 3, 4

✓ a. $800

The following units of a particular item were available for sale during the year:

Beginning inventory	19 units at $46
Sale	15 units at $90
First purchase	32 units at $48
Sale	25 units at $90
Second purchase	40 units at $50
Sale	35 units at $90

The firm uses the perpetual inventory system, and there are 16 units of the item on hand at the end of the year. What is the total cost of the ending inventory according to (a) fifo, (b) lifo?

Exercise 8–12
Identify items missing in determining cost of merchandise sold

Objective 5

For (a) through (d), identify the items designated by "X."

a. Purchases − (X + X) = Net purchases.
b. Net purchases + X = Cost of merchandise purchased.
c. Merchandise inventory (beginning) + Cost of merchandise purchased = X.
d. Merchandise available for sale − X = Cost of merchandise sold.

Exercise 8–13
Cost of merchandise sold and related items

Objective 5

 **SPREADSHEET**

The following data were extracted from the accounting records of My Computers Company for the year ended November 30, 2003:

Merchandise Inventory, December 1, 2002	$ 75,750
Merchandise Inventory, November 30, 2003	88,200
Purchases	625,000
Purchases Returns and Allowances	14,500
Purchases Discounts	12,950
Sales	870,625
Transportation In	6,950

✓ a. Cost of merchandise sold,
$592,050

a. Prepare the cost of merchandise sold section of the income statement for the year ended November 30, 2003, using the periodic inventory method.
b. Determine the gross profit to be reported on the income statement for the year ended November 30, 2003.

Exercise 8–14
Cost of merchandise sold
Objective 5

✓ Correct cost of merchandise sold, $499,700

How many errors can you find in the following schedule of cost of merchandise sold for the current year ended December 31, 2002?

Cost of merchandise sold:			
Merchandise inventory, December 31, 2002			$ 75,000
Purchases		$500,000	
Plus: Purchases returns and allowances	$12,500		
Purchases discounts	6,500	19,000	
Gross purchases		$519,000	
Less transportation in		12,400	
Cost of merchandise purchased			506,600
Merchandise available for sale			$581,600
Less merchandise inventory, January 1, 2002			81,300
Cost of merchandise sold			$500,300

Exercise 8–15
Periodic inventory by three methods
Objectives 3, 5

✓ b. $990

The units of an item available for sale during the year were as follows:

Jan.	1	Inventory	25 units at $24
Feb.	4	Purchase	10 units at $25
July	20	Purchase	30 units at $28
Dec.	30	Purchase	35 units at $30

There are 40 units of the item in the physical inventory at December 31. The periodic inventory system is used. Determine the inventory cost by (a) the first-in, first-out method, (b) the last-in, first-out method, and (c) the average cost method.

Exercise 8–16
Periodic inventory by three methods; cost of merchandise sold
Objectives 3, 5

SPREADSHEET

✓ a. Inventory, $1,254

The units of an item available for sale during the year were as follows:

Jan.	1	Inventory	21 units at $60
Mar.	4	Purchase	29 units at $65
Aug.	7	Purchase	10 units at $68
Nov.	15	Purchase	15 units at $70

There are 18 units of the item in the physical inventory at December 31. The periodic inventory system is used. Determine the inventory cost and the cost of merchandise sold by three methods, presenting your answers in the following form:

	Cost	
Inventory Method	**Merchandise Inventory**	**Merchandise Sold**
a. First-in, first-out	$	$
b. Last-in, first-out		
c. Average cost		

Exercise 8–17
Lower-of-cost-or-market inventory
Objective 7

On the basis of the following data, determine the value of the inventory at the lower of cost or market. Assemble the data in the form illustrated in Exhibit 7.

SPREADSHEET

Commodity	Inventory Quantity	Unit Cost Price	Unit Market Price
X3	9	$300	$320
Y10	16	110	115
A19	12	275	260
J2	15	51	45
J8	25	96	100

Exercise 8–18

Merchandise inventory on the balance sheet

Objective 8

Based on the data in Exercise 8–17 and assuming that cost was determined by the fifo method, show how the merchandise inventory would appear on the balance sheet.

Exercise 8–19

Retail inventory method

Objective 9

A business using the retail method of inventory costing determines that merchandise inventory at retail is $625,750. If the ratio of cost to retail price is 60%, what is the amount of inventory to be reported on the financial statements?

Exercise 8–20

Retail inventory method

Objective 9

SPREADSHEET

On the basis of the following data, estimate the cost of the merchandise inventory at April 30 by the retail method:

		Cost	Retail
April 1	Merchandise inventory	$167,710	$ 270,500
April 1–30	Purchases (net)	651,000	1,050,000
April 1–30	Sales (net)		975,000

✓ Inventory, April 30: $214,210

Exercise 8–21

Gross profit inventory method

Objective 9

The merchandise inventory was destroyed by fire on March 20. The following data were obtained from the accounting records:

Jan. 1	Merchandise inventory	$ 150,000
Jan. 1–Mar. 20	Purchases (net)	900,000
	Sales (net)	1,100,000
	Estimated gross profit rate	40%

a. Estimate the cost of the merchandise destroyed.
b. Briefly describe the situations in which the gross profit method is useful.

Exercise 8–22

Inventory turnover

Objective 10

Real World

The following data were taken from recent annual reports of **Gateway 2000 Inc.**, a vendor of personal computers and related products, and **American Greetings Corporation**, a manufacturer and distributor of greeting cards and related products:

	Gateway 2000	American Greetings
Cost of goods sold	$5,921,651,000	$757,080,000
Inventory, end of year	167,924,000	251,289,000
Inventory, beginning of the year	152,531,000	271,205,000

a. Determine the inventory turnover for Gateway 2000 and American Greetings.
b. Would you expect American Greetings' inventory turnover to be higher or lower than Gateway's? Why?

Exercise 8–23

Inventory turnover and number of days' sales in inventory

Objective 10

The financial statements for **Cisco Systems, Inc.**, are presented in Appendix G at the end of the text. Cisco Systems had inventories of $362,000,000 at July 25, 1998.

a. For the years ended July 29, 2000 and July 31, 1999, determine: (1) the inventory turnover, and (2) the number of days' sales in inventory.
b. ✏️ ► What conclusions can be drawn from these analyses concerning Cisco Systems' efficiency in managing inventory?

PROBLEMS SERIES A

Problem 8–1A

Fifo perpetual inventory

Objectives 3, 4

SPREADSHEET

✓ 3. $7,480

The beginning inventory of floor mats at Eagle Office Supplies and data on purchases and sales for a three-month period are as follows:

Date		Transaction	Number of Units	Per Unit	Total
Sept.	1	Inventory	250	$ 6.10	$1,525
	8	Purchase	750	6.20	4,650
	20	Sale	450	9.00	4,050
	30	Sale	350	9.00	3,150
Oct.	8	Sale	50	9.10	455
	10	Purchase	500	6.10	3,050
	27	Sale	350	9.20	3,220
	31	Sale	200	9.15	1,830
Nov.	5	Purchase	750	6.00	4,500
	13	Sale	350	10.00	3,500
	23	Purchase	400	5.95	2,380
	30	Sale	500	10.00	5,000

Instructions

1. Record the inventory, purchases, and cost of merchandise sold data in a perpetual inventory record similar to the one illustrated in Exhibit 3, using the first-in, first-out method.
2. Determine the total sales and the total cost of floor mats sold for the period. Journalize the entries in the sales and cost of merchandise sold accounts. Assume that all sales were on account.
3. Determine the gross profit from sales for the period.
4. Determine the ending inventory cost.

Problem 8–2A

Lifo perpetual inventory

Objectives 3, 4

✓ 2. Gross profit, $7,510

The beginning inventory of floor mats at Eagle Office Supplies and data on purchases and sales for a three-month period are shown in Problem 8–1A.

Instructions

1. Record the inventory, purchases, and cost of merchandise sold data in a perpetual inventory record similar to the one illustrated in Exhibit 4, using the last-in, first-out method.
2. Determine the total sales, the total cost of floor mats sold, and the gross profit from sales for the period.
3. Determine the ending inventory cost.

Problem 8–3A

Periodic inventory by three methods

Objectives 3, 5

Sixpack Appliances uses the periodic inventory system. Details regarding the inventory of appliances at July 1, 2002, purchases invoices during the year, and the inventory count at June 30, 2003, are summarized as follows:

| Model | Inventory, July 1 | Purchases Invoices | | | Inventory Count, June 30 |
		1st	2nd	3rd	
A103	7 at $242	6 at $250	5 at $260	10 at $259	9
C743	6 at 80	5 at 82	8 at 89	8 at 90	7
F1010	2 at 108	2 at 110	3 at 128	3 at 130	3
H142	8 at 88	4 at 79	3 at 85	6 at 92	8
P813	2 at 250	2 at 260	4 at 271	4 at 272	5
Q661	5 at 160	4 at 170	4 at 175	7 at 180	8
W490	—	4 at 150	4 at 200	4 at 202	5

Instructions

1. Determine the cost of the inventory on June 30, 2003, by the first-in, first-out method. Present data in columnar form, using the following headings:

Model	Quantity	Unit Cost	Total Cost

   If the inventory of a particular model comprises one entire purchase plus a portion of another purchase acquired at a different unit cost, use a separate line for each purchase.

2. Determine the cost of the inventory on June 30, 2003, by the last-in, first-out method, following the procedures indicated in (1).

3. Determine the cost of the inventory on June 30, 2003, by the average cost method, using the columnar headings indicated in (1).

4. ✏︎ Discuss which method (fifo or lifo) would be preferred for income tax purposes in periods of (a) rising prices and (b) declining prices.

If the working papers correlating with this textbook are not used, omit Problem 8–4A.

Problem 8–4A
Lower-of-cost-or-market inventory
Objective 7

Data on the physical inventory of Minish Company as of December 31, 2003, are presented in the working papers. The quantity of each commodity on hand has been determined and recorded on the inventory sheet. Unit market prices have also been determined as of December 31 and recorded on the sheet. The inventory is to be determined at cost and also at the lower of cost or market, using the first-in, first-out method. Quantity and cost data from the last purchases invoice of the year and the next-to-the-last purchases invoice are summarized as follows:

| Description | Last Purchases Invoice | | Next-to-the-Last Purchases Invoice | |
	Quantity Purchased	Unit Cost	Quantity Purchased	Unit Cost
A10	25	$ 60	30	$ 58
B23	30	208	20	205
D82	10	145	25	142
E34	150	25	100	24
F17	10	565	10	560
H99	100	15	100	14
K41	10	387	5	384
M21	500	6	500	6
R72	80	19	50	18
T15	5	255	4	260
BD1	100	20	75	19
MS3	7	701	6	699

Instructions

Record the appropriate unit costs on the inventory sheet, and complete the pricing of the inventory. When there are two different unit costs applicable to an item, proceed as follows:

1. Draw a line through the quantity, and insert the quantity and unit cost of the last purchase.

(continued)

2. On the following line, insert the quantity and unit cost of the next-to-the-last purchase.
3. Total the cost and market columns and insert the lower of the two totals in the Lower of C or M column. The first item on the inventory sheet has been completed as an example.

Problem 8–5A
Retail method; gross profit method

Objective 9

✓ 1. $98,070
✓ 2. a. $163,750

Selected data on merchandise inventory, purchases, and sales for Typhoon Co. and Wheaton Co. are as follows:

	Cost	Retail
Typhoon Co.		
Merchandise inventory, August 1	$ 90,650	$ 129,500
Transactions during August:		
Purchases (net)	735,420	1,050,600
Sales		1,050,000
Sales returns and allowances		10,000
Wheaton Co.		
Merchandise inventory, April 1	$ 147,800	
Transactions during April and May:		
Purchases (net)	1,047,950	
Sales	1,750,000	
Sales returns and allowances	30,000	
Estimated gross profit rate	40%	

Instructions

1. Determine the estimated cost of the merchandise inventory of Typhoon Co. on August 31 by the retail method, presenting details of the computations.
2. a. Estimate the cost of the merchandise inventory of Wheaton Co. on May 31 by the gross profit method, presenting details of the computations.
   b. Assume that Wheaton Co. took a physical inventory on May 31 and discovered that $148,300 of merchandise was on hand. What was the estimated loss of inventory due to theft or damage during April and May?

PROBLEMS SERIES B

Problem 8–1B
Fifo perpetual inventory

Objectives 3, 4

SPREADSHEET

✓ 3. $239,800

The beginning inventory of drift boats at River's Edge Co. and data on purchases and sales for a three-month period are as follows:

Date	Transaction	Number of Units	Per Unit	Total
March 1	Inventory	15	$2,200	$ 33,000
8	Purchase	25	2,250	56,250
11	Sale	10	5,000	50,000
22	Sale	13	5,000	65,000
April 3	Purchase	15	2,300	34,500
10	Sale	10	5,100	51,000
21	Sale	5	5,100	25,500
30	Purchase	25	2,350	58,750
May 5	Sale	20	5,150	103,000
13	Sale	12	5,150	61,800
21	Purchase	20	2,400	48,000
28	Sale	15	5,200	78,000

Instructions

1. Record the inventory, purchases, and cost of merchandise sold data in a perpetual inventory record similar to the one illustrated in Exhibit 3, using the first-in, first-out method.

2. Determine the total sales and the total cost of drift boats sold for the period. Journalize the entries in the sales and cost of merchandise sold accounts. Assume that all sales were on account.
3. Determine the gross profit from sales of drift boats for the period.
4. Determine the ending inventory cost.

Problem 8–2B
Lifo perpetual inventory

Objectives 3, 4

✓ 2. Gross profit, $237,800

The beginning inventory of drift boats and data on purchases and sales for a three-month period are shown in Problem 8–1B.

Instructions

1. Record the inventory, purchases, and cost of merchandise sold data in a perpetual inventory record similar to the one illustrated in Exhibit 4, using the last-in, first-out method.
2. Determine the total sales, the total cost of drift boats sold, and the gross profit from sales for the period.
3. Determine the ending inventory cost.

Problem 8–3B
Periodic inventory by three methods

Objectives 3, 5

✓ 1. $11,580

Yellowstone Appliances uses the periodic inventory system. Details regarding the inventory of appliances at January 1, 2003, purchases invoices during the year, and the inventory count at December 31, 2003, are summarized as follows:

| Model | Inventory, January 1 | Purchases Invoices | | | Inventory Count, December 31 |
		1st	2nd	3rd	
109A	4 at $140	6 at $144	8 at $148	7 at $156	5
110B	3 at 208	3 at 212	5 at 213	4 at 225	5
127X	2 at 520	2 at 527	2 at 530	2 at 535	3
143T	6 at 520	8 at 531	4 at 549	6 at 542	7
144Z	9 at 213	7 at 215	6 at 222	6 at 225	10
160M	6 at 305	3 at 310	3 at 316	4 at 317	5
180X	—	4 at 222	4 at 232	—	2

Instructions

1. Determine the cost of the inventory on December 31, 2003, by the first-in, first-out method. Present data in columnar form, using the following headings:

Model	Quantity	Unit Cost	Total Cost

If the inventory of a particular model comprises one entire purchase plus a portion of another purchase acquired at a different unit cost, use a separate line for each purchase.
2. Determine the cost of the inventory on December 31, 2003, by the last-in, first-out method, following the procedures indicated in (1).
3. Determine the cost of the inventory on December 31, 2003, by the average cost method, using the columnar headings indicated in (1).
4. ▬▬► Discuss which method (fifo or lifo) would be preferred for income tax purposes in periods of (a) rising prices and (b) declining prices.

If the working papers correlating with this textbook are not used, omit Problem 8–4B.

Problem 8–4B
Lower-of-cost-or-market inventory

Objective 7

✓ Total LCM, $38,480

Data on the physical inventory of Trailblazer Co. as of December 31, 2003, are presented in the working papers. The quantity of each commodity on hand has been determined and recorded on the inventory sheet. Unit market prices have also been determined as of December 31 and recorded on the sheet. The inventory is to be determined at cost and also at the lower of cost or market, using the first-in, first-out method. Quantity and cost data from the last purchases invoice of the year and the next-to-the-last purchases invoice are summarized as follows:

| | Last Purchases Invoice | | Next-to-the-Last Purchases Invoice | |
Description	Quantity Purchased	Unit Cost	Quantity Purchased	Unit Cost
A10	25	$ 60	40	$ 58
B23	25	190	15	191
D82	16	143	15	142
E34	150	25	100	27
F17	6	550	15	540
H99	75	14	100	13
K41	8	400	4	398
M21	500	6	500	7
R72	70	17	50	16
T15	5	250	4	260
BD1	120	19	115	17
MS3	8	701	7	699

Instructions

Record the appropriate unit costs on the inventory sheet, and complete the pricing of the inventory. When there are two different unit costs applicable to an item, proceed as follows:

1. Draw a line through the quantity, and insert the quantity and unit cost of the last purchase.
2. On the following line, insert the quantity and unit cost of the next-to-the-last purchase.
3. Total the cost and market columns and insert the lower of the two totals in the Lower of C or M column. The first item on the inventory sheet has been completed as an example.

Problem 8–5B

Retail method; gross profit method

Objective 9

✓ 1. $235,950
✓ 2. a. $287,600

Selected data on merchandise inventory, purchases, and sales for Livingston Co. and Park Co. are as follows:

	Cost	Retail
Livingston Co.		
Merchandise inventory, February 1	$ 184,800	$ 280,000
Transactions during February:		
Purchases (net)	744,150	1,127,500
Sales		1,075,000
Sales returns and allowances		25,000
Park Co.		
Merchandise inventory, July 1	$ 217,500	
Transactions during July and August:		
Purchases (net)	1,491,100	
Sales	2,600,000	
Sales returns and allowances	150,000	
Estimated gross profit rate	42%	

Instructions

1. Determine the estimated cost of the merchandise inventory of Livingston Co. on February 28 by the retail method, presenting details of the computations.
2. a. Estimate the cost of the merchandise inventory of Park Co. on August 31 by the gross profit method, presenting details of the computations.
   b. Assume that Park Co. took a physical inventory on August 31 and discovered that $272,000 of merchandise was on hand. What was the estimated loss of inventory due to theft or damage during July and August?

SPECIAL ACTIVITIES

Activity 8–1
Xanadu Co.
Ethics and professional conduct in business

Xanadu Co. is experiencing a decrease in sales and operating income for the fiscal year ending December 31, 2003. Neil Whyte, controller of Xanadu Co., has suggested that all orders received before the end of the fiscal year be shipped by midnight, December 31, 2003, even if the shipping department must work overtime. Since Xanadu Co. ships all merchandise FOB shipping point, it would record all such shipments as sales for the year ending December 31, 2003, thereby offsetting some of the decreases in sales and operating income.

Discuss whether Neil Whyte is behaving in a professional manner.

Activity 8–2
Walgreen Co.
Fifo vs. lifo

The following footnote was taken from the 1999 financial statements of Walgreen Co.:

Inventories are valued on a . . . last-in, first-out (LIFO) cost . . . basis. At August 31, 1999 and 1998, inventories would have been greater by $536,000,000 and $490,800,000 respectively, if they had been valued on a lower of first-in, first-out (FIFO) cost or market basis.

Additional data are as follows:

Earnings before income taxes, 1999	$1,027,300,000
Total lifo inventories, August 31, 1999	2,462,600,000

Based on the preceding data, determine (a) what the total inventories at August 31, 1999, would have been, using the fifo method, and (b) what the earnings before income taxes for the year ended August 31, 1999, would have been if fifo had been used instead of lifo.

Activity 8–3
Leconte Wholesale Co.
Lifo and inventory flow

The following is an excerpt from a conversation between John Lacy, the warehouse manager for Leconte Wholesale Co., and its accountant, Leanne Huskey. Leconte Wholesale operates a large regional warehouse that supplies produce and other grocery products to grocery stores in smaller communities.

John: Leanne, can you explain what's going on here with these monthly statements?
Leanne: Sure, John. How can I help you?
John: I don't understand this last-in, first-out inventory procedure. It just doesn't make sense.
Leanne: Well, what it means is that we assume that the last goods we receive are the first ones sold. So the inventory is made up of the items we purchased first.
John: Yes, but that's my problem. It doesn't work that way! We always distribute the oldest produce first. Some of that produce is perishable! We can't keep any of it very long or it'll spoil.
Leanne: John, you don't understand. We only *assume* that the products we distribute are the last ones received. We don't actually have to distribute the goods in this way.
John: I always thought that accounting was supposed to show what really happened. It all sounds like "make believe" to me! Why not report what really happens?

Respond to John's concerns.

Activity 8–4
Into the Real World
Observe internal controls over inventory

Select a business in your community and observe its internal controls over inventory. In groups of three or four, identify and discuss the similarities and differences in each business's inventory controls. Prepare a written summary of your findings.

Activity 8–5
Lectern Company
Costing inventory

Lectern Company began operations in 2002 by selling a single product. Data on purchases and sales for the year were as follows:

Purchases:

Date	Units Purchased	Unit Cost	Total Cost
April 8	3,875	$12.20	$ 47,275
May 10	4,125	13.00	53,625
June 4	5,000	13.20	66,000
July 10	5,000	14.00	70,000
August 3	3,400	14.25	48,450
October 5	1,600	14.50	23,200
November 1	1,000	14.95	14,950
December 10	1,000	16.00	16,000
	25,000		$339,500

Sales:

April	2,000 units
May	2,000
June	2,500
July	3,000
August	3,500
September	3,500
October	2,250
November	1,250
December	1,000
Total units	21,000
Total sales	$552,000

On January 3, 2003, the president of the company, Kevin Ivey, asked for your advice on costing the 4,000-unit physical inventory that was taken on December 31, 2002. Moreover, since the firm plans to expand its product line, he asked for your advice on the use of a perpetual inventory system in the future.

1. Determine the cost of the December 31, 2002 inventory under the periodic system, using the (a) first-in, first-out method, (b) last-in, first-out method, and (c) average cost method.
2. Determine the gross profit for the year under each of the three methods in (1).
3. a.   ■▬ Explain varying viewpoints why each of the three inventory costing methods may best reflect the results of operations for 2002.
   b.   ■▬ Which of the three inventory costing methods may best reflect the replacement cost of the inventory on the balance sheet as of December 31, 2002?
   c.   ■▬ Which inventory costing method would you choose to use for income tax purposes? Why?
   d.   ■▬ Discuss the advantages and disadvantages of using a perpetual inventory system. From the data presented in this case, is there any indication of the adequacy of inventory levels during the year?

Activity 8–6
Into the Real World
Compare inventory cost flow assumptions

In groups of three or four, examine the financial statements of a well-known retailing business. You may obtain the financial statements you need from one of the following sources:

1. Your school or local library.
2. The investor relations department of the company.
3. The company's Web site on the Internet.
4. EDGAR (Electronic Data Gathering, Analysis, and Retrieval), the electronic archives of financial statements filed with the Securities and Exchange Commission. SEC documents can be retrieved using the EdgarScan service from **PricewaterhouseCoopers** at

edgarscan.pwcglobal.com. To obtain annual report information, type in a company name in the appropriate space. EdgarScan will list the reports available to you for the company you've selected. Select the most recent annual report filing, identified as a 10-K or 10-K405. EdgarScan provides an outline of the report, including the separate financial statements. You can double-click the income statement and balance sheet for the selected company into an Excel spreadsheet for further analysis.

Determine the cost flow assumption(s) that the company is using for its inventory, and determine whether the company is using the lower-of-cost-or-market rule. Prepare a written summary of your findings.

ANSWERS TO SELF-EXAMINATION QUESTIONS

Matching

1. I
2. B
3. E
4. A
5. F
6. G
7. J
8. C
9. D
10. H

Multiple Choice

1. **D** The overstatement of inventory shrinkage by $7,500 at the end of the year will cause the cost of merchandise sold for the year to be overstated by $7,500, the gross profit for the year to be understated by $7,500, the merchandise inventory to be understated by $7,500, and the net income for the year to be understated by $7,500 (answer D).

2. **A** The fifo method (answer A) is based on the assumption that costs are charged against revenue in the order in which they were incurred. The lifo method (answer B) charges the most recent costs incurred against revenue, and the average cost method (answer C) charges a weighted average of unit costs of items sold against revenue. The perpetual inventory system (answer D) is a system and not a method of costing.

3. **A** The lifo method of costing is based on the assumption that costs should be charged against revenue in the reverse order in which costs were incurred. Thus, the oldest costs are assigned to inventory. Thirty of the 35 units would be assigned a unit cost of $20 (since 110 of the beginning inventory units were sold on the first sale), and the remaining 5 units would be assigned a cost of $23, for a total of $715 (answer A).

4. **D** The fifo method of costing is based on the assumption that costs should be charged against revenue in the order in which they were incurred (first-in, first-out). Thus, the most recent costs are assigned to inventory. The 35 units would be assigned a unit cost of $23 (answer D).

5. **B** When the price level is steadily rising, the earlier unit costs are lower than recent unit costs. Under the fifo method (answer B), these earlier costs are matched against revenue to yield the highest possible net income. The periodic inventory system (answer D) is a system and not a method of costing.

Fixed Assets and Intangible Assets

F9

objectives

After studying this chapter, you should be able to:

1 Define fixed assets and describe the accounting for their cost.

2 Compute depreciation, using the following methods: straight-line method, units-of-production method, and declining-balance method.

3 Classify fixed asset costs as either capital expenditures or revenue expenditures.

4 Journalize entries for the disposal of fixed assets.

5 Define a lease and summarize the accounting rules related to the leasing of fixed assets.

6 Describe internal controls over fixed assets.

7 Compute depletion and journalize the entry for depletion.

8 Journalize the entries for acquiring and amortizing intangible assets, such as patents, copyrights, and goodwill.

9 Describe how depreciation expense is reported in an income statement, and prepare a balance sheet that includes fixed assets and intangible assets.

10 Compute and interpret the ratio of fixed assets to long-term liabilities.

Assume that you are a certified flight instructor and you would like to earn a little extra money by teaching people how to fly. Since you don't own an airplane, one of the pilots at the local airport is willing to let you use her airplane for a fixed fee per year. You will also have to pay your share of the annual operating costs, based on hours flown. The owner will consider your request for upgrading the plane's equipment. At the end of the year, the owner has the right to cancel the agreement.

One of your friends is an airplane mechanic. He is familiar with the plane and has indicated that it needs its annual inspection. There is some structural damage on the right aileron. In addition to this repair, you would like to equip the plane with another radio and a better navigation system.

Since you will not have any ownership in the airplane, it is important for you to distinguish between normal operating costs and costs that add future value or worth to the airplane. These latter costs should be the responsibility of the owner. In this case, you should be willing to pay for part of the cost of the annual inspection. The cost of repairing the structural damage and upgrading the navigation system should be the responsibility of the owner.

Businesses also distinguish between the cost of a fixed asset and the cost of operating the asset. In this chapter, we discuss how to determine the portion of a fixed asset's cost that becomes an expense over a period of time. We also discuss accounting for the disposal of fixed assets and accounting for intangible assets, such as patents and copyrights.

Nature of Fixed Assets

objective 1

Define fixed assets and describe the accounting for their cost.

Businesses use a variety of fixed assets, such as equipment, furniture, tools, machinery, buildings, and land. **Fixed assets** are long-term or relatively permanent assets. They are **tangible assets** because they exist physically. They are owned and used by the business and are not offered for sale as part of normal operations. Other descriptive titles for these assets are **plant assets** or **property, plant, and equipment**.

There is no standard rule for the minimum length of life necessary for an asset to be classified as a fixed asset. Such assets must be capable of providing repeated use or benefit and are normally expected to last more than a year. However, an asset need not actually be used on an ongoing basis or even often. For example, standby equipment for use in the event of a breakdown of regular equipment or for use only during peak periods is included in fixed assets.

Long-term assets acquired for resale in the normal course of business are not classified as fixed assets, regardless of their permanent nature or the length of time they are held. For example, undeveloped land or other real estate acquired as an investment for resale should be listed on the balance sheet in the asset section entitled *Investments*.

The normal costs of using or operating a fixed asset are reported as expenses on a company's income statement. The costs of acquiring a fixed asset become expenses over a period of time. In the next section, we discuss these latter costs and their recognition as expenses.

Q&A *St. Mary's Hospital maintains an auxiliary generator for use in electrical outages. Such outages are rare, and the generator has not been used for the past two years. Should the generator be included as a fixed asset in St. Mary's ledger?*

Yes. Even though the generator has not been used recently, it should be included as a fixed asset.

Glacier Co. is purchasing property (building and land) for use as a warehouse. In purchasing the land, Glacier has agreed to pay the prior owner's delinquent property taxes. Should the cost of paying the delinquent property taxes be included as part of the cost of the property?

Yes. All costs of acquiring the property, including the delinquent property taxes, should be included as part of the total cost of the property.

Costs of Acquiring Fixed Assets

The cost of acquiring a fixed asset includes all amounts spent to get it in place and ready for use. For example, freight costs and the costs of installing equipment are included as part of the asset's total cost. Exhibit 1 summarizes some of the common costs of acquiring fixed assets. These costs should be recorded by debiting the related fixed asset account, such as Land,[1] Building, Land Improvements, or Machinery and Equipment.

Costs *not necessary* for getting a fixed asset ready for use do not increase the asset's usefulness. Such costs should not be included as part of the asset's total cost. For example, the following costs should be debited to an expense account:

- Vandalism
- Mistakes in installation
- Uninsured theft
- Damage during unpacking and installing
- Fines for not obtaining proper permits from government agencies

Nature of Depreciation

As we have discussed in earlier chapters, land has an unlimited life and therefore can provide unlimited services. On the other hand, other fixed assets such as equipment, buildings, and land improvements lose their ability, over time, to provide services. As a result, the costs of equipment, buildings, and land improvements should be transferred to expense accounts in a systematic manner during their expected useful lives. This periodic transfer of cost to expense is called depreciation.

> The adjusting entry to record depreciation debits Depreciation Expense and credits Accumulated Depreciation.

The adjusting entry to record depreciation is usually made at the end of each month or at the end of the year. This entry debits *Depreciation Expense* and credits a *contra asset* account entitled *Accumulated Depreciation* or *Allowance for Depreciation*. The use of a contra asset account allows the original cost to remain unchanged in the fixed asset account.

Factors that cause a decline in the ability of a fixed asset to provide services may be identified as physical depreciation or functional depreciation. **Physical depreciation** occurs from wear and tear while in use and from the action of the weather. **Functional depreciation** occurs when a fixed asset is no longer able to provide services at the level for which it was intended. For example, a personal computer made in the 1980s would not be able to provide an Internet connection. Such advances in technology during this century have made functional depreciation an increasingly important cause of depreciation.

The term *depreciation* as used in accounting is often misunderstood because the same term is also used in business to mean a decline in the market value of an asset. However, the amount of a fixed asset's unexpired cost reported in the balance sheet usually does not agree with the amount that could be realized from its sale. Fixed assets are held for use in a business rather than for sale. It is assumed that the business will continue as a going concern. Thus, a decision to dispose of a fixed asset is based mainly on the usefulness of the asset to the business and not on its market value.

Companies often use different useful lives for similar assets. For example, the primary useful life for buildings is 50 years for JCPenney Co., while the useful life for buildings for Tandy Corporation, which operates Radio Shack, varies from 10 to 40 years.

---

[1] As discussed here, land is assumed to be used only as a location or site. Land acquired for its mineral deposits or other natural resources will be considered later in the chapter.

Exhibit 1 Costs of Acquiring
Fixed Assets

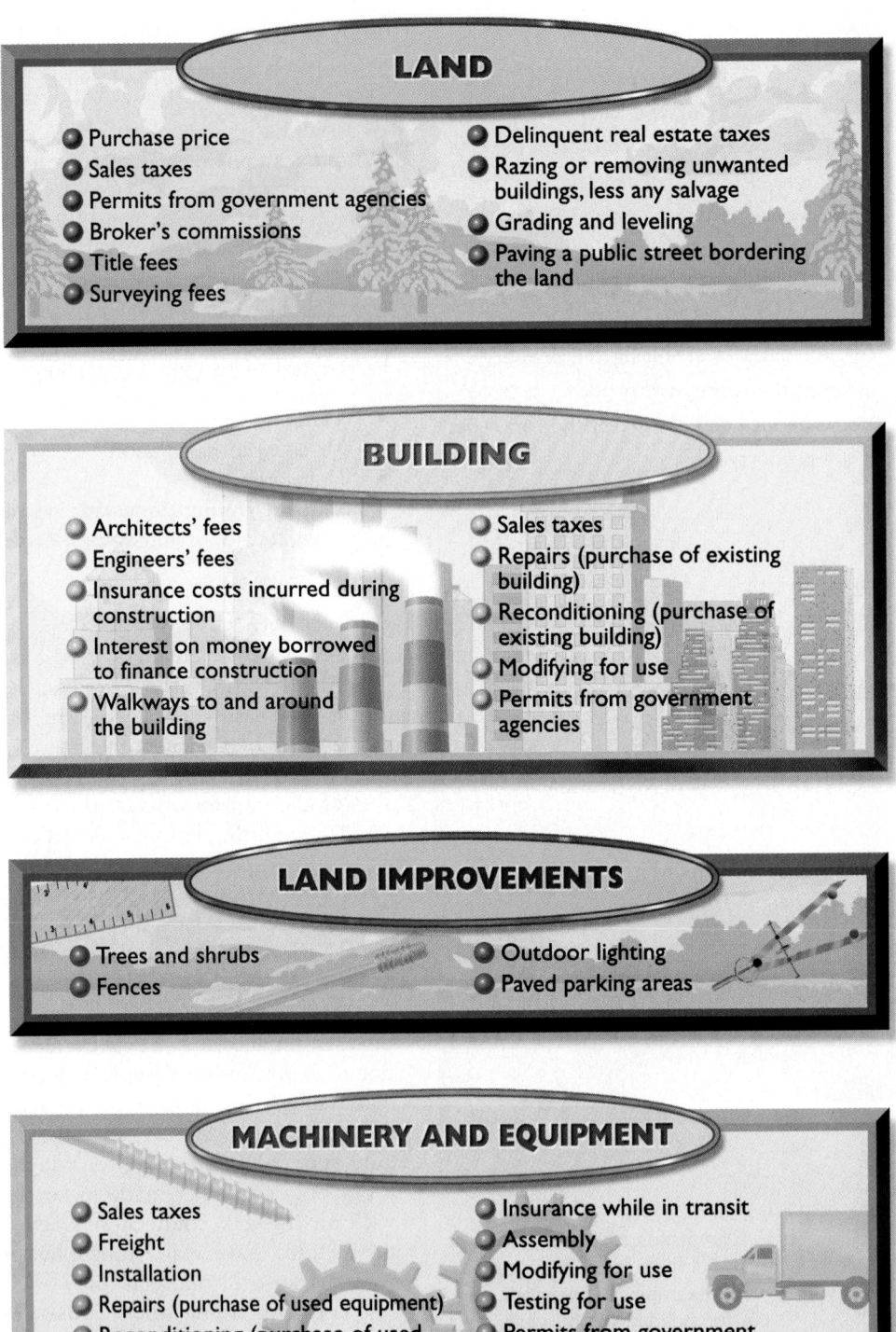

LAND
- Purchase price
- Sales taxes
- Permits from government agencies
- Broker's commissions
- Title fees
- Surveying fees
- Delinquent real estate taxes
- Razing or removing unwanted buildings, less any salvage
- Grading and leveling
- Paving a public street bordering the land

BUILDING
- Architects' fees
- Engineers' fees
- Insurance costs incurred during construction
- Interest on money borrowed to finance construction
- Walkways to and around the building
- Sales taxes
- Repairs (purchase of existing building)
- Reconditioning (purchase of existing building)
- Modifying for use
- Permits from government agencies

LAND IMPROVEMENTS
- Trees and shrubs
- Fences
- Outdoor lighting
- Paved parking areas

MACHINERY AND EQUIPMENT
- Sales taxes
- Freight
- Installation
- Repairs (purchase of used equipment)
- Reconditioning (purchase of used equipment)
- Insurance while in transit
- Assembly
- Modifying for use
- Testing for use
- Permits from government agencies

Point of Interest

Would you have more cash if you depreciated your car? The answer is no. Depreciation does not affect your cash flows. Likewise, depreciation does not affect the cash flows of a business. However, depreciation is subtracted in determining net income.

Another common misunderstanding is that accounting for depreciation provides cash needed to replace fixed assets as they wear out. This misunderstanding probably occurs because depreciation, unlike most expenses, does not require an outlay of cash in the period in which it is recorded. The cash account is neither increased nor decreased by the periodic entries that transfer the cost of fixed assets to depreciation expense accounts.

Accounting for Depreciation

Three factors are considered in determining the amount of depreciation expense to be recognized each period. These three factors are (a) the fixed asset's initial cost, (b) its expected useful life, and (c) its estimated value at the end of its useful life. This third factor is called the **residual value**, **scrap value**, **salvage value**, or **trade-in value**. Exhibit 2 shows the relationship among the three factors and the periodic depreciation expense.

Exhibit 2 Factors that Determine Depreciation Expense

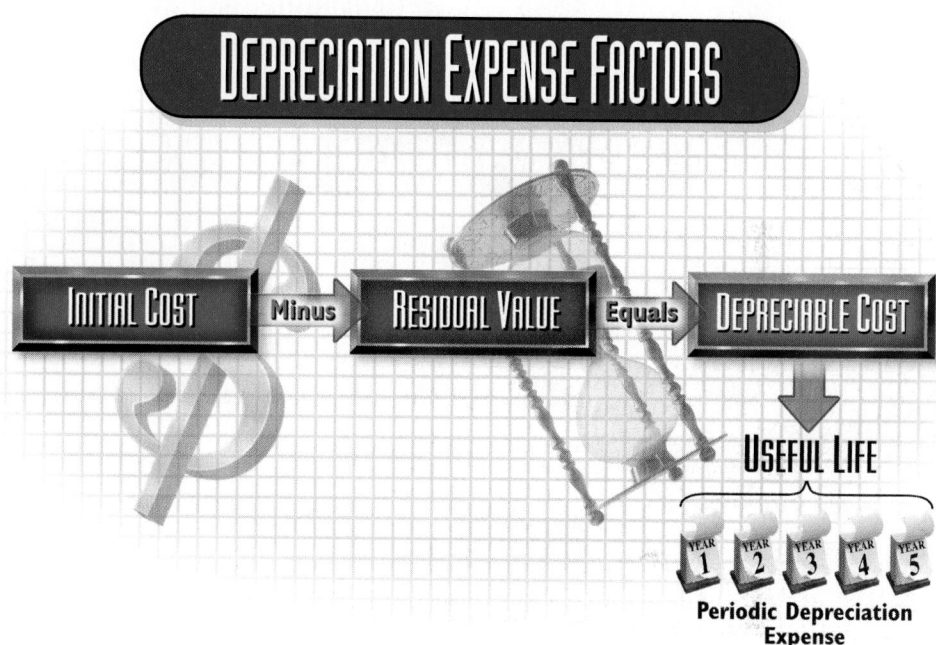

A fixed asset's **residual value** at the end of its expected useful life must be estimated at the time the asset is placed in service. If a fixed asset is expected to have little or no residual value when it is taken out of service, then its initial cost should be spread over its expected useful life as depreciation expense. If, however, a fixed asset is expected to have a significant residual value, the difference between its initial cost and its residual value, called the asset's **depreciable cost**, is the amount that is spread over the asset's useful life as depreciation expense.

A fixed asset's **expected useful life** must also be estimated at the time the asset is placed in service. Estimates of expected useful lives are available from various trade associations and other publications. For federal income tax purposes, the Internal Revenue Service has established guidelines for useful lives. These guidelines may also be helpful in determining depreciation for financial reporting purposes.

The Internal Revenue Service guideline for the useful life of automobiles and light-duty trucks is 5 years, while the designated life for most machinery and equipment is 7 years.

In practice, many businesses use the guideline that all assets placed in or taken out of service during the first half of a month are treated as if the event occurred on the first day of *that* month. That is, these businesses compute depreciation on these assets for the entire month. Likewise, all fixed asset additions and deductions during the second half of a month are treated as if the event occurred on the first day of the *next* month. We will follow this practice in this chapter.

It is not necessary that a business use a single method of computing depreciation for all its depreciable assets. The methods used in the accounts and financial statements may also differ from the methods used in determining income taxes and property taxes. The three methods used most often are (1) straight-line, (2) units-of-production, and (3) declining-balance.[2] Exhibit 3 shows the extent of the use of these methods in financial statements.

Exhibit 3 Use of Depreciation Methods

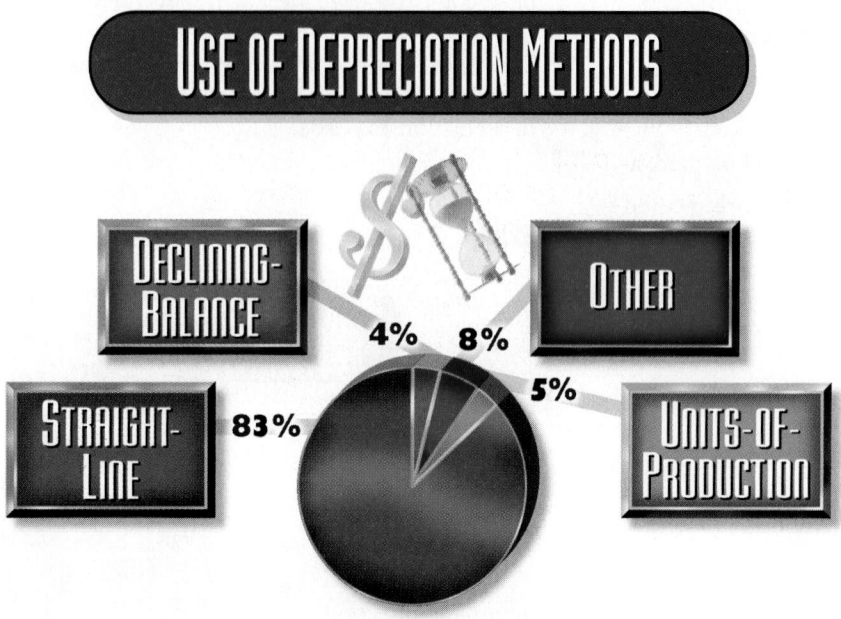

Source: *Accounting Trends & Techniques*, 53rd ed., American Institute of Certified Public Accountants, New York, 1999.

Straight-Line Method

The **straight-line method** provides for the same amount of depreciation expense for each year of the asset's useful life. For example, assume that the cost of a depreciable asset is $24,000, its estimated residual value is $2,000, and its estimated life is 5 years. The annual depreciation is computed as follows:

$$\frac{\$24,000 \text{ cost} - \$2,000 \text{ estimated residual value}}{5 \text{ years estimated life}} = \$4,400 \text{ annual depreciation}$$

When an asset is used for only part of a year, the annual depreciation is prorated. For example, assume that the fiscal year ends on December 31 and that the asset in the above example is placed in service on October 1. The depreciation for the first fiscal year of use would be $1,100 ($4,400 × 3/12).

For ease in applying the straight-line method, the annual depreciation may be converted to a percentage of the depreciable cost. This percentage is determined by dividing 100% by the number of years of useful life. For example, a useful life of 20 years converts to a 5% rate (100%/20), 8 years converts to a 12.5% rate (100%/8), and so on.[3] In the above example, the annual depreciation of $4,400 can be computed by multiplying the depreciable cost of $22,000 by 20% (100%/5).

The straight-line method is simple and is widely used. It provides a reasonable transfer of costs to periodic expense when the asset's use and the related revenues from its use are about the same from period to period.

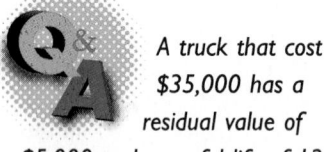

A truck that cost $35,000 has a residual value of $5,000 and a useful life of 12 years. What are (a) the depreciable cost, (b) the straight-line rate, and (c) the annual straight-line depreciation?

(a) $30,000 ($35,000 − $5,000), (b) 8⅓% (¹⁄₁₂), (c) $2,500 ($30,000 × 8⅓%).

---

[2] Another method not often used today, called the *sum-of-the-years-digits method*, is described and illustrated in the appendix at the end of this chapter.

[3] The depreciation rate may also be expressed as a fraction. For example, the annual straight-line rate for an asset with a 3-year useful life is 1/3.

Units-of-Production Method

How would you depreciate a fixed asset when its service is related to use rather than time? When the amount of use of a fixed asset varies from year to year, the units-of-production method is more appropriate than the straight-line method. In such cases, the units-of-production method better matches the depreciation expense with the related revenue.

The **units-of-production method** provides for the same amount of depreciation expense for each unit produced or each unit of capacity used by the asset. To apply this method, the useful life of the asset is expressed in terms of units of productive capacity such as hours or miles. The total depreciation expense for each accounting period is then determined by multiplying the unit depreciation by the number of units produced or used during the period. For example, assume that a machine with a cost of $24,000 and an estimated residual value of $2,000 is expected to have an estimated life of 10,000 operating hours. The depreciation for a unit of one hour is computed as follows:

$$\frac{\$24{,}000 \text{ cost} - \$2{,}000 \text{ estimated residual value}}{10{,}000 \text{ estimated hours}} = \$2.20 \text{ hourly depreciation}$$

Assuming that the machine was in operation for 2,100 hours during a year, the depreciation for that year would be $4,620 ($2.20 × 2,100 hours).

Declining-Balance Method

The **declining-balance method** provides for a declining periodic expense over the estimated useful life of the asset. To apply this method, the annual straight-line depreciation rate is doubled. For example, the declining-balance rate for an asset with an estimated life of 5 years is 40%, which is double the straight-line rate of 20% (100%/5).

For the first year of use, the cost of the asset is multiplied by the declining-balance rate. After the first year, the declining **book value** (cost minus accumulated depreciation) of the asset is multiplied by this rate. To illustrate, the annual declining-balance depreciation for an asset with an estimated 5-year life and a cost of $24,000 is shown below.

Year	Cost	Accum. Depr. at Beginning of Year	Book Value at Beginning of Year	Rate	Depreciation for Year	Book Value at End of Year
1	$24,000		$24,000.00	40%	$9,600.00	$14,400.00
2	24,000	$ 9,600.00	14,400.00	40%	5,760.00	8,640.00
3	24,000	15,360.00	8,640.00	40%	3,456.00	5,184.00
4	24,000	18,816.00	5,184.00	40%	2,073.60	3,110.40
5	24,000	20,889.60	3,110.40	—	1,110.40	2,000.00

You should note that when the declining-balance method is used, the estimated residual value is *not* considered in determining the depreciation rate. It is also ignored in computing the periodic depreciation. However, the asset should not be depreciated below its estimated residual value. In the above example, the estimated residual value was $2,000. Therefore, the depreciation for the fifth year is $1,110.40 ($3,110.40 − $2,000.00) instead of $1,244.16 (40% × $3,110.40).

In the example above, we assumed that the first use of the asset occurred at the beginning of the fiscal year. This is normally not the case in practice, however, and depreciation for the first partial year of use must be computed. For example, assume that the asset above was in service at the end of the *third* month of the fiscal year. In this case, only a portion (9/12) of the first full year's depreciation of $9,600 is allocated to the first fiscal year. Thus, depreciation of $7,200 (9/12 × $9,600) is allocated to the first partial year of use. The depreciation for the second fiscal year would then be $6,720 [40% × ($24,000 − $7,200)].

Comparing Depreciation Methods

The straight-line method provides for the same periodic amounts of depreciation expense over the life of the asset. The units-of-production method provides for periodic amounts of depreciation expense that vary, depending upon the amount the asset is used.

The declining-balance method provides for a higher depreciation amount in the first year of the asset's use, followed by a gradually declining amount. For this reason, the declining-balance method is called an **accelerated depreciation method**. It is most appropriate when the decline in an asset's productivity or earning power is greater in the early years of its use than in later years. Further, using this method is often justified because repairs tend to increase with the age of an asset. The reduced amounts of depreciation in later years are thus offset to some extent by increased repair expenses.

The periodic depreciation amounts for the straight-line method and the declining-balance method are compared in Exhibit 4. This comparison is based on an asset cost of $24,000, an estimated life of 5 years, and an estimated residual value of $2,000.

Exhibit 4 Comparing Depreciation Methods

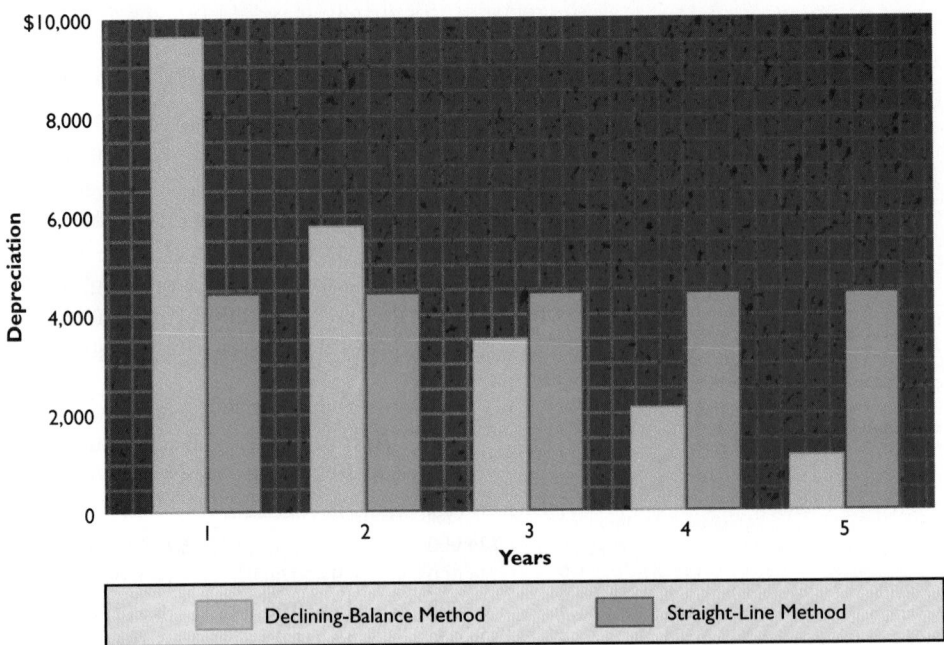

Depreciation for Federal Income Tax

The Internal Revenue Code specifies the *Modified Accelerated Cost Recovery System (MACRS)* for use by businesses in computing depreciation for tax purposes.[4] MACRS specifies eight classes of useful life and depreciation rates for each class. The two most common classes, other than real estate, are the 5-year class and the 7-year class.[5] The 5-year class includes automobiles and light-duty trucks, and the 7-year class includes most machinery and equipment. The depreciation deduction for these two classes is similar to that computed using the declining-balance method.

---

[4] Fixed assets that were acquired before 1987 are allowed to use depreciation methods other than MACRS. These are discussed in tax accounting texts.

[5] Real estate is in 27 1/2-year classes and 31 1/2-year classes and is depreciated by the straight-line method.

In using the MACRS rates, residual value is ignored, and all fixed assets are assumed to be put in and taken out of service in the middle of the year. For the 5-year-class assets, depreciation is spread over six years, as shown in the following MACRS schedule of depreciation rates:

Year	5-Year-Class Depreciation Rates
1	20.0%
2	32.0
3	19.2
4	11.5
5	11.5
6	5.8
	100.0%

What is the third year MACRS depreciation for an automobile that cost $26,000 and has a residual value of $6,500?

$4,992 ($26,000 × 19.2%)

To simplify its record keeping, a business will sometimes use the MACRS method for both financial statement and tax purposes. This is acceptable if MACRS does not result in significantly different amounts than would have been reported using one of the three depreciation methods discussed earlier in this chapter.

Using MACRS for both financial statement and tax purposes may, however, hurt a business. In one case, a business that had used MACRS depreciation for its financial statements lost a $1 million order because its fixed assets had low book values. The bank viewed these low book values as inadequate, so it would not loan the business the amount needed to produce the order.[6]

Revising Depreciation Estimates

Revising the estimates of the residual value and the useful life is normal. When these estimates are revised, they are used to determine the depreciation expense in future periods. They do not affect the amounts of depreciation expense recorded in earlier years.

To illustrate, assume that a fixed asset purchased for $130,000 was originally estimated to have a useful life of 30 years and a residual value of $10,000. The asset has been depreciated for 10 years by the straight-line method. At the end of ten years, the asset's book value (undepreciated cost) is $90,000, determined as follows:

Asset cost	$130,000
Less accumulated depreciation ($4,000 per year × 10 years)	40,000
Book value (undepreciated cost), end of tenth year	$ 90,000

For the $130,000 asset in the example on this page, assume that after 10 more years (20 years in total) its remaining useful life is estimated at 5 years with no residual value. What is the revised depreciation for the twenty-first year?

$11,200 ($130,000 − $40,000 depreciation for years 1–10 = $90,000; $90,000 − $34,000 depreciation for years 11–20 = $56,000; $56,000 divided by 5 years = $11,200)

During the eleventh year, it is estimated that the remaining useful life is 25 years (instead of 20) and that the residual value is $5,000 (instead of $10,000). The depreciation expense for each of the remaining 25 years is $3,400, computed as follows:

Book value (undepreciated cost), end of tenth year	$90,000
Less revised estimated residual value	5,000
Revised remaining depreciable cost	$85,000
Revised annual depreciation expense ($85,000/25)	$ 3,400

[6] Lee Berton, "Do's and Don'ts," *The Wall Street Journal*, June 10, 1988, p. 34R.

Composite-Rate Method

Assets may be grouped according to common traits, such as similar useful lives. For example, a group might include all delivery trucks with useful lives of less than 8 years. Likewise, a group might include all office equipment or all store fixtures. Depreciation may be determined for each group of assets, using a single *composite rate*, rather than a rate for each individual asset. The depreciation computations are similar for groups of assets as for individual assets.

Capital and Revenue Expenditures

objective 3

Classify fixed asset costs as either capital expenditures or revenue expenditures.

The costs of acquiring fixed assets, adding to a fixed asset, improving a fixed asset, or extending a fixed asset's useful life are called **capital expenditures**. Such expenditures are recorded by either debiting the asset account or its related accumulated depreciation account. Costs that benefit only the current period or costs incurred for normal maintenance and repairs are called **revenue expenditures**. Such expenditures are debited to expense accounts. For example, the cost of replacing spark plugs in an automobile or the cost of repainting a building should be debited to an expense account.

To properly match revenues and expenses, it is important to distinguish between capital and revenue expenditures. Capital expenditures will affect the depreciation expense of more than one period, while revenue expenditures will affect the expenses of only the current period.

Types of Capital Expenditures

We have discussed accounting for the initial costs of acquiring fixed assets. Capital expenditures on assets after they have been acquired may be either (a) additions, (b) betterments, or (c) extraordinary repairs.

Additions to Fixed Assets

The cost of an addition to a fixed asset should be debited to the related fixed asset account. For example, the cost of adding a new wing to a building should be debited to the building account. This cost should then be depreciated over its estimated useful life or the remaining useful life of the building, whichever is shorter.

Betterments

An expenditure that improves a fixed asset's operating efficiency or capacity for its remaining useful life is called a **betterment**. Such expenditures should be debited to the related fixed asset account. For example, if the power unit attached to a machine is replaced by one of greater capacity, its cost should be debited to the machine account. Also, the cost and the accumulated depreciation related to the old power unit should be removed from the accounts. The cost of the new power unit should then be depreciated over its estimated useful life or the remaining useful life of the machine, whichever is shorter.

Extraordinary Repairs

An expenditure that increases the useful life of an asset beyond its original estimate is called an **extraordinary repair**. Such expenditures should be debited to the related accumulated depreciation account. In such cases, the repairs are said to *restore* or *make good* a portion of the depreciation recorded in prior years. The depreciation for future periods should be computed on the basis of the revised book value of the asset and the revised estimate of the remaining useful life.

Identify each of the items related to a truck as an addition, a betterment, or an extraordinary repair: (a) a snowplow attachment that allows the truck to be used for snow removal, (b) a new transmission, (c) a hydraulic hitch to replace a manual hitch.

(a) addition, (b) extraordinary repair, (c) betterment.

To illustrate, assume that a machine costing $50,000 has no estimated residual value and an estimated useful life of 10 years. Assume also that the machine has been depreciated for 6 years by the straight-line method ($5,000 annual depreciation). At the beginning of the seventh year, an $11,500 extraordinary repair increases the remaining useful life of the machine to 7 years (instead of 4). The repair of $11,500 should be debited to Accumulated Depreciation. The annual depreciation for the remaining 7 years of use would be $4,500, computed as follows:

Cost of machine		$50,000
Less Accumulated Depreciation balance:		
Depreciation for first 6 years ($5,000 × 6)	$30,000	
Deduct debit for extraordinary repair	11,500	
Balance of Accumulated Depreciation		18,500
Revised book value of machine after extraordinary repair		$31,500
Annual depreciation ($31,500/7 years remaining useful life)		$ 4,500

Summary of Capital and Revenue Expenditures

Exhibit 5 summarizes the accounting for capital and revenue expenditures related to fixed assets.

Exhibit 5 Capital and Revenue Expenditures

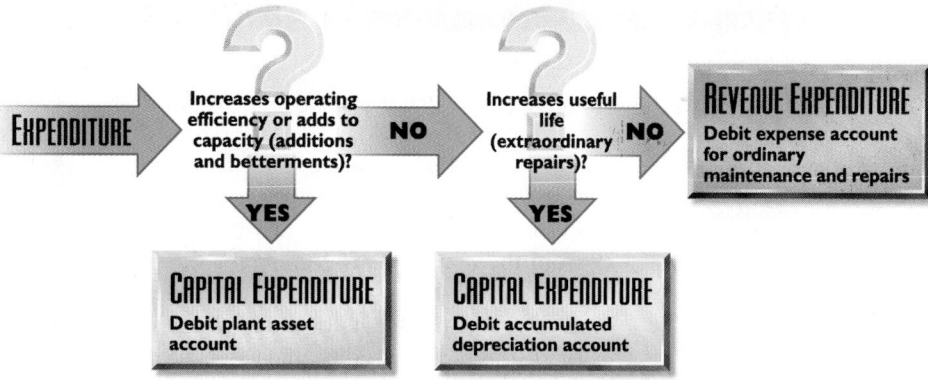

BUSINESS ON STAGE

Running Like a Top

Businesses that use equipment to provide goods or services must maintain that equipment. These businesses usually follow one of three maintenance philosophies: (1) corrective maintenance, (2) preventive maintenance, and (3) predictive maintenance.

• **Corrective maintenance.** Under this philosophy, equipment is repaired when the equipment breaks down. It would be similar to you replacing your car's engine every time it froze up because it needed an an oil change. Compa-

nies that use corrective maintenance don't want to waste time performing maintenance until there is an actual failure. Unfortunately, an unplanned machine failure can cause significant disruptions. Such disruptions include unplanned stops in production, delays in waiting for replacement parts, and additional repair due to broken machine components. Because of this, many consider corrective maintenance a poor philosophy.

- **Preventive maintenance.** Under this philosophy, equipment is repaired under a planned schedule. It would be similar to you changing your car's oil every 6,000 miles. Preventive maintenance is considered superior to corrective maintenance because the maintenance is planned. Therefore, employees can be trained, multiple machines can be repaired, or housekeeping can be performed during the scheduled maintenance. In addition,

replacement parts can be ordered ahead of time, minimizing delays caused by emergencies. Lastly, preventive maintenance may reduce the overall maintenance expenditures, because actual machine failures are minimized.

- **Predictive maintenance.** Under this new maintenance philosophy, equipment is repaired at the exact time it needs to be repaired prior to actual failure. It would be similar to you changing your car's oil when a sensor in the car indicated that the oil had reached a given level of impurity. Predictive maintenance is considered superior to preventive maintenance because maintenance is performed only when it is actually needed. This

may reduce the total amount of time that equipment spends in maintenance during its life, compared to preventive maintenance. At the same time, however, predictive maintenance may still be planned, once it is indicated—so it has the same advantages as preventive maintenance. New sensors and computers are being developed to support predictive maintenance. Vibration sensors are one example. These sensors are placed on machines to measure vibration, which indicates bearing wear. When the vibration levels reach a certain point, bearings are replaced, which is just prior to their failing. ∎

Disposal of Fixed Assets

objective 4

Journalize entries for the disposal of fixed assets.

Fixed assets that are no longer useful may be discarded, sold, or traded for other fixed assets. The details of the entry to record a disposal will vary. In all cases, however, the book value of the asset must be removed from the accounts. The entry for this purpose debits the asset's accumulated depreciation account for its balance on the date of disposal and credits the asset account for the cost of the asset.

A fixed asset should not be removed from the accounts only because it has been fully depreciated. If the asset is still used

> The entry to record the disposal of a fixed asset removes the cost of the asset and its accumulated depreciation from the accounts.

by the business, the cost and accumulated depreciation should remain in the ledger. This maintains accountability for the asset in the ledger. If the book value of the asset was removed from the ledger, the accounts would contain no evidence of the continued existence of the asset. In addition, the cost and the accumulated depreciation data on such assets are often needed for property tax and income tax reports.

Discarding Fixed Assets

When fixed assets are no longer useful to the business and have no residual or market value, they are discarded. To illustrate, assume that an item of equipment acquired at a cost of $25,000 is fully depreciated at December 31, the end of the preceding fiscal year. On February 14, the equipment is discarded. The entry to record this is as follows:

Feb.	14	Accumulated Depreciation—Equipment	25 0 0 0 00		
		Equipment		25 0 0 0 00
		To write off equipment discarded.		

If an asset has not been fully depreciated, depreciation should be recorded prior to removing it from service and from the accounting records. To illustrate, assume that equipment costing $6,000 is depreciated at an annual straight-line rate of 10%. In addition, assume that on December 31 of the preceding fiscal year, the accumulated depreciation balance, after adjusting entries, is $4,750. Finally, assume that the asset is removed from service on the following March 24. The entry to record the depreciation for the three months of the current period prior to the asset's removal from service is as follows:

Mar.	24	Depreciation Expense—Equipment	1 5 0 00		
		Accumulated Depreciation—Equipment		1 5 0 00
		To record current depreciation on		
		equipment discarded ($600 × $^3/_{12}$).		

The discarding of the equipment is then recorded by the following entry:

Mar.	24	Accumulated Depreciation—Equipment	4 9 0 0 00		
		Loss on Disposal of Fixed Assets	1 1 0 0 00		
		Equipment		6 0 0 0 00
		To write off equipment discarded.		

The loss of $1,100 is recorded because the balance of the accumulated depreciation account ($4,900) is less than the balance in the equipment account ($6,000). Losses on the discarding of fixed assets are nonoperating items and are normally reported in the Other Expense section of the income statement.

Selling Fixed Assets

The entry to record the sale of a fixed asset is similar to the entries illustrated above, except that the cash or other asset received must also be recorded. If the selling price is more than the book value of the asset, the transaction results in a gain. If the selling price is less than the book value, there is a loss.

To illustrate, assume that equipment is acquired at a cost of $10,000 and is depreciated at an annual straight-line rate of 10%. The equipment is sold for cash on October 12 of the eighth year of its use. The balance of the accumulated depreciation account as of the preceding December 31 is $7,000. The entry to update the depreciation for the nine months of the current year is as follows:

Oct.	12	Depreciation Expense—Equipment	7 5 0 00		
		Accumulated Depreciation—Equipment		7 5 0 00
		To record current depreciation on		
		equipment sold ($10,000 × $^3/_4$ × 10%).		

After the current depreciation is recorded, the book value of the asset is $2,250 ($10,000 − $7,750). The entries to record the sale, assuming three different selling prices, are as follows:

Sold at book value, for $2,250. No gain or loss.

Oct.	12	Cash	2 2 5 0 00		
		Accumulated Depreciation—Equipment	7 7 5 0 00		
		Equipment		10 0 0 0 00	

Sold below book value, for $1,000. Loss of $1,250.

Oct.	12	Cash	1 0 0 0 00		
		Accumulated Depreciation—Equipment	7 7 5 0 00		
		Loss on Disposal of Fixed Assets	1 2 5 0 00		
		Equipment		10 0 0 0 00	

Sold above book value, for $2,800. Gain of $550.

Oct.	12	Cash	2 8 0 0 00		
		Accumulated Depreciation—Equipment	7 7 5 0 00		
		Equipment		10 0 0 0 00	
		Gain on Disposal of Fixed Assets		5 5 0 00	

Exchanging Similar Fixed Assets

Old equipment is often traded in for new equipment having a similar use. In such cases, the seller allows the buyer an amount for the old equipment traded in. This amount, called the **trade-in allowance**, may be either greater or less than the book value of the old equipment. The remaining balance—the amount owed—is either paid in cash or recorded as a liability. It is normally called **boot**, which is its tax name.

Gains on Exchanges

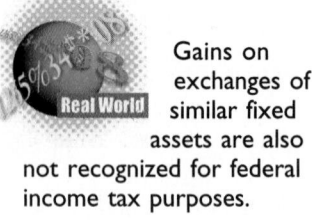

Gains on exchanges of similar fixed assets are also not recognized for federal income tax purposes.

Gains on exchanges of similar fixed assets are not recognized for financial reporting purposes.[7] This is based on the theory that revenue occurs from the production and sale of goods produced by fixed assets and not from the exchange of similar fixed assets.

When the trade-in allowance exceeds the book value of an asset traded in and no gain is recognized, the cost recorded for the new asset can be determined in either of two ways:

> **1. Cost of new asset = List price of new asset − Unrecognized gain**
>
> *or*
>
> **2. Cost of new asset = Cash given (or liability assumed) + Book value of old asset**

---

[7] Gains on exchanges of similar fixed assets are recognized if cash (boot) is received. This topic is discussed in advanced accounting texts.

To illustrate, assume the following exchange:

Similar equipment acquired (new):

List price of new equipment	$5,000
Trade-in allowance on old equipment	1,100
Cash paid at June 19, date of exchange	$3,900

Equipment traded in (old):

Cost of old equipment	$4,000
Accumulated depreciation at date of exchange	3,200
Book value at June 19, date of exchange	$ 800

Recorded cost of new equipment:

Method One:

List price of new equipment		$5,000
Trade-in allowance	$1,100	
Book value of old equipment	800	
Unrecognized gain on exchange		(300)
Cost of new equipment		$4,700

Method Two:

Book value of old equipment	$ 800
Cash paid at date of exchange	3,900
Cost of new equipment	$4,700

Q&A *Equipment with a book value of $14,000 is traded in for similar equipment with a list price of $50,000. A trade-in allowance of $15,000 was allowed on the old equipment. What is the cost of the new equipment to be recorded in the accounts?*

$49,000 ($50,000 − $1,000 gain, or $14,000 + $35,000 boot)

The entry to record this exchange and the payment of cash is as follows:

June	19	Accumulated Depreciation—Equipment	3 2 0 0 00		
		Equipment (new equipment)	4 7 0 0 00		
		Equipment (old equipment)		4 0 0 0 00	
		Cash		3 9 0 0 00	
		To record exchange of equipment.			

Not recognizing the $300 gain ($1,100 trade-in allowance minus $800 book value) at the time of the exchange reduces future depreciation expense. That is, the depreciation expense for the new asset is based on a cost of $4,700 rather than on the list price of $5,000. In effect, the unrecognized gain of $300 reduces the total amount of depreciation taken during the life of the equipment by $300.

Losses on Exchanges

Real World Losses on exchanges of similar fixed assets are *not* recognized for federal income tax purposes.

For financial reporting purposes, losses are recognized on exchanges of similar fixed assets if the trade-in allowance is less than the book value of the old equipment. When there is a loss, the cost recorded for the new asset should be the market (list) price. To illustrate, assume the following exchange:

Similar equipment acquired (new):

List price of new equipment	$10,000
Trade-in allowance on old equipment	2,000
Cash paid at September 7, date of exchange	$ 8,000

Equipment traded in (old):

Cost of old equipment	$ 7,000
Accumulated depreciation at date of exchange	4,600
Book value at September 7, date of exchange	$ 2,400
Trade-in allowance on old equipment	2,000
Loss on exchange	$ 400

The entry to record the exchange is as follows:

Sept.	7	Accumulated Depreciation—Equipment	4 6 0 0 00		
		Equipment	10 0 0 0 00		
		Loss on Disposal of Fixed Assets	4 0 0 00		
		Equipment		7 0 0 0 00
		Cash		8 0 0 0 00
		To record exchange of equipment,		
		with loss.		

Review of Accounting for Exchanges of Similar Fixed Assets

Exhibit 6 reviews the accounting for exchanges of similar fixed assets, using the following data:

List price of new equipment acquired	$15,000
Cost of old equipment traded in	$12,500
Accumulated depreciation at date of exchange	10,100
Book value at date of exchange	$ 2,400

Leasing Fixed Assets

objective 5

Define a lease and summarize the accounting rules related to the leasing of fixed assets.

You are probably familiar with leases. A *lease* is a contract for the use of an asset for a stated period of time. Leases are frequently used in business. For example, automobiles, computers, medical equipment, buildings, and airplanes are often leased.

The two parties to a lease contract are the lessor and the lessee. The *lessor* is the party who owns the asset. The *lessee* is the party to whom the rights to use the asset are granted by the lessor. The lessee is obligated to make periodic rent payments for the lease term. All leases are classified by the lessee as either capital leases or operating leases.

Real World

Delta Air Lines had over $2.3 billion in lease commitments for the year ending June 30, 2000. Of 584 aircraft as of June 30, 1999, 256 were leased.

A **capital lease** is accounted for as if the lessee has, in fact, purchased the asset. The lessee debits an asset account for the fair market value of the asset and credits a long-term lease liability account. The accounting for capital leases and the criteria that a capital lease must satisfy are discussed in more advanced accounting texts.

A lease that is not classified as a capital lease for accounting purposes is classified as an **operating lease**. The lessee records the payments under an operating lease by debiting *Rent Expense* and crediting *Cash*. Neither future lease obligations

Real World

Of the companies surveyed in a recent edition of *Accounting Trends & Techniques*, 91% reported leases.

Exhibit 6 Summary Illustration—Accounting for Exchanges of Similar Fixed Assets

CASE ONE (GAIN): Trade-in allowance is more than book value of asset traded in.

Trade-in allowance, $3,000; cash paid, $12,000 ($15,000 − $3,000)

Cost of new asset	List price of new asset acquired, less unrecognized gain: $14,400 ($15,000 − $600) **or** Cash paid plus book value of asset traded in: $14,400 ($12,000 + $2,400)
Gain recognized	None

Entry	Equipment 14,400
	Accumulated Depreciation 10,100
	    Equipment 12,500
	    Cash 12,000

CASE TWO (LOSS): Trade-in allowance is less than book value of asset traded in.

Trade-in allowance, $2,000; cash paid, $13,000 ($15,000 − $2,000)

Cost of new asset	List price of new asset acquired: $15,000
Loss recognized	$400

Entry	Equipment 15,000
	Accumulated Depreciation 10,100
	Loss on Disposal of Fixed Assets 400
	    Equipment 12,500
	    Cash 13,000

nor the future rights to use the leased asset are recognized in the accounts. However, the lessee must disclose future lease commitments in footnotes to the financial statements.

The asset rentals described in earlier chapters of this text were accounted for as operating leases. To simplify, we will continue to treat asset leases as operating leases.

Internal Control of Fixed Assets

objective 6

Describe internal controls over fixed assets.

Because of their dollar value and long-term nature, it is important to design and apply effective internal controls over fixed assets. Such controls should begin with authorization and approval procedures for the purchase of fixed assets. Controls should also exist to ensure that fixed assets are acquired at the lowest possible costs. One procedure to achieve this objective is to require competitive bids from preapproved vendors.

As soon as a fixed asset is received, it should be inspected and tagged for control purposes and recorded in a subsidiary ledger. This establishes the initial accountability for the asset. Subsidiary ledgers for fixed assets are also useful in determining depreciation expense and recording disposals. Operating data that may be recorded in the subsidiary ledger, such as number of breakdowns, length of time out of service, and cost of repairs, are useful in deciding whether to replace the asset. A company

Subsidiary ledger

that maintains a computerized subsidiary ledger may use bar-coded tags, similar to the one on the back of this textbook, so that fixed asset data can be directly scanned into computer records.

Fixed assets should be insured against theft, fire, flooding, or other disasters. They should also be safeguarded from theft, misuse, or other damage. For example, fixed assets that are highly open to theft, such as computers, should be locked or otherwise protected when not in use. For computers, safeguarding also includes climate controls and special fire-extinguishing equipment. Procedures should also exist for training employees to properly operate fixed assets such as equipment and machinery.

A physical inventory of fixed assets should be taken periodically in order to verify the accuracy of the accounting records. Such an inventory would detect missing, obsolete, or idle fixed assets. In addition, fixed assets should be inspected periodically in order to determine their condition.

Careful control should also be exercised over the disposal of fixed assets. All disposals should be properly authorized and approved. Fully depreciated assets should be retained in the accounting records until disposal has been authorized and they are removed from service.

Natural Resources

objective 7

Compute depletion and journalize the entry for depletion.

The fixed assets of some businesses include timber, metal ores, minerals, or other natural resources. As these businesses harvest or mine and then sell these resources, a portion of the cost of acquiring them must be debited to an expense account. This process of transferring the cost of natural resources to an expense account is called **depletion**. The amount of depletion is determined by multiplying the quantity extracted during the period by the depletion rate. This rate is computed by dividing the cost of the mineral deposit by its estimated size.

Computing depletion is similar to computing units-of-production depreciation. To illustrate, assume that a business paid $400,000 for the mining rights to a mineral deposit estimated at 1,000,000 tons of ore. The depletion rate is $0.40 per ton ($400,000/1,000,000 tons). If 90,000 tons are mined during the year, the periodic depletion is $36,000 (90,000 tons × $0.40). The entry to record the depletion is shown below.

Q&A

A business purchased mineral rights to 250,000 tons of ore for $1,500,000. If 35,000 tons of ore were mined in the first year, what are (a) the depletion rate per ton and (2) the depletion expense for the first year?

(a) **$6 per ton ($1,500,000/ 250,000 tons); (b) $210,000 (35,000 tons × $6)**

			Adjusting Entry								
Dec.	31	Depletion Expense			36 0 0 0 00				
		Accumulated Depletion					36 0 0 0 00

Like the accumulated depreciation account, Accumulated Depletion is a *contra asset* account. It is reported on the balance sheet as a deduction from the cost of the mineral deposit.

Intangible Assets

objective 8

Journalize the entries for acquiring and amortizing intangible assets, such as patents, copyrights, and goodwill.

Patents, copyrights, trademarks, and goodwill are long-term assets that are useful in the operations of a business and are not held for sale. These assets are called **intangible assets** because they do not exist physically.

The basic principles of accounting for intangible assets are like those described earlier for fixed assets. The major concerns are determining (1) the initial cost and (2) the **amortization**—the amount of cost to transfer to expense. Amortization results from the passage of time or a decline in the usefulness of the intangible asset.

Patents

Manufacturers may acquire exclusive rights to produce and sell goods with one or more unique features. Such rights are granted by **patents**, which the federal government issues to inventors. These rights continue in effect for 20 years. A business may purchase patent rights from others, or it may obtain patents developed by its own research and development efforts.

The initial cost of a purchased patent, including any related legal fees, should be debited to an asset account. This cost should be written off, or amortized, over the years of the patent's expected usefulness. This period of time may be less than the remaining legal life of the patent. The estimated useful life of the patent may also change as technology or consumer tastes change.

The straight-line method is normally used to determine the periodic amortization. When the amortization is recorded, it is debited to an expense account and credited directly to the patents account. Not using a separate contra asset account is common for all intangible assets.

To illustrate, assume that at the beginning of its fiscal year a business acquires patent rights for $100,000. The patent had been granted 6 years earlier by the Federal Patent Office. Although the patent will not expire for 14 years, its remaining useful life is estimated as 5 years. The entry to amortize the patent at the end of the fiscal year is as follows:

			Adjusting Entry		
Dec.	31	Amortization Expense—Patents	20 0 0 0 00		
		Patents		20 0 0 0 00	

Rather than purchase patent rights, a business may incur significant costs in developing patents through its own research and development efforts. Such **research and development costs** are usually accounted for as current operating expenses in the period in which they are incurred.

Expensing research and development costs in the period they are incurred is justified for two reasons. First, the future benefits from research and development efforts are highly uncertain. In fact, most research and development efforts do not result in patents. Second, even if a patent is granted, it may be difficult to objectively estimate its cost. If many research projects are in process at the same time, for example, it is difficult to separate the costs of one project from another.

Copyrights and Trademarks

The exclusive right to publish and sell a literary, artistic, or musical composition is granted by a **copyright**. Copyrights are issued by the federal government and extend for 70 years beyond the author's death. The costs of a copyright include all costs of creating the work plus any administrative or legal costs of obtaining the

The **RIAA** (**Recording Industry Association of America**) initiated a copyright infringement suit against **Napster.com**. The RIAA alledged that Napster promoted the piracy of MP3 music files through its file-sharing software.

Coke® is one of the world's most recogniz-able trademarks. As stated in *LIFE*, "Two-thirds of the earth is covered by water; the rest is covered by Coke. If the French are known for wine and the Germans for beer, America achieved global beverage dominance with fizzy water and caramel color."

copyright. A copyright that is purchased from another should be recorded at the price paid for it. Because of the uncertainty regarding the useful life of a copyright, it is normally amortized over a short period of time. For example, the copyright costs of this text are amortized over 3 years.

A **trademark** is a name, term, or symbol used to identify a business and its products. For example, the distinctive red-and-white Coca Cola logo is an example of a trademark. Most businesses identify their trademarks with ® in their advertise-ments and on their products. Under federal law, businesses can protect against others using their trademarks by registering them for 10 years and renewing the registra-tion for 10-year periods thereafter. Like a copyright, the legal costs of registering a trademark with the federal government should be recorded as an asset. Also, if a trademark is purchased from another business, the cost of its purchase would be recorded as an asset. The cost of a trademark should be amortized over its esti-mated useful life, but not more than 40 years.

Goodwill

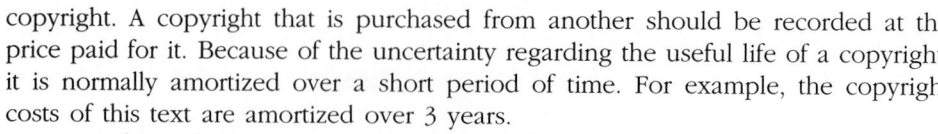

In a recent annual report, **H.J. Heinz Company** reported that it amortizes goodwill, trademarks, and other intangibles over periods ranging from 3 to 40 years.

In business, **goodwill** refers to an intangible asset of a business that is created from such favorable factors as location, product quality, reputation, and managerial skill. Goodwill allows a business to earn a rate of return on its investment that is often in excess of the normal rate for other firms in the same business.

Generally accepted accounting principles permit the recording of goodwill in the accounts only if it is objectively determined by a transaction. An example of a transaction that may justify recording goodwill is the purchase or sale of a business. Goodwill must be amortized over its estimated useful life, which cannot exceed 40 years.[8]

Financial Reporting for Fixed Assets and Intangible Assets

objective 9

Describe how depreciation expense is reported in an income statement, and pre-pare a balance sheet that includes fixed assets and intangible assets.

How should fixed assets and intangible assets be reported in the financial state-ments? The amount of depreciation and amortization expense of a period should be reported separately in the income statement or disclosed in a footnote. A general description of the method or methods used in computing depreciation should also be reported.

The amount of each major class of fixed assets should be disclosed in the bal-ance sheet or in footnotes. The related accumulated depreciation should also be disclosed, either by major class or in total. The fixed assets may be shown at their **book value** (cost less accumulated depreciation), which can also be described as their **net** amount. If there are too many classes of fixed assets, a single amount may be presented in the balance sheet, supported by a separate detailed listing. Fixed assets are normally presented under the more descriptive caption of **property, plant, and equipment**.

The cost of mineral rights or ore deposits is normally shown as part of the fixed assets section of the balance sheet. The related accumulated depletion should also be disclosed. In some cases, the mineral rights are shown net of depletion on the face of the balance sheet, accompanied by a footnote that discloses the amount of the accumulated depletion.

Intangible assets are usually reported in the balance sheet in a separate section immediately following fixed assets. The balance of each major class of intangible as-sets should be disclosed at an amount net of amortization taken to date. Exhibit 7 is a partial balance sheet that shows the reporting of fixed assets and intangible assets.

---

[8] The FASB has proposed that goodwill not be amortized unless the value of the goodwill is determined to be lessened.

Exhibit 7 Fixed Assets and Intangible Assets in the Balance Sheet

Discovery Mining Co.
Balance Sheet
December 31, 20—

Assets

Total current assets . . . . $ 462,500

Property, plant, and equipment:	Cost	Accum. Depr.	Book Value	
Land	$ 30,000	—	$ 30,000	
Buildings	110,000	$ 26,000	84,000	
Factory equipment	650,000	192,000	458,000	
Office equipment	120,000	13,000	107,000	
	$ 910,000	$ 231,000		$679,000

Mineral deposits:	Cost	Accum. Depl.	Book Value	
Alaska deposit	$1,200,000	$ 800,000	$ 400,000	
Wyoming deposit	750,000	200,000	550,000	
	$1,950,000	$1,000,000		950,000

Total property, plant,
and equipment   1,629,000

Intangible assets:

Patents . . . . $ 75,000

Goodwill   50,000

Total intangible assets   125,000

FINANCIAL ANALYSIS AND INTERPRETATION

objective 10

Compute and interpret the ratio of fixed assets to long-term liabilities.

Long-term liabilities are often secured by fixed assets. The ratio of total fixed assets to long-term liabilities provides a solvency measure that indicates the margin of safety to creditors. It also gives an indication of the potential ability of the business to borrow additional funds on a long-term basis. The **ratio of fixed assets to long-term liabilities** is computed as follows:

$$\text{Ratio of fixed assets to long-term liabilities (debt)} = \frac{\text{Fixed assets (net)}}{\text{Long-term liabilities (debt)}}$$

To illustrate, the following data were taken from the 2000 and 1999 financial statements of **Procter & Gamble**:

	(in millions)	
	2000	**1999**
Property, plant, and equipment (net)	$13,692	$12,626
Long-term debt	8,916	6,231

The ratio of fixed assets to long-term liabilities (debt) is 1.5 ($13,692/$8,916) for 2000 and 2.0 ($12,626/$6,231) for 1999. The decrease in the ratio from 1999 to 2000 indicates less of a margin of safety for creditors. As with other financial measures, the interpretation and analysis is enhanced by comparisons over time and with industry averages.

ENCORE

The Ultimate Inventor

Would you like to become an inventor and own patents worth millions? Yoshiro Nakamatsu, who bills himself as the Thomas Edison of Japan, hopes to open a school that will teach people how to create new products. Yoshiro Nakamatsu is the president of Tokyo's **Hi-Tech Innovation Institute** and claims to have 3,042 patents over his inventing career. Nakamatsu's net worth from royalties from his inventions is estimated at $75 million.

At the age of 5, with encouragement from his grandfather, Nakamatsu invented a stabilizer to make planes fly better. He was granted his first patent at age 14. Since then, he has licensed 16 patents to **IBM**, including one for his 1952 invention of the floppy disk for personal computers. Some of Nakamatsu's other inventions and what he claims they do include the following:

- **Yummy TV.** A snack food designed to relieve eye strain caused by watching too much TV.

- **Enerex.** An engine that produces energy from water.
- **Cerebrex Chair.** A chair that uses electronic impulses to both sharpen the mind and rest the body.
- **Nakamatsu Golf Putter.** A putter that has an oversized vibrating handle to make putting 93 percent accurate within 10 feet.
- **Anti-Gravity Floating Vibrating Three-Dimensional Sonic System.** A speaker system for stereo compact disc players and other electronic products.
- **Magnetic Eyeglasses.** Eyeglasses that have magnets attached to them for improving the blood circulation of the eyes.
- **Dr. Nakamatsu's Yummi Nutri Brain Biscuits.** Food for your brain.
- **Nakamatsu's Engine.** An engine that is far more efficient than gasoline or electric engines because it runs on "cosmic" power.

In his lectures, Nakamatsu offers the following advice on how to become a genius and excel at inventing: (1) swim, (2) lift weights, (3) sleep less than six hours a night, (4) work between the hours of midnight and 4 a.m., and (5) never have sex before the age of 24. ■

Source: Dean Takahashi, "Japanese Inventor Nearly Triples Edison's Output," *The Austin American-Statesman,* May 17, 1996.

APPENDIX: SUM-OF-THE-YEARS-DIGITS DEPRECIATION

At one time, the sum-of-the-years-digits method of depreciation was used by many businesses. However, the tax law changes of the 1980s limited its use for tax purposes.

Under the **sum-of-the-years-digits method,** depreciation expense is determined by multiplying the original cost of the asset less its estimated residual value by a smaller fraction each year. Thus, the sum-of-the-years-digits method is similar to the declining-balance method in that the depreciation expense declines each year.

The denominator of the fraction used in determining the depreciation expense is the sum of the digits of the years of the asset's useful life. For example, an asset with a useful life of 5 years would have a denominator of 15 (5 + 4 + 3 + 2 +

A recent edition of *Accounting Trends & Techniques* reported that only 1%–2% of the surveyed companies now use this method for financial reporting purposes.

1).[9] The numerator of the fraction is the number of years of useful life remaining at the beginning of each year for which depreciation is being computed. Thus, the numerator decreases each year by 1. For a useful life of 5 years, the numerator is 5 the first year, 4 the second year, 3 the third year, and so on.

The following depreciation schedule illustrates the sum-of-the-years-digits method for an asset with a cost of $24,000, an estimated residual value of $2,000, and an estimated useful life of 5 years:

Year	Cost Less Residual Value	Rate	Depreciation for Year	Accum. Depr. at End of Year	Book Value at End of Year
1	$22,000	5/15	$7,333.33	$ 7,333.33	$16,666.67
2	22,000	4/15	5,866.67	13,200.00	10,800.00
3	22,000	3/15	4,400.00	17,600.00	6,400.00
4	22,000	2/15	2,933.33	20,533.33	3,466.67
5	22,000	1/15	1,466.67	22,000.00	2,000.00

What if the fixed asset is not placed in service at the beginning of the year? When the date an asset is first put into service is not the beginning of a fiscal year, each full year's depreciation must be allocated between the two fiscal years benefited. To illustrate, assume that the asset in the above example was put into service at the beginning of the fourth month of the first fiscal year. The depreciation for that year would be $5,500 ($9/12 \times 5/15 \times $22,000$). The depreciation for the second year would be $6,233.33, computed as follows:

$3/12 \times 5/15 \times $22,000$	$1,833.33
$9/12 \times 4/15 \times $22,000$	4,400.00
Total depreciation for second fiscal year	$6,233.33

KEY POINTS

1 Define fixed assets and describe the accounting for their cost.

Fixed assets are long-term tangible assets that are owned by the business and are used in the normal operations of the business. Examples of fixed assets are equipment, buildings, and land. The initial cost of a fixed asset includes all amounts spent to get the asset in place and ready for use. For example, sales tax, freight, insurance in transit, and installation costs are all included in the cost of a fixed asset. As time passes, all fixed assets except land lose their ability to provide services. As a result, the cost of a fixed asset should be transferred to an expense account, in a systematic manner, during the asset's expected useful life. This periodic transfer of cost to expense is called depreciation.

2 Compute depreciation, using the following methods: straight-line method, units-of-production method, and declining-balance method.

In computing depreciation, three factors need to be considered: (1) the fixed asset's initial cost, (2) the useful life of the asset, and (3) the residual value of the asset.

The straight-line method spreads the initial cost less the residual value equally over the useful life. The units-of-production method spreads the initial cost less the residual value equally over the units expected to be produced by the asset during its useful life. The declining-balance method is applied by multiplying the declining book value of the asset by twice the straight-line rate.

3 Classify fixed asset costs as either capital expenditures or revenue expenditures.

Costs for additions to fixed assets and other costs related to improving efficiency or capacity are classified as capital expenditures. Costs for additions to an asset and costs that add to the usefulness of the asset for more than one period (called betterments) are also classified as capital expenditures.

[9] The denominator can also be determined from the following formula: $S = N[(N + 1)/2]$, where S = sum of the digits and N = number of years of estimated life.

Costs that increase the useful life of an asset beyond the original estimate are capital expenditures and are called extraordinary repairs. Expenditures that benefit only the current period or that maintain normal operating efficiency are debited to expense accounts and are classified as revenue expenditures.

4 Journalize entries for the disposal of fixed assets.

The journal entries to record disposals of fixed assets will vary. In all cases, however, any depreciation for the current period should be recorded, and the book value of the asset is then removed from the accounts. The entry to remove the book value from the accounts is a debit to the asset's accumulated depreciation account and a credit to the asset account for the cost of the asset. For assets retired from service, a loss may be recorded for any remaining book value of the asset.

When a fixed asset is sold, the book value is removed and the cash or other asset received is also recorded. If the selling price is more than the book value of the asset, the transaction results in a gain. If the selling price is less than the book value, there is a loss.

When a fixed asset is exchanged for another of similar nature, no gain is recognized on the exchange. The acquired asset's cost is adjusted for any gains. A loss on an exchange of similar assets is recorded.

5 Define a lease and summarize the accounting rules related to the leasing of fixed assets.

A lease is a contract for the use of an asset for a period of time. A capital lease is accounted for as if the lessee has purchased the asset. The lease payments under an operating lease are accounted for as rent expense for the lessee.

6 Describe internal controls over fixed assets.

Internal controls over fixed assets should include procedures for authorizing the purchase of assets. Once acquired, fixed assets should be safeguarded from theft, misuse, or damage. A physical inventory of fixed assets should be taken periodically.

7 Compute depletion and journalize the entry for depletion.

The amount of periodic depletion is computed by multiplying the quantity of minerals extracted during the period by a depletion rate. The depletion rate is computed by dividing the cost of the mineral deposit by its estimated size. The entry to record depletion debits a depletion expense account and credits an accumulated depletion account.

8 Journalize the entries for acquiring and amortizing intangible assets, such as patents, copyrights, and goodwill.

Long-term assets that are without physical attributes but are used in the business are classified as intangible assets. Examples of intangible assets are patents, copyrights, trademarks, and goodwill. The initial cost of an intangible asset should be debited to an asset account. This cost should be written off, or amortized, over the years of the asset's expected usefulness by debiting an expense account and crediting the intangible asset account.

9 Describe how depreciation expense is reported in an income statement, and prepare a balance sheet that includes fixed assets and intangible assets.

The amount of depreciation expense and the method or methods used in computing depreciation should be disclosed in the financial statements. In addition, each major class of fixed assets should be disclosed, along with the related accumulated depreciation. Intangible assets are usually presented in the balance sheet in a separate section immediately following fixed assets. Each major class of intangible assets should be disclosed at an amount net of the amortization recorded to date.

10 Compute and interpret the ratio of fixed assets to long-term liabilities.

The ratio of fixed assets to long-term liabilities is a solvency measure that indicates the margin of safety to creditors. It also provides an indication of the ability of a company to borrow additional funds on a long-term basis.

ILLUSTRATIVE PROBLEM

McCollum Company, a furniture wholesaler, acquired new equipment at a cost of $150,000 at the beginning of the fiscal year. The equipment has an estimated life of 5 years and an estimated residual value of $12,000. Ellen McCollum, the president, has requested information regarding alternative depreciation methods.

Instructions

1. Determine the annual depreciation for each of the five years of estimated useful life of the equipment, the accumulated depreciation at the end of each year, and the

book value of the equipment at the end of each year by (a) the straight-line method and (b) the declining-balance method (at twice the straight-line rate).

2. Assume that the equipment was depreciated under the declining-balance method. In the first week of the fifth year, the equipment was traded in for similar equipment priced at $175,000. The trade-in allowance on the old equipment was $10,000, and cash was paid for the balance. Journalize the entry to record the exchange.

Solution

1.

	Year	Depreciation Expense	Accumulated Depreciation, End of Year	Book Value, End of Year
a.	1	$27,600*	$ 27,600	$122,400
	2	27,600	55,200	94,800
	3	27,600	82,800	67,200
	4	27,600	110,400	39,600
	5	27,600	138,000	12,000

*$27,600 = ($150,000 − $12,000) ÷ 5

	Year	Depreciation Expense	Accumulated Depreciation, End of Year	Book Value, End of Year
b.	1	$60,000**	$ 60,000	$ 90,000
	2	36,000	96,000	54,000
	3	21,600	117,600	32,400
	4	12,960	130,560	19,440
	5	7,440***	138,000	12,000

**$60,000 = $150,000 × 40%
***The asset is not depreciated below the estimated residual value of $12,000.

2.

Accumulated Depreciation—Equipment	130 5 6 0 00		
Equipment	175 0 0 0 00		
Loss on Disposal of Fixed Assets	9 4 4 0 00		
Equipment		150 0 0 0 00	
Cash		165 0 0 0 00	

SELF-EXAMINATION QUESTIONS

Answers at End of Chapter

Matching

Match each of the following statements with its proper term. Some terms may not be used.

A. accelerated depreciation method	___ 1. Long-term or relatively permanent tangible assets that are used in the normal business operations.
B. amortization	___ 2. The systematic periodic transfer of the cost of a fixed asset to an expense account during its expected useful life.
C. betterment	
D. book value	___ 3. The estimated value of a fixed asset at the end of its useful life.
E. boot	___ 4. A method of depreciation that provides for equal periodic depreciation expense over the estimated life of a fixed asset.
F. capital expenditures	
G. capital leases	___ 5. A method of depreciation that provides for depreciation expense based on the expected productive capacity of a fixed asset.
H. copyright	
I. declining-balance method	___ 6. A method of depreciation that provides periodic depreciation expense based on the declining book value of a fixed asset over its estimated life.
	___ 7. The cost of a fixed asset minus accumulated depreciation on the asset.

J. depletion

K. depreciation

L. extraordinary repair

M. fixed assets

N. goodwill

O. intangible assets

P. operating leases

Q. patents

R. ratio of fixed assets to long-term liabilities

S. ratio of fixed assets to total assets

T. residual value

U. revenue expenditures

V. straight-line method

W. trade-in allowance

X. trademark

Y. units-of-production method

___ 8. A depreciation method that provides for a higher depreciation amount in the first year of the asset's use, followed by a gradually declining amount of depreciation.

___ 9. The costs of acquiring fixed assets, adding to a fixed asset, improving a fixed asset, or extending a fixed asset's useful life.

___ 10. Costs that benefit only the current period or costs incurred for normal maintenance and repairs of fixed assets.

___ 11. An expenditure that improves a fixed asset's operating efficiency or capacity for its remaining useful life.

___ 12. An expenditure that increases the useful life of an asset beyond its original estimate.

___ 13. The amount a seller allows a buyer for a fixed asset that is traded in for a similar asset.

___ 14. The amount a buyer owes a seller when a fixed asset is traded in on a similar asset.

___ 15. Leases that include one or more provisions that result in treating the leased assets as purchased assets in the accounts.

___ 16. Leases that do not meet the criteria for capital leases and thus are accounted for as operating expenses.

___ 17. The process of transferring the cost of natural resources to an expense account.

___ 18. Long-term assets that are useful in the operations of a business, are not held for sale, and are without physical qualities.

___ 19. The periodic transfer of the cost of an intangible asset to expense.

___ 20. An intangible asset that is created from such favorable factors as location, product quality, reputation, and managerial skill.

___ 21. Exclusive rights to produce and sell goods with one or more unique features.

___ 22. An exclusive right to publish and sell a literary, artistic, or musical composition.

___ 23. A name, term, or symbol used to identify a business and its products.

___ 24. A financial ratio that provides a measure indicating the margin of safety to creditors.

Multiple Choice

1. Which of the following expenditures incurred in connection with acquiring machinery is a proper charge to the asset account?
    A. Freight
    B. Installation costs
    C. Both A and B
    D. Neither A nor B

2. What is the amount of depreciation, using the declining-balance method (twice the straight-line rate) for the second year of use for equipment costing $9,000, with an estimated residual value of $600 and an estimated life of 3 years?
    A. $6,000
    B. $3,000
    C. $2,000
    D. $400

3. An example of an accelerated depreciation method is:
    A. Straight-line
    B. Declining-balance
    C. Units-of-production
    D. Depletion

4. A fixed asset priced at $100,000 is acquired by trading in a similar asset that has a book value of $25,000. Assuming that the trade-in allowance is $30,000 and that $70,000 cash is paid for the new asset, what is the cost of the new asset for financial reporting purposes?
    A. $100,000
    B. $95,000
    C. $70,000
    D. $30,000

5. Which of the following is an example of an intangible asset?
    A. Patents
    B. Goodwill
    C. Copyrights
    D. All of the above

CLASS DISCUSSION QUESTIONS

1. Which of the following qualities are characteristic of fixed assets? (a) tangible, (b) capable of repeated use in the operations of the business, (c) held for sale in the normal course of business, (d) used continuously in the operations of the business, (e) long-lived.

2. Penguin Office Equipment Co. has a fleet of automobiles and trucks for use by salespersons and for delivery of office supplies and equipment. Sioux City Auto Sales Co. has automobiles and trucks for sale. Under what caption would the automobiles and trucks be reported on the balance sheet of (a) Penguin Office Equipment Co., (b) Sioux City Auto Sales Co.?

3. Spiral Co. acquired an adjacent vacant lot with the hope of selling it in the future at a gain. The lot is not intended to be used in Spiral's business operations. Where should such real estate be listed in the balance sheet?

4. Tensile Company solicited bids from several contractors to construct an addition to its office building. The lowest bid received was for $340,000. Tensile Company decided to construct the addition itself at a cost of $325,000. What amount should be recorded in the building account?

5. Are the amounts at which fixed assets are reported in the balance sheet their approximate market values as of the balance sheet date? Discuss.

6. a. Does the recognition of depreciation in the accounts provide a special cash fund for the replacement of fixed assets? Explain.
   b. Describe the nature of depreciation as the term is used in accounting.

7. Name the three factors that need to be considered in determining the amount of periodic depreciation.

8. Trigger Company purchased a machine that has a manufacturer's suggested life of 15 years. The company plans to use the machine on a special project that will last 11 years. At the completion of the project, the machine will be sold. Over how many years should the machine be depreciated?

9. Is it necessary for a business to use the same method of computing depreciation (a) for all classes of its depreciable assets, (b) in the financial statements and in determining income taxes?

10. Of the three common depreciation methods, which is most widely used?

11. a. Under what conditions is the use of an accelerated depreciation method most appropriate?
    b. Why is an accelerated depreciation method often used for income tax purposes?
    c. What is the Modified Accelerated Cost Recovery System (MACRS), and under what conditions is it used?

12. A revision of depreciable fixed asset lives resulted in an increase in the remaining lives of certain fixed assets. The company would like to include, as income of the current period, the cumulative effect of the changes, which reduces the depreciation expense of past periods. Is this in accordance with generally accepted accounting principles? Discuss.

   Source: "Q's and A's Technical Hotline," *Journal of Accountancy,* December 1991, p. 89.

13. Differentiate between the accounting for capital expenditures and revenue expenditures.

14. Immediately after a used truck is acquired, a new motor is installed and the tires are replaced at a total cost of $4,750. Is this a capital expenditure or a revenue expenditure?

15. For some of the fixed assets of a business, the balance in Accumulated Depreciation is exactly equal to the cost of the asset. (a) Is it permissible to record additional depreciation on the assets if they are still useful to the business? Explain. (b) When should an entry be made to remove the cost and the accumulated depreciation from the accounts?

16. In what sections of the income statement are gains and losses from the disposal of fixed assets presented?

17. Differentiate between a capital lease and an operating lease.

18. The financial statements of **La-Z-Boy Chair Company** contain the following footnote:

The Company has several long-term leases covering manufacturing facilities. The lease agreements require the Company to insure and maintain the facilities and provide for annual payments, which include interest. These leases give the Company the option to purchase the facilities for nominal amounts, or in some instances to renew the leases for extended periods at nominal annual rentals.

Would these leases be classified as operating or capital leases? Discuss.

19. Describe the internal controls for acquiring fixed assets.
20. Why is a physical count of fixed assets necessary?
21. What is the term applied to the periodic charge for (a) ore removed from a mine, (b) the use of an intangible asset?
22. a. Over what period of time should the cost of a patent acquired by purchase be amortized?
    b. In general, what is the required treatment for research and development costs?
23. How should (a) fixed assets and (b) intangible assets be reported in the balance sheet?

RESOURCES FOR YOUR SUCCESS ONLINE AT

http://warren.swcollege.com

Remember! If you need additional help, visit South-Western's Web site.
See page F26 for a description of the online and printed materials that are available.

EXERCISES

Exercise 9–1
Costs of acquiring fixed assets

Objective 1

Tracie Klein owns and operates Walcott Print Co. During July, Walcott Print Co. incurred the following costs in acquiring two printing presses. One printing press was new, and the other was used by a business that recently filed for bankruptcy.

Costs related to new printing press:

1. Sales tax on purchase price
2. Insurance while in transit
3. Freight
4. Special foundation
5. New parts to replace those damaged in unloading
6. Fee paid to factory representative for installation

Costs related to secondhand printing press:

7. Freight
8. Installation
9. Repair of vandalism during installation
10. Replacement of worn-out parts
11. Repair of damage incurred in reconditioning the press
12. Fees paid to attorney to review purchase agreement

a. Indicate which costs incurred in acquiring the new printing press should be debited to the asset account.
b. Indicate which costs incurred in acquiring the secondhand printing press should be debited to the asset account.

Exercise 9–2
Determine cost of land

Objective 1

A company has developed a tract of land into a ski resort. The company has cut the trees, cleared and graded the land and hills, and constructed ski lifts. (a) Should the tree cutting, land clearing, and grading costs of constructing the ski slopes be debited to the land account? (b) If such costs are debited to Land, should they be depreciated?

Source: "Technical Issues Feature," *Journal of Accountancy,* December 1987, p. 82.

Exercise 9–3
Determine cost of land

Objective 1

✓ $138,250

Birch Delivery Company acquired an adjacent lot to construct a new warehouse, paying $25,000 and giving a short-term note for $100,000. Legal fees paid were $1,750, delinquent taxes assumed were $7,500, and fees paid to remove an old building from the land were $5,500. Materials salvaged from the demolition of the building were sold for $1,500. A contractor was paid $412,500 to construct a new warehouse. Determine the cost of the land to be reported on the balance sheet.

Exercise 9–4
Nature of depreciation

Objective 1

Yarborough Metal Casting Co. reported $575,000 for equipment and $217,500 for accumulated depreciation—equipment on its balance sheet.

Does this mean (a) that the replacement cost of the equipment is $575,000 and (b) that $217,500 is set aside in a special fund for the replacement of the equipment? Explain.

Exercise 9–5
Straight-line depreciation rates

Objective 2

✓ a. 25%

Convert each of the following estimates of useful life to a straight-line depreciation rate, stated as a percentage, assuming that the residual value of the fixed asset is to be ignored: (a) 4 years, (b) 5 years, (c) 10 years, (d) 20 years, (e) 25 years, (f) 40 years, (g) 50 years.

Exercise 9–6
Straight-line depreciation

Objective 2

✓ $11,750

A refrigerator used by a meat processor has a cost of $112,000, an estimated residual value of $18,000, and an estimated useful life of 8 years. What is the amount of the annual depreciation computed by the straight-line method?

Exercise 9–7
Depreciation by units-of-production method

Objective 2

✓ $3,220

A diesel-powered generator with a cost of $375,000 and estimated residual value of $30,000 is expected to have a useful operating life of 75,000 hours. During November, the generator was operated 700 hours. Determine the depreciation for the month.

Exercise 9–8
Depreciation by units-of-production method

Objective 2

✓ a. Truck #1, credit Accumulated Depreciation, $8,400

Prior to adjustment at the end of the year, the balance in Trucks is $176,600 and the balance in Accumulated Depreciation—Trucks is $60,500. Details of the subsidiary ledger are as follows:

Truck No.	Cost	Estimated Residual Value	Estimated Useful Life	Accumulated Depreciation at Beginning of Year	Miles Operated During Year
1	$75,000	$5,000	250,000 miles	$21,000	30,000 miles
2	38,600	3,600	200,000	31,500	25,000
3	35,000	3,000	100,000	8,000	36,000
4	28,000	4,000	120,000	—	21,000

a. Determine the depreciation rates per mile and the amount to be credited to the accumulated depreciation section of each of the subsidiary accounts for the miles operated during the current year.

b. Journalize the entry to record depreciation for the year.

Exercise 9–9
Depreciation by two methods
Objective 2

✓ a. $15,400

A backhoe acquired on January 2 at a cost of $154,000 has an estimated useful life of 10 years. Assuming that it will have no residual value, determine the depreciation for each of the first two years (a) by the straight-line method and (b) by the declining-balance method, using twice the straight-line rate.

Exercise 9–10
Depreciation by two methods
Objective 2

✓ a. $8,100

A dairy storage tank acquired at the beginning of the fiscal year at a cost of $70,000 has an estimated residual value of $5,200 and an estimated useful life of 8 years. Determine the following: (a) the amount of annual depreciation by the straight-line method and (b) the amount of depreciation for the first and second year computed by the declining-balance method (at twice the straight-line rate).

Exercise 9–11
Partial-year depreciation
Objective 2

✓ a. First year, $7,350

Sandblasting equipment acquired at a cost of $64,000 has an estimated residual value of $5,200 and an estimated useful life of 6 years. It was placed in service on April 1 of the current fiscal year, which ends on December 31. Determine the depreciation for the current fiscal year and for the following fiscal year by (a) the straight-line method and (b) the declining-balance method, at twice the straight-line rate.

Exercise 9–12
Revision of depreciation
Objective 2

✓ a. $12,000

A warehouse with a cost of $500,000 has an estimated residual value of $20,000, an estimated useful life of 40 years, and is depreciated by the straight-line method. (a) What is the amount of the annual depreciation? (b) What is the book value at the end of the twentieth year of use? (c) If at the start of the twenty-first year it is estimated that the remaining life is 15 years and that the residual value is $5,000, what is the depreciation expense for each of the remaining 15 years?

Exercise 9–13
Book value of fixed assets
Objective 2

The following data were taken from recent annual reports of **Interstate Bakeries Corporation (IBC)**. Interstate Bakeries produces, distributes, and sells fresh bakery products nationwide through supermarkets, convenience stores, and its 67 bakeries and 1,500 thrift stores.

	Current Year	Preceding Year
Land and buildings	$388,618,000	$364,773,000
Machinery and equipment	953,625,000	894,533,000
Accumulated depreciation	447,797,000	364,791,000

a. Compute the book value of the fixed assets for the current year and the preceding year and explain the differences, if any.

b. Would you normally expect the book value of fixed assets to increase or decrease during the year?

Exercise 9–14
Capital and revenue expenditures
Objective 3

Yeats Co. incurred the following costs related to trucks and vans used in operating its delivery service:

1. Installed a hydraulic lift to a van.
2. Removed a two-way radio from one of the trucks and installed a new radio with a greater range of communication.
3. Overhauled the engine on one of the trucks that had been purchased four years ago.
4. Changed the oil and greased the joints of all the trucks and vans.
5. Replaced the brakes and alternator on a truck that had been in service for the past 5 years.
6. Installed security systems on three of the newer trucks.

7. Replaced two of the trucks' shock absorbers with new shock absorbers that allow for the delivery of heavier loads.
8. Repaired a flat tire on one of the vans.
9. Rebuilt the transmission on one of the vans that had been driven only 25,000 miles. The van was no longer under warranty.
10. Tinted the back and side windows of one of the vans to discourage theft of contents.

Classify each of the costs as a capital expenditure or a revenue expenditure. For those costs identified as capital expenditures, classify each as an addition, a betterment, or an extraordinary repair.

Exercise 9–15
Capital and revenue expenditures

Objective 3

Faith Inman owns and operates Yellow Ribbon Transport Co. During the past year, Faith incurred the following costs related to her 18-wheel truck.

1. Replaced the hydraulic brake system that had begun to fail during her latest trip through the Smoky Mountains.
2. Overhauled the engine.
3. Replaced a headlight that had burned out.
4. Removed the old CB radio and replaced it with a newer model with a greater range.
5. Replaced a shock absorber that had worn out.
6. Installed fog lights.
7. Installed a wind deflector on top of the cab to increase fuel mileage.
8. Modified the factory-installed turbo charger with a special-order kit designed to add 30 more horsepower to the engine performance.
9. Installed a television in the sleeping compartment of the truck.
10. Replaced the old radar detector with a newer model that detects the KA frequencies now used by many of the state patrol radar guns. The detector is wired directly into the cab, so that it is partially hidden. In addition, Faith fastened the detector to the truck with a locking device that prevents its removal.

Classify each of the costs as a capital expenditure or a revenue expenditure. For those costs identified as capital expenditures, classify each as an addition, a betterment, or an extraordinary repair.

Exercise 9–16
Major repair to fixed asset

Objective 3

✓ a. $22,000
✓ d. $15,000

A number of major structural repairs on a building were completed at the beginning of the current fiscal year at a cost of $50,000. The repairs are expected to extend the life of the building 8 years beyond the original estimate. The original cost of the building was $550,000, and it is being depreciated by the straight-line method for 25 years. The residual value is expected to be negligible and has been ignored. The balance of the related accumulated depreciation account after the depreciation adjustment at the end of the preceding year is $330,000.

a. What has the amount of annual depreciation been in past years?
b. To what account should the cost of repairs ($50,000) be debited?
c. What is the book value of the building after the repairs have been recorded?
d. What is the amount of depreciation for the current year, using the straight-line method (assuming that the repairs were completed at the very beginning of the year)?

Exercise 9–17
Entries for sale of fixed asset

Objective 4

Metal recycling equipment acquired on January 3, 2000, at a cost of $117,500, has an estimated useful life of 8 years, an estimated residual value of $7,500, and is depreciated by the straight-line method.

a. What was the book value of the equipment at December 31, 2003, the end of the fiscal year?
b. Assuming that the equipment was sold on July 1, 2004, for $53,500, journalize the entries to record (1) depreciation for the six months of the current year ending December 31, 2004, and (2) the sale of the equipment.

Exercise 9–18
Disposal of fixed asset

Objective 4

✓ b. $21,250

Equipment acquired on January 3, 2000, at a cost of $71,500, has an estimated useful life of 4 years and an estimated residual value of $4,500.

a. What was the annual amount of depreciation for the years 2000, 2001, and 2002, using the straight-line method of depreciation?
b. What was the book value of the equipment on January 1, 2003? *(continued)*

c. Assuming that the equipment was sold on January 2, 2003, for $18,000, journalize the entry to record the sale.

d. Assuming that the equipment had been sold on January 2, 2003, for $23,000 instead of $18,000, journalize the entry to record the sale.

Exercise 9–19
Asset traded for similar asset
Objective 4

A printing press priced at $220,000 is acquired by trading in a similar press and paying cash for the difference between the trade-in allowance and the price of the new press.

a. Assuming that the trade-in allowance is $35,000, what is the amount of cash given?
b. Assuming that the book value of the press traded in is $18,750, what is the cost of the new press for financial reporting purposes?

Exercise 9–20
Asset traded for similar asset
Objective 4

Assume the same facts as in Exercise 9–19, except that the book value of the press traded in is $41,700. (a) What is the amount of cash given? (b) What is the cost of the new press for financial reporting purposes?

Exercise 9–21
Entries for trade of fixed asset
Objective 4

On April 1, Cascade Co., a water distiller, acquired new bottling equipment with a list price of $285,000. Cascade received a trade-in allowance of $70,000 on the old equipment of a similar type, paid cash of $50,000, and gave a series of five notes payable for the remainder. The following information about the old equipment is obtained from the account in the equipment ledger: cost, $183,500; accumulated depreciation on December 31, the end of the preceding fiscal year, $96,000; annual depreciation, $12,000. Journalize the entries to record (a) the current depreciation of the old equipment to the date of trade-in and (b) the transaction on April 1 for financial reporting purposes.

Exercise 9–22
Entries for trade of fixed asset
Objective 4

On October 1, Rochne Co. acquired a new truck with a list price of $75,000. Rochne received a trade-in allowance of $15,000 on an old truck of similar type, paid cash of $10,000, and gave a series of five notes payable for the remainder. The following information about the old truck is obtained from the account in the equipment ledger: cost, $52,500; accumulated depreciation on December 31, the end of the preceding fiscal year, $36,000; annual depreciation, $4,500. Journalize the entries to record (a) the current depreciation of the old truck to the date of trade-in and (b) the transaction on October 1 for financial reporting purposes.

Exercise 9–23
Depreciable cost of asset acquired by exchange
Objective 4

On the first day of the fiscal year, a delivery truck with a list price of $45,000 was acquired in exchange for an old delivery truck and $28,000 cash. The old truck had a book value of $18,250 at the date of the exchange.

a. Determine the depreciable cost for financial reporting purposes.
b. Assuming that the book value of the old delivery truck was $14,000, determine the depreciable cost for financial reporting purposes.

Exercise 9–24
Internal control of fixed assets
Objective 6

DataNet Co. is a computer software company marketing products in the United States and Canada. While DataNet Co. has over 90 sales offices, all accounting is handled at the company's headquarters in Bozeman, Montana.

DataNet Co. keeps all its fixed asset records on a computerized system. The computer maintains a subsidiary ledger of all fixed assets owned by the company and calculates depreciation automatically. Whenever a manager at one of the ninety sales offices wants to purchase a fixed asset, a purchase request is submitted to headquarters for approval. Upon approval, the fixed asset is purchased and the invoice is sent back to headquarters so that the asset can be entered into the fixed asset system.

A manager who wants to dispose of a fixed asset simply sells or disposes of the asset and notifies headquarters to remove the asset from the system. Company cars and personal computers are frequently purchased by employees when they are disposed of. Most pieces of office equipment are traded in when new assets are acquired.

What internal control weakness exists in the procedures used to acquire and dispose of fixed assets at DataNet Co.?

Exercise 9–25
Depletion entries
Objective 7

Anaconda Co. acquired mineral rights for $30,000,000. The mineral deposit is estimated at 50,000,000 tons. During the current year, 7,500,000 tons were mined and sold for $6,500,000.

a. Determine the amount of depletion expense for the current year.
b. Journalize the adjusting entry to recognize the expense.

Exercise 9–26
Amortization entries
Objective 8

Langohr Company acquired patent rights on January 3, 2000, for $675,000. The patent has a useful life equal to its legal life of 18 years. On January 5, 2003, Langohr successfully defended the patent in a lawsuit at a cost of $45,000.

a. Determine the patent amortization expense for the current year ended December 31, 2003.
b. Journalize the adjusting entry to recognize the amortization.

Exercise 9–27
Balance sheet presentation
Objective 9

How many errors can you find in the following partial balance sheet?

Rosedale Company
Balance Sheet
December 31, 2003

Assets

Total current assets $397,500

	Replacement Cost	Accumulated Depreciation	Book Value
Property, plant, and equipment:			
Land	$ 75,000	$ 20,000	$ 55,000
Buildings	160,000	76,000	84,000
Factory equipment	350,000	192,000	158,000
Office equipment	120,000	77,000	43,000
Patents	80,000	—	80,000
Goodwill	45,000	—	45,000
Total property, plant, and equipment	$830,000	$365,000	465,000

Exercise 9–28
Ratio of fixed assets to long-term liabilities
Objective 10

The following data were taken from recent annual reports of **Intuit Inc.**, a developer and distributor of computer software:

	Current Year	Preceding Year
Property and equipment (net)	$69,413,000	$83,404,000
Long-term notes payable	35,566,000	36,444,000

a. Compute the ratio of fixed assets to long-term liabilities for the current and preceding years. Round to one decimal place.
b. What conclusions can you draw?

Exercise 9–29
Ratio of fixed assets to long-term liabilities
Objective 10

The financial statements of **Cisco Systems, Inc.**, presented in Appendix G at the end of the text, indicate that Cisco Systems has no long-term liabilities.
What conclusions can you draw?

Appendix Exercise 9–30
Sum-of-the-years-digits depreciation

✓ First year: $28,000

Based on the data in Exercise 9–9, determine the depreciation for the backhoe for each of the first two years, using the sum-of-the-years-digits depreciation method.

Appendix Exercise 9–31
Sum-of-the-years-digits depreciation

✓ First year: $14,400

Based on the data in Exercise 9–10, determine the depreciation for the dairy storage tank for each of the first two years, using the sum-of-the-years-digits depreciation method.

Appendix Exercise 9–32
Partial-year depreciation

✓ First year: $12,600

Based on the data in Exercise 9–11, determine the depreciation for the sandblasting equipment for each of the first two years, using the sum-of-the-years-digits depreciation method.

PROBLEMS SERIES A

Problem 9–1A
Allocate payments and receipts to fixed asset accounts

Objective 1

SPREADSHEET

The following payments and receipts are related to land, land improvements, and buildings acquired for use in a wholesale ceramic business. The receipts are identified by an asterisk.

a. Fee paid to attorney for title search	$ 3,500
b. Cost of real estate acquired as a plant site: Land	200,000
Building	55,000
c. Delinquent real estate taxes on property, assumed by purchaser	18,750
d. Cost of razing and removing building	4,800
e. Proceeds from sale of salvage materials from old building	3,100*
f. Special assessment paid to city for extension of water main to the property	5,000
g. Premium on 1-year insurance policy during construction	6,600
h. Cost of filling and grading land	29,700
i. Cost of repairing windstorm damage during construction	1,500
j. Cost of paving parking lot to be used by customers	12,500
k. Cost of trees and shrubbery planted	15,000
l. Architect's and engineer's fees for plans and supervision	40,000
m. Cost of repairing vandalism damage during construction	1,500
n. Interest incurred on building loan during construction	48,000
o. Cost of floodlights installed on parking lot	13,500
p. Money borrowed to pay building contractor	500,000*
q. Payment to building contractor for new building	750,000
r. Proceeds from insurance company for windstorm and vandalism damage	3,000*
s. Refund of premium on insurance policy (g) canceled after 11 months	750*

Instructions

1. Assign each payment and receipt to Land (unlimited life), Land Improvements (limited life), Building, or Other Accounts. Indicate receipts by an asterisk. Identify each item by letter and list the amounts in columnar form, as follows:

Item	Land	Land Improvements	Building	Other Accounts

2. Determine the amount debited to Land, Land Improvements, and Building.
3. ◖▬▬▶ The costs assigned to the land, which is used as a plant site, will not be depreciated, while the costs assigned to land improvements will be depreciated. Explain this seemingly contradictory application of the concept of depreciation.

Problem 9–2A
Compare three depreciation methods

Objective 2

✓ 2002: straight-line depreciation, $105,000

Diamondback Company purchased packaging equipment on January 3, 2002, for $340,000. The equipment was expected to have a useful life of 3 years, or 18,000 operating hours, and a residual value of $25,000. The equipment was used for 7,500 hours during 2002, 6,000 hours in 2003, and 4,500 hours in 2004.

Instructions
Determine the amount of depreciation expense for the years ended December 31, 2002, 2003, and 2004, by (a) the straight-line method, (b) the units-of-production method, and (c) the declining-balance method, using twice the straight-line rate. Also determine the total depreciation expense for the three years by each method. The following columnar headings are suggested for recording the depreciation expense amounts:

	Depreciation Expense		
Year	Straight-Line Method	Units-of-Production Method	Declining-Balance Method

Problem 9–3A
Depreciation by three methods; partial years

Objective 2

SPREADSHEET

✓ a. 2002: $17,000

Newbauer Company purchased plastic laminating equipment on July 1, 2002, for $108,000. The equipment was expected to have a useful life of 3 years, or 13,600 operating hours, and a residual value of $6,000. The equipment was used for 2,400 hours during 2002, 4,500 hours in 2003, 5,000 hours in 2004, and 1,700 hours in 2005.

Instructions
Determine the amount of depreciation expense for the years ended December 31, 2002, 2003, 2004, and 2005, by (a) the straight-line method, (b) the units-of-production method, and (c) the declining-balance method, using twice the straight-line rate.

Problem 9–4A
Depreciation by two methods; trade of fixed asset

Objectives 2, 4

GENERAL LEDGER

✓ 1. b. Year 1: $50,000 depreciation expense
✓ 2. $146,200

New lithographic equipment, acquired at a cost of $125,000 at the beginning of a fiscal year, has an estimated useful life of 5 years and an estimated residual value of $10,000. The manager requested information regarding the effect of alternative methods on the amount of depreciation expense each year. On the basis of the data presented to the manager, the declining-balance method was selected.

In the first week of the fifth year, the equipment was traded in for similar equipment priced at $150,000. The trade-in allowance on the old equipment was $20,000, cash of $30,000 was paid, and a note payable was issued for the balance.

Instructions
1. Determine the annual depreciation expense for each of the estimated 5 years of use, the accumulated depreciation at the end of each year, and the book value of the equipment at the end of each year by (a) the straight-line method and (b) the declining-balance method (at twice the straight-line rate). The following columnar headings are suggested for each schedule:

Year	Depreciation Expense	Accumulated Depreciation, End of Year	Book Value, End of Year

2. For financial reporting purposes, determine the cost of the new equipment acquired in the exchange.
3. Journalize the entry to record the exchange.
4. Journalize the entry to record the exchange, assuming that the trade-in allowance was $15,000 instead of $20,000.

Problem 9–5A

Transactions for fixed assets, including trade

Objectives 1, 3, 4

SPREADSHEET

GENERAL LEDGER

The following transactions, adjusting entries, and closing entries were completed by Trailways Furniture Co. during a 3-year period. All are related to the use of delivery equipment. The declining-balance method (at twice the straight-line rate) of depreciation is used.

2002

Jan. 3. Purchased a used delivery truck for $26,750, paying cash.
      5. Paid $1,250 for a new transmission for the truck. (Debit Delivery Equipment.)
Aug. 16. Paid garage $285 for miscellaneous repairs to the truck.
Dec. 31. Recorded depreciation on the truck for the fiscal year. The estimated useful life of the truck is 4 years, with a residual value of $6,000.
     31. Closed the appropriate accounts to the income summary account.

2003

June 30. Traded in the used truck for a new truck priced at $41,000, receiving a trade-in allowance of $11,500 and paying the balance in cash. (Record depreciation to date in 2003.)
Aug. 10. Paid garage $175 for miscellaneous repairs to the truck.
Dec. 31. Recorded depreciation on the truck. It has an estimated residual value of $7,500 and an estimated life of 5 years.
     31. Closed the appropriate accounts to the income summary account.

2004

Oct. 1. Purchased a new truck for $42,000, paying cash.
      2. Sold the truck purchased June 30, 2003, for $26,750. (Record depreciation for the year.)
Dec. 31. Recorded depreciation on the remaining truck. It has an estimated residual value of $5,000 and an estimated useful life of 8 years.
     31. Closed the appropriate accounts to the income summary account.

Instructions

Journalize the transactions and the adjusting and closing entries. Post to the following accounts in the ledger and determine the balances after each posting:

122	Delivery Equipment
123	Accumulated Depreciation—Delivery Equipment
616	Depreciation Expense—Delivery Equipment
617	Truck Repair Expense
812	Gain on Disposal of Fixed Assets

Problem 9–6A

Amortization and depletion entries

Objectives 7, 8

✓ 1. (a.) $121,600

Data related to the acquisition of timber rights and intangible assets during the current year ended December 31 are as follows:

a. Timber rights on a tract of land were purchased for $480,000 on July 12. The stand of timber is estimated at 1,500,000 board feet. During the current year, 380,000 board feet of timber were cut.
b. Goodwill in the amount of $5,000,000 was purchased on January 3. It is decided to amortize over the maximum period allowable.
c. Governmental and legal costs of $80,000 were incurred on October 2 in obtaining a patent with an estimated economic life of 10 years. Amortization is to be for one-fourth year.

Instructions

1. Determine the amount of the amortization or depletion expense for the current year for each of the foregoing items.
2. Journalize the adjusting entries required to record the amortization or depletion for each item.

Problem 9–1B
Allocate payments and receipts to fixed asset accounts

Objective 1

SPREADSHEET

The following payments and receipts are related to land, land improvements, and buildings acquired for use in a wholesale apparel business. The receipts are identified by an asterisk.

a.	Finder's fee paid to real estate agency	$ 10,000
b.	Cost of real estate acquired as a plant site: Land	250,000
	Building	50,000
c.	Fee paid to attorney for title search	2,500
d.	Delinquent real estate taxes on property, assumed by purchaser	18,500
e.	Cost of razing and removing building	11,250
f.	Proceeds from sale of salvage materials from old building	3,500*
g.	Cost of filling and grading land	15,500
h.	Special assessment paid to city for extension of water main to the property	9,000
i.	Architect's and engineer's fees for plans and supervision	50,000
j.	Premium on 1-year insurance policy during construction	5,700
k.	Cost of repairing windstorm damage during construction	3,500
l.	Cost of repairing vandalism damage during construction	800
m.	Cost of paving parking lot to be used by customers	17,500
n.	Cost of trees and shrubbery planted	20,000
o.	Proceeds from insurance company for windstorm and vandalism damage	4,300*
p.	Interest incurred on building loan during construction	65,000
q.	Money borrowed to pay building contractor	1,000,000*
r.	Payment to building contractor for new building	1,250,000
s.	Refund of premium on insurance policy (j) canceled after 10 months	1,050*

Instructions

1. Assign each payment and receipt to Land (unlimited life), Land Improvements (limited life), Building, or Other Accounts. Indicate receipts by an asterisk. Identify each item by letter and list the amounts in columnar form, as follows:

Item	Land	Land Improvements	Building	Other Accounts

2. Determine the amount debited to Land, Land Improvements, and Building.
3. The costs assigned to the land, which is used as a plant site, will not be depreciated, while the costs assigned to land improvements will be depreciated. Explain this seemingly contradictory application of the concept of depreciation.

Problem 9–2B
Compare three depreciation methods

Objective 2

✓ 2002: straight-line depreciation, $57,500

Sunlight Company purchased waterproofing equipment on January 2, 2002, for $255,000. The equipment was expected to have a useful life of 4 years, or 28,750 operating hours, and a residual value of $25,000. The equipment was used for 8,500 hours during 2002, 8,100 hours in 2003, 7,800 hours in 2004, and 4,350 hours in 2005.

Instructions

Determine the amount of depreciation expense for the years ended December 31, 2002, 2003, 2004, and 2005, by (a) the straight-line method, (b) the units-of-production method, and (c) the declining-balance method, using twice the straight-line rate. Also determine the total depreciation expense for the four years by each method. The following columnar headings are suggested for recording the depreciation expense amounts:

	Depreciation Expense		
Year	Straight-Line Method	Units-of-Production Method	Declining-Balance Method

Problem 9–3B
Depreciation by three methods; partial years

Objective 2

SPREADSHEET

✓ a. 2002, $10,200

Autostock Company purchased tool sharpening equipment on July 1, 2002, for $64,800. The equipment was expected to have a useful life of 3 years, or 15,300 operating hours, and a residual value of $3,600. The equipment was used for 3,100 hours during 2002, 5,000 hours in 2003, 4,900 hours in 2004, and 2,300 hours in 2005.

Instructions
Determine the amount of depreciation expense for the years ended December 31, 2002, 2003, 2004, and 2005, by (a) the straight-line method, (b) the units-of-production method, and (c) the declining-balance method, using twice the straight-line rate.

Problem 9–4B
Depreciation by two methods; trade of fixed asset

Objectives 2, 4

GENERAL LEDGER

✓ 1. b. Year 1, $50,000
depreciation expense

✓ 2. $122,500

New tire retreading equipment, acquired at a cost of $100,000 at the beginning of a fiscal year, has an estimated useful life of 4 years and an estimated residual value of $10,000. The manager requested information regarding the effect of alternative methods on the amount of depreciation expense each year. On the basis of the data presented to the manager, the declining-balance method was selected.

In the first week of the fourth year, the equipment was traded in for similar equipment priced at $125,000. The trade-in allowance on the old equipment was $15,000, cash of $10,000 was paid, and a note payable was issued for the balance.

Instructions

1. Determine the annual depreciation expense for each of the estimated 4 years of use, the accumulated depreciation at the end of each year, and the book value of the equipment at the end of each year by (a) the straight-line method and (b) the declining-balance method (at twice the straight-line rate). The following columnar headings are suggested for each schedule:

Year	Depreciation Expense	Accumulated Depreciation, End of Year	Book Value, End of Year

2. For financial reporting purposes, determine the cost of the new equipment acquired in the exchange.
3. Journalize the entry to record the exchange.
4. Journalize the entry to record the exchange, assuming that the trade-in allowance was $8,000 instead of $15,000.

Problem 9–5B
Transactions for fixed assets, including trade

Objectives 1, 3, 4

SPREADSHEET

GENERAL LEDGER

The following transactions, adjusting entries, and closing entries were completed by Heritage Furniture Co. during a 3-year period. All are related to the use of delivery equipment. The declining-balance method (at twice the straight-line rate) of depreciation is used.

2001
Jan. 2. Purchased a used delivery truck for $18,000, paying cash.
      5. Paid $2,000 to replace the automatic transmission and install new brakes on the truck. (Debit Delivery Equipment.)
April 7. Paid garage $125 for changing the oil, replacing the oil filter, and tuning the engine on the delivery truck.
Dec. 31. Recorded depreciation on the truck for the fiscal year. The estimated useful life of the truck is 8 years, with a residual value of $3,000.
     31. Closed the appropriate accounts to the income summary account.

2002
Mar. 13. Paid garage $180 to tune the engine and make other minor repairs on the truck.
Apr. 30. Traded in the used truck for a new truck priced at $40,000, receiving a trade-in allowance of $15,500 and paying the balance in cash. (Record depreciation to date in 2002.)
Dec. 31. Recorded depreciation on the truck. It has an estimated trade-in value of $4,000 and an estimated life of 10 years.
     31. Closed the appropriate accounts to the income summary account.

2003

Sept. 1. Purchased a new truck for $45,000, paying cash.

2. Sold the truck purchased April 30, 2002, for $30,500. (Record depreciation for the year.)

Dec. 31. Recorded depreciation on the remaining truck. It has an estimated residual value of $4,500 and an estimated useful life of 10 years.

31. Closed the appropriate accounts to the income summary account.

Instructions

Journalize the transactions and the adjusting and closing entries. Post to the following accounts in the ledger and determine the balances after each posting:

122	Delivery Equipment
123	Accumulated Depreciation—Delivery Equipment
616	Depreciation Expense—Delivery Equipment
617	Truck Repair Expense
812	Gain on Disposal of Fixed Assets

Problem 9–6B

Amortization and depletion entries

Objectives 7, 8

✓ 1. (a.) $46,875

Data related to the acquisition of timber rights and intangible assets during the current year ended December 31 are as follows:

a. Goodwill in the amount of $1,875,000 was purchased on January 4. It is decided to amortize over the maximum period allowable.

b. Governmental and legal costs of $75,200 were incurred on July 2 in obtaining a patent with an estimated economic life of 8 years. Amortization is to be for one-half year.

c. Timber rights on a tract of land were purchased for $520,000 on April 2. The stand of timber is estimated at 2,000,000 board feet. During the current year, 250,000 board feet of timber were cut.

Instructions

1. Determine the amount of the amortization or depletion expense for the current year for each of the foregoing items.

2. Journalize the adjusting entries to record the amortization or depletion expense for each item.

SPECIAL ACTIVITIES

Activity 9–1

Tri-State Co.

Ethics and professional conduct in business

Stuart Madden, CPA, is an assistant to the controller of Tri-State Co. In his spare time, Stuart also prepares tax returns and performs general accounting services for clients. Frequently, Stuart performs these services after his normal working hours, using Tri-State Co.'s computers and laser printers. Occasionally, Stuart's clients will call him at the office during regular working hours.

➤ Discuss whether Stuart is performing in a professional manner.

Activity 9–2

Stanza Co.

Financial vs. tax depreciation

The following is an excerpt from a conversation between two employees of Stanza Co., Geoff Haines and Allison Foster. Geoff is the accounts payable clerk, and Allison is the cashier.

Geoff: Allison, could I get your opinion on something?

Allison: Sure, Geoff.

Geoff: Do you know Kris, the fixed assets clerk?

Allison: I know who she is, but I don't know her real well. Why?

Geoff: Well, I was talking to her at lunch last Monday about how she liked her job, etc. You know, the usual . . . and she mentioned something about having to keep two sets of books . . . one for taxes and one for the financial statements. That can't be good accounting, can it? What do you think?

Allison: Two sets of books? It doesn't sound right.

Geoff: It doesn't seem right to me either. I was always taught that you had to use generally accepted accounting principles. How can there be two sets of books? What can be the difference between the two?

How would you respond to Allison and Geoff if you were Kris?

Activity 9–3
Heimlich Construction Co.
Effect of depreciation on net income

Heimlich Construction Co. specializes in building replicas of historic houses. Ami Lamb, president of Heimlich, is considering the purchase of various items of equipment on July 1, 2001, for $150,000. The equipment would have a useful life of 5 years and no residual value. In the past, all equipment has been leased. For tax purposes, Ami is considering depreciating the equipment by the straight-line method. She discussed the matter with her CPA and learned that, although the straight-line method could be elected, it was to her advantage to use the modified accelerated cost recovery system (MACRS) for tax purposes. She asked for your advice as to which method to use for tax purposes.

1. Compute depreciation for each of the years (2001, 2002, 2003, 2004, 2005, and 2006) of useful life by (a) the straight-line method and (b) MACRS. In using the straight-line method, one-half year's depreciation should be computed for 2001 and 2006. Use the MACRS rates presented in the chapter.
2. Assuming that income before depreciation and income tax is estimated to be $150,000 uniformly per year and that the income tax rate is 30%, compute the net income for each of the years 2001, 2002, 2003, 2004, 2005, and 2006, if (a) the straight-line method is used and (b) MACRS is used.
3. What factors would you present for Ami's consideration in the selection of a depreciation method?

Activity 9–4
Into the Real World
Shopping for a delivery truck

You are planning to acquire a delivery truck for use in your business for three years. In groups of three or four, explore a local dealer's purchase and leasing options for the truck. Summarize the costs of purchasing versus leasing, and list other factors that might help you decide whether to buy or lease the truck.

Activity 9–5
Into the Real World
Applying for patents, copyrights, and trademarks

Go to the Internet and review the procedures for applying for a patent, a copyright, and a trademark. One Internet site that is useful for this purpose is:

www.idresearch.com

Prepare a written summary of these procedures.

ANSWERS TO SELF-EXAMINATION QUESTIONS

Matching

1. M	5. Y	9. F	13. W	17. J	21. Q
2. K	6. I	10. U	14. E	18. O	22. H
3. T	7. D	11. C	15. G	19. B	23. X
4. V	8. A	12. L	16. P	20. N	24. R

Multiple Choice

1. **C** All amounts spent to get a fixed asset (such as machinery) in place and ready for use are proper charges to the asset account. In the case of machinery acquired, the freight (answer A) and the installation costs (answer B) are both (answer C) proper charges to the machinery account.

2. **C** The periodic charge for depreciation under the declining-balance method (twice the straight-line rate) for the second year is determined by first computing the depreciation charge for the first year. The depreciation for the first year of $6,000 (answer A) is computed by multiplying the cost of the equipment, $9,000, by 2/3 (the straight-line rate of 1/3 multiplied by 2). The depreciation for the second year of $2,000 (answer C) is then determined by multiplying the book value at the end of the first year, $3,000 (the cost of $9,000 minus the first-year depreciation of $6,000), by 2/3. The third year's depreciation is $400 (answer D). It is determined by multiplying the book value at the end of the second year, $1,000, by 2/3, thus yielding $667. However, the equipment cannot be depreciated below its residual value of $600; thus, the third-year depreciation is $400 ($1,000 − $600).

3. **B** A depreciation method that provides for a higher depreciation amount in the first year of the use of an asset and a gradually declining periodic amount thereafter is called an accelerated depreciation method. The declining-balance method (answer B) is an example of such a method.

4. **B** The acceptable method of accounting for an exchange of similar assets in which the trade-in allowance ($30,000) exceeds the book value of the old asset ($25,000) requires that the cost of the new asset be determined by adding the amount of cash given ($70,000) to the book value of the old asset ($25,000), which totals $95,000. Alternatively, the unrecognized gain ($5,000) can be subtracted from the list price ($100,000).

5. **D** Long-lived assets that are useful in operations, not held for sale, and without physical qualities are called intangible assets. Patents, goodwill, and copyrights are examples of intangible assets (answer D).

Current Liabilities

objectives

After studying this chapter, you should be able to:

1 Define and give examples of current liabilities.

2 Journalize entries for short-term notes payable.

3 Describe the accounting treatment for contingent liabilities and journalize entries for product warranties.

4 Determine employer liabilities for payroll, including liabilities arising from employee earnings and deductions from earnings.

5 Describe payroll accounting systems that use a payroll register, employee earnings records, and a general journal.

6 Journalize entries for employee fringe benefits, including vacation pay and pensions.

7 Use the quick ratio to analyze the ability of a business to pay its current liabilities.

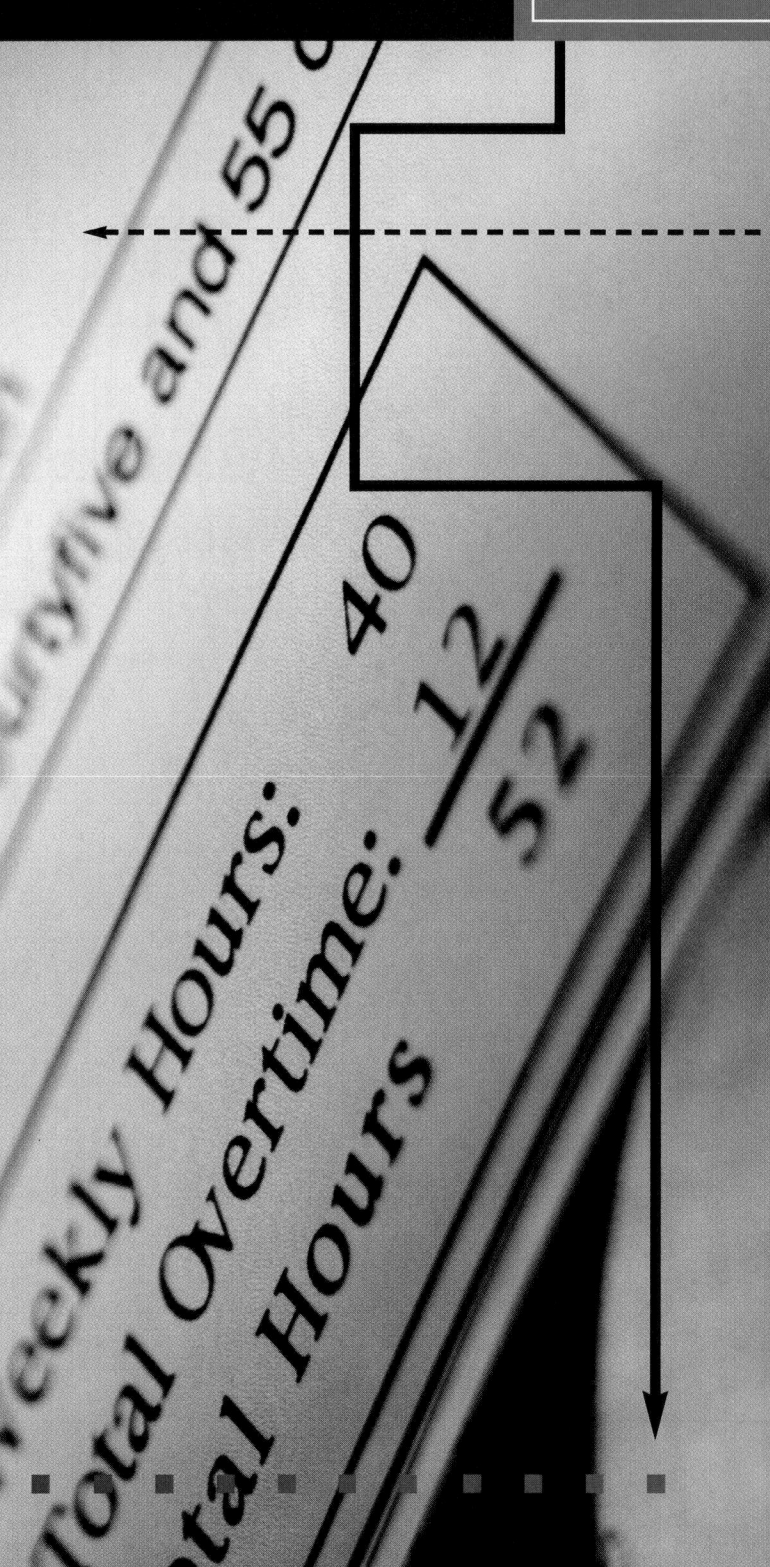

f you are employed, you know that your paycheck is normally less than the total amount you earned because your employer deducted amounts for such items as federal income tax and social security tax. For example, if you worked 20 hours last week at $10 per hour and you are paid weekly, your payroll check could appear as follows:

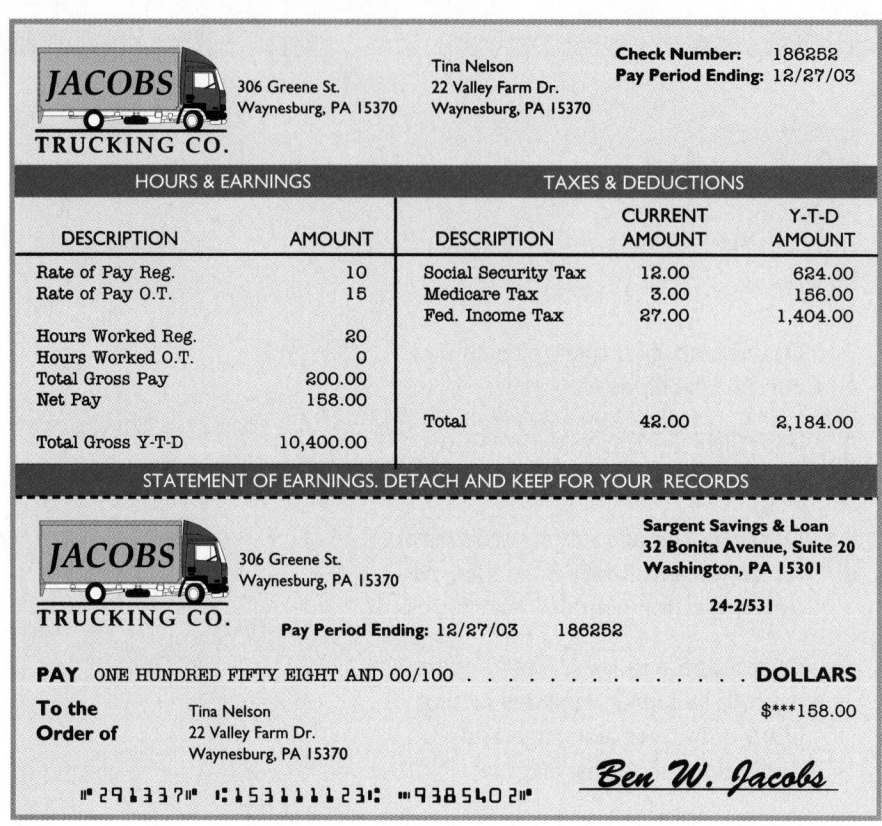

Your employer has a liability to you for your earnings until you are paid. Your employer also has a liability to deposit the taxes withheld. In this chapter, we will discuss liabilities for amounts that must be paid within a short period of time. In addition to liabilities related to payroll and payroll taxes, we will discuss liabilities from notes payable and product warranties.

The Nature of Current Liabilities

objective 1

Define and give examples of current liabilities.

Your credit card balance is probably due within a short time, such as 30 days. Such liabilities that are to be paid out of current assets and are due within a short time, usually within one year, are called **current liabilities**. Most current liabilities arise from two basic transactions:

1. Receiving goods or services prior to making payment.
2. Receiving payment prior to delivering goods or services.

An example of the first type of transaction is **accounts payable** arising from purchases of merchandise for resale. An example of the second type of transaction is **unearned rent** arising from the receipt of rent in advance. Some additional examples of current liabilities that we discussed in previous chapters are:

- Taxes payable—the amount of taxes owed to governmental units
- Interest payable—the amount of interest owed on borrowed funds
- Wages payable—the amount owed to employees

In this chapter, we will introduce some other common current liabilities. These include short-term notes payable, contingencies, payroll liabilities, and employee fringe benefits.

Short-Term Notes Payable

objective 2

Journalize entries for short-term notes payable.

Notes may be issued when merchandise or other assets are purchased. They may also be issued to creditors to temporarily satisfy an account payable created earlier. For example, assume that a business issues a 90-day, 12% note for $1,000, dated August 1, 2003, to Murray Co. for a $1,000 overdue account. The entry to record the issuance of the note is as follows:

Aug.	1	Accounts Payable—Murray Co.	1 0 0 0 00	
		Notes Payable		1 0 0 0 00
		Issued a 90-day, 12% note on account.		

When the note matures, the entry to record the payment of $1,000 principal plus $30 interest ($1,000 × 12% × 90/360) is as follows:

Oct.	30	Notes Payable	1 0 0 0 00	
		Interest Expense	3 0 00	
		Cash		1 0 3 0 00
		Paid principal and interest due on note.		

The interest expense is reported in the Other Expense section of the income statement for the year ended December 31, 2003. The interest expense account is closed at December 31.

The preceding entries for notes payable are similar to those we discussed in an earlier chapter for notes receivable. Notes payable entries are presented from the viewpoint of the borrower, while notes receivable entries are presented from the viewpoint of the creditor or lender. To illustrate, the following entries are journalized for a borrower (Bowden Co.), who issues a note payable to a creditor (Coker Co.):

	Bowden Co. (Borrower)			Coker Co. (Creditor)		

May 1. Bowden Co. purchased merchandise on account from Coker Co., $10,000, 2/10, n/30. The merchandise cost Coker Co. $7,500.	Merchandise Inventory
	  Accounts Payable
		10,000	10,000	Accounts Receivable
				  Sales
				
				Cost of Merchandise Sold
				  Merchandise Inventory
					10,000
					
					7,500
						10,000
						
						7,500

May 31. Bowden Co. issued a 60-day, 12% note for $10,000 to Coker Co. on account.	Accounts Payable
	  Notes Payable
		10,000	10,000	Notes Receivable
				  Accounts Receivable
					10,000	10,000

July 30. Bowden Co. paid Coker Co. the amount due on the note of May 31. Interest: $10,000 × 12% × 60/360.	Notes Payable
	Interest Expense
	  Cash
		10,000
		200
			10,200	Cash
				  Interest Revenue
				  Notes Receivable
					10,200	200
						10,000

Notes may also be issued when money is borrowed from banks. Although the terms may vary, many banks would accept from the borrower an interest-bearing note for the amount of the loan. For example, assume that on September 19 a firm borrows $4,000 from First National Bank by giving the bank a 90-day, 15% note. The entry to record the receipt of cash and the issuance of the note is as follows:

Sep.	19	Cash		4 0 0 0 00	
		Notes Payable			4 0 0 0 00
		Issued a 90-day, 15% note to the bank.			

On the due date of the note (December 18), the borrower owes $4,000, the principal of the note, plus interest of $150 ($4,000 × 15% × 90/360). The entry to record the payment of the note is as follows:

Dec.	18	Notes Payable		4 0 0 0 00	
		Interest Expense		1 5 0 00	
		Cash			4 1 5 0 00
		Paid principal and interest due on note.			

The U.S. Treasury issues short-term treasury bills to investors at a discount.

Sometimes a borrower will issue to a creditor a discounted note rather than an interest-bearing note. Although such a note does not specify an interest rate, the creditor sets a rate of interest and deducts the interest from the face amount of the note. This interest is called the **discount**. The rate used in computing the discount is called the **discount rate**. The borrower is given the remainder, called the **proceeds**.

To illustrate, assume that on August 10, Cary Company issues a $20,000, 90-day note to Seinfeld Company in exchange for inventory. Seinfeld discounts the note at a rate of 15%. The amount of the discount, $750, is debited to *Interest Expense*. The proceeds, $19,250, are debited to *Merchandise Inventory. Notes Payable* is credited for the face amount of the note, which is also its maturity value. This entry is shown on the following page.

In buying a used delivery truck, a business issues an $8,000, 60-day note dated July 15, which the truck's seller discounts at 12%. What is the cost of the truck (the proceeds)?

$7,840 [$8,000 − ($8,000 × 12% × 60/360)]

Aug.	10	Merchandise Inventory	19 2 5 0 00		
		Interest Expense	7 5 0 00		
		Notes Payable		20 0 0 0 00	
		Issued a 90-day note to Seinfeld Co.,			
		discounted at 15%.			

When the note is paid, the following entry is recorded:[1]

Nov.	8	Notes Payable	20 0 0 0 00		
		Cash		20 0 0 0 00	
		Paid note due.			

Contingent Liabilities

objective 3

Describe the accounting treatment for contingent liabilities and journalize entries for product warranties.

Some past transactions will result in liabilities if certain events occur in the future. These potential obligations are called **contingent liabilities**. For example, **Ford Motor Company** would have a contingent liability for the estimated costs associated with warranty work on new car sales. The obligation is contingent upon a *future event*, namely, a customer requiring warranty work on a vehicle. The obligation is the result of a *past transaction*, which is the original sale of the vehicle.

If a contingent liability is *probable* and the amount of the liability can be *reasonably estimated*, it should be recorded in the accounts. **Ford Motor Company's** vehicle warranty costs are an example of a *recordable* contingent liability. The warranty costs are *probable* because it is known that warranty repairs will be required on some vehicles. In addition, the costs can be *estimated* from past warranty experience.

To illustrate, assume that during June a company sells a product for $60,000 on which there is a 36-month warranty for repairing defects. Past experience indicates that the average cost to repair defects is 5% of the sales price over the warranty period. The entry to record the estimated product warranty expense for June is as follows:

A business sells to a customer $120,000 of commercial audio equipment with a one-year repair and replacement warranty. Historically, the average cost to repair or replace is 2% of sales. How is this contingent liability recorded?

Product Warranty Expense   2,400
    Product Warranty Payable   2,400

June	30	Product Warranty Expense	3 0 0 0 00		
		Product Warranty Payable		3 0 0 0 00	
		Warranty expense for June, 5% × $60,000.			

This transaction matches revenues and expenses properly by recording warranty costs in the same period in which the sale is recorded. When the defective product is repaired, the repair costs are recorded by debiting *Product Warranty Payable* and crediting *Cash*, *Supplies*, or other appropriate accounts. Thus, if a customer required a $200 part replacement on August 16, the entry would be:

----

[1] If the accounting period ends before a discounted note is paid, an adjusting entry should record the prepaid (deferred) interest that is not yet an expense. This deferred interest would be deducted from Notes Payable in the Current Liabilities section of the balance sheet.

Aug.	16	Product Warranty Payable			2	0	0	00								
		Supplies								2	0	0	00			
		Replaced defective part under warranty.														

If a contingent liability is probable but cannot be *reasonably estimated* or is only *possible*, then the nature of the contingent liability should be disclosed in the footnotes to the financial statements. Professional judgment is required in distinguishing between contingent liabilities that are probable versus those that are only possible.

Common examples of contingent liabilities disclosed in notes to the financial statements are litigation, environmental matters, guarantees, and sale of receivables. The following example of a contingency disclosure, related to patent infringement litigation, was taken from a recent annual report of **priceline.com**: *A third party patent applicant . . . , Thomas Woolston, . . . had filed . . . a request to declare an interference between (his) patent application . . . describing an electronic market for used and collectible goods and priceline.com's core buyer-driven commerce patent. . . . If an interference is declared and thereafter resolved in favor of Woolston, such resolution could result in an award of some or all of the disputed patent claims to Woolston. If, following such award, Woolston were successful in a patent infringement action against priceline.com, . . . this could require priceline.com to obtain licenses from Woolston at a cost which could significantly adversely affect priceline.com's business.* The accounting treatment of contingent liabilities is summarized in Exhibit 1.

Exhibit 1 Accounting Treatment of Contingent Liabilities

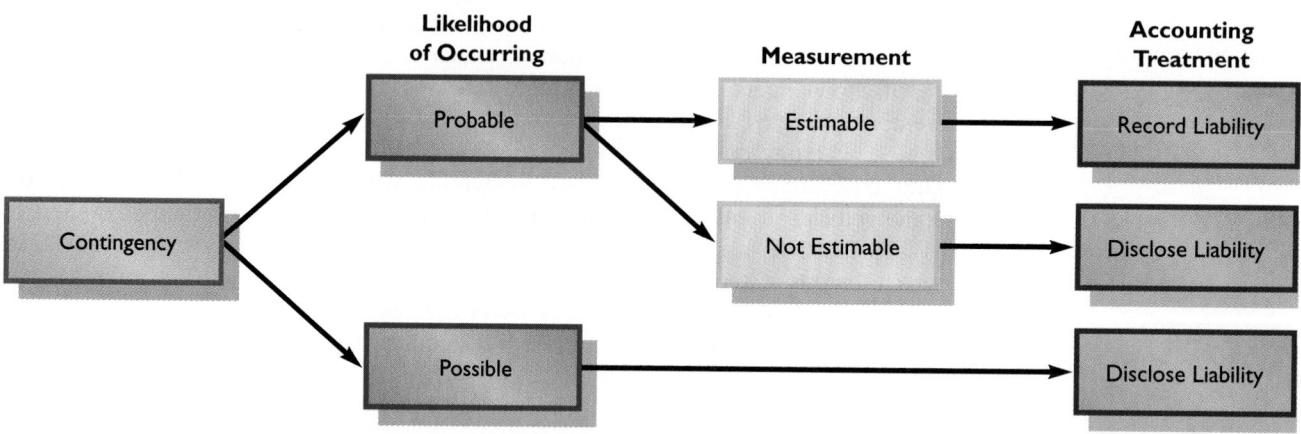

Payroll and Payroll Taxes

objective 4

Determine employer liabilities for payroll, including liabilities arising from employee earnings and deductions from earnings.

We are all familiar with the term payroll. In accounting, the term **payroll** refers to the amount paid to employees for the services they provide during a period. A business's payroll is usually significant for several reasons. First, employees are sensitive to payroll errors and irregularities. Maintaining good employee morale requires that the payroll be paid on a timely, accurate basis. Second, the payroll is subject to various federal and state regulations. Finally, the payroll and related payroll taxes have a significant effect on the net income of most businesses. Although the amount of such expenses varies widely, it is not unusual for a business's payroll and payroll-related expenses to equal nearly one-third of its revenue.

Liability for Employee Earnings

Salaries and wages paid to employees are an employer's labor expenses. The term **salary** usually refers to payment for managerial, administrative, or similar services. The rate of salary is normally expressed in terms of a month or a year. The term **wages** usually refers to payment for manual labor, both skilled and unskilled. The rate of wages is normally stated on an hourly or weekly basis. In practice, the terms salary and wages are often used interchangeably.

The basic salary or wage of an employee may be increased by commissions, profit sharing, or cost-of-living adjustments. Many businesses pay managers an annual bonus in addition to a basic salary. The amount of the bonus is often based on some measure of productivity, such as income or profit of the business. Although payment is usually made by check or in cash, it may be in the form of securities, notes, lodging, or other property or services. Generally, the form of payment has no effect on how salaries and wages are treated by either the employer or the employee.

Salary and wage rates are determined by agreement between the employer and the employees. Businesses engaged in interstate commerce must follow the requirements of the Fair Labor Standards Act. Employers covered by this legislation, which is commonly called the Federal Wage and Hour Law, are required to pay a minimum rate of 1½ times the regular rate for all hours worked in excess of 40 hours per week. Exemptions are provided for executive, administrative, and certain supervisory positions. Premium rates for overtime or for working at night, holidays, or other less desirable times are fairly common, even when not required by law. In some cases, the premium rates may be as much as twice the base rate.

To illustrate computing an employee's earnings, assume that John T. McGrath is employed by McDermott Supply Co. at the rate of $28 per hour. Any hours in excess of 40 hours per week are paid at a rate of 1½ times the normal rate, or $42 ($28 + $14) per hour. For the week ended December 27, McGrath's time card indicates that he worked 42 hours. His earnings for that week are computed as follows:

Earnings at base rate (40 × $28)	$1,120
Earnings at overtime rate (2 × $42)	84
Total earnings	$1,204

Deductions from Employee Earnings

The total earnings of an employee for a payroll period, including bonuses and overtime pay, are called **gross pay**. From this amount is subtracted one or more **deductions** to arrive at the net pay. **Net pay** is the amount the employer must pay the employee. The deductions for federal taxes are usually the largest deduction. Deductions may also be required for state or local income taxes. Other deductions may be made for medical insurance, contributions to pensions, and for items authorized by individual employees.

Income Taxes

Except for certain types of employment, all employers must withhold a portion of employee earnings for payment of the employees' federal income tax. As a basis for determining the amount to be withheld, each employee completes and submits to the employer an "Employee's Withholding Allowance Certificate," often called a W-4. Exhibit 2 is an example of a completed W-4 form.

You may recall filling out a W-4 form. On the W-4, an employee indicates marital status, the number of withholding allowances, and whether any additional withholdings are authorized. A single employee may claim one withholding allowance. A married employee may claim an additional allowance for a spouse. An employee may also claim an allowance for each dependent other than a spouse. Each allowance claimed reduces the amount of federal income tax withheld from the employee's check.

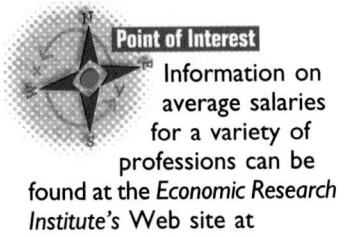

Employee salaries and wages are expenses to an employer.

Point of Interest
Information on average salaries for a variety of professions can be found at the *Economic Research Institute's* Web site at **www.erieri.com**.

Real World
Professional athletes must pay local taxes in each location in which they play their sport.

Exhibit 2 Employee's Withholding Allowance Certificate (W-4 Form)

Cut here and give Form W-4 to your employer. Keep the top part for your records.

Form **W-4**	**Employee's Withholding Allowance Certificate**	OMB No. 1545-0010
Department of the Treasury Internal Revenue Service	► For Privacy Act and Paperwork Reduction Act Notice, see page 2.	**2002**

1 Type or print your first name and middle initial — John T.   Last name — McGrath   **2** Your social security number — 381 48 9120

Home address (number and street or rural route)
1830 4ᵗʰ Street

3 ☒ Single ☐ Married ☐ Married, but withhold at higher Single rate.
Note: If married, but legally separated, or spouse is a nonresident alien, check the Single box.

City or town, state, and ZIP code
Clinton, Iowa 52732-6142

4 If your last name differs from that on your social security card, check here. You must call 1-800-772-1213 for a new card . . . ► ☐

5 Total number of allowances you are claiming (from line H above OR from the applicable worksheet on page 2)   **5**   1

6 Additional amount, if any, you want withheld from each paycheck . . . .   **6** $

7 I claim exemption from withholding for 2002, and I certify that I meet **BOTH** of the following conditions for exemption:
● Last year I had a right to a refund of **ALL** Federal income tax withheld because I had **NO** tax liability **AND**
● This year I expect a refund of **ALL** Federal income tax withheld because I expect to have **NO** tax liability.
If you meet both conditions, write "EXEMPT" here . . . . ► **7**

Under penalties of perjury, I certify that I am entitled to the number of withholding allowances claimed on this certificate, or I am entitled to claim exempt status.
Employee's signature
(Form is not valid
unless you sign it) ► *John T. McGrath*   Date ► June 2, 2002

8 Employer's name and address (Employer: Complete lines 8 and 10 only if sending to the IRS.)   **9** Office code (optional)   **10** Employer identification number

---

Federal income tax withholding tables are available from the Internal Revenue Service as part of Circular E, "Employer's Tax Guide."

The amount that must be withheld for income tax differs, depending upon each employee's gross pay and completed W-4. Most employers use wage bracket withholding tables furnished by the Internal Revenue Service to determine the amount to be withheld.

Exhibit 3 is an example of a wage bracket withholding table. This table is for a single employee who is paid weekly. Other tables are used for employees who are married or who are paid biweekly, semimonthly, monthly, or at other time periods. Unlike social security tax, there is no ceiling on the amount of employee earnings subject to federal income tax withholding.

In using the withholding table, the amount of federal income tax withheld each pay period is indicated where the row showing the employee's wage bracket intersects the column showing the employee's withholding allowances. For example,

Exhibit 3 Wage Bracket Withholding Table

SINGLE Persons—WEEKLY Payroll Period

If the wages are—		And the number of withholding allowances claimed is—										
At least	But less than	0	1	2	3	4	5	6	7	8	9	10
		The amount of income tax to be withheld is—										
900	910	178	163	148	133	118	103	89	74	65	57	49
910	920	180	165	151	136	121	106	91	77	66	58	50
920	930	183	168	153	139	124	109	94	79	68	60	52
930	940	186	171	156	141	127	112	97	82	69	61	53
940	950	189	174	159	144	129	115	100	85	71	63	55
950	960	192	177	162	147	132	117	103	88	73	64	56
960	970	194	179	165	150	135	120	105	91	76	66	58
970	980	197	182	167	153	138	123	108	93	79	67	59
980	990	200	185	170	155	141	126	111	96	81	69	61
990	1,000	203	188	173	158	143	129	114	99	84	70	62
1,000	1,010	206	191	176	161	146	131	117	102	87	72	64
1,010	1,020	208	193	179	164	149	134	119	105	90	75	65
1,020	1,030	211	196	181	167	152	137	122	107	93	78	67
1,030	1,040	214	199	184	169	155	140	125	110	95	81	68
1,040	1,050	217	202	187	172	157	143	128	113	98	83	70
1,050	1,060	220	205	190	175	160	145	131	116	101	86	71
1,060	1,070	222	207	193	178	163	148	133	119	104	89	74
1,070	1,080	225	210	195	181	166	151	136	121	107	92	77
1,080	1,090	228	213	198	183	169	154	139	124	109	95	80
1,090	1,100	231	216	201	186	171	157	142	127	112	97	83
1,100	1,110	234	219	204	189	174	159	145	130	115	100	85
1,110	1,120	236	221	207	192	177	162	147	133	118	103	88
1,120	1,130	239	224	209	195	180	165	150	135	121	106	91
1,130	1,140	242	227	212	197	183	168	153	138	123	109	94
1,140	1,150	245	230	215	200	185	171	156	141	126	111	97
1,150	1,160	248	233	218	203	188	173	159	144	129	114	99
1,160	1,170	252	235	221	206	191	176	161	147	132	117	102
1,170	1,180	255	238	223	209	194	179	164	149	135	120	105
1,180	1,190	258	241	226	211	197	182	167	152	137	123	108
1,190	1,200	261	244	229	214	199	185	170	155	140	125	111
1,200	1,210	264	248	232	217	202	187	173	158	143	128	113
1,210	1,220	267	251	235	220	205	190	175	161	146	131	116
1,220	1,230	270	254	237	223	208	193	178	163	149	134	119
1,230	1,240	273	257	240	225	211	196	181	166	151	137	122
1,240	1,250	276	260	244	228	213	199	184	169	154	139	125

assume that John T. McGrath, who is single and has declared one withholding allowance, made $1,204 for the week ended December 27. Using the withholding table in Exhibit 3, the amount of federal income tax withheld is $248.

In addition to the federal income tax, employees may also be required to pay a state income tax and a city income tax. State and city taxes are withheld from employees' earnings and paid to state and city governments.

FICA Tax

Most of us have FICA tax withheld from our payroll checks by our employers. Employers are required by the Federal Insurance Contributions Act (FICA) to withhold a portion of the earnings of each of the employees. The amount of FICA tax withheld is the employees' contribution to two federal programs. Tax is withheld separately under each program. The first program, called **social security**, is for old age, survivors, and disability insurance (OASDI). The second program, called **Medicare**, is health insurance for senior citizens.

The amount of tax that employers are required to withhold from each employee is normally based on the amount of earnings paid in the *calendar* year. Although both the schedule of future tax rates and the maximum amount subject to tax are revised often by Congress, such changes have little effect on the basic payroll system. In this text, we will use a social security rate of 6% on the first $80,000 of annual earnings and a Medicare rate of 1.5% on all annual earnings.

To illustrate, assume that John T. McGrath's annual earnings prior to the current payroll period total $79,296. Assume also that the current period earnings are $1,204. The total FICA tax of $60.30 is determined as follows:

Earnings subject to 6% social security tax		
($80,000 − $79,296)	$ 704	
Social security tax rate	× 6%	
Social security tax		$42.24
Earnings subject to 1.5% Medicare tax	$1,204	
Medicare tax rate	× 1.5%	
Medicare tax		18.06
Total FICA tax		$60.30

Other Deductions

Neither the employer nor the employee has any choice in deducting taxes from gross earnings. However, employees may choose to have additional amounts deducted for other purposes. For example, you as an employee may authorize deductions for retirement savings, for contributions to charitable organizations, or for premiums on employee insurance. A union contract may also require the deduction of union dues.

Computing Employee Net Pay

Gross earnings less payroll deductions equals the amount to be paid to an employee for the payroll period. This amount is the *net pay*, which is often called the *take-home pay*. Assuming that John T. McGrath authorized deductions for retirement savings and for a United Way contribution, the amount to be paid McGrath for the week ended December 27 is $870.70, as shown at the top of the following page.

Q&A

If an employee earns $6,700 per month and has been employed since January 1 of the current year, what is the total FICA tax deducted from the employee's December paycheck?

Social security tax	
($6,300* × 6%)	$378.00
Medicare tax	
($6,700 × 1.5%)	100.50
Total FICA tax	$478.50

*$80,000 − ($6,700 × 11)

Point of Interest

In 1936, the Social Security Board described how the tax was expected to affect a worker's pay, as follows:

The taxes called for in this law will be paid both by your employer and by you. For the next 3 years you will pay maybe 15 cents a week, maybe 25 cents a week, maybe 30 cents or more, according to what you earn. That is to say, during the next 3 years, beginning January 1, 1937, you will pay 1 cent for every dollar you earn, and at the same time your employer will pay 1 cent for every dollar you earn, up to $3,000 a year. . . .

. . . Beginning in 1940 you will pay, and your employer will pay, 1½ cents for each dollar you earn, up to $3,000 a year . . . and then beginning in 1943, you will pay 2 cents, and so will your employer, for every dollar you earn for the next three years. After that, you and your employer will each pay half a cent more for 3 years, and finally, beginning in 1949, . . . you and your employer will each pay 3 cents on each dollar you earn, up to $3,000 a year. That is the most you will ever pay.

The rate on January 1, 2001, was 7.65 cents per dollar earned (7.65%). The social security portion was 6.20% on the first $80,400 of earnings. The Medicare portion was 1.45% on all earnings.

Source: Arthur Lodge, "That Is the Most You Will Ever Pay," Journal of Accountancy, October 1985, p. 44.

Gross earnings for the week		$1,204.00
Deductions:		
Social security tax	$ 42.24	
Medicare tax	18.06	
Federal income tax	248.00	
Retirement savings	20.00	
United Way	5.00	
Total deductions		333.30
Net pay		$ 870.70

Liability for Employer's Payroll Taxes

So far, we have discussed the payroll taxes that are withheld from the employees' earnings. Most employers are also subject to federal and state payroll taxes based on the amount paid their employees. Such taxes are an operating expense of the business. Exhibit 4 summarizes the responsibility for employee and employer payroll taxes.

Exhibit 4 Responsibility for Tax Payments

The U.S. Government receives income from various taxes, which are spent on a variety of government services. The relative sizes of these incomes and outlays for a recent fiscal year are shown below.

FEDERAL INCOME

Corporate income tax
Estate, gift and other
11%
8%
FICA and FUTA
33%
48%
Personal income tax

FICA Tax

Employers are required to contribute to the social security and Medicare programs for each employee. The employer must match the employee's contribution to each program.

Federal Unemployment Compensation Tax

The Federal Unemployment Tax Act (FUTA) provides for temporary payments to those who become unemployed as a result of layoffs due to economic causes beyond their control. Types of employment subject to this program are similar to those covered by FICA taxes. A tax of 6.2% is levied on employers only, rather than on both employers and employees.[2]

---

[2] This rate may be reduced to 0.8% for credits for state unemployment compensation tax.

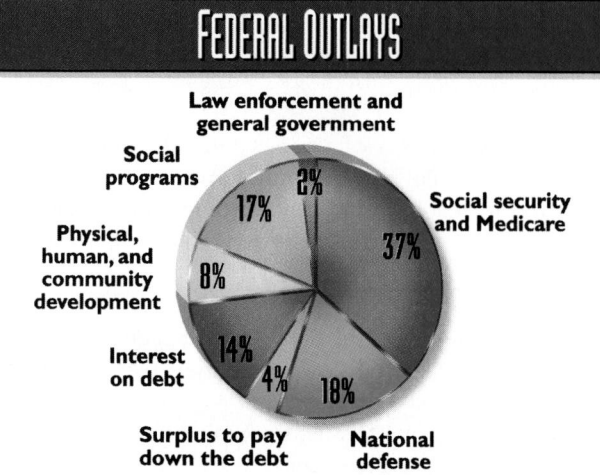

FEDERAL OUTLAYS

Law enforcement and general government — 2%
Social programs — 17%
Physical, human, and community development — 8%
Interest on debt — 14%
Surplus to pay down the debt — 4%
National defense — 18%
Social security and Medicare — 37%

Source: Internal Revenue Service

It is applied to only the first $7,000 of the earnings of each covered employee during a calendar year. Congress often revises the rate and maximum earnings subject to federal unemployment compensation tax. The funds collected by the federal government are not paid directly to the unemployed but are allocated among the states for use in state programs.

State Unemployment Compensation Tax

State Unemployment Tax Acts (SUTA) also provide for payments to unemployed workers. The amounts paid as benefits are obtained, for the most part, from a tax levied upon employers only. A few states require employee contributions also. The rates of tax and the tax bases vary. In most states, employers who provide stable employment for their employees are granted reduced rates. The employment experience and the status of each employer's tax account are reviewed annually, and the tax rates are adjusted accordingly.[3]

[3] As of January 1, 2001, the maximum state rate credited against the federal unemployment rate was 5.4% of the first $7,000 of each employee's earnings during a calendar year.

BUSINESS ON STAGE

Teaming up for High Performance

Picture a factory in your mind. Do you see employees working alone, performing mind-numbing repetitive work? Fortunately, this picture is fast disappearing from the employment landscape. Many companies, such as Procter & Gamble, Hewlett-Packard, and Federal Express, are using teams. Teams typically consist of between 8 to 15 full-time employees. Often team members represent different functions, such as marketing, manufacturing, and finance.

Why are companies using teams? Teams have the following advantages over individual employees:

- Teams are able to put employees' skills together to solve problems, complete projects, and combine tasks that form a process.

- Teams perform the coordination and communication tasks formerly performed by middle management.
- Empowered teams are more creative and more satisfied in their work.
- Teams take on expanded responsibilities, such as ordering materials, conducting quality checks, making team hiring and firing decisions, developing work schedules, and jointly establishing performance targets with management.

One area of challenge is in the area of team compensation and rewards. Popular plans develop individual base pay rates on the basis of skills obtained, rather than just seniority. A recent survey noted that 85% of companies using teams set base pay

rates above the industry average. Additional bonuses are available based on achieving team goals. The same survey noted such bonuses averaged around 10% of base pay.

Team-based management assigns responsibility and authority to the team members and provides rewards for this added work. As one team member put it, "It's a real mind shift. You're used to the expectation that it's your job to have the best idea. But no individual is going to have the best idea. That's not how it works—the best ideas come from the collective intelligence of the team. If you accept that, you're in for a big change in how you think about yourself." ■

Accounting Systems for Payroll and Payroll Taxes

Describe payroll accounting systems that use a payroll register, employee earnings records, and a general journal.

In designing payroll systems, the requirements of various federal, state, and local agencies for payroll data are considered. Payroll data must also be maintained accurately for each payroll period and for each employee. Periodic reports using payroll data must be submitted to government agencies. The payroll data itself must be retained for possible inspection by the various agencies.

Payroll systems must be designed to pay employees on a timely basis. Payroll systems should also be designed to provide useful data for management decision-making needs. Such needs might include settling employee grievances and negotiating retirement or other benefits with employees.

Although payroll systems differ among businesses, the major elements common to most payroll systems are the payroll register, employee's earnings record, and payroll checks. We discuss and illustrate each of these elements next. We have kept the illustrations relatively simple, and they may be modified in practice to meet the needs of each individual business.

Payroll Register

The **payroll register** is a multicolumn form used in assembling and summarizing the data needed for each payroll period. Its design varies according to the number and classes of employees and the extent to which computers are used. Exhibit 5 shows a form suitable for a small number of employees.

The nature of the data appearing in the payroll register is evident from the column headings. The number of hours worked and the earnings and deduction data are inserted in their proper columns. The sum of the deductions for each employee is then subtracted from the total earnings to yield the amount to be paid. The check numbers are recorded in the payroll register as evidence of payment.

The last two columns of the payroll register are used to accumulate the total wages or salaries to be debited to the various expense accounts. This process is usually called **payroll distribution**.

The format of the payroll register in Exhibit 5 aids in determining the mathematical accuracy of the payroll before checks are issued to employees. All column totals should be verified, as shown at the top of the following page.

Exhibit 5 Payroll Register

	Employee Name	Total Hours	Earnings			
			Regular	Overtime	Total	
1	Abrams, Julie S.	40	500.00		500.00	1
2	Elrod, Fred G.	44	392.00	58.80	450.80	2
3	Gomez, Jose C.	40	840.00		840.00	3
4	McGrath, John T.	42	1,120.00	84.00	1,204.00	4
25	Wilkes, Glenn K.	40	480.00		480.00	25
26	Zumpano, Michael W.	40	600.00		600.00	26
27	Total		13,328.00	574.00	13,902.00	27
28						28

Earnings:

Regular	$13,328.00	
Overtime	574.00	
Total		$13,902.00

Deductions:

Social security tax	$ 643.07	
Medicare tax	208.53	
Federal income tax	3,332.00	
Retirement savings	680.00	
United Way	470.00	
Accounts receivable	50.00	
Total		5,383.60

Paid—net amount	$ 8,518.40

Accounts debited:

Sales Salaries Expense	$11,122.00
Office Salaries Expense	2,780.00
Total (as above)	$13,902.00

Recording Employees' Earnings

Amounts in the payroll register may be posted directly to the accounts. An alternative is to use the payroll register as a supporting record for a journal entry. The entry based on the payroll register in Exhibit 5 follows.

Dec.	27	Sales Salaries Expense	11 1 2 2 00		
		Office Salaries Expense	2 7 8 0 00		
		Social Security Tax Payable		6 4 3 07	
		Medicare Tax Payable		2 0 8 53	
		Employees Federal Income Tax Payable		3 3 3 2 00	
		Retirement Savings Deductions Payable		6 8 0 00	
		United Way Deductions Payable		4 7 0 00	
		Accounts Receivable—Fred G. Elrod		5 0 00	
		Salaries Payable		8 5 1 8 40	
		Payroll for week ended December 27.			

Exhibit 5 (concluded)

	Deductions						Paid		Accounts Debited		
	Social Security Tax	Medicare Tax	Federal Income Tax	Retirement Savings	Misc.	Total	Net Amount	Check No.	Sales Salaries Expense	Office Salaries Expense	
1	30.00	7.50	74.00	20.00	UW 10.00	141.50	358.50	6857	500.00		1
2	27.05	6.76	62.00		AR 50.00	145.81	304.99	6858		450.80	2
3	50.40	12.60	131.00	25.00	UW 10.00	229.00	611.00	6859	840.00		3
4	42.24	18.06	248.00	20.00	UW 5.00	333.30	870.70	6860	1,204.00		4
25	28.80	7.20	69.00	10.00		115.00	365.00	6880	480.00		25
26	36.00	9.00	79.00	5.00	UW 2.00	131.00	469.00	6881		600.00	26
27	643.07	208.53	3,332.00	680.00	UW 470.00	5,383.60	8,518.40		11,122.00	2,780.00	27
28					AR 50.00						28

Miscellaneous Deductions: UW—United Way; AR—Accounts Receivable

Recording and Paying Payroll Taxes

The employer's payroll taxes become liabilities when the related payroll is *paid* to employees. In addition, employers are required to compute and report payroll taxes on a *calendar-year* basis, even if a different fiscal year is used for financial reporting and income tax purposes.

To illustrate, assume that Everson Company's fiscal year ends on April 30. Also, assume that Everson Company owes its employees $26,000 of wages on December 31. The following portions of the $26,000 of wages are subject to payroll taxes on December 31:

	Earnings Subject to Payroll Taxes
Social Security Tax (6.0%)	$18,000
Medicare Tax (1.5%)	26,000
State and Federal Unemployment Compensation Tax	1,000

> ### Payroll taxes become a liability to the employer when the payroll is paid.

Real World

Social security contributions (both the employees' and employer's amounts) and federal income taxes must be deposited quarterly in a federal depository bank. An "Employer's Quarterly Federal Tax Return" (Form 941) must also be filed. Unemployment compensation tax returns and payments are required annually by the federal government and most state governments.

If the payroll is paid on December 31, the payroll taxes will be based on the preceding amounts. If the payroll is paid on January 2, however, the *entire* $26,000 will be subject to *all* payroll taxes. This is because the maximum earnings limitation for determining social security and unemployment taxes will not be exceeded at the beginning of the calendar year.

The payroll register for McDermott Supply Co. in Exhibit 5 indicates that the amount of social security tax withheld is $643.07 and Medicare tax withheld is $208.53. Since the employer must match the employees' FICA contributions, the employer's social security payroll tax will also be $643.07, and the Medicare tax will be $208.53. Further, assume that the earnings subject to state and federal unemployment compensation taxes are $2,710. Multiplying this amount by the state (5.4%) and federal (0.8%) rates yields the unemployment compensation taxes shown in the following payroll tax computation:

Social security tax	$ 643.07
Medicare tax	208.53
State unemployment compensation tax (5.4% × $2,710)	146.34
Federal unemployment compensation tax (0.8% × $2,710)	21.68
Total payroll tax expense	$1,019.62

The entry to journalize the payroll tax expense for the week and the liability for the taxes accrued is shown below.

Date		Description	Debit	Credit
Dec.	27	Payroll Tax Expense	1 0 1 9 62	
		Social Security Tax Payable		6 4 3 07
		Medicare Tax Payable		2 0 8 53
		State Unemployment Tax Payable		1 4 6 34
		Federal Unemployment Tax Payable		2 1 68
		Payroll taxes for week ended		
		December 27.		

Employee's Earnings Record

The amount of each employee's earnings to date must be available at the end of each payroll period. This cumulative amount is required in order to compute each employee's social security and Medicare tax withholding and the employer's payroll taxes. It is essential, therefore, that a detailed payroll record be maintained for each employee. This record is called an employee's earnings record.

Exhibit 6 shows a portion of the employee's earnings record for John T. McGrath. The relationship between this record and the payroll register can be seen by tracing the amounts entered on McGrath's earnings record for December 27 back to its source—the fourth line of the payroll register in Exhibit 5.

In addition to spaces for recording data for each payroll period and the cumulative total of earnings, the employee's earnings record has spaces for quarterly totals and the yearly total. These totals are used in various reports for tax, insurance, and other purposes. One such report is the Wage and Tax Statement, commonly called a **Form W-2**. You may recall receiving a W-2 form for use in preparing your individual tax return. This form must be provided annually to each employee as well as to the Social Security Administration. The amounts reported in the Form W-2 shown below were taken from McGrath's employee's earnings record.

a Control number	22222	Void ☐	For Official Use Only ▶ OMB No. 1545-0008		
b Employer's identification number 61-8436524			1 Wages, tips, other compensation 80,500.00		2 Federal income tax withheld 17,710.00
c Employer's name, address, and ZIP code McDermott Supply Co. 415 5th Ave. So. Dubuque, IA 52736-0142			3 Social security wages 80,000.00		4 Social security tax withheld 4,800.00
			5 Medicare wages and tips 80,500.00		6 Medicare tax withheld 1,207.50
			7 Social security tips		8 Allocated tips
d Employee's social security number 381-48-9120			9 Advance EIC payment		10 Dependent care benefits
e Employee's name (first, middle initial, last) John T. McGrath 1830 4th St. Clinton, IA 52732-6142			11 Nonqualified plans		12 Benefits included in box 1
			13 See Instrs. for box 13		14 Other
f Employee's address and ZIP code			15 Statutory employee ☐ Deceased ☐ Pension plan ☐ Legal rep. ☐ Hshld. emp. ☐ Subtotal ☐ Deferred compensation ☐		
16 State IA	Employer's state I.D. No.	17 State wages, tips, etc.	18 State income tax	19 Locality name Dubuque	20 Local wages, tips, etc.	21 Local income tax

Cat. No. 10134D   Department of the Treasury—Internal Revenue Service

Form **W-2** Wage and Tax Statement

For Paperwork Reduction Act Notice, see separate instructions.

Copy A For Social Security Administration

Payroll Checks

At the end of each pay period, **payroll checks** are prepared. Each check includes a detachable statement showing the details of how the net pay was computed. Exhibit 7 on page F412 is a payroll check for John T. McGrath.

The amount paid to employees is normally recorded as a single amount, regardless of the number of employees. There is no need to record each payroll check separately in the journal, since all of the details are available in the payroll register.

For paying their payroll, most employers use payroll checks drawn on a special bank account. After the data for the payroll period have been recorded and summarized in the payroll register, a single check for the total amount to be paid is written on the firm's regular bank account. This check is then deposited in the special payroll bank account. Individual payroll checks are written from the payroll account, and the numbers of the payroll checks are inserted in the payroll register.

An advantage of using a separate payroll bank account is that the task of reconciling the bank statements is simplified. In addition, a payroll bank account establishes control over payroll checks by preventing the theft or misuse of uncashed payroll checks.

Exhibit 6 Employee's
Earnings Record

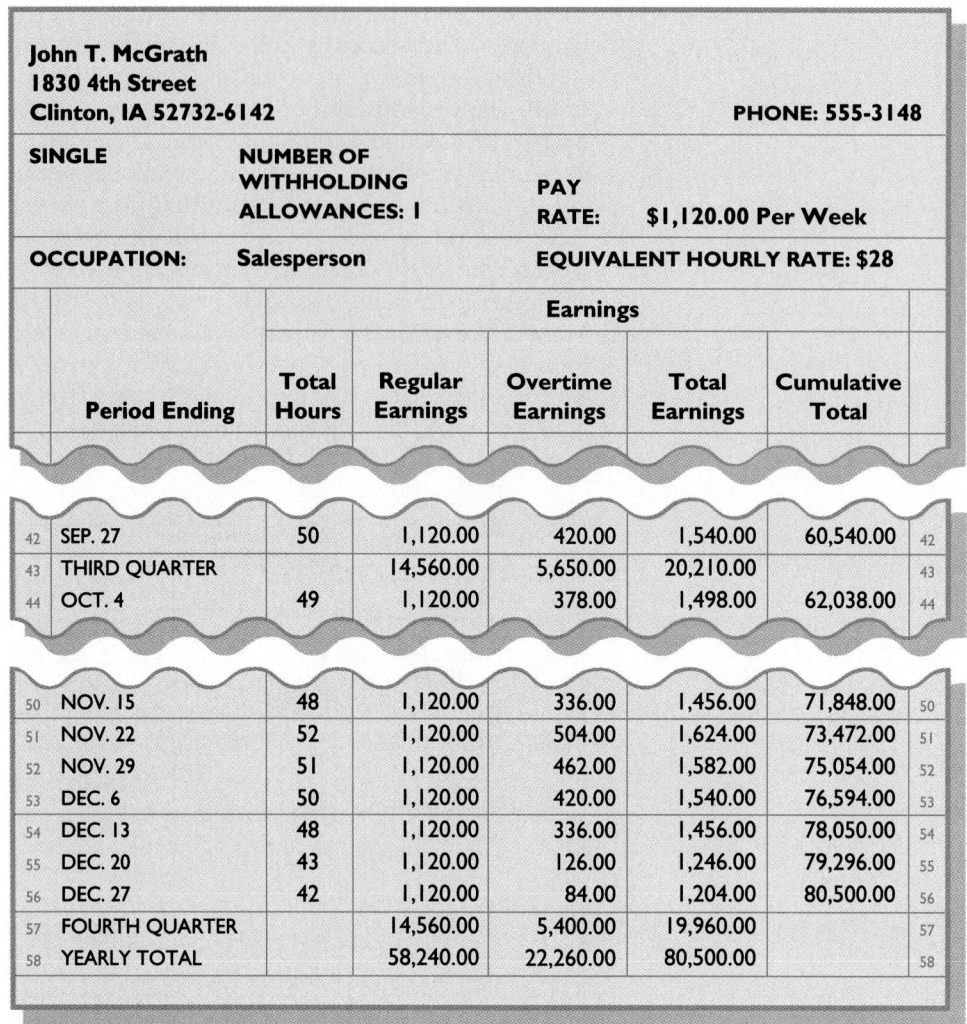

John T. McGrath
1830 4th Street
Clinton, IA 52732-6142   PHONE: 555-3148

SINGLE	NUMBER OF WITHHOLDING ALLOWANCES: 1	PAY RATE:	$1,120.00 Per Week
OCCUPATION:	Salesperson	EQUIVALENT HOURLY RATE: $28	

		Earnings				
	Period Ending	Total Hours	Regular Earnings	Overtime Earnings	Total Earnings	Cumulative Total
42	SEP. 27	50	1,120.00	420.00	1,540.00	60,540.00
43	THIRD QUARTER		14,560.00	5,650.00	20,210.00	
44	OCT. 4	49	1,120.00	378.00	1,498.00	62,038.00
50	NOV. 15	48	1,120.00	336.00	1,456.00	71,848.00
51	NOV. 22	52	1,120.00	504.00	1,624.00	73,472.00
52	NOV. 29	51	1,120.00	462.00	1,582.00	75,054.00
53	DEC. 6	50	1,120.00	420.00	1,540.00	76,594.00
54	DEC. 13	48	1,120.00	336.00	1,456.00	78,050.00
55	DEC. 20	43	1,120.00	126.00	1,246.00	79,296.00
56	DEC. 27	42	1,120.00	84.00	1,204.00	80,500.00
57	FOURTH QUARTER		14,560.00	5,400.00	19,960.00	
58	YEARLY TOTAL		58,240.00	22,260.00	80,500.00	

Currency may be used to pay payroll. However, many employees have their net pay deposited directly in a bank. In these cases, funds are transferred electronically.

Payroll System Diagram

You may find Exhibit 8 useful in following the flow of data within the payroll segment of an accounting system. The diagram indicates the relationships among the primary components of the payroll system we described in this chapter.

Our focus in the preceding discussion has been on the outputs of a payroll system: the payroll register, payroll checks, the employees' earnings records, and tax and other reports. As shown in the diagram in Exhibit 8, the inputs into a payroll system may be classified as either constants or variables.

Constants are data that remain unchanged from payroll to payroll and thus do not need to be entered into the system each pay period. Examples of constants include such data as each employee's name and social security number, marital status, number of income tax withholding allowances, rate of pay, payroll category (office, sales, etc.), and department where employed. The FICA tax rates and various tax tables are also constants that apply to all employees. In a computerized accounting system, constants are stored within a payroll file.

Variables are data that change from payroll to payroll and thus must be entered into the system each pay period. Examples of variables include such data as the

SOC. SEC. NO.: 381-48-9120

EMPLOYEE NO.: 814

DATE OF BIRTH: February 15, 1977

DATE EMPLOYMENT TERMINATED:

	Social Security Tax	Medicare Tax	Federal Income Tax	Retirement Savings	Other		Total	Net Amount	Check No.	
42	92.40	23.10	338.80	20.00			474.30	1,065.70	6175	42
43	1,212.60	303.15	4,446.20	260.00	UW	40.00	6,261.95	13,948.05		43
44	89.88	22.47	329.56	20.00			461.91	1,036.09	6225	44
50	87.36	21.84	320.32	20.00			449.52	1,006.48	6530	50
51	97.44	24.36	357.28	20.00			499.08	1,124.92	6582	51
52	94.92	23.73	348.04	20.00			486.69	1,095.31	6640	52
53	92.40	23.10	338.80	20.00	UW	5.00	479.30	1,060.70	6688	53
54	87.36	21.84	320.32	20.00			449.52	1,006.48	6743	54
55	74.76	18.69	260.00	20.00			373.45	872.55	6801	55
56	42.24	18.06	248.00	20.00	UW	5.00	333.30	870.70	6860	56
57	1,167.60	299.40	4,391.20	260.00	UW	15.00	6,133.20	13,826.80		57
58	4,800.00	1,207.50	17,710.00	1,040.00	UW	100.00	24,857.50	55,642.50		58

Column headers: **Deductions** spanning Social Security Tax, Medicare Tax, Federal Income Tax, Retirement Savings, Other; **Paid** spanning Net Amount, Check No.

Exhibit 6 (concluded)

Point of Interest

In the movie *Superman III*, Gus Gorman embezzled payroll funds by programming the computer to round down each employee's payroll amount to the nearest penny. He then added the amount "rounded out" to his own payroll check. For example, if an employee's total pay was $458.533, the payroll program would pay the employee $458.53 and add the $0.003 to a special account. The total in this special account would be transferred to Gus's paycheck at the end of the processing of the payroll. In this way, Gus's check increased from $143.80 to $85,000 in one pay period!

number of hours or days worked for each employee during the payroll period, days of sick leave with pay, vacation credits, and cumulative earnings and taxes withheld. If salespersons are paid commissions, the amount of their sales would also vary from period to period.

Internal Controls for Payroll Systems

Payroll processing, as we discussed above, requires the input of a large amount of data, along with numerous and sometimes complex computations. These factors, combined with the large dollar amounts involved, require controls to ensure that payroll payments are timely and accurate. In addition, the system must also provide adequate safeguards against theft or other misuse of funds.

The cash payment controls we discussed in the cash chapter also apply to payrolls. Thus, it is normally desirable to use a system that includes procedures for proper authorization and approval of payroll. When a check-signing machine is used, it is important that blank payroll checks and access to the machine be carefully controlled to prevent the theft or misuse of payroll funds.

It is especially important to authorize and approve in writing employee additions and deletions and changes in pay rates. For example, numerous

Exhibit 7 Payroll Check

HOURS & EARNINGS		TAXES & DEDUCTIONS		
DESCRIPTION	**AMOUNT**	**DESCRIPTION**	**CURRENT AMOUNT**	**Y-T-D AMOUNT**
Rate of Pay Reg.	28	Social Security Tax	42.24	4,800.00
Rate of Pay O.T.	42	Medicare Tax	18.06	1,207.50
Hours Worked Reg.	40	Fed. Income Tax	248.00	17,710.00
Hours Worked O.T.	2	U.S. Savings Bonds	20.00	1,040.00
		United Fund	5.00	100.00
Net Pay	870.70			
Total Gross Pay	1,204.00	Total	333.30	24,857.50
Total Gross Y-T-D	80,500.00			

McDermott Supply Co.
415 5th Ave. So.
Dubuque, IA 52736-0142

John T. McGrath
1830 4th St.
Clinton, IA 52732-6142

Check Number: 6860
Pay Period Ending: 12/27/02

STATEMENT OF EARNINGS. DETACH AND KEEP FOR YOUR RECORDS

McDermott Supply Co.
415 5th Ave. So.
Dubuque, IA 52736-0142

LaGesse Savings & Loan
33 Katie Avenue, Suite 33
Clinton, IA 52736-3581

24-2/531

Pay Period Ending: 12/27/02   6860

PAY EIGHT HUNDRED SEVENTY AND 70/100 . . . . **DOLLARS**

To the Order of JOHN T. MCGRATH
1830 4TH ST.
CLINTON, IA 52732-6142

$***870.70

Franklin D. McDermott

⑈6860⑈ ⑆153111123⑆ ⑈938540 2⑈

Exhibit 8 Flow of Data in a Payroll System

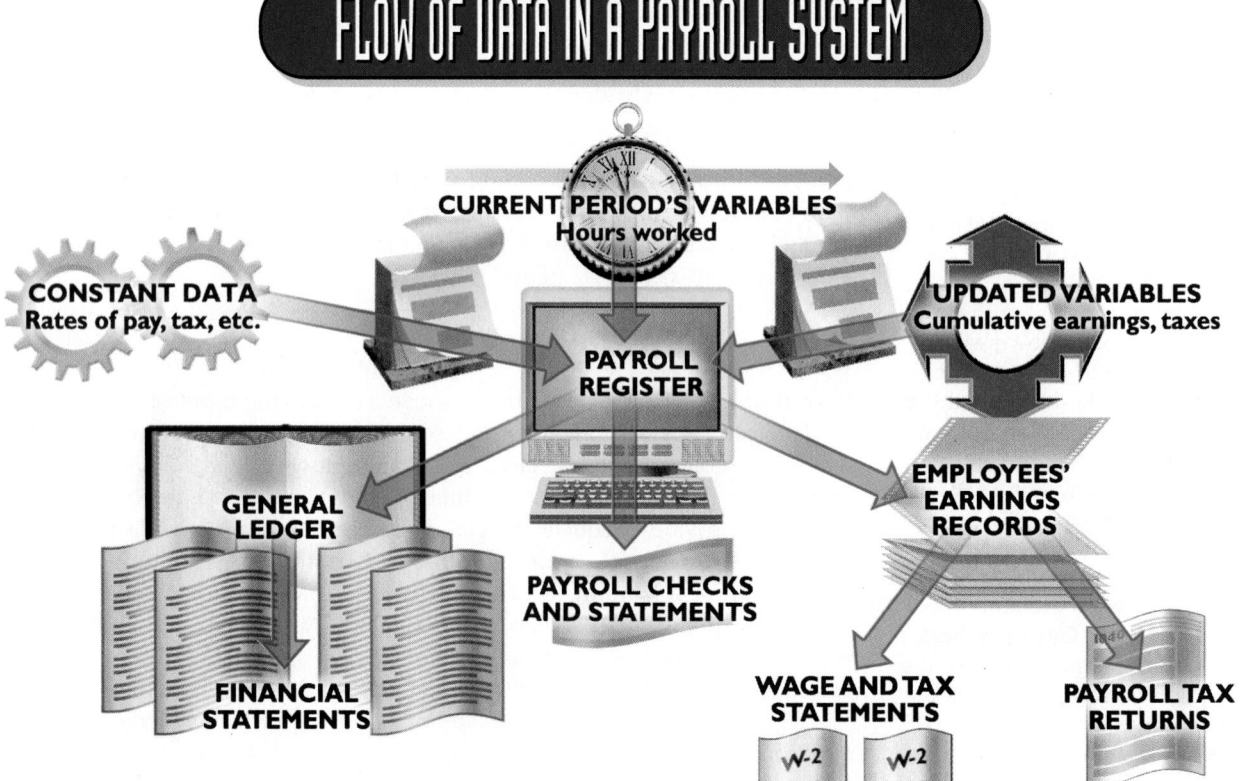

payroll frauds have involved a supervisor adding fictitious employees to the payroll. The supervisor then cashes the fictitious employees' checks. Similar frauds have occurred where employees have been fired but the Payroll Department is not notified. As a result, payroll checks to the fired employees are prepared and cashed by a supervisor.

To prevent or detect frauds such as those we described above, employees' attendance records should be controlled. For example, you may have used an "In and Out" card on which your time of arrival to and departure from work was recorded when you inserted the card into a time clock. A Payroll Department employee may be stationed near the time clock during normal arrival and departure times in order to verify that employees "clock in" only once and only for themselves. Employee identification cards or badges may also be used to verify that only authorized employees are clocking in and are permitted to enter work areas. When payroll checks are distributed, employee identification cards may be used to deter one employee from picking up another's check.

Other controls include verifying and approving all payroll rate changes. In addition, in a computerized system, all program changes should be properly approved and tested by employees who are independent of the payroll system. The use of a special payroll bank account, as we discussed earlier in this chapter, also enhances control over payroll.

Employees' Fringe Benefits

objective 6

Journalize entries for employee fringe benefits, including vacation pay and pensions.

Many companies provide their employees a variety of benefits in addition to salary and wages earned. Such **fringe benefits** may take many forms, including vacations, pension plans, and health, life, and disability insurance. When the employer pays part or all of the cost of the fringe benefits, these costs must be recognized as expenses. To properly match revenues and expenses, the estimated cost of these benefits should be recorded as an expense during the period in which the employee earns the benefit.

Exhibit 9 shows benefit dollars as a percent of total benefits for 864 companies surveyed by the U.S. Chamber of Commerce.

Exhibit 9 Benefit Dollars as a Percent of Total

BENEFIT DOLLARS AS A PERCENT OF TOTAL

Other* 12%

Retirement and savings plans 18%

Medical 25%

*The Other category includes life insurance, educational assistance, breaks, and employee discounts

Social security and Medicare 21%

Vacation and sick pay 24%

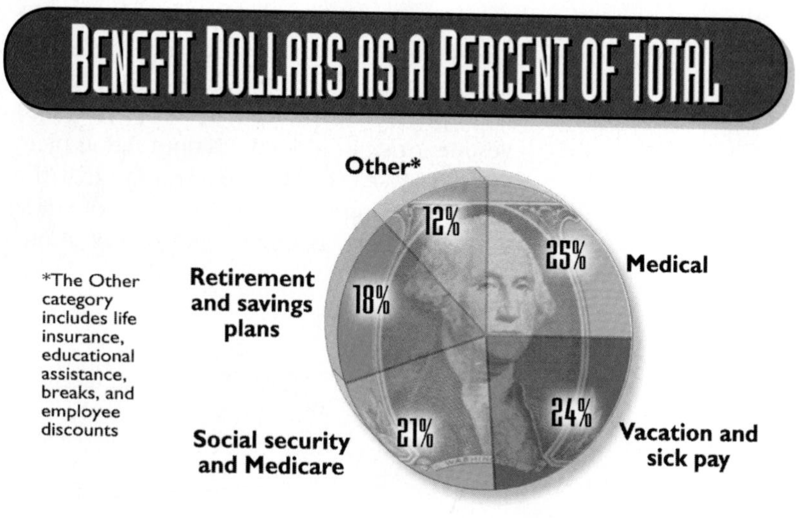

Source: U.S. Chamber of Commerce.

Vacation Pay

Most employers grant vacation rights, sometimes called **compensated absences**, to their employees. Such rights give rise to a recordable contingent liability. The liability for employees' vacation pay should be accrued as a liability as the vacation rights are earned. The entry to accrue vacation pay may be recorded in total at the end of each fiscal year, or it may be recorded at the end of each pay period. To illustrate this latter case, assume that employees earn one day of vacation for each month worked during the year. Assume also that the estimated vacation pay for the payroll period ending May 5 is $2,000. The entry to record the accrued vacation pay for this pay period is shown as follows.

May	5	Vacation Pay Expense	2 0 0 0 00	
		Vacation Pay Payable		2 0 0 0 00
		Vacation pay for week ended May 5.		

If employees are required to take all their vacation time within one year, the vacation pay payable is reported on the balance sheet as a current liability. If employees are allowed to accumulate their vacation time, the estimated vacation pay liability that is applicable to time that will *not* be taken within one year is a long-term liability.

When payroll is prepared for the period in which employees have taken vacations, the vacation pay payable is reduced. The entry debits *Vacation Pay Payable* and credits *Salaries Payable* and the other related accounts for taxes and withholdings.

Pensions

Studies indicate that 57% of all civilian employees work for companies that sponsor pension plans. However, of this amount, only about 75% of the workers actually participate in these plans.

A **pension** represents a cash payment to retired employees. Rights to pension payments are earned by employees during their working years, based on the pension plan established by the employer. One of the fundamental characteristics of such a plan is whether it is a defined contribution plan or a defined benefit plan.

Defined Contribution Plan

A **defined contribution plan** requires that a fixed amount of money be invested for the employee's behalf during the employee's working years. In a defined contribution plan, the employer is required to make annual pension contributions. There is no promise of future pension payments, however, so the employee bears the investment risk in a defined contribution plan. The employer's cost is debited to *Pension Expense*. To illustrate, assume that the pension plan of Flossmoor Industries requires a contribution equal to 10% of employee annual salaries. The entry to record the transaction, assuming $500,000 of annual salaries, is as follows:

Dec.	31	Pension Expense	50 0 0 0 00	
		Cash		50 0 0 0 00
		Contributed 10% of annual salaries to		
		pension plan.		

One of the more popular defined contribution pension plans is the *401K plan*. Under this plan, employees may contribute a limited part of their income to investments, such as mutual funds. A 401K plan offers employees two advantages: (1) the tax on the contribution is deferred (within limits), and (2) future investment earnings are tax deferred until withdrawn at retirement. In addition, for approximately 90% of the 401K plans, the employer matches some portion of the employee's contribution. For example, if the plan has a 50% matching feature, then each $1 contributed by the employee will be matched with a $0.50 contribution by the employer. Many financial planners advise employees to contribute to a 401K plan because of these benefits.

Once Flossmoor makes the annual contribution to the pension fund, its obligation is completed. The employee's final pension will depend on the investment results earned by the pension fund on the contributed balances.

Defined Benefit Plan

Employers may choose to promise employees a fixed annual pension benefit at retirement, based on years of service and compensation levels. An example would be a promise to pay an annual pension based on a formula, such as the following:

1.5% × years of service × average salary for most recent 3 years prior to retirement

Pension benefits based on a formula are termed a **defined benefit plan**. Unlike a defined contribution plan, the employer bears the investment risk in funding a future retirement income benefit. As a result, many companies are replacing their defined benefit plans with defined contribution plans.

The accounting for defined benefit plans is usually very complex due to the uncertainties of projecting future pension obligations. These obligations depend upon such factors as employee life expectancies, employee turnover, expected employee compensation levels, and investment income on pension contributions.

The pension cost of a defined benefit plan is debited to *Pension Expense*. The amount funded is credited to *Cash*. Any unfunded amount is credited to *Unfunded Pension Liability*. For example, assume that the pension plan of Hinkle Co. requires an annual pension cost of $80,000, based on an estimate of the future benefit obligation. Further assume that Hinkle Co. pays $60,000 to the pension fund. The entry to record this transaction is as follows:

Dec.	31	Pension Expense	80 0 0 0 00		
		Cash		60 0 0 0 00	
		Unfunded Pension Liability		20 0 0 0 00	
		To record annual pension cost and			
		contribution to pension plan.			

While 42 million American workers are covered by defined benefit plans, the number of defined contribution plans has been increasing. Over 75% of all new plans are structured as defined contribution plans.

If the unfunded pension liability is to be paid within one year, it will be classified as a current liability. That portion of the liability to be paid beyond one year is a long-term liability.

Postretirement Benefits Other than Pensions

In addition to the pension benefits described above, employees may earn rights to other **postretirement benefits** from their employers. Such benefits may include dental care, eye care, medical care, life insurance, tuition assistance, tax services, and legal services for employees or their dependents. The amount of the annual benefits expense is based upon health statistics of the workforce. This amount is recorded by debiting *Postretirement Benefits Expense*. *Cash* is credited for the same amount if the benefits are fully funded. If the benefits are not fully funded, a postretirement benefits plan liability account is credited. Thus, the accounting for postretirement health benefits is very similar to that of defined benefit pension plans.

A business's financial statements should fully disclose the nature of its postretirement benefit obligations. These disclosures are usually included as footnotes to the financial statements. The complex nature of accounting for postretirement benefits is described in more advanced accounting courses.

FINANCIAL ANALYSIS AND INTERPRETATION

objective 7

Use the quick ratio to analyze the ability of a business to pay its current liabilities.

A business must be able to pay its current liabilities within a short period of time, usually one year. One measure of its ability to make these payments is the **quick ratio** or **acid-test ratio**. The quick ratio is computed as follows:

$$\text{Quick Ratio} = \frac{\text{Quick Assets}}{\text{Current Liabilities}}$$

The quick ratio measures the "instant" debt-paying ability of a company, using quick assets. Quick assets are cash, cash equivalents, and receivables that can quickly be converted into cash. It is often considered desirable to have a quick ratio exceeding 1. A ratio less than 1 would indicate that current liabilities cannot be covered by cash and "near cash" assets.

To illustrate, assume that Noble Co. and Hart Co. have the following quick assets, current liabilities, and quick ratios:

	Noble Co.	Hart Co.
Quick assets:		
Cash	$100,000	$ 55,000
Cash equivalents	47,000	65,000
Accounts receivable (net)	84,000	472,000
Total	$231,000	$592,000
Current liabilities:		
Accounts payable	$125,000	$427,000
Wages payable	65,000	120,000
Employees federal income tax		
payable	18,000	36,000
Social security tax payable	3,025	7,200
Medicare tax payable	975	1,800
Notes payable	8,000	148,000
Total	$220,000	$740,000
Quick ratio	1.05	0.8

As you can see, Noble Co. has quick assets in excess of current liabilities, or a quick ratio of 1.05. The ratio exceeds 1, indicating that the quick assets should be sufficient to meet current liabilities. Hart Co., however, has a quick ratio of 0.8. Its quick assets will not be sufficient to cover the current liabilities. Hart could solve this problem by working with a bank to convert its short-term debt of $148,000 into a long-term obligation. This would remove the notes payable from current liabilities. If Hart did this, then its quick ratio would improve to 1 ($592,000 ÷ $592,000), which would be just sufficient for quick assets to cover current liabilities.

ENCORE

Do You Want to Be a Millionaire?

A recent survey found that 66% of individuals believe that their standard of living at retirement will be the same or higher than during their current working years. Yet, a third of these respondents don't have a formal savings plan for retirement. One-fourth of these respondents believe that they will need to save only $100,000 in order to maintain their lifestyle in retirement. However, experts believe that today's 25-year-old will need savings of $750,000 to $1 million to support a basic retirement, given increased life expectancies and inflation. How do you save this much money? The two keys to savings success are (1) save regularly, such as monthly or quarterly, even if it's a small amount, and (2) start early. For example, to have the same retirement income as a 25-year-old saving $100 per month, a 30-year-old would need to save $200 per month. Waiting until you are 35 years old would require saving $400 per month. Every five years of delay requires doubling the necessary contribution. This is the power of compound interest. Therefore, the worst strategy is to begin retirement saving at middle age. Unfortunately, according to one survey, 41% of workers age 25 to 34 who are eligible for defined contribution pension plans, such as a 401K, do not take advantage of them.

So how much would a 25-year-old need to save monthly to reach the $1 million mark? There are many assumptions that go into such a calculation. Let's assume that an individual begins saving $150 per month at the age of 25, earns 8% on these savings, increases the amount contributed by 5% per year (to match salary increases), and retires at the age of 65. Under these assumptions, the individual would accumulate $975,000 by age 65. What would be the retirement savings if the assumptions were changed so that the savings plan began at age 35, 45, or 55? The graph at the right shows what happens to the savings amount. As you can see, time is money. Beginning just 10 years later at age 35 reduces the accumulated savings by over 60%, to approximately $374,000.

Retirement planning work sheets are available from a number of mutual fund companies on the Internet. One easy-to-use work sheet is provided at the Web site of **T. Rowe Price, www.troweprice.com.** ■

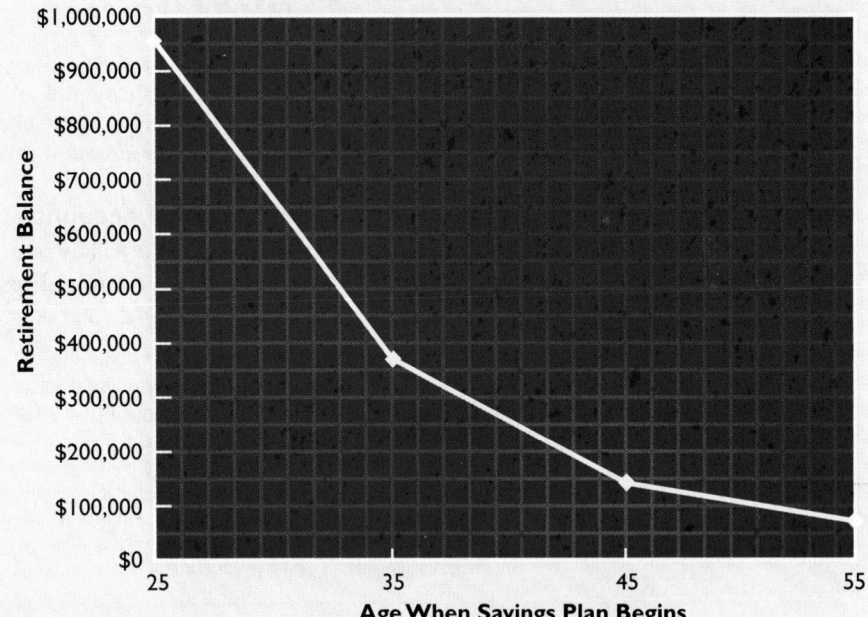

Retirement Balance Under Different Savings Scenarios

KEY POINTS

1 Define and give examples of current liabilities.

Current liabilities are obligations that are to be paid out of current assets and are due within a short time, usually within one year. Current liabilities arise from either (1) receiving goods or services prior to making payment or (2) receiving payment prior to delivering goods or services.

2 Journalize entries for short-term notes payable.

A note issued to a creditor to temporarily satisfy an account payable is recorded as a debit to *Accounts Payable* and a credit to *Notes Payable*. At the time the note is paid, *Notes Payable* and *Interest Expense* are debited and *Cash* is credited. Notes may also be issued to purchase merchandise or other assets or to borrow money from a bank. When a discounted note is issued, *Interest Expense* is debited for the interest deduction at the time of issuance, an asset account is debited for the proceeds, and *Notes Payable* is credited for the face value of the note. The face value and the maturity value of a discounted note are equal.

3 Describe the accounting treatment for contingent liabilities and journalize entries for product warranties.

A contingent liability is a potential obligation that results from a past transaction but depends on a future event. If the contingent liability is both probable and estimable, the liability should be recorded. If the contingent liability is reasonably possible or is not estimable, it should be disclosed in the footnotes to the financial statements. An example of a recordable contingent liability is product warranties. If a company grants a warranty on a product, an estimated warranty expense and liability should be recorded in the period of the sale. The expense and the liability are recorded by debiting *Product Warranty Expense* and crediting *Product Warranty Payable*.

4 Determine employer liabilities for payroll, including liabilities arising from employee earnings and deductions from earnings.

An employer's liability for payroll is calculated by determining employees' total earnings for a payroll period, including overtime pay. From this amount, employee deductions are subtracted to arrive at the net pay to be paid each employee. The employer's liabilities for employee deductions are recognized at the time the payroll is recorded. Most employers also incur liabilities for payroll taxes, such as social security tax, Medicare tax, federal unemployment compensation tax, and state unemployment compensation tax.

5 Describe payroll accounting systems that use a payroll register, employee earnings records, and a general journal.

The payroll register is used in assembling and summarizing the data needed for each payroll period. The data recorded in the payroll register include the number of hours worked and the earnings and deduction data for each employee. The payroll register also includes columns for accumulating total wages or salaries to be debited to the various expense accounts. It is supported by a detailed payroll record for each employee, called an employee's earnings record.

6 Journalize entries for employee fringe benefits, including vacation pay and pensions.

Fringe benefits are expenses of the period in which the employees earn the benefits. Fringe benefits are recorded by debiting an expense account and crediting a liability account. For example, the entry to record accrued vacation pay debits *Vacation Pay Expense* and credits *Vacation Pay Payable*.

7 Use the quick ratio to analyze the ability of a business to pay its current liabilities.

The quick ratio or acid-test ratio is a measure of a business's ability to pay current liabilities within a short period of time. The quick ratio is quick assets divided by current liabilities. A quick ratio exceeding 1 is usually desirable.

ILLUSTRATIVE PROBLEM

Selected transactions of Taylor Company, completed during the fiscal year ended December 31, are as follows:

Mar. 1. Purchased merchandise on account from Kelvin Co., $20,000.
Apr. 10. Issued a 60-day, 12% note for $20,000 to Kelvin Co. on account.
June 9. Paid Kelvin Co. the amount owed on the note of April 10.
Aug. 1. Issued a $50,000, 90-day note to Harold Co. in exchange for a building. Harold Co. discounted the note at 15%.
Oct. 30. Paid Harold Co. the amount due on the note of August 1.
Dec. 27. Journalized the entry to record the biweekly payroll. A summary of the payroll record follows:

Salary distribution:

Sales	$63,400	
Officers	36,600	
Office	10,000	$110,000

Deductions:

Social security tax	$ 5,050	
Medicare tax	1,650	
Federal income tax withheld	17,600	
State income tax withheld	4,950	
Savings bond deductions	850	
Medical insurance deductions	1,120	31,220
Net amount		$ 78,780

Dec. 30. Issued a check in payment of liabilities for employees' federal income tax of $17,600, social security tax of $10,100, and Medicare tax of $3,300.

31. Issued a check for $9,500 to the pension fund trustee to fully fund the pension cost for December.

31. Journalized an entry to record the employees' accrued vacation pay, $36,100.

31. Journalized an entry to record the estimated accrued product warranty liability, $37,240.

Instructions
Journalize the preceding transactions.

Solution

			Debit	Credit
Mar.	1	Merchandise Inventory	20 000 00	
		Accounts Payable—Kelvin Co.		20 000 00
Apr.	10	Accounts Payable—Kelvin Co.	20 000 00	
		Notes Payable		20 000 00
June	9	Notes Payable	20 000 00	
		Interest Expense	4 00 00	
		Cash		20 400 00
Aug.	1	Building	48 125 00	
		Interest Expense	1 875 00	
		Notes Payable		50 000 00
Oct.	30	Notes Payable	50 000 00	
		Cash		50 000 00
Dec.	27	Sales Salaries Expense	63 400 00	
		Officers Salaries Expense	36 600 00	
		Office Salaries Expense	10 000 00	
		Social Security Tax Payable		5 050 00
		Medicare Tax Payable		1 650 00
		Employees Federal Income Tax Payable		17 600 00
		Employees State Income Tax Payable		4 950 00
		Bond Deductions Payable		8 50 00
		Medical Insurance Payable		1 120 00
		Salaries Payable		78 780 00

Dec.	30	Employees Federal Income Tax Payable	17	6	0	0	00									
		Social Security Tax Payable	10	1	0	0	00									
		Medicare Tax Payable	3	3	0	0	00									
		Cash						31	0	0	0	00				
	31	Pension Expense	9	5	0	0	00									
		Cash						9	5	0	0	00				
	31	Vacation Pay Expense	36	1	0	0	00									
		Vacation Pay Payable						36	1	0	0	00				
	31	Product Warranty Expense	37	2	4	0	00									
		Product Warranty Payable						37	2	4	0	00				

SELF-EXAMINATION QUESTIONS

Answers at End of Chapter

Matching

Match each of the following statements with its proper term. Some terms may not be used.

A. defined benefit plan

B. defined contribution plan

C. discount

D. discount rate

E. employee's earnings record

F. FICA tax

G. fringe benefits

H. gross pay

I. net pay

J. payroll

K. payroll register

L. postretirement benefits

M. proceeds

N. quick ratio

___ 1. A detailed record of each employee's earnings.

___ 2. A multicolumn form used to assemble and summarize payroll data at the end of each payroll period.

___ 3. A pension plan that promises employees a fixed annual pension benefit at retirement, based on years of service and compensation levels.

___ 4. Gross pay less payroll deductions; the amount the employer is obligated to pay the employee.

___ 5. The net amount available from discounting a note payable.

___ 6. A pension plan that requires a fixed amount of money to be invested for the employee's behalf during the employee's working years.

___ 7. Benefits provided to employees in addition to wages and salaries.

___ 8. The rate used in computing the interest to be deducted from the maturity value of a note.

___ 9. The total earnings of an employee for a payroll period.

___10. Rights to benefits that employees earn during their term of employment, for themselves and their dependents, after they retire.

___11. The total amount paid to employees for a certain period.

___12. Federal Insurance Contributions Act tax used to finance federal programs for old-age and disability benefits (social security) and health insurance for the aged (Medicare).

___13. A financial ratio that measures the ability to pay current liabilities within a short period of time.

___14. The interest deducted from the maturity value of a note.

Multiple Choice

1. A business issued a $5,000, 60-day, 12% note to the bank. The amount due at maturity is:

A. $4,900

B. $5,000

C. $5,100

D. $5,600

2. A business issued a $5,000, 60-day note to a supplier, which discounted the note at 12%. The proceeds are:

A. $4,400

B. $4,900

C. $5,000

D. $5,100

3. Which of the following taxes are employers usually not required to withhold from employees?
   A. Federal income tax
   B. Federal unemployment compensation tax
   C. Medicare tax
   D. State and local income tax

4. An employee's rate of pay is $20 per hour, with time and a half for all hours worked in excess of 40 during a week. The social security rate is 6.0% on the first $80,000 of annual earnings, and the Medicare rate is 1.5% on all earnings. The following additional data are available:

Hours worked during current week	45
Year's cumulative earnings prior to current week	$79,400
Federal income tax withheld	$212

Based on these data, the amount of the employee's net pay for the current week is:
A. $620.50   C. $666.75
B. $641.50   D. $687.75

5. Within limitations on the maximum earnings subject to the tax, employers do not incur an expense for which of the following payroll taxes?
   A. Social security tax
   B. Federal unemployment compensation tax
   C. State unemployment compensation tax
   D. Employees' federal income tax

CLASS DISCUSSION QUESTIONS

1. What two types of transactions cause most current liabilities?
2. When are short-term notes payable issued?
3. When should the liability associated with a product warranty be recorded? Discuss.
4. **Compaq Computer Corporation** reported $752 million of product warranties in the current liabilities section of a recent balance sheet. How would costs of repairing a defective product be recorded?
5. The "Questions and Answers Technical Hotline" in the *Journal of Accountancy* included the following question:

   Several years ago, Company B instituted legal action against Company A. Under a memorandum of settlement and agreement, Company A agreed to pay Company B a total of $17,500 in three installments—$5,000 on March 1, $7,500 on July 1, and the remaining $5,000 on December 31. Company A paid the first two installments during its fiscal year ended September 30. Should the unpaid amount of $5,000 be presented as a current liability at September 30?

   How would you answer this question?
6. What programs are funded by the FICA (Federal Insurance Contributions Act) tax?
7. a. Identify the federal taxes that most employers are required to withhold from employees.
   b. Give the titles of the accounts to which the amounts withheld are credited.
8. For each of the following payroll-related taxes, indicate whether there is a ceiling on the annual earnings subject to the tax: (a) social security tax, (b) Medicare tax, (c) federal income tax, (d) federal unemployment compensation tax.
9. Why are deductions from employees' earnings classified as liabilities for the employer?
10. Do payroll taxes levied against employers become liabilities at the time the liabilities for wages are incurred or at the time the wages are paid?
11. Taylor Company, with 20 employees, is expanding operations. It is trying to decide whether to hire one employee full-time for $25,000 or two employees part-time for a total of $25,000. Would any of the employer's payroll taxes discussed in this chapter have a bearing on this decision? Explain.
12. For each of the following payroll-related taxes, indicate whether they generally apply to (a) employees only, (b) employers only, (c) both employees and employers:
    1. Social security tax
    2. Medicare tax
    3. Federal income tax
    4. Federal unemployment compensation tax
    5. State unemployment compensation tax
13. What are the principal reasons for using a special payroll checking account?
14. In a payroll system, what type of input data are referred to as (a) constants, (b) variables?

15. To strengthen internal controls, what department should provide written authorizations for the addition of names to the payroll?
16. Explain how a payroll system that is properly designed and operated tends to ensure that (a) wages paid are based on hours actually worked and (b) payroll checks are not issued to fictitious employees.
17. To match revenues and expenses properly, should the expense for employee vacation pay be recorded in the period during which the vacation privilege is earned or during the period in which the vacation is taken? Discuss.
18. Identify several factors that influence the future pension obligation of an employer under a defined benefit pension plan.
19. Where should the unfunded pension liability from a defined benefit pension plan be reported on the balance sheet?
20. What are some examples of postretirement benefits other than pensions that employees may earn for themselves and their dependents?

RESOURCES FOR YOUR SUCCESS ONLINE AT

http://warren.swcollege.com

Remember! If you need additional help, visit South-Western's Web site.
See page F26 for a description of the online and printed materials that are available.

EXERCISES

Exercise 10–1
Current liabilities

Objective 1

✓ Total current liabilities, $218,000

Net World Magazine Inc. sold 4,800 annual subscriptions of *Net World* for $45 during December 2003. These new subscribers will receive monthly issues, beginning in January 2004. In addition, the business had taxable income of $160,000 during the first calendar quarter of 2004. The federal tax rate is 35%. A quarterly tax payment will be made on April 7, 2004.

Prepare the current liabilities section of the balance sheet for Net World Magazine Inc. on March 31, 2004.

Exercise 10–2
Entries for discounting notes payable

Objective 2

National Electric Lighting Co. issues a 90-day note for $500,000 to Home Products Supply Co. for merchandise inventory. Home Products discounts the note at 10%.

a. Journalize National Electric's entries to record:
   1. the issuance of the note.
   2. the payment of the note at maturity.
b. Journalize Home Products' entries to record:
   1. the receipt of the note.
   2. the receipt of the payment of the note at maturity.

Exercise 10–3
Evaluate alternative notes

Objective 2

A borrower has two alternatives for a loan: (1) issue a $60,000, 90-day, 8% note or (2) issue a $60,000, 90-day note that the creditor discounts at 8%.

a. Calculate the amount of the interest expense for each option.
b. Determine the proceeds received by the borrower in each situation.
c. ✏️ Which alternative is more favorable to the borrower? Explain.

Exercise 10–4
Entries for notes payable

Objective 2

A business issued a 60-day, 9% note for $20,000 to a creditor on account. Journalize the entries to record (a) the issuance of the note and (b) the payment of the note at maturity, including interest.

Exercise 10–5
Fixed asset purchases with note
Objective 2

On June 30, Zelda Game Company purchased land for $250,000 and a building for $730,000, paying $380,000 cash and issuing an 8% note for the balance, secured by a mortgage on the property. The terms of the note provide for 20 semiannual payments of $30,000 on the principal plus the interest accrued from the date of the preceding payment. Journalize the entry to record (a) the transaction on June 30, (b) the payment of the first installment on December 31, and (c) the payment of the second installment the following June 30.

Exercise 10–6
Accrued product warranty
Objective 3

Precision Audio Company warrants its products for one year. The estimated product warranty is 3% of sales. Assume that sales were $600,000 for January. In February, a customer received warranty repairs requiring $310 of parts and $460 of labor.

a. Journalize the adjusting entry required at January 31, the end of the first month of the current year, to record the accrued product warranty.
b. Journalize the entry to record the warranty work provided in February.

Exercise 10–7
Accrued product warranty
Objective 2

✓ a. 0.77%

During a recent year, **Motorola, Inc.**, had sales of $29,398,000,000. An analysis of Motorola's product warranty payable account for the year was as follows:

Product warranty payable, January 1	$337,000,000
Product warranty expense	226,000,000
Warranty claims paid	(230,000,000)
Product warranty payable, December 31	$333,000,000

a. Determine the product warranty expense as a percent of sales.
b. Record the adjusting entry for the product warranty expense for the year.

Exercise 10–8
Contingent liabilities
Objective 3

Several months ago, Endurance Battery Company experienced a hazardous materials spill at one of its plants. As a result, the Environmental Protection Agency (EPA) fined the company $170,000. The company is contesting the fine. In addition, an employee is seeking $500,000 damages related to the spill. Lastly, a homeowner has sued the company for $120,000. The homeowner lives 20 miles from the plant but believes that the incident has reduced the home's resale value by $120,000.

Endurance Battery's legal counsel believes that it is probable that the EPA fine will stand. In addition, counsel indicates that an out-of-court settlement of $250,000 has recently been reached with the employee. The final papers will be signed next week. Counsel believes that the homeowner's case is much weaker and will be decided in favor of Endurance. Other litigation related to the spill is possible, but the damage amounts are uncertain.

a. Journalize the contingent liabilities associated with the hazardous materials spill.
b. ✏ Prepare a footnote disclosure relating to this incident.

Exercise 10–9
Contingent liabilities
Objective 3

The following footnote accompanied recent financial statements for **eBAY, Inc.**:

> . . . *The Company was sued by Network Engineering Software, Inc. . . . . for the Company's alleged willful and deliberate violation of a patent. The suit seeks unspecified monetary damages as well as an injunction against the Company's operations. It also seeks treble damages and attorneys' fees and costs. The Company believes that it has meritorious defenses against this suit and intends to vigorously defend itself. The Company could be forced to incur material expenses during this defense and in the event it were to lose this suit, its business would be harmed.*

Was a liability recorded by eBAY, Inc., for this contingent liability? Why or why not?

Exercise 10–10
Calculate payroll
Objective 4

✓ b. Net pay, $989.75

An employee earns $26 per hour and 1½ times that rate for all hours in excess of 40 hours per week. Assume that the employee worked 50 hours during the week, and that the gross pay prior to the current week totaled $62,140. Assume further that the social security tax rate was 6.0% (on earnings up to $80,000), the Medicare tax rate was 1.5%, and federal income tax to be withheld was $333.

a. Determine the gross pay for the week.
b. Determine the net pay for the week.

Exercise 10–11
Calculate payroll

Objective 4

✓ Administrator net pay, $854.50

Prism Business Consultants has three employees—a consultant, a computer programmer, and an administrator. The following payroll information is available for each employee:

	Consultant	Computer Programmer	Administrator
Regular earnings rate	$2,500 per week	$30 per hour	$24 per hour
Overtime earnings rate	Not applicable	1½ times hourly rate	1½ times hourly rate
Gross pay prior to current pay period	$120,000	$79,200	$53,200
Number of withholding allowances	1	0	3

For the current pay period, the computer programmer worked 41 hours and the administrator worked 45 hours. For the current pay period, the federal income tax withheld for the consultant was $670. The federal income tax withheld for the computer programmer and the administrator can be determined from the wage bracket withholding table in Exhibit 3 in the chapter. Assume further that the social security tax rate was 6.0% on the first $80,000 of annual earnings, and the Medicare tax rate was 1.5%.

Determine the gross pay and the net pay for each of the three employees for the current pay period.

Exercise 10–12
Summary payroll data

Objectives 4, 5

✓ a. (3) Total earnings, $211,000

In the following summary of data for a payroll period, some amounts have been intentionally omitted:

Earnings:
1. At regular rate		?
2. At overtime rate		$ 32,500
3. Total earnings		?

Deductions:
4. Social security tax		12,000
5. Medicare tax		3,165
6. Income tax withheld		29,500
7. Medical insurance		3,150
8. Union dues		?
9. Total deductions		50,000
10. Net amount paid		161,000

Accounts debited:
11. Factory Wages		121,600
12. Sales Salaries		?
13. Office Salaries		34,300

a. Calculate the amounts omitted in lines (1), (3), (8), and (12).
b. Journalize the entry to record the payroll accrual.
c. Journalize the entry to record the payment of the payroll.
d. ✏️ From the data given in this exercise and your answer to (a), would you conclude that this payroll was paid sometime during the first few weeks of the calendar year? Explain.

Exercise 10–13
Payroll internal control procedures

Objective 5

Memphis Sounds is a retail store specializing in the sale of jazz compact discs and cassettes. The store employs 3 full-time and 10 part-time workers. The store's weekly payroll averages $2,200 for all 13 workers.

Memphis Sounds uses a personal computer to assist in preparing paychecks. Each week, the store's accountant collects employee time cards and enters the hours worked into the payroll program. The payroll program calculates each employee's pay and prints a paycheck. The accountant uses a check-signing machine to sign the paychecks. Next, the store's owner authorizes the transfer of funds from the store's regular bank account to the payroll account.

For the week of May 10, the accountant accidentally recorded 400 hours worked instead of 40 hours for one of the full-time employees.

➤ Does Memphis Sounds have internal controls in place to catch this error? If so, how will this error be detected?

Exercise 10–14
Internal control procedures
Objective 5

Sure-Grip Tools is a small manufacturer of home workshop power tools. The company employs 30 production workers and 10 administrative persons. The following procedures are used to process the company's weekly payroll:

a.   All employees are required to record their hours worked by clocking in and out on a time clock. Employees must clock out for lunch break. Due to congestion around the time clock area at lunch time, management has not objected to having one employee clock in and out for an entire department.

b.   Whenever a salaried employee is terminated, Personnel authorizes Payroll to remove the employee from the payroll system. However, this procedure is not required when an hourly worker is terminated. Hourly employees only receive a paycheck if their time cards show hours worked. The computer automatically drops an employee from the payroll system when that employee has six consecutive weeks with no hours worked.

c.   Whenever an employee receives a pay raise, the supervisor must fill out a wage adjustment form, which is signed by the company president. This form is used to change the employee's wage rate in the payroll system.

d.   Sure-Grip maintains a separate checking account for payroll checks. Each week, the total net pay for all employees is transferred from the company's regular bank account to the payroll account.

e.   Paychecks are signed by using a check-signing machine. This machine is located in the main office so that it can be easily accessed by anyone needing a check signed.

➤ State whether each of the procedures is appropriate or inappropriate after considering the principles of internal control. If a procedure is inappropriate, describe the appropriate procedure.

Exercise 10–15
Payroll tax entries
Objective 5

According to a summary of the payroll of All Sport Publishing Co., $630,000 was subject to the 6.0% social security tax and $700,000 was subject to the 1.5% Medicare tax. Also, $15,000 was subject to state and federal unemployment taxes.

a.   Calculate the employer's payroll taxes, using the following rates: state unemployment, 4.3%; federal unemployment, 0.8%.
b.   Journalize the entry to record the accrual of payroll taxes.

Exercise 10–16
Payroll procedures
Objective 5

The fiscal year for Country Road Stores Inc. ends on June 30. In addition, the company computes and reports payroll taxes on a fiscal-year basis. Thus, social security and FUTA maximum earnings limitations apply to the fiscal-year payroll.

➤ What is wrong with these procedures for accounting for payroll taxes?

Exercise 10–17
Accrued vacation pay
Objective 6

A business provides its employees with varying amounts of vacation per year, depending on the length of employment. The estimated amount of the current year's vacation pay is $224,400. Journalize the adjusting entry required on January 31, the end of the first month of the current year, to record the accrued vacation pay.

Exercise 10–18
Pension plan entries
Objective 6

Perpetual Images Inc. operates a chain of photography stores. The company maintains a defined contribution pension plan for its employees. The plan requires quarterly installments to be paid to the funding agent, Interstate Insurance Company, by the fifteenth of the month following the end of each quarter. Assuming that the pension cost is $225,000 for the quarter ended December 31, journalize entries to record (a) the accrued pension liability on December 31 and (b) the payment to the funding agent on January 15.

Exercise 10–19
Defined benefit pension plan terms

Objective 6

In a recent year's financial statements, Procter & Gamble Co. showed an unfunded pension liability of $815 million and a periodic pension cost of $173 million.

Explain the meaning of the $815 million unfunded pension liability and the $173 million periodic pension cost.

Exercise 10–20
Quick ratio

Objective 7

The financial statements for Cisco Systems, Inc., are presented in Appendix G at the end of the text.

a. Compute the quick ratio as of July 29, 2000 and July 31, 1999.
b. What conclusions can be drawn from these data as to Cisco Systems' ability to meet its current liabilities?

PROBLEMS SERIES A

Problem 10–1A
Liability transactions

Objectives 2, 3

SPREADSHEET
GENERAL LEDGER

The following items were selected from among the transactions completed by Pride Polymers during the current year:

Apr. 7. Borrowed $15,000 from First Financial Corporation, issuing a 60-day, 12% note for that amount.
May 10. Purchased equipment by issuing a $120,000, 120-day note to Milford Equipment Co., which discounted the note at the rate of 10%.
June 6. Paid First Financial Corporation the interest due on the note of April 7 and renewed the loan by issuing a new 30-day, 16% note for $15,000. (Record both the debit and credit to the notes payable account.)
July 6. Paid First Financial Corporation the amount due on the note of June 6.
Aug. 3. Purchased merchandise on account from Hamilton Co., $36,000, terms, n/30.
Sept. 2. Issued a 60-day, 15% note for $36,000 to Hamilton Co., on account.
7. Paid Milford Equipment Co. the amount due on the note of May 10.
Nov. 1. Paid Hamilton Co. the amount owed on the note of September 2.
15. Purchased store equipment from Shingo Equipment Co. for $100,000, paying $23,000 and issuing a series of seven 12% notes for $11,000 each, coming due at 30-day intervals.
Dec. 15. Paid the amount due Shingo Equipment Co. on the first note in the series issued on November 15.
21. Settled a product liability lawsuit with a customer for $65,000, to be paid in January. Pride Polymers accrued the loss in a litigation claims payable account.

Instructions

1. Journalize the transactions.
2. Journalize the adjusting entry for each of the following accrued expenses at the end of the current year:
   a. Product warranty cost, $11,200.
   b. Interest on the six remaining notes owed to Shingo Equipment Co.

Problem 10–2A
Entries for payroll and payroll taxes

Objectives 4, 5

The following information about the payroll for the week ended December 30 was obtained from the records of Hannah Co.:

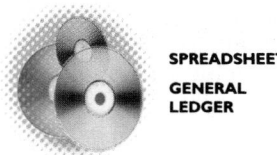

SPREADSHEET

GENERAL LEDGER

✓ 1. (b) Dr. Payroll Taxes
Expense, $41,990

Salaries:		Deductions:	
Sales salaries	$327,000	Income tax withheld	$104,500
Warehouse salaries	87,400	Social security tax withheld	32,600
Office salaries	165,600	Medicare tax withheld	8,700
	$580,000	U.S. savings bonds	24,400
		Group insurance	32,800

Tax rates assumed:
Social security, 6% on first $80,000 of employee annual earnings
Medicare, 1.5%
State unemployment (employer only), 3.8%
Federal unemployment (employer only), 0.8%

Instructions

1. Assuming that the payroll for the last week of the year is to be paid on December 31, journalize the following entries:
   a. December 30, to record the payroll.
   b. December 30, to record the employer's payroll taxes on the payroll to be paid on December 31. Of the total payroll for the last week of the year, $15,000 is subject to unemployment compensation taxes.
2. Assuming that the payroll for the last week of the year is to be paid on January 4 of the following fiscal year, journalize the following entries:
   a. December 30, to record the payroll.
   b. January 4, to record the employer's payroll taxes on the payroll to be paid on January 4.

Problem 10–3A
Wage and tax statement data and employer FICA tax

Objectives 4, 5

✓ 2. (e) $26,348.25

Safety-Haul Distribution Company began business on January 2, 2002. Salaries were paid to employees on the last day of each month, and social security tax, Medicare tax, and federal income tax were withheld in the required amounts. An employee who is hired in the middle of the month receives half the monthly salary for that month. All required payroll tax reports were filed, and the correct amount of payroll taxes was remitted by the company for the calendar year. Early in 2003, before the Wage and Tax Statements (Form W-2) could be prepared for distribution to employees and for filing with the Social Security Administration, the employees' earnings records were inadvertently destroyed.

None of the employees resigned or were discharged during the year, and there were no changes in salary rates. The social security tax was withheld at the rate of 6.0% on the first $80,000 of salary and Medicare tax at the rate of 1.5% on salary. Data on dates of employment, salary rates, and employees' income taxes withheld, which are summarized as follows, were obtained from personnel records and payroll records.

Employee	Date First Employed	Monthly Salary	Monthly Income Tax Withheld
Albright	June 2	$6,200	$1,305.10
Charles	Jan. 2	6,800	1,492.60
Given	Mar. 1	4,100	764.65
Nelson	Jan. 2	3,700	682.65
Quinn	Nov. 15	4,000	740.00
Ramirez	Apr. 15	3,000	535.50
Wu	Jan. 16	7,500	1,676.25

Instructions

1. Calculate the amounts to be reported on each employee's Wage and Tax Statement (Form W-2) for 2002, arranging the data in the following form:

Employee	Gross Earnings	Federal Income Tax Withheld	Social Security Tax Withheld	Medicare Tax Withheld

(continued)

2. Calculate the following employer payroll taxes for the year: (a) social security; (b) Medicare; (c) state unemployment compensation at 3.8% on the first $7,000 of each employee's earnings; (d) federal unemployment compensation at 0.8% on the first $7,000 of each employee's earnings; (e) total.

If the working papers correlating with this textbook are not used, omit Problem 10–4A.

Problem 10–4A
Payroll register

Objectives 4, 5

✓ 3. Dr. Payroll Taxes Expense, $667.58

The payroll register for Chopin Piano Co. for the week ended December 12, 2003, is presented in the working papers.

Instructions

1. Journalize the entry to record the payroll for the week.
2. Journalize the entry to record the issuance of the checks to employees.
3. Journalize the entry to record the employer's payroll taxes for the week. Assume the following tax rates: state unemployment, 3.2%; federal unemployment, 0.8%. Of the earnings, $750 is subject to unemployment taxes.
4. Journalize the entry to record a check issued on December 15 to Second National Bank in payment of employees' income taxes, $1,540.81, social security taxes, $1,020.12, and Medicare taxes, $255.04.

Problem 10–5A
Payroll register

Objectives 4, 5

SPREADSHEET

✓ 1. Total net amount payable, $6,297.25

The following data for Rainbow Paint Co. relate to the payroll for the week ended December 7, 2003:

Employee	Hours Worked	Hourly Rate	Weekly Salary	Federal Income Tax	U.S. Savings Bonds	Accumulated Earnings, Nov. 30
A	48.00	$28.00		$334.88	$15.00	$70,800.00
B	40.00	22.00		176.00		41,500.00
C			$2,100.00	525.00	70.00	100,800.00
D	45.00	18.00		171.00	10.00	43,200.00
E	40.00	15.00		108.00		28,800.00
F	42.00	22.50		203.18	20.00	47,400.00
G	40.00	16.00		108.80	25.00	30,700.00
H			1,100.00	242.00		4,400.00
I	25.00	12.00		36.00	15.00	14,400.00

Employees C and H are office staff, and all of the other employees are sales personnel. All sales personnel are paid 1½ times the regular rate for all hours in excess of 40 hours per week. The social security tax rate is 6.0% on the first $80,000 of each employee's annual earnings, and Medicare tax is 1.5% of each employee's annual earnings. The next payroll check to be used is No. 981.

Instructions

1. Prepare a payroll register for Rainbow Paint Co. for the week ended December 7, 2003.
2. Journalize the entry to record the payroll for the week.

Problem 10–6A
Payroll accounts and year-end entries

Objectives 4, 5, 6

GENERAL LEDGER

The following accounts, with the balances indicated, appear in the ledger of Yellowstone Outdoor Equipment Company on December 1 of the current year:

211	Salaries Payable	—
212	Social Security Tax Payable	$5,278
213	Medicare Tax Payable	1,389
214	Employees Federal Income Tax Payable	8,566
215	Employees State Income Tax Payable	8,334
216	State Unemployment Tax Payable	840
217	Federal Unemployment Tax Payable	210

218	Bond Deductions Payable	$ 1,400
219	Medical Insurance Payable	3,600
611	Sales Salaries Expense	640,200
711	Officers Salaries Expense	283,800
712	Office Salaries Expense	94,600
719	Payroll Taxes Expense	79,114

The following transactions relating to payroll, payroll deductions, and payroll taxes occurred during December:

Dec.   1. Issued Check No. 728 to Pico Insurance Company for $3,600, in payment of the semiannual premium on the group medical insurance policy.

      2. Issued Check No. 729 to First National Bank for $15,233, in payment for $5,278 of social security tax, $1,389 of Medicare tax, and $8,566 of employees' federal income tax due.

      3. Issued Check No. 730 for $1,400 to First National Bank to purchase U.S. savings bonds for employees.

    14. Journalized the entry to record the biweekly payroll. A summary of the payroll record follows:

Salary distribution:		
Sales	$29,000	
Officers	13,200	
Office	4,500	$46,700
Deductions:		
Social security tax	$ 2,569	
Medicare tax	701	
Federal income tax withheld	8,313	
State income tax withheld	2,102	
Savings bond deductions	700	
Medical insurance deductions	600	14,985
Net amount		$31,715

    14. Issued Check No. 738 in payment of the net amount of the biweekly payroll.

    14. Journalized the entry to record payroll taxes on employees' earnings of December 14: social security tax, $2,569; Medicare tax, $701; state unemployment tax, $180; federal unemployment tax, $45.

    17. Issued Check No. 744 to First National Bank for $14,853, in payment for $5,138 of social security tax, $1,402 of Medicare tax, and $8,313 of employees' federal income tax due.

    28. Journalized the entry to record the biweekly payroll. A summary of the payroll record follows:

Salary distribution:		
Sales	$29,500	
Officers	13,100	
Office	4,400	$47,000
Deductions:		
Social security tax	$ 2,538	
Medicare tax	705	
Federal income tax withheld	8,366	
State income tax withheld	2,115	
Savings bond deductions	700	14,424
Net amount		$32,576

    28. Issued Check No. 782 for the net amount of the biweekly payroll.

Dec. 28. Journalized the entry to record payroll taxes on employees' earnings of December 28: social security tax, $2,538; Medicare tax, $705; state unemployment tax, $110; federal unemployment tax, $28.

 30. Issued Check No. 791 for $12,551 to First National Bank, in payment of employees' state income tax due on December 31.

 30. Issued Check No. 792 to First National Bank for $1,400 to purchase U.S. savings bonds for employees.

 31. Paid $61,700 to the employee pension plan. The annual pension cost is $65,000. (Record both the payment and the unfunded pension liability.)

Instructions

1. Journalize the transactions.
2. Journalize the following adjusting entries on December 31:
   a. Salaries accrued: sales salaries, $2,950; officers salaries, $1,310; office salaries, $440. The payroll taxes are immaterial and are not accrued.
   b. Vacation pay, $12,900.

PROBLEMS SERIES B

Problem 10–1B
Liability transactions

Objectives 2, 3

SPREADSHEET

GENERAL
LEDGER

The following items were selected from among the transactions completed by Renaissance Products Co. during the current year:

Feb. 15. Purchased merchandise on account from Ranier Co., $24,000, terms n/30.
Mar. 17. Issued a 30-day, 8% note for $24,000 to Ranier Co., on account.
Apr. 16. Paid Ranier Co. the amount owed on the note of March 17.
July 15. Borrowed $20,000 from Security Bank, issuing a 90-day, 8% note.
 25. Purchased tools by issuing a $90,000, 120-day note to Sun Supply Co., which discounted the note at the rate of 7%.
Oct. 13. Paid Security Bank the interest due on the note of July 15 and renewed the loan by issuing a new 30-day, 9% note for $20,000. (Journalize both the debit and credit to the notes payable account.)
Nov. 12. Paid Security Bank the amount due on the note of October 13.
 22. Paid Sun Supply Co. the amount due on the note of July 25.
Dec. 1. Purchased office equipment from Valley Equipment Co. for $95,000, paying $15,000 and issuing a series of ten 12% notes for $8,000 each, coming due at 30-day intervals.
 17. Settled a product liability lawsuit with a customer for $46,000, payable in January. Renaissance accrued the loss in a litigation claims payable account.
 31. Paid the amount due Valley Equipment Co. on the first note in the series issued on December 1.

Instructions

1. Journalize the transactions.
2. Journalize the adjusting entry for each of the following accrued expenses at the end of the current year: (a) product warranty cost, $18,250; (b) interest on the nine remaining notes owed to Valley Equipment Co.

Problem 10–2B
Entries for payroll and payroll taxes

Objectives 4, 5

GENERAL
LEDGER

The following information about the payroll for the week ended December 30 was obtained from the records of Wong Co.:

Salaries:		Deductions:	
Sales salaries	$205,000	Income tax withheld	$66,000
Warehouse salaries	36,800	Social security tax withheld	19,900
Office salaries	108,200	Medicare tax withheld	5,250
	$350,000	U.S. savings bonds	19,300
		Group insurance	28,700

Tax rates assumed:

Social security, 6% on first $80,000 of employee annual earnings

Medicare, 1.5%

State unemployment (employer only), 4.2%

Federal unemployment (employer only), 0.8%

Instructions

1. Assuming that the payroll for the last week of the year is to be paid on December 31, journalize the following entries:
   a. December 30, to record the payroll.
   b. December 30, to record the employer's payroll taxes on the payroll to be paid on December 31. Of the total payroll for the last week of the year, $12,000 is subject to unemployment compensation taxes.
2. Assuming that the payroll for the last week of the year is to be paid on January 5 of the following fiscal year, journalize the following entries:
   a. December 30, to record the payroll.
   b. January 5, to record the employer's payroll taxes on the payroll to be paid on January 5.

Problem 10–3B

Wage and tax statement data on employer FICA tax

Objectives 4, 5

✓ 2. (e) $26,105.25

Sunrise Bakery Inc. began business on January 2, 2002. Salaries were paid to employees on the last day of each month, and social security tax, Medicare tax, and federal income tax were withheld in the required amounts. An employee who is hired in the middle of the month receives half the monthly salary for that month. All required payroll tax reports were filed, and the correct amount of payroll taxes was remitted by the company for the calendar year. Early in 2003, before the Wage and Tax Statements (Form W-2) could be prepared for distribution to employees and for filing with the Social Security Administration, the employees' earnings records were inadvertently destroyed.

None of the employees resigned or were discharged during the year, and there were no changes in salary rates. The social security tax was withheld at the rate of 6.0% on the first $80,000 of salary and Medicare tax at the rate of 1.5% on salary. Data on dates of employment, salary rates, and employees' income taxes withheld, which are summarized as follows, were obtained from personnel records and payroll records.

Employee	Date First Employed	Monthly Salary	Monthly Income Tax Withheld
Alvarez	Jan. 16	$7,200	$1,548.00
Carver	Nov. 1	3,000	544.20
Felix	Jan. 2	2,600	465.14
Lydall	July 16	3,900	727.35
Porter	Jan. 2	8,400	1,877.40
Song	May 1	4,500	744.75
Walker	Feb. 16	5,400	1,109.16

Instructions

1. Calculate the amounts to be reported on each employee's Wage and Tax Statement (Form W-2) for 2002, arranging the data in the following form:

Employee	Gross Earnings	Federal Income Tax Withheld	Social Security Tax Withheld	Medicare Tax Withheld

2. Calculate the following employer payroll taxes for the year: (a) social security; (b) Medicare; (c) state unemployment compensation at 4.2% on the first $7,000 of each employee's earnings; (d) federal unemployment compensation at 0.8% on the first $7,000 of each employee's earnings; (e) total.

If the working papers correlating with this textbook are not used, omit Problem 10–4B.

Problem 10–4B

Payroll register

Objectives 4, 5

✓ 3. Dr. Payroll Taxes Expense, $692.58

The payroll register for Argentina Leather Goods Co. for the week ended December 12, 2003, is presented in the working papers.

Instructions

1. Journalize the entry to record the payroll for the week.
2. Journalize the entry to record the issuance of the checks to employees.
3. Journalize the entry to record the employer's payroll taxes for the week. Assume the following tax rates: state unemployment, 3.6%; federal unemployment, 0.8%. Of the earnings, $1,250 is subject to unemployment taxes.
4. Journalize the entry to record a check issued on December 15 to Second National Bank in payment of employees' income taxes, $1,540.81, social security taxes, $1,020.12, and Medicare taxes, $255.04.

Problem 10–5B

Payroll register

Objectives 4, 5

SPREADSHEET

✓ 1. Total net amount payable, $6,897.88

The following data for Forever Ready Products Inc. relate to the payroll for the week ended December 7, 2003:

Employee	Hours Worked	Hourly Rate	Weekly Salary	Federal Income Tax	U.S. Savings Bonds	Accumulated Earnings, Nov. 30
M	46.00	$28.00		$301.84	$35.00	$64,200.00
N	20.00	22.00		66.00		12,600.00
O			$1,900.00	456.00	50.00	91,200.00
P	40.00	18.00		144.00	15.00	35,600.00
Q	42.00	20.00		180.60	10.00	40,500.00
R	44.00	18.50		178.71		38,700.00
S	40.00	16.00		121.60	15.00	30,720.00
T			1,000.00	215.00		48,000.00
U	48.00	36.00		430.56	40.00	82,600.00

Employees O and T are office staff, and all of the other employees are sales personnel. All sales personnel are paid 1½ times the regular rate for all hours in excess of 40 hours per week. The social security tax rate is 6.0% on the first $80,000 of each employee's annual earnings, and Medicare tax is 1.5% of each employee's annual earnings. The next payroll check to be used is No. 818.

Instructions

1. Prepare a payroll register for Forever Ready Products Inc. for the week ended December 7, 2003.
2. Journalize the entry to record the payroll for the week.

Problem 10–6B

Payroll accounts and year-end entries

Objectives 4, 5, 6

GENERAL LEDGER

The following accounts, with the balances indicated, appear in the ledger of Mid States CableView Co. on December 1 of the current year:

211	Salaries Payable	—
212	Social Security Tax Payable	$ 7,659
213	Medicare Tax Payable	1,998
214	Employees Federal Income Tax Payable	12,321
215	Employees State Income Tax Payable	11,988
216	State Unemployment Tax Payable	1,180
217	Federal Unemployment Tax Payable	310
218	Bond Deductions Payable	1,200
219	Medical Insurance Payable	6,000
611	Operations Salaries Expense	847,000
711	Officers Salaries Expense	376,200
712	Office Salaries Expense	242,000
719	Payroll Taxes Expense	113,689

The following transactions relating to payroll, payroll deductions, and payroll taxes occurred during December:

Dec. 2. Issued Check No. 728 for $1,200 to First National Bank to purchase U.S. savings bonds for employees.

3. Issued Check No. 729 to First National Bank for $21,978, in payment of $7,659 of social security tax, $1,998 of Medicare tax, and $12,321 of employees' federal income tax due.

14. Journalized the entry to record the biweekly payroll. A summary of the payroll record follows:

Salary distribution:		
Operations	$38,000	
Officers	17,400	
Office	10,800	$66,200
Deductions:		
Social security tax	$ 3,641	
Medicare tax	993	
Federal income tax withheld	11,784	
State income tax withheld	2,979	
Savings bond deductions	600	
Medical insurance deductions	1,000	20,997
Net amount		$45,203

14. Issued Check No. 738 in payment of the net amount of the biweekly payroll.

14. Journalized the entry to record payroll taxes on employees' earnings of December 14: social security tax, $3,641; Medicare tax, $993; state unemployment tax, $285; federal unemployment tax, $75.

17. Issued Check No. 744 to First National Bank for $21,052, in payment of $7,282 of social security tax, $1,986 of Medicare tax, and $11,784 of employees' federal income tax due.

18. Issued Check No. 750 to Pico Insurance Company for $6,000, in payment of the semiannual premium on the group medical insurance policy.

28. Journalized the entry to record the biweekly payroll. A summary of the payroll record follows:

Salary distribution:		
Operations	$39,000	
Officers	17,500	
Office	11,000	$67,500
Deductions:		
Social security tax	$ 3,645	
Medicare tax	1,013	
Federal income tax withheld	12,015	
State income tax withheld	3,038	
Savings bond deductions	600	20,311
Net amount		$47,189

28. Issued Check No. 782 in payment of the net amount of the biweekly payroll.

28. Journalized the entry to record payroll taxes on employees' earnings of December 28: social security tax, $3,645; Medicare tax, $1,013; state unemployment tax, $171; federal unemployment tax, $43.

30. Issued Check No. 791 to First National Bank for $1,200 to purchase U.S. savings bonds for employees.

30. Issued Check No. 792 for $18,005 to First National Bank in payment of employees' state income tax due on December 31.

31. Paid $48,000 to the employee pension plan. The annual pension cost is $50,000. (Record both the payment and unfunded pension liability.)

Instructions

1. Journalize the transactions.
2. Journalize the following adjusting entries on December 31:
   a. Salaries accrued: operations salaries, $3,900; officers salaries, $1,750; office salaries, $1,100. The payroll taxes are immaterial and are not accrued.
   b. Vacation pay, $11,000.

COMPREHENSIVE PROBLEM 3

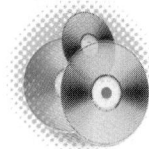

GENERAL LEDGER

✓ 5. Total assets, $994,290

Selected transactions completed by Fore-Most Co. during its first fiscal year ending December 31 were as follows:

Jan. 2. Issued a check to establish a petty cash fund of $600.

Mar. 1. Replenished the petty cash fund, based on the following summary of petty cash receipts: office supplies, $189; miscellaneous selling expense, $125; miscellaneous administrative expense, $205.

Apr. 5. Purchased $9,000 of merchandise on account, terms 1/10, n/30. The perpetual inventory system is used to account for inventory.

May 5. Paid the invoice of April 5 after the discount period had passed.

10. Received cash from daily cash sales for $8,920. The amount indicated by the cash register was $8,960.

June 2. Received a 60-day, 12% note for $60,000 on account.

Aug. 1. Received amount owed on June 2 note, plus interest at the maturity date.

3. Received $900 on account and wrote off the remainder owed on a $1,300 accounts receivable balance. (The allowance method is used in accounting for uncollectible receivables.)

28. Reinstated the account written off on August 3 and received $400 cash in full payment.

Sept. 2. Purchased land by issuing a $90,000, 90-day note to Ace Development Co., which discounted it at 12%.

Oct. 1. Traded office equipment for new equipment with a list price of $160,000. A trade-in allowance of $30,000 was received on the old equipment that had cost $90,000 and had accumulated depreciation of $50,000 as of October 1. A 120-day, 12% note was issued for the balance owed.

Nov. 30. Journalized the monthly payroll for November, based on the following data:

Salaries:		Deductions:	
Sales salaries	$18,500	Income tax withheld	$4,625
Office salaries	6,500	Social security tax	
	$25,000	withheld	1,500
		Medicare tax withheld	375

Unemployment tax rates:	
State unemployment	3.8%
Federal unemployment	0.8%

Amount subject to unemployment taxes:	
State unemployment	$500
Federal unemployment	500

30. Journalized the employer's payroll taxes on the payroll.

Dec. 1. Journalized the payment of the September 2 note at maturity.

30. The pension cost for the year was $45,000, of which $42,800 was paid to the pension plan trustee.

Instructions

1. Journalize the selected transactions.
2. Based on the following data, prepare a bank reconciliation for December of the current year:
   a. Balance according to the bank statement at December 31, $102,610.
   b. Balance according to the ledger at December 31, $85,910.
   c. Checks outstanding at December 31, $29,570.
   d. Deposit in transit, not recorded by bank, $12,600.
   e. Bank debit memorandum for service charges, $70.
   f. A check for $220 in payment of an invoice was incorrectly recorded in the accounts as $20.
3. Based on the bank reconciliation prepared in (2), journalize the entry or entries to be made by Fore-Most Co.
4. Based on the following selected data, journalize the adjusting entries as of December 31 of the current year:
   a. Estimated uncollectible accounts at December 31, $4,760. The balance of Allowance for Doubtful Accounts at December 31 was $800 (debit).
   b. The physical inventory on December 31 indicated an inventory shrinkage of $1,050.
   c. Prepaid insurance expired during the year, $12,200.
   d. Office supplies used during the year, $4,150.
   e. Depreciation is computed as follows:

Asset	Cost	Residual Value	Acquisition Date	Useful Life in Years	Depreciation Method Used
Buildings	$270,000	$ 0	January 2	50	Straight-line
Office Equip.	84,500	12,000	July 1	5	Straight-line
Store Equip.	36,000	10,000	January 3	8	Declining-balance (at twice the straight-line rate)

   f. A patent costing $51,000 when acquired on January 2 has a remaining legal life of 9 years and is expected to have value for 6 years.
   g. The cost of mineral rights was $128,000. Of the estimated deposit of 25,000 tons of ore, 5,000 tons were mined during the year.
   h. Total vacation pay expense for the year, $6,000.
   i. A product warranty was granted beginning December 1 and covering a one-year period. The estimated cost is 3% of sales, which totaled $476,000 in December.
5. Based on the following information and the post-closing trial balance on the next page, prepare a balance sheet in report form at December 31 of the current year.

Notes receivable is a current asset.

The merchandise inventory is stated at cost by the LIFO method.

The product warranty payable is a current liability.

Vacation pay payable:
Current liability	$ 5,000
Long-term liability	1,000

The unfunded pension liability is a long-term liability.

Notes payable:
Current liability	$115,000
Long-term liability	335,000

Fore-Most Co.
Post-Closing Trial Balance
December 31, 2003

Petty Cash	600	
Cash	69,450	
Notes Receivable	50,000	
Accounts Receivable	194,300	
Allowance for Doubtful Accounts		4,760
Merchandise Inventory	40,250	
Prepaid Insurance	24,400	
Office Supplies	6,300	
Land	100,000	
Buildings	270,000	
Accumulated Depreciation—Buildings		5,400
Office Equipment	84,500	
Accumulated Depreciation—Office Equipment		7,250
Store Equipment	36,000	
Accumulated Depreciation—Store Equipment		9,000
Mineral Rights	128,000	
Accumulated Depletion		25,600
Patents	42,500	
Social Security Tax Payable		3,100
Medicare Tax Payable		780
Employees Federal Income Tax Payable		4,700
State Unemployment Tax Payable		45
Federal Unemployment Tax Payable		20
Salaries Payable		26,000
Accounts Payable		94,000
Product Warranty Payable		14,280
Vacation Pay Payable		6,000
Unfunded Pension Liability		2,200
Notes Payable		450,000
Capital Stock		100,000
Retained Earnings		293,165
	1,046,300	1,046,300

6. On February 7 of the following year, the merchandise inventory was destroyed by fire. Based on the following data obtained from the accounting records, estimate the cost of the merchandise destroyed:

Jan. 1 Merchandise inventory	$ 40,250
Jan. 1—Feb. 7 Purchases (net)	246,720
Jan. 1—Feb. 7 Sales (net)	430,000
Estimated gross profit rate	40%

SPECIAL ACTIVITIES

Activity 10–1
Tester and Morris, CPAs

Ethics and professional conduct in business

Marge McMaster is a certified public accountant (CPA) and staff assistant for Tester and Morris, a local CPA firm. It had been the policy of the firm to provide a holiday bonus equal to two weeks' salary to all employees. The firm's new management team announced on November 25 that a bonus equal to only one week's salary would be made available to employees this year. Marge thought that this policy was unfair because she and her co-workers planned on the full two-week bonus. The two-week bonus had been given for ten straight years, so it seemed as though the firm had breached an implied commitment. Thus, Marge decided that she would make up the lost bonus week by working an extra six hours of overtime per week over the next five weeks until the end of the year. Tester and Morris' policy is to pay overtime at 150% of straight time.

Marge's supervisor was surprised to see overtime being reported, since there is generally very little additional or unusual client service demands at the end of the calendar year. However, the overtime was not questioned, since firm employees are on the "honor system" in reporting their overtime.

Discuss whether the firm is acting in an ethical manner by changing the bonus. Is Marge behaving in an ethical manner?

Activity 10–2
ProMatic Company
Recognizing pension expense

What do you think?

The annual examination of ProMatic Company's financial statements by its external public accounting firm (auditors) is nearing completion. The following conversation took place between the controller of ProMatic Company (Peter) and the audit manager from the public accounting firm (Mary).

Mary: You know, Peter, we are about to wrap up our audit for this fiscal year. Yet, there is one item still to be resolved.

Peter: What's that?

Mary: Well, as you know, at the beginning of the year, ProMatic began a defined benefit pension plan. This plan promises your employees an annual payment when they retire, using a formula based on their salaries at retirement and their years of service. I believe that a pension expense should be recognized this year, equal to the amount of pension earned by your employees.

Peter: Wait a minute. I think you have it all wrong. The company doesn't have a pension expense until it actually pays the pension in cash when the employee retires. After all, some of these employees may not reach retirement, and if they don't, the company doesn't owe them anything.

Mary: You're not really seeing this the right way. The pension is earned by your employees during their working years. You actually make the payment much later—when they retire. It's like one long accrual—much like incurring wages in one period and paying them in the next. Thus, I think that you should recognize the expense in the period the pension is earned by the employees.

Peter: Let me see if I've got this straight. I should recognize an expense this period for something that may or may not be paid to the employees in 20 or 30 years, when they finally retire. How am I supposed to determine what the expense is for the current year? The amount of the final retirement depends on many uncertainties: salary levels, employee longevity, mortality rates, and interest earned on investments to fund the pension. I don't think that an amount can be determined, even if I accepted your arguments.

Evaluate Mary's position. Is she right or is Peter correct?

Activity 10–3
Camden Trucking Company
Executive bonuses and accounting methods

Mark Camden, the owner of Camden Trucking Company, initiated an executive bonus plan for his chief executive officer (CEO). The new plan provides a bonus to the CEO equal to 3% of the income before taxes. Upon learning of the new bonus arrangement, the CEO issued instructions to change the company's accounting for trucks. The CEO has asked the controller to make the following two changes:

a. Change from the double-declining-balance method to the straight-line method of depreciation.
b. Add 50% to the useful lives of all trucks.

Why did the CEO ask for these changes? How would you respond to the CEO's request?

Activity 10–4
Into the Real World
Salary survey

Several Internet services provide career guidance, classified employment ads, placement services, résumé posting, career questionnaires, and salary surveys. Select one of the following Internet sites to determine current average salary levels for one of your career options:

**Activity 10–5
Into the Real World**
Payroll forms

Payroll accounting involves the use of government-supplied forms to account for payroll taxes. Three common forms are the W-2, Form 940, and Form 941. Form a team with three of your classmates and retrieve copies of each of these forms. They may be obtained from a local IRS office, a library, or downloaded from the Internet at **www.irs.treas.gov** (go to forms and publications).

a. Briefly describe the purpose of each of the three forms.
b. Fill in the forms using the information provided (leaving blanks where there is no information provided). Assume that your group began a business, called Audit-Proof Tax Services, on November 1 of the current year. Each of you makes a salary of $2,000 per month and claims a single exemption. Salaries were paid on November 30 and December 31. Assume that the withholding tax, social security tax, and Medicare tax are $234, $124, and $29, respectively, per month for each person in the group. Assume further that the federal unemployment tax was $744.

ANSWERS TO SELF-EXAMINATION QUESTIONS

Matching

1.	E	3.	A	5.	M	7.	G	9.	H	11.	J	13.	N
2.	K	4.	I	6.	B	8.	D	10.	L	12.	F	14.	C

Multiple Choice

1. **C** The maturity value is $5,100, determined as follows:

Face amount of note	$5,000
Plus interest ($5,000 × 12% × 60/360)	100
Maturity value	$5,100

2. **B** The net amount available to a borrower from discounting a note payable is called the proceeds. The proceeds of $4,900 (answer B) is determined as follows:

Face amount of note	$5,000
Less discount ($5,000 × 12% × 60/360)	100
Proceeds	$4,900

3. **B** Employers are usually required to withhold a portion of their employees' earnings for payment of federal income taxes (answer A), Medicare tax (answer C), and state and local income taxes (answer D). Generally, federal unemployment compensation taxes (answer B) are levied against the employer only and thus are not deducted from employee earnings.

4. **D** The amount of net pay of $687.75 (answer D) is determined as follows:

Gross pay:		
40 hours at $20	$800.00	
5 hours at $30	150.00	$950.00
Deductions:		
Federal income tax withheld	$212.00	
FICA:		
Social security tax ($600 × 0.06)	$36.00	
Medicare tax ($950 × 0.015) 14.25	50.25	262.25
		$687.75

5. **D** The employer incurs an expense for social security tax (answer A), federal unemployment compensation tax (answer B), and state unemployment compensation tax (answer C). The employees' federal income tax (answer D) is not an expense of the employer. It is withheld from the employees' earnings.

Corporations: Organization, Capital Stock Transactions, and Dividends

F11

o b j e c t i v e s

After studying this chapter, you should be able to:

1 Describe the nature of the corporate form of organization.

2 List the major sources of paid-in capital, including the various classes of stock.

3 Journalize the entries for issuing stock.

4 Journalize the entries for treasury stock transactions.

5 State the effect of stock splits on corporate financial statements.

6 Journalize the entries for cash dividends and stock dividends.

7 Compute and interpret the dividend yield on common stock.

I f you own stock in a corporation, you are interested in how the stock is doing in the market. If you are considering buying stocks, you are interested in your rights as a stockholder and returns that you can expect from the stock. In either case, you should be able to interpret stock market quotations, such as the following:

34^{69}	22^{06}	Walgreen	WAG	.14	.4	50	13406	35^{44}	33^{75}	35^{31}	$+ 0^{13}$
23^{13}	8^{56}	WallaceCS	WCS	.66	6.9	13	1738	9^{81}	9^{25}	9^{63}	$- 0^{13}$
70^{25}	43^{44}	WalMart	WMT	.24	.5	36	49020	50^{13}	49	49^{06}	$- 0^{44}$
13^{69}	7^{25}	WaterInd	WLT	.12	1.5	dd	557	8^{19}	8^{06}	8^{19}	$- 0^{13}$
23^{69}	3^{94}	Warnaco	WAC	.36	7.0	26	733	5^{13}	5	5^{13}	$+ 0^{06}$
29^{44}	21^{75}	WA GasLt	WGL	1.24	4.9	14	422	25^{63}	25	25^{56}	$- 0^{06}$
7^{50}	4^{69}	WA Homes	WHI	...		4	32	7^{19}	7	7^{19}	$+ 0^{13}$

Although you may not own any stocks, you probably buy services or products from corporations, and you may work for a corporation. Understanding the corporate form of organization will help you in your role as a stockholder, a consumer, or an employee. In this chapter, we discuss the characteristics of corporations, as well as how corporations account for stocks.

Nature of a Corporation

objective 1

Describe the nature of the corporate form of organization.

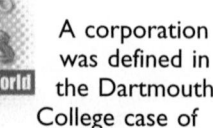

A corporation was defined in the Dartmouth College case of 1819, in which Chief Justice Marshall of the United States Supreme Court stated: "A corporation is an artificial being, invisible, intangible, and existing only in contemplation of the law."

In the preceding chapters, we mentioned that more than 70% of all businesses are proprietorships and 10% are partnerships. Most of these businesses are small businesses. The remaining 20% of businesses are corporations. Many corporations are large and, as a result, they generate more than 90% of the total business dollars in the United States.

Characteristics of a Corporation

A **corporation** is a legal entity, distinct and separate from the individuals who create and operate it. As a legal entity, a corporation may acquire, own, and dispose of property in its own name. It may also incur liabilities and enter into contracts.

Because a corporation is a legal entity, it can sell shares of ownership, called stock, without affecting its operations or continued existence. The stockholders or **shareholders** who own the stock own the corporation. Corporations whose shares of stock are traded in public markets are called **public corporations**. Corporations whose shares are not traded publicly are usually owned by a small group of investors and are called **nonpublic** or **private corporations**.

Corporations can be large because they have the ability to raise large amounts of capital by selling stock. In contrast, a proprietorship's ability to raise capital is limited because it has only one owner. A **partnership** is similar to a proprietorship, except that it has more than one owner. Like a proprietorship, a partnership's ability to raise capital is limited because ownership is not easily transferred.[1]

Stockholders can buy and sell stock without affecting the corporation. In contrast, a proprietorship or a partnership ceases to exist whenever the owner or a partner leaves the business. Likewise, if a new partner is admitted, a new partnership must be formed.

[1] The accounting for partnerships is discussed in Appendix F.

The Coca-Cola Corporation is a well-known public corporation. The Mars Candy Company, which is owned by family members, is a well-known private corporation.

Point of Interest

If you invest in a public corporation, the most you can lose is the amount of your investment, regardless of actions of the corporation.

Point of Interest

If you start a business as a proprietorship or as a partnership with others, your personal assets are at risk for any debts incurred by the business. For example, you could be personally liable for damages awarded in a lawsuit against the business.

The stockholders of a corporation have **limited liability**. This means that a corporation's creditors usually may not go beyond the assets of the corporation to satisfy their claims. Thus, the financial loss that a stockholder may suffer is limited to the amount invested. This feature has contributed to the rapid growth of the corporate form of business.

In contrast, the owner of a proprietorship and the partners of a partnership have **unlimited liability**. They are individually liable to creditors for debts incurred by the business. Thus, if a proprietorship or a partnership is not able to pay its debts, the owner or the partners must contribute personal assets to settle the business debts. This characteristic is significant for partnerships because partners are **mutual agents**, which means that the actions of one partner bind the entire partnership.[2]

A proprietorship is controlled directly by its owner. A partnership is controlled by the partners according to a contract, called the *articles of partnership* or *partnership agreement*. In contrast, the stockholders control a corporation by electing a **board of directors**. This board meets periodically to establish corporate policies. It also selects the chief executive officer (CEO) and other major officers to manage the corporation's day-to-day affairs. Exhibit 1 shows the organizational structure of a corporation.

Exhibit 1 Organizational Structure of a Corporation

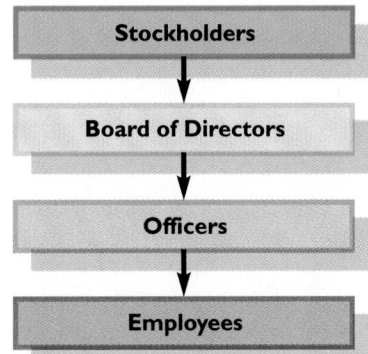

Corporations have a separate legal existence, transferable units of ownership, and limited stockholder liability.

As a separate entity, a corporation is subject to taxes. For example, corporations must pay federal income taxes on their income.[3] Thus, corporate income that is distributed to stockholders in the form of **dividends** has already been taxed. In turn, stockholders must pay income taxes on the dividends they receive. This *double taxation* of corporate earnings is a major disadvantage of the corporate form.[4] In contrast, proprietorships and partnerships are not required to pay federal income taxes. Instead, the owner or partners report their share of the business's income on their personal tax returns.

Forming a Corporation

The first step in forming a corporation is to file an **application of incorporation** with the state. State incorporation laws differ, and corporations often organize in

---

[2] Some states permit limited partnerships, in which the liability of some partners is limited to the amount of their capital investment. However, a limited partnership must have at least one partner who has unlimited liability.

[3] Some states also require corporations to pay income taxes.

[4] Under the *Internal Revenue Code*, a corporation with a few stockholders may elect to be treated like a partnership for income tax purposes. Such corporations are known as Subchapter S corporations.

those states with the more favorable laws. For this reason, more than half of the largest companies are incorporated in Delaware. Exhibit 2 lists some corporations with which you may be familiar, their states of incorporation, and the location of their headquarters.

Corporations may be organized for non-profit reasons, such as recreational, educational, charitable, or humanitarian purposes. Such corporations are not required to pay federal taxes. Examples of nonprofit corporations include the **Sierra Club** and the **National Audubon Society**. However, most corporations are organized to earn a profit and a fair rate of return for their stockholders. Examples of for-profit corporations include **PepsiCo**, **General Motors**, and **Microsoft**.

Exhibit 2 Examples of Corporations and Their States of Incorporation

Corporation	State of Incorporation	Headquarters
Borden, Inc.	New Jersey	New York, N.Y.
Caterpillar, Inc.	Delaware	Peoria, Ill.
Delta Air Lines, Inc.	Delaware	Atlanta, Ga.
Dow Chemical Company	Delaware	Midland, Mich.
General Electric Company	New York	Fairfield, Conn.
The Home Depot	Delaware	Atlanta, Ga.
Kellogg Company	Delaware	Battle Creek, Mich.
3M	Delaware	St. Paul, Minn.
May Department Stores	New York	St. Louis, Mo.
RJR Nabisco	Delaware	New York, N.Y.
Tandy Corporation	Delaware	Ft. Worth, Tex.
The Washington Post Company	Delaware	Washington, D.C.
Whirlpool Corporation	Delaware	Benton Harbor, Mich.

After the application of incorporation has been approved, the state grants a **charter** or **articles of incorporation**. The articles of incorporation formally create the corporation.[5] The corporate management and board of directors then prepare a set of **bylaws**, which are the rules and procedures for conducting the corporation's affairs.

Significant costs may be incurred in organizing a corporation. These costs include legal fees, taxes, state incorporation fees, license fees, and promotional costs. Such costs, referred to as organizational costs or startup costs, should be expensed when they are incurred.

The following entries illustrate the recording of a corporation's organization costs of $8,500 on January 5.

Jan.	5	Organization Costs		8 5 0 0 00			
		Cash				8 5 0 0 00	
		Paid costs of organizing the corporation.					

---

[5] The articles of incorporation may also restrict a corporation's activities in certain areas, such as owning certain types of real estate, conducting certain types of business activities, or purchasing its own stock.

BUSINESS ON STAGE

Stock Exchanges

Stocks are bought and sold through stock exchanges. The New York Stock Exchange and the American Stock Exchange are the two national exchanges. In addition, regional exchanges and the over-the-counter market serve important roles in the trading of stocks.

New York Stock Exchange (**nyse.com**). This exchange, founded in 1792, is located on Wall Street in New York City. It consists of over 1,366 members who own "seats" on the exchange and who are allowed to trade securities. Only stocks listed on the exchange (the "Big Board") can be traded. Currently, stocks of over 3,000 generally older, well-established, larger companies are listed. To qualify for listing, a company must have over 1 million shares outstanding and $2.5 million of pretax profits. Examples of

such companies include General Motors and Alcoa.

American Stock Exchange (**amex.com**). This exchange is similar to the New York Stock Exchange, except that the companies are generally small to medium-size companies. To qualify for listing, a company must have over 500,000 shares outstanding and $750,000 of pretax profits. Currently, about 800 stocks are listed on the American Stock Exchange. As a company grows, it may move from the American Stock Exchange to the New York Stock Exchange. Examples of American Stock Exchange companies include El Paso Electric and TWA.

Regional Exchanges. There are several regional exchanges, including Chicago, Boston, Cincinnati, Philadelphia, and San Francisco. Initially, such exchanges traded mostly in stocks of

local firms. Today, many firms, such as Sears, are traded on both regional and national exchanges.

Nasdaq (**nasdaq.com**). This market refers to a network of brokers who communicate with each other to set prices and trade securities. This system is referred to as the *National Association of Securities Dealers Automated Quotation* system, or more simply by its abbreviation, *Nasdaq*. Larger, actively traded issues are referred to as Nasdaq National Market issues, while less active issues are referred to as Nasdaq Small-Cap issues. Many Internet companies are initially listed on Nasdaq. Examples of Nasdaq companies include Apple Computer, Intel, Cisco Systems, and Amazon.com. ■

Sources of Paid-In Capital

objective 2

List the major sources of paid-in capital, including the various classes of stock.

Some corporations have stopped issuing stock certificates except on special request. In these cases, the corporation maintains records of ownership by using electronic media.

As we discussed and illustrated in earlier chapters, the two main sources of stockholders' equity are paid-in capital (or contributed capital) and retained earnings. The main source of paid-in capital is from issuing stock. In the following paragraphs, we discuss the characteristics of the various classes of stock. We conclude this section with a brief discussion of other sources of paid-in capital.

Stock

The number of shares of stock that a corporation is *authorized* to issue is stated in its charter. The term *issued* refers to the shares issued to the stockholders. A corporation may, under circumstances we discuss later in this chapter, reacquire some of the stock that it has issued. The stock remaining in the hands of stockholders is then called **outstanding stock**. The relationship between authorized, issued, and outstanding stock is shown in the graphic at the right.

Number of shares authorized, issued, and outstanding

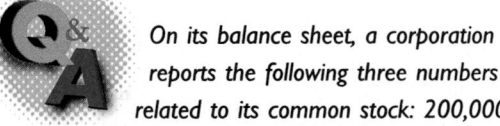

On its balance sheet, a corporation reports the following three numbers related to its common stock: 200,000 shares; 150,000 shares; and 138,000 shares. What is the number of shares authorized, issued, outstanding, and reacquired?

200,000 shares authorized; 150,000 shares issued; 138,000 shares outstanding; 12,000 (150,000 − 138,000) shares reacquired.

The two primary classes of paid-in capital are common stock and preferred stock.

Shares of stock are often assigned a monetary amount, called **par**. Corporations may issue **stock certificates** to stockholders to document their ownership. Printed on a stock certificate is the par value of the stock, the name of the stockholder, and the number of shares owned. Stock may also be issued without par, in which case it is called **no-par stock**. Some states require the board of directors to assign a **stated value** to no-par stock.

Because corporations have limited liability, creditors have no claim against the personal assets of stockholders. However, some state laws require that corporations maintain a minimum **stockholder** contribution to protect creditors. This minimum amount is called *legal capital*. The amount of required legal capital varies among the states, but it usually includes the amount of par or stated value of the shares of stock issued.

The major rights that accompany ownership of a share of stock are as follows:

1. The right to vote in matters concerning the corporation.
2. The right to share in distributions of earnings.
3. The right to share in assets on liquidation.

When only one class of stock is issued, it is called **common stock**. In this case, each share of common stock has equal rights. To appeal to a broader investment market, a corporation may issue one or more classes of stock with various preference rights. A common example of such a right is the preference to dividends. Such a stock is generally called a **preferred stock**.

The dividend rights of preferred stock are usually stated in monetary terms or as a percent of par. For example, *$4 preferred stock* has a right to an annual $4 per share dividend. If the par value of the preferred stock were $50, the same right to dividends could be stated as *8% ($4/$50) preferred stock*.

The board of directors of a corporation has the sole authority to distribute dividends to the stockholders. When such action is taken, the directors are said to *declare* a dividend. Since dividends are normally based on earnings, a corporation cannot guarantee dividends even to preferred stockholders. However, because they have first rights to any dividends, the preferred stockholders have a greater chance of receiving regular dividends than do the common stockholders.

Nonparticipating Preferred Stock

Preferred stockholders' dividend rights are usually limited to a certain amount. Such stock is said to be **nonparticipating preferred stock**.[6] To continue our preceding example, assume that a corporation has 1,000 shares of $4 nonparticipating preferred stock and 4,000 shares of common stock outstanding. Also assume that the net income, amount of earnings retained, and the amount of earnings distributed by the board of directors for the first three years of operations are as follows:

	2002	2003	2004
Net income	$20,000	$55,000	$62,000
Amount retained	10,000	20,000	40,000
Amount distributed	$10,000	$35,000	$22,000

Exhibit 3 shows the earnings distributed each year to the preferred stock and the common stock. In this example, the preferred stockholders received an annual dividend of $4 per share, compared to the common stockholders' dividends of $1.50,

---

[6] In some cases, preferred stock may receive additional dividends if certain conditions are met. Such stock is called *participating preferred stock*. It is rarely used in today's financial markets.

Exhibit 3 Dividends to Nonparticipating Preferred Stock

	2002	2003	2004
Amount distributed	$10,000	$35,000	$22,000
Preferred dividend (1,000 shares)	4,000	4,000	4,000
Common dividend (4,000 shares)	$ 6,000	$31,000	$18,000
Dividends per share:			
Preferred	$ 4.00	$ 4.00	$ 4.00
Common	$ 1.50	$ 7.75	$ 4.50

$7.75, and $4.50 per share. You should note that although preferred stockholders have a greater chance of receiving a regular dividend, common stockholders have a greater chance of receiving larger dividends than do the preferred stockholders.

Romer Corporation has 50,000 shares of $2, $100 par cumulative preferred stock outstanding. Preferred dividends are three years in arrears (not including the current year). What amount of preferred dividends must be paid before any dividends on common shares can be paid?

$400,000 [3 years in arrears (50,000 × $2 × 3) plus the current year's dividend of $100,000]

Cumulative Preferred Stock

Cumulative preferred stock has a right to receive regular dividends that have been passed (not declared) before any common stock dividends are paid. Noncumulative preferred stock does not have this right.

Dividends that have been passed are said to be **in arrears**. Such dividends should be disclosed, normally in a footnote to the financial statements.

To illustrate how dividends on cumulative preferred stock are calculated, assume that the preferred stock in Exhibit 3 is cumulative, and that no dividends were paid in 2002 and 2003. In 2004, the board of directors declares dividends of $22,000. Exhibit 4 shows how the dividends paid in 2004 are distributed between the preferred and common stockholders.

Exhibit 4 Dividends to Cumulative Preferred Stock

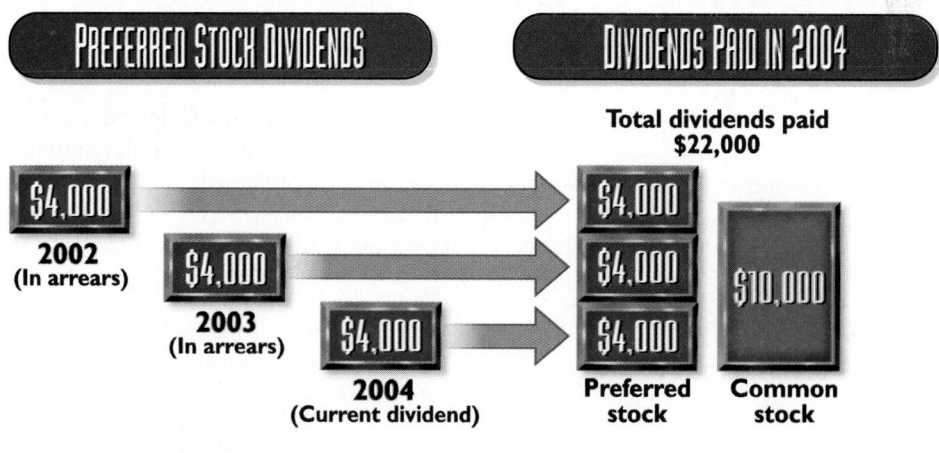

Amount distributed		$22,000
Preferred dividend (1,000 shares):		
2002 dividend in arrears	$4,000	
2003 dividend in arrears	4,000	
2004 dividend	4,000	12,000
Common dividend (4,000 shares)		$10,000
Dividends per share:		
Preferred		$ 12.00
Common		$ 2.50

Other Preferential Rights

In addition to dividend preference, preferred stock may be given preferences to assets if the corporation goes out of business and is liquidated. However, claims of creditors must be satisfied first. Preferred stockholders are next in line to receive any remaining assets, followed by the common stockholders.

Other Sources of Paid-In Capital

In addition to arising from the issuance of stock, paid-in capital may arise from receiving donations of real estate or other assets. Civic groups and municipalities sometimes give land or buildings to a corporation as an incentive to locate or remain in a community. In such cases, the corporation debits the assets for their fair market value and credits *Donated Capital.*

To illustrate, assume that on April 20 the city of Moraine donated land to Merrick Corporation as an incentive for it to relocate its headquarters to Moraine. The land was valued at $500,000. Merrick Corporation would record the land as follows:

Apr.	20	Land	500 0 0 0 00	
		Donated Capital		500 0 0 0 00
		Recorded land donated by the city		
		of Moraine.		

Paid-in capital may also arise when a corporation buys and sells its own stock in the marketplace. Later in this chapter, we will discuss the recording of such transactions.

Issuing Stock

objective 3

Journalize the entries for issuing stock.

A separate account is used for recording the amount of each class of stock issued to investors in a corporation. For example, assume that a corporation is authorized to issue 10,000 shares of preferred stock, $100 par, and 100,000 shares of common stock, $20 par. One-half of each class of authorized shares is issued at par for cash. The corporation's entry to record the stock issue is as follows:[7]

		Cash	1,500 0 0 0 00	
		Preferred Stock		500 0 0 0 00
		Common Stock		1,000 0 0 0 00
		Issued preferred stock and common		
		stock at par for cash.		

Stock is often issued by a corporation at a price other than its par. This is because the par value of a stock is simply its legal capital. The price at which stock can be sold by a corporation depends on a variety of factors, such as:

1.   The financial condition, earnings record, and dividend record of the corporation.
2.   Investor expectations of the corporation's potential earning power.
3.   General business and economic conditions and prospects.

[7] The accounting for investments in stocks from the point of view of the investor is discussed in a later chapter.

When stock is issued for a price that is more than its par, the stock has sold at a **premium**. When stock is issued for a price that is less than its par, the stock has sold at a **discount**. Thus, if stock with a par of $50 is issued for a price of $60, the stock has sold at a premium of $10. If the same stock is issued for a price of $45, the stock has sold at a discount of $5. Many states do not permit stock to be issued at a discount. In others, it may be done only under unusual conditions. Since issuing stock at a discount is rare, we will not illustrate it.

A corporation issuing stock must maintain records of the stockholders in order to issue dividend checks and distribute financial statements and other reports. Large public corporations normally use a financial institution, such as a bank, for this purpose.[8] In such cases, the financial institution is referred to as a *transfer agent* or *registrar*. For example, the transfer agent and registrar for **Coca-Cola Enterprises** is **First Chicago Trust Company of New York**.

Premium on Stock

When stock is issued at a premium, Cash or other asset accounts are debited for the amount received. Common Stock or Preferred Stock is then credited for the par amount. The excess of the amount paid over par is a part of the total investment of the stockholders in the corporation. Therefore, such an amount in excess of par should be classified as a part of the paid-in capital. An account entitled *Paid-In Capital in Excess of Par* is usually credited for this amount.

To illustrate, assume that Caldwell Company issues 2,000 shares of $50 par preferred stock for cash at $55. The entry to record this transaction is as follows:

Cash	110 000 00	
Preferred Stock		100 000 00
Paid-In Capital in Excess of		
Par—Preferred Stock		10 000 00
Issued $50 par preferred stock at $55.		

The following stock quotation for **Wal-Mart Corporation** is taken from *The Wall Street Journal*:

NEW YORK STOCK EXCHANGE

52 Weeks Hi	Lo	Stock	Sym	Div	Yld %	PE	Vol 100s	Hi	Lo	Close	Net Chg
70²⁵	43⁴⁴	WalMart	WMT	.24	.5	36	49020	50¹³	49	49⁰⁶	— 0⁴⁴

The preceding quotation is interpreted as follows:

Hi	Highest price during the past 52 weeks
Lo	Lowest price during the past 52 weeks
Stock	Name of the company
Sym	Stock exchange symbol (WMT for Wal-Mart)
Div	Dividends paid per share during the past year
Yld %	Annual dividend yield per share based on the closing price (Wal-Mart's 0.5% yield on common stock is computed as $0.24/$49.06)
PE	Price-earnings ratio on common stock (price ÷ earnings per share)
Vol	The volume of stock traded in 100s
Hi	Highest price for the day
Lo	Lowest price for the day
Close	Closing price for the day
Net Chg	The net change in price from the previous day

When stock is issued in exchange for assets other than cash, such as land, buildings, and equipment, the assets acquired should be recorded at their fair market value. If this value cannot be objectively determined, the fair market price of the stock issued may be used.

To illustrate, assume that a corporation acquired land for which the fair market value cannot be determined. In exchange, the corporation issued 10,000 shares of its $10 par common. Assuming that the stock has a current market price of $12 per share, this transaction is recorded as follows:

Land	120 000 00	
Common Stock		100 000 00
Paid-In Capital in Excess of Par		20 000 00
Issued $10 par common stock, valued		
at $12 per share, for land.		

---

[8] Small corporations may use a subsidiary ledger, called a *stockholders ledger*. In this case, the stock accounts (Preferred Stock and Common Stock) are controlling accounts for the subsidiary ledger.

No-Par Stock

In most states, both preferred and common stock may be issued without a par value. When no-par stock is issued, the entire proceeds are credited to the stock account. This is true even though the issue price varies from time to time. For example, assume that a corporation issues 10,000 shares of no-par common stock at $40 a share and at a later date issues 1,000 additional shares at $36. The entries to record the no-par stock are as follows:

Cash		400 0 0 0 00	
Common Stock			400 0 0 0 00
Issued 10,000 shares of no-par			
common at $40.			
Cash		36 0 0 0 00	
Common Stock			36 0 0 0 00
Issued 1,000 shares of no-par			
common at $36.			

Some states require that the entire proceeds from the issue of no-par stock be recorded as legal capital. In this case, the preceding entries would be proper. In other states, no-par stock may be assigned a *stated value per share*. The stated value is recorded like a par value, and the excess of the proceeds over the stated value is recorded as follows:

Cash		400 0 0 0 00	
Common Stock			250 0 0 0 00
Paid-In Capital in Excess of Stated Value			150 0 0 0 00
Issued 10,000 shares of no-par common			
at $40; stated value, $25.			
Cash		36 0 0 0 00	
Common Stock			25 0 0 0 00
Paid-In Capital in Excess of Stated Value			11 0 0 0 00
Issued 1,000 shares of no-par common			
at $36; stated value, $25.			

Treasury Stock Transactions

objective 4

Journalize the entries for treasury stock transactions.

A corporation may buy its own stock to provide shares for resale to employees, for reissuing as a bonus to employees, or for supporting the market price of the stock. For example, **General Motors** bought back its common stock and stated that two primary uses of this stock would be for incentive compensation plans and employee savings plans. Such stock that a corporation has once issued and then reacquires is called **treasury stock**.

The 1999 edition of *Accounting Trends & Techniques* indicated that over 65% of the companies surveyed reported treasury stock.

A commonly used method of accounting for the purchase and resale of treasury stock is the **cost method**.[9] When the stock is purchased by the corporation, the account *Treasury Stock* is debited for its cost (the price paid for it). The par value and the price at which the stock was originally issued are ignored. When the stock is resold, Treasury Stock is credited for its cost, and any difference between the cost and the selling price is normally debited or credited to *Paid-In Capital from Sale of Treasury Stock*.

To illustrate, assume that the paid-in capital of a corporation is as follows:

Common stock, $25 par (20,000 shares authorized and issued)	$500,000	
Excess of issue price over par	150,000	$650,000

The purchase and sale of the treasury stock are recorded as follows:

Treasury Stock		45 0 0 0 00	
Cash			45 0 0 0 00
	Purchased 1,000 shares of treasury stock at $45.		
Cash		12 0 0 0 00	
Treasury Stock			9 0 0 0 00
Paid-In Capital from Sale of Treasury Stock			3 0 0 0 00
	Sold 200 shares of treasury stock at $60.		
Cash		8 0 0 0 00	
Paid-In Capital from Sale of Treasury Stock		1 0 0 0 00	
Treasury Stock			9 0 0 0 00
	Sold 200 shares of treasury stock at $40.		

As shown above, a sale of treasury stock may result in a decrease in paid-in capital. To the extent that Paid-In Capital from Sale of Treasury Stock has a credit balance, it should be debited for any decrease. Any remaining decrease should then be debited to the retained earnings account.

At the end of the period, the balance in the treasury stock account is reported as a deduction from the total of the paid-in capital and retained earnings. The balance of Paid-In Capital from Sale of Treasury Stock is reported as part of the paid-in capital, as shown in Exhibit 5.

Exhibit 5 Stockholders' Equity Section with Treasury Stock

Stockholders' Equity		
Paid-in capital:		
Common stock, $25 par (20,000 shares authorized and issued)	$500,000	
Excess of issue price over par	150,000	
From sale of treasury stock	2,000	
Total paid-in capital		$652,000
Retained earnings		130,000
Total		$782,000
Deduct treasury stock (600 shares at cost)		27,000
Total stockholders' equity		$755,000

[9] Another method that is infrequently used, called the *par value method*, is discussed in advanced accounting texts.

Stock Splits

When **Nature's Sunshine Products Inc.** declared a two-for-one stock split, the company president said:

We believe the split will place our stock price in a range attractive to both individual and institutional investors, broadening the market for the stock.

LTM Corporation announced a 4-for-1 stock split of its $50 par value common stock, which is currently trading for $120 per share. What is the new par value and the estimated market price of the stock after the split?

$12.50 ($50/4) par value; $30 ($120/4) estimated market price.

Corporations sometimes reduce the par or stated value of their common stock and issue a proportionate number of additional shares. When this is done, a corporation is said to have *split* its stock, and the process is called a **stock split**.

When stock is split, the reduction in par or stated value applies to all shares, including the unissued, issued, and treasury shares. A major objective of a stock split is to reduce the market price per share of the stock. This, in turn, should attract more investors to enter the market for the stock and broaden the types and numbers of stockholders.

To illustrate a stock split, assume that Rojek Corporation has 10,000 shares of $100 par common stock outstanding with a current market price of $150 per share. The board of directors declares a 5-for-1 stock split, reduces the par to $20, and increases the number of shares to 50,000. The amount of common stock outstanding is $1,000,000 both before and after the stock split. Only the number of shares and the par per share are changed. Each Rojek Corporation shareholder owns the same total par amount of stock before and after the stock split.

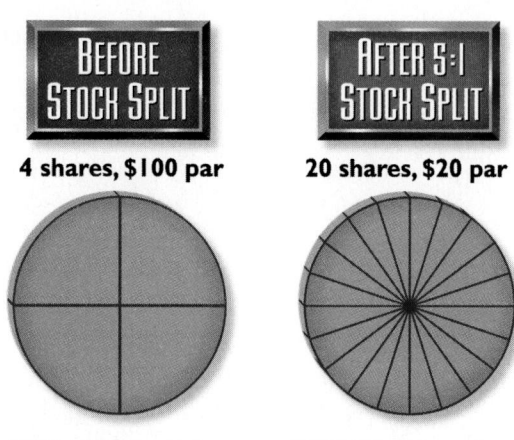

For example, a stockholder who owned 4 shares of $100 par stock before the split (total par of $400) would own 20 shares of $20 par stock after the split (total par of $400).

Since there are more shares outstanding after the stock split, we would expect that the market price of the stock would fall. For example, in the preceding example, there would be 5 times as many shares outstanding after the split. Thus, we would expect the market price of the stock to fall from $150 to approximately $30 ($150/5).

Since a stock split changes only the par or stated value and the number of shares outstanding, it is not recorded by a journal entry. Although the accounts are not affected, the details of stock splits are normally disclosed in the notes to the financial statements.

> **A stock split does not change the balance of any corporation accounts.**

Accounting for Dividends

When a board of directors declares a cash dividend, it authorizes the distribution of a portion of the corporation's cash to stockholders. When a board of directors declares a stock dividend, it authorizes the distribution of a portion of its stock. In both cases, the declaration of a dividend reduces the retained earnings of the corporation.[10]

---

[10] In rare cases, when a corporation is reducing its operations or going out of business, a dividend may be a distribution of paid-in capital. Such a dividend is called a *liquidating dividend*.

Cash Dividends

A cash distribution of earnings by a corporation to its shareholders is called a **cash dividend**. Although dividends may be paid in the form of other assets, cash dividends are the most common form.

There are usually three conditions that a corporation must meet to pay a cash dividend:

1. Sufficient retained earnings
2. Sufficient cash
3. Formal action by the board of directors

A large amount of retained earnings does not always mean that a corporation is able to pay dividends. As we indicated earlier in the chapter, the balance of the cash and retained earnings account are often unrelated. Thus, a large retained earnings account does not mean that there is cash available to pay dividends.

A corporation's board of directors is not required by law to declare dividends. This is true even if both retained earnings and cash are large enough to justify a dividend. However, most corporations try to maintain a stable dividend record in order to make their stock attractive to investors. Although dividends may be paid once a year or semiannually, most corporations pay dividends quarterly. In years of high profits, a corporation may declare a *special* or *extra* dividend.

You may have seen announcements of dividend declarations in financial newspapers or investor services. An example of such an announcement is shown below.

On June 26, the board of directors of **Campbell Soup Co.** *declared a quarterly cash dividend of $0.225 per common share to stockholders of record as of the close of business on July 8, payable on July 31.*

This announcement includes three important dates: the *date of declaration* (June 26), the *date of record* (July 8), and the *date of payment* (July 31). During the period of time between the record date and the payment date, the stock price is usually quoted as selling *ex-dividends*. This means that since the date of record has passed, a new investor will not receive the dividend.

To illustrate, assume that on *December 1* the board of directors of Hiber Corporation declares the following quarterly cash dividends. The date of record is *December 10*, and the date of payment is *January 2*.

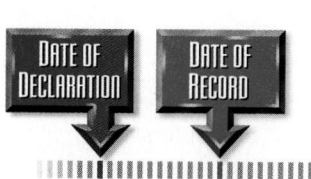

	DATE OF DECLARATION	DATE OF RECORD	DATE OF PAYMENT
	JUNE 26	JULY 8	JULY 31
	Board of Directors takes action to declare dividends.	Ownership of shares determines who receives dividend (no entry required).	Dividend is paid.
	ENTRY: Debit *Cash Dividends* Credit *Cash Dividends Payable*		**ENTRY:** Debit *Cash Dividends Payable* Credit *Cash*

	Dividend per Share	Total Dividends
Preferred stock, $100 par, 5,000 shares outstanding	$2.50	$12,500
Common stock, $10 par, 100,000 shares outstanding	$0.30	30,000
Total		$42,500

Hiber Corporation records the $42,500 liability for the dividends on December 1, the declaration date, as follows:

Dec.	1	Cash Dividends	42 5 0 0 00	
		Cash Dividends Payable		42 5 0 0 00
		Declared cash dividend.		

No entry is required on the date of record, December 10, since this date merely determines which stockholders will receive the dividend. On the date of payment, January 2, the corporation records the $42,500 payment of the dividends as follows:

Jan.	2	Cash Dividends Payable	42 5 0 0 00	
		Cash		42 5 0 0 00
		Paid cash dividend.		

If Hiber Corporation's fiscal year ends December 31, the balance in Cash Dividends will be transferred to Retained Earnings as a part of the closing process by debiting Retained Earnings and crediting Cash Dividends. Cash Dividends Payable will be listed on the December 31 balance sheet as a current liability.

If a corporation that holds treasury stock declares a cash dividend, the dividends are not paid on the treasury shares. To do so would place the corporation in the position of earning income through dealing with itself. For example, if Hiber Corporation in the preceding illustration had held 5,000 shares of its own common stock, the cash dividends on the common stock would have been $28,500 [(100,000 − 5,000) × $0.30] instead of $30,000.

Stock Dividends

A distribution of shares of stock to stockholders is called a **stock dividend**. Usually, such distributions are in common stock and are issued to holders of common stock. Stock dividends are different from cash dividends in that there is no distribution of cash or other assets to stockholders.

The effect of a stock dividend on the stockholders' equity of the issuing corporation is to transfer retained earnings to paid-in capital. For public corporations, the amount transferred from retained earnings to paid-in capital is normally the *fair value* (market price) of the shares issued in the stock dividend.[11] To illustrate, assume that the stockholders' equity accounts of Hendrix Corporation as of December 15 are as follows:

Common Stock, $20 par (2,000,000 shares issued)	$40,000,000
Paid-In Capital in Excess of Par—Common Stock	9,000,000
Retained Earnings	26,600,000

On December 15, the board of directors declares a stock dividend of 5% or 100,000 shares (2,000,000 shares × 5%) to be issued on January 10 to stockholders of record on December 31. The market price of the stock on the declaration date is $31 a share. The entry to record the declaration is as follows:

Dec.	15	Stock Dividends (100,000 × $31 market price)	3,100 0 0 0 00	
		Stock Dividends Distributable		
		(100,000 × $20 Par)		2,000 0 0 0 00
		Paid-In Capital in Excess of		
		Par—Common Stock		1,100 0 0 0 00
		Declared stock dividend.		

---

[11] The use of fair market value is justified as long as the number of shares issued for the stock dividend is small (less than 25% of the shares outstanding).

The $3,100,000 balance in Stock Dividends is closed to Retained Earnings on December 31. The stock dividends distributable account is listed in the Paid-In Capital section of the balance sheet. Thus, the effect of the stock dividend is to transfer $3,100,000 of retained earnings to paid-in capital.

On January 10, the number of shares outstanding is increased by 100,000 by the following entry to record the issue of the stock:

Jan.	10	Stock Dividends Distributable	2,000 0 0 0 00	
		Common Stock		2,000 0 0 0 00
		Issued stock for the stock dividend.		

A stock dividend does not change the assets, liabilities, or total stockholders' equity of the corporation. Likewise, it does not change a stockholder's proportionate interest (equity) in the corporation. For example, if a stockholder owned 1,000 of a corporation's 10,000 shares outstanding, the stockholder owns 10% (1,000/10,000) of the corporation. After declaring a 6% stock dividend, the corporation will issue 600 additional shares (10,000 shares × 6%), and the total shares outstanding will be 10,600. The stockholder of 1,000 shares will receive 60 additional shares and will now own 1,060 shares, which is still a 10% equity.

FINANCIAL ANALYSIS AND INTERPRETATION

objective 7

Compute and interpret the dividend yield on common stock.

The **dividend yield** indicates the rate of return to stockholders in terms of cash dividend distributions. Although the dividend yield can be computed for both preferred and common stock, it is most often computed for common stock. This is because most preferred stock has a stated dividend rate or amount. In contrast, the amount of common stock dividends normally varies with the profitability of the corporation.

The dividend yield is computed by dividing the annual dividends paid per share of common stock by the market price per share at a specific date, as shown below.

$$\text{Dividend Yield} = \frac{\textbf{Dividends per Share of Common Stock}}{\textbf{Market Price per Share of Common Stock}}$$

To illustrate, the market price of **Coca-Cola's** common stock was $58.88 as of the close of business, August 23, 2000. During the past year, Coca-Cola had paid dividends of $0.68 per share. Thus, the dividend yield of Coca-Cola's common stock is 1.2% ($0.68/$58.88). Because the market price of a corporation's stock will vary from day to day, its dividend yield will also vary from day to day.

The dividend yield on common stock is of special interest to investors whose main objective is to receive a current dividend return on their investment. This is in contrast to investors whose main objective is a rapid increase in the market price of their investments. For example, technology companies often do not pay dividends but reinvest their earnings in research and development. The main attraction of such stocks, such as **Microsoft's** common stock, is the expectation of the market price of the stock rising. Since many factors affect stock prices, an investment strategy relying solely on market price increases is more risky than a strategy based on dividend yields.

ENCORE

Would You Like to Own a Sports Team?

The Florida Panthers, a National League Hockey team based in Fort Lauderdale, sold its common stock to the public. At an initial offering price of $10 per share, the stock appeared to be a bargain compared to some of the Panthers' official merchandise. For example, a classic Panthers' cap is $20, a home jersey is $159, and a tire cover is $39.

Like many sports teams, the Panthers are facing some difficult financial issues. For example, the team's margins are being squeezed by players' salaries, which more than doubled in two years. In addition, the Panthers must share equally the franchise fees as well as broadcasting revenues with other NHL clubs. Also, the Panthers must pay $10 million to the NHL's collective bargaining fund by April 2003. The prospectus distributed to potential investors indicates that

the Panthers expected losses and have no plans to pay a dividend "in the foreseeable future."

But what about the thrill of owning a team and voting on draft picks, hiring and firing coaches, and attending games in the owner's box? Not likely. The stock offering was structured so that the current owner, H. Wayne Huizenga, received shares of Class B common stock that entitle him to 10,000 votes for each share of Class A common stock outstanding.

So, are you interested? With no dividend, projected losses, and no voting power, do you think that buying a share of Panthers stock would be a good investment or just end up being a piece of sports memorabilia? In November 1996, the Panthers issued their stock at $10 per share. The stock traded on the NYSE under the symbol PAW until September

1999, when the company changed its name to Boca Resorts, Inc. Boca Resorts, Inc., also owns National Car Rental and such luxury resorts as the Arizona Biltmore Hotel. At the end of trading on August 25, 2000, the stock was trading on the NYSE, under the symbol RST, at $10.88. ■

Source: Tim Carvell, "So You Want to Own a Team?" *Fortune,* November 11, 1996, pp. 46–48.

KEY POINTS

1 Describe the nature of the corporate form of organization.

Corporations have a separate legal existence, transferable units of stock, and limited stockholders' liability. Corporations may be either public or private corporations, and they are subject to federal income taxes.

The documents included in forming a corporation include an application of incorporation, articles of incorporation, and bylaws. Costs often incurred in organizing a corporation include legal fees, taxes, state incorporation fees, and promotional costs. Such costs are

debited to an expense account entitled Organization Costs.

2 List the major sources of paid-in capital, including the various classes of stock.

The main source of paid-in capital is from issuing stock. The two primary classes of stock are common stock and preferred stock. Preferred stock is normally nonparticipating and may be cumulative or noncumulative. In addition to the issuance of stock, paid-in capital may arise from donations of assets and from treasury stock transactions.

3 Journalize the entries for issuing stock.

When a corporation issues stock at par for cash, the cash account is debited and the class of stock issued is credited for its par amount. When a corporation issues stock at more than par, Paid-In Capital in Excess of Par is credited for the difference between the cash received and the par value of the stock. When stock is issued in exchange for assets other than cash, the assets acquired should be recorded at their fair market value.

When no-par stock is issued, the entire proceeds are credited to the stock account. No-par stock may be assigned a stated value per share, and the excess of the proceeds over the stated value may be credited to Paid-In Capital in Excess of Stated Value.

4 Journalize the entries for treasury stock transactions.

When a corporation buys its own stock, the cost method of accounting is normally used. Treasury Stock is debited for its cost, and Cash is credited. If the stock is resold, Treasury Stock is credited for its cost and any difference between the cost and the selling price is normally debited or credited to Paid-In Capital from Sale of Treasury Stock.

5 State the effect of stock splits on corporate financial statements.

When a corporation reduces the par or stated value of its common

stock and issues a proportionate number of additional shares, a stock split has occurred. There are no changes in the balances of any corporation accounts, and no entry is required for a stock split.

6 Journalize the entries for cash dividends and stock dividends.

The entry to record a declaration of cash dividends debits Dividends and credits Dividends Payable for each class of stock. The payment of dividends is recorded in the normal manner. When a stock dividend is declared, Stock Dividends is debited for the fair value of the stock to be issued. Stock Dividends Distributable is credited for the par or stated value of the common stock to be issued. The difference between the fair value of the stock and its par or stated value is credited to Paid-In Capital

in Excess of Par—Common Stock. When the stock is issued on the date of payment, Stock Dividends Distributable is debited and Common Stock is credited for the par or stated value of the stock issued.

7 Compute and interpret the dividend yield on common stock.

The dividend yield indicates the rate of return to stockholders in terms of cash dividend distributions. It is computed by dividing the annual dividends paid per share of common stock by the market price per share at a specific date. This ratio is of special interest to investors whose main objective is to receive a current dividend return on their investment.

ILLUSTRATIVE PROBLEM

Altenburg Inc. is a lighting fixture wholesaler located in Arizona. During its current fiscal year, ended December 31, 2003, Altenburg Inc. completed the following selected transactions:

Feb. 3. Purchased 2,500 shares of its own common stock at $26, recording the stock at cost. (Prior to the purchase, there were 40,000 shares of $20 par common stock outstanding.)

May 1. Declared a semiannual dividend of $1 on the 10,000 shares of preferred stock and a 30¢ dividend on the common stock to stockholders of record on May 31, payable on June 15.

June 15. Paid the cash dividends.

Sept. 23. Sold 1,000 shares of treasury stock at $28, receiving cash.

Nov. 1. Declared semiannual dividends of $1 on the preferred stock and 30¢ on the common stock. In addition, a 5% common stock dividend was declared on the common stock outstanding, to be capitalized at the fair market value of the common stock, which is estimated at $30.

Dec. 1. Paid the cash dividends and issued the certificates for the common stock dividend.

Instructions

Journalize the entries to record the transactions for Altenburg Inc.

Solution

2003 Feb.	3	Treasury Stock		65 0 0 0 00	
		Cash			65 0 0 0 00

May	1	Cash Dividends		21 2 5 0 00	
		Cash Dividends Payable			21 2 5 0 00*
		*(10,000 × $1) + [(40,000 − 2,500) × $0.30]			
June	15	Cash Dividends Payable		21 2 5 0 00	
		Cash			21 2 5 0 00
Sept.	23	Cash		28 0 0 0 00	
		Treasury Stock			26 0 0 0 00
		Paid-In Capital from Sale of Treasury Stock			2 0 0 0 00
Nov.	1	Cash Dividends		21 5 5 0 00*	
		Cash Dividends Payable			21 5 5 0 00
		*(10,000 × $1) + [(40,000 − 1,500) × $0.30]			
	1	Stock Dividends		57 7 5 0 00*	
		Stock Dividends Distributable			38 5 0 0 00
		Paid-In Capital in Excess of Par—Common Stock			19 2 5 0 00
		*(40,000 − 1,500) × 5% × $30			
Dec.	1	Cash Dividends Payable		21 5 5 0 00	
		Stock Dividends Distributable		38 5 0 0 00	
		Cash			21 5 5 0 00
		Common Stock			38 5 0 0 00

SELF-EXAMINATION QUESTIONS   Answers at End of Chapter

Matching

Match each of the following statements with its proper term. Some terms may not be used.

A. cash dividend	___ 1. Shares of ownership of a corporation.
B. common stock	___ 2. The owners of a corporation.
C. cumulative preferred stock	___ 3. The stock in the hands of stockholders.
D. discount	___ 4. A value, similar to par value, approved by the board of directors of a corporation for no-par stock.
E. dividend yield	___ 5. The stock outstanding when a corporation has issued only one class of stock.
F. nonparticipating preferred stock	___ 6. A class of stock with preferential rights over common stock.
G. outstanding stock	___ 7. A class of preferred stock whose dividend rights are usually limited to a certain amount.
H. par	___ 8. A class of preferred stock that has a right to receive regular dividends that have been passed (not declared) before any common stock dividends are paid.
I. preferred stock	___ 9. The excess of the issue price of a stock over its par value.
J. premium	___ 10. The excess of the par value of a stock over its issue price.
K. stated value	

L. stock

M. stock dividend

N. stock split

O. stockholders

P. treasury stock

___11. Stock that a corporation has once issued and then reacquires.

___12. A reduction in the par or stated value of a common stock and the issuance of a proportionate number of additional shares.

___13. A cash distribution of earnings by a corporation to its shareholders.

___14. A distribution of shares of stock to its stockholders.

___15. A ratio, computed by dividing the annual dividends paid per share of common stock by the market price per share at a specific date, that indicates the rate of return to stockholders in terms of cash dividend distributions.

___16. The monetary amount printed on a stock certificate.

Multiple Choice

1. If a corporation has outstanding 1,000 shares of $9 cumulative preferred stock of $100 par and dividends have been passed for the preceding three years, what is the amount of preferred dividends that must be declared in the current year before a dividend can be declared on common stock?
    - A. $ 9,000
    - B. $27,000
    - C. $36,000
    - D. $45,000

2. Paid-in capital for a corporation may arise from which of the following sources?
    - A. Issuing cumulative preferred stock
    - B. Receiving donations of real estate
    - C. Selling the corporation's treasury stock
    - D. All of the above

3. The Stockholders' Equity section of the balance sheet may include:
    - A. Common Stock
    - B. Donated Capital
    - C. Preferred Stock
    - D. All of the above

4. If a corporation reacquires its own stock, the stock is listed on the balance sheet in the:
    - A. Current Assets section.
    - B. Long-Term Liabilities section.
    - C. Stockholders' Equity section.
    - D. Investments section.

5. A corporation has issued 25,000 shares of $100 par common stock and holds 3,000 of these shares as treasury stock. If the corporation declares a $2 per share cash dividend, what amount will be recorded as cash dividends?
    - A. $22,000
    - B. $25,000
    - C. $44,000
    - D. $50,000

CLASS DISCUSSION QUESTIONS

1. Contrast the owners' liability to creditors of (a) a partnership (partners) and (b) a corporation (stockholders).
2. Why is it said that the earnings of a corporation are subject to *double taxation?* Discuss.
3. Why are most large businesses organized as corporations?
4. a. What type of expenditure is charged to the organization costs account?
    b. Give examples of such expenditures.
5. Of two corporations organized at approximately the same time and engaged in competing businesses, one issued $50 par common stock, and the other issued $1 par common stock. Do the par designations provide any indication as to which stock is preferable as an investment? Explain.
6. What are the three basic rights that accompany ownership of a share of common stock?
7. a. Differentiate between common stock and preferred stock.
    b. Describe briefly (1) nonparticipating preferred stock and (2) cumulative preferred stock.
8. A stockbroker advises a client to "buy cumulative preferred stock. . . . With that type of stock, . . . [you] will never have to worry about losing the dividends." Is the broker right?

9. What are some sources of paid-in capital other than the issuance of stock?

10. If a corporation is given land as an inducement to locate in a particular community, (a) how should the amount of the debit to the land account be determined, and (b) what is the title of the account that should be credited for the same amount?

11. If common stock of $100 par is sold for $130, what is the $30 difference between the issue price and par called?

12. What are some of the factors that influence the market price of a corporation's stock?

13. When a corporation issues stock at a premium, is the premium income? Explain.

14. Land is acquired by a corporation for 15,000 shares of its $25 par common stock, which is currently selling for $70 per share on a national stock exchange. What accounts should be credited to record the transaction?

15. Indicate which of the following accounts would be reported as part of paid-in capital on the balance sheet:
    a. Retained Earnings
    b. Common Stock
    c. Donated Capital
    d. Preferred Stock

16. a. In what respect does treasury stock differ from unissued stock?
    b. How should treasury stock be presented on the balance sheet?

17. A corporation reacquires 5,000 shares of its own $40 par common stock for $370,000, recording it at cost. (a) What effect does this transaction have on revenue or expense of the period? (b) What effect does it have on stockholders' equity?

18. The treasury stock in Question 17 is resold for $400,000. (a) What is the effect on the corporation's revenue of the period? (b) What is the effect on stockholders' equity?

19. What is the primary purpose of a stock split?

20. What are the three conditions for the declaration and the payment of a cash dividend?

21. The dates in connection with the declaration of a cash dividend are October 1, November 15, and December 30. Identify each date.

22. A corporation with both cumulative preferred stock and common stock outstanding has a substantial credit balance in its retained earnings account at the beginning of the current fiscal year. Although net income for the current year is sufficient to pay the preferred dividend of $100,000 each quarter and a common dividend of $300,000 each quarter, the board of directors declares dividends only on the preferred stock. Suggest possible reasons for passing the dividends on the common stock.

23. An owner of 200 shares of Dunston Company common stock receives a stock dividend of 4 shares. (a) What is the effect of the stock dividend on the stockholder's proportionate interest (equity) in the corporation? (b) How does the total equity of 204 shares compare with the total equity of 200 shares before the stock dividend?

24. a. Where should a declared but unpaid cash dividend be reported on the balance sheet?
    b. Where should a declared but unissued stock dividend be reported on the balance sheet?

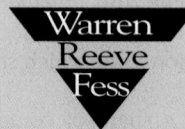

EXERCISES

Exercise 11–1
Dividends per share
Objective 2

✓ Preferred stock, 3rd year: $2.00

Masini Inc., a developer of radiology equipment, has stock outstanding as follows: 20,000 shares of $2 nonparticipating, noncumulative preferred stock of $100 par, and 250,000 shares of $50 par common. During its first five years of operations, the following amounts were distributed as dividends: first year, none; second year, $30,000; third year, $90,000; fourth year, $200,000; fifth year, $240,000. Calculate the dividends per share on each class of stock for each of the five years.

Exercise 11–2
Dividends per share
Objective 2

✓ Preferred stock, 3rd year: $4.00

Mystic.com, a computer software development firm, has stock outstanding as follows: 10,000 shares of $1.50 cumulative, nonparticipating preferred stock of $50 par, and 50,000 shares of $100 par common. During its first five years of operations, the following amounts were distributed as dividends: first year, none; second year, $5,000; third year, $80,000; fourth year, $180,000; fifth year, $75,000. Calculate the dividends per share on each class of stock for each of the five years.

Exercise 11–3
Entries for issuing par stock
Objective 3

On March 10, Candler Inc., a marble contractor, issued for cash 30,000 shares of $20 par common stock at $30, and on August 9, it issued for cash 5,000 shares of $100 par preferred stock at $105.

a. Journalize the entries for March 10 and August 9.
b. What is the total amount invested (total paid-in capital) by all stockholders as of August 9?

Exercise 11–4
Entries for issuing no-par stock
Objective 3

On November 2, Catalpa Corp., a carpet wholesaler, issued for cash 5,000 shares of no-par common stock (with a stated value of $25) at $75, and on December 3, it issued for cash 1,000 shares of $50 par preferred stock at $65.

a. Journalize the entries for November 2 and December 3, assuming that the common stock is to be credited with the stated value.
b. What is the total amount invested (total paid-in capital) by all stockholders as of December 3?

Exercise 11–5
Issuing stock for assets other than cash
Objective 3

On February 27, Sims Corporation, a wholesaler of hydraulic lifts, acquired land in exchange for 4,000 shares of $10 par common stock with a current market price of $73. Journalize the entry to record the transaction.

Exercise 11–6
Selected stock transactions
Objective 3

Koala Corp., an electric guitar retailer, was organized by Nicole West, Shawn Rainey, and Ginger Macke. The charter authorized 100,000 shares of common stock with a par of $20. The following transactions affecting stockholders' equity were completed during the first year of operations:

a. Issued 1,000 shares of stock at par to Rainey for cash.
b. Issued 50 shares of stock at par to West for promotional services provided in connection with the organization of the corporation, and issued 950 shares of stock at par to West for cash.
c. Purchased land and a building from Macke. The building is mortgaged for $125,000 for 25 years at 8%, and there is accrued interest of $1,000 on the mortgage note at the time of the purchase. It is agreed that the land is to be priced at $45,000 and the building at $150,000, and that Macke's equity will be exchanged for stock at par. The corporation agreed to assume responsibility for paying the mortgage note and the accrued interest.

Journalize the entries to record the transactions.

Exercise 11–7
Issuing stock
Objective 3

Gyro.com, with an authorization of 25,000 shares of preferred stock and 100,000 shares of common stock, completed several transactions involving its stock on October 1, the first day of operations. The trial balance at the close of the day follows:

Cash	565,000	
Land	40,000	
Buildings	95,000	
Preferred $5 Stock, $100 par		100,000
Paid-In Capital in Excess of Par—Preferred Stock		35,000
Common Stock, $75 par		450,000
Paid-In Capital in Excess of Par—Common Stock		115,000
	700,000	700,000

All shares within each class of stock were sold at the same price. The preferred stock was issued in exchange for the land and buildings.

Journalize the two entries to record the transactions summarized in the trial balance.

Exercise 11–8
Issuing stock
Objective 3

Fourier Products Inc., a wholesaler of office products, was organized on January 6 of the current year, with an authorization of 50,000 shares of $2 noncumulative preferred stock, $100 par and 250,000 shares of $10 par common stock. The following selected transactions were completed during the first year of operations:

Jan.   6. Issued 25,000 shares of common stock at par for cash.
      11. Issued 150 shares of common stock at par to an attorney in payment of legal fees for organizing the corporation.
Feb. 28. Issued 11,500 shares of common stock in exchange for land, buildings, and equipment with fair market prices of $20,000, $100,000, and $18,000, respectively.
Mar. 15. Issued 5,000 shares of preferred stock at $102 for cash.

Journalize the transactions.

Exercise 11–9
Treasury stock transactions
Objective 4

✓ b. $8,500 credit

Chico Springs Inc. bottles and distributes spring water. On March 1 of the current year, Chico reacquired 5,500 shares of its common stock at $40 per share. On July 8, Chico sold 3,500 of the reacquired shares at $43 per share. The remaining 2,000 shares were sold at $39 per share on December 19.

a. Journalize the transactions of March 1, July 8, and December 19.
b. What is the balance in Paid-In Capital from Sale of Treasury Stock on December 31 of the current year?
c. Where will the balance in Paid-In Capital from Sale of Treasury Stock be reported on the balance sheet?
d. ✏️ For what reasons might Chico Springs have purchased the treasury stock?

Exercise 11–10
Treasury stock transactions
Objective 4

✓ b. $9,000 credit

Aorta Inc. develops and produces spraying equipment for lawn maintenance and industrial uses. On September 6 of the current year, Aorta Inc. reacquired 6,000 shares of its common stock at $90 per share. On November 15, 2,000 of the reacquired shares were sold at $93 per share, and on December 21, 3,000 of the reacquired shares were sold at $91.

a. Journalize the transactions of September 6, November 15, and December 21.
b. What is the balance in Paid-In Capital from Sale of Treasury Stock on December 31 of the current year?
c. What is the balance in Treasury Stock on December 31 of the current year?
d. How will the balance in Treasury Stock be reported on the balance sheet?

Exercise 11–11
Treasury stock transactions

Objective 4

✓ b. $3,000 credit

Heavenly Inc. bottles and distributes spring water. On July 1 of the current year, Heavenly Inc. reacquired 3,000 shares of its common stock at $40 per share. On August 10, Heavenly Inc. sold 1,500 of the reacquired shares at $43 per share. The remaining 1,500 shares were sold at $39 per share on December 19.

a. Journalize the transactions of July 1, August 10, and December 19.
b. What is the balance in Paid-In Capital from Sale of Treasury Stock on December 31 of the current year?
c. Where will the balance in Paid-In Capital from Sale of Treasury Stock be reported on the balance sheet?
d. ✏️ For what reasons might Heavenly Inc. have purchased the treasury stock?

Exercise 11–12
Effect of stock split

Objective 5

Headwaters Corporation wholesales ovens and ranges to restaurants throughout the Northwest. Headwaters Corporation, which had 30,000 shares of common stock outstanding, declared a 3-for-1 stock split (2 additional shares for each share issued).

a. What will be the number of shares outstanding after the split?
b. If the common stock had a market price of $120 per share before the stock split, what would be an approximate market price per share after the split?

Exercise 11–13
Effect of cash dividend and stock split

Objectives 5, 6

Indicate whether the following actions would (+) increase, (−) decrease, or (0) not affect Collier Inc.'s total assets, liabilities, and stockholders' equity:

		Assets	Liabilities	Stockholders' Equity
(1)	Declaring a stock dividend	_____	_____	_____
(2)	Issuing stock certificates for the stock dividend declared in (1)	_____	_____	_____
(3)	Declaring a cash dividend	_____	_____	_____
(4)	Paying the cash dividend declared in (3)	_____	_____	_____
(5)	Authorizing and issuing stock certificates in a stock split	_____	_____	_____

Exercise 11–14
Entries for cash dividends

Objective 6

The dates of importance in connection with a cash dividend of $75,000 on a corporation's common stock are January 4, February 3, and March 5. Journalize the entries required on each date.

Exercise 11–15
Entries for stock dividends

Objective 6

✓ b. (1) $362,500
(3) $833,500

Heartwood Inc. is an HMO for twelve businesses in the Cleveland area. The following account balances appear on the balance sheet of Heartwood: Common stock (100,000 shares authorized), $50 par, $300,000; Paid-in capital in excess of par—common stock, $62,500; and Retained earnings, $471,000. The board of directors declared a 1% stock dividend when the market price of the stock was $76 a share. Heartwood reported no income or loss for the current year.

a. Journalize the entries to record (1) the declaration of the dividend, capitalizing an amount equal to market value, and (2) the issuance of the stock certificates.
b. Determine the following amounts before the stock dividend was declared: (1) total paid-in capital, (2) total retained earnings, and (3) total stockholders' equity.
c. Determine the following amounts after the stock dividend was declared and closing entries were recorded at the end of the year: (1) total paid-in capital, (2) total retained earnings, and (3) total stockholders' equity.

Exercise 11–16
Selected stock and dividend transactions

Objectives 5, 6

Selected transactions completed by Aft Boating Supply Corporation during the current fiscal year are as follows:

Jan. 7. Split the common stock 4 for 1 and reduced the par from $100 to $25 per share. After the split, there were 200,000 common shares outstanding.

Mar. 1. Declared semiannual dividends of $2 on 8,000 shares of preferred stock and $0.10 on the common stock to stockholders of record on March 31, payable on April 15.

Apr. 15. Paid the cash dividends.

Nov. 1. Declared semiannual dividends of $2 on the preferred stock and $0.25 on the common stock (before the stock dividend). In addition, a 1% common stock dividend was declared on the common stock outstanding. The fair market value of the common stock is estimated at $30.

Dec. 15. Paid the cash dividends and issued the certificates for the common stock dividend.

Journalize the transactions.

Exercise 11–17
Dividend yield

Objective 7

The financial statements for **Cisco Systems, Inc.**, are presented in Appendix G at the end of this text.

a. What was the amount of the dividends declared and paid by Cisco Systems, Inc., in 2000 and 1999?
b. Given Cisco Systems' dividend policy, why would an investor be attracted to this company?

Exercise 11–18
Dividend yield

Objective 7

In 1999, **Hershey Foods Corporation** paid dividends of $1.00 per share to its common stockholders (excluding its Class B Common Stock). The market price of Hershey's common stock on December 31, 1999, was $47.44.

a. Determine Hershey's dividend yield on its common stock as of December 31, 1999.
b. What conclusions can you draw from an analysis of Hershey's dividend yield?

PROBLEMS SERIES A

Problem 11–1A
Dividends on preferred and common stock

Objective 2

SPREADSHEET

✓ 1. Common dividends in 2001: $31,000

Magnifico Inc. owns and operates movie theaters throughout Georgia and Mississippi. Magnifico has declared the following annual dividends over a six-year period: 1999, $32,000; 2000, $65,000; 2001, $84,000; 2002, $60,000; 2003, $72,000; and 2004, $95,000. During the entire period, the outstanding stock of the company was composed of 25,000 shares of cumulative, nonparticipating, $2 preferred stock, $100 par, and 50,000 shares of common stock, $7 par.

Instructions

1. Calculate the total dividends and the per-share dividends declared on each class of stock for each of the six years. There were no dividends in arrears on January 1, 1999. Summarize the data in tabular form, using the following column headings:

Year	Total Dividends	Preferred Dividends		Common Dividends	
		Total	Per Share	Total	Per Share
1999	$32,000				
2000	65,000				
2001	84,000				
2002	$60,000				
2003	72,000				
2004	95,000				

2. Calculate the average annual dividend per share for each class of stock for the six-year period.

3. Assuming that the preferred stock was sold at par and common stock was sold at $8 at the beginning of the six-year period, calculate the percentage return on initial shareholders' investment, based on the average annual dividend per share (a) for preferred stock and (b) for common stock.

Problem 11–2A
Stock transactions for corporate expansion

Objective 3

GENERAL
LEDGER

On January 1 of the current year, the following accounts and their balances appear in the ledger of Osaka Corp., a meat processor:

Preferred $4 Stock, $100 par (20,000 shares authorized, 7,500 shares issued)	$ 750,000
Paid-In Capital in Excess of Par—Preferred Stock	150,000
Common Stock, $50 par (100,000 shares authorized, 40,000 shares issued)	2,000,000
Paid-In Capital in Excess of Par—Common Stock	300,000
Retained Earnings	805,000

At the annual stockholders' meeting on February 20, the board of directors presented a plan for modernizing and expanding plant operations at a cost of approximately $1,200,000. The plan provided (a) that a building, valued at $375,000, and the land on which it is located, valued at $75,000, be acquired in accordance with preliminary negotiations by the issuance of 8,000 shares of common stock, (b) that 5,000 shares of the unissued preferred stock be issued through an underwriter, and (c) that the corporation borrow $200,000. The plan was approved by the stockholders and accomplished by the following transactions:

Mar. 7. Issued 8,000 shares of common stock in exchange for land and a building, according to the plan.
21. Issued 5,000 shares of preferred stock, receiving $125 per share in cash from the underwriter.
29. Borrowed $200,000 from US East National Bank, giving a 7% mortgage note.

No other transactions occurred during March.

Instructions
Journalize the entries to record the foregoing transactions.

Problem 11–3A
Selected stock transactions

Objectives 3, 4, 6

GENERAL
LEDGER

The following selected accounts appear in the ledger of Cyma Environmental Corporation on July 1, 2003, the beginning of the current fiscal year:

Preferred 3% Stock, $75 par (10,000 shares authorized, 7,000 shares issued)	$525,000
Paid-In Capital in Excess of Par—Preferred Stock	60,000
Common Stock, $10 par (50,000 shares authorized, 30,000 shares issued)	300,000
Paid-In Capital in Excess of Par—Common Stock	100,000
Retained Earnings	937,000

During the year, the corporation completed a number of transactions affecting the stockholders' equity. They are summarized as follows:

a. Issued 10,000 shares of common stock at $20, receiving cash.
b. Sold 1,000 shares of preferred 3% stock at $90.
c. Purchased 5,000 shares of treasury common for $105,000.
d. Sold 3,000 shares of treasury common for $75,000.
e. Sold 1,000 shares of treasury common for $20,000.
f. Declared cash dividends of $2.25 per share on preferred stock and $0.50 per share on common stock.
g. Paid the cash dividends.

Instructions

Journalize the entries to record the transactions. Identify each entry by letter.

Problem 11–4A
Entries for selected corporate transactions

Objectives 3, 4, 6

SPREADSHEET
GENERAL LEDGER

✓ 3. $3,001,100

Sasquatch Enterprises Inc. manufactures bathroom fixtures. The stockholders' equity accounts of Sasquatch Enterprises Inc., with balances on January 1 of the current fiscal year, are as follows:

Common Stock, $20 stated value (100,000 shares authorized, 80,000 shares issued)	$1,600,000
Paid-In Capital in Excess of Stated Value	300,000
Retained Earnings	625,000
Treasury Stock (4,000 shares, at cost)	120,000

The following selected transactions occurred during the year:

Jan. 10. Received land from the Wilsall City Council as a donation. The land had an estimated fair market value of $100,000.
   30. Paid cash dividends of $1 per share on the common stock. The dividend had been properly recorded when declared on December 30 of the preceding fiscal year for $76,000.
Feb. 19. Issued 10,000 shares of common stock for $350,000.
Apr. 1. Sold all of the treasury stock for $140,000.
July 1. Declared a 5% stock dividend on common stock, to be capitalized at the market price of the stock, which is $42 a share.
Aug. 11. Issued the certificates for the dividend declared on July 1.
Oct. 20. Purchased 7,500 shares of treasury stock for $285,000.
Dec. 27. Declared a $0.90-per-share dividend on common stock.
   31. Closed the credit balance of the income summary account, $369,400.
   31. Closed the two dividends accounts to Retained Earnings.

Instructions

1. Enter the January 1 balances in T accounts for the stockholders' equity accounts listed. Also prepare T accounts for the following: Paid-In Capital from Sale of Treasury Stock; Donated Capital; Stock Dividends Distributable; Stock Dividends; Cash Dividends.
2. Journalize the entries to record the transactions, and post to the nine selected accounts.
3. Determine the total stockholders' equity on December 31.

Problem 11–5A
Entries for selected corporate transactions

Objectives 3, 4, 5, 6

SPREADSHEET
GENERAL LEDGER

Selected transactions completed by Silver Gate Boating Supply Corporation during the current fiscal year are as follows:

Jan. 6. Split the common stock 4 for 1 and reduced the par from $100 to $25 per share. After the split, there were 150,000 common shares outstanding.
Mar. 13. Purchased 7,500 shares of the corporation's own common stock at $35, recording the stock at cost.
May 1. Declared semiannual dividends of $2 on 18,000 shares of preferred stock and $0.60 on the common stock to stockholders of record on May 20, payable on June 1.
June 1. Paid the cash dividends.
Sept. 17. Sold 2,500 shares of treasury stock at $40, receiving cash.
Nov. 2. Declared semiannual dividends of $2 on the preferred stock and $0.60 on the common stock (before the stock dividend). In addition, a 2% common stock dividend was declared on the common stock outstanding. The fair market value of the common stock is estimated at $38.
Dec. 3. Paid the cash dividends and issued the certificates for the common stock dividend.

Instructions

Journalize the transactions.

PROBLEMS SERIES B

Problem 11–1B
Dividends on preferred and common stock

Objective 2

SPREADSHEET

✓ 1. Common dividends in 1999: $10,000

LaMancha Corp. manufactures mountain bikes and distributes them through retail outlets in Idaho and Montana. LaMancha Corp. has declared the following annual dividends over a six-year period: 1999, $25,000; 2000, $8,000; 2001, $10,000; 2002, $4,000; 2003, $50,000; and 2004, $75,500. During the entire period, the outstanding stock of the company was composed of 5,000 shares of cumulative, nonparticipating, $3 preferred stock, $50 par, and 50,000 shares of common stock, $5 par.

Instructions

1. Calculate the total dividends and the per-share dividends declared on each class of stock for each of the six years. There were no dividends in arrears on January 1, 1999. Summarize the data in tabular form, using the following column headings:

Year	Total Dividends	Preferred Dividends Total	Per Share	Common Dividends Total	Per Share
1999	$25,000				
2000	8,000				
2001	10,000				
2002	4,000				
2003	50,000				
2004	75,500				

2. Calculate the average annual dividend per share for each class of stock for the six-year period.
3. Assuming that the preferred stock was sold at par and common stock was sold at $11 at the beginning of the six-year period, calculate the percentage return on initial shareholders' investment, based on the average annual dividend per share (a) for preferred stock and (b) for common stock.

Problem 11–2B
Stock transaction for corporate expansion

Objective 3

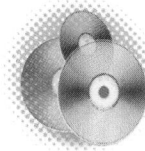

GENERAL LEDGER

Neural Corp. produces medical lasers for use in hospitals. The following accounts and their balances appear in the ledger of Neural Corp. on June 30 of the current year:

Preferred $5 Stock, $100 par (20,000 shares authorized, 10,000 shares issued)	$1,000,000
Paid-In Capital in Excess of Par—Preferred Stock	150,000
Common Stock, $25 par (100,000 shares authorized, 60,000 shares issued)	1,500,000
Paid-In Capital in Excess of Par—Common Stock	200,000
Retained Earnings	915,000

At the annual stockholders' meeting on July 21, the board of directors presented a plan for modernizing and expanding plant operations at a cost of approximately $2,000,000. The plan provided (a) that the corporation borrow $650,000, (b) that 5,000 shares of the unissued preferred stock be issued through an underwriter, and (c) that a building, valued at $750,000, and the land on which it is located, valued at $100,000, be acquired in accordance with preliminary negotiations by the issuance of 20,000 shares of common stock. The plan was approved by the stockholders and accomplished by the following transactions:

Aug. 3. Borrowed $650,000 from First National Bank, giving an 8% mortgage note.
      12. Issued 5,000 shares of preferred stock, receiving $120 per share in cash from the underwriter.
      30. Issued 20,000 shares of common stock in exchange for land and a building, according to the plan.

No other transactions occurred during June.

Instructions

Journalize the entries to record the foregoing transactions.

Problem 11–3B

Selected stock transactions

Objectives 3, 4, 6

GENERAL LEDGER

Cutthroat Corporation sells and services pipe welding equipment in Montana. The following selected accounts appear in the ledger of Cutthroat Corporation on January 1, 2003, the beginning of the current fiscal year:

Preferred 2% Stock, $100 par (40,000 shares authorized, 15,000 shares issued)	$1,500,000
Paid-In Capital in Excess of Par—Preferred Stock	112,500
Common Stock, $10 par (800,000 shares authorized, 400,000 shares issued)	4,000,000
Paid-In Capital in Excess of Par—Common Stock	600,000
Retained Earnings	3,450,000

During the year, the corporation completed a number of transactions affecting the stockholders' equity. They are summarized as follows:

a. Purchased 25,000 shares of treasury common for $550,000.
b. Sold 8,000 shares of treasury common for $192,000.
c. Sold 6,000 shares of preferred 2% stock at $110.
d. Issued 50,000 shares of common stock at $20, receiving cash.
e. Sold 7,000 shares of treasury common for $140,000.
f. Declared cash dividends of $2 per share on preferred stock and $0.25 per share on common stock.
g. Paid the cash dividends.

Instructions

Journalize the entries to record the transactions. Identify each entry by letter.

Problem 11–4B

Entries for selected corporate transactions

Objectives 3, 4, 6

SPREADSHEET

GENERAL LEDGER

✓ 3. $2,232,410

Loran Enterprises Inc. produces aeronautical navigation equipment. The stockholders' equity accounts of Loran Enterprises Inc., with balances on January 1 of the current fiscal year, are as follows:

Common Stock, $10 stated value (100,000 shares authorized, 75,000 shares issued)	$750,000
Paid-In Capital in Excess of Stated Value	150,000
Retained Earnings	597,750
Treasury Stock (5,000 shares, at cost)	90,000

The following selected transactions occurred during the year:

Jan. 15. Paid cash dividends of $0.80 per share on the common stock. The dividend had been properly recorded when declared on December 28 of the preceding fiscal year for $56,000.

Feb. 28. Sold all of the treasury stock for $125,000.

Apr. 5. Issued 10,000 shares of common stock for $300,000.

May 19. Received land from the Lyndon City Council as a donation. The land had an estimated fair market value of $200,000.

July 30. Declared a 3% stock dividend on common stock, to be capitalized at the market price of the stock, which is $28 a share.

Aug. 30. Issued the certificates for the dividend declared on July 30.

Sept. 3. Purchased 4,000 shares of treasury stock for $116,000.

Dec. 30. Declared an $0.80-per-share dividend on common stock.

    31. Closed the credit balance of the income summary account, $382,500.

    31. Closed the two dividends accounts to Retained Earnings.

Instructions

1. Enter the January 1 balances in T accounts for the stockholders' equity accounts listed. Also prepare T accounts for the following: Paid-In Capital from Sale of Treasury Stock; Donated Capital; Stock Dividends Distributable; Stock Dividends; Cash Dividends.

2.   Journalize the entries to record the transactions, and post to the nine selected accounts.
3.   Determine the total stockholders' equity on December 31.

Problem 11–5B
Entries for selected corporate transactions

Objectives 3, 4, 5, 6

SPREADSHEET

GENERAL LEDGER

Ocean Atlantic Corporation manufactures and distributes leisure clothing. Selected transactions completed by Ocean Atlantic during the current fiscal year are as follows:

Jan. 3. Split the common stock 5 for 1 and reduced the par from $50 to $10 per share. After the split, there were 125,000 common shares outstanding.

Mar. 15. Declared semiannual dividends of $3 on 10,000 shares of preferred stock and $0.40 on the 125,000 shares of $10 par common stock to stockholders of record on March 31, payable on April 15.

Apr. 15. Paid the cash dividends.

May 8. Purchased 15,000 shares of the corporation's own common stock at $20, recording the stock at cost.

June 10. Sold 5,000 shares of treasury stock at $23, receiving cash.

Sept. 15. Declared semiannual dividends of $3 on the preferred stock and $0.40 on the common stock (before the stock dividend). In addition, a 2% common stock dividend was declared on the common stock outstanding, to be capitalized at the fair market value of the common stock, which is estimated at $25.

Oct. 15. Paid the cash dividends and issued the certificates for the common stock dividend.

Instructions
Journalize the transactions.

SPECIAL ACTIVITIES

Activity 11–1
Derby Unlimited Inc.
Ethics and professional conduct in business

Holly Abernathy and Garreth Scott are organizing Derby Unlimited Inc. to undertake a high-risk gold-mining venture in Canada. Holly and Garreth tentatively plan to request authorization for 100,000,000 shares of common stock to be sold to the general public. Holly and Garreth have decided to establish par of $1 per share in order to appeal to a wide variety of potential investors. Holly and Garreth feel that investors would be more willing to invest in the company if they received a large quantity of shares for what might appear to be a "bargain" price.

    Discuss whether Holly and Garreth are behaving in a professional manner.

Activity 11–2
Omen Inc.
Issuing stock

What do you think?

Omen Inc. began operations on January 8, 2003, with the issuance of 500,000 shares of $100 par common stock. The sole stockholders of Omen Inc. are Fay Barnes and Dr. Joseph Cawley, who organized Omen Inc. with the objective of developing a new flu vaccine. Dr. Cawley claims that the flu vaccine, which is nearing the final development stage, will protect individuals against 99% of the flu types that have been medically identified. To complete the project, Omen Inc. needs $10,000,000 of additional funds. The local banks have been unwilling to loan the funds because of the lack of sufficient collateral and the riskiness of the business.

    The following is a conversation between Fay Barnes, the chief executive officer of Omen Inc., and Dr. Joseph Cawley, the leading researcher.

Barnes: What are we going to do? The banks won't loan us any more money, and we've got to have $10 million to complete the project. We are so close! It would be a disaster to quit now. The only thing I can think of is to issue additional stock. Do you have any suggestions?

Cawley: I guess you're right. But if the banks won't loan us any more money, how do you think we can find any investors to buy stock?

Barnes: I've been thinking about that. What if we promise the investors that we will pay them 2% of net sales until they have received an amount equal to what they paid for the stock?

Cawley: What happens when we pay back the $10 million? Do the investors get to keep the stock? If they do, it'll dilute our ownership.

Barnes: How about, if after we pay back the $10 million, we make them turn in their stock for $200 per share? That's twice what they paid for it, plus they would have already gotten all their money back. That's a $200 profit per share for the investors.

Cawley: It could work. We get our money, but don't have to pay any interest, dividends, or the $200 until we start generating net sales. At the same time, the investors could get their money back plus $200 per share.

Barnes: We'll need current financial statements for the new investors. I'll get our accountant working on them and contact our attorney to draw up a legally binding contract for the new investors. Yes, this could work.

In late 2003, the attorney and the various regulatory authorities approved the new stock offering, and 100,000 shares of common stock were privately sold to new investors at the stock's par of $100.

In preparing financial statements for 2003, Fay Barnes and Tanya Kuchar, the controller for Omen Inc., have the following conversation.

Kuchar: Fay, I've got a problem.

Barnes: What's that, Tanya?

Kuchar: Issuing common stock to raise that additional $10 million was a great idea. But . . .

Barnes: But what?

Kuchar: I've got to prepare the 2003 annual financial statements, and I am not sure how to classify the common stock.

Barnes: What do you mean? It's common stock.

Kuchar: I'm not so sure. I called the auditor and explained how we are contractually obligated to pay the new stockholders 2% of net sales until $100 per share is paid. Then, we may be obligated to pay them $200 per share.

Barnes: So . . .

Kuchar: So the auditor thinks that we should classify the additional issuance of $10 million as debt, not stock! And, if we put the $10 million on the balance sheet as debt, we will violate our other loan agreements with the banks. And, if these agreements are violated, the banks may call in all our debt immediately. If they do that, we are in deep trouble. We'll probably have to file for bankruptcy. We just don't have the cash to pay off the banks.

1.   ➤ Discuss the arguments for and against classifying the issuance of the $10 million of stock as debt.

2.   ➤ What do you think might be a practical solution to this classification problem?

Activity 11–3
Ball-Peen Inc.
Dividends

Ball-Peen Inc. has paid quarterly cash dividends since 1990. These dividends have steadily increased from $0.05 per share to the latest dividend declaration of $0.40 per share. The board of directors would like to continue this trend and is hesitant to suspend or decrease the amount of quarterly dividends. Unfortunately, sales dropped sharply in the fourth quarter of 2003 because of worsening economic conditions and increased competition. As a result, the board is uncertain as to whether it should declare a dividend for the last quarter of 2003.

On November 1, 2003, Ball-Peen Inc. borrowed $500,000 from City National Bank to use in modernizing its retail stores and to expand its product line in reaction to its competition. The terms of the 10-year, 12% loan require Ball-Peen Inc. to:

a. Pay monthly interest on the last day of the month.
b. Pay $50,000 of the principal each November 1, beginning in 2004.
c. Maintain a current ratio (current assets ÷ current liabilities) of 2.
d. Maintain a minimum balance (a compensating balance) of $25,000 in its City National Bank account.

On December 31, 2003, $125,000 of the $500,000 loan had been disbursed in modernization of the retail stores and in expansion of the product line. Ball-Peen Inc.'s balance sheet as of December 31, 2003, is as follows:

Ball-Peen Inc.
Balance Sheet
December 31, 2003

Assets

Current assets:

Cash		$ 40,000
Marketable securities		375,000
Accounts receivable	$ 91,500	
Less allowance for doubtful accounts	6,500	85,000
Merchandise inventory		125,000
Prepaid expenses		4,500

Total current assets		$ 629,500

Property, plant, and equipment:

Land		$150,000	
Buildings	$950,000		
Less accumulated depreciation	215,000	735,000	
Equipment	$460,000		
Less accumulated depreciation	110,000	350,000	
Total property, plant, and equipment			1,235,000
Total assets			$1,864,500

Liabilities

Current liabilities:

Accounts payable	$ 71,800	
Notes payable (City National Bank)	50,000	
Salaries payable	3,200	
Total current liabilities		$125,000

Long-term liabilities:

Notes payable (City National Bank)		450,000
Total liabilities		$ 575,000

Stockholders' Equity

Paid-in capital:

Common stock, $20 par (50,000 shares authorized,		
25,000 shares issued)	$500,000	
Excess of issue price over par	40,000	
Total paid-in capital	$540,000	
Retained earnings	749,500	
Total stockholders' equity		1,289,500
Total liabilities and stockholders' equity		$1,864,500

The board of directors is scheduled to meet January 6, 2004, to discuss the results of operations for 2003 and to consider the declaration of dividends for the fourth quarter of 2003. The chairman of the board has asked for your advice on the declaration of dividends.

1. What factors should the board consider in deciding whether to declare a cash dividend?
2. The board is considering the declaration of a stock dividend instead of a cash dividend. Discuss the issuance of a stock dividend from the point of view of (a) a stockholder and (b) the board of directors.

Activity 11–4
Into the Real World
Profiling a corporation

Select a public corporation with which you are familiar or which interests you. Using the Internet, your school library, and other sources, develop a short (2 to 5 pages) profile of the corporation. Include in your profile the following information:

1. Name of the corporation.
2. State of incorporation.
3. Nature of its operations.
4. Total assets for the most recent balance sheet.
5. Total revenues for the most recent income statement.
6. Net income for the most recent income statement.
7. Classes of stock outstanding.
8. Market price of the stock outstanding.
9. High and low price of the stock for the past year.
10. Dividends paid for each share of stock during the past year.

In groups of three or four, discuss each corporate profile. Select one of the corporations, assuming that your group has $100,000 to invest in its stock. Summarize why your group selected the corporation it did and how financial accounting information may have affected your decision. Keep track of the performance of your corporation's stock for the remainder of the term.

Note: Most major corporations maintain "home pages" on the Internet. This home page provides a variety of information on the corporation and often includes the corporation's financial statements. In addition, the New York Stock Exchange Web site (**www.nyse.com**) includes links to the home pages of many listed companies. Financial statements can also be accessed using EDGAR, the electronic archives of financial statements filed with the Securities and Exchange Commission (SEC).

SEC documents can also be retrieved using the EdgarScan™ service from **Pricewaterhouse Coopers** at **edgarscan.pwcglobal.com**. To obtain annual report information, key in a company name in the appropriate space. EdgarScan will list the reports, available to you for the company you've selected. Select the most recent annual report filing, identified as a 10-K or 10-K405. EdgarScan provides an outline of the report, including the separate financial statements, which can also be selected in an Excel® spreadsheet.

ANSWERS TO SELF-EXAMINATION QUESTIONS

Matching

1. L	3. G	5. B	7. F	9. J	11. P	13. A	15. E
2. O	4. K	6. I	8. C	10. D	12. N	14. M	16. H

Multiple Choice

1. **C** If a corporation has cumulative preferred stock outstanding, dividends that have been passed for prior years plus the dividend for the current year must be paid before dividends may be declared on common stock. In this case, dividends of $27,000 ($9,000 × 3) have been passed for the preceding three years, and the current year's dividends are $9,000, making a total of $36,000 (answer C) that must be paid to preferred stockholders before dividends can be declared on common stock.

2. **D** Paid-in capital is one of the two major subdivisions of the stockholders' equity of a corporation. It may result from many sources, including the issuance of cumulative preferred stock (answer A), the receipt of donated real estate (answer B), or the sale of a corporation's treasury stock (answer C).

3. **D** The Stockholders' Equity section of corporate balance sheets is divided into two principal subsections: (1) investments contributed by the stockholders and others and (2) net income retained in the business. Included as part of the investments by stockholders and others is the par of common stock (answer A), donated capital (answer B), and the par of preferred stock (answer C).

4. **C** Reacquired stock, known as treasury stock, should be listed in the Stockholders' Equity section (answer C) of the balance sheet. The price paid for the treasury stock is deducted from the total of all the stockholders' equity accounts.

5. **C** If a corporation that holds treasury stock declares a cash dividend, the dividends are not paid on the treasury shares. To do so would place the corporation in the position of earning income through dealing with itself. Thus, the corporation will record $44,000 (answer C) as cash dividends [(25,000 shares issued less 3,000 shares held as treasury stock) × $2 per share dividend].

Corporations: Income and Taxes, Stockholders' Equity, and Investments in Stocks

F12

o b j e c t i v e s

After studying this chapter, you should be able to:

1 Journalize the entries for corporate income taxes, including deferred income taxes.

2 Prepare an income statement reporting the following unusual items: discontinued operations, extraordinary items, and changes in accounting principles.

3 Prepare an income statement reporting earnings per share data.

4 Prepare financial statement presentations of stockholders' equity.

5 Describe the concept and the reporting of comprehensive income.

6 Describe the accounting for investments in stocks.

7 Describe alternative methods of combining businesses and how consolidated financial statements are prepared.

8 Compute and interpret the price-earnings ratio.

f you apply for a bank loan, you will be required to list your assets and liabilities on a loan application. In addition, you will be asked to indicate your monthly income. Assume that the day you were filling out the application, you won $3,000 in the state lottery. The $3,000 lottery winnings increase your assets by $3,000. Should you also show your lottery winnings as part of your monthly income?

The answer, of course, is no. Winning the lottery is an unusual event and, for most of us, a nonrecurring event. In determining whether to grant the loan, the bank is interested in your ability to make monthly loan payments. Such payments depend upon your recurring monthly income.

Businesses also experience unusual and nonrecurring events that affect their financial statements. Such events should be clearly disclosed in the financial statements so that stakeholders in the business will not misinterpret the financial effects of the events. In this chapter, we discuss unusual items that affect corporate income statements and illustrate how such items should be reported.

Corporate Income Taxes

objective 1

Journalize the entries for corporate income taxes, including deferred income taxes.

Under the United States tax code, corporations are taxable entities that must pay federal income taxes. Depending upon where it is located, a corporation may also be required to pay state and local income taxes. Although we limit our discussion to federal income taxes, the basic concepts also apply to other income taxes.

Payment of Income Taxes

Most corporations are required to pay estimated federal income taxes in four installments throughout the year. For example, assume that a corporation with a calendar-year accounting period estimates its income tax expense for the year as $84,000. The entry to record the first of the four estimated tax payments of $21,000 (1/4 of $84,000) is as follows:

Point of Interest

Individuals must pay estimated taxes (on the 15th of January, April, June, and September) if the amount of tax withholding is not sufficient to pay their taxes at the end of the year. This usually occurs when a significant portion of an individual's income is from rent, dividends, or interest.

April	15	Income Tax Expense	21 0 0 0 00	
		Cash		21 0 0 0 00
		To record quarterly payment of		
		estimated income tax.		

At year end, the actual taxable income and the related tax are determined.[1] If additional taxes are owed, the additional liability is recorded. If the total estimated tax payments are greater than the tax liability based on actual taxable income, the overpayment should be debited to a receivable account and credited to *Income Tax Expense.*

---

[1] A corporation's income tax returns and supporting records are subject to audits by taxing authorities, who may assess additional taxes. Because of this possibility, the liability for income taxes is sometimes described in the balance sheet as *Estimated income tax payable.*

Because income taxes are often a significant amount, they are normally reported on the income statement as a special deduction, as shown below in an excerpt from an income statement for **The Procter & Gamble Company**.

Year Ended June 30, 2000	(Amounts in millions)
Net Sales	**$39,951**
Cost of products sold	21,514
Marketing, research, and administrative expenses	12,483
Operating Income	**5,954**
Interest expense	722
Other income, net	304
Earnings Before Income Taxes	**5,536**
Income taxes	1,994
Net Earnings	**$ 3,542**

Allocation of Income Taxes

The taxable income of a corporation is determined according to the tax laws. It is often different from the income before income taxes reported in the income statement according to generally accepted accounting principles. As a result, the *income tax based on taxable income* usually differs from the *income tax based on income before taxes.* This difference may need to be allocated between various financial statement periods, depending on the nature of the items causing the differences.

Some differences between taxable income and income before income taxes are created because items are recognized in one period for tax purposes and in another period for income statement purposes. Such differences, called temporary differences, reverse or turn around in later years. Some examples of items that create temporary differences are listed below.

1. *Revenues or gains are taxed* **after** *they are reported in the income statement.* Example: In some cases, companies who make sales under an installment plan recognize revenue for financial reporting purposes when a sale is made but defer recognizing revenue for tax purposes until cash is collected.
2. *Expenses or losses are deducted in determining taxable income* **after** *they are reported in the income statement.* Example: Product warranty expense estimated and reported in the year of the sale for financial statement reporting is deducted for tax reporting when paid.
3. *Revenues or gains are taxed* **before** *they are reported in the income statement.* Example: Cash received in advance for magazine subscriptions is included in taxable income when received but included in the income statement only when earned in a future period.
4. *Expenses or losses are deducted in determining taxable income* **before** *they are reported in the income statement.* Example: MACRS depreciation is used for tax purposes, and the straight-line method is used for financial reporting purposes.

Since temporary differences reverse in later years, they do not change or reduce the total amount of taxable income over the life of a business. Exhibit 1 illustrates the reversing nature of temporary differences in which a business uses MACRS depreciation for tax purposes and straight-line depreciation for financial statement purposes. MACRS recognizes more depreciation in the early years but less depreciation in the later years. The total depreciation expense is the same for both methods over the life of the asset.

Exhibit 1 Temporary
Differences

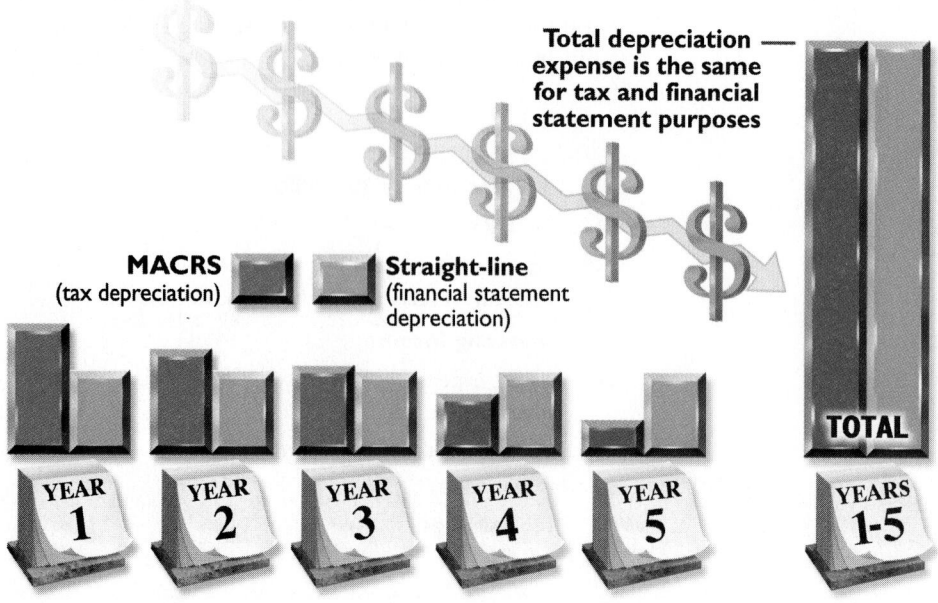

As Exhibit 1 illustrates, temporary differences affect only the timing of when revenues and expenses are recognized for tax purposes. As a result, the total amount of taxes paid does not change. Only the timing of the payment of taxes is affected. In most cases, managers use tax-planning techniques so that temporary differences delay or defer the payment of taxes to later years. As a result, at the end of each year the amount of the current tax liability and the postponed (deferred) liability must be recorded.

To illustrate, assume that at the end of the first year of operations a corporation reports $300,000 income before income taxes on its income statement. If we assume an income tax rate of 40%, the income tax expense reported on the income statement is $120,000 ($300,000 × 40%).[2] However, to reduce the amount owed for current income taxes, the corporation uses tax planning to reduce the taxable income to $100,000. Thus, the income tax actually due for the year is only $40,000 ($100,000 × 40%). The $80,000 ($120,000 − $40,000) difference between the two tax amounts is created by timing differences in recognizing revenue. This amount is deferred to future years. The example is summarized below.

Income tax based on $300,000 reported income at 40%	$120,000
Income tax based on $100,000 taxable income at 40%	40,000
Income tax deferred to future years	$ 80,000

To match the current year's expenses (including income tax) against the current year's revenue on the income statement, income tax is allocated between periods, using the following journal entry:

Income Tax Expense		120 0 0 0 00	
Income Tax Payable			40 0 0 0 00
Deferred Income Tax Payable			80 0 0 0 00
To record income tax for the year.			

A corporation has $300,000 income before income taxes, a 40% tax rate, and $130,000 taxable income. What is the amount of deferred income tax?

$68,000 [($300,000 × 40%) − ($130,000 × 40%)]

----

[2] For purposes of illustration, the 40% rate is assumed to include all federal, state, and local income taxes.

The income tax expense reported on the income statement is the total tax, $120,000, expected to be paid on the income for the year. In future years, the $80,000 in *Deferred Income Tax Payable* will be transferred to *Income Tax Payable* as the timing differences reverse and the taxes become due. For example, if $48,000 of the deferred tax reverses and becomes due in the second year, the following journal entry would be made in the second year:

Deferred Income Tax Payable		48 0 0 0 00		
Income Tax Payable			48 0 0 0 00	
To record current liability for				
deferred tax.				

The balance of *Deferred Income Tax Payable* at the end of a year is reported as a liability. The amount due within one year is classified as a current liability. The remainder is classified as a long-term liability or reported in a Deferred Credits section following the Long-Term Liabilities section.[3]

Differences between taxable income and income (before taxes) reported on the income statement may also arise because certain revenues are exempt from tax and certain expenses are not deductible in determining taxable income.[4] For example, interest income on municipal bonds may be exempt from taxation. Such differences create no special financial reporting problems, since the amount of income tax determined according to the tax laws is the *same* amount reported on the income statement.

Unusual Items that Affect the Income Statement

Three types of unusual items that may affect the current year's net income are:

1. The results of discontinued operations.
2. Extraordinary items that result in a gain or loss.
3. A change from one generally accepted accounting principle to another.

These items are reported separately in the income statement, as shown in the income statement for Jones Corporation in Exhibit 2. Many different terms and formats may be used. For example, the related tax effects of unusual items may be reported with the item with which they are associated or in the notes to the statement.

In the following paragraphs, we briefly discuss each of the three types of unusual items. We assume that these items are material to the financial statements. Immaterial items would not affect the normal financial statement presentation.

Discontinued Operations

A gain or loss from disposing of a business segment is reported on the income statement as a gain or loss from **discontinued operations**. The term **business segment** refers to a major line of business for a company, such as a division or a department or a certain class of customer. For example, assume that Jones Corporation

---

[3] In some cases, a deferred tax asset may arise for tax benefits to be received in the future. Such deferred tax assets are reported as either a current or a long-term asset, depending on when the benefits are expected to be realized.

[4] Such differences, which will not reverse with the passage of time, are sometimes called *permanent differences*.

Exhibit 2 Unusual Items in Income Statement

Jones Corporation Income Statement For the Year Ended December 31, 2003	
Net sales	$9,600,000
Cost of merchandise sold	5,800,000
Gross profit	$3,800,000
Operating expenses	2,490,000
Income from continuing operations before income tax	$1,310,000
Income tax expense	620,000
Income from continuing operations	$ 690,000
Loss on discontinued operations (Note A)	100,000
Income before extraordinary items and cumulative effect of a change in accounting principle	$ 590,000
Extraordinary item:	
Gain on condemnation of land, net of applicable income tax of $65,000	150,000
Cumulative effect on prior years of changing to a different depreciation method (Note B)	92,000
Net income	$ 832,000

Note A.

On July 1 of the current year, the electrical products division of the corporation was sold at a loss of $100,000, net of applicable income tax of $50,000. The net sales of the division for the current year were $2,900,000. The assets sold were composed of inventories, equipment, and plant totaling $2,100,000. The purchaser assumed liabilities of $600,000.

Note B.

Depreciation of all property, plant, and equipment has been computed by the straight-line method in 2003. Prior to 2003, depreciation of equipment for one of the divisions had been computed on the double-declining-balance method. In 2003, the straight-line method was adopted for this division in order to achieve uniformity and to better match depreciation charges with the estimated economic utility of such assets. Consistent with APB Opinion No. 20, this change in depreciation has been applied to prior years. The effect of the change was to increase income by $30,000 before extraordinary items for 2003. The adjustment of $92,000 (after reduction for income tax of $88,000) to apply the new method to prior years is also included in income for 2003.

has separate divisions that produce electrical products, hardware supplies, and lawn equipment. Jones sells its electrical products division at a loss. As shown in Exhibit 2, this loss is deducted from Jones's income from continuing operations (income from its hardware and lawn equipment divisions). In addition, Note A discloses the identity of the segment sold, the disposal date, a description of the segment's assets and liabilities, and the manner of disposal.

Extraordinary Items

Extraordinary items result from events and transactions that (1) are significantly different (unusual) from the typical or the normal operating activities of the business and (2) occur infrequently. The gains and losses that result from natural disasters which occur infrequently, such as floods, earthquakes, and fires, are extraordinary items. Gains or losses from condemning land or buildings for public use are also

Events that are both unusual and infrequent are uncommon. For example, a recent edition of *Accounting Trends & Techniques* indicated that only 74 of 600 companies surveyed reported extraordinary items.

extraordinary. Such gains and losses, other than those from disposing of a business segment, should be reported in the income statement as extraordinary items, as shown in Exhibit 2.

Sometimes extraordinary items result in unusual financial results. For example, **Delta Air Lines** once reported an extraordinary gain of over $5.5 million as the result of the crash of one of its 727s. The plane that crashed was insured for $6.5 million, but its book value in Delta's accounting records was $962,000.

Gains and losses on the disposal of fixed assets are *not* extraordinary items. This is because (1) they are not unusual and (2) they recur from time to time in the normal operations of a business. Likewise, gains and losses from the sale of investments are usual and recurring for most businesses.

Changes in Accounting Principles

A recent edition of *Accounting Trends & Techniques* indicated that the majority of accounting changes were due to adopting a new accounting standard issued by the Financial Accounting Standards Board.

Businesses are often required to change their accounting principles when the Financial Accounting Standards Board (FASB) issues a new accounting standard. In addition, a business may voluntarily change from one generally accepted accounting principle to another. For example, a corporation may change from the fifo to the lifo method of costing inventory to better match revenues and expenses. Changes in generally accepted accounting principles should be disclosed in the financial statements (or in notes to the statements) of the period in which they occur. This disclosure should include the following:

1. The nature of the change.
2. The justification for the change.
3. The effect on the current year's net income.
4. The cumulative effect of the change on the net income of prior periods.

To illustrate, assume that one of Jones Corporation's divisions changes from the double-declining-balance method to the straight-line method of depreciation. As shown in Exhibit 2, the cumulative effect of this change is reported after the extraordinary items. The effect on the prior period is explained in Note B. If financial statements for prior periods are also presented, they should be restated as if the change had been made in the prior periods, and the effect of the restatement should be reported either on the face of the statements or in a note.

Reporting unusual items separately on the income statement allows investors to isolate the effects of these items on income and cash flows. By reporting such items, investors and other users of the financial statements can consider such factors in assessing a business's future income and cash flows.

Earnings per Common Share

objective 3

Prepare an income statement reporting earnings per share data.

The amount of net income is often used by investors and creditors in evaluating a company's profitability. However, net income by itself is difficult to use in comparing companies of different sizes. Also, trends in net income may be difficult to evaluate, using only net income, if there have been significant changes in a company's stockholders' equity. Thus, the profitability of companies is often expressed as earnings per share. **Earnings per common share (EPS)**, sometimes called **basic earnings per share**, is the net income per share of common stock outstanding during a period.

Because of its importance, earnings per share is reported in the financial press and by various investor services, such as **Moody's** and **Standard & Poor's.** Changes in earnings per share can lead to significant changes in the price of a corporation's stock in the marketplace. For example, the stock of **Scientific-Atlanta Inc.** surged by over 13 percent to $39 per share after the company announced earnings per share of 53 cents as compared to 25 cents per share a year earlier. Wall Street analysts had been expecting earnings per share of 41 cents.

Corporations whose stock is traded in a public market must report earnings per common share on their income statements.[5] If no preferred stock is outstanding, the earnings per common share is calculated as follows:

$$\text{Earnings per common share} = \frac{\text{Net income}}{\text{Number of common shares outstanding}}$$

When the number of common shares outstanding has changed during the period, a weighted average number of shares outstanding is used. If a company has preferred stock outstanding, the net income must be reduced by the amount of any preferred dividends, as shown below.

$$\text{Earnings per common share} = \frac{\text{Net income} - \text{Preferred stock dividends}}{\text{Number of common shares outstanding}}$$

Comparing the earnings per share of two or more years, based on only the net incomes of those years, could be misleading. For example, assume that Jones Corporation, whose partial income statement was presented in Exhibit 2, reported $700,000 net income for 2002. Also assume that no extraordinary or other unusual items were reported in 2002. Jones has no preferred stock outstanding and has 200,000 common shares outstanding in 2002 and 2003. The earnings per common share is $3.50 ($700,000/200,000 shares) for 2002 and $4.16 ($832,000/200,000 shares) for 2003. Comparing the two earnings per share amounts suggests that operations have improved. However, the 2003 earnings per share comparable to the $3.50 is $3.45, which is the income from continuing operations of $690,000 divided by 200,000 shares. The latter amount indicates a slight downturn in normal earnings.

When unusual items exist, earnings per common share should be reported for those items. To illustrate, a partial income statement for Jones Corporation, showing earnings per common share, is shown in Exhibit 3. In this income statement, Jones reports all the earnings per common share amounts on the face of the income statement. However, only earnings per share amounts for income from continuing operations and net income are required to be presented on the face of the statement. The other per share amounts may be presented in the notes to the financial statements.[6]

Exhibit 3 Income Statement with Earnings per Share

Jones Corporation
Income Statement
For the Year Ended December 31, 2003

Earnings per common share:	
Income from continuing operations	$3.45
Loss on discontinued operations (Note A)	0.50
Income before extraordinary items and cumulative effect	
of a change in accounting principle	$2.95
Extraordinary item:	
Gain on condemnation of land, net of applicable income	
tax of $65,000	0.75
Cumulative effect on prior years of changing to a different	
depreciation method (Note B)	0.46
Net income	$4.16

---

[5] *Statement of Financial Accounting Standards No. 128,* "Earnings per Share," Financial Accounting Standards Board (Norwalk, Connecticut: 1997).

[6] Ibid., pars. 36 & 37.

In the preceding paragraphs, we have assumed a simple capital structure with only common stock or common stock and preferred stock outstanding. Often, however, corporations have complex capital structures with various types of securities outstanding, such as convertible preferred stock, options, warrants, and contingently issuable shares. In such cases, the possible effects of converting such securities to common stock must be calculated and reported as *earnings per common share assuming dilution* or *diluted earnings per share.*[7] This topic is discussed further in advanced accounting texts.

Reporting Stockholders' Equity

objective 4

Prepare financial statement presentations of stockholders' equity.

As with other sections of the balance sheet, alternative terms and formats may be used in reporting stockholders' equity. In addition, the significant changes in the sources of stockholders' equity—paid-in capital and retained earnings—may be reported in separate statements or notes that support the balance sheet presentation.

Reporting Paid-In Capital

Two alternatives for reporting paid-in capital in the balance sheet are shown in Exhibit 4. In the first example, each class of stock is listed first, followed by its related paid-in capital accounts. In the second example, the stock accounts are listed first. The other paid-in capital accounts are listed as a single item described as *Additional paid-in capital*. These combined accounts could also be described as *Capital in excess of par (or stated value) of shares* or a similar title.

Exhibit 4 Paid-In Capital Section of Stockholders' Equity

Stockholders' Equity

Paid-in capital:			
Preferred $5 stock, cumulative, $50 par (2,000 shares authorized and issued)	$100,000		
Excess of issue price over par	10,000	$ 110,000	
Common stock, $20 par (50,000 shares authorized, 45,000 shares issued)	$900,000		
Excess of issue price over par	132,000	1,032,000	
From donated land		60,000	
Total paid-in capital			$1,202,000

Shareholders' Equity

Contributed capital:		
Preferred 10% stock, cumulative, $50 par (2,000 shares authorized and issued)	$100,000	
Common stock, $20 par (50,000 shares authorized, 45,000 shares issued)	900,000	
Additional paid-in capital	202,000	
Total contributed capital		$1,202,000

[7] Ibid., pars. 11–39.

Significant changes in paid-in capital during a period may be presented either in a *statement of stockholders' equity* or in notes to the financial statements. We describe and illustrate the statement of stockholders' equity later in this section. In addition, relevant rights and privileges of the various classes of stock outstanding must be disclosed.[8] Examples of types of information that must be disclosed include dividend and liquidation preferences, rights to participate in earnings, conversion rights, and redemption rights. Such information may be disclosed on the face of the balance sheet or in the accompanying notes.

Reporting Retained Earnings

The 1999 edition of *Accounting Trends & Techniques* indicated that 2.5% of the companies surveyed presented a separate statement of retained earnings, 1% presented a combined income and retained earnings statement, and 2.6% presented changes in retained earnings in the notes to the financial statements. The other 94% of the companies presented changes in retained earnings in a statement of stockholders' equity.

A corporation may report changes in retained earnings by preparing a separate retained earnings statement, a combined income and retained earnings statement, or a statement of stockholders' equity.

When a separate retained earnings statement is prepared, the beginning balance of retained earnings is reported. The net income is then added (or net loss is subtracted) and any dividends are subtracted to arrive at the ending retained earnings for the period. An example of a such a statement for Adang Corporation is shown in Exhibit 5.

Exhibit 5 Retained Earnings Statement

Adang Corporation Retained Earnings Statement For the Year Ended June 30, 2003		
Retained earnings, July 1, 2002		$350,000
Net income	$280,000	
Less dividends declared	75,000	
Increase in retained earnings		205,000
Retained earnings, June 30, 2003		$555,000

An alternative format for presenting the retained earnings statement is to combine it with the income statement. An advantage of the combined format is that it emphasizes net income as the connecting link between the income statement and the retained earnings portion of stockholders' equity. Since the combined form is not often used, we do not illustrate it.

Appropriations

The 1999 edition of *Accounting Trends & Techniques* reported that 329 of the 600 companies surveyed disclosed dividend restrictions in notes to their financial statements.

The retained earnings available for use as dividends may be restricted by action of a corporation's board of directors. The amount restricted, called an **appropriation**, remains part of the retained earnings. However, it must be disclosed, usually in the notes to the financial statements.

Appropriations may be classified as either legal, contractual, or discretionary. The board of directors may be legally required to restrict retained earnings because of state laws. For example, some state laws require that retained earnings be restricted by the amount of treasury stock purchased, so that legal capital will not be used for dividends. The board may also be required to restrict retained earnings because of contractual requirements. For example, the terms of a bank loan may require restrictions, so that money for repaying the loan will not be used for dividends. Finally, the board

---

[8] *Statement of Financial Accounting Standards No. 129,* "Disclosure Information about Capital Structure," Financial Accounting Standards Board (Norwalk, Connecticut: 1997).

may restrict retained earnings voluntarily. For example, the board may limit dividend distributions so that more money is available for expanding the business.

Prior Period Adjustments

Material errors in a prior period's net income may arise from mathematical mistakes and from mistakes in applying accounting principles. The effect of material errors that are not discovered within the same fiscal period in which they occurred should not be included in determining net income for the current period. Instead, corrections of such errors, called **prior period adjustments**, are reported in the retained earnings statement. These adjustments are reported as an adjustment to the retained earnings balance at the beginning of the period in which the error is discovered and corrected. Because prior period adjustments are rare, we do not illustrate their reporting.

Statement of Stockholders' Equity

Significant changes in stockholders' equity should be reported for the period in which they occur. These changes may be reported in a **statement of stockholders' equity**. This statement is often prepared in a columnar format, where each column represents a major stockholders' equity classification. Changes in each classification are then described in the left-hand column. Exhibit 6 is a statement of stockholders' equity for Telex Inc.

Exhibit 6 Statement of Stockholders' Equity

Telex Inc.
Statement of Stockholders' Equity
For the Year Ended December 31, 2003

	Preferred Stock	Common Stock	Paid-In Capital in Excess of Par—Common Stock	Retained Earnings	Treasury (Common) Stock	Total
Balance, January 1	$5,000,000	$10,000,000	$3,000,000	$2,000,000	$(500,000)	$19,500,000
Net income				850,000		850,000
Dividends on preferred stock				(250,000)		(250,000)
Dividends on common stock				(400,000)		(400,000)
Issuance of additional common stock		500,000	50,000			550,000
Purchase of treasury stock					(30,000)	(30,000)
Balance, December 31	$5,000,000	$10,500,000	$3,050,000	$2,200,000	$(530,000)	$20,220,000

Comprehensive Income

objective 5

Describe the concept and the reporting of comprehensive income.

In 1997, the Financial Accounting Standards Board issued an accounting standard that required the reporting concept referred to as *comprehensive income*.[9] This standard defines **comprehensive income** as all changes in stockholders' equity during

---

[9] *Statement of Financial Accounting Standards No. 130,* "Reporting Comprehensive Income," Financial Accounting Standards Board (Norwalk, Connecticut: 1997).

a period except those resulting from dividends and stockholders' investments. Under this standard, companies must report traditional net income plus or minus other comprehensive income items to arrive at comprehensive income. *Other comprehensive income items* include foreign currency items, pension liability adjustments, and unrealized gains and losses on investments.

To the extent that other comprehensive income items give rise to tax effects, the taxes should be allocated to these items as we illustrated earlier in this chapter. The cumulative effects of other comprehensive income items must be reported separately from retained earnings and paid-in capital on the balance sheet. When other comprehensive income items are not present, the income statement and balance sheet formats are similar to those we have illustrated in this and preceding chapters.

Companies may report comprehensive income on the income statement, in a separate statement of comprehensive income, or in the statement of stockholders' equity. In addition, companies may use terms other than comprehensive income, such as *total nonowner changes in equity.*

You should note that comprehensive income does not affect the determination of net income or retained earnings as we have discussed and illustrated. In the next section, we will illustrate the reporting of unrealized gains and losses on investments as part of other comprehensive income.

Accounting for Investments in Stocks

<table>
<tr><td>

o b j e c t i v e   6

Describe the accounting for investments in stocks.

Warren Buffett became one of the wealthiest men in the world through wise and patient investing. Buffett invests through a public company called **Berkshire Hathaway Inc.**, of which he owns 40%. Berkshire Hathaway started as an old-line textile company. Today, however, it has over $34 billion of equity investment holdings, listed on its balance sheet as "available-for-sale" securities. Some of these investments include **Coca-Cola Company, Gillette Company,** and **American Express**.

</td><td>

Corporations not only issue stock, but they also purchase stocks of other companies for investment purposes. Like individuals, businesses have a variety of reasons for investing in stocks, called **equity securities**. A business may purchase stocks as a means of earning a return (income) on excess cash that it does not need for its normal operations. Such investments are usually for a short period of time. In other cases, a business may purchase the stock of another company as a means of developing or maintaining business relationships with the other company. A business may also purchase common stock as a means of gaining control of another company's operations. In these two latter cases, the business usually intends to hold the investment for a long period of time.

The equity securities in which a business invests may be classified as trading securities or available-for-sale securities. **Trading securities** are securities that management intends to actively trade for profit. Businesses holding trading securities are those whose normal operations involve buying and selling securities. Examples of such businesses include banks and insurance companies. **Available-for-sale securities** are securities that management expects to sell in the future but which are not actively traded for profit. In this section, we describe and illustrate the accounting for available-for-sale equity securities. The accounting for trading securities is described and illustrated in advanced accounting texts.

Short-Term Investments in Stocks

Rather than allow excess cash to be idle until it is needed, a business may invest all or part of it in income-yielding securities. Since these investments can be quickly sold and converted to cash as needed, they are called **temporary investments** or **marketable securities**. Although such investments may be retained for several years, they continue to be classified as temporary, provided they meet two conditions. First, the securities are readily marketable and can be sold for cash at any time. Second, management intends to sell the securities when the business needs cash for operations.

</td></tr>
</table>

Temporary investments are recorded in a current asset account, *Marketable Securities*, at their cost. This cost includes all amounts spent to acquire the securities, such as broker's commissions. Any dividends received on the investment are recorded as a debit to *Cash* and a credit to *Dividend Revenue*.[10]

To illustrate, assume that on June 1 Crabtree Co. purchased 2,000 shares of Inis Corporation common stock at $89.75 per share plus a brokerage fee of $500. On October 1, Inis declared a $0.90 per share cash dividend payable on November 30. Crabtree's entries to record the stock purchase and the receipt of the dividend are as follows:

June	1	Marketable Securities	180 0 0 0 00	
		Cash		180 0 0 0 00
		Purchased 2,000 shares of Inis		
		Corporation common stock		
		($89.75 × 2,000 shares = $179,500;		
		$179,500 + $500 = $180,000).		
Nov.	30	Cash	1 8 0 0 00	
		Dividend Revenue		1 8 0 0 00
		Received dividend on Inis Corporation		
		common stock		
		(2,000 shares × $0.90 = $1,800).		

On the balance sheet, temporary investments are reported at their fair market value. Market values are normally available from stock quotations in financial newspapers, such as *The Wall Street Journal*. Any difference between the fair market values of the securities and their cost is an **unrealized holding gain or loss**. This gain or loss is termed "unrealized" because a transaction (the sale of the securities) is necessary before a gain or loss becomes real (realized).

To illustrate, assume that Crabtree Co.'s portfolio of temporary investments has the following fair market values and unrealized gains and losses on December 31, 2003:

Common Stock	Cost	Market	Unrealized Gain (Loss)
Edwards Inc.	$150,000	$190,000	$40,000
SWS Corp.	200,000	200,000	—
Inis Corporation	180,000	210,000	30,000
Bass Co.	160,000	150,000	(10,000)
Total	$690,000	$750,000	$60,000

If income taxes of $18,000 are allocated to the unrealized gain, Crabtree's temporary investments should be reported at their total cost of $690,000, plus the unrealized gain (net of applicable income tax) of $42,000 ($60,000 − $18,000), as shown in Exhibit 7.

The unrealized gain (net of applicable taxes) of $42,000 should also be reported as an *other comprehensive income item*, as we mentioned in the preceding section. For example, assume that Crabtree Co. has net income of $720,000 for the year ended December 31, 2003. Crabtree elects to report net income and comprehensive income on one financial statement, *Statement of Income and Comprehensive Income*, as shown in Exhibit 8.

---

[10]Stock dividends received on an investment are not journalized, since they have no effect on the investor's assets and revenues.

Exhibit 7 Temporary Investments on the Balance Sheet

Crabtree Co.
Balance Sheet
December 31, 2003

Assets

Current assets:

Cash		$119,500
Temporary investments in marketable securities at cost	$690,000	
Plus unrealized gain (net of applicable income tax of $18,000)	42,000	732,000

Exhibit 8 Statement of Income and Comprehensive Income

Crabtree Co.
Statement of Income and Comprehensive Income
For the Year Ended December 31, 2003

Net income	$720,000
Other comprehensive income:	
Unrealized gain on temporary investments in marketable securities (net of applicable income tax of $18,000)	42,000
Comprehensive income	$762,000

Unrealized losses are reported in a similar manner. Unrealized gains and losses are reported as other comprehensive income items until the related securities are sold. When temporary securities are sold, the unrealized gains or losses become realized and are included in determining net income.[11]

Long-Term Investments in Stocks

Long-term investments in stocks are not intended as a source of cash in the normal operations of the business. They are reported in the balance sheet under the caption **Investments**, which usually follows the Current Assets section.

There are two methods of accounting for long-term investments in stock: (1) the cost method and (2) the equity method. The method used depends on whether the investor (the buyer of the stock) has a significant influence over the operating and financing activities of the company (the investee) whose stock is owned. If the investor does not have a significant influence, the cost method is used. If the investor has a significant influence, the equity method is used. Evidence of such influence includes the percentage of ownership, the existence of intercompany transactions, and the interchange of managerial personnel. Generally, if the investor owns 20% or more of the voting stock of the investee, it is assumed that the investor has significant influence over the investee.

---

[11] To avoid double-counting, realized gains and losses must be removed from comprehensive income. These adjustments are discussed in advanced accounting texts.

Cost Method

Under the **cost method**, the accounting for long-term investments in stocks is similar to that for short-term investments in stocks, which we illustrated in the preceding section. The cost of the stocks is debited to an investment (asset) account. Cash dividends received on the stock are recorded as a debit to *Cash* and a credit to *Dividend Revenue*. On the balance sheet, the stocks are reported at their fair market value net of any applicable income tax effects. In addition, the unrealized gains and losses are reported as part of the comprehensive income.[12]

To illustrate the purchase of stock and the receipt of dividends under the cost method, assume that on March 1, Makowski Corporation purchases 100 shares of Compton Corporation common stock at 59 plus a brokerage fee of $40. On April 30, Compton Corporation declares a $2-per-share dividend, payable on June 15. Makowski's entries to record the investment and the dividend are as follows:

The 1999 edition of *Accounting Trends & Techniques* indicated that 15% of the companies surveyed used the cost method to account for investments.

Mar.	1	Investment in Compton Corp. Stock	5 9 4 0 00	
		Cash		5 9 4 0 00
		Purchased 100 shares of Compton		
		Corp. common stock at 59 plus		
		brokerage fee of $40.		
June	15	Cash	2 0 0 00	
		Dividend Revenue		2 0 0 00
		Received dividend of $2 per share on		
		Compton Corp. common stock.		

Equity Method

Under the **equity method**, a stock purchase is recorded in the same manner as if the cost method were used. The equity method, however, is different from the cost method in the way in which net income and cash dividends of the investee are recorded. The equity method of recording these items is summarized as follows:

The 1999 edition of *Accounting Trends & Techniques* indicated that over 47% of the companies surveyed used the equity method to account for investments.

1. The investor's share of the periodic net income of the investee is recorded as an *increase in the investment account* and as *revenue for the period*. Likewise, the investor's share of an investee's net loss is recorded as a *decrease in the investment account* and as a *loss for the period*.
2. The investor's share of cash dividends from the investee is recorded as an *increase in the cash account* and a *decrease in the investment account*.

To illustrate, assume that on January 2, Hally Inc. pays cash of $350,000 for 40% of the common stock and net assets of Brock Corporation. Assume also that, for the year ending December 31, Brock Corporation reports net income of $105,000 and declares and pays $45,000 in dividends. Using the equity method, Hally Inc. (the investor) records these transactions as follows:

Jan.	2	Investment in Brock Corp. Stock	350 0 0 0 00	
		Cash		350 0 0 0 00
		Purchased 40% of Brock Corp.		
		common stock.		

[12] An exception to reporting unrealized gains and losses as part of comprehensive income is made if the decrease in the market value for a stock is considered permanent. In this case, the cost of the individual stock is written down (decreased), and the amount of the write-down is included in net income.

Dec.	31	Investment in Brock Corp. Stock	42 0 0 0 00	
		Income of Brock Corp.		42 0 0 0 00
		Recorded share (40%) of Brock Corp.		
		net income of $105,000.		
	31	Cash	18 0 0 0 00	
		Investment in Brock Corp. Stock		18 0 0 0 00
		Recorded share (40%) of dividends of		
		$45,000 paid by Brock Corp.		

The combined effect of recording 40% of Brock Corporation's net income and dividends is to increase Hally's interest in the net assets of Brock by $24,000 ($42,000 − $18,000), as shown below.

Assume that Hally Inc. increased its ownership in Brock Corporation to 60% at the beginning of the next year. If Brock Corporation reported net income of $80,000 and declared dividends of $50,000, how much would Hally Inc. debit Investment in Brock Corp. Stock?

$18,000 [($80,000 × 60%) − ($50,000 × 60%)]

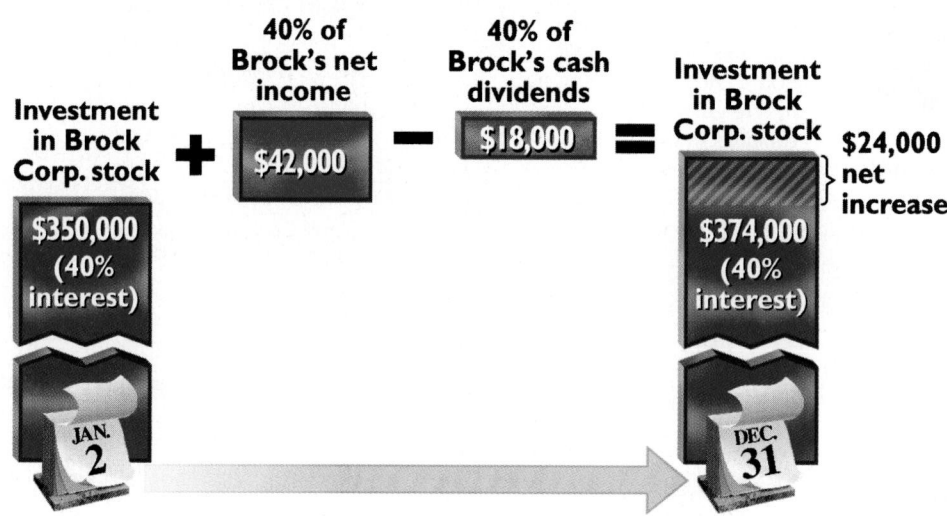

Sale of Investments in Stocks

The accounting for the sale of stock is the same for both short-term and long-term investments. When shares of stock are sold, the investment account is credited for the carrying amount (book value) of the shares sold. The cash or receivables account is debited for the proceeds (sales price less commission and other selling costs). Any difference between the proceeds and the carrying amount is recorded as a gain or loss on the sale and is included in the determination of net income.

To illustrate, assume that an investment in Drey Inc. stock has a carrying amount of $15,700 when it is sold on March 1. If the proceeds from the sale of the stock are $17,500, the entry to record the transaction is as follows:

Mar.	1	Cash	17 5 0 0 00	
		Investment in Drey Inc. Stock		15 7 0 0 00
		Gain on Sale of Investments		1 8 0 0 00
		Sold investment in Drey Inc. stock.		

BUSINESS ON STAGE

Buying and Selling Stocks

After you have evaluated a business and identified companies in which you would like to make an investment, how would you go about making the purchase? The most common method is to purchase common stock through a stockbroker, or account representative. A *stockbroker* is a person who executes trades on the major stock exchanges on your behalf. Stockbrokers can be associated with large "full-service" firms, such as Merrill Lynch; "discount" brokerage firms, such as OLDE Discount Brokers; or regional and local firms.

Once you've selected your stockbroker, you begin by opening an account. This usually involves placing money in the account. After your account is opened, you can place an order for the purchase of your selected stocks. There are two basic types of purchase orders—a market order and a limit order.

A *market order* instructs the broker to buy the stock at the best possible price. If the stock is actively traded, the buy price will usually be close to the last traded price prior to the order. Stockbrokers usually execute trades within minutes of taking an order. A *limit order* instructs the broker to buy the stock at a specified price or lower. An example of a limit order would be to buy 50 shares of Coca-Cola common stock at $60 or lower. The limit order prohibits the broker from purchasing the stock at a price higher than $60.

When you decide to sell, you can place a stop-loss order. With a *stop-loss order*, you set a selling market price below the current price. If the market price drops to your limit, then the sale is executed, thus limiting your loss. After your trade is executed, you will receive a statement confirming your trade, which shows your investment, the number of shares bought or sold, the dollar value, and the stockbroker's commission. These statements should be kept for tax purposes.

Internet trading is an alternative to using a stockbroker. For more information, see E*TRADE's home page at **www.etrade.com**. ∎

Business Combinations

objective 7

Describe alternative methods of combining businesses and how consolidated financial statements are prepared.

Each year, many businesses combine in order to produce more efficiently or to diversify product lines. Business combinations often involve complex accounting principles and terminology. Our objective in this section is to introduce you to some of the unique terminology and concepts related to business combinations. We also briefly describe the use and preparation of consolidated financial statements.

Mergers and Consolidations

One corporation may acquire all the assets and liabilities of another corporation, which is then dissolved. This joining of two corporations is called a **merger**. The acquiring company may use cash, debt, or its own stock as the payment. Whatever the form of payment, the amount received by the dissolving corporation is distributed to its stockholders in final liquidation.

A new corporation may be created, and the assets and liabilities of two or more existing corporations transferred to it. This type of combination is called a **consolidation**. The new corporation usually issues its own stock in exchange for the net assets acquired. The original corporations are then dissolved. For example, **ExxonMobil Corporation** became the new consolidated company that resulted from the combining of the individual corporations—Exxon and Mobil.

Parent and Subsidiary Corporations

Boeing Co. acquired McDonnell Douglas Corporation for $15 billion in mid-1997. The merged company became the United States' biggest aerospace company, with projected sales of more than $38 billion. As a result of the merger, McDonnell Douglas no longer exists as a separate company.

Business combinations may also occur when one corporation buys a controlling share of the outstanding voting stock of one or more other corporations. In this case, none of the corporations dissolve. The corporations continue as separate legal entities in a parent-subsidiary relationship. The corporation owning all or a majority of the voting stock of the other corporation is called the **parent company**. The corporation that is controlled is called the **subsidiary company**. Two or more corporations closely related through stock ownership are sometimes called **affiliated** companies. An example of an affiliated company is Waldenbooks, a subsidiary of Kmart.

A corporation may acquire the controlling share of the voting common stock of another corporation by paying cash, exchanging other assets, issuing debt, or using some combination of these methods. The stockholders of the acquired company, in turn, transfer their stock to the parent corporation. In such cases, the transaction is recorded like a normal purchase of assets, and the combination is accounted for by the **purchase method**.

A parent-subsidiary relationship may be created by exchanging the voting common stock of the acquiring corporation (the parent) for the common stock of the acquired corporation (the subsidiary). If at least 90% of the stock of the subsidiary is acquired in this way, the transaction is a pooling of interests, and the combination is accounted for by the **pooling-of-interests method**. In a pooling of interests, the stockholders of the acquired company (the subsidiary) become stockholders of the acquiring company (the parent).

The 1999 edition of *Accounting Trends & Techniques* reported that 92% of the business combinations surveyed were accounted for by the purchase method.

The accounting for a purchase and a pooling of interests are significantly different. A purchase is accounted for as a *sale-purchase transaction*, whereas a pooling of interests is accounted for as a *joining of ownership interests*. Because businesses must meet very strict criteria to use the pooling-of-interests method, the vast majority of business combinations are accounted for by using the purchase method.[13]

Consolidated Financial Statements

Although parent and subsidiary corporations may operate as a single economic unit, they continue to maintain separate accounting records and prepare their own periodic financial statements. At the end of the year, the financial statements of the parent and subsidiary are combined and reported as a single company. These combined financial statements are called **consolidated financial statements**. Such statements are usually identified by adding "and subsidiary(ies)" to the name of the parent corporation or by adding "consolidated" to the statement title.

To the stockholders of the parent company, consolidated financial statements are more meaningful than separate statements for each corporation. This is because the parent company, in substance, controls the subsidiaries, even though the parent and its subsidiaries are separate entities.

When a business combination is accounted for as a purchase, the subsidiary's net assets are reported in the consolidated balance sheet at their fair market value at the time of the purchase. In some cases, a parent may pay more than the fair market value of a subsidiary's net assets because the subsidiary has prospects for high future earnings. The difference between the amount paid by the parent and the fair market value of the subsidiary's net assets is reported on the consolidated balance sheet as an intangible asset. This asset is identified as **Goodwill** or **Excess of cost of business acquired over related net assets**.

When a consolidated balance sheet is prepared, the ownership interest of the parent in the subsidiary's stock, which is the balance in the parent's investment in subsidiary account, must be eliminated. This is done by eliminating the parent's investment in subsidiary account against the balances of the subsidiary's stockholders' equity accounts.

---

[13]The FASB has proposed a standard that would eliminate the pooling-of-interests method.

A recent edition of *Accounting Trends & Techniques* indicates that most of the companies surveyed reported minority interest in the long-term liabilities (noncurrent) section of the consolidated balance sheet.

If the parent owns less than 100% of the subsidiary stock, the subsidiary stock owned by outsiders is *not* eliminated but is normally reported immediately preceding the consolidated stockholders' equity. This amount is described as the **minority interest**.

When the data on the financial statements of the parent and its subsidiaries are combined to form the consolidated statements, intercompany transactions are given special attention. An example of such a transaction is the parent purchasing goods from the subsidiary or the subsidiary loaning money to the parent. These transactions affect the individual accounts of the parent and subsidiary and thus the financial statements of both companies.[14] To illustrate, assume that P Inc. (the parent) sold merchandise to S Inc. (the subsidiary) for $90,000. The merchandise cost P Inc. $50,000. In turn, S Inc. sold the merchandise to a customer for $120,000.

The individual income statements for P Inc. and S Inc. are shown in Exhibit 9. The consolidated (combined) income statement is shown in Exhibit 10. The consolidated income statement presents the income statements for P Inc. and S Inc. as if they were one operating entity. Thus, the $90,000 sale (P Inc.) and the $90,000 cost of merchandise sold (S Inc.) are eliminated. This is because the consolidated entity cannot sell to itself or buy from itself.

Exhibit 9 Income Statements for P Inc. and S Inc.

	P Inc.		S Inc.	
Sales		$950,000		$400,000
Cost of merchandise sold		625,000		240,000
Gross profit		$325,000		$160,000
Operating expenses:				
Selling expenses	$155,000		$55,000	
Administrative expenses	85,000	240,000	35,000	90,000
Net income		$ 85,000		$ 70,000

Exhibit 10 Consolidated Income Statement for P Inc. and S Inc.

Sales		$1,260,000*
Cost of merchandise sold		775,000**
Gross profit		$ 485,000
Operating expenses:		
Selling expenses	$210,000	
Administrative expenses	120,000	330,000
Net income		$ 155,000

*$950,000 − $90,000 + $400,000
**$625,000 + $240,000 − $90,000

General Motors Corporation is a multinational company that consolidates the financial statements of its foreign subsidiaries, such as the European *Opel* division, into U.S. dollars.

Many U.S. corporations own subsidiaries in foreign countries. Such corporations are often called *multinational corporations*. The financial statements of the foreign subsidiary are usually prepared in the foreign currency. Before the financial statements of foreign subsidiaries are consolidated with their domestic parent's financial statements, the amounts shown on the statements for the foreign companies must be converted to U.S. dollars.

[14] Examples of accounts often affected by intercompany transactions include *Accounts Receivable* and *Accounts Payable*, *Interest Receivable* and *Interest Payable*, and *Interest Expense* and *Interest Revenue*.

FINANCIAL ANALYSIS AND INTERPRETATION

objective 8

Compute and interpret the price-earnings ratio.

The assessment of a firm's growth potential and future earnings prospects is indicated by how much the market is willing to pay per dollar of a company's earnings. This ratio, called the **price-earnings ratio**, or **P/E ratio**, is commonly included in stock market quotations reported by the financial press. A high P/E ratio indicates that the market expects high growth and earnings in the future. Likewise, a low P/E ratio indicates lower growth and earnings expectations.

The price-earnings ratio on common stock is computed by dividing the stock's market price per share at a specific date by the company's annual earnings per share, as shown below.

$$\text{Price-earnings ratio} = \frac{\textbf{Market price per share of common stock}}{\textbf{Earnings per share of common stock}}$$

To illustrate, assume that Harper Inc. reported earnings per share of $1.64 in 2003 and $1.35 in 2002. The market prices per common share are $20.50 at the end of 2003 and $13.50 at the end of 2002. The price-earnings ratio on this stock is computed as follows:

	Price-Earnings Ratio
Year 2003	12.5 ($20.50/$1.64)
Year 2002	10.0 ($13.50/$1.35)

The price-earnings ratio indicates that a share of Harper Inc.'s common stock was selling for 10 times the amount of earnings per share at the end of 2002. At the end of 2003, the common stock was selling for 12.5 times the amount of earnings per share. These results would indicate a generally improving expectation of growth and earnings for Harper Inc. However, a prospective investor should also consider the price-earnings ratios for competing firms in the same industry.

ENCORE

Monster Eats into Mattell's Profits

Mattell Inc., one of the largest toy makers in the world, is best known for its Barbie dolls, Fisher-Price infant and preschool toys, Hot Wheels die-cast cars, and its Cabbage Patch dolls. It is estimated that over 80 million Cabbage Patch dolls have been sold since they were introduced in 1983.

In the late 1990s, Mattell decided to introduce a new version of the Cabbage Patch dolls, called Snacktime Kids. The Snacktime Kids came with pieces of plastic shaped carrots, pretzels, biscuits, and licorice that could be put into the doll's mechanical mouth. Once in the doll's mouth, a battery-driven motor "chewed" them and ejected them into a pack on the doll's back.

Unfortunately, the dolls could not discern between the plastic snacks and other small objects provided by its owner, such as hair and fingers. One young father demonstrated how he was forced to decapitate a Snacktime Kid after it "attacked" his daughter. Evidently, the doll began devouring the little girl's hair as if it were spaghetti. Fearing the worst, the father terminated the ravenous toy *with extreme*

prejudice. Similar hair-gobbling incidents were reported across the country.

Mattell announced a refund program for the dolls, offering to buy back Snacktime Kids from parents for $40 a doll. Mattell estimated that 500,000 Snacktime Kids had been sold and another 200,000 dolls were still on the shelves. The buyback of the monster dolls cost Mattell $10 million in sales and $8 million in after-tax earnings. In addition, at least one lawsuit claiming grievous psychological trauma was filed against Mattell. The lawsuit asked for $25 million in punitive damages.

Although Mattell hoped that the buyback program would have a non-recurring impact on its profits, it wasn't the first time that Mattell had had to pull a toy from the market. In the early 1990s, Mattell pulled Teacher Barbie from stores after the talking doll was criticized by educators, who said it set a bad example with comments like, "Math class is tough." Teacher Barbie was "reeducated," however, and put back on the market. ■

KEY POINTS

1 Journalize the entries for corporate income taxes, including deferred income taxes.

Corporations are subject to federal income tax and are required to make estimated payments throughout the year. To record the payment of estimated tax, Income Tax is debited and Cash is credited. If additional taxes are owed at the end of the year, Income Tax is debited and Income Tax Payable is credited for the amount owed. If the estimated tax payments are greater than the actual tax liability, a receivable account is debited and Income Tax is credited.

The tax effects of temporary differences between taxable income and income before income taxes must be allocated between periods. The journal entry for such allocations normally debits Income Tax and credits Income Tax Payable and Deferred Income Tax Payable.

2 Prepare an income statement reporting the following unusual items: discontinued operations, extraordinary items, and changes in accounting principles.

A gain or loss resulting from the disposal of a business segment should be identified on the income statement, net of related income tax. The results of continuing operations should also be identified.

Gains and losses may result from events and transactions that are unusual and occur infrequently. Such extraordinary items, net of related income tax, should be identified on the income statement.

A change in an accounting principle results from the adoption of a generally accepted accounting principle different from the one used previously for reporting purposes. The effect of the change in principle on net income in the current period, as well as the cumulative effect on income of prior periods, should be disclosed in the financial statements. The effects of a change in an accounting principle should be reported net of related income tax.

3 Prepare an income statement reporting earnings per share data.

Earnings per share is reported on the income statements of public corporations. If there are unusual items on the income statement, the per share amount should be presented for each of these items as well as net income.

4 Prepare financial statement presentations of stockholders' equity.

Significant changes in the sources of stockholders' equity—paid-in capital and retained earnings—may be reported in separate statements or notes that support the balance sheet presentation. Changes in retained earnings may be reported by preparing a separate retained earnings statement, a combined income and retained earnings statement, or a statement of stockholders' equity. Restrictions to retained earnings, called appropriations, must be disclosed, usually in the notes to the financial statements. Material errors in a prior period's net income, called prior-period adjustments, are reported in the retained earnings statement. Significant changes in stockholders' equity may also be reported in a statement of stockholders' equity.

5 Describe the concept and the reporting of comprehensive income.

Comprehensive income is all changes in stockholders' equity during a period except those resulting from dividends and stockholders' investments. Companies must report traditional net income plus or minus other comprehensive income items to arrive at comprehensive income. Other comprehensive income items include transactions and events that are excluded from net income, such as unrealized gains and losses on certain investments in debt and equity securities.

6 Describe the accounting for investments in stocks.

A business may purchase stocks as a means of earning a return (income) on excess cash that it does not need for its normal operations. Such investments are recorded in a marketable securities account. Their cost includes all amounts spent to acquire the securities. Any dividends received on an investment are recorded as a debit to Cash and a credit to Dividend Revenue. On the balance sheet, temporary investments are reported at their fair market values. Any difference between the fair market values of the securities and their cost is an unrealized holding gain or loss (net of applicable taxes) that is reported as an other comprehensive income item.

Long-term investments in stocks are not intended as a source of cash in the normal operations of the business. They are reported in the balance sheet under the caption Investments. Two methods of accounting for long-term investments in stock are (1) the cost method and (2) the equity method.

The accounting for the sale of stock is the same for both short-term and long-term investments. The investment account is credited for the carrying amount (book value) of the shares sold, the cash or receivables account is debited for the proceeds, and any difference between the proceeds and the carrying amount is recorded as a gain or loss on the sale.

7 Describe alternative methods of combining businesses and how consolidated financial statements are prepared.

Businesses may combine in a merger or a consolidation. Business combinations may also occur when one corporation acquires a controlling share of the outstanding voting stock of another corporation. In this case, a parent-subsidiary relationship exists, and the companies are called affiliated or associated companies.

Although the corporations that make up a parent-subsidiary affiliation may operate as a single economic unit, they usually continue to maintain separate accounting records and prepare their own periodic financial statements. The financial statements prepared by combining the parent and subsidiary statements are called consolidated financial statements.

When a parent corporation purchases less than 100% of the subsidiary's stock, the remaining stockholders' equity is identified as minority interest. The minority interest is reported on the consolidated balance sheet, usually preceding stockholders' equity.

In preparing consolidated income statements for a parent and its subsidiary, all amounts from intercompany transactions, such as intercompany sales of merchandise and cost of merchandise sold, are eliminated.

8 Compute and interpret the price-earnings ratio.

The assessment of a firm's growth potential and future earnings prospects is indicated by the price-earnings ratio, or P/E ratio. It is computed by dividing the stock's market price per share at a specific date by the company's annual earnings per share.

ILLUSTRATIVE PROBLEM

The following data were selected from the records of Botanica Greenhouses Inc. for the current fiscal year ended August 31:

Administrative expenses	$ 82,200
Cost of merchandise sold	750,000
Gain on condemnation of land	25,000
Income tax:	
Applicable to continuing operations	27,200
Applicable to gain on condemnation of land	10,000
Applicable to loss from disposal of a segment of the business (reduction)	24,000
Interest expense	15,200
Loss from disposal of a segment of the business	60,200
Sales	1,097,500
Selling expenses	182,100

Instructions

Prepare a multiple-step income statement, concluding with a section for earnings per share in the form illustrated in this chapter. There were 10,000 shares of common stock (no preferred) outstanding throughout the year. Assume that the gain on condemnation of land is an extraordinary item.

Solution

Botanica Greenhouses Inc.
Income Statement
For the Year Ended August 31, 2003

Sales		$1,097,500
Cost of merchandise sold		750,000
Gross profit		$ 347,500
Operating expenses:		
Selling expenses	$182,100	
Administrative expenses	82,200	
Total operating expenses		264,300
Income from operations		$ 83,200
Other expense:		
Interest expense		15,200
Income from continuing operations before		
income tax		$ 68,000
Income tax expense		27,200
Income from continuing operations		$ 40,800
Loss from disposal of a segment of the		
business	$ 60,200	
Less applicable income tax	24,000	36,200
Income before extraordinary item		$ 4,600
Extraordinary item:		
Gain on condemnation of land	$ 25,000	
Less applicable income tax	10,000	15,000
Net income		$ 19,600
Earnings per share:		
Income from continuing operations		$4.08
Loss on discontinued operations		3.62
Income before extraordinary item		$0.46
Extraordinary item		1.50
Net income		$1.96

SELF-EXAMINATION QUESTIONS

Answers at End of Chapter

Matching

Match each of the following statements with its proper term. Some terms may not be used.

A. appropriation

B. available-for-sale securities

C. balance sheet

D. comprehensive income

____ 1. The income according to the tax laws that is used as a base for determining the amount of taxes owed.

____ 2. Differences between taxable income and income before income taxes, created because items are recognized in one period for tax purposes and in another period for income statement purposes. Such differences reverse or turn around in later years.

____ 3. Operations of a major line of business for a company, such as a division, a department, or a certain class of customer, that have been disposed of.

E. consolidated financial statements

F. consolidation

G. cost method

H. discontinued operations

I. earnings per common share (EPS)

J. equity method

K. equity per share

L. equity security

M. extraordinary items

N. investments

O. merger

P. minority interest

Q. parent company

R. permanent differences

S. pooling-of-interests method

T. price-earnings ratio

U. prior period adjustments

V. purchase method

W. statement of cash flows

X. statement of stockholders' equity

Y. subsidiary company

Z. taxable income

AA. temporary differences

BB. temporary investments

CC. trading securities

DD. unrealized holding gain or loss

___ 4. Events and transactions that (1) are significantly different (unusual) from the typical or the normal operating activities of a business and (2) occur infrequently.

___ 5. Net income per share of common stock outstanding during a period.

___ 6. The amount of retained earnings that has been restricted and therefore is unavailable for use as dividends.

___ 7. Errors in a prior period's net income that arise from mathematical mistakes or from mistakes in applying accounting principles.

___ 8. A statement summarizing significant changes in stockholders' equity that have occurred during a period.

___ 9. All changes in stockholders' equity during a period except those resulting from dividends and stockholders' investments.

___ 10. Preferred or common stock.

___ 11. Securities that management intends to actively trade for profit.

___ 12. Securities that management expects to sell in the future but which are not actively traded for profit.

___ 13. The balance sheet caption used to report investments in income-yielding securities that can be quickly sold and converted to cash as needed.

___ 14. The difference between the fair market values of the securities and their cost.

___ 15. The balance sheet caption used to report long-term investments in stocks not intended as a source of cash in the normal operations of the business.

___ 16. A method of accounting for an investment in common stock by which the investor recognizes as income its share of cash dividends of the investee.

___ 17. A method of accounting for an investment in common stock by which the investment account is adjusted for the investor's share of periodic net income and cash dividends of the investee.

___ 18. The joining of two corporations in which one company acquires all the assets and liabilities of another corporation, which is then dissolved.

___ 19. The creation of a new corporation by the transfer of assets and liabilities of two or more existing corporations, which are then dissolved.

___ 20. The corporation owning all or a majority of the voting stock of the other corporation.

___ 21. The corporation that is controlled by a parent company.

___ 22. The accounting method used when a corporation acquires the controlling share of the voting common stock of another corporation by paying cash, exchanging other assets, issuing debt, or some combination of these methods.

___ 23. The accounting method used when a corporation acquires the controlling share of the voting common stock of another corporation by exchanging the voting common stock of the acquiring corporation for the common stock of the acquired corporation.

___ 24. Financial statements resulting from combining parent and subsidiary statements.

___ 25. The portion of a subsidiary corporation's stock owned by outsiders.

___ 26. The ratio computed by dividing a corporation's stock market price per share at a specific date by the company's annual earnings per share.

Multiple Choice

1. During its first year of operations, a corporation elected to use the straight-line method of depreciation for financial reporting purposes and MACRS in determining taxable income. If the income tax is 40% and the amount of depreciation expense is $60,000 under the straight-line method and $100,000 under MACRS, what is the amount of income tax deferred to future years?

A. $16,000   C. $40,000

B. $24,000   D. $60,000

2. A material gain resulting from condemning land for public use would be reported on the income statement as:
   A. an extraordinary item
   B. an other income item
   C. revenue from sales
   D. a change in estimate

3. Gwinnett Corporation's temporary investments cost $100,000 and have a market value of $120,000 at the end of the accounting period. Assuming a tax rate of 40%, the difference between the cost and market value would be reported as a:
   A. $12,000 realized gain
   B. $12,000 unrealized gain
   C. $20,000 realized gain
   D. $20,000 unrealized gain

4. Parker Corporation, which owns 100% of Sweeney Company, sold merchandise costing $50,000 to Sweeney Company for $75,000. Sweeney then sold the merchandise to a customer for $100,000. Before consolidation, Parker and Sweeney reported the following sales, cost of merchandise sold, and gross profit:

	Parker Corporation	Sweeney Company
Sales	$980,000	$600,000
Cost of merchandise sold	500,000	360,000
Gross profit	$480,000	$240,000

What is the total sales and cost of merchandise sold that should be reported on the consolidated income statement?
   A. Sales: $1,505,000; cost of merchandise sold: $785,000
   B. Sales: $1,505,000; cost of merchandise sold: $860,000
   C. Sales: $1,580,000; cost of merchandise sold: $785,000
   D. Sales: $1,580,000; cost of merchandise sold: $860,000

5. Cisneros Corporation owns 75% of Harrell Inc. During the current year, Harrell Inc. reported net income of $150,000 and declared dividends of $40,000. How much would Cisneros Corporation increase Investment in Harrell Inc. Stock for the current year?
   A. $0   C. $82,500
   B. $30,000   D. $112,500

CLASS DISCUSSION QUESTIONS

1. A corporation has paid estimated federal income tax during the year on the basis of its estimated income. Indicate the accounts that would be debited and credited at the end of the year if the corporation (a) owes an additional tax; (b) overpaid its tax.

2. How would the amount of deferred income tax payable be reported in the balance sheet if (a) it is payable within one year and (b) it is payable beyond one year?

3. What two criteria must be met to classify an item as an extraordinary item on the income statement?

4. During the current year, 40 acres of land that cost $200,000 were condemned for construction of an interstate highway. Assuming that an award of $350,000 in cash was received and that the applicable income tax on this transaction is 40%, how would this information be presented in the income statement?

5. Corporation X realized a material gain when its facilities at a designated floodway were acquired by the urban renewal agency. How should the gain be reported in the income statement?

Source: "Technical Hotline," *Journal of Accountancy*, June 1989, p. 32.

6. An annual report of **Sears, Roebuck and Co.** disclosed the discontinuance of several business segments, including **Coldwell Banker Residential Services**. The estimated loss on disposal of these operations was $64 million, including $22 million of tax expense. Indicate how the loss from discontinued operations should be reported by Sears, Roebuck and Co. on its income statement.

7. If significant changes are made in the accounting principles applied from one period to the next, why should the effect of these changes be disclosed in the financial statements?

8. A corporation reports earnings per share of $1.38 for the most recent year and $1.10 for the preceding year. The $1.38 includes a $0.45-per-share gain from insurance proceeds related to a fully depreciated asset that was destroyed by fire. (a) Should the composition of the $1.38 be disclosed in the financial reports? (b) On the basis of the limited information presented, would you conclude that operations had improved or declined?

9. What is the primary advantage of combining the retained earnings statement with the income statement?

10. What are the three classifications of appropriations and how are appropriations normally reported in the financial statements?

11. Indicate how prior period adjustments would be reported on the financial statements presented only for the current period.

12. Describe the format of the statement of stockholders' equity.

13. How is comprehensive income determined?

14. a. List some examples of other comprehensive income items.
    b. Does the reporting of comprehensive income affect the determination of net income and retained earnings?

15. Why might a business invest in another company's stock?

16. How are temporary investments in marketable securities reported on the balance sheet?

17. How are unrealized gains and losses on temporary investments in marketable securities reported on the statement of income and comprehensive income?

18. a. What are two methods of accounting for long-term investments in stock?
    b. Under what caption are long-term investments in stock reported on the balance sheet?

19. Plaster Inc. received a $0.15-per-share cash dividend on 50,000 shares of Gestalt Corporation common stock, which Plaster Inc. carries as a long-term investment. (a) Assuming that Plaster Inc. uses the cost method of accounting for its investment in Gestalt Corporation, what account would be credited for the receipt of the $7,500 dividend? (b) Assuming that Plaster Inc. uses the equity method of accounting for its investment in Gestalt Corporation, what account would be credited for the receipt of the $7,500 dividend?

20. Which method of accounting for long-term investments in stock (cost or equity) should be used by the parent company in accounting for its investments in stock of subsidiaries?

21. What are the two methods of accounting for the creation of a parent-subsidiary relationship?

22. Polska Company purchases the entire common stock of Strabo Corporation for $30,000,000. What accounts are eliminated on Strabo's balance sheet and Polska's balance sheet upon consolidation?

23. Parent Corporation owns 90% of the outstanding common stock of Subsidiary Corporation, which has no preferred stock. (a) What is the term applied to the remaining 10% interest? (b) On the consolidated balance sheet, where is the amount of Subsidiary's book equity allocable to outsiders reported?

24. An annual report of **The Campbell Soup Company** reported on its income statement $2.4 million as "equity in earnings of affiliates." Journalize the entry that Campbell would have made to record this equity in earnings of affiliates.

EXERCISES

Exercise 12–1
Income tax entries

Objective 1

Journalize the entries to record the following selected transactions of Supernal Grave Markers Inc.:

Apr. 15. Paid the first installment of the estimated income tax for the current fiscal year ending December 31, $80,000. No entry had been made to record the liability.
June 15. Paid the second installment of $80,000.

Sept. 15. Paid the third installment of $80,000.

Dec. 31. Recorded the estimated income tax liability for the year just ended and the deferred income tax liability, based on the preceding transactions and the following data:

Income tax rate	40%
Income before income tax	$1,200,000
Taxable income according to tax return	850,000

Jan. 15. Paid the fourth installment of $100,000.

Exercise 12–2
Extraordinary item
Objective 2

A company received life insurance proceeds on the death of its president before the end of its fiscal year. It intends to report the amount in its income statement as an extraordinary item.

➤ Would this be in conformity with generally accepted accounting principles? Discuss.

Source: "Technical Hotline," *Journal of Accountancy*, June 1989, p. 31.

Exercise 12–3
Extraordinary item
Objective 2

On May 11, 1996, **ValuJet** tragically lost its Flight 592 en route from Miami to Atlanta. One hundred and ten people lost their lives. The crash cost ValuJet millions of dollars, including $2 million the company paid to the Federal Aviation Administration (FAA) to compensate it for the costs of the special inspections that were conducted. Do you believe that the costs related to this crash should be reported as an extraordinary item on the 1996 income statement of ValuJet?

Exercise 12–4
Identifying extraordinary items
Objective 2

Assume that the amount of each of the following items is material to the financial statements. Classify each item as either normally recurring (NR) or extraordinary (E).

a. Interest revenue on notes receivable.
b. Uninsured flood loss. (Flood insurance is unavailable because of periodic flooding in the area.)
c. Loss on sale of fixed assets.
d. Salaries of corporate officers.
e. Gain on sale of land condemned for public use.
f. Uncollectible accounts expense.
g. Uninsured loss on building due to hurricane damage. The firm was organized in 1920 and had not previously incurred hurricane damage.
h. Loss on disposal of equipment considered to be obsolete because of development of new technology.

Exercise 12–5
Income statement
Objectives 2, 3

✓ Net income, $77,000

Trafalgar Inc. produces and distributes equipment for sailboats. On the basis of the following data for the current fiscal year ended June 30, 2003, prepare a multiple-step income statement for Trafalgar Inc., including an analysis of earnings per share in the form illustrated in this chapter. There were 10,000 shares of $150 par common stock outstanding throughout the year.

Administrative expenses	$ 26,750
Cost of merchandise sold	684,500
Cumulative effect on prior years of changing to a different depreciation method (decrease in income)	60,000
Gain on condemnation of land (extraordinary item)	37,750
Income tax reduction applicable to change in depreciation method	18,200
Income tax applicable to gain on condemnation of land	7,750
Income tax reduction applicable to loss from discontinued operations	56,000
Income tax applicable to ordinary income	105,200
Loss on discontinued operations	125,000
Sales	1,050,000
Selling expenses	75,750

Exercise 12–6
Income statement

Objectives 2, 3

✓ Correct EPS for net income,
$8.55

Boss Sound Inc. sells automotive and home stereo equipment. It has 50,000 shares of $100 par common stock and 10,000 shares of $2, $100 par cumulative preferred stock outstanding as of December 31, 2003. It also holds 10,000 shares of common stock as treasury stock as of December 31, 2003. How many errors can you find in the following income statement for the year ended December 31, 2003?

Boss Sound Inc.
Income Statement
For the Year Ended December 31, 2003

Net sales		$9,450,000
Cost of merchandise sold		7,100,000
Gross profit		$2,350,000
Operating expenses:		
Selling expenses	$920,000	
Administrative expenses	380,000	1,300,000
Income from continuing operations before income tax		$1,050,000
Income tax expense		420,000
Income from continuing operations		$ 730,000
Cumulative effect on prior years' income (decrease) of changing to a different depreciation method (net of applicable income tax of $86,000)		(204,000)
Correction of error (understatement) in December 31, 2002 physical inventory (net of applicable income tax of $20,000)		30,000
Income before condemnation of land and discontinued operations		$ 556,000
Extraordinary item:		
Gain on condemnation of land, net of applicable income tax of $80,000		120,000
Loss on discontinued operations (net of applicable income tax of $76,000)		(184,000)
Net income		$ 492,000
Earnings per common share:		
Income from continuing operations		$14.60
Cumulative effect on prior years' income (decrease) of changing to a different depreciation method		(4.08)
Correction of error (understatement) in December 31, 2002 physical inventory		0.60
Income before extraordinary item and discontinued operations		$11.12
Extraordinary item		2.40
Loss on discontinued operations		(3.68)
Net income		$ 9.84

Exercise 12–7
Reporting paid-in capital

Objective 4

The following accounts and their balances were selected from the unadjusted trial balance of Vintage Inc., a freight forwarder, at December 31, the end of the current fiscal year:

Preferred $2 Stock, $100 par	$1,000,000
Paid-In Capital in Excess of Par—Preferred Stock	120,000
Common Stock, no par, $5 stated value	750,000
Paid-In Capital in Excess of Stated Value—Common Stock	100,000
Paid-In Capital from Sale of Treasury Stock	85,000
Donated Capital	270,000
Retained Earnings	2,230,000

Prepare the Paid-In Capital portion of the Stockholders' Equity section of the balance sheet. There are 300,000 shares of common stock authorized and 70,000 shares of preferred stock authorized.

Exercise 12–8
Stockholders' equity section of balance sheet

Objective 4

✓ Total stockholders' equity, $1,082,500

The following accounts and their balances appear in the ledger of Siphon Inc. on April 30 of the current year:

Common Stock, $10 par	$375,000
Paid-In Capital in Excess of Par	60,000
Paid-In Capital from Sale of Treasury Stock	12,500
Retained Earnings	675,000
Treasury Stock	40,000

Prepare the Stockholders' Equity section of the balance sheet as of April 30. Fifty thousand shares of common stock are authorized, and 1,000 shares have been reacquired.

Exercise 12–9
Stockholders' equity section of balance sheet

Objective 4

✓ Total stockholders' equity, $4,327,500

Motor Toys Inc. retails racing products for BMWs, Porsches, and Ferraris. The following accounts and their balances appear in the ledger of Motor Toys Inc. on December 31, the end of the current year:

Common Stock, $5 par	$ 500,000
Paid-In Capital in Excess of Par—Common Stock	175,000
Paid-In Capital in Excess of Par—Preferred Stock	65,000
Paid-In Capital from Sale of Treasury Stock—Common	35,000
Preferred $2 Stock, $100 par	400,000
Retained Earnings	3,252,500
Treasury Stock—Common	100,000

Ten thousand shares of preferred and 350,000 shares of common stock are authorized. There are 4,000 shares of common stock held as treasury stock.

Prepare the Stockholders' Equity section of the balance sheet as of December 31, the end of the current year.

Exercise 12–10
Retained earnings statement

Objective 4

✓ Retained earnings, Aug. 31, $1,627,600

Mohawk Corporation, a manufacturer of industrial pumps, reports the following results for the year ending August 31, 2003:

Retained earnings, September 1, 2002	$1,475,600
Net income	372,000
Cash dividends declared	120,000
Stock dividends declared	100,000

Prepare a retained earnings statement for the fiscal year ended August 31, 2003.

Exercise 12–11
Stockholders' equity section of balance sheet

Objective 4

✓ Corrected total stockholders' equity, $2,228,000

How many errors can you find in the following Stockholders' Equity section of the balance sheet prepared as of the end of the current year?

Stockholders' Equity

Paid-in capital:		
Preferred $2 stock, cumulative, $100 par		
(3,500 shares authorized and issued)	$ 350,000	
Excess of issue price over par	60,000	$ 410,000
Retained earnings		540,000
Treasury stock (4,000 shares at cost)		75,000
Dividends payable		100,000
Total paid-in capital		$1,125,000
Common stock, $25 par (50,000 shares		
authorized, 40,000 shares issued)	$1,278,000	
Donated capital	75,000	
Organization costs	80,000	1,433,000
Total stockholders' equity		$2,558,000

Exercise 12–12
Statement of stockholders' equity

Objective 4

✓ Total stockholders' equity,
Dec. 31, $2,270,000

The stockholders' equity accounts of Galapagos Corporation for the current fiscal year ended December 31, 2003, are as follows:

ACCOUNT *Common Stock, $2 Par*

Date		Item	Debit	Credit	Balance Debit	Balance Credit
2003						
Jan.	1	Balance				500,000
March	13	Issued 50,000 shares		100,000		600,000

ACCOUNT *Paid-In Capital in Excess of Par*

Date		Item	Debit	Credit	Balance Debit	Balance Credit
2003						
Jan.	1	Balance				400,000
March	13	Issued 50,000 shares		45,000		445,000

ACCOUNT *Treasury Stock*

Date		Item	Debit	Credit	Balance Debit	Balance Credit
2003						
April	30	Purchased 10,000 shares	25,000		25,000	

ACCOUNT *Retained Earnings*

Date		Item	Debit	Credit	Balance Debit	Balance Credit
2003						
Jan.	1	Balance				1,075,000
Dec.	31	Income summary		220,000		1,295,000
	31	Cash dividends	45,000			1,250,000

ACCOUNT *Cash Dividends*

Date		Item	Debit	Credit	Balance Debit	Balance Credit
2003						
June	30		22,500		22,500	
Dec.	30		22,500		45,000	
	31	Closing		45,000	—	—

Prepare a statement of stockholders' equity for the fiscal year ended December 31, 2003.

Exercise 12–13
Temporary investments in marketable securities

Objective 6

During its first year of operations, Genotype Corporation purchased the following securities as a temporary investment:

Security	Shares Purchased	Cost	Cash Dividends Received
Research Inc.	1,000	$25,000	$ 800
Crisp Corp.	2,500	36,000	1,200

a. Journalize the purchase of the temporary investments for cash.
b. Journalize the receipt of the dividends.

Exercise 12–14
Financial statement reporting of temporary investments

Objectives 5, 6

✓ b. Comprehensive income, $81,200

Using the data for Genotype Corporation in Exercise 12–13, assume that as of December 31, 2003, the Research Inc. stock had a market value of $28 per share and the Crisp Corp. stock had a market value of $14 per share. For the year ending December 31, 2003, Genotype Corporation had net income of $80,000. Its tax rate is 40%.

a. Prepare the balance sheet presentation for the temporary investments.
b. Prepare a statement of income and comprehensive income presentation for the temporary investments.

Exercise 12–15
Entries for investment in stock, receipt of dividends, and sale of shares

Objective 6

On February 27, Gourmet Corporation acquired 3,000 shares of the 50,000 outstanding shares of Goulash Co. common stock at 58 plus commission charges of $420. On July 8, a cash dividend of $1 per share and a 2% stock dividend were received. On December 7, 1,000 shares were sold at 62, less commission charges of $375. Journalize the entries to record (a) the purchase of the stock, (b) the receipt of dividends, and (c) the sale of the 1,000 shares.

Exercise 12–16
Equity method

Objective 6

The following note to the consolidated financial statements for **The Goodyear Tire and Rubber Co.** relates to the principles of consolidation used in preparing the financial statements:

The Company's investments in 20% to 50% owned companies in which it has the ability to exercise significant influence over operating and financial policies are accounted for by the equity method. Accordingly, the Company's share of the earnings of these companies is included in consolidated net income.

Is it a requirement that Goodyear use the equity method in this situation? Explain.

Exercise 12–17
Entries using equity method for stock investment

Objective 6

At a total cost of $13,500,000, Southern Corporation acquired 150,000 shares of Northern Corp. common stock as a long-term investment. Southern Corporation uses the equity method of accounting for this investment. Northern Corp. has 500,000 shares of common stock outstanding, including the shares acquired by Southern Corporation. Journalize the entries by Southern Corporation to record the following information:

a. Northern Corp. reports net income of $8,500,000 for the current period.
b. A cash dividend of $1.25 per common share is paid by Northern Corp. during the current period.

Exercise 12–18
Eliminations for consolidated income statement

Objective 7

✓ a. (1) $80,000
✓ b. $1,950,000

For the current year ended June 30, the results of operations of Iowa Corporation and its wholly owned subsidiary, Hawkee Enterprises, are as follows:

	Iowa Corporation		Hawkee Enterprises	
Sales		$8,150,000		$750,000
Cost of merchandise sold	$5,000,000		$440,000	
Selling expenses	800,000		75,000	
Administrative expenses	600,000		35,000	
Interest expense (revenue)	(30,000)	6,370,000	30,000	580,000
Net income		$1,780,000		$170,000

During the year, Iowa sold merchandise to Hawkee for $80,000. The merchandise was sold by Hawkee to nonaffiliated companies for $120,000. Iowa's interest revenue was realized from a long-term loan to Hawkee.

a. Determine the amounts to be eliminated from the following items in preparing a consolidated income statement for the current year: (1) sales and (2) cost of merchandise sold.
b. Determine the consolidated net income.

Exercise 12–19
Price-earnings ratio

Objective 8

Real World

The financial statements for **Cisco Systems, Inc.**, are presented in Appendix G at the end of the text.

a. Determine the price-earnings ratio for Cisco Systems for 2000 and 1999. The high market price of Cisco Systems' common stock was $33.53 in the fourth quarter of fiscal year 1999 and $71.44 in the fourth quarter of fiscal year 2000.

b. ✏️➡ What conclusions can you reach by considering the price-earnings ratio?

PROBLEMS SERIES A

Problem 12–1A
Income tax allocation

Objective 1

SPREADSHEET

✓ 1. Year-end balance, 3rd year, $72,000

Differences between the accounting methods applied to accounts and financial reports and those used in determining taxable income yielded the following amounts for the first four years of a corporation's operations:

	First Year	Second Year	Third Year	Fourth Year
Income before income taxes	$300,000	$450,000	$400,000	$500,000
Taxable income	250,000	300,000	420,000	510,000

The income tax rate for each of the four years was 40% of taxable income, and each year's taxes were promptly paid.

Instructions

1. Determine for each year the amounts described by the following captions, presenting the information in the form indicated:

Year	Income Tax Deducted on Income Statement	Income Tax Payments for the Year	Deferred Income Tax Payable	
			Year's Addition (Deduction)	Year-End Balance

2. Total the first three amount columns.

Problem 12–2A
Income tax; income statement

Objectives 1, 2, 3

✓ Net income, $57,000

The following data were selected from the records of Mantra Greenhouses Inc. for the current fiscal year ended June 30, 2003:

Advertising expense	$ 40,000
Cost of merchandise sold	266,000
Depreciation expense—office equipment	5,000
Depreciation expense—store equipment	29,000
Gain from disposal of a segment of the business	37,500
Income tax:	
Applicable to continuing operations	32,000
Applicable to gain from disposal of a segment of the business	15,000
Applicable to loss on condemnation of land (reduction)	9,000
Insurance expense	8,000
Interest expense	15,000
Loss on condemnation of land	22,500
Miscellaneous administrative expense	6,000
Miscellaneous selling expense	5,000

Office salaries expense	$ 50,000
Rent expense	21,000
Sales	665,000
Sales commissions expense	140,000

Instructions

Prepare a multiple-step income statement, concluding with a section for earnings per share in the form illustrated in this chapter. There were 75,000 shares of common stock (no preferred) outstanding throughout the year. Assume that the loss on condemnation of land is an extraordinary item.

Problem 12–3A
Income statement, retained earnings statement, balance sheet

Objectives 1, 2, 3, 4

SPREADSHEET

✓ Net income, $313,500

The following data were taken from the records of Pushkin Corporation for the year ended October 31, 2003:

Income statement data:

Administrative expenses	$ 100,000
Cost of merchandise sold	732,000
Gain on condemnation of land	30,000
Income tax:	
Applicable to continuing operations	234,000
Applicable to loss from disposal of a segment of the business	37,000
Applicable to gain on condemnation of land	12,000
Interest expense	8,000
Interest revenue	5,000
Loss from disposal of a segment of the business	92,500
Sales	1,820,000
Selling expenses	400,000

Retained earnings and balance sheet data:

Accounts payable	$ 149,500
Accounts receivable	309,050
Accumulated depreciation	3,050,000
Allowance for doubtful accounts	21,500
Cash	145,500
Common stock, $15 par (400,000 shares authorized; 152,000 shares issued)	2,280,000
Deferred income taxes payable (current portion, $4,700)	25,700
Dividends:	
Cash dividends for common stock	120,000
Cash dividends for preferred stock	75,000
Stock dividends for common stock	60,000
Dividends payable	30,000
Equipment	9,541,050
Income tax payable	55,900
Interest receivable	2,500
Merchandise inventory (October 31, 2003), at lower of cost (fifo) or market	425,000
Notes receivable	77,500
Organization costs	55,000
Paid-in capital from sale of treasury stock	16,000
Paid-in capital in excess of par—common stock	666,250
Paid-in capital in excess of par—preferred stock	240,000
Preferred 5% stock, $100 par (30,000 shares authorized; 15,000 shares issued)	1,500,000
Prepaid expenses	15,900
Retained earnings, November 1, 2002	2,548,150
Treasury stock (2,000 shares of common stock at cost of $35 per share)	70,000

Instructions

1. Prepare a multiple-step income statement for the year ended October 31, 2003, concluding with earnings per share. In computing earnings per share, assume that the average number of common shares outstanding was 150,000 and preferred dividends were $75,000. Assume that the gain on condemnation of land is an extraordinary item.
2. Prepare a retained earnings statement for the year ended October 31, 2003.
3. Prepare a balance sheet in report form as of October 31, 2003.

Problem 12–4A

Entries for investments in stock

Objective 6

SPREADSHEET

Thematic Company is a wholesaler of men's hair products. The following transactions relate to certain securities acquired by Thematic Company, whose fiscal year ends on December 31:

2001
Jan. 3. Purchased 3,000 shares of the 40,000 outstanding common shares of Perch Corporation at 89 plus commission and other costs of $594.
July 2. Received the regular cash dividend of $1 a share on Perch Corporation stock.
Dec. 5. Received the regular cash dividend of $1 a share plus an extra dividend of $0.10 a share on Perch Corporation stock.
(Assume that all intervening transactions have been recorded properly and that the number of shares of stock owned have not changed from December 31, 2001, to December 31, 2003.)

2004
Jan. 2. Purchased controlling interest in Villard Inc. for $890,000 by purchasing 60,000 shares directly from the estate of the founder of Villard. There are 80,000 shares of Villard Inc. stock outstanding.
July 6. Received the regular cash dividend of $1 a share and a 3% stock dividend on the Perch Corporation stock.
Oct. 23. Sold 750 shares of Perch Corporation stock at 90. The broker deducted commission and other costs of $140, remitting the balance.
Dec. 10. Received a cash dividend at the new rate of $1.10 a share on the Perch Corporation stock.
    31. Received $24,000 of cash dividends on Villard Inc. stock. Villard Inc. reported net income of $315,000 in 2004. Thematic uses the equity method of accounting for its investment in Villard Inc.

Instructions

Journalize the entries for the preceding transactions.

PROBLEMS SERIES B

Problem 12–1B

Income tax allocation

Objective 1

SPREADSHEET

✓ 1. Year-end balance, 3rd year, $56,000

Differences between the accounting methods applied to accounts and financial reports and those used in determining taxable income yielded the following amounts for the first four years of a corporation's operations:

	First Year	Second Year	Third Year	Fourth Year
Income before income taxes	$350,000	$440,000	$520,000	$695,000
Taxable income	270,000	350,000	550,000	710,000

The income tax rate for each of the four years was 40% of taxable income, and each year's taxes were promptly paid.

Instructions

1. Determine for each year the amounts described by the following captions, presenting the information in the form indicated:

	Income Tax Deducted on Income Statement	Income Tax Payments for the Year	Deferred Income Tax Payable	
Year			Year's Addition (Deduction)	Year-End Balance

2. Total the first three amount columns.

Problem 12–2B
Income tax; income statement

Objectives 1, 2, 3

✓ Net income, $51,500

SUV Inc. produces and sells off-road motorcycles and jeeps. The following data were selected from the records of SUV Inc. for the current fiscal year ended October 31, 2003:

Advertising expense	$ 60,000
Cost of merchandise sold	553,500
Depreciation expense—office equipment	6,000
Depreciation expense—store equipment	21,500
Gain on condemnation of land	31,250
Income tax:	
Applicable to continuing operations	36,250
Applicable to loss from disposal of a segment of the business (reduction)	5,000
Applicable to gain on condemnation of land	12,500
Interest revenue	7,500
Loss from disposal of a segment of the business	26,000
Miscellaneous administrative expense	10,000
Miscellaneous selling expense	4,500
Office salaries expense	68,000
Rent expense	20,000
Sales	950,000
Sales salaries expense	120,000
Store supplies expense	4,000

Instructions

Prepare a multiple-step income statement, concluding with a section for earnings per share (rounded to the nearest cent) in the form illustrated in this chapter. There were 25,000 shares of common stock (no preferred) outstanding throughout the year. Assume that the gain on condemnation of land is an extraordinary item.

Problem 12–3B
Income statement, retained earnings statement, balance sheet

Objectives 1, 2, 3, 4

SPREADSHEET

✓ Net income, $255,000

The following data were taken from the records of Onyx Corporation for the year ended July 31, 2003:

Income statement data:

Administrative expenses	$ 130,000
Cost of merchandise sold	884,000
Gain on condemnation of land	25,000
Income tax:	
Applicable to continuing operations	220,000
Applicable to loss from disposal of a segment of the business	54,000
Applicable to gain on condemnation of land	10,000
Interest expense	7,500
Interest revenue	1,500
Loss from disposal of a segment of the business	134,000
Sales	2,100,000
Selling expenses	540,000

Retained earnings and balance sheet data:

Accounts payable	$ 149,500
Accounts receivable	276,050

Accumulated depreciation	$ 3,050,000
Allowance for doubtful accounts	11,500
Cash	125,500
Common stock, $10 par (500,000 shares authorized;	
251,000 shares issued)	2,510,000
Deferred income taxes payable (current portion, $4,700)	25,700
Dividends:	
Cash dividends for common stock	80,000
Cash dividends for preferred stock	120,000
Stock dividends for common stock	40,000
Dividends payable	25,000
Equipment	11,064,050
Income tax payable	55,900
Interest receivable	2,500
Merchandise inventory (July 31, 2003), at lower of	
cost (fifo) or market	522,500
Organization costs	55,000
Paid-in capital from sale of treasury stock	5,000
Paid-in capital in excess of par—common stock	437,500
Paid-in capital in excess of par—preferred stock	240,000
Preferred 8% stock, $100 par (30,000 shares authorized;	
15,000 shares issued)	1,500,000
Prepaid expenses	15,900
Retained earnings, August 1, 2002	4,076,400
Treasury stock (1,000 shares of common stock at cost	
of $40 per share)	40,000

Instructions

1. Prepare a multiple-step income statement for the year ended July 31, 2003, con-
    cluding with earnings per share. In computing earnings per share, assume that the
    average number of common shares outstanding was 250,000 and preferred dividends
    were $120,000. Assume that the gain on condemnation of land is an extraordinary
    item.
2. Prepare a retained earnings statement for the year ended July 31, 2003.
3. Prepare a balance sheet in report form as of July 31, 2003.

Problem 12–4B

Entries for investments in stock

Objective 6

SPREADSHEET

Wilhelm Company produces and sells theater costumes. The following transactions
relate to certain securities acquired by Wilhelm Company, whose fiscal year ends on
December 31:

2001

Feb. 10. Purchased 4,000 shares of the 150,000 outstanding common shares of Moore
         Corporation at 42 plus commission and other costs of $300.

June 15. Received the regular cash dividend of $0.80 a share on Moore Corporation
         stock.

Dec. 15. Received the regular cash dividend of $0.80 a share plus an extra dividend
         of $0.05 a share on Moore Corporation stock.
         (Assume that all intervening transactions have been recorded properly and
         that the number of shares of stock owned have not changed from December
         31, 2001, to December 31, 2003.)

2004

Jan. 3. Purchased controlling interest in Sirloin Inc. for $750,000 by purchasing
         40,000 shares directly from the estate of the founder of Sirloin. There are
         50,000 shares of Sirloin Inc. stock outstanding.

Apr. 1. Received the regular cash dividend of $0.80 a share and a 2% stock dividend
         on the Moore Corporation stock.

July 20. Sold 1,000 shares of Moore Corporation stock at 43. The broker deducted
         commission and other costs of $150, remitting the balance.

Dec. 15. Received a cash dividend at the new rate of $0.90 a share on the Moore Corporation stock.

    31. Received $30,000 of cash dividends on Sirloin Inc. stock. Sirloin Inc. reported net income of $245,000 in 2004. Wilhelm uses the equity method of accounting for its investment in Sirloin Inc.

Instructions

Journalize the entries for the preceding transactions.

SPECIAL ACTIVITIES

Activity 12–1
Mojave Inc.
Ethics and professional conduct in business

At a recent dinner party, you met Steph Melick, the controller for Mojave Inc. Steph has worked for Mojave for the past seven years. During your conversation, you complained about having to pay your third-quarter estimated taxes on Monday, September 15. In response, Steph indicated that she always *underpays* her estimated taxes. That way, she can use her money as long as possible. Is it appropriate to deliberately underpay your estimated taxes?

Activity 12–2
Ratchet Corporation
Ethics and professional conduct in business

Reed Osborn is the president and chief operating officer of Ratchet Corporation, a developer of personal financial planning software. During the past year, Ratchet Corporation was forced to sell ten acres of land to the city of Houston for expansion of a freeway exit. The corporation fought the sale, but after condemnation hearings, a judge ordered it to sell the land. Because of the location of the land and the fact that Ratchet Corporation had purchased the land over 15 years ago, the corporation recorded a $0.20-per-share gain on the sale. Always looking to turn a negative into a positive, Reed Osborn has decided to announce the corporation's earnings per share of $1.05, without identifying the $0.20 impact of selling the land. Although he will retain majority ownership, Reed plans on selling 20,000 of his shares in the corporation sometime within the next month. Are Reed's plans to announce earnings per share of $1.05 without mentioning the $0.20 impact of selling the land ethical and professional?

Activity 12–3
Ulster Inc.
Reporting extraordinary item

Ulster Inc. is in the process of preparing its annual financial statements. Ulster Inc. is a large citrus grower located in central Florida. The following is a discussion between Jason Kirk, the controller, and April Gwinn, the chief executive officer and president of Ulster Inc.

April: Jason, I've got a question about your rough draft of this year's income statement.
Jason: Sure, April. What's your question?
April: Well, your draft shows a net loss of $750,000.
Jason: That's right. We'd have had a profit, except for this year's frost damage. I figured that the frost destroyed over 30 percent of our crop. We had a good year otherwise.
April: That's my concern. I estimated that if we eliminate the frost damage, we'd show a profit of . . . let's see . . . about $250,000.
Jason: That sounds about right.
April: This income statement seems misleading. Why can't we show the loss on the frost damage separately? That way the bank and our outside investors will be able to see that this year's loss is just temporary. I'd hate to get them upset over nothing.
Jason: Maybe we can do something. I recall from my accounting courses something about showing unusual items separately. Let's see . . . yes, I remember. They're called extraordinary items.
April: Well, we haven't had any frost damage in over five years. This year's damage is certainly extraordinary. Let's do it!

Discuss the appropriateness of revising Ulster Inc.'s income statement to report the frost damage separately as an extraordinary item.

Activity 12–4
Charlene Seymour
Consolidated financial statements

Charlene Seymour, your grandmother, recently retired, sold her condominium in New York City, and moved to a retirement community in Florida. With some of the proceeds from the sale of her condominium, she is considering investing $800,000 in the stock market.

In the process of selecting among alternative stock investments, your grandmother collected annual reports from fifteen different companies. In reviewing these reports, however, she has become confused and has questions concerning several items that appear in the financial reports. She has asked for your help and has written down the following questions for you to answer:

a. *In reviewing the annual reports, I noticed many references to "consolidated financial statements." What are consolidated financial statements?*

b. *"Excess of cost of business acquired over related net assets" appears on the consolidated balance sheets in several annual reports. What does this mean? Is it an asset (it appears with other assets)?*

c. *What is minority interest?*

d. *A footnote to one of the consolidated statements indicated interest and the amount of a loan from one company to another had been eliminated. Is this good accounting? A loan is a loan. How can a company just eliminate a loan that hasn't been paid off?*

e. *How can financial statements for an American company (in dollars) be combined with a German subsidiary (in marks)?*

1. ▬▬► Briefly respond to each of your grandmother's questions.

2. ▬▬► While discussing the items in (1) with your grandmother, she asked for your advice on whether she should limit her investment to one stock. What would you advise?

Activity 12–5
Into the Real World
Extraordinary items and discontinued operations

In groups of three or four students, search company annual reports, news releases, or the Internet for extraordinary items and announcements of discontinued operations. Identify the most unusual extraordinary item in your group. Also, select a discontinued operation of a well-known company that might be familiar to other students or might interest them.

Prepare a brief analysis of the earnings per share impact of both the extraordinary item and the discontinued operation. Estimate the *potential* impact on the company's market price by multiplying the current price-earnings ratio by the earnings per share amount of each item.

One Internet site that has annual reports is EDGAR (Electronic Data Gathering, Analysis, and Retrieval), the electronic archives of financial statements filed with the Securities and Exchange Commission. SEC documents can be retrieved using the EdgarScan service from **PricewaterhouseCoopers** at **edgarscan.pwcglobal.com**.

To obtain annual report information, type in a company name in the appropriate space. EdgarScan will list the reports available to you for the company you've selected. Select the most recent annual report filing, identified as a 10-K or 10-K405. EdgarScan provides an outline of the report, including the separate financial statements. You can double click the income statement and balance sheet for the selected company into an Excel™ spreadsheet for further analysis.

ANSWERS TO SELF-EXAMINATION QUESTIONS

Matching

1. Z	5. I	9. D	13. BB	17. J	21. Y	25. P
2. AA	6. A	10. L	14. DD	18. O	22. V	26. T
3. H	7. U	11. CC	15. N	19. F	23. S	
4. M	8. X	12. B	16. G	20. Q	24. E	

Multiple Choice

1. **A** The amount of income tax deferred to future years is $16,000 (answer A), determined as follows:

Depreciation expense, MACRS	$100,000
Depreciation expense, straight-line method	60,000
Excess expense in determining taxable income ..	$ 40,000
Income tax rate	× 40%
Income tax deferred to future years	$ 16,000

2. **A** Events and transactions that are distinguished by their unusual nature and by the infrequency of their occurrence, such as a gain on condemning land for public use, are reported in the income statement as extraordinary items (answer A).

3. **B** The difference between the cost of temporary investments held as available-for-sale securities and their market value is reported as an unrealized gain, net of applicable income taxes, as shown below:

Market value of investments	$120,000
Cost of investments	100,000
	$ 20,000
Applicable taxes (40%)	8,000
Unrealized gain, net of taxes	$ 12,000

The unrealized gain of $12,000 (answer B) is reported on the balance sheet as an addition to the cost of the investments and as part of other comprehensive income.

4. **A** The consolidated income statement should report the incomes of Parker and Sweeney as if they were one operating entity. Because an entity cannot sell to itself or buy from itself, the $75,000 sale from Parker to Sweeney must be eliminated. In addition, the $75,000 purchase by Sweeney must be eliminated from Sweeney's cost of merchandise sold. Thus, sales of $1,505,000 ($980,000 − $75,000 + $600,000) and cost of merchandise sold of $785,000 ($500,000 + $360,000 − $75,000) would be reported on the consolidated income statement (answer A).

5. **C** Under the equity method of accounting for investments in stocks, Cisneros Corporation records its share of both net income and dividends of Harrell Inc. in Investment in Harrell Inc. Stock. Thus, Investment in Harrell Inc. Stock would increase by $82,500 [($150,000 × 75%) − ($40,000 × 75%)] for the current year. $30,000 (answer B) is only Cisneros Corporation's share of Harrell's dividends for the current year. $112,500 (answer D) is only Cisneros Corporation's share of Harrell's net income for the year.

Bonds Payable and Investments in Bonds

After studying this chapter, you should be able to:

1 Compute the potential impact of long-term borrowing on the earnings per share of a corporation.

2 Describe the characteristics of bonds.

3 Compute the present value of bonds payable.

4 Journalize entries for bonds payable.

5 Describe bond sinking funds.

6 Journalize entries for bond redemptions.

7 Journalize entries for the purchase, interest, discount and premium amortization, and sale of bond investments.

8 Prepare a corporation balance sheet.

9 Compute and interpret the number of times interest charges are earned.

You have just inherited $50,000 from a distant relative, and you are considering some options for investing the money. Some of your friends have suggested that you invest it in long-term bonds. As a result, you have scanned *The Wall Street Journal's* November 16, 2000 listing of New York Exchange Bonds. You've identified the following two listings as possible bond investments:

- AT&T (American Telephone & Telegraph) 7¾% Bonds, maturing in 2007
- HewlPkd (Hewlett-Packard) Zero, maturing in 2017

The AT&T bonds are selling for 100½, while the Hewlett-Packard bonds are selling for only 55. The AT&T bonds are selling for over one and one-half times the price of the Hewlett-Packard bonds. Does this mean that the Hewlett-Packard bonds are a better buy? Does the 7¾% mean that if you buy the AT&T bonds you can actually earn 7¾% interest? What does the "zero" mean? Does it have anything to do with the fact that the Hewlett-Packard bonds are selling for only 55?

In this chapter, we will answer each of these questions. We first discuss the advantages and disadvantages of financing a corporation's operations by issuing debt rather than equity. We then discuss the accounting principles related to issuing long-term debt. Finally, we discuss the accounting for investments in bonds.

Financing Corporations

objective 1

Compute the potential impact of long-term borrowing on the earnings per share of a corporation.

Point of Interest

Bonds of major corporations are actively traded on bond exchanges. You can purchase bonds through a financial services firm, such as **Merrill Lynch** or **A. G. Edwards & Sons**.

Most of you have financed (purchased on credit) an automobile, a home, or a computer. Similarly, corporations often finance their operations by purchasing on credit and issuing notes or bonds. We have discussed accounts payable and notes payable in earlier chapters. A **bond** is simply a form of an interest-bearing note. Like a note, a bond requires periodic interest payments, and the face amount must be repaid at the maturity date. Bondholders are creditors of the issuing corporation, and their claims on the assets of the corporation rank ahead of stockholders.

One of the many factors that influence the decision to issue debt or equity is the effect of each alternative on earnings per share. To illustrate the possible effects, assume that a corporation's board of directors is considering the following alternative plans for financing a $4,000,000 company:

Plan 1: 100% financing from issuing common stock, $10 par

Plan 2: 50% financing from issuing preferred 9% stock, $50 par
50% financing from issuing common stock, $10 par

Plan 3: 50% financing from issuing 12% bonds
25% financing from issuing preferred 9% stock, $50 par
25% financing from issuing common stock, $10 par

In each case, we assume that the stocks or bonds are issued at their par or face amount. The corporation is expecting to earn $800,000 annually, before deducting interest on the bonds and income taxes estimated at 40% of income. Exhibit 1 shows the effect of the three plans on the income of the corporation and the earnings per share on common stock.

Exhibit 1 indicates that Plan 3 yields the highest earnings per share on common stock and is thus the most attractive for common stockholders. If the estimated earnings are more than $800,000, the difference between the earnings per share to com-

Exhibit 1 Effect of Alternative Financing Plans—$800,000 Earnings

	Plan 1	Plan 2	Plan 3
12% bonds	—	—	$2,000,000
Preferred 9% stock, $50 par	—	$2,000,000	1,000,000
Common stock, $10 par	$4,000,000	2,000,000	1,000,000
Total	$4,000,000	$4,000,000	$4,000,000
Earnings before interest and income tax	$ 800,000	$ 800,000	$ 800,000
Deduct interest on bonds	—	—	240,000
Income before income tax	$ 800,000	$ 800,000	$ 560,000
Deduct income tax	320,000	320,000	224,000
Net income	$ 480,000	$ 480,000	$ 336,000
Dividends on preferred stock	—	180,000	90,000
Available for dividends on common stock	$ 480,000	$ 300,000	$ 246,000
Shares of common stock outstanding	÷ 400,000	÷ 200,000	÷ 100,000
Earnings per share on common stock	$ 1.20	$ 1.50	$ 2.46

mon stockholders under Plan 1 and Plan 3 is even greater.[1] However, if smaller earnings occur, Plans 2 and 3 become less attractive to common stockholders. To illustrate, the effect of earnings of $440,000 rather than $800,000 is shown in Exhibit 2.

Exhibit 2 Effect of Alternative Financing Plans—$440,000 Earnings

	Plan 1	Plan 2	Plan 3
12% bonds	—	—	$2,000,000
Preferred 9% stock, $50 par	—	$2,000,000	1,000,000
Common stock, $10 par	$4,000,000	2,000,000	1,000,000
Total	$4,000,000	$4,000,000	$4,000,000
Earnings before interest and income tax	$ 440,000	$ 440,000	$ 440,000
Deduct interest on bonds	—	—	240,000
Income before income tax	$ 440,000	$ 440,000	$ 200,000
Deduct income tax	176,000	176,000	80,000
Net income	$ 264,000	$ 264,000	$ 120,000
Dividends on preferred stock	—	180,000	90,000
Available for dividends on common stock	$ 264,000	$ 84,000	$ 30,000
Shares of common stock outstanding	÷ 400,000	÷ 200,000	÷ 100,000
Earnings per share on common stock	$ 0.66	$ 0.42	$ 0.30

Real World When interest rates are low, corporations usually finance their operations with debt. For example, as interest rates fell in the early 1990s, corporations rushed to issue new debt. In one day alone, more than $4.5 billion of debt was issued.

In addition to the effect on earnings per share, the board of directors should consider other factors in deciding whether to issue debt or equity. For example, once bonds are issued, periodic interest payments and repayment of the face value of the bonds are beyond the control of the corporation. That is, if these payments are not made, the bondholders could seek court action and could force the company into bankruptcy. In contrast, a corporation is not legally obligated to pay dividends.

---

[1] The higher earnings per share under Plan 1 is due to a finance concept known as **leverage**. This concept is discussed further in a later chapter.

Characteristics of Bonds Payable

objective 2

Describe the characteristics of bonds.

AT&T 7½% bonds maturing in 2006 were listed as selling for 100½ on September 7, 2000.

A corporation that issues bonds enters into a contract, called a **bond indenture** or **trust indenture**, with the bondholders. A bond issue is normally divided into a number of individual bonds. Usually, the face value of each bond, called the **principal**, is $1,000 or a multiple of $1,000. The interest on bonds may be payable annually, semiannually, or quarterly. Most bonds pay interest semiannually.

The prices of bonds are quoted as a percentage of the bonds' face value. Thus, investors could purchase or sell **TimeWarner** bonds quoted at 109⅞ for $1,098.75. Likewise, bonds quoted at 109 could be purchased or sold for $1,090.

When all bonds of an issue mature at the same time, they are called **term bonds**. If the maturities are spread over several dates, they are called **serial bonds**. For example, one-tenth of an issue of $1,000,000 bonds, or $100,000, may mature 16 years from the issue date, another $100,000 in the 17th year, and so on until the final $100,000 matures in the 25th year.

Bonds that may be exchanged for other securities, such as common stock, are called **convertible bonds**. Bonds that a corporation reserves the right to redeem before their maturity are called **callable bonds**. Bonds issued on the basis of the general credit of the corporation are called **debenture bonds**.

BUSINESS ON STAGE

Bond Ratings

Bonds are rated as to their riskiness as investments by such independent financial reporting services as Moody's (www.moodys.com) and Standard and Poor's (www.standardandpoors.com). These services rely heavily on analysis of the financial statements and the terms of the bond indenture in setting the credit rating. This credit rating, in turn, influences how much the bonds will sell for in the marketplace. Moody's and Standard and Poor's rate bonds slightly differently. The following table shows all but the lowest ratings and their accompanying interpretation.

Moody's will use a "+" sign or "−" sign to indicate the relative strength of a bond within a general rating category. For example, AAA+ indicates that a bond is at the high end of the AAA category.

Instead of using a "+" or "−" sign to indicate relative strength within a rating category, Standard & Poor's uses 1, 2, and 3. For example, Aaa1 indicates that a bond is in the upper third of the Aaa category, while Aaa3 indicates that a bond is in the bottom third. ■

Moody's Rating	Standard and Poor's Rating	Interpretation
AAA	Aaa	Highest rating; ability to pay interest and principal is very secure.
AA	Aa	High quality; differs from highest-rated bonds only to a small degree.
A	A	Upper-medium quality; interest and principal may be in jeopardy if a long, deep economic downturn (recession) occurs.
BBB	Baa	Medium grade; adequate ability to pay interest and principal in normal economic conditions.
BB	Ba	Quite risky; modest ability to pay interest and principal.
B	B	Poor investment; highly speculative; ability to pay interest and principal over a long period is small.

The Present-Value Concept and Bonds Payable

objective 3

Compute the present value of bonds payable.

When a corporation issues bonds, the price that buyers are willing to pay for the bonds depends upon the following three factors:

1. The face amount of the bonds, which is the amount due at the maturity date.
2. The periodic interest to be paid on the bonds.
3. The market rate of interest.

The face amount and the periodic interest to be paid on the bonds are identified in the bond indenture. The periodic interest is expressed as a percentage of the face amount of the bond. This percentage or rate of interest is called the **contract rate** or **coupon rate**.

The **market** or **effective rate of interest** is determined by transactions between buyers and sellers of similar bonds. The market rate of interest is affected by a variety of factors, including investors' assessment of current economic conditions as well as future expectations.

If the contract rate of interest equals the market rate of interest, the bonds will sell at their face amount. If the market rate is higher than the contract rate, the bonds will sell at a **discount**, or less than their face amount. Why is this the case? Buyers are not willing to pay the face amount for bonds whose contract rate is lower than the market rate. The discount, in effect, represents the amount necessary to make up for the difference in the market and the contract interest rates. In contrast, if the market rate is lower than the contract rate, the bonds will sell at a **premium**, or more than their face amount. In this case, buyers are willing to pay more than the face amount for bonds whose contract rate is higher than the market rate.

The face amount of the bonds and the periodic interest on the bonds represent cash to be received by the buyer in the future. The buyer determines how much to pay for the bonds by computing the present value of these future cash receipts, using the market rate of interest. The concept of present value is based on the time value of money.

The time value of money concept recognizes that an amount of cash to be received today is worth more than the same amount of cash to be received in the future. For example, what would you rather have: $100 today or $100 one year from now? You would rather have the $100 today because it could be invested to earn income. For example, if the $100 could be invested to earn 10% per year, the $100 will accumulate to $110 ($100 plus $10 earnings) in one year. In this sense, you can think of the $100 in hand today as the **present value** of $110 to be received a year from today. This present value is illustrated in the following time line:

MARKET RATE = CONTRACT RATE

Selling price of bond = $1,000

$1,000 Bond

MARKET RATE > CONTRACT RATE

Selling price of bond < $1,000

$1,000 Bond − Discount

MARKET RATE < CONTRACT RATE

Selling price of bond > $1,000

$1,000 Bond + Premium

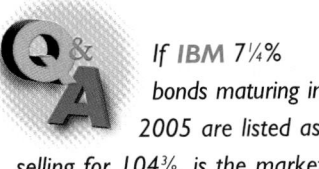

Q & A

If IBM 7¼% bonds maturing in 2005 are listed as selling for 104⅜, is the market rate of interest higher or lower than that for similar bonds?

Lower

Present value of $110 to be received one year from today

$100

TODAY

(Interest rate of 10%)

Future value of $100 to be received one year from today

$110

ONE YEAR FROM TODAY

What is the future value of $100 to be received in two years, assuming an interest rate of 10%?

$121 ($100 × 1.10 × 1.10)

A related concept to present value is **future value**. In the preceding illustration, the $110 to be received a year from today is the future value of $100 today, assuming an interest rate of 10%.

Present Value of the Face Amount of Bonds

The present value of the face amount of bonds is the value today of the amount to be received at a future maturity date. For example, assume that you are to receive the face value of a $1,000 bond in one year. If the market rate of interest is 10%, the present value of the face value of the $1,000 bond is $909.09 ($1,000/1.10). This present value is illustrated in the following time line:

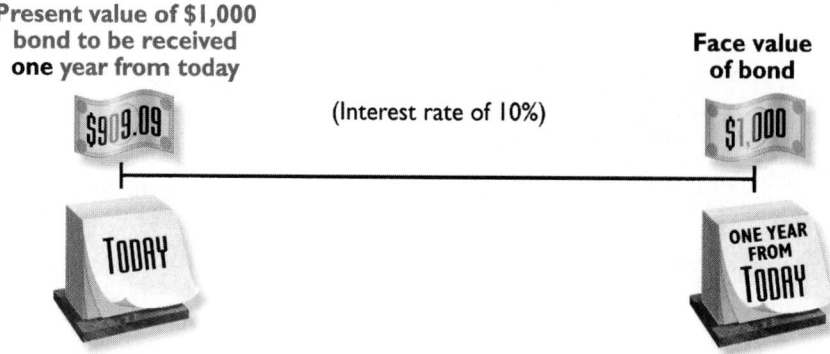

If you are to receive the face value of a $1,000 bond in two years, with interest of 10% compounded at the end of the first year, the present value is $826.45 ($909.09/1.10).[2] We illustrate this present value in the following time line:

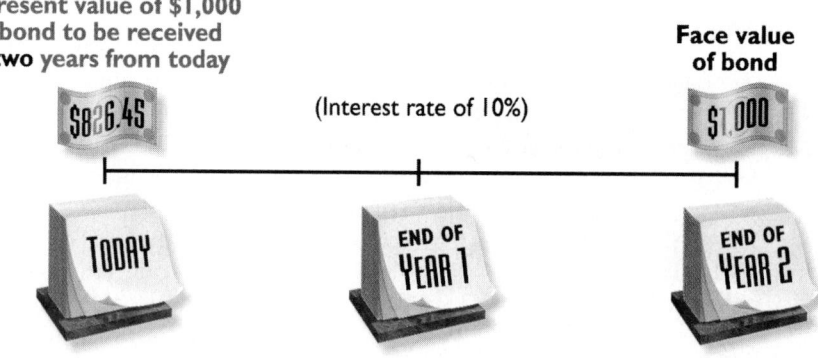

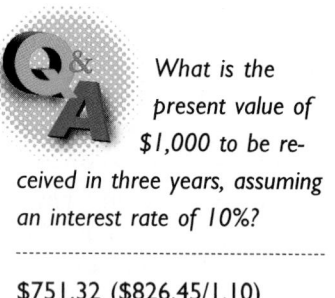

What is the present value of $1,000 to be received in three years, assuming an interest rate of 10%?

$751.32 ($826.45/1.10)

Point of Interest
Spreadsheet software with built-in present value functions can be used to calculate present values.

You can determine the present value of the face amount of bonds to be received in the future by a time line and a series of divisions. In practice, however, it is easier to use a table of present values. The *present value of $1 table* can be used to find the present-value factor for $1 to be received after a number of periods in the future. The face amount of the bonds is then multiplied by this factor to determine its present value. Exhibit 3 is a partial table of the present value of $1.[3]

---

[2] Note that the future value of $826.45 in two years, at an interest rate of 10% compounded annually, is $1,000.

[3] To simplify the illustrations and homework assignments, the tables presented in this chapter are limited to 10 periods for a small number of interest rates, and the amounts are carried to only five decimal places. Computer programs are available for determining present value factors for any number of interest rates, decimal places, or periods. More complete interest tables, including future value tables, are presented in Appendix A.

Exhibit 3 Present Value of $1 at Compound Interest

Periods	5%	5½%	6%	6½%	7%	10%	11%	12%	13%	14%
1	0.95238	0.94787	0.94340	0.93897	0.93458	0.90909	0.90090	0.89286	0.88496	0.87719
2	0.90703	0.89845	0.89000	0.88166	0.87344	0.82645	0.81162	0.79719	0.78315	0.76947
3	0.86384	0.85161	0.83962	0.82785	0.81630	0.75132	0.73119	0.71178	0.69305	0.67497
4	0.82270	0.80722	0.79209	0.77732	0.76290	0.68301	0.65873	0.63552	0.61332	0.59208
5	0.78353	0.76513	0.74726	0.72988	0.71299	0.62092	0.59345	0.56743	0.54276	0.51937
6	0.74622	0.72525	0.70496	0.68533	0.66634	0.56447	0.53464	0.50663	0.48032	0.45559
7	0.71068	0.68744	0.66506	0.64351	0.62275	0.51316	0.48166	0.45235	0.42506	0.39964
8	0.67684	0.65160	0.62741	0.60423	0.58201	0.46651	0.43393	0.40388	0.37616	0.35056
9	0.64461	0.61763	0.59190	0.56735	0.54393	0.42410	0.39092	0.36061	0.33288	0.30751
10	0.61391	0.58543	0.55840	0.53273	0.50835	0.38554	0.35218	0.32197	0.29459	0.26974

What is the present value of $3,000 to be received in 5 years at a market rate of interest of 14% compounded annually?

$1,558.11 ($3,000 × 0.51937)

Exhibit 3 indicates that the present value of $1 to be received in two years with a market rate of interest of 10% a year is 0.82645. Multiplying the $1,000 face amount of the bond in the preceding example by 0.82645 yields $826.45.

In Exhibit 3, the Periods column represents the number of compounding periods, and the percentage columns represent the compound interest rate per period. For example, 10% for two years compounded *annually*, as in the preceding example, is 10% for two periods. Likewise, 10% for two years compounded *semiannually* would be 5% (10% per year/2 semiannual periods) for four periods (2 years × 2 semiannual periods). Similarly, 10% for three years compounded semiannually would be 5% (10%/2) for six periods (3 years × 2 semiannual periods).

Present Value of the Periodic Bond Interest Payments

The present value of the periodic bond interest payments is the value today of the amount of interest to be received at the end of each interest period. Such a series of equal cash payments at fixed intervals is called an **annuity**.

The **present value of an annuity** is the sum of the present values of each cash flow. To illustrate, assume that the $1,000 bond in the preceding example pays interest of 10% annually and that the market rate of interest is also 10%. In addition, assume that the bond matures at the end of two years. The present value of the two interest payments of $100 ($1,000 × 10%) is $173.56, as shown in the time line at the left. It can be determined by using the present value table shown in Exhibit 3.

Instead of using present value of amount tables, such as Exhibit 3, separate present value tables are normally used for annuities. Exhibit 4 is a partial table of the *present value of an annuity of $1* at compound interest. It shows the present value of $1 to be received at the end of each period for various compound rates of interest. For example, the present

Interest payment $100   Interest payment $100

TODAY   END OF YEAR 1   END OF YEAR 2

$90.91 $100 x 0.90909

$82.65 $100 x 0.82645

$173.56

Present value of $100 interest payments to be received each year for 2 years (rounded to the nearest cent)

value of $100 to be received at the end of each of the next two years at 10% compound interest per period is $173.55 ($100 × 1.73554). This amount is the same amount that we computed previously, except for rounding.

Exhibit 4 Present Value of Annuity of $1 at Compound Interest

Periods	5%	5½%	6%	6½%	7%	10%	11%	12%	13%	14%
1	0.95238	0.94787	0.94340	0.93897	0.93458	0.90909	0.90090	0.89286	0.88496	0.87719
2	1.85941	1.84632	1.83339	1.82063	1.80802	1.73554	1.71252	1.69005	1.66810	1.64666
3	2.72325	2.69793	2.67301	2.64848	2.62432	2.48685	2.44371	2.40183	2.36115	2.32163
4	3.54595	3.50515	3.46511	3.42580	3.38721	3.16987	3.10245	3.03735	2.97447	2.91371
5	4.32948	4.27028	4.21236	4.15568	4.10020	3.79079	3.69590	3.60478	3.51723	3.43308
6	5.07569	4.99553	4.91732	4.84101	4.76654	4.35526	4.23054	4.11141	3.99755	3.88867
7	5.78637	5.68297	5.58238	5.48452	5.38929	4.86842	4.71220	4.56376	4.42261	4.28830
8	6.46321	6.33457	6.20979	6.08875	5.97130	5.33493	5.14612	4.96764	4.79677	4.63886
9	7.10782	6.95220	6.80169	6.65610	6.51523	5.75902	5.53705	5.32825	5.13166	4.94637
10	7.72174	7.53763	7.36009	7.18883	7.02358	6.14457	5.88923	5.65022	5.42624	5.21612

What is the present value of a $10,000, 7%, 5-year bond that pays interest annually, assuming a market rate of interest of 7%?

$10,000 [($10,000 × 0.71299) + ($700 × 4.10020)]

As we stated earlier, the amount buyers are willing to pay for a bond is the sum of the present value of the face value and the periodic interest payments, calculated by using the market rate of interest. In our example, this calculation is as follows:

Present value of face value of $1,000 due in 2 years at 10% compounded annually: $1,000 × 0.82645 (present value factor of $1 for 2 periods at 10%)	$ 826.45
Present value of 2 annual interest payments of $100 at 10% compounded annually: $100 × 1.73554 (present value of annuity of $1 for 2 periods at 10%)	173.55
Total present value of bonds	$1,000.00

In this example, the market rate and the contract rate of interest are the same. Thus, the present value is the same as the face value.

Accounting for Bonds Payable

objective 4

Journalize entries for bonds payable.

In the preceding section, we described and illustrated how present value concepts are used in determining how much buyers are willing to pay for bonds. In this section, we describe and illustrate how corporations record the issuance of bonds and the payment of bond interest.

Bonds Issued at Face Amount

To illustrate the journal entries for issuing bonds, assume that on January 1, 2002, a corporation issues for cash $100,000 of 12%, five-year bonds, with interest of $6,000 payable *semiannually*. The market rate of interest at the time the bonds are issued is 12%. Since the contract rate and the market rate of interest are the same, the bonds will sell at their face amount. This amount is the sum of (1) the present value of the face amount of $100,000 to be repaid in five years and (2) the present value of ten *semiannual* interest payments of $6,000 each. This computation and a time line are shown below.

Present value of face amount of $100,000 due in 5 years,
    at 12% compounded semiannually: $100,000 × 0.55840
    (present value of $1 for 10 periods at 6%) .... $ 55,840
Present value of 10 semiannual interest payments of $6,000,
    at 12% compounded semiannually: $6,000 × 7.36009
    (present value of annuity of $1 for 10 periods at 6%) 44,160*

Total present value of bonds $100,000

*Because the present-value tables are rounded to five decimal places, minor rounding differences may appear in the illustrations.

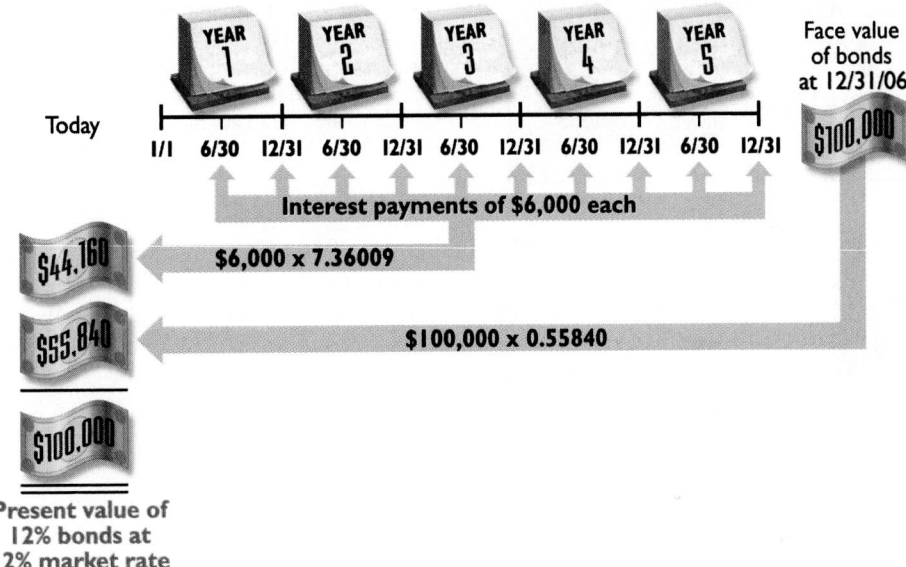

Present value of
12% bonds at
12% market rate

The following entry records the issuing of the $100,000 bonds at their face amount:

2002 Jan.	1	Cash	100 0 0 0 00		
		Bonds Payable		100 0 0 0 00	
		Issued $100,000 bonds payable at			
		face amount.			

Every six months after the bonds have been issued, interest payments of $6,000 are made. The first interest payment is recorded as shown below.

June	30	Interest Expense	6 0 0 0 00		
		Cash		6 0 0 0 00	
		Paid six months' interest on bonds.			

At the maturity date, the payment of the principal of $100,000 is recorded as follows:

2006 Dec.	31	Bonds Payable	100 0 0 0 00	
		Cash		100 0 0 0 00
		Paid bond principal at maturity		
		date.		

Bonds Issued at a Discount

What if the market rate of interest is higher than the contract rate of interest? If the market rate of interest is 13% and the contract rate is 12% on the five-year, $100,000 bonds, the bonds will sell at a discount. The present value of these bonds is calculated as follows:

> **Bonds will sell at a discount when the market rate of interest is higher than the contract rate.**

Present value of face amount of $100,000 due in 5 years, at 13% compounded semiannually: $100,000 × 0.53273 (present value of $1 for 10 periods at 6½%)	$53,273
Present value of 10 semiannual interest payments of $6,000, at 13% compounded semiannually: $6,000 × 7.18883 (present value of an annuity of $1 for 10 periods at 6½%)	43,133
Total present value of bonds	$96,406

The two present values that make up the total are both less than the related amounts in the preceding example. This is because the market rate of interest was 12% in the first example, while the market rate of interest is 13% in this example. The present value of a future amount becomes less and less as the interest rate used to compute the present value increases.

The entry to record the issuing of the $100,000 bonds at a discount is shown below.

What is the present value of a $100,000, 6%, 5-year bond paying semiannual interest if the market rate of interest is 10%?

$84,556 [($100,000 × 0.61391) + ($3,000 × 7.72174)]

2002 Jan.	1	Cash	96 4 0 6 00	
		Discount on Bonds Payable	3 5 9 4 00	
		Bonds Payable		100 0 0 0 00
		Issued $100,000 bonds at discount.		

The $3,594 discount may be viewed as the amount that is needed to entice investors to accept a contract rate of interest that is below the market rate. You may think of the discount as the market's way of adjusting a bond's contract rate of interest to the higher market rate of interest. Using this logic, generally accepted accounting principles require that bond discounts be amortized as interest expense over the life of the bond.

Amortizing a Bond Discount

There are two methods of amortizing a bond discount: (1) the **straight-line method** and (2) the effective interest rate method, often called the **interest method**. Both methods amortize the same total amount of discount over the life of the bonds. The interest method is required by generally accepted accounting principles. However, the straight-line method is acceptable if the results obtained do not materially differ from the results that would be obtained by using the interest method. Because the straight-line method illustrates the basic concept of amortizing discounts and is simpler, we will use it in this chapter. We illustrate the interest method in an appendix to this chapter.

The straight-line method of amortizing a bond discount provides for amortization in equal periodic amounts. Applying this method to the preceding example yields amortization of ¹⁄₁₀ of $3,594, or $359.40, each half year. The amount of the interest expense on the bonds is the same, $6,359.40 ($6,000 + $359.40) for each half year. The entry to record the first interest payment and the amortization of the related discount is shown below.

2002 June	30	Interest Expense	6 3 5 9 40		
		Discount on Bonds Payable		3 5 9 40	
		Cash			6 0 0 0 00
		Paid semiannual interest and			
		amortized ¹⁄₁₀ of bond discount.			

Bonds Issued at a Premium

If the market rate of interest is 11% and the contract rate is 12% on the five-year, $100,000 bonds, the bonds will sell at a premium. The present value of these bonds is computed as follows:

> **Bonds will sell at a premium when the market rate of interest is less than the contract rate.**

Present value of face amount of $100,000 due in 5 years, at 11% compounded semiannually: $100,000 × 0.58543 (present value of $1 for 10 periods at 5½%)	$ 58,543
Present value of 10 semiannual interest payments of $6,000, at 11% compounded semiannually: $6,000 × 7.53763 (present value of an annuity of $1 for 10 periods at 5½%)	45,226
Total present value of bonds	$103,769

The entry to record the issuing of the bonds is as follows:

2002 Jan.	1	Cash	103 7 6 9 00		
		Bonds Payable		100 0 0 0 00	
		Premium on Bonds Payable		3 7 6 9 00	
		Issued $100,000 bonds at a			
		premium.			

Amortizing a Bond Premium

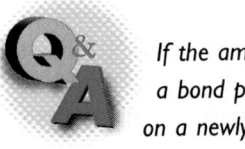

The amortization of bond premiums is basically the same as that for bond discounts, except that interest expense is decreased. In the above example, the straight-line method yields amortization of ¹⁄₁₀ of $3,769, or $376.90, each half year. The entry to record the first interest payment and the amortization of the related premium is as follows:

2002 June	30	Interest Expense	5 6 2 3 10		
		Premium on Bonds Payable	3 7 6 90		
		Cash			6 0 0 0 00
		Paid semiannual interest and			
		amortized ¹⁄₁₀ of bond premium.			

Zero-Coupon Bonds

Some corporations issue bonds that provide for only the payment of the face amount at the maturity date. Such bonds are called **zero-coupon bonds**. Because they do not provide for interest payments, these bonds sell at a large discount. For example, **Hewlett-Packard's** zero-coupon bonds maturing in 2017 were selling for 55 on November 16, 2000.

 Some bonds with high contract rates, as well as some zero-coupon bonds, are issued by weak companies. Because such bonds are high-risk bonds, they are called **junk bonds**.

The issuing price of zero-coupon bonds is the present value of their face amount. To illustrate, if the market rate of interest is 13%, the present value of $100,000 zero-coupon, five-year bonds is calculated as follows:

Present value of $100,000 due in 5 years, at 13%
  compounded semiannually: $100,000 × 0.53273
  (present value of $1 for 10 periods at 6½%) $53,273

The accounting for zero-coupon bonds is similar to that for interest-bearing bonds that have been sold at a discount. The discount is amortized as interest expense over the life of the bonds. The entry to record the issuing of the bonds is as follows:

2002						
Jan.	1	Cash	53 2 7 3 00	
		Discount on Bonds Payable	46 7 2 7 00	
		Bonds Payable		100 0 0 0 00
		Issued $100,000 zero-coupon		
		bonds.		

Bond Sinking Funds

A bond indenture may restrict dividend payments to stockholders as a means of increasing the likelihood that the bonds will be paid at maturity. In addition to or instead of this restriction, the bond indenture may require that funds for the payment of the face value of the bonds at maturity be set aside over the life of the bond issue. The amounts set aside are kept separate from other assets in a special fund called a sinking fund.

When cash is transferred to the sinking fund, it is recorded in an account called *Sinking Fund Cash*. When investments are purchased with the sinking fund cash, they are recorded in an account called *Sinking Fund Investments*. As income (interest or dividends) is received, it is recorded in an account called *Sinking Fund Revenue*.

Sinking fund revenue represents earnings of the corporation and is reported in the income statement as Other Income. The cash and the securities making up the sinking fund are reported in the balance sheet as Investments, immediately below the Current Assets section.

Bond Redemption

objective 6

Journalize entries for bond redemptions.

Indo Rayon issued 5-year, 10% bonds, callable after 3 years.

A corporation may call or redeem bonds before they mature. This is often done if the market rate of interest declines significantly after the bonds have been issued. In this situation, the corporation may sell new bonds at a lower interest rate and use the funds to redeem the original bond issue. The corporation can thus save on future interest expenses.

A corporation often issues callable bonds to protect itself against significant declines in future interest rates. However, callable bonds are more risky for investors, who may not be able to replace the called bonds with investments paying an equal amount of interest.

Callable bonds can be redeemed by the issuing corporation within the period of time and at the price stated in the bond indenture. Normally, the call price is above the face value. A corporation may also redeem its bonds by purchasing them on the open market.

A corporation usually redeems its bonds at a price different from that of the carrying amount (or book value) of the bonds. The **carrying amount** of bonds payable is the balance of the bonds payable account (face amount of the bonds) less any unamortized discount or plus any unamortized premium. If the price paid for redemption is below the bond carrying amount, the difference in these two amounts is recorded as a gain. If the price paid for the redemption is above the carrying amount, a loss is recorded. Gains and losses on the redemption of bonds are reported as an extraordinary item on the income statement.

To illustrate, assume that on June 30 a corporation has a bond issue of $100,000 outstanding, on which there is an unamortized premium of $4,000. Assuming that the corporation purchases one-fourth ($25,000) of the bonds for $24,000 on June 30, the entry to record the redemption is as follows:

2002					
June	30	Bonds Payable	25 0 0 0 00		
		Premium on Bonds Payable	1 0 0 0 00		
		Cash		24 0 0 0 00	
		Gain on Redemption of Bonds		2 0 0 0 00	
		Redeemed $25,000 bonds for			
		$24,000.			

In the preceding entry, only a portion of the premium relating to the redeemed bonds is written off. The difference between the carrying amount of the bonds purchased, $26,000 ($25,000 + $1,000), and the price paid for the redemption, $24,000, is recorded as a gain.

If the corporation calls the entire bond issue for $105,000 on June 30, the entry to record the redemption is as follows:

Q&A *A $250,000 bond issue on which there is an unamortized discount of $20,000 is redeemed for $235,000. What is the gain or loss on the redemption of the bonds?*

$5,000 loss ($250,000 − $20,000 − $235,000)

2002					
June	30	Bonds Payable	100 0 0 0 00		
		Premium on Bonds Payable	4 0 0 0 00		
		Loss on Redemption of Bonds	1 0 0 0 00		
		Cash		105 0 0 0 00	
		Redeemed $100,000 bonds for			
		$105,000.			

Investments in Bonds

objective 7

Journalize entries for the purchase, interest, discount and premium amortization, and sale of bond investments.

Loews' 3⅛% bonds maturing in 2007 were listed as selling for 92¾ on September 7, 2000.

Throughout this chapter, we have discussed bonds and the related transactions of the issuing corporation (the debtor). However, these transactions also affect investors. In this section, we discuss the accounting for bonds from the point of view of investors.

Accounting for Bond Investments—Purchase, Interest, and Amortization

Bonds may be purchased either directly from the issuing corporation or through an organized bond exchange. Bond exchanges publish daily bond quotations. These quotations normally include the bond interest rate, maturity date, volume of sales, and the high, low, and closing prices for each corporation's bonds traded during the day. Prices for bonds are quoted as a percentage of the face amount. Thus, the price of a $1,000 bond quoted at 99½ would be $995, while the price of a bond quoted at 104¼ would be $1,042.50.

As with other assets, the cost of a bond investment includes all costs related to the purchase. For example, for bonds purchased through an exchange, the amount paid as a broker's commission should be included as part of the cost of the investment.

When bonds are purchased between interest dates, the buyer normally pays the seller the interest accrued from the last interest payment date to the date of purchase. The amount of the interest paid is normally debited to *Interest Revenue*, since it is an offset against the amount that will be received at the next interest date.

To illustrate, assume that an investor purchases a $1,000 bond at 102 plus a brokerage fee of $5.30 and accrued interest of $10.20. The investor records the transaction as follows:

2002 Apr.	2	Investment in Lewis Co. Bonds		1 0 2 5 30		
		Interest Revenue		1 0 20		
		Cash			1 0 3 5 50

A premium or discount on a bond investment is recorded in the investment account and is amortized over the remaining life of the bonds.

The cost of the bond is recorded in a single investment account. The face amount of the bond and the premium (or discount) are normally not recorded in separate accounts. This is different from the accounting for bonds payable. Separate premium and discount accounts are usually not used by investors, because they usually do not hold bond investments until the bonds mature.

When bonds held as long-term investments are purchased at a price other than the face amount, the premium or discount should be amortized over the remaining life of the bonds. The amortization of premiums and discounts affects the investment and interest accounts as shown below.

Premium Amortization:			*Discount Amortization:*		
Interest Revenue	XXX		Investment in Bonds	XXX	
Investment in Bonds		XXX	Interest Revenue		XXX

The amount of the amortization can be determined by using either the straight-line or interest methods. Unlike bonds payable, the amortization of premiums and discounts on bond investments is usually recorded at the end of the period, rather than when interest is received.

To illustrate the accounting for bond investments, assume that on July 1, 2002, Crenshaw Inc. purchases $50,000 of 8% bonds of Deitz Corporation, due in 8¾ years. Crenshaw Inc. purchases the bonds directly from Deitz Corporation to yield an effective interest rate of 11%. The purchase price is $41,706 plus interest of $1,000 ($50,000 × 8% × 3/12) accrued from April 1, 2002, the date of the last semiannual interest payment. Entries in the accounts of Crenshaw Inc. at the time of purchase and for the remainder of the fiscal period ending December 31, 2002, are as follows:

2002					
July	1	Investment in Deitz Corp. Bonds		41 7 0 6 00	
		Interest Revenue		1 0 0 0 00	
		Cash			42 7 0 6 00
		Purchased investment in bonds,			
		plus accrued interest:			
		Cost of $50,000 of Deitz			
		Corp. bonds $41,706			
		Interest accrued ($50,000			
		× 8% × 3/12) 1,000			
		Total $42,706			
Oct.	1	Cash		2 0 0 0 00	
		Interest Revenue			2 0 0 0 00
		Received semiannual interest for			
		April 1 to October 1 ($50,000 ×			
		8% × 6/12).			
Dec.	31	Interest Receivable		1 0 0 0 00	
		Interest Revenue			1 0 0 0 00
		Adjusting entry for interest			
		accrued from October 1 to			
		December 31 ($50,000 ×			
		8% × 3/12).			
	31	Investment in Deitz Corp. Bonds		4 7 4 00	
		Interest Revenue			4 7 4 00
		Adjusting entry for amortization of			
		discount for July 1 to December 31:			
		Face value of bonds $50,000			
		Cost of bond			
		investment 41,706			
		Discount on bond			
		investment $ 8,294			
		Number of months to			
		maturity (8¾ years			
		× 12) 105 months			
		Monthly amortization			
		($8,294/105 months,			
		rounded to nearest			
		dollar) $79 per mo.			
		Amortization for 6			
		months ($79 × 6) $474			

The effect of these entries on the interest revenue account is shown below.

Interest Revenue

July 1	1,000	Oct. 1	2,000		
		Dec. 31	1,000		
		31	474		
	Bal. 2,474		*3,474*		

Accounting for Bond Investments—Sale

Many long-term investments in bonds are sold before their maturity date. When this occurs, the seller receives the sales price (less commissions and other selling costs) plus any accrued interest since the last interest payment date. Before recording the cash proceeds, the seller should amortize any discount or premium for the current period up to the date of sale. Any gain or loss on the sale is then recorded when the cash proceeds are recorded. Such gains and losses are normally reported in the Other Income section of the income statement.

To illustrate, assume that the Deitz Corporation bonds in the preceding example are sold for $47,350 plus accrued interest on June 30, 2009. The *carrying amount* of the bonds (cost plus amortized discount) as of January 1, 2009 (78 months after their purchase) is $47,868 [$41,706 + ($79 per month × 78 months)]. The entries to amortize the discount for the current year and to record the sale of the bonds are as follows:

2009					
June	30	Investment in Deitz Corp. Bonds		4 7 4 00	
		Interest Revenue			4 7 4 00
		Amortized discount for current			
		year ($79 × 6 months).			
	30	Cash		48 3 5 0 00	
		Loss on Sale of Investments		9 9 2 00	
		Interest Revenue			1 0 0 0 00
		Investment in Deitz Corp. Bonds			48 3 4 2 00
		Received interest and proceeds			
		from sale of bonds.			
		Interest for April 1 to June 30 =			
		$50,000 × 8% × $^3/_{12}$ = $1,000			
		Carrying amount of			
		bonds on Jan. 1, 2009 $47,868			
		Discount amortized,			
		Jan. 1 to June 30, 2009 474			
		Carrying amount of			
		bonds on June 30, 2009 $48,342			
		Proceeds of sale 47,350			
		Loss on sale $ 992			

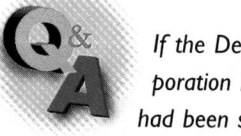

If the Deitz Corporation bonds had been sold on September 30 instead of June 30, what would have been the amount of the loss?

$1,229 {$47,350 − [$48,342 + ($79 × 3 months)]}

Corporation Balance Sheet

objective 8

Prepare a corporation balance sheet.

In previous chapters, we illustrated the income statement and retained earnings statement for a corporation. The consolidated balance sheet in Exhibit 5 illustrates the presentation of many of the items discussed in this and preceding chapters. These items include bond sinking funds, investments in bonds, goodwill, deferred income taxes, bonds payable and unamortized discount, and minority interest in subsidiaries.

Exhibit 5 Balance Sheet of a Corporation

Escoe Corporation and Subsidiaries
Consolidated Balance Sheet
December 31, 2003

Assets

Current assets:

Cash and cash equivalents			$ 407,500
Accounts and notes receivable		$ 722,000	
Less allowance for doubtful receivables		37,000	685,000
Inventories, at lower of cost (first-in, first-out) or market			917,500
Prepaid expenses			70,000
Total current assets			$2,080,000

Investments:

Bond sinking fund (market value, $473,000)			$ 422,500
Investment in bonds of Dalton Company			
(market value, $231,000)			240,000
Total investments			662,500

	Cost	Accumulated Depreciation	Book Value	
Property, plant, and equipment (depreciated by the straight-line method):				
Land	$ 250,000	—	$ 250,000	
Buildings	920,000	$ 379,955	540,045	
Machinery and equipment	2,764,400	766,200	1,998,200	
Total property, plant, and equipment	$3,934,400	$1,146,155		2,788,245
Intangible assets:				
Goodwill			$ 300,000	
Organization costs			50,000	
Total intangible assets				350,000
Total assets				$5,880,745

Liabilities

Current liabilities:

Accounts payable			$ 508,810
Income tax payable			120,500
Dividends payable			94,000
Accrued liabilities			81,400
Deferred income tax payable			10,000
Total current liabilities			$ 814,710

Long-term liabilities:

Debenture 8% bonds payable, due December 31, 2018			
(market value, $950,000)		$1,000,000	
Less unamortized discount		60,000	$ 940,000
Minority interest in subsidiaries			115,000
Total long-term liabilities			1,055,000

Deferred credits:

Deferred income tax payable			85,500
Total liabilities			$1,955,210

Stockholders' Equity

Paid-in capital:

Common stock, $20 par (250,000 shares authorized,			
100,000 shares issued)		$2,000,000	
Excess of issue price over par		320,000	
Total paid-in capital			$2,320,000
Retained earnings			1,605,535
Total stockholders' equity			3,925,535
Total liabilities and stockholders' equity			$5,880,745

Balance Sheet Presentation of Bonds Payable

In Exhibit 5, Escoe Corporation's bonds payable are reported as long-term liabilities. If there were two or more bond issues, the details of each would be reported on the balance sheet or in a supporting schedule or note. Separate accounts are normally maintained for each bond issue.

When the balance sheet date is within one year of the maturity date of the bonds, the bonds may be classified as a current liability. This would be the case if the bonds are to be paid out of current assets. If the bonds are to be paid from a sinking fund or if they are to be refinanced with another bond issue, they should remain in the noncurrent category. In this case, the details of the retirement of the bonds are normally disclosed in a note to the financial statements.

The balance in Escoe's discount on bonds payable account is reported as a *deduction* from the bonds payable. Conversely, the balance in a bond premium account would be reported as an *addition* to the related bonds payable. Either on the face of the financial statements or in accompanying notes, a description of the bonds (terms, due date, and effective interest rate) and other relevant information such as sinking fund requirements should be disclosed.[4] Finally, the market (fair) value of the bonds payable should also be disclosed.

Balance Sheet Presentation of Bond Investments

Investments in bonds or other debt securities that management intends to hold to their maturity are called **held-to-maturity securities**. Such securities are classified as long-term investments under the caption Investments. These investments are reported at their cost less any amortized premium or plus any amortized discount. In addition, the market (fair) value of the bond investments should be disclosed, either on the face of the balance sheet or in an accompanying note.

FINANCIAL ANALYSIS AND INTERPRETATION

objective 9

Compute and interpret the number of times interest charges are earned.

Some corporations, such as railroads and public utilities, have a high ratio of debt to stockholders' equity. For such corporations, analysts often assess the relative risk of the debtholders in terms of the **number of times the interest charges are earned** during the year. The higher the ratio, the greater the chance that interest payments will continue to be made if earnings decrease.[5]

The amount available to make interest payments is not affected by taxes on income. This is because interest is deductible in determining taxable income. To illustrate, the following data were taken from the 1999 annual report of **Briggs & Stratton Corporation**:

Interest expense $17,024,000
Income before income tax $169,771,000

The number of times interest charges are earned, 10.97, is calculated below.

$$\text{Number of times interest charges earned} = \frac{\text{Income before income tax} + \text{Interest expense}}{\text{Interest expense}}$$

---

[4] *Statement of Financial Accounting Standards No. 129*, "Disclosure Information About Capital Structure," Financial Accounting Standards Board (Norwalk, Connecticut: 1997).

[5] A similar analysis can also be applied to dividends on preferred stock. In such cases, net income would be divided by the amount of preferred dividends to yield the number of times preferred dividends were earned. This measure gives an indication of the relative assurance of continued dividend payments to preferred stockholders.

$$\text{Number of times interest charges earned} = \frac{\$169,771,000 + \$17,024,000}{\$17,024,000} = 10.97$$

The number of times interest charges are earned indicates that the debtholders of Briggs & Stratton have adequate protection against a potential drop in earnings jeopardizing their receipt of interest payments. However, a final assessment should include a review of trends of past years and a comparison with industry averages.

ENCORE

Let's Dance—A Bond with a Tune

How would you like to tune into some of the royalties from David Bowie's hit song, *Let's Dance*? The British rock star has offered bonds backed by future royalties from his hit songs and albums recorded prior to 1990. In addition to *Let's Dance*, other songs include *Jean Genie, A Space Oddity, Changes, Diamond Dogs*, and *Rebel*.

Bowie's bonds, which have an average maturity of 10 years, pay 7.9% annual interest. Such asset-backed bonds have grown in popularity. However, this is the first time that a popular artist has made use of future royalties as asset backing. The Bowie Bonds, which are officially called Class-A royalty-backed securities, were rated AAA—the highest rating—by Moody's Investors Service.

Bowie is one of the most financially savvy rock stars in the world, with a well-chosen art collection and an appreciation for market trends. Bowie's principal residence is a $3.4 million, 640-acre estate in County Wicklow, Ireland, a noted tax haven. He lives there with his second wife, the supermodel and actress Iman. Still, Bowie's business manager said that when he approached him with the bond idea, "he [Bowie] kind of looked at me cross-eyed and said, 'What?'"

Potential investors were reassured by the fact that Bowie never sells fewer than a million albums a year. At the time of the offering, Bowie's album, "Earthling," was near the top of the European charts. In addition, the month before the offering, he performed for a sold-out concert at New York's Madison Square Garden.

Prudential Insurance Co. isn't kidding when it says you can own a piece of the *rock*. In a private placement, Prudential purchased all of David Bowie's $55 million bonds for its general investment fund, in which the money of life insurance policyholders is invested.

In addition to Bowie, other musicians who have issued royalty-backed bonds include James Brown and the heavy-metal band Iron Maiden. The Iron Maiden bonds were successfully sold for $30 million. ■

APPENDIX—EFFECTIVE INTEREST RATE METHOD OF AMORTIZATION

The effective interest rate method of amortizing discounts and premiums provides for a constant rate of interest on the carrying amount of the bonds at the beginning of each period. This is in contrast to the straight-line method, which provides for a constant amount of interest expense.

The interest rate used in the interest method of amortization is the market rate on the date the bonds are issued. The carrying amount of the bonds to which the interest rate is applied is the face amount of the bonds minus any unamortized discount or plus any unamortized premium. Under the interest method, the interest expense to be reported on the income statement is computed by multiplying the effective interest rate by the carrying amount of the bonds. The difference between the interest expense computed in this way and the periodic interest payment is the amount of discount or premium to be amortized for the period.

Amortization of Discount by the Interest Method

To illustrate the interest method for amortizing bond discounts, we assume the following data from the chapter illustration of issuing $100,000 bonds at a discount:

Face value of 12%, 5-year bonds, interest compounded semiannually	$100,000
Present value of bonds at effective (market) rate of interest of 13%	96,406
Discount on bonds payable	$ 3,594

Applying the interest method to these data yields the amortization table in Exhibit 6. You should note the following items in this table:

1. The interest paid (Column A) remains constant at 6% of $100,000, the face amount of the bonds.
2. The interest expense (Column B) is computed at 6½% of the bond carrying amount at the beginning of each period. This results in an increasing interest expense each period.
3. The excess of the interest expense over the interest payment of $6,000 is the amount of discount to be amortized (Column C).
4. The unamortized discount (Column D) decreases from the initial balance, $3,594, to a zero balance at the maturity date of the bonds.
5. The carrying amount (Column E) increases from $96,406, the amount received for the bonds, to $100,000 at maturity.

Exhibit 6 Amortization of Discount on Bonds Payable

Interest Payment	A Interest Paid (6% of Face Amount)	B Interest Expense (6½% of Bond Carrying Amount)	C Discount Amortization (B − A)	D Unamortized Discount (D − C)	E Bond Carrying Amount ($100,000 − D)
				$3,594	$ 96,406
1	$6,000	$6,266 (6½% of $96,406)	$266	3,328	96,672
2	6,000	6,284 (6½% of $96,672)	284	3,044	96,956
3	6,000	6,302 (6½% of $96,956)	302	2,742	97,258
4	6,000	6,322 (6½% of $97,258)	322	2,420	97,580
5	6,000	6,343 (6½% of $97,580)	343	2,077	97,923
6	6,000	6,365 (6½% of $97,923)	365	1,712	98,288
7	6,000	6,389 (6½% of $98,288)	389	1,323	98,677
8	6,000	6,414 (6½% of $98,677)	414	909	99,091
9	6,000	6,441 (6½% of $99,091)	441	468	99,532
10	6,000	6,470 (6½% of $99,532)	468*	—	100,000

*Cannot exceed unamortized discount.

The entry to record the first interest payment on June 30, 2002, and the related discount amortization is as follows:

	2002 June	30	Interest Expense			6 2 6 6 00		
			Discount on Bonds Payable				2 6 6 00	
			Cash				6 0 0 0 00	
			Paid semiannual interest and					
			amortized bond discount for					
			one-half year.					

If the amortization is recorded only at the end of the year, the amount of the discount amortized on December 31 would be $550. This is the sum of the first two semiannual amortization amounts ($266 and $284) from Exhibit 6.

Amortization of Premium by the Interest Method

To illustrate the interest method for amortizing bond premiums, we assume the following data from the chapter illustration of issuing $100,000 bonds at a premium:

Present value of bonds at effective (market) rate of interest of 11% $103,769

Face value of 12%, 5-year bonds, interest compounded semiannually   100,000

Premium on bonds payable $ 3,769

Using the interest method to amortize the above premium yields the amortization table in Exhibit 7.

Exhibit 7 Amortization of Premium on Bonds Payable

Interest Payment	A Interest Paid (6% of Face Amount)	B Interest Expense (5½% of Bond Carrying Amount)	C Premium Amortization (A − B)	D Unamortized Premium (D − C)	E Bond Carrying Amount ($100,000 + D)
				$3,769	$103,769
1	$6,000	$5,707 (5½% of $103,769)	$293	3,476	103,476
2	6,000	5,691 (5½% of $103,476)	309	3,167	103,167
3	6,000	5,674 (5½% of $103,167)	326	2,841	102,841
4	6,000	5,656 (5½% of $102,841)	344	2,497	102,497
5	6,000	5,637 (5½% of $102,497)	363	2,134	102,134
6	6,000	5,617 (5½% of $102,134)	383	1,751	101,751
7	6,000	5,596 (5½% of $101,751)	404	1,347	101,347
8	6,000	5,574 (5½% of $101,347)	426	921	100,921
9	6,000	5,551 (5½% of $100,921)	449	472	100,472
10	6,000	5,526 (5½% of $100,472)	472*	—	100,000

*Cannot exceed unamortized premium.

You should note the following items in this table:

1. The interest paid (Column A) remains constant at 6% of $100,000, the face amount of the bonds.
2. The interest expense (Column B) is computed at 5½% of the bond carrying amount at the beginning of each period. This results in a decreasing interest expense each period.
3. The excess of the periodic interest payment of $6,000 over the interest expense is the amount of premium to be amortized (Column C).

4. The unamortized premium (Column D) decreases from the initial balance, $3,769, to a zero balance at the maturity date of the bonds.
5. The carrying amount (Column E) decreases from $103,769, the amount received for the bonds, to $100,000 at maturity.

The entry to record the first interest payment on June 30, 2002, and the related premium amortization is as follows:

2002						
June	30	Interest Expense	5 7 0 7 00	
		Premium on Bonds Payable	2 9 3 00	
		Cash		6 0 0 0 00
		Paid semiannual interest and		
		amortized bond premium for		
		one-half year.		

If the amortization is recorded only at the end of the year, the amount of the premium amortized on December 31, 2002, would be $602. This is the sum of the first two semiannual amortization amounts ($293 and $309) from Exhibit 7.

KEY POINTS

1 Compute the potential impact of long-term borrowing on the earnings per share of a corporation.
Three alternative plans for financing a corporation by issuing common stock, preferred stock, or bonds are illustrated in Exhibits 1 and 2. The effects of alternative financing on the earnings per share vary significantly, depending upon the level of earnings.

2 Describe the characteristics of bonds.
The characteristics of bonds depend upon the type of bonds issued by a corporation. Bonds that may be issued include term bonds, serial bonds, convertible bonds, callable bonds, and debenture bonds.

3 Compute the present value of bonds payable.
The concept of present value is based on the time value of money. That is, an amount of cash to be received at some date in the future is worth less than

the same amount of cash held today. For example, if $100 cash today can be invested to earn 10% per year, the $100 today is referred to as the present value amount that is equal to $110 to be received a year from today.

A price that a buyer is willing to pay for a bond is the sum of (1) the present value of the face amount of the bonds at the maturity date and (2) the present value of the periodic interest payments.

4 Journalize entries for bonds payable.
The journal entry for issuing bonds payable debits Cash for the proceeds received and credits Bonds Payable for the face amount of the bonds. Any difference between the face amount of the bonds and the proceeds is debited to Discount on Bonds Payable or credited to Premium on Bonds Payable.

A discount or premium on bonds payable is amortized to interest expense over the life of

the bonds. The entry to amortize a discount debits Interest Expense and credits Discount on Bonds Payable. The entry to amortize a premium debits Premium on Bonds Payable and credits Interest Expense.

5 Describe bond sinking funds.
A bond indenture may require that funds for the payment of the bonds at maturity be set aside over the life of the bonds. The amounts set aside are kept separate from other assets in a special fund called a sinking fund. A sinking fund is reported as an investment on the balance sheet. Income from a sinking fund is reported as Other Income on the income statement.

6 Journalize entries for bond redemptions.
When a corporation redeems bonds, Bonds Payable is debited for the face amount of the bonds, the premium (discount) on bonds account is debited (credited) for

its balance, Cash is credited, and any gain or loss on the redemption is recorded.

7 Journalize entries for the purchase, interest, discount and premium amortization, and sale of bond investments.

A long-term investment in bonds is recorded by debiting Investment in Bonds. When bonds are purchased between interest dates, the amount of the interest paid should be debited to Interest Revenue. Any discount or premium on bond investments should be amortized, using the straight-line or effective interest rate methods. The amortization of a discount is recorded by debiting Investment in Bonds and crediting Interest Revenue. The amortization of a premium is recorded by debiting Interest Revenue and crediting Investment in Bonds.

When bonds held as long-term investments are sold, any discount or premium for the current period should first be amortized. Cash is then debited for the proceeds of the sale, Investment in Bonds is credited for its balance, and any gain or loss is recorded.

8 Prepare a corporation balance sheet.

The corporation balance sheet may include bond sinking funds, investments in bonds, goodwill, deferred income taxes, bonds payable and unamortized premium or discount, and minority interest in subsidiaries.

Bonds payable are usually reported as long-term liabilities.

A discount on bonds should be reported as a deduction from the related bonds payable. A premium on bonds should be reported as an addition to the related bonds payable. Investments in bonds that are held-to-maturity securities are reported as investments at cost less any amortized premium or plus any amortized discount.

9 Compute and interpret the number of times interest charges are earned.

The number of times interest charges are earned during the year is a measure of the risk that interest payments to debtholders will continue to be made if earnings decrease. It is computed by dividing income before income tax plus interest expense by interest expense.

ILLUSTRATIVE PROBLEM

The fiscal year of Russell Inc., a manufacturer of acoustical supplies, ends December 31. Selected transactions for the period 2002 through 2009, involving bonds payable issued by Russell Inc., are as follows:

2002
June 30. Issued $2,000,000 of 25-year, 7% callable bonds dated June 30, 2002, for cash of $1,920,000. Interest is payable semiannually on June 30 and December 31.
Dec. 31. Paid the semiannual interest on the bonds.
    31. Recorded straight-line amortization of $1,600 of discount on the bonds.
    31. Closed the interest expense account.

2003
June 30. Paid the semiannual interest on the bonds.
Dec. 31. Paid the semiannual interest on the bonds.
    31. Recorded straight-line amortization of $3,200 of discount on the bonds.
    31. Closed the interest expense account.

2009
June 30. Recorded the redemption of the bonds, which were called at 101½. The balance in the bond discount account is $57,600 after the payment of interest and amortization of discount have been recorded. (Record the redemption only.)

Instructions

1. Journalize entries to record the preceding transactions.
2. Determine the amount of interest expense for 2002 and 2003.
3. Estimate the effective annual interest rate by dividing the interest expense for 2002 by the bond carrying amount at the time of issuance and multiplying by 2.
4. Determine the carrying amount of the bonds as of December 31, 2003.

Solution

1.

2002 June	30	Cash		1,920 0 0 0 00	
		Discount on Bonds Payable		80 0 0 0 00	
		Bonds Payable			2,000 0 0 0 00
Dec.	31	Interest Expense		70 0 0 0 00	
		Cash			70 0 0 0 00
	31	Interest Expense		1 6 0 0 00	
		Discount on Bonds Payable			1 6 0 0 00
	31	Income Summary		71 6 0 0 00	
		Interest Expense			71 6 0 0 00
2003 June	30	Interest Expense		70 0 0 0 00	
		Cash			70 0 0 0 00
Dec.	31	Interest Expense		70 0 0 0 00	
		Cash			70 0 0 0 00
	31	Interest Expense		3 2 0 0 00	
		Discount on Bonds Payable			3 2 0 0 00
	31	Income Summary		143 2 0 0 00	
		Interest Expense			143 2 0 0 00
2009 June	30	Bonds Payable		2,000 0 0 0 00	
		Loss on Redemption of Bonds Payable		87 6 0 0 00	
		Discount on Bonds Payable			57 6 0 0 00
		Cash			2,030 0 0 0 00

2. a. 2002—$71,600
   b. 2003—$143,200

3. $71,600 ÷ $1,920,000 = 3.73% rate for six months of a year
   3.73% × 2 = 7.46% annual rate

4.
Initial carrying amount of bonds	$1,920,000
Discount amortized on December 31, 2002	1,600
Discount amortized on December 31, 2003	3,200
Carrying amount of bonds, December 31, 2003	$1,924,800

SELF-EXAMINATION QUESTIONS   Answers at End of Chapter

Matching

Match each of the following statements with its proper term. Some terms may not be used.

A. annuity

B. available-for-sale securities

___ 1. A form of an interest-bearing note used by corporations to borrow on a long-term basis.

___ 2. The contract between a corporation issuing bonds and the bondholders.

C. bond

D. bond fund

E. bond indenture

F. carrying amount

G. contract rate

H. discount

I. dividend yield

J. effective interest rate method

K. effective rate of interest

L. future value

M. held-to-maturity securities

N. number of times interest charges earned

O. premium

P. present value

Q. present value of an annuity

R. sinking fund

___ 3. The periodic interest to be paid on the bonds that is identified in the bond indenture; expressed as a percentage of the face amount of the bond.

___ 4. A series of equal cash flows at fixed intervals.

___ 5. The sum of the present values of a series of equal cash flows to be received at fixed intervals.

___ 6. The estimated worth today of an amount of cash to be received (or paid) in the future.

___ 7. The estimated worth in the future of an amount of cash on hand today invested at a fixed rate of interest.

___ 8. The excess of the face amount of bonds over their issue price.

___ 9. The excess of the issue price of bonds over their face amount.

___ 10. A fund in which cash or assets are set aside for the purpose of paying the face amount of the bonds at maturity.

___ 11. The balance of the bonds payable account (face amount of the bonds) less any unamortized discount or plus any unamortized premium.

___ 12. Investments in bonds or other debt securities that management intends to hold to their maturity.

___ 13. A ratio that measures the risk that interest payments to debtholders will continue to be made if earnings decrease.

___ 14. The market rate of interest at the time bonds are issued.

Multiple Choice

1. If a corporation plans to issue $1,000,000 of 12% bonds at a time when the market rate for similar bonds is 10%, the bonds can be expected to sell at:
   A. their face amount
   B. a premium
   C. a discount
   D. a price below their face amount

2. If the bonds payable account has a balance of $500,000 and the discount on bonds payable account has a balance of $40,000, what is the carrying amount of the bonds?
   A. $460,000   C. $540,000
   B. $500,000   D. $580,000

3. The cash and securities that make up the sinking fund established for the payment of bonds at maturity are classified on the balance sheet as:

   A. current assets   C. long-term liabilities
   B. investments   D. current liabilities

4. If a firm purchases $100,000 of bonds of X Company at 101 plus accrued interest of $2,000 and pays broker's commissions of $50, the amount debited to Investment in X Company Bonds would be:
   A. $100,000   C. $103,000
   B. $101,050   D. $103,050

5. The balance in the discount on bonds payable account would usually be reported in the balance sheet in the:
   A. Current Assets section
   B. Current Liabilities section
   C. Long-Term Liabilities section
   D. Investments section

CLASS DISCUSSION QUESTIONS

1. Describe the two distinct obligations incurred by a corporation when issuing bonds.
2. Explain the meaning of each of the following terms as they relate to a bond issue: (a) convertible, (b) callable, and (c) debenture.
3. What is meant by the "time value of money"?
4. What has the higher present value: (a) $5,000 to be received at the end of two years, or (b) $2,500 to be received at the end of each of the next two years?

5. If you asked your broker to purchase for you a 6% bond when the market interest rate for such bonds was 7%, would you expect to pay more or less than the face amount for the bond? Explain.

6. A corporation issues $10,000,000 of 6% bonds to yield interest at the rate of 5%. (a) Was the amount of cash received from the sale of the bonds greater or less than $10,000,000? (b) Identify the following terms related to the bond issue: (1) face amount, (2) market or effective rate of interest, (3) contract rate of interest, and (4) maturity amount.

7. If bonds issued by a corporation are sold at a premium, is the market rate of interest greater or less than the contract rate?

8. The following data relate to a $1,000,000, 6% bond issue for a selected semiannual interest period:

Bond carrying amount at beginning of period	$1,150,000
Interest paid at end of period	30,000
Interest expense allocable to the period	28,750

(a) Were the bonds issued at a discount or at a premium? (b) What is the unamortized amount of the discount or premium account at the beginning of the period? (c) What account was debited to amortize the discount or premium?

9. Assume that Abacus Co. amortizes premiums and discounts on bonds payable at the end of the year rather than when interest is paid. What accounts would be debited and credited to record (a) the amortization of a discount on bonds payable and (b) the amortization of a premium on bonds payable?

10. Would a zero-coupon bond ever sell for its face amount?

11. What is the purpose of a bond sinking fund?

12. How are earnings from investments in a sinking fund reported on the income statement?

13. How are cash and securities comprising a sinking fund classified on the balance sheet?

14. Assume that two 15-year, 7% bond issues are identical, except that one bond issue is callable at its face amount at the end of 10 years. Which of the two bond issues do you think will sell for a lower value?

15. Bonds Payable has a balance of $750,000, and Discount on Bonds Payable has a balance of $12,500. If the issuing corporation redeems the bonds at 99, is there a gain or loss on the bond redemption?

16. How are gains or losses on bond redemptions reported on the income statement?

17. Assume that a company purchases bonds between interest dates. What accounts would normally be debited?

18. Indicate how the following accounts should be reported on the balance sheet: (a) Premium on Bonds Payable and (b) Discount on Bonds Payable.

19. Where are investments in bonds that are classified as held-to-maturity securities reported on the balance sheet?

20. At what amount are held-to-maturity investments in bonds reported on the balance sheet?

EXERCISES

Exercise 13–1
Effect of financing on earnings per share

Objective 1

✓ a. $0.30

Compatriot Co., which produces and sells skiing equipment, is financed as follows:

Bonds payable, 8% (issued at face amount)	$5,000,000
Preferred $3 stock (nonparticipating), $50 par	5,000,000
Common stock, $25 par	5,000,000

Income tax is estimated at 40% of income.

Determine the earnings per share of common stock, assuming that the income before bond interest and income tax is (a) $1,000,000, (b) $1,500,000, and (c) $2,500,000.

Exercise 13–2
Evaluate alternative financing plans

Objective 1

■──▶ Based upon the data in Exercise 13–1, discuss factors other than earnings per share that should be considered in evaluating such financing plans.

Exercise 13–3
Corporate financing

Objective 1

Real World

The financial statements for **Cisco Systems, Inc.**, are presented in Appendix G at the end of the text.

a. What is the major source of financing for Cisco Systems?
b. Why would you expect that Cisco Systems has not used any long-term debt in its financing?

Exercise 13–4
Present value of amounts due

Objective 3

Determine the present value of $10,000 to be received in three years, using an interest rate of 6%, compounded annually, as follows:

a. By successive divisions. (Round to the nearest dollar.)
b. By using the present value table in Exhibit 3.

Exercise 13–5
Present value of annuity

Objective 3

Determine the present value of $6,000 to be received at the end of each of four years, using an interest rate of 5%, compounded annually, as follows:

a. By successive computations, using the present value table in Exhibit 3.
b. By using the present value table in Exhibit 4.

Exercise 13–6
Present value of an annuity

Objective 3

On January 1, 2003, you win $10,000,000 in the state lottery. The $10,000,000 prize will be paid in equal installments of $400,000 over 25 years. The payments will be made on December 31 of each year, beginning on December 31, 2003. If the current interest rate is 7%, determine the present value of your winnings. Use the present value tables in Appendix A.

Exercise 13–7
Present value of an annuity

Objective 3

Assume the same data as in Exercise 13–6, except that the current interest rate is 14%.
■──▶ Will the present value of your winnings using an interest rate of 14% be one-half the present value of your winnings using an interest rate of 7%? Why or why not?

Exercise 13–8
Present value of bonds payable; discount

Objectives 3, 4

Czerny Co. produces and sells bottle capping equipment for soft drink and spring water bottlers. To finance its operations, Czerny Co. issued $8,000,000 of five-year, 9% bonds with interest payable semiannually at an effective interest rate of 10%. Determine the present value of the bonds payable, using the present value tables in Exhibits 3 and 4. Round to the nearest dollar.

Exercise 13–9
Present value of bonds payable; premium

Objectives 3, 4

Descartes Alarms Co. issued $10,000,000 of five-year, 12% bonds with interest payable semiannually, at an effective interest rate of 11%. Determine the present value of the bonds payable, using the present value tables in Exhibits 3 and 4. Round to the nearest dollar.

Exercise 13–10
Bond price

Objectives 3, 4

IBM Corporation 7½% bonds due in 2013 were reported in *The Wall Street Journal* as selling for 102⅝ on September 7, 2000.

➡ Were the bonds selling at a premium or at a discount on September 7, 2000? Explain.

Exercise 13–11
Entries for issuing bonds

Objective 4

Elba Co. produces and distributes fiber optic cable for use by telecommunications companies. Elba Co. issued $12,000,000 of 15-year, 9% bonds on April 1 of the current year, with interest payable on April 1 and October 1. The fiscal year of the company is the calendar year. Journalize the entries to record the following selected transactions for the current year:

Apr. 1. Issued the bonds for cash at their face amount.
Oct. 1. Paid the interest on the bonds.
Dec. 31. Recorded accrued interest for three months.

Exercise 13–12
Entries for issuing bonds and amortizing discount by straight-line method

Objective 4

✓ b. $513,065

On the first day of its fiscal year, Electrokinetics Company issued $5,000,000 of five-year, 8% bonds to finance its operations of producing and selling home electronics equipment. Interest is payable semiannually. The bonds were issued at an effective interest rate of 11%, resulting in Electrokinetics Company receiving cash of $4,434,676.

a. Journalize the entries to record the following:
  1. Sale of the bonds.
  2. First semiannual interest payment. (Amortization of discount is to be recorded annually.)
  3. Second semiannual interest payment.
  4. Amortization of discount at the end of the first year, using the straight-line method. (Round to the nearest dollar.)
b. Determine the amount of the bond interest expense for the first year.

Exercise 13–13
Computing bond proceeds, entries for bond issuing, and amortizing premium by straight-line method

Objectives 3, 4

Fajitas Corporation wholesales oil and grease products to equipment manufacturers. On March 1, 2003, Fajitas Corporation issued $10,000,000 of five-year, 11% bonds at an effective interest rate of 10%. Interest is payable semiannually on March 1 and September 1. Journalize the entries to record the following:

a. Sale of bonds on March 1, 2003. (Use the tables of present values in Exhibits 3 and 4 to determine the bond proceeds.)
b. First interest payment on September 1, 2003, and amortization of bond premium for six months, using the straight-line method. (Round to the nearest dollar.)

Exercise 13–14
Entries for issuing and calling bonds; loss

Objectives 4, 6

Farouk Corp., a wholesaler of office furniture, issued $15,000,000 of 30-year, 8% callable bonds on March 1, 2003, with interest payable on March 1 and September 1. The fiscal year of the company is the calendar year. Journalize the entries to record the following selected transactions:

2003
Mar. 1. Issued the bonds for cash at their face amount.
Sept. 1. Paid the interest on the bonds.
2007
Sept. 1. Called the bond issue at 101, the rate provided in the bond indenture. (Omit entry for payment of interest.)

Exercise 13–15
Entries for issuing and calling bonds; gain

Objectives 4, 6

Gehrig Corp. produces and sells automotive and aircraft safety belts. To finance its operations, Gehrig Corp. issued $20,000,000 of 25-year, 9% callable bonds on June 1, 2003, with interest payable on June 1 and December 1. The fiscal year of the company is the calendar year. Journalize the entries to record the following selected transactions:

2003
June 1. Issued the bonds for cash at their face amount.
Dec. 1. Paid the interest on the bonds.
2008
Dec. 1. Called the bond issue at 99, the rate provided in the bond indenture. (Omit entry for payment of interest.)

Exercise 13–16
Reporting bonds

Objectives 5, 6, 8

At the beginning of the current year, two bond issues (A and B) were outstanding. During the year, bond issue A was redeemed and a significant loss on the redemption of bonds was reported as Other Expense on the income statement. At the end of the year, bond issue B was reported as a current liability because its maturity date was early in the following year. A sinking fund of cash and securities sufficient to pay the series B bonds was reported in the balance sheet as *Investments*.

Can you find any flaws in the reporting practices related to the two bond issues?

Exercise 13–17
Amortizing discount on bond investment

Objective 7

A company purchased a $1,000, 20-year zero-coupon bond for $189 to yield 8.5% to maturity. How is the interest revenue computed?

Source: "Technical Hotline," *Journal of Accountancy*, January 1989, p. 100.

Exercise 13–18
Entries for purchase and sale of investment in bonds; loss

Objective 7

Gloucester Co. sells optical supplies to opticians and ophthalmologists. Journalize the entries to record the following selected transactions of Gloucester Co.:

a. Purchased for cash $300,000 of Glitz Co. 8% bonds at 102½ plus accrued interest of $6,000.
b. Received first semiannual interest.
c. At the end of the first year, amortized $250 of the bond premium.
d. Sold the bonds at 98½ plus accrued interest of $2,000. The bonds were carried at $302,500 at the time of the sale.

Exercise 13–19
Entries for purchase and sale of investment in bonds; gain

Objective 7

Nelson Company develops and sells graphics software for use by architects. Journalize the entries to record the following selected transactions of Nelson Company:

a. Purchased for cash $180,000 of Sequoyah Co. 5% bonds at 96 plus accrued interest of $1,500.
b. Received first semiannual interest.
c. Amortized $1,440 on the bond investment at the end of the first year.
d. Sold the bonds at 99 plus accrued interest of $3,000. The bonds were carried at $176,300 at the time of the sale.

Exercise 13–20
Number of times interest charges earned

Objective 9

The following data were taken from recent annual reports of **Mirage Resorts, Inc.,** which owns and operates casino-based entertainment resorts in Las Vegas and Laughlin, Nevada.

	Current Year	Preceding Year
Interest expense	$130,598,000	$ 70,350,000
Income before income tax	135,178,000	329,079,000

a. Determine the number of times interest charges were earned for the current and preceding years. Round to one decimal place.

b. What conclusions can you draw?

Appendix Exercise 13–21
Amortize discount by interest method

✓ b. $490,229

On the first day of its fiscal year, Electrokinetics Company issued $5,000,000 of five-year, 8% bonds to finance its operations of producing and selling home electronics equipment. Interest is payable semiannually. The bonds were issued at an effective interest rate of 11%, resulting in Electrokinetics Company receiving cash of $4,434,676.

a. Journalize the entries to record the following:
   1. Sale of the bonds.
   2. First semiannual interest payment. (Amortization of discount is to be recorded annually.)
   3. Second semiannual interest payment.
   4. Amortization of discount at the end of the first year, using the interest method. (Round to the nearest dollar.)

b. Compute the amount of the bond interest expense for the first year.

Appendix Exercise 13–22
Amortize premium by interest method

✓ b. $1,037,071

Fajitas Corporation wholesales oil and grease products to equipment manufacturers. On March 1, 2003, Fajitas Corporation issued $10,000,000 of five-year, 11% bonds at an effective interest rate of 10%, receiving cash of $10,386,057. Interest is payable semiannually on March 1 and September 1. Fajitas Corporation's fiscal year begins on March 1.

a. Journalize the entries to record the following:
   1. First interest payment on September 1, 2003. (Amortization of premium is to be recorded annually.)
   2. Second interest payment on March 1, 2004.
   3. Amortization of premium at the end of the first year, using the interest method. (Round to the nearest dollar.)

b. Determine the bond interest expense for the first year.

Appendix Exercise 13–23
Compute bond proceeds, amortizing premium by interest method, and interest expense

✓ a. $25,942,195
✓ b. $73,179

Pyrite Co. produces and sells spray painting equipment for construction contractors. On the first day of its fiscal year, Pyrite Co. issued $25,000,000 of five-year, 12% bonds at an effective interest rate of 11%, with interest payable semiannually. Compute the following, presenting figures used in your computations.

a. The amount of cash proceeds from the sale of the bonds. (Use the tables of present values in Exhibits 3 and 4.)

b. The amount of premium to be amortized for the first semiannual interest payment period, using the interest method. (Round to the nearest dollar.)

c. The amount of premium to be amortized for the second semiannual interest payment period, using the interest method. (Round to the nearest dollar.)

d. The amount of the bond interest expense for the first year.

Appendix Exercise 13–24
Compute bond proceeds, amortizing discount by interest method, and interest expense

Viceroy Co. produces and sells concrete mixing equipment. On the first day of its fiscal year, Viceroy Co. issued $14,000,000 of five-year, 10% bonds at an effective interest rate of 12%, with interest payable semiannually. Compute the following, presenting figures used in your computations.

a. The amount of cash proceeds from the sale of the bonds. (Use the tables of present values in Exhibits 3 and 4.)

b. The amount of discount to be amortized for the first semiannual interest payment period, using the interest method. (Round to the nearest dollar.)

✓ a. $12,969,663
✓ b. $78,180

c. The amount of discount to be amortized for the second semiannual interest payment period, using the interest method. (Round to the nearest dollar.)
d. The amount of the bond interest expense for the first year.

PROBLEMS SERIES A

Problem 13–1A
Effect of financing on earnings per share

Objective 1

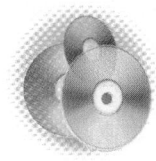

SPREADSHEET

✓ 1. Plan 3: $5.20

Three different plans for financing a $15,000,000 corporation are under consideration by its organizers. Under each of the following plans, the securities will be issued at their par or face amount, and the income tax rate is estimated at 40% of income.

	Plan 1	Plan 2	Plan 3
12% bonds			$ 6,250,000
Preferred $4 stock, $50 par		$ 7,500,000	5,000,000
Common stock, $30 par	$15,000,000	7,500,000	3,750,000
Total	$15,000,000	$15,000,000	$15,000,000

Instructions

1. Determine for each plan the earnings per share of common stock, assuming that the income before bond interest and income tax is $2,500,000.
2. Determine for each plan the earnings per share of common stock, assuming that the income before bond interest and income tax is $1,500,000.
3. ✏️ Discuss the advantages and disadvantages of each plan.

Problem 13–2A
Present value; bond premium; entries for bonds payable transactions

Objectives 3, 4

GENERAL LEDGER

✓ 3. $415,075

Moresby Inc. produces and sells voltage regulators. On July 1, 2002, Moresby Inc. issued $8,000,000 of ten-year, 11% bonds at an effective interest rate of 10%. Interest on the bonds is payable semiannually on December 31 and June 30. The fiscal year of the company is the calendar year.

Instructions

1. Journalize the entry to record the amount of the cash proceeds from the sale of the bonds. Use the tables of present values in Appendix A to compute the cash proceeds, rounding to the nearest dollar.
2. Journalize the entries to record the following:
   a. The first semiannual interest payment on December 31, 2002, including the amortization of the bond premium, using the straight-line method.
   b. The interest payment on June 30, 2003, and the amortization of the bond premium, using the straight-line method.
3. Determine the total interest expense for 2002.
4. ✏️ Will the bond proceeds always be greater than the face amount of the bonds when the contract rate is greater than the market rate of interest? Explain.

Problem 13–3A
Present value; bond discount; entries for bonds payable transactions

Objectives 3, 4

GENERAL LEDGER

On July 1, 2002, Cucumber Communications Equipment Inc. issued $10,000,000 of ten-year, 9% bonds at an effective interest rate of 10%. Interest on the bonds is payable semiannually on December 31 and June 30. The fiscal year of the company is the calendar year.

Instructions

1. Journalize the entry to record the amount of the cash proceeds from the sale of the bonds. Use the tables of present values in Appendix A to compute the cash proceeds, rounding to the nearest dollar.

(continued)

✓ 3. $481,155

2. Journalize the entries to record the following:
   a. The first semiannual interest payment on December 31, 2002, and the amortization of the bond discount, using the straight-line method. (Round to the nearest dollar.)
   b. The interest payment on June 30, 2003, and the amortization of the bond discount, using the straight-line method.
3. Determine the total interest expense for 2002.
4.  Will the bond proceeds always be less than the face amount of the bonds when the contract rate is less than the market rate of interest? Explain.

Problem 13–4A
Entries for bonds payable transactions

Objectives 4, 6

SPREADSHEET
GENERAL
LEDGER

✓ 2. a. $1,252,787

Downing Co. produces and sells synthetic string for tennis rackets. The following transactions were completed by Downing Co., whose fiscal year is the calendar year:

2002
July 1. Issued $20,000,000 of 5-year, 14% callable bonds dated July 1, 2002, at an effective rate of 12%, receiving cash of $21,472,126. Interest is payable semiannually on December 31 and June 30.
Dec. 31. Paid the semiannual interest on the bonds.
     31. Recorded bond premium amortization of $147,213, which was determined by using the straight-line method.
     31. Closed the interest expense account.
2003
June 30. Paid the semiannual interest on the bonds.
Dec. 31. Paid the semiannual interest on the bonds.
     31. Recorded bond premium amortization of $294,425, which was determined by using the straight-line method.
     31. Closed the interest expense account.
2004
July 1. Recorded the redemption of the bonds, which were called at 102. The balance in the bond premium account is $883,275 after the payment of interest and amortization of premium have been recorded. (Record the redemption only.)

Instructions

1. Journalize the entries to record the foregoing transactions.
2. Indicate the amount of the interest expense in (a) 2002 and (b) 2003.
3. Determine the carrying amount of the bonds as of December 31, 2003.

Problem 13–5A
Entries for bond investments

Objective 7

SPREADSHEET
GENERAL
LEDGER

The following selected transactions relate to certain securities acquired by Custom Blueprints Inc., whose fiscal year ends on December 31:

2002
Sept. 1. Purchased $500,000 of Donner Company 20-year, 9% bonds dated July 1, 2002, directly from the issuing company, for $482,150 plus accrued interest of $7,500.
Dec. 31. Received the semiannual interest on the Donner Company bonds.
     31. Recorded bond discount amortization of $300 on the Donner Company bonds. The amortization amount was determined by using the straight-line method.

(Assume that all intervening transactions and adjustments have been properly recorded and that the number of bonds owned has not changed from December 31, 2002, to December 31, 2006.)

2007
June 30. Received the semiannual interest on the Donner Company bonds.
Oct. 31. Sold one-half of the Donner Company bonds at 96½ plus accrued interest. The broker deducted $400 for commission, etc., remitting the balance. Prior to the sale, $375 of discount on one-half of the bonds was amortized, increasing the carrying amount of those bonds to $243,400.
Dec. 31. Received the semiannual interest on the Donner Company bonds.
     31. Recorded bond discount amortization of $450 on the Donner Company bonds.

Instructions
Journalize the entries to record the foregoing transactions.

Appendix
Problem 13–6A
Entries for bonds payable transactions; interest method of amortizing bond premium

✓ 2. $424,925

Moresby Inc. produces and sells voltage regulators. On July 1, 2002, Moresby Inc. issued $8,000,000 of ten-year, 11% bonds at an effective interest rate of 10%, receiving proceeds of $8,498,492. Interest on the bonds is payable semiannually on December 31 and June 30. The fiscal year of the company is the calendar year.

Instructions

1. Journalize the entries to record the following:
   a. The first semiannual interest payment on December 31, 2002, and the amortization of the bond premium, using the interest method. (Round to nearest dollar.)
   b. The interest payment on June 30, 2003, and the amortization of the bond premium, using the interest method. (Round to nearest dollar.)
2. Determine the total interest expense for 2002.

Appendix
Problem 13–7A
Entries for bonds payable transactions; interest method of amortizing bond discount

✓ 2. $468,845

On July 1, 2002, Cucumber Communications Equipment Inc. issued $10,000,000 of ten-year, 9% bonds at an effective interest rate of 10%, receiving proceeds of $9,376,895. Interest on the bonds is payable semiannually on December 31 and June 30. The fiscal year of the company is the calendar year.

Instructions

1. Journalize the entries to record the following:
   a. The first semiannual interest payment on December 31, 2002, and the amortization of the bond discount, using the interest method.
   b. The interest payment on June 30, 2003, and the amortization of the bond discount, using the interest method.
2. Determine the total interest expense for 2002.

PROBLEMS SERIES B

Problem 13–1B
Effect of financing on earnings per share

Objective 1

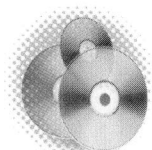
SPREADSHEET

✓ 1. Plan 3: $10.30

Three different plans for financing a $10,000,000 corporation are under consideration by its organizers. Under each of the following plans, the securities will be issued at their par or face amount, and the income tax rate is estimated at 40% of income.

	Plan 1	Plan 2	Plan 3
10% bonds			$ 5,000,000
Preferred 5% stock, $100 par		$ 5,000,000	2,500,000
Common stock, $10 par	$10,000,000	5,000,000	2,500,000
Total	$10,000,000	$10,000,000	$10,000,000

Instructions

1. Determine for each plan the earnings per share of common stock, assuming that the income before bond interest and income tax is $5,000,000.
2. Determine for each plan the earnings per share of common stock, assuming that the income before bond interest and income tax is $800,000.
3. ✏️ Discuss the advantages and disadvantages of each plan.

Problem 13–2B
Present value; bond premium; entries for bonds payable transactions

Objectives 3, 4

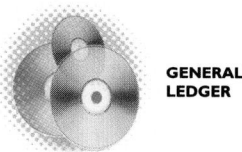
GENERAL LEDGER

Parnell Corporation produces and sells burial vaults. On July 1, 2003, Parnell Corporation issued $12,000,000 of ten-year, 12% bonds at an effective interest rate of 10%. Interest on the bonds is payable semiannually on December 31 and June 30. The fiscal year of the company is the calendar year.

Instructions

1. Journalize the entry to record the amount of the cash proceeds from the sale of the bonds. Use the tables of present values in Appendix A to compute the cash proceeds, rounding to the nearest dollar. *(continued)*

✓ 3. $645,226

2. Journalize the entries to record the following:
    a. The first semiannual interest payment on December 31, 2003, and the amortization of the bond premium, using the straight-line method. (Round to the nearest dollar.)
    b. The interest payment on June 30, 2004, and the amortization of the bond premium, using the straight-line method.
3. Determine the total interest expense for 2003.
4. 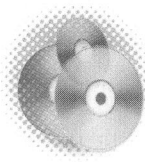➤ Will the bond proceeds always be greater than the face amount of the bonds when the contract rate is greater than the market rate of interest? Explain.

Problem 13–3B

Present value; bond discount; entries for bonds payable transactions

Objectives 3, 4

GENERAL LEDGER

✓ 3. $418,010

On July 1, 2002, Raptor Corporation, a wholesaler of used robotic equipment, issued $7,500,000 of ten-year, 10% bonds at an effective interest rate of 12%. Interest on the bonds is payable semiannually on December 31 and June 30. The fiscal year of the company is the calendar year.

Instructions

1. Journalize the entry to record the amount of the cash proceeds from the sale of the bonds. Use the tables of present values in Appendix A to compute the cash proceeds, rounding to the nearest dollar.
2. Journalize the entries to record the following:
    a. The first semiannual interest payment on December 31, 2002, and the amortization of the bond discount, using the straight-line method. (Round to the nearest dollar.)
    b. The interest payment on June 30, 2003, and the amortization of the bond discount, using the straight-line method.
3. Determine the total interest expense for 2002.
4. ➤ Will the bond proceeds always be less than the face amount of the bonds when the contract rate is less than the market rate of interest? Explain.

Problem 13–4B

Entries for bonds payable transactions

Objectives 4, 6

SPREADSHEET
GENERAL LEDGER

✓ 2. a. $477,220

The following transactions were completed by Shadwell Inc., whose fiscal year is the calendar year:

2002
July 1. Issued $10,000,000 of 5-year, 8% callable bonds dated July 1, 2002, at an effective rate of 10%, receiving cash of $9,227,796. Interest is payable semiannually on December 31 and June 30.
Dec. 31. Paid the semiannual interest on the bonds.
     31. Recorded bond discount amortization of $77,220, which was determined by using the straight-line method.
     31. Closed the interest expense account.
2003
June 30. Paid the semiannual interest on the bonds.
Dec. 31. Paid the semiannual interest on the bonds.
     31. Recorded bond discount amortization of $154,440, which was determined by using the straight-line method.
     31. Closed the interest expense account.
2004
June 30. Recorded the redemption of the bonds, which were called at 98½. The balance in the bond discount account is $463,324 after payment of interest and amortization of discount have been recorded. (Record the redemption only.)

Instructions

1. Journalize the entries to record the foregoing transactions.
2. Indicate the amount of the interest expense in (a) 2002 and (b) 2003.
3. Determine the carrying amount of the bonds as of December 31, 2003.

Problem 13–5B

Entries for bond investments

Objective 7

Genesis Inc. develops and leases databases of publicly available information. The following selected transactions relate to certain securities acquired as a long-term investment by Genesis Inc., whose fiscal year ends on December 31:

SPREADSHEET

GENERAL LEDGER

2002

Sept. 1. Purchased $240,000 of Joshua Company 10-year, 8% bonds dated July 1, 2002, directly from the issuing company, for $247,375 plus accrued interest of $3,200.

Dec. 31. Received the semiannual interest on the Joshua Company bonds.

31. Recorded bond premium amortization of $250 on the Joshua Company bonds. The amortization amount was determined by using the straight-line method.

(Assume that all intervening transactions and adjustments have been properly recorded and that the number of bonds owned has not changed from Dec. 31, 2002, to Dec. 31, 2007.)

2008

June 30. Received the semiannual interest on the Joshua Company bonds.

Aug. 31. Sold one-half of the Joshua Company bonds at 102 plus accrued interest. The broker deducted $500 for commission, etc., remitting the balance. Prior to the sale, $250 of premium on one-half of the bonds is to be amortized, reducing the carrying amount of those bonds to $121,438.

Dec. 31. Received the semiannual interest on the Joshua Company bonds.

31. Recorded bond premium amortization of $375 on the Joshua Company bonds.

Instructions

Journalize the entries to record the foregoing transactions.

Appendix
Problem 13–6B

Entries for bonds payable transactions; interest method of amortizing bond premium

✓ 2. $674,774

Parnell Corporation produces and sells burial vaults. On July 1, 2003, Parnell Corporation issued $12,000,000 of ten-year, 12% bonds at an effective interest rate of 10%, receiving proceeds of $13,495,471. Interest on the bonds is payable semiannually on December 31 and June 30. The fiscal year of the company is the calendar year.

Instructions

1. Journalize the entries to record the following:
   a. The first semiannual interest payment on December 31, 2003, and the amortization of the bond premium, using the interest method. (Round to nearest dollar.)
   b. The interest payment on June 30, 2004, and the amortization of the bond premium, using the interest method. (Round to nearest dollar.)
2. Determine the total interest expense for 2003.

Appendix
Problem 13–7B

Entries for bonds payable transactions; interest method of amortizing bond discount

✓ 2. $398,388

On July 1, 2002, Raptor Corporation, a wholesaler of used robotic equipment, issued $7,500,000 of ten-year, 10% bonds at an effective interest rate of 12%, receiving proceeds of $6,639,795. Interest on the bonds is payable semiannually on December 31 and June 30. The fiscal year of the company is the calendar year.

Instructions

1. Journalize the entries to record the following:
   a. The first semiannual interest payment on December 31, 2002, and the amortization of the bond discount, using the interest method. (Round to nearest dollar.)
   b. The interest payment on June 30, 2003, and the amortization of the bond discount, using the interest method. (Round to nearest dollar.)
2. Determine the total interest expense for 2002.

COMPREHENSIVE PROBLEM 4

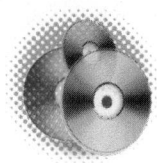

GENERAL LEDGER

Selected transactions completed by Heywood Products Inc. during the fiscal year ending July 31, 2003, were as follows:

a. Issued 12,000 shares of $25 par common stock at $45, receiving cash.
b. Issued 7,500 shares of $100 par preferred 8% stock at $120, receiving cash.

✓ 2.a. Net income, $163,000

c. Issued $6,000,000 of 10-year, 11% bonds at an effective interest rate of 10%, with interest payable semiannually. Use the present value tables in Appendix A to determine the bond proceeds. Round to the nearest dollar.
d. Declared a dividend of $0.25 per share on common stock and $2 per share on preferred stock. On the date of record, 100,000 shares of common stock were outstanding, no treasury shares were held, and 15,000 shares of preferred stock were outstanding.
e. Paid the cash dividends declared in (d).
f. Redeemed $500,000 of 8-year, 12% bonds at 101. The balance in the bond premium account is $6,150 after the payment of interest and amortization of premium have been recorded. (Record only the redemption of the bonds payable.)
g. Purchased 5,000 shares of treasury common stock at $42 per share.
h. Declared a 2% stock dividend on common stock and a $2 cash dividend per share on preferred stock. On the date of declaration, the market value of the common stock was $41 per share. On the date of record, 100,000 shares of common stock had been issued, 5,000 shares of treasury common stock were held, and 15,000 shares of preferred stock had been issued.
i. Issued the stock certificates for the stock dividends declared in (h) and paid the cash dividends to the preferred stockholders.
j. Purchased $100,000 of Key West Sports Inc. 10-year, 15% bonds, directly from the issuing company, for $97,000 plus accrued interest of $3,750.
k. Sold, at $48 per share, 3,000 shares of treasury common stock purchased in (g).
l. Recorded the payment of semiannual interest on the bonds issued in (c) and the amortization of the premium for six months. The amortization was determined using the straight-line method. (Round the amortization to the nearest dollar.)
m. Accrued interest for four months on the Key West Sports Inc. bonds purchased in (j). Also recorded amortization of $100.

Instructions

1. Journalize the selected transactions.
2. After all of the transactions for the year ended July 31, 2003, had been posted (including the transactions recorded in (1) and all adjusting entries), the following data were taken from the records of Heywood Products Inc.:

Income statement data:

Advertising expense	$ 75,000
Cost of merchandise sold	1,890,000
Delivery expense	17,000
Depreciation expense—office buildings and equipment	13,100
Depreciation expense—store buildings and equipment	45,000
Gain on redemption of bonds	1,150
Income tax:	
Applicable to continuing operations	156,043
Applicable to loss from disposal of a segment of the business	48,000
Applicable to gain from redemption of bonds	150
Interest expense	311,307
Interest revenue	1,350
Loss from disposal of a segment of the business	120,000
Miscellaneous administrative expenses	1,600
Miscellaneous selling expenses	5,000
Office rent expense	25,000
Office salaries expense	85,000
Office supplies expense	5,300
Sales	3,150,000
Sales commissions	98,000
Sales salaries expense	180,000
Store supplies expense	10,000

Retained earnings and balance sheet data:

Accounts payable	$ 149,500
Accounts receivable	280,500
Accumulated depreciation—office buildings and equipment	835,250
Accumulated depreciation—store buildings and equipment	2,214,750
Allowance for doubtful accounts	21,500
Bonds payable, 11%, due 2013	6,000,000
Cash	125,500
Common stock, $25 par (400,000 shares authorized; 101,900 shares outstanding)	2,547,500
Deferred income tax payable (current portion, $4,700)	25,700
Dividends:	
Cash dividends for common stock	55,000
Cash dividends for preferred stock	105,000
Stock dividends for common stock	77,900
Dividends payable	30,000
Income tax payable	55,900
Interest receivable	5,000
Investment in Key West Sports Inc. bonds (long-term)	97,100
Merchandise inventory (July 31, 2003), at lower of cost (fifo) or market	425,000
Notes receivable	77,500
Office buildings and equipment	3,762,329
Paid-in capital from sale of treasury stock	18,000
Paid-in capital in excess of par—common stock	560,000
Paid-in capital in excess of par—preferred stock	240,000
Preferred 8% stock, $100 par (30,000 shares authorized; 15,000 shares issued)	1,500,000
Premium on bonds payable	355,176
Prepaid expenses	15,900
Retained earnings, August 1, 2002	677,124
Store buildings and equipment	10,282,671
Treasury stock (2,000 shares of common stock at cost of $42 per share)	84,000

a. Prepare a multiple-step income statement for the year ended July 31, 2003, concluding with earnings per share. In computing earnings per share, assume that the average number of common shares outstanding was 100,000 and preferred dividends were $105,000.
b. Prepare a retained earnings statement for the year ended July 31, 2003.
c. Prepare a balance sheet in report form as of July 31, 2003.

SPECIAL ACTIVITIES

Activity 13–1
Fun Inc.

Ethics and professional conduct in business

Fun Inc. produces and sells water slides for theme parks. Fun Inc. has outstanding a $50,000,000, 25-year, 10% debenture bond issue dated July 1, 1998. The bond issue is due June 30, 2023. The bond indenture requires a sinking fund, which has a balance of $6,000,000 as of July 1, 2003. Fun Inc. is currently experiencing a shortage of funds due to a recent plant expansion. Lee Noel, treasurer of Fun Inc., has suggested using the sinking fund cash to temporarily relieve the shortage of funds. Noel's brother-in-law, who is trustee of the sinking fund, is willing to loan Fun Inc. the necessary funds from the sinking fund.

Discuss whether Lee Noel is behaving in a professional manner.

Activity 13–2
Carlisle Distributors Inc.
Present values

Carlisle Distributors Inc. is a wholesaler of oriental rugs. The following is a luncheon conversation between Jenny Wilder, the assistant controller, and Peter Isaacs, an assistant financial analyst for Carlisle.

Peter: Jenny, do you mind if I spoil your lunch and ask you an accounting question?
Jenny: No, go ahead. This chicken salad sandwich is pretty bad. It smells like it's three days old, and I've already picked three bones out of it.
Peter: Well, as you know, in finance we use present values for capital budgeting analysis, assessing financing alternatives, etc. It's probably the most important concept that I learned in school that I actually use.
Jenny: So . . . ?
Peter: I was just wondering why accountants don't use present values more.
Jenny: What do you mean?
Peter: Well, it seems to me that you ought to value all the balance sheet liabilities at their present values.

➤ How would you respond if you were Jenny?

Activity 13–3
Daffodil Inc.
Preferred stock vs. bonds

Daffodil Inc. has decided to expand its operations to owning and operating theme parks. The following is an excerpt from a conversation between the chief executive officer, JoAnn Hanson, and the vice-president of finance, Chris Fowler.

JoAnn: Chris, have you given any thought to how we're going to finance the acquisition of WaterWave Corporation?
Chris: Well, the two basic options, as I see it, are to issue either preferred stock or bonds. The equity market is a little depressed right now. The rumor is that the Federal Reserve Bank's going to increase the interest rates either this month or next.
JoAnn: Yes, I've heard the rumor. The problem is that we can't wait around to see what's going to happen. We'll have to move on this next week if we want any chance to complete the acquisition of WaterWave.
Chris: Well, the bond market is strong right now. Maybe we should issue debt this time around.
JoAnn: That's what I would have guessed as well. WaterWave's financial statements look pretty good, except for the volatility of their income and cash flows. But that's characteristic of their industry.

➤ Discuss the advantages and disadvantages of issuing preferred stock versus bonds.

Activity 13–4
Into the Real World
Investing in bonds

Select a bond from listings that appear daily in *The Wall Street Journal*, and summarize the information related to the bond you select. Include the following information in your summary:

1. Contract rate of interest
2. Year when the bond matures
3. Current yield (effective rate of interest)
4. Closing price of bond (indicate date)
5. Other information noted about the bond, such as whether it is a zero-coupon bond (see the Explanatory Notes to the listings)

In groups of three or four, share the information you developed about the bond you selected. As a group, select one bond to invest $100,000 in and prepare a justification for your choice for presentation to the class. For example, your justification should include a consideration of risk and return.

Activity 13–5
Inman Bottling Co.
Financing business expansion

You hold a 25% common stock interest in the family-owned business, a soft drink bottling distributorship. Your sister, who is the manager, has proposed an expansion of plant facilities at an expected cost of $5,000,000. Two alternative plans have been suggested as methods of financing the expansion. Each plan is briefly described as follows:

Plan 1. Issue $5,000,000 of 20-year, 8% notes at face amount.
Plan 2. Issue an additional 70,000 shares of $20 par common stock at $25 per share, and $3,250,000 of 20-year, 8% notes at face amount.

The balance sheet as of the end of the previous fiscal year is as follows:

Inman Bottling Co.
Balance Sheet
December 31, 2003

Assets

Current assets	$2,350,000
Property, plant, and equipment	5,150,000
Total assets	$7,500,000

Liabilities and Stockholders' Equity

Liabilities	$2,000,000
Common stock, $20	800,000
Paid-in capital in excess of par	80,000
Retained earnings	4,620,000
Total liabilities and stockholders' equity	$7,500,000

Net income has remained relatively constant over the past several years. The expansion program is expected to increase yearly income before bond interest and income tax from $500,000 in the previous year to $700,000 for this year. Your sister has asked you, as the company treasurer, to prepare an analysis of each financing plan.

1. Prepare a table indicating the expected earnings per share on the common stock under each plan. Assume an income tax rate of 40%.
2. a. ✏️ Discuss the factors that should be considered in evaluating the two plans.
   b. ✏️ Which plan offers the greater benefit to the present stockholders? Give reasons for your opinion.

Activity 13–6
Into the Real World
Bond ratings

Moody's Investors Service maintains a Web site at **www.Moodys.com**. One of the services offered at this site is a listing of announcements of recent bond rating changes. Visit this site and read over some of these announcements. Write down several of the reasons provided for rating downgrades and upgrades. If you were a bond investor or bond issuer, would you care if Moody's changed the rating on your bonds? Why or why not?

ANSWERS TO SELF-EXAMINATION QUESTIONS

Matching

1. C	3. G	5. Q	7. L	9. O	11. F	13. N
2. E	4. A	6. P	8. H	10. R	12. M	14. K

Multiple Choice

1. **B** Since the contract rate on the bonds is higher than the prevailing market rate, a rational investor would be willing to pay more than the face amount, or a premium (answer B), for the bonds. If the contract rate and the market rate were equal, the bonds could be expected to sell at their face amount (answer A). Likewise, if the market rate is higher than the contract rate, the bonds would sell at a price below their face amount (answer D) or at a discount (answer C).

2. **A** The bond carrying amount is the face amount plus unamortized premium or less unamortized discount. For this question, the carrying amount is $500,000 less $40,000, or $460,000 (answer A).

3. **B** Although the sinking fund may consist of cash as well as securities, the fund is listed on the balance sheet as an investment (answer B) because it is to be used to pay the long-term liability at maturity.

4. **B** The amount debited to the investment account is the cost of the bonds, which includes the amount paid to the seller for the bonds (101% × $100,000) plus broker's commissions ($50), or $101,050 (answer B). The $2,000 of accrued interest that is paid to the seller should be debited to Interest Revenue, since it is an offset against the amount that will be received as interest at the next interest date.

5. **C** The balance of Discount on Bonds Payable is usually reported as a deduction from Bonds Payable in the Long-Term Liabilities section (answer C) of the balance sheet. Likewise, a balance in a premium on bonds payable account would usually be reported as an addition to Bonds Payable in the Long-Term Liabilities section of the balance sheet.

Statement of Cash Flows

objectives

After studying this chapter, you should be able to:

1 Explain why the statement of cash flows is one of the basic financial statements.

2 Summarize the types of cash flow activities reported in the statement of cash flows.

3 Prepare a statement of cash flows, using the indirect method.

4 Prepare a statement of cash flows, using the direct method.

5 Calculate and interpret the free cash flow.

ow much cash do you have in the bank or in your wallet or purse? How much cash did you have at the beginning of the month? The difference between these two amounts is the net change in your cash during the month. Knowing the reasons for the change in cash may be useful in evaluating whether your financial position has improved and whether you will be able to pay your bills in the future.

For example, assume that you had $200 at the beginning of the month and $550 at the end of the month. The net change in cash is $350. Based on this net change, it appears that your financial position has improved. However, this conclusion may or may not be valid, depending upon how the change of $350 was created. If you borrowed $1,000 during the month and spent $650 on living expenses, your cash would have increased by $350 by living off borrowed funds. On the other hand, if you earned $1,000 and spent $650 on living expenses, your cash would have also increased by $350, but your financial position is improved compared to the first scenario.

In previous chapters, we have used the income statement, balance sheet, and retained earnings statement and other information to analyze the effects of management decisions on a business's financial position and operating performance. In this chapter, we present how to prepare and use the statement of cash flows.

Purpose of the Statement of Cash Flows

objective 1

Explain why the statement of cash flows is one of the basic financial statements.

The **statement of cash flows** reports a firm's major cash inflows and outflows for a period.[1] It provides useful information about a firm's ability to generate cash from operations, maintain and expand its operating capacity, meet its financial obligations, and pay dividends.

The statement of cash flows is one of the basic financial statements. It is useful to managers in evaluating past operations and in planning future investing and financing activities. It is useful to investors, creditors, and others in assessing a firm's profit potential. In addition, it is a basis for assessing the firm's ability to pay its maturing debt.

Reporting Cash Flows

objective 2

Summarize the types of cash flow activities reported in the statement of cash flows.

The statement of cash flows reports cash flows by three types of activities:

1. **Cash flows from operating activities** are cash flows from transactions that affect net income. Examples of such transactions include the purchase and sale of merchandise by a retailer.
2. **Cash flows from investing activities** are cash flows from transactions that affect the investments in noncurrent assets. Examples of such transactions include the sale and purchase of fixed assets, such as equipment and buildings.

[1] As used in this chapter, cash refers to cash and cash equivalents. Examples of cash equivalents include marketable securities, certificates of deposit, U.S. Treasury bills, and money market funds.

3. **Cash flows from financing activities** are cash flows from transactions that affect the equity and debt of the business. Examples of such transactions include issuing or retiring equity and debt securities.

> The statement of cash flows reports cash flows from operating, investing, and financing activities.

The cash flows from operating activities is normally presented first, followed by the cash flows from investing activities and financing activities. The total of the net cash flow from these activities is the net increase or decrease in cash for the period. The cash balance at the beginning of the period is added to the net increase or decrease in cash, resulting in the cash balance at the end of the period. The ending cash balance on the statement of cash flows equals the cash reported on the balance sheet.

Exhibit 1 shows common cash flow transactions reported in each of the three sections of the statement of cash flows. By reporting cash flows by operating, investing, and financing activities, significant relationships within and among the activities can be evaluated. For example, the cash receipts from issuing bonds can be related to repayments of borrowings when both are reported as financing activities. Also, the impact of each of the three activities (operating, investing, and financing) on cash flows can be identified. This allows investors and creditors to evaluate the effects of cash flows on a firm's profits and ability to pay debt.

Exhibit 1 Cash Flows

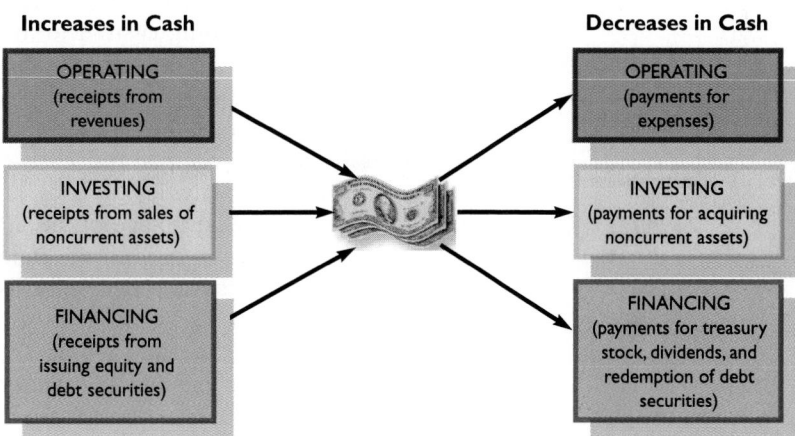

BUSINESS ON STAGE

Focus on Cash Flow

In the past, investors and creditors have relied heavily on a company's earnings information in judging the company's performance. Now, more and more investors and creditors are also focusing on cash flows for providing additional information, as described below.

As the term suggests, cash flow is basically a measure of the money flowing into—or out of—a business. If large companies were run like lemonade stands, on a cash

basis, earnings and cash flow would be identical.

Every major corporation, however, keeps its books on an accrual basis.... [This] can give a truer picture of corporate profitability, but sometimes it obscures important developments.

Take a company that spent $140 million on new machinery last year. If it depreciates the equipment over a seven-year period, it will be subtracting $20 million from reported profits each year.

But if the machines will stay up to date and useful for 25 years, the company's reported earnings may understate its true strength....

Sometimes the reverse is true. If a company has been neglecting capital spending, its earnings may look good. But on a cash-flow basis, it will look no better...than its competitors. ∎

Source: John R. Dorfman, "Stock Analysts Increase Focus on Cash Flow," *The Wall Street Journal*, February 17, 1987, Section 2, p. 1.

Cash Flows from Operating Activities

The most important cash flows of a business often relate to operating activities. There are two alternative methods for reporting cash flows from operating activities in the statement of cash flows. These methods are (1) the direct method and (2) the indirect method.

Which U.S. industrial companies have the largest cash balances? A recent list is as follows:

	In millions
Ford Motor Co.	$24,773
General Motors	20,024
Microsoft	13,927
Intel	7,626
IBM	5,768

These companies have had substantial cash flows from operations over the past 3–5 years, and as a result, have been able to build large cash balances (in the billions!). These balances can be used to cushion future business downturns, as would be the case for businesses subject to boom and bust cycles, such as Ford and GM. Alternatively, the cash can be used to expand the business or move into new markets, as would be the case for technology companies, such as Microsoft, Intel, and IBM.

The **direct method** reports the sources of operating cash and the uses of operating cash. The major source of operating cash is cash received from customers. The major uses of operating cash include cash paid to suppliers for merchandise and services and cash paid to employees for wages. The difference between these operating cash receipts and cash payments is the net cash flow from operating activities.

The primary advantage of the direct method is that it reports the sources and uses of cash in the statement of cash flows. Its primary disadvantage is that the necessary data may not be readily available and may be costly to gather.

The **indirect method** reports the operating cash flows by beginning with net income and adjusting it for revenues and expenses that do not involve the receipt or payment of cash. In other words, accrual net income is adjusted to determine the net amount of cash flows from operating activities.

A major advantage of the indirect method is that it focuses on the differences between net income and cash flows from operations. In this sense, it shows the relationship between the income statement, the balance sheet, and the statement of cash flows. Because the data are readily available, the indirect method is normally less costly to use than the direct method. Because of these advantages, most firms use the indirect method to report cash flows from operations.

Exhibit 2 illustrates the cash flow from operating activities section of the statement of cash flows under the direct and indirect methods. Both statements are for NetSolutions for the month ended November 2002. Both methods show the same amount of net cash flow from operating activities, regardless of the method. We will illustrate both methods in detail later in this chapter.

Cash Flows from Investing Activities

Cash inflows from investing activities normally arise from selling fixed assets, investments, and intangible assets. Cash outflows normally include payments to acquire fixed assets, investments, and intangible assets.

Cash flows from investing activities are reported on the statement of cash flows by first listing the cash inflows. The cash outflows are then presented. If the inflows

Exhibit 2 Cash Flow from Operations: Direct and Indirect Methods

Direct Method	
Cash flows from operating activities:	
Cash received from customers	$7,500
Deduct cash payments for expenses	
and payments to creditors	4,600
Net cash flow from operating activities	$2,900

Indirect Method	
Cash flows from operating activities:	
Net income, per income statement	$3,050
Add increase in accounts payable	400
	$3,450
Deduct increase in supplies	550
Net cash flow from operating activities	$2,900

The Walt Disney Company recently invested $3.3 billion to develop new action and animated films and $2.3 billion to design and develop new theme park attractions and resort properties, such as Disney's California Adventure and the Disney Cruise Line.

are greater than the outflows, **net cash flow provided by investing activities** is reported. If the inflows are less than the outflows, **net cash flow used for investing activities** is reported.

The cash flows from investing activities section in the statement of cash flows for NetSolutions is shown below.

Cash flows from investing activities:
Cash payments for acquiring land . . . . $(20,000)

Cash Flows from Financing Activities

Cash inflows from financing activities normally arise from issuing debt or equity securities. Examples of such inflows include issuing bonds, notes payable, and preferred and common stocks. Cash outflows from financing activities include paying cash dividends, repaying debt, and acquiring treasury stock.

Cash flows from financing activities are reported on the statement of cash flows by first listing the cash inflows. The cash outflows are then presented. If the inflows are greater than the outflows, **net cash flow provided by financing activities** is reported. If the inflows are less than the outflows, **net cash flow used for financing activities** is reported.

The cash flows from financing activities section in the statement of cash flows for NetSolutions is shown below.

Intel Corp. plans to keep enough cash on hand to build two computer chip factories and to repurchase common stock (treasury stock).

Cash flows from financing activities:
Cash received as owner's investment $25,000
Deduct cash withdrawal by owner 2,000
Net cash flow from financing activities $23,000

Noncash Investing and Financing Activities

A business may enter into investing and financing activities that do not directly involve cash. For example, it may issue common stock to retire long-term debt. Such a transaction does not have a direct effect on cash. However, the transaction does eliminate the need for future cash payments to pay interest and retire the bonds. Thus, because of their future effect on cash flows, such transactions should be reported to readers of the financial statements.

When noncash investing and financing transactions occur during a period, their effect is reported in a separate schedule. This schedule usually appears at the bottom of the statement of cash flows. For example, in such a schedule, **Amazon.com** disclosed the issuance of $217 million in common stock for Internet acquisitions. Other examples of noncash investing and financing transactions include acquiring fixed assets by issuing bonds or capital stock and issuing common stock in exchange for convertible preferred stock.

BUSINESS ON STAGE

Seasonal Cash Management

A business must manage its cash position so that there is enough cash on hand to pay bills and other liabilities. Cash management is particularly important for seasonal businesses, which use cash in one part of the year and generate it in another. For example, consider this assumed cash position from operations for Smart Toys, Inc., a toy retailer, in the chart below.

Smart Toys uses cash to purchase inventory prior to the winter holiday season. It is able to generate surplus cash by selling its inventory throughout the holiday season and into the early part of the calendar year.

If the cash required to purchase inventory exceeds Smart Toys' ability to generate operating cash flow, it may experience a cash shortage. In such a case, it must obtain short-term credit, which may be structured as a line of credit from a bank. A line of credit is an agreement that allows the business to borrow an unsecured amount of money up to some stated limit. For example, Smart Toys has a line of credit of $60,000, of which $40,000 was used during the year. Amounts drawn on a line of credit must usually be paid back within a year.

Seasonal businesses must be careful to avoid overextending their cash position during the "down cycle." For example, if Smart Toys purchases items that do not sell, a cash surplus will not be generated during the selling season. ■

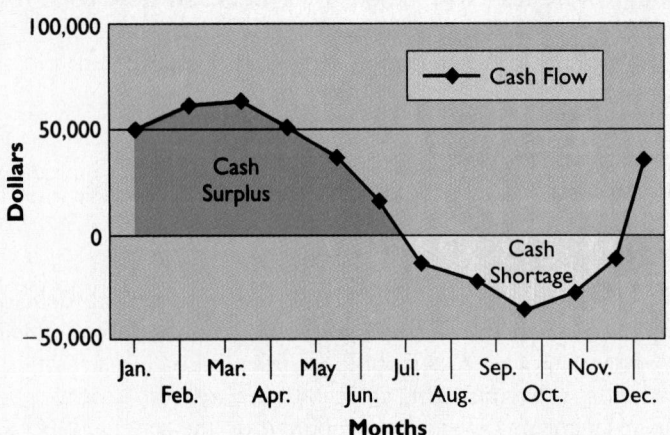

No Cash Flow per Share

The term *cash flow per share* is sometimes reported in the financial press. Often, the term is used to mean "cash flow from operations per share." Such reporting may be misleading to users of the financial statements. For example, users might interpret cash flow per share as the amount available for dividends. This would not be the case if most of the cash generated by operations is required for repaying loans or for reinvesting in the business. Users might also think that cash flow per share is equivalent or perhaps superior to earnings per share. For these reasons, the financial statements, including the statement of cash flows, should not report cash flow per share.

Statement of Cash Flows—The Indirect Method

The indirect method of reporting cash flows from operating activities is normally less costly and more efficient than the direct method. In addition, when the direct method is used, the indirect method must also be used in preparing a supplemental reconciliation of net income with cash flows from operations. The 1999 edition of *Accounting Trends & Techniques* reported that 99% of the companies surveyed used the indirect method. For these reasons, we will discuss first the indirect method of preparing the statement of cash flows.

To collect the data for the statement of cash flows, all the cash receipts and cash payments for a period could be analyzed. However, this procedure is expensive and time-consuming. A more efficient approach is to analyze the changes in the noncash balance sheet accounts. The logic of this approach is that a change in any balance sheet account (including cash) can be analyzed in terms of changes in the other balance sheet accounts. To illustrate, the accounting equation is rewritten below to focus on the cash account:

$$\textbf{Assets} = \textbf{Liabilities} + \textbf{Stockholders' Equity}$$
$$\textbf{Cash} + \textbf{Noncash Assets} = \textbf{Liabilities} + \textbf{Stockholders' Equity}$$
$$\textbf{Cash} = \textbf{Liabilities} + \textbf{Stockholders' Equity} - \textbf{Noncash Assets}$$

Any change in the cash account results in a change in one or more noncash balance sheet accounts. That is, if the cash account changes, then a liability, stockholders' equity, or noncash asset account must also change.

Additional data are also obtained by analyzing the income statement accounts and supporting records. For example, since the net income or net loss for the period is closed to *Retained Earnings*, a change in the retained earnings account can be partially explained by the net income or net loss reported on the income statement.

There is no order in which the noncash balance sheet accounts must be analyzed. However, it is usually more efficient to analyze the accounts in the reverse order in which they appear on the balance sheet. Thus, the analysis of retained earnings provides the starting point for determining the cash flows from operating activities, which is the first section of the statement of cash flows.

The comparative balance sheet for Rundell Inc. on December 31, 2003 and 2002, is used to illustrate the indirect method. This balance sheet is shown in Exhibit 3. Selected ledger accounts and other data are presented as needed.[2]

Retained Earnings

The comparative balance sheet for Rundell Inc. shows that retained earnings increased $80,000 during the year. Analyzing the entries posted to the retained earnings account indicates how this change occurred. The retained earnings account for Rundell Inc. is shown below.

ACCOUNT *Retained Earnings*						ACCOUNT NO.	
						Balance	
Date		Item	Debit	Credit		Debit	Credit
2003 Jan.	1	Balance					202,300
Dec.	31	Net income		108,000			310,300
	31	Cash dividends	28,000				282,300

The retained earnings account must be carefully analyzed because some of the entries to retained earnings may not affect cash. For example, a decrease in retained earnings resulting from issuing a stock dividend does not affect cash. Such transactions are not reported on the statement of cash flows.

---

[2] An appendix that discusses using a work sheet as an aid in assembling data for the statement of cash flows is presented at the end of this chapter. This appendix illustrates a work sheet that can be used with the indirect method and a work sheet that can be used with the direct method of reporting cash flows from operating activities.

Exhibit 3 Comparative
Balance Sheet

Rundell Inc.
Comparative Balance Sheet
December 31, 2003 and 2002

Assets	2003	2002	Increase Decrease*
Cash	$ 97,500	$ 26,000	$ 71,500
Accounts receivable (net)	74,000	65,000	9,000
Inventories	172,000	180,000	8,000*
Land	80,000	125,000	45,000*
Building	260,000	200,000	60,000
Accumulated depreciation—building	(65,300)	(58,300)	(7,000)
Total assets	$618,200	$537,700	$ 80,500
Liabilities			
Accounts payable (merchandise creditors)	$ 43,500	$ 46,700	$ 3,200*
Accrued expenses payable (operating expenses)	26,500	24,300	2,200
Income taxes payable	7,900	8,400	500*
Dividends payable	14,000	10,000	4,000
Bonds payable	100,000	150,000	50,000*
Total liabilities	$191,900	$239,400	$ 47,500*
Stockholders' Equity			
Common stock ($2 par)	$ 24,000	$ 16,000	$ 8,000
Paid-in capital in excess of par	120,000	80,000	40,000
Retained earnings	282,300	202,300	80,000
Total stockholders' equity	$426,300	$298,300	$128,000
Total liabilities and stockholders' equity	$618,200	$537,700	$ 80,500

For Rundell Inc., the retained earnings account indicates that the $80,000 change resulted from net income of $108,000 and cash dividends declared of $28,000. The effect of each of these items on cash flows is discussed in the following sections.

Cash Flows from Operating Activities

The net income of $108,000 reported by Rundell Inc. normally is not equal to the amount of cash generated from operations during the period. This is because net income is determined using the accrual method of accounting.

Under the accrual method of accounting, revenues and expenses are recorded at different times from when cash is received or paid. For example, merchandise may be sold on account and the cash received at a later date.

Likewise, insurance expense represents the amount of insurance expired during the period. The premiums for the insurance may have been paid in a prior period. Thus, the net income reported on the income statement must be adjusted in determining cash flows from operating activities. The typical adjustments to net income are summarized in Exhibit 4.[3]

---

[3] Other items that also require adjustments to net income to obtain cash flow from operating activities include amortization of bonds payable discounts (add), losses on debt retirement (add), amortization of bonds payable premium (deduct), and gains on retirement of debt (deduct).

Exhibit 4 Adjustments to Net Income—Indirect Method

Net income, per income statement		$XX
Add: Depreciation of fixed assets and amortization of intangible assets ..	$XX	
Decreases in current assets (receivables, inventories, prepaid expenses)	XX	
Increases in current liabilities (accounts and notes payable, accrued liabilities)	XX	
Losses on disposal of assets	XX	XX
Deduct: Increases in current assets (receivables, inventories, prepaid expenses)	$XX	
Decreases in current liabilities (accounts and notes payable, accrued liabilities)	XX	
Gains on disposal of assets	XX	XX
Net cash flow from operating activities		$XX

Some of the adjustment items in Exhibit 4 are for expenses that affect noncurrent accounts but not cash. For example, depreciation of fixed assets and amortization of intangible assets are deducted from revenue but do not affect cash.

Some of the adjustment items in Exhibit 4 are for revenues and expenses that affect current assets and current liabilities but not cash flows. For example, a sale of $10,000 on account increases accounts receivable by $10,000. However, cash is not affected. Thus, the increase in accounts receivable of $10,000 between two balance sheet dates is deducted from net income in arriving at cash flows from operating activities.

Cash flows from operating activities should not include investing or financing transactions. For example, assume that land costing $50,000 was sold for $90,000 (a gain of $40,000). The sale should be reported as an investing activity: "Cash receipts from the sale of land, $90,000." However, the $40,000 gain on the sale of the land is included in net income on the income statement. Thus, the $40,000 gain is deducted from net income in determining cash flows from operations in order to avoid "double counting" the cash flow from the gain. Losses from the sale of fixed assets are added to net income in determining cash flows from operations.

The effect of dividends payable on cash flows from operating activities is omitted from Exhibit 4. Dividends payable is omitted because dividends do not affect net income. Later in the chapter, we will discuss how dividends are reported in the statement of cash flows. In the following paragraphs, we will discuss each of the adjustments that change Rundell Inc.'s net income to "Cash flows from operating activities."

Depreciation

The comparative balance sheet in Exhibit 3 indicates that Accumulated Depreciation—Building increased by $7,000. As shown below, this account indicates that depreciation for the year was $7,000 for the building.

ACCOUNT *Accumulated Depreciation—Building*					ACCOUNT NO.	
					Balance	
Date		**Item**	**Debit**	**Credit**	**Debit**	**Credit**
2003 Jan.	1	Balance				58,300
Dec.	31	Depreciation for year		7,000		65,300

The $7,000 of depreciation expense reduced net income but did not require an outflow of cash. Thus, the $7,000 is added to net income in determining cash flows from operating activities, as follows:

Cash flows from operating activities:		
Net income	$108,000	
Add depreciation	7,000	$115,000

Current Assets and Current Liabilities

As shown in Exhibit 4, decreases in noncash current assets and increases in current liabilities are added to net income. In contrast, increases in noncash current assets and decreases in current liabilities are deducted from net income. The current asset and current liability accounts of Rundell Inc. are as follows:

		December 31	Increase
Accounts	**2003**	**2002**	**Decrease***
Accounts receivable (net)	$ 74,000	$ 65,000	$9,000
Inventories	172,000	180,000	8,000*
Accounts payable (merchandise creditors)	43,500	46,700	3,200*
Accrued expenses payable (operating expenses)	26,500	24,300	2,200
Income taxes payable	7,900	8,400	500*

The $9,000 increase in **accounts receivable** indicates that the sales on account during the year are $9,000 more than collections from customers on account. The amount reported as sales on the income statement therefore includes $9,000 that did not result in a cash inflow during the year. Thus, $9,000 is deducted from net income.

The $8,000 decrease in **inventories** indicates that the merchandise sold exceeds the cost of the merchandise purchased by $8,000. The amount deducted as cost of merchandise sold on the income statement therefore includes $8,000 that did not require a cash outflow during the year. Thus, $8,000 is added to net income.

The $3,200 decrease in **accounts payable** indicates that the amount of cash payments for merchandise exceeds the merchandise purchased on account by $3,200. The amount reported on the income statement for cost of merchandise sold therefore excludes $3,200 that required a cash outflow during the year. Thus, $3,200 is deducted from net income.

The $2,200 increase in **accrued expenses payable** indicates that the amount incurred during the year for operating expenses exceeds the cash payments by $2,200. The amount reported on the income statement for operating expenses therefore includes $2,200 that did not require a cash outflow during the year. Thus, $2,200 is added to net income.

The $500 decrease in **income taxes payable** indicates that the amount paid for taxes exceeds the amount incurred during the year by $500. The amount reported on the income statement for income tax therefore is less than the amount paid by $500. Thus, $500 is deducted from net income.

Gain on Sale of Land

The ledger or income statement of Rundell Inc. indicates that the sale of land resulted in a gain of $12,000. As we discussed previously, the sale proceeds, which include the gain and the carrying value of the land, are included in cash flows from investing activities.[4] The gain is also included in net income. Thus, to avoid double

-----

[4] The reporting of the proceeds (cash flows) from the sale of land as part of investing activities is discussed later in this chapter.

reporting, the gain of $12,000 is deducted from net income in determining cash flows from operating activities, as shown below.

Cash flows from operating activities:
Net income $108,000
Deduct gain on sale of land 12,000

Reporting Cash Flows from Operating Activities

We have now presented all the necessary adjustments to convert the net income to cash flows from operating activities for Rundell Inc. These adjustments are summarized in Exhibit 5 in a format suitable for the statement of cash flows.

Exhibit 5 Cash Flows from Operating Activities—Indirect Method

Cash flows from operating activities:		
Net income		$108,000
Add: Depreciation	$ 7,000	
Decrease in inventories	8,000	
Increase in accrued expenses	2,200	17,200
		$125,200
Deduct: Increase in accounts receivable	$ 9,000	
Decrease in accounts payable	3,200	
Decrease in income taxes payable	500	
Gain on sale of land	12,000	24,700
Net cash flow from operating activities		$100,500

Cash Flows Used for Payment of Dividends

According to the retained earnings account of Rundell Inc., shown earlier in the chapter, cash dividends of $28,000 were declared during the year. However, the dividends payable account, shown below, indicates that dividends of only $24,000 were paid during the year.

ACCOUNT *Dividends Payable*					ACCOUNT NO.	
					Balance	
Date		**Item**	**Debit**	**Credit**	**Debit**	**Credit**
2003 Jan.	1	Balance				10,000
	10	Cash paid	10,000		—	—
June	20	Dividends declared		14,000		14,000
July	10	Cash paid	14,000		—	—
Dec.	20	Dividends declared		14,000		14,000

The $24,000 of dividend payments represents a cash outflow that is reported in the financing activities section as follows:

Cash flows from financing activities:
Cash paid for dividends $24,000

Common Stock

The common stock account increased by $8,000, and the paid-in capital in excess of par—common stock account increased by $40,000, as shown below. These increases result from issuing 4,000 shares of common stock for $12 per share.

ACCOUNT Common Stock					ACCOUNT NO.	
					Balance	
Date		**Item**	**Debit**	**Credit**	**Debit**	**Credit**
2003 Jan.	1	Balance				16,000
Nov.	1	4,000 shares issued for cash		8,000		24,000

ACCOUNT Paid-In Capital in Excess of Par—Common Stock					ACCOUNT NO.	
					Balance	
Date		**Item**	**Debit**	**Credit**	**Debit**	**Credit**
2003 Jan.	1	Balance				80,000
Nov.	1	4,000 shares issued for cash		40,000		120,000

This cash inflow is reported in the financing activities section as follows:

Cash flows from financing activities:
    Cash received from sale of common stock **$48,000**

Bonds Payable

The bonds payable account decreased by $50,000, as shown below. This decrease results from retiring the bonds by a cash payment for their face amount.

ACCOUNT Bonds Payable					ACCOUNT NO.	
					Balance	
Date		**Item**	**Debit**	**Credit**	**Debit**	**Credit**
2003 Jan.	1	Balance				150,000
June	30	Retired by payment of cash at face amount	50,000			100,000

This cash outflow is reported in the financing activities section as follows:

Cash flows from financing activities:
    Cash paid to retire bonds payable **$50,000**

Building

The building account increased by $60,000, and the accumulated depreciation—building account increased by $7,000, as shown below.

ACCOUNT **Building**					ACCOUNT NO.	
					Balance	
Date		**Item**	**Debit**	**Credit**	**Debit**	**Credit**
2003 Jan.	1	Balance			200,000	
Dec.	27	Purchased for cash	60,000		260,000	

ACCOUNT **Accumulated Depreciation—Building**					ACCOUNT NO.	
					Balance	
Date		**Item**	**Debit**	**Credit**	**Debit**	**Credit**
2003 Jan.	1	Balance				58,300
Dec.	31	Depreciation for the year		7,000		65,300

A building with a cost of $145,000 and accumulated depreciation of $35,000 was sold for a $10,000 gain. How much cash was generated from this investing activity?

$120,000 ($145,000 − $35,000 + $10,000)

The purchase of a building for cash of $60,000 is reported as an outflow of cash in the investing activities section, as follows:

Cash flows from investing activities:
   Cash paid for purchase of building $60,000

The credit in the accumulated depreciation—building account, shown earlier, represents depreciation expense for the year. This depreciation expense of $7,000 on the building has already been considered as an addition to net income in determining cash flows from operating activities, as reported in Exhibit 5.

Land

The $45,000 decline in the land account resulted from two separate transactions, as shown below.

ACCOUNT **Land**					ACCOUNT NO.	
					Balance	
Date		**Item**	**Debit**	**Credit**	**Debit**	**Credit**
2003 Jan.	1	Balance			125,000	
June	8	Sold for $72,000 cash		60,000	65,000	
Oct.	12	Purchased for $15,000 cash	15,000		80,000	

The first transaction is the sale of land with a cost of $60,000 for $72,000 in cash. The $72,000 proceeds from the sale are reported in the investing activities section, as follows:

Cash flows from investing activities:
   Cash received from sale of land (includes $12,000 gain reported
    in net income) $72,000

The proceeds of $72,000 include the $12,000 gain on the sale of land and the $60,000 cost (book value) of the land. As shown in Exhibit 5, the $12,000 gain is also deducted from net income in the cash flows from operating activities section. This is necessary so that the $12,000 cash inflow related to the gain is not included twice as a cash inflow.

The second transaction is the purchase of land for cash of $15,000. This transaction is reported as an outflow of cash in the investing activities section, as follows:

Cash flows from investing activities:
    Cash paid for purchase of land $15,000

Preparing the Statement of Cash Flows

The statement of cash flows for Rundell Inc. is prepared from the data assembled and analyzed above, using the indirect method. Exhibit 6 shows the statement of cash flows prepared by Rundell Inc. The statement indicates that the cash position increased by $71,500 during the year. The most significant increase in net cash flows, $100,500, was from operating activities. The most significant use of cash, $26,000, was for financing activities.

Exhibit 6 Statement of Cash Flows—Indirect Method

Rundell Inc. Statement of Cash Flows For the Year Ended December 31, 2003			
Cash flows from operating activities:			
Net income		$108,000	
Add: Depreciation	$ 7,000		
Decrease in inventories	8,000		
Increase in accrued expenses	2,200	17,200	
		$125,200	
Deduct: Increase in accounts receivable	$ 9,000		
Decrease in accounts payable	3,200		
Decrease in income taxes payable	500		
Gain on sale of land	12,000	24,700	
Net cash flow from operating activities			$100,500
Cash flows from investing activities:			
Cash from sale of land		$ 72,000	
Less: Cash paid to purchase land	$15,000		
Cash paid for purchase of building	60,000	75,000	
Net cash flow used for investing activities			(3,000)
Cash flows from financing activities:			
Cash received from sale of common stock		$ 48,000	
Less: Cash paid to retire bonds payable	$50,000		
Cash paid for dividends	24,000	74,000	
Net cash flow used for financing activities			(26,000)
Increase in cash			$ 71,500
Cash at the beginning of the year			26,000
Cash at the end of the year			$ 97,500

Statement of Cash Flows—The Direct Method

objective 4

Prepare a statement of cash flows, using the direct method.

As we discussed previously, the manner of reporting cash flows from investing and financing activities is the same under the direct and indirect methods. In addition, the direct method and the indirect method will report the same amount of cash flows from operating activities. However, the methods differ in how the cash flows from operating activities data are obtained, analyzed, and reported.

To illustrate the direct method, we will use the comparative balance sheet and the income statement for Rundell Inc. In this way, we can compare the statement of cash flows under the direct method and the indirect method.

Exhibit 7 shows the changes in the current asset and liability account balances for Rundell Inc. The income statement in Exhibit 7 shows additional data for Rundell Inc.

Exhibit 7 Balance Sheet and Income Statement Data for Direct Method

Rundell Inc.
Schedule of Changes in Current Accounts

Accounts	December 31 2003	December 31 2002	Increase Decrease*
Cash	$ 97,500	$ 26,000	$71,500
Accounts receivable (net)	74,000	65,000	9,000
Inventories	172,000	180,000	8,000*
Accounts payable (merchandise creditors)	43,500	46,700	3,200*
Accrued expenses payable (operating expenses)	26,500	24,300	2,200
Income taxes payable	7,900	8,400	500*
Dividends payable	14,000	10,000	4,000

Rundell Inc.
Income Statement
For the Year Ended December 31, 2003

Sales		$1,180,000
Cost of merchandise sold		790,000
Gross profit		$ 390,000
Operating expenses:		
Depreciation expense	$ 7,000	
Other operating expenses	196,000	
Total operating expenses		203,000
Income from operations		$ 187,000
Other income:		
Gain on sale of land	$ 12,000	
Other expense:		
Interest expense	8,000	4,000
Income before income tax		$ 191,000
Income tax expense		83,000
Net income		$ 108,000

The direct method reports cash flows from operating activities by major classes of operating cash receipts and operating cash payments. The difference between the major classes of total operating cash receipts and total operating cash payments is the net cash flow from operating activities.

Cash Received from Customers

The $1,180,000 of sales for Rundell Inc. is reported by using the accrual method. To determine the cash received from sales to customers, the $1,180,000 must be adjusted. The adjustment necessary to convert the sales reported on the income statement to the cash received from customers is summarized below.

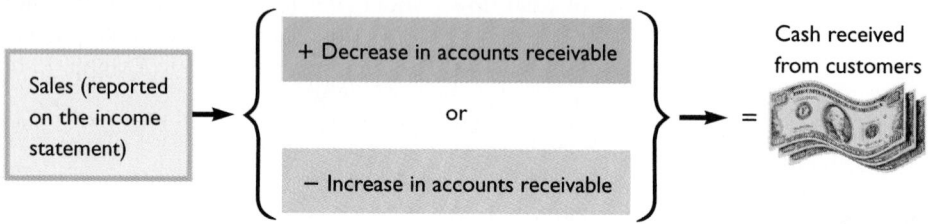

For Rundell Inc., the cash received from customers is $1,171,000, as shown below.

Sales	$1,180,000
Less increase in accounts receivable	9,000
Cash received from customers	$1,171,000

The additions to **accounts receivable** for sales on account during the year were $9,000 more than the amounts collected from customers on account. Sales reported on the income statement therefore included $9,000 that did not result in a cash inflow during the year. In other words, the increase of $9,000 in accounts receivable during 2003 indicates that sales on account exceeded cash received from customers by $9,000. Thus, $9,000 is deducted from sales to determine the cash received from customers. The $1,171,000 of cash received from customers is reported in the cash flows from operating activities section of the cash flow statement.

Cash Payments for Merchandise

The $790,000 of cost of merchandise sold is reported on the income statement for Rundell Inc., using the accrual method. The adjustments necessary to convert the cost of merchandise sold to cash payments for merchandise during 2003 are summarized below.

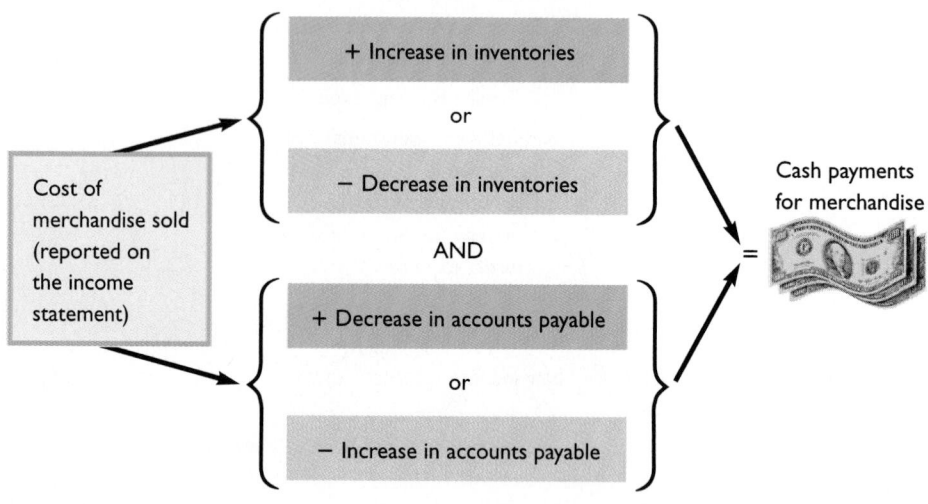

Q&A

Sales reported on the income statement were $350,000. The accounts receivable balance declined $8,000 over the year. What was the amount of cash received from customers?

$358,000 ($350,000 + $8,000)

For Rundell Inc., the amount of cash payments for merchandise is $785,200, as determined below.

Cost of merchandise sold	$790,000
Deduct decrease in inventories	(8,000)
Add decrease in accounts payable	3,200
Cash payments for merchandise	$785,200

The $8,000 decrease in **inventories** indicates that the merchandise sold exceeded the cost of the merchandise purchased by $8,000. The amount reported on the income statement for cost of merchandise sold therefore includes $8,000 that did not require a cash outflow during the year. Thus, $8,000 is deducted from the cost of merchandise sold in determining the cash payments for merchandise.

The $3,200 decrease in **accounts payable** (merchandise creditors) indicates a cash outflow that is excluded from cost of merchandise sold. In other words, the decrease in accounts payable indicates that cash payments for merchandise were $3,200 more than the purchases on account during 2003. Thus, $3,200 is added to the cost of merchandise sold in determining the cash payments for merchandise.

Cash Payments for Operating Expenses

The $7,000 of depreciation expense reported on the income statement did not require a cash outflow. Thus, under the direct method, it is not reported on the statement of cash flows. The $196,000 reported for other operating expenses is adjusted to reflect the cash payments for operating expenses, as summarized below.

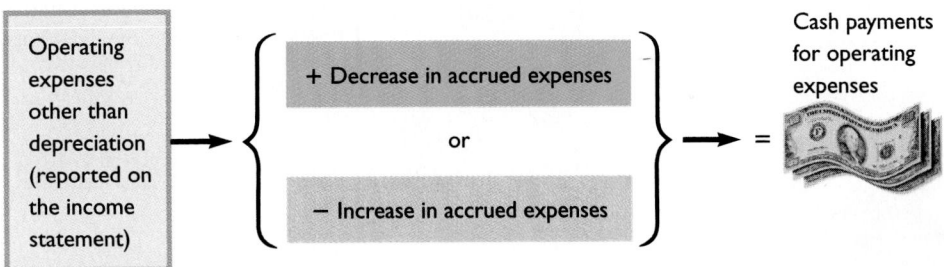

For Rundell Inc., the amount of cash payments for operating expenses is $193,800, determined as follows:

Operating expenses other than depreciation	$196,000
Deduct increase in accrued expenses	2,200
Cash payments for operating expenses	$193,800

The increase in **accrued expenses** (operating expenses) indicates that operating expenses include $2,200 for which there was no cash outflow (payment) during the year. In other words, the increase in accrued expenses indicates that the cash payments for operating expenses were $2,200 less than the amount reported as an expense during the year. Thus, $2,200 is deducted from the operating expenses on the income statement in determining the cash payments for operating expenses.

Gain on Sale of Land

The income statement for Rundell Inc. in Exhibit 7 reports a gain of $12,000 on the sale of land. As we discussed previously, the gain is included in the proceeds from the sale of land, which is reported as part of the cash flows from investing activities.

Interest Expense

The income statement for Rundell Inc. in Exhibit 7 reports interest expense of $8,000. The interest expense is related to the bonds payable that were outstanding during the year. We assume that interest on the bonds is paid on June 30 and December 31. Thus, $8,000 cash outflow for interest expense is reported on the statement of cash flows as an operating activity.

If interest payable had existed at the end of the year, the interest expense would be adjusted for any increase or decrease in interest payable from the beginning to the end of the year. That is, a decrease in interest payable would be added to interest expense and an increase in interest payable would be subtracted from interest expense. This is similar to the adjustment for changes in income taxes payable, which we will illustrate in the following paragraphs.

Cash Payments for Income Taxes

The adjustment to convert the income tax reported on the income statement to the cash basis is summarized below.

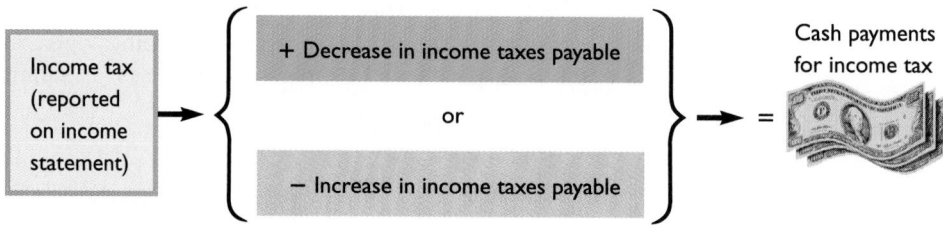

For Rundell Inc., cash payments for income tax are $83,500, determined as follows:

Income tax	$83,000
Add decrease in income taxes payable	500
Cash payments for income tax	$83,500

The cash outflow for income taxes exceeded the income tax deducted as an expense during the period by $500. Thus, $500 is added to the amount of income tax reported on the income statement in determining the cash payments for income tax.

Reporting Cash Flows from Operating Activities— Direct Method

Exhibit 8 is a complete statement of cash flows for Rundell Inc., using the direct method for reporting cash flows from operating activities. The portions of this statement that differ from the indirect method are highlighted in color. Exhibit 8 also includes the separate schedule reconciling net income and net cash flow from operating activities. This schedule must accompany the statement of cash flows when the direct method is used. This schedule is similar to the cash flows from operating activities section of the statement of cash flows prepared using the indirect method.

Dell Computer Corporation is one of the few companies that has a *negative cash conversion cycle*. This means that Dell receives payment for a computer before it pays for the parts that went into that computer. This can only be done by collecting the sale with a credit card, maintaining very little inventory, and holding accounts payable open for 30 days.

Exhibit 8 Statement of Cash Flows—Direct Method

Rundell Inc.
Statement of Cash Flows
For the Year Ended December 31, 2003

Cash flows from operating activities:			
Cash received from customers			$1,171,000
Deduct: Cash payments for merchandise	$785,200		
Cash payments for operating expenses	193,800		
Cash payments for interest	8,000		
Cash payments for income taxes	83,500	1,070,500	
Net cash flow from operating activities			$100,500
Cash flows from investing activities:			
Cash from sale of land		$ 72,000	
Less: Cash paid to purchase land	$ 15,000		
Cash paid for purchase of building	60,000	75,000	
Net cash flow used for investing activities			(3,000)
Cash flows from financing activities:			
Cash received from sale of common stock		$ 48,000	
Less: Cash paid to retire bonds payable	$ 50,000		
Cash paid for dividends	24,000	74,000	
Net cash flow used for financing activities			(26,000)
Increase in cash			$ 71,500
Cash at the beginning of the year			26,000
Cash at the end of the year			$ 97,500

Schedule Reconciling Net Income with Cash Flows from Operating Activities:

Net income, per income statement			$108,000
Add: Depreciation		$ 7,000	
Decrease in inventories		8,000	
Increase in accrued expenses		2,200	17,200
			$125,200
Deduct: Increase in accounts receivable		$ 9,000	
Decrease in accounts payable		3,200	
Decrease in income taxes payable		500	
Gain on sale of land		12,000	24,700
Net cash flow from operating activities			$100,500

FINANCIAL ANALYSIS AND INTERPRETATION

objective 5

Calculate and interpret the free cash flow.

A valuable tool for evaluating the cash position of a business is free cash flow. **Free cash flow** is a measure of operating cash flow available for corporate purposes after providing sufficient fixed asset additions to maintain current productive capacity and dividends. Thus, free cash flow can be calculated as follows:

Cash flow from operating activities
Less: Cash used to purchase fixed assets to maintain productive capacity used up in producing income during the period
Less: Cash used for dividends
Free cash flow

Many high technology firms must aggressively reinvest in new technology to remain competitive. This can reduce free cash flow. For example, **Motorola's** free cash flow is less than 10% of the cash flow from operating activities. In contrast, **Coca-Cola's** free cash flow is approximately 75% of the cash flow from operating activities.

To illustrate, assume that O'Brien Company had cash flow from operating activities of $1,400,000. O'Brien Company invested $450,000 in fixed assets to maintain productive capacity, and another $300,000 to expand capacity. Dividends were $100,000. Thus, free cash flow is as follows:

Cash flow from operating activities		$1,400,000
Less: Cash invested in fixed assets to		
maintain productive capacity	$450,000	
Cash for dividends	100,000	550,000
Free cash flow		$ 850,000

A company that has free cash flow is able to fund internal growth, retire debt, and enjoy financial flexibility. A company with no free cash flow is unable to maintain current productive capacity or dividend payouts to stockholders. Lack of free cash flow can be an early indicator of liquidity problems. Indeed, as stated by one analyst, "Free cash flow gives the company firepower to reduce debt and ultimately generate consistent, actual income."[5]

ENCORE

Cash Is King for the Pack

The **Green Bay Packers** is the only team in the NFL to be owned by the fans (over 109,000 of them). Indeed, over 10,000 fans show up in early July at Lambeau Field for the shareholders' meeting, the largest shareholders' meeting in corporate America. Unfortunately, the recent financial news has not been good. Although the club had a profit of $1 million, it had a negative cash flow of $10.7 million (excluding a one-time expansion team payment). Why did the cash decline in the face of positive earnings? The answer is simple. The Packers have paid over $32 million in player-signing bonuses, while continuing to make improvements to Lambeau Field. John Underwood, treasurer, stated, "We really need to focus our attention on generating higher levels of cash. In the business we're in, cash is king. And every dollar we make in

this franchise goes to only one of two purposes: the football team or the facilities." While the Packers place 15th out of 31 teams in total revenue, the president predicts that they will fall to last place by 2003 if Lambeau Field is not renovated. A stadium renovation will allow the Packers to:

- expand the concourse for additional retail shops and concession space.
- build a stadium club that can be used for banquets and events.
- expand Lambeau's rather small 61,000-seat capacity by 8,000 seats.
- rebuild the luxury boxes.

The added cash flow from stadium improvements is the key to financial success in professional football. The question is how to come up with $150

million for stadium renovations. The team is presently considering a one-time, $1,000 per-seat user fee to be assessed to the season ticket holders to cover part of it. Apparently, if you're a stockholder who also holds season tickets, the news is doubly bad. ■

[5] Jill Krutick, *Fortune*, March 30, 1998, p. 106.

A work sheet may be useful in assembling data for the statement of cash flows. Whether or not a work sheet is used, the concepts of cash flow and the statements of cash flows presented in this chapter are not affected. In this appendix, we will describe and illustrate the use of work sheets for the indirect method and the direct method.

Work Sheet—Indirect Method

We will use the data for Rundell Inc., presented in Exhibit 3, as a basis for illustrating the work sheet for the indirect method. The procedures used in preparing this work sheet, shown in Exhibit 9, are outlined at the top of the next page.

Exhibit 9 Work Sheet for Statement of Cash Flows—Indirect Method

Rundell Inc.
Work Sheet for Statement of Cash Flows
For the Year Ended December 31, 2003

	Accounts	Balance Dec. 31, 2002	Transactions Debit	Transactions Credit	Balance Dec. 31, 2003	
1	Cash	26,000	(o) 71,500		97,500	1
2	Accounts receivable (net)	65,000	(n) 9,000		74,000	2
3	Inventories	180,000		(m) 8,000	172,000	3
4	Land	125,000	(k) 15,000	(l) 60,000	80,000	4
5	Building	200,000	(j) 60,000		260,000	5
6	Accumulated depreciation—building	(58,300)		(i) 7,000	(65,300)	6
7	Accounts payable (merchandise creditors)	(46,700)	(h) 3,200		(43,500)	7
8	Accrued expenses payable (operating expenses)	(24,300)		(g) 2,200	(26,500)	8
9	Income taxes payable	(8,400)	(f) 500		(7,900)	9
10	Dividends payable	(10,000)		(e) 4,000	(14,000)	10
11	Bonds payable	(150,000)	(d) 50,000		(100,000)	11
12	Common stock	(16,000)		(c) 8,000	(24,000)	12
13	Paid-in capital in excess of par	(80,000)		(c) 40,000	(120,000)	13
14	Retained earnings	(202,300)	(b) 28,000	(a) 108,000	(282,300)	14
15	Totals	0	237,200	237,200	0	15
16	Operating activities:					16
17	Net income		(a) 108,000			17
18	Depreciation of building		(i) 7,000			18
19	Decrease in inventories		(m) 8,000			19
20	Increase in accrued expenses		(g) 2,200			20
21	Increase in accounts receivable			(n) 9,000		21
22	Decrease in accounts payable			(h) 3,200		22
23	Decrease in income taxes payable			(f) 500		23
24	Gain on sale of land			(l) 12,000		24
25	Investing activities:					25
26	Sale of land		(l) 72,000			26
27	Purchase of land			(k) 15,000		27
28	Purchase of building			(j) 60,000		28
29	Financing activities:					29
30	Issued common stock		(c) 48,000			30
31	Retired bonds payable			(d) 50,000		31
32	Declared cash dividends		—	(b) 28,000		32
33	Increase in dividends payable		(e) 4,000			33
34	Net increase in cash			(o) 71,500		34
35	Totals		249,200	249,200		35

1. List the title of each balance sheet account in the Accounts column. For each account, enter its balance as of December 31, 2002, in the first column and its balance as of December 31, 2003, in the last column. Place the credit balances in parentheses. The column totals should equal zero, since the total of the debits in a column should equal the total of the credits in a column.
2. Analyze the change during the year in each account to determine the net increase (decrease) in cash and the cash flows from operating activities, investing activities, financing activities, and the noncash investing and financing activities. Show the effect of the change on cash flows by making entries in the Transactions columns.

Analyzing Accounts

An efficient method of analyzing cash flows is to determine the type of cash flow activity that led to changes in balance sheet accounts during the period. As we analyze each noncash account, we will make entries on the work sheet for specific types of cash flow activities related to the noncash accounts. After we have analyzed all the noncash accounts, we will make an entry for the increase (decrease) in cash during the period. These entries, however, are not posted to the ledger. They only aid in assembling the data on the work sheet.

The order in which the accounts are analyzed is unimportant. However, it is more efficient to begin with the retained earnings account and proceed upward in the account listing.

Retained Earnings. The work sheet shows a Retained Earnings balance of $202,300 at December 31, 2002, and $282,300 at December 31, 2003. Thus, Retained Earnings increased $80,000 during the year. This increase resulted from two factors: (1) net income of $108,000 and (2) declaring cash dividends of $28,000. To identify the cash flows by activity, we will make two entries on the work sheet. These entries also serve to account for or explain, in terms of cash flows, the increase of $80,000.

In closing the accounts at the end of the year, the retained earnings account was credited for the net income of $108,000. The $108,000 is reported on the statement of cash flows as "cash flows from operating activities." The following entry is made in the Transactions columns on the work sheet. This entry (1) accounts for the credit portion of the closing entry (to Retained Earnings) and (2) identifies the cash flow in the bottom portion of the work sheet.

| (a) | Operating Activities—Net Income | 108,000 | |
| | Retained Earnings | | 108,000 |

In closing the accounts at the end of the year, the retained earnings account was debited for dividends declared of $28,000. The $28,000 is reported as a financing activity on the statement of cash flows. The following entry on the work sheet (1) accounts for the debit portion of the closing entry (to Retained Earnings) and (2) identifies the cash flow in the bottom portion of the work sheet.

| (b) | Retained Earnings | 28,000 | |
| | Financing Activities—Declared Cash Dividends | | 28,000 |

The $28,000 of declared dividends will be adjusted later for the actual amount of cash dividends paid during the year.

Other Accounts. The entries for the other accounts are made in the work sheet in a manner similar to entries (a) and (b). A summary of these entries is as follows:

(c)	Financing Activities—Issued Common Stock	48,000	
	Common Stock		8,000
	Paid-In Capital in Excess of Par—Common Stock		40,000

(d)	Bonds Payable	50,000	
	Financing Activities—Retired Bonds Payable		50,000
(e)	Financing Activities—Increase in Dividends Payable	4,000	
	Dividends Payable		4,000
(f)	Income Taxes Payable	500	
	Operating Activities—Decrease in Income Taxes Payable		500
(g)	Operating Activities—Increase in Accrued Expenses	2,200	
	Accrued Expenses Payable		2,200
(h)	Accounts Payable	3,200	
	Operating Activities—Decrease in Accounts Payable		3,200
(i)	Operating Activities—Depreciation of Building	7,000	
	Accumulated Depreciation—Building		7,000
(j)	Building	60,000	
	Investing Activities—Purchase of Building		60,000
(k)	Land	15,000	
	Investing Activities—Purchase of Land		15,000
(l)	Investing Activities—Sale of Land	72,000	
	Operating Activities—Gain on Sale of Land		12,000
	Land		60,000
(m)	Operating Activities—Decrease in Inventories	8,000	
	Inventories		8,000
(n)	Accounts Receivable	9,000	
	Operating Activities—Increase in Accounts Receivable		9,000
(o)	Cash	71,500	
	Net Increase in Cash		71,500

Completing the Work Sheet

After we have analyzed all the balance sheet accounts and made the entries on the work sheet, all the operating, investing, and financing activities are identified in the bottom portion of the work sheet. The accuracy of the work sheet entries is verified by the equality of each pair of the totals of the debit and credit Transactions columns.

Preparing the Statement of Cash Flows

The statement of cash flows prepared from the work sheet is identical to the statement in Exhibit 6. The data for the three sections of the statement are obtained from the bottom portion of the work sheet.

In the cash flows from operating activities section, the effect of depreciation is normally presented first. The effects of increases and decreases in current assets and current liabilities are then presented. The effects of any gains and losses on operating activities are normally reported last. The cash paid for dividends is reported as $24,000 instead of the amount of dividends declared ($28,000) less the increase in dividends payable ($4,000). Any noncash investing and financing activities are usually reported in a separate schedule at the bottom of the statement.

Work Sheet—Direct Method

As a basis for illustrating the direct method work sheet, we will use the balance sheet data for Rundell Inc. in Exhibit 3 and the income statement data in Exhibit 7. The procedures used in preparing the work sheet are outlined below and following Exhibit 10.

1. List the title of each balance sheet account in the Accounts column. For each account, enter its balance as of December 31, 2002, in the first column and its balance as of December 31, 2003, in the last column. Place the credit balances in parentheses. The column totals should equal zero, since the total of the debits in a column should equal the total of the credits in a column.

Exhibit 10 Work Sheet for Statement of Cash Flows—Direct Method

<table>
<thead>
<tr><th colspan="7">Rundell Inc.
Work Sheet for Statement of Cash Flows
For the Year Ended December 31, 2003</th></tr>
<tr><th rowspan="2">Accounts</th><th rowspan="2">Balance
Dec. 31, 2002</th><th colspan="2">Transactions</th><th rowspan="2">Balance
Dec. 31, 2003</th><th></th></tr>
<tr><th>Debit</th><th>Credit</th><th></th></tr>
</thead>
<tbody>
<tr><td>1 **Balance Sheet**</td><td></td><td></td><td></td><td></td><td>1</td></tr>
<tr><td>2 Cash ....</td><td>26,000</td><td>(t) 71,500</td><td></td><td>97,500</td><td>2</td></tr>
<tr><td>3 Accounts receivable (net) ....</td><td>65,000</td><td>(s) 9,000</td><td></td><td>74,000</td><td>3</td></tr>
<tr><td>4 Inventories ....</td><td>180,000</td><td></td><td>(r) 8,000</td><td>172,000</td><td>4</td></tr>
<tr><td>5 Land ....</td><td>125,000</td><td>(q) 15,000</td><td>(e) 60,000</td><td>80,000</td><td>5</td></tr>
<tr><td>6 Building ....</td><td>200,000</td><td>(p) 60,000</td><td></td><td>260,000</td><td>6</td></tr>
<tr><td>7 Accumulated depreciation—building ....</td><td>(58,300)</td><td></td><td>(c) 7,000</td><td>(65,300)</td><td>7</td></tr>
<tr><td>8 Accounts payable (merchandise creditors) ....</td><td>(46,700)</td><td>(o) 3,200</td><td></td><td>(43,500)</td><td>8</td></tr>
<tr><td>9 Accrued expenses payable (operating expenses) ..</td><td>(24,300)</td><td></td><td>(n) 2,200</td><td>(26,500)</td><td>9</td></tr>
<tr><td>10 Income taxes payable ....</td><td>(8,400)</td><td>(m) 500</td><td></td><td>(7,900)</td><td>10</td></tr>
<tr><td>11 Dividends payable ....</td><td>(10,000)</td><td></td><td>(l) 4,000</td><td>(14,000)</td><td>11</td></tr>
<tr><td>12 Bonds payable ....</td><td>(150,000)</td><td>(k) 50,000</td><td></td><td>(100,000)</td><td>12</td></tr>
<tr><td>13 Common stock ....</td><td>(16,000)</td><td></td><td>(j) 8,000</td><td>(24,000)</td><td>13</td></tr>
<tr><td>14 Paid-in capital in excess of par ....</td><td>(80,000)</td><td></td><td>(j) 40,000</td><td>(120,000)</td><td>14</td></tr>
<tr><td>15 Retained earnings ....</td><td>(202,300)</td><td>(i) 28,000</td><td>(h) 108,000</td><td>(282,300)</td><td>15</td></tr>
<tr><td>16 Totals ....</td><td>0</td><td>237,200</td><td>237,200</td><td>0</td><td>16</td></tr>
<tr><td>17 **Income Statement**</td><td></td><td></td><td></td><td></td><td>17</td></tr>
<tr><td>18 Sales ....</td><td></td><td></td><td>(a)1,180,000</td><td></td><td>18</td></tr>
<tr><td>19 Cost of merchandise sold ....</td><td></td><td>(b) 790,000</td><td></td><td></td><td>19</td></tr>
<tr><td>20 Depreciation expense ....</td><td></td><td>(c) 7,000</td><td></td><td></td><td>20</td></tr>
<tr><td>21 Other operating expenses ....</td><td></td><td>(d) 196,000</td><td></td><td></td><td>21</td></tr>
<tr><td>22 Gain on sale of land ....</td><td></td><td></td><td>(e) 12,000</td><td></td><td>22</td></tr>
<tr><td>23 Interest expense ....</td><td></td><td>(f) 8,000</td><td></td><td></td><td>23</td></tr>
<tr><td>24 Income taxes ....</td><td></td><td>(g) 83,000</td><td></td><td></td><td>24</td></tr>
<tr><td>25 Net income ....</td><td></td><td>(h) 108,000</td><td></td><td></td><td>25</td></tr>
<tr><td>26 **Cash Flows**</td><td></td><td></td><td></td><td></td><td>26</td></tr>
<tr><td>27 Operating activities:</td><td></td><td></td><td></td><td></td><td>27</td></tr>
<tr><td>28   Cash received from customers ....</td><td></td><td>(a)1,180,000</td><td>(s) 9,000</td><td></td><td>28</td></tr>
<tr><td>29   Cash payments:</td><td></td><td></td><td></td><td></td><td>29</td></tr>
<tr><td>30   Merchandise ....</td><td></td><td>(r) 8,000</td><td>(b) 790,000</td><td></td><td>30</td></tr>
<tr><td>31</td><td></td><td></td><td>(o) 3,200</td><td></td><td>31</td></tr>
<tr><td>32   Operating expenses ....</td><td></td><td>(n) 2,200</td><td>(d) 196,000</td><td></td><td>32</td></tr>
<tr><td>33   Interest ....</td><td></td><td></td><td>(f) 8,000</td><td></td><td>33</td></tr>
<tr><td>34   Income taxes ....</td><td></td><td></td><td>(g) 83,000</td><td></td><td>34</td></tr>
<tr><td>35</td><td></td><td></td><td>(m) 500</td><td></td><td>35</td></tr>
<tr><td>36 Investing activities:</td><td></td><td></td><td></td><td></td><td>36</td></tr>
<tr><td>37   Sale of land ....</td><td></td><td>(e) 72,000</td><td></td><td></td><td>37</td></tr>
<tr><td>38   Purchase of land ....</td><td></td><td></td><td>(q) 15,000</td><td></td><td>38</td></tr>
<tr><td>39   Purchase of building ....</td><td></td><td></td><td>(p) 60,000</td><td></td><td>39</td></tr>
<tr><td>40 Financing activities:</td><td></td><td></td><td></td><td></td><td>40</td></tr>
<tr><td>41   Issued common stock ....</td><td></td><td>(j) 48,000</td><td></td><td></td><td>41</td></tr>
<tr><td>42   Retired bonds payable ....</td><td></td><td></td><td>(k) 50,000</td><td></td><td>42</td></tr>
<tr><td>43   Declared cash dividends ....</td><td></td><td></td><td>(i) 28,000</td><td></td><td>43</td></tr>
<tr><td>44   Increase in dividends payable ....</td><td></td><td>(l) 4,000</td><td></td><td></td><td>44</td></tr>
<tr><td>45 Net increase in cash ....</td><td></td><td></td><td>(t) 71,500</td><td></td><td>45</td></tr>
<tr><td>46 Totals ....</td><td></td><td>2,506,200</td><td>2,506,200</td><td></td><td>46</td></tr>
</tbody>
</table>

2. List the title of each income statement account and "Net income" on the work sheet.
3. Analyze the effect of each income statement item on cash flows from operating activities. Beginning with sales, enter the balance of each item in the proper Transactions column. Complete the entry in the Transactions columns to show the effect on cash flows.
4. Analyze the change during the year in each balance sheet account to determine the net increase (decrease) in cash and the cash flows from operating activities, investing activities, financing activities, and the noncash investing and financing activities. Show the effect of the change on cash flows by making entries in the Transactions columns.

Analyzing Accounts

Under the direct method of reporting cash flows from operating activities, analyzing accounts begins with the income statement. As we analyze each income statement account, we will make entries on the work sheet that show the effect on cash flows from operating activities. After we have analyzed the income statement accounts, we will analyze changes in the balance sheet accounts.

The order in which the balance sheet accounts are analyzed is unimportant. However, it is more efficient to begin with the retained earnings account and proceed upward in the account listing. As each noncash balance sheet account is analyzed, we will make entries on the work sheet for the related cash flow activities. After we have analyzed all the noncash accounts, we will make an entry for the increase (decrease) in cash during the period.

Sales. The income statement for Rundell Inc. shows sales of $1,180,000 for the year. Sales for cash provide cash when the sale is made. Sales on account provide cash when customers pay their bills. The entry on the work sheet is as follows:

| (a) | Operating Activities—Receipts from Customers | 1,180,000 | |
| | Sales | | 1,180,000 |

Cost of Merchandise Sold. The income statement for Rundell Inc. shows cost of merchandise sold of $790,000 for the year. The cost of merchandise sold requires cash payments for cash purchases of merchandise. For purchases on account, cash payments are made when the invoices are due. The entry on the work sheet is as follows:

| (b) | Cost of Merchandise Sold | 790,000 | |
| | Operating Activities—Payments for Merchandise | | 790,000 |

Depreciation Expense. The income statement for Rundell Inc. shows depreciation expense of $7,000. Depreciation expense does not require a cash outflow and thus is not reported on the statement of cash flows. The entry on the work sheet to fully account for the depreciation expense is as follows:

| (c) | Depreciation Expense | 7,000 | |
| | Accumulated Depreciation—Building | | 7,000 |

Other Accounts. The entries for the other accounts are made on the work sheet in a manner similar to entries (a), (b), and (c). A summary of these entries is as follows:

| (d) | Other Operating Expenses | 196,000 | |
| | Operating Activities—Paid Operating Expenses | | 196,000 |

(e)	Investing Activities—Sale of Land	72,000	
	Land		60,000
	Gain on Sale of Land		12,000
(f)	Interest Expense	8,000	
	Operating Activities—Paid Interest		8,000
(g)	Income Taxes	83,000	
	Operating Activities—Paid Income Taxes		83,000
(h)	Net Income	108,000	
	Retained Earnings		108,000
(i)	Retained Earnings	28,000	
	Financing Activities—Declared Cash Dividends		28,000
(j)	Financing Activities—Issued Common Stock	48,000	
	Common Stock		8,000
	Paid-In Capital in Excess of Par—Common Stock		40,000
(k)	Bonds Payable	50,000	
	Financing Activities—Retired Bonds Payable		50,000
(l)	Financing Activities—Increase in Dividends Payable	4,000	
	Dividends Payable		4,000
(m)	Income Taxes Payable	500	
	Operating Activities—Cash Paid for Income Taxes		500
(n)	Operating Activities—Cash Paid for Operating Expenses	2,200	
	Accrued Expenses Payable		2,200
(o)	Accounts Payable	3,200	
	Operating Activities—Cash Paid for Merchandise		3,200
(p)	Building	60,000	
	Investing Activities—Purchase of Building		60,000
(q)	Land	15,000	
	Investing Activities—Purchase of Land		15,000
(r)	Operating Activities—Cash Paid for Merchandise	8,000	
	Inventories		8,000
(s)	Accounts Receivable	9,000	
	Operating Activities—Cash Received from Customers		9,000
(t)	Cash	71,500	
	Net Increase in Cash		71,500

Completing the Work Sheet

After we have analyzed all the income statement and balance sheet accounts and have made the entries on the work sheet, all the operating, investing, and financing activities are identified in the bottom portion of the work sheet. The mathematical accuracy of the work sheet entries is verified by the equality of each pair of the totals of the debit and credit Transactions columns.

Preparing the Statement of Cash Flows

The statement of cash flows prepared from the work sheet is identical to the statement in Exhibit 8. The data for the three sections of the statement are obtained from the bottom portion of the work sheet. Some of these data may not be reported exactly as they appear on the work sheet. The cash paid for dividends is reported as $24,000 instead of the amount of dividends declared ($28,000) less the increase in the dividends payable ($4,000).

HEY POINTS

1 Explain why the statement of cash flows is one of the basic financial statements.
The statement of cash flows reports useful information about a firm's ability to generate cash from operations, maintain and expand its operating capacity, meet its financial obligations, and pay dividends. This information assists investors, creditors, and others in assessing the firm's profit potential and its ability to pay its maturing debt. The statement of cash flows is also useful to managers in evaluating past operations and in planning future operating, investing, and financing activities.

2 Summarize the types of cash flow activities reported in the statement of cash flows.
The statement of cash flows reports cash receipts and cash payments by three types of activities: operating activities, investing activities, and financing activities.

Cash flows from operating activities are cash flows from transactions that affect net income. There are two methods of reporting cash flows from operating activities: (1) the direct method and (2) the indirect method.

Cash inflows from investing activities are cash flows from the sale of investments, fixed assets, and intangible assets. Cash outflows generally include payments to acquire investments, fixed assets, and intangible assets.

Cash inflows from financing activities include proceeds from issuing equity securities, such as preferred and common stock. Cash inflows also arise from issuing bonds, mortgage notes payable, and other long-term debt. Cash outflows from financing activities arise from paying cash dividends, purchasing treasury stock, and repaying amounts borrowed.

Investing and financing for a business may be affected by transactions that do not involve cash. The effect of such transactions should be reported in a separate schedule accompanying the statement of cash flows.

Because it may be misleading, cash flow per share is not reported in the statement of cash flows.

3 Prepare a statement of cash flows, using the indirect method.
To prepare the statement of cash flows, changes in the noncash balance sheet accounts are analyzed. This logic relies on the fact that a change in any balance sheet account can be analyzed in terms of changes in the other balance sheet accounts. Thus, by analyzing the noncash balance sheet accounts, those activities that resulted in cash flows can be identified. Although the noncash balance sheet accounts may be analyzed in any order, it is usually more efficient to begin with retained earnings. Additional data are obtained by analyzing the income statement accounts and supporting records.

4 Prepare a statement of cash flows, using the direct method.
The direct method and the indirect method will report the same amount of cash flows from operating activities. Also, the manner of reporting cash flows from investing and financing activities is the same under both methods. The methods differ in how the cash flows from operating activities data are obtained, analyzed, and reported. The direct method reports cash flows from operating activities by major classes of operating cash receipts and cash payments. The difference between the major classes of total operating cash receipts and total operating cash payments is the net cash flow from operating activities.

The data for reporting cash flows from operating activities by the direct method can be obtained by analyzing the cash flows related to the revenues and expenses reported on the income statement. The revenues and expenses are adjusted from the accrual basis of accounting to the cash basis for purposes of preparing the statement of cash flows.

When the direct method is used, a reconciliation of net income and net cash flow from operating activities is reported in a separate schedule. This schedule is similar to the cash flows from operating activities section of the statement of cash flows prepared using the indirect method.

5 Calculate and interpret the free cash flow.
Free cash flow is the amount of operating cash flow remaining after replacing current productive capacity and maintaining current dividends. Free cash flow is the amount of cash available to reduce debt, expand the business, or return to shareholders through increased dividends or treasury stock purchases.

ILLUSTRATIVE PROBLEM

The comparative balance sheet of Dowling Company for December 31, 2004 and 2003, is as follows:

Dowling Company
Comparative Balance Sheet
December 31, 2004 and 2003

	2004	2003
Assets		
Cash	$ 140,350	$ 95,900
Accounts receivable (net)	95,300	102,300
Inventories	165,200	157,900
Prepaid expenses	6,240	5,860
Investments (long-term)	35,700	84,700
Land	75,000	90,000
Buildings	375,000	260,000
Accumulated depreciation—buildings	(71,300)	(58,300)
Machinery and equipment	428,300	428,300
Accumulated depreciation—machinery and equipment	(148,500)	(138,000)
Patents	58,000	65,000
Total assets	$1,159,290	$1,093,660
Liabilities and Stockholders' Equity		
Accounts payable (merchandise creditors)	$ 43,500	$ 46,700
Accrued expenses (operating expenses)	14,000	12,500
Income taxes payable	7,900	8,400
Dividends payable	14,000	10,000
Mortgage note payable, due 2004	40,000	0
Bonds payable	150,000	250,000
Common stock, $30 par	450,000	375,000
Excess of issue price over par—common stock	66,250	41,250
Retained earnings	373,640	349,810
Total liabilities and stockholders' equity	$1,159,290	$1,093,660

The income statement for Dowling Company is shown below.

Dowling Company
Income Statement
For the Year Ended December 31, 2004

Sales		$1,100,000
Cost of merchandise sold		710,000
Gross profit		$ 390,000
Operating expenses:		
Depreciation expense	$ 23,500	
Patent amortization	7,000	
Other operating expenses	196,000	
Total operating expenses		226,500
Income from operations		$ 163,500
Other income:		
Gain on sale of investments	$ 11,000	
Other expense:		
Interest expense	26,000	(15,000)
Income before income tax		$ 148,500
Income tax expense		50,000
Net income		$ 98,500

An examination of the accounting records revealed the following additional information applicable to 2004:

a. Land costing $15,000 was sold for $15,000.
b. A mortgage note was issued for $40,000.
c. A building costing $115,000 was constructed.
d. 2,500 shares of common stock were issued at 40 in exchange for the bonds payable.
e. Cash dividends declared were $74,670.

Instructions

1. Prepare a statement of cash flows, using the indirect method of reporting cash flows from operating activities.
2. Prepare a statement of cash flows, using the direct method of reporting cash flows from operating activities.

Solution

1.

Dowling Company
Statement of Cash Flows—Indirect Method
For the Year Ended December 31, 2004

Cash flows from operating activities:			
Net income, per income statement		$ 98,500	
Add: Depreciation	$23,500		
Amortization of patents	7,000		
Decrease in accounts receivable	7,000		
Increase in accrued expenses	1,500	39,000	
		$137,500	
Deduct: Increase in inventories	$ 7,300		
Increase in prepaid expenses	380		
Decrease in accounts payable	3,200		
Decrease in income taxes payable	500		
Gain on sale of investments	11,000	22,380	
Net cash flow from operating activities			$115,120
Cash flows from investing activities:			
Cash received from sale of:			
Investments	$60,000		
Land	15,000	$ 75,000	
Less: Cash paid for construction of building		115,000	
Net cash flow used for investing activities			(40,000)
Cash flows from financing activities:			
Cash received from issuing mortgage note payable		$ 40,000	
Less: Cash paid for dividends		70,670	
Net cash flow used for financing activities			(30,670)
Increase in cash			$ 44,450
Cash at the beginning of the year			95,900
Cash at the end of the year			$140,350

Schedule of Noncash Investing and
Financing Activities:

Issued common stock to retire bonds payable	$100,000

2.

Dowling Company
Statement of Cash Flows—Direct Method
For the Year Ended December 31, 2004

Cash flows from operating activities:			
Cash received from customers[1]		$1,107,000	
Deduct: Cash paid for merchandise[2]	$720,500		
Cash paid for operating expenses[3]	194,880		
Cash paid for interest expense	26,000		
Cash paid for income tax[4]	50,500	991,880	
Net cash flow from operating activities			$115,120
Cash flows from investing activities:			
Cash received from sale of:			
Investments	$ 60,000		
Land	15,000	$ 75,000	
Less: Cash paid for construction of building		115,000	
Net cash flow used for investing activities			(40,000)
Cash flows from financing activities:			
Cash received from issuing mortgage note payable ...		$ 40,000	
Less: Cash paid for dividends[5]		70,670	
Net cash flow used for financing activities			(30,670)
Increase in cash			$ 44,450
Cash at the beginning of the year			95,900
Cash at the end of the year			$140,350

Schedule of Noncash Investing and Financing Activities:

Issued common stock to retire bonds payable	$100,000

Computations:

[1]$1,100,000 + $7,000 = $1,107,000

[2]$710,000 + $3,200 + $7,300 = $720,500

[3]$196,000 + $380 − $1,500 = $194,880

[4]$50,000 + $500 = $50,500

[5]$74,670 + $10,000 − $14,000 = $70,670

SELF-EXAMINATION QUESTIONS   Answers at End of Chapter

Matching

Match each of the following statements with its proper term. Some terms may not be used.

A. cash flows from financing activities

B. cash flows from investing activities

C. cash flows from operating activities

D. decrease in accounts payable

E. decrease in accounts receivable

___ 1. An addition to sales under the direct method for determining cash flows from operating activities.

___ 2. A statement of cash flows disclosure item.

___ 3. The section of the statement of cash flows that reports cash flows from transactions affecting the equity and debt of the business.

___ 4. A financing activity that increases cash.

___ 5. An addition to net income under the indirect method for determining cash flows from operating activities.

___ 6. The section of the statement of cash flows that reports cash flows from transactions affecting investments in noncurrent assets.

F. direct method

G. dividends declared

H. free cash flow

I. loss on sale of land

J. indirect method

K. issuance of common stock

L. purchase of land with common stock

M. sale of land

N. statement of cash flows

___ 7. A summary of the major cash receipts and cash payments for a period.

___ 8. A deduction from net income under the indirect method for determining cash flows from operating activities.

___ 9. A method of reporting the cash flows from operating activities as the difference between the operating cash receipts and the operating cash payments.

___ 10. The section of the statement of cash flows that reports the cash transactions affecting the determination of net income.

___ 11. A method of reporting the cash flows from operating activities as the net income from operations adjusted for all deferrals of past cash receipts and payments and all accruals of expected future cash receipts and payments.

___ 12. An investing activity.

___ 13. The amount of operating cash flow remaining after replacing current productive capacity and maintaining current dividends.

Multiple Choice

1. An example of a cash flow from an operating activity is:
   A. receipt of cash from the sale of stock
   B. receipt of cash from the sale of bonds
   C. payment of cash for dividends
   D. receipt of cash from customers on account

2. An example of a cash flow from an investing activity is:
   A. receipt of cash from the sale of equipment
   B. receipt of cash from the sale of stock
   C. payment of cash for dividends
   D. payment of cash to acquire treasury stock

3. An example of a cash flow from a financing activity is:
   A. receipt of cash from customers on account
   B. receipt of cash from the sale of equipment
   C. payment of cash for dividends
   D. payment of cash to acquire land

4. Which of the following methods of reporting cash flows from operating activities adjusts net income for revenues and expenses not involving the receipt or payment of cash?

   A. Direct method   C. Reciprocal method
   B. Purchase method   D. Indirect method

5. The net income reported on the income statement for the year was $55,000, and depreciation of fixed assets for the year was $22,000. The balances of the current asset and current liability accounts at the beginning and end of the year are as follows:

	End	Beginning
Cash	$ 65,000	$ 70,000
Accounts receivable	100,000	90,000
Inventories	145,000	150,000
Prepaid expenses	7,500	8,000
Accounts payable (merchandise creditors)	51,000	58,000

The total amount reported for cash flows from operating activities in the statement of cash flows, using the indirect method, is:

A. $33,000   C. $65,500
B. $55,000   D. $77,000

CLASS DISCUSSION QUESTIONS

1. What is the principal disadvantage of the direct method of reporting cash flows from operating activities?
2. What are the major advantages of the indirect method of reporting cash flows from operating activities?
3. A corporation issued $200,000 of common stock in exchange for $200,000 of fixed assets. Where would this transaction be reported on the statement of cash flows?
4. a. What is the effect on cash flows of declaring and issuing a stock dividend?
   b. Is the stock dividend reported on the statement of cash flows?
5. A retail business, using the accrual method of accounting, owed merchandise creditors (accounts payable) $290,000 at the beginning of the year and $315,000 at the end of the year. How would the $25,000 increase be used to adjust net income in

determining the amount of cash flows from operating activities by the indirect method? Explain.

6. If salaries payable was $75,000 at the beginning of the year and $65,000 at the end of the year, should $10,000 be added to or deducted from income to determine the amount of cash flows from operating activities by the indirect method? Explain.

7. A long-term investment in bonds with a cost of $75,000 was sold for $80,000 cash. (a) What was the gain or loss on the sale? (b) What was the effect of the transaction on cash flows? (c) How should the transaction be reported in the statement of cash flows if cash flows from operating activities are reported by the indirect method?

8. A corporation issued $5,000,000 of 20-year bonds for cash at 105. How would the transaction be reported on the statement of cash flows?

9. Fully depreciated equipment costing $55,000 was discarded. What was the effect of the transaction on cash flows if (a) $5,000 cash is received, (b) no cash is received?

10. For the current year, Accord Company decided to switch from the indirect method to the direct method for reporting cash flows from operating activities on the statement of cash flows. Will the change cause the amount of net cash flow from operating activities to be (a) larger, (b) smaller, or (c) the same as if the indirect method had been used? Explain.

11. Name five common major classes of operating cash receipts or operating cash payments presented on the statement of cash flows when the cash flows from operating activities are reported by the direct method.

12. In a recent annual report, **PepsiCo, Inc.**, reported that during the year it issued stock of $438 million for acquisitions. How would this be reported on the statement of cash flows?

RESOURCES FOR YOUR SUCCESS ONLINE AT

http://warren.swcollege.com

Remember! If you need additional help, visit South-Western's Web site.
See page F26 for a description of the online and printed materials that are available.

EXERCISES

Exercise 14–1
Cash flows from operating activities—net loss

Objective 2

On its income statement for a recent year, **Amazon.com, Inc.**, reported a net loss of $124 million from operations. On its statement of cash flows, it reported $31 million of cash flows from operating activities.

➤ Explain this apparent contradiction between the loss and the positive cash flows.

Exercise 14–2
Effect of transactions on cash flows

Objective 2

✓ b. Cash payment, $501,000

State the effect (cash receipt or payment and amount) of each of the following transactions, considered individually, on cash flows:

a. Purchased a building by paying $30,000 cash and issuing a $90,000 mortgage note payable.

b. Retired $500,000 of bonds, on which there was $2,500 of unamortized discount, for $501,000.

c. Paid dividends of $1.50 per share. There were 30,000 shares issued and 5,000 shares of treasury stock.
d. Sold a new issue of $100,000 of bonds at 101.
e. Purchased 5,000 shares of $30 par common stock as treasury stock at $50 per share.
f. Purchased land for $120,000 cash.
g. Sold equipment with a book value of $42,500 for $41,000.
h. Sold 5,000 shares of $30 par common stock for $45 per share.

Exercise 14–3
Classifying cash flows
Objective 2

Identify the type of cash flow activity for each of the following events (operating, investing, or financing):

a. Issued bonds.
b. Issued common stock.
c. Sold long-term investments.
d. Paid cash dividends.
e. Redeemed bonds.
f. Issued preferred stock.
g. Net income.
h. Sold equipment.
i. Purchased treasury stock.
j. Purchased buildings.
k. Purchased patents.

Exercise 14–4
Cash flows from operating activities—indirect method
Objective 3

Indicate whether each of the following would be added to or deducted from net income in determining net cash flow from operating activities by the indirect method:

a. Loss on disposal of fixed assets
b. Decrease in accounts payable
c. Decrease in salaries payable
d. Depreciation of fixed assets
e. Amortization of patent
f. Decrease in accounts receivable
g. Gain on retirement of long-term debt
h. Increase in merchandise inventory
i. Decrease in prepaid expenses
j. Increase in notes receivable due in 90 days from customers
k. Amortization of goodwill
l. Increase in notes payable due in 90 days to vendors

Exercise 14–5
Cash flows from operating activities—indirect method
Objectives 2, 3

✓ a. Cash flows from operating activities, $196,150

The net income reported on the income statement for the current year was $167,900. Depreciation recorded on equipment and a building amounted to $41,300 for the year. Balances of the current asset and current liability accounts at the beginning and end of the year are as follows:

	End of Year	Beginning of Year
Cash	$ 27,900	$ 30,900
Accounts receivable (net)	75,100	70,250
Inventories	120,400	110,900
Prepaid expenses	5,800	6,000
Accounts payable (merchandise creditors)	67,200	65,300
Salaries payable	7,150	7,950

a. Prepare the cash flows from operating activities section of the statement of cash flows, using the indirect method.
b. ◄━━━━► If the direct method had been used, would the net cash flow from operating activities have been the same? Explain.

Exercise 14–6
Cash flows from operating activities—indirect method
Objective 3

The net income reported on the income statement for the current year was $489,000. Depreciation recorded on store equipment for the year amounted to $135,700. Balances of the current asset and current liability accounts at the beginning and end of the year are as follows:

	End of Year	Beginning of Year
Cash	$420,400	$509,000
Accounts receivable (net)	625,100	693,200
Merchandise inventory	724,600	704,700
Prepaid expenses	32,000	30,500
Accounts payable (merchandise creditors)	432,700	452,500
Wages payable	40,600	35,000

Prepare the cash flows from operating activities section of the statement of cash flows, using the indirect method.

Exercise 14–7
Determining cash payments to stockholders
Objective 3

The board of directors declared cash dividends totaling $280,000 during the current year. The comparative balance sheet indicates dividends payable of $60,000 at the beginning of the year and $70,000 at the end of the year. What was the amount of cash payments to stockholders during the year?

Exercise 14–8
Reporting changes in equipment on statement of cash flows
Objective 3

An analysis of the general ledger accounts indicates that office equipment, which had cost $200,000 and on which accumulated depreciation totaled $95,000 on the date of sale, was sold for $125,000 during the year. Using this information, indicate the items to be reported on the statement of cash flows.

Exercise 14–9
Reporting changes in equipment on statement of cash flows
Objective 3

An analysis of the general ledger accounts indicates that delivery equipment, which had cost $50,000 and on which accumulated depreciation totaled $23,000 on the date of sale, was sold for $24,000 during the year. Using this information, indicate the items to be reported on the statement of cash flows.

Exercise 14–10
Reporting land transactions on statement of cash flows
Objective 3

On the basis of the details of the following fixed asset account, indicate the items to be reported on the statement of cash flows:

ACCOUNT *Land*   **ACCOUNT NO.**

Date		Item	Debit	Credit	Balance Debit	Balance Credit
2003						
Jan.	1	Balance			400,000	
Feb.	5	Purchased for cash	200,000		600,000	
Oct.	30	Sold for $105,000		80,000	520,000	

Exercise 14–11
Reporting stockholders' equity items on statement of cash flows
Objective 3

On the basis of the following stockholders' equity accounts, indicate the items, exclusive of net income, to be reported on the statement of cash flows. There were no unpaid dividends at either the beginning or the end of the year.

ACCOUNT *Common Stock, $10 Par*   **ACCOUNT NO.**

Date		Item	Debit	Credit	Balance Debit	Balance Credit
2003						
Jan.	1	Balance, 50,000 shares				500,000
Feb.	11	6,000 shares issued for cash		60,000		560,000
June	30	2,750-share stock dividend		27,500		587,500

ACCOUNT **Paid-In Capital in Excess of Par—Common Stock**   ACCOUNT NO.

Date		Item	Debit	Credit	Balance Debit	Balance Credit
2003						
Jan.	1	Balance				90,000
Feb.	11	6,000 shares issued for cash		240,000		330,000
June	30	Stock dividend		137,500		467,500

ACCOUNT **Retained Earnings**   ACCOUNT NO.

Date		Item	Debit	Credit	Balance Debit	Balance Credit
2003						
Jan.	1	Balance				475,000
June	30	Stock dividend	165,000			310,000
Dec.	30	Cash dividend	180,000			130,000
	31	Net income		450,000		580,000

Exercise 14–12

Reporting land acquisition for cash and mortgage note on statement of cash flows

Objective 3

On the basis of the details of the following fixed asset account, indicate the items to be reported on the statement of cash flows:

ACCOUNT **Land**   ACCOUNT NO.

Date		Item	Debit	Credit	Balance Debit	Balance Credit
2003						
Jan.	1	Balance			450,000	
Feb.	10	Purchased for cash	210,000		660,000	
Nov.	20	Purchased with long-term mortgage note	250,000		910,000	

Exercise 14–13

Determining net income from net cash flow from operating activities

Objective 3

Tiger Golf Inc. reported a net cash flow from operating activities of $93,200 on its statement of cash flows for the year ended December 31, 2003. The following information was reported in the cash flows from operating activities section of the statement of cash flows, using the indirect method:

Decrease in income taxes payable	$ 1,600
Decrease in inventories	7,400
Depreciation	12,500
Gain on sale of investments	2,350
Increase in accounts payable	3,200
Increase in prepaid expenses	1,500
Increase in accounts receivable	4,850

Determine the net income reported by Tiger Golf Inc. for the year ended December 31, 2003.

Exercise 14–14

Cash flows from operating activities

Objective 3

Selected data derived from the income statement and balance sheet of **Intel Corp.** for a recent year are as follows:

Income Statement Data (dollars in millions)

Net earnings	$6,068
Depreciation	2,807
Loss on sale of property, plant, and equipment	282
Other noncash expenses	242

Balance Sheet Data (dollars in millions)

Increase in accounts receivable	$ 38
Decrease in inventories	167
Decrease in other operating assets	37
Decrease in accounts payable and accrued expenses	163
Decrease in income tax payable	211

Prepare the cash flows from operating activities section of the statement of cash flows (using the indirect method) for Intel Corp., for the year.

Exercise 14–15
Cash flows from operating activities—direct method

Objective 4

The cash flows from operating activities are reported by the direct method on the statement of cash flows. Determine the following:

a. If sales for the current year were $685,000 and accounts receivable decreased by $38,000 during the year, what was the amount of cash received from customers?
b. If income tax expense for the current year was $72,000 and income tax payable decreased by $4,500 during the year, what was the amount of cash payments for income tax?

Exercise 14–16
Cash paid for merchandise purchases

Objective 4

The cost of merchandise sold for **Toys 'R' Us, Inc.**, for a recent year was $8,191 million. The balance sheet showed the following current account balances (in millions):

	Balance, End of Year	Balance, Beginning of Year
Merchandise inventories	$1,902	$2,464
Accounts payable	1,415	1,280

Determine the amount of cash payments for merchandise.

Exercise 14–17
Determining selected amounts for cash flows from operating activities—direct method

Objective 4

Selected data taken from the accounting records of Zippy Electronics Company for the current year ended December 31 are as follows:

	Balance December 31	Balance January 1
Accrued expenses (operating expenses)	$ 5,800	$ 6,200
Accounts payable (merchandise creditors)	35,700	39,100
Inventories	25,000	27,400
Prepaid expenses	3,000	3,500

During the current year, the cost of merchandise sold was $315,000 and the operating expenses other than depreciation were $87,600. The direct method is used for presenting the cash flows from operating activities on the statement of cash flows.

Determine the amount reported on the statement of cash flows for (a) cash payments for merchandise and (b) cash payments for operating expenses.

Exercise 14–18
Cash flows from operating activities—direct method

Objective 4

The income statement of Tender Memories Greeting Card Company for the current year ended June 30 is as follows:

Sales		$358,000
Cost of merchandise sold		163,400
Gross profit		$194,600
Operating expenses:		
Depreciation expense	$ 32,500	
Other operating expenses	142,600	
Total operating expenses		175,100
Income before income tax		$ 19,500
Income tax expense		7,300
Net income		$ 12,200

Changes in the balances of selected accounts from the beginning to the end of the current year are as follows:

	Increase Decrease*
Accounts receivable (net)	$17,000*
Inventories	5,300
Prepaid expenses	3,100*
Accounts payable (merchandise creditors)	13,600*
Accrued expenses (operating expenses)	8,300
Income tax payable	2,400*

Prepare the cash flows from operating activities section of the statement of cash flows, using the direct method.

Exercise 14–19

Cash flows from operating activities—direct method

Objective 4

✓ Cash flows from operating activities, $130,100

The income statement for Wholly Donut Company for the current year ended June 30 and balances of selected accounts at the beginning and the end of the year are as follows:

Sales		$935,600
Cost of merchandise sold		534,200
Gross profit		$401,400
Operating expenses:		
Depreciation expense	$ 54,200	
Other operating expenses	195,700	
Total operating expenses		249,900
Income before income tax		$151,500
Income tax expense		65,300
Net income		$ 86,200

	End of Year	Beginning of Year
Accounts receivable (net)	$ 96,500	$ 93,000
Inventories	143,200	132,700
Prepaid expenses	7,500	8,900
Accounts payable (merchandise creditors)	102,300	98,400
Accrued expenses (operating expenses)	12,400	14,000
Income tax payable	2,000	2,000

Prepare the cash flows from operating activities section of the statement of cash flows, using the direct method.

Exercise 14–20

Analysis of statement of cash flows

Objectives 3, 5

The financial statements for **Cisco Systems, Inc.**, are presented in Appendix G at the end of the text.

a. From Cisco Systems' statement of cash flows, determine the free cash flow for 1999 and 2000. Assume that 40% of the acquisition of property and equipment and 20% of the acquisition of technology licenses are used to maintain productive capacity. The remaining 60% and 80%, respectively, add to productive capacity.

b. ✏ What conclusions can you draw from your analysis?

Exercise 14–21

Statement of cash flows

Objective 3

The comparative balance sheet of Maria's Memories Inc. for December 31, 2003 and 2002, is as follows:

	Dec. 31, 2003	Dec. 31, 2002
Assets		
Cash	$ 54	$ 34
Accounts receivable (net)	23	27
Inventories	16	14
Land	20	30
Equipment	26	12
Accumulated depreciation—equipment	(8)	(5)
Total	$131	$112
Liabilities and Stockholders' Equity		
Accounts payable (merchandise creditors)	$ 17	$ 18
Dividends payable	8	6
Common stock, $1 par	3	2
Paid-in capital in excess of par—common stock	15	10
Retained earnings	88	76
Total	$131	$112

The following additional information is taken from the records:

a. Land was sold for $17.
b. Equipment was acquired for cash.
c. There were no disposals of equipment during the year.
d. The common stock was issued for cash.
e. There was a $25 credit to Retained Earnings for net income.
f. There was a $13 debit to Retained Earnings for cash dividends declared.

Prepare a statement of cash flows, using the indirect method of presenting cash flows from operating activities.

Exercise 14–22
Statement of cash flows
Objective 3

What's Wrong With This?

List the errors you find in the following statement of cash flows. The cash balance at the beginning of the year was $70,700. All other figures are correct, except the cash balance at the end of the year.

Cyber-Master Games Inc.
Statement of Cash Flows
For the Year Ended December 31, 2003

Cash flows from operating activities:			
Net income, per income statement		$100,500	
Add: Depreciation	$ 49,000		
Increase in accounts receivable	11,500		
Gain on sale of investments	7,000	67,500	
		$168,000	
Deduct: Increase in accounts payable	$ 4,400		
Increase in inventories	18,300		
Decrease in accrued expenses	1,600	24,300	
Net cash flow from operating activities			$143,700
Cash flows from investing activities:			
Cash received from sale of investments		$ 85,000	
Less: Cash paid for purchase of land	$ 90,000		
Cash paid for purchase of equipment	150,100	240,100	
Net cash flow used for investing activities			(155,100)
Cash flows from financing activities:			
Cash received from sale of common stock		$107,000	
Cash paid for dividends		36,800	
Net cash flow provided by financing activities			143,800
Increase in cash			$132,400
Cash at the end of the year			105,300
Cash at the beginning of the year			$237,700

PROBLEMS SERIES A

Problem 14–1A
*Statement of cash flows—
indirect method*

Objective 3

✓ Net cash flow from operating
activities, $139,800

The comparative balance sheet of Everlast Flooring Co. for June 30, 2003 and 2002, is as follows:

	June 30, 2003	June 30, 2002
Assets		
Cash	$124,200	$ 67,900
Accounts receivable (net)	102,400	97,600
Inventories	142,700	123,500
Investments	0	58,000
Land	124,000	0
Equipment	373,400	201,400
Accumulated depreciation	(79,400)	(58,900)
	$787,300	$489,500
Liabilities and Stockholders' Equity		
Accounts payable (merchandise creditors)	$ 93,200	$ 84,600
Accrued expenses (operating expenses)	13,000	12,300
Dividends payable	15,000	12,500
Common stock, $10 par	120,000	80,000
Paid-in capital in excess of par—common stock	310,000	130,000
Retained earnings	236,100	170,100
	$787,300	$489,500

The following additional information was taken from the records of Everlast Flooring Co.:

a. Equipment and land were acquired for cash.
b. There were no disposals of equipment during the year.
c. The investments were sold for $50,000 cash.
d. The common stock was issued for cash.
e. There was a $126,000 credit to Retained Earnings for net income.
f. There was a $60,000 debit to Retained Earnings for cash dividends declared.

Instructions

Prepare a statement of cash flows, using the indirect method of presenting cash flows from operating activities.

Problem 14–2A
*Statement of cash flows—
indirect method*

Objective 3

SPREADSHEET

✓ Net cash flow from operating
activities, $151,800

The comparative balance sheet of Bon Voyage Luggage Company at December 31, 2003 and 2002, is as follows:

	Dec. 31, 2003	Dec. 31, 2002
Assets		
Cash	$ 155,400	$ 134,600
Accounts receivable (net)	192,400	176,400
Inventories	287,500	312,300
Prepaid expenses	8,500	6,000
Land	100,000	100,000
Buildings	550,000	415,000
Accumulated depreciation—buildings	(201,500)	(176,000)
Machinery and equipment	295,700	295,700
Accumulated depreciation—machinery & equipment	(119,800)	(84,600)
Patents	37,400	40,000
	$1,305,600	$1,219,400

(continued)

	Dec. 31, 2003	Dec. 31, 2002
Liabilities and Stockholders' Equity		
Accounts payable (merchandise creditors)	$ 131,400	$ 146,700
Dividends payable	12,000	10,000
Salaries payable	10,500	12,800
Mortgage note payable, due 2004	50,000	—
Bonds payable	—	164,000
Common stock, $1 par	19,000	15,000
Paid-in capital in excess of par—common stock	210,000	50,000
Retained earnings	872,700	820,900
	$1,305,600	$1,219,400

An examination of the income statement and the accounting records revealed the following additional information applicable to 2003:

a. Net income, $99,800.
b. Depreciation expense reported on the income statement: buildings, $25,500; machinery and equipment, $35,200.
c. Patent amortization reported on the income statement, $2,600.
d. A building was constructed for $135,000.
e. A mortgage note for $50,000 was issued for cash.
f. 4,000 shares of common stock were issued at $41 in exchange for the bonds payable.
g. Cash dividends declared, $48,000.

Instructions

Prepare a statement of cash flows, using the indirect method of presenting cash flows from operating activities.

Problem 14–3A

Statement of cash flows— indirect method

Objective 3

✓ Net cash flow from operating activities, ($1,500)

The comparative balance sheet of Union Wholesale Supply Co. at December 31, 2003 and 2002, is as follows:

	Dec. 31, 2003	Dec. 31, 2002
Assets		
Cash	$ 24,900	$ 27,400
Accounts receivable (net)	113,100	94,600
Inventories	194,000	176,500
Prepaid expenses	3,400	4,000
Land	60,000	80,000
Buildings	265,000	155,000
Accumulated depreciation—buildings	(55,800)	(43,500)
Equipment	195,600	185,600
Accumulated depreciation—equipment	(71,500)	(74,500)
	$728,700	$605,100
Liabilities and Stockholders' Equity		
Accounts payable (merchandise creditors)	$140,000	$143,700
Income tax payable	4,000	3,800
Bonds payable	50,000	—
Common stock, $1 par	26,000	25,000
Paid-in capital in excess of par—common stock	350,000	280,000
Retained earnings	158,700	152,600
	$728,700	$605,100

The noncurrent asset, the noncurrent liability, and the stockholders' equity accounts for 2003 are as follows:

ACCOUNT *Land*   **ACCOUNT NO.**

Date		Item	Debit	Credit	Balance Debit	Balance Credit
2003						
Jan.	1	Balance			80,000	
April	20	Realized $34,000 cash				
		from sale		20,000	60,000	

ACCOUNT *Buildings*   **ACCOUNT NO.**

Date		Item	Debit	Credit	Balance Debit	Balance Credit
2003						
Jan.	1	Balance			155,000	
April	20	Acquired for cash	110,000		265,000	

ACCOUNT *Accumulated Depreciation—Buildings*   **ACCOUNT NO.**

Date		Item	Debit	Credit	Balance Debit	Balance Credit
2003						
Jan.	1	Balance				43,500
Dec.	31	Depreciation for year		12,300		55,800

ACCOUNT *Equipment*   **ACCOUNT NO.**

Date		Item	Debit	Credit	Balance Debit	Balance Credit
2003						
Jan.	1	Balance			185,600	
	26	Discarded, no salvage		30,000	155,600	
Aug.	11	Purchased for cash	40,000		195,600	

ACCOUNT *Accumulated Depreciation—Equipment*   **ACCOUNT NO.**

Date		Item	Debit	Credit	Balance Debit	Balance Credit
2003						
Jan.	1	Balance				74,500
	26	Equipment discarded	30,000			44,500
Dec.	31	Depreciation for year		27,000		71,500

ACCOUNT *Bonds Payable*   **ACCOUNT NO.**

Date		Item	Debit	Credit	Balance Debit	Balance Credit
2003						
May	1	Issued 20-year bonds		50,000		50,000

ACCOUNT *Common Stock, $1 Par*   **ACCOUNT NO.**

Date		Item	Debit	Credit	Balance Debit	Balance Credit
2003						
Jan.	1	Balance				25,000
Dec.	7	Issued 1,000 shares of common				
		stock for $71 per share		1,000		26,000

ACCOUNT *Paid-In Capital in Excess of Par—Common Stock*   **ACCOUNT NO.**

Date		Item	Debit	Credit	Balance Debit	Balance Credit
2003						
Jan.	1	Balance				280,000
Dec.	7	Issued 1,000 shares of common				
		stock for $71 per share		70,000		350,000

ACCOUNT *Retained Earnings*   **ACCOUNT NO.**

Date		Item	Debit	Credit	Balance Debit	Balance Credit
2003						
Jan.	1	Balance				152,600
Dec.	31	Net income		12,100		164,700
	31	Cash dividends	6,000			158,700

Instructions

Prepare a statement of cash flows, using the indirect method of presenting cash flows from operating activities.

Problem 14–4A

Statement of cash flows—direct method

Objective 4

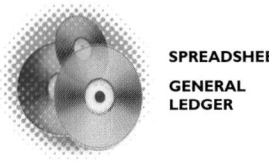

SPREADSHEET
GENERAL LEDGER

✓ Net cash flow from operating activities, $99,900

The comparative balance sheet of Green Thumb Nursery Inc. for December 31, 2003 and 2004, is as follows:

	Dec. 31, 2004	Dec. 31, 2003
Assets		
Cash	$ 154,700	$176,500
Accounts receivable (net)	261,300	243,200
Inventories	317,800	303,300
Investments	—	65,000
Land	95,000	—
Equipment	365,000	275,000
Accumulated depreciation	(123,700)	(103,200)
	$1,070,100	$959,800
Liabilities and Stockholders' Equity		
Accounts payable (merchandise creditors)	$ 248,300	$235,700
Accrued expenses (operating expenses)	10,900	12,500
Dividends payable	24,000	20,000
Common stock, $1 par	15,000	12,000
Paid-in capital in excess of par—common stock	185,000	110,000
Retained earnings	586,900	569,600
	$1,070,100	$959,800

The income statement for the year ended December 31, 2004, is as follows:

Sales		$1,250,000
Cost of merchandise sold		759,000
Gross profit		$ 491,000
Operating expenses:		
Depreciation expense	$ 20,500	
Other operating expenses	284,500	
Total operating expenses		305,000
Operating income		$ 186,000
Other income:		
Gain on sale of investments		14,000
Income before income tax		$ 200,000
Income tax expense		85,000
Net income		$ 115,000

The following additional information was taken from the records:

a. Equipment and land were acquired for cash.
b. There were no disposals of equipment during the year.
c. The investments were sold for $79,000 cash.
d. The common stock was issued for cash.
e. There was a $97,700 debit to Retained Earnings for cash dividends declared.

Instructions

Prepare a statement of cash flows, using the direct method of presenting cash flows from operating activities.

Problem 14–5A

*Statement of cash flows—
direct method applied to
Problem 14–1A*

Objective 4

✓ Net cash flow from operating
activities, $139,800

The comparative balance sheet of Everlast Flooring Co. for June 30, 2003 and 2002, is as follows:

	June 30, 2003	June 30, 2002
Assets		
Cash	$124,200	$ 67,900
Accounts receivable (net)	102,400	97,600
Inventories	142,700	123,500
Investments	0	58,000
Land	124,000	0
Equipment	373,400	201,400
Accumulated depreciation	(79,400)	(58,900)
	$787,300	$489,500
Liabilities and Stockholders' Equity		
Accounts payable (merchandise creditors)	$ 93,200	$ 84,600
Accrued expenses (operating expenses)	13,000	12,300
Dividends payable	15,000	12,500
Common stock, $10 par	120,000	80,000
Paid-in capital in excess of par—common stock	310,000	130,000
Retained earnings	236,100	170,100
	$787,300	$489,500

The income statement for the year ended June 30, 2003, is as follows:

Sales		$543,800
Cost of merchandise sold		198,200
Gross profit		$345,600
Operating expenses:		
Depreciation expense	$ 20,500	
Other operating expenses	110,300	
Total operating expenses		130,800
Operating income		$214,800
Other expenses:		
Loss on sale of investments		8,000
Income before income tax		$206,800
Income tax expense		80,800
Net income		$126,000

The following additional information was taken from the records:

a. Equipment and land were acquired for cash.
b. There were no disposals of equipment during the year.
c. The investments were sold for $50,000 cash.
d. The common stock was issued for cash.
e. There was a $60,000 debit to Retained Earnings for cash dividends declared.

Instructions

Prepare a statement of cash flows, using the direct method of presenting cash flows from operating activities.

PROBLEMS SERIES B

Problem 14–1B
Statement of cash flows—indirect method

Objective 3

✓ Net cash flow from operating activities, $368,900

The comparative balance sheet of Idaho Al's Golf Shops Co. for December 31, 2003 and 2002, is as follows:

	Dec. 31, 2003	Dec. 31, 2002
Assets		
Cash	$ 524,300	$ 313,400
Accounts receivable (net)	132,500	126,700
Inventories	342,600	332,100
Investments	0	90,000
Land	125,000	0
Equipment	755,000	535,000
Accumulated depreciation—equipment	(189,000)	(158,000)
	$1,690,400	$1,239,200
Liabilities and Stockholders' Equity		
Accounts payable (merchandise creditors)	$ 85,200	$ 80,300
Accrued expenses (operating expenses)	4,300	7,400
Dividends payable	24,000	20,000
Common stock, $10 par	80,000	50,000
Paid-in capital in excess of par—common stock	335,000	200,000
Retained earnings	1,161,900	881,500
	$1,690,400	$1,239,200

The following additional information was taken from the records:

a. The investments were sold for $114,000 cash.
b. Equipment and land were acquired for cash.
c. There were no disposals of equipment during the year.
d. The common stock was issued for cash.
e. There was a $376,400 credit to Retained Earnings for net income.
f. There was a $96,000 debit to Retained Earnings for cash dividends declared.

Instructions

Prepare a statement of cash flows, using the indirect method of presenting cash flows from operating activities.

Problem 14–2B
Statement of cash flows—indirect method

Objective 3

SPREADSHEET

✓ Net cash flow from operating activities, $262,100

The comparative balance sheet of Gold Medal Athletic Apparel Co. at December 31, 2003 and 2002, is as follows:

	Dec. 31, 2003	Dec. 31, 2002
Assets		
Cash	$ 232,500	$ 257,900
Accounts receivable (net)	497,800	532,500
Merchandise inventory	635,200	621,300
Prepaid expenses	17,000	15,000
Equipment	720,000	600,000
Accumulated depreciation—equipment	(265,000)	(297,500)
	$1,837,500	$1,729,200
Liabilities and Stockholders' Equity		
Accounts payable (merchandise creditors)	$ 423,100	$ 397,600
Mortgage note payable	0	205,000
Common stock, $10 par	120,000	70,000
Paid-in capital in excess of par—common stock	820,000	620,000
Retained earnings	474,400	436,600
	$1,837,500	$1,729,200

Additional data obtained from the income statement and from an examination of the accounts in the ledger for 2003 are as follows:

a. Net income, $125,800.
b. Depreciation reported on the income statement, $92,000.
c. Equipment was purchased at a cost of $244,500, and fully depreciated equipment costing $124,500 was discarded, with no salvage realized.
d. The mortgage note payable was not due until 2006, but the terms permitted earlier payment without penalty.
e. 5,000 shares of common stock were issued at $50 for cash.
f. Cash dividends declared and paid, $88,000.

Instructions
Prepare a statement of cash flows, using the indirect method of presenting cash flows from operating activities.

Problem 14–3B
*Statement of cash flows—
indirect method*

Objective 3

✓ Net cash flow from operating
activities, ($131,800)

The comparative balance sheet of Handyman's Helper Hardware Company at December 31, 2003 and 2002, is as follows:

	Dec. 31, 2003	Dec. 31, 2002
Assets		
Cash	$ 263,400	$ 275,400
Accounts receivable (net)	375,200	356,800
Inventories	543,200	512,400
Prepaid expenses	8,500	9,000
Land	95,000	120,000
Buildings	470,000	350,000
Accumulated depreciation—buildings	(182,300)	(170,000)
Equipment	198,700	185,500
Accumulated depreciation—equipment	(44,000)	(48,000)
	$1,727,700	$1,591,100
Liabilities and Stockholders' Equity		
Accounts payable (merchandise creditors)	$ 367,900	$ 377,100
Bonds payable	60,000	0
Common stock, $1 par	90,000	70,000
Paid-in capital in excess of par—common stock	450,000	250,000
Retained earnings	759,800	894,000
	$1,727,700	$1,591,100

The noncurrent asset, the noncurrent liability, and the stockholders' equity accounts for 2003 are as follows:

ACCOUNT *Land* **ACCOUNT NO.**

Date		Item	Debit	Credit	Balance Debit	Balance Credit
2003						
Jan.	1	Balance			120,000	
April	20	Realized $38,000 cash from sale		25,000	95,000	

ACCOUNT *Buildings* **ACCOUNT NO.**

Date		Item	Debit	Credit	Balance Debit	Balance Credit
2003						
Jan.	1	Balance			350,000	
April	20	Acquired for cash	120,000		470,000	

ACCOUNT *Accumulated Depreciation—Buildings*   **ACCOUNT NO.**

Date		Item	Debit	Credit	Balance Debit	Balance Credit
2003						
Jan.	1	Balance				170,000
Dec.	31	Depreciation for year		12,300		182,300

ACCOUNT *Equipment*   **ACCOUNT NO.**

Date		Item	Debit	Credit	Balance Debit	Balance Credit
2003						
Jan.	1	Balance			185,500	
	26	Discarded, no salvage		45,000	140,500	
Aug.	11	Purchased for cash	58,200		198,700	

ACCOUNT *Accumulated Depreciation—Equipment*   **ACCOUNT NO.**

Date		Item	Debit	Credit	Balance Debit	Balance Credit
2003						
Jan.	1	Balance				48,000
	26	Equipment discarded	45,000			3,000
Dec.	31	Depreciation for year		41,000		44,000

ACCOUNT *Bonds Payable*   **ACCOUNT NO.**

Date		Item	Debit	Credit	Balance Debit	Balance Credit
2003						
May	1	Issued 20-year bonds		60,000		60,000

ACCOUNT *Common Stock, $1 Par*   **ACCOUNT NO.**

Date		Item	Debit	Credit	Balance Debit	Balance Credit
2003						
Jan.	1	Balance				70,000
Dec.	7	Issued 20,000 shares of common stock for $11 per share		20,000		90,000

ACCOUNT *Paid-In Capital in Excess of Par—Common Stock*   **ACCOUNT NO.**

Date		Item	Debit	Credit	Balance Debit	Balance Credit
2003						
Jan.	1	Balance				250,000
Dec.	7	Issued 20,000 shares of common stock for $11 per share		200,000		450,000

ACCOUNT *Retained Earnings*   **ACCOUNT NO.**

Date		Item	Debit	Credit	Balance Debit	Balance Credit
2003						
Jan.	1	Balance				894,000
Dec.	31	Net loss	114,200			779,800
	31	Cash dividends	20,000			759,800

Instructions

Prepare a statement of cash flows, using the indirect method of presenting cash flows from operating activities.

Problem 14–4B

Statement of cash flows— direct method

Objective 4

The comparative balance sheet of Nature's Bounty Markets, Inc., for December 31, 2004 and 2003, is as follows:

SPREADSHEET

GENERAL LEDGER

✓ Net cash flow from operating activities, $70,900

	Dec. 31, 2004	Dec. 31, 2003
Assets		
Cash	$ 65,800	$ 83,500
Accounts receivable (net)	101,200	95,800
Inventories	132,400	125,700
Investments	—	45,000
Land	70,500	—
Equipment	300,500	210,500
Accumulated depreciation	(65,900)	(45,600)
	$604,500	$514,900
Liabilities and Stockholders' Equity		
Accounts payable (merchandise creditors)	$ 93,500	$ 86,700
Accrued expenses (operating expenses)	10,200	12,000
Dividends payable	6,000	4,000
Common stock, $1 par	17,000	15,000
Paid-in capital in excess of par—common stock	200,000	150,000
Retained earnings	277,800	247,200
	$604,500	$514,900

The income statement for the year ended December 31, 2004, is as follows:

Sales		$545,000
Cost of merchandise sold		294,000
Gross profit		$251,000
Operating expenses:		
Depreciation expense	$ 20,300	
Other operating expenses	152,500	
Total operating expenses		172,800
Operating income		$ 78,200
Other expense:		
Loss on sale of investments		4,000
Income before income tax		$ 74,200
Income tax expense		20,500
Net income		$ 53,700

The following additional information was taken from the records:

a. Equipment and land were acquired for cash.
b. There were no disposals of equipment during the year.
c. The investments were sold for $41,000 cash.
d. The common stock was issued for cash.
e. There was a $23,100 debit to Retained Earnings for cash dividends declared.

Instructions

Prepare a statement of cash flows, using the direct method of presenting cash flows from operating activities.

Problem 14–5B
Statement of cash flows—direct method applied to Problem 14–1B

Objective 4

The comparative balance sheet of Idaho Al's Golf Shops Co. for December 31, 2003 and 2002, is as follows:

✓ Net cash flow from operating
activities, $368,900

	Dec. 31, 2003	Dec. 31, 2002
Assets		
Cash	$ 524,300	$ 313,400
Accounts receivable (net)	132,500	126,700
Inventories	342,600	332,100
Investments	0	90,000
Land	125,000	0
Equipment	755,000	535,000
Accumulated depreciation—equipment	(189,000)	(158,000)
	$1,690,400	$1,239,200
Liabilities and Stockholders' Equity		
Accounts payable (merchandise creditors)	$ 85,200	$ 80,300
Accrued expenses (operating expenses)	4,300	7,400
Dividends payable	24,000	20,000
Common stock, $10 par	80,000	50,000
Paid-in capital in excess of par—common stock	335,000	200,000
Retained earnings	1,161,900	881,500
	$1,690,400	$1,239,200

The income statement for the year ended December 31, 2003, is as follows:

Sales		$1,096,500
Cost of merchandise sold		401,200
Gross profit		$ 695,300
Operating expenses:		
Depreciation expense	$ 31,000	
Other operating expenses	163,400	
Total operating expenses		194,400
Operating income		$ 500,900
Other income:		
Gain on sale of investments		24,000
Income before income tax		$ 524,900
Income tax expense		148,500
Net income		$ 376,400

The following additional information was taken from the records:

a. The investments were sold for $114,000 cash.
b. Equipment and land were acquired for cash.
c. There were no disposals of equipment during the year.
d. The common stock was issued for cash.
e. There was a $96,000 debit to Retained Earnings for cash dividends declared.

Instructions

Prepare a statement of cash flows, using the direct method of presenting cash flows from operating activities.

SPECIAL ACTIVITIES

Activity 14–1
Fine Fashions Inc.
Ethics and professional conduct in business

Toni Lance, president of Fine Fashions Inc., believes that reporting operating cash flow per share on the income statement would be a useful addition to the company's just completed financial statements. The following discussion took place between Toni Lance and Fine Fashions' controller, Tom Kee, in January, after the close of the fiscal year.

Toni: I have been reviewing our financial statements for the last year. I am disappointed that our net income per share has dropped by 10% from last year. This is not going to look good to our shareholders. Isn't there anything we can do about this?

Tom: What do you mean? The past is the past, and the numbers are in. There isn't much that can be done about it. Our financial statements were prepared according to generally accepted accounting principles, and I don't see much leeway for significant change at this point.

Toni: No, no. I'm not suggesting that we "cook the books." But look at the cash flow from operating activities on the statement of cash flows. The cash flow from operating activities has increased by 20%. This is very good news—and, I might add, useful information. The higher cash flow from operating activities will give our creditors comfort.

Tom: Well, the cash flow from operating activities is on the statement of cash flows, so I guess users will be able to see the improved cash flow figures there.

Toni: This is true, but somehow I feel that this information should be given a much higher profile. I don't like this information being "buried" in the statement of cash flows. You know as well as I do that many users will focus on the income statement. Therefore, I think we ought to include an operating cash flow per share number on the face of the income statement—someplace under the earnings per share number. In this way users will get the complete picture of our operating performance. Yes, our earnings per share dropped this year, but our cash flow from operating activities improved! And all the information is in one place where users can see and compare the figures. What do you think?

Tom: I've never really thought about it like that before. I guess we could put the operating cash flow per share on the income statement, under the earnings per share. Users would really benefit from this disclosure. Thanks for the idea—I'll start working on it.

Toni: Glad to be of service.

How would you interpret this situation? Is Tom behaving in an ethical and professional manner?

Activity 14–2
VideoToGo.com Inc.
Using the statement of cash flows

You are considering an investment in a new start-up Internet company, VideoToGo.com Inc. A review of the company's financial statements reveals a negative retained earnings. In addition, it appears as though the company has been running a negative cash flow from operating activities since the company's inception.

How is the company staying in business under these circumstances? Could this be a good investment?

Activity 14–3
Biltmore Company
Analysis of cash flow from operations

The Retailing Division of Biltmore Company provided the following information on its cash flow from operations:

Net income	$ 450,000
Increase in accounts receivable	(340,000)
Increase in inventory	(300,000)
Decrease in accounts payable	(90,000)
Depreciation	100,000
Cash flow from operating activities	$(180,000)

The manager of the Retailing Division provided the accompanying memo with this report:

From: Senior Vice President, Retailing Division

I am pleased to report that we had earnings of $450,000 over the last period. This resulted in a return on invested capital of 10%, which is near our targets for this division. I have been aggressive in building the revenue volume in the division. As a result, I am happy to report that we have increased the number of new credit card customers as a result of an aggressive marketing campaign. In addition, we have found some excellent merchandise opportunities. Some of our suppliers have made some of their apparel merchandise available at a deep discount. We have purchased as much of these goods as possible in order to improve profitability. I'm also happy to report that our vendor payment problems have improved. We are nearly caught up on our overdue payables balances.

Comment on the senior vice president's memo in light of the cash flow information.

Activity 14–4
Elite Cabinets, Inc.
Analysis of statement of cash flows

Alan Hart is the president and majority shareholder of Elite Cabinets, Inc., a small retail store chain. Recently, Hart submitted a loan application for Elite Cabinets, Inc., to Montvale National Bank. It called for a $200,000, 11%, ten-year loan to help finance the construction of a building and the purchase of store equipment, costing a total of $250,000, to enable Elite Cabinets, Inc., to open a store in Montvale. Land for this purpose was acquired last year. The bank's loan officer requested a statement of cash flows in addition to the most recent income statement, balance sheet, and retained earnings statement that Hart had submitted with the loan application.

As a close family friend, Hart asked you to prepare a statement of cash flows. From the records provided, you prepared the following statement.

Elite Cabinets, Inc.
Statement of Cash Flows
For the Year Ended December 31, 2003

Cash flows from operating activities:			
Net income, per income statement		$ 86,400	
Add: Depreciation	$31,000		
Decrease in accounts receivable	11,500	42,500	
		$128,900	
Deduct: Increase in inventory	$12,000		
Increase in prepaid expenses	1,500		
Decrease in accounts payable	3,000		
Gain on sale of investments	7,500	24,000	
Net cash flow from operating activities			$104,900
Cash flows from investing activities:			
Cash received from investments sold		$ 42,500	
Less: Cash paid for purchase of store equipment		31,000	
Net cash flow from investing activities			11,500
Cash flows from financing activities:			
Cash paid for dividends		$ 40,000	
Net cash flow used for financing activities			(40,000)
Increase in cash			$ 76,400
Cash at the beginning of the year			27,500
Cash at the end of the year			$103,900

Schedule of Noncash Financing and Investing Activities:

Issued common stock at par for land			$ 40,000

After reviewing the statement, Hart telephoned you and commented, "Are you sure this statement is right?" Hart then raised the following questions:

1. "How can depreciation be a cash flow?"
2. "Issuing common stock for the land is listed in a separate schedule. This transaction has nothing to do with cash! Shouldn't this transaction be eliminated from the statement?"
3. "How can the gain on sale of investments be a deduction from net income in determining the cash flow from operating activities?"
4. "Why does the bank need this statement anyway? They can compute the increase in cash from the balance sheets for the last two years."

After jotting down Hart's questions, you assured him that this statement was "right." However, to alleviate Hart's concern, you arranged a meeting for the following day.

a.   How would you respond to each of Hart's questions?
b.   Do you think that the statement of cash flows enhances the chances of Elite Cabinets, Inc., receiving the loan? Discuss.

Activity 14–5
Into the Real World
Statement of cash flows

This activity will require two teams to retrieve cash flow statement information from the Internet. One team is to obtain the most recent year's statement of cash flows for **Philip Morris Companies**, and the other team the most recent year's statement of cash flows for **Loral Space & Communications, LTD.**, a satellite-based mobile phone company.

The statement of cash flows is included as part of the annual report information that is a required disclosure to the Securities and Exchange Commission (SEC). The SEC, in turn, provides this information online through its EDGAR service. EDGAR (Electronic Data Gathering, Analysis, and Retrieval) is the electronic archive of financial statements filed with the Securities and Exchange Commission (SEC). SEC documents can be retrieved using the EdgarScan service from **PricewaterhouseCoopers** at **edgarscan.pwcglobal.com**.

To obtain annual report information, type in a company name in the appropriate space. EdgarScan will list the reports available to you for the company you've selected. Select the most recent annual report filing, identified as a 10-K or 10-K405. EdgarScan provides an outline of the report, including the separate financial statements. You can double-click the income statement and balance sheet for the selected company into an Excel™ spreadsheet for further analysis.

As a group, compare the two statements of cash flows. How are Philip Morris and Loral Space & Communications similar or different regarding cash flows?

ANSWERS TO SELF-EXAMINATION QUESTIONS

Matching

1. E	3. A	5. I	7. N	9. F	11. J	13. H
2. L	4. K	6. B	8. D	10. C	12. M	

Multiple Choice

1. **D** Cash flows from operating activities affect transactions that enter into the determination of net income, such as the receipt of cash from customers on account (answer D). Receipts of cash from the sale of stock (answer A) and the sale of bonds (answer B) and payments of cash for dividends (answer C) are cash flows from financing activities.

2. **A** Cash flows from investing activities include receipts from the sale of noncurrent assets, such as equipment (answer A), and payments to acquire noncurrent assets. Receipts of cash from the sale of stock (answer B)

and payments of cash for dividends (answer C) and to acquire treasury stock (answer D) are cash flows from financing activities.

3. **C** Payment of cash dividends (answer C) is an example of a financing activity. The receipt of cash from customers on account (answer A) is an operating activity. The receipt of cash from the sale of equipment (answer B) is an investing activity. The payment of cash to acquire land (answer D) is an example of an investing activity.

4. **D** The indirect method (answer D) reports cash flows from operating activities by beginning with net income and adjusting it for revenues and expenses not involving the receipt or payment of cash.

5. **C** The cash flows from operating activities section of the statement of cash flows would report net cash flow from operating activities of $65,500, determined as follows:

Net income		$55,000
Add: Depreciation	$22,000	
Decrease in inventories	5,000	
Decrease in prepaid expenses	500	27,500
		$82,500
Deduct: Increase in accounts receivable	$10,000	
Decrease in accounts payable	7,000	17,000
Net cash flow from operating activities		$65,500

Financial Statement Analysis

F15

objectives

After studying this chapter, you should be able to:

1 List basic financial statement analytical procedures.

2 Apply financial statement analysis to assess the solvency of a business.

3 Apply financial statement analysis to assess the profitability of a business.

4 Summarize the uses and limitations of analytical measures.

5 Describe the contents of corporate annual reports.

T

he Wall Street Journal (September 18, 2000) reported that the common stock of **Microsoft Corporation** was selling for $64.19 per share. If you had funds to invest, would you invest in Microsoft common stock?

Microsoft is a well-known, international company. However, **Eastern Airlines**, **Pan Am**, **Montgomery Ward**, **Woolworth's**, and **Planet Hollywood** were also well-known companies. These latter companies share the common characteristic of having declared bankruptcy!

Obviously, being well-known is not necessarily a good basis for investing. Knowledge that a company has a good product, by itself, may also be an inadequate basis for investing in the company. Even with a good product, a company may go bankrupt for a variety of reasons, such as inadequate financing. For example, Planet Hollywood sought bankruptcy protection, even though it was owned and promoted by such prominent Hollywood stars as Bruce Willis, Whoopi Goldberg, and Arnold Schwarzenegger.

How, then, does one decide on the companies in which to invest? This chapter describes and illustrates common financial data that can be analyzed to assist you in making investment decisions. In addition, the contents of corporate annual reports are also discussed.

Basic Analytical Procedures

objective 1

List basic financial statement analytical procedures.

The basic financial statements provide much of the information users need to make economic decisions about businesses. In this chapter, we illustrate how to perform a complete analysis of these statements by integrating individual analytical measures.

Analytical procedures may be used to compare items on a current statement with related items on earlier statements. For example, cash of $150,000 on the current balance sheet may be compared with cash of $100,000 on the balance sheet of a year earlier. The current year's cash may be expressed as 1.5 or 150% of the earlier amount, or as an increase of 50% or $50,000.

Analytical procedures are also widely used to examine relationships within a financial statement. To illustrate, assume that cash of $50,000 and inventories of $250,000 are included in the total assets of $1,000,000 on a balance sheet. In relative terms, the cash balance is 5% of the total assets, and the inventories are 25% of the total assets.

In this chapter, we will illustrate a number of common analytical measures. The measures are not ends in themselves. They are only guides in evaluating financial and operating data. Many other factors, such as trends in the industry and general economic conditions, should also be considered.

Horizontal Analysis

The percentage analysis of increases and decreases in related items in comparative financial statements is called **horizontal analysis**. The amount of each item on the most recent statement is compared with the related item on one or more earlier statements. The amount of increase or decrease in the item is listed, along with the percent of increase or decrease.

Horizontal analysis may compare two statements. In this case, the earlier statement is used as the base. Horizontal analysis may also compare three or more statements. In this case, the earliest date or period may be used as the base for comparing all later dates or periods. Alternatively, each statement may be compared to the immediately preceding statement. Exhibit 1 is a condensed comparative balance sheet for two years for Lincoln Company, with horizontal analysis.

We cannot fully evaluate the significance of the various increases and decreases in the items shown in Exhibit 1 without additional information. Although total assets at the end of 2003 were $91,000 (7.4%) less than at the beginning of the year, liabilities were reduced by $133,000 (30%), and stockholders' equity increased $42,000 (5.3%). It appears that the reduction of $100,000 in long-term liabilities was achieved mostly through the sale of long-term investments.

Exhibit 1 Comparative Balance Sheet—Horizontal Analysis

Lincoln Company Comparative Balance Sheet December 31, 2003 and 2002			Increase (Decrease)	
	2003	2002	Amount	Percent
Assets				
Current assets	$ 550,000	$ 533,000	$ 17,000	3.2%
Long-term investments	95,000	177,500	(82,500)	(46.5%)
Property, plant, and equipment (net)	444,500	470,000	(25,500)	(5.4%)
Intangible assets	50,000	50,000	—	
Total assets	$1,139,500	$1,230,500	$ (91,000)	(7.4%)
Liabilities				
Current liabilities	$ 210,000	$ 243,000	$ (33,000)	(13.6%)
Long-term liabilities	100,000	200,000	(100,000)	(50.0%)
Total liabilities	$ 310,000	$ 443,000	$(133,000)	(30.0%)
Stockholders' Equity				
Preferred 6% stock, $100 par	$ 150,000	$ 150,000	—	—
Common stock, $10 par	500,000	500,000	—	—
Retained earnings	179,500	137,500	$ 42,000	30.5%
Total stockholders' equity	$ 829,500	$ 787,500	$ 42,000	5.3%
Total liabilities and stockholders' equity	$1,139,500	$1,230,500	$ (91,000)	(7.4%)

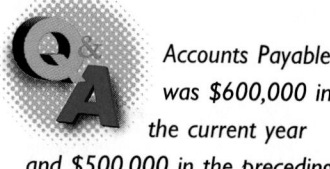

Accounts Payable was $600,000 in the current year and $500,000 in the preceding year. What is the amount and the percentage of increase or decrease that would be shown in a balance sheet with horizontal analysis?

$100,000 or 20% ($100,000/ $500,000) increase

The balance sheet in Exhibit 1 may be expanded to include the details of the various categories of assets and liabilities. An alternative is to present the details in separate schedules. Exhibit 2 is a supporting schedule with horizontal analysis.

The decrease in accounts receivable may be due to changes in credit terms or improved collection policies. Likewise, a decrease in inventories during a period of increased sales may indicate an improvement in the management of inventories.

The changes in the current assets in Exhibit 2 appear favorable. This assessment is supported by the 24.8% increase in net sales shown in Exhibit 3.

An increase in net sales may not have a favorable effect on operating performance. The percentage increase in Lincoln Company's net sales is accompanied by a greater percentage increase in the cost of goods (merchandise) sold.[1] This has the

---
[1] The term *cost of goods sold* is often used in practice in place of *cost of merchandise sold*. Such usage is followed in this chapter.

Exhibit 2 Comparative Schedule of Current Assets —Horizontal Analysis

Lincoln Company
Comparative Schedule of Current Assets
December 31, 2003 and 2002

	2003	2002	Increase (Decrease) Amount	Percent
Cash	$ 90,500	$ 64,700	$ 25,800	39.9%
Marketable securities	75,000	60,000	15,000	25.0%
Accounts receivable (net)	115,000	120,000	(5,000)	(4.2%)
Inventories	264,000	283,000	(19,000)	(6.7%)
Prepaid expenses	5,500	5,300	200	3.8%
Total current assets	$550,000	$533,000	$ 17,000	3.2%

Exhibit 3 Comparative Income Statement— Horizontal Analysis

Lincoln Company
Comparative Income Statement
For the Years Ended December 31, 2003 and 2002

	2003	2002	Increase (Decrease) Amount	Percent
Sales	$1,530,500	$1,234,000	$296,500	24.0%
Sales returns and allowances	32,500	34,000	(1,500)	(4.4%)
Net sales	$1,498,000	$1,200,000	$298,000	24.8%
Cost of goods sold	1,043,000	820,000	223,000	27.2%
Gross profit	$ 455,000	$ 380,000	$ 75,000	19.7%
Selling expenses	$ 191,000	$ 147,000	$ 44,000	29.9%
Administrative expenses	104,000	97,400	6,600	6.8%
Total operating expenses	$ 295,000	$ 244,400	$ 50,600	20.7%
Income from operations	$ 160,000	$ 135,600	$ 24,400	18.0%
Other income	8,500	11,000	(2,500)	(22.7%)
	$ 168,500	$ 146,600	$ 21,900	14.9%
Other expense	6,000	12,000	(6,000)	(50.0%)
Income before income tax	$ 162,500	$ 134,600	$ 27,900	20.7%
Income tax expense	71,500	58,100	13,400	23.1%
Net income	$ 91,000	$ 76,500	$ 14,500	19.0%

effect of reducing gross profit. Selling expenses increased significantly, and administrative expenses increased slightly. Overall, operating expenses increased by 20.7%, whereas gross profit increased by only 19.7%.

The increase in income from operations and in net income is favorable. However, a study of the expenses and additional analyses and comparisons should be made before reaching a conclusion as to the cause.

Exhibit 4 illustrates a comparative retained earnings statement with horizontal analysis. It reveals that retained earnings increased 30.5% for the year. The increase is due to net income of $91,000 for the year, less dividends of $49,000.

Exhibit 4 Comparative
Retained Earnings Statement
—Horizontal Analysis

Lincoln Company Comparative Retained Earnings Statement December 31, 2003 and 2002			Increase (Decrease)	
	2003	**2002**	**Amount**	**Percent**
Retained earnings, January 1	$137,500	$100,000	$37,500	37.5%
Net income for the year	91,000	76,500	14,500	19.0%
Total	$228,500	$176,500	$52,000	29.5%
Dividends:				
On preferred stock	$ 9,000	$ 9,000	—	—
On common stock	40,000	30,000	$10,000	33.3%
Total	$ 49,000	$ 39,000	$10,000	25.6%
Retained earnings, December 31	$179,500	$137,500	$42,000	30.5%

At the end of the current year, Accounts Payable was $600,000 and total liabilities and stockholders' equity was $1,200,000. What percent would be shown for Accounts Payable in a balance sheet with vertical analysis?

50% ($600,000/$1,200,000)

Vertical Analysis

A percentage analysis may also be used to show the relationship of each component to the total within a single statement. This type of analysis is called **vertical analysis**. Like horizontal analysis, the statements may be prepared in either detailed or condensed form. In the latter case, additional details of the changes in individual items may be presented in supporting schedules. In such schedules, the percentage analysis may be based on either the total of the schedule or the statement total. Although vertical analysis is limited to an individual statement, its significance may be improved by preparing comparative statements.

In vertical analysis of the balance sheet, each asset item is stated as a percent of the total assets. Each liability and stockholders' equity item is stated as a percent of the total liabilities and stockholders' equity. Exhibit 5 is a condensed comparative balance sheet with vertical analysis for Lincoln Company.

The major percentage changes in Lincoln Company's assets are in the current asset and long-term investment categories. In the Liabilities and Stockholders' Equity sections of the balance sheet, the greatest percentage changes are in long-term liabilities and retained earnings. Stockholders' equity increased from 64% to 72.8% of total liabilities and stockholders' equity in 2003. There is a comparable decrease in liabilities.

In a vertical analysis of the income statement, each item is stated as a percent of net sales. Exhibit 6 is a condensed comparative income statement with vertical analysis for Lincoln Company.

We must be careful when judging the significance of differences between percentages for the two years. For example, the decline of the gross profit rate from 31.7% in 2002 to 30.4% in 2003 is only 1.3 percentage points. In terms of dollars of potential gross profit, however, it represents a decline of approximately $19,500 (1.3% × $1,498,000).

Common-Size Statements

Horizontal and vertical analyses with both dollar and percentage amounts are useful in assessing relationships and trends in financial conditions and operations of a business. Vertical analysis with both dollar and percentage amounts is also useful in comparing one company with another or with industry averages. Such comparisons are easier to make with the use of common-size statements. In a **common-size statement**, all items are expressed in percentages.

Exhibit 5 Comparative
Balance Sheet—Vertical
Analysis

Lincoln Company
Comparative Balance Sheet
December 31, 2003 and 2002

	2003		2002	
	Amount	**Percent**	**Amount**	**Percent**
Assets				
Current assets	$ 550,000	48.3%	$ 533,000	43.3%
Long-term investments	95,000	8.3	177,500	14.4
Property, plant, and				
equipment (net)	444,500	39.0	470,000	38.2
Intangible assets	50,000	4.4	50,000	4.1
Total assets	$1,139,500	100.0%	$1,230,500	100.0%
Liabilities				
Current liabilities	$ 210,000	18.4%	$ 243,000	19.7%
Long-term liabilities	100,000	8.8	200,000	16.3
Total liabilities	$ 310,000	27.2%	$ 443,000	36.0%
Stockholders' Equity				
Preferred 6% stock, $100 par	$ 150,000	13.2%	$ 150,000	12.2%
Common stock, $10 par	500,000	43.9	500,000	40.6
Retained earnings	179,500	15.7	137,500	11.2
Total stockholders' equity	$ 829,500	72.8%	$ 787,500	64.0%
Total liabilities and				
stockholders' equity	$1,139,500	100.0%	$1,230,500	100.0%

Exhibit 6 Comparative
Income Statement—Vertical
Analysis

Lincoln Company
Comparative Income Statement
For the Years Ended December 31, 2003 and 2002

	2003		2002	
	Amount	**Percent**	**Amount**	**Percent**
Sales	$1,530,500	102.2%	$1,234,000	102.8%
Sales returns and allowances	32,500	2.2	34,000	2.8
Net sales	$1,498,000	100.0%	$1,200,000	100.0%
Cost of goods sold	1,043,000	69.6	820,000	68.3
Gross profit	$ 455,000	30.4%	$ 380,000	31.7%
Selling expenses	$ 191,000	12.8%	$ 147,000	12.3%
Administrative expenses	104,000	6.9	97,400	8.1
Total operating expenses	$ 295,000	19.7%	$ 244,400	20.4%
Income from operations	$ 160,000	10.7%	$ 135,600	11.3%
Other income	8,500	0.6	11,000	0.9
	$ 168,500	11.3%	$ 146,600	12.2%
Other expense	6,000	0.4	12,000	1.0
Income before income tax	$ 162,500	10.9%	$ 134,600	11.2%
Income tax expense	71,500	4.8	58,100	4.8
Net income	$ 91,000	6.1%	$ 76,500	6.4%

The percentages of gross profit and net income to sales for fiscal year-end 1999 for **Kmart Corp.** and **Wal-Mart Stores Inc.** are shown below.

	Kmart Corp.	Wal-Mart Stores Inc.
Gross profit to sales	21.8%	21.0%
Net income to sales	1.5%	3.3%

Wal-Mart has a slightly lower gross profit margin than Kmart, which is likely due to lower prices. However, Wal-Mart has a much leaner operating expense structure, so it is able to earn an overall higher percentage of net income to sales.

Common-size statements are useful in comparing the current period with prior periods, individual businesses, or one business with industry percentages. Industry data are often available from trade associations and financial information services. Exhibit 7 is a comparative common-size income statement for two businesses.

Exhibit 7 indicates that Lincoln Company has a slightly higher rate of gross profit than Madison Corporation. However, this advantage is more than offset by Lincoln Company's higher percentage of selling and administrative expenses. As a result, the income from operations of Lincoln Company is 10.7% of net sales, compared with 14.4% for Madison Corporation—an unfavorable difference of 3.7 percentage points.

Other Analytical Measures

In addition to the preceding analyses, other relationships may be expressed in ratios and percentages. Often, these items are taken from the financial statements and thus are a type of vertical analysis. Comparing these items with items from earlier periods is a type of horizontal analysis.

Exhibit 7 Common-Size Income Statement

Lincoln Company and Madison Corporation
Condensed Common-Size Income Statement
For the Year Ended December 31, 2003

	Lincoln Company	Madison Corporation
Sales	102.2%	102.3%
Sales returns and allowances	2.2	2.3
Net sales	100.0%	100.0%
Cost of goods sold	69.6	70.0
Gross profit	30.4%	30.0%
Selling expenses	12.8%	11.5%
Administrative expenses	6.9	4.1
Total operating expenses	19.7%	15.6%
Income from operations	10.7%	14.4%
Other income	0.6	0.6
	11.3%	15.0%
Other expense	0.4	0.5
Income before income tax	10.9%	14.5%
Income tax expense	4.8	5.5
Net income	6.1%	9.0%

Solvency Analysis

objective 2

Apply financial statement analysis to assess the solvency of a business.

Some aspects of a business's financial condition and operations are of greater importance to some users than others. However, all users are interested in the ability of a business to pay its debts as they are due and to earn income. The ability of a business to meet its financial obligations (debts) is called **solvency**. The ability of a business to earn income is called **profitability**.

The factors of solvency and profitability are interrelated. A business that cannot pay its debts on a timely basis may experience difficulty in obtaining credit. A lack of available credit may, in turn, lead to a decline in the business's profitability. Eventually, the business may be forced into bankruptcy. Likewise, a business that is less profitable than its competitors is likely to be at a disadvantage in obtaining credit or new capital from stockholders.

In the following paragraphs, we discuss various types of financial analyses that are useful in evaluating the solvency of a business. In the next section, we discuss various types of profitability analyses. The examples in both sections are based on Lincoln Company's financial statements presented earlier. In some cases, data from Lincoln Company's financial statements of the preceding year and from other sources are also used. These historical data are useful in assessing the past performance of a business and in forecasting its future performance. The results of financial analyses may be even more useful when they are compared with those of competing businesses and with industry averages.

Solvency analysis focuses on the ability of a business to pay or otherwise satisfy its current and noncurrent liabilities. It is normally assessed by examining balance sheet relationships, using the following major analyses:

1. Current position analysis
2. Accounts receivable analysis
3. Inventory analysis
4. The ratio of fixed assets to long-term liabilities
5. The ratio of liabilities to stockholders' equity
6. The number of times interest charges are earned

> **Solvency analysis focuses on the ability of a business to pay or otherwise satisfy its current and noncurrent liabilities.**

Current Position Analysis

To be useful in assessing solvency, a ratio or other financial measure must relate to a business's ability to pay or otherwise satisfy its liabilities. Using measures to assess a business's ability to pay its current liabilities is called **current position analysis**. Such analysis is of special interest to short-term creditors.

An analysis of a firm's current position normally includes determining the working capital, the current ratio, and the acid-test ratio. The current and acid-test ratios are most useful when analyzed together and compared to previous periods and other firms in the industry.

Working Capital

The excess of the current assets of a business over its current liabilities is called **working capital**. The working capital is often used in evaluating a company's ability to meet currently maturing debts. It is especially useful in making monthly or other period-to-period comparisons for a company. However, amounts of working capital are difficult to assess when comparing companies of different sizes or in comparing such amounts with industry figures. For example, working capital of $250,000 may be adequate for a small local hardware store, but it would be inadequate for all of **Home Depot**.

Current Ratio

Another means of expressing the relationship between current assets and current liabilities is the **current ratio**. This ratio is sometimes called the **working capital ratio** or **bankers' ratio**. The ratio is computed by dividing the total current assets by the total current liabilities. For Lincoln Company, working capital and the current ratio for 2003 and 2002 are as follows:

	2003	2002
Current assets	$550,000	$533,000
Current liabilities	210,000	243,000
Working capital	$340,000	$290,000
Current ratio	2.6	2.2

The **Wm. Wrigley Company** maintains a high current ratio—3.9 for a recent year. Wrigley's stable and profitable chewing gum business has allowed it to develop a strong cash position coupled with no short-term notes payable.

The current ratio is a more reliable indicator of solvency than is working capital. To illustrate, assume that as of December 31, 2003, the working capital of a competitor is much greater than $340,000, but its current ratio is only 1.3. Considering these facts alone, Lincoln Company, with its current ratio of 2.6, is in a more favorable position to obtain short-term credit than the competitor, which has the greater amount of working capital.

Acid-Test Ratio

The working capital and the current ratio do not consider the makeup of the current assets. To illustrate the importance of this consideration, the current position data for Lincoln Company and Jefferson Corporation as of December 31, 2003, are as follows:

	Lincoln Company	Jefferson Corporation
Current assets:		
Cash	$ 90,500	$ 45,500
Marketable securities	75,000	25,000
Accounts receivable (net)	115,000	90,000
Inventories	264,000	380,000
Prepaid expenses	5,500	9,500
Total current assets	$550,000	$550,000
Current liabilities	210,000	210,000
Working capital	$340,000	$340,000
Current ratio	2.6	2.6

Both companies have a working capital of $340,000 and a current ratio of 2.6. But the ability of each company to pay its current debts is significantly different. Jefferson Corporation has more of its current assets in inventories. Some of these inventories must be sold and the receivables collected before the current liabilities can be paid in full. Thus, a large amount of time may be necessary to convert these inventories into cash. Declines in market prices and a reduction in demand could also impair its ability to pay current liabilities. In contrast, Lincoln Company has cash and current assets (marketable securities and accounts receivable) that can generally be converted to cash rather quickly to meet its current liabilities.

A ratio that measures the "instant" debt-paying ability of a company is called the **acid-test ratio** or **quick ratio**. It is the ratio of the total quick assets to the total current liabilities. **Quick assets** are cash and other current assets that can be quickly converted to cash. Quick assets normally include cash, marketable securities, and receivables. The acid-test ratio data for Lincoln Company are as follows:

A balance sheet shows $300,000 of cash, marketable securities, and receivables, and $250,000 of inventories. Current liabilities are $200,000. What are (a) the current ratio and (b) the acid-test ratio?

(a) 2.75 ($550,000/$200,000);
(b) 1.5 ($300,000/$200,000)

	2003	2002
Quick assets:		
Cash	$ 90,500	$ 64,700
Marketable equity securities	75,000	60,000
Accounts receivable (net)	115,000	120,000
Total quick assets	$280,500	$244,700
Current liabilities	$210,000	$243,000
Acid-test ratio	1.3	1.0

Accounts Receivable Analysis

The size and makeup of accounts receivable change constantly during business operations. Sales on account increase accounts receivable, whereas collections from customers decrease accounts receivable. Firms that grant long credit terms usually have larger accounts receivable balances than those granting short credit terms. Increases or decreases in the volume of sales also affect the balance of accounts receivable.

It is desirable to collect receivables as promptly as possible. The cash collected from receivables improves solvency. In addition, the cash generated by prompt collections from customers may be used in operations for such purposes as purchasing merchandise in large quantities at lower prices. The cash may also be used for payment of dividends to stockholders or for other investing or financing purposes. Prompt collection also lessens the risk of loss from uncollectible accounts.

Accounts Receivable Turnover

The relationship between credit sales and accounts receivable may be stated as the **accounts receivable turnover**. This ratio is computed by dividing net sales on account by the average net accounts receivable. It is desirable to base the average on monthly balances, which allows for seasonal changes in sales. When such data are not available, it may be necessary to use the average of the accounts receivable balance at the beginning and the end of the year. If there are trade notes receivable as well as accounts, the two may be combined. The accounts receivable turnover data for Lincoln Company are as follows. All sales were made on account.

	2003	2002
Net sales on account	$1,498,000	$1,200,000
Accounts receivable (net):		
Beginning of year	$ 120,000	$ 140,000
End of year	115,000	120,000
Total	$ 235,000	$ 260,000
Average (Total ÷ 2)	$ 117,500	$ 130,000
Accounts receivable turnover	12.7	9.2

The increase in the accounts receivable turnover for 2003 indicates that there has been an improvement in the collection of receivables. This may be due to a change in the granting of credit or in collection practices or both.

Number of Days' Sales in Receivables

Another measure of the relationship between credit sales and accounts receivable is the **number of days' sales in receivables**. This ratio is computed by dividing the net accounts receivable at the end of the year by the average daily sales on account. Average daily sales on account is determined by dividing net sales on account by 365 days. The number of days' sales in receivables is computed for Lincoln Company as follows:

	2003	2002
Accounts receivable (net), end of year	$115,000	$120,000
Net sales on account	$1,498,000	$1,200,000
Average daily sales on account (sales ÷ 365)	$4,104	$3,288
Number of days' sales in receivables	28.0*	36.5*

*Accounts receivable ÷ Average daily sales on account

The number of days' sales in receivables is an estimate of the length of time (in days) the accounts receivable have been outstanding. Comparing this measure with

Sales were $1,200,000, of which 80% were on account. The accounts receivable balance at the beginning of the year was $56,000, and at the end of the year it was $40,000. What are (a) the accounts receivable turnover and (b) the number of days' sales in receivables?

(a) 20 [(0.80 × $1,200,000)/($56,000 + $40,000)/2]; (b) 15.2 days [$40,000/ ($960,000/365)]

the credit terms provides information on the efficiency in collecting receivables. For example, assume that the number of days' sales in receivables for Grant Inc. is 40. If Grant Inc.'s credit terms are n/45, then its collection process appears to be efficient. On the other hand, if Grant Inc.'s credit terms are n/30, its collection process does not appear to be efficient. A comparison with other firms in the same industry and with prior years also provides useful information. Such comparisons may indicate efficiency of collection procedures and trends in credit management.

Inventory Analysis

A business should keep enough inventory on hand to meet the needs of its customers and its operations. At the same time, however, an excessive amount of inventory reduces solvency by tying up funds. Excess inventories also increase insurance expense, property taxes, storage costs, and other related expenses. These expenses further reduce funds that could be used elsewhere to improve operations. Finally, excess inventory also increases the risk of losses because of price declines or obsolescence of the inventory. Two measures that are useful for evaluating the management of inventory are the inventory turnover and the number of days' sales in inventory.

Inventory Turnover

The relationship between the volume of goods (merchandise) sold and inventory may be stated as the **inventory turnover**. It is computed by dividing the cost of goods sold by the average inventory. If monthly data are not available, the average of the inventories at the beginning and the end of the year may be used. The inventory turnover for Lincoln Company is computed as follows:

	2003	2002
Cost of goods sold	$1,043,000	$820,000
Inventories:		
Beginning of year	$ 283,000	$311,000
End of year	264,000	283,000
Total	$ 547,000	$594,000
Average (Total ÷ 2)	$ 273,500	$297,000
Inventory turnover	3.8	2.8

The inventory turnover of **McDonald's Corporation** for a recent year was 39, while for **Toys "R" Us Inc.**, it was 4.3. McDonald's inventory turnover is higher because it sells perishable food products, while toys can sit on the shelf longer without "spoiling."

The inventory turnover improved for Lincoln Company because of an increase in the cost of goods sold and a decrease in the average inventories. Differences across inventories, companies, and industries are too great to allow a general statement on what is a good inventory turnover. For example, a firm selling food should have a higher turnover than a firm selling furniture or jewelry. Likewise, the perishable foods department of a supermarket should have a higher turnover than the soaps and cleansers department. However, for each business or each department within a business, there is a reasonable turnover rate. A turnover lower than this rate could mean that inventory is not being managed properly.

Number of Days' Sales in Inventory

Another measure of the relationship between the cost of goods sold and inventory is the **number of days' sales in inventory**. This measure is computed by dividing the inventory at the end of the year by the average daily cost of goods sold (cost of goods sold divided by 365). The number of days' sales in inventory for Lincoln Company is computed as follows:

	2003	2002
Inventories, end of year	$264,000	$283,000
Cost of goods sold	$1,043,000	$820,000
Average daily cost of goods sold (COGS ÷ 365 days)	$2,858	$2,247
Number of days' sales in inventory	92.4	125.9

The number of days' sales in inventory is a rough measure of the length of time it takes to acquire, sell, and replace the inventory. For Lincoln Company, there is a major improvement in the number of days' sales in inventory during 2003. However, a comparison with earlier years and similar firms would be useful in assessing Lincoln Company's overall inventory management.

Ratio of Fixed Assets to Long-Term Liabilities

Long-term notes and bonds are often secured by mortgages on fixed assets. The **ratio of fixed assets to long-term liabilities** is a solvency measure that indicates the margin of safety of the noteholders or bondholders. It also indicates the ability of the business to borrow additional funds on a long-term basis. The ratio of fixed assets to long-term liabilities for Lincoln Company is as follows:

	2003	2002
Fixed assets (net)	$444,500	$470,000
Long-term liabilities	$100,000	$200,000
Ratio of fixed assets to long-term liabilities	4.4	2.4

The major increase in this ratio at the end of 2003 is mainly due to liquidating one-half of Lincoln Company's long-term liabilities. If the company needs to borrow additional funds on a long-term basis in the future, it is in a strong position to do so.

Ratio of Liabilities to Stockholders' Equity

Claims against the total assets of a business are divided into two groups: (1) claims of creditors and (2) claims of owners. The relationship between the total claims of the creditors and owners—the **ratio of liabilities to stockholders' equity**—is a solvency measure that indicates the margin of safety for creditors. It also indicates the ability of the business to withstand adverse business conditions. When the claims of creditors are large in relation to the equity of the stockholders, there are usually significant interest payments. If earnings decline to the point where the company is unable to meet its interest payments, the business may be taken over by the creditors.

The relationship between creditor and stockholder equity is shown in the vertical analysis of the balance sheet. For example, the balance sheet of Lincoln Company in Exhibit 5 indicates that on December 31, 2003, liabilities represented 27.2% and stockholders' equity represented 72.8% of the total liabilities and stockholders' equity (100.0%). Instead of expressing each item as a percent of the total, this relationship may be expressed as a ratio of one to the other, as follows:

The ratio of liabilities to stockholders' equity varies across industries. For example, recent annual reports of some selected companies showed the following ratio of liabilities to stockholders' equity:

Continental Airlines	4.31
Procter & Gamble	1.85
Circuit City Stores	0.93

The airline industry generally uses more debt financing than the consumer product or retail industries. Thus, the airline industry is generally considered more risky.

	2003	2002
Total liabilities	$310,000	$443,000
Total stockholders' equity	$829,500	$787,500
Ratio of liabilities to stockholders' equity	0.37	0.56

The balance sheet of Lincoln Company shows that the major factor affecting the change in the ratio was the $100,000 decrease in long-term liabilities during 2003. The ratio at the end of both years shows a large margin of safety for the creditors.

Number of Times Interest Charges Earned

Corporations in some industries, such as airlines, normally have high ratios of debt to stockholders' equity. For such corporations, the relative risk of the debtholders is normally measured as the **number of times interest charges are earned** during the year. The higher the ratio, the lower the risk that interest payments will not be made if earnings decrease. In other words, the higher the ratio, the greater the assurance that interest payments will be made on a continuing basis. This measure also indicates the general financial strength of the business, which is of interest to stockholders and employees as well as creditors.

The amount available to meet interest charges is not affected by taxes on income. This is because interest is deductible in determining taxable income. Thus, the number of times interest charges are earned is computed as shown below.

What would be the number of times interest charges are earned for a company with $1,500,000, 10% debt; net income of $120,000; and a corporate tax rate of 40%?

$$\frac{[\$120{,}000/(1.0 - 0.4)] + \$150{,}000}{\$150{,}000} = 2.33$$

	2003	2002
Income before income tax	$ 900,000	$ 800,000
Add interest expense	300,000	250,000
Amount available to meet interest charges	$1,200,000	$1,050,000
Number of times interest charges earned	4	4.2

Analysis such as this can also be applied to dividends on preferred stock. In such a case, net income is divided by the amount of preferred dividends to yield the **number of times preferred dividends are earned**. This measure indicates the risk that dividends to preferred stockholders may not be paid.

Profitability Analysis

objective 3

Apply financial statement analysis to assess the profitability of a business.

The ability of a business to earn profits depends on the effectiveness and efficiency of its operations as well as the resources available to it. Profitability analysis, therefore, focuses primarily on the relationship between operating results as reported in the income statement and resources available to the business as reported in the balance sheet. Major analyses used in assessing profitability include the following:

1. Ratio of net sales to assets
2. Rate earned on total assets
3. Rate earned on stockholders' equity
4. Rate earned on common stockholders' equity
5. Earnings per share on common stock
6. Price-earnings ratio
7. Dividends per share
8. Dividend yield

> **Profitability analysis focuses on the relationship between operating results and the resources available to a business.**

Ratio of Net Sales to Assets

The **ratio of net sales to assets** is a profitability measure that shows how effectively a firm utilizes its assets. For example, two competing businesses have equal amounts of assets. If the sales of one are twice the sales of the other, the business with the higher sales is making better use of its assets.

In computing the ratio of net sales to assets, any long-term investments are excluded from total assets, because such investments are unrelated to normal operations involving the sale of goods or services. Assets may be measured as the total at the end of the year, the average at the beginning and end of the year, or the average of monthly totals. The basic data and the computation of this ratio for Lincoln Company are as follows:

	2003	2002
Net sales	$1,498,000	$1,200,000
Total assets (excluding long-term investments):		
Beginning of year	$1,053,000	$1,010,000
End of year	1,044,500	1,053,000
Total	$2,097,500	$2,063,000
Average (Total ÷ 2)	$1,048,750	$1,031,500
Ratio of net sales to assets	1.4	1.2

This ratio improved during 2003, primarily due to an increase in sales volume. A comparison with similar companies or industry averages would be helpful in assessing the effectiveness of Lincoln Company's use of its assets.

Rate Earned on Total Assets

The **rate earned on total assets** measures the profitability of total assets, without considering how the assets are financed. This rate is therefore not affected by whether the assets are financed primarily by creditors or stockholders.

The rate earned on total assets is computed by adding interest expense to net income and dividing this sum by the average total assets. Adding interest expense to net income eliminates the effect of whether the assets are financed by debt or equity. The rate earned by Lincoln Company on total assets is computed as follows:

	2003	2002
Net income	$ 91,000	$ 76,500
Plus interest expense	6,000	12,000
Total	$ 97,000	$ 88,500
Total assets:		
Beginning of year	$1,230,500	$1,187,500
End of year	1,139,500	1,230,500
Total	$2,370,000	$2,418,000
Average (Total ÷ 2)	$1,185,000	$1,209,000
Rate earned on total assets	8.2%	7.3%

The rate earned on total assets of Lincoln Company during 2003 improved over that of 2002. A comparison with similar companies and industry averages would be useful in evaluating Lincoln Company's profitability on total assets.

Sometimes it may be desirable to compute the **rate of income from operations to total assets**. This is especially true if significant amounts of nonoperating income and expense are reported on the income statement. In this case, any assets related to the nonoperating income and expense items should be excluded from total assets in computing the rate. In addition, using income from operations (which is before tax) has the advantage of eliminating the effects of any changes in the tax structure on the rate of earnings. When evaluating published data on rates earned on assets, you should be careful to determine the exact nature of the measure that is reported.

Rate Earned on Stockholders' Equity

Another measure of profitability is the **rate earned on stockholders' equity**. It is computed by dividing net income by average total stockholders' equity. In contrast to the rate earned on total assets, this measure emphasizes the rate of income earned on the amount invested by the stockholders.

The total stockholders' equity may vary throughout a period. For example, a business may issue or retire stock, pay dividends, and earn net income. If monthly amounts are not available, the average of the stockholders' equity at the beginning and the end of the year is normally used to compute this rate. For Lincoln Company, the rate earned on stockholders' equity is computed as follows:

	2003	2002
Net income	$ 91,000	$ 76,500
Stockholders' equity:		
Beginning of year	$ 787,500	$ 750,000
End of year	829,500	787,500
Total	$1,617,000	$1,537,500
Average (Total ÷ 2)	$ 808,500	$ 768,750
Rate earned on stockholders' equity	11.3%	10.0%

The rate earned by a business on the equity of its stockholders is usually higher than the rate earned on total assets. This occurs when the amount earned on assets acquired with creditors' funds is more than the interest paid to creditors. This difference in the rate on stockholders' equity and the rate on total assets is called **leverage**.

Lincoln Company's rate earned on stockholders' equity for 2003, 11.3%, is greater than the rate of 8.2% earned on total assets. The leverage of 3.1% (11.3% − 8.2%) for 2003 compares favorably with the 2.7% (10.0% − 7.3%) leverage for 2002. Exhibit 8 shows the 2003 and 2002 leverages for Lincoln Company.

Exhibit 8 Leverage

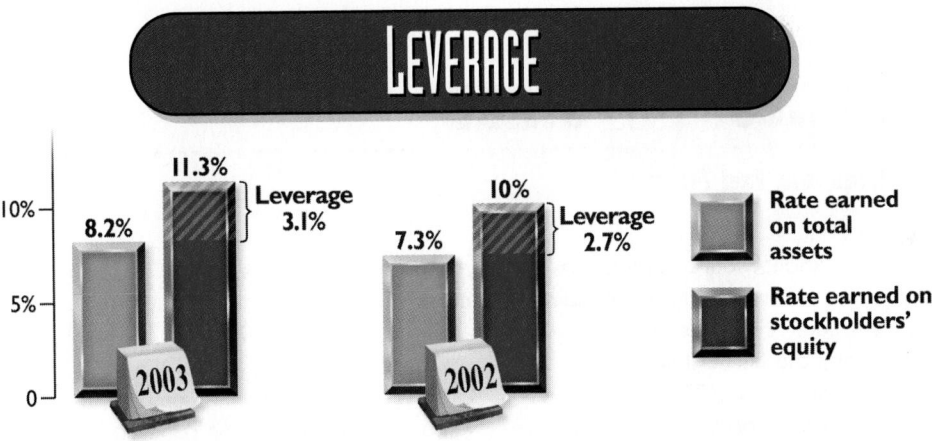

Rate Earned on Common Stockholders' Equity

A corporation may have both preferred and common stock outstanding. In this case, the common stockholders have the residual claim on earnings. The **rate earned on common stockholders' equity** focuses only on the rate of profits earned on the amount invested by the common stockholders. It is computed by subtracting preferred dividend requirements from the net income and dividing by the average common stockholders' equity.

The approximate rates earned on assets and stockholders' equity for **Adolph Coors Company** and **Anheuser-Busch Companies** for a recent fiscal year are shown below.

	Adolph Coors	Anheuser-Busch
Rate earned on assets	5%	13%
Rate earned on stockholders' equity	9%	30%

Anheuser-Busch has been more profitable and has benefited from a greater use of leverage than has Adolph Coors.

Lincoln Company has $150,000 of 6% nonparticipating preferred stock outstanding on December 31, 2003 and 2002. Thus, the annual preferred dividend requirement is $9,000 ($150,000 × 6%). The common stockholders' equity equals the total stockholders' equity, including retained earnings, less the par of the preferred stock ($150,000). The basic data and the rate earned on common stockholders' equity for Lincoln Company are as follows:

	2003	2002
Net income	$ 91,000	$ 76,500
Preferred dividends	9,000	9,000
Remainder—identified with common stock	$ 82,000	$ 67,500
Common stockholders' equity:		
Beginning of year	$ 637,500	$ 600,000
End of year	679,500	637,500
Total	$1,317,000	$1,237,500
Average (Total ÷ 2)	$ 658,500	$ 618,750
Rate earned on common stockholders' equity	12.5%	10.9%

The rate earned on common stockholders' equity differs from the rates earned by Lincoln Company on total assets and total stockholders' equity. This occurs if there are borrowed funds and also preferred stock outstanding, which rank ahead of the common shares in their claim on earnings. Thus, the concept of leverage, as we discussed in the preceding section, can also be applied to the use of funds from the sale of preferred stock as well as borrowing. Funds from both sources can be used in an attempt to increase the return on common stockholders' equity.

BUSINESS ON STAGE

Analysis and Red Flags

An additional source of information about a corporation is the independent auditor's report, which must accompany the financial statements of a public corporation. The purpose of this report is to provide assurance to investors that the financial statements are fairly presented in conformity with generally accepted accounting principles.

The auditor's report may raise "red flags" indicating that profitability and solvency measures should be analyzed further. In such cases, an investor should read the auditor's report carefully to see if the "reliability" of these measures has been affected by one or more of the following factors:

1. There may be substantial doubt as to the ability of the company to continue as a going concern beyond one year.
2. An unusual accounting practice is being followed.
3. The company changed accounting principles from prior years.
4. The auditor wants to call your attention to a specific matter of importance.
5. The financial statements do not conform to generally accepted accounting principles.

The date of the auditor's report is also significant. It represents the last date that the auditor searched for events occurring subsequent to the date of the financial statements—events that might be significant to the interpretation of those statements. For example, the company may have sold a subsidiary after year-end or suffered a substantial loss as a result of some disaster. Such events should be disclosed in notes to the financial statements. ■

Earnings per Share on Common Stock

One of the profitability measures often quoted by the financial press is **earnings per share (EPS) on common stock**. It is also normally reported in the income statement in corporate annual reports. If a company has issued only one class of stock, the earnings per share is computed by dividing net income by the number of shares of stock outstanding. If preferred and common stock are outstanding, the net income is first reduced by the amount of preferred dividend requirements.[2]

The data on the earnings per share of common stock for Lincoln Company are as follows:

	2003	2002
Net income	$91,000	$76,500
Preferred dividends	9,000	9,000
Remainder—identified with common stock	$82,000	$67,500
Shares of common stock outstanding	50,000	50,000
Earnings per share on common stock	$1.64	$1.35

Price-Earnings Ratio

Another profitability measure quoted by the financial press is the **price-earnings (P/E) ratio** on common stock. The price-earnings ratio is an indicator of a firm's future earnings prospects. It is computed by dividing the market price per share of common stock at a specific date by the annual earnings per share. To illustrate, assume that the market prices per common share are 41 at the end of 2003 and 27 at the end of 2002. The price-earnings ratio on common stock of Lincoln Company is computed as follows:

	2003	2002
Market price per share of common stock	$41.00	$27.00
Earnings per share on common stock	÷ 1.64	÷ 1.35
Price-earnings ratio on common stock	25	20

The price-earnings ratio indicates that a share of common stock of Lincoln Company was selling for 20 times the amount of earnings per share at the end of 2002. At the end of 2003, the common stock was selling for 25 times the amount of earnings per share.

P/E ratios that are much higher than the market averages are generally associated with companies with fast-growing profits. P/E ratios that are much lower than the market averages are generally associated with "out of favor" or declining profit companies.

Dividends per Share and Dividend Yield

Since the primary basis for dividends is earnings, **dividends per share** and earnings per share on common stock are commonly used by investors in assessing alternative stock investments. The dividends per share for Lincoln Company were $0.80 ($40,000 ÷ 50,000 shares) for 2003 and $0.60 ($30,000 ÷ 50,000 shares) for 2002.

Dividends per share can be reported with earnings per share to indicate the relationship between dividends and earnings. Comparing these two per share amounts indicates the extent to which the corporation is retaining its earnings for use in operations. Exhibit 9 shows these relationships for Lincoln Company:

The **dividend yield** on common stock is a profitability measure that shows the rate of return to common stockholders in terms of cash dividends. It is of special interest to investors whose main investment objective is to receive current returns

---

[2] Additional details related to earnings per share were discussed in a previous chapter.

Exhibit 9 Dividends and Earnings per Share of Common Stock

The dividend per share, dividend yield, and P/E ratio of a common stock are normally quoted on the daily listing of stock prices in *The Wall Street Journal* and other financial publications.

(dividends) on an investment rather than an increase in the market price of the investment. The dividend yield is computed by dividing the annual dividends paid per share of common stock by the market price per share on a specific date. To illustrate, assume that the market price was 41 at the end of 2003 and 27 at the end of 2002. The dividend yield on common stock of Lincoln Company is as follows:

	2003	2002
Dividends per share of common stock	$ 0.80	$ 0.60
Market price per share of common stock	÷ 41.00	÷ 27.00
Dividend yield on common stock	1.95%	2.22%

Summary of Analytical Measures

objective 4

Summarize the uses and limitations of analytical measures.

Exhibit 10 presents a summary of the analytical measures that we have discussed. These measures can be computed for most medium-size businesses. Depending on the specific business being analyzed, some measures might be omitted or additional measures could be developed. The type of industry, the capital structure, and the diversity of the business's operations usually affect the measures used. For example, analysis for an airline might include revenue per passenger mile and cost per available seat as measures. Likewise, analysis for a hotel might focus on occupancy rates.

Percentage analyses, ratios, turnovers, and other measures of financial position and operating results are useful analytical measures. They are helpful in assessing a business's past performance and predicting its future. They are not, however, a substitute for sound judgment. In selecting and interpreting analytical measures, conditions peculiar to a business or its industry should be considered. In addition, the influence of the general economic and business environment should be considered.

In determining trends, the interrelationship of the measures used in assessing a business should be carefully studied. Comparable indexes of earlier periods should also be studied. Data from competing businesses may be useful in assessing the efficiency of operations for the firm under analysis. In making such comparisons, however, the effects of differences in the accounting methods used by the businesses should be considered.

Exhibit 10 Summary of Analytical Measures

	Method of Computation	Use
Solvency measures:		
Working capital	Current assets − Current liabilities	To indicate the ability to meet currently maturing obligations
Current ratio	$\dfrac{\text{Current assets}}{\text{Current liabilities}}$	
Acid-test ratio	$\dfrac{\text{Quick assets}}{\text{Current liabilities}}$	To indicate instant debt-paying ability
Accounts receivable turnover	$\dfrac{\text{Net sales on account}}{\text{Average accounts receivable}}$	To assess the efficiency in collecting receivables and in the management of credit
Numbers of days' sales in receivables	$\dfrac{\text{Accounts receivable, end of year}}{\text{Average daily sales on account}}$	
Inventory turnover	$\dfrac{\text{Cost of goods sold}}{\text{Average inventory}}$	To assess the efficiency in the management of inventory
Number of days' sales in inventory	$\dfrac{\text{Inventory, end of year}}{\text{Average daily cost of goods sold}}$	
Ratio of fixed assets to long-term liabilities	$\dfrac{\text{Fixed assets (net)}}{\text{Long-term liabilities}}$	To indicate the margin of safety to long-term creditors
Ratio of liabilities to stockholders' equity	$\dfrac{\text{Total liabilities}}{\text{Total stockholders' equity}}$	To indicate the margin of safety to creditors
Number of times interest charges earned	$\dfrac{\text{Income before}\ \text{income tax} + \text{Interest expense}}{\text{Interest expense}}$	To assess the risk to debtholders in terms of number of times interest charges were earned
Profitability measures:		
Ratio of net sales to assets	$\dfrac{\text{Net sales}}{\text{Average total assets (excluding long-term investments)}}$	To assess the effectiveness in the use of assets
Rate earned on total assets	$\dfrac{\text{Net income} + \text{Interest expense}}{\text{Average total assets}}$	To assess the profitability of the assets
Rate earned on stockholders' equity	$\dfrac{\text{Net income}}{\text{Average total stockholders' equity}}$	To assess the profitability of the investment by stockholders
Rate earned on common stockholders' equity	$\dfrac{\text{Net income} - \text{Preferred dividends}}{\text{Average common stockholders' equity}}$	To assess the profitability of the investment by common stockholders
Earnings per share on common stock	$\dfrac{\text{Net income} - \text{Preferred dividends}}{\text{Shares of common stock outstanding}}$	
Price-earnings ratio	$\dfrac{\text{Market price per share of common stock}}{\text{Earnings per share of common stock}}$	To indicate future earnings prospects, based on the relationship between market value of common stock and earnings
Dividends per share of common stock	$\dfrac{\text{Dividends}}{\text{Shares of common stock outstanding}}$	To indicate the extent to which earnings are being distributed to common stockholders
Dividend yield	$\dfrac{\text{Dividends per share of common stock}}{\text{Market price per share of common stock}}$	To indicate the rate of return to common stockholders in terms of dividends

Corporate Annual Reports

Corporations normally issue annual reports to their stockholders and other interested parties. Such reports summarize the corporation's operating activities for the past year and plans for the future. There are many variations in the order and form for presenting the major sections of annual reports. However, one section of the annual report is devoted to the financial statements, including the accompanying notes. In addition, annual reports usually include the following sections:

1. Financial Highlights
2. President's Letter to the Stockholders
3. Management Discussion and Analysis
4. Independent Auditors' Report
5. Historical Summary

In the following paragraphs, we describe these sections. Each section, as well as the financial statements, is illustrated in the 2000 annual report for **Cisco Systems, Inc.**, in Appendix G.

Financial Highlights

The Financial Highlights section summarizes the operating results for the last year or two. It is sometimes called *Results in Brief*. It is usually presented on the first one or two pages of the annual report.

There are many variations in the format and content of the Financial Highlights section. Such items as sales, net income, net income per common share, cash dividends paid, cash dividends per common share, and the amount of capital expenditures are typically presented. In addition to these data, information about the financial position at the end of the year may be presented. The Financial Highlights section for Cisco Systems, Inc., includes the year-end amounts of stockholders' equity, common shares outstanding, net income, and working capital.

President's Letter to the Stockholders

A letter from the company president to the stockholders is also presented in most annual reports. These letters usually discuss such items as reasons for an increase or decrease in net income, changes in existing plants, purchase or construction of new plants, significant new financing commitments, social responsibility issues, and future plans. The President's Letter for Cisco Systems, Inc., mentions the importance of the Internet to the company's growth.

Management Discussion and Analysis

A required disclosure in the annual report filed with the Securities and Exchange Commission is the **Management Discussion and Analysis (MDA)**. The MDA provides critical information in interpreting the financial statements and assessing the future of the company.

The MDA includes an analysis of the results of operations and discusses management's opinion about future performance. It compares the prior year's income statement with the current year's to explain changes in sales, significant expenses, gross profit, and income from operations. For example, an increase in sales may be explained by referring to higher shipment volume or stronger prices.

The MDA also includes an analysis of the company's financial condition. It compares significant balance sheet items between successive years to explain changes in liquidity and capital resources. In addition, the MDA discusses significant risk exposure. For example, Cisco Systems has identified fluctuations in foreign currencies, credit risk, and worldwide economic conditions among its risk factors.

The largest companies in the U.S. and in most parts of the world are audited by one of five large international accounting firms: **Arthur Andersen, Pricewater-houseCoopers, Deloitte & Touche, Ernst & Young,** and **KPMG Peat Marwick.**

Independent Auditors' Report

Before issuing annual statements, all publicly held corporations are required to have an independent audit (examination) of their financial statements. For the financial statements of most companies, the CPAs who conduct the audit render an opinion on the fairness of the statements, as shown in the Independent Auditors' Report for Cisco Systems, Inc.

Historical Summary

The Historical Summary section reports selected financial and operating data of past periods, usually for five or ten years. It is usually presented near the financial statements for the current year. There are wide variations in the types of data reported and the title of this section. In the annual report for Cisco Systems, Inc., this section is called "Selected Financial Data" and includes data for five years.

ENCORE

Bricks vs. Clicks

Online retailing has surged as consumers have begun purchasing items on the Internet. One of the largest online retailers is **Amazon.com, Inc.**, which began as an online bookseller. Amazon competes with such traditional retailers as **Borders** and **Barnes & Noble**. Amazon promises to provide cheaper products than the traditional retailer, because they are able to replace expensive "bricks" with less expensive "clicks." The financial statements can give us some clues as to how this business strategy is working. The charts shown were prepared from recent (1998) annual reports for Amazon.com and Barnes & Noble.

First, notice the chart labeled "Asset Efficiency." Here we see that Amazon generates over $5 of sales for each dollar of assets. This compares to Barnes & Noble, which generates only around $1.70 for each dollar of assets. This means that Amazon does not require the same amount of assets to generate sales. This makes sense, because Amazon doesn't have real estate and stores (bricks), as does Barnes & Noble. Amazon has computers (clicks), but they are not as costly as the traditional retail infrastructure. As further evidence, consider the inventory turnover. The inventory turnover for Amazon is over 15,

while for Barnes & Noble it's around 2. Barnes & Noble must stock its stores with inventory, while Amazon just passes electronic orders to publishers and thus avoids holding much inventory.

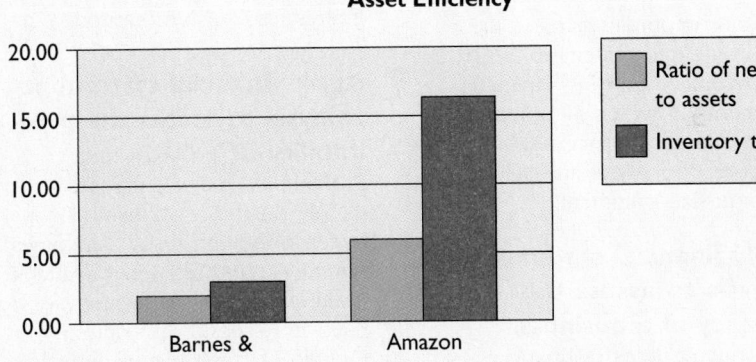

Asset Efficiency

Legend: Ratio of net sales to assets; Inventory turnover

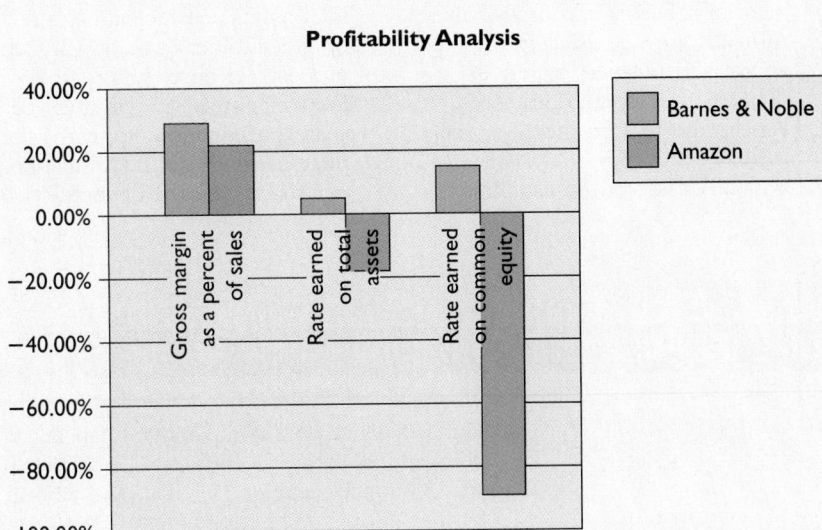

Profitability Analysis

Legend: Barnes & Noble; Amazon

Axis labels: Gross margin as a percent of sales; Rate earned on total assets; Rate earned on common equity

Now let's look at the profitability of the two companies in the chart labeled "Profitability Analysis." First, a vertical analysis of the income statement indicates that the gross margin as a percent of sales for Barnes & Noble is nearly 29%, while for Amazon, it is only 22%. This means that Amazon is selling its products at a lower price than Barnes & Noble, since we assume that the two companies pay the same amount for their sold goods. This is consistent with Amazon's business strategy to undercut the traditional "bricks and mortar" competition. Unfortunately, at the time of this writing, Amazon has not been able to earn an operating profit. Both the rate earned on total assets and common equity are negative, while Barnes & Noble is profitable. Indeed, comparing Amazon's rate earned on total assets to the rate earned on common equity indicates that Amazon is also highly leveraged. The reason for Amazon's losses is the high operating expenses incurred to grow the business. Amazon's revenue grew over 4,000% over the three-year reporting period. Eventually, however, Amazon will need to earn a profit. This may require improving the gross margin percentage or reducing expenditures for growth. Either way, Amazon has a fundamentally different business model than does the traditional retailer. It remains to be seen if this model can become profitable. ■

HEY POINTS

1 List basic financial statement analytical procedures.

The analysis of percentage increases and decreases in related items in comparative financial statements is called horizontal analysis. The analysis of percentages of component parts to the total in a single statement is called vertical analysis. Financial statements in which all amounts are expressed in percentages for purposes of analysis are called common-size statements.

2 Apply financial statement analysis to assess the solvency of a business.

The primary focus of financial statement analysis is the assessment of solvency and profitability. All users are interested in the ability of a business to pay its debts as they come due (solvency) and to earn income (profitability). Solvency analysis is normally assessed by examining the following balance sheet relationships: (1) current position analysis, (2) accounts receivable analysis, (3) inventory analysis, (4) the ratio of fixed assets to long-term liabilities, (5) the ratio of liabilities to stockholders' equity, and (6) the number of times interest charges are earned.

3 Apply financial statement analysis to assess the profitability of a business.

Profitability analysis focuses mainly on the relationship between operating results (income statement) and resources available (balance sheet). Major analyses used in assessing profitability include (1) the ratio of net sales to assets, (2) the rate earned on total assets, (3) the rate earned on stockholders' equity, (4) the rate earned on common stockholders' equity, (5) earnings per share on common stock, (6) the price-earnings ratio, (7) dividends per share, and (8) dividend yield.

4 Summarize the uses and limitations of analytical measures.

In selecting and interpreting analytical measures, conditions peculiar to a business or its industry should be considered. For example, the type of industry, capital structure, and diversity of the business's operations affect the measures used. In addition, the influence of the general economic and business environment should be considered.

5 Describe the contents of corporate annual reports.

Corporate annual reports normally include financial statements and the following sections: Financial Highlights, President's Letter to the Stockholders, Management Discussion and Analysis, Independent Auditors' Report, and Historical Summary.

ILLUSTRATIVE PROBLEM

Rainbow Paint Co.'s comparative financial statements for the years ending December 31, 2003 and 2002, are as follows. The market price of Rainbow Paint Co.'s common stock was $30 on December 31, 2002, and $25 on December 31, 2003.

Rainbow Paint Co.
Comparative Income Statement
For the Years Ended December 31, 2003 and 2002

	2003	2002
Sales (all on account)	$5,125,000	$3,257,600
Sales returns and allowances	125,000	57,600
Net sales	$5,000,000	$3,200,000
Cost of goods sold	3,400,000	2,080,000
Gross profit	$1,600,000	$1,120,000
Selling expenses	$ 650,000	$ 464,000
Administrative expenses	325,000	224,000
Total operating expenses	$ 975,000	$ 688,000
Income from operations	$ 625,000	$ 432,000
Other income	25,000	19,200
	$ 650,000	$ 451,200
Other expense (interest)	105,000	64,000
Income before income tax	$ 545,000	$ 387,200
Income tax expense	300,000	176,000
Net income	$ 245,000	$ 211,200

Rainbow Paint Co.
Comparative Retained Earnings Statement
For the Years Ended December 31, 2003 and 2002

	2003	2002
Retained earnings, January 1	$723,000	$581,800
Add net income for year	245,000	211,200
Total	$968,000	$793,000
Deduct dividends:		
On preferred stock	$ 40,000	$ 40,000
On common stock	45,000	30,000
Total	$ 85,000	$ 70,000
Retained earnings, December 31	$883,000	$723,000

Rainbow Paint Co.
Comparative Balance Sheet
December 31, 2003 and 2002

	2003	2002
Assets		
Current assets:		
Cash	$ 175,000	$ 125,000
Marketable securities	150,000	50,000
Accounts receivable (net)	425,000	325,000
Inventories	720,000	480,000
Prepaid expenses	30,000	20,000
Total current assets	$1,500,000	$1,000,000
Long-term investments	250,000	225,000
Property, plant, and equipment (net)	2,093,000	1,948,000
Total assets	$3,843,000	$3,173,000

(continued)

Liabilities

Current liabilities	$ 750,000	$ 650,000
Long-term liabilities:		
Mortgage note payable, 10%, due 2006	$ 410,000	—
Bonds payable, 8%, due 2009	800,000	$ 800,000
Total long-term liabilities	$1,210,000	$ 800,000
Total liabilities	$1,960,000	$1,450,000

Stockholders' Equity

Preferred 8% stock, $100 par	$ 500,000	$ 500,000
Common stock, $10 par	500,000	500,000
Retained earnings	883,000	723,000
Total stockholders' equity	$1,883,000	$1,723,000
Total liabilities and stockholders' equity	$3,843,000	$3,173,000

Instructions

Determine the following measures for 2003:

1. Working capital
2. Current ratio
3. Acid-test ratio
4. Accounts receivable turnover
5. Number of days' sales in receivables
6. Inventory turnover
7. Number of days' sales in inventory
8. Ratio of fixed assets to long-term liabilities
9. Ratio of liabilities to stockholders' equity
10. Number of times interest charges earned
11. Number of times preferred dividends earned
12. Ratio of net sales to assets
13. Rate earned on total assets
14. Rate earned on stockholders' equity
15. Rate earned on common stockholders' equity
16. Earnings per share on common stock
17. Price-earnings ratio
18. Dividends per share of common stock
19. Dividend yield

Solution

(Ratios are rounded to the nearest single digit after the decimal point.)

1. Working capital: $750,000
   $1,500,000 − $750,000
2. Current ratio: 2.0
   $1,500,000 ÷ $750,000
3. Acid-test ratio: 1.0
   $750,000 ÷ $750,000
4. Accounts receivable turnover: 13.3
   $5,000,000 ÷ [($425,000 + $325,000) ÷ 2]
5. Number of days' sales in receivables: 31 days
   $5,000,000 ÷ 365 = $13,699
   $425,000 ÷ $13,699
6. Inventory turnover: 5.7
   $3,400,000 ÷ [($720,000 + $480,000) ÷ 2]
7. Number of days' sales in inventory: 77.3 days
   $3,400,000 ÷ 365 = $9,315
   $720,000 ÷ $9,315
8. Ratio of fixed assets to long-term liabilities: 1.7
   $2,093,000 ÷ $1,210,000
9. Ratio of liabilities to stockholders' equity: 1.0
   $1,960,000 ÷ $1,883,000

10. Number of times interest charges earned: 6.2
   ($545,000 + $105,000) ÷ $105,000
11. Number of times preferred dividends earned: 6.1
   $245,000 ÷ $40,000
12. Ratio of net sales to assets: 1.5
   $5,000,000 ÷ [($3,593,000 + $2,948,000) ÷ 2]
13. Rate earned on total assets: 10.0%
   ($245,000 + $105,000) ÷ [($3,843,000 + $3,173,000) ÷ 2]
14. Rate earned on stockholders' equity: 13.6%
   $245,000 ÷ [($1,883,000 + $1,723,000) ÷ 2]
15. Rate earned on common stockholders' equity: 15.7%
   ($245,000 − $40,000) ÷ [($1,383,000 + $1,223,000) ÷ 2]
16. Earnings per share on common stock: $4.10
   ($245,000 − $40,000) ÷ 50,000
17. Price-earnings ratio: 6.1
   $25 ÷ $4.10
18. Dividends per share of common stock: $0.90
   $45,000 ÷ 50,000 shares
19. Dividend yield: 3.6%
   $0.90 ÷ $25

SELF-EXAMINATION QUESTIONS
Answers at End of Chapter

Matching

Match each of the following statements with its proper term. Some terms may not be used.

A. **accounts receivable turnover**
B. **acid-test ratio**
C. **common-size statement**
D. **current ratio**
E. **dividend yield**
F. **dividends per share**
G. **earnings per share (EPS) on common stock**
H. **horizontal analysis**
I. **inventory turnover**
J. **leverage**
K. **Management Discussion and Analysis (MDA)**
L. **number of days' sales in inventory**
M. **number of days' sales in receivables**
N. **number of times interest charges are earned**
O. **price-earnings (P/E) ratio**
P. **profitability**
Q. **quick assets**
R. **rate earned on common stockholders' equity**
S. **rate earned on stockholders' equity**

___ 1. The percentage of increases and decreases in corresponding items in comparative financial statements.

___ 2. The sum of cash, receivables, and marketable securities.

___ 3. The relationship between the volume of sales and inventory, computed by dividing the inventory at the end of the year by the average daily cost of goods sold.

___ 4. The ability of a firm to pay its debts as they come due.

___ 5. The relationship between credit sales and accounts receivable, computed by dividing the net accounts receivable at the end of the year by the average daily sales on account.

___ 6. The relationship between credit sales and accounts receivable, computed by dividing net sales on account by the average net accounts receivable.

___ 7. The tendency of the rate earned on stockholders' equity to vary from the rate earned on total assets because the amount earned on assets acquired through the use of funds provided by creditors varies from the interest paid to these creditors.

___ 8. A financial statement in which all items are expressed only in relative terms.

___ 9. A measure of profitability computed by dividing net income by total stockholders' equity.

___ 10. The excess of total current assets over total current liabilities at some point in time.

___ 11. The ratio of the market price per share of common stock, at a specific date, to the annual earnings per share.

___ 12. A measure of the profitability of assets, without regard to the equity of creditors and stockholders in the assets.

___ 13. The profitability ratio of net income available to common shareholders to the number of common shares outstanding.

___ 14. The ratio of the sum of cash, receivables, and marketable securities to current liabilities.

T.	**rate earned on total assets**
U.	**ratio of fixed assets to long-term liabilities**
V.	**ratio of liabilities to stockholders' equity**
W.	**ratio of net sales to assets**
X.	**solvency**
Y.	**vertical analysis**
Z.	**working capital**

___ 15. The percentage analysis of component parts in relation to the total of the parts in a single financial statement.

___ 16. A measure of profitability computed by dividing net income, reduced by preferred dividend requirements, by common stockholders' equity.

___ 17. The ratio of current assets to current liabilities.

___ 18. The relationship between the volume of goods sold and inventory, computed by dividing the cost of goods sold by the average inventory.

___ 19. The ability of a firm to earn income.

___ 20. An annual report disclosure that provides an analysis of the results of operations and financial condition.

Multiple Choice

1. What type of analysis is indicated by the following?

	Amount	Percent
Current assets	$100,000	20%
Property, plant, and equipment	400,000	80
Total assets	$500,000	100%

  A. Vertical analysis   C. Profitability analysis
  B. Horizontal analysis   D. Contribution margin analysis

2. Which of the following measures indicates the ability of a firm to pay its current liabilities?
  A. Working capital   C. Acid-test ratio
  B. Current ratio   D. All of the above

3. The ratio determined by dividing total current assets by total current liabilities is:
  A. current ratio   C. bankers' ratio
  B. working capital ratio   D. all of the above

4. The ratio of the quick assets to current liabilities, which indicates the "instant" debt-paying ability of a firm, is:
  A. current ratio   C. acid-test ratio
  B. working capital ratio   D. bankers' ratio

5. A measure useful in evaluating the efficiency in the management of inventories is:
  A. working capital ratio
  B. acid-test ratio
  C. number of days' sales in inventory
  D. ratio of fixed assets to long-term liabilities

CLASS DISCUSSION QUESTIONS

1. What is the difference between horizontal and vertical analysis of financial statements?
2. What is the advantage of using comparative statements for financial analysis rather than statements for a single date or period?
3. The current year's amount of net income (after income tax) is 15% larger than that of the preceding year. Does this indicate an improved operating performance? Discuss.
4. How would you respond to a horizontal analysis that showed an expense increasing by over 100%?
5. a. Name the major ratios useful in assessing solvency and profitability.
   b. Why is it important not to rely on only one ratio or measure in assessing the solvency or profitability of a business?
6. How would the current and acid-test ratios of a service business compare?
7. For Lindsay Corporation, the working capital at the end of the current year is $5,000 greater than the working capital at the end of the preceding year, reported as follows:

	Current Year	Preceding Year
Current assets:		
Cash, marketable securities, and receivables	$34,000	$30,000
Inventories	51,000	32,500
Total current assets	$85,000	$62,500
Current liabilities	42,500	25,000
Working capital	$42,500	$37,500

Has the current position improved? Explain.

8. A company that grants terms of n/30 on all sales has a yearly accounts receivable turnover, based on monthly averages, of 6. Is this a satisfactory turnover? Discuss.

9. What does an increase in the number of days' sales in receivables ordinarily indicate about the credit and collection policy of the firm?

10. a. Why is it advantageous to have a high inventory turnover?
    b. Is it possible for the inventory turnover to be too high? Discuss.
    c. Is it possible to have a high inventory turnover and a high number of days' sales in inventory? Discuss.

11. What do the following data taken from a comparative balance sheet indicate about the company's ability to borrow additional funds on a long-term basis in the current year as compared to the preceding year?

	Current Year	Preceding Year
Fixed assets (net)	$175,000	$170,000
Total long-term liabilities	70,000	85,000

12. What does a decrease in the ratio of liabilities to stockholders' equity indicate about the margin of safety for a firm's creditors and the ability of the firm to withstand adverse business conditions?

13. In computing the ratio of net sales to assets, why are long-term investments excluded in determining the amount of the total assets?

14. In determining the number of times interest charges are earned, why are interest charges added to income before income tax?

15. In determining the rate earned on total assets, why is interest expense added to net income before dividing by total assets?

16. a. Why is the rate earned on stockholders' equity by a thriving business ordinarily higher than the rate earned on total assets?
    b. Should the rate earned on common stockholders' equity normally be higher or lower than the rate earned on total stockholders' equity? Explain.

17. The net income (after income tax) of A. L. Gibson Inc. was $25 per common share in the latest year and $40 per common share for the preceding year. At the beginning of the latest year, the number of shares outstanding was doubled by a stock split. There were no other changes in the amount of stock outstanding. What were the earnings per share in the preceding year, adjusted for comparison with the latest year?

18. The price-earnings ratio for the common stock of Essian Company was 10 at December 31, the end of the current fiscal year. What does the ratio indicate about the selling price of the common stock in relation to current earnings?

19. Why would the dividend yield differ significantly from the rate earned on common stockholders' equity?

20. Favorable business conditions may bring about certain seemingly unfavorable ratios, and unfavorable business operations may result in apparently favorable ratios. For example, Sanchez Company increased its sales and net income substantially for the current year, yet the current ratio at the end of the year is lower than at the beginning of the year. Discuss some possible causes of the apparent weakening of the current position, while sales and net income have increased substantially.

21. a. What are the major components of an annual report?
    b. Indicate the purpose of the Financial Highlights section and the Management Discussion and Analysis.

EXERCISES

Exercise 15–1
Vertical analysis of income statement

Objective 1

✓ 2003 net income: $77,000; 10% of sales

Revenue and expense data for Murry Cabinet Co. are as follows:

	2003	2002
Sales	$770,000	$700,000
Cost of goods sold	415,800	350,000
Selling expenses	138,600	140,000
Administrative expenses	84,700	105,000
Income tax expense	53,900	49,000

a. Prepare an income statement in comparative form, stating each item for both 2003 and 2002 as a percent of sales.
b. Comment on the significant changes disclosed by the comparative income statement.

Exercise 15–2
Vertical analysis of income statement

Objective 1

✓ a. Fiscal year 1998 income from operations, 11.2% of revenues

The following comparative income statement (in thousands of dollars) for the fiscal years 1999 and 1998 was adapted from the annual report of **Dell Computer Corporation**:

	Fiscal Year 1999	Fiscal Year 1998
Revenues	$25,265	$18,243
Costs and expenses:		
Cost of sales	20,047	14,137
Gross profit	$ 5,218	$ 4,106
Operating expenses	2,955	2,060
Income from operations	$ 2,263	$ 2,046

a. Prepare a comparative income statement for fiscal years 1999 (ended January 28, 2000) and 1998 (ended January 29, 1999) in vertical form, stating each item as a percent of revenues. Round to one digit after the decimal place.
b. Comment on the significant changes.

Exercise 15–3
Common-size income statement

Objective 1

✓ a. Keystone net income: $218,500; 9.1% of sales

Revenue and expense data for the current calendar year for Keystone Publishing Company and for the publishing industry are as follows. The Keystone Publishing Company data are expressed in dollars. The publishing industry averages are expressed in percentages.

	Keystone Publishing Company	Publishing Industry Average
Sales	$2,450,000	101.0%
Sales returns and allowances	24,500	1.0
Cost of goods sold	850,000	40.0
Selling expenses	970,000	39.0
Administrative expenses	280,000	10.5
Other income	30,000	1.2
Other expense	40,000	1.7
Income tax expense	97,000	4.0

a. Prepare a common-size income statement comparing the results of operations for Keystone Publishing Company with the industry average. Round to one digit after the decimal place.
b. As far as the data permit, comment on significant relationships revealed by the comparisons.

Exercise 15–4
Vertical analysis of balance sheet

Objective 1

✓ Retained earnings, Dec. 31, 2003, 37.27%

Balance sheet data for Atlas Fitness Equipment Company on December 31, the end of the fiscal year, are as follows:

	2003	2002
Current assets	$180,000	$150,000
Property, plant, and equipment	340,000	330,000
Intangible assets	30,000	35,000
Current liabilities	120,000	125,000
Long-term liabilities	175,000	150,000
Common stock	50,000	40,000
Retained earnings	205,000	200,000

Prepare a comparative balance sheet for 2003 and 2002, stating each asset as a percent of total assets and each liability and stockholders' equity item as a percent of the total liabilities and stockholders' equity. Round to two digits after the decimal place.

Exercise 15–5
Horizontal analysis of the income statement

Objective 1

✓ a. Net income decrease, 31.67%

Income statement data for Neon Flashlight Company for the years ended December 31, 2003 and 2002, are as follows:

	2003	2002
Sales	$400,000	$460,000
Cost of goods sold	170,000	200,000
Gross profit	$230,000	$260,000
Selling expenses	$ 70,000	$ 60,000
Administrative expenses	50,000	40,000
Total operating expenses	$120,000	$100,000
Income before income tax	$110,000	$160,000
Income tax expense	28,000	40,000
Net income	$ 82,000	$120,000

a. Prepare a comparative income statement with horizontal analysis, indicating the increase (decrease) for 2003 when compared with 2002. Round to two digits after the decimal place.
b. What conclusions can be drawn from the horizontal analysis?

Exercise 15–6
Current position analysis

Objective 2

✓ Current year working capital, $1,085,000

The following data were taken from the balance sheet of Precision Gears Company:

	Current Year	Preceding Year
Cash	$280,000	$265,000
Marketable securities	131,000	121,000
Accounts and notes receivable (net)	395,000	384,000
Inventories	570,000	555,000
Prepaid expenses	19,000	40,000
Accounts and notes payable (short-term)	250,000	285,700
Accrued liabilities	60,000	64,300

a. Determine for each year (1) the working capital, (2) the current ratio, and (3) the acid-test ratio.
b. What conclusions can be drawn from these data as to the company's ability to meet its currently maturing debts?

Exercise 15–7
Current position analysis

Objective 2

PepsiCo, the parent company of Frito-Lay snack foods and Pepsi beverages, had the following current assets and current liabilities at the end of two recent years:

	Current Year (in millions)	Preceding Year (in millions)
Cash	$ 311	$1,928
Marketable securities	83	955
Accounts and notes receivable (net)	2,453	2,150
Inventories	1,016	732
Prepaid expenses	499	486
Short-term borrowings	3,921	—
Accounts and notes payable (short-term)	3,870	3,617
Income taxes payable	123	640

✓ a. (1) Current year's current ratio, 0.55

a. Determine the (1) current ratio and (2) acid-test ratio for both years. Round to two digits after the decimal place.
b. What conclusions can you draw from these data?

Exercise 15–8
Current position analysis
Objective 2

The bond indenture for the 10-year, 9½% debenture bonds dated January 2, 2002, required working capital of $350,000, a current ratio of 1.5, and an acid-test ratio of 1 at the end of each calendar year until the bonds mature. At December 31, 2003, the three measures were computed as follows:

1. Current assets:
Cash	$245,000	
Marketable securities	123,000	
Accounts and notes receivable (net)	172,000	
Inventories	295,000	
Prepaid expenses	35,000	
Goodwill	150,000	
Total current assets		$1,020,000
Current liabilities:		
Accounts and short-term notes payable	$350,000	
Accrued liabilities	250,000	
Total current liabilities		600,000
Working capital		$ 420,000

2. Current ratio = 1.7 ($1,020,000 ÷ $600,000)
3. Acid-test ratio = 1.54 ($540,000 ÷ $350,000), rounded

a. Can you find any errors in the determination of the three measures of current position analysis?
b. Is the company satisfying the terms of the bond indenture?

Exercise 15–9
Accounts receivable analysis
Objective 2

The following data are taken from the financial statements of Northern Expressions Company. Terms of all sales are 1/10, n/60.

✓ a. Accounts receivable turnover, current year, 7.0

	Current Year	Preceding Year
Accounts receivable, end of year	$ 222,466	$ 235,068
Monthly average accounts receivable (net)	207,143	216,667
Net sales on account	1,450,000	1,300,000

a. Determine for each year (1) the accounts receivable turnover and (2) the number of days' sales in receivables. Round to one digit after the decimal place.
b. What conclusions can be drawn from these data concerning accounts receivable and credit policies?

Exercise 15–10
Accounts receivable analysis
Objective 2

Sears and **JCPenney** are two of the largest department store chains in the United States. Both companies offer credit to their customers through their own credit card operations. Information from the financial statements for both companies for two recent years is as follows (all numbers are in millions):

	Sears	JCPenney
Sales—recent year	$41,332	$30,678
Credit card receivables—recent year balance	18,946	4,415
Credit card receivables—previous year balance	20,956	3,819

Real World

✓ a. (1) Sears' accounts receivable turnover, 2.1

a. Determine the (1) accounts receivable turnover and (2) the number of days' sales in receivables for both companies. Round to one digit after the decimal place.
b. Compare the two companies with regard to their credit card policies.

Exercise 15–11
Inventory analysis

Objective 2

✓ a. Inventory turnover, current year, 6.0

The following data were extracted from the income statement of Sierra Instruments Inc.:

	Current Year	Preceding Year
Sales	$3,600,000	$3,900,000
Beginning inventories	310,000	290,000
Cost of goods sold	2,010,000	2,400,000
Ending inventories	360,000	310,000

a. Determine for each year (1) the inventory turnover and (2) the number of days' sales in inventory. Round to two digits after the decimal place.
b. What conclusions can be drawn from these data concerning the inventories?

Exercise 15–12
Inventory analysis

Objective 2

Real World

✓ a. (1) Dell inventory turnover, 55.9

Dell Computer Corporation and **Compaq Computer Corporation** compete with each other in the personal computer market. Dell's strategy is to assemble computers to customer orders, rather than for inventory. Thus, for example, Dell will build and deliver a computer within four days of a customer entering an order on a Web page. Compaq, on the other hand, builds some computers prior to receiving an order, then sells from this inventory once an order is received. Below is selected financial information for both companies from a recent year's financial statements (in millions):

	Dell Computer Corporation	Compaq Computer Corporation
Sales	$18,243	$31,169
Cost of goods sold	14,137	23,980
Inventory, beginning of period	233	1,570
Inventory, end of period	273	2,005

a. Determine for both companies (1) the inventory turnover and (2) the number of days' sales in inventory. Round to one digit after the decimal place.
b. Interpret the inventory ratios by considering Dell's and Compaq's operating strategies.

Exercise 15–13
Ratio of liabilities to stockholders' equity and number of times interest charges earned

Objective 2

✓ a. Ratio of liabilities to stockholders' equity, Dec. 31, 2003, 0.63

The following data were taken from the financial statements of Clear Spring Water Co. for December 31, 2003 and 2002:

	December 31, 2003	December 31, 2002
Accounts payable	$ 150,000	$ 204,000
Current maturities of serial bonds payable	300,000	300,000
Serial bonds payable, 8%, issued 1998, due 2008	1,800,000	2,100,000
Common stock, $1 par value	100,000	100,000
Paid-in capital in excess of par	800,000	800,000
Retained earnings	2,700,000	2,200,000

The income before income tax was $252,000 and $216,000 for the years 2003 and 2002, respectively.

a. Determine the ratio of liabilities to stockholders' equity at the end of each year. Round to two digits after the decimal place. *(continued)*

    b.   Determine the number of times the bond interest charges are earned during the year for both years.

    c.   What conclusions can be drawn from these data as to the company's ability to meet its currently maturing debts?

Exercise 15–14
Profitability ratios

Objective 3

✓ a. Rate earned on total assets, 2004, 18.7%

The following selected data were taken from the financial statements of Central States Transportation Co. for December 31, 2004, 2003, and 2002:

	December 31, 2004	December 31, 2003	December 31, 2002
Total assets	$3,200,000	$2,800,000	$2,200,000
Notes payable (10% interest)	400,000	400,000	400,000
Common stock	900,000	900,000	900,000
Preferred $12 stock, $100 par, cumulative, nonparticipating (no change during year)	500,000	500,000	500,000
Retained earnings	1,330,000	870,000	330,000

The 2004 net income was $520,000, and the 2003 net income was $600,000. No dividends on common stock were declared between 2002 and 2004.

    a.   Determine the rate earned on total assets, the rate earned on stockholders' equity, and the rate earned on common stockholders' equity for the years 2003 and 2004. Round to one digit after the decimal place.

    b.   What conclusions can be drawn from these data as to the company's profitability?

Exercise 15–15
Profitability ratios

Objective 3

✓ a. 1999 rate earned on total assets, 7.87%

Ann Taylor Stores Corporation sells professional women's apparel through company-owned retail stores. Recent financial information for Ann Taylor is provided below (all numbers in thousands):

	Fiscal Year Ended	
	Jan. 31, 1999	Jan. 31, 1998
Net income	$39,324	$11,824
Interest expense	18,117	19,989

	Jan. 31, 1999	Jan. 31, 1998	Jan. 31, 1997
Total assets	$775,417	$683,661	$688,139
Total stockholders' equity	432,699	384,107	370,582

An analysis of 50 apparel retail companies indicates an industry average rate earned on total assets of 24.4% and an average rate earned on stockholders' equity of 53.03%.

    a.   Determine the rate earned on total assets for Ann Taylor for the fiscal years ended January 31, 1999, and January 31, 1998. Round to two digits after the decimal place.

    b.   Determine the rate earned on stockholders' equity for Ann Taylor for the fiscal years ended January 31, 1999, and January 31, 1998. Round to two digits after the decimal place.

    c.   Evaluate the two-year trend for the profitability ratios determined in (a) and (b).

    d.   Evaluate Ann Taylor's profit performance relative to the industry.

Exercise 15–16
Six measures of solvency or profitability

Objectives 2, 3

✓ c. Ratio of net sales to assets, 1.14

The following data were taken from the financial statements of Austin Labs Inc. for the current fiscal year:

Property, plant, and equipment (net)		$2,500,000
Liabilities:		
Current liabilities	$ 100,000	
Mortgage note payable, 7.5%, issued 1993, due 2008	1,200,000	
Total liabilities		$1,300,000

(continued)

Stockholders' equity:

Preferred $8 stock, $100 par, cumulative, nonparticipating (no change during year)			$ 600,000
Common stock, $10 par (no change during year)			1,600,000
Retained earnings:			
Balance, beginning of year	$900,000		
Net income	500,000	$1,400,000	
Preferred dividends	$ 48,000		
Common dividends	52,000	100,000	
Balance, end of year			1,300,000
Total stockholders' equity			$3,500,000
Net sales			$5,000,000
Interest expense			$ 90,000

Assuming that long-term investments totaled $200,000 throughout the year and that total assets were $4,400,000 at the beginning of the year, determine the following: (a) ratio of fixed assets to long-term liabilities, (b) ratio of liabilities to stockholders' equity, (c) ratio of net sales to assets, (d) rate earned on total assets, (e) rate earned on stockholders' equity, and (f) rate earned on common stockholders' equity. Round to two digits after the decimal place.

Exercise 15–17

Five measures of solvency or profitability

Objectives 2, 3

✓ d. Price-earnings ratio, 20

The balance sheet for Aspen Properties Inc. at the end of the current fiscal year indicated the following:

Bonds payable, 12% (issued in 1993, due in 2013)	$3,000,000
Preferred $10 stock, $100 par	500,000
Common stock, $20 par	5,000,000

Income before income tax was $800,000, and income taxes were $200,000 for the current year. Cash dividends paid on common stock during the current year totaled $220,000. The common stock was selling for $44 per share at the end of the year. Determine each of the following: (a) number of times bond interest charges were earned, (b) number of times preferred dividends were earned, (c) earnings per share on common stock, (d) price-earnings ratio, (e) dividends per share of common stock, and (f) dividend yield. Round to two digits after the decimal place.

Exercise 15–18

Earnings per share, price-earnings ratio, dividend yield

Objective 3

✓ b. Price-earnings ratio, 30

The following information was taken from the financial statements of Arctic Air Conditioners Inc. for December 31 of the current fiscal year:

Common stock, $12 par value (no change during the year)	$4,800,000
Preferred $9 stock, $100 par, cumulative, nonparticipating (no change during year) . . .	1,200,000

The net income was $588,000 and the declared dividends on the common stock were $500,000 for the current year. The market price of the common stock is $36 per share.

For the common stock, determine the (a) earnings per share, (b) price-earnings ratio, (c) dividends per share, and (d) dividend yield. Round to two digits after the decimal place.

Exercise 15–19

Earnings per share

Objective 3

✓ b. Earnings per share on common stock, $8.64

The net income reported on the income statement of Southern Pulp and Paper Co. was $2,800,000. There were 250,000 shares of $20 par common stock and 80,000 shares of $8 cumulative preferred stock outstanding throughout the current year. The income statement included two extraordinary items: a $400,000 gain from condemnation of land and a $600,000 loss arising from flood damage, both after applicable income tax. Determine the per share figures for common stock for (a) income before extraordinary items and (b) net income.

PROBLEMS SERIES A

Problem 15–1A

Horizontal analysis for income statement

Objective 1

GENERAL LEDGER

✓ 1. Sales, 30% increase

For 2003, Better Biscuit Company reported its most significant increase in net income in years. At the end of the year, John Newton, the president, is presented with the following condensed comparative income statement:

Better Biscuit Company
Comparative Income Statement
For the Years Ended December 31, 2003 and 2002

	2003	2002
Sales	$715,000	$550,000
Sales returns and allowances	5,000	5,000
Net sales	$710,000	$545,000
Cost of goods sold	281,250	225,000
Gross profit	$428,750	$320,000
Selling expenses	$136,400	$110,000
Administrative expenses	42,350	35,000
Total operating expenses	$178,750	$145,000
Income from operations	$250,000	$175,000
Other income	3,500	3,000
Income before income tax	$253,500	$178,000
Income tax expense	85,000	60,000
Net income	$168,500	$118,000

Instructions

1. Prepare a comparative income statement with horizontal analysis for the two-year period, using 2002 as the base year. Round to two digits after the decimal place.
2. To the extent the data permit, comment on the significant relationships revealed by the horizontal analysis prepared in (1).

Problem 15–2A

Vertical analysis for income statement

Objective 1

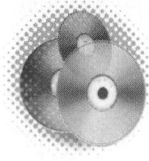

SPREADSHEET
GENERAL LEDGER

✓ 1. Net income, 2003, 8.55%

For 2003, Stainless Flow Systems Inc. initiated a sales promotion campaign that included the expenditure of an additional $50,000 for advertising. At the end of the year, Eduardo Gonzalez, the president, is presented with the following condensed comparative income statement:

Stainless Flow Systems Inc.
Comparative Income Statement
For the Years Ended December 31, 2003 and 2002

	2003	2002
Sales	$810,000	$775,000
Sales returns and allowances	5,000	5,000
Net sales	$805,000	$770,000
Cost of goods sold	438,700	416,000
Gross profit	$366,300	$354,000
Selling expenses	$165,800	$115,800
Administrative expenses	96,600	93,400
Total operating expenses	$262,400	$209,200
Income from operations	$103,900	$144,800
Other income	2,000	1,800
Income before income tax	$105,900	$146,600
Income tax expense	37,000	51,000
Net income	$ 68,900	$ 95,600

Instructions

1. Prepare a comparative income statement for the two-year period, presenting an analysis of each item in relationship to net sales for each of the years. Round to two digits after the decimal place.
2. To the extent the data permit, comment on the significant relationships revealed by the vertical analysis prepared in (1).

Problem 15–3A
Effect of transactions on current position analysis

Objective 2

✓ 1. c. Acid-test ratio, 1.45

Data pertaining to the current position of Flintstone Aggregates Inc. are as follows:

Cash	$150,000
Marketable securities	64,000
Accounts and notes receivable (net)	221,000
Inventories	294,000
Prepaid expenses	11,000
Accounts payable	204,000
Notes payable (short-term)	66,000
Accrued expenses	30,000

Instructions

1. Compute (a) the working capital, (b) the current ratio, and (c) the acid-test ratio. Round to two digits after the decimal place.
2. List the following captions on a sheet of paper:

Transaction	Working Capital	Current Ratio	Acid-Test Ratio

Compute the working capital, the current ratio, and the acid-test ratio after each of the following transactions, and record the results in the appropriate columns. Consider each transaction separately and assume that only that transaction affects the data given above. Round to two digits after the decimal point.

a. Sold marketable securities at no gain or loss, $34,000.
b. Paid accounts payable, $60,000.
c. Purchased goods on account, $40,000.
d. Paid notes payable, $20,000.
e. Declared a cash dividend, $25,000.
f. Declared a common stock dividend on common stock, $16,500.
g. Borrowed cash from bank on a long-term note, $120,000.
h. Received cash on account, $86,000.
i. Issued additional shares of stock for cash, $100,000.
j. Paid cash for prepaid expenses, $9,000.

Problem 15–4A
Nineteen measures of solvency and profitability

Objectives 2, 3

SPREADSHEET

✓ 9. Ratio of liabilities to stockholders' equity, 0.7

The comparative financial statements of Integrity Technologies Inc. are as follows. The market price of Integrity Technologies Inc. common stock was $80 on December 31, 2003.

Integrity Technologies Inc.
Comparative Retained Earnings Statement
For the Years Ended December 31, 2003 and 2002

	Dec. 31, 2003	Dec. 31, 2002
Retained earnings, January 1	$ 964,000	$ 689,000
Add net income for year	503,000	435,000
Total	$1,467,000	$1,124,000
Deduct dividends:		
On preferred stock	$ 48,000	$ 40,000
On common stock	120,000	120,000
Total	$ 168,000	$ 160,000
Retained earnings, December 31	$1,299,000	$ 964,000

Integrity Technologies Inc.
Comparative Income Statement
For the Years Ended December 31, 2003 and 2002

	2003	2002
Sales (all on account)	$6,130,000	$5,640,000
Sales returns and allowances	30,000	40,000
Net sales	$6,100,000	$5,600,000
Cost of goods sold	2,800,000	2,550,000
Gross profit	$3,300,000	$3,050,000
Selling expenses	$1,450,000	$1,440,000
Administrative expenses	1,000,000	910,000
Total operating expenses	$2,450,000	$2,350,000
Income from operations	$ 850,000	$ 700,000
Other income	40,000	30,000
	$ 890,000	$ 730,000
Other expense (interest)	157,000	85,000
Income before income tax	$ 733,000	$ 645,000
Income tax expense	230,000	210,000
Net income	$ 503,000	$ 435,000

Integrity Technologies Inc.
Comparative Balance Sheet
December 31, 2003 and 2002

	Dec. 31, 2003	Dec. 31, 2002
Assets		
Current assets:		
Cash	$ 200,000	$ 180,000
Marketable securities	923,000	215,000
Accounts receivable (net)	350,000	365,000
Inventories	500,000	480,000
Prepaid expenses	26,000	24,000
Total current assets	$1,999,000	$1,264,000
Long-term investments	700,000	500,000
Property, plant, and equipment (net)	3,100,000	2,600,000
Total assets	$5,799,000	$4,364,000
Liabilities		
Current liabilities	$ 600,000	$ 400,000
Long-term liabilities:		
Mortgage note payable, 9%, due 2008	$ 800,000	—
Bonds payable, 8.5%, due 2012	1,000,000	$1,000,000
Total long-term liabilities	$1,800,000	$1,000,000
Total liabilities	$2,400,000	$1,400,000
Stockholders' Equity		
Preferred $8 stock, $100 par	$ 600,000	$ 500,000
Common stock, $10 par	1,500,000	1,500,000
Retained earnings	1,299,000	964,000
Total stockholders' equity	$3,399,000	$2,964,000
Total liabilities and stockholders' equity	$5,799,000	$4,364,000

Instructions

Determine the following measures for 2003, rounding to the nearest single digit after the decimal point:

1. Working capital
2. Current ratio
3. Acid-test ratio
4. Accounts receivable turnover
5. Number of days' sales in receivables
6. Inventory turnover
7. Number of days' sales in inventory
8. Ratio of fixed assets to long-term liabilities
9. Ratio of liabilities to stockholders' equity
10. Number of times interest charges earned
11. Number of times preferred dividends earned
12. Ratio of net sales to assets
13. Rate earned on total assets
14. Rate earned on stockholders' equity
15. Rate earned on common stockholders' equity
16. Earnings per share on common stock
17. Price-earnings ratio
18. Dividends per share of common stock
19. Dividend yield

Problem 15–5A

Solvency and profitability trend analysis

Objectives 2, 3

Jupiter Company has provided the following comparative information:

	2003	2002	2001	2000	1999
Net income	$ 100,000	$ 150,000	$ 150,000	$ 200,000	$ 250,000
Income tax expense	30,000	45,000	45,000	60,000	75,000
Interest	144,000	138,000	138,000	126,000	120,000
Average total assets	2,300,000	2,150,000	2,000,000	1,750,000	1,500,000
Average total stockholders' equity	1,100,000	1,000,000	850,000	700,000	500,000

You have been asked to evaluate the historical performance of the company over the last five years.

Selected industry ratios have remained relatively steady for the last five years at the following levels:

	1999–2003
Rate earned on total assets	12%
Rate earned on stockholders' equity	15%
Number of times interest charges earned	3.0
Ratio of liabilities to stockholders' equity	1.5

Instructions

1. Prepare four line graphs, with the ratio on the vertical axis and the years on the horizontal axis for the following four ratios (round to two digits after the decimal place):
   a. Rate earned on total assets
   b. Rate earned on stockholders' equity
   c. Number of times interest charges earned
   d. Ratio of liabilities to stockholders' equity (using average balances)
   Display both the company ratio and the industry benchmark on each graph (each graph should have two lines).
2. Prepare an analysis of the graphs in (1).

Problem 15–1B
Horizontal analysis for income statement

Objective 1

GENERAL LEDGER

✓ 1. Sales, 15% increase

For 2003, Chow Company reported its most significant decline in net income in years. At the end of the year, Hai Chow, the president, is presented with the following condensed comparative income statement:

Chow Company
Comparative Income Statement
For the Years Ended December 31, 2003 and 2002

	2003	2002
Sales	$690,000	$600,000
Sales returns and allowances	5,000	2,000
Net sales	$685,000	$598,000
Cost of goods sold	341,600	280,000
Gross profit	$343,400	$318,000
Selling expenses	$147,000	$105,000
Administrative expenses	81,250	65,000
Total operating expenses	$228,250	$170,000
Income from operations	$115,150	$148,000
Other income	2,500	2,000
Income before income tax	$117,650	$150,000
Income tax expense	32,000	40,000
Net income	$ 85,650	$110,000

Instructions

1. Prepare a comparative income statement with horizontal analysis for the two-year period, using 2002 as the base year. Round to two digits after the decimal place.
2. To the extent the data permit, comment on the significant relationships revealed by the horizontal analysis prepared in (1).

Problem 15–2B
Vertical analysis for income statement

Objective 1

SPREADSHEET
GENERAL LEDGER

✓ 1. Net income, 2003, 13.58%

For 2003, Guardian Home Security Company initiated a sales promotion campaign that included the expenditure of an additional $10,000 for advertising. At the end of the year, Gordon Kincaid, the president, is presented with the following condensed comparative income statement:

Guardian Home Security Company
Comparative Income Statement
For the Years Ended December 31, 2003 and 2002

	2003	2002
Sales	$595,000	$485,000
Sales returns and allowances	6,000	5,000
Net sales	$589,000	$480,000
Cost of goods sold	253,000	216,000
Gross profit	$336,000	$264,000
Selling expenses	$153,000	$136,500
Administrative expenses	71,000	64,500
Total operating expenses	$224,000	$201,000
Income from operations	$112,000	$ 63,000
Other income	2,500	2,000
Income before income tax	$114,500	$ 65,000
Income tax expense	34,500	20,000
Net income	$ 80,000	$ 45,000

Instructions

1. Prepare a comparative income statement for the two-year period, presenting an analysis of each item in relationship to net sales for each of the years. Round to two digits after the decimal place.
2. To the extent the data permit, comment on the significant relationships revealed by the vertical analysis prepared in (1).

Problem 15–3B
Effect of transactions on current position analysis

Objective 2

✓ 1. b. Current ratio, 1.96

Data pertaining to the current position of Porter Glass Company are as follows:

Cash	$221,000
Marketable securities	95,000
Accounts and notes receivable (net)	345,000
Inventories	410,000
Prepaid expenses	22,000
Accounts payable	412,000
Notes payable (short-term)	100,000
Accrued expenses	45,000

Instructions

1. Compute (a) the working capital, (b) the current ratio, and (c) the acid-test ratio. Round to two digits after the decimal place.
2. List the following captions on a sheet of paper:

Transaction	Working Capital	Current Ratio	Acid-Test Ratio

Compute the working capital, the current ratio, and the acid-test ratio after each of the following transactions, and record the results in the appropriate columns. Consider each transaction separately and assume that only that transaction affects the data given above. Round to two digits after the decimal point.

a. Sold marketable securities at no gain or loss, $56,000.
b. Paid accounts payable, $60,000.
c. Purchased goods on account, $80,000.
d. Paid notes payable, $40,000.
e. Declared a cash dividend, $25,000.
f. Declared a common stock dividend on common stock, $28,500.
g. Borrowed cash from bank on a long-term note, $120,000.
h. Received cash on account, $164,000.
i. Issued additional shares of stock for cash, $250,000.
j. Paid cash for prepaid expenses, $10,000.

Problem 15–4B
Nineteen measures of solvency and profitability

Objectives 2, 3

SPREADSHEET

✓ 5. Number of days' sales in receivables, 45.4

The comparative financial statements of Victor Audio Company are as follows. The market price of Victor Audio Company common stock was $105 on December 31, 2003.

Victor Audio Company
Comparative Retained Earnings Statement
For the Years Ended December 31, 2003 and 2002

	Dec. 31, 2003	Dec. 31, 2002
Retained earnings, January 1	$394,000	$ 50,000
Add net income for year	420,000	378,000
Total	$814,000	$428,000
Deduct dividends:		
On preferred stock	$ 30,000	$ 18,000
On common stock	16,000	16,000
Total	$ 46,000	$ 34,000
Retained earnings, December 31	$768,000	$394,000

Victor Audio Company
Comparative Income Statement
For the Years Ended December 31, 2003 and 2002

	2003	2002
Sales (all on account)	$2,170,000	$1,960,000
Sales returns and allowances	70,000	60,000
Net sales	$2,100,000	$1,900,000
Cost of goods sold	840,000	770,000
Gross profit	$1,260,000	$1,130,000
Selling expenses	$ 410,000	$ 370,000
Administrative expenses	305,000	290,000
Total operating expenses	$ 715,000	$ 660,000
Income from operations	$ 545,000	$ 470,000
Other income	20,000	15,000
	$ 565,000	$ 485,000
Other expense (interest)	104,000	72,000
Income before income tax	$ 461,000	$ 413,000
Income tax expense	41,000	35,000
Net income	$ 420,000	$ 378,000

Victor Audio Company
Comparative Balance Sheet
December 31, 2003 and 2002

	Dec. 31, 2003	Dec. 31, 2002
Assets		
Current assets:		
Cash	$ 87,000	$ 176,000
Marketable securities	258,000	335,000
Accounts receivable (net)	261,000	235,000
Inventories	212,000	190,000
Prepaid expenses	25,000	18,000
Total current assets	$ 843,000	$ 954,000
Long-term investments	1,000,000	400,000
Property, plant, and equipment (net)	1,675,000	1,050,000
Total assets	$3,518,000	$2,404,000
Liabilities		
Current liabilities	$ 450,000	$ 310,000
Long-term liabilities:		
Mortgage note payable, 8%, due 2008	$ 400,000	—
Bonds payable, 12%, due 2012	600,000	$ 600,000
Total long-term liabilities	$1,000,000	$ 600,000
Total liabilities	$1,450,000	$ 910,000
Stockholders' Equity		
Preferred $6 stock, $100 par	$ 500,000	$ 300,000
Common stock, $10 par	800,000	800,000
Retained earnings	768,000	394,000
Total stockholders' equity	$2,068,000	$1,494,000
Total liabilities and stockholders' equity	$3,518,000	$2,404,000

Instructions
Determine the following measures for 2003, rounding to the nearest single digit after the decimal point:

1. Working capital
2. Current ratio
3. Acid-test ratio
4. Accounts receivable turnover
5. Number of days' sales in receivables
6. Inventory turnover
7. Number of days' sales in inventory
8. Ratio of fixed assets to long-term liabilities
9. Ratio of liabilities to stockholders' equity
10. Number of times interest charges earned
11. Number of times preferred dividends earned
12. Ratio of net sales to assets
13. Rate earned on total assets
14. Rate earned on stockholders' equity
15. Rate earned on common stockholders' equity
16. Earnings per share on common stock
17. Price-earnings ratio
18. Dividends per share of common stock
19. Dividend yield

Problem 15–5B
Solvency and profitability trend analysis

Objectives 2, 3

Nova Company has provided the following comparative information:

	2003	2002	2001	2000	1999
Net income	$ 400,000	$ 300,000	$ 200,000	$ 100,000	$ 50,000
Income tax expense	100,000	75,000	50,000	25,000	12,500
Interest	88,000	72,000	56,000	48,000	40,000
Average total assets	2,600,000	2,000,000	1,500,000	1,200,000	1,000,000
Average total stockholders' equity	1,500,000	1,100,000	800,000	600,000	500,000

You have been asked to evaluate the historical performance of the company over the last five years. Selected industry ratios have remained relatively steady for the last five years at the following levels:

	1999–2003
Rate earned on total assets	14%
Rate earned on stockholders' equity	18%
Number of times interest charges earned	5.0
Ratio of liabilities to stockholders' equity	0.9

Instructions

1. Prepare four line graphs, with the ratio on the vertical axis and the years on the horizontal axis for the following four ratios (rounded to two digits after the decimal place):
   a. Rate earned on total assets
   b. Rate earned on stockholders' equity
   c. Number of times interest charges earned
   d. Ratio of liabilities to stockholders' equity (using average balances)
   Display both the company ratio and the industry benchmark on each graph (each graph should have two lines).
2. Prepare an analysis of the graphs in (1).

CISCO SYSTEMS, INC. PROBLEM

Financial Statement Analysis

The financial statements for **Cisco Systems, Inc.**, are presented in Appendix G at the end of the text. The following additional information is available:

Accounts receivable at July 25, 1998	$1,303,000,000
Inventories at July 25, 1998	362,000,000
Total assets at July 25, 1998	9,043,000,000
Stockholders' equity at July 25, 1998	7,197,000,000

Assume that all sales are credit sales.

Instructions

1. Determine the following measures for 2000 and 1999, rounding to two digits after the decimal place.
   a. Working capital
   b. Current ratio
   c. Acid-test ratio
   d. Accounts receivable turnover
   e. Number of days' sales in receivables
   f. Inventory turnover
   g. Number of days' sales in inventory
   h. Ratio of liabilities to stockholders' equity
   i. Ratio of net sales to average total assets
   j. Rate earned on average total assets
   k. Rate earned on average common stockholders' equity
   l. Price-earnings ratio, assuming that the market price was $30.00 per share on July 31, 1999 and $62.75 on July 29, 2000
   m. Percentage relationship of net income to net sales
2. What conclusions can be drawn from these analyses?

SPECIAL ACTIVITIES

Activity 15–1 Camden Equipment Co.

Ethics and professional conduct in business

Lee Camden, president of Camden Equipment Co., prepared a draft of the President's Letter to be included with Camden Equipment Co.'s 2003 annual report. The letter mentions a 10% increase in sales and a recent expansion of plant facilities but fails to mention the net loss of $180,000 for the year. You have been asked to review the letter for inclusion in the annual report.

How would you respond to the omission of the net loss of $180,000? Specifically, is such an action ethical?

**Activity 15–2
Crest Brewery**
*Analysis of financing
corporate growth*

Assume that the president of Crest Brewery made the following statement in the President's Letter to Shareholders:

"The founding family and majority shareholders of the company do not believe in using debt to finance future growth. The founding family learned from hard experience during Prohibition and the Great Depression that debt can cause loss of flexibility and eventual loss of corporate control. The company will not place itself at such risk. As such, all future growth will be financed either by stock sales to the public or by internally generated resources."

➤ As a public shareholder of this company, how would you respond to this policy?

**Activity 15–3
Imex Computer
Company**
*Receivables and inventory
turnover*

Imex Computer Company has completed its fiscal year on December 31, 2003. The auditor, Sandra Blake, has approached the CFO, Travis Williams, regarding the year-end receivables and inventory levels of Imex. The following conversation takes place:

Sandra: We are beginning our audit of Imex and have prepared ratio analyses to determine if there have been significant changes in operations or financial position. This helps us guide the audit process. These analyses indicate that the inventory turnover has decreased from 5 to 2.8, while the accounts receivable turnover has decreased from 12 to 8. I was wondering if you could explain this change in operations.

Travis: There is little need for concern. The inventory represents computers that we were unable to sell during the holiday buying season. We are confident, however, that we will be able to sell these computers as we move into the next fiscal year.

Sandra: What gives you this confidence?

Travis: We will increase our advertising and provide some very attractive price concessions to move these machines. We have no choice. Newer technology is already out there, and we have to unload this inventory.

Sandra: . . . and the receivables?

Travis: As you may be aware, the company is under tremendous pressure to expand sales and profits. As a result, we lowered our credit standards to our commercial customers so that we would be able to sell products to a broader customer base. As a result of this policy change, we have been able to expand sales by 35%.

Sandra: Your responses have not been reassuring to me.

Travis: I'm a little confused. Assets are good, right? Why don't you look at our current ratio? It has improved, hasn't it? I would think that you would view that very favorably.

➤ Why is Sandra concerned about the inventory and accounts receivable turnover ratios and Travis's responses to them? What action may Sandra need to take? How would you respond to Travis's last comment?

**Activity 15–4
Apple Computer and
Dell Computer**
Vertical analysis

The condensed income statements through income from operations for **Apple Computer Co.** and **Dell Computer Corporation** are reproduced below for recent fiscal years (numbers in millions):

	Dell Computer Corporation For the Year Ended January 29, 1999	Apple Computer Co. For the Year Ended September 25, 1999
Sales (net)	$18,243	$6,134
Cost of sales	14,137	4,438
Gross profit	$ 4,106	$1,696
Selling, general, and administrative expense	$ 1,788	$ 314
Research and development	272	1,023
Operating expenses	$ 2,060	$1,337
Income from operations	$ 2,046	$ 359

Prepare comparative vertical analyses, rounding to two digits after the decimal point. Interpret the analyses.

Activity 15–5
Into the Real World
Horizontal analysis and profitability analysis

Go to the **Microsoft** Web site at **www.microsoft.com** and download Microsoft's comparative income statements for the last two fiscal years as an Excel® file. The most recent downloadable annual report can be found in the "Investor Relations" area of Microsoft's Web environment. Next, go to *The Wall Street Journal* and look up Microsoft in the NASDAQ National Market pages. Under this listing, report the price-earnings ratio and dividend yield for Microsoft.

Use the comparative income statement Excel file to prepare a horizontal analysis for the last two fiscal years. Use Microsoft's balance sheet and income statement information to determine the rate earned on stockholders' equity for the latest fiscal year. How do these analyses reconcile with Microsoft's price-earnings ratio and dividend yield?

Activity 15–6
Into the Real World
Solvency and profitability analysis

One team should obtain the latest annual report for **Wal-Mart Stores Inc.**, and the other team should obtain the latest **Kmart Corp.** annual report. These annual reports can be obtained from a library or the SEC's EDGAR service.

EDGAR (Electronic Data Gathering, Analysis, and Retrieval) is the electronic archive of financial statements filed with the Securities and Exchange Commission (SEC). SEC documents can be retrieved using the EdgarScan service from **PricewaterhouseCoopers** at **edgarscan.pwcglobal.com**. To obtain annual report information, type in a company name in the appropriate space. EdgarScan will list the reports available to you for the company you've selected. Select the most recent annual report filing, identified as a 10-K or 10-K405. EdgarScan provides an outline of the report, including the separate financial statements. You can double-click the income statement and balance sheet for the selected company into an Excel spreadsheet for further analysis.

Each team should compute the following for their company:

a. Current ratio
b. Inventory turnover
c. Rate earned on stockholders' equity
d. Rate earned on total assets
e. Net income as a percentage of sales
f. Ratio of liabilities to stockholders' equity

As a class, prepare a report comparing the two companies for the latest fiscal period.

ANSWERS TO SELF-EXAMINATION QUESTIONS

Matching

1. H	4. X	7. J	10. Z	13. G	16. R	19. P
2. Q	5. M	8. C	11. O	14. B	17. D	20. K
3. L	6. A	9. S	12. T	15. Y	18. I	

Multiple Choice

1. **A** Percentage analysis indicating the relationship of the component parts to the total in a financial statement, such as the relationship of current assets to total assets (20% to 100%) in the question, is called vertical analysis (answer A). Percentage analysis of increases and decreases in corresponding items in comparative financial statements is called horizontal analysis (answer B). An example of horizontal analysis would be the presentation of the amount of current assets in the preceding balance sheet, along with the amount of current assets at the end of the current year, with the increase or decrease in current assets between the periods expressed as a percentage. Profitability analysis (answer C) is the analysis of a firm's ability to earn income. Contribution margin analysis (answer D) is discussed in a later managerial accounting chapter.

2. **D** Various solvency measures, categorized as current position analysis, indicate a firm's ability to meet currently maturing obligations. Each measure contributes in the analysis of a firm's current position and is most useful when viewed with other measures and when compared with similar measures for other periods and for other firms. Working capital (answer A) is the excess of current assets over current liabilities; the current ratio (answer B) is the ratio of current assets to current liabilities; and the acid-test ratio (answer C) is the ratio of the sum of cash, receivables, and marketable securities to current liabilities.

3. **D** The ratio of current assets to current liabilities is usually called the current ratio (answer A). It is sometimes called the working capital ratio (answer B) or bankers' ratio (answer C).

4. **C** The ratio of the sum of cash, receivables, and marketable securities (sometimes called quick assets) to current liabilities is called the acid-test ratio (answer C) or quick ratio. The current ratio (answer A), working capital ratio (answer B), and bankers' ratio (answer D) are terms that describe the ratio of current assets to current liabilities.

5. **C** The number of days' sales in inventory (answer C), which is determined by dividing the inventories at the end of the year by the average daily cost of goods sold, expresses the relationship between the cost of goods sold and inventory. It indicates the efficiency in the management of inventory. The working capital ratio (answer A) indicates the ability of the business to meet currently maturing obligations (debt). The acid-test ratio (answer B) indicates the "instant" debt-paying ability of the business. The ratio of fixed assets to long-term liabilities (answer D) indicates the margin of safety for long-term creditors.

Introduction to Managerial Accounting and Job Order Cost Systems

M1

objectives

After studying this chapter, you should be able to:

1. Describe the differences between managerial and financial accounting.

2. Evaluate the organizational role of management accountants.

3. Define and illustrate materials, factory labor, and factory overhead costs.

4. Describe accounting systems used by manufacturing businesses.

5. Describe and prepare summary journal entries for a job order cost accounting system.

6. Use job order cost information for decision making.

7. Diagram the flow of costs for a service business that uses a job order cost accounting system.

S uppose you go down to the local bakery and buy a bagel and coffee before class. How much should the bakery charge you? The purchase price must be greater than the costs of producing and serving the bagel and coffee. Moreover, the bakery needs to be able to answer additional questions, such as:

- How many bagels must be sold in a given month and at given prices to cover costs?
- How should the price for a single bagel differ from the price for a dozen bagels?
- How many employees should be in the shop at different times of the week?
- How much should be charged for delivery service?
- Would a larger oven be a good investment?
- Should the shop stay open 24 hours per day?

All of these questions can be answered with the aid of cost information. In this chapter you will be introduced to cost concepts used in managerial accounting, which help answer questions like those above. In addition, we will see how cost information is developed and used when work is performed on a specified quantity of product.

We will begin this chapter by describing managerial (or management) accounting and its relationship to financial accounting. Following this overview, we will describe the organizational role of management accountants in the management process. Lastly, we will introduce you to the basic cost terms and apply them within a job order cost system.

The Differences Between Managerial and Financial Accounting

objective 1

Describe the differences between managerial and financial accounting.

Although economic information can be classified in many ways, accountants often divide accounting information into two types: financial and managerial. The diagram in Exhibit 1 illustrates the relationship between financial accounting and managerial accounting. Understanding this relationship is useful in understanding the information needs of management.

Financial accounting information is reported in statements that are useful for persons or institutions who are "outside" or external to the organization. Examples of such users include shareholders, creditors, government agencies, and the general public. To the extent that management uses the financial statements in directing current operations and planning future operations, the two areas of accounting overlap. For example, in planning future operations, management often begins by evaluating the results of past activities as reported in the financial statements. The financial statements objectively and periodically report the results of past operations and the financial condition of the business according to generally accepted accounting principles (GAAP).

Managerial accounting information includes both historical and estimated data used by management in conducting daily operations, planning future operations, and developing overall business strategies. The characteristics of managerial accounting are influenced by the varying needs of management. First, managerial accounting reports provide both objective measures of past operations and subjective estimates about future decisions. Using subjective estimates in managerial accounting reports assists management in responding to business opportunities. Second, managerial

Exhibit 1 Financial Accounting and Managerial Accounting

FINANCIAL ACCOUNTING

Financial Statements

MANAGERIAL ACCOUNTING

Management Reports

Users:

External Users and Management

Management

Characteristics:

FINANCIAL ACCOUNTING	MANAGERIAL ACCOUNTING
Objective	Objective and subjective
Prepared according to GAAP	Prepared according to management needs
Prepared periodically	Prepared periodically, or as needed
Business entity	Business entity or segment

Steve Ballmer, CEO of **Microsoft**, has the following five tips for managing a company:

1. Narrow and simplify goals.
2. Continue improving products and services.
3. Know key employees and be dedicated to their well-being.
4. Keep all employees informed and pay attention to their concerns.
5. See customers; keep them informed.

Source: Rebecca Buckman, "Keeping on Course in a Crisis," *The Wall Street Journal,* June 9, 2000.

reports need not be prepared according to generally accepted accounting principles. Since only management uses managerial accounting information, the accountant can provide the information according to management's needs. Third, managerial accounting reports may be provided periodically, as with financial accounting, or at any time management needs information. For example, if senior management is deciding on a geographical expansion, a managerial accounting report can be developed in a format and within a time frame to assist management in the decision. Lastly, managerial accounting reports can be prepared to report information for the business entity or a segment of the entity, such as a division, product, project, or territory.

BUSINESS ON STAGE

The Management Process

The management process consists of planning, directing, controlling, and improving. *Planning* is used by management to develop the organization's objectives (goals) and to translate those objectives into courses of action. *Strategic planning* is developing long-range courses of action, called strate-

gies, to achieve goals. For example, **Toyota Motor Company** has established an assembly facility in the United States as a strategy to capture a greater North American market share (the goal) by avoiding import controls and currency fluctuations. *Operational planning,* sometimes called

tactical planning, is the short-term planning used for achieving operational goals. For example, Toyota's operational plans for its Georgetown, Kentucky assembly plant are to hire and train employees to support an operational goal of increasing the annual production target.

Directing is the process by which managers, given their assigned level of responsibilities, run day-to-day operations. Examples of directing include a production supervisor's efforts to keep the production line moving smoothly throughout a work shift and the credit manager's efforts to assess the credit standing of potential customers.

Once managers have planned the goals and directed the action, there comes the need to assess how well the plan is working. This is termed *controlling*. Controlling consists of monitoring the operating results of implemented plans and comparing the actual results with the expected results. This feedback allows management to isolate significant departures from plan for further investigation and possible corrective action. It may also lead to revising future plans.

Feedback can also be used by managers to support improvement in business processes. *Continuous process improvement* is the business philosophy of continually improving employees, business processes, and products by using process information to eliminate the source of process problems. This philosophy requires managers to be responsible for permanent process improvement, rather than temporary solutions that fail to address the root cause of a problem. ■

The Management Accountant in the Organization

In most large organizations, departments or similar units are assigned responsibilities for specific functions or activities. This operating structure of an organization can be diagrammed in an organization chart. Exhibit 2 is a partial organization chart for **Callaway Golf Company**, the manufacturer and distributor of Big Bertha® woods and irons.

The individual reporting units in an organization can be viewed as having either (1) line responsibilities or (2) staff responsibilities. A **line** department or unit is one directly involved in the basic objectives of the organization. For Callaway Golf, the vice-president of manufacturing and the manager of the Carlsbad plant occupy line positions because they are responsible for manufacturing Callaway's products. Likewise, the vice-president of U.S. sales and other sales managers are in line positions because they are directly responsible for generating revenues.

A **staff** department or unit is one that provides services, assistance, and advice to the departments with line or other staff responsibilities. A staff department has no direct authority over a line department. For example, the manager of pro tour

Exhibit 2 Partial Organization Chart for Callaway Golf Company

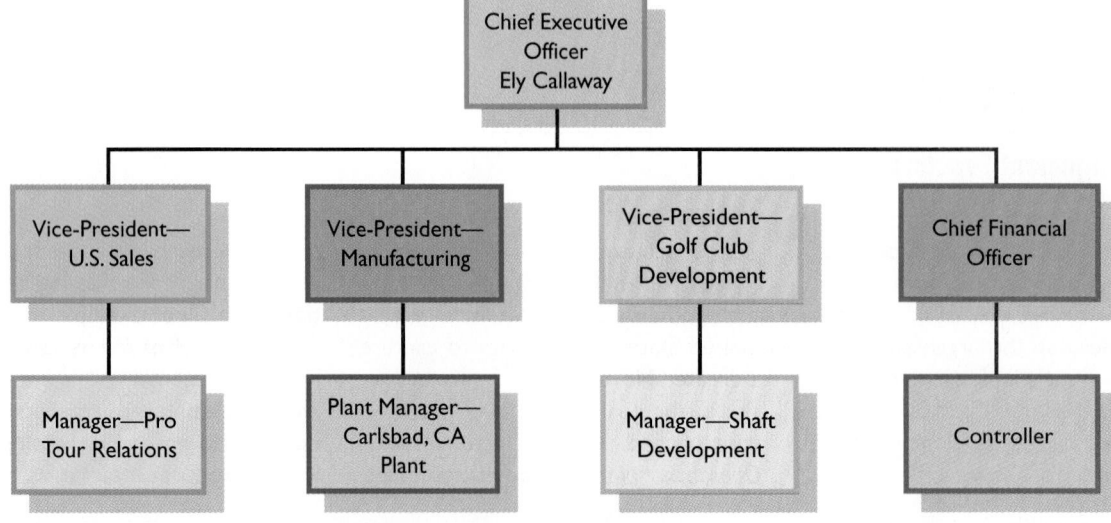

The terms *line* and *staff* may be applied to service organizations. For example, the line positions in a hospital would be the nurses, doctors, and other caregivers. Staff positions would include admissions and records. The line positions for a professional basketball team, such as the Boston Celtics, would be the basketball players and coaches, since they are directly involved in the basic objectives of the organization—playing professional basketball. Staff positions would include public relations, player development and recruiting, legal staff, and accounting. These positions serve and advise the players and coaches.

relations is a staff position supporting the sales organization. In addition, the vice-president of golf club development occupies a staff position because new products are developed to support sales and manufacturing. Likewise, the vice-president of finance (sometimes called the chief financial officer) occupies a staff position, to which the controller reports. In most business organizations, the **controller** is the chief management accountant.

The controller's staff often consists of several management accountants. Each accountant is responsible for a specialized accounting function, such as systems and procedures, general accounting, budgets and budget analysis, special reports and analysis, taxes, and cost accounting.

Experience in managerial accounting is often an excellent training ground for senior management positions. One poll indicated that over 21% of the chief executive officers (CEOs) of the largest 1,000 companies in the United States have career paths that began with accounting or finance. More CEOs started out in these areas than in any other functional business area.[1] This is not surprising, since accounting and finance bring an individual into contact with all phases of operations.

Manufacturing Cost Terms

objective 3

Define and illustrate materials, factory labor, and factory overhead costs.

Managers rely on managerial accountants to provide useful *cost* information to support decision making. What is a cost? A **cost** is a payment of cash or its equivalent or the commitment to pay cash in the future for the purpose of generating revenues. A cost provides a benefit that is used immediately or deferred to a future period of time. If the benefit is used immediately, then the cost is an expense, such as salary expense. If the benefit is deferred, then the cost is an asset, such as equipment. As the asset is used, an expense, such as depreciation expense, is recognized.

In this section, we will illustrate manufacturing costs for Goodwell Printers, a manufacturing firm. A **manufacturing business** converts materials into a finished product through the use of machinery and labor. Goodwell Printers prints textbooks, like the one you are using now. Exhibit 3 provides an overview of Goodwell Printers' textbook printing operations. The Printing Department feeds large rolls of paper into printing presses. The printing presses use electricity and ink. From the Printing Department, the printed pages are stacked and moved to the Binding Department. In the Binding Department, the pages are cut, separated, stacked, and bound to book covers. A finished book is the final output of the Binding Department.

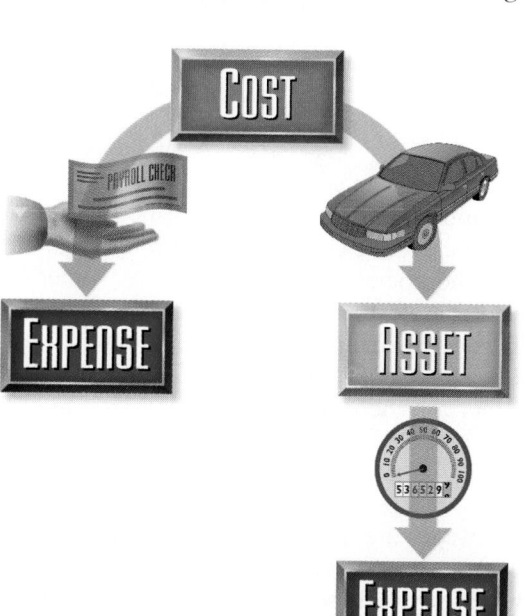

Materials

The cost of materials that are an integral part of the product is classified as **direct materials cost**. For example, the direct materials cost for Goodwell Printers would include paper and book covers.

As a practical matter, a direct materials cost must not only be

 Some service companies also have direct materials costs. For example, fuel is a direct materials cost to a flight for an airline, while medicines are a direct materials cost to a patient in a hospital.

---

[1] "Corporate Elite Career Path," *Business Week*, October 11, 1993, p. 65.

Exhibit 3 Textbook Printing Operations of Goodwell Printers

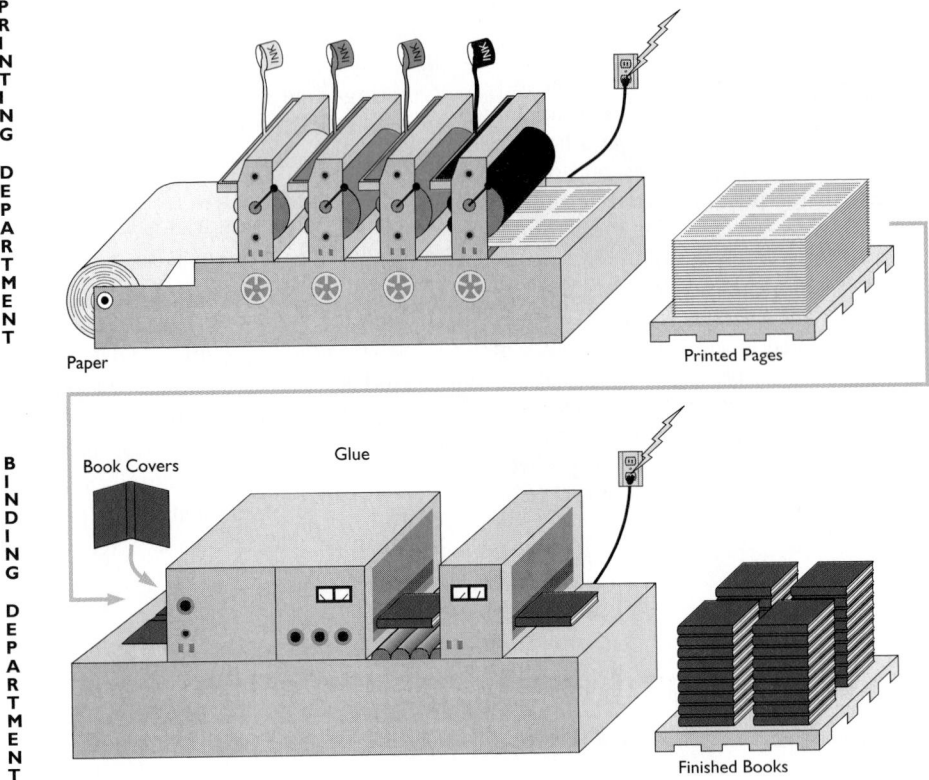

PRINTING DEPARTMENT

Paper

Printed Pages

BINDING DEPARTMENT

Book Covers   Glue

Finished Books

EXAMPLES OF DIRECT MATERIALS

TELEVISION MANUFACTURER

GOODWELL PRINTERS

AUTOMOBILE MANUFACTURER

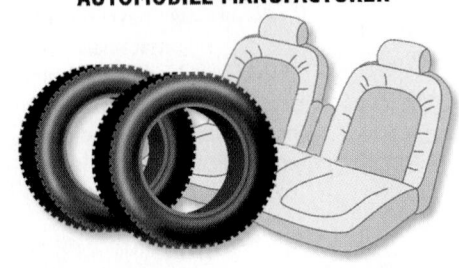

an integral part of the finished product, but it must also be a significant portion of the total cost of the product. Other examples of direct materials costs are the cost of electronic components for a TV manufacturer and tires for an automobile manufacturer.

The costs of materials that are not a significant portion of the total product cost are termed **indirect materials**. Indirect materials are considered a part of factory overhead, which we discuss later. For Goodwell Printers, the costs of ink and binding glue are classified as indirect materials.

Factory Labor

The cost of wages of employees who are directly involved in converting materials into the manufactured product is classified as **direct labor cost**. The direct labor cost of Goodwell Printers includes the wages of the employees who operate the printing presses. Other examples of direct labor costs are carpenters' wages for a construction contractor, mechanics' wages in an automotive repair shop, machine operators' wages in a tool manufacturing plant, and assemblers' wages in a microcomputer assembly plant.

As a practical matter, a direct labor cost must not only be an integral part of the finished product, but it must also be a significant portion of the total cost of the product. For Goodwell Printers, the printing press operators' wages are a significant portion of the total cost of each book. Labor costs that do not enter directly into the manufacture of a product are termed **indirect labor** and are recorded as factory overhead. Indirect labor for Goodwell Printers might include the salaries of maintenance, plant management, and quality control personnel.

Identify whether the following costs are direct materials, direct labor, or factory overhead for an automobile assembler: tires, quality engineering salaries, assembly wages, coil steel, painter wages, plant manager salary, cleaning fluids.

Tires and coil steel—direct materials; assembly wages and painter wages—direct labor; quality engineering salaries, plant manager's salary, and cleaning fluids—factory overhead.

Factory Overhead Cost

Costs other than direct materials cost and direct labor cost incurred in the manufacturing process are classified as factory overhead cost. Factory overhead is sometimes called **manufacturing overhead** or **factory burden**. Examples of factory overhead costs, in addition to indirect materials and indirect labor, are machine depreciation, factory utilities, factory supplies, and factory insurance. In addition, payments to employees for overtime and nonproductive time (such as idle time) are considered factory overhead. For many industries, factory overhead costs are becoming a larger portion of the costs of a product as manufacturing processes become more automated.

The direct materials, direct labor, and factory overhead costs are considered product costs, because they are associated with making a product. The costs of converting the materials into finished products consist of direct labor and factory overhead costs, which are commonly called conversion costs.

> **Direct materials, direct labor, and factory overhead costs are product costs.**

Cost Accounting System Overview

objective 4

Describe accounting systems used by manufacturing businesses.

Warner Bros. and other movie studios use job order cost systems to accumulate movie production and distribution costs. Costs such as actor salaries, production costs, movie print costs, and marketing costs are accumulated in a job account for a particular movie. Cost information from the job cost report can be used to control the costs of the movie while it is being produced and to determine the profitability of the movie after it has been exhibited.

An objective of a cost accounting system is to accumulate product costs. Product cost information is used by managers to establish product prices, control operations, and develop financial statements. In addition, the cost accounting system improves control by supplying data on the costs incurred by each manufacturing department or process.

There are two main types of cost accounting systems for manufacturing operations: job order cost systems and process cost systems. Each of the two systems is widely used, and any one manufacturer may use more than one type. In this chapter, we will illustrate the job order cost system. In the next chapter, we will illustrate the process cost system.

A **job order cost system** provides a separate record for the cost of each quantity of product that passes through the factory. A particular quantity of product is termed a *job*. A job order cost system is best suited to industries that manufacture custom goods to fill special orders from customers or that produce a high variety of products for stock. Manufacturers that use a job order cost system are sometimes called **job shops**. An example of a job shop would be an apparel manufacturer, such as **Levi Strauss**.

Many service firms also use job order cost systems to accumulate the costs associated with providing client services. For example, an accounting firm will accumulate all of the costs associated with a particular client engagement, such as accountant time, copying charges, and travel costs. Recording costs in this manner helps the accounting firm control costs during a client engagement and determines client billing and profitability.

Name two types of cost systems and a typical user of each system.

Job order cost system: cabinet manufacturer, law practice, movie studio. Process cost system: food processing, paper processing, metal processing, petroleum refining.

Under a **process cost system**, costs are accumulated for each of the departments or processes within the factory. A process system is best suited for manufacturers of units of product that are not distinguishable from each other during a continuous production process. An example would be an oil refinery.

Exhibit 4 summarizes a survey of manufacturers, showing the breakdown between the use of job order and process costing. Exhibit 4 indicates that over 50% of the respondents use some other type of cost system. Although not indicated in this survey, these other respondents probably use a hybrid system that combines features of a job order and a process cost system.

Exhibit 4 Cost Accounting Practices by Major Industries

Industry Group	% Using Job Order Costing	% Using Process Costing
Metal, chemical, oil, gas, paper	21	41
Machinery	35	15
Automobile	11	8
Aerospace	45	10
Electronics	24	15
High technology	33	43
Other industrial products	13	23
Consumer products	2	33
Diverse products	50	31
Average of all respondents	20%	23%

Source: R. A. Howell, J. D. Brown, S. R. Soucy, and A. H. Seed, *Management Accounting in the New Manufacturing Environment,* IMA/CAM-I, 1987, p. 36.

Job Order Cost Systems for Manufacturing Businesses

objective 5

Describe and prepare summary journal entries for a job order cost accounting system.

The work in process inventory consists of direct materials, direct labor, and factory overhead costs of products not yet completed.

In this section, we will illustrate the job order cost system for a manufacturing firm, Goodwell Printers. The job order system accumulates manufacturing costs by job, as shown in Exhibit 5. The **materials inventory**, sometimes called **raw materials inventory**, consists of the costs of the direct and indirect materials that have not yet entered the manufacturing process. For Goodwell Printers, the materials inventory would consist of paper, ink, glue, and book covers. The **work in process inventory** consists of direct materials costs, direct labor costs, and factory overhead costs that have entered the manufacturing process but are associated with products that have not been completed. Examples are the costs of Jobs 71 and 72 that are still in the printing process in Exhibit 5. Completed jobs that have not been sold are termed **finished goods inventory**. Examples are completed printed books from Jobs 69 and 70 shown in Exhibit 5. Upon sale, a manufacturer will record the cost of the sale as **cost of goods sold**. An example is the case of *Physics* books sold to the bookstore in Exhibit 5. The *cost of goods sold* for a manufacturer is comparable to the *cost of merchandise sold* for a merchandising business.

In a job order cost accounting system, perpetual inventory controlling accounts and subsidiary ledgers are maintained for materials, work in process, and finished goods inventories. Each inventory account is debited for all additions and is credited for all deductions. The balance of each account thus represents the balance on hand.

Exhibit 5 Manufacturing Costs and Jobs

FLOW OF MANUFACTURING COSTS

- **Direct Labor**
- **Factory Overhead**

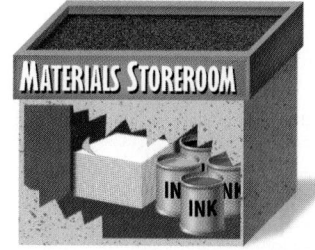

Materials Inventory	Work In Process Inventory	Finished Goods Inventory	Cost of Goods Sold

Materials

The procedures used to purchase, store, and issue materials to production often differ among manufacturers. Exhibit 6 shows the basic information and cost flows for the paper received and issued to production by Goodwell Printers.

Purchased materials are first received and inspected by the Receiving Department. The Receiving Department personnel prepare a **receiving report**, showing the quantity received and its condition. Some organizations now use bar code scanning devices in place of receiving reports to record and electronically transmit incoming materials data. The receiving information and invoice are used to record the receipt and control the payment for purchased items. The journal entry to record Receiving Report No. 196 in Exhibit 6 is:

a.	Materials		10 5 0 0 00	
	Accounts Payable			10 5 0 0 00
	Materials purchased during			
	December.			

The materials account in the general ledger is a controlling account. A separate account for each type of material is maintained in a subsidiary **materials ledger**. Details as to the quantity and cost of materials received are recorded in the materials ledger on the basis of the receiving reports. A typical form of a materials ledger account is illustrated in Exhibit 6.

Materials are released from the storeroom to the factory in response to **materials requisitions** from the Production Department. An illustration of a materials requisition is in Exhibit 6. The completed requisition for each job serves as the basis for posting quantities and dollar data to the job cost sheets in the case of direct materials or to factory overhead in the case of indirect materials. **Job cost sheets**, which are illustrated in Exhibit 6, are the work in process subsidiary ledger. For Goodwell Printers, Job 71 is for 1,000 textbooks titled *American History*, while Job 72 is for 4,000 textbooks titled *Algebra*.

In Exhibit 6, the first-in, first-out costing method is used. A summary of the materials requisitions completed during the month is the basis for transferring the

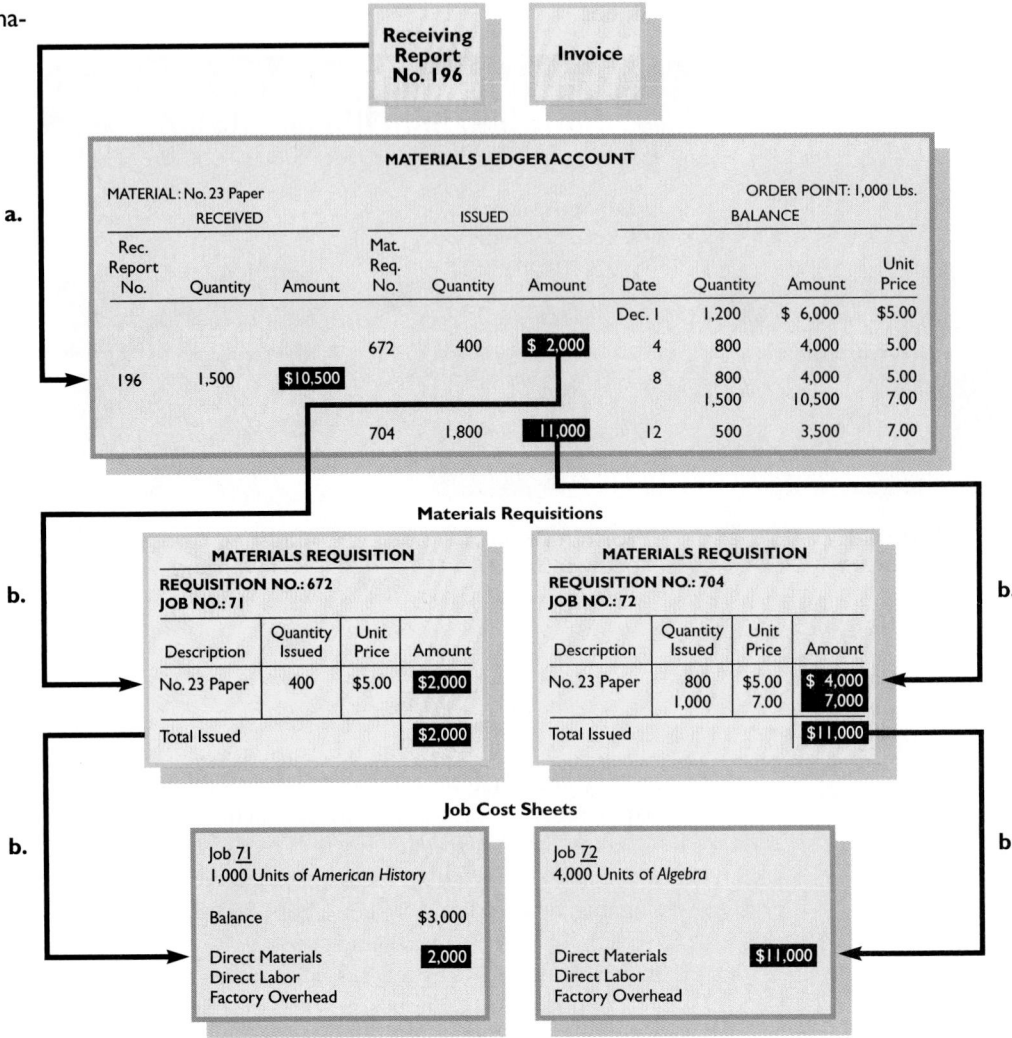

Exhibit 6 Materials Information and Cost Flows

For many manufacturing firms, the direct materials cost can be greater than 50% of the total cost to manufacture a product. This is why controlling materials costs is very important.

cost of the direct materials from the materials account in the general ledger to the controlling account for work in process. The flow of materials from the materials storeroom into production ($2,000 + $11,000) is recorded by the following entry:

	b.	Work in Process		13 0 0 0 00			
		Materials				13 0 0 0 00
		Materials requisitioned to jobs.					

Many organizations are using computerized information processes that account for the flow of materials. In a computerized setting, the storeroom manager would record the release of materials into a computer, which would automatically update the subsidiary materials records.

Factory Labor

There are two primary objectives in accounting for factory labor. One objective is to determine the correct amount to be paid each employee for each payroll period. A second objective is to properly allocate factory labor costs to factory overhead and individual job orders.

The amount of time spent by an employee in the factory is usually recorded on **clock cards** or **in-and-out cards**. The amount of time spent by each employee and the labor cost incurred for each individual job are recorded on **time tickets**. Exhibit 7 shows typical time ticket forms and cost flows for direct labor for Goodwell Printers.

Exhibit 7 Labor Information and Cost Flows

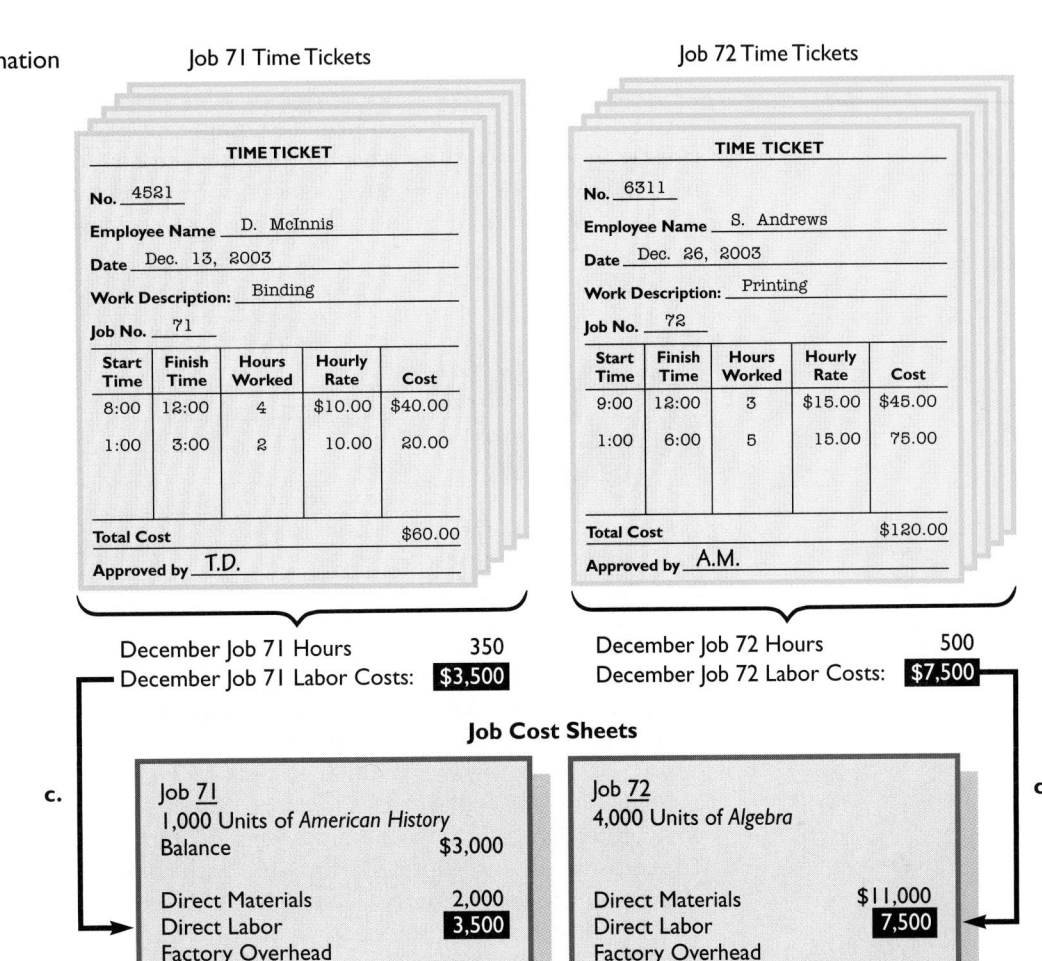

A summary of the time tickets at the end of each month is the basis for recording the direct and indirect labor costs incurred in production. Direct labor is posted to each job cost sheet, while indirect labor is debited to Factory Overhead.[2] Goodwell Printers incurred 850 direct labor hours on Jobs 71 and 72 during December. The total direct labor costs were $11,000, divided into $3,500 for Job 71 and $7,500 for Job 72. The labor costs that flow into production are recorded by the following summary entry to the work in process controlling account:

c.	Work in Process	11 0 0 0 00	
	Wages Payable		11 0 0 0 00
	Factory labor used in production		
	of jobs.		

[2] There are a variety of methods for recording direct labor costs. In the approach illustrated in this chapter, we assume that labor costs are automatically recorded to jobs or factory overhead when incurred. Alternatively, wages could first be debited to Factory Labor when incurred and then later distributed to jobs and factory overhead.

Shell Oil Company Real World uses a magnetic system to track the work of maintenance crews in its refineries.

As with recording materials, many organizations are automating the labor recording process. For example, in companies that build very large products, such as submarines, jet aircraft, or space vehicles, direct labor employees can be given magnetic cards, much like credit cards. These cards can be used to log in and log out of particular work assignments on particular jobs by running the card through a magnetic reader at any number of remote computer terminals.

Factory Overhead Cost

Factory overhead includes all manufacturing costs except direct materials and direct labor. Debits to Factory Overhead come from various sources, such as indirect materials, indirect labor, factory power, and factory depreciation. For example, the factory overhead of $4,600 incurred in December for Goodwell Printers would be recorded as follows:

d.	Factory Overhead		4 6 0 0 00		
	Materials			5 0 0 00	
	Wages Payable			2 0 0 0 00	
	Utilities Payable			9 0 0 00	
	Accumulated Depreciation			1 2 0 0 00	
	Factory overhead incurred in				
	production.				

Allocating Factory Overhead

Factory overhead is much different from direct labor and direct materials because it is indirectly related to the jobs. How, then, do the jobs get assigned a portion of overhead costs? The answer is through cost allocation. **Cost allocation** is the process of assigning factory overhead costs to a cost object, such as a job. The factory overhead costs are assigned to the jobs on the basis of some known measure about each job. The measure used to allocate factory overhead is frequently called an **activity base**, **allocation base**, or **activity driver**. The estimated activity base should be a measure that reflects the consumption or use of factory overhead cost. For example, the direct labor is recorded for each job using time tickets. Thus, direct labor could be used to allocate production-related factory overhead costs to each job. Likewise, direct materials costs are known about each job through the materials requisitions. Thus, materials-related factory overhead, such as Purchasing Department salaries, could logically be allocated to the job on the basis of direct materials cost.

Predetermined Factory Overhead Rate

In order that job costs may be currently available, factory overhead may be allocated or applied to production using a **predetermined factory overhead rate**. The predetermined factory overhead rate is calculated by dividing the estimated amount of factory overhead for the forthcoming year by the estimated activity base, such as machine hours, direct materials costs, direct labor costs, or direct labor hours.

To illustrate calculating a predetermined overhead rate, assume that Goodwell Printers estimates the total factory overhead cost to be $50,000 for the year and the activity base to be 10,000 direct labor hours. The predetermined factory overhead rate would be calculated as $5 per direct labor hour, as follows:

$$\text{Predetermined factory overhead rate} = \frac{\text{Estimated total factory overhead costs}}{\text{Estimated activity base}}$$

$$\text{Predetermined factory overhead rate} = \frac{\$50,000}{10,000 \text{ direct labor hours}} = \$5 \text{ per direct labor hour}$$

A variety of activity bases may be used to allocate factory overhead to jobs. One survey reported the following activity bases used by manufacturers:

Description of Activity Base (Driver)	Percentage of Survey Respondents Indicating Usage*
Direct labor hours	61%
Direct labor dollars	54
Machine hours	54
Direct material dollars	26
Other	25

*Note: The percentages total more than 100% because many firms use more than one activity base in different parts of their operations.

Source: James A. Hendricks, "Applying Cost Accounting to Factory Automation," *Management Accounting*, December 1988, pp. 24–30.

Why is the predetermined overhead rate calculated from estimated numbers at the beginning of the period? The answer is to ensure timely information. If a company waited until the end of an accounting period when all overhead costs are known, the allocated factory overhead would be accurate but not timely. If the cost system is to have maximum usefulness, cost data should be available as each job is completed, even though there may be a small sacrifice in accuracy. Only through timely reporting can management make needed adjustments in pricing or in manufacturing methods and achieve the best possible combination of revenue and cost on future jobs.

A number of companies are using a new product-costing approach called activity-based costing. **Activity-based costing** is a method of accumulating and allocating factory overhead costs to products using many overhead rates. Each rate is related to separate factory activities, such as inspecting, moving, and machining. Activity-based costing is discussed and illustrated in a later chapter.

A survey conducted by the Cost Management Group of the Institute for Management Accountants found that 43% of survey respondents had adopted activity-based costing and 39% were considering it.

Applying Factory Overhead to Work in Process

As factory overhead costs are incurred, they are debited to the factory overhead account, as shown previously in transaction (d). For Goodwell Printers, factory overhead costs are applied to production at the rate of $5 per direct labor hour. The amount of factory overhead applied to each job would be recorded in the job cost sheets as shown in Exhibit 8. For example, the 850 direct labor hours used in Goodwell's December operations would all be traced to individual jobs. Job 71 used 350 labor hours, so $1,750 (350 × $5) of factory overhead would be applied to Job 71. Similarly, $2,500 (500 × $5) of factory overhead would be applied to Job 72.

The factory overhead costs applied to production are periodically debited to the work in process account and credited to the factory overhead account. The summary entry to apply the $4,250 ($1,750 + $2,500) of factory overhead is as follows:

Factory overhead costs are estimated to be $120,000. Direct labor hours are estimated to be 20,000 hours. Determine (a) the predetermined factory overhead rate and (b) the amount of factory overhead applied to a job with 30 direct labor hours.

	e.	Work in Process	4 2 5 0 00		
		Factory Overhead		4 2 5 0 00
		Factory overhead applied to jobs		
		according to the predetermined		
		overhead rate.		

(a) $6 per hour ($120,000/20,000); (b) $180 ($6 × 30 hours)

The factory overhead costs applied and the actual factory overhead costs incurred during a period will usually differ. If the amount applied exceeds the actual costs incurred, the factory overhead account will have a credit balance. This credit is described as **overapplied** or **overabsorbed** **factory overhead**. If the amount applied is less than the actual costs incurred, the account will have a debit balance.

Exhibit 8 Assigning Factory Overhead to Jobs

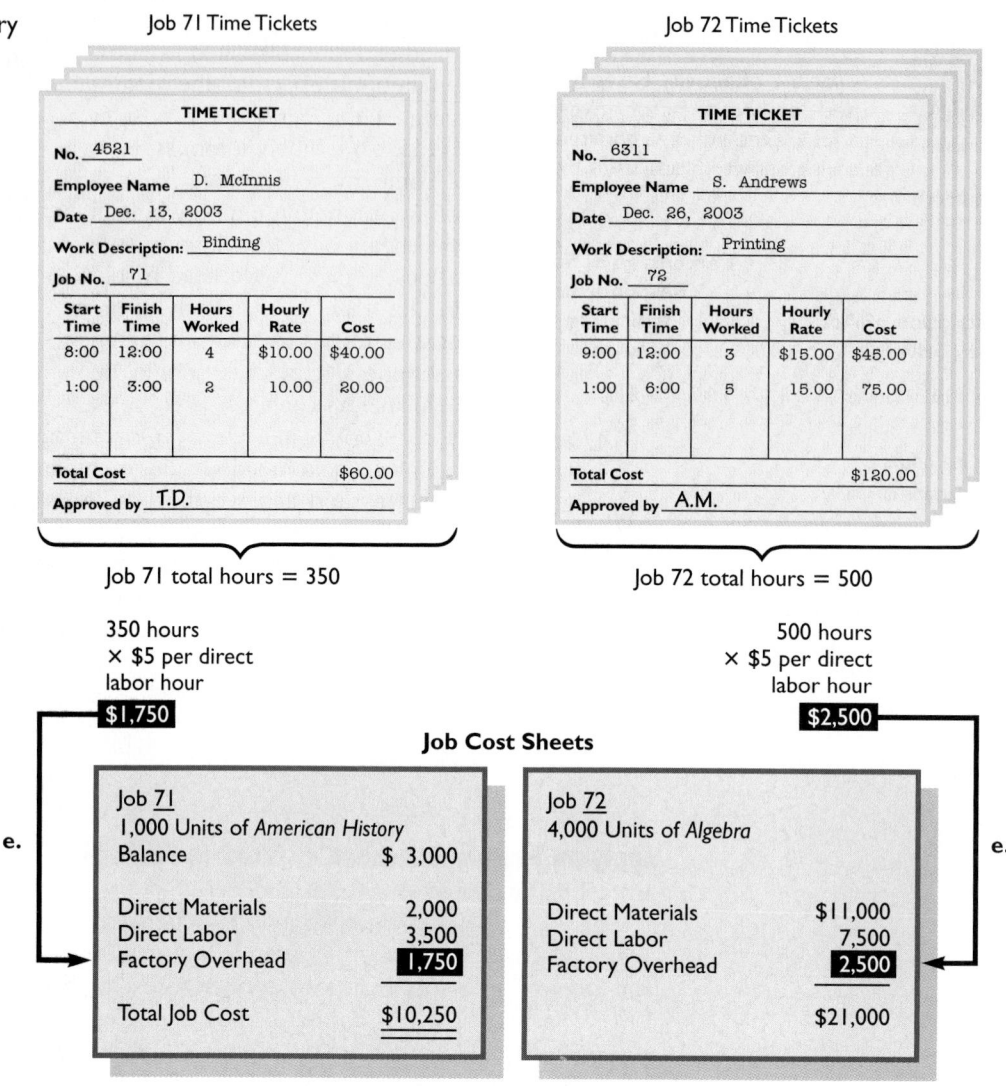

This debit is described as **underapplied** or **underabsorbed** factory overhead. Both cases are illustrated in the following account for Goodwell Printers:

ACCOUNT *Factory Overhead*					ACCOUNT NO.	
Date	Item	Post Ref.	Debit	Credit	Balance Debit	Balance Credit
Dec. 1	Balance					200
31	Factory overhead cost incurred		4,600		4,400	
31	Factory overhead cost applied			4,250	150	

Underapplied balance
Overapplied balance

If the underapplied or overapplied balance increases in only one direction and it becomes large, the balance and the overhead rate should be investigated. For example, if a large balance is caused by changes in manufacturing methods or in production goals, the factory overhead rate should be revised. On the other hand, a large underapplied balance may indicate a serious control problem caused by inefficiencies in production methods, excessive costs, or a combination of factors.

Disposal of Factory Overhead Balance

The balance in the factory overhead account is carried forward from month to month. It is reported on interim balance sheets as a deferred debit or credit. This balance should not be carried over to the next year, however, since it applies to the operations of the year just ended.

One approach for disposing of the balance of factory overhead at the end of the year is to transfer the entire balance to the cost of goods sold account.[3] To illustrate, the journal entry to eliminate Goodwell Printers' underapplied overhead balance of $150 at the end of the calendar year would be:

f.	Cost of Goods Sold			1 5 0 00	
	Factory Overhead				1 5 0 00
		Closed underapplied factory			
		overhead to cost of goods sold.			

Work in Process

Costs incurred for the various jobs are debited to Work in Process. Goodwell Printers' job costs described in the preceding sections may be summarized as follows:

- **Direct materials, $13,000**—Work in Process debited and Materials credited (transaction b); data obtained from summary of materials requisitions.
- **Direct labor, $11,000**—Work in Process debited and Wages Payable credited (transaction c); data obtained from summary of time tickets.
- **Factory overhead, $4,250**—Work in Process debited and Factory Overhead credited (transaction e); data obtained from summary of time tickets.

The details concerning the costs incurred on each job order are accumulated in the job cost sheets. Exhibit 9 illustrates the relationship between the job cost sheets and the work in process controlling account.

In this example, Job 71 was started in November and completed in December. The beginning December balance for Job 71 represents the costs carried over from the end of November. Job 72 was started in December but was not yet completed at the end of the month. Thus, the balance of the incomplete Job 72, or $21,000, will be shown on the balance sheet on December 31 as work in process inventory.

When Job 71 was completed, the direct materials costs, the direct labor costs, and the factory overhead costs were totaled and divided by the number of units produced to determine the cost per unit. If we assume that 1,000 units of a textbook titled *American History* were produced for Job 71, then the unit cost would be $10.25 ($10,250 ÷ 1,000).

Upon completing Job 71, the job cost sheet was removed from the cost ledger and filed for future reference. At the end of the accounting period (December), the total costs for all completed jobs during the period are determined, and the following entry is made:

g.	Finished Goods			10 2 5 0 00	
	Work in Process				10 2 5 0 00
		Job 71 completed in December.			

---

[3] Alternatively, the balance may be allocated among the work in process, finished goods, and cost of goods sold balances. This approach brings the accounts into agreement with the costs actually incurred. Since this approach is a more complex calculation that adds little additional accuracy, it will not be used in this text.

Exhibit 9 Job Cost Sheets and the Work in Process Controlling Account

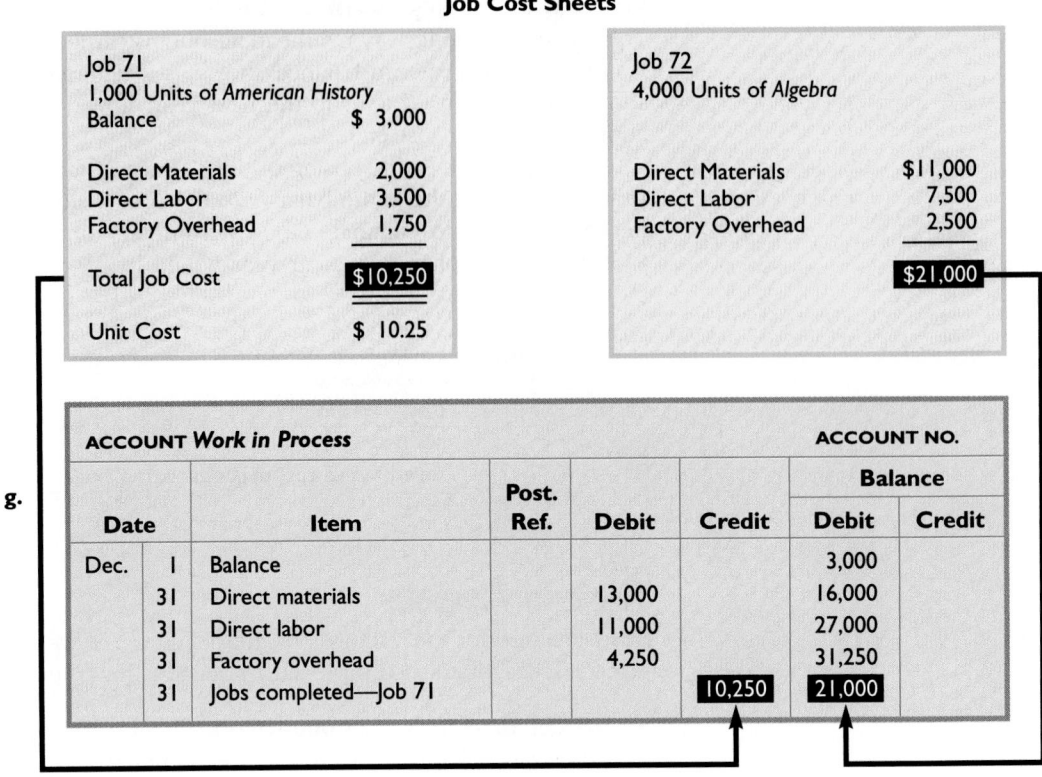

Job Cost Sheets

Job 71	
1,000 Units of *American History*	
Balance	$ 3,000
Direct Materials	2,000
Direct Labor	3,500
Factory Overhead	1,750
Total Job Cost	$10,250
Unit Cost	$ 10.25

Job 72	
4,000 Units of *Algebra*	
Direct Materials	$11,000
Direct Labor	7,500
Factory Overhead	2,500
	$21,000

g.

ACCOUNT Work in Process						ACCOUNT NO.	
Date		Item	Post. Ref.	Debit	Credit	Balance Debit	Balance Credit
Dec.	1	Balance				3,000	
	31	Direct materials		13,000		16,000	
	31	Direct labor		11,000		27,000	
	31	Factory overhead		4,250		31,250	
	31	Jobs completed—Job 71			10,250	21,000	

Finished Goods and Cost of Goods Sold

The finished goods account is a controlling account. Its related subsidiary ledger, which has an account for each product, is called the **finished goods ledger** or **stock ledger**. Each account in the finished goods ledger contains cost data for the units manufactured, units sold, and units on hand. Exhibit 10 illustrates an account in the finished goods ledger.

Exhibit 10 Finished Goods Ledger Account

ITEM: *American History*									
Manufactured			Shipped			Balance			
Job Order No.	Quantity	Amount	Ship Order No.	Quantity	Amount	Date	Quantity	Amount	Unit Cost
						Dec. 1	2,000	$20,000	$10.00
			643	2,000	$20,000	9	—	—	—
71	1,000	$10,250				31	1,000	10,250	10.25

Just as there are various methods of costing materials entering into production, there are various methods of determining the cost of the finished goods sold. In Exhibit 10, the first-in, first-out method is used. A summary of the cost data for the units shipped ($20,000) becomes the basis for the following entry:

Boxer Company completed 80,000 units at a cost of $680,000. The beginning finished goods inventory was 10,000 units at $80,000. What is the cost of goods sold for 60,000 units, assuming a FIFO cost flow?

$505,000 [$80,000 + (50,000 × $8.50)]

h.	Cost of Goods Sold		20 0 0 0 00		
	Finished Goods			20 0 0 0 00
	Cost of 2,000 *American History*			
	textbooks sold.			

Sales

The selling price of the goods sold is recorded by debiting Accounts Receivable (or Cash) and crediting Sales. To illustrate, assume that Goodwell Printers sold the 2,000 *American History* textbooks during December for $14 per unit.[4] The entry to the accounts receivable controlling account would be:

i.	Accounts Receivable		28 0 0 0 00		
	Sales			28 0 0 0 00
	Revenue received from textbooks			
	sold.			

Period Costs

In addition to product costs (direct materials, direct labor, and factory overhead), businesses also have period costs. **Period costs** are expenses that are used in generating revenue during the current period and are not involved in the manufacturing process. Period costs are generally classified into two categories: selling and administrative. **Selling expenses** are incurred in marketing the product and delivering the sold product to customers. **Administrative expenses** are incurred in the administration of the business and are not related to the manufacturing or selling functions.

EXAMPLES OF PERIOD COSTS

SELLING EXPENSES
- Advertising expenses
- Sales salaries expenses
- Commission expenses

ADMINISTRATIVE EXPENSES
- Office salaries expenses
- Office supplies expenses
- Depreciation expense—office buildings and equipment

---

[4] The price of the textbook is the amount paid by the textbook publisher for printing the book. Printing is one small part of the total cost of the textbook. The publisher must also pay royalties, development and production costs, and selling expenses. Thus, the price of the textbook to the final user will be higher than $14.

Service companies, such as telecommunications, insurance, banking, broadcasting, and hospitality, typically have a large portion of their total costs as period costs. This is because most service companies do not have products that can be inventoried, and hence, they do not have product costs.

For Goodwell Printers, the following period expenses were recorded for December:

	j.	Sales Salaries Expense		2 0 0 0 00				
		Office Salaries Expense		1 5 0 0 00				
		Accounts Payable				3 5 0 0 00		
		Recorded December period costs.						

Summary of Cost Flows for Goodwell Printers

Exhibit 11 shows the cost flow through the manufacturing accounts, together with summary details of the subsidiary ledgers for Goodwell Printers. Entries in the accounts are identified by letters that refer to the summary journal entries introduced in the preceding section.

The balances of the general ledger controlling accounts are supported by their respective subsidiary ledgers. The balances of the three inventory accounts—Finished Goods, Work in Process, and Materials—represent the respective ending inventories of December 31 on the balance sheet. These balances are as follows:

Materials	$ 3,500
Work in process	21,000
Finished goods	10,250

The income statement for Goodwell Printers would be as shown in Exhibit 12.

Exhibit 12 Income Statement of Goodwell Printers

Goodwell Printers
Income Statement
For the Month Ended December 31, 2003

Sales		$28,000
Cost of goods sold		20,150
Gross profit		$ 7,850
Selling and administrative expenses:		
Sales salaries expense	$2,000	
Office salaries expense	1,500	
Total selling and administrative expenses		3,500
Income from operations		$ 4,350

Job Order Costing for Decision Making

objective 6

Use job order cost information for decision making.

The job order cost system that we developed in the previous sections can be used to evaluate an organization's cost performance. The unit costs for similar jobs can be compared over time to determine if costs are staying within expected ranges. If costs increase for some unexpected reason, the details in the job cost sheets can help discover the reasons.

Exhibit 11 Flow of Manufacturing Costs for Goodwell Printers

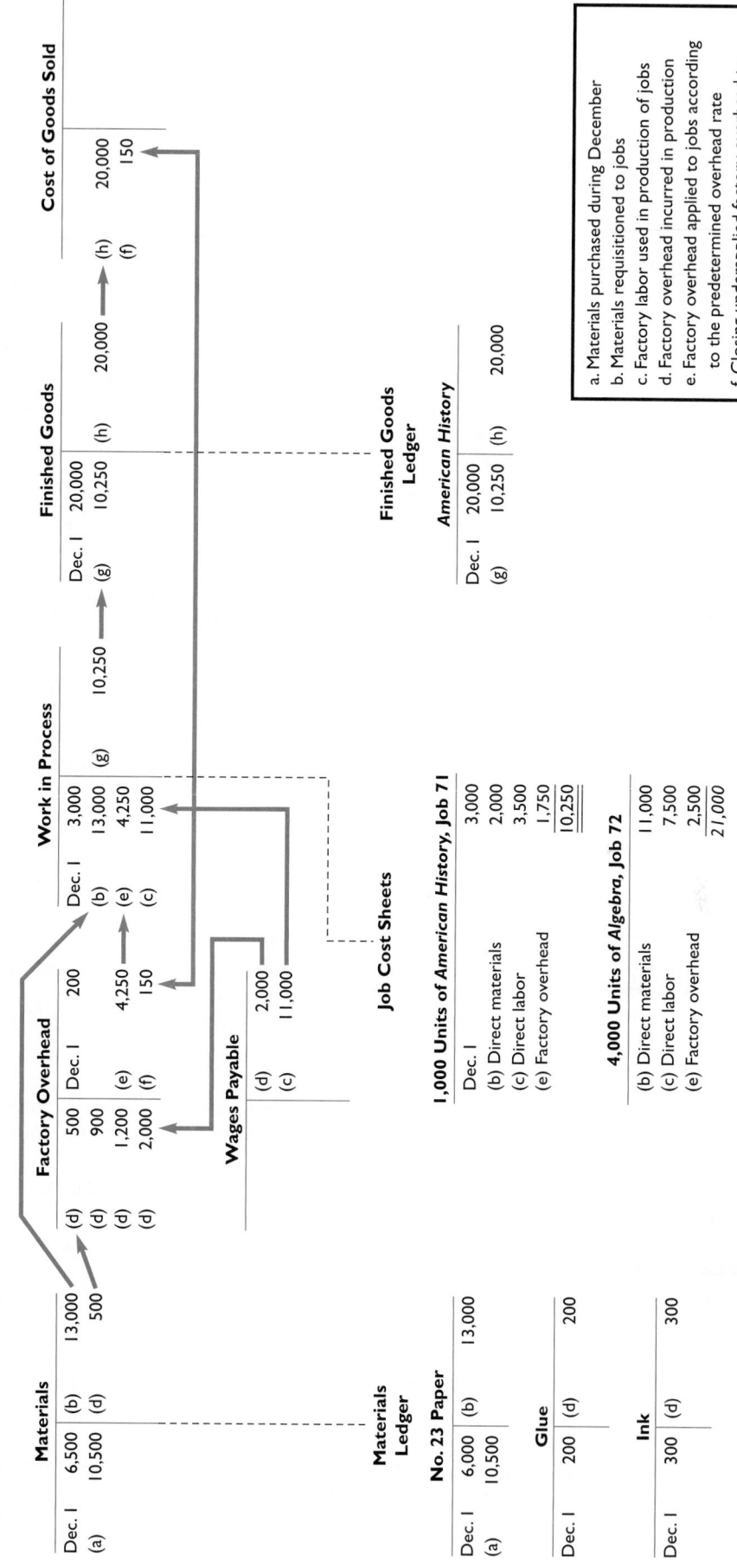

To illustrate, Exhibit 13 shows the direct materials on the job cost sheets for Jobs 144 and 163 for a furniture company. Since both job cost sheets refer to the same type and number of chairs, the direct materials cost per unit should be about the same. However, the materials cost per chair for Job 144 is $28, while for Job 163 it is $35. For some reason, materials costs have increased since the folding chairs were produced for Job 144.

Exhibit 13 Comparing Data from Job Cost Sheets

Job 144
Item: 200 folding chairs

	Materials Quantity (board feet)	Materials Price	Materials Amount
Direct materials:			
Wood	1,600	$3.50	$5,600
Direct materials per chair			$28

Job 163
Item: 200 folding chairs

	Materials Quantity (board feet)	Materials Price	Materials Amount
Direct materials:			
Wood	2,000	$3.50	$7,000
Direct materials per chair			$35

Major electric utilities such as **Tennessee Valley Authority**, **Consolidated Edison**, and **Pacific Gas and Electric** use job order accounting to control the costs associated with major repairs and overhauls that occur during forced or planned outages. A forced outage is an unexpected shutdown of a power plant, whereas a planned outage is a scheduled shutdown.

Job cost sheets can be used to investigate possible reasons for the increased cost. First, you should note that the rate for direct materials did not change. Thus, the cost increase is not related to increasing prices. What about the wood consumption? This tells us a different story. The quantity of wood used to produce 200 chairs in Job 144 is 1,600 board feet. However, Job 163 required 2,000 board feet. How can this be explained? Any one of the following explanations is possible and could be investigated further:

1. There was a new employee who was not adequately trained for cutting the wood for chairs. As a result, the employee improperly cut and scrapped many pieces.
2. The lumber was of poor quality. As a result, the cutting operator ended up using and scrapping additional pieces of lumber.
3. The cutting tools were in need of repair. As a result, the cutting operators miscut and scrapped many pieces of wood.
4. The operator was careless. As a result of poor work, many pieces of cut wood had to be scrapped.
5. The instructions attached to the job were incorrect. The operator cut wood according to the instructions but discovered that the pieces would not fit. As a result, many pieces had to be scrapped.

You should note that many of these explanations are not necessarily related to operator error. Poor cost performance may be the result of root causes that are outside the control of the operator.

Job Order Cost Systems for Professional Service Businesses

A job order cost accounting system may be useful to the management of a professional service business in planning and controlling operations. For example, an advertising agency, an attorney, and a physician all share the common characteristic of providing services to individual customers, clients, or patients. In such cases, the customer, client, or patient can be viewed as an individual job for which costs are accumulated.

Since the "product" of a service business is service, management's focus is on direct labor and overhead costs. The cost of any materials or supplies used in rendering services for a client is usually small and is normally included as part of the overhead.

The direct labor and overhead costs of rendering services to clients are accumulated in a work in process account. This account is supported by a cost ledger. A job cost sheet is used to accumulate the costs for each client's job. When a job is completed and the client is billed, the costs are transferred to a cost of services account. This account is similar to the cost of merchandise sold account for a merchandising business or the cost of goods sold account for a manufacturing business. A finished goods account and related finished goods ledger are not necessary, since the revenues associated with the services are recorded after the services have been provided. The flow of costs through a service business using a job order cost accounting system is shown in Exhibit 14.

Exhibit 14 Flow of Costs Through a Service Business

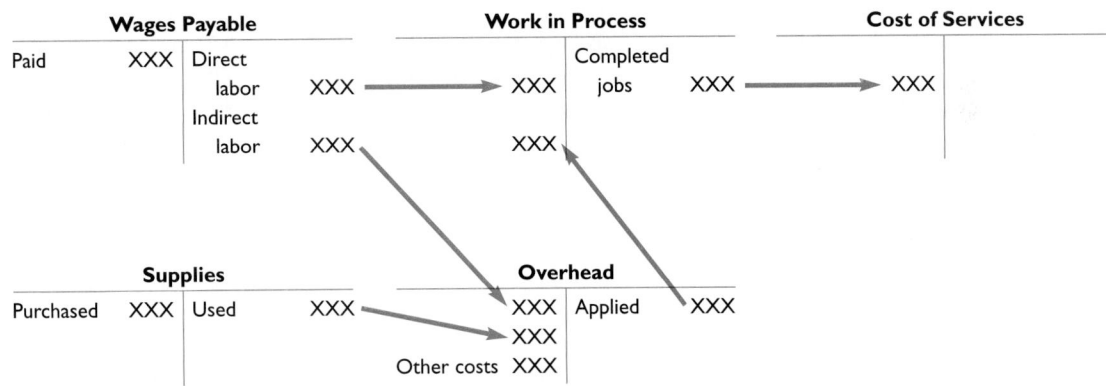

In practice, additional accounting considerations unique to service businesses may need to be considered. For example, a service business may bill clients on a weekly or monthly basis rather than waiting until a job is completed. In these situations, a portion of the costs related to each billing should be transferred from the work in process account to the cost of services account. A service business may also have advance billings that would be accounted for as deferred revenue until the services have been completed.

ENCORE

Reel Profits in Hollywood

Winston Groom, the author of *Forrest Gump*, was promised $350,000 and 3% of the net profits of the *Forrest Gump* movie. We would think that Winston Groom is a lucky man. After all, *Forrest Gump* grossed $670 million in worldwide ticket sales, ranking its revenues as one of the highest in movie history. Unfortunately, Groom has yet to see any money from participating in the profits, because the movie has yet to make a profit. Instead, Paramount Studios estimated that the movie had a loss of $62 million! Or how about Arthur Sarkissian, who had a 10% net profit participation deal for screenwriting *While You Were Sleeping*. Walt Disney Company reports that the picture grossed over $300 million in revenues but has lost $20 million and isn't expected to make a profit. It looks as if Sarkissian is also going to strike out. What's happening here?

These results can be explained by the unique form of job order costing used in Hollywood, termed *contract accounting*. Under contract accounting, all the costs associated with the movie

are accumulated by each movie project, including overhead allocations. Many are critical of some of the overhead allocation practices. For example, it is common to add in a distribution fee to the cost of the movie. This fee compensates the studio for maintaining its distribution arm. In the case of *Forrest Gump*, Paramount included a distribution fee equal to 32% of the gross revenue. Critics argue that the actual cost of distribution is closer to 10% of the gross revenue. For example, in *Coming To America*, the distribution fee for this one film ($42 million) more than covered Paramount's entire distribution costs for the whole year. All this raises an interesting question: Is it possible under contract accounting for a hit movie to ever show a profit? Or as Arnold Schwarzenegger stated regarding *Titanic*, "Its box office may grow so large that it will actually show a profit that no accountant can hide."

The accounting rule-makers are responding to Hollywood's accounting tactics by standardizing how profitability is determined. For example, one suggestion is to write off the cost of

abandoned scripts and projects as an expense of the period, rather than being placed in the overhead pool to be allocated to successful pictures. This is an example of properly defining period versus product costs.

Regardless, it looks as if Groom has wised up to the ways of Hollywood accounting. Groom has made a new seven-figure deal with Paramount for *Gump & Co.*, the sequel to *Forrest Gump*. In this deal, Groom takes a percentage of the gross revenues, *before expenses*. Under this contract, Groom won't care about "distribution fees" and other cost allocations. ■

KEY POINTS

1 Describe the differences between managerial and financial accounting.
Managerial accounting and financial accounting serve different needs and, as such, have different characteristics. Managerial accounting serves the reporting needs of managers in meeting strategic and operational goals. Managerial accounting is not bound by a set of generally accepted accounting principles, as is financial account-

ing. As a result, the practice of managerial accounting is as diverse as are organizations. This additional complexity in understanding the structure of managerial accounting is offset by the degree of creativity that can be applied to managerial information needs.

2 Evaluate the organizational role of management accountants.

The financial function is generally a staff function of the organization. The chief accountant is often called the controller. The controller's function includes providing a variety of reports to support management decision making.

3 Define and illustrate materials, factory labor, and factory overhead costs.

A manufacturer converts materials into a finished product by using machinery and labor. The cost of materials that are an integral part of the manufactured product is direct materials cost. The cost of wages of employees who are involved in converting materials into the manufactured product is direct labor cost. Costs other than direct materials and direct labor costs are factory overhead costs, including indirect materials and labor. Direct labor and factory overhead are termed conversion costs. Direct materials, direct labor, and factory overhead costs are associated with products and are called product costs.

4 Describe accounting systems used by manufacturing businesses.

A cost accounting system accumulates product costs. The cost accounting system is used by management to determine the proper product cost for inventory valuation on the financial statements, to support product pricing decisions, and to identify opportunities for cost reduction and improved production efficiency. The two primary cost accounting systems are job order and process cost systems.

5 Describe and prepare summary journal entries for a job order cost accounting system.

A job order cost system provides for a separate record of the cost of each particular quantity of product that passes through the factory. Direct materials, direct labor, and factory overhead costs are accumulated in a subsidiary cost ledger, in which each account is represented by a job cost sheet. Work in Process is the controlling account for the cost ledger. As a job is finished, its costs are transferred to the finished goods ledger, for which Finished Goods is the controlling account.

6 Use job order cost information for decision making.

Job order cost information can support pricing and cost analysis. Managers can use job cost information to identify unusual trends and areas for cost improvement.

7 Diagram the flow of costs for a service business that uses a job order cost accounting system.

A cost flow diagram for a service business using a job order cost accounting system is shown in Exhibit 14. For a service business, the cost of materials or supplies used is normally included as part of the overhead. The direct labor and overhead costs of rendering services are accumulated in a work in process account. When a job is completed and the client is billed, the costs are transferred to a cost of services account.

ILLUSTRATIVE PROBLEM

Derby Music Company specializes in producing and packaging compact discs (CDs) for the music recording industry. Derby uses a job order cost system. The following data summarize the operations related to production for March, the first month of operations:

a. Materials purchased on account, $15,500.
b. Materials requisitioned and labor used:

	Materials	Factory Labor
Job No. 100	$2,650	$1,770
Job No. 101	1,240	650
Job No. 102	980	420
Job No. 103	3,420	1,900
Job No. 104	1,000	500
Job No. 105	2,100	1,760
For general factory use	450	650

c. Factory overhead costs incurred on account, $2,700.
d. Depreciation of machinery, $1,750.
e. Factory overhead is applied at a rate of 70% of direct labor cost.
f. Jobs completed: Nos. 100, 101, 102, 104.
g. Jobs 100, 101, and 102 were shipped, and customers were billed for $8,100, $3,800, and $3,500, respectively.

Instructions

1. Journalize the entries to record the transactions identified above.
2. Determine the account balances for Work in Process and Finished Goods.
3. Prepare a schedule of unfinished jobs to support the balance in the work in process account.
4. Prepare a schedule of completed jobs on hand to support the balance in the finished goods account.

Solution

1.

a.	Materials	15,500	
	Accounts Payable		15,500
b.	Work in Process	11,390	
	Materials		11,390
	Work in Process	7,000	
	Wages Payable		7,000
	Factory Overhead	1,100	
	Materials		450
	Wages Payable		650
c.	Factory Overhead	2,700	
	Accounts Payable		2,700
d.	Factory Overhead	1,750	
	Accumulated Depreciation—Machinery		1,750
e.	Work in Process	4,900	
	Factory Overhead (70% of $7,000)		4,900
f.	Finished Goods	11,548	
	Work in Process		11,548

Computation of the cost of jobs finished:

Job	Direct Materials	Direct Labor	Factory Overhead	Total
Job No. 100	$2,650	$1,770	$1,239	$ 5,659
Job No. 101	1,240	650	455	2,345
Job No. 102	980	420	294	1,694
Job No. 104	1,000	500	350	1,850
				$11,548

g.	Accounts Receivable	15,400	
	Sales		15,400
	Cost of Goods Sold	9,698	
	Finished Goods		9,698

Cost of jobs sold computation:

Job No. 100	$5,659
Job No. 101	2,345
Job No. 102	1,694
	$9,698

2. Work in Process: $11,742 ($11,390 + $7,000 + $4,900 − $11,548)
Finished Goods: $1,850 ($11,548 − $9,698)

3.

Schedule of Unfinished Jobs

Job	Direct Materials	Direct Labor	Factory Overhead	Total
Job No. 103	$3,420	$1,900	$1,330	$ 6,650
Job No. 105	2,100	1,760	1,232	5,092
Balance of Work in Process, March 31				$11,742

4.

Schedule of Completed Jobs

Job No. 104:

Direct materials	$1,000
Direct labor	500
Factory overhead	350
Balance of Finished Goods, March 31	$1,850

SELF-EXAMINATION QUESTIONS

Answers at End of Chapter

Matching

Match each of the following statements with its proper term. Some terms may not be used.

A.	**activity base**
B.	**activity-based costing**
C.	**controller**
D.	**conversion costs**
E.	**cost**
F.	**cost accounting system**
G.	**cost allocation**
H.	**cost of goods sold**
I.	**direct labor cost**
J.	**direct materials cost**
K.	**factory overhead cost**
L.	**financial accounting**
M.	**finished goods inventory**
N.	**finished goods ledger**
O.	**job cost sheet**
P.	**job order cost system**
Q.	**managerial accounting**
R.	**materials inventory**
S.	**materials ledger**
T.	**materials requisitions**
U.	**overapplied factory overhead**
V.	**period costs**

___ 1. The chief management accountant of a division or other segment of a business.

___ 2. The branch of accounting that is concerned with the recording of transactions using generally accepted accounting principles (GAAP) for a business or other economic unit and with a periodic preparation of various statements from such records.

___ 3. The branch of accounting that uses both historical and estimated data in providing information that management uses in conducting daily operations, in planning future operations, and in developing overall business strategies.

___ 4. A payment of cash (or a commitment to pay cash in the future) for the purpose of generating revenues.

___ 5. A system used to accumulate manufacturing costs for decision-making and financial reporting purposes.

___ 6. A type of cost accounting system that provides for a separate record of the cost of each particular quantity of product that passes through the factory.

___ 7. All of the costs of operating the factory except for direct materials and direct labor.

___ 8. The cost of materials that are an integral part of the finished product.

___ 9. Wages of factory workers who are directly involved in converting materials into a finished product.

___ 10. The combination of direct labor and factory overhead costs.

___ 11. The three components of manufacturing cost: direct materials, direct labor, and factory overhead costs.

___ 12. The direct materials costs, the direct labor costs, and the factory overhead costs that have entered into the manufacturing process but are associated with products that have not been finished.

___ 13. An account in the work in process subsidiary ledger in which the costs charged to a particular job order are recorded.

___ 14. The form or electronic transmission used by a manufacturing department to authorize the issuance of materials from the storeroom.

W. **predetermined factory overhead rate**

X. **process cost system**

Y. **product costs**

Z. **receiving report**

AA. **time tickets**

BB. **underapplied factory overhead**

CC. **work in process inventory**

___ 15. The cost of materials that have not yet entered into the manufacturing process.

___ 16. The cost of the manufactured product sold.

___ 17. The subsidiary ledger containing the individual accounts for each type of material.

___ 18. The form or electronic transmission used by the receiving personnel to indicate that materials have been received and inspected.

___ 19. The form on which the amount of time spent by each employee and the labor cost incurred for each individual job, or for factory overhead, are recorded.

___ 20. The process of assigning indirect costs to a cost object, such as a job.

___ 21. A measure of activity that is related to changes in cost and is used in the denominator in calculating the predetermined factory overhead rate to assign factory overhead costs to cost objects.

___ 22. The rate used to apply factory overhead costs to the goods manufactured. The rate is determined from budgeted overhead cost and estimated activity usage data at the beginning of the fiscal period.

___ 23. The amount of factory overhead applied in excess of the actual factory overhead costs incurred for production during a period.

___ 24. An accounting framework based on determining the cost of activities.

___ 25. The subsidiary ledger that contains the individual accounts for each kind of commodity or product produced.

___ 26. The cost of finished products on hand that have not been sold.

___ 27. Those costs that are used up in generating revenue during the current period and that are not involved in the manufacturing process.

___ 28. A type of cost accounting system in which costs are accumulated by department or process within a factory.

Multiple Choice

1. Which of the following best describes the difference between financial and managerial accounting?
   A. Managerial accounting provides information to support decisions, while financial accounting does not.
   B. Managerial accounting is not restricted to generally accepted accounting principles (GAAP), while financial accounting is restricted to GAAP.
   C. Managerial accounting does not result in financial reports, while financial accounting does result in financial reports.
   D. Managerial accounting is concerned solely with the future and does not record events from the past, while financial accounting records only events from past transactions.

2. Which of the following is *not* considered a cost of manufacturing a product?
   A. Direct materials cost　C. Sales salaries
   B. Factory overhead cost　D. Direct labor cost

3. Which of the following costs would be included as part of the factory overhead costs of a microcomputer manufacturer?
   A. The cost of memory chips
   B. Depreciation of testing equipment
   C. Wages of computer assemblers
   D. The cost of disk drives

4. For which of the following would the job order cost system be appropriate?
   A. Antique furniture repair shop
   B. Rubber manufacturer
   C. Coal mining
   D. All of the above

5. If the factory overhead account has a credit balance, factory overhead is said to be:
   A. underapplied　　　C. underabsorbed
   B. overapplied　　　D. in error

CLASS DISCUSSION QUESTIONS

1. What are the major differences between managerial accounting and financial accounting?

2. a. Differentiate between a department with line responsibility and a department with staff responsibility.

   b. In an organization that has a Sales Department and a Personnel Department, among others, which of the two departments has (1) line responsibility and (2) staff responsibility?

3. a. What is the role of the controller in a business organization?

   b. Does the controller have a line or staff responsibility?

4. For a company that produces microcomputers, would memory chips be considered a direct or an indirect materials cost of each microcomputer produced?

5. What three costs make up the cost of manufacturing a product?

6. If the cost of wages paid to employees who are directly involved in converting raw materials into a manufactured end product is not a significant portion of the total product cost, how would the wages cost be classified as to type of manufacturing cost?

7. Name the three inventory accounts for a manufacturing business and describe what each balance represents at the end of an accounting period.

8. For a manufacturer, what is comparable to a merchandising business's cost of merchandise sold?

9. How is product cost information used by managers?

10. a. Name two principal types of cost accounting systems.

   b. Which system provides for a separate record of each particular quantity of product that passes through the factory?

   c. Which system accumulates the costs for each department or process within the factory?

11. What kind of firm would use a job order cost system?

12. **Hewlett-Packard Company** assembles printed circuit boards in which a high volume of standardized units are assembled and tested. Is the job order cost system appropriate in this situation?

13. Which account is used in a job order cost system to accumulate direct materials, direct labor, and factory overhead applied to production costs for individual jobs?

14. What is a job cost sheet?

15. How does the use of the materials requisition help control the issuance of materials from the storeroom?

16. a. Differentiate between the clock card and the time ticket.

   b. Why should the total time reported on an employee's time tickets for a payroll period be compared with the time reported on the employee's clock cards for the same period?

17. What document serves as the basis for posting to (a) the direct materials section of the job cost sheet and (b) the direct labor section of the job cost sheet?

18. Describe the source of the data for debiting Work in Process for (a) direct materials, (b) direct labor, and (c) factory overhead.

19. Discuss how the predetermined factory overhead rate can be used in job order cost accounting to assist management in pricing jobs.

20. a. How is a predetermined factory overhead rate calculated?

   b. Name three common bases used in calculating the rate.

21. a. What is (1) overapplied factory overhead and (2) underapplied factory overhead?

   b. If the factory overhead account has a debit balance, was factory overhead under-applied or overapplied?

   c. If the factory overhead account has a credit balance at the end of the first month of the fiscal year, where will the amount of this balance be reported on the interim balance sheet?

22. At the end of the fiscal year, there was a relatively minor balance in the factory overhead account. What procedure can be used for disposing of the balance in the account?

23. What account is the controlling account for (a) the materials ledger, (b) the job cost sheets, and (c) the finished goods ledger or stock ledger?

24. What is the difference between a product cost and a period cost?

25. How can job cost information be used to identify cost improvement opportunities?

26. What account is debited for completed service jobs?

A TRADITION OF INNOVATION

Innovation. Motivation. Results.

Thank you for joining the thousands of other students who have achieved outstanding results using this innovative text. To help you even further, we have developed incredible resources to make learning accounting even easier. You can purchase these supplements by visiting

http://warren.swcollege.com.

Here are numerous resources to help you get the results you want:

Personal WebTutor Advantage
GO TO THIS URL TO PURCHASE THIS PRODUCT:
pwt.swcollege.com

- Automatic and immediate feedback from quizzes and exams.
- Interactive, multimedia rich explanation of concepts.
- Online exercises that reinforce what you've learned.
- Flashcards that include audio support.
- Greater interaction and involvement through online discussion forums.

General Ledger Software
0-324-05462-9

- This software package teaches you the basics of a computerized accounting system in an easy-to-use environment.
- You will get hints and tips completing end-of-chapter problems.
- You will get immediate feedback to determine if you have done the problems correctly.

Personal Trainer
FINANCIAL & MANAGERIAL ACCOUNTING
0-324-12384-1
CORPORATE FINANCIAL ACCOUNTING
0-324-12381-7
MANAGERIAL ACCOUNTING
0-324-12377-9

- This online tutorial will help you complete the end-of-chapter exercises from the textbook, with hints.
- You will get immediate feedback to determine if you have done the exercises correctly.
- This product will not only save you time on your homework but will help you learn the concepts.

Spreadsheet Applications Software
CORPORATE FINANCIAL 0-324-05464-5
MANAGERIAL 0-324-05465-3

- You will learn how Excel is used in accounting situations.

Study Guide
CORPORATE FINANCIAL 0-324-05460-2
MANAGERIAL 0-324-05461-0

- This guide will give you quiz and test hints.
- You can practice the concepts you learn through numerous multiple choice, fill-in-the-blank, true-false questions, and exercises, all with solutions.

Working Papers
CORPORATE FINANCIAL 0-324-05456-4
MANAGERIAL 0-324-05457-2

- This supplement contains forms that help you organize your solutions.

Working Papers Plus
CORPORATE FINANCIAL 0-324-05458-0
MANAGERIAL 0-324-05459-9

- This special edition of Working Papers integrates the Working Papers forms with exercises and selected problems from the text.

INTACCT
(Internet Accounting Tutor)
FINANCIAL 0-324-01592-5
MANAGERIAL 0-324-01613-1
rama.swcollege.com

- This product, designed to be used with any introductory accounting textbook, will give you reinforcement of key accounting concepts in an interactive format.
- You can see how to apply the concepts with practice problems and demonstration problems.
- You can email your INTACCT homework problems to your instructor to grade.

Save on these products by purchasing online a

http://warren.swcollege.com

EXERCISES

Exercise 1–1
Classify costs as materials, labor, or factory overhead

Objective 3

Indicate whether each of the following costs of a furniture manufacturer would be classified as direct materials cost, direct labor cost, or factory overhead cost:

a. Supervisor salaries
b. Saw blades
c. Furniture hardware
d. Wages of wood cutters
e. Wood
f. Assembly wages
g. Depreciation on woodworking machinery
h. Inspector salaries

Exercise 1–2
Classify costs as materials, labor, or factory overhead

Objective 3

Indicate whether each of the following costs of the Procter & Gamble Company would be classified as direct materials cost, direct labor cost, or factory overhead cost:

a. Salary of process engineers
b. Depreciation on disposable diaper converting machines
c. Scents and fragrances
d. Wages of Making Department employees
e. Pulp for towel and tissue products
f. Plant manager salary of the Lima, Ohio, liquid soap plant
g. Packaging materials
h. Maintenance supplies
i. Wages paid to Packing Department employees
j. Depreciation on the St. Bernard (Cincinnati) soap plant

Exercise 1–3
Classify costs as product or period costs

Objectives 3, 5

Classify the following costs for Ford Motor Company as either a product cost or a period cost.

a. Steel
b. Stamping Department employee wages
c. Utility costs used in executive building
d. Travel costs used by sales personnel
e. Shipping costs
f. Property taxes on Kansas City, Missouri, assembly plant
g. Glass
h. Maintenance supplies
i. Depreciation on Atlanta, Georgia, assembly plant
j. Plant manager's salary
k. CEO's salary
l. Depreciation of Dearborn, Michigan, executive building
m. Salary of marketing executive
n. Assembly employee wages
o. Tires
p. Advertising

Exercise 1–4
Classify factory overhead costs

Objective 3

Which of the following items are properly classified as part of factory overhead for John Deere & Co.?

a. Factory supplies used in the Loudon, Tennessee, skid loader factory
b. Consultant fees for surveying production employee morale
c. Interest expense on debt
d. Amortization of patents on a new welding process
e. Sales incentive fees to dealers
f. Steel plate
g. Chief financial officer's salary
h. Property taxes on Ankeny, Iowa, components plant
i. Depreciation on Moline, Illinois, headquarters building
j. Plant manager's salary at Greenville, Tennessee, turf care products plant

Exercise 1–5
Concepts and terminology
Objectives 3, 5

From the choices presented in the parentheses, choose the appropriate term for completing each of the following sentences:

a.   An example of factory overhead is (plant depreciation, sales office depreciation).
b.   Materials that are an integral part of the manufactured product are classified as (direct materials, materials inventory).
c.   The balance sheet of a manufacturer would include an account for (cost of goods sold, work in process inventory).
d.   Advertising expenses are usually viewed as (period, product) costs.
e.   Payments of cash or its equivalent or the commitment to pay cash in the future for the purpose of generating revenues are (costs, expenses).
f.   Implementing automatic factory robotics equipment normally (increases, decreases) the factory overhead component of product costs.
g.   Direct labor costs combined with factory overhead costs are called (product, conversion) costs.
h.   The wages of an assembly worker are normally considered a (period, product) cost.

Exercise 1–6
Transactions in a job order cost system
Objective 5

Five selected transactions for the current month are indicated by letters in the following T accounts in a job order cost accounting system:

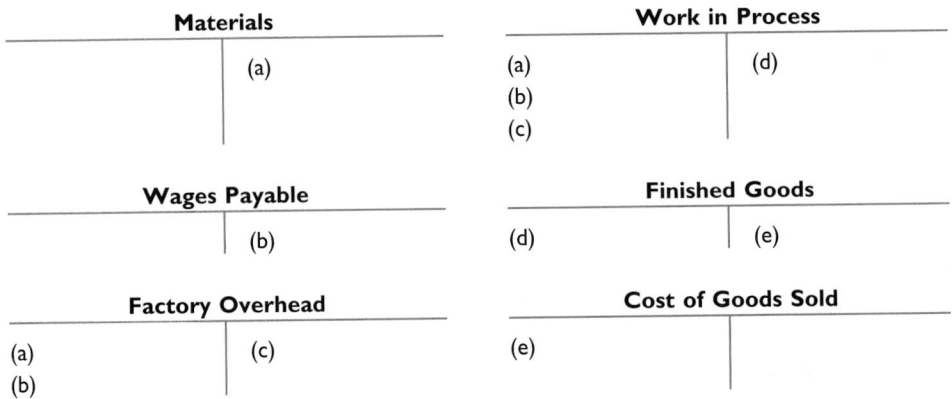

Describe each of the five transactions.

Exercise 1–7
Cost flow relationships
Objective 5

✓ c. $343,000

The following information is available for the first month of operations of Asian Arts Inc., a manufacturer of craft items:

Sales	$710,000
Gross profit	220,000
Indirect labor	15,000
Indirect materials	25,000
Other factory overhead	12,000
Materials purchased	180,000
Total manufacturing costs for the period	530,000
Materials inventory, end of period	20,000

Using the above information, determine the following missing amounts:

a.   Cost of goods sold
b.   Direct materials cost
c.   Direct labor cost

Exercise 1–8
Cost of materials issuances by FIFO method
Objective 5

An incomplete subsidiary ledger of wire cable for May is as follows:

SPREADSHEET

✓ b. $1,100

	RECEIVED			ISSUED			BALANCE			
Receiving Report Number	Quantity	Unit Price	Materials Requisition Number	Quantity	Amount	Date	Quantity	Amount	Unit Price
						May 1	150	$2,700	$18.00
23	210	$20.00				May 3			
			104	250		May 5			
29	140	22.00				May 19			
			117	200		May 25			

a. Complete the materials issuances and balances for the wire cable subsidiary ledger under FIFO.
b. Determine the balance of wire cable at the end of May.
c. Journalize the summary entry to transfer materials to work in process.
d. ✏️ Explain how the materials ledger might be used as an aid in maintaining inventory quantities on hand.

Exercise 1–9
Entry for issuing materials
Objective 5

Materials issued for the current month are as follows:

Requisition No.	Material	Job No.	Amount
711	Steel	511	$ 9,500
712	Copper	514	6,300
713	Plastic	526	900
714	Abrasives	Indirect	150
715	Titanium alloy	533	36,400

Journalize the entry to record the issuance of materials.

Exercise 1–10
Entries for materials
Objective 5

✓ c. Fabric, $97,600

Hermitage Furniture Company (HFC) manufactures furniture. HFC uses a job order cost system. Balances on June 1 from the materials ledger are as follows:

Fabric	$45,800
Polyester filling	9,200
Lumber	95,800
Glue	2,200

The materials purchased during June are summarized from the receiving reports as follows:

Fabric	$568,500
Polyester filling	165,500
Lumber	842,200
Glue	19,100

Materials were requisitioned to individual jobs as follows:

	Fabric	Polyester Filling	Lumber	Glue	Total
Job 11	$276,700	$ 85,400	$454,800		$ 816,900
Job 12	35,800	12,300	78,900		127,000
Job 13	204,200	66,300	340,800		611,300
Factory overhead—indirect materials				$17,900	17,900
Total	$516,700	$164,000	$874,500	$17,900	$1,573,100

The glue is not a significant cost, so it is treated as indirect materials (factory overhead).

a. Journalize the entry to record the purchase of materials in June.
b. Journalize the entry to record the requisition of materials in June.
c. Determine the June 30 balances that would be shown in the materials ledger accounts.

Exercise 1–11
Entry for factory labor costs

Objective 5

A summary of the time tickets for the current month follows:

Job No.	Amount	Job No.	Amount
101	$1,540	141	$ 1,540
122	1,610	Indirect labor	10,100
133	870	143	3,240
139	3,550	147	2,480

Journalize the entry to record the factory labor costs.

Exercise 1–12
Entries for direct labor and factory overhead

Objective 5

Colonial Homes Inc. manufactures log homes. Colonial uses a job order cost system. The time tickets from September jobs are summarized below.

Job 502	$1,680
Job 503	784
Job 504	490
Job 505	1,078
Factory supervision	1,670

Factory overhead is applied to jobs on the basis of a predetermined overhead rate of $22 per direct labor hour. The direct labor rate is $14 per hour.

a. Journalize the entry to record the factory labor costs.
b. Journalize the entry to apply factory overhead to production for September.

Exercise 1–13
Factory overhead rates, entries, and account balance

Objective 5

✓ b. $25 per direct labor hour

Digital Pictures Inc. operates two factories. The company applies factory overhead to jobs on the basis of machine hours in Factory 1 and on the basis of direct labor hours in Factory 2. Estimated factory overhead costs, direct labor hours, and machine hours are as follows:

	Factory 1	Factory 2
Estimated factory overhead cost for fiscal year beginning April 1	$270,000	$235,000
Estimated direct labor hours for year		9,400
Estimated machine hours for year	15,000	
Actual factory overhead costs for April	$21,900	$19,400
Actual direct labor hours for April		770
Actual machine hours for April	1,260	

a. Determine the factory overhead rate for Factory 1.
b. Determine the factory overhead rate for Factory 2.
c. Journalize the entries to apply factory overhead to production in each factory for April.
d. Determine the balances of the factory accounts for each factory as of April 30, and indicate whether the amounts represent overapplied or underapplied factory overhead.

Exercise 1–14
Predetermined factory overhead rate

Objective 5

The AutoCare Body Shop uses a job order cost system to determine the cost of performing automotive body and repair work. Estimated costs and expenses for the coming period are as follows:

Auto parts	$ 520,000
Shop direct labor	384,000
Shop and repair equipment depreciation	14,800
Shop supervisor salaries	82,400
Shop property tax	23,200
Shop supplies	12,400
Advertising expense	15,200
Administrative office salaries	54,800
Administrative office depreciation expense	10,000
Total costs and expenses	$1,116,800

The average shop direct labor rate is $12 per hour.

Determine the predetermined shop overhead rate per direct labor hour.

Exercise 1–15

Predetermined factory overhead rate

Objective 5

✓ a. $175 per hour

Elk City Medical Center has a single operating room that is used by local physicians to perform surgical procedures. The cost of using the operating room is accumulated by each patient procedure and includes the direct materials costs (drugs and medical devices), physician surgical time, and operating room overhead. On January 1 of the current year, the annual operating room overhead is estimated to be:

Disposable supplies	$ 65,000
Depreciation expense	22,000
Utilities	16,300
Nurse salaries	168,800
Technician wages	95,400
Total operating room overhead	$367,500

The overhead costs will be assigned to procedures based on the number of surgical room hours. The Medical Center expects to use the operating room an average of seven hours per day, six days per week. In addition, the operating room will be shut down two weeks per year for general repairs.

a. Determine the predetermined operating room overhead rate for the year.

b. LeVar Wilson had a 3-hour procedure on January 10. How much operating room overhead would be charged to his procedure, using the rate determined in (a)?

c. During January, the operating room was used 190 hours. The actual overhead costs incurred for January were $31,800. Determine the overhead under- or overapplied for the period.

Exercise 1–16

Entry for jobs completed; cost of unfinished jobs

Objective 5

✓ b. $27,500

The following account appears in the ledger after only part of the postings have been completed for March:

Work in Process	
Balance, March 1	$ 19,200
Direct materials	121,400
Direct labor	52,500
Factory overhead	74,600

Jobs finished during March are summarized as follows:

Job 320	$52,100	Job 327	$28,400
Job 326	72,500	Job 350	87,200

a. Journalize the entry to record the jobs completed.

b. Determine the cost of the unfinished jobs at March 31.

Exercise 1–17
Entries for factory costs and jobs completed

Objective 5

✓ d. $22,570

Palm Printing Company began manufacturing operations on May 1. Jobs 1 and 2 were completed during the month, and all costs applicable to them were recorded on the related cost sheets. Jobs 3 and 4 are still in process at the end of the month, and all applicable costs except factory overhead have been recorded on the related cost sheets. In addition to the materials and labor charged directly to the jobs, $960 of indirect materials and $6,300 of indirect labor were used during the month. The cost sheets for the four jobs entering production during the month are as follows, in summary form:

Job 1	
Direct materials	5,400
Direct labor	1,250
Factory overhead	1,500
Total	8,150

Job 2	
Direct materials	9,800
Direct labor	2,100
Factory overhead	2,520
Total	14,420

Job 3	
Direct materials	7,200
Direct labor	1,600
Factory overhead	

Job 4	
Direct materials	1,200
Direct labor	350
Factory overhead	

Journalize the summary entry to record each of the following operations for May (one entry for each operation):

a. Direct and indirect materials used.
b. Direct and indirect labor used.
c. Factory overhead applied (a single overhead rate is used based on direct labor *cost*).
d. Completion of Jobs 1 and 2.

Exercise 1–18
Financial statements of a manufacturing firm

Objective 5

✓ a. Income from operations, $97,100

The following events took place for Comet Shoe Company during May 2003, the first month of operations as a producer of athletic shoes:

• Purchased $124,000 of materials.
• Used $111,300 of direct materials in production.
• Incurred $84,700 of direct labor wages.
• Applied factory overhead at a rate of 80% of direct labor cost.
• Transferred $257,000 of work in process to finished goods.
• Sold goods with a cost of $246,500.
• Sold goods for $450,000.
• Incurred $65,000 of selling expenses.
• Incurred $41,400 of administrative expenses.

a. Prepare the May income statement for Comet Shoe Company. Assume that Comet Shoe uses the perpetual inventory method.
b. Determine the inventory balances at the end of the first month of operations.

Exercise 1–19
Decision making with job order costs

Objective 6

Yokohama Manufacturing Company is a job shop. The management of Yokohama uses the cost information from the job sheets to assess their cost performance. Information on the total cost, product type, and quantity of items produced is as follows:

Date	Job No.	Quantity	Product	Amount
Jan. 1	1	400	XXY	$ 4,800
Jan. 29	26	1,200	AAB	18,000
Feb. 15	43	600	AAB	9,600
Mar. 10	64	450	XXY	6,300
Mar. 31	75	900	MM	19,800
May 10	91	1,000	MM	21,000
June 20	104	400	XXY	6,800
Aug. 2	112	1,500	MM	25,500
Sept. 20	114	400	AAB	6,000
Nov. 1	126	600	XXY	10,800
Dec. 3	133	850	MM	12,750

a. Develop a graph for *each* product (three graphs), with Job No. (in date order) on the horizontal axis and unit cost on the vertical axis. Use this information to determine Yokohama's cost performance over time for the three products.

b. ✏️➤ What additional information would you require to investigate Yokohama's cost performance more precisely?

Exercise 1–20
Decision making with job order costs
Objective 6

Brass Plaque Company uses a job order cost system for determining the cost to manufacture award products (plaques and trophies). Among the company's products is an engraved plaque that is awarded to participants who complete an executive education program at a local university. The company sells the plaque to the university for $12 each.

Each plaque has a brass plate engraved with the name of the participant. Engraving requires approximately 10 minutes per name. Improperly engraved names must be redone. The plate is screwed to a walnut backboard. This assembly takes approximately 5 minutes per unit. Improper assembly must be redone using a new walnut backboard.

During the first half of the year, the university had two separate executive education classes. The job cost sheets for the two separate jobs indicated the following information:

Job 223   **March 28**

	Cost per Unit	Units	Job Cost
Direct materials:			
Wood	$1.20/unit	36 units	$ 43.20
Brass	1.50/unit	36 units	54.00
Engraving labor	12.00/hr.	6.0 hrs.	72.00
Assembly labor	12.00/hr.	3.0 hrs.	36.00
Factory overhead	20.00/hr.	9.0 hrs.	180.00
			$385.20
Plaques shipped			÷ 36
Cost per plaque			$ 10.70

Job 275   **May 16**

	Cost per Unit	Units	Job Cost
Direct materials:			
Wood	$1.20/unit	42 units	$ 50.40
Brass	1.50/unit	45 units	67.50
Engraving labor	12.00/hr.	7.5 hrs.	90.00
Assembly labor	12.00/hr.	3.5 hrs.	42.00
Factory overhead	20.00/hr.	11.0 hrs.	220.00
			$469.90
Plaques shipped			÷ 40
Cost per plaque			$ 11.75

a. Why did the cost per plaque increase from $10.70 to $11.75?

b. What improvements would you recommend for Brass Plaque Company?

Exercise 1–21
Job order cost accounting entries for a service business
Objective 7

New Media Solutions provides advertising services for clients across the nation. New Media Solutions is presently working on four projects, each for a different client. New Media Solutions accumulates costs for each account (client) on the basis of both direct costs and allocated indirect costs. The direct costs include the charged time of professional personnel and media purchases (air time and ad space). Overhead is allocated to each project as a percentage of media purchases. The predetermined overhead rate is 30% of media purchases.

On March 1, the four advertising projects had the following accumulated costs:

March 1 Balances	
Stone Beverage	$120,000
Hampshire Bank	160,000
All-Right Rentals	60,000
SleepEzz Hotel	12,000

✓ d. Dr. Cost of Services, $665,000

During March, New Media Solutions incurred the following direct labor and media purchase costs related to preparing advertising for each of the four accounts:

	Direct Labor	Media Purchases
Stone Beverage	$ 48,000	$150,000
Hampshire Bank	25,000	90,000
All-Right Rentals	67,000	105,000
SleepEzz Hotel	70,000	155,000
Total	$210,000	$500,000

At the end of March, both the Stone Beverage and Hampshire Bank campaigns were completed. The cost of completed campaigns are debited to the cost of services account.
Journalize the summary entry to record each of the following for the month:

a.   Direct labor costs
b.   Media purchases
c.   Overhead applied
d.   Completion of Stone Beverage and Hampshire Bank campaigns

PROBLEMS SERIES A

Problem 1–1A

Classify costs

Objectives 3, 5

The following is a list of costs that were incurred in the production and sale of boats:

a.   Steering wheels.
b.   Commissions to sales representatives, based upon the number of boats sold.
c.   Wood paneling for use in interior boat trim.
d.   Straight-line depreciation on factory equipment.
e.   Oil to lubricate factory equipment.
f.   Hourly wages of assembly-line workers.
g.   Cost of paving the employee parking lot.
h.   Masks for use by sanders in smoothing boat hulls.
i.   Cost of normal scrap from defective hulls.
j.   Premiums on business interruption insurance in case of a natural disaster.
k.   Yearly cost of maintenance contract for robotics equipment.
l.   Power used by sanding equipment.
m.   Cost of metal hardware for boats, such as ornaments and tie-down grasps.
n.   Fiberglass for producing the boat hull.
o.   Salary of president of company.
p.   Paint for boats.
q.   Legal department costs for the year.
r.   Annual fee for Jim Bo Wilks, a famous fisherman, to promote the boats.
s.   Decals for boat hulls.
t.   Salary of shop supervisor.
u.   Executive end-of-year bonuses.
v.   Cost of electrical wiring for boats.
w.   Navigation and fishing instruments for boats.
x.   Memberships for key executives in the Bass World Association.
y.   Cost of boat for "grand prize" promotion in local bass tournament.
z.   Special advertising campaign in *Bass World*.

Instructions

Classify each cost as either a product cost or a period cost. Indicate whether each product cost is a direct materials cost, a direct labor cost, or a factory overhead cost. Indicate whether each period cost is a selling expense or an administrative expense. Use the following tabular headings for your answer, placing an "X" in the appropriate column.

Product Costs			Period Costs	
Direct Materials Cost	Direct Labor Cost	Factory Overhead Cost	Selling Expense	Admin. Expense

Problem 1–2A

Entries for costs in a job order cost system

Objective 5

GENERAL LEDGER

Beachwear Apparel Company uses a job order cost system. The following data summarize the operations related to production for June:

a. Materials purchased on account, $107,600.
b. Materials requisitioned, $108,600, of which $3,200 was for general factory use.
c. Factory labor used, $134,200, of which $18,300 was factory overhead.
d. Other costs incurred on account were for factory overhead, $66,600; selling expenses, $39,600; and administrative expenses, $29,000.
e. Prepaid expenses expired for factory overhead were $2,400; for selling expenses, $800; and for administrative expenses, $650.
f. Depreciation of factory equipment was $11,200; of office equipment, $8,400; and of store equipment, $1,500.
g. Factory overhead costs applied to jobs, $102,500.
h. Jobs completed, $320,600.
i. Cost of goods sold, $316,400.

Instructions

Journalize the entries to record the summarized operations.

Problem 1–3A

Entries and schedules for unfinished jobs and completed jobs

Objective 5

GENERAL LEDGER

✓ 3. Work in Process balance, $87,700

Industrial Fittings Inc. uses a job order cost system. The following data summarize the operations related to production for June, 2003, the first month of operations:

a. Materials purchased on account, $150,500.
b. Materials requisitioned and factory labor used:

Job	Materials	Factory Labor
No. 601	$32,400	$19,300
No. 602	18,500	14,200
No. 603	21,300	15,200
No. 604	10,400	8,900
No. 605	15,200	11,300
No. 606	28,400	17,500
For general factory use	5,300	32,400

c. Factory overhead costs incurred on account, $27,500.
d. Depreciation of machinery and equipment, $5,100.
e. The factory overhead rate is $50 per machine hour. Machine hours used:

Job	Machine Hours
No. 601	320
No. 602	205
No. 603	225
No. 604	150
No. 605	180
No. 606	300
Total	1,380

f. Jobs completed: 601, 602, 603, and 605.
g. Jobs were shipped and customers were billed as follows: Job 601, $83,200; Job 602, $54,200; Job 605, $49,100.

Instructions

1. Journalize the entries to record the summarized operations.
2. Post the appropriate entries to T accounts for Work in Process and Finished Goods, using the identifying letters as dates. Insert memorandum account balances as of the end of the month.
3. Prepare a schedule of unfinished jobs to support the balance in the work in process account.
4. Prepare a schedule of completed jobs on hand to support the balance in the finished goods account.

If the working papers correlating with the textbook are not used, omit Problem 1–4A.

Problem 1–4A

Job order cost sheet

Objectives 5, 6

Nathan Hale Furniture Company refinishes and reupholsters furniture. Nathan Hale uses a job order cost system. When a prospective customer asks for a price quote on a job, the estimated cost data are inserted on an unnumbered job cost sheet. If the offer is accepted, a number is assigned to the job, and the costs incurred are recorded in the usual manner on the job cost sheet. After the job is completed, reasons for the variances between the estimated and actual costs are noted on the sheet. The data are then available to management in evaluating the efficiency of operations and in preparing quotes on future jobs. On September 1, an estimate of $910.00 for reupholstering two chairs and a couch was given to Kendra Brown. The estimate was based on the following data:

Estimated direct materials:	
14 meters at $18 per meter	$252.00
Estimated direct labor:	
20 hours at $16 per hour	320.00
Estimated factory overhead (40% of direct labor cost)	128.00
Total estimated costs	$700.00
Markup (30% of production costs)	210.00
Total estimate	$910.00

On September 4, the chairs and couch were picked up from the residence of Kendra Brown, 1244 Merchants Drive, Columbus, with a commitment to return them on October 13. The job was completed on October 10.

The related materials requisitions and time tickets are summarized as follows:

Materials Requisition No.	Description	Amount
3480	9 meters at $18	$162
3492	8 meters at $18	144

Time Ticket No.	Description	Amount
H143	12 hours at $16	$192
H151	10 hours at $16	160

Instructions

1. Complete that portion of the job order cost sheet that would be prepared when the estimate is given to the customer.
2. ▬▶ Assign number 00-10-23 to the job, record the costs incurred, and complete the job order cost sheet. Comment on the reasons for the variances between actual costs and estimated costs. For this purpose, assume that 3 meters of materials were spoiled, the factory overhead rate has been proved to be satisfactory, and an inexperienced employee performed the work.

Problem 1–5A

Analyzing manufacturing cost accounts

Objective 5

Sawtooth Golf Equipment Company manufactures golf club sets in a wide variety of lengths and weights. The following incomplete ledger accounts refer to transactions that are summarized for August:

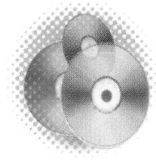

SPREADSHEET

✓ G. $215,865

Materials

Aug.	1	Balance	8,000	Aug. 31	Requisitions		(A)
	31	Purchases	100,000				

Work in Process

Aug.	1	Balance	(B)	Aug. 31	Completed jobs	(F)
	31	Materials	(C)			
	31	Direct labor	(D)			
	31	Factory overhead applied	(E)			

Finished Goods

Aug.	1	Balance	0	Aug. 31	Cost of goods sold	(G)
	31	Completed jobs	(F)			

Wages Payable

				Aug. 31	Wages incurred	90,000

Factory Overhead

Aug.	1	Balance	2,000	Aug. 31	Factory overhead applied	(E)
	31	Indirect labor	(H)			
	31	Indirect materials	2,500			
	31	Other overhead	35,000			

In addition, the following information is available:

a. Materials and direct labor were applied to six jobs in August:

Job No.	Style	Quantity	Direct Materials	Direct Labor
Job 111	DL-8	110	$ 20,380	$15,600
Job 112	DL-18	120	25,450	19,500
Job 113	DL-11	50	14,120	11,400
Job 114	SL-101	150	9,400	4,200
Job 115	SL-110	70	27,500	24,300
Job 116	DL-14	75	4,000	3,000
Total		575	$100,850	$78,000

b. Factory overhead is applied to each job at a rate of 70% of direct labor cost.
c. The August 1 Work in Process balance consisted of two jobs, as follows:

Job No.	Style	Work in Process, Aug. 1
Job 111	DL-8	$18,000
Job 112	DL-18	35,000
Total		$53,000

d. Customer jobs completed and units sold in August were as follows:

Job No.	Style	Completed in August	Units Sold in August
Job 111	DL-8	X	90
Job 112	DL-18	X	105
Job 113	DL-11	X	40

Job No.	Style	Completed in August	Units Sold in August
Job 114	SL-101		0
Job 115	SL-110	X	55
Job 116	DL-14		0

Instructions

1. Determine the missing amounts associated with each letter. Provide supporting calculations by completing a table with the following headings:

Job No.	Quantity	Aug. 1 Work in Process	Direct Materials	Direct Labor	Factory Overhead	Total Cost	Unit Cost	Units Sold	Cost of Goods Sold

2. Determine the August 31 balances for each of the inventory accounts and factory overhead.

Problem 1–6A

Flow of costs and income statement

Objective 5

✓ 1. Income from operations, $1,335,200

Advent Technologies Inc. (AT) is a designer, manufacturer, and distributor of software for microcomputers. A new product, *Wordsmith 2003*, was released for production and distribution in early 2003. In January, $450,000 was spent to design print advertisement. For the first six months of 2003, the company spent $1,500,000 promoting *Wordsmith 2003* in computer trade magazines. The product was ready for manufacture on January 21, 2003.

AT uses a job order cost system to accumulate costs associated with each software title. Direct materials unit costs are:

Blank disk	$ 8.00
Packaging	5.00
Manual	10.00
Total	$23.00

The actual production process for the software product is fairly straightforward. First, blank disks are brought to a disk-copying machine. The copying machine requires 1 hour per 1,000 disks.

After the program is copied onto the disk, the disk is brought to assembly, where assembly personnel pack the disk and manual for shipping. The direct labor cost for this work is $0.80 per unit.

The completed packages are then sold to retail outlets through a sales force. The sales force is compensated by a 10% commission on the wholesale price for all sales. In addition, salespersons are trained at a cost of $500 per individual.

Total completed production was 30,000 units during the year. Other information is as follows:

Number of salespersons	1,500
Number of software units sold in 2003	26,000
Wholesale price per unit	$200

Factory overhead cost is applied to jobs at the rate of $1,000 per copy machine hour. There were an additional 500 copied CDs, packaging, and manuals waiting to be assembled on December 31, 2003.

Instructions

1. Prepare an annual income statement for the *Wordsmith 2003* product, including supporting calculations, from the information above.
2. Determine the balances in the finished goods and work in process inventory for the *Wordsmith 2003* product on December 31, 2003.

PROBLEMS SERIES B

Problem 1–1B
Classify costs

Objectives 3, 5

The following is a list of costs that were incurred in the production and sale of lawn mowers.

a. Straight-line depreciation on the robotics machinery used to manufacture the lawn mowers.
b. Maintenance costs for new factory robotics equipment, based upon hours of usage.
c. Attorney fees for drafting a new lease for headquarters offices.
d. Engine oil used in mower engines prior to shipment.
e. Cash paid to outside firm for janitorial services for factory.
f. Rivets, bolts, and other fasteners used in lawn mowers.
g. Payroll taxes on hourly assembly-line employees.
h. Filter for spray gun used to paint the lawn mowers.
i. Cost of boxes used in storing and shipping lawn mowers.
j. Premiums on insurance policy for factory buildings.
k. Gasoline engines used for lawn mowers.
l. Salary of factory supervisor.
m. Tires for lawn mowers.
n. Cost of advertising in a national magazine.
o. Plastic for outside housing of lawn mowers.
p. Salary of quality control supervisor who inspects each lawn mower before it is shipped.
q. Telephone charges for controller's office.
r. Lawn mower throttle controls.
s. Steel used in producing the lawn mowers.
t. Commissions paid to sales representatives, based upon the number of lawn mowers sold.
u. Electricity used to run the robotics machinery.
v. Factory cafeteria cashier's wages.
w. Property taxes on the factory building and equipment.
x. Salary of vice-president of marketing.
y. Hourly wages of operators of robotics machinery used in production.
z. License fees for use of patent for lawn mower blade, based upon the number of lawn mowers produced.

Instructions

Classify each cost as either a product cost or a period cost. Indicate whether each product cost is a direct materials cost, a direct labor cost, or a factory overhead cost. Indicate whether each period cost is a selling expense or an administrative expense. Use the following tabular headings for your answer, placing an "X" in the appropriate column.

Product Costs			Period Costs	
Direct Materials Cost	Direct Labor Cost	Factory Overhead Cost	Selling Expense	Admin. Expense

Problem 1–2B
Entries for costs in a job order cost system

Objective 5

GENERAL LEDGER

Hilton Industries Inc. uses a job order cost system. The following data summarize the operations related to production for June:

a. Materials purchased on account, $116,500.
b. Materials requisitioned, $109,200, of which $2,600 was for general factory use.
c. Factory labor used, $205,000, of which $24,500 was factory overhead.
d. Other costs incurred on account were for factory overhead, $95,800; selling expenses, $57,800; and administrative expenses, $44,400.
e. Prepaid expenses expired for factory overhead were $1,200; for selling expenses, $350; and for administrative expenses, $300.
f. Depreciation of factory equipment was $6,000; of office equipment, $1,600; and of store equipment, $1,700.
g. Factory overhead costs applied to jobs, $130,000.
h. Jobs completed, $402,500.
i. Cost of goods sold, $405,100.

Instructions

Journalize the entries to record the summarized operations.

Problem 1–3B

Entries and schedules for unfinished jobs and completed jobs

Objective 5

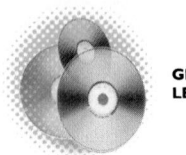

GENERAL LEDGER

✓ 3. Work in Process balance, $5,720

Creative Graphics Printing Company uses a job order cost system. The following data summarize the operations related to production for April, 2003, the first month of operations:

a. Materials purchased on account, $8,200.
b. Materials requisitioned and factory labor used:

Job	Materials	Factory Labor
No. 101	$1,340	$ 950
No. 102	950	740
No. 103	2,310	1,640
No. 104	520	540
No. 105	690	525
No. 106	1,420	1,080
For general factory use	380	2,310

c. Factory overhead costs incurred on account, $4,100.
d. Depreciation of machinery and equipment, $900.
e. The factory overhead rate is $120 per machine hour. Machine hours used:

Job	Machine Hours
No. 101	11.0
No. 102	9.5
No. 103	20.0
No. 104	5.5
No. 105	7.0
No. 106	12.5
Total	65.5

f. Jobs completed: 101, 102, 103, and 105.
g. Jobs were shipped and customers were billed as follows: Job 101, $5,000; Job 102, $3,900; Job 103, $10,500.

Instructions

1. Journalize the entries to record the summarized operations.
2. Post the appropriate entries to T accounts for Work in Process and Finished Goods, using the identifying letters as dates. Insert memorandum account balances as of the end of the month.
3. Prepare a schedule of unfinished jobs to support the balance in the work in process account.
4. Prepare a schedule of completed jobs on hand to support the balance in the finished goods account.

If the working papers correlating with the textbook are not used, omit Problem 1–4B.

Problem 1–4B

Job order cost sheet

Objectives 5, 6

Olde English Furniture Company refinishes and reupholsters furniture. Olde English uses a job order cost system. When a prospective customer asks for a price quote on a job, the estimated cost data are inserted on an unnumbered job cost sheet. If the offer is accepted, a number is assigned to the job, and the costs incurred are recorded in the usual manner on the job cost sheet. After the job is completed, reasons for the variances between the estimated and actual costs are noted on the sheet. The data are then available to management in evaluating the efficiency of operations and in preparing quotes on future jobs. On June 10, an estimate of $567.84 for reupholstering a chair and couch was given to Jamal Price. The estimate was based on the following data:

Estimated direct materials:

14 meters at $20 per meter $280.00

Estimated direct labor:

8 hours at $14 per hour 112.00

Estimated factory overhead (40% of direct labor cost) 44.80

Total estimated costs $436.80

Markup (30% of production costs) 131.04

Total estimate $567.84

On June 16, the chair and couch were picked up from the residence of Jamal Price, 1900 Peachtree, Atlanta, with a commitment to return it on July 16. The job was completed on July 11.

The related materials requisitions and time tickets are summarized as follows:

Materials Requisition No.	Description	Amount
U642	9 meters at $20	$180
U651	7 meters at $20	140

Time Ticket No.	Description	Amount
1519	5 hours at $14	$ 70
1520	5 hours at $14	70

Instructions

1. Complete that portion of the job order cost sheet that would be prepared when the estimate is given to the customer.

2. Assign number 00-8-38 to the job, record the costs incurred, and complete the job order cost sheet. Comment on the reasons for the variances between actual costs and estimated costs. For this purpose, assume that two meters of materials were spoiled, the factory overhead rate has been proved to be satisfactory, and an inexperienced employee performed the work.

Problem 1–5B

Analyzing manufacturing cost accounts

Objective 5

SPREADSHEET

✓ G. $253,300

Swiss Ski Company manufactures snow skis in a wide variety of lengths and styles. The following incomplete ledger accounts refer to transactions that are summarized for January:

Materials

Jan. 1	Balance	10,000	Jan. 31	Requisitions	(A)
31	Purchases	190,000			

Work in Process

Jan. 1	Balance	(B)	Jan. 31	Completed jobs	(F)
31	Materials	(C)			
31	Direct labor	(D)			
31	Factory overhead applied	(E)			

Finished Goods

Jan. 1	Balance	0	Jan. 31	Cost of goods sold	(G)
31	Completed jobs	(F)			

Wages Payable

		Jan. 31	Wages incurred	100,000

Factory Overhead

Jan. 1	Balance	4,000	Jan. 31	Factory overhead applied	(E)
31	Indirect labor	(H)			
31	Indirect materials	3,000			
31	Other overhead	105,000			

In addition, the following information is available:

a. Materials and direct labor were applied to six jobs in January:

Job No.	Style	Quantity	Direct Materials	Direct Labor
Job 51	V-100	240	$ 28,000	$14,800
Job 52	V-200	260	40,300	18,500
Job 53	V-500	200	19,000	11,500
Job 54	A-200	220	27,500	12,500
Job 55	V-400	280	42,300	28,500
Job 56	A-100	100	10,000	5,400
Total		1,300	$167,100	$91,200

b. Factory overhead is applied to each job at a rate of 120% of direct labor cost.
c. The January 1 Work in Process balance consisted of two jobs, as follows:

Job No.	Style	Work in Process, Jan. 1
Job 51	V-100	$ 4,000
Job 52	V-200	10,000
Total		$14,000

d. Customer jobs completed and units sold in January were as follows:

Job No.	Style	Completed in January	Units Sold in January
Job 51	V-100	X	200
Job 52	V-200	X	170
Job 53	V-500		0
Job 54	A-200	X	200
Job 55	V-400	X	240
Job 56	A-100		0

Instructions

1. Determine the missing amounts associated with each letter. Provide supporting calculations by completing a table with the following headings:

Job No.	Quantity	Jan. 1 Work in Process	Direct Materials	Direct Labor	Factory Overhead	Total Cost	Unit Cost	Units Sold	Cost of Goods Sold

2. Determine the January 31 balances for each of the inventory accounts and factory overhead.

Problem 1–6B
Flow of costs and income statement

Objective 5

✓ 1. Income from operations, $775,000

Jam N Records is in the business of developing, promoting, and selling musical talent on compact disc (CD). The company signed a new musical act, called *Silk*, on January 1, 2003. For the first six months of 2003, the company spent $1,000,000 on a media campaign for *Silk* and $300,000 in legal costs. The CD production began on February 22, 2003.

Jam N uses a job order cost system to accumulate costs associated with a CD title. The unit direct materials cost for the CD is:

Blank CD	$5.00
Jewel case	0.50
Song lyric insert	0.25

The production process is straightforward. First, the blank CDs are brought to a production area where the digital soundtrack is copied onto the CD. The copying machine requires one hour per 1,000 CDs.

After the CDs are copied, they are brought to an assembly area where an employee packs the CD with a jewel case and song lyric insert. The direct labor cost is $0.50 per unit.

The CDs are sold to record stores. Each record store is given promotional materials, such as posters and aisle displays. Promotional materials cost $10 per record store. In addition, shipping costs average $0.25 per CD.

Total completed production was 800,000 units during the year. Other information is as follows:

Number of customers (record stores)	40,000
Number of CDs sold	750,000
Wholesale price (to record store) per CD	$10

Factory overhead cost is applied to jobs at the rate of $200 per copy machine hour. There were an additional 10,000 copied CDs, packages, and inserts waiting to be assembled on December 31, 2003.

Instructions

1. Prepare an annual income statement for the *Silk* CD, including supporting calculations, from the information above.
2. Determine the balances in the work in process and finished goods inventory for the *Silk* CD on December 31, 2003.

SPECIAL ACTIVITIES

Activity 1–1
Oak Enterprises
Ethics and professional conduct in business

Oak Enterprises allows employees to purchase, at cost, manufacturing materials, such as metal and lumber, for personal use. To purchase materials for personal use, an employee must complete a materials requisition form, which must then be approved by the employee's immediate supervisor. Cheryl Long, an assistant cost accountant, charges the employee an amount based on Oak's net purchase cost.

Cheryl Long is in the process of replacing a deck on her home and has requisitioned lumber for personal use, which has been approved in accordance with company policy. In computing the cost of the lumber, Long reviewed all the purchase invoices for the past year. She then used the lowest price to compute the amount due the company for the lumber.

➤ Discuss whether Cheryl behaved in an ethical manner.

Activity 1–2
Kitty Hawk Aerospace Company
Financial vs. managerial accounting

The following statement was made by the vice-president of finance of Kitty Hawk Aerospace Company: "The managers of a company should use the same information as the shareholders of the firm. When managers use the same information in guiding their internal operations as shareholders use in evaluating their investments, the managers will be aligned with the stockholders' profit objectives."

➤ Respond to the vice-president's statement.

Activity 1–3
Reliable TV Repairs
Classifying costs

Reliable TV Repairs provides TV repair services for the community. Gail Song's TV was not working, and she called Reliable for a home repair visit. The Reliable technician arrived at 2:00 P.M. to begin work. By 4:00 P.M. the problem was diagnosed as a failed circuit board. Unfortunately, the technician did not have a new circuit board in the truck, since the technician's previous customer had the same problem, and a board was used on that visit. Replacement boards were available back at the Reliable shop. Therefore, the technician drove back to the shop to retrieve a replacement board. From 4:00 to 5:00 P.M., the Reliable technician drove the round trip to retrieve the replacement board from the shop.

At 5:00 P.M. the technician was back on the job at Song's home. The replacement procedure is somewhat complex, since a variety of tests must be performed once the board is installed. The job was completed at 6:00 P.M.

Gail Song's repair bill showed the following:

Circuit board	$ 50
Labor charges	140
Total	$190

Gail Song was surprised at the size of the bill and asked for some greater detail supporting the calculations. Reliable responded with the following explanations.

Cost of materials:	
Purchase price of circuit board	$40
Markup on purchase price to cover storage and handling	10
Total materials charge	$50

The labor charge per hour is detailed as follows:

2:00–3:00 P.M.	$ 30
3:00–4:00 P.M.	25
4:00–5:00 P.M.	35
5:00–6:00 P.M.	50
Total labor charge	$140

Further explanations in the differences in the hourly rates are as follows:

First hour:	
Base labor rate	$15
Fringe benefits	5
Overhead (other than storage and handling)	5
Total base labor rate	$25
Additional charge for first hour of any job to cover the cost of vehicle depreciation, fuel, and employee time in transit. A 30-minute transit time is assumed.	5
	$30

Third hour:	
Base labor rate	$25
The trip back to the shop includes vehicle depreciation and fuel; therefore, a charge was added to the hourly rate to cover these costs. The round trip took an hour.	10
	$35

Fourth hour:

Base labor rate	$25
Overtime premium for time worked in excess of an eight-hour day (starting at 5:00 P.M.) is equal to the base rate. ...	25
	$50

1.   ▬✏➤ If you were in Gail Song's position, how would you respond to the bill? Are there parts of the bill that appear incorrect to you? If so, what argument would you employ to convince Reliable that the bill is too high?

2.   Use the headings below to construct a table. Fill in the table by first listing the costs identified in the activity in the left-hand column. For each cost, place a check mark in the appropriate column identifying the correct cost classification. Assume that each service call is a job.

Cost	Direct Materials	Direct Labor	Overhead

Activity 1–4
Texas Molding
Company
Managerial analysis

The controller of the plant of Texas Molding Company prepared a graph of the unit costs from the job cost reports for Product XD. The graph appeared as follows:

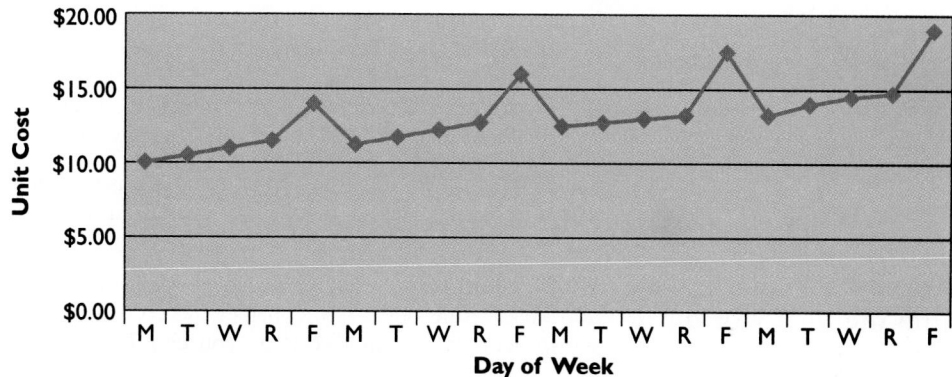

▬✏➤ How would you interpret this information? What further information would you request?

Activity 1–5
Silicon Inc.
Factory overhead rate

Silicon Inc., an electronics instrument manufacturer, uses a job order costing system. The overhead is allocated to jobs on the basis of direct labor hours. The overhead rate is now $1,000 per direct labor hour. The design engineer thinks that this is illogical. The design engineer has stated the following:

Our accounting system doesn't make any sense to me. It tells me that every labor hour carries an additional burden of $1,000. This means that direct labor makes up only 5% of our total product cost, yet it drives all our costs. In addition, these rates give my design engineers incentives to "design out" direct labor by using machine technology. Yet, over the past years as we have had less and less direct labor, the overhead rate keeps going up and up. I won't be surprised if next year the rate is $1,200 per direct labor hour. I'm also concerned because small errors in our estimates of the direct labor content can have a large impact on our estimated costs. Just a 30-minute error in our estimate of assembly time is worth $500. Small mistakes in our direct labor time estimates really swing our bids around. I think this puts us at a disadvantage when we are going after business.

1.   ▬✏➤ What is the engineer's concern about the overhead rate going "up and up"?

2.   ▬✏➤ What did the engineer mean about the large overhead rate being a disadvantage when placing bids and seeking new business?

3.   ▬✏➤ What do you think is a possible solution?

Activity 1–6
Delightful Inc.
Recording manufacturing costs

Jeff Flowers just began working as a cost accountant for Delightful Inc., which manufactures gift items. Flowers is preparing to record summary journal entries for the month. Flowers begins by recording the factory wages as follows:

| Wages Expense | 15,000 | |
| Wages Payable | | 15,000 |

Then the factory depreciation:

| Depreciation Expense—Factory Machinery | 4,000 | |
| Accumulated Depreciation—Factory Machinery | | 4,000 |

Flowers' supervisor, Hanna Tully, walks by and notices the entries. The following conversation takes place.

Hanna: That's a very unusual way to record our factory wages and depreciation for the month.

Jeff: What do you mean? This is exactly the way we were taught to record wages and depreciation in school. You know, debit an expense and credit Cash or payables, or in the case of depreciation, credit Accumulated Depreciation.

Hanna: Well, it's not the credits I'm concerned about. It's the debits—I don't think you've recorded the debits correctly. I wouldn't mind if you were recording the administrative wages or office equipment depreciation this way, but I've got real questions about recording factory wages and factory machinery depreciation this way.

Jeff: Now I'm really confused. You mean this is correct for administrative costs, but not for factory costs? Well, what am I supposed to do—and why?

1. Play the role of Hanna and answer Jeff's questions.
2. Why would Hanna accept the journal entries if they were for administrative costs?

Activity 1–7
Into the Real World
Classifying costs

With a group of students, visit a local copy and graphics shop or a pizza restaurant. As you observe the operation, consider the costs associated with running the business. As a group, identify as many costs as you can and classify them according to the following table headings:

Cost	Direct Materials	Direct Labor	Overhead	Selling Expenses

Matching

1.	C	5.	F	9.	I	13.	O	17.	S	21.	A	25.	N
2.	L	6.	P	10.	D	14.	T	18.	Z	22.	W	26.	M
3.	Q	7.	K	11.	Y	15.	R	19.	AA	23.	U	27.	V
4.	E	8.	J	12.	CC	16.	H	20.	G	24.	B	28.	X

Multiple Choice

1. **B** Both financial and managerial accounting support decision making (answer A). Financial accounting is mostly concerned with the decision making of external users, while managerial accounting supports decision making of management. Both financial and managerial accounting can result in financial reports (answer C). Managerial accounting reports are developed for internal use by managers at various levels in the organization. Both managerial and financial accounting record events from the past (answer D); however, managerial

accounting can also include information about the future in the form of budgets and cash flow projections. It is true that managerial accounting is not restricted to generally accepted accounting principles, as is financial accounting (answer B).

2. **C** Sales salaries (answer C) is a selling expense and is not considered a cost of manufacturing a product. Direct materials cost (answer A), factory overhead cost (answer B), and direct labor cost (answer D) are costs of manufacturing a product.

3. **B** Depreciation of testing equipment (answer B) is included as part of the factory overhead costs of the microcomputer manufacturer. The cost of memory chips (answer A) and the cost of disk drives (answer D) are both considered a part of direct materials cost. The wages of microcomputer assemblers (answer C) are part of direct labor costs.

4. **A** Job order cost systems are best suited to businesses manufacturing special orders from customers, such as would be the case for a repair shop for antique furniture (answer A). A process cost system is best suited for manufacturers of homogeneous units of product, such as rubber (answer B) and coal (answer C).

5. **B** If the amount of factory overhead applied during a particular period exceeds the actual overhead costs, the factory overhead account will have a credit balance and is said to be overapplied (answer B) or overabsorbed. If the amount applied is less than the actual costs, the account will have a debit balance and is said to be underapplied (answer A) or underabsorbed (answer C). Since an "estimated" predetermined overhead rate is used to apply overhead, a credit balance does not necessarily represent an error (answer D).

Process Cost Systems

M2

objectives

After studying this chapter, you should be able to:

1 Distinguish between job order costing and process costing systems.

2 Explain and illustrate the physical flows and cost flows for a process manufacturer.

3 Calculate and interpret the accounting for completed and partially completed units under the fifo method.

4 Prepare a cost of production report.

5 Prepare journal entries for transactions of a process manufacturer.

6 Use cost of production reports for decision making.

7 Contrast just-in-time processing with conventional manufacturing practices.

I f you bake cookies, the ingredients would include flour, sugar, and shortening. These ingredients would all be added at the beginning of the baking process by mixing them in a bowl. After mixing, do you have cookies? No. Why? Because they aren't baked (converted). But are they 100% complete with respect to materials? Yes, all the materials have been added to the baking process. When will they be cookies? When they are 100% complete with respect to materials *and* baking.

Now, assume that you ask the question, "How much cost have I incurred in baking cookies after 15 minutes (out of 30 minutes) of baking time?" The answer would require that you separate the ingredients and the electricity costs. These two costs are incurred in the baking process at different rates, and so it is convenient to identify them separately. The ingredient costs have all been incurred, since they were all introduced at the beginning of the process. The electricity costs, however, are a different story. Since the baking is only 50% complete, only 50% of the electricity costs (for the oven) have been incurred in the baking process. Therefore, the answer to the question is that all the materials costs and half the electricity costs have been incurred in the baking process after 15 minutes of baking.

In this chapter, we apply these concepts to manufacturers that use a process cost system. After introducing process costing, we discuss decision making with process cost system reports. We conclude the chapter with a brief discussion of just-in-time cost systems.

Comparing Job Order Costing and Process Costing

objective 1

Distinguish between job order costing and process costing systems.

As we discussed in the previous chapter, the job order cost system is best suited to industries that make special orders for customers or manufacture different products in groups. Industries that may use job order cost systems include special-order printing, custom-made tailoring, furniture manufacturing, shipbuilding, aircraft building, and construction. Process manufacturing is different from job-order manufacturing. **Process manufacturers** typically use large machines to process a flow of raw materials into a finished state. For example, a petrochemical business processes crude oil through numerous refining steps to produce higher grades of oil until gasoline is produced. The cost accounting system used by process manufacturers is called the **process cost system**.

In some ways, the process cost and job order cost systems are similar. Both systems accumulate product costs—direct materials, direct labor, and factory overhead—and allocate these costs to the units produced. Both systems maintain perpetual inventory accounts with subsidiary ledgers for materials, work in process, and finished goods. Both systems also provide product cost data to management for planning, directing, improving, controlling, and decision making. The main difference between the two systems is the form in which the product costs are accumulated and reported.

Exhibit 1 illustrates the main differences between the job order and process cost systems. In a job order cost system, product costs are accumulated by job and are summarized on job cost sheets. The job cost sheets provide unit cost information and can be used by management for product pricing, cost control, and inventory valuation. The process manufacturer does not manufacture according to "jobs." Thus, costs are accumulated

Industries and examples of companies that may use process cost systems are:

Industry	Example Company
Automobile	General Motors
Beverages	Coca-Cola
Chemicals	Dow Chemical
Food	Campbell Soup
Forest and paper products	Georgia Pacific
Metals	Alcoa
Petroleum refining	ExxonMobil
Pharmaceuticals	Merck
Soap and cosmetics	Procter & Gamble

Exhibit 1 Job Order and Process Cost Systems Compared

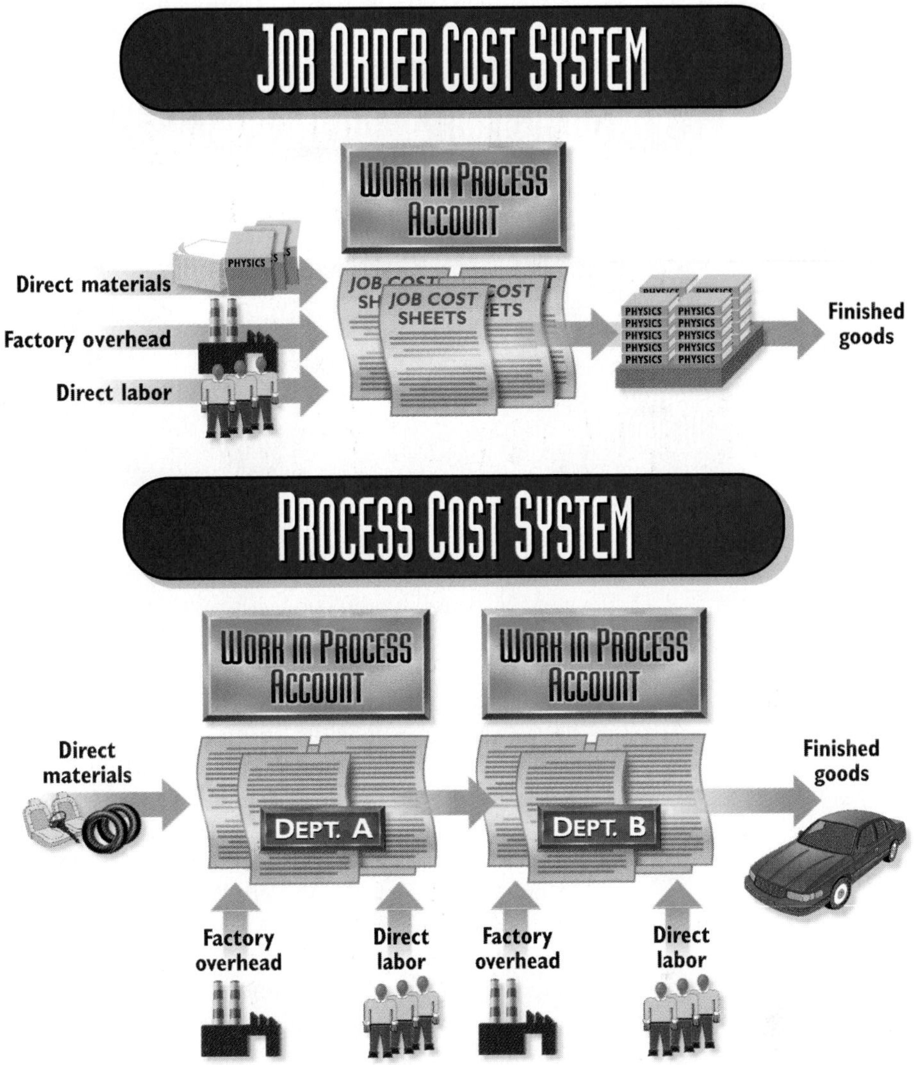

by department. Each unit of product that passes through the department is similar. Thus, the production costs reported by each department provide unit cost information that can be used by management for cost control. In a job order cost system, the work in process inventory at the end of the accounting period is the sum of the job cost sheets for partially completed jobs. In a process cost system, the amount of work in process inventory is determined by allocating costs between completed and partially completed units within a department.

> **Process manufacturers accumulate costs by department.**

Physical Flows and Cost Flows for a Process Manufacturer

objective 2

Explain and illustrate the physical flows and cost flows for a process manufacturer.

Materials costs are a large portion of the costs for most process manufacturers. Often, the materials costs can be as high as 70% of the total manufacturing costs. Thus, accounting for materials costs is very important for process operations.

Exhibit 2 illustrates the physical flow of materials for a steel processor. Direct materials in the form of scrap metal are placed into a furnace in the Melting Department. The Melting Department uses conversion costs (direct labor and factory overhead) during the melting process. The molten metal is then transferred to the

Exhibit 2 Physical Flows for a Process Manufacturer

Casting Department, where it is poured into an ingot casting. The Casting Department also uses conversion costs during the casting process. The ingot castings are transferred to the finished goods inventory for shipment to customers.

The cost flows in a process cost system reflect the physical materials flows and are illustrated in Exhibit 3. Purchased materials are debited to Materials (a) and credited to Accounts Payable (not shown). Direct materials (scrap metal) used by the Melting Department are debited to Work in Process—Melting and credited to Materials (b). In addition, indirect materials and other overhead incurred are debited to department factory overhead accounts and credited to Materials (d) and other accounts. Direct labor in the Melting Department is debited to the department's work in process account (c) and credited to Wages Payable (not shown). Applied factory overhead is debited to Work in Process—Melting, using a predetermined overhead rate (e). The cost of completed production from the Melting Department is transferred to the Casting Department by debiting Work in Process—Casting and crediting Work in Process—Melting (f). The transferred costs include the direct materials and conversion costs for completed production of the Melting Department. The direct labor and applied factory overhead costs in the Casting Department are debited to Work in Process—Casting (g and h). The cost of the finished ingots is transferred out of the Casting Department by debiting Finished Goods and crediting Work in Process—Casting (i). The cost of ingots sold to customers is transferred out of finished goods with a debit to Cost of Goods Sold and a credit to Finished Goods (j).

Exhibit 3 Cost Flows for a Process Manufacturer

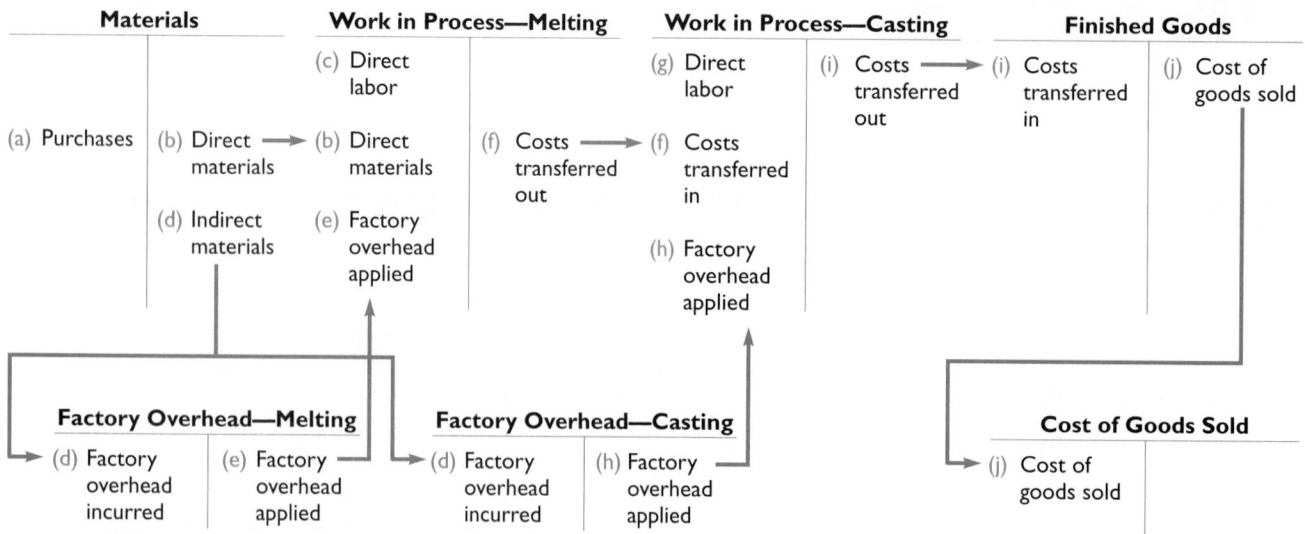

BUSINESS ON STAGE

What Is a Product?

In manufacturing, inputs are processed into a product with physical attributes. In business, however, a product is often thought of in terms other than just its physical attributes. For example, why a customer buys a product usually impacts how a business markets the product. Other considerations, such as warranty needs, servicing needs, and perceived quality, also affect business strategies.

Four types of products are (1) convenience products, (2) shopping products, (3) specialty products, and (4) unsought products. To illustrate, consider the following four products:

1. Convenience product: Snickers candy bar
2. Shopping product: Sony television
3. Specialty product: Diamond ring
4. Unsought product: Prearranged funeral

For each of these products, the frequency of purchase, the profit per unit, and the number of retailers differ. As a result, the sales and marketing approach for each product differs as shown below. ■

Product	Frequency of Purchase	Profit per Unit	Number of Retailers	Sales/Marketing Approach
Snickers	often	low	many	mass advertising
Sony TV	occasional	moderate	many	mass advertising; personal selling
Diamond ring	seldom	high	few	personal selling
Prearranged funeral	rare	high	few	aggressive personal selling

The First-In, First-Out (Fifo) Method

objective 3

Calculate and interpret the accounting for completed and partially completed units under the fifo method.

In a process cost system, the accountant determines the cost transferred out and thus the amount remaining in inventory for each department. For many manufacturing processes, materials are added at the beginning of production, and the units are moved through the production processes in a **first-in, first-out (fifo)** flow. That is, the first units entering the production process are the first to be completed.[1]

Most process manufacturers have more than one department. In the illustrations that follow, McDermott Steel Inc. has two departments, Melting and Casting. McDermott melts scrap metal and then pours the molten metal into an ingot casting.

To illustrate the first-in, first-out method, we will simplify by using only the Melting Department of McDermott Steel Inc. The following data for the Melting Department are for July of the current year:

Inventory in process, July 1, 500 tons:		
Direct materials cost, for 500 tons	$24,550	
Conversion costs, for 500 tons, 70% completed	3,600	
Total inventory in process, July 1		$28,150
Direct materials cost for July, 1,000 tons		50,000
Conversion costs for July		9,690
Goods transferred to Casting in July (includes units in process on July 1), 1,100 tons		?
Inventory in process, July 31, 400 tons, 25% completed as to conversion costs		?

We assume that all materials used in the department are added at the beginning of the process, and conversion costs (direct labor and factory overhead) are incurred

---

[1] An alternative method—the average cost method—is discussed in advanced textbooks.

evenly throughout the melting process. The objective is to determine the cost of goods completed and the ending inventory valuation, which are represented by the question marks. We determine these amounts by using the following four steps:

1. Determine the units to be assigned costs.
2. Calculate equivalent units of production.
3. Determine the cost per equivalent unit.
4. Allocate costs to transferred and partially completed units.

Step 1: Determine the Units to Be Assigned Costs

The first step in our illustration is to determine the units to be assigned costs. A unit can be any measure of completed production, such as tons, gallons, pounds, barrels, or cases. We use tons as the definition for units in McDermott Steel.

McDermott Steel had 1,500 tons of direct materials charged to production in the Melting Department for July, as shown below.

Total tons charged to production:

In process, July 1	500 tons
Received from materials storeroom	1,000
Total units accounted for by the Melting Department	1,500 tons

There are three categories of units to be assigned costs for an accounting period: **(A)** units in beginning in-process inventory, **(B)** units started and completed during the period, and **(C)** units in ending in-process inventory. Exhibit 4 illustrates these categories in the Melting Department for July. The 500-ton beginning inventory **(A)** was completed and transferred to the Casting Department. McDermott Steel started another 1,000 tons of material into the process during July. Of the 1,000 tons introduced in July, 400 tons were left incomplete at the end of the month **(C)**. Thus, only 600 of the 1,000 tons were actually started and completed in July **(B)**.

Exhibit 4 July Units to Be Costed—Melting Department

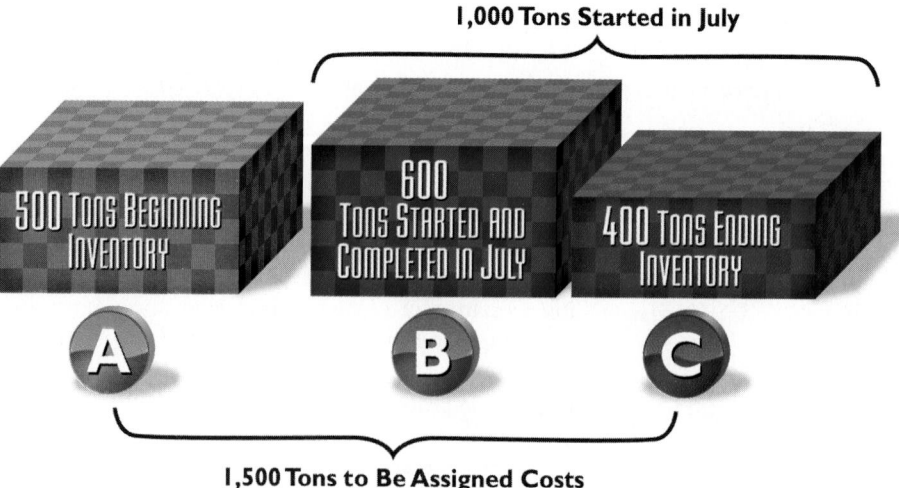

The total units (tons) to be assigned costs for McDermott Steel can be summarized as shown below.

(A)	Inventory in process, July 1, completed in July	500 tons
(B)	Started and completed in July	600
	Transferred out to the Casting Department in July	1,100
(C)	Inventory in process, July 31	400
	Total tons to be assigned costs	1,500 tons

Department 2 received 2,400 tons from Department 1. During the period, Department 2 completed 2,600 tons and had 600 tons of work in process at the beginning of the period. The ending work in process inventory was 400 tons. How many tons were started and completed during the period?

2,000 tons (2,400 − 400, or 2,600 − 600)

Note that the total tons to be assigned costs equals the total tons accounted for by the department. The three unit categories (**A**, **B**, and **C**) are used in the remaining steps to determine the cost transferred to the Casting Department and the cost remaining in work in process inventory at the end of the period.

Step 2: Calculate Equivalent Units of Production

Process manufacturers often have some partially processed materials remaining in production at the end of a period. In these cases, the costs of production must be allocated between the units that have been completed and transferred to the next process (or finished goods) and those that are only partially completed and remain within the department. This allocation can be determined by using the equivalent units of production.

The **equivalent units of production** are the number of units that *could have been* completed within a given accounting period. In contrast, **whole units** are the number of units in production during a period, whether or not completed. For example, assume that 800 whole units are in work in process at the end of a period. If the units are 60% complete, the number of equivalent units in process is 480 (800 × 60%).

Equivalent units for materials and conversion costs are usually determined separately because they are often introduced at different times or at different rates in the production process. In contrast, direct labor and factory overhead are combined together as conversion costs because they are often incurred in production at the same time and rate.

> **The equivalent units of production are the number of units that could have been completed during a period.**

Materials Equivalent Units

To allocate materials costs between the completed and partially completed units, it is necessary to determine how materials are added during the manufacturing process. In the case of McDermott Steel, the materials are added at the beginning of the melting process. In other words, the melting process cannot begin without the scrap metal. The equivalent unit computation for materials in July is as follows:

	Total Whole Units	Percent Materials Added in July	Equivalent Units for Direct Materials
Inventory in process, July 1	500	0%	0
Started and completed in July (1,100 − 500)	600	100%	600
Transferred out to Casting Dept. in July	1,100	—	600
Inventory in process, July 31	400	100%	400
Total tons to be assigned cost	1,500		1,000

Department 3 had 400 tons in beginning work in process inventory (30% complete). During the period, 5,800 tons were completed. The ending work in process inventory was 600 tons (60% complete). What are the equivalent units for direct materials if materials are added at the beginning of the process?

6,000 tons (5,800 − 400 + 600)

The whole units from Step 1 are multiplied by the percentage of materials that are added in July for the in-process inventories and units started and completed. The equivalent units for direct materials are illustrated in Exhibit 5.

The direct materials for the 500 tons of July 1 in-process inventory were introduced in June. Thus, no materials units were added in July for the inventory in process on July 1. All of the 600 tons started and completed in July were 100% complete with respect to materials. Thus, 600 equivalent units of materials were added in July. All the materials for the July 31 in-process inventory were introduced at the beginning of the process. Thus, 400 equivalent units of material for the July 31 in-process inventory were added in July.

Exhibit 5 Direct Materials Equivalent Units

DIRECT MATERIALS EQUIVALENT UNITS

Inventory in process, July 1

500 tons beginning inventory

500 EQUIVALENT UNITS OF MATERIALS

100% materials added in June

No materials equivalent units added to beginning inventory for July

600 tons started and completed

600 EQUIVALENT UNITS OF MATERIALS

100% materials added in July

Started and completed

400 tons ending inventory

400 EQUIVALENT UNITS OF MATERIALS

100% materials added in July

No materials equivalent units added to beginning inventory for August

Inventory in process, July 31

1,000 Equivalent Units in July

Conversion Equivalent Units

The conversion costs are usually incurred evenly throughout a process. For example, direct labor, utilities, and machine depreciation are usually used uniformly during processing. Thus, the conversion equivalent units are added in July in direct relation to the percentage of processing completed in July. The computations for July are as follows:

	Total Whole Units	Percent Conversion Completed in July	Equivalent Units for Conversion
Inventory in process, July 1	500	30%	150
Started and completed in July (1,100 − 500)	600	100%	600
Transferred out to Casting Dept. in July	1,100	—	750
Inventory in process, July 31	400	25%	100
Total tons to be assigned cost	1,500		850

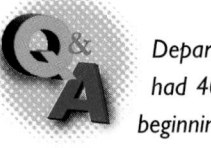

Department 3 had 400 tons in beginning work in process inventory (30% complete). During the period, 5,800 tons were completed. The ending work in process inventory was 600 tons (60% complete). What are the equivalent units for conversion costs?

6,040 tons [(70% × 400) + (5,800 − 400) + (60% × 600)]

The whole units from Step 1 are multiplied by the percentage of conversion completed in July for the in-process inventories and units started and completed. The equivalent units for conversion are illustrated in Exhibit 6.

The conversion equivalent units of the July 1 in-process inventory are 30% of the 500 tons, or 150 equivalent units. Since 70% of the conversion had been completed on July 1, only 30% of the conversion effort for these tons was incurred in July. All the units started and completed used converting effort in July. Thus, conversion equivalent units are 100% of these tons. The equivalent units for the July 31 in-process inventory are 25% of the 400 tons because only 25% of the converting has been completed with respect to these tons in July.

Exhibit 6 Conversion Equivalent Units

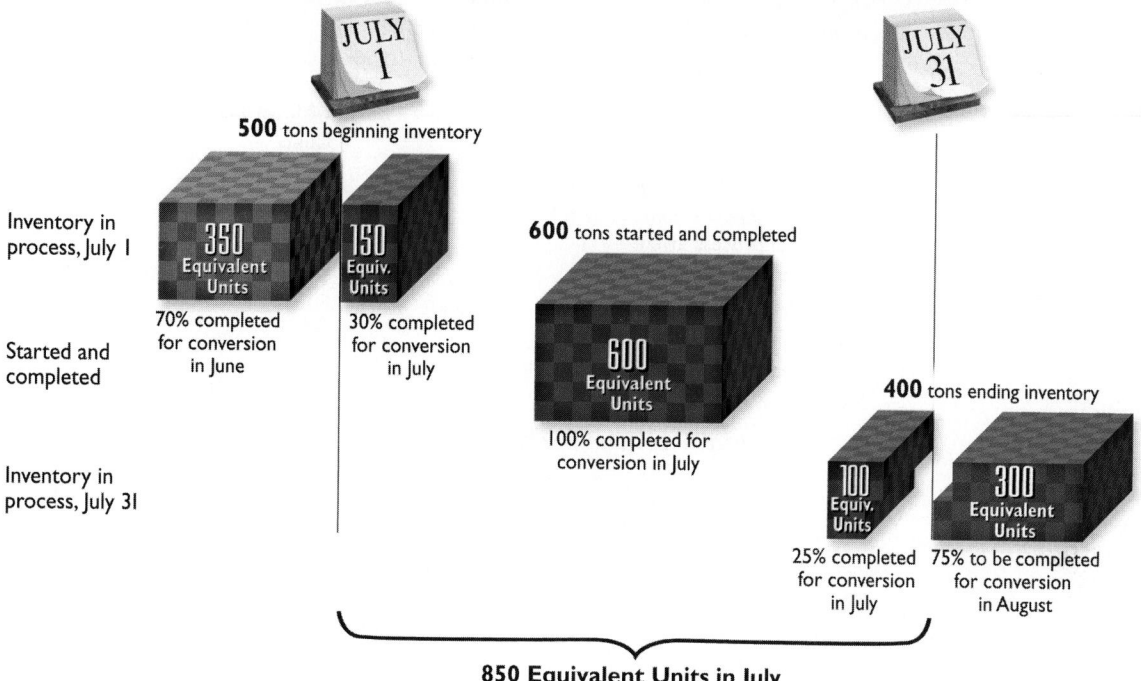

CONVERSION EQUIVALENT UNITS

JULY 1

JULY 31

500 tons beginning inventory

Inventory in process, July 1

350 Equivalent Units
70% completed for conversion in June

150 Equiv. Units
30% completed for conversion in July

600 tons started and completed

600 Equivalent Units
100% completed for conversion in July

400 tons ending inventory

Started and completed

Inventory in process, July 31

100 Equiv. Units
25% completed for conversion in July

300 Equivalent Units
75% to be completed for conversion in August

850 Equivalent Units in July

Step 3: Determine the Cost per Equivalent Unit

In Step 3, we calculate the cost per equivalent unit. The July equivalent unit totals for McDermott Steel's Melting Department are reproduced from Step 2 as follows:

	Equivalent Units	
	Direct Materials	**Conversion**
Inventory in process, July 1	0	150
Started and completed in July (1,100 − 500)	600	600
Transferred out to Casting Dept. in July	600	750
Inventory in process, July 31	400	100
Total tons to be assigned cost	1,000	850

The **cost per equivalent unit** is determined by dividing the direct materials and conversion costs incurred in July by the respective total equivalent units for direct materials and conversion costs. The direct materials and conversion costs were given at the beginning of this illustration. These calculations are as follows:

Equivalent unit cost for direct materials:

$$\frac{\$50,000 \text{ direct materials cost}}{1,000 \text{ direct materials equivalent units}} = \frac{\$50.00 \text{ per equivalent}}{\text{unit of direct materials}}$$

Equivalent unit cost for conversion:

$$\frac{\$9,690 \text{ conversion cost}}{850 \text{ conversion equivalent units}} = \frac{\$11.40 \text{ per equivalent}}{\text{unit of conversion}}$$

We will use these rates in Step 4 to allocate the direct materials and conversion costs to the completed and partially completed units.

Step 4: Allocate Costs to Transferred and Partially Completed Units

In Step 4, we multiply the equivalent unit rates by their respective equivalent units of production in order to determine the cost of transferred and partially completed units. The cost of the July 1 in-process inventory, completed and transferred out to the Casting Department, is determined as follows:

What costs are included in the $28,150 beginning work in process inventory for McDermott Steel?

·····································

70% of the conversion cost and all of the materials costs for 500 tons.

	Direct Materials Costs	Conversion Costs	Total Costs
Inventory in process, July 1 balance			$28,150
Equivalent units for completing the July 1 in-process inventory	0	150	
Equivalent unit cost	×$50.00	×$11.40	
Cost of completed July 1 in-process inventory	0	$1,710	1,710
Cost of July 1 in-process inventory transferred to Casting Department			$29,860

The July 1 in-process inventory cost of $28,150 is carried over from June and will be transferred to Casting. The cost required to finish the July 1 in-process inventory is $1,710, which consists of conversion costs required to complete the remaining 30% of the processing. This total does not include direct materials costs, since these costs were added at the beginning of the process in June. The conversion costs required to complete the beginning inventory are added to the balance carried over from the previous month to yield a total cost of the completed July 1 in-process inventory of $29,860.

The 600 units started and completed in July receive 100% of their direct materials and conversion costs in July. The costs associated with the units started and completed are determined by multiplying the equivalent units in Step 2 by the unit costs in Step 3, as follows:

	Direct Materials Costs	Conversion Costs	Total Costs
Units started and completed in July	600	600	
Equivalent unit cost	×$50.00	×$11.40	
Cost to complete the units started and completed in July	$ 30,000	$ 6,840	$36,840

The total cost transferred to the Casting Department is the sum of the beginning inventory cost from the previous period ($28,150), the additional costs incurred in July to complete the beginning inventory ($1,710), and the costs incurred for the units started and completed in July ($36,840). Thus, the total cost transferred to Casting is $66,700.

The units of ending inventory have not been transferred, so they must be valued at July 31. The costs associated with the partially completed units in the ending inventory are determined by multiplying the equivalent units in Step 2 by the unit costs in Step 3, as follows:

	Direct Materials Costs	Conversion Costs	Total Costs
Equivalent units in ending inventory	400	100	
Equivalent unit cost	×$50.00	×$11.40	
Cost of ending inventory	$ 20,000	$ 1,140	$21,140

The units in the ending inventory have received 100% of their materials in July. Thus, the materials cost incurred in July for the ending inventory is $20,000, or 400 equivalent units of materials multiplied by $50. The conversion cost incurred in July for the ending inventory is $1,140, which is 100 equivalent units of conversion (400 units, 25% complete) for the ending inventory multiplied by $11.40. Summing the conversion and materials costs, the total ending inventory cost is $21,140.

Bringing It All Together: The Cost of Production Report

objective 4

Prepare a cost of production report.

A **cost of production report** is normally prepared for each processing department at periodic intervals. The July cost of production report for McDermott Steel's Melting Department is shown in Exhibit 7. As can be seen on the report, the two question marks from page M55 can now be determined. The cost of goods transferred to the Casting Department in July was $66,700, while the cost of the ending work in process in the Melting Department on July 31 is $21,140.

Exhibit 7 Cost of Production Report for McDermott Steel's Melting Department—FIFO

McDermott Steel Inc.
Cost of Production Report—Melting Department
For the Month Ended July 31, 2003

UNITS	Whole Units (Step 1)	Equivalent Units (Step 2) Direct Materials	Conversion
Units charged to production:			
Inventory in process, July 1	500		
Received from materials storeroom	1,000		
Total units accounted for by the Melting Dept.	1,500		
Units to be assigned cost:			
Inventory in process, July 1 (70% completed)	500	0	150
Started and completed in July	600	600	600
Transferred to Casting Department in July	1,100	600	750
Inventory in process, July 31 (25% complete)	400	400	100
Total units to be assigned cost	1,500	1,000	850

COSTS	Costs Direct Materials	Conversion	Total Costs
Unit costs (Step 3):			
Total costs for July in Melting Dept.	$50,000	$9,690	
Total equivalent units (from Step 2 above)	÷ 1,000	÷ 850	
Cost per equivalent unit	$ 50.00	$11.40	
Costs charged to production:			
Inventory in process, July 1			$28,150
Costs incurred in July			59,690
Total costs accounted for by the Melting Dept.			$87,840
Costs allocated to completed and partially completed units (Step 4):			
Inventory in process, July 1—balance			$28,150
To complete inventory in process, July 1	$ 0	$1,710[a]	1,710
Started and completed in July	30,000[b]	6,840[c]	36,840
Transferred to Casting Dept. in July			$66,700
Inventory in process, July 31	$20,000[d]	$1,140[e]	21,140
Total costs assigned by the Melting Dept.			$87,840

[a]150 units × $11.40 = $1,710   [c]600 units × $11.40 = $6,840   [e]100 units × $11.40 = $1,140
[b]600 units × $50.00 = $30,000   [d]400 units × $50.00 = $20,000

The report summarizes the four previous steps by providing the following production quantity and cost data:

1. The units for which the department is accountable and the disposition of those units.
2. The production costs incurred by the department and the allocation of those costs between completed and partially completed units.

The cost of production report is also used to control costs. Each department manager is responsible for the units entering production and the costs incurred in the department. Any failure to account for all costs and any significant differences in unit product costs from one month to another should be investigated.

Journal Entries for a Process Cost System

objective 5

Prepare journal entries for transactions of a process manufacturer.

To illustrate the journal entries to record the cost flows in a process costing system, we will use the July transactions for McDermott Steel. The entries in summary form for these transactions are shown here and on the following page. In practice, transactions would be recorded daily.

JOURNAL

Date		Description	Post. Ref.	Debit	Credit
	a.	Materials		62,000.00	
		Accounts Payable			62,000.00
		Materials purchased on account.			
	b.	Work in Process—Melting		50,000.00	
		Factory Overhead—Melting		4,000.00	
		Factory Overhead—Casting		3,000.00	
		Materials			57,000.00
		Materials requisitioned.			
	c.	Work in Process—Melting		5,000.00	
		Work in Process—Casting		4,500.00	
		Wages Payable			9,500.00
		Direct labor used.			
	d.	Factory Overhead—Melting		1,000.00	
		Factory Overhead—Casting		7,000.00	
		Accumulated Depreciation			8,000.00
		Depreciation expenses.			
	e.	Work in Process—Melting		4,690.00	
		Work in Process—Casting		9,640.00	
		Factory Overhead—Melting			4,690.00
		Factory Overhead—Casting			9,640.00
		Factory overhead applied.			

f.	Work in Process—Casting	66 7 0 0 00	
	Work in Process—Melting		66 7 0 0 00
	Melting Department transferred		
	$66,700 to Casting Department		
	(from Exhibit 7).		
g.	Finished Goods	78 6 0 0 00	
	Work in Process—Casting		78 6 0 0 00
	Casting Department transferred		
	$78,600 to Finished Goods.		
h.	Cost of Goods Sold	73 7 0 0 00	
	Finished Goods		73 7 0 0 00
	Goods sold.		

Exhibit 8 shows the flow of costs for each transaction. Note that the highlighted amounts in Exhibit 8 were determined from assigning the costs charged to production in the Melting Department. These amounts were computed and are shown at the bottom of the cost of production report for the Melting Department in Exhibit 7. Likewise, the amount transferred out of the Casting Department to Finished Goods would have also been determined from a cost of production report for the Casting Department.

Exhibit 8 McDermott Steel's Cost Flows

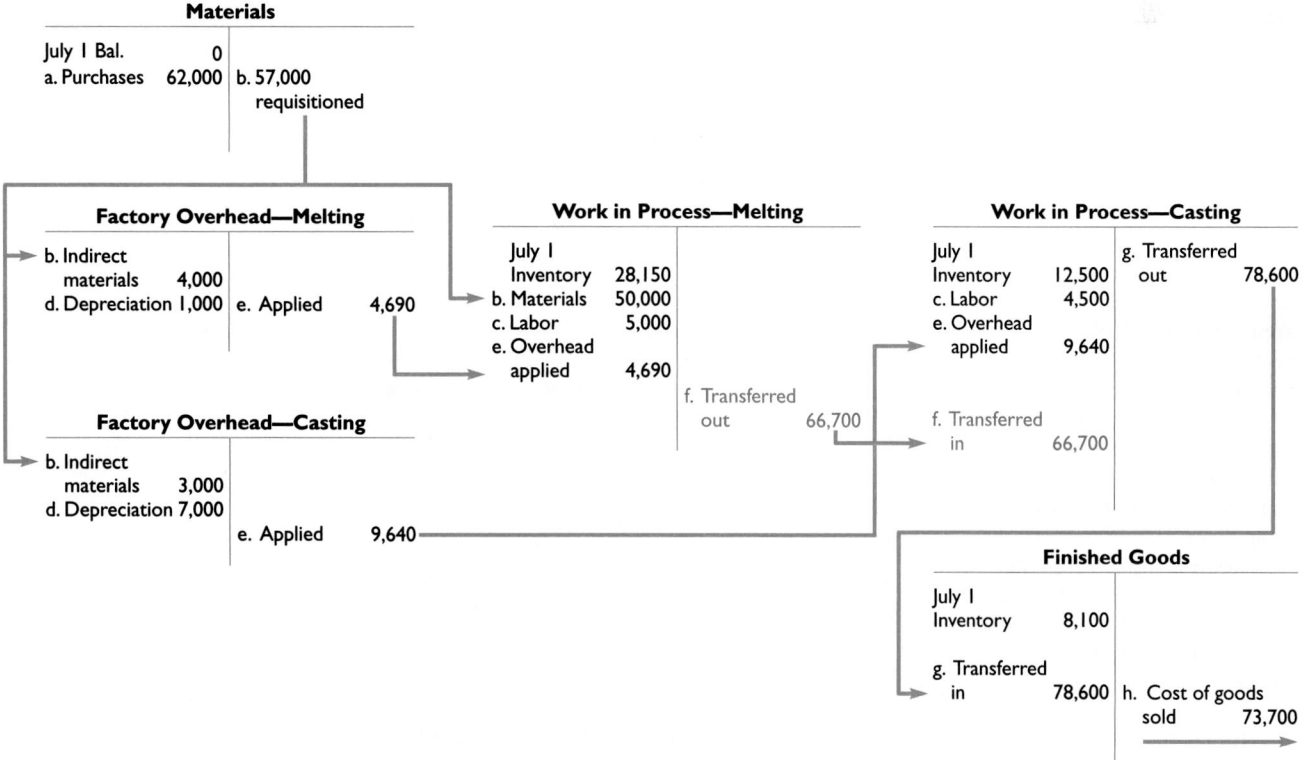

Using the Cost of Production Report for Decision Making

objective 6

Use cost of production reports for decision making.

The cost of production report is one source of information that may be used by managers to control and improve operations. A cost of production report will normally list costs in greater detail than in Exhibit 7. This greater detail helps management isolate problems and opportunities. To illustrate, assume that the Blending Department of Holland Beverage Company prepared cost of production reports for April and May. In addition, assume that the Blending Department had no beginning or ending work in process inventory either month. Thus, in this simple case, there is no need to determine equivalent units of production for allocating costs between completed and partially completed units. The cost of production reports for April and May in the Blending Department are as follows:

Cost of Production Reports
Holland Beverage Company—Blending Department
For the Months Ended April 30 and May 31, 2003

	April	May
Direct materials	$ 20,000	$ 40,600
Direct labor	15,000	29,400
Energy	8,000	20,000
Repairs	4,000	8,000
Tank cleaning	3,000	8,000
Total	$ 50,000	$ 106,000
Units completed	÷100,000	÷200,000
Cost per unit	$ 0.50	$ 0.53

Note that the preceding reports provide more cost detail than simply reporting direct materials and conversion costs. The May results indicate that total unit costs have increased from $0.50 to $0.53, or 6% from the previous month. What caused this increase? To determine the possible causes for this increase, the cost of production report may be restated in per-unit terms, as shown below.

Blending Department Per-Unit
Expense Comparisons

	April	May	% Change
Direct materials	$0.200	$0.203	1.50%
Direct labor	0.150	0.147	−2.00%
Energy	0.080	0.100	25.00%
Repairs	0.040	0.040	0.00%
Tank cleaning	0.030	0.040	33.33%
Total	$0.500	$0.530	6.00%

Both energy and tank cleaning per-unit costs have increased dramatically in May. Further investigation should focus on these costs. For example, an increasing trend in energy may indicate that the machines are losing fuel efficiency, thereby requiring the company to purchase an increasing amount of fuel. This unfavorable trend could motivate management to repair the machines. The tank cleaning costs could be investigated in a similar fashion.

In addition to unit production cost trends, managers of process manufacturers are also concerned about yield trends. **Yield** is the ratio of the materials output quantity to the input quantity. A yield less than one occurs when the output quantity is less than the input quantity due to materials losses during the process. For

Middle Tennessee Lumber Company produces cabinet and furniture panels from various hardwoods. The company purchased new computer and sawing technology that improved the cutting yield by approximately 10%. The cutting yield is the ratio of finished panel board feet to the number of board feet input to the sawing operation. The new equipment scans the rough-cut lumber with a laser beam. The scanned information is input to a software program that calculates the optimum cutting pattern for minimizing trim waste. The wood is then sent to a computer-controlled saw, which proceeds to cut the board according to the calculations from the laser scan.

example, if 1,000 pounds of sugar entered the packing operation, and only 980 pounds of sugar were packed, the yield would be 98%. Two percent or 20 pounds of sugar were lost or spilled during the packing process.

Just-in-Time Processing

objective 7

Contrast just-in-time processing with conventional manufacturing practices.

The objective of many companies is to produce products with high quality, low cost, and instant availability. One approach to achieving this objective is to implement just-in-time processing. **Just-in-time processing (JIT)** is a philosophy that focuses on reducing time and cost and eliminating poor quality. A JIT system achieves production efficiencies and flexibility by reorganizing the traditional production process.

In a traditional production process (illustrated in Exhibit 9), a product moves from process to process as each function or step is completed. Each worker is assigned a specific job, which is performed repeatedly as unfinished products are received from the preceding department. For example, a furniture manufacturer might use seven production departments to perform the operating functions necessary to manufacture furniture, as shown in the diagram in Exhibit 9.

Exhibit 9 Traditional Production Line— Furniture Manufacturer

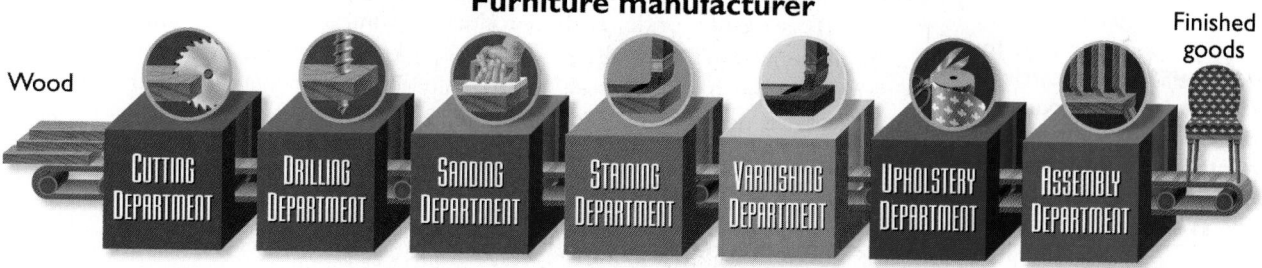

TRADITIONAL PRODUCTION LINE

Furniture manufacturer

Wood

CUTTING DEPARTMENT · DRILLING DEPARTMENT · SANDING DEPARTMENT · STAINING DEPARTMENT · VARNISHING DEPARTMENT · UPHOLSTERY DEPARTMENT · ASSEMBLY DEPARTMENT

Finished goods

Point of Interest

The Internet complements a just-in-time processing strategy. **Ford Motor Company** states that the impact of the Internet is the equivalent of "the moving assembly line of the 21st Century." This is because the Internet will connect the whole supply chain—from customers to suppliers—to create a fast and efficient manufacturing system. As stated by William Clay Ford, Chairman of Ford Motor, "The automobile is about to undergo the most profound and revolutionary changes it's seen since the Model T first hit the streets."

For the furniture maker in the illustration, manufacturing would begin in the Cutting Department, where the wood would be cut to design specifications. Next, the Drilling Department would perform the drilling function, after which the Sanding Department would sand the wood, the Staining Department would stain the furniture, and the Varnishing Department would apply varnish and other protective coatings. Then, the Upholstery Department would add fabric and other materials. Finally, the Assembly Department would assemble the furniture to complete the process.

In the traditional production process, production supervisors attempt to enter enough materials into the process to keep all the manufacturing departments operating. Some departments, however, may process materials more rapidly than others. In addition, if one department stops production because of machine breakdowns, for example, the preceding departments usually continue production in order to avoid idle time. This may result in a build-up of work in process inventories in some departments.

In a just-in-time system, processing functions are combined into work centers, sometimes called manufacturing cells. For example, the seven departments just illustrated for the furniture manufacturer might be reorganized into three work centers. As shown in the diagram in Exhibit 10, Work Center One would perform the cutting, drilling, and sanding functions, Work Center Two would perform the staining and varnishing functions, and Work Center Three would perform the upholstery and assembly functions.

Exhibit 10 Just-in-Time Production Line— Furniture Manufacturer

JUST-IN-TIME PRODUCTION LINE

Furniture manufacturer

Finished goods

Wood

WORK CENTER ONE — Cutting, drilling, and sanding

WORK CENTER TWO — Staining and varnishing

WORK CENTER THREE — Upholstery and assembly

American auto-makers are continuing to look for ways to be more efficient and catch up with their Japanese counterparts. One basis for comparison is the number of workers needed to make one vehicle a day, as shown in the table below:

	1995	1999
Ford	3.11	2.97
General Motors	3.64	3.04
Honda	2.53	2.46
Toyota	2.62	2.73

Source: Keith Bradsher, "Efficiency on Wheels," *The New York Times,* June 16, 2000.

In the traditional production line, a worker typically performs only one function. However, in a work center in which several functions take place, the workers are often cross-trained to perform more than one function. Research has indicated that workers who perform several manufacturing functions identify better with the end product. This creates pride in the product and improves quality and productivity.

Implementing JIT may also result in reorganizing service activities. Specifically, the service activities may be assigned to individual work centers, rather than to centralized service departments. For example, each work center may be assigned the responsibility for the repair and maintenance of its machinery and equipment. Accepting this responsibility creates an environment in which workers gain a better understanding of the production process and the machinery. In turn, workers tend to take better care of the machinery, which decreases repairs and maintenance costs, reduces machine downtime, and improves product quality.

In a JIT system, wasted motion from moving the product and materials is reduced. The product is often placed on a movable carrier that is centrally located in the work center. After the workers in a work center have completed their activities with the product, the entire carrier and any additional materials are moved just in time to satisfy the demand or need of the next work center. In this sense, the product is said to be "pulled through." Each work center is connected to other work centers through information contained on Kanbans, which is a Japanese term for cards.

The experience of Caterpillar Inc. illustrates the impact of JIT. Before implementing JIT, an average transmission would travel 10 miles through the factory and require 1,000 pieces of paper for materials, labor, and movement transactions. After implementing JIT, Caterpillar improved manufacturing so that an average transmission traveled only 200 feet and required only 10 pieces of paper.

In summary, the primary benefit of JIT systems is the increased efficiency of operations, which is achieved by eliminating waste and simplifying the production process. At the same time, JIT systems emphasize continuous improvement in the manufacturing process and the improvement of product quality.

ENCORE

P & G's "Pit Stops"

What do **Procter & Gamble** and Formula One racing have in common? The answer begins with P&G's Packing Department, which is where detergents and other products are filled on a "pack line." Containers move down the pack line and are filled with products from a multihead packing machine. When it was time to change from a 36-oz. to a 54-oz. *Tide* box, for example, the changeover involved stopping the line, adjusting guide rails, retrieving items from the tool room, placing items back in the tool room, changing and cleaning the pack heads, and performing routine maintenance. Changing the pack line could be a very difficult process and typically took up to eight hours. Management realized that it was important to reduce this time significantly in order to become more flexible and cost efficient in packing products. Where could they learn how to do changeovers faster? They turned to Formula One racing, reasoning that a pit stop was much

like a changeover. As a result, P&G videotaped actual Formula One pit stops. These videos were used to form the following principles for conducting a fast changeover:

- Position the tools near their point of use on the line prior to stopping the line, to reduce time going back and forth to the tool room.
- Arrange the tools in the exact order of work, so that no time is wasted looking for a tool.
- Have each employee perform a very specific task during the changeover.
- Design the workflow so that employees don't interfere with each other.
- Have each employee in position at the moment the line is stopped.
- Train each employee, and practice, practice, practice.
- Put a stop watch on the changeover process.

- Plot improvements over time on a visible chart.

As a result of these changes, P&G was able to reduce pack-line changeover time from eight hours to 20 minutes. This allowed them to produce a much larger variety of products every day and to improve the cost performance of the Packing Department. ■

KEY POINTS

1 Distinguish between job order costing and process costing systems.

The process cost system is best suited for industries that mass-produce identical units of a product that often have passed through a sequence of processes on a continuous basis. In process cost accounting, costs are charged to processing departments, and the cost of the finished unit is determined by dividing the total cost incurred in each process by the number of units produced.

2 Explain and illustrate the physical flows and cost flows for a process manufacturer.

Materials are introduced, converted, and passed from one department to the next department or to finished goods. The accumulated costs transferred from preceding departments and the costs of direct materials and direct labor incurred in each processing department are debited to the related work in process account in a process cost system. Each

work in process account is also debited for the factory overhead applied.

3 Calculate and interpret the accounting for completed and partially completed units under the fifo method.

Frequently, partially processed materials remain in various stages of production in a department at the end of a period. In this case, the manufacturing costs must be allocated between the units that have been completed and those that are only partially completed and remain within the department. To allocate processing costs between the output completed and the inventory of goods within the department under fifo, it is necessary to determine the number of equivalent units of production during the period for the beginning inventory, units started and completed currently, and the ending inventory.

4 Prepare a cost of production report.

A cost of production report is prepared periodically for each processing department. It summarizes (1) the units for which the department is accountable and the disposition of those units and (2) the production costs incurred by the department and the allocation of those costs. The report is used to control costs and improve the process.

5 Prepare journal entries for transactions of a process manufacturer.

Summary journal entries for common process manufacturer transactions are illustrated for McDermott Steel in the text. Basic entries include debiting the processing department work in process account for direct materials, direct labor, and applied factory overhead costs incurred in production. Costs for completed units are credited to the transferring department's work in process account and debited to the receiving department's work in process account.

6 Use cost of production reports for decision making.

The cost of production report provides information for controlling and improving operations. Most cost of production reports include the detailed manufacturing costs incurred for completing production during the period. Analyzing trends in each of these costs over time can provide insights about process performance.

7 Contrast just-in-time processing with conventional manufacturing practices.

The just-in-time processing philosophy focuses on reducing time, cost, and poor quality within the process. This is accomplished by combining process functions into work centers, assigning overhead services directly to the cells, involving the employees in process improvement efforts, eliminating wasteful activities, and reducing the amount of work in process inventory required to fulfill production targets.

ILLUSTRATIVE PROBLEM

Southern Aggregate Company manufactures concrete by a series of four processes. All materials are introduced in Crushing. From Crushing, the materials pass through Sifting, Baking, and Mixing, emerging as finished concrete. All inventories are costed by the first-in, first-out method.

The balances in the accounts Work in Process—Mixing and Finished Goods were as follows on May 1, 2003:

Work in Process—Mixing (2,000 units, 1/4 completed)	$13,700
Finished Goods (1,800 units at $8.00 a unit)	14,400

The following costs were charged to Work in Process—Mixing during May:

Direct materials transferred from Baking:	
15,200 units at $6.50 a unit	$98,800
Direct labor	17,200
Factory overhead	11,780

During May, 16,000 units of concrete were completed, and 15,800 units were sold. Inventories on May 31 were as follows:

Work in Process—Mixing: 1,200 units, 1/2 completed
Finished Goods: 2,000 units

Instructions

1. Prepare a cost of production report for the Mixing Department.
2. Determine the cost of goods sold (indicate number of units and unit costs).
3. Determine the finished goods inventory, May 31, 2003.

Solution

1.

Southern Aggregate Company
Cost of Production Report—Mixing Department
For the Month Ended May 31, 2003

UNITS	Whole Units	Equivalent Units Direct Materials	Equivalent Units Conversion
Units charged to production:			
Inventory in process, May 1	2,000		
Received from Baking	15,200		
Total units accounted for by the Mixing Dept.	17,200		
Units to be assigned cost:			
Inventory in process, May 1 (25% completed)	2,000	0	1,500
Started and completed in May	14,000	14,000	14,000
Transferred to finished goods in May	16,000	14,000	15,500
Inventory in process, May 31 (50% complete)	1,200	1,200	600
Total units to be assigned cost	17,200	15,200	16,100

COSTS	Costs Direct Materials	Costs Conversion	Total Costs
Unit costs:			
Total cost for May in Mixing	$ 98,800	$ 28,980	
Total equivalent units (from above)	÷15,200	÷16,100	
Cost per equivalent unit	$ 6.50	$ 1.80	
Costs charged to production:			
Inventory in process, May 1			$ 13,700
Costs incurred in May			127,780
Total costs accounted for by the Mixing Dept.			$141,480

	Direct Materials	Conversion	Total Costs
Costs allocated to completed and partially completed units:			
Inventory in process, May 1—balance			$ 13,700
To complete inventory in process, May 1	$ 0	$ 2,700 (a)	2,700
Started and completed in May	91,000 (b)	25,200 (c)	116,200
Transferred to finished goods in May			$132,600
Inventory in process, May 31	$ 7,800 (d)	$ 1,080 (e)	8,880
Total costs assigned by the Mixing Department			$141,480

(a) 1,500 × $1.80 = $2,700   (c) 14,000 × $1.80 = $25,200   (e) 600 × $1.80 = $1,080
(b) 14,000 × $6.50 = $91,000   (d) 1,200 × $6.50 = $7,800

2. Cost of goods sold:

1,800 units at $8.00	$ 14,400	(from finished goods beginning inventory)
2,000 units at $8.20*	16,400	(from work in process beginning inventory)
12,000 units at $8.30**	99,600	(from May production started and completed)
15,800 units	$130,400	

*($13,700 + $2,700) ÷ 2,000
**$116,200 ÷ 14,000

3. Finished goods inventory, May 31:

2,000 units at $8.30 $16,600

SELF-EXAMINATION QUESTIONS
Answers at End of Chapter

Matching
Match each of the following statements with its proper term. Some terms may not be used.

A.	cost of production report
B.	cost per equivalent unit
C.	equivalent units of production
D.	first-in, first-out (FIFO) cost method
E.	just-in-time processing
F.	manufacturing cells
G.	oil refinery
H.	process cost system
I.	process manufacturers
J.	transferred-out costs
K.	yield

___ 1. A type of cost system that accumulates costs for each of the various departments within a manufacturing facility.

___ 2. Manufacturers that use large machines to process a continuous flow of raw materials through various stages of completion into a finished state.

___ 3. The number of production units that could have been completed within a given accounting period, given the resources consumed.

___ 4. A method of inventory costing that assumes the unit product costs should be determined separately for each period in the order in which the costs were incurred.

___ 5. The rate used to allocate costs between completed and partially completed production.

___ 6. A report prepared periodically by a processing department, summarizing the costs incurred by the department and the allocation of those costs between completed and incomplete production.

___ 7. A measure of materials usage efficiency.

___ 8. A grouping of processes where employees are cross-trained to perform more than one function.

___ 9. A processing approach that focuses on eliminating time, cost, and poor quality within manufacturing and nonmanufacturing processes.

Multiple Choice

1. For which of the following businesses would the process cost system be most appropriate?
   A. Custom furniture manufacturer
   B. Commercial building contractor
   C. Crude oil refinery
   D. Automobile repair shop

2. There were 2,000 pounds in process at the beginning of the period in the Packing Department. Packing received 24,000 pounds from the Blending Department during the month, of which 3,000 pounds were in process at the end of the month. How many pounds were completed and transferred to finished goods from the Packing Department?
   A. 23,000   C. 26,000
   B. 21,000   D. 29,000

3. Information relating to production in Department A for May is as follows:

May 1	Balance, 1,000 units, 3/4 completed	$22,150
31	Direct materials, 5,000 units	75,000
31	Direct labor	32,500
31	Factory overhead	16,250

   If 500 units were one-fourth completed at May 31, 5,500 units were completed during May, and inventories are costed by the first-in, first-out method, what was the number of equivalent units of production with respect to conversion costs for May?
   A. 4,500   C. 5,500
   B. 4,875   D. 6,000

4. Based on the data presented in Question 3, what is the conversion cost per equivalent unit?
   A. $10   C. $25
   B. $15   D. $32

5. Information from the accounting system revealed the following:

	Day 1	Day 2	Day 3	Day 4	Day 5
Materials	$ 20,000	$18,000	$ 22,000	$ 20,000	$ 20,000
Electricity	2,500	3,000	3,500	4,000	4,700
Maintenance	4,000	3,800	3,400	3,000	2,800
Total costs	$ 26,500	$24,800	$ 28,900	$ 27,000	$ 27,500
Pounds produced	÷10,000	÷9,000	÷11,000	÷10,000	÷10,000
Cost per unit	$ 2.65	$ 2.75	$ 2.63	$ 2.70	$ 2.75

Which of the following statements best interprets this information?

A. The total costs are out of control.
B. The product costs have steadily increased because of higher electricity costs.
C. Electricity costs have steadily increased because of lack of maintenance.
D. The unit costs reveal a significant operating problem.

CLASS DISCUSSION QUESTIONS

1. Which type of cost system, process or job order, would be best suited for each of the following: (a) custom jewelry manufacturer, (b) paper manufacturer, (c) automobile repair shop, (d) building contractor, (e) TV assembler? Give reasons for your answers.

2. Are perpetual inventory accounts for materials, work in process, and finished goods generally used for (a) job order and (b) process cost systems?

3. In job order cost accounting, the three elements of manufacturing cost are charged directly to job orders. Why is it not necessary to charge manufacturing costs in process cost accounting to job orders?

4. In a job order cost system, direct labor and factory overhead applied are debited to individual jobs. How are these items treated in a process cost system and why?

5. What two groups of manufacturing costs are referred to as conversion costs?

6. What are transferred-out materials?

7. What account for a production department receives the debit for "transferred-in materials"?

8. What are the four steps for determining the cost of goods completed and the ending inventory?

9. What is meant by the term *equivalent units*?

10. Why is the cost per equivalent unit often determined separately for direct materials and conversion costs?

11. What is the purpose for determining the cost per equivalent unit?

12. Domingo Company is a process manufacturer with two production departments, Departments A and B. All direct materials are introduced in Department A from the materials store area. What is included in the cost transferred to Department B?

13. How is actual factory overhead accounted for in a process manufacturer?

14. What data are summarized in the two principal sections of the cost of production report?

15. What is the most important purpose of the cost of production report?

16. How are cost of production reports used for controlling and improving operations?

17. How is "yield" determined for a process manufacturer?

18. What is just-in-time processing?

19. How does just-in-time processing differ from the conventional manufacturing process?

RESOURCES FOR YOUR SUCCESS ONLINE AT

http://warren.swcollege.com

Remember! If you need additional help, visit South-Western's Web site.
See page M28 for a description of the online and printed materials that are available.

EXERCISES

Exercise 2–1

Flowchart of accounts related to service and processing departments

Objective 2

Alcoa Inc. is the world's largest producer of aluminum products. One product that Alcoa manufactures is aluminum sheet products for the aerospace industry. The entire output of the Smelting Department is transferred to the Rolling Department. Part of the fully processed goods from the Rolling Department are sold as rolled sheet, and the remainder of the goods are transferred to the Converting Department for further processing into sheared sheet.

Prepare a chart of the flow of costs from the processing department accounts into the finished goods accounts and then into the cost of goods sold account. The relevant accounts are as follows:

Cost of Goods Sold	Finished Goods—Rolled Sheet
Materials	Finished Goods—Sheared Sheet
Factory Overhead—Smelting Department	Work in Process—Smelting Department
Factory Overhead—Rolling Department	Work in Process—Rolling Department
Factory Overhead—Converting Department	Work in Process—Converting Department

Exercise 2–2

Entries for materials cost flows in a process cost system

Objective 2

Hershey Foods Corporation manufactures chocolate confectionery products. The three largest raw materials are cocoa beans, sugar, and dehydrated milk. These raw materials first go into the Blending Department. The blended product is then sent to the Molding Department, where the bars of candy are formed. The candy is then sent to the Packing Department, where the bars are wrapped and boxed. The boxed candy is then sent to the distribution center, where it is eventually sold to food brokers and retailers.

Show the accounts debited and credited for each of the following business events:

a.   Materials used by the Blending Department.
b.   Transfer of blended product to the Molding Department.
c.   Transfer of candy to the Packing Department.
d.   Transfer of boxed candy to the distribution center.
e.   Sale of boxed candy.

Exercise 2–3

Entries for flow of factory costs for process cost system

Objectives 2, 5

The **Domino Sugar Corporation** manufactures a sugar product by a continuous process, involving three production departments. Assume that records indicate that direct materials, direct labor, and applied factory overhead for the first department, Refining, were $145,000, $102,000, and $31,600, respectively. Also, work in process in the Refining Department at the beginning of the period totaled $14,000, and work in process at the end of the period totaled $45,000.

Journalize the entries to record (a) the flow of costs into the Refining Department during the period for (1) direct materials, (2) direct labor, and (3) factory overhead, and (b) the transfer of production costs to the second department, Sifting.

Exercise 2–4

Factory overhead rate, entry for applying factory overhead, and factory overhead account balance

Objectives 2, 5

✓ a. 130%

The chief cost accountant for Topps Beverage Co. estimated that total factory overhead cost for the Blending Department for the coming fiscal year beginning April 1 would be $520,000, and total direct labor costs would be $400,000. During April, the actual direct labor cost totaled $34,500, and factory overhead cost incurred totaled $44,000.

a.   What is the predetermined factory overhead rate based on direct labor cost?
b.   Journalize the entry to apply factory overhead to production for April.
c.   What is the April 30 balance of the account Factory Overhead—Blending Department?
d.   Does the balance in (c) represent overapplied or underapplied factory overhead?

Exercise 2–5

Equivalent units of production

Objective 3

✓ Direct materials, 9,900 units

The Converting Department of Zhao Napkin Company had 1,200 units in work in process at the beginning of the period, which were 60% complete. During the period, 10,500 units were completed and transferred to the Packing Department. There were 600 units in process at the end of the period, which were 30% complete. Direct materials are placed into the process at the beginning of production. Determine the number of equivalent units of production with respect to direct materials and conversion costs.

Exercise 2–6

Equivalent units of production

Objective 3

✓ a. Conversion, 75,400 units

Units of production data for the two departments of Southern Cable and Wire Company for October of the current fiscal year are as follows:

	Drawing Department	Winding Department
Work in process, October 1	2,000 units, 65% completed	1,400 units, 30% completed
Completed and transferred to next processing department during October	74,000 units	73,000 units
Work in process, October 31	3,600 units, 75% completed	2,400 units, 20% completed

If all direct materials are placed in process at the beginning of production, determine the direct materials and conversion equivalent units of production for October for (a) the Drawing Department and (b) the Winding Department.

Exercise 2–7

Equivalent units of production

Objectives 2, 3

✓ b. Conversion, 100,400

The following information concerns production in the Finishing Department for March. All direct materials are placed in process at the beginning of production.

ACCOUNT **Work in Process—Finishing Department**   ACCOUNT NO.

Date		Item	Debit	Credit	Balance Debit	Balance Credit
Mar.	1	Bal., 14,000 units, ²/₅ completed			38,000	
	31	Direct materials, 103,000 units	240,000		278,000	
	31	Direct labor	68,000		346,000	
	31	Factory overhead	40,800		386,800	
	31	Goods finished, 89,500 units		304,842	81,958	
	31	Bal.—units, ³/₅ completed			81,958	

a. Determine the number of units in work in process inventory at the end of the month.
b. Determine the equivalent units of production for direct materials and conversion costs in March.

Exercise 2–8

Equivalent units of production

Objectives 2, 3

The **Kellogg Company** manufactures cold cereal products, such as *Frosted Flakes* and *Special K*. Assume that the Inventory in Process for February 1 for the Packing Department included 1,200 pounds of cereal in the packing machine hopper. In addition, there were 800 empty 24-oz. boxes held in the package carousel of the packing machine. During February, 15,000 boxes of 24-oz. cereal were packaged. Conversion costs are incurred when a box is filled with cereal. On February 28, the packing machine hopper held 300 pounds of cereal, and the package carousel held 200 empty 24-oz. boxes. Assume that once a box is filled with cereal, it is immediately transferred to the finished goods warehouse.

Determine the equivalent units of production for cereal, boxes, and conversion costs for February. An equivalent unit is defined as "pounds" for cereal and "24-oz. boxes" for boxes and conversion costs.

Exercise 2–9

Costs per equivalent unit

Objective 3

✓ c. $5.50

Northern Pine Wood Products Inc. completed and transferred 32,000 particle board units of production from the Pressing Department. There was no beginning inventory in process in the department. The ending in-process inventory was 900 units, which were ²/₃ complete as to conversion cost. All materials are added at the beginning of the process. Direct materials cost incurred was $180,950, direct labor cost incurred was $30,000, and factory overhead applied was $18,900.

Determine the following for the Pressing Department:

a. Total conversion cost
b. Conversion cost per equivalent unit
c. Direct materials cost per equivalent unit

Exercise 2–10
Equivalent units of production and related costs

Objective 3

SPREADSHEET

✓ b. Conversion, $1.05

The charges to Work in Process—Baking Department for a period, together with information concerning production, are as follows. All direct materials are placed in process at the beginning of production.

Work in Process—Baking Department			
Bal., 8,000 units, 70% completed	75,000	To Finished Goods, 75,400 units	296,570
Direct materials, 67,400 units @ $2.20	148,280		
Direct labor	35,000		
Factory overhead	38,290		

Determine the following:

a. Equivalent units of production for direct materials and conversion.
b. Costs per equivalent unit for direct materials and conversion.

Exercise 2–11
Errors in equivalent unit computation

Objective 3

What's Wrong With This?

West Texas Oil Refining Company processes gasoline. At June 1 of the current year, 3,000 units were ⅖ completed in the Blending Department. During June, 16,500 units entered the Blending Department from the Refining Department. During June, the units in process at the beginning of the month were completed. Of the 16,500 units entering the department, all were completed except 3,900 units that were ⅓ completed. The equivalent units for conversion costs for June for the Blending Department were computed as follows:

Equivalent units of production in June:

To process units in inventory on June 1: 3,000 × ⅖	1,200
To process units started and completed in June: 16,500 − 3,000	13,500
To process units in inventory on June 30: 3,900 × ⅓	1,300
Equivalent units of production	16,000

List the errors in the computation of equivalent units for conversion costs for the Blending Department for June.

Exercise 2–12
Cost per equivalent unit

Objectives 2, 3

✓ Conversion, $4.50

The following information concerns production in the Forging Department for September. All direct materials are placed into the process at the beginning of production, and conversion costs are incurred evenly throughout the process. The beginning inventory consists of $43,000 of direct materials and $10,000 of conversion costs.

ACCOUNT Work in Process—Forging Department					ACCOUNT NO.	
					Balance	
Date		Item	**Debit**	**Credit**	**Debit**	**Credit**
Sept.	1	Bal., 5,500 units, 40% completed			53,000	
	30	Direct materials, 36,000 units	284,400		337,400	
	30	Direct labor	83,385		420,785	
	30	Factory overhead	83,385		504,170	
	30	Goods transferred, 38,300 units		474,570	29,600	
	30	Bal., 3,200 units, 30% completed			29,600	

Determine the cost per equivalent unit of direct materials and conversion.

Exercise 2–13
Cost of production report

Objective 4

The debits to Work in Process—Cooking Department for Better Beans Company for January 2003, together with information concerning production, are as follows:

✓ d. $750

Work in process, January 1, 800 pounds, 30% complete	$ 1,050
Beans added during January, 48,600 pounds	58,320
Conversion costs during January	24,480
Work in process, January 31, 500 pounds, 60% completed	—
Goods finished during January, 48,900 pounds	—

All direct materials are placed in process at the beginning of production. Prepare a cost of production report, presenting the following computations:

a. Direct materials and conversion equivalent units of production for the period.
b. Direct materials and conversion cost per equivalent unit for the period.
c. Cost of goods finished during the period.
d. Cost of work in process at the end of the period.

Exercise 2–14
Cost of production report

Objective 4

✓ Conversion rate, $0.70

Prepare a cost of production report for the Cutting Department of Arizona Carpet Company for July 2003, using the following data and assuming that all materials are added at the beginning of the process:

Work in process, July 1, 10,000 units, 70% complete	$ 50,000
Materials added during July from Weaving Dept., 182,000 units	837,200
Direct labor for July	71,160
Factory overhead for July	50,500
Goods finished during July (includes goods in process, July 1), 178,000 units	—
Work in process, July 31, 14,000 units, 20% completed	—

Exercise 2–15
Cost of production and journal entries

Objectives 2, 3, 5

Ventura Metal Works Company casts blades for turbine engines. Within the Casting Department, alloy is first melted in a crucible, then poured into molds to produce the castings. On March 1, there were 400 pounds of alloy in process, which were 65% complete as to conversion. The Work in Process balance for these 400 pounds was $20,000. During March, the Casting Department was charged $420,000 for 12,000 pounds of alloy and $140,000 for direct labor. Factory overhead is applied to the department at a rate of 90% of direct labor. The department transferred out 11,500 pounds of finished castings to the Machining Department. The March 31 inventory in process was 36% complete as to conversion.

Prepare the following March journal entries for the Casting Department:

a. The materials charged to production.
b. The conversion costs charged to production.
c. The completed production transferred to the Machining Department. Round to the nearest dollar.

Exercise 2–16
Decision making

Objective 6

Denver Bottling Company bottles popular beverages. The beverages are produced by blending concentrate with water and sugar. The concentrate is purchased from a concentrate producer. The concentrate producer sets higher prices for the more popular concentrate flavors. Below is a simplified cost of production report separating the cost of bottling the four flavors.

	Orange	Cola	Lemon-Lime	Root Beer
Concentrate	$ 3,600	$33,000	$21,000	$1,800
Water	1,200	9,000	6,000	600
Sugar	2,000	15,000	10,000	1,000
Bottles	4,400	33,000	22,000	2,200
Flavor changeover	3,000	1,800	1,200	3,000
Conversion cost	1,600	7,500	5,000	800
Total cost	$15,800	$99,300	$65,200	$9,400
Number of cases	2,000	15,000	10,000	1,000

Beginning and ending work in process inventories are negligible, so they are omitted from the cost of production report. The flavor changeover cost represents the cost of cleaning the bottling machines between production runs of different flavors.

▬▬▶ Prepare a memo to the production manager analyzing this comparative cost information. In your memo, provide recommendations for further action, along with supporting schedules showing the total cost per case and cost per case by cost element.

Exercise 2–17
Decision making
Objective 6

Forever Images Inc. produces film products for cameras. One of the processes for this operation is a coating (solvent spreading) operation, where chemicals are coated on to film stock. There has been some concern about the cost performance of this operation. As a result, you have begun an investigation. You first discover that all input prices have not changed for the last six months. If there is a problem, it is related to the quantity of input. You have discovered three possible problems from some of the operating personnel whose quotes follow:

Operator 1: "I've been keeping an eye on my operating room instruments. I feel as though our energy consumption is becoming less efficient."
Operator 2: "Every time the coating machine goes down, we produce waste on shutdown and subsequent startup. It seems as if during the last half year we have had more unscheduled machine shutdowns than in the past. Thus, I feel as though our yields must be dropping."
Operator 3: "My sense is that our coating costs are going up. It seems to me that we are spreading a thicker coating than we should. Perhaps the coating machine needs to be recalibrated."

The Coating Department had no beginning or ending inventories for any month during the study period. The following data from the cost of production report is made available:

	January	February	March	April	May	June
Transferred-in materials	$53,760	$67,200	$60,480	$50,400	$53,760	$67,200
Coating cost	$15,360	$21,120	$21,600	$20,160	$22,272	$30,720
Conversion cost (incl. energy)	$38,400	$48,000	$43,200	$36,000	$38,400	$48,000
Pounds input to the process	80,000	100,000	90,000	75,000	80,000	100,000
Pounds transferred out	76,800	96,000	86,400	72,000	76,800	96,000

Use the preceding information to discover the problem in the operation.

Exercise 2–18
Just-in-time manufacturing
Objective 7

The following are some quotes provided by a number of managers at Manning Machining Company regarding the company's planned move toward a just-in-time manufacturing system:

Director of Purchasing: *I'm very concerned about moving to a just-in-time system for materials. What would happen if one of our suppliers were unable to make a shipment? A supplier could fall behind in production or have a quality problem. Without some safety stock in our materials, our whole plant would shut down.*

Director of Manufacturing: *If we go to just-in-time, I think our factory output will drop. We need in-process inventory in order to "smooth out" the inevitable problems that occur during manufacturing. For example, if a machine that is used to process a product breaks down, I would starve the next machine if I don't have in-process inventory between the two machines. If I have in-process inventory, then I can keep the next operation busy while I fix the broken machine. Thus, the in-process inventories give me a safety valve that I can use to keep things running when things go wrong.*

Director of Sales: *I'm afraid we'll miss some sales if we don't keep a large stock of items on hand just in case demand increases. It only makes sense to me to keep large inventories in order to assure product availability for our customers.*

▬▬▶ How would you respond to these managers?

PROBLEMS SERIES A

Problem 2–1A
Entries for process cost system

Objectives 2, 5

GENERAL LEDGER

✓ 2. Materials March 31 balance, $25,900

Aladdin Carpet Company manufactures carpets. Fiber is placed in process in the Spinning Department, where it is spun into yarn. The output of the Spinning Department is transferred to the Tufting Department, where carpet backing is added at the beginning of the process and the process is completed. On March 1, Aladdin Carpet Company had the following inventories:

Finished Goods	$32,600
Work in Process—Spinning Department	5,800
Work in Process—Tufting Department	24,300
Materials	18,600

Departmental accounts are maintained for factory overhead, and both have zero balances on March 1.

Manufacturing operations for March are summarized as follows:

a.	Materials purchased on account	$732,400
b.	Materials requisitioned for use:	
	Fiber—Spinning Department	$489,300
	Carpet backing—Tufting Department	192,300
	Indirect materials—Spinning Department	34,000
	Indirect materials—Tufting Department	9,500
c.	Labor used:	
	Direct labor—Spinning Department	$234,200
	Direct labor—Tufting Department	165,700
	Indirect labor—Spinning Department	92,300
	Indirect labor—Tufting Department	54,200
d.	Depreciation charged on fixed assets:	
	Spinning Department	$63,200
	Tufting Department	31,200
e.	Expired prepaid factory insurance:	
	Spinning Department	$14,000
	Tufting Department	12,000
f.	Applied factory overhead:	
	Spinning Department	$205,000
	Tufting Department	105,000
g.	Production costs transferred from Spinning Dept. to Tufting Dept.	$914,300
h.	Production costs transferred from Tufting Dept. to Finished Goods	$1,380,100
i.	Cost of goods sold during the period	$1,393,000

Instructions

1. Journalize the entries to record the operations, identifying each entry by letter.
2. Compute the March 31 balances of the inventory accounts.
3. Compute the March 31 balances of the factory overhead accounts.

Problem 2–2A
Entries for process cost system

Objectives 2, 5

GENERAL LEDGER

Tasty Bakery Company manufactures cookies. Materials are placed in production in the Baking Department and after processing are transferred to the Packing Department, where packing materials are added. The finished products emerge from the Packing Department.

There were no inventories of work in process at the beginning or at the end of March, 2003. Finished goods inventory at March 1 was 500 cases of cookies at a total cost of $22,500.

Transactions related to manufacturing operations for March are summarized as follows:

a. Materials purchased on account, $280,000.
b. Materials requisitioned for use: Baking Department, $222,000 ($215,000 entered directly into the product); Packing Department, $50,000 ($45,000 entered directly into the product).

c. Labor costs incurred: Baking Department, $97,500 ($91,000 entered directly into the product); Packing Department, $73,200 ($70,000 entered directly into the product).

d. Miscellaneous costs and expenses incurred on account: Baking Department, $10,300; Packing Department, $4,300.

e. Depreciation charged on fixed assets: Baking Department, $15,500; Packing Department, $7,300.

f. Expiration of various prepaid expenses: Baking Department, $2,400; Packing Department, $1,100.

g. Factory overhead applied to production, based on machine hours: $42,000 for Baking and $21,000 for Packing.

h. Output of Baking Department: 11,000 cases.

i. Output of Packing Department: 11,000 cases of cookies.

j. Sales on account: 11,200 cases of cookies at $70. Credits to the finished goods account are to be made according to the first-in, first-out method.

Instructions

Journalize the entries to record the transactions, identifying each by letter. Include as an explanation for entry (j) the number of cases and the cost per case of cookies sold.

Problem 2–3A
Cost of production report
Objectives 3, 4

✓ Conversion cost per equivalent unit, $3.60

Valdez Coffee Company roasts and packs coffee beans. The process begins by placing coffee beans into the Roasting Department. From the Roasting Department, coffee beans are then transferred to the Packing Department. The following is a partial work in process account of the Roasting Department at March 31, 2003:

ACCOUNT Work in Process—Roasting Department					ACCOUNT NO.	
					Balance	
Date		**Item**	**Debit**	**Credit**	**Debit**	**Credit**
Mar.	1	Bal., 13,800 units, ⁴/₅ completed			114,600	
	31	Direct materials, 258,000 units	1,444,800		1,559,400	
	31	Direct labor	335,000		1,894,400	
	31	Factory overhead	571,192		2,465,592	
	31	Goods finished, 260,500 units		?		
	31	Bal. ? units, ¹/₅ completed			?	

Instructions

Prepare a cost of production report, and identify the missing amounts for the Work in Process—Roasting Department account.

Problem 2–4A
Equivalent units and related costs; cost of production report; entries
Objectives 3, 4, 5

SPREADSHEET

✓ 1. Transferred to Packaging Dept., $996,177

Baker's Choice Flour Company manufactures flour by a series of three processes, beginning with wheat grain being introduced in the Milling Department. From the Milling Department, the materials pass through the Sifting and Packaging Departments, emerging as packaged refined flour.

The balance in the account Work in Process—Sifting Department was as follows on July 1, 2003:

Work in Process—Sifting Department (25,800 units, 3/4 completed) $38,700

The following costs were charged to Work in Process—Sifting Department during July:

Direct materials transferred from Milling Department: 640,000 units at $1.15 a unit	$736,000
Direct labor	148,742
Factory overhead	92,406

During July, 650,000 units of flour were completed. Work in Process—Sifting Department on July 31 was 15,800 units, ¼ completed.

Instructions

1. Prepare a cost of production report for the Sifting Department for July.
2. Journalize the entries for costs transferred from Milling to Sifting and the costs transferred from Sifting to Packaging.
3. ◼━━► Discuss the uses of the cost of production report.

Problem 2–5A
Work in process account data for two months; cost of production reports

Objectives 2, 3, 4, 5

✓ 1. c. Transferred to finished goods in July, $648,900

Camden Soup Co. uses a process cost system to record the costs of processing soup, which requires a series of three processes. The inventory of Work in Process—Filling on July 1 and debits to the account during July 2003 were as follows:

Bal., 1,500 units, 35% completed	$ 9,225
From Cooking Dept., 90,000 units	486,000
Direct labor	100,346
Factory overhead	61,393

During July, 1,500 units in process on July 1 were completed, and of the 90,000 units entering the department, all were completed except 1,400 units that were 20% completed. Charges to Work in Process—Filling for August were as follows:

From Cooking Dept., 85,000 units	$467,500
Direct labor	101,199
Factory overhead	61,916

During August, the units in process at the beginning of the month were completed, and of the 85,000 units entering the department, all were completed except 1,350 units that were 80% completed.

Instructions

1. Enter the balance as of July 1, 2003, in a four-column account for Work in Process—Filling. Record the debits and the credits in the account for July. Construct a cost of production report, and present computations for determining (a) equivalent units of production for materials and conversion, (b) equivalent costs per unit, (c) cost of goods finished, differentiating between units started in the prior period and units started and finished in July, and (d) work in process inventory.
2. Provide the same information for August by recording the August transactions in the four-column work in process account. Construct a cost of production report, and present the August computations (a through d) listed in (1).

PROBLEMS SERIES B

Problem 2–1B
Entries for process cost system

Objectives 2, 5

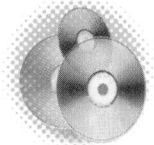
GENERAL LEDGER

✓ 2. Materials October 31 balance, $7,530

DirtAway Soap Company manufactures powdered detergent. Phosphate is placed in process in the Making Department, where it is turned into granulars. The output of Making is transferred to the Packing Department, where packaging is added at the beginning of the process. On October 1, DirtAway Soap Company had the following inventories:

Finished Goods	$15,800
Work in Process—Making	3,580
Work in Process—Packing	6,450
Materials	2,400

Departmental accounts are maintained for factory overhead, which both have zero balances on October 1.

Manufacturing operations for October are summarized as follows:

a.	Materials purchased on account	$158,900
b.	Materials requisitioned for use:	
	Phosphate—Making Department	$112,400
	Packaging—Packing Department	36,700
	Indirect materials—Making Department	3,200
	Indirect materials—Packing Department	1,470
c.	Labor used:	
	Direct labor—Making Department	$67,900
	Direct labor—Packing Department	42,700
	Indirect labor—Making Department	14,300
	Indirect labor—Packing Department	23,700
d.	Depreciation charged on fixed assets:	
	Making Department	$12,500
	Packing Department	9,400
e.	Expired prepaid factory insurance:	
	Making Department	$2,600
	Packing Department	1,000
f.	Applied factory overhead:	
	Making Department	$32,000
	Packing Department	36,000
g.	Production costs transferred from Making Dept. to Packing Dept.	$210,470
h.	Production costs transferred from Packing Dept. to finished goods	$324,700
i.	Cost of goods sold during the period	$330,500

Instructions

1. Journalize the entries to record the operations, identifying each entry by letter.
2. Compute the October 31 balances of the inventory accounts.
3. Compute the October 31 balances of the factory overhead accounts.

Problem 2–2B

Entries for process cost system

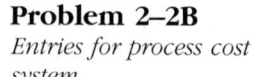

Objectives 2, 5

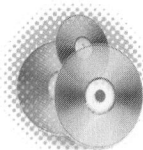

GENERAL LEDGER

Black Gold Refining Company processes gasoline. Petroleum is placed in production in the Refining Department and, after processing, is transferred to the Blending Department, where detergents are added. The finished blended gasoline emerges from the Blending Department.

There were no inventories of work in process at the beginning or at the end of July, 2003. Finished goods inventory at July 1 was 5,000 barrels of gasoline at a total cost of $200,000.

Transactions related to manufacturing operations for July are summarized as follows:

a. Materials purchased on account, $485,200.
b. Materials requisitioned for use: Refining, $417,500 ($412,300 entered directly into the product); Blending, $57,600 ($54,200 entered directly into the product).
c. Labor costs incurred: Refining, $106,300 ($83,200 entered directly into the product); Blending, $44,600 ($31,400 entered directly into the product).
d. Miscellaneous costs and expenses incurred on account: Refining, $13,200; Blending, $4,300.
e. Expiration of various prepaid expenses: Refining, $4,000; Blending, $1,500.
f. Depreciation charged on plant assets: Refining, $35,400; Blending, $12,300.
g. Factory overhead applied to production, based on processing hours: $82,000 for Refining and $34,275 for Blending.
h. Output of Refining: 17,500 barrels.
i. Output of Blending: 17,500 barrels of gasoline.
j. Sales on account: 20,000 barrels of gasoline at $45 per barrel. Credits to the finished goods account are to be made according to the first-in, first-out method.

Instructions

Journalize the entries to record the transactions, identifying each by letter. Include as an explanation for entry (j) the number of barrels and the cost per barrel of gasoline sold.

Problem 2–3B
Cost of production report
Objectives 3, 4

✓ Conversion rate per equivalent unit, $1.70

Wonder Chocolate Company processes chocolate into candy bars. The process begins by placing direct materials (raw chocolate, milk, and sugar) into the Blending Department. All materials are placed into production at the beginning of the blending process. After blending, the milk chocolate is then transferred to the Molding Department, where the milk chocolate is formed into candy bars. The following is a partial work in process account of the Blending Department at December 31, 2003:

ACCOUNT Work in Process—Blending Department					ACCOUNT NO.	
					Balance	
Date		Item	Debit	Credit	Debit	Credit
Dec.	1	Bal., 3,500 units, 40% completed			17,000	
	31	Direct materials, 145,000 units	638,000		655,000	
	31	Direct labor	94,500		749,500	
	31	Factory overhead	149,977		899,477	
	31	Goods finished, 143,800 units		?		
	31	Bal. ? units, 30% completed			?	

Instructions
Prepare a cost of production report, and identify the missing amounts for the Work in Process—Blending Department account.

Problem 2–4B
Equivalent units and related costs; cost of production report; entries
Objectives 3, 4, 5

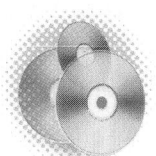 **SPREADSHEET**

✓ Transferred to finished goods, $565,982

Coastal Chemical Company manufactures specialty chemicals by a series of three processes, all materials being introduced in the Distilling Department. From the Distilling Department, the materials pass through the Reaction and Filling Departments, emerging as finished chemicals.

The balance in the account Work in Process—Filling was as follows on October 1, 2003:

Work in Process—Filling Department
(800 units, 60% completed) $15,520

The following costs were charged to Work in Process—Filling during October:

Direct materials transferred from Reaction	
Department: 24,500 units at $14.40 a unit	$352,800
Direct labor	74,498
Factory overhead	146,996

During October, 24,100 units of specialty chemicals were completed. Work in Process—Filling Department on October 31 was 1,200 units, 60% completed.

Instructions
1. Prepare a cost of production report for the Filling Department for October.
2. Journalize the entries for costs transferred from Reaction to Filling and the cost of goods transferred to finished goods.
3. ▬▬► Discuss the uses of the cost of production report.

Problem 2–5B
Work in process account data for two months; cost of production reports
Objectives 2, 3, 4, 5

✓ 1. c. Transferred to finished goods in September, $6,920,015

International Aluminum Company uses a process cost system to record the costs of manufacturing rolled aluminum, which requires a series of four processes. The inventory of Work in Process—Rolling on September 1, 2003, and debits to the account during September were as follows:

Bal., 3,700 units, 10% completed	$ 183,150
From Smelting Dept., 114,500 units	5,152,500
Direct labor	459,123
Factory overhead	1,348,642

During September, 3,700 units in process on September 1 were completed, and of the 114,500 units entering the department, all were completed except 4,000 units that were 70% completed.

Charges to Work in Process—Rolling for October were as follows:

From Smelting Department, 120,200 units	$5,589,300
Direct labor	458,373
Factory overhead	1,346,427

During October, the units in process at the beginning of the month were completed, and of the 120,200 units entering the department, all were completed except 5,400 units that were 80% completed.

Instructions

1. Enter the balance as of September 1, 2003, in a four-column account for Work in Process—Rolling. Record the debits and the credits in the account for September. Construct a cost of production report and present computations for determining (a) equivalent units of production for materials and conversion, (b) equivalent costs per unit, (c) cost of goods finished, differentiating between units started in the prior period and units started and finished in September, and (d) work in process inventory.
2. Provide the same information for October by recording the October transactions in the four-column work in process account. Construct a cost of production report, and present the October computations (a through d) listed in (1).

SPECIAL ACTIVITIES

Activity 2–1
Auntie M's Cookie Company
Ethics and professional conduct in business

You are the division controller for Auntie M's Cookie Company. Auntie M has introduced a new chocolate chip cookie called Chock Full of Chips, and it is a success. As a result, the product manager responsible for the launch of this new cookie was promoted to division vice-president and became your boss. A new product manager, Davis, has been brought in to replace the promoted manager. Davis notices that the Chock Full of Chips cookie uses a lot of chips, which increases the cost of the cookie. As a result, Davis has ordered that the amount of chips used in the cookies be reduced by 5%. The manager believes that a 5% reduction in chips will not adversely affect sales, but will reduce costs, and hence improve margins. The increased margins would help Davis meet profit targets for the period.

You are looking over some cost of production reports segmented by cookie line. You notice that there is a drop in the materials costs for Chock Full of Chips. On further investigation, you discover why the chip costs have declined (fewer chips). Both you and Davis report to the division vice-president, who was the original product manager for Chock Full of Chips. You are trying to decide what to do, if anything.

➤ Discuss the options you might consider.

Activity 2–2
International Paper, Inc.
Accounting for materials costs

In papermaking operations for companies such as **International Paper, Inc.**, wet pulp is fed into paper machines, which press and dry pulp into a continuous sheet of paper. The paper is formed at very high speeds (60 mph). Once the paper is formed, the paper is rolled onto a reel at the back end of the paper machine. One of the characteristics of paper making is the creation of "broke" paper. Broke is paper that fails to satisfy quality standards and is therefore rejected for final shipment to customers. Broke is recycled back to the beginning of the process by combining the recycled paper with virgin (new) pulp material. The combination of virgin pulp and recycled broke is sent to the paper machine for papermaking. Broke is fed into this recycle process continuously from all over the facility.

In this industry it is typical to charge the papermaking operation with the cost of direct materials, which is a mixture of virgin materials and broke. Broke has a much lower cost than does virgin pulp. Therefore, the more broke in the mixture, the lower the average cost of direct materials to the department. Papermaking managers will frequently comment on the importance of broke for keeping their direct materials costs down.

a. ■───► How do you react to this accounting procedure?
b. ■───► What "hidden costs" are not considered when accounting for broke as described above?

Activity 2–3
Pittsburgh Can
Company
Analyzing unit costs

Pittsburgh Can Company manufactures cans for the canned food industry. The operations manager of a can manufacturing operation wants to conduct a cost study investigating the relationship of tin content in the material (can stock) to the energy cost for enameling the cans. The enameling was necessary to prepare the cans for labeling. A higher percentage of tin content in the can stock increases the cost of material. The operations manager believed there was a relationship between the tin content and energy costs for enameling. During the analysis period the amount of tin content in the steel can stock was increased for every week, from week 1 to week 6. The following operating reports were available from the controller:

	Week 1	Week 2	Week 3	Week 4	Week 5	Week 6
Energy	$ 1,300	$ 2,880	$ 2,420	$ 1,400	$ 1,620	$ 1,500
Materials	1,200	3,000	2,860	1,890	2,520	2,900
Total cost	$ 2,500	$ 5,880	$ 5,280	$ 3,290	$ 4,140	$ 4,400
Units produced	÷10,000	÷24,000	÷22,000	÷14,000	÷18,000	÷20,000
Cost per unit	$ 0.250	$ 0.245	$ 0.240	$ 0.235	$ 0.230	$ 0.220

Differences in materials unit costs were entirely related to the amount of tin content. ■───► Interpret this information and report to the operations manager your recommendations with respect to tin content.

Activity 2–4
Ranier Paper Company
Decision making

Fred Greenbar, plant manager of Ranier Paper Company's papermaking mill, was looking over the cost of production reports for October and November for the Papermaking Department. The reports revealed the following:

	October	November
Pulp and chemicals	$300,000	$307,000
Conversion cost	150,000	153,000
Total cost	$450,000	$460,000
Number of tons	÷ 625	÷ 575
Cost per ton	$ 720	$ 800

Fred was concerned about the growth in the cost per ton from the output of the department. As a result, he asked the plant controller to perform a study to help explain these results. The controller, Sally Kramer, began the analysis by performing some interviews of key plant personnel in order to understand what the problem might be. Excerpts from an interview with Ferris Miles, a paper machine operator, follow:

Ferris: We have two papermaking machines in the department. I have no data, but I think paper machine 1 is applying too much pulp, and thus is wasting both conversion and materials resources. We haven't had repairs on paper machine 1 in a while. Maybe this is the problem.
Sally: How does too much pulp result in wasted resources?
Ferris: Well, you see, if too much pulp is applied, then we will waste pulp material. The customer will not pay for the extra weight. Thus, we just lose that amount of material. Also, when there is too much pulp, the machine must be slowed down in order to complete the drying process. This results in a waste of conversion costs.
Sally: Do you have any other suspicions?

Ferris: Well, as you know, we have two products—red paper and blue paper. They are identical except for the color. The color is added to the paper-making process in the paper machine. I think that during November these two color papers have been behaving very differently. I don't have any data, but it just seems as though the amount of waste associated with the red paper has increased.

Sally: Why is this?

Ferris: I understand that there has been a change in specifications for the red paper starting near the beginning of November. This change could be causing the machines to run poorly when making red paper. If this is the case, the cost per ton would increase for red paper.

Sally also asked for a computer printout providing greater detail on November's operating results.

Computer run: 42
December 4
Requested by: Sally Kramer

Papermaking Department—November detail

Paper Machine	Color	Materials Costs	Conversion Costs	Tons
1	Red	35,800	17,400	60
1	Blue	41,700	21,200	70
1	Red	44,600	22,500	75
1	Blue	36,100	18,100	60
2	Red	38,300	18,800	80
2	Blue	41,300	19,900	85
2	Red	35,600	18,100	75
2	Blue	33,600	17,000	70
Total		307,000	153,000	575

Assuming that you're Sally Kramer, write a memo to Fred Greenbar with a recommendation to management. You should analyze the November data to determine whether the paper machine or the paper color explains the increase in the unit cost from October. Include any supporting schedules that are appropriate.

Activity 2–5
Into the Real World
Process costing companies

The following categories represent typical process manufacturing industries:

Beverages	Metals
Chemicals	Petroleum refining
Food	Pharmaceuticals
Forest and paper products	Soap and cosmetics

In each category, identify one company (following your instructor's specific instructions) and determine the following:

1. Typical products manufactured by the selected company, including brand names.
2. Typical raw materials used by the selected company.
3. Types of processes used by the selected company.

Use annual reports, the Internet, or library resources in doing this activity.

ANSWERS TO SELF-EXAMINATION QUESTIONS

Matching
1. H   2. I   3. C   4. D   5. B   6. A   7. K   8. F   9. E

Multiple Choice

1. **C** The process cost system is most appropriate for a business where manufacturing is conducted by continuous operations and involves a series of uniform production processes, such as the processing of crude oil (answer C). The job order cost system is most appropriate for a business where the product is made to customers' specifications, such as custom furniture manufacturing (answer A), commercial building construction (answer B), or automobile repair shop (answer D).

2. **A** The total pounds transferred to finished goods (23,000) are the 2,000 in-process pounds at the beginning of the period plus the number of pounds started and completed during the month, 21,000 (24,000 − 3,000). Answer B incorrectly assumes that the beginning inventory is not transferred during the month. Answer C assumes that all 24,000 pounds started during the month are transferred to finished goods, instead of only the portion started and completed. Answer D incorrectly adds all the numbers together.

3. **B** The number of units that could have been produced from start to finish during a period is termed equivalent units. The 4,875 equivalent units (answer B) is determined as follows:

To process units in inventory on May 1 (1,000 × 1/4)	250
To process units started and completed in May (5,500 units − 1,000 units)	4,500
To process units in inventory on May 31 (500 units × 1/4)	125
Equivalent units of production in May	4,875

4. **A** The conversion costs (direct labor and factory overhead) totaling $48,750 are divided by the number of equivalent units (4,875) to determine the unit conversion cost of $10 (answer A).

5. **C** The electricity costs have increased, and maintenance costs have decreased. Answer C would be a reasonable explanation for these results. The total costs, materials costs, and costs per unit do not reveal any type of pattern over the time period. In fact, the materials costs have stayed at exactly $2.00 per pound over the time period. This demonstrates that aggregated numbers can sometimes hide underlying information that can be used to improve the process.

Cost Behavior and Cost-Volume-Profit Analysis

M3

objectives

After studying this chapter, you should be able to:

1 Classify costs by their behavior as variable costs, fixed costs, or mixed costs.

2 Compute the contribution margin, the contribution margin ratio, and the unit contribution margin, and explain how they may be useful to managers.

3 Using the unit contribution margin, determine the break-even point and the volume necessary to achieve a target profit.

4 Using a cost-volume-profit chart and a profit-volume chart, determine the break-even point and the volume necessary to achieve a target profit.

5 Calculate the break-even point for a business selling more than one product.

6 Compute the margin of safety and the operating leverage, and explain how managers use these concepts.

7 List the assumptions underlying cost-volume-profit analysis.

hat are the costs of operating your car? You will normally pay a license plate (tag) fee once a year. This cost does not change, regardless of the number of miles you drive. On the other hand, the total amount you spend on gasoline during the year changes on a day-to-day basis as you drive. The more you drive, the more you spend on gasoline.

How does such operating cost information affect you? Information on how your car's operating costs behave could be relevant in planning a summer vacation. For example, you might be trying to decide between taking an airline flight or driving your car to your vacation destination. In this case, your license plate fee and annual car insurance costs will not change, regardless of whether you drive your car or fly. Thus, these costs would not affect your decision. However, the estimated cost of gasoline and routine maintenance would affect your decision.

As in operating your car, all of the costs of operating a business do not behave in the same way. In this chapter, we discuss commonly used methods for classifying costs according to how they change. We also discuss how management uses cost-volume-profit analysis as a tool in making decisions.

Cost Behavior

objective 1

Classify costs by their behavior as variable costs, fixed costs, or mixed costs.

Knowing how costs behave is useful to management for a variety of purposes. For example, knowing how costs behave allows managers to predict profits as sales and production volumes change. Knowing how costs behave is also useful for estimating costs. Estimated costs, in turn, affect a variety of management decisions, such as whether to use excess machine capacity to produce and sell a product at a reduced price.

Cost behavior refers to the manner in which a cost changes as a related activity changes. To understand cost behavior, two factors must be considered. First, we must identify the activities that are thought to cause the cost to be incurred. Such activities are called **activity bases** (or **activity drivers**). Second, we must specify the range of activity over which the changes in the cost are of interest. This range of activity is called the **relevant range**.

To illustrate, hospital administrators must plan and control hospital food costs. To fully understand why food costs change, the activity that causes cost to be incurred must be identified. In the case of food costs, the feeding of patients is a major cause of these costs. The number of patients *treated* by the hospital would not be a good activity base, since some patients are outpatients who do not stay in the hospital. The number of patients who *stay* in the hospital, however, is a good activity base for studying food costs. Once the proper activity base is identified, food costs can then be analyzed over the range of the number of patients who normally stay in the hospital (the relevant range).

Three of the most common classifications of cost behavior are variable costs, fixed costs, and mixed costs.

Variable Costs

When the level of activity is measured in units produced, direct materials and direct labor costs are generally classified as variable costs. **Variable costs** are costs that vary in proportion to changes in the level of activity. For example, assume that

Jason Inc. produces stereo sound systems under the brand name of J-Sound. The parts for the stereo systems are purchased from outside suppliers for $10 per unit and are assembled in Jason Inc.'s Waterloo plant. The direct materials costs for Model JS-12 for the relevant range of 5,000 to 30,000 units of production are shown below.

Number of Units of Model JS-12 Produced	Direct Materials Cost per Unit	Total Direct Materials Cost
5,000 units	$10	$ 50,000
10,000	10	100,000
15,000	10	150,000
20,000	10	200,000
25,000	10	250,000
30,000	10	300,000

Variable costs are the same per unit, while the total variable cost changes in proportion to changes in the activity base. For Model JS-12, for example, the direct materials cost for 10,000 units ($100,000) is twice the direct materials cost for 5,000 units ($50,000). The total direct materials cost varies in proportion to the number of units produced because the direct materials cost per unit ($10) is the same for all levels of production. Thus, producing 20,000 additional units of JS-12 will increase the direct materials cost by $200,000 (20,000 × $10), producing 25,000 additional units will increase the materials cost by $250,000, and so on.

Exhibit 1 illustrates how the variable costs for direct materials for Model JS-12 behave in total and on a per-unit basis as production changes.

Exhibit 1 Variable Cost Graphs

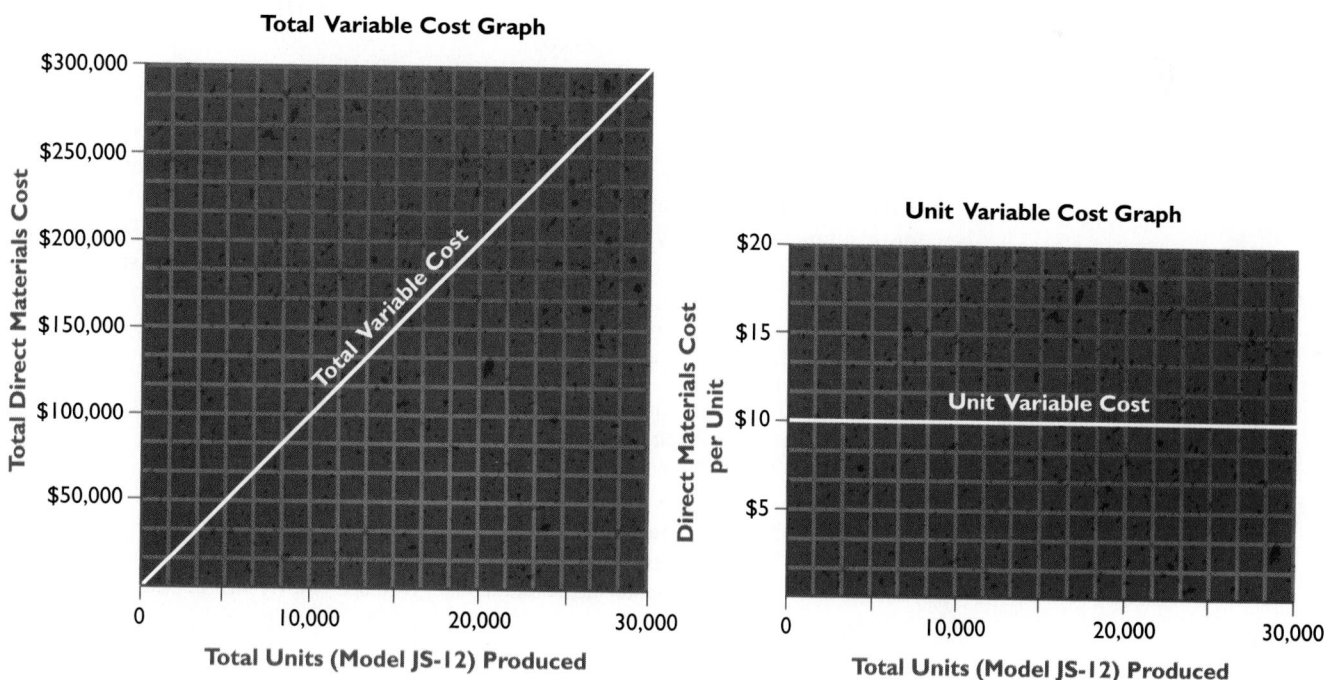

There are a variety of activity bases used by managers for evaluating cost behavior. The following list provides some examples of variable costs, along with their related activity bases for various types of businesses.

Type of Business	Cost	Activity Base
University	Instructor salaries	Number of classes
Passenger airline	Fuel	Number of miles flown
Manufacturing	Direct materials	Number of units produced
Hospital	Nurse wages	Number of patients
Hotel	Maid wages	Number of guests
Bank	Teller wages	Number of banking transactions
Insurance	Claim processing salaries	Number of claims

Fixed Costs

Fixed costs are costs that remain the same in total dollar amount as the level of activity changes. To illustrate, assume that Minton Inc. manufactures, bottles, and distributes La Fleur Perfume at its Los Angeles plant. The production supervisor at the Los Angeles plant is Jane Sovissi, who is paid a salary of $75,000 per year. The relevant range of activity for a year is 50,000 to 300,000 bottles of perfume. Sovissi's salary is a fixed cost that does not vary with the number of units produced. Regardless of the number of bottles produced within the range of 50,000 to 300,000 bottles, Sovissi receives a salary of $75,000.

Although the total fixed cost remains the same as the number of bottles produced changes, the fixed cost per bottle changes. As more bottles are produced, the total fixed costs are spread over a larger number of bottles, and thus the fixed cost per bottle decreases. This relationship is shown below for Jane Sovissi's $75,000 salary.

Number of Bottles of Perfume Produced	Total Salary for Jane Sovissi	Salary per Bottle of Perfume Produced
50,000 bottles	$75,000	$1.500
100,000	75,000	0.750
150,000	75,000	0.500
200,000	75,000	0.375
250,000	75,000	0.300
300,000	75,000	0.250

Exhibit 2 illustrates how the fixed cost of Jane Sovissi's salary behaves in total and on a per-unit basis as production changes. When units produced is the measure of activity, examples of fixed costs include straight-line depreciation of factory equipment, insurance on factory plant and equipment, and salaries of factory supervisors. Other examples of fixed costs and their activity bases for a variety of businesses are as follows:

Type of Business	Fixed Cost	Activity Base
University	Building depreciation	Number of students
Passenger airline	Airplane depreciation	Number of passengers
Manufacturing	Plant manager salary	Number of units produced
Hospital	Property insurance	Number of patients
Hotel	Property taxes	Number of guests
Bank	Branch manager salary	Number of customer accounts
Insurance	Computer depreciation	Number of insurance policies

Mixed Costs

A mixed cost has characteristics of both a variable and a fixed cost. For example, over one range of activity, the total mixed cost may remain the same. It thus behaves as a fixed cost. Over another range of activity, the mixed cost may change in proportion to changes in the level of activity. It thus behaves as a variable cost. Mixed costs are sometimes called *semivariable* or *semifixed* costs.

Exhibit 2 Fixed Cost Graphs

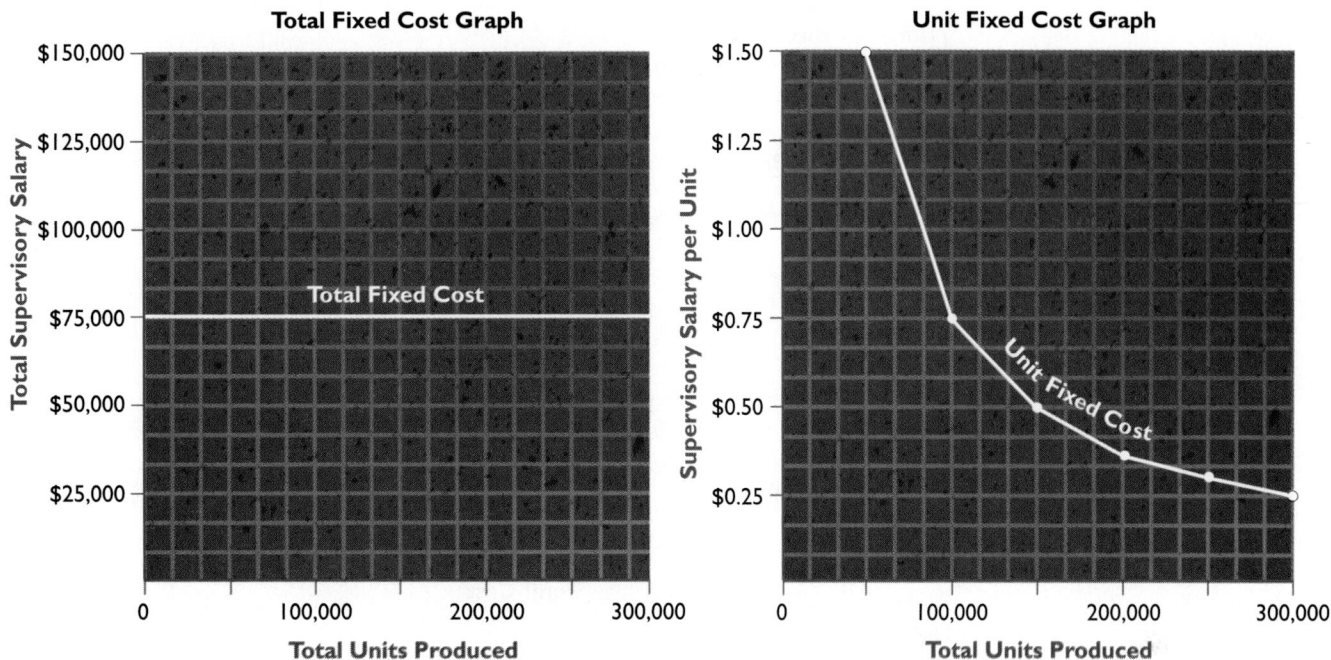

Total Fixed Cost Graph

Total Supervisory Salary

$150,000

$125,000

$100,000

Total Fixed Cost

$75,000

$50,000

$25,000

0   100,000   200,000   300,000

Total Units Produced

Unit Fixed Cost Graph

Supervisory Salary per Unit

$1.50

$1.25

$1.00

$0.75

Unit Fixed Cost

$0.50

$0.25

0   100,000   200,000   300,000

Total Units Produced

To illustrate, assume that Simpson Inc. manufactures sails, using rented machinery. The rental charges are $15,000 per year, plus $1 for each machine hour used over 10,000 hours. If the machinery is used 8,000 hours, the total rental charge is $15,000. If the machinery is used 20,000 hours, the total rental charge is $25,000 [$15,000 + (10,000 hours × $1)], and so on. Thus, if the level of activity is measured in machine hours and the relevant range is 0 to 40,000 hours, the rental charges are a fixed cost up to 10,000 hours and a variable cost thereafter. This mixed cost behavior is shown graphically in Exhibit 3.

Exhibit 3 Mixed Costs

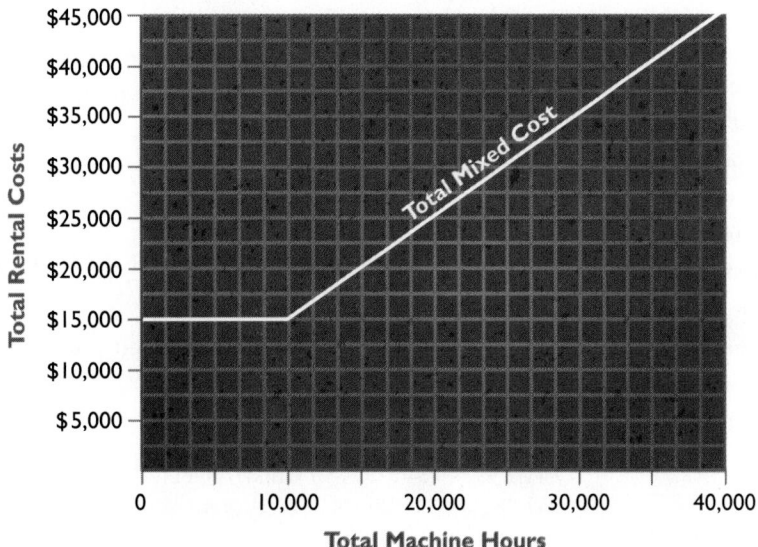

Total Rental Costs

$45,000

$40,000

$35,000

$30,000

$25,000

$20,000

Total Mixed Cost

$15,000

$10,000

$5,000

0   10,000   20,000   30,000   40,000

Total Machine Hours

In analyses, mixed costs are usually separated into their fixed and variable components. The **high-low method** is a cost estimation technique that may be used for this purpose.[1] The high-low method uses the highest and lowest activity levels and their related costs to estimate the variable cost per unit and the fixed cost component of mixed costs.

To illustrate, assume that the Equipment Maintenance Department of Kason Inc. incurred the following costs during the past five months:

	Production	Total Cost
June	1,000 units	$45,550
July	1,500	52,000
August	2,100	61,500
September	1,800	57,500
October	750	41,250

The number of units produced is the measure of activity, and the number of units produced between June and October is the relevant range of production. For Kason Inc., the difference between the number of units produced and the difference between the total cost at the highest and lowest levels of production are as follows:

	Production	Total Cost
Highest level	2,100 units	$61,500
Lowest level	750	41,250
Difference	1,350 units	$20,250

Since the total fixed cost does not change with changes in volume of production, the $20,250 difference in the total cost is the change in the total variable cost. Hence, dividing the difference in the total cost by the difference in production provides an estimate of the variable cost per unit. For Kason Inc., this estimate is $15, as shown below.

$$\textbf{Variable cost per unit} = \frac{\textbf{Difference in total cost}}{\textbf{Difference in production}}$$

$$\text{Variable cost per unit} = \frac{\$20,250}{1,350 \text{ units}} = \$15$$

The fixed cost will be the same at both the highest and the lowest levels of production. Thus, the fixed cost can be estimated at either of these levels. This is done by subtracting the estimated total variable cost from the total cost, using the following total cost equation:

Total cost = (Variable cost per unit × Units of production) + Fixed cost

Highest level:
$61,500 = ($15 × 2,100 units) + Fixed cost
$61,500 = $31,500 + Fixed cost
$30,000 = Fixed cost
Lowest level:
$41,250 = ($15 × 750 units) + Fixed cost
$41,250 = $11,250 + Fixed cost
$30,000 = Fixed cost

The manufacturing cost at the highest production level of 2,500 units is $125,000. The manufacturing cost at the lowest production level of 1,000 units is $80,000. Using the high-low method, what are (a) the variable cost per unit and (b) the total fixed cost?

- -

(a) $30 per unit [($125,000 − $80,000) ÷ (2,500 − 1,000)]; (b) $50,000 [$125,000 − ($30 × 2,500)]

---

[1] Other methods of estimating costs, such as the scattergraph method and the least squares method, are discussed in cost accounting textbooks.

The total equipment maintenance cost for Kason Inc. can thus be analyzed as a $30,000 fixed cost and a $15-per-unit variable cost. Using these amounts in the total cost equation, the total equipment maintenance cost at other levels of production can be estimated.

Summary of Cost Behavior Concepts

Examples of common variable, fixed, and mixed costs when the number of units produced is the activity base are:

Variable Cost	Fixed Cost	Mixed Cost
Direct materials	Depreciation expense	Quality Control Department salaries
Direct labor	Property taxes	Purchasing Department salaries
Electricity expense	Officer salaries	Maintenance expenses
Sales commissions	Insurance expense	Warehouse expenses

Mixed costs contain a fixed cost component that is incurred even if nothing is produced. For analyses, the fixed and variable cost components of mixed costs should be separated.

The following table summarizes the cost behavior attributes of variable costs and fixed costs:

Cost	Effect of Changing Activity Level	
	Total Amount	**Per-Unit Amount**
Variable	Increases and decreases proportionately with activity level.	Remains the same regardless of activity level.
Fixed	Remains the same regardless of activity level.	Increases and decreases inversely with activity level.

BUSINESS ON STAGE

Cost Behavior and Employee Compensation

There are several methods for compensating employees, each of which has a different cost behavior. The most common form is a *wage* based on the number of hours worked. This type of compensation causes wages to be variable to the number of hours worked. Alternatively, some industries, such as the garment industry, use a *piecework* system to pay their employees. Under this type of plan, the employee is paid a given amount for each unit completed. The compensation is variable to the number of units produced. In contrast, many staff employees are paid a weekly or monthly *salary*. A salaried employee's compensation does not depend on the number of hours worked or the actual number of units produced or sold. Thus, a salary is fixed to the underlying level of production or sales. In between these two extremes are several plans that have both fixed and variable elements and, as such, are mixed costs. Examples include pay for salespeople based on a straight salary plus a *commission* based on sales. In manufacturing settings, *gain-sharing* plans are becoming very popular. Under these plans, employees receive a straight wage plus a bonus for achieving production targets or other efficiency gains. In a *profit-sharing* plan, employees receive a wage or salary plus a periodic bonus based on the profits earned by the business. Compensation plans that use variable compensation attempt to provide employees incentives for achieving specific goals. ■

Reporting Variable and Fixed Costs

Separating costs into their variable and fixed components for reporting purposes can be useful for decision making. One method of reporting variable and fixed costs is called **variable costing** or **direct costing**. Under variable costing, only the variable manufacturing costs (direct materials, direct labor, and variable factory overhead) are included in the product cost. The fixed factory overhead is an expense of the period in which it is incurred.[2]

Cost-Volume-Profit Relationships

objective 2

Compute the contribution margin, the contribution margin ratio, and the unit contribution margin, and explain how they may be useful to managers.

After costs have been classified as fixed and variable, their effect on revenues, volume, and profits can be studied by using cost-volume-profit analysis. **Cost-volume-profit analysis** is the systematic examination of the relationships among selling prices, sales and production volume, costs, expenses, and profits.

Cost-volume-profit analysis provides management with useful information for decision making. For example, cost-volume-profit analysis may be used in setting selling prices, selecting the mix of products to sell, choosing among marketing strategies, and analyzing the effects of changes in costs on profits. In today's business environment, management must make such decisions quickly and accurately. As a result, the importance of cost-volume-profit analysis has increased in recent years.

Contribution Margin Concept

One relationship among cost, volume, and profit is the contribution margin. The **contribution margin** is the excess of sales revenues over variable costs. The contribution margin concept is especially useful in business planning because it gives insight into the profit potential of a firm. To illustrate, the income statement of Lambert Inc. in Exhibit 4 has been prepared in a contribution margin format.

Exhibit 4 Contribution Margin Income Statement

Sales	$1,000,000
Variable costs	600,000
Contribution margin	$ 400,000
Fixed costs	300,000
Income from operations	$ 100,000

Contribution Margin

Income from Operations

The contribution margin of $400,000 is available to cover the fixed costs of $300,000. Once the fixed costs are covered, any remaining amount adds directly to the income from operations of the company. Think of the fixed costs as a bucket and the contribution margin as water filling the bucket. Once the bucket is filled, the overflow represents income from operations. Up until the point of overflow, however, the contribution margin contributes to fixed costs (filling the bucket).

---

[2] The variable costing concept is discussed more fully in the next chapter.

Contribution Margin Ratio

The contribution margin can also be expressed as a percentage. The contribution margin ratio, sometimes called the **profit-volume ratio**, indicates the percentage of each sales dollar available to cover the fixed costs and to provide income from operations. For Lambert Inc., the contribution margin ratio is 40%, as computed below.

$$\text{Contribution margin ratio} = \frac{\text{Sales} - \text{Variable costs}}{\text{Sales}}$$

$$\text{Contribution margin ratio} = \frac{\$1,000,000 - \$600,000}{\$1,000,000} = 40\%$$

The contribution margin ratio measures the effect on income from operations of an increase or a decrease in sales volume. For example, assume that the management of Lambert Inc. is studying the effect of adding $80,000 in sales orders. Multiplying the contribution margin ratio (40%) by the change in sales volume ($80,000) indicates that income from operations will increase $32,000 if the additional orders are obtained. The validity of this analysis is illustrated by the following contribution margin income statement of Lambert Inc.:

Sales	$1,080,000
Variable costs ($1,080,000 × 60%)	648,000
Contribution margin ($1,080,000 × 40%)	$ 432,000
Fixed costs	300,000
Income from operations	$ 132,000

Variable costs as a percentage of sales are equal to 100% minus the contribution margin ratio. Thus, in the above income statement, the variable costs are 60% (100% − 40%) of sales, or $648,000 ($1,080,000 × 60%). The total contribution margin, $432,000, can also be computed directly by multiplying the sales by the contribution margin ratio ($1,080,000 × 40%).

In using the contribution margin ratio in analysis, factors other than sales volume, such as variable cost per unit and sales price, are assumed to remain constant. If such factors change, their effect must be considered.

The contribution margin ratio is also useful in setting business policy. For example, if the contribution margin ratio of a firm is large and production is at a level below 100% capacity, a large increase in income from operations can be expected from an increase in sales volume. A firm in such a position might decide to devote more effort to sales promotion because of the large change in income from operations that will result from changes in sales volume. In contrast, a firm with a small contribution margin ratio will probably want to give more attention to reducing costs before attempting to promote sales.

Unit Contribution Margin

The unit contribution margin is also useful for analyzing the profit potential of proposed projects. The unit contribution margin is the dollars from each unit of sales available to cover fixed costs and provide income from operations. For example, if Lambert Inc.'s unit selling price is $20 and its unit variable cost is $12, the unit contribution margin is $8 ($20 − $12).

Sales are 20,000 units at $12 per unit, variable costs are $9 per unit, and fixed costs are $25,000. What are (a) the contribution margin ratio, (b) the unit contribution margin, and (c) the income from operations?

(a) 25% [($240,000 − $180,000) ÷ $240,000]; (b) $3 per unit ($12 − $9); (c) $35,000 ($240,000 − $180,000 − $25,000)

A $200-per-night room at the Ritz Carlton may have a variable cost, including maids' salaries, linens, towels, soap, and utilities, of only $25 per night and thus a high contribution margin per room. Likewise, the contribution margin per unit for Microsoft software will also be very high. The variable costs per unit include packaging, CDs, and copying costs. These costs are small relative to the price. In both these cases, the high contribution margin per unit is necessary to cover other costs. In the case of the hotel, the fixed costs for the hotel must be covered by the high contribution margin per unit, while for Microsoft, the high contribution margin is necessary to fund software development expenditures.

The *contribution margin ratio* is most useful when the increase or decrease in sales volume is measured in sales dollars. The *unit contribution margin* is most useful when the increase or decrease in sales volume is measured in sales units (quantities). To illustrate, assume that Lambert Inc. sold 50,000 units. Its income from operations is $100,000, as shown in the following contribution margin income statement:

Sales (50,000 units × $20)	$1,000,000
Variable costs (50,000 units × $12)	600,000
Contribution margin (50,000 units × $8)	$ 400,000
Fixed costs	300,000
Income from operations	$ 100,000

If Lambert Inc.'s sales could be increased by 15,000 units, from 50,000 units to 65,000 units, its income from operations would increase by $120,000 (15,000 units × $8), as shown below.

Sales (65,000 units × $20)	$1,300,000
Variable costs (65,000 units × $12)	780,000
Contribution margin (65,000 units × $8)	$ 520,000
Fixed costs	300,000
Income from operations	$ 220,000

Unit contribution margin analyses can provide useful information for managers. The preceding illustration indicates, for example, that Lambert could spend up to $120,000 for special advertising or other product promotions to increase sales by 15,000 units.

Mathematical Approach to Cost-Volume-Profit Analysis

objective 3

Using the unit contribution margin, determine the break-even point and the volume necessary to achieve a target profit.

Accountants use various approaches for expressing the relationship of costs, sales (volume), and income from operations (operating profit). The mathematical approach is one approach that is used often in practice.

The mathematical approach to cost-volume-profit analysis uses equations (1) to determine the units of sales necessary to achieve the break-even point in operations or (2) to determine the units of sales necessary to achieve a target or desired profit. We will next describe and illustrate these equations and their use by management in profit planning.

Break-Even Point

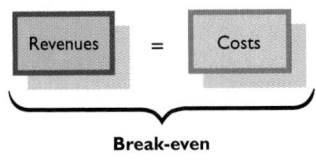

Break-even

The **break-even point** is the level of operations at which a business's revenues and expired costs are exactly equal. At break-even, a business will have neither an income nor a loss from operations. The break-even point is useful in business planning, especially when expanding or decreasing operations.

To illustrate the computation of the break-even point, assume that the fixed costs for Barker Corporation are estimated to be $90,000. The unit selling price, unit variable cost, and unit contribution margin for Barker Corporation are as follows:

Unit selling price	$25
Unit variable cost	15
Unit contribution margin	$10

The break-even point is 9,000 units, which can be computed by using the following equation:

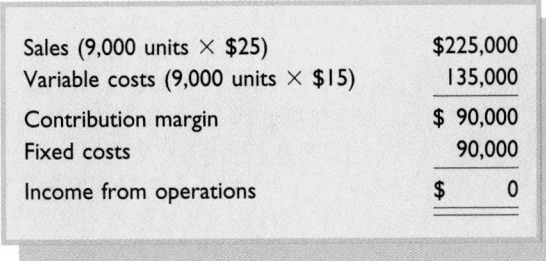

$$\text{Break-even sales (units)} = \frac{\text{Fixed costs}}{\text{Unit contribution margin}}$$

$$\text{Break-even sales (units)} = \frac{\$90,000}{\$10} = 9,000 \text{ units}$$

The following income statement verifies the preceding computation:

Sales (9,000 units × $25)	$225,000
Variable costs (9,000 units × $15)	135,000
Contribution margin	$ 90,000
Fixed costs	90,000
Income from operations	$ 0

The break-even point is affected by changes in the fixed costs, unit variable costs, and the unit selling price. Next, we will briefly describe the effect of each of these factors on the break-even point.

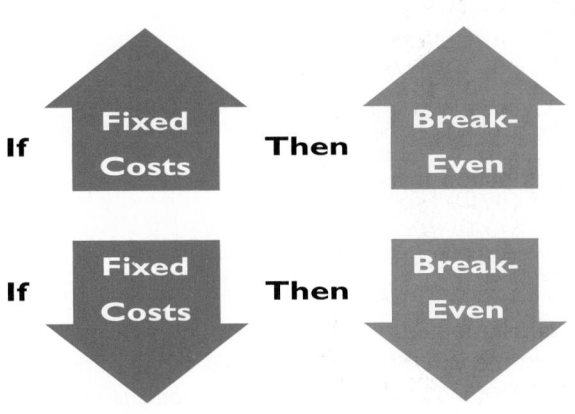

Effect of Changes in Fixed Costs

Although fixed costs do not change in total with changes in the level of activity, they may change because of other factors. For example, changes in property tax rates or factory supervisors' salaries change fixed costs. Increases in fixed costs will raise the break-even point. Likewise, decreases in fixed costs will lower the break-even point. For example, **General Motors** closed 21 plants and eliminated 74,000 jobs to lower its break-even from approximately 7 million to 5 million automobiles through the 1990s.

To illustrate, assume that Bishop Co. is evaluating a proposal to budget an additional $100,000 for advertising. Fixed costs before the additional advertising are estimated at

Warner Books agreed to pay $7.1 million for the publishing rights to the memoirs of Jack Welch, the legendary **General Electric** chairman and CEO. To make money on the deal, Warner Books estimates it must sell about 1.5 million hardback books.

$600,000, and the unit contribution margin is $20. The break-even point before the additional expense is 30,000 units, computed as follows:

$$\text{Break-even sales (units)} = \frac{\text{Fixed costs}}{\text{Unit contribution margin}}$$

$$\text{Break-even sales (units)} = \frac{\$600,000}{\$20} = 30,000 \text{ units}$$

If the additional amount is spent, the fixed costs will increase by $100,000 and the break-even point will increase to 35,000 units, computed as follows:

$$\text{Break-even sales (units)} = \frac{\text{Fixed costs}}{\text{Unit contribution margin}}$$

$$\text{Break-even sales (units)} = \frac{\$700,000}{\$20} = 35,000 \text{ units}$$

The $100,000 increase in the fixed costs requires an additional 5,000 units ($100,000 ÷ $20) of sales to break even. In other words, an increase in sales of 5,000 units is required in order to generate an additional $100,000 of total contribution margin (5,000 units × $20) to cover the increased fixed costs.

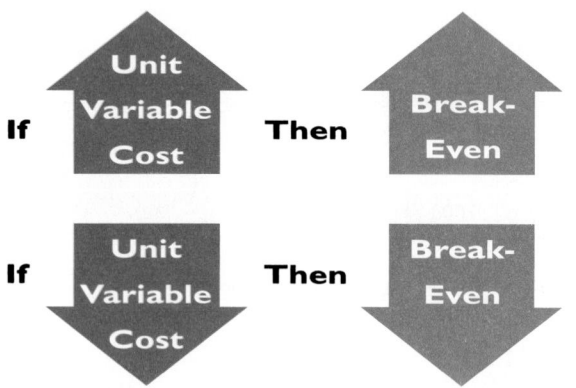

Effect of Changes in Unit Variable Costs

Although unit variable costs are not affected by changes in volume of activity, they may be affected by other factors. For example, changes in the price of direct materials and the wages for factory workers providing direct labor change unit variable costs. Increases in unit variable costs will raise the break-even point. Likewise, decreases in unit variable costs will lower the break-even point. For example, when fuel prices rise or decline, there is a direct impact on the break-even passenger load for **American Airlines**.

To illustrate, assume that Park Co. is evaluating a proposal to pay an additional 2% commission on sales to its salespeople as an incentive to increase sales. Fixed costs are estimated at $840,000, and the unit selling price, unit variable cost, and unit contribution margin before the additional 2% commission are as follows:

Unit selling price	$250
Unit variable cost	145
Unit contribution margin	$105

The break-even point is 8,000 units, computed as follows:

$$\text{Break-even sales (units)} = \frac{\text{Fixed costs}}{\text{Unit contribution margin}}$$

$$\text{Break-even sales (units)} = \frac{\$840,000}{\$105} = 8,000 \text{ units}$$

If the sales commission proposal is adopted, variable costs will increase by $5 per unit ($250 × 2%). This increase in the variable costs will decrease the unit contribution margin by $5 (from $105 to $100). Thus, the break-even point is raised to 8,400 units, computed as follows:

$$\text{Break-even sales (units)} = \frac{\text{Fixed costs}}{\text{Unit contribution margin}}$$

$$\text{Break-even sales (units)} = \frac{\$840,000}{\$100} = 8,400 \text{ units}$$

At the original break-even point of 8,000 units, the new unit contribution margin of $100 would provide only $800,000 to cover fixed costs of $840,000. Thus, an additional 400 units of sales will be required in order to provide the additional $40,000 (400 units × $100) contribution margin necessary to break even.

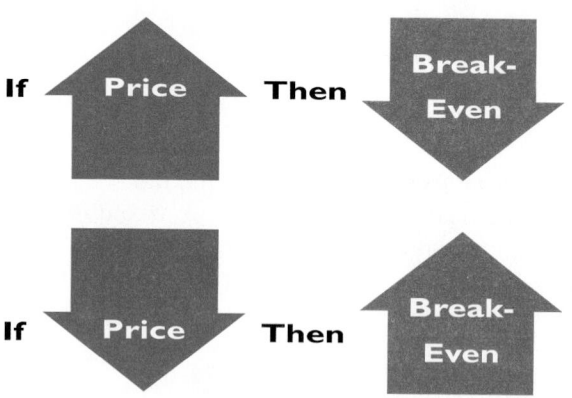

Effect of Changes in the Unit Selling Price

Increases in the unit selling price will lower the break-even point, while decreases in the unit selling price will raise the break-even point. For example, when **The Golf Channel** went from a premium cable service price of $6.95 per month to a much lower basic cable price, its break-even point increased from 6 million to 19 million subscribers.

To illustrate, assume that Graham Co. is evaluating a proposal to increase the unit selling price of its product from $50 to $60. The following data have been gathered:

	Current	Proposed
Unit selling price	$50	$60
Unit variable cost	30	30
Unit contribution margin	$20	$30
Total fixed costs	$600,000	$600,000

The break-even point based on the current selling price is 30,000 units, computed as follows:

$$\text{Break-even sales (units)} = \frac{\text{Fixed costs}}{\text{Unit contribution margin}}$$

$$\text{Break-even sales (units)} = \frac{\$600,000}{\$20} = 30,000 \text{ units}$$

If the selling price is increased by $10 per unit, the break-even point is decreased to 20,000 units, computed as follows:

$$\text{Break-even sales (units)} = \frac{\text{Fixed costs}}{\text{Unit contribution margin}}$$

$$\text{Break-even sales (units)} = \frac{\$600,000}{\$30} = 20,000 \text{ units}$$

The increase of $10 per unit in the selling price increases the unit contribution margin by $10. Thus, the break-even point decreases by 10,000 units (from 30,000 units to 20,000 units).

Summary of Effects of Changes on Break-Even Point

The break-even point in sales (units) moves in the same direction as changes in the variable cost per unit and fixed costs. In contrast, the break-even point in sales (units)

Q&A

The selling price for a product is $60 per unit. The variable cost is $35 per unit, while fixed costs are $80,000. What are the following amounts: (a) the break-even point in sales units and (b) the break-even point if the selling price were increased to $67 per unit?

(a) 3,200 units [$80,000 ÷ ($60 − $35)]; (b) 2,500 units [$80,000 ÷ ($67 − $35)]

moves in the opposite direction to changes in the sales price per unit. A summary of the impact of these changes on the break-even point in sales (units) is shown below.

Type of Change	Direction of Change	Effect of Change on Break-Even Sales (Units)
Fixed cost	Increase	Increase
	Decrease	Decrease
Variable cost per unit	Increase	Increase
	Decrease	Decrease
Unit sales price	Increase	Decrease
	Decrease	Increase

Target Profit

At the break-even point, sales and costs are exactly equal. However, the break-even point is not the goal of most businesses. Rather, managers seek to maximize profits. By modifying the break-even equation, the sales volume required to earn a target or desired amount of profit may be estimated. For this purpose, target profit is added to the break-even equation as shown below.

$$\text{Sales (units)} = \frac{\text{Fixed costs} + \text{Target profit}}{\text{Unit contribution margin}}$$

To illustrate, assume that fixed costs are estimated at $200,000, and the desired profit is $100,000. The unit selling price, unit variable cost, and unit contribution margin are as follows:

Unit selling price	$75
Unit variable cost	45
Unit contribution margin	$30

The sales volume necessary to earn the target profit of $100,000 is 10,000 units, computed as follows:

$$\text{Sales (units)} = \frac{\text{Fixed costs} + \text{Target profit}}{\text{Unit contribution margin}}$$

$$\text{Sales (units)} = \frac{\$200,000 + \$100,000}{\$30} = 10,000 \text{ units}$$

The following income statement verifies this computation:

Sales (10,000 units × $75)	$750,000
Variable costs (10,000 units × $45)	450,000
Contribution margin (10,000 units × $30)	$300,000
Fixed costs	200,000
Income from operations	$100,000	← Target profit

The sales price is $140 per unit, variable costs are $60 per unit, and fixed costs are $240,000. What would be (a) the break-even point in sales units and (b) the break-even point in sales units if a target profit of $50,000 is desired?

- -

(a) 3,000 units [$240,000 ÷ ($140 − $60)]; (b) 3,625 units [($240,000 + $50,000) ÷ ($140 − $60)]

Graphic Approach to Cost-Volume-Profit Analysis

objective 4

Using a cost-volume-profit chart and a profit-volume chart, determine the break-even point and the volume necessary to achieve a target profit.

Cost-volume-profit analysis can be presented graphically as well as in equation form. Many managers prefer the graphic format because the income or loss from operations (operating profit or loss) for different levels of sales can readily be determined. Next, we describe two graphic approaches that managers find useful.

Cost-Volume-Profit (Break-Even) Chart

A **cost-volume-profit chart**, sometimes called a **break-even chart**, may assist management in understanding relationships among costs, sales, and operating profit or loss. To illustrate, the cost-volume-profit chart in Exhibit 5 is based on the following data:

Unit selling price	$50
Unit variable cost	30
Unit contribution margin	$20
Total fixed costs	$100,000

Exhibit 5 Cost-Volume-Profit Chart

Sales and Costs

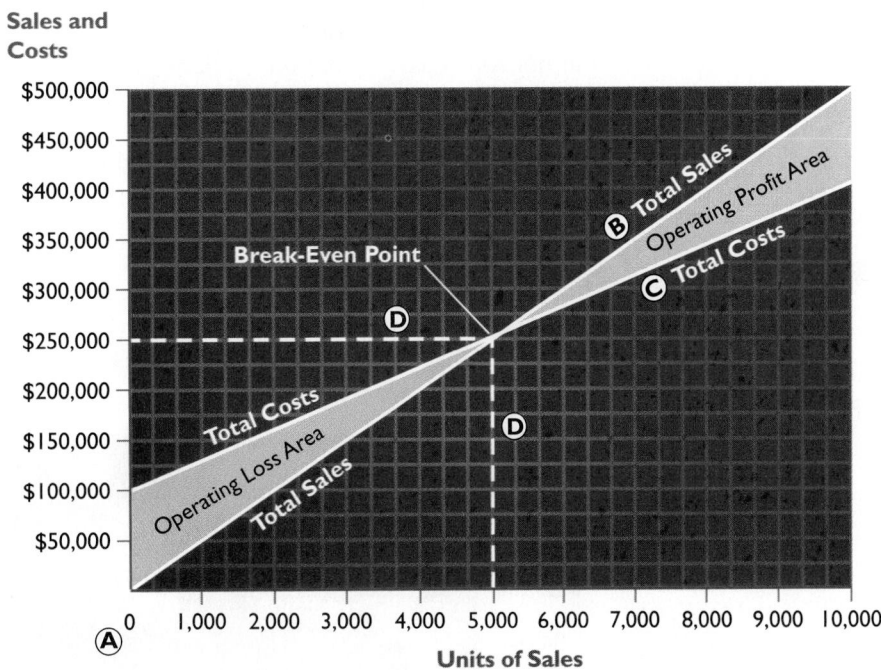

Units of Sales

We constructed the cost-volume-profit chart in Exhibit 5 as follows:

A. Volume expressed in units of sales is indicated along the horizontal axis. The range of volume shown on the horizontal axis should reflect the *relevant range* in which the business expects to operate. Dollar amounts representing total sales and costs are indicated along the vertical axis.

B. A sales line is plotted by beginning at zero on the left corner of the graph. A second point is determined by multiplying any units of sales on the horizontal axis by the unit sales price of $50. For example, for 10,000 units of sales, the total sales would be $500,000 (10,000 units × $50). The sales line is drawn upward to the right from zero through the $500,000 point.

C. A cost line is plotted by beginning with total fixed costs, $100,000, on the vertical axis. A second point is determined by multiplying any units of sales on the horizontal axis by the unit variable costs and adding the fixed costs. For example, for 10,000 units of sales, the total estimated costs would be $400,000 [(10,000 units × $30) + $100,000]. The cost line is drawn upward to the right from $100,000 on the vertical axis through the $400,000 point.

D. Horizontal and vertical lines are drawn at the point of intersection of the sales and cost lines, which is the break-even point, and the areas representing operating profit and operating loss are identified.

In Exhibit 5, the dotted lines drawn from the point of intersection of the total sales line and the total cost line identify the break-even point in total sales dollars and units. The break-even point is $250,000 of sales, which represents a sales volume of 5,000 units. Operating profits will be earned when sales levels are to the right of the break-even point (operating profit area). Operating losses will be incurred when sales levels are to the left of the break-even point (operating loss area).

Changes in the unit selling price, total fixed costs, and unit variable costs can be analyzed by using a cost-volume-profit chart. Using the data in Exhibit 5, assume that a proposal to reduce fixed costs by $20,000 is to be evaluated. In this case, the total fixed costs would be $80,000 ($100,000 − $20,000). As shown in Exhibit 6, the total cost line should be redrawn, starting at the $80,000 point (total fixed costs) on the vertical axis. A second point is determined by multiplying any units of sales on the horizontal axis by the unit variable costs and adding the fixed costs. For example, for 10,000 units of sales, the total estimated costs would be $380,000 [(10,000 units × $30) + $80,000]. The cost line is drawn upward to the right from $80,000 on the vertical axis through the $380,000 point. The revised cost-volume-profit chart in Exhibit 6 indicates that the break-even point decreases to $200,000 or 4,000 units of sales.

Exhibit 6 Revised Cost-Volume-Profit Chart

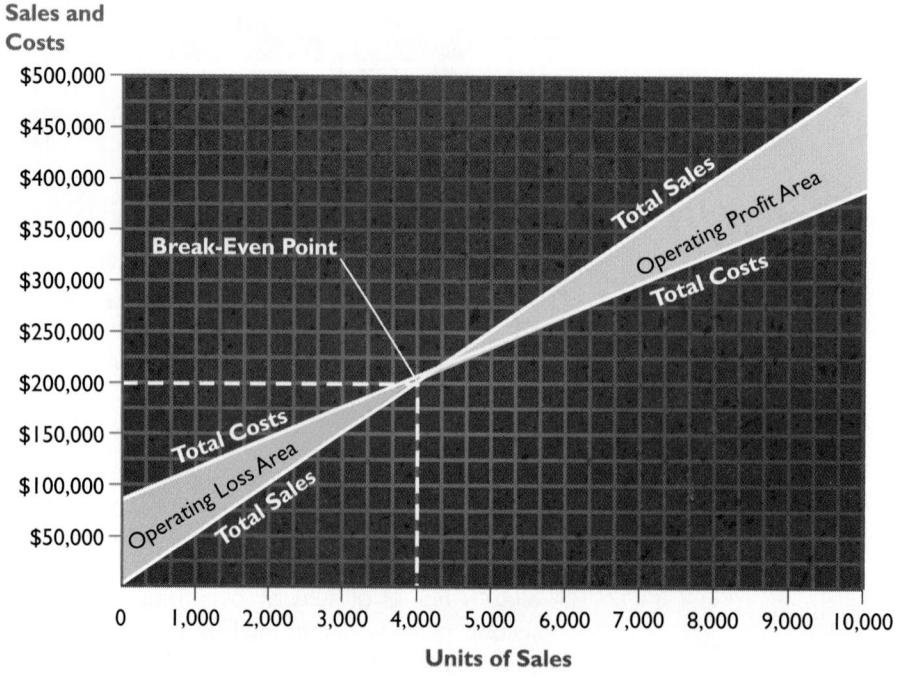

Profit-Volume Chart

Another graphic approach to cost-volume-profit analysis, the **profit-volume chart**, focuses on profits. This is in contrast to the cost-volume-profit chart, which focuses on sales and costs. The profit-volume chart plots only the difference between total sales and total costs (or profits). In this way, the profit-volume chart allows managers to determine the operating profit (or loss) for various levels of operations.

To illustrate, assume that the profit-volume chart in Exhibit 7 is based on the same data as used in Exhibit 5. These data are as follows:

Unit selling price	$50
Unit variable cost	30
Unit contribution margin	$20
Total fixed costs	$100,000

The maximum operating loss is equal to the fixed costs of $100,000. Assuming that the maximum unit sales within the relevant range is 10,000 units, the maximum operating profit is $100,000, computed as follows:

Sales (10,000 units × $50)	$500,000
Variable costs (10,000 units × $30)	300,000
Contribution margin (10,000 units × $20)	$200,000
Fixed costs	100,000
Operating profit	$100,000	← Maximum profit

Exhibit 7 Profit-Volume Chart

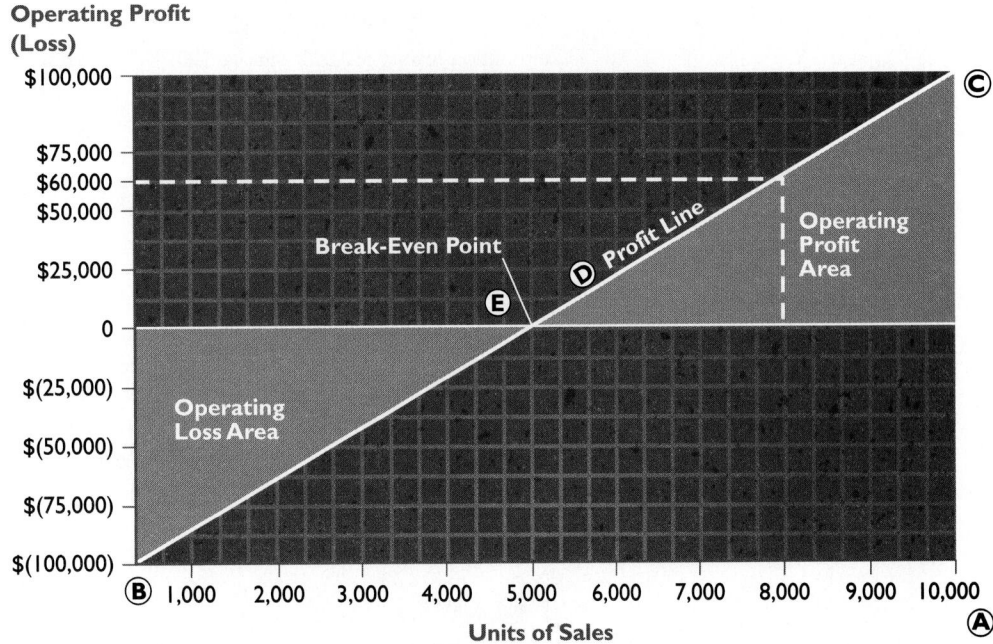

We constructed the profit-volume chart in Exhibit 7 as follows:

A. Volume expressed in units of sales is indicated along the horizontal axis. The range of volume shown on the horizontal axis should reflect the *relevant range*

Many NBA franchises, such as the **Los Angeles Lakers**, state that their financial goal is to break even during the regular season and to make their profit during the playoffs, or basketball's so called "second season." The deeper the team goes into the playoffs, the greater the operating profit earned above break-even from additional ticket sales and TV revenues.

in which the business expects to operate. In this illustration, the maximum number of sales units within the relevant range is assumed to be 10,000 units. Dollar amounts indicating operating profits and losses are shown along the vertical axis.

B. A point representing the maximum operating loss is plotted on the vertical axis at the left. This loss is equal to the total fixed costs at the zero level of sales.
C. A point representing the maximum operating profit within the relevant range is plotted on the right.
D. A diagonal profit line is drawn connecting the maximum operating loss point with the maximum operating profit point.
E. The profit line intersects the horizontal zero operating profit line at the break-even point expressed in units of sales, and the areas indicating operating profit and loss are identified.

In Exhibit 7, the break-even point is 5,000 units of sales, which is equal to total sales of $250,000 (5,000 units × $50). Operating profit will be earned when sales levels are to the right of the break-even point (operating profit area). Operating losses will be incurred when sales levels are to the left of the break-even point (operating loss area). For example, at sales of 8,000 units, an operating profit of $60,000 will be earned, as shown in Exhibit 7.

The effect of changes in the unit selling price, total fixed costs, and unit variable costs on profit can be analyzed using a profit-volume chart. To illustrate, using the data in Exhibit 7, we will evaluate the effect on profit of an increase of $20,000 in fixed costs. In this case, the total fixed costs would be $120,000 ($100,000 + $20,000), and the maximum operating loss would also be $120,000. If the maximum sales within the relevant range is 10,000 units, the maximum operating profit would be $80,000, computed as follows:

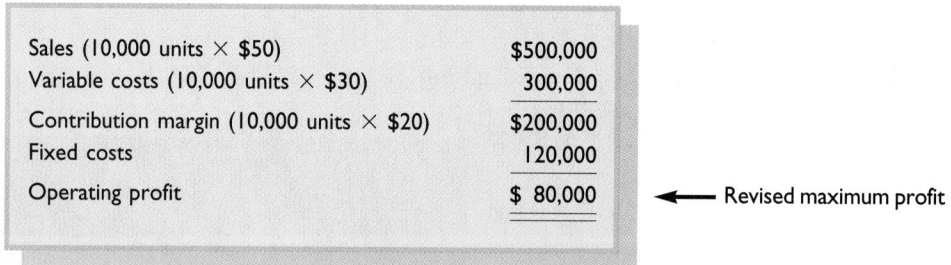

Sales (10,000 units × $50)	$500,000
Variable costs (10,000 units × $30)	300,000
Contribution margin (10,000 units × $20)	$200,000
Fixed costs	120,000
Operating profit	$ 80,000

⟵ Revised maximum profit

A revised profit-volume chart is constructed by plotting the maximum operating loss and maximum operating profit points and drawing the revised profit line. The original and the revised profit-volume charts are shown in Exhibit 8.

The revised profit-volume chart indicates that the break-even point is 6,000 units of sales. This is equal to total sales of $300,000 (6,000 units × $50). The operating loss area of the chart has increased, while the operating profit area has decreased under the proposed change in fixed costs.

Use of Computers in Cost-Volume-Profit Analysis

With computers, the graphic approach and the mathematical approach to cost-volume-profit analysis are easy to use. Managers can vary assumptions regarding selling prices, costs, and volume and can immediately see the effects of each change on the break-even point and profit. Such an analysis is called a **"what if" analysis** or **sensitivity analysis**.

Exhibit 8 Original Profit-Volume Chart and Revised Profit-Volume Chart

Original Chart

Revised Chart

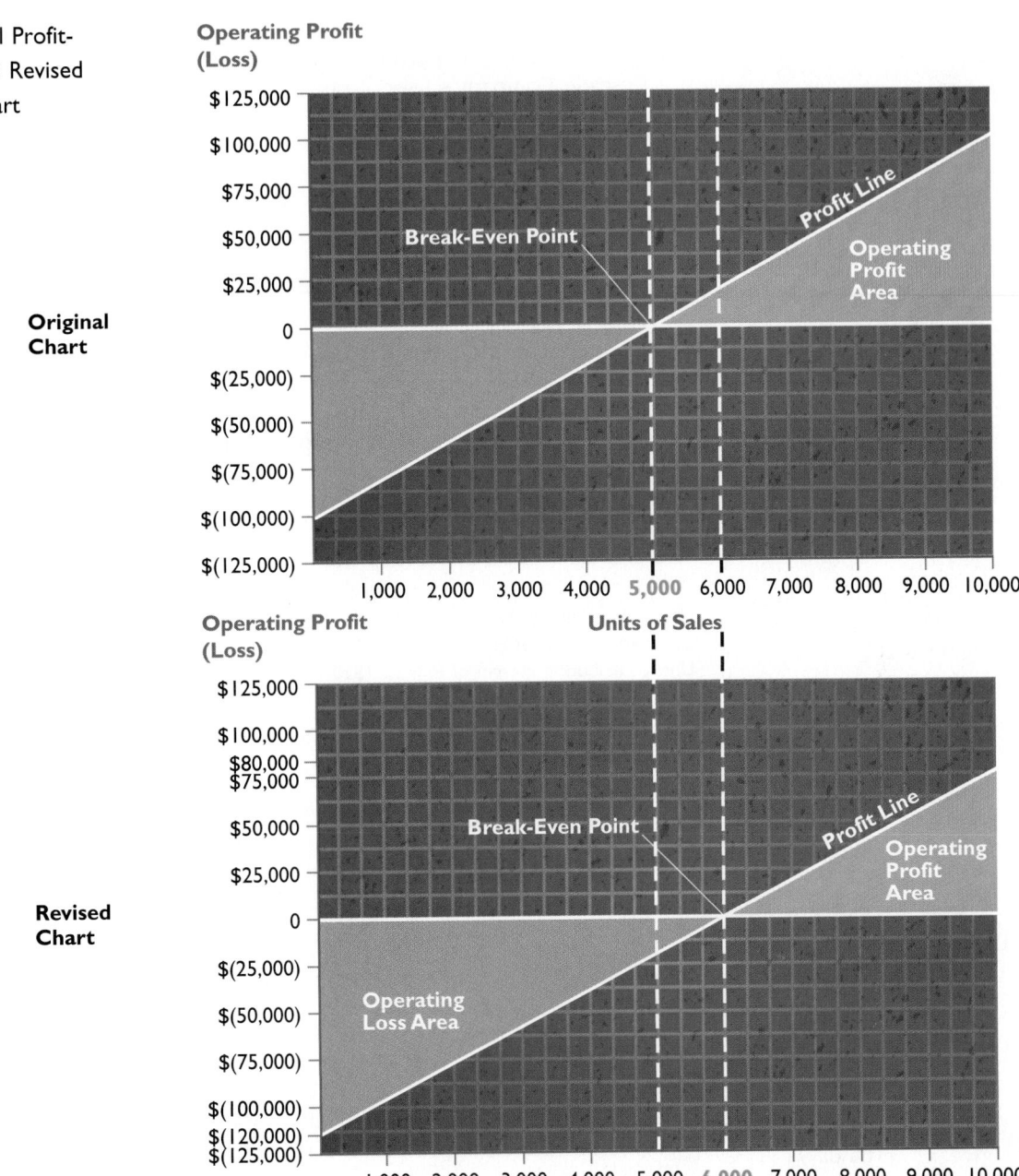

Sales Mix Considerations

objective 5

Calculate the break-even point for a business selling more than one product.

In most businesses, more than one product is sold at varying selling prices. In addition, the products often have different unit variable costs, and each product makes a different contribution to profits. Thus, the sales volume necessary to break even or to earn a target profit for a business selling two or more products depends upon the sales mix. The **sales mix** is the relative distribution of sales among the various products sold by a business.

To illustrate the calculation of the break-even point for a company that sells more than one product, assume that Cascade Company sold 8,000 units of Product A

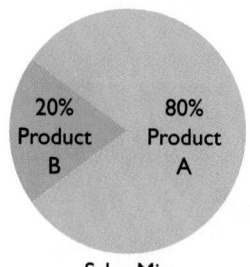

Sales Mix

and 2,000 units of Product B during the past year. The sales mix for products A and B can be expressed as percentages (80% and 20%) or as a ratio (80:20).

Cascade Company's fixed costs are $200,000. The unit selling prices, unit variable costs, and unit contribution margins for products A and B are as follows:

Product	Unit Selling Price	Unit Variable Cost	Unit Contribution Margin
A	$ 90	$70	$20
B	140	95	45

In computing the break-even point, it is useful to think of the individual products as components of one overall enterprise product. For Cascade Company, this overall enterprise product is called E. We can think of the unit selling price of E as equal to the total of the unit selling prices of products A and B, multiplied by their sales mix percentages. Likewise, we can think of the unit variable cost and unit contribution margin of E as equal to the total of the unit variable costs and unit contribution margins of products A and B, multiplied by the sales mix percentages. These computations are as follows:

Unit selling price of E: ($90 × 0.8) + ($140 × 0.2) = $100
Unit variable cost of E: ($70 × 0.8) + ($ 95 × 0.2) = $ 75
Unit contribution margin of E: ($20 × 0.8) + ($ 45 × 0.2) = $ 25

The break-even point of 8,000 units of E can be determined in the normal manner as follows:

$$\text{Break-even sales (units)} = \frac{\text{Fixed costs}}{\text{Unit contribution margin}}$$

$$\text{Break-even sales (units)} = \frac{\$200,000}{\$25} = 8,000 \text{ units}$$

Since the sales mix for products A and B is 80% and 20%, the break-even quantity of A is 6,400 units (8,000 units × 80%) and B is 1,600 units (8,000 units × 20%). This analysis can be verified in the following income statement:

	Product A	Product B	Total
Sales:			
6,400 units × $90	$576,000		$576,000
1,600 units × $140		$224,000	224,000
Total sales	$576,000	$224,000	$800,000
Variable costs:			
6,400 units × $70	$448,000		$448,000
1,600 units × $95		$152,000	152,000
Total variable costs	$448,000	$152,000	$600,000
Contribution margin	$128,000	$ 72,000	$200,000
Fixed costs			200,000
Income from operations			$ 0	⟵ Break-even point

The daily break-even attendance at **Universal Studios** theme areas depends on how many tickets were sold at an advance purchase discount rate vs. the full gate rate. Likewise, the break-even point for an overseas flight of **Delta Air Lines** will be influenced by the number of first class, business class, and economy class tickets sold for the flight. The weekly break-even number of long distance minutes for **AT&T** depends on the number of minutes called during day, evening, and weekend rates.

The effects of changes in the sales mix on the break-even point can be determined by repeating this analysis, assuming a different sales mix.

Special Cost-Volume-Profit Relationships

Some additional relationships useful to managers can be developed from cost-volume-profit data. Two of these relationships are the margin of safety and operating leverage.

Margin of Safety

The difference between the current sales revenue and the sales at the break-even point is called the margin of safety. It indicates the possible decrease in sales that may occur before an operating loss results. For example, if the margin of safety is low, even a small decline in sales revenue may result in an operating loss.

If sales are $250,000, the unit selling price is $25, and sales at the break-even point are $200,000, the margin of safety is 20%, computed as follows:

$$\text{Margin of safety} = \frac{\text{Sales} - \text{Sales at break-even point}}{\text{Sales}}$$

$$\text{Margin of safety} = \frac{\$250,000 - \$200,000}{\$250,000} = 20\%$$

The margin of safety may also be stated in terms of units. In this illustration, for example, the margin of safety of 20% is equivalent to $50,000 ($250,000 × 20%). In units, the margin of safety is 2,000 units ($50,000 ÷ $25). Thus, the current sales of $250,000 may decline $50,000 or 2,000 units before an operating loss occurs.

Operating Leverage

The relative mix of a business's variable costs and fixed costs is measured by the operating leverage. It is computed as follows:

$$\text{Operating leverage} = \frac{\text{Contribution margin}}{\text{Income from operations}}$$

One type of business that has high operating leverage is what is called a "network" business—one in which service is provided over a network that moves either goods or information. Examples of network businesses include **United Airlines**, **USWEST**, **Yahoo!**, and **Union Pacific**.

Since the difference between contribution margin and income from operations is fixed costs, companies with large amounts of fixed costs will generally have a high operating leverage. Thus, companies in capital-intensive industries, such as the airline and automotive industries, will generally have a high operating leverage. A low operating leverage is normal for companies in industries that are labor-intensive, such as professional services.

Managers can use operating leverage to measure the impact of changes in sales on income from operations. A high operating leverage indicates that a small increase in sales will yield a large percentage increase in income from operations. In contrast, a low operating leverage indicates that a large increase in sales is necessary to significantly increase income from operations. To illustrate, assume the following operating data for Jones Inc. and Wilson Inc.:

	Jones Inc.	Wilson Inc.
Sales	$400,000	$400,000
Variable costs	300,000	300,000
Contribution margin	$100,000	$100,000
Fixed costs	80,000	50,000
Income from operations	$ 20,000	$ 50,000

Q&A

What is the operating leverage for a company with sales of $410,000, variable costs of $250,000, and fixed costs of $80,000?

2.0 [($410,000 − $250,000) ÷ ($410,000 − $250,000 − $80,000)]

Both companies have the same sales, the same variable costs, and the same contribution margin. Jones Inc. has larger fixed costs than Wilson Inc. and, as a result, a lower income from operations and a higher operating leverage. The operating leverage for each company is computed as follows:

Jones Inc.	Wilson Inc.
$$\text{Operating leverage} = \frac{\$100,000}{\$20,000} = 5$$	$$\text{Operating leverage} = \frac{\$100,000}{\$50,000} = 2$$

Jones Inc.'s operating leverage indicates that, for each percentage point change in sales, income from operations will change five times that percentage. In contrast, for each percentage point change in sales, the income from operations of Wilson Inc. will change only two times that percentage. For example, if sales increased by 10% ($40,000) for each company, income from operations will increase by 50% (10% × 5), or $10,000 (50% × $20,000), for Jones Inc. The sales increase of $40,000 will increase income from operations by only 20% (10% × 2), or $10,000 (20% × $50,000), for Wilson Inc. The validity of this analysis is shown as follows:

HIGH OPERATING LEVERAGE

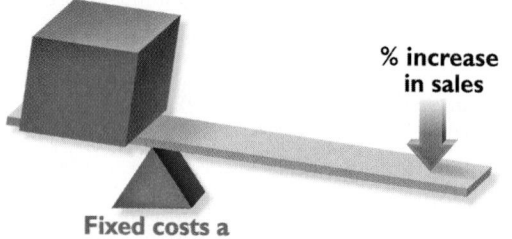

% increase in income from operations

% increase in sales

Fixed costs a large % of total costs

LOW OPERATING LEVERAGE

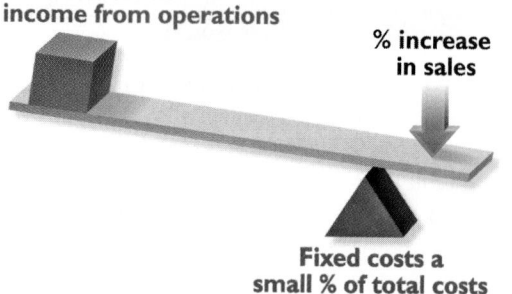

% increase in income from operations

% increase in sales

Fixed costs a small % of total costs

	Jones Inc.	Wilson Inc.
Sales	$440,000	$440,000
Variable costs	330,000	330,000
Contribution margin	$110,000	$110,000
Fixed costs	80,000	50,000
Income from operations	$ 30,000	$ 60,000

For Jones Inc., even a small increase in sales will generate a large percentage increase in income from operations. Thus, Jones's managers may be motivated to think of ways to increase sales. In contrast, Wilson's managers might attempt to increase operating leverage by reducing variable costs and thereby change the cost structure.

Assumptions of Cost-Volume-Profit Analysis

objective 7

List the assumptions underlying cost-volume-profit analysis.

The reliability of cost-volume-profit analysis depends upon the validity of several assumptions. The primary assumptions are as follows:

1. Total sales and total costs can be represented by straight lines.
2. Within the relevant range of operating activity, the efficiency of operations does not change.
3. Costs can be accurately divided into fixed and variable components.

4. The sales mix is constant.
5. There is no change in the inventory quantities during the period.

These assumptions simplify cost-volume-profit analysis. Since they are often valid for the relevant range of operations, cost-volume-profit analysis is useful to decision making.[3]

[3] The impact of violating these assumptions is discussed in advanced accounting texts.

ENCORE

Online Music Challenges the Recording Industry

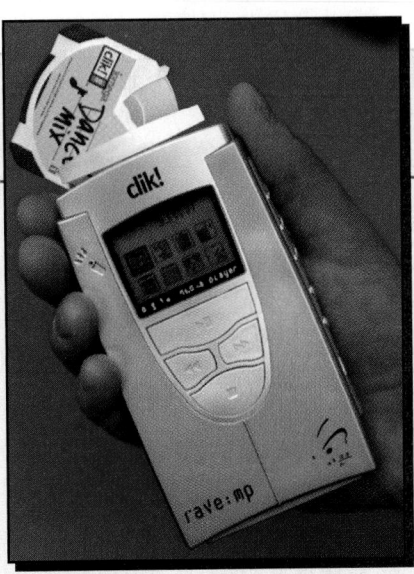

The recording industry is consolidated around a number of powerhouse labels, such as **EMI, Warner Bros., RCA,** and **Sony.** As a result, they have a lot of clout when negotiating a record deal with an artist. Say you've got a band and want to sign a record deal. If the label is interested, you'll end up signing a long-term contract that will lock you into royalties of around 10% of sales. In addition, you'll have to pay back the label for its fixed costs of recording and launching your CD. Thus, it's estimated you won't make any money until over 500,000 copies are sold! With such a high break-even point, many artists make most of their money from performing and merchandise sales, not from CD sales. Most of the money from CD sales goes to the label.

In comes a new company, **MP3.com, Inc.** MP3 offers music over the Internet. MP3 files can be downloaded right from your computer, so that the cost of pressing and selling a CD through the old "bricks and mortar" distribution system is eliminated. This radically changes the economics of the business. Since the variable cost per copy is next to nothing, the break-even point is now much lower for anyone who wishes to offer music to the public. Indeed, many emerging artists are offering their music on the Net *for free.* And why not? If the labels retain most of the profits from the CDs, why not bypass them and offer music directly to the public. In this way, artists are gaining control over their own music while building a loyal fan base that wouldn't mind paying for concert tickets and merchandise, which is where the artists will make their money. ■

KEY POINTS

1 Classify costs by their behavior as variable costs, fixed costs, or mixed costs.
Cost behavior refers to the manner in which a cost changes as a related activity changes. Variable costs are costs that vary in total in proportion to changes in the level of activity. Fixed costs are costs that remain the same in total dollar amount as the level of activity changes. A mixed cost has attributes of both a variable and a fixed cost.

2 Compute the contribution margin, the contribution margin ratio, and the unit contribution margin, and explain how they may be useful to managers.

The contribution margin concept is useful in business planning because it gives insight into the profit potential of a firm. The contribution margin is the excess of sales revenues over variable costs. The contribution margin ratio is computed as follows:

Contribution margin ratio =

$$\frac{\textbf{Sales} - \textbf{Variable costs}}{\textbf{Sales}}$$

The unit contribution margin is the excess of the unit selling price over the unit variable cost.

3 Using the unit contribution margin, determine the break-even point and the volume necessary to achieve a target profit.

The mathematical approach to cost-volume-profit analysis uses the unit contribution margin concept and the following equations to determine the break-even point and the volume necessary to achieve a target profit for a business:

Break-even sales (units) =

$$\frac{\text{Fixed costs}}{\text{Unit contribution margin}}$$

Sales (units) =

$$\frac{\text{Fixed costs + Target profit}}{\text{Unit contribution margin}}$$

4 Using a cost-volume-profit chart and a profit-volume chart, determine the break-even point and the volume necessary to achieve a target profit.

A cost-volume-profit chart focuses on the relationships among costs, sales, and operating profit or loss. Preparing and using a cost-volume-profit chart to determine the break-even point and the volume

necessary to achieve a target profit are illustrated in this chapter.

The profit-volume chart focuses on profits rather than on revenues and costs. Preparing and using a profit-volume chart to determine the break-even point and the volume necessary to achieve a target profit are illustrated in this chapter.

5 Calculate the break-even point for a business selling more than one product.

Calculating the break-even point for a business selling two or more products is based upon a specified sales mix. Given the sales mix, the break-even point can be computed, using the methods illustrated for Cascade Company in this chapter.

6 Compute the margin of safety and the operating leverage, and explain how managers use these concepts.

The margin of safety as a percentage of current sales is computed as follows:

Margin of safety =

$$\frac{\text{Sales} - \text{Sales at break-even point}}{\text{Sales}}$$

The margin of safety is useful in evaluating past operations and in planning future operations. For example, if the margin of safety

is low, even a small decline in sales revenue will result in an operating loss.

Operating leverage is computed as follows:

Operating leverage =

$$\frac{\text{Contribution margin}}{\text{Income from operations}}$$

Operating leverage is useful in measuring the impact of changes in sales on income from operations without preparing formal income statements. For example, a high operating leverage indicates that a small increase in sales will yield a large percentage increase in income from operations.

7 List the assumptions underlying cost-volume-profit analysis.

The primary assumptions underlying cost-volume-profit analysis are as follows:

1. Total sales and total costs can be represented by straight lines.
2. Within the relevant range of operating activity, the efficiency of operations does not change.
3. Costs can be accurately divided into fixed and variable components.
4. The sales mix is constant.
5. There is no change in the inventory quantities during the period.

ILLUSTRATIVE PROBLEM

Wyatt Inc. expects to maintain the same inventories at the end of the year as at the beginning of the year. The estimated fixed costs for the year are $288,000, and the estimated variable costs per unit are $14. It is expected that 60,000 units will be sold at a price of $20 per unit. Maximum sales within the relevant range are 70,000 units.

Instructions

1. What is (a) the contribution margin ratio and (b) the unit contribution margin?
2. Determine the break-even point in units.
3. Construct a cost-volume-profit chart, indicating the break-even point.
4. Construct a profit-volume chart, indicating the break-even point.
5. What is the margin of safety?

Solution

1. a. Contribution margin ratio $= \dfrac{\text{Sales} - \text{Variable costs}}{\text{Sales}}$

Contribution margin ratio $= \dfrac{(60{,}000 \text{ units} \times \$20) - (60{,}000 \text{ units} \times \$14)}{(60{,}000 \text{ units} \times \$20)}$

Contribution margin ratio $= \dfrac{\$1{,}200{,}000 - \$840{,}000}{\$1{,}200{,}000} = \dfrac{\$360{,}000}{\$1{,}200{,}000}$

Contribution margin ratio $= 30\%$

b. Unit contribution margin $=$ Unit selling price $-$ Unit variable costs
Unit contribution margin $= \$20 - \$14 = \$6$

2. Break-even sales (units) $= \dfrac{\text{Fixed costs}}{\text{Unit contribution margin}}$

Break-even sales (units) $= \dfrac{\$288{,}000}{\$6} = 48{,}000$ units

3. **Sales and Costs**

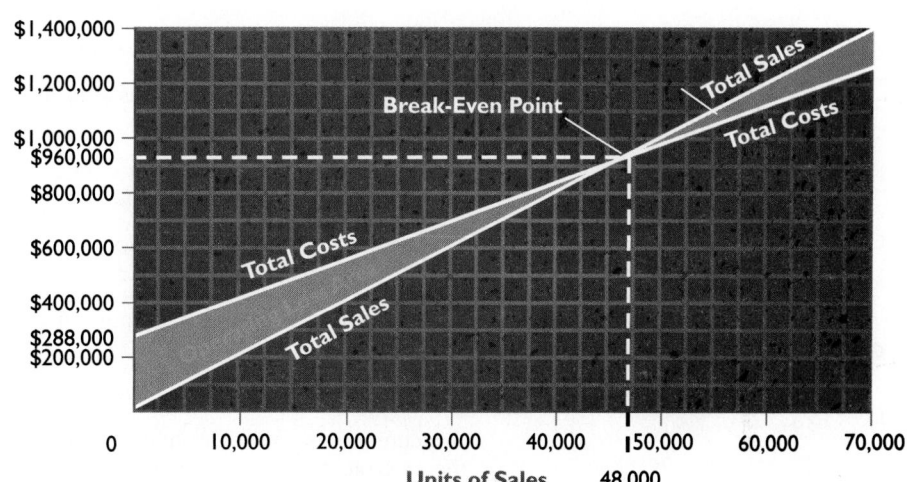

4. **Operating Profit (Loss)**

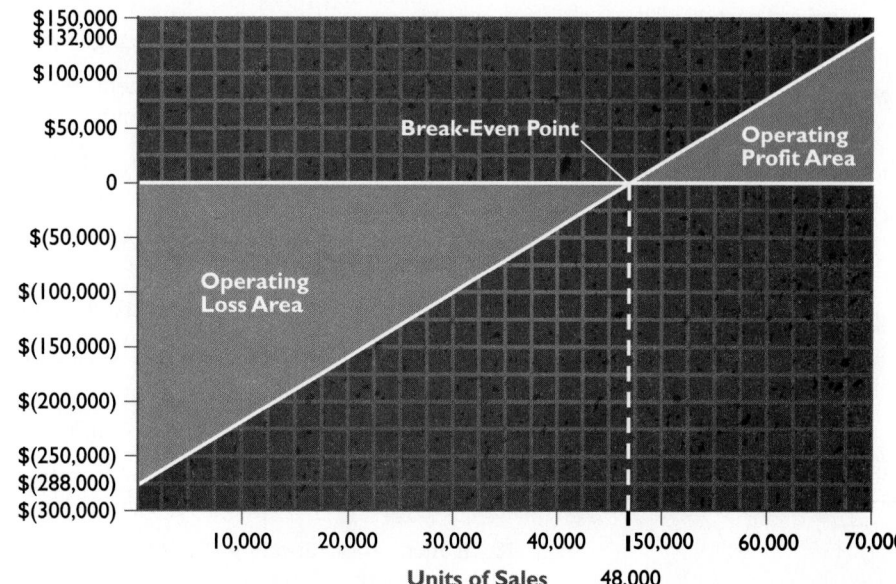

5. Margin of safety:

Expected sales (60,000 units × $20)	$1,200,000
Break-even point (48,000 units × $20)	960,000
Margin of safety	$ 240,000

or

$$\text{Margin of safety} = \frac{\text{Sales} - \text{Sales at break-even point}}{\text{Sales}}$$

$$\text{Margin of safety} = \frac{\$240,000}{\$1,200,000} = 20\%$$

SELF-EXAMINATION QUESTIONS
Answers at End of Chapter

Matching

Match each of the following statements with its proper term. Some terms may not be used.

A. activity bases (drivers)

B. break-even point

C. contribution margin

D. contribution margin ratio

E. cost behavior

F. cost-volume-profit analysis

G. cost-volume-profit chart

H. fixed costs

I. high-low method

J. income from operations

K. margin of safety

L. mixed cost

M. operating leverage

N. profit-volume chart

O. relevant range

P. sales mix

Q. unit contribution margin

R. variable costing

S. variable costs

___ 1. Costs that vary in total dollar amount as the level of activity changes.

___ 2. Sales less variable cost of goods sold and variable selling and administrative expenses.

___ 3. A measure of activity that is thought to cause a cost; used in analyzing and classifying cost behavior.

___ 4. The percentage of each sales dollar that is available to cover the fixed costs and provide income from operations.

___ 5. Costs that tend to remain the same in amount, regardless of variations in the level of activity.

___ 6. The range of activity over which changes in cost are of interest to management.

___ 7. A technique that uses the highest and lowest total cost as a basis for estimating the variable cost per unit and the fixed cost component of a mixed cost.

___ 8. The level of business operations at which revenues and expired costs are equal.

___ 9. The systematic examination of the relationships among costs, expenses, sales, and operating profit or loss.

___10. The manner in which a cost changes in relation to its activity base (driver).

___11. A chart used to assist management in understanding the relationships among costs, expenses, sales, and operating profit or loss.

___12. The dollars available from each unit of sales to cover fixed costs and provide income from operations.

___13. A chart used to assist management in understanding the relationship between profit and volume.

___14. A cost with both variable and fixed characteristics.

___15. The difference between current sales revenue and the sales at the break-even point.

___16. The relative distribution of sales among the various products available for sale.

___17. A measure of the relative mix of a business's variable costs and fixed costs, computed as contribution margin divided by income from operations.

___18. A method of reporting variable and fixed costs that includes only the variable manufacturing costs in the cost of the product.

Multiple Choice

1. Which of the following statements describes variable costs?
   A. Costs that vary on a per-unit basis as the level of activity changes.
   B. Costs that vary in total in direct proportion to changes in the level of activity.
   C. Costs that remain the same in total dollar amount as the level of activity changes.
   D. Costs that vary on a per-unit basis but remain the same in total as the level of activity changes.

2. If sales are $500,000, variable costs are $200,000, and fixed costs are $240,000, what is the contribution margin ratio?
   A. 40%   C. 52%
   B. 48%   D. 60%

3. If the unit selling price is $16, the unit variable cost is $12, and fixed costs are $160,000, what are the break-even sales (units)?

   A. 5,714 units   C. 13,333 units
   B. 10,000 units   D. 40,000 units

4. Based on the data presented in Question 3, how many units of sales would be required to realize income from operations of $20,000?
   A. 11,250 units   C. 40,000 units
   B. 35,000 units   D. 45,000 units

5. Based on the following operating data, what is the operating leverage?

Sales	$600,000
Variable costs	240,000
Contribution margin	$360,000
Fixed costs	160,000
Income from operations	$200,000

   A. 0.8   B. 1.2   C. 1.8   D. 4.0

CLASS DISCUSSION QUESTIONS

1. What are the three most common classifications of cost behavior?
2. Describe how total variable costs and unit variable costs behave with changes in the level of activity.
3. How would each of the following costs be classified if units produced is the activity base?
   a. Direct labor costs
   b. Direct materials cost
   c. Electricity costs of $0.20 per kilowatt-hour
4. Describe the behavior of (a) total fixed costs and (b) unit fixed costs as the level of activity increases.
5. How would each of the following costs be classified if units produced is the activity base?
   a. Straight-line depreciation of plant and equipment
   b. Salary of factory supervisor ($80,000 per year)
   c. Property insurance premiums of $5,000 per month on plant and equipment
6. In cost analyses, how are mixed costs treated?
7. Which of the following graphs illustrates how total variable costs behave with changes in total units produced?

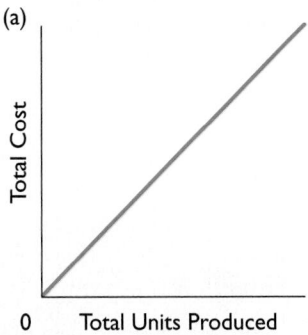

(a)

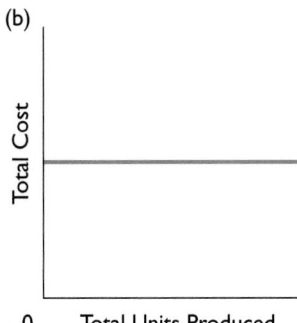

(b)

8. Which of the following graphs illustrates how unit variable costs behave with changes in total units produced?

(a)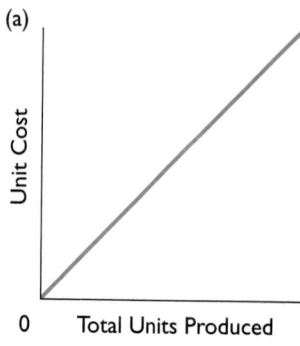

(b)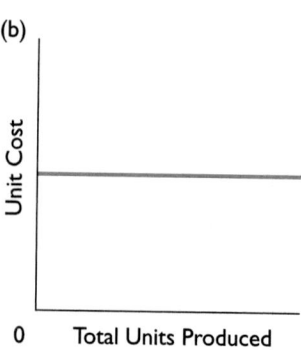

9. Which of the following graphs best illustrates fixed costs per unit as the activity base changes?

(a)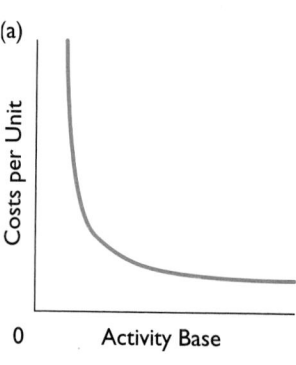

(b)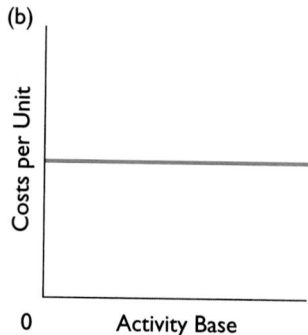

10. In applying the high-low method of cost estimation, how is the total fixed cost estimated?

11. How is contribution margin calculated?

12. If fixed costs increase, what would be the impact on the (a) contribution margin? (b) income from operations?

13. An examination of the accounting records of Hudson Company disclosed a high contribution margin ratio and production at a level below maximum capacity. Based on this information, suggest a likely means of improving income from operations. Explain.

14. What equation is used to determine the break-even point in sales units?

15. If the unit cost of direct materials is decreased, what effect will this change have on the break-even point?

16. If insurance rates are increased, what effect will this change in fixed costs have on the break-even point?

17. Both Simmons Company and Pate Company had the same sales, total costs, and income from operations for the current fiscal year; yet Simmons Company had a lower break-even point than Pate Company. Explain the reason for this difference in break-even points.

18. How does the sales mix affect the calculation of the break-even point?

19. How is the margin of safety calculated?

20. a. How is operating leverage computed?
    b. What does operating leverage measure?

EXERCISES

Exercise 3–1
Classify costs

Objective 1

Following is a list of various costs incurred in producing frozen pizzas. With respect to the production and sale of frozen pizzas, classify each cost as either variable, fixed, or mixed.

1. Pepperoni
2. Salary of plant manager
3. Electricity costs, $0.08 per kilowatt-hour
4. Tomato paste
5. Rent on warehouse, $5,000 per month plus $5 per square foot of storage used
6. Janitorial costs, $3,000 per month
7. Hourly wages of machine operators
8. Dough
9. Hourly wages of inspectors
10. Pension cost, $0.50 per employee hour on the job
11. Property taxes, $50,000 per year on factory building and equipment
12. Property insurance premiums, $1,500 per month plus $0.005 for each dollar of property over $3,000,000
13. Packaging
14. Straight-line depreciation on the production equipment
15. Refrigerant used in refrigeration equipment

Exercise 3–2
Identify cost graphs

Objective 1

The following cost graphs illustrate various types of cost behavior:

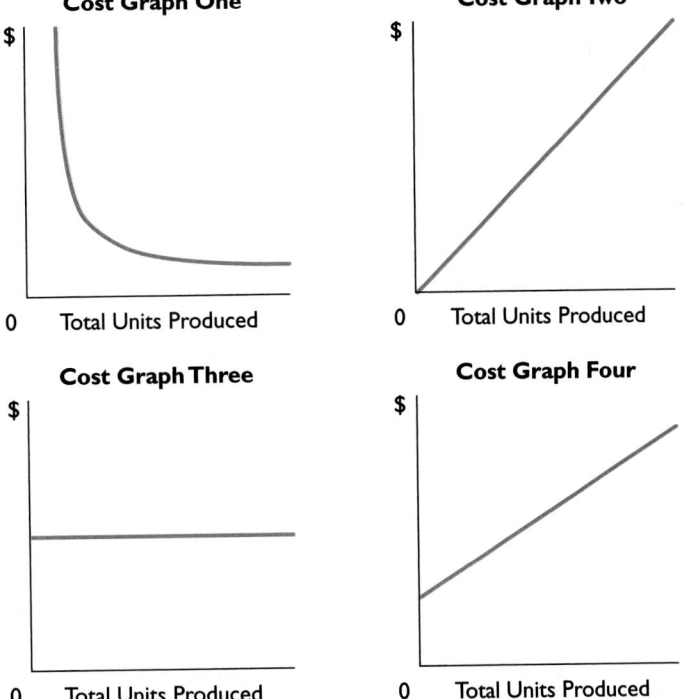

For each of the following costs, identify the cost graph that best illustrates its cost behavior as the number of units produced increases.

a. Per-unit cost of straight-line depreciation on factory equipment
b. Per-unit direct labor cost
c. Electricity costs of $2,000 per month plus $0.02 per kilowatt-hour
d. Salary of quality control supervisor, $4,000 per month
e. Total direct materials cost

Exercise 3–3
Identify activity bases
Objective 1

For **Ohio State University**, match each cost in the following table with the activity base most appropriate to it. An activity base may be used more than once, or not used at all.

Cost:
1. Financial aid office salaries
2. Instructor salaries
3. Supplies
4. Housing personnel wages
5. Record office salaries
6. Admissions office salaries

Activity Base:
a. Number of enrollment applications
b. Number of financial aid applications
c. Student credit hours
d. Number of enrolled students and alumni
e. Number of students living on campus
f. Number of student/athletes

Exercise 3–4
Identify activity bases
Objective 1

From the following list of activity bases for an automobile dealership, select the base that would be most appropriate for each of these costs: (1) preparation costs (cleaning, oil, and gasoline costs) for each car received, (2) salespersons' commission of 3% for each car sold, and (3) administrative costs for ordering cars.

a. Number of cars sold
b. Number of cars ordered
c. Number of cars on hand
d. Number of cars received
e. Dollar amount of cars ordered
f. Dollar amount of cars received
g. Dollar amount of cars on hand
h. Dollar amount of cars sold

Exercise 3–5
Identify fixed and variable costs
Objective 1

Intuit Inc. develops and sells software products for the personal finance market, including popular titles such as Quicken® and TurboTax®. Classify each of the following costs and expenses for this company as either variable or fixed to the number of units produced and sold:

a. President's salary
b. User's guides
c. Property taxes on general offices
d. Wages of telephone order assistants
e. Shipping expenses
f. Straight-line depreciation of computer equipment
g. Advertising
h. Sales commissions
i. Disks
j. Salaries of customer support personnel
k. Salaries of software developers
l. Packaging costs

Exercise 3–6
Relevant range and fixed and variable costs
Objective 1

SPREADSHEET

✓ a. $7.00

Tru-View Video Inc. manufactures video cassette cartridges within a relevant range of 200,000 to 400,000 cassettes per year. Within this range, the following partially completed manufacturing cost schedule has been prepared:

Cassettes produced	200,000	300,000	400,000
Total costs:			
Total variable costs	$1,400,000	(d)	(j)
Total fixed costs	600,000	(e)	(k)
Total costs	$2,000,000	(f)	(l)
Cost per unit:			
Variable cost per unit	(a)	(g)	(m)
Fixed cost per unit	(b)	(h)	(n)
Total cost per unit	(c)	(i)	(o)

Complete the cost schedule, identifying each cost by the appropriate letter (a) through (o).

Exercise 3–7
High-low method
Objective 1

✓ a. $26.50 per unit

Tiempo Watch Company has decided to use the high-low method to estimate the total cost and the fixed and variable cost components of the total cost. The data for the highest and lowest levels of production are as follows:

	Units Produced	Total Costs
Highest level	15,000	$557,500
Lowest level	5,000	$292,500

a. Determine the variable cost per unit and the fixed cost.
b. Based on (a), estimate the total cost for 12,000 units of production.

Exercise 3–8
High-low method for service company
Objective 1

✓ Fixed cost, $620,000

Bi-Coast Railroad decided to use the high-low method and operating data from the past six months to estimate the fixed and variable components of transportation costs. The activity base used by Bi-Coast Railroad is a measure of railroad operating activity, termed "gross-ton miles," which is the total number of tons multiplied by the miles moved.

	Transportation Costs	Gross-Ton Miles
January	$1,710,000	450,000
February	2,090,000	580,000
March	1,632,500	405,000
April	2,105,000	600,000
May	1,900,000	520,000
June	2,145,000	610,000

Determine the variable cost per gross-ton mile and the fixed cost.

Exercise 3–9
Contribution margin ratio
Objective 2

✓ a. 25%

(a) Banner Company budgets sales of $480,000, fixed costs of $90,000, and variable costs of $360,000. What is the contribution margin ratio for Banner Company?
(b) If the contribution margin ratio for Manville Company is 32%, sales were $850,000, and fixed costs were $190,000, what was the income from operations?

Exercise 3–10
Contribution margin and contribution margin ratio
Objective 2

✓ b. 52.46%

For a recent year, **McDonald's Corporation** had the following sales and expenses (in millions):

Sales	$12,421
Food	$ 2,997
Payroll	2,220
Occupancy (rent, depreciation, etc.)	2,722
General, selling, and administrative expenses	1,720
	$ 9,659
Income from operations	$ 2,762

Assume that the variable costs consist of food, payroll, and 40% of the general, selling, and administrative expenses.

a. What is McDonald's contribution margin?
b. What is McDonald's contribution margin ratio?
c. How much would income from operations increase if same-store sales increased by $280 million for the coming year, with no change in the contribution margin ratio or fixed costs?

Exercise 3–11
Break-even sales and sales to realize income from operations

Objective 3

✓ b. 15,775 units

For the current year ending March 31, Yin Company expects fixed costs of $437,600, a unit variable cost of $48, and a unit selling price of $80.

a. Compute the anticipated break-even sales (units).
b. Compute the sales (units) required to realize income from operations of $67,200.

Exercise 3–12
Break-even sales

Objective 3

✓ a. 66,905,206 barrels

The **Anheuser Busch Corporation** reported the following operating information for a recent year (in millions):

Net sales	$11,246
Cost of goods sold	$ 7,162
Marketing and distribution	1,958
	$ 9,120
Income from operations	$ 2,126

In addition, Anheuser Busch sold 111 million barrels of beer during the year. Assume that variable costs were 70% of the cost of goods sold and 45% of marketing and distribution expenses. Assume that the remaining costs are fixed. For the following year, assume that Anheuser Busch expects all revenue and costs to remain constant, except that a new computer system and general office facility are expected to increase fixed costs by $40 million.

Rounding to the nearest cent:
a. Compute the break-even sales (barrels) for the current year.
b. Compute the anticipated break-even (barrels) for the following year.

Exercise 3–13
Break-even sales

Objective 3

✓ a. 11,250 units

Currently, the unit selling price of a product is $165, the unit variable cost is $105, and the total fixed costs are $675,000. A proposal is being evaluated to increase the unit selling price to $180.

a. Compute the current break-even sales (units).
b. Compute the anticipated break-even sales (units), assuming that the unit selling price is increased and all costs remain constant.

Exercise 3–14
Break-even analysis

Objective 3

America Online (AOL) has fueled its growth by using aggressive promotion strategies. One of these strategies is to send CD disks to potential customers, offering free AOL service for a period of time. If AOL mailed 500,000 disks to prospective customers, offering three months free service, how many people would need to sign up for the service in order to break even on the cost of this campaign? Assume the following in forming your response:

Cost per disk (including mailing)	$2.50
Number of months an average new customer stays with the service	36 months
Revenue per month per account	$20

In addition, assume that the monthly variable cost of providing the AOL service to an individual customer is insignificant.

Exercise 3–15
Break-even analysis

Objective 3

Nextel Communications Inc. is one of the largest digital wireless service providers in the United States. In a recent year, it had 3.6 million subscribers that generated revenue of $1,846,758,000. Costs and expenses for the year were as follows:

Cost of revenue	$ 516,393,000
Selling, general, and administrative expenses	1,550,323,000
Depreciation	832,299,000

Assume that 20% of the cost of revenue and 40% of the selling, general, and administrative expenses are variable to the number of subscribers.

a. What is Nextel's break-even number of subscribers, using the data and assumptions above? Round per-unit calculations to the nearest dollar.
b. How much revenue per subscriber would be sufficient for Nextel to break even if the number of subscribers remained constant?

Exercise 3–16
Cost-volume-profit chart
Objective 4

✓ b. $800,000

For the coming year, Peters Inc. anticipates fixed costs of $300,000, a unit variable cost of $25, and a unit selling price of $40. The maximum sales within the relevant range are $1,600,000.

a. Construct a cost-volume-profit chart.
b. Estimate the break-even sales (dollars) by using the cost-volume-profit chart constructed in (a).
c. ✏️ What is the main advantage of presenting the cost-volume-profit analysis in graphic form rather than equation form?

Exercise 3–17
Profit-volume chart
Objective 4

✓ b. $300,000

Using the data for Peters Inc. in Exercise 3–16, (a) determine the maximum possible operating loss, (b) compute the maximum possible income from operations, (c) construct a profit-volume chart, and (d) estimate the break-even sales (units) by using the profit-volume chart constructed in (c).

Exercise 3–18
Break-even chart
Objective 4

Name the following chart, and identify the items represented by the letters (a) through (f).

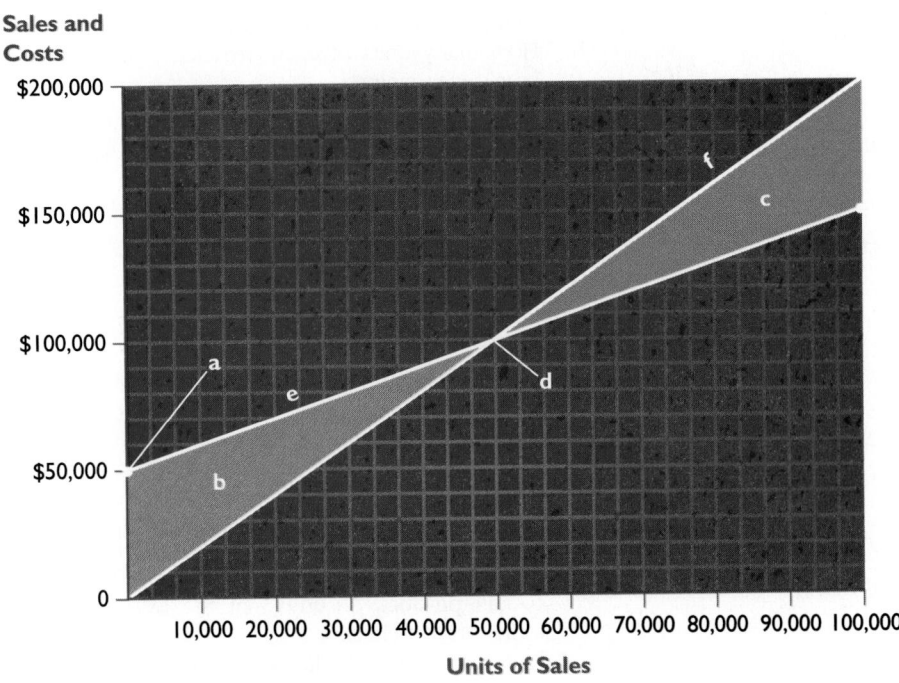

Exercise 3–19
Break-even chart
Objective 4

Name the following chart, and identify the items represented by the letters (a) through (f).

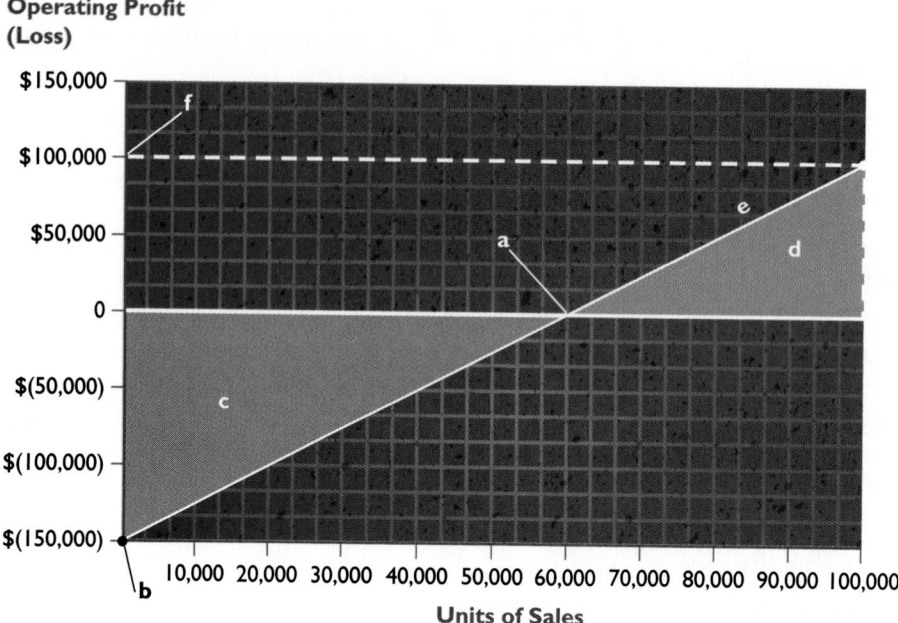

Operating Profit (Loss)

Units of Sales

Exercise 3–20
Sales mix and break-even sales

Objective 5

SPREADSHEET

✓ a. 250,000 units

Tasty Snacks Inc. manufactures and sells two products, potato chips and pretzels. The fixed costs are $167,500, and the sales mix is 70% potato chips and 30% pretzels. The unit selling price and the unit variable cost for each product are as follows:

Products	Unit Selling Price	Unit Variable Cost
Potato Chips	$2.20	$1.50
Pretzels	1.70	1.10

a. Compute the break-even sales (units) for the overall product, E.
b. How many units of each product, potato chips and pretzels, would be sold at the break-even point?

Exercise 3–21
Break-even sales and sales mix for a service company

Objective 5

✓ a. 48 seats

Eastern Airways provides air transportation services between New York and Miami. A single New York to Miami round-trip flight has the following operating statistics:

Fuel	$6,520
Flight crew salaries	3,400
Airplane depreciation	1,600
Variable cost per passenger—business class	58
Variable cost per passenger—tourist class	34
One-way ticket price—business class	400
One-way ticket price—tourist class	240

It is assumed that the fuel, crew salaries, and airplane depreciation are fixed, regardless of the number of seats sold for the round-trip flight.

a. Compute the break-even number of seats sold on a single round-trip flight for the overall product. Assume that the overall product is 25% business class and 75% tourist class tickets.
b. How many business class and tourist class seats would be sold at the break-even point?

Exercise 3–22
Margin of safety

Objective 6

✓ a. 1. $50,000

a. If Kelvin Company, with a break-even point at $350,000 of sales, has actual sales of $400,000, what is the margin of safety expressed (1) in dollars and (2) as a percentage of sales?
b. If the margin of safety for Moore Company was 25%, fixed costs were $600,000, and variable costs were 60% of sales, what was the amount of actual sales (dollars)? (Hint: Determine the break-even in sales dollars first.)

Exercise 3–23
Break-even and margin of safety relationships

Objective 6

At a recent staff meeting, the question of discontinuing Product Q from the product line was being discussed. The chief financial analyst reported the following current monthly data for Product Q:

Units of sales	20,000
Break-even units	23,000
Margin of safety in units	3,000

For what reason would you question the validity of these data?

Exercise 3–24
Operating leverage

Objective 6

✓ a. Duncan, 1.50

Duncan Inc. and Chow Inc. have the following operating data:

	Duncan	Chow
Sales	$550,000	$525,000
Variable costs	400,000	250,000
Contribution margin	$150,000	$275,000
Fixed costs	50,000	225,000
Income from operations	$100,000	$ 50,000

a. Compute the operating leverage for Duncan Inc. and Chow Inc.
b. How much would income from operations increase for each company if the sales of each increased by 20%?
c. Why is there a difference in the increase in income from operations for the two companies? Explain.

PROBLEMS SERIES A

Problem 3–1A
Classify costs

Objective 1

Franklin Furniture Company manufactures sofas for distribution to several major retail chains. The following costs are incurred in the production and sale of sofas:

a. Salesperson's salary, $12,000 plus 5% of the selling price of each sofa sold
b. Janitorial supplies, $10 for each sofa produced
c. Consulting fee of $15,000 paid to efficiency specialists
d. Rent on experimental equipment, $25 for every sofa produced
e. Springs
f. Employer's FICA taxes on controller's salary of $75,000
g. Insurance premiums on property, plant, and equipment, $5,000 per year plus $20 per $10,000 of insured value over $8,000,000
h. Salary of production vice-president
i. Fabric for sofa coverings
j. Cartons used to ship sofas
k. Straight-line depreciation on factory equipment
l. Electricity costs of $0.02 per kilowatt-hour
m. Property taxes on property, plant, and equipment
n. Hourly wages of sewing machine operators
o. Sewing supplies
p. Foam rubber for cushion fillings
q. Salary of designers
r. Wood for framing the sofas
s. Rental costs of warehouse, $10,000 per month
t. Legal fees paid to attorneys in defense of the company in a patent infringement suit, $10,000 plus $75 per hour

Instructions

Classify the preceding costs as either fixed, variable, or mixed. Use the following tabular headings and place an "X" in the appropriate column. Identify each cost by letter in the Cost column.

Cost	Fixed Cost	Variable Cost	Mixed Cost

Problem 3–2A

Break-even sales under present and proposed conditions

Objectives 2, 3

SPREADSHEET

✓ 3. 210,000 units

Good Earth Garden Tools Inc., operating at full capacity, sold 292,000 units at a price of $45 per unit during 2003. Its income statement for 2003 is as follows:

Sales		$13,140,000
Cost of goods sold		8,000,000
Gross profit		$ 5,140,000
Operating expenses:		
Selling expenses	$1,500,000	
Administrative expenses	2,000,000	
Total operating expenses		3,500,000
Income from operations		$ 1,640,000

The division of costs between fixed and variable is as follows:

	Fixed	Variable
Cost of sales	25%	75%
Selling expenses	40%	60%
Administrative expenses	80%	20%

Management is considering a plant expansion program that will permit an increase of $2,250,000 in yearly sales. The expansion will increase fixed costs by $600,000, but will not affect the relationship between sales and variable costs.

Instructions

1. Determine for 2003 the total fixed costs and the total variable costs.
2. Determine for 2003 (a) the unit variable cost and (b) the unit contribution margin.
3. Compute the break-even sales (units) for 2003.
4. Compute the break-even sales (units) under the proposed program.
5. Determine the amount of sales (units) that would be necessary under the proposed program to realize the $1,640,000 of income from operations that was earned in 2003.
6. Determine the maximum income from operations possible with the expanded plant.
7. If the proposal is accepted and sales remain at the 2003 level, what will the income or loss from operations be for 2004?
8. ✏→ Based on the data given, would you recommend accepting the proposal? Explain.

Problem 3–3A

Break-even sales and cost-volume-profit chart

Objectives 3, 4

✓ 1. 18,000 units

For the coming year, Colorado Shoe Company anticipates a unit selling price of $80, a unit variable cost of $50, and fixed costs of $540,000.

Instructions

1. Compute the anticipated break-even sales (units).
2. Compute the sales (units) required to realize income from operations of $84,000.
3. Construct a cost-volume-profit chart, assuming maximum sales of 40,000 units within the relevant range.
4. Determine the probable income (loss) from operations if sales total 23,000 units.

Problem 3–4A

Break-even sales and cost-volume-profit chart

Objectives 3, 4

Last year, Lansing Company had sales of $225,000, based on a unit selling price of $180. The variable cost per unit was $100, and fixed costs were $120,000. The maximum sales within Lansing Company's relevant range are 3,000 units. Lansing Company is considering a proposal to spend an additional $40,000 on billboard advertising during the current year in an attempt to increase sales and utilize unused capacity.

✓ 1. 1,500 units

Instructions

1. Construct a cost-volume-profit chart indicating the break-even sales for last year.
2. Using the cost-volume-profit chart prepared in (1), determine (a) the income from operations for last year and (b) the maximum income from operations that could have been realized during the year.
3. Construct a cost-volume-profit chart indicating the break-even sales for the current year, assuming that a noncancelable contract is signed for the additional billboard advertising. No changes are expected in the selling price or other costs.
4. Using the cost-volume-profit chart prepared in (3), determine (a) the income from operations if sales total 2,500 units and (b) the maximum income from operations that could be realized during the year.

Problem 3–5A
Sales mix and break-even sales

Objective 5

✓ 1. 55,000 units

Data related to the expected sales of CDs and cassette tapes for Bliss Music Inc. for the current year, which is typical of recent years, are as follows:

Products	Unit Selling Price	Unit Variable Cost	Sales Mix
CDs	$18.00	$11.00	75%
Cassette tapes	12.00	7.00	25%

The estimated fixed costs for the current year are $357,500.

Instructions

1. Determine the estimated units of sales of the overall product necessary to reach the break-even point for the current year.
2. Based on the break-even sales (units) in (1), determine the unit sales of both CDs and cassette tapes for the current year.
3. ✎ Assume that the sales mix was 25% CDs and 75% cassette tapes. Compare the break-even point with that in (1). Why is it so different?

Problem 3–6A
Contribution margin, break-even sales, cost-volume-profit chart, margin of safety, and operating leverage

Objectives 2, 3, 4, 6

✓ 2. 50%

Jarvis Inc. expects to maintain the same inventories at the end of 2003 as at the beginning of the year. The total of all production costs for the year is therefore assumed to be equal to the cost of goods sold. With this in mind, the various department heads were asked to submit estimates of the costs for their departments during 2003. A summary report of these estimates is as follows:

	Estimated Fixed Cost	Estimated Variable Cost (per unit sold)
Production costs:		
Direct materials	—	$ 6.80
Direct labor	—	3.20
Factory overhead	$ 83,500	1.40
Selling expenses:		
Sales salaries and commissions	37,300	0.80
Advertising	12,500	—
Travel	3,200	—
Miscellaneous selling expense	4,200	0.50
Administrative expenses:		
Office and officers' salaries	75,400	—
Supplies	5,000	0.20
Miscellaneous administrative expense	3,900	2.10
Total	$225,000	$15.00

It is expected that 20,000 units will be sold at a price of $30 a unit. Maximum sales within the relevant range are 30,000 units.

Instructions

1. Prepare an estimated income statement for 2003.
2. What is the expected contribution margin ratio?
3. Determine the break-even sales in units.
4. Construct a cost-volume-profit chart indicating the break-even sales.
5. What is the expected margin of safety?
6. Determine the operating leverage.

PROBLEMS SERIES B

Problem 3–1B
Classify costs

Objective 1

Highlands Company manufactures blue jeans for distribution to several major retail chains. The following costs are incurred in the production and sale of blue jeans:

a. Insurance premiums on property, plant, and equipment, $10,000 per year plus $3 per $10,000 of insured value over $5,000,000
b. Blue dye
c. Thread
d. Property taxes on property, plant, and equipment
e. Sewing supplies
f. Shipping boxes used to ship orders
g. Rent on experimental equipment, $25,000 per year
h. Leather for patches identifying each jean style
i. Straight-line depreciation on sewing machines
j. Salary of production vice-president
k. Janitorial supplies, $2,000 per month
l. Hourly wages of sewing machine operators
m. Blue denim fabric
n. Electricity costs of $0.07 per kilowatt-hour
o. Legal fees paid to attorneys in defense of the company in a patent infringement suit, $20,000 plus $100 per hour
p. Consulting fee of $50,000 paid to industry specialist for marketing advice
q. Brass buttons
r. Rental costs of warehouse, $2,000 per month plus $1 per square foot of storage used
s. Salesperson's salary, $12,000 plus 3% of the total sales
t. Salary of designers

Instructions
Classify the preceding costs as either fixed, variable, or mixed. Use the following tabular headings and place an "X" in the appropriate column. Identify each cost by letter in the cost column.

Cost	Fixed Cost	Variable Cost	Mixed Cost

Problem 3–2B
Break-even sales under present and proposed conditions

Objectives 2, 3

SPREADSHEET

✓ 2. a. $75

Radiance Lighting Company, operating at full capacity, sold 60,000 units at a price of $125 per unit during 2003. Its income statement for 2003 is as follows:

Sales		$7,500,000
Cost of goods sold		4,000,000
Gross profit		$3,500,000
Operating expenses:		
Selling expenses	$2,400,000	
Administrative expenses	600,000	
Total operating expenses		3,000,000
Income from operations		$ 500,000

The division of costs between fixed and variable is as follows:

	Fixed	Variable
Cost of sales	40%	60%
Selling expenses	25%	75%
Administrative expenses	50%	50%

Management is considering a plant expansion program that will permit an increase of $1,200,000 in yearly sales. The expansion will increase fixed costs by $300,000, but will not affect the relationship between sales and variable costs.

Instructions

1. Determine for 2003 the total fixed costs and the total variable costs.
2. Determine for 2003 (a) the unit variable cost and (b) the unit contribution margin.
3. Compute the break-even sales (units) for 2003.
4. Compute the break-even sales (units) under the proposed program.
5. Determine the amount of sales (units) that would be necessary under the proposed program to realize the $500,000 of income from operations that was earned in 2003.
6. Determine the maximum income from operations possible with the expanded plant.
7. If the proposal is accepted and sales remain at the 2003 level, what will the income or loss from operations be for 2004?
8. ◀▬▬▶ Based on the data given, would you recommend accepting the proposal? Explain.

Problem 3–3B
Break-even sales and cost-volume-profit chart

Objectives 3, 4

✓ 1. 10,000 units

For the coming year, Doctors' Medical Equipment Company anticipates a unit selling price of $400, a unit variable cost of $280, and fixed costs of $1,200,000.

Instructions

1. Compute the anticipated break-even sales (units).
2. Compute the sales (units) required to realize income from operations of $120,000.
3. Construct a cost-volume-profit chart, assuming maximum sales of 16,000 units within the relevant range.
4. Determine the probable income (loss) from operations if sales total 11,500 units.

Problem 3–4B
Break-even sales and cost-volume-profit chart

Objectives 3, 4

✓ 1. 4,000 units

Last year, Carter Company had sales of $375,000, based on a unit selling price of $75. The variable cost per unit was $54, and fixed costs were $84,000. The maximum sales within Carter Company's relevant range are 10,000 units. Carter Company is considering a proposal to spend an additional $42,000 on billboard advertising during the current year in an attempt to increase sales and utilize unused capacity.

Instructions

1. Construct a cost-volume-profit chart indicating the break-even sales for last year.
2. Using the cost-volume-profit chart prepared in (1), determine (a) the income from operations for last year and (b) the maximum income from operations that could have been realized during the year.
3. Construct a cost-volume-profit chart indicating the break-even sales for the current year, assuming that a noncancelable contract is signed for the additional billboard advertising. No changes are expected in the unit selling price or other costs.
4. Using the cost-volume-profit chart prepared in (3), determine (a) the income from operations if sales total 9,000 units and (b) the maximum income from operations that could be realized during the year.

Problem 3–5B
Sales mix and break-even sales

Objective 5

✓ 1. 21,000 units

Data related to the expected sales of golf balls and tennis balls for Sports Inc. for the current year, which is typical of recent years, are as follows:

Products	Unit Selling Price	Unit Variable Cost	Sales Mix
Golf balls	$24.00	$15.50	36%
Tennis balls	6.50	3.00	64%

The estimated fixed costs for the current year are $111,300.

Instructions

1. Determine the estimated units of sales of the overall product necessary to reach the break-even point for the current year.
2. Based on the break-even sales (units) in (1), determine the unit sales of both golf balls and tennis balls for the current year.
3. ━━━► Assume that the sales mix was 70% golf balls and 30% tennis balls. Compare the break-even point with that in (1). Why is it so different?

Problem 3–6B
Contribution margin, break-even sales, cost-volume-profit chart, margin of safety, and operating leverage

Objectives 2, 3, 4, 6

✓ 2. 40%

Universal Products Inc. expects to maintain the same inventories at the end of 2003 as at the beginning of the year. The total of all production costs for the year is therefore assumed to be equal to the cost of goods sold. With this in mind, the various department heads were asked to submit estimates of the costs for their departments during 2003. A summary report of these estimates is as follows:

	Estimated Fixed Cost	Estimated Variable Cost (per unit sold)
Production costs:		
Direct materials	—	$122.30
Direct labor	—	105.50
Factory overhead	$264,000	20.30
Selling expenses:		
Sales salaries and commissions	245,000	10.70
Advertising	75,000	—
Travel	39,500	—
Miscellaneous selling expense	24,500	6.70
Administrative expenses:		
Office and officers' salaries	220,000	—
Supplies	15,000	2.30
Miscellaneous administrative expense	17,000	2.20
Total	$900,000	$270.00

It is expected that 6,250 units will be sold at a price of $450 a unit. Maximum sales within the relevant range are 10,000 units.

Instructions

1. Prepare an estimated income statement for 2003.
2. What is the expected contribution margin ratio?
3. Determine the break-even sales in units.
4. Construct a cost-volume-profit chart indicating the break-even sales.
5. What is the expected margin of safety?
6. Determine the operating leverage.

SPECIAL ACTIVITIES

Activity 3–1
Golden Properties Inc.
Ethics and professional conduct in business

Howard Skinner is a financial consultant to Golden Properties Inc., a real estate syndicate. Golden Properties Inc. finances and develops commercial real estate (office buildings). The completed projects are then sold as limited partnership interests to individual investors. The syndicate makes a profit on the sale of these partnership interests. Howard provides financial information for the offering prospectus, which is a document that provides the financial and legal details of the limited partnership offerings. In one of the projects, the bank has financed the construction of a commercial office building at a rate of 6% for the first four years, after which time the rate jumps to 10% for the remaining

26 years of the mortgage. The interest costs are one of the major ongoing costs of a real estate project. Howard has reported prominently in the prospectus that the break-even occupancy for the first four years is 60%. This is the amount of office space that must be leased to cover the interest and general upkeep costs over the first four years. The 60% break-even is very low and thus communicates a low risk to potential investors. Howard uses the 60% break-even rate as a major marketing tool in selling the limited partnership interests. Buried in the fine print of the prospectus is additional information that would allow an astute investor to determine that the break-even occupancy will jump to 85% after the fourth year because of the contracted increase in the mortgage interest rate. Howard believes prospective investors are adequately informed as to the risk of the investment.

➤ Comment on the ethical considerations of this situation.

Activity 3–2
U.S. Airlines
Break-even sales, contribution margin

"For a student, a grade of 65 percent is nothing to write home about. But for the airline . . . [industry], filling 65 percent of the seats . . . is the difference between profit and loss.

The [economy] might be just strong enough to sustain all the carriers on a cash basis, but not strong enough to bring any significant profitability to the industry. . . . For the airlines . . . , the emphasis will be on trying to consolidate routes and raise ticket prices. . . ."

➤ The airline industry is notorious for boom and bust cycles. Why is airline profitability very sensitive to these cycles? Do you think that during a down cycle the strategy to consolidate routes and raise ticket prices is reasonable? What would make this strategy succeed or fail? Why?

Source: Edwin McDowell, "Empty Seats, Empty Beds, Empty Pockets," *New York Times*, January 6, 1992, p. C3.

Activity 3–3
Galaxy Studios
Break-even analysis

Galaxy Studios has finished a new VCR movie offering, *Keeping in Balance*. Management is now considering its marketing strategies. The following information is available:

Anticipated sales price per unit	$25
Variable cost per unit*	$5
Anticipated volume	750,000
Movie production costs	$10,000,000
Anticipated advertising	$5,000,000

*The cost of the VCR tape, packaging, and copying costs.

Two managers, Julie Wilson and Steve Harris, had the following discussion of ways to increase the profitability of this new offering.

Julie: I think we need to think of some way to increase our profitability. Do you have any ideas?

Steve: Well, I think the best strategy would be to become aggressive on price.

Julie: How aggressive?

Steve: If we drop the price to $20 per unit and maintain our advertising budget at $5,000,000, I think we will generate sales of 1,600,000 units.

Julie: I think that's the wrong way to go. You're giving too much up on price. Instead, I think we need to follow an aggressive advertising strategy.

Steve: How aggressive?

Julie: If we increase our advertising to a total of $8,000,000, we should be able to increase sales volume to 1,500,000 units without any change in price.

Steve: I don't think that's reasonable. We'll never cover the increased advertising costs.

➤ Which strategy is best: Do nothing? Follow the advice of Julie Wilson? Or follow Steve Harris's strategy?

Activity 3–4
Image4U Inc.
Variable costs and activity bases in decision making

The owner of Image4U Inc., a T-shirt printing company, is planning direct labor needs for the upcoming year. The owner has provided you with the following information for next year's plans:

	One Color	Two Color	Three Color	Four Color	Total
Number of T-shirts	300	800	900	1,000	3,000

Each color on the T-shirt must be printed one at a time. Thus, for example, a four-color T-shirt will need to be run through the silk screen operation four separate times. The total production volume last year was 2,000 T-shirts, as shown below.

	One Color	Two Color	Three Color	Total
Number of T-shirts	300	800	900	2,000

As you can see, the four-color T-shirt is a new product offering for the upcoming year. The owner believes that the expected 1,000-unit increase in volume from last year means that direct labor expenses should increase by 50% (1,000/2,000). What do you think?

Activity 3–5
Hassid Company
Variable costs and activity bases in decision making

Sales volume has been dropping at Hassid Company. During this time, however, the Shipping Department manager has been under severe financial constraints. The manager knows that most of the Shipping Department's effort is related to pulling inventory from the warehouse for each order and performing the paperwork. The paperwork involves preparing shipping documents for each order. Thus, the pulling and paperwork effort associated with each sales order is essentially the same, regardless of the size of the order. The Shipping Department manager has discussed the financial situation with senior management. Senior management has responded by pointing out that sales volume has been dropping, so that the amount of work in the Shipping Department should be dropping. Thus, senior management told the Shipping Department manager that costs should be decreasing in the department.

The Shipping Department manager prepared the following information:

Month	Sales Volume	Number of Customer Orders	Sales Volume per Order
January	$95,000	500	$190
February	93,600	520	180
March	90,100	530	170
April	90,000	600	150
May	89,900	620	145
June	85,000	625	136
July	81,900	630	130
August	80,000	640	125

Given this information, how would you respond to senior management?

Activity 3–6
Into the Real World
Break-even analysis

Break-even analysis is one of the most fundamental tools for managing any kind of business unit. Consider the management of your school. In a group, brainstorm some applications of break-even analysis at your school. Identify three areas where break-even analysis might be used. For each area, identify the revenues, variable costs, and fixed costs that would be used in the calculation.

Activity 3–7
Into the Real World
Cost-volume-profit analysis

Access the portion of **Microsoft's** Web site at **www.microsoft.com/msft** that deals with investor relations. There are a number of features accessible from this contents page. Go to the online analysis tools. One of these tools is a Microsoft Excel® "what-if" model.

Download this model, and use Excel® (or the Excel Viewer if you don't have Excel) to open the model.

a. Use the model to project next year's net income, based on the following assumptions:*

Revenue to change by	0.12
Cost of revenue to change by	0.10
Sales and marketing to change by	0.10
Research and development to change by	0.11
General and administrative expenses to change by	0.08
Investment income	$2,000 million
Other expenses to be	$100 million
Tax rate to be	0.30
Average number of shares to be	5,500 million

*If the model has changed since this text was written, complete the projection by filling in your own assumptions required by the model.

b. Why did your net income increase a different percentage than did sales?

ANSWERS TO SELF-EXAMINATION QUESTIONS

Matching

1.	S	4.	D	7.	I	10.	E	13.	N	16.	P
2.	C	5.	H	8.	B	11.	G	14.	L	17.	M
3.	A	6.	O	9.	F	12.	Q	15.	K	18.	R

Multiple Choice

1. **B** Variable costs vary in total in direct proportion to changes in the level of activity (answer B). Costs that vary on a per-unit basis as the level of activity changes (answer A) or remain constant in total dollar amount as the level of activity changes (answer C), or both (answer D), are fixed costs.

2. **D** The contribution margin ratio indicates the percentage of each sales dollar available to cover the fixed costs and provide income from operations and is determined as follows:

$$\text{Contribution margin ratio} = \frac{\text{Sales} - \text{Variable costs}}{\text{Sales}}$$

$$\text{Contribution margin ratio} = \frac{\$500,000 - \$200,000}{\$500,000}$$

$$= 60\%$$

3. **D** The break-even sales of 40,000 units (answer D) is computed as follows:

$$\text{Break-even sales (units)} = \frac{\text{Fixed costs}}{\text{Unit contribution margin}}$$

$$\text{Break-even sales (units)} = \frac{\$160,000}{\$4} = 40,000 \text{ units}$$

4. **D** Sales of 45,000 units are required to realize income from operations of $20,000, computed as follows:

$$\text{Sales (units)} = \frac{\text{Fixed costs} + \text{Target profit}}{\text{Unit contribution margin}}$$

$$\text{Sales (units)} = \frac{\$160,000 + \$20,000}{\$4} = 45,000 \text{ units}$$

5. **C** The operating leverage is 1.8, computed as follows:

$$\text{Operating leverage} = \frac{\text{Contribution margin}}{\text{Income from operations}}$$

$$\text{Operating leverage} = \frac{\$360,000}{\$200,000} = 1.8$$

Profit Reporting for Management Analysis

objectives

After studying this chapter, you should be able to:

1. Describe and illustrate income reporting under variable costing and absorption costing.

2. Describe and illustrate income analysis under variable costing and absorption costing.

3. Describe and illustrate management's use of variable costing and absorption costing for controlling costs, pricing products, planning production, analyzing market segments, and analyzing contribution margins.

S ay you are interested in obtaining a temporary job during the summer, and you have three different job options. How would you evaluate these options? Naturally, there are many things to consider, including how much income each job would provide.

Determining the income from each job may not be as simple as comparing the rates of pay per hour. For example, a job as an office clerk at a local company pays $7 per hour. A job delivering pizza pays $10 per hour (including estimated tips), although you must use your own transportation. A job working in a store located in a beach resort over 500 miles away from your home pays $8 per hour. All three jobs offer work for 40 hours per week for the whole summer. If these options were ranked according to their pay per hour, the pizza delivery job would appear to be the most attractive. However, the costs associated with each job must also be evaluated. For example, the office job may require that you pay for downtown parking and purchase office clothes. The pizza delivery job will require you to pay for gas and maintenance for your car. The resort job will require you to move to the resort city and incur additional living costs. Only by considering the direct costs for each job will you be able to determine which job will provide you the most income.

Just as you should evaluate the relative financial impact of various choices, so must a business evaluate the financial impact of its choices. In this chapter we will discuss how businesses measure profitability, using absorption costing and variable costing. After illustrating and comparing these concepts, we discuss how businesses use them for controlling costs, pricing products, planning production, analyzing market segments, and analyzing contribution margins.

The Income Statement Under Variable Costing and Absorption Costing

objective 1

Describe and illustrate income reporting under variable costing and absorption costing.

One of the most important items affecting a business's net income is the cost of goods sold. In many cases, the cost of goods sold is larger than all of the other expenses combined. The cost of goods sold can be determined under either the absorption costing or variable costing concept.

Under **absorption costing**, all manufacturing costs are included in finished goods and remain there as an asset until the goods are sold. Absorption costing is necessary in determining historical costs for financial reporting to external users and for tax reporting.

ABSORPTION COSTING

COST OF GOODS MANUFACTURED
- Direct materials
- Direct labor
- Variable factory overhead
- Fixed factory overhead

INVENTORY

VARIABLE COSTING

COST OF GOODS MANUFACTURED
- Direct materials
- Direct labor
- Variable factory overhead

INVENTORY

PERIOD EXPENSE ➝ ● Fixed factory overhead

Variable costing may be more useful to management in making decisions. In **variable costing**, which is also called **direct costing**, the cost of goods manufactured is composed only of *variable* manufacturing costs—costs that increase or decrease as the volume of production rises or falls. These costs are the direct materials, direct labor, and only those factory overhead costs that vary with the rate of production. The remaining factory overhead costs, which are fixed or nonvariable costs, are generally related to the productive capacity of the manufacturing plant and are not affected by changes in the quantity of product manufactured. Thus, the fixed factory overhead does not become a part of the cost of goods manufactured but is treated as an expense of the period in which it is incurred.

To illustrate the difference between the variable costing income statement and the absorption costing income statement, assume that Belling Co. manufactured 15,000 units at the following costs:

	Total Cost	Number of Units	Unit Cost
Manufacturing costs:			
Variable	$375,000	15,000	$25
Fixed	150,000	15,000	10
Total	$525,000		$35
Selling and administrative expenses:			
Variable ($5 per unit sold)	$ 75,000		
Fixed	50,000		
Total	$125,000		

> The variable costing income statement includes only variable manufacturing costs in the cost of goods sold.

The units sell at a price of $50, as shown in the variable costing income statement for Belling Co. in Exhibit 1. In this income statement, variable costs are separated from fixed costs. The variable cost of goods sold, which includes the variable manufacturing costs, is deducted from sales to yield the **manufacturing margin** of $375,000. The variable selling and administrative expenses of $75,000 are deducted from the manufacturing margin to yield the contribution margin of $300,000. Thus, the **contribution margin** is sales less variable costs, as we defined in the previous chapter. The income from operations of $100,000 is then determined by deducting fixed costs of $200,000 from the contribution margin.

Exhibit 1 Variable Costing Income Statement

Sales (15,000 × $50)		$750,000
Variable cost of goods sold (15,000 × $25)		375,000
Manufacturing margin		$375,000
Variable selling and administrative expenses		75,000
Contribution margin		$300,000
Fixed costs:		
Fixed manufacturing costs	$150,000	
Fixed selling and administrative expenses	50,000	200,000
Income from operations		$100,000

Q&A

A company has sales of $450,000, cost of goods sold of $300,000, variable cost of goods sold of $220,000, and variable selling expenses of $50,000. What are (a) its manufacturing margin and (b) its contribution margin?

(a) $230,000 ($450,000 − $220,000);
(b) $180,000 ($230,000 − $50,000)

Exhibit 2 shows the absorption costing income statement prepared for Belling Co. The absorption costing income statement does not distinguish between variable and fixed costs. All manufacturing costs are included in the cost of goods sold. Deducting cost of goods sold from sales yields the $225,000 gross profit. Deducting selling and administrative expenses then yields income from operations of $100,000.

Exhibit 2 Absorption Costing Income Statement

Sales (15,000 × $50)	$750,000
Cost of goods sold (15,000 × $35)	525,000
Gross profit	$225,000
Selling and administrative expenses ($75,000 + $50,000)	125,000
Income from operations	$100,000

Different parts of the world emphasize different approaches to reporting income. For example, Scandinavian companies have a strong variable costing tradition, while German cost accountants have developed some of the most advanced absorption costing practices.

Income from Operations When Units Manufactured Equal Units Sold

In Exhibits 1 and 2, 15,000 units were manufactured and sold. Both the variable and the absorption costing income statements reported the same income from operations of $100,000. Thus, when the number of units manufactured equals the number of units sold, income from operations will be the same under both methods.

Income from Operations When Units Manufactured Exceed Units Sold

When the number of units manufactured exceeds the number of units sold, the variable costing income from operations will be *less* than the absorption costing income from operations. To illustrate, assume that in the preceding example only 12,000 units of the 15,000 units manufactured were sold. Exhibit 3 shows the two income statements that result.

Exhibit 3 Units Manufactured Exceed Units Sold

Variable Costing Income Statement		
Sales (12,000 × $50)		$600,000
Variable cost of goods sold:		
Variable cost of goods manufactured (15,000 × $25)	$375,000	
Less ending inventory (3,000 × $25)	75,000	
Variable cost of goods sold		300,000
Manufacturing margin		$300,000
Variable selling and administrative expenses (12,000 × $5)		60,000
Contribution margin		$240,000
Fixed costs:		
Fixed manufacturing costs	$150,000	
Fixed selling and administrative expenses	50,000	200,000
Income from operations		$ 40,000

Exhibit 3 (Concluded)

Fixed costs are $40 per unit and variable costs are $120 per unit. Production exceeded sales by 5,000 units. What is the difference in the variable costing and absorption costing income from operations?

Variable costing income from operations will be $200,000 ($40 per unit × 5,000) less than absorption costing income from operations.

Absorption Costing Income Statement		
Sales (12,000 × $50)		$600,000
Cost of goods sold:		
Cost of goods manufactured (15,000 × $35)	$525,000	
Less ending inventory (3,000 × $35)	105,000	
Cost of goods sold		420,000
Gross profit		$180,000
Selling and administrative expenses ($60,000 + $50,000)		110,000
Income from operations		$ 70,000

The $30,000 difference ($70,000 − $40,000) in the amount of income from operations is due to the different treatment of the fixed manufacturing costs. The entire amount of the $150,000 of fixed manufacturing costs is included as an expense of the period in the variable costing statement. The ending inventory in the absorption costing statement includes $30,000 (3,000 units × $10) of fixed manufacturing costs. This $30,000 is excluded from the current cost of goods sold in the absorption costing statement and is thus deferred to a future period.

Income from Operations When Units Manufactured Are Less than Units Sold

When the number of units manufactured is less than the number of units sold, the variable costing income from operations will be *greater* than the absorption costing income from operations. To illustrate, assume that 5,000 units of inventory were on hand at the beginning of a period, 10,000 units were manufactured during the period, and 15,000 units were sold (10,000 units manufactured during the period plus the 5,000 units on hand at the beginning of the period) at $50 per unit. The manufacturing costs and selling and administrative expenses are as follows. Exhibit 4 shows the two income statements prepared from this information.

	Total Cost	Number of Units	Unit Cost
Beginning inventory:			
Manufacturing costs:			
Variable	$125,000	5,000	$25
Fixed	50,000	5,000	10
Total	$175,000		$35
Current period:			
Manufacturing costs:			
Variable	$250,000	10,000	$25
Fixed	150,000	10,000	15
Total	$400,000		$40
Selling and administrative expenses:			
Variable ($5 per unit sold)	$ 75,000		
Fixed	50,000		
Total	$125,000		

Exhibit 4 Units Manufactured Are Less than Units Sold

Variable Costing Income Statement		
Sales (15,000 × $50)		$750,000
Variable cost of goods sold:		
Beginning inventory (5,000 × $25)	$125,000	
Variable cost of goods manufactured (10,000 × $25)	250,000	
Variable cost of goods sold		375,000
Manufacturing margin		$375,000
Variable selling and administrative expenses (15,000 × $5)		75,000
Contribution margin		$300,000
Fixed costs:		
Fixed manufacturing costs	$150,000	
Fixed selling and administrative expenses	50,000	200,000
Income from operations		$100,000

Q&A *The beginning inventory is 8,000 units, all of which are sold during the period. The beginning inventory fixed costs are $60 per unit, and variable costs are $300 per unit. What is the difference in the variable costing and absorption costing income from operations, assuming no ending inventory?*

Variable costing income from operations will be $480,000 ($60 per unit × 8,000) greater than absorption costing income from operations.

Absorption Costing Income Statement		
Sales (15,000 × $50)		$750,000
Cost of goods sold:		
Beginning inventory (5,000 × $35)	$175,000	
Cost of goods manufactured (10,000 × $40)	400,000	
Cost of goods sold		575,000
Gross profit		$175,000
Selling and administrative expenses ($75,000 + $50,000)		125,000
Income from operations		$ 50,000

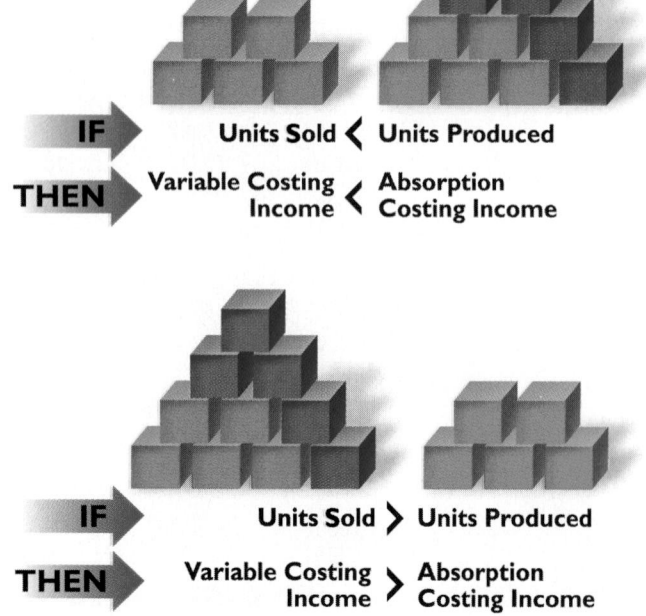

The $50,000 difference ($100,000 − $50,000) in the income from operations is caused by the different treatment of the fixed manufacturing costs. The beginning inventory in the absorption costing income statement includes $50,000 (5,000 units × $10) of fixed manufacturing costs incurred in the preceding period. By being included in the beginning inventory, this $50,000 is included in the cost of goods sold for the current period. Under variable costing, however, this $50,000 was included as an expense in an income statement of a prior period. Therefore, none of it is included as an expense in the current income statement.

Comparing Income from Operations Under the Two Concepts

The two preceding examples illustrate the effects of the variable costing and absorption costing concepts on income from operations when the number of units sold do *not* equal the number of units produced. These effects are summarized at the left.

Income Analysis Under Variable Costing and Absorption Costing

objective 2

Describe and illustrate income analysis under variable costing and absorption costing.

As we have illustrated, the income from operations under variable costing can differ from the income from operations under absorption costing. This difference results from changes in the quantity of the finished goods inventory, which are caused by differences in the levels of sales and production. In analyzing and evaluating operations, management should be aware of the possible effects of changing inventory levels under the two concepts. To illustrate, assume that Frand Manufacturing Company has no beginning inventory and sales are estimated to be 20,000 units at $75 per unit, regardless of production levels. Assume further that the following two proposed production levels are being evaluated by the management of Frand Manufacturing Company:

Proposal 1: 20,000 Units to Be Manufactured and Sold

	Total Cost	Number of Units	Unit Cost
Manufacturing costs:			
Variable	$ 700,000	20,000	$35
Fixed	400,000	20,000	20
Total costs	$1,100,000		$55
Selling and administrative expenses:			
Variable ($5 per unit sold)	$ 100,000		
Fixed	100,000		
Total expenses	$ 200,000		

Proposal 2: 25,000 Units to Be Manufactured; 20,000 Units to Be Sold

	Total Cost	Number of Units	Unit Cost
Manufacturing costs:			
Variable	$ 875,000	25,000	$35
Fixed	400,000	25,000	16
Total costs	$1,275,000		$51
Selling and administrative expenses:			
Variable ($5 per unit sold)	$ 100,000		
Fixed	100,000		
Total expenses	$ 200,000		

If Frand Manufacturing Company manufactures 20,000 units, which is an amount equal to the estimated sales, income from operations under absorption costing would be $200,000. However, the income from operations could be increased by $80,000 by manufacturing 25,000 units and adding 5,000 units to the finished goods inventory. The absorption costing income statements illustrating this effect are shown in Exhibit 5.

Exhibit 5 Absorption Costing Income Statements for Two Production Levels

Frand Manufacturing Company Absorption Costing Income Statements		
	20,000 Units Manufactured	**25,000 Units Manufactured**
Sales (20,000 units × $75)	$1,500,000	$1,500,000
Cost of goods sold:		
Cost of goods manufactured:		
(20,000 units × $55)	$1,100,000	
(25,000 units × $51)		$1,275,000
Less ending inventory:		
(5,000 units × $51)		255,000
Cost of goods sold	$1,100,000	$1,020,000
Gross profit	$ 400,000	$ 480,000
Selling and administrative expenses ($100,000 + $100,000)	200,000	200,000
Income from operations	$ 200,000	$ 280,000

Variable costs are $100 per unit, and fixed costs are $50,000. Sales are estimated to be 4,000 units. (a) How much would absorption costing income from operations differ between a plan to produce 4,000 units and 5,000 units? (b) How much would variable costing income from operations differ between the two production plans?

(a) $10,000 greater for 5,000 units of production [1,000 units × ($50,000 ÷ 5,000), or 4,000 units × ($12.50 − $10.00)]; (b) There would be no difference in income from operations.

The $80,000 increase in income from operations would be caused by allocating the fixed manufacturing costs of $400,000 over a greater number of units of production. Specifically, an increase in production from 20,000 units to 25,000 units meant that the fixed manufacturing costs per unit decreased from $20 ($400,000 ÷ 20,000 units) to $16 ($400,000 ÷ 25,000 units). Thus, the cost of goods sold when 25,000 units are manufactured would be $4 per unit less, or $80,000 less in total (20,000 units sold × $4). Since the cost of goods sold is less, income from operations is $80,000 more when 25,000 units rather than 20,000 units are manufactured.

Under variable costing, income from operations would have been $200,000, regardless of the amount by which units manufactured exceeded sales, because no fixed manufacturing costs are allocated to the units manufactured. To illustrate, Exhibit 6 presents the variable costing income statements for Frand Manufacturing Company for the production of 20,000 units, 25,000 units, and 30,000 units. In each case, the income from operations is $200,000.

As illustrated, if absorption costing is used, management should be careful in analyzing income from operations when large changes in inventory levels occur. Managers could misinterpret increases or decreases in income from operations, due to mere changes in inventory levels, to be the result of business events, such as changes in sales volume, prices, or costs.

Many accountants believe that variable costing should be used for evaluating operating performance because absorption costing encourages management to produce inventory. This is because producing inventory absorbs fixed costs and causes the income from operations to appear higher, as we have illustrated above. In the long run, building inventory without the promise of future sales may lead to higher handling, storage, financing, and obsolescence costs.

Exhibit 6 Variable Costing Income Statements for Three Production Levels

Frand Manufacturing Company Variable Costing Income Statements			
	20,000 Units Manufactured	25,000 Units Manufactured	30,000 Units Manufactured
Sales (20,000 units × $75)	$1,500,000	$1,500,000	$1,500,000
Variable cost of goods sold:			
Variable cost of goods manufactured:			
(20,000 units × $35)	$ 700,000		
(25,000 units × $35)		$ 875,000	
(30,000 units × $35)			$1,050,000
Less ending inventory:			
(0 units × $35)	0		
(5,000 units × $35)		175,000	
(10,000 units × $35)			350,000
Variable cost of goods sold	$ 700,000	$ 700,000	$ 700,000
Manufacturing margin	$ 800,000	$ 800,000	$ 800,000
Variable selling and administrative expenses	100,000	100,000	100,000
Contribution margin	$ 700,000	$ 700,000	$ 700,000
Fixed costs:			
Fixed manufacturing costs	$ 400,000	$ 400,000	$ 400,000
Fixed selling and administrative expenses	100,000	100,000	100,000
Total fixed costs	$ 500,000	$ 500,000	$ 500,000
Income from operations	$ 200,000	$ 200,000	$ 200,000

Management's Use of Variable Costing and Absorption Costing

objective 3

Describe and illustrate management's use of variable costing and absorption costing for controlling costs, pricing products, planning production, analyzing market segments, and analyzing contribution margins.

Managerial accountants should carefully analyze each situation in evaluating whether variable costing or absorption costing reports would be more useful to management. In many situations, preparing reports under both concepts provides useful insights. In the following paragraphs, we discuss such reports and their advantages and disadvantages to management in making decisions related to the items identified in Exhibit 7.

Controlling Costs

All costs are controllable in the long run by someone within a business, but they are not all controllable at the same level of management. For example, plant supervisors, as members of operating management, are responsible for controlling the use of direct materials in their departments. They have no control, however, of insurance costs related to the buildings housing their departments. For a specific level of management, **controllable costs** are costs that can be influenced by management at that level, and **noncontrollable costs** are costs that another level of management controls. This distinction is useful in fixing the responsibility for incurring costs and for reporting costs to those responsible for their control.

Exhibit 7 Accounting Reports and Management Decisions

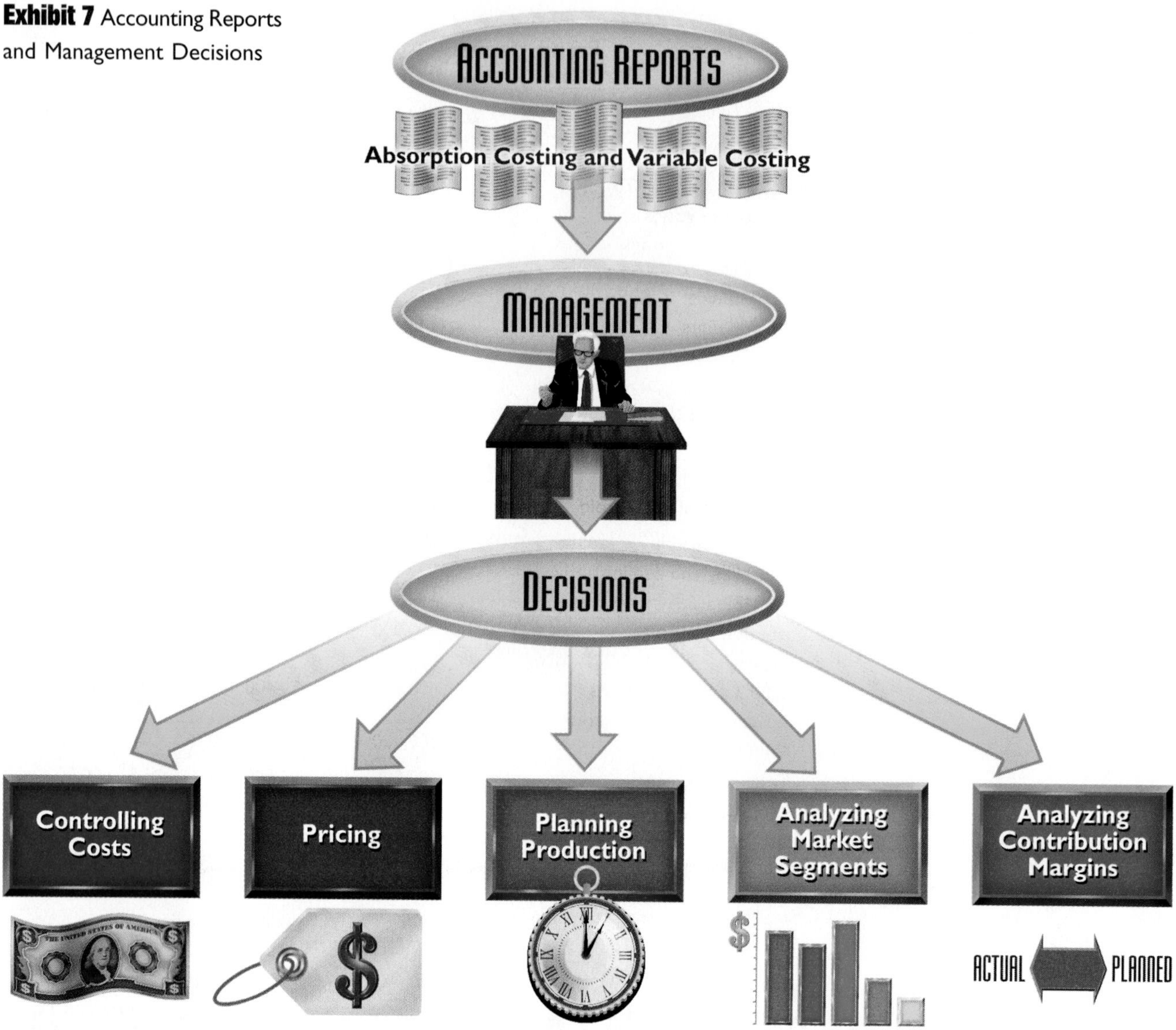

ACCOUNTING REPORTS

Absorption Costing and Variable Costing

MANAGEMENT

DECISIONS

Controlling Costs	Pricing	Planning Production	Analyzing Market Segments	Analyzing Contribution Margins

ACTUAL ⟷ PLANNED

Most chemical companies, such as **Union Carbide** or **Dow Chemical,** use variable costing to evaluate the profitability of their operations. These approaches prevent fixed costs outside of managers' control to be used for evaluation purposes.

Variable manufacturing costs are controlled at the operating level. If the product's cost includes only variable manufacturing costs, the cost can be controlled by operating management. The fixed factory overhead costs are normally the responsibility of a higher level of management. When the fixed factory overhead costs are reported as a separate item in the variable costing income statement, they are easier to identify and control than when they are spread among units of product, as they are under absorption costing.

As in the case with the fixed and variable manufacturing costs, the control of the variable and fixed operating expenses is usually the responsibility of different levels of management. Under variable costing, the variable selling and administrative expenses are reported separately from the fixed selling and administrative expenses. Because they are reported in this manner, both types of operating expenses are easier to identify and control than is the case under absorption costing.

Pricing Products

Many factors enter into determining the selling price of a product. The cost of making the product is clearly significant. Microeconomic theory states that income

Major hotel chains, such as **Marriott, Hilton,** and **Hyatt,** often provide "weekend getaway" packages, which provide discounts for weekend stays in their city hotels. As long as the weekend rates exceed the variable costs, the "weekend getaway" pricing will contribute to the hotel's short-run profitability. However, the revenues earned for all rooms across all the days of the week must be high enough to cover all costs of operation, including fixed costs, in order for the hotel to achieve long-run profitability.

is maximized by expanding output to the volume where the revenue realized by the sale of an additional unit (marginal revenue) equals the cost of that unit (marginal cost). Although the degree of accuracy assumed in economic theory is rarely achieved, the concepts of marginal revenue and marginal cost are useful in setting selling prices.

In the short run, a business is committed to its existing manufacturing facilities. The pricing decision should be based upon making the best use of such capacity. The fixed costs cannot be avoided, but the variable costs can be eliminated if the company does not manufacture the product. The selling price of a product, therefore, should at least be equal to the variable costs of making and selling it. Any price above this minimum selling price contributes an amount toward covering fixed costs and providing income. Variable costing procedures yield data that emphasize these relationships.

In the long run, plant capacity can be increased or decreased. If a business is to continue operating, the selling prices of its products must cover all costs and provide a reasonable income. Hence, in establishing pricing policies for the long run, information provided by absorption costing procedures is needed.

The results of a research study indicated that the companies studied used absorption costing in making routine pricing decisions. However, these companies regularly used variable costing as a basis for setting prices in many short-run situations.[1]

There are no simple solutions to most pricing problems. Consideration must be given to many factors of varying importance. Accounting can contribute by preparing analyses of various pricing plans for both the short run and the long run. Additional analyses useful for product pricing are further described and illustrated in a later chapter.

Planning Production

Planning production also has both short-run and long-run implications. In the short run, production is limited to existing capacity. Operating decisions must be made quickly before opportunities are lost. For example, a company manufacturing products with a seasonal demand may have an opportunity to obtain an off-season order that will not interfere with its production schedule nor reduce the sales of its other products. The relevant factors for such a short-run decision are the additional revenues and the additional variable costs associated with the off-season order. If the revenues from the special order will provide a contribution margin, the order should be accepted because it will increase the company's income from operations. For long-run planning, management must also consider the fixed costs.

Grocery retailers, such as **Safeway,** are using "loyalty" programs to track consumer spending habits in their stores. In these programs, consumers use store-provided magnetic cards to record their purchases. This information can help the stores identify the direct profitability of their customers.

Analyzing Market Segments

Market analysis is performed by the sales and marketing function in order to determine the profit contributed by market segments. A **market segment** is a portion of business that can be assigned to a manager for profit responsibility. Examples of market segments include sales territories, products, salespersons, and customer distribution channels. Variable costing can provide significant insight to decision making regarding such segments.

To illustrate, assume the following data for the month of March 2003 for Camelot Fragrance Company. Camelot Fragrance Company manufactures and markets the Gwenevere perfume line for women and the Lancelot cologne line for men.

[1] Thomas M. Bruegelmann, Gaile A. Haessly, Michael Schiff, and Clair P. Wolfangel, *The Use of Variable Costing in Pricing Decisions*, National Association of Accountants (Montvale, New Jersey, 1986), p. vii.

	Northern Territory	Southern Territory	Total
Sales:			
Gwenevere	$60,000	$30,000	$ 90,000
Lancelot	20,000	50,000	70,000
Total territory sales	$80,000	$80,000	$160,000
Variable production costs:			
Gwenevere (12% of sales)	$ 7,200	$ 3,600	$ 10,800
Lancelot (12% of sales)	2,400	6,000	8,400
Total variable production cost by territory ...	$ 9,600	$ 9,600	$ 19,200
Promotion costs:			
Gwenevere (variable at 30% of sales)	$18,000	$ 9,000	$ 27,000
Lancelot (variable at 20% of sales)	4,000	10,000	14,000
Total promotion cost by territory	$22,000	$19,000	$ 41,000
Sales commissions:			
Gwenevere (variable at 20% of sales)	$12,000	$ 6,000	$ 18,000
Lancelot (variable at 10% of sales)	2,000	5,000	7,000
Total sales commissions by territory	$14,000	$11,000	$ 25,000

This information can be used by Camelot Fragrance Company to prepare a sales territory, product, and salesperson profitability analysis. Each of these is discussed on the following pages.

Sales Territory Profitability Analysis

An income statement presenting the contribution margin by sales territories is often useful to management in evaluating past performance and in directing future sales efforts. Sales territory profitability analysis may lead management to reduce costs in lower-profit sales territories or to increase sales effort in higher-profit territories. For example, the Coca-Cola Company earns over 75% of its total corporate profits outside of the United States. This information motivates the Coca-Cola management to continue expanding operations and sales efforts around the world.

There are many possible explanations for profit differences between territories, including differences in pricing, sales unit volumes, media rates, selling costs, and the types of products sold. To illustrate the analysis of profit differences by sales territory, Exhibit 8 shows the contribution margin by sales territory for Camelot Fragrance Company.

The contribution margin for each territory consists of the sales less the variable costs associated with producing and selling products in each territory. In addition to the contribution margin, the contribution margin ratio (contribution margin divided by sales) for each territory is useful in evaluating sales territories and directing operations toward more profitable activities. For the Northern Territory, the contribution margin ratio is 43% ($34,400 ÷ $80,000), and for the Southern Territory the ratio is 50.5% ($40,400 ÷ $80,000). Although each territory had the same sales, the contribution margin ratios are different. Why is this?

In this case, the difference in territory profit performance can be explained by the difference in sales mix between the two territories. Sales mix, sometimes referred to as *product mix*, is defined as the relative distribution of sales among the various products sold. From the assumed information, the Southern Territory had a higher relative proportion of Lancelot sales than did the Northern Territory. If the

Exhibit 8 Contribution Margin by Sales Territory Report

Camelot Fragrance Company
Contribution Margin by Sales Territory
For the Month Ended March 31, 2003

	Northern Territory		Southern Territory	
Sales		$80,000		$80,000
Variable cost of goods sold		9,600		9,600
Manufacturing margin		$70,400		$70,400
Variable selling expenses:				
Promotion costs	$22,000		$19,000	
Sales commissions	14,000	36,000	11,000	30,000
Contribution margin		$34,400		$40,400
Contribution margin ratio		43%		50.5%

Customer, territory, product, and salesperson profit analysis is done by using a "data warehouse." A data warehouse is a relational database of revenue and cost information that can be divided into many different profit views. For example, **Johnson and Johnson's** data warehouse, called Darwin, enables managers from fifty countries around the world to see various profit views at the click of a mouse.

Lancelot line is more profitable than the Gwenevere line, then we would expect the Southern Territory's overall profitability to be higher than the Northern Territory's, as shown in Exhibit 8. To verify the difference between the profitabilities of the two products, product profitability analysis may be performed.

Product Profitability Analysis

Management should focus its sales efforts on those products that will provide the maximum total contribution margin. An income statement presenting the contribution margin by products is often used by management to guide product-related sales and promotional efforts. For example, **Ford's** *Explorer* sport utility vehicle is one of its most profitable models. Ford uses this information to motivate higher production levels and promotion effort for this brand.

Some products are more profitable than others due to differences with respect to pricing, manufacturing costs, advertising support, or salesperson support. To illustrate the analysis of these differences, Exhibit 9 shows the contribution margin by product for Camelot Fragrance Company.

As you can see, Lancelot's contribution margin ratio is greater than Gwenevere's, even though both product lines have the same manufacturing margin as a percent

Exhibit 9 Contribution Margin by Product Line Report

Camelot Fragrance Company
Contribution Margin by Product Line
For the Month Ended March 31, 2003

	Gwenevere		Lancelot	
Sales		$90,000		$70,000
Variable cost of goods sold		10,800		8,400
Manufacturing margin		$79,200		$61,600
Variable selling expenses:				
Promotion costs	$27,000		$14,000	
Sales commissions	18,000	45,000	7,000	21,000
Contribution margin		$34,200		$40,600
Contribution margin ratio		38%		58%

of sales. The higher contribution margin ratio is the result of Lancelot's lower promotion costs and sales commissions as a percent of sales. The sales territory profitability analysis and the product profitability analysis both indicate the superior profit performance of the Lancelot line. Thus, management should emphasize the Lancelot product line in its marketing plans, try to reduce the promotion and sales commission expenses associated with Gwenevere sales, or increase the price of Gwenevere.

Salesperson Profitability Analysis

In addition to the sales territory and product profitability analyses, sales managers may wish to evaluate the performance of salespersons. This may be done with a salesperson profitability analysis.

A report to management for use in evaluating the sales performance of each salesperson could include total sales, variable cost of goods sold, variable selling expenses, contribution margin, and contribution margin ratio. Exhibit 10 illustrates such a report for three salespersons in the Northern Territory of Camelot Fragrance Company.

Exhibit 10 Contribution Margin by Salesperson Report

Camelot Fragrance Company **Contribution Margin by Salesperson—Northern Territory** **For the Month Ended March 31, 2003**			
	Inez Rodriguez	**Tom Ginger**	**Beth Williams**	**Northern Territory— Total**
Sales	$20,000	$20,000	$40,000	$80,000
Variable cost of goods sold ...	2,400	2,400	4,800	9,600
Manufacturing margin	$17,600	$17,600	$35,200	$70,400
Variable selling expenses:				
Promotion costs	$ 5,000	$ 5,000	$12,000	$22,000
Sales commissions	3,000	3,000	8,000	14,000
	$ 8,000	$ 8,000	$20,000	$36,000
Contribution margin	$ 9,600	$ 9,600	$15,200	$34,400
Contribution margin ratio	48%	48%	38%	43%
Sales mix (% Lancelot sales) ..	50%	50%	0	25%

The total sales and costs of all three salespersons agree with the sales and costs for the Northern Territory in Exhibit 8. Thus, this report provides the Northern Territory manager with a more detailed analysis of the territory's performance. The report indicates that Beth Williams produced the greatest contribution margin for the company but had the lowest contribution margin ratio. Beth Williams sold $40,000 of product, which is twice as much product as the other two salespersons. However, Beth Williams sold only the Gwenevere product line, which has the lowest contribution margin ratio (from Exhibit 9). The other two salespersons sold equal amounts of Gwenevere and Lancelot. These two salespersons had higher contribution margin ratios because of the sales of the higher-margin Lancelot line. The territory manager could use this report to encourage Rodriguez and Ginger to sell more total product, while encouraging Williams to place more selling effort on the Lancelot line.

Other factors should also be considered in evaluating the performance of salespersons. For example, sales growth rates, years of experience, customer service, size of the territory, and actual performance compared to budgeted performance may also be important.

BUSINESS ON STAGE

Finding the Right Niche

Businesses often attempt to divide a market into its unique characteristics, called market segmentation. Once a market segment is identified, product, price, promotion, and location strategies are tailored to fit that market. This is a better approach for many products and services than following a "one size fits all" strategy. For example, the **McDonald's** "Happy Meal" is targeted to the children's market segment, while the "Quarter Pounder" is targeted to more adult segments. The following table lists popular forms of segmentation and their common characteristics:

Form of Segmentation	Characteristics
Demographic	Age, education, gender, income, race
Geographic	Region, city, country
Psychographic	Lifestyle, values, attitudes
Benefit	Benefits provided
Volume	Light vs. heavy use

Examples for each of these forms of segmentation are as follows:

Demographic: **Cadillac** automobiles are targeted to an older, more affluent segment.

Geographic: Pro sports teams offer merchandise in their home cities.

Psychographic: **The Body Shop** markets all-natural beauty products to consumers who value cosmetic products that have not been animal-tested.

Benefit: **TCBY** frozen yogurt shops market a low-fat product that tastes good.

Volume: **Delta Air Lines** provides additional benefits, such as class upgrades, free air travel, and boarding priority, to its frequent fliers. ■

Analyzing Contribution Margins

Another use of the contribution margin concept to assist management in planning and controlling operations focuses on differences between planned and actual contribution margins. However, mere knowledge of the differences is insufficient. Management needs information about the causes of the differences. The systematic examination of the differences between planned and actual contribution margins is termed **contribution margin analysis**.

Since contribution margin is the excess of sales over variable costs, a difference between the planned and actual contribution margin can be caused by (1) an increase or decrease in the amount of sales or (2) an increase or decrease in the amount of variable costs. An increase or decrease in either element may in turn be due to (1) an increase or decrease in the number of units sold or (2) an increase or decrease in the unit sales price or unit cost. The effect of these two factors on either sales or variable costs may be stated as follows:

1. **Quantity factor**—the effect of a difference in the number of units sold, assuming no change in unit sales price or unit cost. The quantity factor is the difference between the actual quantity sold and the planned quantity sold, multiplied by the planned unit sales price or unit cost.

2. **Unit price factor** or **unit cost factor**—the effect of a difference in unit sales price or unit cost on the number of units sold. The unit price or unit cost factor is the difference between the actual unit price or unit cost and the planned unit price or unit cost, multiplied by the actual quantity sold.

We will use the following data for Noble Inc. for the year ended December 31, 2003, as a basis for illustrating contribution margin analysis. For the sake of simplicity, we will assume a single commodity. The analysis would be more complex if several different commodities were sold, but the basic principles would not be affected.

	Actual	Planned	Increase or (Decrease)
Sales	$937,500	$800,000	$137,500
Less: Variable cost of goods sold	$425,000	$350,000	$ 75,000
Variable selling and administrative expenses	162,500	125,000	37,500
Total	$587,500	$475,000	$112,500
Contribution margin	$350,000	$325,000	$ 25,000
Number of units sold	125,000	100,000	
Per unit:			
Sales price	$7.50	$8.00	
Variable cost of goods sold	$3.40	$3.50	
Variable selling and administrative expenses	$1.30	$1.25	

The analysis of these data in Exhibit 11 shows that the favorable increase of $25,000 in the contribution margin was due in large part to an increase in the number of units sold. This increase was partially offset by a decrease in the unit sales price and an increase in the unit cost for variable selling and administrative expenses. The decrease in the unit cost for the variable cost of goods sold was an additional favorable result of 2003 operations.

The information presented in the contribution margin analysis report is useful to management in evaluating past performance and in planning future operations. For example, the impact of the $0.50 reduction in the unit sales price on the number of units sold and on the total sales for the year is useful information that management can use in determining whether further price reductions might be desirable. The contribution margin analysis report also highlights the impact of changes in unit variable costs and expenses. For example, the $0.05 increase in the unit variable selling and administrative expenses might be a result of increased advertising expenditures. If so, the increase in the number of units sold in 2003 could be attributed to both the $0.50 price reduction and the increased advertising.

Q&A

If the actual price was $48 per unit, the planned price was $40 per unit, and the volume sold increased by 5,000 units, to a total of 60,000 units, what would be (a) the quantity factor and (b) the price factor for sales?

(a) $200,000 (5,000 units × $40 per unit);
(b) $480,000 ($8 × 60,000 units)

Exhibit 11 Contribution Margin Analysis Report

Noble Inc.
Contribution Margin Analysis
For the Year Ended December 31, 2003

Increase in amount of sales attributed to:			
Quantity factor:			
Increase in number of units sold in 2003		25,000	
Planned sales price in 2003		× $8.00	$200,000
Price factor:			
Decrease in unit sales price in 2003		$(0.50)	
Number of units sold in 2003		×125,000	(62,500)
Net increase in amount of sales			$137,500
Increase in amount of variable cost of goods sold attributed to:			
Quantity factor:			
Increase in number of units sold in 2003	25,000		
Planned unit cost in 2003	× $3.50	$ 87,500	
Unit cost factor:			
Decrease in unit cost in 2003	$(0.10)		
Number of units sold in 2003	×125,000	(12,500)	
Net increase in amount of variable cost of goods sold		$ 75,000	
Increase in amount of variable selling and administrative expenses attributed to:			
Quantity factor:			
Increase in number of units sold in 2003	25,000		
Planned unit cost in 2003	× $1.25	$ 31,250	
Unit cost factor:			
Increase in unit cost in 2003	$0.05		
Number of units sold in 2003	×125,000	6,250	
Net increase in the amount of variable selling and administrative expenses . . .		$ 37,500	
Net increase in amount of variable costs			112,500
Increase in contribution margin			$ 25,000

ENCORE

Green Products Provide Green Profit

There are significant societal and legal pressures for managers to consider the environmental consequences of their decisions. In response, managers recognize that becoming "green" is not only good for society but also good for business. Given this trend, managers need information to help them assess the environmental impact of their decisions. Thus, new accounting measures are emerging under the label "full environmental costing." Under this approach, environmental costs are associated with the products that cause these costs, thus providing a more complete product profit picture.

Environmental costs fall into three basic categories:

1. *Current costs related to previous production.* These are the current costs of cleanup and remediation associated with decades-old production. An example is the remediation costs incurred by **Champion Paper Company** to clean up the Pigeon River in Tennessee.

2. *Current costs related to current production.* These are the current environmental cleanup costs, such as waste cleanup and disposal, associated with current production. For example, **Eastman Chemical Company** expends significant amounts to safeguard its chemical processes against spills and other environmental events.

3. *Future costs associated with current production.* These are the costs associated with product "take-back," such as recycling, disposal, and remanufacturing costs. For example, **Bristol-Myers Squibb** redesigned *Ban Roll-On* to fit tightly in a carton, which saved 600 tons of recycled paperboard per year.

Few companies have attempted full environmental costing. However, for those who have, the results have been positive overall. Including environmental costs in profit analysis has the following effects:

• Production managers become sensitive to wasted materials in the process, since it is costly to recycle the waste.

• Design managers begin to design products so that it will be easy to take the product back when the consumer is done with it.

• Materials managers begin to save money by using inexpensive recycled materials in current production as a replacement for expensive virgin materials.

Monsanto executives concluded that . . . "the first company to learn how to expand the boundaries of traditional accounting into (product) life cycle assessments, will be in a position to set critical worldwide standards for sustainable growth." ∎

Source: Marc J. Epstein, "Accounting for Product Take-Back," *Management Accounting*, August 1996.

KEY POINTS

1 Describe and illustrate income reporting under variable costing and absorption costing.

Under absorption costing, direct materials, direct labor, and factory overhead become part of the cost of goods manufactured. Under variable costing, the cost of goods manufactured is composed of only variable costs—the direct materials, direct labor, and only those factory overhead costs that vary with the rate of production. The fixed factory overhead costs do not become a part of the cost of goods manufactured but are considered an expense of the period.

Deducting the variable cost of goods sold from sales in the variable costing income statement yields the manufacturing margin. Deducting the variable selling and administrative expenses from the manufacturing margin yields the contribution margin. Deducting the fixed costs from the contribution margin yields the income from operations.

The difference in the income reported under variable costing and absorption costing is summarized in the following table:

Units manufactured:	
Equal units sold	Variable costing income equals absorption costing income.
Exceed units sold	Variable costing income is less than absorption costing income.
Less than units sold	Variable costing income is greater than absorption costing income.

2 Describe and illustrate income analysis under variable costing and absorption costing.

Management should be aware of the effects of changes in inventory levels on income from operations reported under variable costing and absorption costing. If absorption costing is used, managers could misinterpret increases or decreases in income from operations due to changes in inventory levels to be the result of operating efficiencies or inefficiencies.

3 Describe and illustrate management's use of variable costing and absorption costing for controlling costs, pricing products, planning production, analyzing market segments, and analyzing contribution margins.

Variable costing is especially useful at the operating level of management because the amount of variable manufacturing costs are controllable at this level. The fixed factory overhead costs are ordinarily controllable by a higher level of management.

In the short run, variable costing may be useful in establishing the selling price of a product. This price should be at least equal to the variable costs of making and selling the product. In the long run, however, absorption costing is useful in establishing selling prices because all costs must be covered and a reasonable amount of operating income must be earned.

Variable costing can make a significant contribution to management decision making in analyzing and evaluating market segments, such as territories, products, salespersons, and customers.

Contribution margin analysis is the systematic examination of differences between planned and actual contribution margins. These differences can be caused by (1) an increase or decrease in the amount of sales or (2) an increase or decrease in the amount of variable costs. An increase or decrease in either element may in turn be due to (1) an increase or decrease in the number of units sold or (2) an increase or decrease in the unit sales price or unit cost. The effect of these two factors on either sales or variable costs may be stated as follows:

1. **Quantity factor**—the effect of a difference in the number of units sold, assuming no change in unit sales price or unit cost. The quantity factor is the difference between the actual quantity sold and the planned quantity sold, multiplied by the planned unit sales price or unit cost.

2. **Unit price or unit cost factor** —the effect of a difference in unit sales price or unit cost on the number of units sold. The unit price or unit cost factor is the difference between the actual unit price or unit cost and the planned unit price or unit cost, multiplied by the actual quantity sold.

ILLUSTRATIVE PROBLEM

During the current period, McLaughlin Company sold 60,000 units of product at $30 per unit. At the beginning of the period, there were 10,000 units in inventory and McLaughlin Company manufactured 50,000 units during the period. The manufacturing costs and selling and administrative expenses were as follows:

	Total Cost	Number of Units	Unit Cost
Beginning inventory:			
Direct materials	$ 67,000	10,000	$ 6.70
Direct labor	155,000	10,000	15.50
Variable factory overhead	18,000	10,000	1.80
Fixed factory overhead	20,000	10,000	2.00
Total	$ 260,000		$26.00
Current period costs:			
Direct materials	$ 350,000	50,000	$ 7.00
Direct labor	810,000	50,000	16.20
Variable factory overhead	90,000	50,000	1.80
Fixed factory overhead	100,000	50,000	2.00
Total	$1,350,000		$27.00
Selling and administrative expenses:			
Variable	$ 65,000		
Fixed	45,000		
Total	$ 110,000		

Instructions

1. Prepare an income statement based on the variable costing concept.
2. Prepare an income statement based on the absorption costing concept.
3. Give the reason for the difference in the amount of income from operations in 1 and 2.

Solution

1.

Variable Costing Income Statement

Sales (60,000 × $30)		$1,800,000
Variable cost of goods sold:		
Beginning inventory (10,000 × $24)	$ 240,000	
Variable cost of goods manufactured (50,000 × $25)	1,250,000	
Variable cost of goods sold		1,490,000
Manufacturing margin		$ 310,000
Variable selling and administrative expenses		65,000
Contribution margin		$ 245,000
Fixed costs:		
Fixed manufacturing costs	$ 100,000	
Fixed selling and administrative expenses	45,000	145,000
Income from operations		$ 100,000

2.

Absorption Costing Income Statement

Sales (60,000 × $30)		$1,800,000
Cost of goods sold:		
Beginning inventory (10,000 × $26)	$ 260,000	
Cost of goods manufactured (50,000 × $27)	1,350,000	
Cost of goods sold		1,610,000
Gross profit		$ 190,000
Selling and administrative expenses ($65,000 + $45,000)		110,000
Income from operations		$ 80,000

3. The difference of $20,000 ($100,000 − $80,000) in the amount of income from operations is attributable to the different treatment of the fixed manufacturing costs. The beginning inventory in the absorption costing income statement includes $20,000 (10,000 units × $2) of fixed manufacturing costs incurred in the preceding period. This $20,000 was included as an expense in a variable costing income statement of a prior period. Therefore, none of it is included as an expense in the current period variable costing income statement.

SELF-EXAMINATION QUESTIONS
Answers at End of Chapter

Matching
Match each of the following statements with its proper term. Some terms may not be used.

A. absorption costing

B. contribution margin

___ 1. The concept that considers the cost of products manufactured to be composed only of those manufacturing costs that increase or decrease as the volume of production rises or falls (direct materials, direct labor, and variable factory overhead).

C. contribution margin analysis

D. controllable cost

E. conversion cost

F. manufacturing margin

G. market segment

H. noncontrollable cost

I. price factor

J. quantity factor

K. sales mix

L. units manufactured exceed units sold

M. variable costing

___ 2. The concept that considers the cost of manufactured products to be composed of direct materials, direct labor, and factory overhead.

___ 3. Sales less variable cost of goods sold and variable selling and administrative expenses.

___ 4. Sales less variable cost of goods sold.

___ 5. Variable costing income is less than absorption costing income.

___ 6. For a specific level of management, a cost that cannot be directly controlled.

___ 7. A portion of business that is assigned to a manager for profit responsibility.

___ 8. For a specific level of management, a cost that can be directly controlled.

___ 9. The relative distribution of sales among the various products available for sale.

___ 10. The systematic examination of the differences between planned and actual contribution margin.

___ 11. The effect of a difference in unit sales price or unit cost from plan.

___ 12. The effect of a difference in the number of units sold from plan.

Multiple Choice

1. Sales were $750,000, the variable cost of goods sold was $400,000, the variable selling and administrative expenses were $90,000, and fixed costs were $200,000. The contribution margin was:
   A. $60,000
   B. $260,000
   C. $350,000
   D. none of the above

2. During a year in which the number of units manufactured exceeded the number of units sold, the income from operations reported under the absorption costing concept would be:
   A. larger than the income from operations reported under the variable costing concept.
   B. smaller than the income from operations reported under the variable costing concept.
   C. the same as the income from operations reported under the variable costing concept.
   D. none of the above.

3. The beginning inventory consists of 6,000 units, all of which are sold during the period. The beginning inventory fixed costs are $20 per unit, and variable costs are $90 per unit. What is the difference in income from operations between variable and absorption costing?

   A. Variable costing income from operations is $540,000 less than under absorption costing.
   B. Variable costing income from operations is $660,000 greater than under absorption costing.
   C. Variable costing income from operations is $120,000 less than under absorption costing.
   D. Variable costing income from operations is $120,000 greater than under absorption costing.

4. Variable costs are $70 per unit and fixed costs are $150,000. Sales are estimated to be 10,000 units. How much would absorption costing income from operations differ between a plan to produce 10,000 units and 12,000 units?
   A. $150,000 greater for 12,000 units
   B. $150,000 less for 12,000 units
   C. $25,000 greater for 12,000 units
   D. $25,000 less for 12,000 units

5. If actual sales totaled $800,000 for the current year (80,000 units at $10 each) and planned sales were $765,000 (85,000 units at $9 each), the difference between actual and planned sales due to the quantity factor is:
   A. a $50,000 increase
   B. a $35,000 increase
   C. a $45,000 decrease
   D. none of the above

CLASS DISCUSSION QUESTIONS

1. What types of costs are customarily included in the cost of manufactured products under (a) the absorption costing concept and (b) the variable costing concept?

2. Which type of manufacturing cost (direct materials, direct labor, variable factory overhead, fixed factory overhead) is included in the cost of goods manufactured under the absorption costing concept but is excluded from the cost of goods manufactured under the variable costing concept?

3. Which of the following costs would be included in the cost of a manufactured product according to the variable costing concept: (a) direct labor, (b) depreciation on factory building, (c) salary of factory supervisor, (d) electricity purchased to operate factory equipment, (e) property taxes on factory building, (f) rent on factory building, (g) direct materials?

4. In the following equations, based on the variable costing income statement, identify the items designated by X:
   a. Net sales − X = manufacturing margin
   b. Manufacturing margin − X = contribution margin
   c. Contribution margin − X = income from operations

5. In the variable costing income statement, how are the fixed manufacturing costs reported and how are the fixed selling and administrative expenses reported?

6. If the quantity of the ending inventory is larger than that of the beginning inventory, will the amount of income from operations determined by absorption costing be more than or less than the amount determined by variable costing? Explain.

7. Since all costs of operating a business are controllable, what is the significance of the term *noncontrollable cost*?

8. Discuss how financial data prepared on the basis of variable costing can assist management in the development of short-run pricing policies.

9. How might management analyze sales territory profitability?

10. Why might management analyze product profitability?

11. Explain why rewarding sales personnel on the basis of total sales might not be in the best interests of a business whose goal is to maximize profits.

12. Discuss the two factors affecting both sales and variable costs, to which a change in contribution margin can be attributed.

13. How is the quantity factor for an increase or decrease in the amount of sales computed in using contribution margin analysis?

14. How is the unit cost factor for an increase or decrease in the amount of variable cost of goods sold computed in using contribution margin analysis?

EXERCISES

Exercise 4–1

Inventory valuation under absorption costing and variable costing

Objective 1

✓ b. Inventory, $147,000

At the end of the first year of operations, 3,000 units remained in the finished goods inventory. The unit manufacturing costs during the year were as follows:

Direct materials	$34.00
Direct labor	12.40
Fixed factory overhead cost	3.80
Variable factory overhead cost	2.60

What would be the cost of the finished goods inventory reported on the balance sheet under (a) the absorption costing concept and (b) the variable costing concept?

Exercise 4–2
Income statements under absorption costing and variable costing

Objective 1

✓ a. Income from operations, $483,000

Audio Impressions Inc. assembles and sells CD players. The company began operations on May 1, 2003, and operated at 100% of capacity during the first month. The following data summarize the results for May:

Sales (17,000 units)		$2,975,000
Production costs (20,000 units):		
Direct materials	$1,200,000	
Direct labor	680,000	
Variable factory overhead	284,000	
Fixed factory overhead	176,000	2,340,000
Selling and administrative expenses:		
Variable selling and administrative expenses	$ 408,000	
Fixed selling and administrative expenses	95,000	503,000

a. Prepare an income statement according to the absorption costing concept.
b. Prepare an income statement according to the variable costing concept.
c. ◀▬▬▶ What is the reason for the difference in the amount of income from operations reported in (a) and (b)?

Exercise 4–3
Income statements under absorption costing and variable costing

Objective 1

✓ b. Income from operations, $1,400,000

Paris Fashions Inc. manufactures and sells women's clothes. The company began operations on August 1, 2003, and operated at 100% of capacity (40,000 units) during the first month, creating an ending inventory of 4,000 units. During September, the company produced 36,000 garments during the month but sold 40,000 units at $125 per unit. The September manufacturing costs and selling and administrative expenses were as follows:

	Total Cost	Number of Units Produced	Unit Cost
Manufacturing costs in Sept. beginning inventory:			
Variable	$ 184,000	4,000	$46.00
Fixed	54,000	4,000	13.50
Total	$ 238,000		$59.50
September manufacturing costs:			
Variable	$1,656,000	36,000	$46.00
Fixed	540,000	36,000	15.00
Total	$2,196,000		$61.00
Selling and administrative expenses:			
Variable ($24.50 per unit sold)	$ 980,000		
Fixed	240,000		
Total	$1,220,000		

a. Prepare an income statement according to the absorption costing concept for September.
b. Prepare an income statement according to the variable costing concept for September.
c. ◀▬▬▶ What is the reason for the difference in the amount of income from operations reported in (a) and (b)?

Exercise 4–4
Cost of goods manufactured, using variable costing and absorption costing

Objective 1

✓ b. Unit cost of goods manufactured, $35,500

On August 31, the end of the first year of operations, Atlas Equipment Company manufactured 850 units and sold 800 units. The following income statement was prepared, based on the variable costing concept:

Atlas Equipment Company
Variable Costing Income Statement
For the Year Ended August 31, 2003

Sales		$38,400,000
Variable cost of goods sold:		
Variable cost of goods manufactured	$20,825,000	
Less inventory, August 31	1,225,000	
Variable cost of goods sold		19,600,000
Manufacturing margin		$18,800,000
Variable selling and administrative expenses		4,300,000
Contribution margin		$14,500,000
Fixed costs:		
Fixed manufacturing costs	$ 9,350,000	
Fixed selling and administrative expenses	2,800,000	12,150,000
Income from operations		$ 2,350,000

Determine the unit cost of goods manufactured, based on (a) the variable costing concept and (b) the absorption costing concept.

Exercise 4–5

Variable costing income statement

Objective 1

SPREADSHEET

✓ Income from operations, $6,650

On April 30, the end of the first month of operations, South Fork Petroleum Company prepared the following income statement, based on the absorption costing concept:

South Fork Petroleum Company
Absorption Costing Income Statement
For the Month Ended April 30, 2003

Sales (3,100 units)		$77,500
Cost of goods sold:		
Cost of goods manufactured (3,500 units)	$52,500	
Less inventory, April 30 (400 units)	6,000	
Cost of goods sold		46,500
Gross profit		$31,000
Selling and administrative expenses		22,550
Income from operations		$ 8,450

If the fixed manufacturing costs were $15,750 and the variable selling and administrative expenses were $6,500, prepare an income statement according to the variable costing concept.

Exercise 4–6

Absorption costing income statement

Objective 1

✓ Income from operations, $43,150

On September 30, the end of the first month of operations, Rattan Furniture Company prepared the following income statement, based on the variable costing concept:

Rattan Furniture Company
Variable Costing Income Statement
For the Month Ended September 30, 2004

Sales (9,000 units)		$360,000
Variable cost of goods sold:		
Variable cost of goods manufactured	$229,500	
Less inventory, September 30 (1,200 units)	27,000	
Variable cost of goods sold		202,500
Manufacturing margin		$157,500
Variable selling and administrative expenses		34,000
Contribution margin		$123,500
Fixed costs:		
Fixed manufacturing costs	$ 65,280	
Fixed selling and administrative expenses	22,750	88,030
Income from operations		$ 35,470

Prepare an income statement under absorption costing.

Exercise 4–7
Variable costing income statement

Objective 1

✓ a. Income from operations, $6,253

The following data were adapted from a recent income statement of **Procter & Gamble Company**:

	(in millions)
Net sales	$38,125
Operating costs:	
Cost of products sold	$21,206
Marketing, administrative, and other expenses	10,666
Operating costs	$31,872
Income from operations	$ 6,253

Assume that the variable amount of each category of operating costs is as follows:

	(in millions)
Cost of products sold	$15,000
Marketing, administrative, and other expenses	6,400

a. Based on the above data, prepare a variable costing income statement for Procter & Gamble Company, assuming that the company maintained constant inventory levels during the period.

b. ➤ If Procter & Gamble reduced its inventories during the period, what impact would that have on the income from operations determined under absorption costing?

Exercise 4–8
Estimated income statements, using absorption and variable costing

Objectives 1, 2

✓ a. 1. Income from operations, $34,575 (8,500 units)

Prior to the first month of operations ending March 31, 2003, Carbide Products Inc. estimated the following operating results:

Sales (8,500 × $95)	$807,500
Manufacturing costs (8,500 units):	
Direct materials	493,000
Direct labor	119,000
Variable factory overhead	44,625
Fixed factory overhead	73,100
Fixed selling and administrative expenses	14,300
Variable selling and administrative expenses	28,900

The company is evaluating a proposal to manufacture 10,000 units instead of 8,500 units, thus creating an ending inventory of 1,500 units. Manufacturing the additional units will not change sales, unit variable factory overhead costs, total fixed factory overhead cost, and total selling and administrative expenses.

a. Prepare an estimated income statement, comparing operating results if 8,500 and 10,000 units are manufactured, in the (1) absorption costing format and (2) variable costing format.

b. ➤ What is the reason for the difference in income from operations reported for the two levels of production by the absorption costing income statement?

Exercise 4–9
Change in sales mix and contribution margin

Objective 3

Mountain Pen Company manufactures ballpoint and fountain pens and is operating at less than full capacity. Market research indicates that 4,000 additional ballpoint pens and 6,000 additional fountain pens could be sold. The income from operations by unit of product is as follows:

	Ballpoint Pen	Fountain Pen
Sales price	$5.50	$15.00
Variable cost of goods sold	2.80	8.30
Manufacturing margin	$2.70	$ 6.70
Variable selling and administrative expenses	1.00	2.50
Contribution margin	$1.70	$ 4.20
Fixed manufacturing costs	0.50	1.00
Income from operations	$1.20	$ 3.20

Prepare an analysis indicating the increase or decrease in total profitability if 4,000 additional ballpoint pens and 6,000 additional fountain pens are produced and sold, assuming that there is sufficient capacity for the additional production.

Exercise 4–10

Product profitability analysis

Objective 3

✓ Console contribution margin, $112,200

Digital Image Inc. manufactures and sells two styles of televisions, table top and console, from a single manufacturing facility. The manufacturing facility operates at 100% of capacity. The following per unit information is available for the two products:

	Table Top	Console
Sales price	$260	$440
Variable cost of goods sold	145	232
Manufacturing margin	$115	$208
Variable selling expenses	50	76
Contribution margin	$ 65	$132
Fixed expenses	25	92
Income from operations	$ 40	$ 40

In addition, the following unit volume information for the period is as follows:

	Table Top	Console
Sales unit volume	1,600	850

a. Prepare a contribution margin report by product.
b. What advice would you give to the management of Digital Image Inc.?

Exercise 4–11

Variable and absorption costing

Objectives 2, 3

Tahoe Boot Company manufactures and sells three types of boots. The income statements prepared under the absorption costing method for the three boots are as follows:

Tahoe Boot Company
Product Income Statements—Absorption Costing
For the Year Ended December 31, 2003

	Hiking Boots	Fishing Boots	Ski Boots
Revenues	$590,000	$500,000	$430,000
Cost of goods sold	310,000	230,000	250,000
Gross profit	$280,000	$270,000	$180,000
Selling and administrative expenses	200,000	150,000	210,000
Income from operations	$ 80,000	$120,000	$ (30,000)

In addition, you have determined the following information with respect to allocated fixed costs:

	Hiking Boots	Fishing Boots	Ski Boots
Fixed costs:			
Cost of goods sold	$70,000	$55,000	$60,000
Selling and administrative expenses	60,000	50,000	70,000

These fixed costs are used to support all three product lines. In addition, you have determined that the inventory is negligible.

The management of the company has deemed unacceptable the profit performance of the ski boot line. As a result, they have decided to eliminate the ski boot line. Management does not expect to be able to increase sales in the other two lines. However, as a result of eliminating the ski boot line, management expects the profits of the company to increase by $30,000.

a.   ✏️━▶   Do you agree with management's decision and conclusions?
b.   Prepare a profit report under the variable costing approach for the three products.
c.   Use the report in (b) to determine the profit impact of eliminating the ski boot line, assuming no other changes.

Exercise 4–12
Variable and absorption costing

Objective 1

✓ a. Contribution margin, $3,731.50

Whirlpool Corporation had the following abbreviated income statement for a recent year:

	(in millions)
Net sales	$10,323
Cost of goods sold	$ 7,805
Selling and administrative expenses	1,830
Total expenses	$ 9,635
Income from operations	$ 688

The company reported depreciation of $400 million for the recent year. Assume that 65% of the depreciation was related to manufacturing property, plant, and equipment. In addition, assume that there were an additional $2,100 million fixed manufacturing costs and $500 million fixed general, selling, and administrative costs for the year.

The finished goods inventories at the beginning and end of the year from the balance sheet were as follows:

January 1	$1,105 million
December 31	$ 960 million

Assume that 30% of the beginning and ending inventory consists of fixed costs.

a.   Prepare an income statement according to the variable costing concept for Whirlpool Corporation for the recent year.
b.   ✏️━▶   What is the reason for the difference in the amount of income from operations reported under the absorption costing and variable costing concepts?

Exercise 4–13
Territory and product profitability analysis

Objective 3

✓ a. France contribution margin, $2,325,000

Open Road Bicycle Company manufactures and sells two styles of bicycles, touring and mountain. These bicycles are sold in two countries, the Netherlands and France. Information about the two bicycles is as follows:

	Touring Bike	Mountain Bike
Sales price	$550	$370
Variable cost of goods sold per unit	210	225
Manufacturing margin per unit	$340	$145
Variable selling expense per unit	260	70
Contribution margin per unit	$ 80	$ 75

The sales unit volume for the territories and products for the period is as follows:

	Netherlands	France
Touring Bike	30,000	15,000
Mountain Bike	0	15,000

a. Prepare a contribution margin report by sales territory.
b.  What advice would you give to the management of Open Road Bicycle Company?

Exercise 4–14
Sales territory and salesperson profitability analysis

Objective 3

✓ a. Luis A. contribution margin, $345,600

Home Helper Hardware Company manufactures and sells a wide variety of hardware products to retailers in the Eastern and Western regions. There are two salespersons assigned to each territory. Higher commission rates go to the most experienced salespersons. The following sales statistics are available for each salesperson:

	Eastern		Western	
	Connie M.	Luis A.	Wendy L.	Kalifa T.
Average per unit:				
Sales price	$85.00	$80.00	$90.00	$75.00
Variable cost of goods sold	42.50	32.00	45.00	30.00
Commission rate	8%	12%	12%	8%
Units sold	9,000	9,000	6,500	12,000
Manufacturing margin ratio	50%	60%	50%	60%

a. 1. Prepare a contribution margin by salesperson report.
   2. Interpret the report.
b. 1. Prepare a contribution margin by territory report. Round to two decimal places.
   2. Interpret the report.

Exercise 4–15
Segment profitability analysis

Objective 3

✓ a. North America contribution margin, $1,565.60

Provided below are the equipment and machinery segment sales for **Caterpillar, Inc.** for a recent year.

Caterpillar, Inc.
Equipment and Machinery Segment Sales
(in millions)

	Asia/Pacific	Europe/Africa/ Middle East (EAME)	Latin America	Power Products	North America
Sales	$1,093	$3,289	$1,763	$5,300	$7,414

The Power Products segment designs, manufactures, and markets engines. The geographic segments sell Caterpillar equipment to their respective regions.
Assume that the following information is also available:

	Asia/Pacific	Europe/Africa/ Middle East (EAME)	Latin America	Power Products	North America
Variable cost of goods sold as a percent of sales	50%	60%	45%	60%	52%
Dealer commissions as a percent of sales	8%	12%	8%	5%	8%
Variable promotion expenses (in millions)	$300	$500	$400	$800	$1,400

a. Use the sales information and the additional assumed information to prepare a segment contribution margin statement. Round to two decimal places.
b. Prepare a table showing the manufacturing margin, dealer commissions, and variable promotion expenses as a percent of sales for each territory. Round to two decimal places.
c.  Use the information in (a) and (b) to interpret the segment performance.

Exercise 4–16
Segment contribution margin analysis

Objective 3

Real World

✓ a. Video, $1,362.70; 35%

The operating revenues of the four largest business segments for **Viacom, Inc.** for a recent year are shown below. Each segment includes a number of businesses, of which the largest is indicated in parentheses.

Viacom, Inc.
Segment Revenues
(in millions)

Video (Blockbuster Video)	$3,893.40
Entertainment (Paramount Pictures)	4,757.80
Networks (MTV)	2,607.90
Publishing (Simon & Schuster)	564.60

Assume that the variable costs as a percent of sales for each segment are as follows:

Video (Blockbuster Video)	65%
Entertainment (Paramount Pictures)	15%
Networks (MTV)	10%
Publishing (Simon & Schuster)	60%

a. Determine the contribution margin and contribution margin ratio for each segment from the above information.
b. ━━▶ Why are the contribution margin ratios for the entertainment and network segments larger than for the publishing and video segments?
c. ━━▶ Does your answer to (a) mean that the entertainment and network segments are more profitable businesses than the video or publishing segments?

Exercise 4–17
Contribution margin analysis—sales

Objective 3

The Crystal Sound Music Company sells recorded CD music. Management decided early in the year to reduce the price of the CD in order to increase sales volume. As a result, for the year ended December 31, 2003, the sales increased by $21,000 from the planned level of $204,000. The following information is available from the accounting records for the year ended December 31, 2003:

	Actual	Planned	Difference— Increase (Decrease)
Sales	$225,000	$204,000	$21,000
Number of units sold	15,000	12,000	3,000
Sales price	$15.00	$17.00	$ (2.00)

a. Prepare an analysis of the sales quantity and price factors.
b. ━━▶ Did the price decrease generate sufficient volume to result in a net increase in contribution margin if the actual variable cost per unit was $6, as planned?

Exercise 4–18
Contribution margin analysis—sales

Objective 3

✓ Sales quantity factor, $(78,000)

The following data for Zephyr Building Products Inc. are available:

	For the Year Ended December 31, 2003		
	Actual	Planned	Difference— Increase or (Decrease)
Sales	$2,310,000	$2,223,000	$ 87,000
Less:			
Variable cost of goods sold	$1,364,000	$1,254,000	$110,000
Variable selling and administrative expenses ...	176,000	190,380	(14,380)
Total variable costs	$1,540,000	$1,444,380	$ 95,620
Contribution margin	$ 770,000	$ 778,620	$ (8,620)
Number of units sold	11,000	11,400	
Per unit:			
Sales price	$210.00	$195.00	
Variable cost of goods sold	$124.00	$110.00	
Variable selling and administrative expenses ...	$16.00	$16.70	

Prepare an analysis of the sales quantity and price factors.

Exercise 4–19
Contribution margin analysis—variable costs

Objective 3

✓ Variable cost of goods sold price factor, $154,000

Based upon the data in Exercise 4–18, prepare a contribution analysis of the variable costs for Zephyr Building Products Inc. for the year ended December 31, 2003.

PROBLEMS SERIES A

Problem 4–1A
Absorption and variable costing income statements

Objectives 1, 2

✓ 2. Contribution margin, $131,250

During the first month of operations ended June 30, 2003, Revere Pager Company manufactured 8,800 pagers, of which 7,500 were sold. Operating data for the month are summarized as follows:

Sales		$637,500
Manufacturing costs:		
Direct materials	$343,200	
Direct labor	70,400	
Variable manufacturing cost	105,600	
Fixed manufacturing cost	30,800	550,000
Selling and administrative expenses:		
Variable	$ 63,750	
Fixed	15,000	78,750

Instructions

1. Prepare an income statement based on the absorption costing concept.
2. Prepare an income statement based on the variable costing concept.
3. ✏ Explain the reason for the difference in the amount of income from operations reported in (1) and (2).

Problem 4–2A
Income statements under absorption costing and variable costing

Objectives 1, 2

✓ 2. Contribution margin, $125,400

The demand for shampoo, one of numerous products manufactured by Soft and Silky Inc., has dropped sharply because of recent competition from a similar product. The company's chemists are currently completing tests of various new formulas, and it is anticipated that the manufacture of a superior product can be started on March 1, one month hence. No changes will be needed in the present production facilities to manufacture the new product because only the mixture of the various materials will be changed.

The controller has been asked by the president of the company for advice on whether to continue production during February or to suspend the manufacture of shampoo until March 1. The controller has assembled the following pertinent data:

Soft and Silky Inc.
Income Statement—Shampoo
For the Month Ended January 31, 2003

Sales (95,000 units)	$912,000
Cost of goods sold	732,000
Gross profit	$180,000
Selling and administrative expenses	206,000
Loss from operations	$ (26,000)

The production costs and selling and administrative expenses, based on production of 95,000 units in January, are as follows:

Direct materials	$ 1.90 per unit
Direct labor	2.60 per unit
Variable manufacturing cost	1.10 per unit
Variable selling and administrative expenses	1.80 per unit
Fixed manufacturing costs	200,000 for January
Fixed selling and administrative expenses	35,000 for January

Sales for February are expected to drop about 40% below those of the preceding month. No significant changes are anticipated in the fixed costs or variable costs per unit. No extra costs will be incurred in discontinuing operations in the portion of the plant associated with shampoo. The inventory of shampoo at the beginning and end of February is expected to be inconsequential.

Instructions

1. Prepare an estimated income statement in absorption costing form for February for shampoo, assuming that production continues during the month.
2. Prepare an estimated income statement in variable costing form for February for shampoo, assuming that production continues during the month.
3. What would be the estimated loss in income from operations if the shampoo production were temporarily suspended for February?
4. ▬▬► What advice should the controller give to management?

Problem 4–3A

Absorption and variable costing income statements for two months and analysis

Objectives 1, 2

SPREADSHEET

✓ 2. a. Manufacturing margin, $8,400

During the first month of operations ended May 31, 2003, Celebration Cake Company baked 1,700 cakes, of which 1,600 were sold. Operating data for the month are summarized as follows:

Sales		$20,000
Baking costs:		
Direct materials	$5,780	
Direct labor	3,995	
Variable manufacturing cost	2,550	
Fixed manufacturing cost	2,295	14,620
Selling and administrative expenses:		
Variable	$1,440	
Fixed	960	2,400

During June, Celebration Cake Company baked 1,500 cakes and sold 1,600 cakes. Operating data for June are summarized as follows:

Sales		$20,000
Baking costs:		
Direct materials	$5,100	
Direct labor	3,525	
Variable manufacturing cost	2,250	
Fixed manufacturing cost	2,295	13,170
Selling and administrative expenses:		
Variable	$1,440	
Fixed	960	2,400

Instructions

1. Using the absorption costing concept, prepare income statements for (a) May and (b) June.
2. Using the variable costing concept, prepare income statements for (a) May and (b) June.
3. a. ▬▬► Explain the reason for the differences in the amount of income from operations in (1) and (2) for May.
   b. ▬▬► Explain the reason for the differences in the amount of income from operations in (1) and (2) for June. *(continued)*

4. ━━▶ Based upon your answers to (1) and (2), did Celebration Cake Company operate more profitably in May or in June? Explain.

Problem 4–4A

Salespersons' report and analysis

Objective 3

✓ 1. Marvin contribution margin ratio, 26.2%

Dakota Apparel Company employs seven salespersons to sell and distribute its product throughout the state. Data taken from reports received from the salespersons during the year ended June 30, 2004, are as follows:

Salesperson	Total Sales	Variable Cost of Goods Sold	Variable Selling Expenses
Cooper	$310,000	$150,000	$ 70,000
Eastwood	480,000	200,000	85,000
Ladd	350,000	165,000	80,000
Marvin	420,000	210,000	100,000
Newman	450,000	190,000	120,000
Redford	570,000	250,000	110,000
Wayne	470,000	205,000	105,000

Instructions

1. Prepare a table indicating contribution margin, variable cost of goods sold as a percent of sales, variable selling expenses as a percent of sales, and contribution margin ratio by salesperson (round to nearest tenth of a percent).
2. Which salesperson generated the highest contribution margin ratio for the year and why?
3. ━━▶ Briefly list factors other than contribution margin that should be considered in evaluating the performance of salespersons.

Problem 4–5A

Variable costing income statement and effect on income of change in operations

Objective 3

✓ 3. Income from operations, $55,500

Portable Chair Company manufactures three sizes of folding chairs, small (S), medium (M), and large (L). The income statement has consistently indicated a net loss for the M size, and management is considering three proposals: (1) continue Size M, (2) discontinue Size M and reduce total output accordingly, or (3) discontinue Size M and conduct an advertising campaign to expand the sales of Size S so that the entire plant capacity can continue to be used.

If Proposal 2 is selected and Size M is discontinued and production curtailed, the annual fixed production costs and fixed operating expenses could be reduced by $110,000 and $50,000 respectively. If Proposal 3 is selected, it is anticipated that an additional annual expenditure of $60,000 for the salary of an assistant brand manager (classified as a fixed operating expense) would yield an increase of 150% in Size S sales volume. It is also assumed that the increased production of Size S would utilize the plant facilities released by the discontinuance of Size M.

The sales and costs have been relatively stable over the past few years, and they are expected to remain so for the foreseeable future. The income statement for the past year ended January 31, 2003, is as follows:

	Size			
	S	**M**	**L**	**Total**
Sales	$960,000	$1,450,000	$1,225,000	$3,635,000
Cost of goods sold:				
Variable costs	$500,000	$ 840,000	$ 605,000	$1,945,000
Fixed costs	215,000	360,000	310,000	885,000
Total cost of goods sold	$715,000	$1,200,000	$ 915,000	$2,830,000
Gross profit	$245,000	$ 250,000	$ 310,000	$ 805,000
Less operating expenses:				
Variable expenses	$125,000	$ 195,000	$ 165,000	$ 485,000
Fixed expenses	72,000	120,000	100,000	292,000
Total operating expenses	$197,000	$ 315,000	$ 265,000	$ 777,000
Income from operations	$ 48,000	$ (65,000)	$ 45,000	$ 28,000

Instructions

1. Prepare an income statement for the past year in the variable costing format. Use the following headings:

Size			
S	M	L	Total

Data for each style should be reported through contribution margin. The fixed costs should be deducted from the total contribution margin, as reported in the "Total" column, to determine income from operations.

2. Based on the income statement prepared in (1) and the other data presented above, determine the amount by which total annual income from operations would be reduced below its present level if Proposal 2 is accepted.

3. Prepare an income statement in the variable costing format, indicating the projected annual income from operations if Proposal 3 is accepted. Use the following headings:

Size		
S	L	Total

Data for each style should be reported through contribution margin. The fixed costs should be deducted from the total contribution margin as reported in the "Total" column. For purposes of this problem, the additional expenditure of $60,000 for the assistant brand manager's salary can be added to the fixed operating expenses.

4. By how much would total annual income increase above its present level if Proposal 3 is accepted? Explain.

Problem 4–6A
Contribution margin analysis

Objective 3

SPREADSHEET

✓ 1. Sales price factor, ($51,000)

Sigma Electronics Company manufactures only one product. For the year ended December 31, 2003, the contribution margin decreased by $34,950 from the planned level of $139,500. The president of Sigma Electronics Company has expressed serious concern about the size of this decrease and has requested a follow-up report.

The following data have been gathered from the accounting records for the year ended December 31, 2003:

	Actual	Planned	Difference— Increase or (Decrease)
Sales	$433,500	$427,500	$ 6,000
Less:			
Variable cost of goods sold	$244,800	$225,000	$ 19,800
Variable selling and administrative expenses	84,150	63,000	21,150
Total	$328,950	$288,000	$ 40,950
Contribution margin	$104,550	$139,500	$(34,950)
Number of units sold	5,100	4,500	
Per unit:			
Sales price	$85.00	$95.00	
Variable cost of goods sold	48.00	50.00	
Variable selling and administrative expenses	16.50	14.00	

Instructions

1. Prepare a contribution margin analysis report for the year ended December 31, 2003.

2. At a meeting of the board of directors on January 30, 2004, the president, after reviewing the contribution margin analysis report, made the following comment:

(continued)

"It looks as if the price decrease of $10.00 had the effect of increasing sales. However, we lost control over the variable cost of goods sold and variable selling and administrative expenses. Let's look into these expenses and get them under control! Also, let's consider decreasing the sales price to $80 to increase sales further."

➤ Do you agree with the president's comment? Explain.

PROBLEMS SERIES B

Problem 4–1B
Absorption and variable costing income statements

Objectives 1, 2

✓ 2. Income from operations, $211,850

During the first month of operations ended August 31, 2004, Techno Appliance Company manufactured 1,560 refrigerators, of which 1,490 were sold. Operating data for the month are summarized as follows:

Sales		$923,800
Manufacturing costs:		
Direct materials	$327,600	
Direct labor	132,600	
Variable manufacturing cost	70,200	
Fixed manufacturing cost	93,600	624,000
Selling and administrative expenses:		
Variable	$ 74,500	
Fixed	37,250	111,750

Instructions

1. Prepare an income statement based on the absorption costing concept.
2. Prepare an income statement based on the variable costing concept.
3. ➤ Explain the reason for the difference in the amount of income from operations reported in (1) and (2).

Problem 4–2B
Income statements under absorption costing and variable costing

Objectives 1, 2

✓ 2. Contribution margin, $32,916

The demand for solvent, one of numerous products manufactured by Corning Products Inc., has dropped sharply because of recent competition from a similar product. The company's chemists are currently completing tests of various new formulas, and it is anticipated that the manufacture of a superior product can be started on November 1, one month hence. No changes will be needed in the present production facilities to manufacture the new product because only the mixture of the various materials will be changed.

The controller has been asked by the president of the company for advice on whether to continue production during October or to suspend the manufacture of solvent until November 1. The controller has assembled the following pertinent data:

Corning Products Inc.
Income Statement—Solvent
For the Month Ended September 30, 2004

Sales (1,950 units)	$167,700
Cost of goods sold	159,855
Gross profit	$ 7,845
Selling and administrative expenses	30,700
Loss from operations	$ (22,855)

The production costs and selling and administrative expenses, based on production of 1,950 units in September, are as follows:

Direct materials	$ 36.00 per unit
Direct labor	12.50 per unit
Variable manufacturing cost	10.40 per unit
Variable selling and administrative expenses	6.00 per unit
Fixed manufacturing costs	45,000 for September
Fixed selling and administrative expenses	19,000 for September

Sales for October are expected to drop about 20% below those of the preceding month. No significant changes are anticipated in the fixed costs or variable costs per unit. No extra costs will be incurred in discontinuing operations in the portion of the plant associated with solvent. The inventory of solvent at the beginning and end of October is expected to be inconsequential.

Instructions

1. Prepare an estimated income statement in absorption costing form for October for solvent, assuming that production continues during the month.
2. Prepare an estimated income statement in variable costing form for October for solvent, assuming that production continues during the month.
3. What would be the estimated loss in income from operations if the solvent production were temporarily suspended for October?
4. ◀▬▬▶ What advice should the controller give to management?

Problem 4–3B

Absorption and variable costing income statements for two months and analysis

Objectives 1, 2

SPREADSHEET

✓ 1. b. Income from operations, $88,080

During the first month of operations ended July 31, 2003, CleanNote Tape Company produced 41,600 cassette tapes, of which 40,000 were sold. Operating data for the month are summarized as follows:

Sales		$368,000
Manufacturing costs:		
Direct materials	$141,440	
Direct labor	54,080	
Variable manufacturing cost	33,280	
Fixed manufacturing cost	24,960	253,760
Selling and administrative expenses:		
Variable	$ 20,000	
Fixed	14,000	34,000

During August, CleanNote Tape Company produced 38,400 cassette tapes and sold 40,000 tapes. Operating data for August are summarized as follows:

Sales		$368,000
Manufacturing costs:		
Direct materials	$130,560	
Direct labor	49,920	
Variable manufacturing cost	30,720	
Fixed manufacturing cost	24,960	236,160
Selling and administrative expenses:		
Variable	$ 20,000	
Fixed	14,000	34,000

Instructions

1. Using the absorption costing concept, prepare income statements for (a) July and (b) August.
2. Using the variable costing concept, prepare income statements for (a) July and (b) August.
3. a. ◀▬▬▶ Explain the reason for the differences in the amount of income from operations in (1) and (2) for July.
   b. ◀▬▬▶ Explain the reason for the differences in the amount of income from operations in (1) and (2) for August.
4. ◀▬▬▶ Based upon your answers to (1) and (2), did CleanNote Tape Company operate more profitably in July or in August? Explain.

Problem 4–4B

Salespersons' report and analysis

Objective 3

River City Band Instrument Company employs seven salespersons to sell and distribute its product throughout the state. Data taken from reports received from the salespersons during the year ended December 31, 2004, are as follows:

Salesperson	Total Sales	Variable Cost of Goods Sold	Variable Selling Expenses
Alpert	$400,000	$255,000	$ 85,000
Armstrong	550,000	330,000	125,000
Goodman	420,000	260,000	90,000
Hirt	415,000	290,000	85,000
Kenny G.	600,000	360,000	125,000
Marsalis	520,000	300,000	100,000
Severinsen	510,000	320,000	120,000

Instructions

1. Prepare a table indicating contribution margin, variable cost of goods sold as a percent of sales, variable selling expenses as a percent of sales, and contribution margin ratio by salesperson. Round to the nearest tenth of a percent.
2. Which salesperson generated the highest contribution margin ratio for the year and why?
3. ✏️ Briefly list factors other than contribution margin that should be considered in evaluating the performance of salespersons.

Problem 4–5B
Variable costing income statement and effect on income of change in operations

Objective 3

Siberian Coat Company manufactures three sizes of winter coats, small (S), medium (M), and large (L). The income statement has consistently indicated a net loss for the M size, and management is considering three proposals: (1) continue Size M, (2) discontinue Size M and reduce total output accordingly, or (3) discontinue Size M and conduct an advertising campaign to expand the sales of Size S so that the entire plant capacity can continue to be used.

If Proposal 2 is selected and Size M is discontinued and production curtailed, the annual fixed production costs and fixed operating expenses could be reduced by $40,000 and $32,000, respectively. If Proposal 3 is selected, it is anticipated that an additional annual expenditure of $45,000 for the salary of an assistant brand manager would yield an increase of 120% in Size S sales volume. It is also assumed that the increased production of Size S would utilize the plant facilities released by the discontinuance of Size M.

The sales and costs have been relatively stable over the past few years, and they are expected to remain so for the foreseeable future. The income statement for the past year ended June 30, 2003, is as follows:

	Size S	Size M	Size L	Total
Sales	$560,000	$670,000	$860,000	$2,090,000
Cost of goods sold:				
Variable costs	$245,000	$340,000	$395,000	$ 980,000
Fixed costs	60,000	95,000	130,000	285,000
Total cost of goods sold	$305,000	$435,000	$525,000	$1,265,000
Gross profit	$255,000	$235,000	$335,000	$ 825,000
Less operating expenses:				
Variable expenses	$115,000	$155,000	$175,000	$ 445,000
Fixed expenses	65,000	95,000	125,000	285,000
Total operating expenses	$180,000	$250,000	$300,000	$ 730,000
Income from operations	$ 75,000	$(15,000)	$ 35,000	$ 95,000

Instructions

1. Prepare an income statement for the past year in the variable costing format. Use the following headings:

	Size		
S	**M**	**L**	**Total**

Data for each style should be reported through contribution margin. The fixed costs should be deducted from the total contribution margin, as reported in the "Total" column, to determine income from operations.

2. Based on the income statement prepared in (1) and the other data presented, determine the amount by which total annual income from operations would be reduced below its present level if Proposal 2 is accepted.

3. Prepare an income statement in the variable costing format, indicating the projected annual income from operations if Proposal 3 is accepted. Use the following headings:

	Size	
S	**L**	**Total**

Data for each style should be reported through contribution margin. The fixed costs should be deducted from the total contribution margin as reported in the "Total" column. For purposes of this problem, the additional expenditure of $45,000 for the assistant brand manager's salary can be added to the fixed operating expenses.

4. By how much would total annual income increase above its present level if Proposal 3 is accepted? Explain.

Problem 4–6B
Contribution margin analysis

Objective 3

SPREADSHEET

✓ 1. Sales quantity factor, ($55,500)

Gladwell Industries Inc. manufactures only one product. For the year ended December 31, 2003, the contribution margin decreased by $6,000 from the planned level of $114,000. The president of Gladwell Industries Inc. has expressed some concern about this decrease and has requested a follow-up report.

The following data have been gathered from the accounting records for the year ended December 31, 2003:

	Actual	Planned	Difference—Increase (Decrease)
Sales	$352,000	$351,500	$ 500
Less: Variable cost of goods sold	$148,000	$161,500	$(13,500)
Variable selling and administrative expense: ...	96,000	76,000	20,000
Total	$244,000	$237,500	$ 6,500
Contribution margin	$108,000	$114,000	$ (6,000)
Number of units sold	8,000	9,500	
Per unit:			
Sales price	$44.00	$37.00	
Variable cost of goods sold	18.50	17.00	
Variable selling and administrative expenses	12.00	8.00	

Instructions

1. Prepare a contribution margin analysis report for the year ended December 31, 2003.
2. At a meeting of the board of directors on January 30, 2004, the president, after reviewing the contribution margin analysis report, made the following comment:

It looks as if the price increase of $7.00 had the effect of decreasing sales volume. However, this was a favorable tradeoff. The variable cost of goods sold was less than planned. Apparently, we are efficiently managing our variable cost of goods sold. However, the variable selling and administrative expenses appear out of control. Let's look into these expenses and get them under control! Also, let's consider increasing the sales price to $48 and continue this favorable tradeoff between higher price and lower volume.

➤ Do you agree with the president's comment? Explain.

SPECIAL ACTIVITIES

Activity 4–1
Deerfield Inc.
Ethics and professional conduct in business

The Sporting Goods Division of Deerfield Inc. uses absorption costing for profit reporting. The general manager of the Sporting Goods Division is concerned about meeting the income objectives of the division. At the beginning of the reporting period, the division had an adequate supply of inventory. The general manager has decided to increase production of goods in the plant in order to allocate fixed manufacturing cost over a greater number of units. Unfortunately, the increased production cannot be sold and will increase the inventory. However, the impact on earnings will be positive, because the lower cost per unit will be matched against sales. The general manager has come to Les Carroll, the controller, to determine exactly how much additional production is required in order to increase net income enough to meet the division's profit objectives. Carroll analyzes the data and determines that the inventory will need to be increased by 30% in order to absorb enough fixed costs and meet the income objective. Carroll reports this information to the division manager.

> Discuss whether Carroll is acting in an ethical manner.

Activity 4–2
BusBar Enterprises
Inventories under absorption costing

BusBar Enterprises manufactures power converters for the electronics industry and has just completed its first year of operations. The following discussion took place between the controller, Joel Andrews, and the company president, Sara Jenkins:

Sara: I've been looking over our first year's performance by quarters. Our earnings have been increasing each quarter, even though our sales have been flat and our prices and costs have not changed. Why is this?

Joel: Our actual sales have stayed even throughout the year, but we've been increasing the utilization of our factory every quarter. By keeping our factory utilization high, we will keep our costs down by allocating the fixed plant costs over a greater number of units. Naturally, this causes our cost per unit to be lower than it would be otherwise.

Sara: Yes, but what good is it if we have been unable to sell everything that we make? Our inventory is also increasing.

Joel: This is true. However, our unit costs are lower because of the additional production. When these lower costs are matched against sales, it has a positive impact on our earnings.

Sara: Are you saying that we are able to create additional earnings merely by building inventory? Can this be true?

Joel: Well, I've never thought about it quite that way . . . but I guess so.

Sara: And another thing. What will happen if we begin to reduce our production in order to liquidate the inventory? Don't tell me our earnings will go down even though our production effort drops!

Joel: Well . . .

Sara: There must be a better way. I'd like our quarterly income statements to reflect what's really going on. I don't want our income reports to reward building inventory and penalize reducing inventory.

Joel: I'm not sure what I can do—we have to follow generally accepted accounting principles.

1.   Why does reporting income under generally accepted accounting principles "reward" building inventory and "penalize" reducing inventory?
2.   What advice would you give to Joel in responding to Sara's concern about the present method of profit reporting?

Activity 4–3
Cardiovascular Systems Inc.
Margin analysis

Cardiovascular Systems Inc. manufactures and sells devices used in cardiovascular surgery. The company has two salespersons, Kimble and Monroe.

A contribution margin by salesperson report was prepared as follows:

Cardiovascular Systems Inc.
Contribution Margin by Salesperson

	Kimble	Monroe
Sales	$240,000	$300,000
Variable cost of goods sold	96,000	210,000
Manufacturing margin	$144,000	$ 90,000
Variable promotion expenses	$ 80,000	$ 10,000
Variable sales commission expenses	40,000	50,000
	$120,000	$ 60,000
Contribution margin	$ 24,000	$ 30,000
Manufacturing margin as a percent of sales (manufacturing margin ratio)	60.00%	30.00%
Contribution margin ratio	10.00%	10.00%

Interpret the report, and provide recommendations to the two salespersons for improving profitability.

Activity 4–4
Kitchen Helper Company
Margin analysis

Kitchen Helper Company manufactures and sells kitchen cooking products throughout the state. The company employs four salespersons. The following contribution margin by salesperson analysis was prepared:

Kitchen Helper Company
Contribution Margin Analysis by Salesperson

	Childs	Tipton	Huang	Chavez
Sales	$120,000	$150,000	$140,000	$100,000
Variable cost of goods sold	48,000	75,000	70,000	50,000
Manufacturing margin	$ 72,000	$ 75,000	$ 70,000	$ 50,000
Variable selling expenses:				
Commissions	$ 6,000	$ 7,500	$ 7,000	$ 5,000
Promotion expenses	24,000	45,000	42,000	30,000
Total variable selling expenses	$ 30,000	$ 52,500	$ 49,000	$ 35,000
Contribution margin	$ 42,000	$ 22,500	$ 21,000	$ 15,000

1. Calculate the manufacturing margin as a percent of sales and the contribution margin ratio for each salesperson.
2. Explain the results of the analysis.

Activity 4–5
Impression Art Supply Company
Contribution margin analysis

Impression Art Supply Company sells artistic supplies to retailers in three different sales territories, Northeast, Southeast, and Midwest. The following profit analysis by territory was prepared by the company:

	Northeast	Southeast	Midwest
Revenue	$320,000	$380,000	$300,000
Cost of goods sold	160,000	200,000	150,000
Gross profit	$160,000	$180,000	$150,000
Selling expenses	100,000	80,000	50,000
Income from operations	$ 60,000	$100,000	$100,000

The following fixed costs have also been provided:

	Northeast	Southeast	Midwest
Fixed manufacturing costs	$70,000	$40,000	$40,000
Fixed selling expenses	60,000	30,000	20,000

In addition, assume that inventories have been negligible.

Management believes it could increase territory sales by 25%, without increasing any of the fixed costs, by spending an additional $10,000 on territory advertising.

1. Prepare a contribution margin by territory report for Impression Art Supply Company.
2. Determine how much territory operating profit will be generated for an additional $10,000 of territory advertising.
3. ✏️➤ Which territory will provide the greatest profit return for a $10,000 increase in advertising? Why?

Activity 4–6
Neyland Company
Absorption costing

Group Activity

Neyland Company is a family-owned business in which you own 20% of the common stock and your brothers and sisters own the remaining shares. The employment contract of Neyland's new president, Ellen Edwards, stipulates a base salary of $75,000 per year plus 7% of income from operations in excess of $1,000,000. Neyland uses the absorption costing method of reporting income from operations, which has averaged approximately $1,000,000 for the past several years.

Sales for 2003, Edwards' first year as president of Neyland Company, are estimated at 100,000 units at a selling price of $60 per unit. To maximize the use of Neyland's productive capacity, Edwards has decided to manufacture 150,000 units, rather than the 100,000 units of estimated sales. The beginning inventory at January 1, 2003, is insignificant in amount, and the manufacturing costs and selling and administrative expenses for the production of 100,000 and 150,000 units are as follows:

100,000 Units to Be Manufactured

	Total Cost	Number of Units	Unit Cost
Manufacturing costs:			
Variable	$3,200,000	100,000	$32
Fixed	600,000	100,000	6
Total	$3,800,000		$38
Selling and administrative expenses:			
Variable	$ 900,000		
Fixed	300,000		
Total	$1,200,000		

150,000 Units to Be Manufactured

	Total Cost	Number of Units	Unit Cost
Manufacturing costs:			
Variable	$4,800,000	150,000	$32
Fixed	600,000	150,000	4
Total	$5,400,000		$36
Selling and administrative expenses:			
Variable	$ 900,000		
Fixed	300,000		
Total	$1,200,000		

1. In one group, prepare an absorption costing income statement for the year ending December 31, 2003, based upon sales of 100,000 units and the manufacture of 100,000 units. In the other group, conduct the same analysis, assuming production of 150,000 units.

2.  Explain the difference in the income from operations reported in (1).

3. Compute Edwards' total salary for the year 2003, based on sales of 100,000 units and the manufacture of 100,000 units (Group 1) and 150,000 units (Group 2). Compare your answers.

4.  In addition to maximizing the use of Neyland Company's productive capacity, why might Edwards wish to manufacture 150,000 units rather than 100,000 units?

5.  Can you suggest an alternative way in which Edwards' salary could be determined, using a base salary of $75,000 and 7% of income from operations in excess of $1,000,000, so that the salary could not be increased by simply manufacturing more units?

Activity 4–7
Into the Real World
Revenue report by product and channel

Go to **Microsoft Corporation's** Web site at **www.microsoft.com/msft**. This is the portion of Microsoft's Web site for stockholders. Find the page for "analysis tools" and select the "financial history Pivot Table." This tool will allow you to construct a revenue report by product group and by channel.

1. In one group, construct a bar chart of revenue by product group for the last fiscal year.

2. In the other group, construct a bar chart of revenue by channel for the last fiscal year.

3. Interpret the charts.

ANSWERS TO SELF-EXAMINATION QUESTIONS

Matching

1. M	3. B	5. L	7. G	9. K	11. I
2. A	4. F	6. H	8. D	10. C	12. J

Multiple Choice

1. **B** The contribution margin of $260,000 (answer B) is determined by deducting all of the variable costs ($400,000 + $90,000) from sales ($750,000).

2. **A** In a period in which the number of units manufactured exceeds the number of units sold, the income from operations reported under the absorption costing concept is larger than the income from operations reported under the variable costing concept (answer A). This is because a portion of the fixed manufacturing costs are deferred when the absorption costing concept is used. This deferment has the effect of excluding a portion of the fixed manufacturing costs from the current cost of goods sold.

3. **D** (6,000 units × $20 per unit). Answer A incorrectly calculates the difference in income from operations using the variable cost per unit, while Answer B incorrectly calculates the difference in income from operations using the total cost per unit. Answer C is incorrect because variable costing income from operations will be greater than absorption costing income from operations when units manufactured is less than units sold.

4. **C** [2,000 units × ($150,000 ÷ 12,000)]. Answers A and B incorrectly calculate the difference in income from operations using variable cost per unit. When production exceeds sales, absorption costing will in-clude fixed costs in the ending inventory, which causes cost of goods sold to decline and income from operations to increase. Thus, income from operations would not decline (answer D) for a production level of 12,000 units.

5. **C** A difference between planned and actual sales can be attributed to a unit price factor. The $45,000 decrease (answer C) attributed to the quantity factor is determined as follows:

Decrease in number of units sold	5,000
Planned unit sales price	× $9
Quantity factor—decrease	$45,000

The unit price factor can be determined as follows:

Increase in unit sales price	$1
Actual number of units sold	× 80,000
Price factor—increase	$80,000

The increase of $80,000 attributed to the price factor less the decrease of $45,000 attributed to the quantity factor accounts for the $35,000 increase in total sales.

Budgeting

After studying this chapter, you should be able to:

1 Describe budgeting, its objectives, and its impact on human behavior.

2 Describe the basic elements of the budget process, the two major types of budgeting, and the use of computers in budgeting.

3 Describe the master budget for a manufacturing business.

4 Prepare the basic income statement budgets for a manufacturing business.

5 Prepare balance sheet budgets for a manufacturing business.

Y ou may have financial goals for your life. To achieve these goals, it is necessary to plan for future expenses. For example, you may consider taking a part-time job to save money for school expenses for the coming school year. How much money would you need to earn and save in order to pay these expenses? One way to answer this question would be to prepare a budget. For example, a budget would show an estimate of your expenses associated with school, such as tuition, fees, and books. In addition, you would have expenses for day-to-day living, such as rent, food, and clothing. You might also have expenses for travel and entertainment. Once the school year begins, you can use the budget as a tool for guiding your spending priorities during the year.

The budget is used in businesses in much the same way as it can be used in personal life. For example, **DaimlerChrysler** uses budgeting to determine the number of cars to be produced, number of shifts to operate, number of people to be employed, and amount of material to be purchased. The budget provides the company a "game plan" for the year. In this chapter, you will see how budgets can be used for financial planning and control.

Nature and Objectives of Budgeting

objective 1

Describe budgeting, its objectives, and its impact on human behavior.

If you were driving across the country, you might plan your trip with the aid of a road map. The road map would lay out your route across the country, identify stopovers, and reduce your chances of getting lost. In the same way, a **budget** charts a course for a business by outlining the plans of the business in financial terms. Like the road map, the budget can help a company navigate through the year and reduce negative outcomes.

 A recent U.S. government budget showed a $70 billion surplus, or about 4% of the total budget.

Although budgets are normally associated with profit-making businesses, they also play an important role in operating most units of government. For example, budgets are important in managing rural school districts and small villages as well as agencies of the federal government. Budgets are also important for managing the operations of churches, hospitals, and other nonprofit institutions. Individuals and families also use budgeting techniques in managing their financial affairs. In this chapter, we discuss the principles of budgeting in the context of a business organized for profit.

Point of Interest
The chart below shows the estimated portion of your total monthly income that should be budgeted for various living expenses.

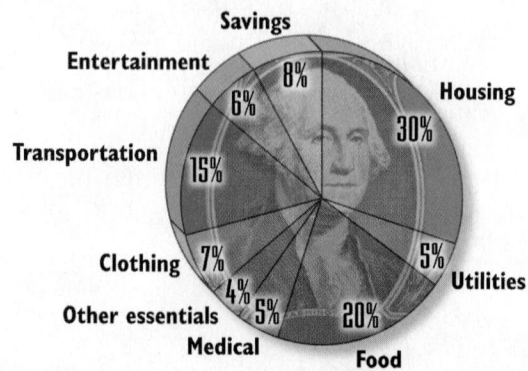

Savings 8%
Entertainment 6%
Housing 30%
Transportation 15%
Clothing 7%
Utilities 5%
Other essentials 4% 5%
Medical
Food 20%

Source: Consumer Credit Counseling Service

Objectives of Budgeting

Budgeting involves (1) establishing specific goals, (2) executing plans to achieve the goals, and (3) periodically comparing actual results with the goals. These goals include both the overall business goals as well as the specific goals for the individual units within the business. Establishing specific goals for future operations is part of the *planning* function of management, while executing actions to meet the goals is the *directing* function of management. Periodically comparing actual results with these goals and taking appropriate action is the *controlling* function of management. The relationships of these functions are illustrated in Exhibit 1.

Exhibit 1 Planning, Directing, and Controlling

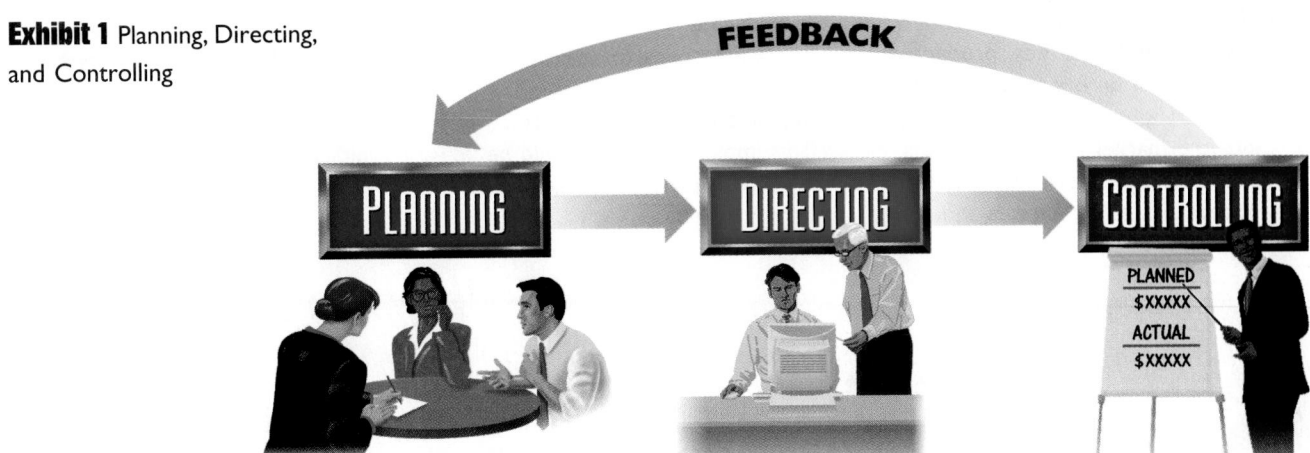

Planning

A set of goals is often necessary to guide and focus individual and group actions. For example, students set academic goals, athletes set athletic goals, employees set career goals, and businesses set financial goals. In the same way, budgeting supports the planning process by requiring all organizational units to establish their goals for the upcoming period. These goals, in turn, motivate individuals and groups to perform at high levels. For example, **Florida Power and Light (FP&L)**, an electric utility, announced plans to reduce costs by 8% of its total budget in order to maintain its target profitability. Using the budget to communicate these expectations throughout the organization helped FP&L to reach its target. Without the budget establishing this clear expectation, these results would have been very difficult to achieve.

Planning not only motivates employees to attain goals but also improves overall decision making. During the planning phase of the budget process, all viewpoints are considered, options identified, and cost reduction opportunities assessed. This effort leads to better decision making for the organization. As a result, the budget process may reveal opportunities or threats that were not known prior to the budget planning process. For example, the financial planning process helped **General Motors** identify the high costs associated with its far-flung parts operations. As a result, GM decided to sell over 45 lines of businesses (radiator caps, vacuum pumps, electric motors, etc.) in order to focus on its core auto-making business.

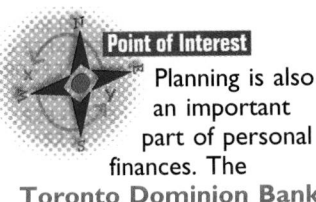

Point of Interest

Planning is also an important part of personal finances. The **Toronto Dominion Bank** offers a student budget planner and budget worksheet on the Internet at **www.tdbank.ca/student**. Visit this site if you would like to prepare a budget or download helpful budgeting tips.

BUSINESS ON STAGE

Strategic Planning

Strategic planning is essential for successful business. The strategic plan, which is the starting point for developing operating budgets, involves five steps:

1. Define the company's purpose, vision, and mission. The purpose of the company is the reason it exists. For most companies, this purpose is to maximize shareholder value by maximizing profits. The vision of a company is how it plans to achieve its purpose. The mission of a company represents the specific manner in which the company plans to achieve its purpose and vision.

2. Set specific performance goals that are consistent with the company's purpose, vision, and mission. For example, a specific performance goal might be to earn an 18% rate of return on stockholders' equity for the coming year.

3. Formulate a strategic plan by analyzing the company's strengths, weaknesses, opportunities, and threats. For example, a proven management team is a strength;

obsolete machinery is a weakness; demand for a new product or service is an opportunity; and the entry of new competitors into the market is a threat. The analysis of strengths, weaknesses, opportunities, and threats should provide the company with alternative strategies to achieve its purpose, vision, and mission.

4. Implement the strategic plan. This implementation should be reflected in the company's operating budgets.

5. Continually reevaluate the strategic plan and make any necessary changes. For example, new legislation might create new opportunities for services or products. ■

Georgia Tech introduced what it terms a "responsibility center approach" (RCA) to financial management in its athletic department. The approach required each sport to be responsible for its own budgeted revenues and outlays. Thus, for example, budgeted outlays were compared to budgeted revenues to determine anticipated surplus and deficits in each sport. This new approach provided coaches with incentives to control costs and seek revenue possibilities. For example, the baseball program took advantage of revenue-growing opportunities by developing the "Grand Slam Club," leasing scoreboard advertising, and increasing baseball yearbook advertising.

Source: C. David Strupeck, Ken Milani, and James E. Murphy, "Financial Management at Georgia Tech," *Management Accounting,* February 1993, pp. 58–63.

Directing

Once the budget plans are in place, they can be used to direct and coordinate operations in order to achieve the stated goals. For example, your goal to receive an "A" in a course would result in certain activities, such as reading the book, completing assignments, participating in class, and studying for exams. Such actions are fairly easy to direct and coordinate. A business, however, is much more complex and requires more formal direction and coordination. The budget is one way to direct and coordinate business activities and units to achieve stated goals. The budgetary units of an organization are called **responsibility centers**. Each responsibility center is led by a manager who has the authority over and responsibility for the unit's performance.

If there is a change in the external environment, the budget process can also be used by unit managers to readjust the operations. For example, **SKI Ltd.** uses weather information to plan expenditures at its Killington and Mt. Snow ski resorts in Vermont. When the weather is forecasted to turn cold and dry, the company increases expenditures in snow-making activities and adds to the staff in order to serve a greater number of skiers.

Controlling

As time passes, the actual performance of an operation can be compared against the planned goals. This provides prompt feedback to employees about their performance. If necessary, employees can use such **feedback** to adjust their activities in the future. For example, a salesperson may be given a quota to achieve $100,000 in sales for the period. If the actual sales are only $75,000, the salesperson can use this feedback about underperformance to change sales tactics and improve future sales. Feedback is not only helpful to individuals, but it can also redirect a complete organization. For example, **The Coca-Cola Company** slashed its workforce by 20%, or 6,000 employees, as a result of the company reporting its first quarterly earnings loss in a decade.

Comparing actual results to the plan also helps prevent unplanned expenditures. The budget encourages employees to establish their spending priorities. For example, departments in universities have budgets to support faculty travel to conferences and meetings. The travel budget communicates to the faculty the upper limit on travel. Often, desired travel exceeds the budget. Thus, the budget requires the faculty to prioritize travel-related opportunities. In the next chapter, we will discuss comparing actual costs with budgeted costs in greater detail.

Human Behavior and Budgeting

In the budgeting process, business, team, and individual goals are established. Human behavior problems can arise if (1) the budget goal is unachievable (too tight), (2) the budget goal is very easy to achieve (too loose), or (3) the budget goals of the business conflict with the objectives of employees (goal conflict).

Setting Budget Goals too Tightly

People can become discouraged if performance expectations are set too high. For example, would you be inspired or discouraged by a guitar instructor expecting you to play like Eric Clapton after only a few lessons? You'd probably be discouraged. This same kind of problem can occur in businesses if employees view budget goals as unrealistic or unachievable. In such a case, the budget discourages employees from achieving the goals. On the other hand, aggressive but attainable goals are likely to inspire employees to achieve the goals. Therefore, it is important that employees (managers and nonmanagers) be involved in establishing reasonable budget estimates.

Involving all employees encourages cooperation both within and among departments. It also increases awareness of each department's importance to the overall objectives of the company. Employees view budgeting more positively when they have an opportunity to participate in the budget-setting process. This is because employees with a greater sense of control over the budget process will have a greater commitment to achieving its goals. In such cases, budgets are valuable planning tools that increase the possibility of achieving business goals.

Setting Budget Goals too Loosely

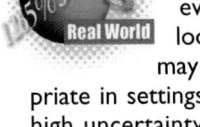

There is strong evidence that loose budgets may be appropriate in settings involving high uncertainty, such as research and development. The loose budget acts as a sort of "shock absorber," giving managers maneuvering room to minimize work disruptions.

Although it is desirable to establish attainable goals, it is undesirable to plan lower goals than may be possible. Such budget "padding" is termed **budgetary slack**. An example of budgetary slack is including spare employees in the plan. Managers may plan slack in the budget in order to provide a "cushion" for unexpected events or improve the appearance of operations. Budgetary slack can be avoided if lower- and mid-level managers are required to support their spending requirements with operational plans.

Slack budgets can cause employees to develop a "spend it or lose it" mentality. This often occurs at the end of the budget period when actual spending is much less than the budget. Employees may attempt to spend the remaining budget (purchase equipment, hire consultants, purchase supplies) in order to avoid having the budget cut next period.

Setting Conflicting Budget Goals

Goal conflict occurs when individual self-interest differs from business objectives. To illustrate, the manager of the Transportation Department of one company was instructed to stay within the department's budget. To meet the budget goal, the manager stopped transporting all shipments for the last two weeks of the period. Though the Transportation Department budget was met, customers were upset because they did not receive their orders. As a result, many customers stopped doing business with the company or demanded price discounts that far exceeded the additional transportation costs that should have been spent. In this example, the budget pressure caused the Transportation Department manager to make a decision that appeared correct from the department's view but was harmful to the business. Goal conflict can be avoided if budget goals are carefully designed for consistency across all areas of the organization.

Budgeting Systems

objective 2

Describe the basic elements of the budget process, the two major types of budgeting, and the use of computers in budgeting.

Budgeting systems vary among businesses because of such factors as organizational structure, complexity of operations, and management philosophy. Differences in budget systems are even more significant among different types of businesses, such as manufacturers and service businesses. The details of a budgeting system used by an automobile manufacturer such as Ford would obviously differ from a service company such as American Airlines. However, the basic budgeting concepts illustrated in the following paragraphs apply to all types of businesses and organizations.

Sprint Corporation was spending twice as many resources producing budgets as it was analyzing them. As a result, Sprint reengineered its budget process by replacing its annual budget with quarterly reviews of six-quarter rolling forecasts of key business drivers, coupled with exception-based monitoring. The new process shortened the budget process from 137 days to less than two months and gave Sprint the ability to respond faster to changes in business conditions.

The budgetary period for operating activities normally includes the fiscal year of a business. A year is short enough that future operations can be estimated fairly accurately, yet long enough that the future can be viewed in a broad context. However, to achieve effective control, the annual budgets are usually subdivided into shorter time periods, such as quarters of the year, months, or weeks.

A variation of fiscal-year budgeting, called **continuous budgeting**, maintains a twelve-month projection into the future. The twelve-month budget is continually revised by removing the data for the period just ended and adding estimated budget data for the same period next year, as shown in Exhibit 2.

Exhibit 2 Continuous Budgeting

Lockheed Martin Corporation used a zero-based budgeting approach, called risk-based budgeting, to identify cost savings during the downsizing of some of its military and weapons programs. Lockheed Martin divided its operations into core and supplemental activities. Core activities were spared from deep budget cuts, but supplemental activities were evaluated for possible budget reductions.

Developing budgets for the next fiscal year usually begins several months prior to the end of the current year. This responsibility is normally assigned to a budget committee. Such a committee often consists of the budget director and such high-level executives as the controller, the treasurer, the production manager, and the sales manager. Once the budget has been approved, the budget process is monitored and summarized by the Accounting Department, which reports to the committee.

There are several methods of developing budget estimates. One method, termed **zero-based budgeting**, requires managers to estimate sales, production, and other operating data as though operations are being started for the first time. This approach has the benefit of taking a fresh view of operations each year. A more common approach is to start with last year's budget and revise it for actual results and expected changes for the coming year. Two major budgets using this approach are the static budget and the flexible budget.

Static Budget

A **static budget** shows the expected results of a responsibility center for only one activity level. Once the budget has been determined, it is not changed, even if the activity changes. Static budgeting is used by many service companies and for some administrative functions of manufacturing companies, such as purchasing, engineering, and accounting. For example, the Assembly Department manager for Colter Manufacturing Company prepared the static budget for the upcoming year, shown in Exhibit 3.

Exhibit 3 Static Budget

Colter Manufacturing Company Assembly Department Budget For the Year Ending July 31, 2003	
Direct labor	$40,000
Electric power	5,000
Supervisor salaries	15,000
Total department costs	$60,000

A disadvantage of static budgets is that they do not adjust for changes in activity levels. For example, assume that the actual amounts spent by the Assembly Department of Colter Manufacturing totaled $72,000, which is $12,000 or 20% ($12,000 ÷ $60,000) more than budgeted. Is this good news or bad news? At first you might think that this is a bad result. However, this conclusion may not be valid, since static budget results may be difficult to interpret. To illustrate, assume that the assembly manager constructed the budget based on plans to assemble *8,000* units during the year. However, *10,000* units were actually produced, which represents 25% (2,000 ÷ 8,000) more work than expected. Should the additional $12,000 in spending in excess of the budget be considered "bad news"? Maybe not. The Assembly Department provided 25% more output for only 20% additional cost.

Flexible Budget

Flexible budgets show expected results for several activity levels.

Unlike static budgets, **flexible budgets** show the expected results of a responsibility center for several activity levels. You can think of a flexible budget as a series of static budgets for different levels of activity. Such budgets are especially useful in estimating and controlling factory costs and operating expenses. Exhibit 4 is a flexible budget for the annual manufacturing expense in the Assembly Department of Colter Manufacturing Company.

When constructing a flexible budget, we first identify the relevant activity levels. In Exhibit 4, there are 8,000, 9,000, and 10,000 units of production. Alternative activity bases, such as machine hours or direct labor hours, may be used in measuring the volume of activity. Second, we identify the fixed and variable cost components of the costs being budgeted. For example, in Exhibit 4, the electric power cost is separated into its fixed cost ($1,000 per month) and variable cost ($0.50 per unit). Lastly, we prepare the budget for each activity level by multiplying the variable cost per unit by the activity level and then adding the monthly fixed cost.

Real World

Many hospitals use flexible budgeting to plan the number of nurses for patient floors. These budgets use a measure termed "relative value units." A relative value unit is a measure of effort related to a nursing activity, such as feeding the patient or verifying vital signs. The total relative value units for a floor can be determined from a computer simulation, based on the number of patients on the floor and the type of illnesses. Naturally, the more patients and the more severe their illnesses, the higher the total relative value units. The total relative units can then be translated into the number of nurses required to support the patients.

With a flexible budget, the department manager can be evaluated by comparing actual expenses to the budgeted amount for actual activity. For example, if Colter Manufacturing Company's Assembly Department actually spent $72,000 to produce

Exhibit 4 Flexible Budget

Colter Manufacturing Company **Assembly Department Budget** **For the Year Ending July 31, 2003**			
Units of production	8,000	9,000	10,000
Variable cost:			
Direct labor ($5 per unit)	$40,000	$45,000	$50,000
Electric power ($0.50 per unit)	4,000	4,500	5,000
Total variable cost	$44,000	$49,500	$55,000
Fixed cost:			
Electric power	$ 1,000	$ 1,000	$ 1,000
Supervisor salaries	15,000	15,000	15,000
Total fixed cost	$16,000	$16,000	$16,000
Total department costs	$60,000	$65,500	$71,000

Q&A *At the beginning of the period, the Assembly Department budgeted direct labor of $45,000 and supervisor salaries of $30,000 for 5,000 hours of production. The department actually completed 6,000 hours of production. What is the appropriate total budget for the department, assuming that it uses flexible budgeting?*

$84,000 [($9 × 6,000) + $30,000]

10,000 units, the manager would be considered over budget by $1,000 ($72,000 − $71,000). Under the static budget in Exhibit 3, the department was $12,000 over budget. This comparison is illustrated in Exhibit 5. The flexible budget for the Assembly Department is much more accurate than the static budget, because budget amounts adjust for changes in activity.

Computerized Budgeting Systems

In developing budgets, many firms use computerized budgeting systems. Such systems speed up and reduce the cost of preparing the budget. This is especially true when large quantities of data need to be processed. Computers are also useful in continuous budgeting. Reports that compare actual results with amounts budgeted can also

Exhibit 5 Static and Flexible Budgets

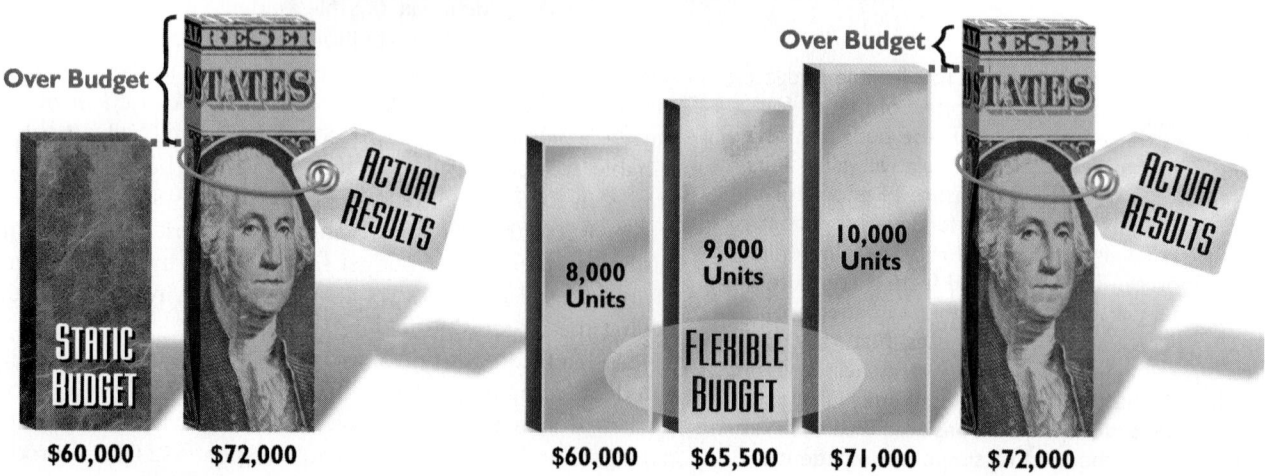

be prepared on a timely basis through the use of computerized systems. For example, **Fujitsu** used Enterprise Resource Planning (ERP) software to streamline its budgeting process from 6–8 weeks down to 10 to 15 days.

Managers often use computer spreadsheets or simulation models to represent the operating and budget relationships. By using computer simulation models, the impact of various operating alternatives on the budget can be assessed. For example, the budget can be revised to show the impact of a proposed change in indirect labor wage rates. Likewise, the budgetary effect of a proposed product line can be determined.

A common objective of using computer-based budgeting is to tie all the budgets of the organization together. In the next section, we will illustrate how a company ties its budgets together to develop a complete plan.

Master Budget

objective 3

Describe the master budget for a manufacturing business.

Manufacturing operations require a series of budgets that are linked together in a **master budget**. The major parts of the master budget are as follows:

Budgeted Income Statement	**Budgeted Balance Sheet**
Sales budget	Cash budget
Cost of goods sold budget:	Capital expenditures budget
Production budget	
Direct materials purchases budget	
Direct labor cost budget	
Factory overhead cost budget	
Selling and administrative expenses budget	

Exhibit 6 shows the relationship among the income statement budgets. The budget process begins by estimating sales. The sales information is then provided to the various units for estimating the production and selling and administrative expenses budgets. The production budgets are used to prepare the direct materials purchases, direct labor cost, and factory overhead cost budgets. These three budgets are used to develop the cost of goods sold budget. Once these budgets and the selling and administrative expenses budget have been completed, the budgeted income statement can be prepared.

After the budgeted income statement has been developed, the budgeted balance sheet can be prepared. Two major budgets comprising the budgeted balance sheet are the cash budget and the capital expenditures budget.

Income Statement Budgets

objective 4

Prepare the basic income statement budgets for a manufacturing business.

In the following sections, we will illustrate the major elements of the income statement budget. We will use a small manufacturing business, Elite Accessories Inc., as the basis for our illustration.

Exhibit 6 Income Statement
Budgets

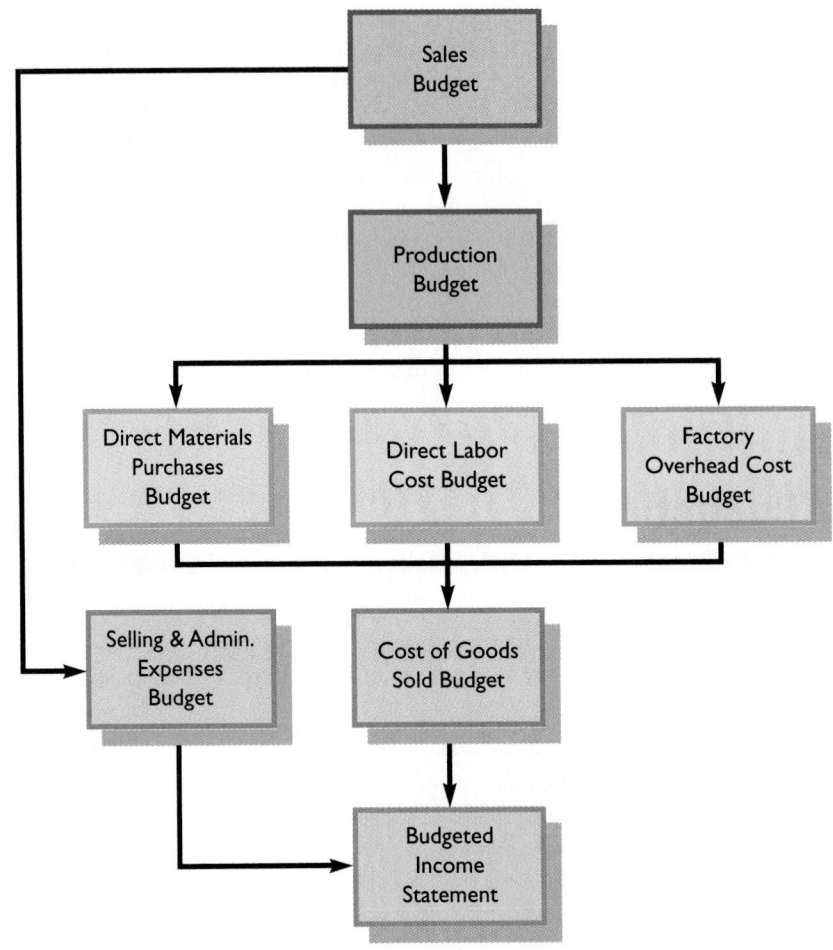

Sales Budget

The **sales budget** normally indicates for each product (1) the quantity of estimated sales and (2) the expected unit selling price. These data are often reported by regions or by sales representatives.

In estimating the quantity of sales for each product, past sales volumes are often used as a starting point. These amounts are revised for factors that are expected to affect future sales, such as the factors listed below.

- backlog of unfilled sales orders
- planned advertising and promotion
- expected industry and general economic conditions
- productive capacity
- projected pricing policy
- findings of market research studies

Once an estimate of the sales volume is obtained, the expected sales revenue can be determined by multiplying the volume by the expected unit sales price. Exhibit 7 is the sales budget for Elite Accessories Inc.

For control purposes, management can compare actual sales and budgeted sales by product, region, or sales representative. Management would investigate any significant differences and take possible corrective actions.

Exhibit 7 Sales Budget

Elite Accessories Inc. Sales Budget For the Year Ending December 31, 2003			
Product and Region	**Unit Sales Volume**	**Unit Selling Price**	**Total Sales**
Wallet:			
East	287,000	$12.00	$ 3,444,000
West	241,000	12.00	2,892,000
Total	528,000		$ 6,336,000
Handbag:			
East	156,400	$25.00	$ 3,910,000
West	123,600	25.00	3,090,000
Total	280,000		$ 7,000,000
Total revenue from sales			$13,336,000

Sales of 45,000 units are budgeted for the period. The estimated beginning inventory is 3,000 units, and the desired ending inventory is 5,000 units. What is the budgeted production (in units) for the period?

47,000 units (45,000 units + 5,000 units − 3,000 units)

Production Budget

Production should be carefully coordinated with the sales budget to ensure that production and sales are kept in balance during the period. The number of units to be manufactured to meet budgeted sales and inventory needs for each product is set forth in the **production budget**. The budgeted volume of production is determined as follows:

   Expected units to be sold
+ Desired units in ending inventory
− Estimated units in beginning inventory

   Total units to be produced

Exhibit 8 is the production budget for Elite Accessories Inc.

Exhibit 8 Production Budget

Elite Accessories Inc. Production Budget For the Year Ending December 31, 2003		
	Units	
	Wallet	**Handbag**
Expected units to be sold (from Exhibit 7)	528,000	280,000
Plus desired ending inventory, December 31, 2003	80,000	60,000
Total	608,000	340,000
Less estimated beginning inventory, January 1, 2003	88,000	48,000
Total units to be produced	520,000	292,000

Direct Materials Purchases Budget

The production budget is the starting point for determining the estimated quantities of direct materials to be purchased. Multiplying these quantities by the expected unit purchase price determines the total cost of direct materials to be purchased.

Materials required for production
+ Desired ending materials inventory
− Estimated beginning materials inventory
───────────────────────────────
Direct materials to be purchased

In Elite Accessories Inc.'s production operations, leather and lining are required for wallets and handbags. The quantity of direct materials expected to be used for each unit of product is as follows:

Wallet:
Leather: 0.30 square yard per unit
Lining: 0.10 square yard per unit

Handbag:
Leather: 1.25 square yards per unit
Lining: 0.50 square yard per unit

Based on these data and the production budget, the **direct materials purchases budget** is prepared. As shown in the budget in Exhibit 9, for Elite Accessories Inc. to produce 520,000 wallets, 156,000 square yards (520,000 units × 0.30 square yard per unit) of leather are needed. Likewise, to produce 292,000 handbags, 365,000 square yards (292,000 units × 1.25 square yards per unit) of leather are needed. We can compute the needs for lining in a similar manner. Then adding the desired ending inventory for each material and deducting the estimated beginning inventory determines the amount of each material to be purchased. Multiplying these amounts by the estimated cost per square yard yields the total materials purchase cost.

The direct materials purchases budget helps management maintain inventory levels within reasonable limits. For this purpose, the timing of the direct materials purchases should be coordinated between the purchasing and production departments.

Exhibit 9 Direct Materials Purchases Budget

Elite Accessories Inc.
Direct Materials Purchases Budget
For the Year Ending December 31, 2003

	Direct Materials		
	Leather	Lining	Total
Square yards required for production:			
Wallet (Note A)	156,000	52,000	
Handbag (Note B)	365,000	146,000	
Plus desired inventory, December 31, 2003	20,000	12,000	
Total	541,000	210,000	
Less estimated inventory, January 1, 2003	18,000	15,000	
Total square yards to be purchased	523,000	195,000	
Unit price (per square yard)	× $4.50	× $1.20	
Total direct materials to be purchased	$2,353,500	$234,000	$2,587,500

Note A: Leather: 520,000 units × 0.30 sq. yd. per unit = 156,000 sq. yds.
Lining: 520,000 units × 0.10 sq. yd. per unit = 52,000 sq. yds.

Note B: Leather: 292,000 units × 1.25 sq. yds. per unit = 365,000 sq. yds.
Lining: 292,000 units × 0.50 sq. yd. per unit = 146,000 sq. yds.

Direct Labor Cost Budget

The production budget also provides the starting point for preparing the direct labor cost budget. For Elite Accessories Inc., the labor requirements for each unit of product are estimated as follows:

Wallet:

    Cutting Department: 0.10 hour per unit
    Sewing Department: 0.25 hour per unit

Handbag:

    Cutting Department: 0.15 hour per unit
    Sewing Department: 0.40 hour per unit

Based on these data and the production budget, Elite Accessories Inc. prepares the direct labor budget. As shown in the budget in Exhibit 10, for Elite Accessories Inc. to produce 520,000 wallets, 52,000 hours (520,000 units × 0.10 hour per unit) of labor in the Cutting Department are required. Likewise, to produce 292,000 handbags, 43,800 hours (292,000 units × 0.15 hour per unit) of labor in the Cutting Department are required. In a similar manner, we can determine the direct labor hours needed in the Sewing Department to meet the budgeted production. Multiplying the direct labor hours for each department by the estimated department hourly rate yields the total direct labor cost for each department.

Exhibit 10 Direct Labor Cost Budget

Elite Accessories Inc.
Direct Labor Cost Budget
For the Year Ending December 31, 2003

	Cutting	Sewing	Total
Hours required for production:			
Wallet (Note A)	52,000	130,000	
Handbag (Note B)	43,800	116,800	
Total	95,800	246,800	
Hourly rate	× $12.00	× $15.00	
Total direct labor cost	$1,149,600	$3,702,000	$4,851,600

Note A: Cutting Department: 520,000 units × 0.10 hour per unit = 52,000 hours
           Sewing Department: 520,000 units × 0.25 hour per unit = 130,000 hours

Note B: Cutting Department: 292,000 units × 0.15 hour per unit = 43,800 hours
           Sewing Department: 292,000 units × 0.40 hour per unit = 116,800 hours

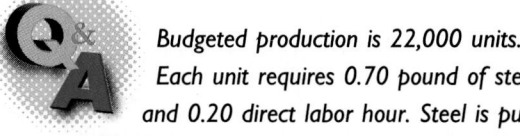

Budgeted production is 22,000 units. Each unit requires 0.70 pound of steel and 0.20 direct labor hour. Steel is purchased for $45 per pound, and direct labor is $18 per hour. Steel has an estimated beginning inventory of 700 units and a desired ending inventory of 200 units. For the period, what is the budgeted (a) direct materials purchases and (b) direct labor cost?

(a) $670,500 {[(22,000 units × 0.70 lb.) + 200 lbs. − 700 lbs.] × $45}; (b) $79,200 (22,000 units × 0.20 hr. × $18)

The direct labor needs should be coordinated between the production and personnel departments. This ensures that there will be enough labor available for production.

Factory Overhead Cost Budget

The estimated factory overhead costs necessary for production make up the factory overhead cost budget. This budget usually includes the total estimated cost for each item of factory overhead, as shown in Exhibit 11.

A business may prepare supporting departmental schedules, in which the factory overhead costs are separated into their fixed and variable cost elements. Such schedules enable department managers to direct their attention to those costs for which they are responsible and to evaluate performance.

Exhibit 11 Factory Overhead Cost Budget

Elite Accessories Inc. Factory Overhead Cost Budget For the Year Ending December 31, 2003	
Indirect factory wages	$ 732,800
Supervisor salaries	360,000
Power and light	306,000
Depreciation of plant and equipment	288,000
Indirect materials	182,800
Maintenance	140,280
Insurance and property taxes	79,200
Total factory overhead cost	$2,089,080

Cost of Goods Sold Budget

The direct materials purchases budget, direct labor cost budget, and factory overhead cost budget are the starting point for preparing the **cost of goods sold budget**. To illustrate, these data are combined with the desired ending inventory and the estimated beginning inventory data below to determine the budgeted cost of goods sold shown in Exhibit 12.

Estimated inventories on January 1, 2003:		Desired inventories on December 31, 2003:	
Finished goods	$1,095,600	Finished goods	$1,565,000
Work in process	214,400	Work in process	220,000

Exhibit 12 Cost of Goods Sold Budget

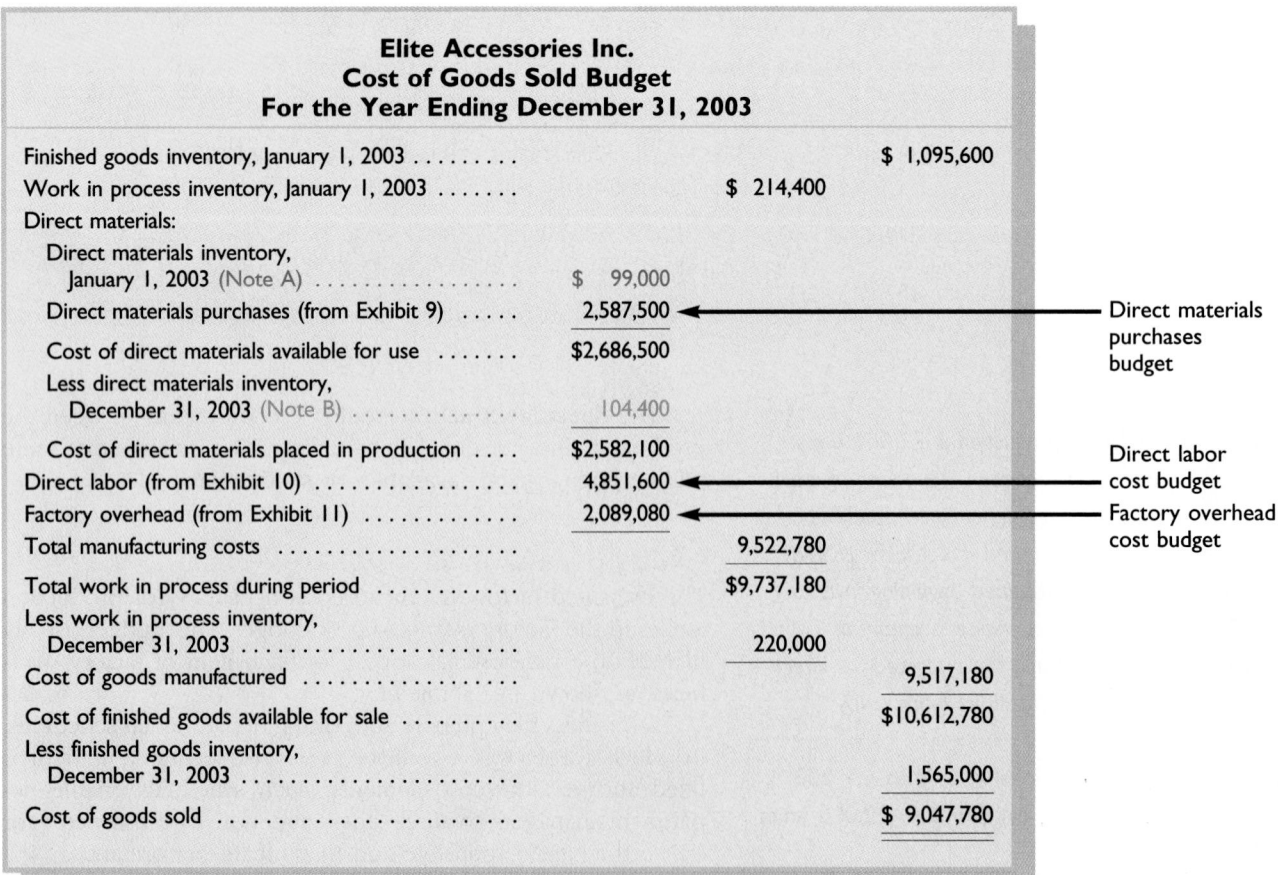

Elite Accessories Inc. Cost of Goods Sold Budget For the Year Ending December 31, 2003			
Finished goods inventory, January 1, 2003			$ 1,095,600
Work in process inventory, January 1, 2003		$ 214,400	
Direct materials:			
Direct materials inventory, January 1, 2003 (Note A)	$ 99,000		
Direct materials purchases (from Exhibit 9)	2,587,500		
Cost of direct materials available for use	$2,686,500		
Less direct materials inventory, December 31, 2003 (Note B)	104,400		
Cost of direct materials placed in production	$2,582,100		
Direct labor (from Exhibit 10)	4,851,600		
Factory overhead (from Exhibit 11)	2,089,080		
Total manufacturing costs		9,522,780	
Total work in process during period		$9,737,180	
Less work in process inventory, December 31, 2003		220,000	
Cost of goods manufactured			9,517,180
Cost of finished goods available for sale			$10,612,780
Less finished goods inventory, December 31, 2003			1,565,000
Cost of goods sold			$ 9,047,780

Direct materials purchases budget

Direct labor cost budget

Factory overhead cost budget

Exhibit 12 (Concluded)

Note A:	Leather:	18,000 sq. yds. × $4.50 per sq. yd.	$ 81,000
	Lining:	15,000 sq. yds. × $1.20 per sq. yd.	18,000
	Direct materials inventory, January 1, 2003		$ 99,000
Note B:	Leather:	20,000 sq. yds. × $4.50 per sq. yd.	$ 90,000
	Lining:	12,000 sq. yds. × $1.20 per sq. yd.	14,400
	Direct materials inventory, December 31, 2003		$104,400

Many companies are implementing software to link their business processes within the organization. Such software is termed ERP (enterprise resource planning) software. A recent study found that 49% of the implementations came in on time and on budget. For the remaining 51%, the general expense budgets failed to keep the costs under control because of unplanned difficulties in the implementation. These budget overruns have been a major criticism of ERP implementations.

Selling and Administrative Expenses Budget

The sales budget is often used as the starting point for estimating the selling and administrative expenses. For example, a budgeted increase in sales may require more advertising. Exhibit 13 is a selling and administrative expenses budget for Elite Accessories Inc.

Detailed supporting schedules are often prepared for major items in the selling and administrative expenses budget. For example, an advertising expense schedule for the Marketing Department should include the advertising media to be used (newspaper, direct mail, television), quantities (column inches, number of pieces, minutes), and the cost per unit. Attention to such details results in realistic budgets. Effective control results from assigning responsibility for achieving the budget to department supervisors.

Exhibit 13 Selling and Administrative Expenses Budget

Elite Accessories Inc.
Selling and Administrative Expenses Budget
For the Year Ending December 31, 2003

Selling expenses:		
Sales salaries expense	$715,000	
Advertising expense	360,000	
Travel expense	115,000	
Total selling expenses		$1,190,000
Administrative expenses:		
Officers' salaries expense	$360,000	
Office salaries expense	258,000	
Office rent expense	34,500	
Office supplies expense	17,500	
Miscellaneous administrative expenses	25,000	
Total administrative expenses		695,000
Total selling and administrative expenses		$1,885,000

Budgeted Income Statement

The budgets for sales, cost of goods sold, and selling and administrative expenses, combined with the data on other income, other expense, and income tax, are used to prepare the budgeted income statement. Exhibit 14 is a budgeted income statement for Elite Accessories Inc.

Exhibit 14 Budgeted Income Statement

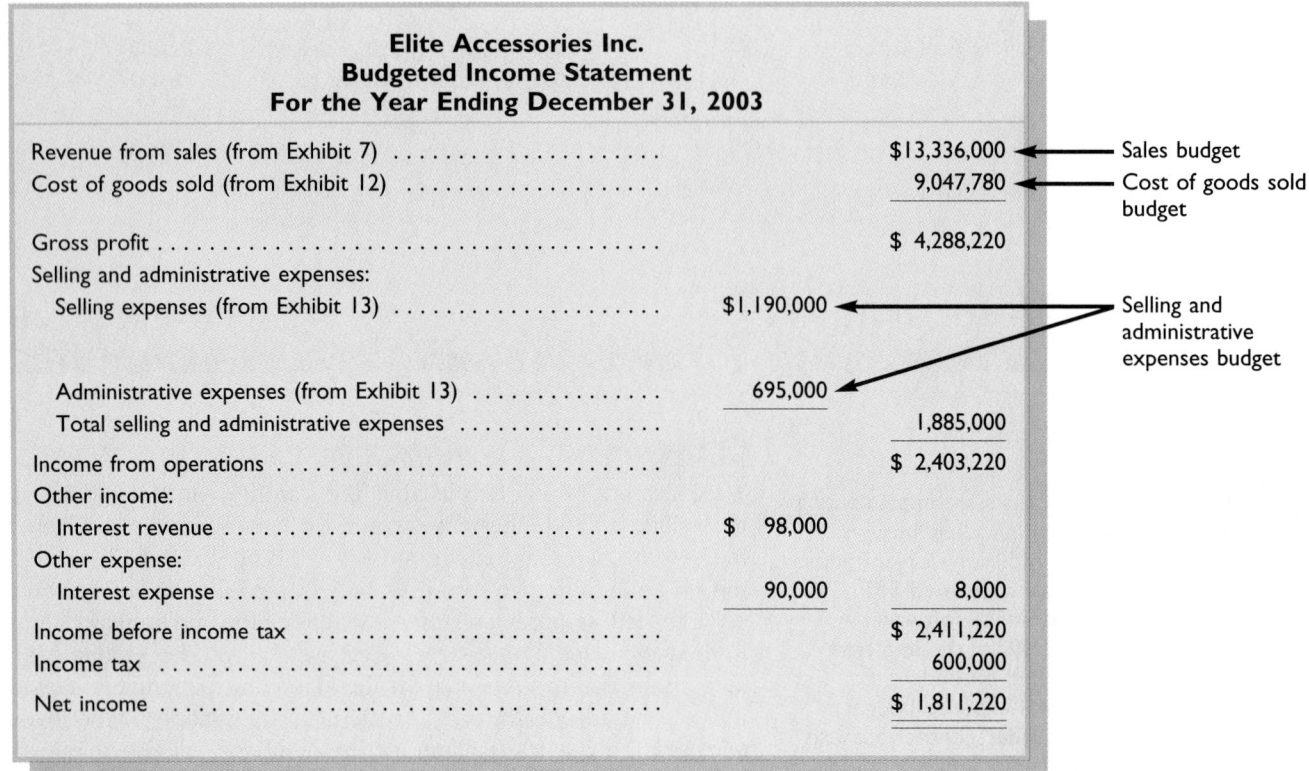

The budgeted income statement summarizes the estimates of all phases of operations. This allows management to assess the effects of the individual budgets on profits for the year. If the budgeted net income is too low, management could review and revise operating plans in an attempt to improve income.

Balance Sheet Budgets

Balance sheet budgets are used by managers to plan financing, investing, and cash objectives for the firm. The balance sheet budgets illustrated for Elite Accessories Inc. in the following sections are the cash budget and the capital expenditures budget.

Cash Budget

The **cash budget** is one of the most important elements of the budgeted balance sheet. The cash budget presents the expected receipts (inflows) and payments (outflows) of cash for a period of time.

Information from the various operating budgets, such as the sales budget, the direct materials purchases budget, and the selling and administrative expenses budget, affects the cash budget. In addition, the capital expenditures budget, dividend policies, and plans for equity or long-term debt financing also affect the cash budget.

We illustrate the monthly cash budget for January, February, and March 2003, for Elite Accessories Inc. We begin by developing the estimated cash receipts and estimated cash payments portion of the cash budget.

> The cash budget presents the expected receipts and payments of cash for a period of time.

Estimated Cash Receipts

Estimated cash receipts are planned additions to cash from sales and other sources, such as issuing securities or collecting interest. A supporting schedule can be used in determining the collections from sales. To illustrate this schedule, assume the following information for Elite Accessories Inc.:

Accounts receivable, January 1, 2003 . . . . $370,000

	January	February	March
Budgeted sales	$1,080,000	$1,240,000	$970,000

Elite Accessories Inc. expects to sell 10% of its merchandise for cash. Of the remaining 90% of the sales on account, 60% are expected to be collected in the month of the sale and the remainder in the next month.

Using this information, we prepare the schedule of collections from sales, shown in Exhibit 15. The cash receipts from sales on account are determined by adding the amounts collected from credit sales earned in the current period (60%) and the amounts accrued from sales in the previous period as accounts receivable (40%).

Exhibit 15 Schedule of Collections from Sales

Elite Accessories Inc.
Schedule of Collections from Sales
For the Three Months Ending March 31, 2003

	January	February	March
Receipts from cash sales:			
Cash sales (10% × current month's sales—Note A)	$108,000	$ 124,000	$ 97,000
Receipts from sales on account:			
Collections from prior month's sales (40% of previous month's credit sales—Note B)	$370,000	$ 388,800	$446,400
Collections from current month's sales (60% of current month's credit sales—Note C)	583,200	669,600	523,800
Total receipts from sales on account	$953,200	$1,058,400	$970,200

Note A: $108,000 = $1,080,000 × 10%
         $124,000 = $1,240,000 × 10%
         $ 97,000 = $ 970,000 × 10%

Note B: $370,000, given as January 1, 2003 Accounts Receivable balance
         $388,800 = $1,080,000 × 90% × 40%
         $446,400 = $1,240,000 × 90% × 40%

Note C: $583,200 = $1,080,000 × 90% × 60%
         $669,600 = $1,240,000 × 90% × 60%
         $523,800 = $ 970,000 × 90% × 60%

Q&A A company collects 25% of its sales in the month of the sale and 75% in the month following the sale. If sales are budgeted to be $750,000 for March and $900,000 for April, what are the budgeted cash receipts for April?

- -

$787,500 [($750,000 × 0.75) + ($900,000 × 0.25)]

Estimated Cash Payments

Estimated cash payments are planned reductions in cash from manufacturing costs, selling and administrative expenses, capital expenditures, and other sources, such as buying securities or paying interest or dividends. A supporting schedule can be used in estimating the cash payments for manufacturing costs. To illustrate, assume the following information for Elite Accessories Inc.:

Accounts payable, January 1, 2003 . . . . $190,000

	January	February	March
Manufacturing costs	$840,000	$780,000	$812,000

Depreciation expense on machines is estimated to be $24,000 per month and is included in the manufacturing costs. The accounts payable were incurred for manufacturing costs. Elite Accessories Inc. expects to pay 75% of the manufacturing costs in the month in which they are incurred and the balance in the next month.

Using this information, we can prepare the schedule of payments for manufacturing costs, as shown in Exhibit 16.

Exhibit 16 Schedule of Payments for Manufacturing Costs

Elite Accessories Inc.
Schedule of Payments for Manufacturing Costs
For the Three Months Ending March 31, 2003

	January	February	March
Payments of prior month's manufacturing costs {[25% × previous month's manufacturing costs (less depreciation)]—Note A}	$190,000	$204,000	$189,000
Payments of current month's manufacturing costs {[75% × current month's manufacturing costs (less depreciation)]—Note B}	612,000	567,000	591,000
Total payments	$802,000	$771,000	$780,000

Note A: $190,000, given as January 1, 2003 Accounts Payable balance
$204,000 = ($840,000 − $24,000) × 25%
$189,000 = ($780,000 − $24,000) × 25%

Note B: $612,000 = ($840,000 − $24,000) × 75%
$567,000 = ($780,000 − $24,000) × 75%
$591,000 = ($812,000 − $24,000) × 75%

In Exhibit 16, the cash payments are determined by adding the amounts paid from costs incurred in the current period (75%) and the amounts accrued as a liability from costs in the previous period (25%). The $24,000 of depreciation must be excluded from all calculations, since depreciation is a noncash expense that should not be included in the cash budget.

Completing the Cash Budget

To complete the cash budget for Elite Accessories Inc., as shown in Exhibit 17, assume that Elite Accessories Inc. is expecting the following:

Cash balance on January 1	$280,000
Quarterly taxes paid on March 31	150,000
Quarterly interest expense paid on January 10	22,500
Quarterly interest revenue received on March 21	24,500
Sewing equipment purchased in February	274,000

In addition, monthly selling and administrative expenses, which are paid in the month incurred, are estimated as follows:

	January	February	March
Selling and administrative expenses	$160,000	$165,000	$145,000

We can compare the estimated cash balance at the end of the period with the minimum balance required by operations. Assuming that the minimum cash balance for Elite Accessories Inc. is $340,000, we can determine any expected excess or deficiency.

Exhibit 17 Cash Budget

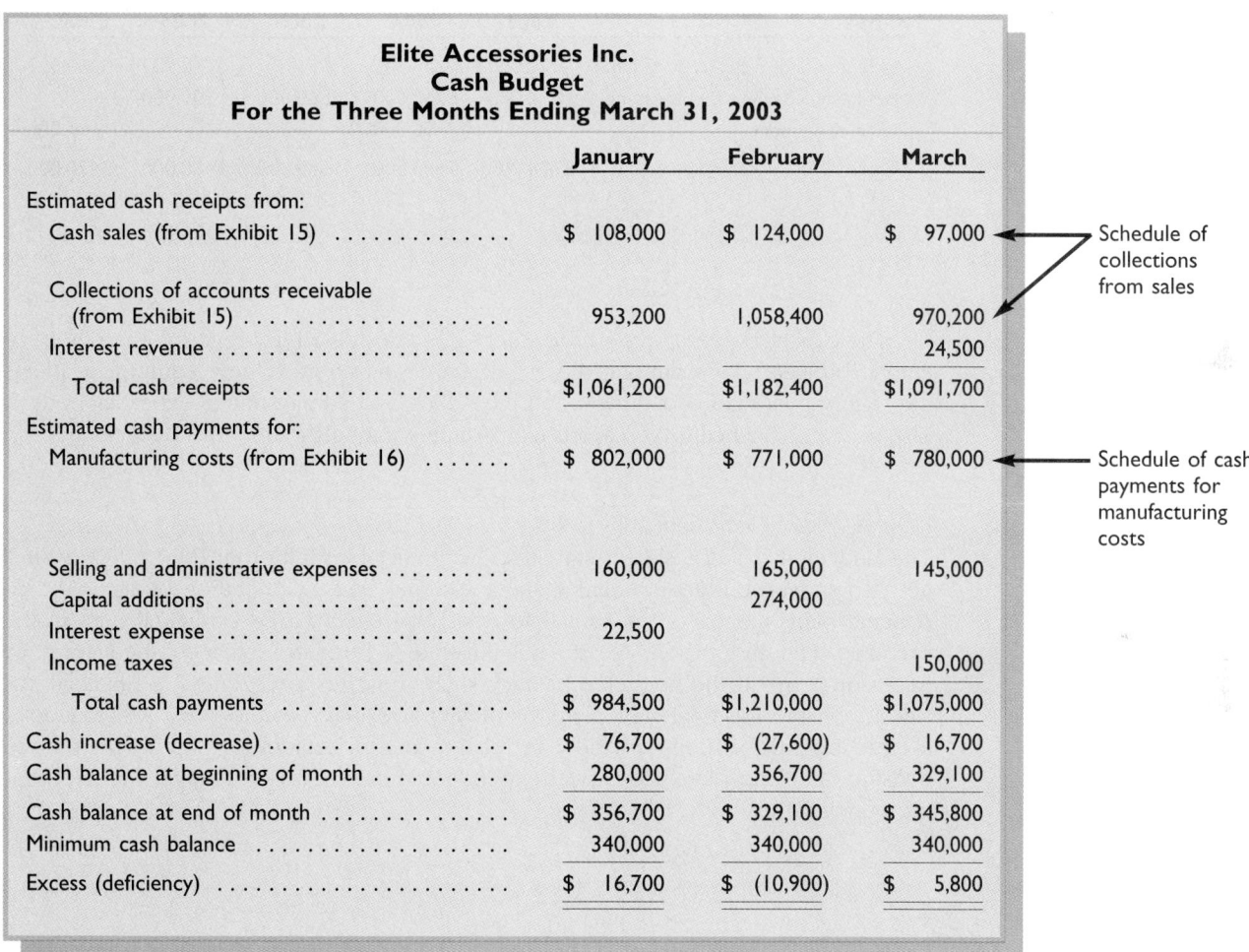

Elite Accessories Inc.
Cash Budget
For the Three Months Ending March 31, 2003

	January	February	March	
Estimated cash receipts from:				
Cash sales (from Exhibit 15)	$ 108,000	$ 124,000	$ 97,000	Schedule of collections from sales
Collections of accounts receivable (from Exhibit 15)	953,200	1,058,400	970,200	
Interest revenue			24,500	
Total cash receipts	$1,061,200	$1,182,400	$1,091,700	
Estimated cash payments for:				
Manufacturing costs (from Exhibit 16)	$ 802,000	$ 771,000	$ 780,000	Schedule of cash payments for manufacturing costs
Selling and administrative expenses	160,000	165,000	145,000	
Capital additions		274,000		
Interest expense	22,500			
Income taxes			150,000	
Total cash payments	$ 984,500	$1,210,000	$1,075,000	
Cash increase (decrease)	$ 76,700	$ (27,600)	$ 16,700	
Cash balance at beginning of month	280,000	356,700	329,100	
Cash balance at end of month	$ 356,700	$ 329,100	$ 345,800	
Minimum cash balance	340,000	340,000	340,000	
Excess (deficiency)	$ 16,700	$ (10,900)	$ 5,800	

The minimum cash balance protects against variations in estimates and for unexpected cash emergencies. For effective cash management, much of the minimum cash balance should be deposited in income-producing securities that can be readily converted to cash. U.S. Treasury Bills or Notes are examples of such securities.

Capital Expenditures Budget

The **capital expenditures budget** summarizes plans for acquiring fixed assets. Such expenditures are necessary as machinery and other fixed assets wear out, become obsolete, or for other reasons need to be replaced. In addition, expanding plant facilities may be necessary to meet increasing demand for a company's product.

The useful life of many fixed assets extends over long periods of time. In addition, the amount of the expenditures for such assets may vary from year to year. It is normal to project the plans for a number of periods into the future in preparing the capital expenditures budget. Exhibit 18 is a five-year capital expenditures budget for Elite Accessories Inc.

Exhibit 18 Capital Expenditures Budget

Elite Accessories Inc. Capital Expenditures Budget For the Five Years Ending December 31, 2007					
Item	2003	2004	2005	2006	2007
Machinery—Cutting Department	$400,000			$280,000	$360,000
Machinery—Sewing Department	274,000	$260,000	$560,000	200,000	
Office equipment		90,000			60,000
Total	$674,000	$350,000	$560,000	$480,000	$420,000

The capital expenditures budget should be considered in preparing the other operating budgets. For example, the estimated depreciation of new equipment affects the factory overhead cost budget and the selling and administrative expenses budget. The plans for financing the capital expenditures may also affect the cash budget.

Budgeted Balance Sheet

The budgeted balance sheet estimates the financial condition at the end of a budget period. The budgeted balance sheet assumes that all operating budgets and financing plans are met. It is similar to a balance sheet based on actual data in the accounts. For this reason, we do not illustrate a budgeted balance sheet for Elite Accessories Inc. If the budgeted balance sheet indicates a weakness in financial position, revising the financing plans or other plans may be necessary. For example, a large amount of long-term debt in relation to stockholders' equity might require revising financing plans for capital expenditures. Such revisions might include issuing equity rather than debt.

Buzz for E-Biz

Many companies create budgets for advertising, but what would you think of a company that:

• budgets 20% of its net assets on advertising costs.
• creates an ad budget greater than five times revenue.

• budgets half of its initial financing on Super Bowl ads.
• increases its advertising budget by 12 times from the previous year.

Well, welcome to the world of the dot.coms, where advertising budgets like these are commonplace. Why would a young company spend so much on advertising, or in other cases, bet the whole company on Super Bowl ads? The answer is that many dot.com sites need "eyeballs," or visitors. More visitors means more advertising revenue to be earned from banner ads or more fees to be earned from Internet consumers. Either way, Internet companies need to create buzz for their businesses, or they will become lost in cyberspace. The dot.coms are effectively buying their way into survival.

Just how much buzz for the bucks? LifeMinders.com placed a $2.2 million ad for a 30-second spot in the Super Bowl and added over

700,000 new members in the week following the Super Bowl. Other multimillion dollar Super Bowl ads helped WebMD.com record 500,000 unique visitors to its site, OurBeginning.com boost its unique visitors by 5,000%, and Monster.com add a record 11,300 new resumes to its job listing site. The initial evidence is that advertising is working for some companies. This is why Amazon.com is increasing its ad budget by 12 times, and E*Trade is budgeting over $400 million in advertising.

One fall-out is that ad rates have been increasing while ad space has declined. The dot.coms are eating up

the prime advertising space. The manager of Shell's corporate communications states, "As if the higher rates weren't bad enough, there were basically no prime spots available to buy. Morning news, evening news, and prime news were basically gone."

The question, however, is when will the public be saturated with Internet ads and the ads cease to be effective? Some express concern that that moment has arrived. As one ad manager expressed, it's no longer "Here's $25 million and spend it on television and build a brand; it's here's $10 million and I want (financial) results quickly." ■

KEY POINTS

1 Describe budgeting, its objectives, and its impact on human behavior.
Budgeting involves (1) establishing specific goals, (2) executing plans to achieve the goals, and (3) periodically comparing actual results with these goals. In addition, budget goals should be established to avoid problems in human behavior. Thus, budgets should not be set too tightly, too loosely, or with goal conflict.

2 Describe the basic elements of the budget process, the two major types of budgeting, and the use of computers in budgeting.
The budget process is initiated by a budget committee. The annual estimates received by the budget committee should be carefully studied, analyzed, revised, and

finally integrated together into the budget. Two major types of budgets are the static budget and the flexible budget. The static budget does not adjust with changes in activity, while the flexible budget does adjust with changes in activity. Computers can be useful in speeding up the budgetary process and in preparing timely budget performance reports. In addition, simulation models can be used to determine the impact of operating alternatives on various budgets.

3 Describe the master budget for a manufacturing business.
The master budget consists of the budgeted income statement and budgeted balance sheet. These two budgets are developed from detailed budgets that are described in the next two objectives.

4 Prepare the basic income statement budgets for a manufacturing business.
The basic income statement budgets are the sales budget, production budget, direct materials purchases budget, direct labor cost budget, factory overhead cost budget, cost of goods sold budget, and selling and administrative expenses budget.

5 Prepare balance sheet budgets for a manufacturing business.
Both the cash budget and the capital expenditures budget can be used in preparing the budgeted balance sheet. The cash budget consists of budgeted cash receipts and budgeted cash payments. The capital expenditures budget is an important tool for planning expenditures for fixed assets.

ILLUSTRATIVE PROBLEM

Selected information concerning sales and production for Cabot Co. for July 2003 are summarized as follows:

a. Estimated sales:

Product K: 40,000 units at $30.00 per unit
Product L: 20,000 units at $65.00 per unit

b. Estimated inventories, July 1, 2003:

Material A: 4,000 lbs.	Product K: 3,000 units at $17 per unit	$ 51,000
Material B: 3,500 lbs.	Product L: 2,700 units at $35 per unit	94,500
	Total	$145,500

There were no work in process inventories estimated for July 1, 2003.

c. Desired inventories at July 31, 2003:

Material A: 3,000 lbs.	Product K: 2,500 units at $17 per unit	$ 42,500
Material B: 2,500 lbs.	Product L: 2,000 units at $35 per unit	70,000
	Total	$112,500

There were no work in process inventories desired for July 31, 2003.

d. Direct materials used in production:

	Product K	Product L
Material A:	0.7 lb. per unit	3.5 lbs. per unit
Material B:	1.2 lbs. per unit	1.8 lbs. per unit

e. Unit costs for direct materials:

Material A: $4.00 per lb.
Material B: $2.00 per lb.

f. Direct labor requirements:

	Department 1	Department 2
Product K	0.4 hour per unit	0.15 hour per unit
Product L	0.6 hour per unit	0.25 hour per unit

g.

	Department 1	Department 2
Direct labor rate	$12.00 per hour	$16.00 per hour

h. Estimated factory overhead costs for July:

Indirect factory wages	$200,000
Depreciation of plant and equipment	40,000
Power and light	25,000
Indirect materials	34,000
Total	$299,000

Instructions

1. Prepare a sales budget for July.
2. Prepare a production budget for July.
3. Prepare a direct materials purchases budget for July.
4. Prepare a direct labor cost budget for July.
5. Prepare a cost of goods sold budget for July.

Solution

1.

Cabot Co.
Sales Budget
For the Month Ending July 31, 2003

Product	Unit Sales Volume	Unit Selling Price	Total Sales
Product K	40,000	$30.00	$1,200,000
Product L	20,000	65.00	1,300,000
Total revenue from sales ...			$2,500,000

2.

Cabot Co.
Production Budget
For the Month Ending July 31, 2003

	Units	
	Product K	**Product L**
Sales	40,000	20,000
Plus desired inventories at July 31, 2003	2,500	2,000
Total	42,500	22,000
Less estimated inventories, July 1, 2003	3,000	2,700
Total production	39,500	19,300

3.

Cabot Co.
Direct Materials Purchases Budget
For the Month Ending July 31, 2003

	Direct Materials		
	Material A	**Material B**	**Total**
Units required for production:			
Product K (39,500 × lbs. per unit)	27,650 lbs.*	47,400 lbs.*	
Product L (19,300 × lbs. per unit)	67,550**	34,740**	
Plus desired units of inventory, July 31, 2003	3,000	2,500	
Total	98,200 lbs.	84,640 lbs.	
Less estimated units of inventory, July 1, 2003	4,000	3,500	
Total units to be purchased	94,200 lbs.	81,140 lbs.	
Unit price	× $4.00	× $2.00	
Total direct materials purchases	$376,800	$162,280	$539,080

*27,650 = 39,500 × 0.7   47,400 = 39,500 × 1.2
**67,550 = 19,300 × 3.5   34,740 = 19,300 × 1.8

4.

Cabot Co. Direct Labor Cost Budget For the Month Ending July 31, 2003			
	Department 1	**Department 2**	**Total**
Hours required for production:			
Product K (39,500 × hours per unit) . . .	15,800*	5,925*	
Product L (19,300 × hours per unit)	11,580**	4,825**	
Total	27,380	10,750	
Hourly rate	× $12.00	× $16.00	
Total direct labor cost	$328,560	$172,000	$500,560

*15,800 = 39,500 × 0.4   5,925 = 39,500 × 0.15
**11,580 = 19,300 × 0.6   4,825 = 19,300 × 0.25

5.

Cabot Co. Cost of Goods Sold Budget For the Month Ending July 31, 2003		
Finished goods inventory, July 1, 2003		$ 145,500
Direct materials:		
Direct materials inventory, July 1, 2003—(Note A)	$ 23,000	
Direct materials purchases	539,080	
Cost of direct materials available for use	$562,080	
Less direct materials inventory, July 31, 2003—(Note B)	17,000	
Cost of direct materials placed in production	$545,080	
Direct labor	500,560	
Factory overhead	299,000	
Cost of goods manufactured		1,344,640
Cost of finished goods available for sale		$1,490,140
Less finished goods inventory, July 31, 2003		112,500
Cost of goods sold		$1,377,640

Note A:
Material A   4,000 lbs.   at $4.00 per lb. $16,000
Material B   3,500 lbs.   at $2.00 per lb.   7,000
Direct materials inventory, July 1, 2003 $23,000

Note B:
Material A   3,000 lbs.   at $4.00 per lb. $12,000
Material B   2,500 lbs.   at $2.00 per lb.   5,000
Direct materials inventory, July 31, 2003 $17,000

Matching

Match each of the following statements with its proper term. Some terms may not be used.

A. **budget**

B. **capital expenditures budget**

C. **cash budget**

D. **continuous budgeting**

E. **cost of goods sold budget**

F. **direct materials purchases budget**

G. **flexible budget**

H. **goal conflict**

I. **master budget**

J. **production budget**

K. **responsibility center**

L. **sales budget**

M. **static budget**

N. **zero-based budgeting**

___ 1. The comprehensive budget plan linking all the individual budgets related to sales, cost of goods sold, operating expenses, projects, capital expenditures, and cash.

___ 2. A method of budgeting that provides for maintaining a twelve-month projection into the future.

___ 3. A concept of budgeting that requires all levels of management to start from zero and estimate budget data as if there had been no previous activities in their units.

___ 4. An accounting device used to plan and control resources of operational departments and divisions.

___ 5. A budget that uses the production budget as a starting point.

___ 6. The budget summarizing future plans for acquiring plant facilities and equipment.

___ 7. A budget of the estimated direct materials, direct labor, and factory overhead consumed by sold products.

___ 8. A budget of estimated unit production.

___ 9. A budget that does not adjust to changes in activity levels.

___ 10. A budget that adjusts for varying rates of activity.

___ 11. A budget of estimated cash receipts and payments.

___ 12. An organizational unit for which a manager is assigned responsibility over costs, revenues, or assets.

Multiple Choice

1. A tight budget may create:
   A. budgetary slack
   B. discouragement
   C. a flexible budget
   D. a "spend it or lose it" mentality

2. The first step of the budget process is:
   A. plan   C. control
   B. direct   D. feedback

3. Static budgets are often used by:
   A. production departments
   B. administrative departments
   C. responsibility centers
   D. capital projects

4. The total estimated sales for the coming year is 250,000 units. The estimated inventory at the beginning of the year is 22,500 units, and the desired inventory at the end of the year is 30,000 units. The total production indicated in the production budget is:
   A. 242,500 units   C. 280,000 units
   B. 257,500 units   D. 302,500 units

5. Dixon Company expects $650,000 of credit sales in March and $800,000 of credit sales in April. Dixon historically collects 70% of its sales in the month of sale and 30% in the following month. How much cash does Dixon expect to collect in April?
   A. $800,000   C. $755,000
   B. $560,000   D. $1,015,000

1. What are the three major objectives of budgeting?
2. What is the manager's role in a responsibility center?
3. Briefly describe the type of human behavior problems that might arise if budget goals are set too tightly.

4. Why should all levels of management and all departments participate in preparing and submitting budget estimates?
5. Give an example of budgetary slack.
6. What behavioral problems are associated with setting a budget too loosely?
7. What behavioral problems are associated with establishing conflicting goals within the budget?
8. When would a company use zero-based budgeting?
9. Under what circumstances would a static budget be appropriate?
10. How do computerized budgeting systems aid firms in the budgeting process?
11. What is the first step in preparing a master budget?
12. Why should the production requirements set forth in the production budget be carefully coordinated with the sales budget?
13. Why should the timing of direct materials purchases be closely coordinated with the production budget?
14. In preparing the budget for the cost of goods sold, what are the three budgets from which data on relevant estimates of quantities and costs are combined with data on estimated inventories?
15. a. Discuss the purpose of the cash budget.
    b. If the cash for the first quarter of the fiscal year indicates excess cash at the end of each of the first two months, how might the excess cash be used?
16. How does a schedule of collections from sales assist in preparing the cash budget?
17. Give an example of how the capital expenditures budget affects other operating budgets.

Warren Reeve Fess

RESOURCES FOR YOUR SUCCESS ONLINE AT

http://warren.swcollege.com

Remember! If you need additional help, visit South-Western's Web site.
See page M28 for a description of the online and printed materials that are available.

E X E R C I S E S

Exercise 5–1
Personal cash budget

Objectives 2, 5

SPREADSHEET

✓ December 31 cash balance, $220

At the beginning of the 2003 school year, Jennifer Bell decided to prepare a cash budget for the months of September, October, November, and December. The following information relates to the budget:

Cash balance, September 1	$5,000
Purchase season football tickets in September	180
Additional entertainment for each month	250
Pay semester tuition on September 3	4,000
Pay rent at the beginning of each month	480
Pay for food each month	320
Pay apartment deposit on September 2 (to be returned December 15)	500
Part-time job earnings each month (net of taxes)	900

a. Prepare a cash budget for September, October, November, and December.
b. Are the budgets prepared as static budgets or flexible budgets?
c. ✏ What are the budget implications for Jennifer Bell?

Exercise 5–2
Flexible budget for selling and administrative expenses

Objectives 2, 4

✓ Total selling and administrative expenses at $200,000 sales, $56,500

Medico Medical Supply Company uses flexible budgets that are based on the following data:

Sales commissions	5% of sales
Advertising expense	12% of sales
Miscellaneous selling expense	$2,000 plus 3% of sales
Office salaries expense	$8,000 per month
Office supplies expense	2% of sales
Miscellaneous administrative expense	$500 per month plus 1% of sales

Prepare a flexible selling and administrative expenses budget for May 2003, for sales volumes of $120,000, $160,000, and $200,000. (Use Exhibit 4 as a model.)

Exercise 5–3
Static budget vs. flexible budget

Objectives 2, 4

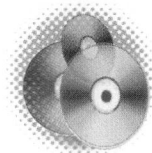

GENERAL LEDGER

✓ b. Excess of actual over budget for March, $65,000

The production supervisor of the Welding Department for Nunly Company agreed to the following monthly static budget for the upcoming year:

**Nunly Company
Welding Department
Monthly Production Budget**

Wages	$450,000
Utilities	100,000
Depreciation	50,000
Total	$600,000

The actual amount spent for the first three months of the year 2003 in the Welding Department was as follows:

January	$560,000
February	520,000
March	500,000

The Welding Department supervisor has been very pleased with this performance, since actual expenditures have been less than the monthly budget. However, the plant manager believes that the budget should not remain fixed for every month but should "flex" or adjust to the volume of work that is produced in the Welding Department. Additional budget information for the Welding Department is as follows:

Wages per hour	$18.00
Utility cost per direct labor hour	$4.00
Direct labor hours per unit	0.50
Planned unit production	50,000

The actual units produced in the Welding Department were as follows:

January	45,000 units
February	40,000
March	35,000

a. Prepare a flexible budget for the actual units produced for January, February, and March in the Welding Department.
b. ◄━━► Compare the flexible budget with the actual expenditures for the first three months. What does this comparison suggest?

Exercise 5–4
Flexible budget for Fabrication Department

Objective 2

Steelcase Corporation is one of the largest manufacturers of office furniture in the United States. In Grand Rapids, Michigan, it produces filing cabinets in two departments: Fabrication and Trim Assembly. Assume the following information for the Fabrication Department:

✓ Total department cost at 10,000 units, $588,500

Steel per filing cabinet	35 pounds
Direct labor per filing cabinet	36 minutes
Supervisor salaries	$12,000 per month
Depreciation	$2,500 per month
Direct labor rate	$14 per hour
Steel cost	$1.40 per pound

Prepare a flexible budget for 10,000, 11,000, and 12,000 filing cabinets for the month of May 2003, similar to Exhibit 4, assuming that inventories are not significant.

Exercise 5–5
Sales and production budgets

Objective 4

✓ b. Model CR1 total production, 8,160 units

Grand Electronics Company manufactures two models of clock radios, CR1 and CR2. Based on the following production and sales data for September 2004, prepare (a) a sales budget and (b) a production budget.

	CR1	CR2
Estimated inventory (units), September 1	350	120
Desired inventory (units), September 30	410	100
Expected sales volume (units):		
East Region	4,700	3,200
West Region	3,400	2,400
Unit sales price	$65.00	$80.00

Exercise 5–6
Professional fees budget

Objective 4

✓ Total professional fees, $15,259,500

Garcia and Berry, CPAs, offer three types of services to clients: auditing, tax, and computer consulting. Based on experience and projected growth, the following billable hours have been estimated for the year ending December 31, 2003:

	Billable Hours
Audit Department:	
Staff	36,000
Partners	5,200
Tax Department:	
Staff	30,600
Partners	4,100
Computer Consulting Department:	
Staff	40,200
Partners	15,800

The average billing rate for staff is $90 per hour, and the average billing rate for partners is $225 per hour. Prepare a professional fees budget for Garcia and Berry, CPAs, for the year ending December 31, 2003, using the following column headings and showing the estimated professional fees by type of service rendered:

Billable Hours   Hourly Rate   Total Revenue

Exercise 5–7
Professional labor cost budget

Objective 4

✓ Staff total labor cost, $4,272,000

Based on the data in Exercise 5–6 and assuming that the average compensation per hour for staff is $40 and for partners is $120, prepare a professional labor cost budget for Garcia and Berry, CPAs, for the year ending December 31, 2003. Use the following column headings:

Billable Hours Required

Staff   Partners

Exercise 5–8
Direct materials purchases budget
Objective 4

✓ Total cheese purchases, $157,992

Mama Leona's Frozen Pizza Inc. has determined from its production budget the following estimated production volumes for 12″ and 16″ frozen pizzas for August 2003:

	Units	
	12″ Pizza	**16″ Pizza**
Budgeted production volume	28,500	41,800

There are three direct materials used in producing the two types of pizza. The quantities of direct materials expected to be used for each pizza are as follows:

	12″ Pizza	**16″ Pizza**
Direct materials:		
Dough	1.00 lb. per unit	1.50 lbs. per unit
Tomato	0.50	0.80
Cheese	0.70	1.10

In addition, Mama Leona's has determined the following information about each material:

	Dough	**Tomato**	**Cheese**
Estimated inventory, August 1, 2003	500 lbs.	200 lbs.	450 lbs.
Desired inventory, August 31, 2003	450 lbs.	240 lbs.	350 lbs.
Price per pound	$1.30	$2.10	$2.40

Prepare August's direct materials purchases budget for Mama Leona's Frozen Pizza Inc.

Exercise 5–9
Direct materials purchases budget
Objective 4

✓ Concentrate budgeted purchases, $89,820

Coca-Cola Enterprises is the largest bottler of Coca-Cola® in North America. The company purchases Coke® and Sprite® concentrate from **The Coca-Cola Company**, dilutes and mixes the concentrate with carbonated water, and then fills the blended beverage into cans or plastic 2-liter bottles. Assume the estimated production for Coke and Sprite 2-liter bottles at the Chattanooga, Tennessee, bottling plant are as follows for the month of September:

Coke   155,000 two-liter bottles
Sprite   126,000 two-liter bottles

In addition, assume that the concentrate costs $90 per pound for both Coke and Sprite and is used at a rate of 0.2 pound per 100 liters of carbonated water in blending Coke and 0.15 pound per 100 liters of carbonated water in blending Sprite. Assume that two-liter bottles cost $0.09 per bottle and carbonated water costs $0.04 per liter.

Prepare a direct materials purchases budget for September 2003, assuming no changes between beginning and ending inventories for all three materials.

Exercise 5–10
Direct materials purchases budget
Objective 4

✓ Total steel belt purchases, $617,600

Anticipated sales for SureGrip Tire Company were 30,000 passenger car tires and 10,000 truck tires. There were no anticipated beginning finished goods inventories for either product. The planned ending finished goods inventories were 2,000 units for each product. Rubber and steel belts are used in producing passenger car and truck tires according to the following table:

	Passenger Car	**Truck**
Rubber	25 lbs. per unit	60 lbs. per unit
Steel belts	3 lbs. per unit	8 lbs. per unit

The purchase prices of rubber and steel are $2.00 and $3.20 per pound, respectively. The desired ending inventories of rubber and steel belts are 40,000 and 6,000 pounds, respectively. The estimated beginning inventories for rubber and steel belts are 70,000 and 5,000 pounds, respectively.

The following materials purchases budget was prepared for SureGrip Tire Company:

SureGrip Tire Company
Direct Materials Purchases Budget
For the Year Ending December 31, 2003

	Rubber	Steel Belts	Total
Units required for production:			
Passenger tires	750,000 lbs.	90,000 lbs.	
Truck tires	600,000	80,000	
Total	$1,350,000 lbs.	170,000 lbs.	
Unit price	× $2.00	× $3.20	
Total direct materials purchases	$2,700,000	$544,000	$3,244,000

Correct the direct materials purchases budget for SureGrip Tire Company.

Exercise 5–11
Direct labor cost budget
Objective 4

✓ Total direct labor cost, Finishing, $154,620

Ace Racket Company manufactures two types of tennis rackets, the Junior and Pro-Striker models. The production budget for August for the two rackets is as follows:

	Junior	Pro-Striker
Production budget	4,300 units	14,600 units

Both rackets are produced in two departments, Molding and Finishing. The direct labor hours required for each racket are estimated as follows:

	Molding Department	Finishing Department
Junior	0.20 hour per unit	0.30 hour per unit
Pro-Striker	0.30 hour per unit	0.50 hour per unit

The direct labor rate for each department is as follows:

Molding Department	$15.00 per hour
Finishing Department	$18.00 per hour

Prepare the direct labor cost budget for August 2003.

Exercise 5–12
Production and direct labor cost budgets
Objective 4

✓ a. Total production of 501 Jeans, 49,560

Levi Strauss & Co. manufactures jeans and slacks under a variety of brand names, such as Dockers® and 501 Jeans®. Slacks and jeans are assembled by a variety of different sewing operations. Assume that the sales budget for Dockers and 501 Jeans shows estimated sales of 25,400 and 49,600 pairs, respectively, for March 2003. The finished goods inventory is assumed as follows:

	Dockers	501 Jeans
March 1 estimated inventory	300	140
March 31 desired inventory	250	100

Assume the following direct labor data per 10 pairs of Dockers and 501 Jeans for four different sewing operations:

	Direct Labor per 10 Pairs	
	Dockers	501 Jeans
Inseam	15 minutes	12 minutes
Outerseam	20	14
Pockets	5	8
Zipper	6	6
Total	46 minutes	40 minutes

a. Prepare a production budget for March.
b. Prepare the March direct labor cost budget for the four sewing operations, assuming a $9 wage per hour for the inseam and outerseam sewing operations and a $10 wage per hour for the pocket and zipper sewing operations.

Exercise 5–13
Factory overhead cost budget

Objective 4

✓ Total variable factory overhead costs, $237,000

Hans Watch Company budgeted the following costs for anticipated production for January 2003:

Advertising expenses	$260,000
Manufacturing supplies	12,000
Power and light	45,000
Sales commissions	280,000
Factory insurance	20,000
Supervisor wages	123,000
Production control salaries	32,000
Executive officer salaries	210,000
Materials management salaries	25,000
Factory depreciation	19,000

Prepare a factory overhead cost budget, separating variable and fixed costs. Assume that factory insurance and depreciation are the only fixed costs.

Exercise 5–14
Cost of goods sold budget

Objective 4

✓ Cost of goods sold, $342,050

The controller of Model Ceramic Company wishes to prepare a cost of goods sold budget for June. The controller assembled the following information for constructing the cost of goods sold budget:

Direct materials:

	Enamel	Paint	Porcelain	Total
Total direct materials purchases budgeted for June	$28,580	$5,340	$96,400	$130,320
Estimated inventory, June 1, 2003	1,250	2,400	4,540	8,190
Desired inventory, June 30, 2003	2,000	2,150	5,000	9,150

Direct labor cost:

	Kiln Department	Decorating Department	Total
Total direct labor cost budgeted for June	$36,500	$105,800	$142,300

Finished goods inventories:

	Dish	Bowl	Figurine	Total
Estimated inventory, June 1, 2003	$4,180	$3,270	$2,580	$10,030
Desired inventory, June 30, 2003	3,250	3,940	3,100	10,290

Work in process inventories:

Estimated inventory, June 1, 2003	$2,900
Desired inventory, June 30, 2003	1,350

Budgeted factory overhead costs for June:

Indirect factory wages	$45,800
Depreciation of plant and equipment	14,600
Power and light	5,300
Indirect materials	3,400
Total	$69,100

Use the preceding information to prepare a cost of goods sold budget for June 2003.

Exercise 5–15
Schedule of cash collections of accounts receivable

Objective 5

✓ Total cash collected in May, $525,700

Trevor Company was organized on March 1, 2003. Projected sales for each of the first three months of operations are as follows:

March	$480,000
April	590,000
May	505,000

The company expects to sell 10% of its merchandise for cash. Of sales on account, 60% are expected to be collected in the month of the sale, 30% in the month following the sale, and the remainder in the second month following the sale.

Prepare a schedule indicating cash collections from sales for March, April, and May.

Exercise 5–16
Schedule of cash payments

Objective 5

✓ Total cash payments in August, $136,925

Tutor.com Inc. was organized on May 31, 2003. Projected selling and administrative expenses for each of the first three months of operations are as follows:

June	$ 95,400
July	126,800
August	156,300

Depreciation, insurance, and property taxes represent $12,000 of the estimated monthly expenses. The annual insurance premium was paid on May 31, and property taxes for the year will be paid in December. Three-fourths of the remainder of the expenses are expected to be paid in the month in which they are incurred, with the balance to be paid in the following month.

Prepare a schedule indicating cash payments for selling and administrative expenses for June, July, and August.

Exercise 5–17
Schedule of cash payments

Objective 5

✓ Total cash payments in December, $123,980

The Sea Breeze Hotel is planning its cash payments for operations for the fourth quarter (October–December), 2004. The Accrued Expenses Payable balance on October 1 is $18,400. The budgeted expenses for the next three months are as follows:

	October	November	December
Salaries	$ 57,400	$ 68,900	$ 75,600
Utilities	5,000	5,400	6,100
Other operating expenses	43,200	51,300	62,300
Total	$105,600	$125,600	$144,000

Other operating expenses include $13,500 of monthly depreciation expense and $1,000 of monthly insurance expense that was prepaid for the year on March 1 of the current year. Of the remaining expenses, 70% are paid in the month in which they are incurred, with the remainder paid in the following month. The Accrued Expenses Payable balance on October 1 relates to the expenses incurred in September.

Prepare a schedule of cash payments for operations for October, November, and December.

Exercise 5–18
Capital expenditures budget

Objective 5

✓ Total capital expenditures in 2005, $5,000,000

On January 1, 2002, the controller of Minter Manufacturing Company is planning capital expenditures for the years 2002–2005. The following interviews helped the controller collect the necessary information for the capital expenditures budget.

Director of Facilities: A construction contract was signed in late 2001 for the construction of a new factory building at a contract cost of $10,000,000. The construction is scheduled to begin in 2002 and be completed in 2003.

Vice-President of Manufacturing: Once the new factory building is finished, we plan to purchase $1.6 million in equipment in late 2003. I expect that an additional $300,000 will be needed early in the following year (2004) to test and install the equipment before we can begin production. If sales continue to grow, I expect we'll need to invest another million in equipment in 2005.

Vice-President of Marketing: We have really been growing lately. I wouldn't be sur-prised if we need to expand the size of our new factory building in 2005 by at least 40%. Fortunately, we expect inflation to have minimal impact on construc-tion costs over the next four years.

Director of Information Systems: We need to upgrade our information systems to local area network (LAN) technology. It doesn't make sense to do this until after the new factory building is completed and producing product. During 2004, once the factory is up and running, we should equip the whole facility with LAN technology. I think it would cost us $1,800,000 today to install the technology. However, prices have been dropping by 20% per year, so it should be less expensive at a later date.

President: I am excited about our long-term prospects. My only short-term concern is financing the $6,000,000 of construction costs on the portion of the new factory building scheduled to be completed in 2002.

Use the interview information above to prepare a capital expenditures budget for Minter Manufacturing Company for the years 2002–2005.

PROBLEMS SERIES A

Problem 5–1A

Forecast sales volume and sales budget

Objective 4

✓ 3. Total revenue from sales, $1,393,000

Renoir Frame Company prepared the following sales budget for the current year:

Renoir Frame Company
Sales Budget
For the Year Ending December 31, 2003

Product and Area	Unit Sales Volume	Unit Selling Price	Total Sales
8″ × 10″ Frame:			
East	25,000	$8.00	$ 200,000
Central	32,000	8.00	256,000
West	12,000	8.00	96,000
Total	69,000		$ 552,000
12″ × 16″ Frame:			
East	20,000	$15.00	$ 300,000
Central	25,000	15.00	375,000
West	10,000	15.00	150,000
Total	55,000		$ 825,000
Total revenue from sales			$1,377,000

At the end of December 2003, the following unit sales data were reported for the year:

	Unit Sales	
	8″ × 10″ Frame	12″ × 16″ Frame
East	26,125	20,600
Central	32,640	26,375
West	11,448	9,500

For the year ending December 31, 2004, unit sales are expected to follow the pat-terns established during the year ending December 31, 2003. The unit selling price for the 8″ × 10″ frame is expected to change to $9, and the unit selling price for the 12″ × 16″ frame is expected to decline to $13, effective January 1, 2004.

Instructions

1. Compute the increase or decrease of actual unit sales for the year ended December 31, 2003, over budget. Place your answers in a columnar table with the following format:

	Unit Sales, Year Ended 2003		Increase (Decrease) Actual Over Budget	
	Budget	Actual Sales	Amount	Percent
8″ × 10″ Frame:				
East				
Central				
West				
12″ × 16″ Frame:				
East				
Central				
West				

2. Assuming that the trend of sales indicated in (1) is to continue in 2004, compute the unit sales volume to be used for preparing the sales budget for the year ending December 31, 2004. Place your answers in a columnar table with the following format. Round budgeted units to the nearest thousand.

	2003 Actual Units	Percentage Increase (Decrease)	2004 Budgeted Units
8″ × 10″ Frame:			
East			
Central			
West			
12″ × 16″ Frame:			
East			
Central			
West			

3. Prepare a sales budget for the year ending December 31, 2004.

Problem 5–2A

Sales, production, direct materials, and direct labor budgets

Objective 4

SPREADSHEET

✓ 3. Total direct materials purchases, $5,662,360

The budget director of Summertime Grill Company requests estimates of sales, production, and other operating data from the various administrative units every month. Selected information concerning sales and production for May 2003 is summarized as follows:

a. Estimated sales for May by sales territory:

Maine:
Backyard Chef . . . .   3,500 units at $550 per unit
Master Chef . . . .   1,800 units at $1,300 per unit
Vermont:
Backyard Chef . . . .   2,800 units at $500 per unit
Master Chef . . . .   1,500 units at $1,200 per unit
New Hampshire:
Backyard Chef . . . .   4,000 units at $600 per unit
Master Chef . . . .   2,900 units at $1,500 per unit

b. Estimated inventories at May 1:

Direct materials:
Grates . . . .   1,000 units
Stainless steel . . . .   2,500 lbs.
Burner subassemblies . . . .   600 units
Shelves . . . .   400 units
Finished products:
Backyard Chef . . . .   1,500 units
Master Chef . . . .   400 units

c. Desired inventories at May 31:

Direct materials:
Grates . . . .   800 units
Stainless steel . . . .   1,900 lbs.
Burner subassemblies . . . .   800 units
Shelves . . . .   480 units
Finished products:
Backyard Chef . . . .   1,200 units
Master Chef . . . .   500 units

d. Direct materials used in production:

In manufacture of Backyard Chef:
Grates . . . .   2 units per unit of product
Stainless steel . . . .   25 lbs. per unit of product
Burner subassemblies . . . .   1 unit per unit of product
Shelves . . . .   2 units per unit of product
In manufacture of Master Chef:
Grates . . . .   6 units per unit of product
Stainless steel . . . .   65 lbs. per unit of product
Burner subassemblies . . . .   4 units per unit of product
Shelves . . . .   3 units per unit of product

e. Anticipated purchase price for direct materials:

Grates . . . . $15 per unit
Stainless steel . . . . $3 per lb.
Burner subassemblies . . . . $72 per unit
Shelves . . . . $7 per unit

f. Direct labor requirements:

Backyard Chef:
Stamping Department . . . .   0.50 hour at $12 per hour
Forming Department . . . .   0.75 hour at $10 per hour
Assembly Department . . . .   1.50 hours at $9 per hour
Master Chef:
Stamping Department . . . .   0.60 hour at $12 per hour
Forming Department . . . .   1.50 hours at $10 per hour
Assembly Department . . . .   2.50 hours at $9 per hour

Instructions

1. Prepare a sales budget for May.
2. Prepare a production budget for May.
3. Prepare a direct materials purchases budget for May.
4. Prepare a direct labor cost budget for May.

Problem 5–3A
*Budgeted income statement
and supporting budgets*

Objective 4

✓ 4. Total direct labor cost in
Slitting Dept., $205,120

The budget director of Instant Memories Film Company, with the assistance of the controller, treasurer, production manager, and sales manager, has gathered the following data for use in developing the budgeted income statement for October 2003:

a. Estimated sales for October:

Instant Image . . . .   26,800 units at $65 per unit
Pro Image . . . .   20,400 units at $90 per unit

b. Estimated inventories at October 1:

Direct materials: Finished products:
Celluloid . . . . 2,700 lbs.   Instant Image . . . . . 4,800 units at $35 per unit
Silver . . . . 3,000 ozs.   Pro Image . . . . 2,400 units at $55 per unit

c. Desired inventories at October 31:

Direct materials:		Finished products:	
Celluloid	3,400 lbs.	Instant Image	5,400 units at $35 per unit
Silver	2,900 ozs.	Pro Image	1,900 units at $55 per unit

d. Direct materials used in production:

In manufacture of Instant Image:
    Celluloid . . . .   0.40 lb. per unit of product
    Silver . . . .   2.50 ozs. per unit of product
In manufacture of Pro Image:
    Celluloid . . . .   0.60 lb. per unit of product
    Silver . . . .   4.00 ozs. per unit of product

e. Anticipated cost of purchases and beginning and ending inventory of direct materials:

Celluloid . . . . $1.50 per lb.   Silver . . . . $6 per oz.

f. Direct labor requirements:

Instant Image:
    Coating Department . . . .   0.20 hour at $14 per hour
    Slitting Department . . . .   0.25 hour at $16 per hour
Pro Image:
    Coating Department . . . .   0.40 hour at $14 per hour
    Slitting Department . . . .   0.30 hour at $16 per hour

g. Estimated factory overhead costs for October:

Indirect factory wages	$525,000
Depreciation of plant and equipment	145,000
Power and light	46,000
Insurance and property tax	18,400

h. Estimated operating expenses for October:

Sales salaries expense	$225,000
Advertising expense	146,500
Office salaries expense	120,800
Depreciation expense—office equipment	5,300
Telephone expense—selling	5,000
Telephone expense—administrative	1,900
Travel expense—selling	38,500
Office supplies expense	3,000
Miscellaneous administrative expense	4,200

i. Estimated other income and expense for October:

Interest revenue	$16,700
Interest expense	12,300

j. Estimated tax rate: 40%

Instructions

1. Prepare a sales budget for October.
2. Prepare a production budget for October.
3. Prepare a direct materials purchases budget for October.
4. Prepare a direct labor cost budget for October.
5. Prepare a factory overhead cost budget for October.

6. Prepare a cost of goods sold budget for October. Work in process at the beginning of October is estimated to be $28,500, and work in process at the end of October is estimated to be $34,200.
7. Prepare a selling and administrative expenses budget for October.
8. Prepare a budgeted income statement for October.

Problem 5–4A
Cash budget

Objective 5

SPREADSHEET

✓ 1. October deficiency, $41,000

The controller of Butler Boat Company instructs you to prepare a monthly cash budget for the next three months. You are presented with the following budget information:

	August	September	October
Sales	$590,000	$650,000	$750,000
Manufacturing costs	300,000	340,000	390,000
Selling and administrative expenses	150,000	170,000	200,000
Capital expenditures			120,000

The company expects to sell about 10% of its merchandise for cash. Of sales on account, 60% are expected to be collected in full in the month following the sale and the remainder the following month. Depreciation, insurance, and property tax expense represent $30,000 of the estimated monthly manufacturing costs. The annual insurance premium is paid in July, and the annual property taxes are paid in November. Of the remainder of the manufacturing costs, 80% are expected to be paid in the month in which they are incurred and the balance in the following month.

Current assets as of August 1 include cash of $55,000, marketable securities of $85,000, and accounts receivable of $594,000 ($442,000 from July sales and $152,000 from June sales). Current liabilities as of August 1 include a $100,000, 10%, 90-day note payable due October 20 and $60,000 of accounts payable incurred in July for manufacturing costs. All selling and administrative expenses are paid in cash in the period they are incurred. It is expected that $1,500 in dividends will be received in August. An estimated income tax payment of $42,000 will be made in September. Butler's regular quarterly dividend of $15,000 is expected to be declared in September and paid in October. Management desires to maintain a minimum cash balance of $45,000.

Instructions

1. Prepare a monthly cash budget and supporting schedules for August, September, and October.
2. ✏️▸ On the basis of the cash budget prepared in (1), what recommendation should be made to the controller?

Problem 5–5A
Budgeted income statement and balance sheet

Objectives 4, 5

✓ 1. Net income, $131,600

As a preliminary to requesting budget estimates of sales, costs, and expenses for the fiscal year beginning January 1, 2004, the following tentative trial balance as of December 31, 2003, is prepared by the Accounting Department of Little Suzie Cake Co.:

Cash	$ 85,000	
Accounts Receivable	104,700	
Finished Goods	74,800	
Work in Process	25,600	
Materials	46,700	
Prepaid Expenses	2,400	
Plant and Equipment	340,000	
Accumulated Depreciation—Plant and Equipment		$135,200
Accounts Payable		59,000
Common Stock, $10 par		200,000
Retained Earnings		285,000
	$679,200	$679,200

Factory output and sales for 2004 are expected to total 250,000 units of product, which are to be sold at $4.20 per unit. The quantities and costs of the inventories (lifo method) at December 31, 2004, are expected to remain unchanged from the balances at the beginning of the year.

Budget estimates of manufacturing costs and operating expenses for the year are summarized as follows:

	Estimated Costs and Expenses	
	Fixed (Total for Year)	Variable (Per Unit Sold)
Cost of goods manufactured and sold:		
Direct materials	—	$1.20
Direct labor	—	0.45
Factory overhead:		
Depreciation of plant and equipment	$14,000	—
Other factory overhead	8,000	0.28
Selling expenses:		
Sales salaries and commissions	45,000	0.30
Advertising	60,000	—
Miscellaneous selling expense	4,300	0.10
Administrative expenses:		
Office and officers salaries	65,100	0.15
Supplies	4,000	0.05
Miscellaneous administrative expense	3,000	0.07

Balances of accounts receivable, prepaid expenses, and accounts payable at the end of the year are not expected to differ significantly from the beginning balances. Federal income tax of $65,000 on 2004 taxable income will be paid during 2004. Regular quarterly cash dividends of $0.50 a share are expected to be declared and paid in March, June, September, and December. It is anticipated that fixed assets will be purchased for $50,000 cash in May.

Instructions

1. Prepare a budgeted income statement for 2004.
2. Prepare a budgeted balance sheet as of December 31, 2004, with supporting calculations.

PROBLEMS SERIES B

Problem 5–1B
Forecast sales volume and sales budget

Objective 4

✓ 3. Total revenue from sales, $29,000,000

HomeGuard Security Devices Inc. prepared the following sales budget for the current year:

HomeGuard Security Devices Inc.
Sales Budget
For the Year Ending December 31, 2003

Product and Area	Unit Sales Volume	Unit Selling Price	Total Sales
Home Alert System:			
United States	18,500	$260	$ 4,810,000
Europe	5,400	260	1,404,000
Asia	3,700	260	962,000
Total	27,600		$ 7,176,000
Business Alert System:			
United States	10,500	$900	$ 9,450,000
Europe	8,600	900	7,740,000
Asia	4,200	900	3,780,000
Total	23,300		$20,970,000
Total revenue from sales			$28,146,000

At the end of December 2003, the following unit sales data were reported for the year:

	Unit Sales	
	Home Alert System	Business Alert System
United States	19,055	10,752
Europe	5,022	8,987
Asia	3,885	4,011

For the year ending December 31, 2004, unit sales are expected to follow the patterns established during the year ending December 31, 2003. The unit selling price for the Home Alert System is expected to increase to $280, and the unit selling price for the Business Alert System is expected to be reduced to $870, effective January 1, 2004.

Instructions

1. Compute the increase or decrease of actual unit sales for the year ended December 31, 2003, over budget. Place your answers in a columnar table with the following format:

	Unit Sales, Year Ended 2003		Increase (Decrease) Actual Over Budget	
	Budget	Actual Sales	Amount	Percent
Home Alert System:				
United States				
Europe				
Asia				
Business Alert System:				
United States				
Europe				
Asia				

2. Assuming that the trend of sales indicated in (1) is to continue in 2004, compute the unit sales volume to be used for preparing the sales budget for the year ending December 31, 2004. Place your answers in a columnar table with the following format. Round budgeted units to the nearest thousand.

	2003 Actual Units	Percentage Increase (Decrease)	2004 Budgeted Units
Home Alert System:			
United States			
Europe			
Asia			
Business Alert System:			
United States			
Europe			
Asia			

3. Prepare a sales budget for the year ending December 31, 2004.

Problem 5–2B

Sales, production, direct materials, and direct labor budgets

Objective 4

The budget director of Dalen Furniture Company requests estimates of sales, production, and other operating data from the various administrative units every month. Selected information concerning sales and production for July 2003 is summarized as follows:

SPREADSHEET

✓ 3. Total direct materials
purchases, $3,213,028

a.   Estimated sales of King and Prince chairs for July by sales territory:

Northern Domestic:
King . . . .   7,300 units at $450 per unit
Prince . . . .   5,250 units at $310 per unit
Southern Domestic:
King . . . .   6,400 units at $430 per unit
Prince . . . .   5,100 units at $300 per unit
International:
King . . . .   1,500 units at $500 per unit
Prince . . . .   900 units at $350 per unit

b.   Estimated inventories at July 1:

Direct materials:
Fabric . . . .   4,300 sq. yds.
Wood . . . .   6,300 lineal ft.
Filler . . . .   2,500 cu. ft.
Springs . . . .   7,500 units
Finished products:
King . . . .   840 units
Prince . . . .   280 units

c.   Desired inventories at July 31:

Direct materials:
Fabric . . . .   4,500 sq. yds.
Wood . . . .   5,700 lineal ft.
Filler . . . .   2,700 cu. ft.
Springs . . . .   7,000 units
Finished products:
King . . . .   700 units
Prince . . . .   300 units

d.   Direct materials used in production:

In manufacture of King:
Fabric . . . .   4 sq. yds. per unit of product
Wood . . . .   30 lineal ft. per unit of product
Filler . . . .   3.5 cu. ft. per unit of product
Springs . . . .   12 units per unit of product
In manufacture of Prince:
Fabric . . . .   3.2 sq. yds. per unit of product
Wood . . . .   20 lineal ft. per unit of product
Filler . . . .   3.0 cu. ft. per unit of product
Springs . . . .   10 units per unit of product

e.   Anticipated purchase price for direct materials:

Fabric . . . . $7.00 per square yard
Wood . . . .   2.50 per lineal foot
Filler . . . .   3.00 per cubic foot
Springs . . . .   2.00 per unit

f.   Direct labor requirements:

King:
Framing Department . . . .   2.0 hours at $10 per hour
Cutting Department . . . .   0.5 hour at $12 per hour
Upholstery Department . . . .   2.5 hours at $15 per hour
Prince:
Framing Department . . . .   1.5 hours at $10 per hour
Cutting Department . . . .   0.4 hour at $12 per hour
Upholstery Department . . . .   1.8 hours at $15 per hour

Instructions

1. Prepare a sales budget for July.
2. Prepare a production budget for July.
3. Prepare a direct materials purchases budget for July.
4. Prepare a direct labor cost budget for July.

Problem 5–3B
Budgeted income statement and supporting budgets

Objective 4

✔ 4. Total direct labor cost in Assembly Dept., $510,240

The budget director of Safety Sports Inc., with the assistance of the controller, treasurer, production manager, and sales manager, has gathered the following data for use in developing the budgeted income statement for August 2003:

a. Estimated sales for August:

Batting helmet	25,800 units at $40 per unit
Football helmet	54,100 units at $75 per unit

b. Estimated inventories at August 1:

Direct materials:		Finished products:	
Plastic	9,500 lbs.	Batting helmet	2,450 units at $21 per unit
Foam lining	4,700 lbs.	Football helmet ...	3,900 units at $40 per unit

c. Desired inventories at August 31:

Direct materials:		Finished products:	
Plastic	11,400 lbs.	Batting helmet	2,400 units at $21 per unit
Foam lining	4,500 lbs.	Football helmet ...	3,500 units at $40 per unit

d. Direct materials used in production:

In manufacture of batting helmet:	
Plastic	1.40 lbs. per unit of product
Foam lining	0.60 lb. per unit of product
In manufacture of football helmet:	
Plastic	3.20 lbs. per unit of product
Foam lining	1.20 lbs. per unit of product

e. Anticipated cost of purchases and beginning and ending inventory of direct materials:

Plastic	$6.50 per lb.
Foam lining	$3.00 per lb.

f. Direct labor requirements:

Batting helmet:	
Molding Department	0.16 hour at $14 per hour
Assembly Department	0.40 hour at $12 per hour
Football helmet:	
Molding Department	0.25 hour at $14 per hour
Assembly Department	0.60 hour at $12 per hour

g. Estimated factory overhead costs for August:

Indirect factory wages	$250,000
Depreciation of plant and equipment	63,000
Power and light	24,000
Insurance and property tax	9,700

h. Estimated operating expenses for August:

Sales salaries expense	$505,700
Advertising expense	350,800
Office salaries expense	145,800

(continued)

Depreciation expense—office equipment	$ 6,200
Telephone expense—selling	4,700
Telephone expense—administrative	900
Travel expense—selling	42,100
Office supplies expense	4,000
Miscellaneous administrative expense	5,000

i. Estimated other income and expense for August:

Interest revenue	$12,500
Interest expense	15,700

j. Estimated tax rate: 40%

Instructions

1. Prepare a sales budget for August.
2. Prepare a production budget for August.
3. Prepare a direct materials purchases budget for August.
4. Prepare a direct labor cost budget for August.
5. Prepare a factory overhead cost budget for August.
6. Prepare a cost of goods sold budget for August. Work in process at the beginning of August is estimated to be $43,600, and work in process at the end of August is estimated to be $37,800.
7. Prepare a selling and administrative expenses budget for August.
8. Prepare a budgeted income statement for August.

Problem 5–4B

Cash budget

Objective 5

SPREADSHEET

✓ 1. June deficiency, $8,700

The controller of Lightning Blade N'Skate Company instructs you to prepare a monthly cash budget for the next three months. You are presented with the following budget information:

	April	May	June
Sales	$300,000	$360,000	$380,000
Manufacturing costs	150,000	180,000	200,000
Selling and administrative expenses	100,000	120,000	125,000
Capital expenditures	—	—	90,000

The company expects to sell about 10% of its merchandise for cash. Of sales on account, 70% are expected to be collected in full in the month following the sale and the remainder the following month. Depreciation, insurance, and property tax expense represent $20,000 of the estimated monthly manufacturing costs. The annual insurance premium is paid in July, and the annual property taxes are paid in November. Of the remainder of the manufacturing costs, 80% are expected to be paid in the month in which they are incurred and the balance in the following month.

Current assets as of April 1 include cash of $40,000, marketable securities of $65,000, and accounts receivable of $370,000 ($280,000 from March sales and $90,000 from February sales). Current liabilities as of April 1 include a $50,000, 12%, 90-day note payable due June 20 and $25,000 of accounts payable incurred in March for manufacturing costs. All selling and administrative expenses are paid in cash in the period they are incurred. It is expected that $3,000 in dividends will be received in April. An estimated income tax payment of $32,000 will be made in May. Lightning's regular quarterly dividend of $10,000 is expected to be declared in May and paid in June. Management desires to maintain a minimum cash balance of $35,000.

Instructions

1. Prepare a monthly cash budget and supporting schedules for April, May, and June.
2. ▬▬► On the basis of the cash budget prepared in (1), what recommendation should be made to the controller?

Problem 5–5B

Budgeted income statement and balance sheet

Objectives 4, 5

✓ 1. Net income, $746,200

As a preliminary to requesting budget estimates of sales, costs, and expenses for the fiscal year beginning January 1, 2004, the following tentative trial balance as of December 31, 2003, is prepared by the Accounting Department of Cody Camera Company:

Cash	$ 122,500	
Accounts Receivable	246,700	
Finished Goods	157,800	
Work in Process	37,800	
Materials	57,800	
Prepaid Expenses	4,500	
Plant and Equipment	620,000	
Accumulated Depreciation—Plant and Equipment		$ 267,000
Accounts Payable		184,500
Common Stock, $15 par		450,000
Retained Earnings		345,600
	$1,247,100	$1,247,100

Factory output and sales for 2004 are expected to total 30,000 units of product, which are to be sold at $120 per unit. The quantities and costs of the inventories (lifo method) at December 31, 2004, are expected to remain unchanged from the balances at the beginning of the year.

Budget estimates of manufacturing costs and operating expenses for the year are summarized as follows:

	Estimated Costs and Expenses	
	Fixed **(Total for Year)**	**Variable** **(Per Unit Sold)**
Cost of goods manufactured and sold:		
Direct materials	—	$35.00
Direct labor	—	12.50
Factory overhead:		
Depreciation of plant and equipment	$ 55,000	—
Other factory overhead	20,000	5.20
Selling expenses:		
Sales salaries and commissions	84,500	10.80
Advertising	105,800	—
Miscellaneous selling expense	11,500	2.50
Administrative expenses:		
Office and officers salaries	84,500	6.40
Supplies	4,700	1.50
Miscellaneous administrative expense	2,000	1.10

Balances of accounts receivable, prepaid expenses, and accounts payable at the end of the year are not expected to differ significantly from the beginning balances. Federal income tax of $235,800 on 2004 taxable income will be paid during 2004. Regular quarterly cash dividends of $2.50 a share are expected to be declared and paid in March, June, September, and December. It is anticipated that fixed assets will be purchased for $180,000 cash in May.

Instructions

1. Prepare a budgeted income statement for 2004.
2. Prepare a budgeted balance sheet as of December 31, 2004, with supporting calculations.

SPECIAL ACTIVITIES

Activity 5–1
Apex Software Company
Ethics and professional conduct in business

The director of marketing for Apex Software Company, Connie Keller, had the following discussion with the company controller, Josh Johnson, on July 26 of the current year:

Connie: Josh, it looks like I'm going to spend much less than indicated on my July budget.

Josh: I'm glad to hear it.

Connie: Well, I'm not so sure it's good news. I'm concerned that the president will see that I'm under budget and reduce my budget in the future. The only reason that I look good is that we've delayed an advertising campaign. Once the campaign hits in September, I'm sure my actual expenditures will go up. You see, we are also having our sales convention in September. Having the advertising campaign and the convention at the same time is going to kill my September numbers.

Josh: I don't think that's anything to worry about. We all expect some variation in actual spending month to month. What's really important is staying within the budgeted targets for the year. Does that look as if it's going to be a problem?

Connie: I don't think so, but just the same, I'd like to be on the safe side.

Josh: What do you mean?

Connie: Well, this is what I'd like to do. I want to pay the convention-related costs in advance this month. I'll pay the hotel for room and convention space and purchase the airline tickets in advance. In this way, I can charge all these expenditures to July's budget. This would cause my actual expenses to come close to budget for July. Moreover, when the big advertising campaign hits in September, I won't have to worry about expenditures for the convention on my September budget as well. The convention costs will already be paid. Thus, my September expenses should be pretty close to budget.

Josh: I can't tell you when to make your convention purchases, but I'm not too sure that it should be expensed on July's budget.

Connie: What's the problem? It looks like "no harm, no foul" to me. I can't see that there's anything wrong with this—it's just smart management.

How should Josh Johnson respond to Connie Keller's request to expense the advanced payments for convention-related costs against July's budget?

Activity 5–2
Elgin Sweeper Company
Evaluating budgeting systems

Elgin Sweeper Company began an overhaul of its planning and control system. This overhaul is described in the following excerpt from an article in *Management Accounting*:

> *How could we bring responsibility for and management of costs to the individual department managers? For two years before we began our efforts, the annual budget had been prepared substantially by the accounting department with little ownership for results felt by persons outside top management.*
>
> *Our first step was to modify the budget responsibility reports to reflect only those costs controllable by the department manager.... The next step was the actual budget preparation.... [Expense] accounts did not segregate variable and fixed costs. When volume-adjusted numbers were required for either budget preparation or budget-to-actual comparison, we merely would use an "executive judgment" percentage to adjust the appropriate expenses. Needless to say, this system resulted in some unusual variations, which sometimes required "innovative" explanations.*

Source: J. P. Callan, W. N. Tredup, and R. S. Wisinger, "Elgin Sweeper Company's Journey Toward Cost Management," *Management Accounting*, July 1991, pp. 24–27.

What are the behavioral ramifications of including expenses within a responsibility center for which a manager has no control? Did Elgin previously use static budgeting or flexible budgeting? What type of budgeting will Elgin use in the future?

Activity 5–3
Acorn Bancorp
Service company static decision making

A bank manager of Acorn Bancorp uses the managerial accounting system to track the costs of operating the various departments within the bank. The departments include Cash Management, Trust Commercial Loans, Mortgage Loans, Operations, Credit Card, and Branch Services. The budget and actual results for the Operations Department are as follows:

Resources	Budget	Actual
Salaries	$150,000	$150,000
Benefits	30,000	30,000
Supplies	45,000	42,000
Travel	20,000	30,000
Training	25,000	30,000
Overtime	25,000	20,000
Total	$295,000	$302,000
Excess of actual over budget	$ 7,000	

a.   ✏️ What information is provided by the budget? Specifically, what questions can the bank manager ask of the Operations Department manager?

b.   ✏️ What information does the budget fail to provide? Specifically, could the budget information be presented differently to provide even more insight for the bank manager?

Activity 5–4
Webvan Group, Inc.
Objectives of the master budget

Webvan is an Internet company that prepares and delivers meals, groceries, and other items to customers in a particular metropolitan area. Webvan began in the San Francisco area and has expanded to other cities, including Chicago and Atlanta. As stated by one of its executives:

Webvan's chef-prepared meals are the ultimate time saver for families and professionals on the go. We have our own chefs on-site who develop the recipes and prepare the meals. Everyday, our team will be busy concocting a broad selection of delicious and nutritious meals for the home or office. Customers simply point and click, and these high-quality prepared meals are conveniently delivered with a Webvan order.

After making a selection, the meal is delivered to the customer's door within 30 minutes, using a fleet of vans and $14-per-hour drivers.

✏️ Go to **Webvan.com** and learn about Webvan's business and operations. How would a master budget support planning, directing, and control for Webvan Group?

Activity 5–5
SRC
Behavioral aspects of financial goals

One aspect of motivating line employees is to provide them financial improvement targets. The following excerpt describes this approach:

For managers and line workers to be similarly focused on bottom-line issues, it's critical that all employees are first well-trained in understanding the financials. . . . While training is important, what makes Bottom Line Powered Management so powerful is that financial and performance data are presented to employees to be used as direct, practical feedback for operations. At SRC, for example, financial and performance data become critical to individual performance when the profit-and-loss statement is broken down for all operations—that is, for all employee teams and work groups. Each employee team then knows if it is on target and can make the appropriate corrections. If sales to a particular customer are off track, that is immediately investigated. If the team's overhead is above the projection, that is attacked. Moreover, this information is provided weekly, letting the employees quickly pounce on any problem. . . . To ensure that financial data are actually used, [they are given] numbers the employees can understand and influence.

Source: Willard I. Zangwill, "Focusing All Eyes on the Bottom Line," *The Wall Street Journal*, March 21, 1994, p. A12.

✏️ Identify the critical characteristics of the Bottom Line Powered Management (BLPM) approach and explain how they appear to affect human behavior.

Activity 5–6
Ben Knight
Objectives of budgeting

At the beginning of the year, Ben Knight decided to prepare a cash budget for the year, based upon anticipated cash receipts and payments. The estimates in the budget represent a "best guess." The budget is as follows:

Expected annual cash receipts:	
Salary from part-time job	$10,000
Salary from summer job	4,000
Total receipts	$14,000
Expected annual cash payments:	
Tuition	$ 4,500
Books	400
Rent	3,500
Food	2,500
Utilities	800
Entertainment	4,000
Total payments	15,700
Net change in cash	$ (1,700)

1. ✏️ What does this budget suggest? In what ways is this information useful to Ben?
2. a. ✏️ Some items in the budget are more certain than are others. Which items are the most certain? Which items are the most uncertain? What are the implications of these different levels of certainty to Ben's planning?
   b. ✏️ Some payment items are more controllable than others. Assuming that Ben plans to go to school, classify the items as controllable, partially controllable, or not controllable. What are the implications of controllable items to planning?
3. ✏️ What actions could Ben take in order to avoid having the anticipated shortfall of $1,700 at the end of the year?
4. ✏️ What does this budget fail to consider, and what are the implications of these omissions to Ben's planning?

Activity 5–7
Into the Real World
Budget for a state government

In a group, find the home page of the state in which you presently live. The state's home page, if it has one, will be in the form: **www.state.*stateabbreviation*.us/**. At the home page site, search for annual budget information. If you are unable to find the budget of your state, then go to the state of Ohio's budget page at **www.state.oh.us/obm/** to complete this activity.

1. What are the budgeted sources of revenue and their percentage breakdown?
2. What are the major categories of budgeted expenditures (or appropriations) and their percentage breakdown?
3. Is the projected budget in balance?

ANSWERS TO SELF-EXAMINATION QUESTIONS

Matching
1. I
2. D
3. N
4. A
5. F
6. B
7. E
8. J
9. M
10. G
11. C
12. K

Multiple Choice

1. **B** Individuals can be discouraged with budgets that appear too tight or unobtainable. Flexible budgeting (answer C) provides a series of budgets for varying rates of activity and thereby builds into the budgeting system the effect of fluctuations in the level of activity.

Budgetary slack (answer A) comes from a loose budget, not a tight budget. A "spend it or lose it" mentality (answer D) is often associated with loose budgets.

2. **A** The first step of the budget process is to develop a plan. Once plans are established, management may

direct actions (answer B). The results of actions can be controlled (answer C) by comparing them to the plan. This feedback (answer D) can be used by management to change plans or redirect actions.

3. **B** Administrative departments (answer B), such as Purchasing or Human Resources, will often use static budgeting. Production departments (answer A) frequently use flexible budgets. Responsibility centers (answer C) can use either static or flexible budgeting. Capital expenditure budgets are used to plan capital projects (answer D).

4. **B** The total production indicated in the production budget is 257,500 units (answer B), which is computed as follows:

Sales	250,000 units
Plus desired ending inventory	30,000 units
Total	280,000 units
Less estimated beginning inventory	22,500 units
Total production	257,500 units

5. **C** Dixon expects to collect 70% of April sales ($560,000) plus 30% of the March sales ($195,000) in April, for a total of $755,000 (answer C). Answer A is 100% of April sales. Answer B is 70% of April sales. Answer D adds 70% of both March and April sales.

Performance Evaluation Using Variances from Standard Costs

M6

W hen you play a sport, you are evaluated with respect to how well you perform compared to a standard or to a competitor. In bowling, for example, your score is compared to a perfect score of 300 or to the score of your competitors. In this class, you are compared to performance standards. These standards are often described in terms of letter grades, which provide a measure of how well you achieved the class objectives. On your job, you are also evaluated according to performance standards.

Just as your class performance is evaluated, managers are evaluated according to goals and plans. Performance is often measured as the difference between actual results and planned results. In this chapter, we will discuss and illustrate the ways in which business performance is evaluated.

Standards

objective 1

Describe the types of standards and how they are established for businesses.

What are standards? **Standards** are performance goals. Service, merchandising, and manufacturing businesses may all use standards to evaluate and control operations. For example, long-haul drivers for United Parcel Service are expected to drive a standard distance per day. Salespersons for The Limited are expected to meet sales standards.

Manufacturers normally use standard costs for each of the three manufacturing costs: direct materials, direct labor, and factory overhead. Accounting systems that use standards for these costs are called **standard cost systems**. These systems enable management to determine how much a product should cost (**standard cost**), how much it does cost (actual cost), and the causes of any difference (**cost variances**). When actual costs are compared with standard costs, only the exceptions or variances are reported for cost control. This reporting by the *principle of exceptions* allows management to focus on correcting the variances. Thus, using standard costs assists management in controlling costs and in motivating employees to focus on costs.

Standard cost systems are commonly used with job order and process systems. One survey of manufacturing firms reported that 87% of the firms use some form of standard costing.[1] Automated manufacturing operations may also integrate standard cost data with the computerized system that directs operations. Such systems detect and report variances automatically and make adjustments to operations in progress.

Setting Standards

Setting standards is both an art and a science. The standard-setting process normally requires the joint efforts of accountants, engineers, and other management personnel. The accountant plays an essential role by expressing in dollars and cents the results of judgments and studies. Engineers contribute to the standard-setting process by identifying the materials, labor, and machine requirements needed to produce the product. For example, engineers determine the direct materials requirements by studying the materials specifications for products and estimating normal spoilage in production. Time and motion studies may be used to determine the length of time required for each manufacturing operation. Engineering studies may also be used to determine standards for factory overhead, such as the amount of power needed to operate machinery.

[1] B. R. Gaumnitz and F. P. Kollaritsch, "Manufacturing Variances: Current Trends and Practice," *Journal of Cost Management*, Spring 1991, pp. 58–63.

Setting standards often begins with analyzing past operations. However, standards are not just an extension of past costs, and caution must be used in relying on past cost data. For example, inefficiencies may be contained within past costs. In addition, changes in technology, machinery, or production methods may make past costs irrelevant for future operations.

Types of Standards

Standards imply an acceptable level of production efficiency. One of the major objectives in setting standards is to motivate workers to achieve efficient operations.

Like the budgets we discussed earlier, tight, unrealistic standards may have a negative impact on performance. This is because workers may become frustrated with an inability to meet the standards and may give up trying to do their best. Such standards can be achieved only under perfect operating conditions, such as no idle time, no machine breakdowns, and no materials spoilage. These standards are called **theoretical standards** or **ideal standards**. Although ideal standards are not widely used, a few firms use ideal standards to motivate changes and improvement. Such an approach is termed "Kaizen costing." Kaizen is a Japanese term meaning "continuous improvement."

Standards that are too loose might not motivate employees to perform at their best. This is because the standard level of performance can be reached too easily. As a result, operating performance may be lower than what could be achieved.

Most companies use **currently attainable standards** (sometimes called **normal standards**). These standards can be attained with reasonable effort. Such standards allow for normal production difficulties and mistakes, such as materials spoilage and machine breakdowns. When reasonable standards are used, employees become more focused on cost and are more likely to put forth their best efforts.

An example from the game of golf illustrates the distinction between ideal and normal standards. In golf, "par" is an *ideal* standard for most players. Each player's **USGA** (United States Golf Association) handicap is the player's *normal* standard. The motivation of average players is to beat their handicaps because they may view beating par as unrealistic. Normal and ideal standards are illustrated as follows:

Mohawk Forest Products had a normal standard cost for a premium grade paper of $2,900 per ton, while the ideal cost was $1,342 per ton. The company used the ideal standard to motivate cost improvement. The resulting improvements allowed the company to reduce the normal standard cost to $1,738 per ton.

Currently attainable (personal best)

Ideal (world record)

Reviewing and Revising Standards

Standard costs should be continuously reviewed and should be revised when they no longer reflect operating conditions. Inaccurate standards may distort management decision making and may weaken management's ability to plan and control operations.

Standards should not be revised, however, just because they differ from actual costs. They should be revised only when they no longer reflect the operating conditions that they were intended to measure. For example, the direct labor standard would not be revised simply because workers were unable to meet properly determined standards. On the other hand, standards should be revised when prices, product designs, labor rates, or manufacturing methods change. For example, when aluminum beverage cans were redesigned to taper slightly at the top of the can, manufacturers reduced the standard amount of aluminum per can because less aluminum was required for the top piece of the tapered can.

Support and Criticism of Standards

Standards are used to value inventory and to plan and control costs. As evidence of the increasing importance of standards, one survey indicates that companies are now using standards to assess performance at lower levels of the organization, for shorter accounting periods, and for an increasing number of costs.[2]

Using standards for performance evaluation has been criticized by some. For example, critics assert that standards limit improvement of operations by discouraging improvement beyond the standard. Regardless of this criticism, standards are widely used. One survey reports that managers strongly support standard cost systems and that they regard standards as critical for running large businesses efficiently.[3]

Budgetary Performance Evaluation

objective 2

Explain and illustrate how standards are used in budgeting.

As we discussed in the previous chapter, the master budget assists a company in planning, directing, and controlling performance. In the remainder of this chapter, we will discuss using the master budget for control purposes. The control function, or budgetary performance evaluation, compares the actual performance against the budget.

We illustrate budget performance evaluation using Western Rider Inc., a manufacturer of blue jeans. Western Rider Inc. uses standard manufacturing costs in its budgets. The standards for direct materials, direct labor, and factory overhead are separated into two components: (1) a price standard and (2) a quantity standard. Multiplying these two elements together yields the standard cost per unit for a given manufacturing cost category, as shown for style XL jeans in Exhibit 1.

Exhibit 1 Standard Cost for XL Jeans

Manufacturing Costs	Standard Price	×	Standard Quantity per Pair	=	Standard Cost per Pair of XL Jeans
Direct materials	$5.00 per square yard		1.5 square yards		$ 7.50
Direct labor	$9.00 per hour		0.80 hour per pair		7.20
Factory overhead	$6.00 per hour		0.80 hour per pair		4.80
Total standard cost per pair					$19.50

[2] *Ibid.*
[3] C. Graham, D. Lydall, and A. G. Puxty, "Cost Control: The Manager's Perspective," *Management Accounting*, UK, October 1992, pp. 26–27.

The standard price and quantity are separated because the means of controlling them are normally different. For example, the direct materials price per square yard is controlled by the Purchasing Department, and the direct materials quantity per pair is controlled by the Production Department.

As we illustrated in the previous chapter, the budgeted costs at planned volumes are included in the master budget at the beginning of the period. The standard amounts budgeted for materials purchases, direct labor, and factory overhead are determined by multiplying the standard costs per unit by the *planned* level of production. At the end of the month, the standard costs per unit are multiplied by the *actual* production and compared to the actual costs. To illustrate, assume that Western Rider produced and sold 5,000 pairs of XL jeans. It incurred direct materials costs of $40,150, direct labor costs of $38,500, and factory overhead costs of $22,400. The **budget performance report** shown in Exhibit 2 summarizes the actual costs, the standard amounts for the actual level of production achieved, and the differences between the two amounts. These differences are called **cost variances**. A *favorable* cost variance occurs when the actual cost is less than the standard cost (at actual volumes). An *unfavorable* variance occurs when the actual cost exceeds the standard cost (at actual volumes).

Based on the information in the budget performance report, management can investigate major differences and take corrective action. In Exhibit 2, for example, the direct materials cost variance is an unfavorable $2,650. There are two possible explanations for this variance: (1) the amount of blue denim used per pair of blue jeans was different than expected, and/or (2) the purchase price of blue denim was different than expected. In the

What is the amount of standard cost per unit of a product that has 3 standard pounds of material at a standard cost of $12 per pound, 4.5 standard direct labor hours at a standard cost of $11 per direct labor hour, and standard factory overhead of $7 per direct labor hour?

$117 [($12 × 3 pounds) + ($11 × 4.5 hours) + ($7 × 4.5 hours)]

Actual cost < Standard cost at actual volumes: Favorable cost variance

Actual cost > Standard cost at actual volumes: Unfavorable cost variance

Exhibit 2 Budget Performance Report

Western Rider Inc.
Budget Performance Report
For the Month Ended June 30, 2003

Manufacturing Costs	Actual Costs	Standard Cost at Actual Volume (5,000 pairs of XL Jeans)*	Cost Variance— (Favorable) Unfavorable
Direct materials	$ 40,150	$37,500	$2,650
Direct labor	38,500	36,000	2,500
Factory overhead	22,400	24,000	(1,600)
Total manufacturing costs	$101,050	$97,500	$3,550

*5,000 pairs × $7.50 per pair = $37,500
5,000 pairs × $7.20 per pair = $36,000
5,000 pairs × $4.80 per pair = $24,000

next sections, we will illustrate how to separate the price and quantity variances for direct materials, the rate and time variances for direct labor, and the controllable and volume variances for factory overhead.

The relationship of these variances to the total manufacturing cost variance is shown below.

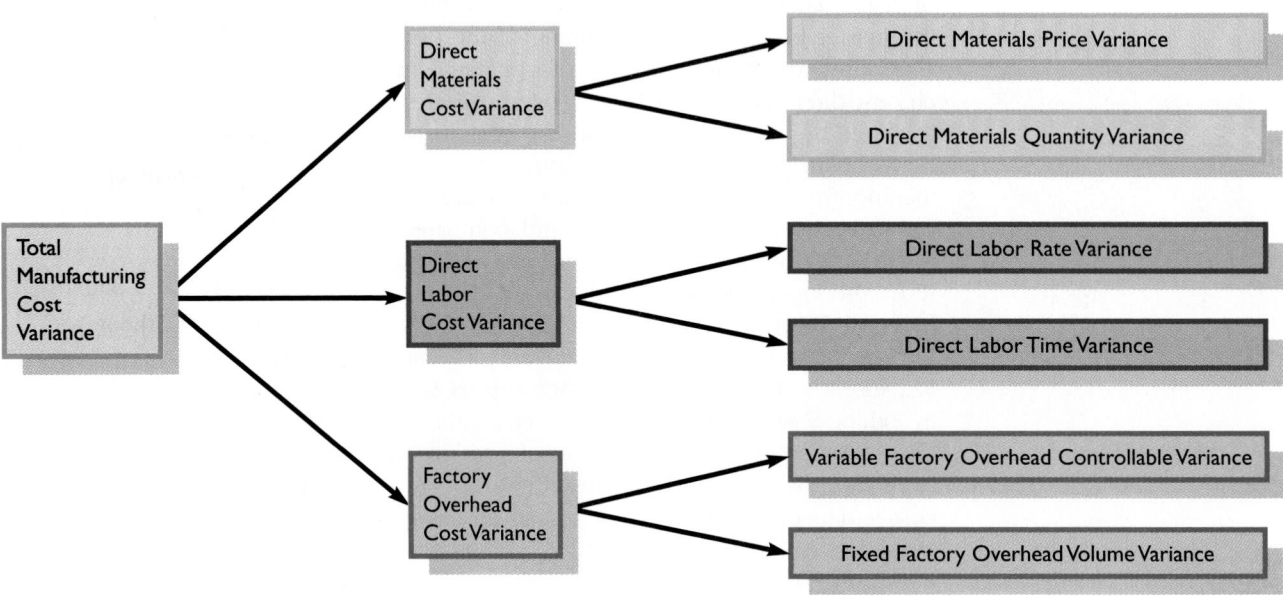

Direct Materials Variances

What caused Western Rider Inc.'s unfavorable materials variance of $2,650? Recall that the direct materials standards from Exhibit 1 are as follows:

Price standard: $5.00 per square yard
Quantity standard: 1.5 square yards per pair of XL jeans

To determine the number of standard square yards of denim budgeted, multiply the actual production for June 2003 (5,000 pairs) by the quantity standard (1.5 square yards per pair). Then multiply the standard square yards by the standard price per square yard ($5.00) to determine the *standard* budgeted cost at the actual volume. The calculation is shown as follows:

Standard square yards per pair of jeans	1.5 sq. yards
Actual units produced	× 5,000 pairs of jeans
Standard square yards of denim budgeted for actual production	7,500 sq. yards
Standard price per square yard	× $5.00
Standard direct materials cost at actual production (same as Exhibit 2)	$37,500

This calculation assumes that there is no change in the beginning and ending materials inventories. Thus, the amount of materials budgeted for production equals the amount purchased.

Assume that the *actual* total cost for denim used during June 2003 was as follows:

Actual quantity of denim used in production	7,300 sq. yards
Actual price per square yard	× $5.50
Total actual direct materials cost (same as Exhibit 2)	$40,150

The total unfavorable cost variance of $2,650 ($40,150 − $37,500) results from an excess price per square yard of $0.50 and using 200 fewer square yards of denim. These two reasons can be reported as two separate variances, as shown in the next sections.

Direct Materials Price Variance

The **direct materials price variance** is the difference between the actual price per unit ($5.50) and the standard price per unit ($5.00), multiplied by the actual quantity used (7,300 square yards). If the actual price per unit exceeds the standard price per unit, the variance is unfavorable, as shown for Western Rider Inc. If the actual price per unit is less than the standard price per unit, the variance is favorable. The calculation for Western Rider Inc. is as follows:

Price variance:

Actual price per unit	$5.50 per square yard
Standard price per unit	5.00 per square yard
Price variance—unfavorable	$0.50 per square yard × actual qty., 7,300 sq. yds. = $3,650 U

Direct Materials Quantity Variance

The **direct materials quantity variance** is the difference between the actual quantity used (7,300 square yards) and the standard quantity at actual production (7,500 square yards), multiplied by the standard price per unit ($5.00). If the actual quantity of materials used exceeds the standard quantity budgeted, the variance is unfavorable. If the actual quantity of materials used is less than the standard quantity, the variance is favorable, as shown for Western Rider Inc.:

Quantity variance:

Actual quantity	7,300 square yards
Standard quantity at actual production	7,500
Quantity variance—favorable	(200) square yards × standard price, $5.00 = ($1,000) F

Direct Materials Variance Relationships

The direct materials variances can be illustrated by making the three calculations shown in Exhibit 3.

Reporting Direct Materials Variances

The direct materials quantity variance should be reported to the proper operating management level for corrective action. For example, an unfavorable quantity variance might have been caused by malfunctioning equipment that has not been properly maintained or operated. However, unfavorable materials quantity variances are not always caused by operating departments. For example, the excess materials usage may be caused by purchasing inferior raw materials. In this case, the Purchasing Department should be held responsible for the variance.

Most restaurants use standards to control the amount of food served to customers. For example, Darden Restaurants Inc., the operator of the Red Lobster chain, establishes standards for the number of shrimp, scallops, or clams on a seafood plate. In the same way, Keystone Foods, Inc., a major food supplier to McDonald's, uses standards to carefully control the size and weight of chicken nuggets.

A product requires 6 standard pounds per unit. The standard price is $4.50 per pound. If 3,000 units required 18,500 pounds, which were purchased at $4.35 per pound, what is the direct materials (1) price variance and (2) quantity variance?

---

(1) $2,775 favorable [($4.35 − $4.50) × 18,500 lbs.]; (2) $2,250 unfavorable [(18,500 lbs. − 18,000 lbs.) × $4.50]

Exhibit 3 Direct Materials
Variance Relationships

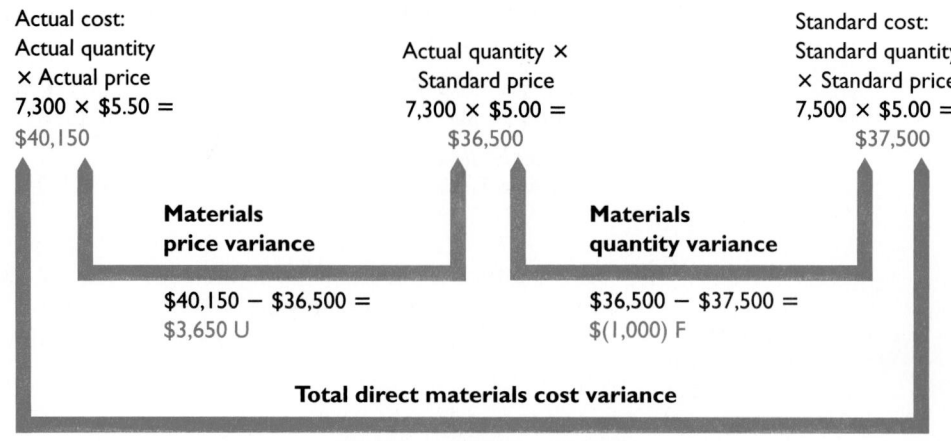

Actual cost: Actual quantity × Actual price 7,300 × $5.50 = $40,150	Actual quantity × Standard price 7,300 × $5.00 = $36,500	Standard cost: Standard quantity × Standard price 7,500 × $5.00 = $37,500

Materials
price variance

$40,150 − $36,500 =
$3,650 U

Materials
quantity variance

$36,500 − $37,500 =
$(1,000) F

Total direct materials cost variance

$40,150 − $37,500 = $2,650 U

The materials price variance should normally be reported to the Purchasing Department, which may or may not be able to control this variance. If materials of the same quality could have been purchased from another supplier at the standard price, the variance was controllable. On the other hand, if the variance resulted from a marketwide price increase, the variance may not be controllable.

Direct Labor Variances

objective 4

Calculate and interpret direct labor rate and time variances.

Western Rider Inc.'s direct labor cost variance can also be separated into two parts. Recall that the direct labor standards from Exhibit 1 are as follows:

Rate standard: $9.00 per hour
Time standard: 0.80 hour per pair of XL jeans

The actual production (5,000 pairs) is multiplied by the time standard (0.80 hour per pair) to determine the number of standard direct labor hours budgeted. The standard direct labor hours are then multiplied by the standard rate per hour ($9.00) to determine the *standard* direct labor cost at actual volumes. These calculations are shown below.

Standard direct labor hours per pair of XL jeans	0.80 direct labor hours
Actual units produced	× 5,000 pairs of jeans
Standard direct labor hours budgeted for actual production	4,000 direct labor hours
Standard rate per direct labor hour	× $9.00
Standard direct labor cost at actual production (same as Exhibit 2)	$36,000

Assume that the *actual* total cost for direct labor during June 2003 was as follows:

Actual direct labor hours used in production	3,850 direct labor hours
Actual rate per direct labor hour	× $10.00
Total actual direct labor cost (same as Exhibit 2)	$ 38,500

The total unfavorable cost variance $2,500 ($38,500 − $36,000) results from an excess rate of $1.00 per direct labor hour and using 150 fewer direct labor hours. These two reasons can be reported as two separate variances, as we discuss next.

Direct Labor Rate Variance

The **direct labor rate variance** is the difference between the actual rate per hour ($10.00) and the standard rate per hour ($9.00), multiplied by the actual hours worked (3,850 hours). If the actual rate per hour is less than the standard rate per hour, the variance is favorable. If the actual rate per hour exceeds the standard rate per hour, the variance is unfavorable, as shown below for Western Rider Inc.

Rate variance:

Actual rate	$10.00 per hour
Standard rate	9.00
Rate variance—unfavorable	$ 1.00 per hour × actual time, 3,850 hours = $3,850 U

Direct Labor Time Variance

The **direct labor time variance** is the difference between the actual hours worked (3,850 hours) and the standard hours at actual production (4,000 hours), multiplied by the standard rate per hour ($9.00). If the actual hours worked exceed the standard hours, the variance is unfavorable. If the actual hours worked are less than the standard hours, the variance is favorable, as shown below for Western Rider Inc.

Time variance:

Actual hours	3,850 direct labor hours
Standard hours at actual production	4,000
Time variance—favorable	(150) direct labor hours × standard rate, $9.00 = ($1,350) F

Direct Labor Variance Relationships

The direct labor variances can be illustrated by making the three calculations shown in Exhibit 4.

Reporting Direct Labor Variances

Controlling direct labor cost is normally the responsibility of the production supervisors. To aid them, reports analyzing the cause of any direct labor variance may be

---

Hospitals are now developing cost standards for various categories of procedures. Variances from standard cost can be accumulated by procedure, by patient, or by doctor. Doctor variances occur when a doctor consistently prescribes treatment that varies from the standard. Doctors who have consistent unfavorable variances may be asked to review their treatment decisions.

A product requires 2.5 standard hours per unit at a standard hourly rate of $12 per hour. If 800 units required 1,920 hours at an hourly rate of $12.30 per hour, what is the direct labor (1) rate variance and (2) time variance?

(1) $576 unfavorable [($12.30 − $12.00) × 1,920 hours]; (2) $960 favorable [(1,920 hrs. − 2,000 hrs.) × $12.00]

Exhibit 4 Direct Labor Variance Relationships

In highly automated industries, such as chemical, metal, food, and paper processing, direct labor variances are rarely used. This is because factory employees run and maintain equipment, and thus the cost of their labor is part of factory overhead.

prepared. Differences between standard direct labor hours and actual direct labor hours can be investigated. For example, a time variance may be incurred because of the shortage of skilled workers. Such variances may be uncontrollable unless they are related to high turnover rates among employees, in which case the cause of the high turnover should be investigated.

Likewise, differences between the rates paid for direct labor and the standard rates can be investigated. For example, unfavorable rate variances may be caused by the improper scheduling and use of workers. In such cases, skilled, highly paid workers may be used in jobs that are normally performed by unskilled, lower-paid workers. In this case, the unfavorable rate variance should be reported for corrective action to the managers who schedule work assignments.

BUSINESS ON STAGE

Measuring the Performance of Teams

Many organizations are using cross-functional teams in order to foster higher cooperation in achieving objectives. For example, **Procter & Gamble** has a "Wal-Mart" team that is designed to support its largest customer by integrating the sales, logistical, and customer service functions. Manufacturing companies such as **Northern Telecom** and **Harley-Davidson** have created self-directed work teams on the manufacturing floor to reduce waste and improve cost. When a company uses teams, how should performance be measured?

The following three concepts are relevant to team measurement:

1. Identify team performance targets and standards.
2. Identify individual contributions required to achieve team targets.

3. Establish the relative weights between individual and team goals.

If a company has developed a manufacturing cell that uses a team of individuals from a variety of functional areas, the team goals should address performance of the complete team. Examples include overall quality goals, productivity standards, and cost targets. To illustrate, a team goal would be to achieve 100% of required output of the cell per day.

Because a team is made up of individuals, individual goals should be established to support the team goals. In this way, individuals will be less likely to "free ride" on the team's performance. Individual goals focus more on what an individual can directly control. To illustrate, an individual objective for a machinist would be to scrap less

than 1% of the machined parts. This individual goal contributes to the team's overall quality and cost targets.

Once the team and individual goals are determined, weights should be established between the various goals in determining an individual's performance. For example, a team member may have 60% of his or her evaluation based on achieving team goals and the remaining 40% on achieving individual goals. The actual weighting depends on how much management wishes to reward team versus individual performance.

Once the performance system is in place, the measures should be used to provide feedback to the team. Such feedback can be used to monitor and adjust team and individual performance relative to expectations. ■

Factory Overhead Variances

objective 5

Calculate and interpret factory overhead controllable and volume variances.

Factory overhead costs are more difficult to manage than are direct labor and materials costs. This is because the relationship between production volume and indirect costs is not easy to determine. For example, when production is increased, the direct materials will increase. But what about the Engineering Department overhead? The relationship between production volume and cost is less clear for the

Engineering Department. Companies normally respond to this difficulty by separating factory overhead into variable and fixed costs. For example, manufacturing supplies are considered variable to production volume, whereas straight-line plant depreciation is considered fixed. In the following sections, we discuss the approaches used to budget and control factory overhead by separating overhead into fixed and variable components.

The Factory Overhead Flexible Budget

A flexible budget may be used to determine the impact of changing production on fixed and variable factory overhead costs. The standard overhead rate is determined by dividing the budgeted factory overhead costs by the standard amount of productive activity, such as direct labor hours. Exhibit 5 is a flexible factory overhead budget for Western Rider Inc.

Exhibit 5 Factory Overhead Cost Budget Indicating Standard Factory Overhead Rate

Western Rider Inc.
Factory Overhead Cost Budget
For the Month Ending June 30, 2003

	80%	90%	100%	110%
Percent of normal capacity	80%	90%	100%	110%
Units produced	5,000	5,625	6,250	6,875
Direct labor hours (0.80 hour per unit)	4,000	4,500	5,000	5,500
Budgeted factory overhead:				
Variable costs:				
Indirect factory wages	$ 8,000	$ 9,000	$10,000	$11,000
Power and light	4,000	4,500	5,000	5,500
Indirect materials	2,400	2,700	3,000	3,300
Total variable cost	$14,400	$16,200	$18,000	$19,800
Fixed costs:				
Supervisory salaries	$ 5,500	$ 5,500	$ 5,500	$ 5,500
Depreciation of plant and equipment	4,500	4,500	4,500	4,500
Insurance and property taxes	2,000	2,000	2,000	2,000
Total fixed cost	$12,000	$12,000	$12,000	$12,000
Total factory overhead cost	$26,400	$28,200	$30,000	$31,800

Factory overhead rate per direct labor hour, $30,000 ÷ 5,000 = $6.00

In Exhibit 5, the standard factory overhead cost rate is $6.00. It is determined by dividing the total budgeted cost of 100% of normal capacity by the standard hours required at 100% of normal capacity, or $30,000 ÷ 5,000 hours = $6.00 per hour. This rate can be subdivided into $3.60 per hour for variable factory overhead ($18,000 ÷ 5,000 hours) and $2.40 per hour for fixed factory overhead ($12,000 ÷ 5,000 hours).

Variances from standard for factory overhead cost result from:

1. Actual variable factory overhead cost greater or less than budgeted variable factory overhead for actual production.
2. Actual production at a level above or below 100% of normal capacity.

The first factor results in the controllable variance for variable overhead costs. The second factor results in a volume variance for fixed overhead costs. We will discuss each of these variances next.

Variable Factory Overhead Controllable Variance

The variable factory overhead controllable variance is the difference between the actual variable overhead incurred and the budgeted variable overhead for actual production. The controllable variance measures the *efficiency* of using variable overhead resources. Thus, if the actual variable overhead is less than the budgeted variable overhead, the variance is favorable. If the actual variable overhead exceeds the budgeted variable overhead, the variance is unfavorable.

To illustrate, recall that Western Rider Inc. produced 5,000 pairs of XL jeans in June. Each pair requires 0.80 standard labor hour for production. As a result, Western Rider Inc. had 4,000 standard hours at actual production (5,000 jeans × 0.80 hour). This represents 80% of normal productive capacity (4,000 hours ÷ 5,000 hours). The standard variable overhead at 4,000 hours worked, according to the budget in Exhibit 5, was $14,400 (4,000 direct labor hours × $3.60). The following actual factory overhead costs were incurred in June:

Actual costs:

Variable factory overhead	$10,400
Fixed factory overhead	12,000
Total actual factory overhead	$22,400

The controllable variance can be calculated as follows:

Controllable variance:

Actual variable factory overhead	$10,400
Budgeted variable factory overhead for actual amount produced (4,000 hrs. × $3.60)	14,400
Variance—favorable	$ (4,000) F

The variable factory overhead controllable variance indicates management's ability to keep the factory overhead costs within the budget limits. Since variable factory overhead costs are normally controllable at the department level, responsibility for controlling this variance usually rests with department supervisors.

Fixed Factory Overhead Volume Variance

Using currently attainable standards, Western Rider Inc. set its budgeted normal capacity at 5,000 direct labor hours. This is the amount of expected capacity that management believes will be used under normal business conditions. You should note that this amount may be much less than the total available capacity if management believes demand will be low.

The fixed factory overhead volume variance is the difference between the budgeted fixed overhead at 100% of normal capacity and the standard fixed overhead for the actual production achieved during the period. The volume variance measures the use of fixed overhead resources. If the standard fixed overhead exceeds the budgeted overhead at 100% of normal capacity, the variance is favorable. Thus, the firm used its plant and equipment more than would be expected under normal operating conditions. If the standard fixed overhead is less than the budgeted overhead at 100% of normal capacity, the variance is unfavorable. Thus, the company used its plant and equipment less than would be expected under normal operating conditions.

The volume variance for Western Rider Inc. is shown in the following calculation:

100% of normal capacity	5,000 direct labor hours
Standard hours at actual production	4,000
Capacity not used	1,000 direct labor hours
Standard fixed overhead rate	× $2.40
Volume variance—unfavorable	$ 2,400 U

A company produced 1,500 units of product that required 3.5 standard hours per unit. The standard variable and fixed overhead cost is $2.20 and $0.90 per hour, respectively, at 5,500 hours, which is 100% of normal capacity. The actual variable overhead was $12,000. What are (1) the variable factory overhead controllable variance and (2) the fixed factory overhead volume variance?

(1) $450 unfavorable [$12,000 − ($2.20 × 5,250 hrs.)];
(2) $225 unfavorable [$0.90 × (5,500 hrs. − 5,250 hrs.)]

Exhibit 6 illustrates the volume variance graphically. For Western Rider Inc., the budgeted fixed overhead is $12,000 at all levels. The standard fixed overhead at 5,000 hours is also $12,000. This is the point at which the standard fixed overhead line intersects the budgeted fixed cost line. For actual volume greater than 100% of normal capacity, the volume variance is favorable. For volume at less than 100% of normal volume, the volume variance is unfavorable. For Western Rider Inc., the volume variance is unfavorable because the actual production is 4,000 standard hours, or 80% of normal volume. The amount of the volume variance, $2,400, can be viewed as the cost of the unused capacity (1,000 hours).

Exhibit 6 Graph of Fixed Overhead Volume Variance

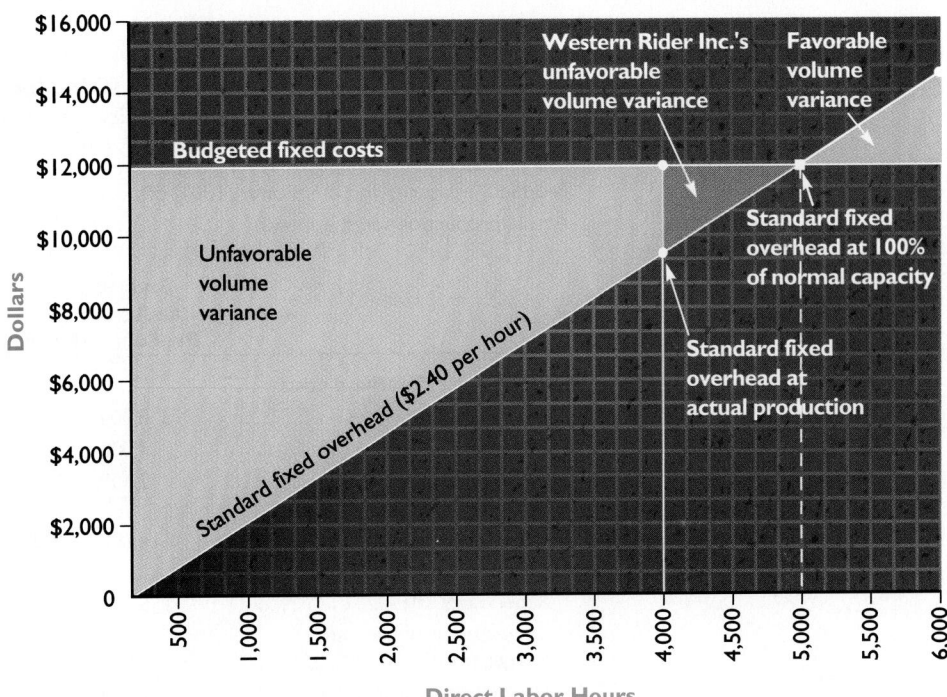

An unfavorable volume variance may be due to such factors as failure to maintain an even flow of work, machine breakdowns, repairs causing work stoppages, and failure to obtain enough sales orders to keep the factory operating at normal capacity. Management should determine the causes of the unfavorable variance and consider taking corrective action. A volume variance caused by an uneven flow of work, for example, can be remedied by changing operating procedures. Volume variances caused by lack of sales orders may be corrected through increased advertising or other sales effort.

Volume variances tend to encourage manufacturing managers to run the factory above the normal capacity. This is favorable when the additional production can be sold. However, if the additional production cannot be sold and must be stored as inventory, favorable volume variances may actually be harmful. For example, one paper company ran paper machines above normal volume in order to create favorable volume variances. Unfortunately, this created a six months' supply of finished goods inventory that had to be stored in public warehouses. The "savings" from the favorable volume variances were exceeded by the additional inventory carrying costs. By creating incentives for manufacturing managers to overproduce, the volume variances produced *goal conflicts*, as we described in a preceding chapter.

Many companies develop customized variances to fit their business. For example, **Parker Hannifin Corporation** reports a "standard run quantity variance" (which measures the difference between actual lot size and ideal lot size), "material substitution variance" (which measures the financial impact of substituted material), and "method variance" (which measures the financial impact of a change in processing methods).

Reporting Factory Overhead Variances

The total factory overhead cost variance is the difference between the actual factory overhead and the total overhead applied to production. This calculation is as follows:

Total actual factory overhead	$22,400
Factory overhead applied (4,000 hours × $6.00 per hour)	24,000
Total factory overhead cost variance—favorable	$(1,600) F

The factory overhead cost variance may be broken down by each variable factory overhead cost and fixed factory overhead cost element in a **factory overhead cost variance report**. Such a report, which is useful to management in controlling costs, is shown in Exhibit 7. The report indicates both the controllable variance and the volume variance.

Exhibit 7 Factory Overhead Cost Variance Report

Western Rider Inc.
Factory Overhead Cost Variance Report
For the Month Ended June 30, 2003

Productive capacity for the month (100% of normal)	5,000 hours			
Actual production for the month	4,000 hours			

	Budget (at Actual Production)	Actual	Variances Favorable	Variances Unfavorable
Variable factory overhead costs:				
Indirect factory wages	$ 8,000	$ 5,100	$2,900	
Power and light	4,000	4,200		$ 200
Indirect materials	2,400	1,100	1,300	
Total variable factory overhead cost	$14,400	$10,400		
Fixed factory overhead costs:				
Supervisory salaries	$ 5,500	$ 5,500		
Depreciation of plant and equipment	4,500	4,500		
Insurance and property taxes ...	2,000	2,000		
Total fixed factory overhead cost	$12,000	$12,000		
Total factory overhead cost	$26,400	$22,400		
Total controllable variances			$4,200	$ 200
Net controllable variance—favorable				$4,000
Volume variance—unfavorable:				
Capacity not used at the standard rate for fixed factory overhead—1,000 × $2.40				2,400
Total factory overhead cost variance—favorable				$1,600

It is also possible to break down many of the individual factory overhead cost variances into quantity and price variances, similar to direct materials and direct labor. For example, the indirect factory wages variance may include both time and rate variances. Likewise, the indirect materials variance may include both a quantity variance and a price variance. Such variances are illustrated in advanced textbooks.

Recording and Reporting Variances from Standards

objective 6

Journalize the entries for recording standards in the accounts and prepare an income statement that includes variances from standard.

Standard costs can be used solely as a management tool separate from the accounts in the general ledger. However, many companies include both standard costs and variances, in addition to actual costs, in their accounts. In doing so, one approach is to record the standard costs and variances at the same time the actual manufacturing costs are recorded in the accounts. To illustrate, assume that Western Rider Inc. purchased, on account, the 7,300 square yards of blue denim used at $5.50 per square yard. The standard price for direct materials is $5.00 per square yard. The entry to record the purchase and the unfavorable direct materials price variance is as follows:

	Materials (7,300 sq. yds. × $5.00)		36	5	0	0	00				
	Direct Materials Price Variance		3	6	5	0	00				
	Accounts Payable (7,300 sq. yds. × $5.50)							40	1	5	0	00

The materials account is debited for the actual quantity purchased at the standard price, $36,500 (7,300 square yards × $5.00). Accounts Payable is credited for the $40,150 actual cost. The unfavorable direct materials price variance is $3,650 [($5.50 actual price per square yard − $5.00 standard price per square yard) × 7,300 square yards purchased]. It is recorded by debiting Direct Materials Price Variance. If the variance had been favorable, Direct Materials Price Variance would have been credited for the amount of the variance.

The direct materials quantity variance is recorded in a similar manner. For example, Western Rider Inc. used 7,300 square yards of blue denim to produce 5,000 pairs of XL jeans, compared to a standard of 7,500 square yards. The entry to record the materials used is as follows:

	Work in Process (7,500 sq. yds. × $5.00)		37	5	0	0	00				
	Direct Materials Quantity Variance							1	0	0	0	00
	Materials (7,300 sq. yds. × $5.00)							36	5	0	0	00

The work in process account is debited for the standard price of the standard amount of direct materials required, $37,500 (7,500 square yards × $5.00). Materials is credited for the actual amount of materials used at the standard price, $36,500 (7,300 square yards × $5.00). The favorable direct materials quantity variance of $1,000 [(7,500 standard square yards − 7,300 actual square yards) × $5.00 standard price per square yard] is credited to Direct Materials Quantity Variance. If the variance had been unfavorable, Direct Materials Quantity Variance would have been debited for the amount of the variance.

The entries for direct labor are recorded in a manner similar to direct materials. Thus, the work in process account is debited for the standard cost of direct labor and direct materials, as well as factory overhead. Likewise, the work in process account is credited for the standard cost of the product completed and transferred to the finished goods account.

In a given period, it is possible to have both favorable and unfavorable variances. At the end of the period, the balances of the variance accounts will indicate the net favorable or unfavorable variance for the period.

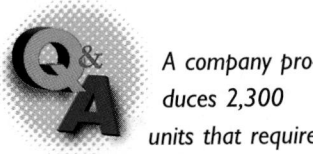

A company produces 2,300 units that require 2.4 standard hours per unit. The standard direct labor cost is $9 per hour. The actual direct labor cost totaled $50,670. What is the amount of direct labor debited to Work in Process?

$49,680 (2,300 units × 2.4 hrs. × $9 per hr.)

Boeing Company specifically identifies sources of waste in the uses of machine capacity, such as setup, teardown, inspection, and out of service, in explaining its unfavorable volume variances.

Variances from standard costs are usually not reported to stockholders and others outside the business. If standards are recorded in the accounts, however, the variances may be reported in income statements prepared for management's use. Exhibit 8 is an example of such an income statement prepared for Western Rider Inc.'s internal use. In this exhibit, we assume a sales price of $28 per pair of jeans, selling expenses of $14,500, and administrative expenses of $11,225.

At the end of the fiscal year, the variances from standard are usually transferred to the cost of goods sold account. However, if the variances are significant or if many of the products manufactured are still in inventory, the variances should be allocated to the work in process, finished goods, and cost of goods sold accounts. Such an allocation converts these account balances from standard cost to actual cost.

Exhibit 8 Variances from Standards in Income Statement

Western Rider Inc.
Income Statement
For the Month Ended June 30, 2003

	Favorable	Unfavorable	
Sales			$140,000[1]
Cost of goods sold—at standard			97,500[2]
Gross profit—at standard			$ 42,500
Less variances from standard cost:			
Direct materials price		$ 3,650	
Direct materials quantity	$1,000		
Direct labor rate		3,850	
Direct labor time	1,350		
Factory overhead controllable	4,000		
Factory overhead volume		2,400	3,550
Gross profit			$ 38,950
Operating expenses:			
Selling expenses		$14,500	
Administrative expenses		11,225	25,725
Income before income tax			$ 13,225

[1] 5,000 × $28
[2] $37,500 + $36,000 + $24,000 (from Exhibit 2), or 5,000 × $19.50 (from Exhibit 1)

Standards for Nonmanufacturing Expenses

objective 7

Explain how standards may be used for nonmanufacturing expenses.

Using standards for nonmanufacturing expenses, such as service, selling, and administrative expenses, is not as common as using standards for manufacturing costs. This is often due to many nonmanufacturing expenses not directly relating to a unit of output or other measure of activity. For example, the administrative expenses associated with the work of the office manager are not easily related to a measurable output. In these cases, nonmanufacturing expenses are normally controlled by using static budgets.

However, when nonmanufacturing activities are repetitive and produce a common output, standards can be applied. In these cases, the use of standards is similar to that described for a manufactured product. For example, standards can be applied to the work of office personnel who process sales orders. A standard cost for processing a sales order (the output) could be developed. The variance between the actual cost of processing a sales order and the standard cost could then be used to control sales order processing costs.

Nonfinancial Performance Measures

objective 8

Explain and provide examples of nonfinancial performance measures.

Real World

U.S. airlines use a variety of nonfinancial measures, such as on-time performance, lost baggage, and customer complaints. These nonfinancial measures are used to balance customer satisfaction with cost reduction. Many airlines have admitted going too far in cutting costs. For example, **Northwest Airlines** increased the frequency of steam-cleaning its planes' lavatories from every 14 days to every 9 days. **America West** upgraded food and installed in-flight phones. **Delta Air Lines** added baggage handlers and gate agents to reduce waiting time during arrivals and departures.

Many managers believe that financial performance measures, such as variances from standard, should be supplemented with nonfinancial measures of performance. Measuring both financial and nonfinancial performance helps employees consider multiple, and sometimes conflicting, performance objectives. For example, one company had a machining operation that was measured according to a direct labor time standard. Employees did their work quickly in order to create favorable direct labor time variances. Unfortunately, the fast work resulted in poor quality that, in turn, created difficulty in the assembly operation. The company decided to use both a labor time standard *and* a quality standard in order to encourage employees to consider both the speed and quality of their work.

In the preceding example, nonfinancial performance measures brought additional perspectives, such as quality of work, to evaluating performance. Some additional examples of nonfinancial performance measures are as follows:

Nonfinancial Performance Measures[4]

Inventory turnover (82%)
On-time delivery (41%)
Elapsed time between a customer order and product delivery (35%)
Customer preference rankings compared to competitors
Response time to a service call
Time to develop new products
Employee satisfaction
Number of customer complaints

Nonfinancial measures can relate to either inputs or outputs to an activity or process, shown as follows:

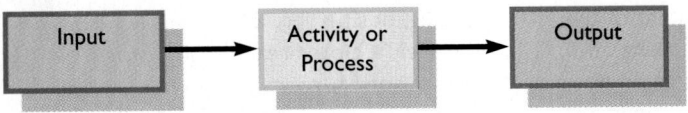

For example, consider the counter service activity of a fast food restaurant. The following input/output relationship could be identified:

---

[4] The first three examples indicate the percentage of firms using the nonfinancial performance measure, taken from a survey by Forrest B. Green and Felix E. Amenkhienan, "Accounting Innovations: A Cross-Sectional Survey of Manufacturing Firms," *Journal of Cost Management*, Spring 1992, pp. 58–64.

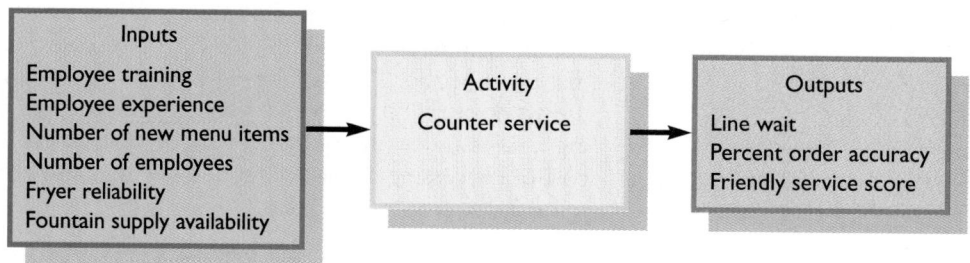

Inputs
- Employee training
- Employee experience
- Number of new menu items
- Number of employees
- Fryer reliability
- Fountain supply availability

Activity
Counter service

Outputs
- Line wait
- Percent order accuracy
- Friendly service score

The outputs of the counter service activity include the customer line wait, order accuracy, and service experience. The inputs that impact these outputs include the number of employees, level of employee experience and training, reliability of the french fryer, menu complexity, fountain drink supply, and the like. Additionally, note that the inputs for one activity could be the outputs of another. For example, fryer reliability is an input to the counter service activity, but is an output of the french frying activity. Moving back, fryer maintenance would be an input to the french frying activity. Thus, a chain of inputs and outputs can be developed between a set of connected activities or processes. The fast food restaurant can develop a set of linked nonfinancial performance measures across the chain of inputs and outputs. The output measures tell management how the activity is performing, such as keeping the line wait to a minimum. The input measures are the *levers* that impact the activity's performance. Thus, if the fast food restaurant line wait is too long, then the input measures might indicate a need for more training, more employees, or better fryer reliability.

ENCORE

Frederick Taylor and "Scientific Management"

The use of standards has its roots in the work of Frederick Taylor, who in the late 1800s proposed what he termed scientific management. *Scientific management* is, in part, a philosophy of improving operations by breaking work down into its components, measuring the work content of the components, and then making improvements. Taylor illustrated his concept with a pig-iron loading operation. In this operation, workers were to move 92-lb. ingots 36 feet up an incline and drop the load into a railcar. By studying, measuring, and standardizing the work elements of this operation, Taylor was able to improve the daily loading rate from 12.5 tons to 47.5 tons per man.

Many criticize scientific management for dehumanizing work and treating workers as if they were mere machines. This criticism resulted from the apparent focus by these early engineers on specializing and measuring labor for repetitive tasks, such as grasping, positioning, and moving. However, a closer reading of Taylor's original work suggests a man who was ahead of his time. The four principles of scientific management as described by Taylor are:

1. Develop a science for each element of a person's work.
2. Select, train, and develop each worker.

3. Encourage a close cooperation between workers and management.
4. Share responsibility and rewards for success between workers and management.

The first principle was widely embraced in the early part of the twentieth century and is often considered the sum and substance of scientific management. However, Taylor considered the last three principles as equally important. Unfortunately, it has taken nearly one hundred years before these latter principles have taken root in business. Today, these latter principles go by such names as *just-in-time*, *team-based management*, *total quality management*, and *gainsharing*. ■

HEY POINTS

1 Describe the types of standards and how they are established for businesses.

Standards represent performance benchmarks that can be compared to actual results in evaluating performance. Standards are developed, reviewed, and revised by accountants and engineers, based upon studies of operations. Standards are established so that they are neither too high nor too low, but are attainable.

2 Explain and illustrate how standards are used in budgeting.

Budgets are prepared by multiplying the standard cost per unit by the planned production. To measure performance, the standard cost per unit is multiplied by the actual number of units produced, and the actual results are compared with the standard cost at actual volumes (cost variance).

3 Calculate and interpret direct materials price and quantity variances.

The direct materials cost variance can be separated into a direct materials price and quantity variance. The direct materials price variance is calculated by multiplying the actual quantity by the difference between the actual and standard price. The direct materials quantity variance is calculated by multiplying the standard price by the difference between the actual materials used and the standard materials at actual volumes.

4 Calculate and interpret direct labor rate and time variances.

The direct labor cost variance can be separated into a direct labor rate and time variance. The direct labor rate variance is calculated by multiplying the actual hours worked by the difference between the actual labor rate and the standard labor rate. The direct labor time variance is calculated by multiplying the standard labor rate by the difference between the actual labor hours worked and the standard labor hours at actual volumes.

5 Calculate and interpret factory overhead controllable and volume variances.

The factory overhead cost variance can be separated into a variable factory overhead controllable variance and a fixed factory overhead volume variance. The controllable variance is calculated by subtracting the actual variable factory overhead from the budgeted variable factory overhead at actual volumes. The volume variance is determined by multiplying the fixed factory overhead rate by the difference between the budgeted hours at 100% of normal capacity and the standard hours used at actual production.

6 Journalize the entries for recording standards in the accounts and prepare an income statement that includes variances from standard.

Standard costs and variances can be recorded in the accounts at the same time the manufacturing costs are recorded in the accounts. For example, the purchase of direct materials on account is recorded as a debit to Materials for the standard cost of materials and a credit to Accounts Payable for the actual cost. Any difference is debited or credited to the direct materials price variance account.

The entries for direct labor, factory overhead, and other variances are recorded in a manner similar to the entries for direct materials. The work in process account is debited for the standard costs of direct labor and factory overhead as well as direct materials. Likewise, the work in process account is credited for the standard cost of the product completed and transferred to the finished goods account.

Under a standard cost system, the cost of goods sold will be reported at standard cost. Manufacturing variances can be disclosed on the income statement to adjust the gross profit at standard to the actual gross profit. Such a disclosure is generally limited for use by management. At the end of the year, the variances from standard are usually transferred to the cost of goods sold account.

7 Explain how standards may be used for nonmanufacturing expenses.

Standards may be used for nonmanufacturing expenses when

nonmanufacturing activities are repetitive and related to an activity base. Such standards may be useful to managers in planning, directing, and controlling nonmanufacturing expenses.

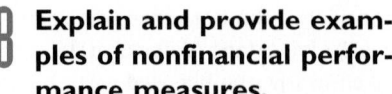 **Explain and provide examples of nonfinancial performance measures.**
Many companies use a combination of financial and nonfinancial measures in order for multiple

perspectives to be incorporated in evaluating performance. Combining financial and nonfinancial measures helps employees balance cost efficiency with quality and customer service performance.

ILLUSTRATIVE PROBLEM

Hawley Inc. manufactures Product S for national distribution. The standard costs for the manufacture of Product S were as follows:

	Standard Costs	**Actual Costs**
Direct materials	1,500 pounds at $35	1,600 pounds at $32
Direct labor	4,800 hours at $11	4,500 hours at $11.80
Factory overhead	Rates per labor hour, based on 100% of normal capacity of 5,500 labor hours:	
	Variable cost, $2.40	$12,300 variable cost
	Fixed cost, $3.50	$19,250 fixed cost

Instructions

1. Determine the quantity variance, price variance, and total direct materials cost variance for Product S.
2. Determine the time variance, rate variance, and total direct labor cost variance for Product S.
3. Determine the controllable variance, volume variance, and total factory overhead cost variance for Product S.

Solution

1.

Direct Materials Cost Variance

Quantity variance:			
Actual quantity	1,600 pounds		
Standard quantity	1,500		
Variance—unfavorable	100 pounds × standard price, $35		$ 3,500
Price variance:			
Actual price	$32.00 per pound		
Standard price	35.00		
Variance—favorable	$ (3.00) per pound × actual quantity, 1,600		(4,800)
Total direct materials cost variance—favorable			$(1,300)

2.

Direct Labor Cost Variance

Time variance:			
Actual time	4,500 hours		
Standard time	4,800 hours		
Variance—favorable	(300) hours × standard rate, $11		$(3,300)
Rate variance:			
Actual rate	$11.80		
Standard rate	11.00		
Variance—unfavorable	$ 0.80 per hour × actual time, 4,500 hrs.		3,600
Total direct labor cost variance—unfavorable			$ 300

3.

Factory Overhead Cost Variance

Variable factory overhead—controllable variance:		
Actual variable factory overhead cost incurred	$12,300	
Budgeted variable factory overhead for 4,800 hours	11,520*	
Variance—unfavorable		$ 780
Fixed factory overhead—volume variance:		
Budgeted hours at 100% of normal capacity	5,500 hours	
Standard hours for actual production	4,800	
Productive capacity not used	700 hours	
Standard fixed factory overhead cost rate	× $3.50 hours	
Variance—unfavorable		2,450
Total factory overhead cost variance—unfavorable		$ 3,230

*4,800 hrs. × $2.40 = $11,520

SELF-EXAMINATION QUESTIONS
Answers at End of Chapter

Matching
Match each of the following statements with its proper term. Some terms may not be used.

A. **budget performance report**

B. **controllable variance**

C. **cost variance**

D. **currently attainable standards**

E. **direct labor rate variance**

F. **direct labor time variance**

G. **direct materials price variance**

H. **direct materials quantity variance**

I. **nonfinancial performance measures**

J. **standard cost**

K. **standard cost systems**

L. **theoretical standards**

M. **volume variance**

___ 1. Standards that represent levels of operation that can be obtained with reasonable effort.

___ 2. The cost associated with the difference between the standard quantity and the actual quantity of direct materials used in producing a commodity.

___ 3. A report comparing actual results with budget figures.

___ 4. Standards that represent levels of performance that can be achieved only under perfect operating conditions.

___ 5. A detailed estimate of what a product should cost.

___ 6. The difference between the budgeted fixed overhead at 100% of normal capacity and the standard fixed overhead for the actual production achieved during the period.

___ 7. The cost associated with the difference between the standard hours and the actual hours of direct labor spent producing a commodity.

___ 8. The difference between the actual amount of variable factory overhead cost incurred and the amount of variable factory overhead budgeted for actual production.

___ 9. The cost associated with the difference between the standard price and the actual price of direct materials used in producing a commodity.

___ 10. The difference between the actual cost and the standard cost at actual volumes.

___ 11. The cost associated with the difference between the standard rate and the actual rate paid for direct labor used in producing a commodity.

___ 12. Accounting systems that use standards for each manufacturing cost entering into the finished product.

Multiple Choice

1. The actual and standard direct materials costs for producing a specified quantity of product are as follows:
   Actual: 51,000 pounds at $5.05 $257,550
   Standard: 50,000 pounds at $5.00 $250,000

   The direct materials price variance is:
   A. $50 unfavorable   C. $2,550 unfavorable
   B. $2,500 unfavorable   D. $7,550 unfavorable

2. Bower Company produced 4,000 units of product. Each unit requires 0.5 standard hour. The standard labor rate is $12 per hour. Actual direct labor for the period was $22,000 (2,200 hours × $10 per hour). The direct labor time variance is:
   A. 200 hours unfavorable
   B. $2,000 unfavorable
   C. $4,000 favorable
   D. $2,400 unfavorable

3. The actual and standard factory overhead costs for producing a specified quantity of product are as follows:

   Actual: Variable factory overhead $72,500
            Fixed factory overhead   40,000 $112,500

   Standard: 19,000 hours at $6
            ($4 variable and $2 fixed)   114,000

   If 1,000 hours were unused, the fixed factory overhead volume variance would be:
   A. $1,500 favorable
   B. $2,000 unfavorable
   C. $4,000 unfavorable
   D. $6,000 unfavorable

4. Ramathan Company produced 6,000 units of product Y, which is 80% of capacity. Each unit required 0.25 standard machine hour for production. The standard variable factory overhead rate is $5.00 per machine hour. The actual variable factory overhead incurred during the period was $8,000. The variable factory overhead controllable variance is:
   A. $500 favorable
   B. $500 unfavorable
   C. $1,875 favorable
   D. $1,875 unfavorable

5. Applegate Company has a normal budgeted capacity of 200 machine hours. Applegate produced 600 units. Each unit requires a standard 0.2 machine hour to complete. The standard fixed factory overhead is $12.00 per hour, determined at normal capacity. The fixed factory overhead volume variance is:
   A. $4,800 unfavorable
   B. $4,800 favorable
   C. $960 favorable
   D. $960 unfavorable

CLASS DISCUSSION QUESTIONS

1. What are the basic objectives in the use of standard costs?
2. How can standards be used by management to help control costs?
3. What is meant by reporting by the "principle of exceptions," as the term is used in reference to cost control?
4. How often should standards be revised?
5. How are standards used in budgetary performance evaluation?
6. a. What are the two variances between the actual cost and the standard cost for direct materials?
   b. Discuss some possible causes of these variances.
7. The materials cost variance report for Nickols Inc. indicates a large favorable materials price variance and a significant unfavorable materials quantity variance. What might have caused these offsetting variances?
8. a. What are the two variances between the actual cost and the standard cost for direct labor?
   b. Who generally has control over the direct labor cost?
9. A new assistant controller recently was heard to remark: "All the assembly workers in this plant are covered by union contracts, so there should be no labor variances." Was the controller's remark correct? Discuss.
10. a. Describe the two variances between the actual costs and the standard costs for factory overhead.
    b. What is a factory overhead cost variance report?
11. What are budgeted fixed costs at normal volume?
12. If variances are recorded in the accounts at the time the manufacturing costs are incurred, what does a debit balance in Direct Materials Price Variance represent?
13. If variances are recorded in the accounts at the time the manufacturing costs are incurred, what does a credit balance in Direct Materials Quantity Variance represent?
14. Are variances from standard costs usually reported in financial statements issued to stockholders and others outside the firm?
15. Assuming that the variances from standards are not significant at the end of the period, to what account are they transferred?
16. Would the use of standards be appropriate in a nonmanufacturing setting, such as a fast food restaurant?
17. Briefly explain why firms might use nonfinancial performance measures.

RESOURCES FOR YOUR SUCCESS ONLINE AT

http://warren.swcollege.com

Remember! If you need additional help, visit South-Western's Web site.
See page M28 for a description of the online and printed materials that are available.

EXERCISES

Exercise 6–1
Standard direct materials cost per unit

Objective 2

Belgian Delight Chocolate Company produces chocolate bars. The primary materials used in producing chocolate bars are cocoa, sugar, and milk. The standard costs for a batch of chocolate (1,000 bars) are as follows:

Ingredient	Quantity	Price
Cocoa	260 pounds	$0.25 per pound
Sugar	100 pounds	$0.45 per pound
Milk	60 gallons	$1.50 per gallon

Determine the standard direct materials cost per bar of chocolate.

Exercise 6–2
Standard product cost

Objective 2

Pine Hill Furniture Company manufactures unfinished oak furniture. Pine Hill uses a standard cost system. The direct labor, direct materials, and factory overhead standards for an unfinished dining room table are as follows:

Direct labor:	standard rate	$12.00 per hour
	standard time per unit	4.80 hours
Direct materials (oak):	standard price	$24.00 per board foot
	standard quantity	20 board feet
Variable factory overhead:	standard rate	$4.00 per direct labor hour
Fixed factory overhead:	standard rate	$1.50 per direct labor hour

Determine the standard cost per dining room table.

Exercise 6–3
Budget performance report

Objective 2

SPREADSHEET

✓ b. Direct labor cost variance,
$150 F

Baker Bottle Company (BBC) manufactures plastic 2-liter bottles for the beverage industry. The cost standards per 100 2-liter bottles are as follows:

Cost Category	Standard Cost per 100 2-Liter Bottles
Direct labor	$1.80
Direct materials	7.20
Factory overhead	0.50
Total	$9.50

At the beginning of May, BBC management planned to produce 400,000 bottles. The actual number of bottles produced for May was 450,000 bottles. The actual costs for May of the current year were as follows:

| | Actual Cost for the |
Cost Category	Month Ended May 31, 2003
Direct labor	$ 7,950
Direct materials	33,100
Factory overhead	2,500
Total	$43,550

a.   Prepare the May manufacturing standard cost budget (direct labor, direct materials, and factory overhead) for BBC, assuming planned production.
b.   Prepare a budget performance report for manufacturing costs, showing the total cost variances for direct materials, direct labor, and factory overhead for May.
c.   ◖━━► Interpret the budget performance report.

Exercise 6–4
Direct materials variances

Objective 3

✓ a. Price variance, $12,680 F

The following data relate to the direct materials cost for the production of 4,000 automobile tires:

| Actual: | 126,800 pounds at $1.90 | $240,920 |
| Standard: | 125,000 pounds at $2.00 | $250,000 |

a.   Determine the price variance, quantity variance, and total direct materials cost variance.
b.   ◖━━► To whom should the variances be reported for analysis and control?

Exercise 6–5
Standard direct materials cost per unit from variance data

Objectives 2, 3

The following data relating to direct materials cost for August of the current year are taken from the records of Big Toys Inc., a manufacturer of plastic toys:

Quantity of direct materials used	40,000 pounds
Actual unit price of direct materials	$1.40 per pound
Units of finished product manufactured	6,000 units
Standard direct materials per unit of finished product	6.25 pounds
Direct materials quantity variance—unfavorable	$3,400
Direct materials price variance—unfavorable	$1,600

Determine the standard direct materials cost per unit of finished product, assuming that there was no inventory of work in process at either the beginning or the end of the month.

Exercise 6–6
Standard product cost, direct materials variance

Objectives 2, 3

Real World

✓ a. $0.80 per pound

H.J. Heinz Company uses standards to control its materials costs. Assume that a batch of ketchup (1,500 pounds) has the following standards:

	Standard Quantity	Standard Price
Whole tomatoes	2,000 pounds	$0.35 per pound
Vinegar	104 gallons	2.50 per gallon
Corn syrup	15 gallons	8.50 per gallon
Salt	50 pounds	2.25 per pound

The actual materials in a batch may vary from the standard due to tomato characteristics. Assume that the actual quantity of materials for batch A-24 were:

2,050 pounds of tomatoes
  100 gallons of vinegar
   16 gallons of corn syrup
   48 pounds of salt

a.   Determine the standard unit materials cost per pound for a standard batch.
b.   Determine the direct materials quantity variance for batch A-24.

Exercise 6–7
Direct labor variances

Objective 4

✓ a. Rate variance, $3,360 U

The following data relate to labor cost for production of 6,000 cellular telephones:

Actual: 8,400 hours at $16.40 $137,760
Standard: 9,000 hours at $16.00 $144,000

a. Determine the rate variance, time variance, and total direct labor cost variance.
b. ◀▬▬▶ Discuss what might have caused these variances.

Exercise 6–8
Direct labor variances

Objective 4

✓ a. Time variance, $500 F

High Mountain Bicycle Company manufactures mountain bikes. The following data for March of the current year are available:

Quantity of direct labor used	1,860 hours
Actual rate for direct labor	$13.00 per hour
Bicycles completed in March	250
Standard direct labor per bicycle	7.60 hours
Standard rate for direct labor	$12.50 per hour
Planned bicycles for March	200

a. Determine the direct labor rate and time variance.
b. How much direct labor should be debited to Work in Process?

Exercise 6–9
Direct materials and direct labor variances

Objectives 2, 3, 4

✓ Direct materials quantity variance, $1,250 F

At the beginning of September, Academic Printers Company budgeted 22,000 books to be printed in September at standard direct materials and direct labor costs as follows:

Direct materials	$28,600
Direct labor	24,200
Total	$52,800

The standard materials price is $0.50 per pound. The standard direct labor rate is $11 per hour. At the end of September, the actual direct materials and direct labor costs were as follows:

Actual direct materials	$31,250
Actual direct labor	28,100
Total	$59,350

There were no direct materials price or direct labor rate variances for September. In addition, assume no changes in the direct materials inventory balances in September. Academic Printers Company actually produced 25,000 units during September.
Determine the direct materials quantity and direct labor time variances.

Exercise 6–10
Flexible overhead budget

Objective 5

✓ Total factory overhead, 8,000 hrs: $88,000

Paul Bunyan Wood Products Company prepared the following factory overhead cost budget for the Press Department for August 2003, during which it expected to require 6,000 hours of productive capacity in the department:

Variable overhead cost:		
Indirect factory labor	$16,800	
Power and light	2,700	
Indirect materials	13,200	
Total variable cost		$32,700
Fixed overhead cost:		
Supervisory salaries	$21,600	
Depreciation of plant and equipment	18,000	
Insurance and property taxes	4,800	
Total fixed cost		44,400
Total factory overhead cost		$77,100

Assuming that the estimated costs for September are the same as for August, prepare a flexible factory overhead cost budget for the Press Department for September for 4,000, 6,000, and 8,000 hours of production.

Exercise 6–11
Factory overhead cost variances

Objective 5

✓ Volume variance, $19,200 U

The following data relate to factory overhead cost for the production of 20,000 micro-computers:

Actual:	Variable factory overhead	$448,000
	Fixed factory overhead	115,200
Standard:	30,000 hours at $18.80	564,000

If productive capacity of 100% was 36,000 hours and the factory overhead cost budgeted at the level of 30,000 standard hours was $583,200, determine the variable factory overhead controllable variance, fixed factory overhead volume variance, and total factory overhead cost variance. The fixed factory overhead rate was $3.20 per hour.

Exercise 6–12
Factory overhead cost variances

Objective 5

✓ a. $400 U

Tennessee Textiles Corporation began March with a budget for 40,000 hours of production in the Weaving Department. The department has a full capacity of 50,000 hours under normal business conditions. The budgeted overhead at the planned volumes at the beginning of March was as follows:

Variable overhead	$164,000
Fixed overhead	77,500
Total	$241,500

The actual factory overhead was $262,400 for March. The actual fixed factory overhead was as budgeted. During March, the Weaving Department had standard hours at actual production volume of 45,000 hours.

a. Determine the variable factory overhead controllable variance.
b. Determine the fixed factory overhead volume variance.

Exercise 6–13
Factory overhead cost variance report

Objective 5

✓ Net controllable variance, $13,300 F

Murphy Molded Products Inc. prepared the following factory overhead cost budget for the Trim Department for May 2003, during which it expected to use 12,000 hours for production:

Variable overhead cost:		
Indirect factory labor	$ 33,600	
Power and light	4,200	
Indirect materials	22,200	
Total variable cost		$ 60,000
Fixed overhead cost:		
Supervisory salaries	$114,200	
Depreciation of plant and equipment	39,200	
Insurance and property taxes	6,600	
Total fixed cost		160,000
Total factory overhead cost		$220,000

Murphy Molded Products has available 20,000 hours of monthly productive capacity in the Trim Department under normal business conditions. During May, the Trim Department actually used 15,000 hours for production. The actual fixed costs were as budgeted. The actual variable overhead for May was as follows:

Actual variable factory overhead cost:	
Indirect factory labor	$35,200
Power and light	4,000
Indirect materials	22,500
Total variable cost	$61,700

Construct a factory overhead cost variance report for the Trim Department for May.

Exercise 6–14
Recording standards in accounts

Objective 6

SPREADSHEET

Cedrick Manufacturing Company incorporates standards in the accounts and identifies variances at the time the manufacturing costs are incurred. Journalize the entries to record the following transactions:

a. Purchased 800 units of copper tubing on account at $42.50 per unit. The standard price is $41.00 per unit.
b. Used 520 units of copper tubing in the process of manufacturing 90 air conditioners. Six units of copper tubing are required, at standard, to produce one air conditioner.

Exercise 6–15
Income statement indicating standard cost variance

Objective 6

✓ Income before income tax, $168,000

The following data were taken from the records of Cumberland Company for January, 2003:

Administrative expenses	$ 44,000
Cost of goods sold (at standard)	650,000
Direct materials price variance—favorable	1,200
Direct materials quantity variance—favorable	2,200
Direct labor rate variance—unfavorable	800
Direct labor time variance—unfavorable	3,000
Variable factory overhead controllable variance—favorable	3,800
Fixed factory overhead volume variance—unfavorable	8,000
Interest expense	1,900
Sales	960,000
Selling expenses	91,500

Prepare an income statement for presentation to management.

Exercise 6–16
Variance calculations

Objective 5

What's Wrong With This?

The data related to Big Fish Sporting Goods Company's factory overhead cost for the production of 70,000 units of product are as follows:

Actual:	Variable factory overhead	$385,700
	Fixed factory overhead	280,000
Standard:	60,000 hours at $10 ($6.50 for variable factory overhead)	600,000

Productive capacity at 100% of normal was 80,000 hours, and the factory overhead cost budgeted at the level of 60,000 standard hours was $670,000. Based upon these data, the chief cost accountant prepared the following variance analysis:

Variable factory overhead controllable variance:		
Actual variable factory overhead cost incurred	$385,700	
Budgeted variable factory overhead for 60,000 hours	390,000	
Variance—favorable		$ (4,300)
Fixed factory overhead volume variance:		
Normal productive capacity at 100%	80,000 hours	
Standard for amount produced	60,000	
Productive capacity not used	20,000 hours	
Standard variable factory overhead rate	× $6.50	
Variance—unfavorable		130,000
Total factory overhead cost variance—unfavorable		$125,700

Identify the errors in the factory overhead cost variance analysis.

Exercise 6–17
Standards for nonmanufacturing expenses

Objective 7

✓ a. $1,200

Mercy Hospital began using standards to evaluate its Admissions Department. The standard was broken into two types of admissions as follows:

Type of Admission	Standard Time to Complete Admission Record
Unscheduled admission	36 minutes
Scheduled admission	18 minutes

The unscheduled admission took longer, since name, address, and insurance information needed to be determined at the time of admission. Information was collected on scheduled admissions prior to the admissions, which was less time consuming.

The Admissions Department employs two full-time people (40 productive hours per week, with no overtime) at $15 per hour. For the most recent week, the department handled 45 unscheduled and 180 scheduled admissions.

a. How much was actually spent on labor for the week?
b. What are the standard hours for the actual volume for the week?
c. Calculate a time variance, and report how well the department performed for the week.

Exercise 6–18
Standards for nonmanufacturing operations

Objectives 2, 4, 7

✓ b. $3,200 U

One of the operations in the **U.S. Post Office** is a mechanical mail sorting operation. In this operation, letter mail is sorted at a rate of one letter per second. The letter is mechanically sorted from a three-digit code input by an operator sitting at a keyboard. The manager of the mechanical sorting operation wishes to determine the number of temporary employees to hire for December. The manager estimates that there will be an additional 25.92 million pieces of mail in December, due to the upcoming holiday season.

Assume that the sorting operators are temporary employees. The union contract requires that temporary employees be hired for one month at a time. Each temporary employee is hired to work 160 hours in the month.

a. How many temporary employees should the manager hire for December?
b. If each employee earns a standard $16 per hour, what would be the labor time variance if there were only 25.2 million additional letters sorted in December?

Exercise 6–19
Nonfinancial performance measures

Objective 8

Concord University wishes to monitor the efficiency and quality of its course registration process.

a. Identify three input and three output measures for this process.
b. Why would Concord University use nonfinancial measures for monitoring this process?

Exercise 6–20
Nonfinancial performance measures

Objective 8

WinnersEdge.com is an Internet retailer of sporting good products. Customers order sporting goods from the company, using an online catalog. The company processes these orders and delivers the requested product from the company's warehouse. The company wants to provide customers with an excellent purchase experience in order to expand the business with favorable word-of-mouth and to drive repeat business. To help monitor performance, the company developed a set of performance measures for its order placement and delivery process.

Number of misfilled orders
Average computer response time to customer "clicks"
System capacity divided by customer demands
Elapsed time between customer order and product delivery
Number of page faults or errors due to software programming errors
Server (computer) downtime
Training dollars per programmer
Dollar amount of returned goods
Number of orders per warehouse employee
Number of customer complaints divided by the number of orders
Maintenance dollars divided by hardware investment

From the list above, classify the measures as either input or output measures related to the order placement and delivery process.

Problem 6–1A
Direct materials and direct labor variance analysis

Objectives 2, 3, 4

✓ c. Rate variance, $351 U

Dresses by Linda, Inc. manufactures silk dresses in a small manufacturing facility. Manufacturing has 13 employees. Each employee presently provides 36 hours of productive labor per week. Information about a production week is as follows:

Standard wage per hour	$10.00
Standard labor time per dress	18 minutes
Standard number of yards of silk per dress	4.2 yards
Standard price per yard of silk	$6.00
Actual price per yard of silk	$6.20
Actual yards of silk used during the week	6,100 yards
Number of dresses produced during the week	1,500
Actual wage per hour	$10.75
Actual hours per week	468 hours

Instructions
Determine (a) the standard cost per dress for direct materials and direct labor, (b) the price variance, quantity variance, and total direct materials cost variance, and (c) the rate variance, time variance, and total direct labor cost variance.

Problem 6–2A
Flexible budgeting and variance analysis

Objectives 2, 3, 4

✓ 1. a. Direct materials quantity variance, $1,900 F

Venus Chocolate Company makes dark chocolate and light chocolate. Both products require cocoa and sugar. The following planning information has been made available:

	Standard Quantity		
	Dark Chocolate	**Light Chocolate**	**Standard Price per Pound**
Cocoa	12 lbs.	8 lbs.	$10.00
Sugar	10 lbs.	16 lbs.	$ 3.00
Standard labor time	0.25 hr.	0.40 hr.	
Planned production	2,400 cases	5,400 cases	
Standard labor rate	$14.00 per hour	$14.00 per hour	

Venus Chocolate does not expect there to be any beginning or ending inventories of cocoa or sugar.

At the end of the budget year, Venus Chocolate had the following actual results:

	Dark Chocolate	Light Chocolate
Actual production (cases)	2,800	6,000

	Actual Price per Pound	Actual Pounds Purchased and Used
Cocoa	$9.50	80,900
Sugar	3.20	125,700

	Actual Labor Rate	Actual Labor Hours Used
Dark chocolate	$14.40	725
Light chocolate	14.40	2,310

Instructions

1. Prepare the following variance analyses, based on the actual results and production levels at the end of the budget year:
   a. Direct materials price, quantity, and total variance.
   b. Direct labor rate, time, and total variance.
2. ✏️ Why are the standard amounts in (1) based on the actual production for the year instead of the planned production for the year?

Problem 6–3A
Direct materials, direct labor, and factory overhead cost variance analysis

Objectives 3, 4, 5

SPREADSHEET

✓ c. Controllable variance, $150 F

Bayou Resins Company processes a base chemical into plastic. Standard costs and actual costs for direct materials, direct labor, and factory overhead incurred for the manufacture of 1,500 units of product were as follows:

	Standard Costs	Actual Costs
Direct materials	6,000 pounds at $3.40	5,930 pounds at $3.50
Direct labor	1,125 hours at $18.00	1,140 hours at $18.50
Factory overhead	Rates per direct labor hour, based on 100% of normal capacity of 1,100 direct labor hours:	
	Variable cost, $4.80	$5,250 variable cost
	Fixed cost, $12.00	$13,200 fixed cost

Each unit requires 0.75 hours of direct labor.

Instructions
Determine (a) the price variance, quantity variance, and total direct materials cost variance, (b) the rate variance, time variance, and total direct labor cost variance, and (c) variable factory overhead controllable variance, the fixed factory overhead volume variance, and total factory overhead cost variance.

Problem 6–4A
Standard factory overhead variance report

Objective 5

GENERAL LEDGER

✓ Volume variance, $3,300 F

Wells Inc., a manufacturer of construction equipment, prepared the following factory overhead cost budget for the Welding Department for May 2003. The company expected to operate the department at 100% of normal capacity of 3,000 hours.

Variable costs:		
Indirect factory wages	$22,800	
Power and light	3,750	
Indirect materials	10,200	
Total variable cost		$ 36,750
Fixed costs:		
Supervisory salaries	$67,500	
Depreciation of plant and equipment	26,400	
Insurance and property taxes	5,100	
Total fixed cost		99,000
Total factory overhead cost		$135,750

During May, the department operated at 3,100 hours, and the factory overhead costs incurred were: indirect factory wages, $23,450; power and light, $3,980; indirect materials, $10,600; supervisory salaries, $67,500; depreciation of plant and equipment, $26,400; and insurance and property taxes, $5,100.

Instructions
Prepare a factory overhead cost variance report for May. To be useful for cost control, the budgeted amounts should be based on 3,100 hours.

Problem 6–5A
Standards for nonmanufacturing expenses

Objectives 4, 7, 8

✓ 3. $960 U

Verimax Software Company does software development. One important activity in software development is writing software code. The manager of the WordPro Development Team determined that the average software programmer could write 30 lines of code in an hour. The plan for the first week in July called for 4,500 lines of code to be written on the WordPro product. The WordPro Team has four programmers. Each programmer is hired from an employment firm that requires that temporary employees be hired for a minimum of a 40-hour week. Programmers are paid $20.00 per hour. The manager offered a bonus if the team could generate more than 4,800 lines for the week, without overtime. Due to a project emergency, the programmers wrote more code in the first week of July than planned. The actual amount of code written in the first week of July was 5,280 lines, without overtime. As a result, the bonus caused the average programmer's hourly rate to increase to $26.00 per hour during the first week in July.

Instructions

1. If the team generated 4,500 lines of code according to the original plan, what would have been the labor time variance?
2. What was the actual labor time variance as a result of generating 5,280 lines of code?
3. What was the labor rate variance as a result of the bonus?
4. The manager is trying to determine if a better decision would have been to hire a temporary programmer to meet the higher programming demand in the first week of July, rather than paying out the bonus. If another employee was hired from the employment firm, what would have been the labor time variance in the first week?
5. ▬▬► Which decision is better, paying the bonus or hiring another programmer?
6. ▬▬► Are there any performance-related issues that the labor time and rate variances fail to consider? Explain.

PROBLEMS SERIES B

Problem 6–1B
Direct materials and direct labor variance analysis

Objectives 2, 3, 4

✓ c. Direct labor time variance, $1,560 F

Gilded Fixtures Company manufactures faucets in a small manufacturing facility. The faucets are made from zinc. Manufacturing has 13 employees. Each employee presently provides 40 hours of labor per week. Information about a production week is as follows:

Standard wage per hour	$13.00
Standard labor time per faucet	12 minutes
Standard number of pounds of zinc	2.5 pounds
Standard price per pound of zinc	$8.50
Actual price per pound of zinc	$8.25
Actual pounds of zinc used during the week	8,140 lbs.
Number of faucets produced during the week	3,200
Actual wage per hour	$12
Actual hours per week	520 hours

Instructions

Determine (a) the standard cost per unit for direct materials and direct labor, (b) the price variance, quantity variance, and total direct materials cost variance, and (c) the rate variance, time variance, and total direct labor cost variance.

Problem 6–2B
Flexible budgeting and variance analysis

Objectives 2, 3, 4

✓ 1. b. Time variance, $120 U

Polar Coat Company makes women's and men's coats. Both products require filler and lining material. The following planning information has been made available:

	Standard Quantity		
	Women's Coats	**Men's Coats**	**Standard Price per Unit**
Filler	2 lbs.	3.5 lbs.	$25.00
Liner	5 yds.	8 yds.	$ 8.00
Standard labor time	0.20 hr.	0.30 hr.	
Planned production	2,000 units	3,500 units	
Standard labor rate	$12.00 per hour	$12.00 per hour	

Polar Coat does not expect there to be any beginning or ending inventories of filler and lining material.

At the end of the budget year, Polar Coat experienced the following actual results:

	Women's Coats	Men's Coats
Actual production	1,800	3,200

	Actual Price per Unit	Actual Quantity Purchased and Used
Filler	$24.60	15,200
Liner	8.20	34,000

	Actual Labor Rate	Actual Labor Hours Used
Woman's Coat	$11.75	380
Man's Coat	12.10	950

The expected beginning inventory and desired ending inventory were realized.

Instructions

1. Prepare the following variance analyses, based on the actual results and production levels at the end of the budget year:
    a. Direct materials price, quantity, and total variance.
    b. Direct labor rate, time, and total variance.
2. ✏︎ Why are the standard amounts in (1) based on the actual production at the end of the year instead of the planned production at the beginning of the year?

Problem 6–3B
Direct materials, direct labor, and factory overhead cost variance analysis

Objectives 3, 4, 5

SPREADSHEET

✓ a. Price variance, $1,825 F

Comfort Ride Tire Co. manufactures automobile tires. Standard costs and actual costs for direct materials, direct labor, and factory overhead incurred for the manufacture of 14,000 tires were as follows:

	Standard Costs	Actual Costs
Direct materials	36,000 pounds at $3.40	36,500 pounds at $3.35
Direct labor	3,500 hours at $16.00	3,580 hours at $16.20
Factory overhead	Rates per direct labor hour, based on 100% of normal capacity of 4,000 direct labor hours:	
	Variable cost, $1.80	$6,270 variable cost
	Fixed cost, $2.50	$10,000 fixed cost

Each tire requires 0.25 hour of direct labor.

Instructions

Determine (a) the price variance, quantity variance, and total direct materials cost variance, (b) the rate variance, time variance, and total direct labor cost variance, and (c) variable factory overhead controllable variance, the fixed factory overhead volume variance, and total factory overhead cost variance.

Problem 6–4B
Standard factory overhead variance report

Objective 5

GENERAL LEDGER

✓ Net controllable variance, $60 F

HealthGuard Company, a manufacturer of disposable medical supplies, prepared the following factory overhead cost budget for the Assembly Department for July 2003. The company expected to operate the department at 100% of normal capacity of 5,000 hours.

Variable costs:		
Indirect factory wages	$ 9,000	
Power and light	2,500	
Indirect materials	6,000	
Total variable cost		$17,500
Fixed costs:		
Supervisory salaries	$16,400	
Depreciation of plant and equipment	4,800	
Insurance and property taxes	1,800	
Total fixed cost		23,000
Total factory overhead cost		$40,500

During July, the department operated at 4,600 hours, and the factory overhead costs incurred were: indirect factory wages, $8,150; power and light, $2,390; indirect materials, $5,500; supervisory salaries, $16,400; depreciation of plant and equipment, $4,800; and insurance and property taxes, $1,800.

Instructions

Prepare a factory overhead cost variance report for July. To be useful for cost control, the budgeted amounts should be based on 4,600 hours.

Problem 6–5B
Standards for
nonmanufacturing expenses

Objectives 4, 7, 8

✓ 2. $72 F

The Radiology Department provides imaging services for Hope Medical Center. One important activity in the Radiology Department is transcribing tape-recorded analyses of images into a written report. The manager of the Radiology Department determined that the average transcriptionist could type 450 lines of a report in an hour. The plan for the first week in May called for 45,000 typed lines to be written. The Radiology Department has three transcriptionists. Each transcriptionist is hired from an employment firm that requires that temporary employees be hired for a minimum of a 40-hour week. Transcriptionists are paid $12.00 per hour. The manager offered a bonus if the department could type more than 54,000 lines for the week, without overtime. Due to high service demands, the transcriptionists typed more lines in the first week of May than planned. The actual amount of lines typed in the first week of May was 56,700 lines, without overtime. As a result, the bonus caused the average transcriptionist hourly rate to increase to $15.00 per hour during the first week in May.

Instructions

1. If the department typed 45,000 lines according to the original plan, what would have been the labor time variance?
2. What was the labor time variance as a result of typing 56,700 lines?
3. What was the labor rate variance as a result of the bonus?
4. The manager is trying to determine if a better decision would have been to hire a temporary transcriptionist to meet the higher typing demands in the first week of May, rather than paying out the bonus. If another employee was hired from the employment firm, what would have been the labor time variance in the first week?
5. ▬▶ Which decision is better, paying the bonus or hiring another transcriptionist?
6. ▬▶ Are there any performance-related issues that the labor time and rate variances fail to consider? Explain.

SPECIAL ACTIVITIES

Activity 6–1
Cambridge Insurance
Company
Ethics and professional
conduct in business

Dan Hendrix is a cost analyst with Cambridge Insurance Company. Cambridge is applying standards to its claims payment operation. Claims payment is a repetitive operation that could be evaluated with standards. Dan used time and motion studies to identify a theoretical standard of 25 claims processed per hour. The Claims Processing Department manager, Angie Street, has rejected this standard and has argued that the standard should be 20 claims processed per hour. Angie and Dan were unable to agree, so they decided to discuss this matter openly at a joint meeting with the vice-president of operations, who would arbitrate a final decision. Prior to the meeting, Dan wrote the following memo to the VP.

To: Kim Jan, Vice-President of Operations
From: Dan Hendrix
Re: Standards in the Claims Processing Department

As you know, Angie and I are scheduled to meet with you to discuss our disagreement with respect to the appropriate standards for the Claims Processing Department. I have conducted time and motion studies and have determined that the theoretical standard is 25 claims processed per hour. Angie argues that 20 claims processed per hour would be more appropriate. I believe she is trying to "pad" the budget with some slack. I'm not sure what she is trying to get away with, but I believe a tight standard will drive efficiency up in her area. I hope you will agree when we meet with you next week.

▬▶ Discuss the ethical and professional issues in this situation.

Activity 6–2
Lang Company
Nonfinancial performance measures

The senior management of Lang Company has proposed the following three performance measures for the company:

1. Net income as a percent of stockholders' equity
2. Revenue growth
3. Employee satisfaction

Management believes these three measures combine both financial and nonfinancial measures and are thus superior to using just financial measures.

✏️→ What advice would you give Lang Company for improving on its performance measurement system?

Activity 6–3
Rogers Corporation
Nonfinancial performance measures

At the Soladyne Division of **Rogers Corporation**, the controller used a number of measures to provide managers information about the performance of a just-in-time (JIT) manufacturing operation. Three measures used by the company are:

- Orders Past Due: Sales dollar value of orders that were scheduled for shipment, but were not shipped during the period.
- Buyer Misery Index: Number of different customers that have orders that are late (scheduled for shipment, but not shipped).
- Scrap Index: The sales dollar value of scrap for the period.

1. ✏️→ How is the "orders past due" measure different from the "buyer's misery index," or are the two measures just measuring the same thing?
2. ✏️→ Why do you think the scrap index is measured at sales dollar value, rather than at cost?

Source: John W. Schmitthenner, "Metrics," *Management Accounting*, May 1993, pp. 27–30.

Activity 6–4
S-Scape Electronics Inc.
Variance interpretation

You have been asked to investigate some cost problems in the Assembly Department of S-Scape Electronics Inc., a consumer electronics company. To begin your investigation, you have obtained the following budget performance report for the department for the last quarter:

S-Scape Electronics Inc.—Assembly Department
Quarterly Budget Performance Report

	Standard Quantity at Standard Rates	Actual Quantity at Standard Rates	Quantity Variances
Direct labor	$ 45,000	$ 65,000	$20,000 U
Direct materials	85,000	110,000	25,000 U
Total	$130,000	$175,000	$45,000 U

The following reports were also obtained:

S-Scape Electronics Inc.—Purchasing Department
Quarterly Budget Performance Report

	Actual Quantity at Standard Rates	Actual Quantity at Actual Rates	Price Variance
Direct materials	$125,000	$110,000	$15,000 F

S-Scape Electronics Inc.—Fabrication Department
Quarterly Budget Performance Report

	Standard Quantity at Standard Rates	Actual Quantity at Standard Rates	Quantity Variances
Direct labor	$ 70,000	$ 58,000	$12,000 F
Direct materials	40,000	40,000	0
Total	$110,000	$ 98,000	$12,000 F

You also interviewed the Assembly Department supervisor. Excerpts from the interview follow.

Q: *What explains the poor performance in your department?*
A: *Listen, you've got to understand what it's been like in this department recently. Lately, it seems no matter how hard we try, we can't seem to make the standards. I'm not sure what is going on, but we've been having a lot of problems lately.*
Q: *What kind of problems?*
A: *Well, for instance, all this quarter we've been requisitioning purchased parts from the material storeroom, and the parts just didn't fit together very well. I'm not sure what is going on, but during most of this quarter we've had to scrap and sort purchased parts—just to get our assemblies put together. Naturally, all this takes time and material. And that's not all.*
Q: *Go on.*
A: *All this quarter, the work that we've been receiving from the Fabrication Department has been shoddy. I mean, maybe around 20% of the stuff that comes in from Fabrication just can't be assembled. The fabrication is all wrong. As a result, we've had to scrap and rework a lot of the stuff. Naturally, this has just shot our quantity variances.*

Interpret the variance reports in light of the comments by the Assembly Department supervisor.

Activity 6–5
TruNote Company
Variance interpretation

TruNote Company is a small manufacturer of electronic musical instruments. The plant manager received the following variable factory overhead report for the period:

	Actual	Budgeted Variable Factory Overhead at Actual Production
Supplies	$21,000	$20,000
Power and light	9,000	8,000
Indirect factory wages	50,000	40,000
Total	$80,000	$68,000

Actual units produced: 4,000 (90% of practical capacity)

The plant manager is not pleased with the $12,000 unfavorable variable factory overhead controllable variance and has come to discuss the matter with the controller. The following discussion occurred:

Plant Manager: I just received this factory report for the latest month of operation. I'm not very pleased with these figures. Before these numbers go to headquarters, you and I will need to reach an understanding.
Controller: Go ahead, what's the problem?
Plant Manager: What's the problem? Well, everything. Look at the variance. It's too large. If I understand the accounting approach being used here, you are assuming that my costs are variable to the units produced. Thus, as the production volume declines, so should these costs. Well, I don't believe that these costs are variable at all. I think they are fixed costs. As a result, when we operate below capacity, the costs really don't go down at all. I'm being penalized for costs I have no control over at all. I need this report to be redone to reflect this fact. If anything, the difference between actual and budget is essentially a volume variance. Listen, I know that you're a team player. You really need to reconsider your assumptions on this one.

If you were in the controller's position, how would you respond to the plant manager?

Activity 6–6
Into the Real World
Government performance review

The **U.S. General Services Administration (GSA)** provides a one-stop source for information related to the development and use of performance measures for public service agencies. The portal for these activities is titled "Performance Pathways" and is located at **http://www.itpolicy.gsa.gov/mkm/pathways/pathways.htm**. Go to this Web site and locate the "sample performance measures" link. This link leads to examples of performance measures used by different types of public service agencies, such as police, parks and recreation, health care, property management, and information technology. Select one of the listed agencies, or if you are in a group, have different members of the group select several different agencies. List the nonfinancial measures used by your selected agency. For each performance measure, create a table showing whether the performance measure is related to service performance (to the public), internal efficiency, or employee satisfaction. Be prepared to report your findings back to your class.

ANSWERS TO SELF-EXAMINATION QUESTIONS

Matching

1. D	3. A	5. J	7. F	9. G	11. E
2. H	4. L	6. M	8. B	10. C	12. K

Multiple Choice

1. **C** The unfavorable direct materials price variance of $2,550 is determined as follows:

Actual price	$5.05 per pound
Standard price	5.00
Price variance—unfavorable	$0.05 per pound

$0.05 × 51,000 actual pounds = $2,550

2. **D** The unfavorable direct labor time variance of $2,400 is determined as follows:

Actual direct labor time	2,200
Standard direct labor time	2,000
Direct labor time variance—unfavorable	200 × $12 standard rate = $2,400

3. **B** The unfavorable factory overhead volume variance of $2,000 is determined as follows:

Productive capacity not used	1,000 hours
Standard fixed factory overhead cost rate	× $2
Factory overhead volume variance—unfavorable	$2,000

4. **B** The controllable variable factory overhead variance is determined as follows:

6,000 units × 0.25 hour = 1,500 hours
1,500 hours × $5.00 per hour = $7,500

Actual variable overhead:	$8,000
Less: Budgeted variable overhead at actual volume	7,500
Unfavorable controllable variance	$ 500

5. **D** The fixed factory overhead volume variance can be determined as follows:

Actual production in standard hours:
    600 units × 0.2 machine hour = 120 machine hours

Practical capacity	200 machine hours
Standard hours at actual production	120
Idle capacity	80 machine hours

80 hours × $12.00 = $960 unfavorable volume variance

Performance Evaluation for Decentralized Operations

M7

objectives

After studying this chapter, you should be able to:

1 List and explain the advantages and disadvantages of decentralized operations.

2 Prepare a responsibility accounting report for a cost center.

3 Prepare responsibility accounting reports for a profit center.

4 Compute and interpret the rate of return on investment, the residual income, and the balanced scorecard for an investment center.

5 Explain how the market price, negotiated price, and cost price approaches to transfer pricing may be used by decentralized segments of a business.

ave you ever wondered if there is an economic reason why large retail stores, such as **JCPenney Co.** and **Sears**, are divided into departments? Typically, these stores include a Men's Department, Women's Department, Appliances Department, Home Entertainment Department, and Sporting Goods Department. Each department usually has a manager who is responsible for the financial performance of the department. The store may be the responsibility of a store manager, and a group of stores within a particular geographic area may be the responsibility of a division or district manager. If you were to be hired by a department store chain, you would probably begin your career in a department. Running a department would be a valuable experience before becoming responsible for a complete store. Likewise, responsibility for a complete store provides excellent training for other management positions.

In this chapter, we will focus on the role of accounting in assisting managers in planning and controlling organizational units, such as divisions, stores, and departments.

Centralized and Decentralized Operations

objective 1

List and explain the advantages and disadvantages of decentralized operations.

A **centralized** business is one in which all major planning and operating decisions are made by top management. For example, a one-person, owner/manager-operated business is centralized because all plans and decisions are made by one person. In a small owner/manager-operated business, centralization may be desirable. This is because the owner/manager's close supervision ensures that the business will be operated in the way the owner/manager wishes.

Separating a business into **divisions** or operating units and delegating responsibility to unit managers is called **decentralization**. In a decentralized business, the unit managers are responsible for planning and controlling the operations of their units.

Divisions are often structured around common functions, products, customers, or regions. For example, **Delta Air Lines** is organized around *functions*, such as the Flight Operations Division. The **Procter & Gamble Company** is organized around common *products*, such as the Soap Division, which sells a wide array of cleaning products.

There is no one best amount of decentralization for all businesses. In some companies, division managers have authority over all operations, including fixed asset acquisitions and retirements. In other companies, division managers have authority over profits but not fixed asset acquisitions and retirements. The proper amount of decentralization for a company depends on its advantages and disadvantages for the company's unique circumstances.

Advantages of Decentralization

As a business grows, it becomes more difficult for top management to maintain close daily contact with all operations. In such cases, delegating authority to managers closest to the operations usually results in better decisions. These managers often anticipate and react to operating data more quickly than could top management. In addition, as a company expands into a wide range of products and services, it

Real World

A trend among large international companies is to decentralize into smaller customer-focused units, while maintaining the advantage of a big company. For example, **Siemens**, the giant $60 billion German electronics company, divided responsibility into 16 minicorporations, each with its own CEO and board of directors. To streamline decision making and enhance financial accountability, **Aluminum Company of America (Alcoa)** restructured its centrally managed divisions into 26 autonomous business units.

Real World

Nucor Corporation, a $4 billion steel company, practices a highly decentralized form of management, with only 30 people on its headquarters staff.

AOL Time Warner is a major media and entertainment empire that is decentralized into net services, publishing, cable networks, music, and movie production units. The net services division is AOL. The publishing division produces a number of popular magazines, including *Time, People, Sports Illustrated,* and *Money.* The cable network division consists of Turner Broadcasting, which produces CNN. The music division records and distributes music for such artists as Sugar Ray, Red Hot Chili Peppers, and GooGoo Dolls. The movie production division produces Warner Brothers films, such as *The Matrix.* These divisions are treated as separate units, with their own financial performance targets.

becomes more difficult for top management to maintain operating expertise in all product lines and services. Decentralization allows managers to focus on acquiring expertise in their areas of responsibility. For example, in a company that maintains operations in insurance, banking, and health care, managers could become "experts" in their area of operation and responsibility.

Decentralized decision making also provides excellent training for managers. This may be a factor in helping a company retain quality managers. Since the art of management is best acquired through experience, delegating responsibility allows managers to acquire and develop managerial expertise early in their careers.

Businesses that work closely with customers, such as hotels, are often decentralized. This helps managers create good customer relations by responding quickly to customers' needs. In addition, because managers of decentralized operations tend to identify with customers and with operations, they are often more creative in suggesting operating and product improvements.

BUSINESS ON STAGE

Generating Creativity in Business

One of the advantages of decentralized operations is that it brings a wide variety of managers' ideas and insights together to solve business problems and issues. Several methods often used in business to generate creative solutions to problems and issues are described below.

- **Brainstorming** involves bringing a small group of people together in a room, presenting them with a problem or issue, and directing them to follow four rules. First, no ideas can be criticized. Second, any idea, no matter how wild or unconventional, is considered. Third, the more ideas the better. Fourth, each participant should try to improve on others' ideas and thus create a chain of inspiration. Many businesses use brainstorming to come up with new products and customer service opportunities. For example, the fuel-efficient engine for the *Honda Civic* was developed through brainstorming.

- **Retroduction** challenges the assumptions about the way things are and thus forces managers to look at problems and issues from a different perspective. For example, some Citicorp managers challenged the widespread assumption that customers prefer to bank with human tellers. This led to the use of automatic teller machines by Citicorp.

- **Listing** involves identifying alternative ways a business might use something it already has. Often, a checklist of idea-spurring questions is used, such as SCAMPER, which stands for *Substitute, Combine, Adapt, Modify* or *magnify, Put to other uses, Eliminate* or *reduce, Reverse* or *rearrange.* For example, Kiichiro Toyoda, the founder of Toyota, sought ways to eliminate large inventories and the need for warehouses. He was fascinated by how American supermarkets sold vast amounts of food that might spoil if large inventories were kept at each store. He adapted this observation into the just-in-time approach to manufacturing automobiles. ■

Disadvantages of Decentralization

A primary disadvantage of decentralized operations is that decisions made by one manager may negatively affect the profitability of the entire company. For example, the Pizza Hut chain added chicken to its menu and ended up taking business away from KFC. Then KFC retaliated with a blistering ad campaign against Pizza Hut. This happened even though both chains are part of the same company, **Tricon Global Restaurants**!

Another potential disadvantage of decentralized operations is duplicating assets and costs in operating divisions. For example, each manager of a product line might have a separate sales force and administrative office staff. Centralizing these personnel could save money.

Responsibility Accounting

In a decentralized business, an important function of accounting is to assist unit managers in evaluating and controlling their areas of responsibility, called **responsibility centers**. **Responsibility accounting** is the process of measuring and reporting operating data by responsibility center. Three common types of responsibility centers are cost centers, profit centers, and investment centers. These three responsibility centers differ in their scope of responsibility, as shown below.

Q&A A department in a manufacturing facility would likely be what type of performance center?

Cost center

Cost Center	Profit Center	Investment Center
	Revenue	Revenue
Cost	− Cost	− Cost
	Profit	Profit
		Investment in assets

Responsibility Accounting for Cost Centers

objective 2

Prepare a responsibility accounting report for a cost center.

In a **cost center**, the unit manager has responsibility and authority for controlling the costs incurred. For example, the supervisor of the Power Department has responsibility for the costs incurred in providing power. A cost center manager does not make decisions concerning sales or the amount of fixed assets invested in the center. Cost centers may vary in size from a small department to an entire manufacturing plant. In addition, cost centers may exist within other cost centers. For example, we could view an entire university as a cost center, and each college and department within the university could also be a cost center, as shown in Exhibit 1.

Exhibit 1 Cost Centers in a University

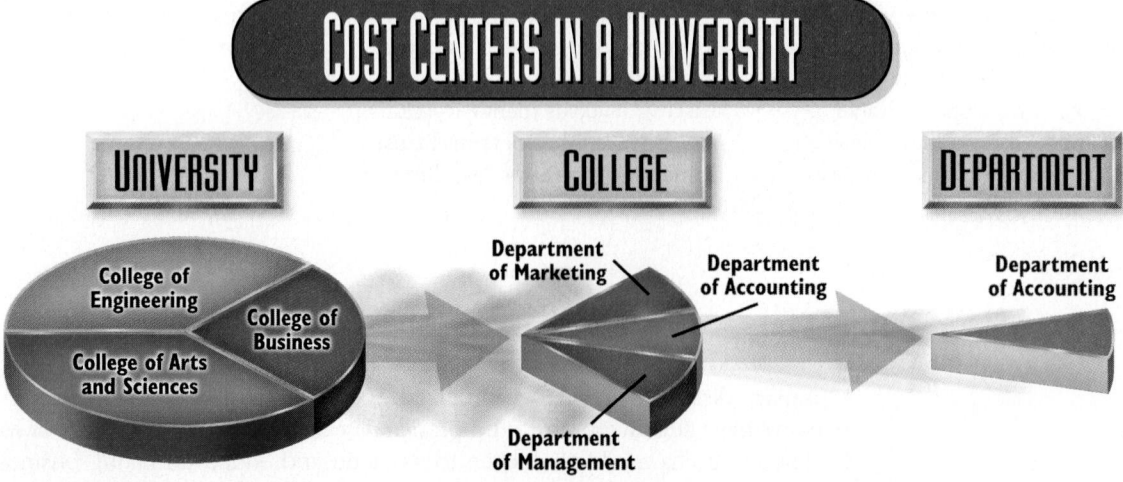

Since managers of cost centers have responsibility and authority over costs, responsibility accounting for cost centers focuses on costs. To illustrate, the budget performance reports in Exhibit 2 are part of a responsibility accounting system. These reports aid the managers in controlling costs.

Exhibit 2 Responsibility Accounting Reports for Cost Centers

Budget Performance Report
Vice-President, Production
For the Month Ended October 31, 2003

	Budget	Actual	Over Budget	Under Budget
Administration	$ 19,500	$ 19,700	$ 200	
Plant A	467,475	470,330	2,855	
Plant B	395,225	394,300		$925
	$882,200	$884,330	$3,055	$925

Budget Performance Report
Manager, Plant A
For the Month Ended October 31, 2003

	Budget	Actual	Over Budget	Under Budget
Administration	$ 17,500	$ 17,350		$150
Department 1	109,725	111,280	$1,555	
Department 2	190,500	192,600	2,100	
Department 3	149,750	149,100		650
	$467,475	$470,330	$3,655	$800

Budget Performance Report
Supervisor, Department 1—Plant A
For the Month Ended October 31, 2003

	Budget	Actual	Over Budget	Under Budget
Factory wages	$ 58,100	$ 58,000		$100
Materials	32,500	34,225	$1,725	
Supervisory salaries	6,400	6,400		
Power and light	5,750	5,690		60
Depreciation of plant and equipment	4,000	4,000		
Maintenance	2,000	1,990		10
Insurance and property taxes	975	975		
	$109,725	$111,280	$1,725	$170

Organizational chart:
- Vice-President Production
  - Plant A / Plant B
  - Manager Plant A
    - Dept. 1 / Dept. 2 / Dept. 3
    - Supervisor Dept. 1

In Exhibit 2, the reports prepared for the department supervisors show the budgeted and actual manufacturing costs for their departments. The supervisors can use these reports to focus on areas of significant difference, such as the difference between the budgeted and actual materials cost. The supervisor of Department 1 in Plant A may use additional information from a scrap report to determine why materials are over budget. Such a report might show that materials were scrapped as a result of machine malfunctions, improper use of machines by employees, or low quality materials.

For higher levels of management, responsibility accounting reports are usually more summarized than for lower levels of management. In Exhibit 2, for example, the budget performance report for the plant manager summarizes budget and actual cost data for the departments under the manager's supervision. This report enables the plant manager to identify the department supervisors responsible for major differences. Likewise, the report for the vice-president of production summarizes the cost data for each plant. The plant managers can thus be held responsible for major differences in budgeted and actual costs in their plants.

Responsibility Accounting for Profit Centers

objective 3

Prepare responsibility accounting reports for a profit center.

Profit centers may be divisions, departments, or products.

In a **profit center**, the unit manager has the responsibility and the authority to make decisions that affect both costs and revenues (and thus profits). Profit centers may be divisions, departments, or products. For example, a consumer products company might organize its brands (product lines) as divisional profit centers. The manager of each brand could have responsibility for product cost and decisions regarding revenues, such as setting sales prices. The manager of a profit center does not make decisions concerning the fixed assets invested in the center. For example, the brand manager of a consumer products company does not make the decision to expand the plant capacity for the brand.

Profit centers are often viewed as an excellent training assignment for new managers. For example, Lester B. Korn, Chairman and Chief Executive Officer of **Korn/Ferry International**, offered the following strategy for young executives en route to top management positions:

Get Profit-Center Responsibility—Obtain a position where you can prove yourself as both a specialist with particular expertise and a generalist who can exercise leadership, authority, and inspire enthusiasm among colleagues and subordinates.

Responsibility accounting reports usually show the revenues, expenses, and income from operations for the profit center. The profit center income statement should include only revenues and expenses that are controlled by the manager. **Controllable revenues** are revenues earned by the profit center. **Controllable expenses** are costs that can be influenced (controlled) by the decisions of profit center managers. For example, the manager of the Men's Department at **Nordstrom** most likely controls the salaries of department personnel but does not control the property taxes of the store.

Service Department Charges

We will illustrate profit center income reporting for the Nova Entertainment Group (NEG). Assume that NEG is a diversified entertainment company with two operating divisions organized as profit centers: the Theme Park Division and the Movie Production Division. The revenues and operating expenses for the two divisions are shown on the following page. The operating expenses consist of the direct expenses, such as the wages and salaries of a division's employees.

	Theme Park Division	Movie Production Division
Revenues	$6,000,000	$2,500,000
Operating expenses	2,495,000	405,000

In addition to direct expenses, divisions may also have expenses for services provided by internal centralized **service departments**. These service departments are often more efficient at providing service than are outside service providers. Examples of such service departments include the following:

Which of the following departments—Legal Department, Fabrication Department, MIS Department, Maintenance Department— are examples of service departments?

Legal Department, MIS Department, and Maintenance Department

- Research and Development
- Government Relations
- Telecommunications
- Publications and Graphics
- Facilities Management
- Purchasing
- Information Systems
- Payroll Accounting
- Transportation
- Personnel Administration

A profit center's income from operations should reflect the cost of any internal services used by the center. To illustrate, assume that NEG established a Payroll Accounting Department. The costs of the payroll services, called **service department charges**, are charged to NEG's profit centers, as shown in Exhibit 3.

Exhibit 3 Payroll Accounting Department Charges to NEG's Theme Park and Movie Production Divisions

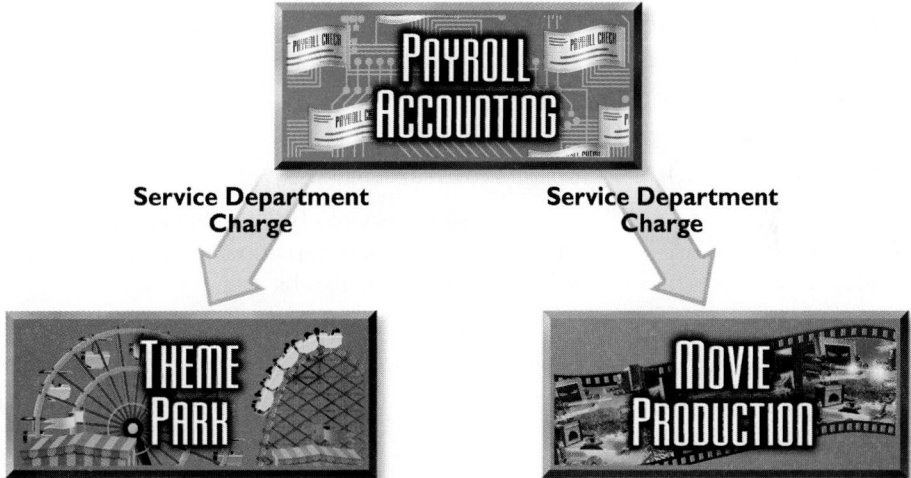

Service department charges are *indirect expenses* to a profit center. They are similar to the expenses that would be incurred if the profit center had purchased the services from a source outside the company. A profit center manager has control over such expenses if the manager is free to choose *how much* service is used from the service department.

To illustrate service department charges, assume that NEG has two other service departments—Purchasing and Legal, in addition to Payroll Accounting. The expenses for the year ended December 31, 2003, for each service department are as follows:

Employees of IBM speak of "green money" and "blue money." Green money comes from customers. Blue money comes from providing services to other IBM departments via service department charges. IBM employees note that blue money is easier to earn than green money; yet from the stockholders' perspective, green money is the only money that counts.

Purchasing	$400,000
Payroll Accounting	255,000
Legal	250,000
Total	$905,000

An **activity base** for each service department is used to charge service department expenses to the Theme Park and Movie Production Divisions. The activity base for each service department is a measure of the services performed. For NEG, the service department activity bases are as follows:

Department	Activity Base
Purchasing	Number of purchase requisitions
Payroll Accounting	Number of payroll checks
Legal	Number of billed hours

The use of services by the Theme Park and Movie Production Divisions is as follows:

	Service Usage		
	Purchasing	Payroll Accounting	Legal
Theme Park Division	25,000 purchase requisitions	12,000 payroll checks	100 billed hours
Movie Production Division	15,000	3,000	900
Total	40,000 purchase requisitions	15,000 payroll checks	1,000 billed hours

The rates at which services are charged to each division are called **service department charge rates**. These rates are determined by dividing each service department's expenses by the total service usage as follows:

Purchasing: $\dfrac{\$400,000}{40,000 \text{ purchase requisitions}} = \$10$ per purchase requisition

Payroll Accounting: $\dfrac{\$255,000}{15,000 \text{ payroll checks}} = \$17$ per payroll check

Legal: $\dfrac{\$250,000}{1,000 \text{ hours}} = \$250$ per hour

The use of services by the Theme Park and Movie Production Divisions is multiplied by the service department charge rates to determine the charges to each division, as shown in Exhibit 4.

The centralized payroll department has expenses of $120,000. The department processed a total of 25,000 payroll checks for the period. If the Eastern Division has 6,000 payroll checks for the period, how much should it be charged for payroll services?

$28,800 [($120,000/25,000) × 6,000]

Exhibit 4 Service Department Charges to NEG Divisions

Nova Entertainment Group Service Department Charges to NEG Divisions For the Year Ended December 31, 2003		
Service Department	Theme Park Division	Movie Production Division
Purchasing (Note A)	$250,000	$150,000
Payroll Accounting (Note B)	204,000	51,000
Legal (Note C)	25,000	225,000
Total service department charges	$479,000	$426,000

Note A:
25,000 purchase requisitions × $10 per purchase requisition = $250,000
15,000 purchase requisitions × $10 per purchase requisition = $150,000
Note B:
12,000 payroll checks × $17 per check = $204,000
3,000 payroll checks × $17 per check = $51,000
Note C:
100 hours × $250 per hour = $25,000
900 hours × $250 per hour = $225,000

Some companies require service departments to measure the quality of their service. For example, the Weyerhaeuser human resource, accounting, and quality control service departments must measure the quality of their services to line departments, such as sales, marketing, and production. So while the internal line departments "pay" for service in the form of service department charges, they also provide feedback on the service quality. In this way, the line departments are treated like customers.

The Theme Park Division employs many temporary and part-time employees who are paid weekly. This is in contrast to the Movie Production Division, which has a more permanent payroll that is paid on a monthly basis. As a result, the Theme Park Division requires 12,000 payroll checks. This results in a large service charge from Payroll Accounting to the Theme Park Division. In contrast, the Movie Production Division uses many legal services for contract negotiations. Thus, there is a large service charge from Legal to the Movie Production Division.

Profit Center Reporting

The divisional income statements for NEG are presented in Exhibit 5. These statements show the service department charges to the divisions.

Exhibit 5 Divisional Income Statements—NEG

If sales are $500,000, the cost of goods sold is $285,000, selling expenses are $85,000, and service department charges are $53,000, what is the income from operations?

$77,000 ($500,000 − $285,000 − $85,000 − $53,000)

Nova Entertainment Group
Divisional Income Statements
For the Year Ended December 31, 2003

	Theme Park Division	Movie Production Division
Revenues*	$6,000,000	$2,500,000
Operating expenses	2,495,000	405,000
Income from operations before service department charges	$3,505,000	$2,095,000
Less service department charges:		
Purchasing	$ 250,000	$ 150,000
Payroll Accounting	204,000	51,000
Legal	25,000	225,000
Total service department charges	$ 479,000	$ 426,000
Income from operations	$3,026,000	$1,669,000

*For a profit center that sells products, the income statement would show: Net sales − Cost of goods sold = Gross profit. The operating expenses would be deducted from the gross profit to get the income from operations before service department charges.

The **income from operations** is a measure of a manager's performance. In evaluating the profit center manager, the income from operations should be compared over time to a budget. It should not be compared across profit centers, since the profit centers are usually different in terms of size, products, and customers.

Responsibility Accounting for Investment Centers

objective 4

Compute and interpret the rate of return on investment, the residual income, and the balanced scorecard for an investment center.

In an **investment center**, the unit manager has the responsibility and the authority to make decisions that affect not only costs and revenues but also the assets invested in the center. Investment centers are widely used in highly diversified companies organized by divisions.

The manager of an investment center has more authority and responsibility than the manager of a cost center or a profit center. The manager of an investment center occupies a position similar to that of a chief operating officer or president of a company and is evaluated in much the same way.

Since investment center managers have responsibility for revenues and expenses, income from operations is an important part of investment center reporting. In addition, because the manager has responsibility for the assets invested in the center, two additional measures of performance are often used. These measures are the rate of return on investment and residual income. Top management often compares these measures across investment centers to reward performance and assess investment in the centers.

To illustrate, assume that DataLink Inc. is a cellular phone company that has three regional divisions, Northern, Central, and Southern. Condensed divisional income statements for the investment centers are shown in Exhibit 6.

Exhibit 6 Divisional Income Statements—DataLink Inc.

DataLink Inc. Divisional Income Statements For the Year Ended December 31, 2003			
	Northern Division	**Central Division**	**Southern Division**
Revenues	$560,000	$672,000	$750,000
Operating expenses	336,000	470,400	562,500
Income from operations before service department charges	$224,000	$201,600	$187,500
Service department charges	154,000	117,600	112,500
Income from operations . . .	$ 70,000	$ 84,000	$ 75,000

Using only income from operations, the Central Division is the most profitable division. However, income from operations does not reflect the amount of assets invested in each center. For example, if the amount of assets invested in the Central Division is twice that of the other divisions, then the Central Division would be the least profitable in terms of the rate of return on these assets.

Rate of Return on Investment

Since investment center managers also control the amount of assets invested in their centers, they should be held accountable for the use of these assets. One measure that considers the amount of assets invested is the **rate of return on investment** (ROI) or **rate of return on assets**. It is one of the most widely used measures for investment centers and is computed as follows:

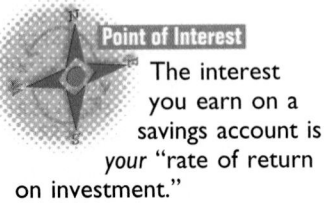

Point of Interest

The interest you earn on a savings account is *your* "rate of return on investment."

$$\text{Rate of return on investment (ROI)} = \frac{\textbf{Income from operations}}{\textbf{Invested assets}}$$

The rate of return on investment is useful because the three factors subject to control by divisional managers (revenues, expenses, and invested assets) are used in its computation. By measuring profitability relative to the amount of assets invested in each division, the rate of return on investment can be used to compare divisions. The higher the rate of return on investment, the better the division utilizes its assets to generate income. To illustrate, the rate of return on investment for each division of DataLink Inc., based on the book value of invested assets, is as follows:

	Northern Division	Central Division	Southern Division
Income from operations	$ 70,000	$ 84,000	$ 75,000
Invested assets	$350,000	$700,000	$500,000
Rate of return on investment	20%	12%	15%

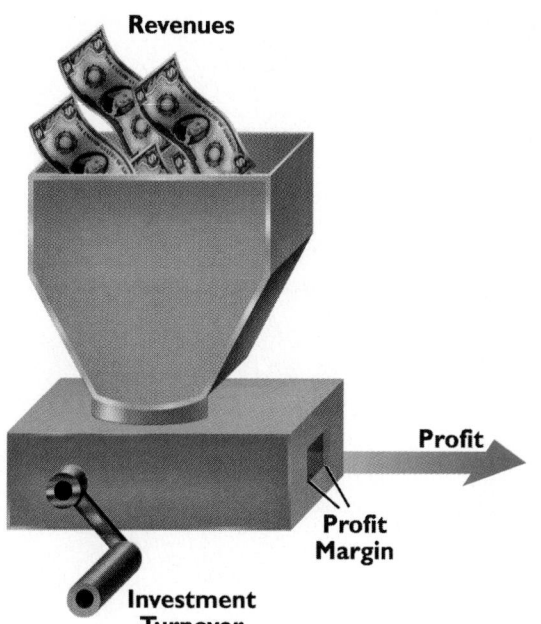

Revenues

Profit

Profit Margin

Investment Turnover

Although the Central Division generated the largest income from operations, its rate of return on investment (12%) is the lowest. Hence, relative to the assets invested, the Central Division is the least profitable division. In comparison, the rate of return on investment of the Northern Division is 20% and the Southern Division is 15%. These differences in the rates of return on investment can be further analyzed using an expanded formula for the rate of return on investment.

In the expanded formula, the rate of return on investment is the product of two factors. The first factor is the ratio of income from operations to sales, often called the **profit margin**. The second factor is the ratio of sales to invested assets, often called the **investment turnover**. In the illustration at the left, profits can be earned by either increasing the investment turnover (turning the crank faster), by increasing the profit margin (increasing the size of the opening), or both.

Using the expanded expression yields the same rate of return on investment for the Northern Division, 20%, as computed previously.

Rate of return on investment (ROI) = Profit margin × Investment turnover

$$\text{Rate of return on investment (ROI)} = \frac{\text{Income from operations}}{\text{Sales}} \times \frac{\text{Sales}}{\text{Invested assets}}$$

$$\text{ROI} = \frac{\$\,70{,}000}{\$560{,}000} \times \frac{\$560{,}000}{\$350{,}000}$$

$$\text{ROI} = 12.5\% \times 1.6$$

$$\text{ROI} = 20\%$$

The expanded expression for the rate of return on investment is useful in evaluating and controlling divisions. This is because the profit margin and the investment turnover focus on the underlying operating relationships of each division.

The profit margin component focuses on profitability by indicating the rate of profit earned on each sales dollar. If a division's profit margin increases, and all other factors remain the same, the division's rate of return on investment will increase. For example, a division might add more profitable products to its sales mix and thereby increase its overall profit margin and rate of return on investment.

The investment turnover component focuses on efficiency in using assets and indicates the rate at which sales are generated for each dollar of invested assets. The more sales per dollar invested, the greater the efficiency in using the assets. If a division's investment turnover increases, and all other factors remain the same, the division's rate of return on investment will increase. For example, a division might attempt to increase sales through special sales promotions or reduce inventory assets by using just-in-time principles, either of which would increase investment turnover.

The rate of return on investment, using the expanded expression for each division of DataLink Inc., is summarized as follows:

> The profit margin indicates the rate of profit on each sales dollar, while the investment turnover indicates the rate of sales on each dollar of invested assets.

$$\text{Rate of return on investment (ROI)} = \frac{\text{Income from operations}}{\text{Sales}} \times \frac{\text{Sales}}{\text{Invested assets}}$$

$$\textbf{Northern Division (ROI)} = \frac{\$\ 70,000}{\$560,000} \times \frac{\$560,000}{\$350,000}$$

$$\text{ROI} = 12.5\% \times 1.6$$
$$\text{ROI} = 20\%$$

$$\textbf{Central Division (ROI)} = \frac{\$\ 84,000}{\$672,000} \times \frac{\$672,000}{\$700,000}$$

$$\text{ROI} = 12.5\% \times 0.96$$
$$\text{ROI} = 12\%$$

$$\textbf{Southern Division (ROI)} = \frac{\$\ 75,000}{\$750,000} \times \frac{\$750,000}{\$500,000}$$

$$\text{ROI} = 10\% \times 1.5$$
$$\text{ROI} = 15\%$$

Income from operations is $35,000, invested assets are $140,000, and sales are $437,500. What is the (a) profit margin, (b) investment turnover, and (c) rate of return on investment?

(a) 8% ($35,000/$437,500); (b) 3.125 ($437,500/$140,000); (c) 25% (8% × 3.125, or $35,000/$140,000)

Although the Northern and Central Divisions have the same profit margins, the Northern Division investment turnover (1.6) is larger than that of the Central Division (0.96). Thus, by using its invested assets more efficiently, the Northern Division's rate of return on investment is higher than the Central Division's. The Southern Division's profit margin of 10% and investment turnover of 1.5 are lower than those of the Northern Division. The product of these factors results in a return on investment of 15% for the Southern Division, compared to 20% for the Northern Division.

To determine possible ways of increasing the rate of return on investment, the profit margin and investment turnover for a division may be analyzed. For example, if the Northern Division is in a highly competitive industry in which the profit margin cannot be easily increased, the division manager might focus on increasing the investment turnover. To illustrate, assume that the revenues of the Northern Division could be increased by $56,000 through increasing operating expenses, such as advertising, to $385,000. The Northern Division's income from operations will increase from $70,000 to $77,000, as shown below.

Revenues ($560,000 + $56,000)	$616,000
Operating expenses	385,000
Income from operations before service department charges	$231,000
Service department charges	154,000
Income from operations	$ 77,000

The rate of return on investment for the Northern Division, using the expanded expression, is recomputed as follows:

$$\text{Rate of return on investment (ROI)} = \frac{\text{Income from operations}}{\text{Sales}} \times \frac{\text{Sales}}{\text{Invested assets}}$$

$$\textbf{Northern Division revised ROI} = \frac{\$\ 77,000}{\$616,000} \times \frac{\$616,000}{\$350,000}$$

$$\text{ROI} = 12.5\% \times 1.76$$
$$\text{ROI} = 22\%$$

Although the Northern Division's profit margin remains the same (12.5%), the investment turnover has increased from 1.6 to 1.76, an increase of 10% (0.16 ÷ 1.6).

The 10% increase in investment turnover also increases the rate of return on investment by 10% (from 20% to 22%).

In addition to using it as a performance measure, the rate of return on investment may assist management in other ways. For example, in considering a decision to expand the operations of DataLink Inc., management might consider giving priority to the Northern Division because it earns the highest rate of return on investment. If the current rates of return on investment are maintained in the future, an investment in the Northern Division will return 20 cents (20%) on each dollar invested. In contrast, investments in the Central Division will earn only 12 cents per dollar invested, and investments in the Southern Division will return only 15 cents per dollar.

A disadvantage of the rate of return on investment as a performance measure is that it may lead divisional managers to reject new investments that could be profitable for the company as a whole. For example, the Northern Division of DataLink Inc. has an overall rate of return on investment of 20%. The minimum acceptable rate of return on investment for DataLink Inc. is 10%. The manager of the Northern Division has the opportunity of investing in a new project that is estimated will earn a 17% rate of return. If the manager of the Northern Division invests in the project, however, the Northern Division's overall rate of return will decrease from 20%. Thus, the division manager might decide to reject the project, even though the investment would exceed DataLink's minimum acceptable rate of return on investment. The CFO of **Millennium Chemicals Inc.** referred to a similar situation by stating: "We had too many divisional executives who failed to spend money on capital projects with more than satisfactory returns because those projects would have lowered the average return on assets of their particular business."

Residual Income

An additional measure of evaluating divisional performance—residual income—is useful in overcoming some of the disadvantages associated with the rate of return on investment. **Residual income** is the excess of income from operations over a minimum acceptable income from operations, as illustrated below.

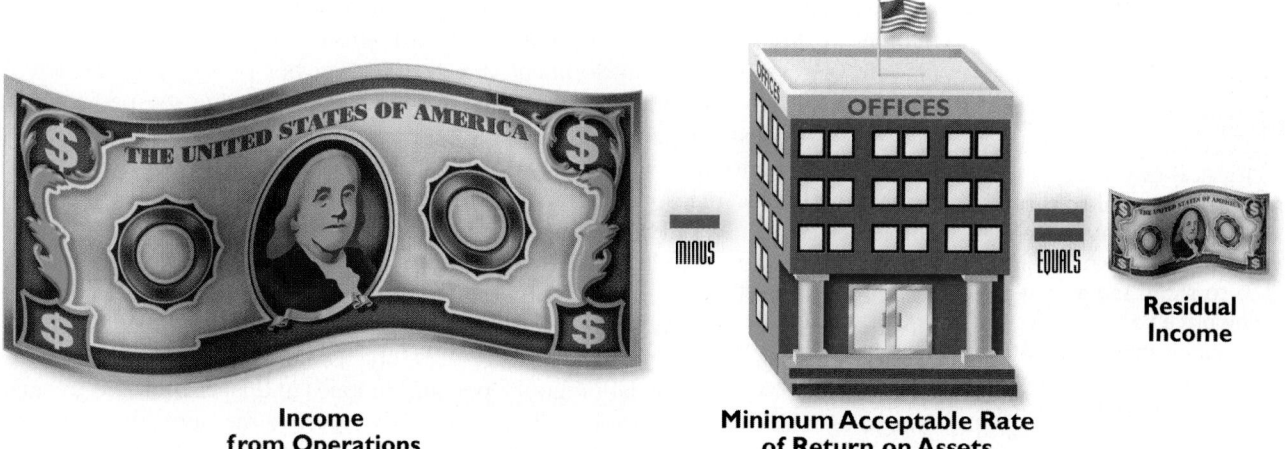

Income from Operations   mINUS   **Minimum Acceptable Rate of Return on Assets**   EQUALS   **Residual Income**

The minimum acceptable income from operations is normally computed by multiplying a minimum rate of return by the amount of divisional assets. The minimum rate is set by top management, based on such factors as the cost of financing the business operations. To illustrate, assume that DataLink Inc. has established 10% as the minimum acceptable rate of return on divisional assets. The residual incomes for the three divisions are as follows:

	Northern Division	Central Division	Southern Division
Income from operations	$70,000	$84,000	$75,000
Minimum acceptable income from operations as a percent of assets:			
$350,000 × 10%	35,000		
$700,000 × 10%		70,000	
$500,000 × 10%			50,000
Residual income	$35,000	$14,000	$25,000

The Northern Division has more residual income than the other divisions, even though it has the least amount of income from operations. This is because the assets on which to earn a minimum acceptable rate of return are less for the Northern Division than for the other divisions.

The major advantage of residual income as a performance measure is that it considers both the minimum acceptable rate of return and the total amount of the income from operations earned by each division. Residual income encourages division managers to maximize income from operations in excess of the minimum. This provides an incentive to accept any project that is expected to have a rate of return in excess of the minimum. Thus, the residual income number supports both divisional and overall company objectives.

The Balanced Scorecard[1]

In addition to financial divisional performance measures, many companies are also relying on nonfinancial divisional measures. One popular evaluation approach is the **balanced scorecard**. The balanced scorecard is a set of financial and nonfinancial measures that reflect multiple performance dimensions of a business. A common balanced scorecard design measures performance in the innovation and learning, customer, internal, and financial dimensions of a business. These four areas can be diagrammed as shown in Exhibit 7.

The innovation and learning perspective measures the amount of innovation in an organization. For example, a drug company, such as **Merck**, would measure the number of drugs in its FDA (Food and Drug Administration) approval pipeline, the amount of research and development (R&D) spending per period, and the length of time it takes to turn ideas into marketable products. Managing the performance of its R&D processes is critical to Merck's longer-term prospects and thus would be an additional performance perspective beyond the financial numbers. The customer perspective would measure customer satisfaction, loyalty, and perceptions. For example, **Amazon.com** measures the number of repeat visitors to its Web site as a measure of customer loyalty. Amazon.com needs repeat business because the costs to acquire a new customer are very high. The internal process perspective measures the effectiveness and efficiency of internal business processes. For example, **Daimler-Chrysler** measures quality by the average warranty claims per automobile, measures efficiency by the average labor hours per automobile, and measures the average time to assemble each automobile. The financial perspective measures the economic performance of the responsibility center as we have illustrated in the previous sections of this chapter. All companies will use financial measures. For example, one survey found that over 70% of companies use income from operations as a percent of sales, 62% use rate of return on investment, and 13% use residual income as financial performance measures.[2]

[1] The balanced scorecard was developed by R. S. Kaplan and D. P. Norton and explained in *The Balanced Scorecard: Translating Strategy into Action* (Cambridge: Harvard Business School Press, 1996).
[2] Robert A. Howell, James D. Brown, Stephen R. Soucy, and Allen H. Seed, *Management Accounting in the New Manufacturing Environment*, National Association of Accountants, Montvale, New Jersey, 1987.

Exhibit 7 The Balanced Scorecard

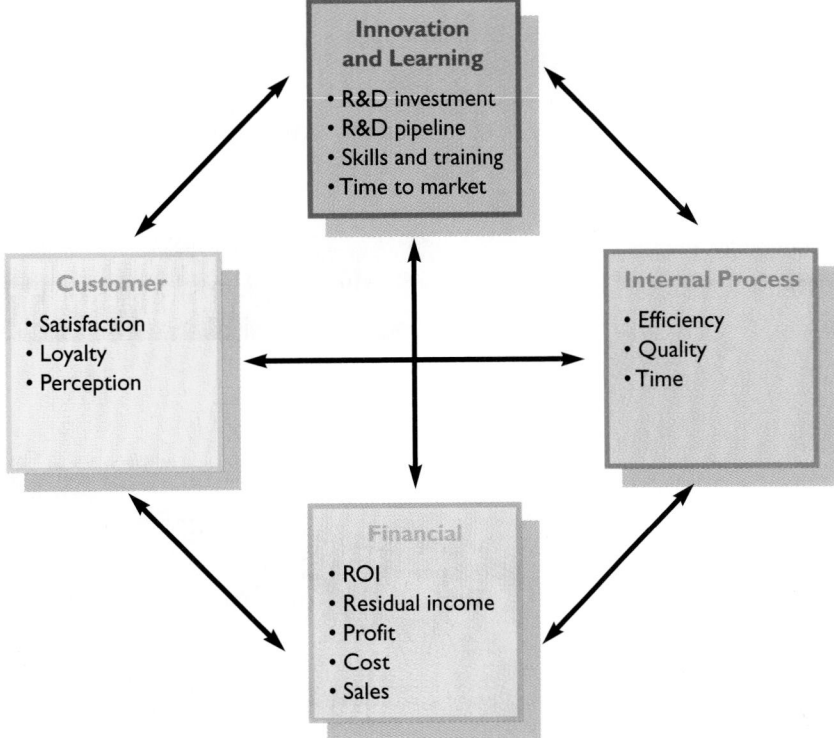

The balanced scorecard is designed to reveal the underlying nonfinancial drivers, or causes, of financial performance. For example, if a business improves customer satisfaction, this will likely lead to improved financial performance. In addition, the balanced scorecard helps managers consider trade-offs between short- and long-term performance. For example, additional investment in research and development (R&D) would penalize the short-term financial perspective, because R&D is an expense that reduces income from operations. However, the innovation perspective would measure additional R&D expenditures favorably, because current R&D expenditures will lead to future profits from new products. The balanced scorecard will motivate the manager to invest in new R&D, even though it is recognized as a current period expense. A recent survey has indicated that 40% of the companies use or are planning to use the balanced scorecard.[3] Thus, the balanced scorecard is gaining acceptance because of its ability to reveal the underlying causes of financial performance, while helping managers consider the short- and long-term implications of their decisions.

Transfer Pricing

[3] Mark L. Frigo and Kip R. Krumwiede, "The Balanced Scorecard," *Strategic Finance* (January 2000), pp. 50–54.

objective 5

Explain how the market price, negotiated price, and cost price approaches to transfer pricing may be used by decentralized segments of a business.

When divisions transfer products or render services to each other, a **transfer price** is used to charge for the products or services. Since transfer prices affect the goals for both divisions, setting these prices is a sensitive matter for division managers.

Transfer prices should be set so that overall company income is increased when goods are transferred between divisions. As we will illustrate, however, transfer prices may be misused in such a way that overall company income suffers.

In the following paragraphs, we discuss various approaches to setting transfer prices. Exhibit 8 shows the range of prices that results from common approaches to setting transfer prices.[4] Transfer prices can be set as low as the variable cost per unit or as high as the market price. Often, transfer prices are negotiated at some point between variable cost per unit and market price.

Exhibit 8 Commonly Used Transfer Prices

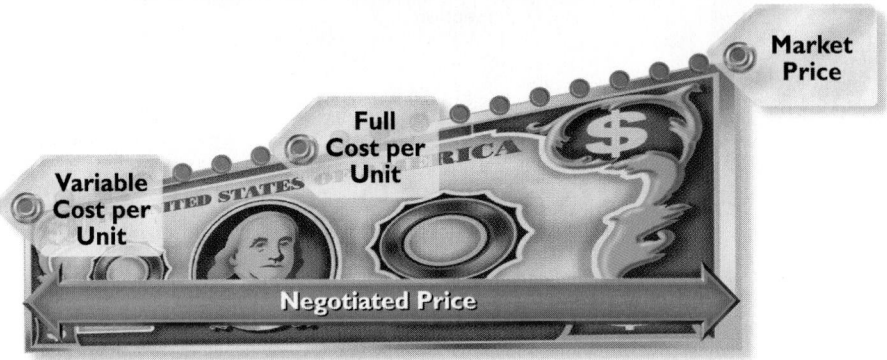

A survey of transfer pricing practices has reported the following usage:

Cost price (variable or full)	46%
Market price	37
Negotiated price	17

Source: Roger Y. W. Tang, "Transfer Pricing in the 1990's," *Management Accounting*, February 1992, pp. 22–26.

Transfer prices may be used when decentralized units are organized as cost, profit, or investment centers. To illustrate, we will use a packaged snack food company (Wilson Company) with no service departments and two operating divisions (Eastern and Western) organized as investment centers. Condensed divisional income statements for Wilson Company, assuming no transfers between divisions, are shown in Exhibit 9.

Market Price Approach

Using the **market price approach**, the transfer price is the price at which the product or service transferred could be sold to outside buyers. If an outside market exists for the product or service transferred, the current market price may be a proper transfer price.

To illustrate, assume that materials used by Wilson Company in producing snack food in the Western Division are currently purchased from an outside supplier at $20 per unit. The same materials are produced by the Eastern Division. The Eastern Division is operating at full capacity of 50,000 units and can sell all it produces to either the Western Division or to outside buyers. A transfer price of $20 per unit (the market price) has no effect on the Eastern Division's income or total company income. The Eastern Division will earn revenues of $20 per unit on all its production and sales, regardless of who buys its product. Likewise, the Western Division

---

[4] The discussion in this chapter highlights the essential concepts of transfer pricing. In-depth discussion of transfer pricing can be found in advanced texts.

Exhibit 9 Income Statement
—No Transfers Between
Divisions

Wilson Company
Divisional Income Statements
For the Year Ended December 31, 2003

	Eastern Division	Western Division	Total
Sales:			
50,000 units × $20 per unit	$1,000,000		$1,000,000
20,000 units × $40 per unit		$800,000	800,000
			$1,800,000
Expenses:			
Variable:			
50,000 units × $10 per unit . . .	$ 500,000		$ 500,000
20,000 units × $30* per unit . . .		$600,000	600,000
Fixed	300,000	100,000	400,000
Total expenses	$ 800,000	$700,000	$1,500,000
Income from operations	$ 200,000	$100,000	$ 300,000

*$20 of the $30 per unit represents materials costs, and the remaining $10 per unit represents other variable conversion expenses incurred within the Western Division.

Transfer prices can be used by multinational corporations to shift tax burdens across different countries. For example, assume that a multinational corporation has one division in the United States and another division outside the U.S. The two divisions sell goods to each other. If the tax rate is lower outside the U.S., the corporation may want to shift income to the division outside the U.S. This can be done by setting the U.S. division's purchase transfer prices high and selling transfer prices low. For example, a recent Government Accounting Office (GAO) report found some American subsidiaries bought safety pins at $29 apiece and toothbrushes at $8 each and sold pianos for $50 each and tractor tires for $7.89 each. To change this behavior, the tax codes in the United States and most other countries require transfer prices to be set at "Basic Arm's-Length Standard" (BALS), which is often interpreted as market price. Due to their subjectivity, transfer pricing practices are frequently audited by the Internal Revenue Service (IRS).

will pay $20 per unit for materials (the market price). Thus, the use of the market price as the transfer price has no effect on the Eastern Division's income or total company income. In this situation, the use of the market price as the transfer price is proper. The condensed divisional income statements for Wilson Company in this case are also shown in Exhibit 9.

Negotiated Price Approach

If unused or excess capacity exists in the supplying division (the Eastern Division), and the transfer price is equal to the market price, total company profit may not be maximized. This is because the manager of the Western Division will be indifferent toward purchasing materials from the Eastern Division or from outside suppliers. Thus, the Western Division may purchase the materials from outside suppliers. If, however, the Western Division purchases the materials from the Eastern Division, the difference between the market price of $20 and the variable costs of the Eastern Division can cover fixed costs and contribute to company profits. When the negotiated price approach is used in this situation, the manager of the Western Division is encouraged to purchase the materials from the Eastern Division.

The **negotiated price approach** allows the managers of decentralized units to agree (negotiate) among themselves as to the transfer price. The only constraint on the negotiations is that the transfer price be less than the market price but greater than the supplying division's variable costs per unit.

To illustrate the use of the negotiated price approach, assume that instead of a capacity of 50,000 units, the Eastern Division's capacity is 70,000 units. In addition, assume that the Eastern Division can continue to sell only 50,000 units to outside buyers. A transfer price less than $20 would encourage the manager of the Western Division to purchase from the Eastern Division. This is because the Western Division's materials cost per unit would decrease, and its income from operations would increase. At the same time, a transfer price above the Eastern Division's variable costs per unit of $10 (from Exhibit 9) would encourage the manager of the Eastern Division to use the excess capacity to supply materials to the Western Division. In doing so, the Eastern Division's income from operations would increase.

We continue the illustration with the aid of Exhibit 10, assuming that Wilson Company's division managers agree to a transfer price of $15 for the Eastern Division's product. By purchasing from the Eastern Division, the Western Division's materials cost would be $5 per unit less. At the same time, the Eastern Division would increase its sales by $300,000 (20,000 units × $15 per unit) and increase its income by $100,000 ($300,000 sales − $200,000 variable costs). The effect of reducing the Western Division's materials cost by $100,000 (20,000 units × $5 per unit) is to increase its income by $100,000. Therefore, Wilson Company's income is increased by $200,000 ($100,000 reported by the Eastern Division and $100,000 reported by the Western Division), as shown in the condensed income statements in Exhibit 10.

Exhibit 10 Income Statements—Negotiated Transfer Price

Wilson Company
Divisional Income Statements
For the Year Ended December 31, 2003

	Eastern Division	Western Division	Total
Sales:			
50,000 units × $20 per unit	$1,000,000		$1,000,000
20,000 units × $15 per unit	300,000		300,000
20,000 units × $40 per unit		$800,000	800,000
	$1,300,000	$800,000	$2,100,000
Expenses:			
Variable:			
70,000 units × $10 per unit ...	$ 700,000		$ 700,000
20,000 units × $25* per unit ...		$500,000	500,000
Fixed	300,000	100,000	400,000
Total expenses	$1,000,000	$600,000	$1,600,000
Income from operations	$ 300,000	$200,000	$ 500,000

*$10 of the $25 are variable conversion expenses incurred solely within the Western Division, and $15 per unit represents the transfer price per unit from the Eastern Division.

In this illustration, any transfer price less than the market price of $20 but greater than the Eastern Division's unit variable costs of $10 would increase each division's income. In addition, overall company profit would increase by $200,000. By establishing a range of $20 to $10 for the transfer price, each division manager has an incentive to negotiate the transfer of the materials.

Cost Price Approach

Under the **cost price approach**, cost is used to set transfer prices. With this approach, a variety of cost concepts may be used. For example, cost may refer to either total product cost per unit or variable product cost per unit. If total product cost per unit is used, direct materials, direct labor, and factory overhead are included in the transfer price. If variable product cost per unit is used, the fixed factory overhead component of total product cost is excluded from the transfer price.

Either actual costs or standard (budgeted) costs may be used in applying the cost price approach. If actual costs are used, inefficiencies of the producing division are transferred to the purchasing division. Thus, there is little incentive for the producing division to control costs carefully. For this reason, most companies use standard costs in the cost price approach. In this way, differences between actual and standard costs remain with the producing division for cost control purposes.

When division managers have responsibility for cost centers, the cost price approach to transfer pricing is proper and is often used. The cost price approach may not be proper, however, for decentralized operations organized as profit or investment centers. In profit and investment centers, division managers have responsibility for both revenues and expenses. The use of cost as a transfer price ignores the supplying division manager's responsibility for revenues. When a supplying division's sales are all intracompany transfers, for example, using the cost price approach prevents the supplying division from reporting any income from operations. A cost-based transfer price may therefore not motivate the division manager to make intracompany transfers, even though they are in the best interests of the company.

ENCORE

Turning a Cost Center into a Profit Center

Over the last 20 years, Richard Sasso has turned the production department at *Scientific American* into a profit center. Under Sasso's leadership, the production department (normally a boring "nuts and bolts" operation) has been a constant source of innovation and experimentation.

In 1975, Sasso began to use computers to typeset the magazine electronically. As the computer revolution advanced through the 1980s, so did Sasso's production department. The department purchased Apple McIntoshes and QuarkXPress software. This allowed Sasso to convert the entire production process to computers, using what is termed "direct to plate" technologies. This marked the turning point, because now the magazine's content became available in digital form. Once in digital form, it could be made available through media other than print form. Sasso says, "We want to be in position to take all of our products and make

the information available on a variety of platforms."

The first product developed by Sasso was *Scidex*, an electronic index of *Scientific American*, which sold 6,500 copies at nearly $50 a piece, more than paying for itself. Next, in 1993, *Scientific American* became the first magazine to publish simultaneously a print and CD version of the "Ancient Cities" issue. A recent Sasso success was the "Computer in the 21st Century" issue. In this issue, Apple Computer became the sole advertiser. All advertising was submitted electronically, so that the complete magazine was printed without using any advertising "film" in the production process. This was the first complete electronic print run of a major magazine. The issue was a public relations and financial bonanza. Sasso has embraced technology by launching new electronic magazines, such as *The Cancer Journal* and *Science & Medicine*. In addition, excerpts from *Scientific*

American are posted on SA's Web site.

For all this hard work and creativity, Sasso was promoted to Vice-President, Technology, a newly created position to fit the expanding world of electronic production and publishing. The publisher, John Moeling, states, "The role of the production director may be changing. It certainly has at *Scientific American*." ■

Source: Hanna Rubin, "Ink in His Veins," Folio: The Magazine for Magazine Management, June 15, 1995.

KEY POINTS

1 **List and explain the advantages and disadvantages of decentralized operations.**

The advantages of decentralization may include better decisions by the managers closest to the operations, more time for top management

to focus on strategic planning, training for managers, improved ability to serve customers and respond to their needs, and improved manager morale. The disadvantages of decentralization may include failure of the company to maximize profits because decisions made by one manager may affect other managers in such a way that the profitability of the entire company may suffer.

2 Prepare a responsibility accounting report for a cost center.

Since managers of cost centers have responsibility and authority to make decisions regarding costs, responsibility accounting for cost centers focuses on costs. The primary accounting tools for planning and controlling costs for a cost center are budgets and budget performance reports. An example of a budget performance report is shown in Exhibit 2.

3 Prepare responsibility accounting reports for a profit center.

In preparing a profitability report for a profit center, operating expenses are subtracted from revenues in order to determine the income from operations before service department charges. Service department charges are then subtracted in order to determine the income from operations of the profit center. An example of a divisional income statement is shown in Exhibit 5.

4 Compute and interpret the rate of return on investment, the residual income, and the balanced scorecard for an investment center.

The rate of return on investment for an investment center is the income from operations divided by invested assets. The rate of return on investment may also be computed as the product of (1) the profit margin and (2) the investment turnover. Residual income for an investment center is the excess of income from operations over a minimum amount of desired income from operations. The balanced scorecard combines nonfinancial measures in order to help managers consider the underlying causes of financial performance and tradeoffs between short-term and long-term performance.

5 Explain how the market price, negotiated price, and cost price approaches to transfer pricing may be used by decentralized segments of a business.

Under the market price approach, the transfer price is the price at which the product or service transferred could be sold to outside buyers. Market price should be used when the supplier division is able to sell to outsiders and is operating at capacity.

Under the negotiated price approach, the managers of decentralized units agree (negotiate) among themselves as to the transfer price. Negotiated prices should be used when the supplier division is operating below capacity.

Under the cost price approach, cost is used as the basis for setting transfer prices. A variety of cost concepts may be used, such as total product cost per unit or variable product cost per unit. In addition, actual costs or standard (budgeted) costs may be used. The cost price approach should be used for supplier divisions that are organized as cost centers.

ILLUSTRATIVE PROBLEM

Quinn Company has two divisions, Domestic and International. Invested assets and condensed income statement data for each division for the past year ended December 31 are as follows:

	Domestic Division	International Division
Revenues	$675,000	$480,000
Operating expenses	450,000	372,400
Service department charges	90,000	50,000
Invested assets	600,000	384,000

Instructions

1. Prepare condensed income statements for the past year for each division.
2. Using the expanded expression, determine the profit margin, investment turnover, and rate of return on investment for each division.
3. If management's minimum acceptable rate of return is 10%, determine the residual income for each division.

Solution

1.

Quinn Company
Divisional Income Statements
For the Year Ended December 31, 2003

	Domestic Division	International Division
Revenues	$675,000	$480,000
Operating expenses	450,000	372,400
Income from operations before service department charges	$225,000	$107,600
Service department charges	90,000	50,000
Income from operations	$135,000	$ 57,600

2.

$$\text{Rate of return on investment (ROI)} = \text{Profit margin} \times \text{Investment turnover}$$

$$\text{Rate of return on investment (ROI)} = \frac{\text{Income from operations}}{\text{Sales}} \times \frac{\text{Sales}}{\text{Invested assets}}$$

$$\text{Domestic Division: ROI} = \frac{\$135,000}{\$675,000} \times \frac{\$675,000}{\$600,000}$$

$$\text{ROI} = 20\% \quad \times 1.125$$

$$\text{ROI} = 22.5\%$$

$$\text{International Division: ROI} = \frac{\$ 57,600}{\$480,000} \times \frac{\$480,000}{\$384,000}$$

$$\text{ROI} = 12\% \quad \times 1.25$$

$$\text{ROI} = 15\%$$

3. Domestic Division: $75,000 [$135,000 − (10% × $600,000)]
International Division: $19,200 [$57,600 − (10% × $384,000)]

SELF-EXAMINATION QUESTIONS

Answers at End of Chapter

Matching

Match each of the following statements with its proper term. Some terms may not be used.

A.	**balanced scorecard**
B.	**controllable expenses**
C.	**cost center**
D.	**cost price approach**
E.	**cost variance**
F.	**decentralization**
G.	**division**
H.	**income from operations**
I.	**investment center**
J.	**investment turnover**

____ 1. A measure of managerial efficiency in the use of investments in assets, computed as income from operations divided by invested assets.

____ 2. An approach to transfer pricing that uses the price at which the product or service transferred could be sold to outside buyers as the transfer price.

____ 3. Revenues less operating expenses and service department charges for a profit or investment center.

____ 4. The costs of services provided by an internal service department and transferred to a responsibility center.

____ 5. An approach to transfer pricing that uses cost as the basis for setting the transfer price.

____ 6. A decentralized unit in which the manager has the responsibility and authority to make decisions that affect not only costs and revenues but also the fixed assets available to the center.

K.   **market price approach**

L.   **negotiated price approach**

M.   **profit center**

N.   **profit margin**

O.   **rate of return on investment**

P.   **residual income**

Q.   **responsibility accounting**

R.   **service department charges**

S.   **transfer price**

___ 7. Costs that can be influenced by the decisions of a manager.

___ 8. An approach to transfer pricing that allows managers of decentralized units to agree (negotiate) among themselves as to the transfer price.

___ 9. A component of the rate of return on investment, computed as the ratio of income from operations to sales.

___ 10. The price charged one decentralized unit by another for the goods or services provided.

___ 11. The separation of a business into more manageable operating units.

___ 12. The excess of divisional income from operations over a "minimum" acceptable income from operations.

___ 13. A decentralized unit in which the manager has the responsibility and the authority to make decisions that affect both costs and revenues (and thus profits).

___ 14. A decentralized unit that is structured around a common function, product, customer, or geographical territory.

___ 15. The process of measuring and reporting operating data by areas of responsibility.

___ 16. A decentralized unit in which the department or division manager has responsibility for the control of costs incurred and the authority to make decisions that affect these costs.

___ 17. A component of the rate of return on investment, computed as the ratio of sales to invested assets.

___ 18. A performance evaluation approach that incorporates multiple performance dimensions by combining financial and nonfinancial measures.

Multiple Choice

1. When the manager has the responsibility and authority to make decisions that affect costs and revenues but no responsibility for or authority over assets invested in the department, the department is called:
    A. a cost center   C. an investment center
    B. a profit center   D. a service department

2. The Accounts Payable Department has expenses of $600,000 and makes 150,000 payments to the various vendors who provide products and services to the divisions. Division A has income from operations of $900,000, before service department charges, and requires 60,000 payments to vendors. If the Accounts Payable Department is treated as a service department, what is Division A's income from operations?
    A. $300,000   C. $660,000
    B. $900,000   D. $540,000

3. Division A of Kern Co. has sales of $350,000, cost of goods sold of $200,000, operating expenses of $30,000, and invested assets of $600,000. What is the rate of return on investment for Division A?
    A. 20%   C. 33%
    B. 25%   D. 40%

4. Division L of Liddy Co. has a rate of return on investment of 24% and an investment turnover of 1.6. What is the profit margin?
    A. 6%   C. 24%
    B. 15%   D. 38%

5. Which approach to transfer pricing uses the price at which the product or service transferred could be sold to outside buyers?
    A. Cost price approach
    B. Negotiated price approach
    C. Market price approach
    D. Standard cost approach

CLASS DISCUSSION QUESTIONS

1. Name three common types of responsibility centers for decentralized operations.
2. Differentiate between a cost center and a profit center.
3. Differentiate between a profit center and an investment center.

4. In what major respect would budget performance reports prepared for the use of plant managers of a manufacturing business with cost centers differ from those prepared for the use of the various department supervisors who report to the plant managers?

5. For what decisions is the manager of a cost center *not* responsible?

6. How are service department costs charged to responsibility centers?

7. How is a service department charge rate determined?

8. **Weyerhaeuser Company** developed a system that assigns service department expenses to user divisions on the basis of actual services consumed by the division. Here are a number of Weyerhaeuser's activities in its central financial services department:

   - Payroll
   - Accounts payable
   - Accounts receivable
   - Database administration—report preparation

   For each activity, identify an output measure that could be used to charge user divisions for service.

9. Name two performance measures useful in evaluating investment centers.

10. What is the major shortcoming of using income from operations as a performance measure for investment centers?

11. Why should the factors under the control of the investment center manager (revenues, expenses, and invested assets) be considered in computing the rate of return on investment?

12. What are two ways of expressing the rate of return on investment?

13. In evaluating investment centers, what does multiplying the profit margin by the investment turnover equal?

14. In a decentralized company in which the divisions are organized as investment centers, how could a division be considered the least profitable even though it earned the largest amount of income from operations?

15. Which component of the rate of return on investment (profit margin or investment turnover) focuses on efficiency in the use of assets and indicates the rate at which sales are generated for each dollar of invested assets?

16. How does using the rate of return on investment facilitate comparability between divisions of decentralized companies?

17. The rates of return on investment for Harmon Co.'s three divisions, A, B, and C, are 20%, 17%, and 15%, respectively. In expanding operations, which of Harmon Co.'s divisions should be given priority? Explain.

18. How is the residual income computed?

19. Why would a firm use a balanced scorecard in evaluating divisional performance?

20. What is the objective of transfer pricing?

21. When is the negotiated price approach preferred over the market price approach in setting transfer prices?

22. If division managers cannot agree among themselves on a transfer price when using the negotiated price approach, how is the transfer price established?

23. When using the negotiated price approach to transfer pricing, within what range should the transfer price be established?

EXERCISES

Exercise 7–1
Budget performance reports for cost centers

Objective 2

✓ c. $2,300

Partially completed budget performance reports for Handy Company, a manufacturer of air conditioners, are provided below.

Handy Company
Budget Performance Report—Vice-President, Production
For the Month Ended April 30, 2003

Plant	Budget	Actual	Over Budget	Under Budget
St. Louis Plant	$523,700	$521,400		$2,300
Tempe Plant	810,000	805,200		4,800
Syracuse Plant	(g)	(h)	$ (i)	
	$ (j)	$ (k)	$ (l)	$7,100

Handy Company
Budget Performance Report—Manager, Syracuse Plant
For the Month Ended April 30, 2003

Department	Budget	Actual	Over Budget	Under Budget
Compressor Assembly	$ (a)	$ (b)	$ (c)	
Electronic Assembly	125,700	125,750	50	
Final Assembly	204,800	204,500		$300
	$ (d)	$ (e)	$ (f)	$300

Handy Company
Budget Performance Report—Supervisor, Compressor Assembly
For the Month Ended April 30, 2003

Costs	Budget	Actual	Over Budget	Under Budget
Factory wages	$ 34,800	$ 36,300	$1,500	
Materials	93,600	93,300		$300
Power and light	8,400	8,900	500	
Maintenance	14,800	15,400	600	
	$151,600	$153,900	$2,600	$300

a. Complete the budget performance reports by determining the correct amounts for the lettered spaces.
b. ✏️ Compose a memo to Karen Poling, vice-president of production for Handy Company, explaining the performance of the production division for April.

Exercise 7–2
Divisional income statements

Objective 3

SPREADSHEET

✓ Residential Division income from operations, $53,700

The following data were summarized from the accounting records for Circle D Electrical Equipment Company for the year ended June 30, 2003:

Cost of goods sold:
Residential Division	$305,000
Industrial Division	425,000

Administrative expenses:
Residential Division	90,500
Industrial Division	164,800

Service department charges:
Residential Division	25,800
Industrial Division	75,200

Net sales:
Residential Division	475,000
Industrial Division	825,000

Prepare divisional income statements for Circle D Electrical Equipment Company.

Exercise 7–3
Service department charges

Objective 3

✓ a. Commercial payroll, $34,650

In divisional income statements prepared for Owen Paving Company, the Payroll Department costs are charged back to user divisions on the basis of the number of payroll checks, and the Purchasing Department costs are charged back on the basis of the number of purchase requisitions. The Payroll Department had expenses of $149,520, and the Purchasing Department had expenses of $59,640 for the year. The following annual data for Residential, Commercial, and Highway Divisions were obtained from corporate records:

	Residential	Commercial	Highway
Sales	$2,400,000	$2,600,000	$3,000,000
Number of employees:			
Weekly payroll (52 weeks per year)	120	60	80
Monthly payroll	20	15	25
Number of purchase requisitions per year	1,600	1,400	1,200

a. Determine the annual amount of payroll and purchasing costs charged back to the Residential, Commercial, and Highway Divisions from payroll and purchasing services.

b. ✎➤ Why does the Residential Division have a larger service department charge than the other two divisions even though its sales are lower?

Exercise 7–4
Service department charges and activity bases

Objective 3

For each of the following service departments, identify an activity base that could be used for charging the expense to the profit center.

a. Duplication services
b. Accounts receivable
c. Electronic data processing
d. Central purchasing
e. Legal
f. Telecommunications

Exercise 7–5
Activity bases for service department charges

Objective 3

For each of the following service departments, select the activity base listed that is most appropriate for charging service expenses to responsible units.

Service Department	Activity Base
a. Accounts Receivable	1. Number of purchase requisitions
b. Conferences	2. Number of travel claims
c. Payroll Accounting	3. Number of conference attendees
d. Telecommunications	4. Number of payroll checks
e. Employee Travel	5. Number of telephone lines
f. Computer Support	6. Number of computers
g. Training	7. Number of employees trained
h. Central Purchasing	8. Number of sales invoices

Exercise 7–6
Service department charges and activity bases

Objective 3

✓ b. Help Desk, $16,704

Harris Corporation, a manufacturer of electronics and communications systems, uses a service department charge system to charge profit centers with Computing and Communications Services (CCS) service department costs. The following table identifies an abbreviated list of service categories and activity bases used by the CCS department. The table also includes some assumed cost and activity base quantity information for each service for March.

CCS Service Category	Activity Base	Assumed Cost	Assumed Activity Base Quantity
Help desk	Number of calls	$156,000	6,500
Network center	Number of devices monitored	547,560	10,800
Electronic mail	Number of user accounts	180,000	30,000
Local voice support	Number of phone extensions	416,560	25,400

One of the profit centers for Harris Corporation is the Communication Systems (COMM) sector. Assume the following information for the COMM sector:

• The sector has 5,800 employees, of whom 50% are office employees.
• All the office employees have a phone, and 80% of them have a computer on the network.

- Ninety percent of the employees with a computer also have an e-mail account.
- The average number of help desk calls for March was 0.30 calls per individual with a computer.
- There are 300 additional printers, servers, and peripherals on the network beyond the personal computers.

a. Determine the service charge rate for the four CCS service categories for March.
b. Determine the charges to the COMM sector for the four CCS service categories for March.

Exercise 7–7
Divisional income statements with service department charges

Objective 3

✓ Audio income from operations, $655,250

Acadia Electronics Company has two divisions, Video and Audio, and two corporate service departments, Computer Support and Accounts Payable. The corporate expenses for the year ended December 31, 2003, are as follows:

Computer Support Department	$360,000
Accounts Payable Department	125,000
Other corporate administrative expenses	215,000
Total corporate expense	$700,000

The other corporate administrative expenses include officers' salaries and other expenses required by the corporation. The Computer Support Department charges the divisions for services rendered, based on the number of computers in the department, and the Accounts Payable Department charges divisions for services, based on the number of checks issued. The usage of service by the two divisions is as follows:

Video Division	325 computers	4,500 checks
Audio Division	175	5,500
Total	500 computers	10,000 checks

The service department charges of the Computer Support Department and the Accounts Payable Department are considered controllable by the divisions. Corporate administrative expenses are not considered controllable by the divisions. The revenues, cost of goods sold, and operating expenses for the two divisions are as follows:

	Video	Audio
Revenues	$3,500,000	$2,750,000
Cost of goods sold	2,800,000	1,500,000
Operating expenses	250,000	400,000

Prepare the divisional income statements for the two divisions.

Exercise 7–8
Corrections to service department charges

Objective 3

What's Wrong With This?

✓ b. Income from operations, Cargo Division, $1,184,000

Atlantic Airlines Inc. has two divisions organized as profit centers, the Passenger Division and the Cargo Division. The following divisional income statements were prepared:

Atlantic Airlines Inc.
Divisional Income Statements
For the Year Ended October 31, 2003

	Passenger Division		Cargo Division	
Revenues		$6,500,000		$6,500,000
Operating expenses		5,500,000		5,000,000
Income from operations before service department charges		$1,000,000		$1,500,000
Less service department charges:				
Training	$150,000		$150,000	
Flight scheduling	200,000		200,000	
Reservations	300,000	650,000	300,000	650,000
Income from operations		$ 350,000		$ 850,000

The service department charge rate for the service department costs was based on revenues. Since the revenues of the two divisions were the same, the service department charges to each division were also the same.

The following additional information is available:

	Passenger Division	Cargo Division	Total
Number of flight personnel trained	160	40	200
Number of flights	180	320	500
Number of reservations requested	30,000	—	30,000

a. Does the income from operations for the two divisions accurately measure performance?
b. Correct the divisional income statements, using the activity bases provided above in revising the service department charges.

Exercise 7–9
Profit center responsibility reporting
Objectives 3, 5

SPREADSHEET

✓ Income from operations,
Camping Equipment Division,
$70,250

Tahoe Sporting Goods Co. operates two divisions—the Camping Equipment Division and the Ski Equipment Division. The following income and expense accounts were provided from the trial balance as of June 30, 2003, the end of the current fiscal year, after all adjustments, including those for inventories, were recorded and posted:

Sales—Camping Equipment Division	$460,000
Sales—Ski Equipment Division	745,000
Cost of Goods Sold—Camping Equipment Division	215,000
Cost of Goods Sold—Ski Equipment Division	385,000
Sales Expense—Camping Equipment Division	80,000
Sales Expense—Ski Equipment Division	105,000
Administrative Expense—Camping Equipment Division	45,400
Administrative Expense—Ski Equipment Division	66,800
Advertising Expense	19,900
Transportation Expense	22,050
Accounts Receivable Collection Expense	3,600
Warehouse Expense	45,000

The bases to be used in allocating expenses, together with other essential information, are as follows:

a. Advertising expense—incurred at headquarters, charged back to divisions on the basis of usage: Camping Equipment Division, $7,400; Ski Equipment Division, $12,500.
b. Transportation expense—charged back to divisions at a transfer price of $4.50 per bill of lading: Camping Equipment Division, 2,300 bills of lading; Ski Equipment Division, 2,600 bills of lading.
c. Accounts receivable collection expense—incurred at headquarters, charged back to divisions at a transfer price of $0.80 per invoice: Camping Equipment Division, 2,000 sales invoices; Ski Equipment Division, 2,500 sales invoices.
d. Warehouse expense—charged back to divisions on the basis of floor space used in storing division products: Camping Equipment Division, 10,000 square feet; Ski Equipment Division, 5,000 square feet.

Prepare a divisional income statement with two column headings: Camping Equipment Division and Ski Equipment Division. Provide supporting schedules for determining service department charges.

Exercise 7–10
Rate of return on investment
Objective 4

✓ a. Milk Division, 20%

The income from operations and the amount of invested assets in each division of Green Bay Dairy Company are as follows:

	Income from Operations	Invested Assets
Cheese Division	$133,000	$ 950,000
Milk Division	104,000	520,000
Butter Division	182,400	1,140,000

a.   Compute the rate of return on investment for each division.
b.   Which division is the most profitable per dollar invested?

Exercise 7–11
Residual income
Objective 4

✓ a. Cheese Division, $19,000

Based on the data in Exercise 7–10, assume that management has established a 12% minimum acceptable rate of return for invested assets.

a.   Determine the residual income for each division.
b.   Which division has the most residual income?

Exercise 7–12
Rate of return on investment
Objective 4

Real World

The Walt Disney Corporation has three major sectors, as follows:

- **Creative Content:** produces live action and animated motion pictures, manages licensing, and operates the Disney Stores.
- **Broadcasting:** operates the ABC broadcasting network.
- **Theme Parks and Resorts:** operates the Disney entertainment and vacation properties, including Disney World and Disney Land.

Disney recently reported sector income from operations, revenue, and invested assets (in millions) as follows:

	Income from Operations	Revenue	Invested Assets
Creative Content	$1,403	$10,302	$ 9,509
Broadcasting	1,325	7,142	20,099
Theme Parks and Resorts	1,287	5,532	9,214

a.   Use the expanded formula to determine the rate of return on investment for the three Disney sectors. Round to two decimal places.
b.   ▬▬➤   How do the three sectors differ in their profit margin, investment turnover, and rate of return on investment?

Exercise 7–13
Determining missing items in rate of return computation
Objective 4

✓ d. 1.4

One item is omitted from each of the following computations of the rate of return on investment:

Rate of return on investment	=	Profit margin	×	Investment turnover
27%	=	18%	×	(a)
(b)	=	12%	×	2.0
18%	=	(c)	×	0.75
21%	=	15%	×	(d)
(e)	=	8%	×	1.75

Determine the missing items, identifying each by the appropriate letter.

Exercise 7–14
Profit margin, investment turnover, and rate of return on investment
Objective 4

✓ a. ROI, 18.4%

The condensed income statement for the New England Division of CinePlex Cinemas Inc. is as follows (assuming no service department charges):

Sales	$500,000
Cost of goods sold	320,000
Gross profit	$180,000
Administrative expenses	65,000
Income from operations	$115,000

The manager of the New England Division is considering ways to increase the rate of return on investment.

a.   Using the expanded expression for rate of return on investment, determine the profit margin, investment turnover, and rate of return on investment of the New England

Division, assuming that $625,000 of assets have been invested in the New England Division.

b. If expenses could be reduced by $20,000 without decreasing sales, what would be the impact on the profit margin, investment turnover, and rate of return on investment for the New England Division?

Exercise 7–15
Determining missing items in rate of return and residual income computations

Objective 4

✓ c. $9,000

Data for Black Gold Drilling Company is presented in the following table of rates of return on investment and residual incomes:

Invested Assets	Income from Operations	Rate of Return on Investment	Minimum Rate of Return	Minimum Acceptable Income from Operations	Residual Income
$450,000	$54,000	(a)	10%	(b)	(c)
220,000	(d)	14%	(e)	$35,200	$(4,400)
335,000	(f)	(g)	(h)	$50,250	$16,750
515,000	$77,250	(i)	12%	(j)	(k)

Determine the missing items, identifying each item by the appropriate letter.

Exercise 7–16
Determining missing items from computations

Objective 4

✓ a. (e) 15%

Data for the North, East, South, and West Divisions of Mountain Power and Light Company are as follows:

	Sales	Income from Operations	Invested Assets	Rate of Return on Investment	Profit Margin	Investment Turnover
North	$850,000	$119,000	$680,000	(a)	(b)	(c)
East	$326,000	(d)	$407,500	12%	(e)	(f)
South	(g)	$60,000	(h)	(i)	12.5%	0.64
West	$365,000	(j)	(k)	20%	16%	(l)

a. Determine the missing items, identifying each by the letters (a) through (l).
b. Determine the residual income for each division, assuming that the minimum acceptable rate of return established by management is 10%.
c. Which division is the most profitable in terms of (a) return on investment and (b) residual income?

Exercise 7–17
Balanced scorecard

Objective 4

The **American Express Company** is a major financial services company, noted for its American Express® card. Below are some of the performance measures used by the company in its balanced scorecard.

Average cardmember spending
Cards in force
Earnings growth
Hours of credit consultant training
Investment in information technology
Number of Internet features
Number of merchant signings
Number of card choices
Number of new card launches
Return on equity
Revenue growth

For each measure, identify whether the measure best fits the innovation, customer, internal process, or financial dimension of the balanced scorecard.

Exercise 7–18
Balanced scorecard
Objective 4

Several years ago, **United Parcel Service (UPS)** believed that the Internet was going to change the parcel delivery market and would require UPS to become a more nimble and customer-focused organization. As a result, UPS replaced its old measurement system, which was 90% oriented toward financial performance, with a balanced scorecard. The scorecard emphasized four "point of arrival" measures, which were:

1. Customer satisfaction index—a measure of customer satisfaction.
2. Employee relations index—a measure of employee sentiment and morale.
3. Competitive position—delivery performance relative to competition.
4. Time in transit—the time from order entry to delivery.

a. ◖▬▬► Why did UPS introduce a balanced scorecard and nonfinancial measures in its new performance measurement system?
b. ◖▬▬► Why do you think UPS included a factor measuring employee sentiment?

Exercise 7–19
Decision on transfer pricing
Objective 5

✓ a. $2,800,000

Materials used by the Truck Division of Structure Motors are currently purchased from outside suppliers at a cost of $260 per unit. However, the same materials are available from the Component Division. The Component Division has unused capacity and can produce the materials needed by the Truck Division at a variable cost of $190 per unit.

a. If a transfer price of $230 per unit is established and 40,000 units of materials are transferred, with no reduction in the Component Division's current sales, how much would Structure Motors' total income from operations increase?
b. How much would the Truck Division's income from operations increase?
c. How much would the Component Division's income from operations increase?

Exercise 7–20
Decision on transfer pricing
Objective 5

✓ b. $400,000

Based on the Structure Motors data in Exercise 7–19, assume that a transfer price of $250 has been established and that 40,000 units of materials are transferred, with no reduction in the Component Division's current sales.

a. How much would Structure Motors' total income from operations increase?
b. How much would the Truck Division's income from operations increase?
c. How much would the Component Division's income from operations increase?
d. ◖▬▬► If the negotiated price approach is used, what would be the range of acceptable transfer prices and why?

PROBLEMS SERIES A

Problem 7–1A
Budget performance report for a cost center
Objective 2

SPREADSHEET
GENERAL
LEDGER

The Eastern District of Mobile-One Communications Inc. is organized as a cost center. The budget for the Eastern District of Mobile-One Communications Inc. for the month ended September 30, 2003, is as follows:

Sales salaries	$ 625,700
Network administration salaries	321,900
Customer service salaries	173,400
Billing salaries	61,300
Maintenance	162,000
Depreciation of plant and equipment	58,000
Insurance and property taxes	31,400
Total	$1,433,700

During September, the costs incurred in the Eastern District were as follows:

Sales salaries	$ 623,700
Network administration salaries	320,100
Customer service salaries	189,200
Billing salaries	60,800
Maintenance	162,800
Depreciation of plant and equipment	58,000
Insurance and property taxes	31,600
Total	$1,446,200

Instructions

1. Prepare a budget performance report for the manager of the Eastern District of Mobile-One Communications Inc. for the month of September.
2. ◖▬▬► For which costs might the supervisor be expected to request supplemental reports?

Problem 7–2A
Profit center responsibility reporting
Objective 3

✓ 1. Income from operations, Northern Division, $444,000

Continental Railroad Company organizes its three divisions, the Northwest, Western, and Northern Regions, as profit centers. The CEO evaluates divisional performance, using income from operations as a percent of revenues. The following quarterly income and expense accounts were provided from the trial balance as of December 31, 2004:

Revenues—NW Region	$1,850,000
Revenues—W Region	2,830,000
Revenues—N Region	2,180,000
Operating Expenses—NW Region	900,000
Operating Expenses—W Region	1,750,000
Operating Expenses—N Region	1,430,000
Corporate Expenses—Dispatching	420,000
Corporate Expenses—Equipment	510,000
Corporate Expenses—Officers' Salaries	650,000
Corporate Expenses—Internal Auditing	350,000

The company operates three service departments: the Dispatching Department, the Equipment Department, and the Internal Auditing Department. The Dispatching Department manages the scheduling and releasing of complete trains. The Equipment Department manages the railroad car inventories. It makes sure the right freight cars are at the right place at the right time. The Internal Auditing Department conducts a variety of audit services for the company as a whole. The following additional information has been gathered:

	Northwest	Western	Northern
Number of scheduled trains	550	850	600
Number of railroad cars in inventory	5,000	6,000	6,000

Instructions

1. Prepare quarterly income statements showing income from operations for the three divisions. Use three column headings: Northwest, Western, and Northern.
2. Which division would the CEO identify as the most successful? Round to two decimal places.
3. ◖▬▬► Provide a recommendation to the CEO for a better method for evaluating the performance of the divisions. In your recommendation, identify the major weakness of the present method.

Problem 7–3A
Divisional income statements and rate of return on investment analysis
Objective 4

Union Trust Inc. is a diversified financial services company with three operating divisions organized as investment centers. Condensed data taken from the records of the three divisions for the year ended December 31, 2003, are as follows:

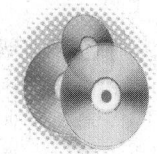

SPREADSHEET

✓ 2. Retail Broker Division ROI, 8.8%

	Retail Broker Division	E-trade Division	Mutual Fund Division
Fee revenue	$ 625,000	$250,000	$ 860,000
Operating expenses	350,000	225,000	705,200
Invested assets	3,125,000	125,000	1,000,000

The management of Union Trust Inc. is evaluating each division as a basis for planning a future expansion of operations.

Instructions

1. Prepare condensed divisional income statements for the three divisions, assuming that there were no service department charges.
2. Using the expanded expression for rate of return on investment, compute the profit margin, investment turnover, and rate of return on investment for each division.
3. ◄■■■► If available funds permit the expansion of operations of only one division, which of the divisions would you recommend for expansion, based on (1) and (2)? Explain.

Problem 7–4A
Effect of proposals on divisional performance

Objective 4

✓ 3. Proposal 3 ROI, 18%

A condensed income statement for the Golf Equipment Division of St. Andrews Inc. for the year ended January 31, 2003, is as follows:

Sales	$4,800,000
Cost of goods sold	2,650,000
Gross profit	$2,150,000
Operating expenses	1,454,000
Income from operations	$ 696,000

Assume that the Golf Equipment Division received no charges from service departments.

The president of St. Andrews Inc. has indicated that the division's rate of return on a $4,000,000 investment must be increased to at least 20% by the end of the next year if operations are to continue. The division manager is considering the following three proposals:

Proposal 1: Reduce invested assets by discontinuing a product line. This action would eliminate sales of $500,000, cost of goods sold of $323,000, and operating expenses of $40,000. Assets of $560,000 would be transferred to other divisions at no gain or loss.

Proposal 2: Transfer equipment with a book value of $1,000,000 to other divisions at no gain or loss and lease similar equipment. The annual lease payments would exceed the amount of depreciation expense on the old equipment by $72,000. This increase in expense would be included as part of the cost of goods sold. Sales would remain unchanged.

Proposal 3: Purchase new and more efficient machinery and thereby reduce the cost of goods sold by $168,000. Sales would remain unchanged, and the old machinery, which has no remaining book value, would be scrapped at no gain or loss. The new machinery would increase invested assets by $800,000 for the year.

Instructions

1. Using the expanded expression for rate of return on investment, determine the profit margin, investment turnover, and rate of return on investment for the Golf Equipment Division for the past year.
2. Prepare condensed estimated income statements and calculate the invested assets for each proposal.
3. Using the expanded expression for rate of return on investment, determine the profit margin, investment turnover, and rate of return on investment for each proposal.
4. Which of the three proposals would meet the required 20% rate of return on investment?

5. If the Golf Equipment Division were in an industry where the profit margin could not be increased, how much would the investment turnover have to increase to meet the president's required 20% rate of return on investment?

Problem 7–5A
Divisional performance analysis and evaluation

Objective 4

✓ 2. Office Division ROI, 12%

The vice-president of operations of Van Horne Commercial Furniture Company is evaluating the performance of two divisions organized as investment centers. Invested assets and condensed income statement data for the past year for each division are as follows:

	Office Division	Hotel Division
Sales	$ 6,500,000	$5,000,000
Cost of goods sold	3,200,000	2,200,000
Operating expenses	1,350,000	1,300,000
Invested assets	16,250,000	6,250,000

Instructions

1. Prepare condensed divisional income statements for the year ended July 31, 2003, assuming that there were no service department charges.
2. Using the expanded expression for rate of return on investment, determine the profit margin, investment turnover, and rate of return on investment for each division.
3. If management's minimum acceptable rate of return is 10%, determine the residual income for each division.
4. ✏️ Discuss the evaluation of the two divisions, using the performance measures determined in (1), (2), and (3).

Problem 7–6A
Transfer pricing

Objective 5

✓ 4. Instruments Division, $140,000

Fisher Instrument Company is a diversified aerospace company, with two operating divisions, Electronics and Instruments Divisions. Condensed divisional income statements, which involve no intracompany transfers and which include a breakdown of expenses into variable and fixed components, are as follows:

Fisher Instrument Company
Divisional Income Statements
For the Year Ended December 31, 2003

	Electronics Division	Instruments Division	Total
Sales:			
700 units × $2,500 per unit	$1,750,000		$1,750,000
1,200 units × $5,500 per unit		$6,600,000	6,600,000
			$8,350,000
Expenses:			
Variable:			
700 units × $1,570 per unit	$1,099,000		$1,099,000
1,200 units × $4,200* per unit		$5,040,000	5,040,000
Fixed	430,000	735,000	1,165,000
Total expenses	$1,529,000	$5,775,000	$7,304,000
Income from operations	$ 221,000	$ 825,000	$1,046,000

*$2,500 of the $4,200 per unit represents materials costs, and the remaining $1,700 per unit represents other variable conversion expenses incurred within the Instruments Division.

The Electronics Division is presently producing 700 units out of a total capacity of 900 units. Materials used in producing the Instruments Division's product are currently purchased from outside suppliers at a price of $2,500 per unit. The Electronics Division is able to produce the components used by the Instruments Division. Except for the possible transfer of materials between divisions, no changes are expected in sales and expenses.

Instructions

1.   ✏️➤ Would the market price of $2,500 per unit be an appropriate transfer price for Fisher Instrument Company? Explain.
2.   ✏️➤ If the Instruments Division purchases 200 units from the Electronics Division, rather than externally, at a negotiated transfer price of $2,000 per unit, how much would the income from operations of each division and total company income from operations increase?
3.   Prepare condensed divisional income statements for Fisher Instrument Company, based on the data in (2).
4.   ✏️➤ If a transfer price of $1,800 per unit is negotiated, how much would the income from operations of each division and total company income from operations increase?
5.   a.   ✏️➤ What is the range of possible negotiated transfer prices that would be acceptable for Fisher Instrument Company?
       b.   Assuming that the managers of the two divisions cannot agree on a transfer price, what price would you suggest as the transfer price?

PROBLEMS SERIES B

Problem 7–1B
Budget performance report for a cost center

Objective 2

SPREADSHEET
GENERAL
LEDGER

AudioNet.Com sells music CDs over the Internet. The International Division is organized as a cost center. The budget for the International Division for the month ended April 30, 2003, is as follows:

Software engineer salaries	$185,000
Customer service salaries	95,800
Logistics salaries	165,000
Marketing salaries	225,000
Warehouse wages	115,500
Equipment depreciation	35,000
Insurance and property taxes	28,000
Total	$849,300

During April, the costs incurred in the International Division were as follows:

Software engineer salaries	$183,400
Customer service salaries	124,700
Logistics salaries	163,700
Marketing salaries	248,000
Warehouse wages	115,000
Equipment depreciation	36,000
Insurance and property taxes	27,800
Total	$898,600

Instructions

1. Prepare a budget performance report for the director of the International Division for the month of April.
2. For which costs might the director be expected to request supplemental reports?

Problem 7–2B
Profit center responsibility reporting

Objective 3

Appalachian Gas Company has three regional divisions organized as profit centers. The CEO evaluates divisional performance, using income from operations as a percent of revenues. The following quarterly income and expense accounts were provided from the trial balance as of December 31, 2003:

Revenues—Central Division	$485,000
Revenues—Coastal Division	732,000
Revenues—Metro Division	940,000
Operating Expenses—Central Division	282,400
Operating Expenses—Coastal Division	432,500
Operating Expenses—Metro Division	575,000
Corporate Expenses—Shareholder Relations	35,000
Corporate Expenses—Customer Support	78,000
Corporate Expenses—Central Accounting	94,900
General Corporate Officers' Salaries	190,000

The company operates three service departments, Shareholder Relations, Customer Support, and Central Accounting. The Shareholder Relations Department conducts a variety of services for shareholders of the company. The Customer Support Department is the company's telephone point of contact for new service, complaints, and requests for repair. The department believes that the number of customer calls is an activity base for this work. The Central Accounting Department provides reports for division management. The department believes that the number of reports is an activity base for this work. The following additional information has been gathered:

	Central	Coastal	Metro
Number of customer calls	2,000	2,500	5,500
Number of accounting reports	8,400	10,500	7,100

Instructions

1. Prepare quarterly income statements showing income from operations for the three divisions. Use three column headings: Central, Coastal, and Metro.
2. Which division would the CEO identify as the most successful? Round to two decimal places.
3. ✏ Provide a recommendation to the CEO for a better method for evaluating the performance of the divisions. In your recommendation, identify the major weakness of the present method.

Problem 7–3B
Divisional income statements and rate of return on investment analysis

Objective 4

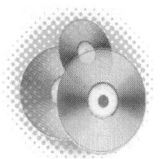
SPREADSHEET

Rise 'N Shine Food Company is a diversified food products company with three operating divisions organized as investment centers. Condensed data taken from the records of the three divisions for the year ended June 30, 2003, are as follows:

	Cereal Division	Fruit Juice Division	Bread Division
Sales	$1,000,000	$1,500,000	$625,000
Cost of goods sold	630,000	950,000	350,000
Operating expenses	120,000	400,000	120,000
Invested assets	1,250,000	2,000,000	500,000

The management of Rise 'N Shine Food Company is evaluating each division as a basis for planning a future expansion of operations.

Instructions

1. Prepare condensed divisional income statements for the three divisions, assuming that there were no service department charges.
2. Using the expanded expression for rate of return on investment, compute the profit margin, investment turnover, and rate of return on investment for each division.
3. ✏ If available funds permit the expansion of operations of only one division, which of the divisions would you recommend for expansion, based on (1) and (2)? Explain.

Problem 7–4B

Effect of proposals on divisional performance

Objective 4

✓ I. ROI, 17.60%

A condensed income statement for the Music Division of Hollywood Entertainment Inc. for the year ended December 31, 2003, is as follows:

Sales	$820,000
Cost of goods sold	355,000
Gross profit	$465,000
Operating expenses	374,800
Income from operations	$ 90,200

Assume that the Music Division received no charges from service departments. The president of Hollywood Entertainment has indicated that the division's rate of return on a $512,500 investment must be increased to at least 20% by the end of the next year if operations are to continue. The division manager is considering the following three proposals:

Proposal 1: Reduce invested assets by discontinuing a label. This action would eliminate sales of $140,000, cost of goods sold of $70,000, and operating expenses of $75,000. Assets of $87,500 would be transferred to other divisions at no gain or loss.

Proposal 2: Transfer recording equipment with a book value of $102,500 to other divisions at no gain or loss and lease similar equipment. The annual lease payments would exceed the amount of depreciation expense on the old equipment by $24,600. This increase in expense would be included as part of the cost of goods sold. Sales would remain unchanged.

Proposal 3: Purchase new and more efficient disk reproduction equipment and thereby reduce the cost of goods sold by $106,600. Sales would remain unchanged, and the old equipment, which has no remaining book value, would be scrapped at no gain or loss. The new equipment would increase invested assets by an additional $512,500 for the year.

Instructions

1. Using the expanded expression for rate of return on investment, determine the profit margin, investment turnover, and rate of return on investment for the Music Division for the past year.
2. Prepare condensed estimated income statements and calculate the invested assets for each proposal.
3. Using the expanded expression for rate of return on investment, determine the profit margin, investment turnover, and rate of return on investment for each proposal.
4. Which of the three proposals would meet the required 20% rate of return on investment?
5. If the Music Division were in an industry where the profit margin could not be increased, how much would the investment turnover have to increase to meet the president's required 20% rate of return on investment?

Problem 7–5B

Divisional performance analysis and evaluation

Objective 4

✓ 2. Men's Division ROI, 18.75%

The vice-president of operations of Fleet Shoe Company is evaluating the performance of two divisions organized as investment centers. Invested assets and condensed income statement data for the past year for each division are as follows:

	Men's Division	Women's Division
Sales	$3,000,000	$2,400,000
Cost of goods sold	1,800,000	1,250,000
Operating expenses	450,000	718,000
Invested assets	4,000,000	1,920,000

Instructions

1. Prepare condensed divisional income statements for the year ended December 31, 2003, assuming that there were no service department charges.

2. Using the expanded expression for rate of return on investment, determine the profit margin, investment turnover, and rate of return on investment for each division.
3. If management desires a minimum acceptable rate of return of 16%, determine the residual income for each division.
4. ✏️ Discuss the evaluation of the two divisions, using the performance measures determined in (1), (2), and (3).

Problem 7–6B
Transfer pricing
Objective 5

✓ 3. Total income from operations, $337,000

Oxford Container Company manufactures cardboard and container products, with two operating divisions, the Cardboard and Box Divisions. Condensed divisional income statements, which involve no intracompany transfers and which include a breakdown of expenses into variable and fixed components, are as follows:

Oxford Container Company
Divisional Income Statements
For the Year Ended December 31, 2003

	Cardboard Division	Box Division	Total
Sales:			
10,000 units × $86 per case	$860,000		$ 860,000
15,000 units × $164 per case		$2,460,000	2,460,000
			$3,320,000
Expenses:			
Variable:			
10,000 units × $60 per case	$600,000		$ 600,000
15,000 units × $128* per case		$1,920,000	1,920,000
Fixed	155,000	360,000	515,000
Total expenses	$755,000	$2,280,000	$3,035,000
Income from operations	$105,000	$ 180,000	$ 285,000

*$86 of the $128 per case represents materials costs, and the remaining $42 per case represents other variable conversion expenses incurred within the Box Division.

The Cardboard Division is presently producing 10,000 cases out of a total capacity of 12,000 cases. Materials used in producing the Box Division's product are currently purchased from outside suppliers at a price of $86 per case. The Cardboard Division is able to produce the materials used by the Box Division. Except for the possible transfer of materials between divisions, no changes are expected in sales and expenses.

Instructions

1. ✏️ Would the market price of $86 per case be an appropriate transfer price for Oxford Container Company? Explain.
2. ✏️ If the Box Division purchases 2,000 cases from the Cardboard Division, rather than externally, at a negotiated transfer price of $70 per case, how much would the income from operations of each division and the total company income from operations increase?
3. Prepare condensed divisional income statements for Oxford Container Company, based on the data in (2).
4. ✏️ If a transfer price of $65 per case is negotiated, how much would the income from operations of each division and the total company income from operations increase?
5. a. ✏️ What is the range of possible negotiated transfer prices that would be acceptable for Oxford Container Company?
   b. Assuming that the managers of the two divisions cannot agree on a transfer price, what price would you suggest as the transfer price?

SPECIAL ACTIVITIES

Activity 7–1
Jolly Giant Company
Ethics and professional conduct in business

Jolly Giant Company has two divisions, the Can Division and the Food Division. The Food Division may purchase cans from the Can Division or from outside suppliers. The Can Division sells can products both internally and externally. The market price for cans is $100 per 1,000 cans. Lee Tazwell is the controller of the Food Division, and Tracy Ford is the controller of the Can Division. The following conversation took place between Lee and Tracy:

Lee: I hear you are having problems selling cans out of your division. Maybe I can help.

Tracy: You've got that right. We're producing and selling at only 70% of our capacity to outsiders. Last year we were selling all we could make. It would help a great deal if your division would divert some of your purchases to our division so we could use up our capacity. After all, we are part of the same company.

Lee: What kind of price could you give me?

Tracy: Well, you know as well as I that we are under strict profit responsibility in our divisions, so I would expect to get market price, $100 for 1,000 cans.

Lee: I'm not so sure we can swing that. I was expecting a price break from a "sister" division.

Tracy: Hey, I can only take this "sister" stuff so far. If I give you a price break, our profits will fall from last year's levels. I don't think I could explain that. I'm sorry, but I must remain firm—market price. After all, it's only fair—that's what you would have to pay from an external supplier.

Lee: Fair or not, I think we'll pass. Sorry we couldn't have helped.

➤ Was Lee behaving ethically by trying to force the Can Division into a price break? Comment on Tracy's reactions.

Activity 7–2
Milford University
Service department charges

The Accounting Department of Milford University asked the Publications Department to prepare a brochure for the Masters of Accountancy program. The Publications Department delivered the brochures and charged the Accounting Department a rate that was 20% higher than could be obtained from an outside printing company. The policy of the university required the Accounting Department to use the internal publications group for brochures. The Publications Department claimed that they had a drop in demand for their services during the fiscal year, so they had to charge higher prices in order to recover their payroll and fixed costs.

➤ Should the cost of the brochure be transferred to the Accounting Department in order to hold the department head accountable for the cost of the brochure? What changes in policy would you recommend?

Activity 7–3
World Media Enterprises
Evaluating divisional performance

The three divisions of World Media Enterprises are Broadcasting, Music, and Publications. The divisions are structured as investment centers. The following responsibility reports were prepared for the three divisions for the prior year:

	Broadcasting	Music	Publications
Revenues	$ 600,000	$1,400,000	$500,000
Operating expenses	240,000	800,000	100,000
Income from operations before service department charges	$ 360,000	$ 600,000	$400,000
Service department charges:			
Promotion	$ 100,000	$ 200,000	$200,000
Legal	50,000	40,000	80,000
	$ 150,000	$ 240,000	$280,000
Income from operations	$ 210,000	$ 360,000	$120,000
Invested assets	$1,500,000	$3,000,000	$800,000

1. Which division is making the best use of invested assets and thus should be given priority for future capital investments?
2. ◖▬▬▶ Assuming that the minimum acceptable rate of return on new projects is 10%, would all investments that produce a return in excess of 10% be accepted by the divisions?
3. ◖▬▬▶ Can you identify opportunities for improving the company's financial performance?

**Activity 7–4
Nature's Garden Food Co.**
Evaluating division performance over time

The Snack Foods Division of Nature's Garden Food Co. has been experiencing revenue and profit growth during the years 2002–2004. The divisional income statements are provided below.

Nature's Garden Food Co.
Divisional Income Statements, Snack Foods Division
For the Years Ended December 31, 2002–2004

	2002	2003	2004
Sales	$420,000	$540,000	$650,000
Cost of goods sold	264,000	310,000	342,500
Gross profit	$156,000	$230,000	$307,500
Operating expenses	93,000	116,600	145,000
Income from operations	$ 63,000	$113,400	$162,500

Assume that there are no charges from service departments. The vice-president of the division, Harlan Tyson, is proud of his division's performance over the last three years. The president of Nature's Garden Food Co., Janice Gleason, is discussing the division's performance with Harlan, as follows:

Harlan: As you can see, we've had a successful three years in the Snack Foods Division.
Janice: I'm not too sure.
Harlan: What do you mean? Look at our results. Our income from operations has nearly tripled, while our profit margins are improving.
Janice: I am looking at your results. However, your income statements fail to include one very important piece of information; namely, the invested assets. You have been investing a great deal of assets into the division. You had $210,000 in invested assets in 2002, $540,000 in 2003, and $1,000,000 in 2004.
Harlan: You are right. I've needed the assets in order to upgrade our technologies and expand our operations. The additional assets are one reason we have been able to grow and improve our profit margins. I don't see that this is a problem.
Janice: The problem is that we must maintain a 20% rate of return on invested assets.

1. Determine the profit margins for the Snack Foods Division for 2002–2004.
2. Calculate the investment turnover for the Snack Foods Division for 2002–2004.
3. Calculate the rate of return on investment for the Snack Foods Division for 2002–2004.
4. ◖▬▬▶ Evaluate the division's performance over the 2002–2004 time period. Why was Janice concerned about the performance?

**Activity 7–5
Outdoor Life Inc.**
Evaluating division performance

Your father is president of Outdoor Life Inc., a privately held diversified company with five separate divisions organized as investment centers. A condensed income statement for the Sporting Goods Division for the past year, assuming no service department charges, is as follows:

Outdoor Life Inc.—Sporting Goods Division
Income Statement
For the Year Ended December 31, 2003

Sales	$16,000,000
Cost of goods sold	10,100,000
Gross profit	$ 5,900,000
Operating expenses	1,900,000
Income from operations	$ 4,000,000

The manager of the Sporting Goods Division was recently presented with the opportunity to add an additional product line, which would require invested assets of $12,000,000. A projected income statement for the new product line is as follows:

New Product Line
Projected Income Statement
For the Year Ended December 31, 2003

Sales	$7,500,000
Cost of goods sold	4,200,000
Gross profit	$3,300,000
Operating expenses	2,100,000
Income from operations	$1,200,000

The Sporting Goods Division currently has $20,000,000 in invested assets, and Outdoor Life Inc.'s overall rate of return on investment, including all divisions, is 8%. Each division manager is evaluated on the basis of divisional rate of return on investment, and a bonus equal to $5,000 for each percentage point by which the division's rate of return on investment exceeds the company average is awarded each year.

Your father is concerned that the manager of the Sporting Goods Division rejected the addition of the new product line, when all estimates indicated that the product line would be profitable and would increase overall company income. You have been asked to analyze the possible reasons why the Sporting Goods Division manager rejected the new product line.

1. Determine the rate of return on investment for the Sporting Goods Division for the past year.
2. Determine the Sporting Goods Division manager's bonus for the past year.
3. Determine the estimated rate of return on investment for the new product line.
4. ✏➤ Why might the manager of the Sporting Goods Division decide to reject the new product line?
5. ✏➤ Can you suggest an alternative performance measure for motivating division managers to accept new investment opportunities that would increase the overall company income and rate of return on investment?

Activity 7–6
Into the Real World
The balanced scoreboard and EVA

Divide responsibilities between two groups, with one group going to the home page of Renaissance Worldwide at **www.rens.com**, and the second group going to the home page of **Stern Stewart & Co.** at **www.eva.com**. Renaissance Worldwide, is a consulting firm that helped develop the "balanced scorecard" concept. Stern Stewart & Co. is a consulting firm that developed the concept of "economic value added" (EVA), another method of measuring corporate and divisional performance, similar to residual income.

In the home page of Renaissance Worldwide, type "balanced scorecard" in the site search field. After reading about the balanced scorecard from selected documents, prepare a brief report describing the balanced scorecard and its claimed advantages. In the Stern group, use links in the home page of Stern Stewart & Co. to learn about EVA. After reading about EVA, prepare a brief report describing EVA and its claimed advantages. After preparing these reports, both groups should discuss their research and prepare a brief analysis comparing and contrasting these two approaches to corporate and divisional performance measurement.

ANSWERS TO SELF-EXAMINATION QUESTIONS

Matching

1.	O	4.	R	7.	B	10.	S	13.	M	16.	C
2.	K	5.	D	8.	L	11.	F	14.	G	17.	J
3.	H	6.	I	9.	N	12.	P	15.	Q	18.	A

Multiple Choice

1. **B** The manager of a profit center (answer B) has responsibility for and authority over costs and revenues. If the manager has responsibility for only costs, the department is called a cost center (answer A). If the responsibility and authority extend to the investment in assets as well as costs and revenues, it is called an investment center (answer C). A service department (answer D) provides services to other departments. A service department could be a cost center, profit center, or investment center.

2. **C** $600,000/150,000 = $4 per payment. Division A anticipates 60,000 payments or $240,000 (60,000 × $4) in service department charges from the Accounts Payable Department. Income from operations is thus $900,000 − $240,000, or $660,000. Answer A assumes that all of the service department overhead is assigned to Division A, which would be incorrect, since Division A does not use all of the accounts payable service. Answer B incorrectly assumes that there are no service department charges from Accounts Payable. Answer D incorrectly determines the accounts payable transfer rate from Division A's income from operations.

3. **A** The rate of return on investment for Division A is 20% (answer A), computed as follows:

$$\text{Rate of return on investment (ROI)} = \frac{\text{Income from operations}}{\text{Invested assets}}$$

$$\text{ROI} = \frac{\$350,000 - \$200,000 - \$30,000}{\$600,000} = 20\%$$

4. **B** The profit margin for Division L of Liddy Co. is 15% (answer B), computed as follows:

$$\text{Rate of return on investment (ROI)} = \text{Profit margin} \times \text{Investment turnover}$$

$$24\% = \text{Profit margin} \times 1.6$$
$$15\% = \text{Profit margin}$$

5. **C** The market price approach (answer C) to transfer pricing uses the price at which the product or service transferred could be sold to outside buyers. The cost price approach (answer A) uses cost as the basis for setting transfer prices. The negotiated price approach (answer B) allows managers of decentralized units to agree (negotiate) among themselves as to the proper transfer price. The standard cost approach (answer D) is a version of the cost price approach that uses standard costs in setting transfer prices.

Differential Analysis and Product Pricing

objectives

After studying this chapter, you should be able to:

1 Prepare a differential analysis report for decisions involving leasing or selling equipment, discontinuing an unprofitable segment, manufacturing or purchasing a needed part, replacing usable fixed assets, processing further or selling an intermediate product, or accepting additional business at a special price.

2 Determine the selling price of a product, using the total cost, product cost, and variable cost concepts.

3 Calculate the relative profitability of products in bottleneck production environments.

Many of the decisions that you make depend on comparing the estimated costs of alternatives. The payoff from such comparisons is described in the following report from a University of Michigan study.

Richard Nisbett and two colleagues quizzed Michigan faculty members and university seniors on such questions as how often they walk out on a bad movie, refuse to finish a bad meal, start over on a weak term paper, or abandon a research project that no longer looks promising. They believe that people who cut their losses this way are following sound economic rules: calculating the net benefits of alternative courses of action, writing off past costs that can't be recovered, and weighing the opportunity to use future time and effort more profitably elsewhere.

They find that among faculty members, those who use cost-benefit reasoning in this fashion—being more likely to give up on research that isn't getting anywhere or using labor-saving devices as often as possible—have higher salaries relative to their age and departments. Not surprisingly, economists are more likely to apply the approach than professors of humanities or biology.

Among students, those who have learned to use cost-benefit analysis frequently are apt to have far better grades than their Scholastic Aptitude Test scores would have predicted. Again, the more economics courses the students have, the more likely they are to apply cost-benefit analysis outside the classroom.

Dr. Nisbett concedes that for many Americans, cost-benefit rules often appear to conflict with such traditional principles as "never give up" and "waste not, want not."

Managers must also consider the effects of alternative decisions on their businesses. In this chapter, we discuss differential analysis, which reports the effects of alternative decisions on total revenues and costs. We also describe and illustrate practical approaches to setting product prices. Finally, we discuss how production bottlenecks influence product mix and pricing decisions.

Source: Alan L. Otten, "Economic Perspective Produces Steady Yields," from People Patterns, *The Wall Street Journal,* March 31, 1992, p. B1.

Differential Analysis

objective 1

Prepare a differential analysis report for decisions involving leasing or selling equipment, discontinuing an unprofitable segment, manufacturing or purchasing a needed part, replacing usable fixed assets, processing further or selling an intermediate product, or accepting additional business at a special price.

Planning for future operations involves decision making. For some decisions, revenue and cost data from the accounting records may be useful. However, the revenue and cost data for use in evaluating courses of future operations or choosing among competing alternatives are often not available in the accounting records and must be estimated.

Consider:

- The decision by **General Motors** to purchase on-board communications products from **Delphi Automotive Systems** instead of making them internally.
- The decision by **Marriott** hotels to accept a special price from a bid placed on **priceline.com**.
- The decision by **TWA** to discontinue service to Rome, Madrid, and Barcelona.

In each of these decisions, the estimated revenues and costs were **relevant**. The relevant revenues and costs focus on the differences between each alternative. Costs that have been incurred in the past are not relevant to the decision. These costs are called **sunk costs**.

The irrelevancy of sunk cost is sometimes difficult to apply in practice. Psychologists believe this is because acknowledging a sunk cost is the same as admitting to a past mistake. For example, one study compared the playing time of players selected in the first round of the **NBA** draft with other players. The study found that poor-performing first-round draftees received more court time than players with better performance but smaller contracts. Apparently, the owners felt that they had to prove that the big contract wasn't wasted, even though it meant having the wrong players on the court.

Decision	Differential Analysis
Alternative A	
or	**Differential revenue**
	− Differential costs
	Differential income or loss
Alternative B	

Differential revenue is the amount of increase or decrease in revenue expected from a course of action as compared with an alternative. To illustrate, assume that certain equipment is being used to manufacture calculators, which are expected to generate revenue of $150,000. If the equipment could be used to make digital clocks, which would generate revenue of $175,000, the differential revenue from making and selling digital clocks is $25,000.

Differential cost is the amount of increase or decrease in cost that is expected from a course of action as compared with an alternative. For example, if an increase in advertising expenditures from $100,000 to $150,000 is being considered, the differential cost of the action is $50,000.

Differential income or loss is the difference between the differential revenue and the differential costs. Differential income indicates that a particular decision is expected to be profitable, while a differential loss indicates the opposite.

Differential analysis focuses on the effect of alternative courses of action on the relevant revenues and costs. For example, if a manager must decide between two alternatives, differential analysis would involve comparing the differential revenues of the two alternatives with the differential costs.

In this chapter, we will discuss the use of differential analysis in analyzing the following alternatives:

1. Leasing or selling equipment.
2. Discontinuing an unprofitable segment.
3. Manufacturing or purchasing a needed part.
4. Replacing usable fixed assets.
5. Processing further or selling an intermediate product.
6. Accepting additional business at a special price.

Lease or Sell

Management may have a choice between leasing or selling a piece of equipment that is no longer needed in the business. In deciding which option is best, management may use differential analysis. To illustrate, assume that Marcus Company is considering disposing of equipment that cost $200,000 and has $120,000 of accumulated depreciation to date. Marcus Company can sell the equipment through a broker for $100,000 less a 6% commission. Alternatively, Potamkin Company (the lessee) has offered to lease the equipment for five years for a total of $160,000. At the end of the fifth year of the lease, the equipment is expected to have no residual value. During the period of the lease, Marcus Company (the lessor) will incur repair, insurance, and property tax expenses estimated at $35,000. Exhibit 1 shows Marcus Company's analysis of whether to lease or sell the equipment.

Note that in Exhibit 1, the $80,000 book value ($200,000 − $120,000) of the equipment is a sunk cost and is not considered in the analysis. The $80,000 is a cost that resulted from a previous decision. It is not affected by the alternatives now being considered in leasing or selling the equipment. The relevant factors to be considered are the differential revenues and differential costs associated with the lease or sell decision. This analysis is verified by the traditional analysis in Exhibit 2.

Marcus Company

Sell Equipment to OR **Lease Equipment to**

Broker   **Potamkin Company**

Exhibit 1 Differential
Analysis Report—Lease
or Sell

Proposal to Lease or Sell Equipment June 22, 2003		
Differential revenue from alternatives:		
Revenue from lease	$160,000	
Revenue from sale	100,000	
Differential revenue from lease		$60,000
Differential cost of alternatives:		
Repair, insurance, and property tax expenses	$ 35,000	
Commission expense on sale	6,000	
Differential cost of lease		29,000
Net differential income from the lease alternative		**$31,000**

Exhibit 2 Traditional
Analysis

Lease or Sell		
Lease alternative:		
Revenue from lease		$160,000
Depreciation expense for remaining five years	$80,000	
Repair, insurance, and property tax expenses	35,000	115,000
Net gain		$45,000
Sell alternative:		
Sales price		$100,000
Book value of equipment	$80,000	
Commission expense	6,000	86,000
Net gain		14,000
Net differential income from the lease alternative		**$31,000**

Many compa-
nies that
manufacture
expensive equip-
ment give customers the
choice of leasing the equipment. For example, con-
struction equipment from
Caterpillar Inc. can either
be purchased outright or
leased through Caterpillar's
financial services subsidiary.
IBM makes its large main-
frame computers available
by lease, as does Xerox
with its copy machines.

The alternatives presented in Exhibits 1 and 2 were relatively simple. However, regardless of the complexity, the approach to differential analysis is basically the same. Two additional factors that often need to be considered are (1) differential revenue from investing the funds generated by the alternatives and (2) any income tax differential. In Exhibit 1, there could be differential interest revenue related to investing the cash flows from the two alternatives. Any income tax differential would be related to the differences in the timing of the income from the alternatives and the differences in the amount of investment income. In the next chapter, we will consider these factors on management decisions.

Discontinue a Segment or Product

When a product or a department, branch, territory, or other segment of a business is generating losses, management may consider eliminating the product or segment. It is often assumed, sometimes in error, that the total income from operations of a business would be increased if the operating loss could be eliminated. Discontinu-ing the product or segment usually eliminates all of the product or segment's vari-able costs (direct materials, direct labor, sales commissions, and so on). However, if the product or segment is a relatively small part of the business, the fixed costs (depreciation, insurance, property taxes, and so on) may not be decreased by dis-continuing it. It is possible in this case for the total operating income of a company to decrease rather than increase by eliminating the product or segment. To illustrate, the income statement for Battle Creek Cereal Co. presented in Exhibit 3 is for a normal year ending August 31, 2003.

Exhibit 3 Income (Loss) by Product

Battle Creek Cereal Co. Condensed Income Statement For the Year Ended August 31, 2003				
	Corn Flakes	Toasted Oats	Bran Flakes	Total
Sales	$500,000	$400,000	$100,000	$1,000,000
Cost of goods sold:				
Variable costs	$220,000	$200,000	$ 60,000	$ 480,000
Fixed costs	120,000	80,000	20,000	220,000
Total cost of goods sold	$340,000	$280,000	$ 80,000	$ 700,000
Gross profit	$160,000	$120,000	$ 20,000	$ 300,000
Operating expenses:				
Variable expenses	$ 95,000	$ 60,000	$ 25,000	$ 180,000
Fixed expenses	25,000	20,000	6,000	51,000
Total operating expenses . . .	$120,000	$ 80,000	$ 31,000	$ 231,000
Income (loss) from operations . . .	$ 40,000	$ 40,000	$(11,000)	$ 69,000

Product A has a loss from operations of $18,000 and fixed costs of $25,000. Product B has a loss from operations of $12,000 and fixed costs of $8,000. All remaining products have income from operations of $75,000 and fixed costs of $30,000. (1) Which product(s) should be discontinued, and (2) what would be the estimated income from operations if the action in (1) is taken?

----

(1) Product B; (2) $49,000 ($75,000 − $18,000 − $8,000)

Because Bran Flakes incurs annual losses, management is considering discontinuing it. Total annual operating income of $80,000 ($40,000 Toasted Oats + $40,000 Corn Flakes) might seem to be indicated by the income statement in Exhibit 3 if Bran Flakes is discontinued.

Discontinuing Bran Flakes, however, would actually decrease operating income by $15,000, to $54,000 ($69,000 − $15,000). This is shown by the differential analysis report in Exhibit 4, in which we assume that discontinuing Bran Flakes would have no effect on fixed costs and expenses.

Exhibit 4 Differential Analysis Report—Discontinue an Unprofitable Segment

Proposal to Discontinue Bran Flakes September 29, 2003		
Differential revenue from annual sales of Bran Flakes:		
Revenue from sales		$100,000
Differential cost of annual sales of Bran Flakes:		
Variable cost of goods sold	$60,000	
Variable operating expenses	25,000	85,000
Annual differential income from sales of Bran Flakes . . .		**$ 15,000**

The traditional analysis in Exhibit 5 verifies the preceding differential analysis. In Exhibit 5, only the short-term (one year) effects of discontinuing Bran Flakes are

Exhibit 5 Traditional Analysis

Proposal to Discontinue Bran Flakes **September 29, 2003**			
	Bran Flakes, Toasted Oats, and Corn Flakes	Discontinue Bran Flakes*	Toasted Oats and Corn Flakes
Sales	$1,000,000	$100,000	$900,000
Cost of goods sold:			
Variable costs	$ 480,000	$ 60,000	$420,000
Fixed costs	220,000	—	220,000
Total cost of goods sold	$ 700,000	$ 60,000	$640,000
Gross profit	$ 300,000	$ 40,000	$260,000
Operating expenses:			
Variable expenses	$ 180,000	$ 25,000	$155,000
Fixed expenses	51,000	—	51,000
Total operating expenses	$ 231,000	$ 25,000	$206,000
Income (loss) from operations	**$ 69,000**	**$15,000**	**$ 54,000**

*Fixed costs do not decline with the discontinuance of Bran Flakes.

considered. When eliminating a product or segment, management may also consider the long-term effects. For example, the plant capacity made available by discontinuing Bran Flakes might be eliminated. This could reduce fixed costs. Some employees may have to be laid off, and others may have to be relocated and re-trained. Further, there may be a related decrease in sales of more profitable products to those customers who were attracted by the discontinued product.

Make or Buy

The assembly of many parts is often a major element in manufacturing some products, such as automobiles. These parts may be made by the product's manufacturer, or they may be purchased. For example, some of the parts for an automobile, such as the motor, may be produced by the automobile manufacturer. Other parts, such as tires, may be purchased from other manufacturers. In addition, in manufacturing motors, such items as spark plugs and nuts and bolts may be acquired from suppliers.

Management uses differential costs to decide whether to make or buy a part. For example, if a part is purchased, management has concluded that it is less costly to buy the part than to manufacture it. Make or buy options often arise when a manufacturer has excess productive capacity in the form of unused equipment, space, and labor.

The differential analysis is similar, whether management is considering making a part that is currently being purchased or purchasing a part that is currently

Nike, Inc., does not make shoes but buys 100% of its shoe manufacturing from outside suppliers. Nike, Inc., believes that its strengths are in designing, marketing, distributing, and selling athletic shoes. Thus, Nike focuses on the parts of the business where it believes that it adds the greatest value to the customer and thus the greatest profitability to the company.

being made. To illustrate, assume that an automobile manufacturer has been purchasing instrument panels for $240 a unit. The factory is currently operating at 80% of capacity, and no major increase in production is expected in the near future. The cost per unit of manufacturing an instrument panel internally, including fixed costs, is estimated as follows:

Direct materials	$ 80
Direct labor	80
Variable factory overhead	52
Fixed factory overhead	68
Total cost per unit	$280

Q&A *Part K can be purchased for $30 per unit. Part K can be manufactured internally using $7.50 of direct materials and 0.75 hour of direct labor at $12 per direct labor hour (dlh). Factory overhead is applied at a rate of $20 per direct labor hour. ($7 per dlh is fixed.) What is the cost savings or penalty from manufacturing the part internally?*

$3.75 cost savings {$30 − [$7.50 + (0.75 × $12) + (0.75 × $13)]}

If the *make* price of $280 is simply compared with the *buy* price of $240, the decision is to buy the instrument panel. However, if unused capacity could be used in manufacturing the part, there would be no increase in the total amount of fixed factory overhead costs. Thus, only the variable factory overhead costs need to be considered. The relevant costs are summarized in the differential report in Exhibit 6.

Exhibit 6 Differential Analysis Report—Make or Buy

Proposal to Manufacture Instrument Panels **February 15, 2003**		
Purchase price of an instrument panel		$240.00
Differential cost to manufacture:		
Direct materials	$80.00	
Direct labor	80.00	
Variable factory overhead	52.00	212.00
Cost savings from manufacturing an instrument panel		$ 28.00

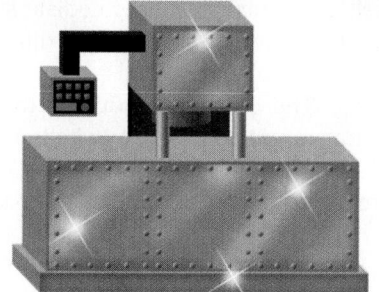

Other possible effects of a decision to manufacture the instrument panel should also be considered. For example, increasing production in the future might require using the currently idle capacity. This decision may affect employees. It may also affect future business relations with the instrument panel supplier, who may provide other essential parts. The company's decision to manufacture instrument panels might jeopardize the timely delivery of these other parts.

Replace Equipment

The usefulness of fixed assets may be reduced long before they are considered to be worn out. For example, equipment may no longer be efficient for the purpose for which it is used. On the other hand, the equipment may not have reached the point of complete inadequacy. Decisions to replace usable fixed assets should be based on relevant costs. The relevant costs are the future costs of continuing to use the equipment versus replacement. The book values of the fixed assets being replaced are sunk costs and are irrelevant.

To illustrate, assume that a business is considering the disposal of several identical machines having a total book value of $100,000 and an estimated remaining life of five years. The old machines can be sold for $25,000. They can be replaced by a single high-speed machine at a cost of $250,000. The new machine has an estimated useful life of five years and no residual value. Analyses indicate an estimated annual reduction in variable manufacturing costs from $225,000 with the old machine to $150,000 with the new machine. No other changes in the manufacturing costs or the operating expenses are expected. The relevant costs are summarized in the differential report in Exhibit 7.

Exhibit 7 Differential Analysis Report—Replace Equipment

Proposal to Replace Equipment November 28, 2003		
Annual variable costs—present equipment	$225,000	
Annual variable costs—new equipment	150,000	
Annual differential decrease in cost	$ 75,000	
Number of years applicable	× 5	
Total differential decrease in cost	$375,000	
Proceeds from sale of present equipment	25,000	$400,000
Cost of new equipment		250,000
Net differential decrease in cost, 5-year total		$150,000
Annual net differential decrease in cost—new equipment ..		**$ 30,000**

Other factors are often important in equipment replacement decisions. For example, differences between the remaining useful life of the old equipment and the estimated life of the new equipment could exist. In addition, the new equipment might improve the overall quality of the product, resulting in an increase in sales volume. Additional factors could include the time value of money and other uses for the cash needed to purchase the new equipment.[1]

The amount of income that is forgone from an alternative use of an asset, such as cash, is called an **opportunity cost**. For example, your opportunity cost of attending school is the income forgone from lost work hours. Although the opportunity cost does not appear as a part of historical accounting data, it is useful in analyzing alternative courses of action. To illustrate, assume that the cash outlay of $250,000 for the new equipment, less the $25,000 proceeds from the sale of the present equipment, could be invested to yield a 10% return. Thus, the annual opportunity cost related to the purchase of the new equipment is $22,500 (10% × $225,000).

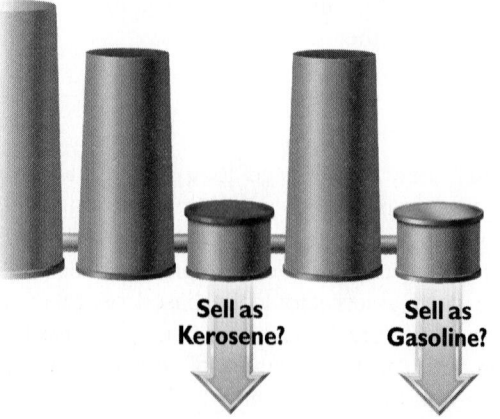

Sell as Kerosene?

Sell as Gasoline?

Process or Sell

When a product is manufactured, it progresses through various stages of production. Often a product can be sold at an intermediate stage of production, or it can be processed further and then sold. In deciding whether to sell a product at an intermediate stage or to process it further, differential analysis is useful. The differential revenues from further processing are compared to the differential costs of further processing. The costs of producing the intermediate product do not change, regardless of whether the intermediate product is sold or processed further. Thus, these costs are not differential costs and are irrelevant to the decision to process further.

[1] The importance of the time value of money in equipment replacement decisions is discussed in a later chapter.

After initial release, film studios "process" movies further by releasing them in DVD format for the home market. Items that are relevant to making this decision are the copying and packaging costs for the disk, marketing costs associated with promoting the disk, and anticipated revenues from selling the disk. The original movie production costs are not relevant to the decision.

Product T is produced for $2.50 per gallon ($1.00 fixed cost) and can be sold without additional processing for $3.50 per gallon. Product T can be processed further into Product V at a cost of $1.60 per gallon ($0.90 fixed). Product V can be sold for $4.00 per gallon. What is the differential income or loss per gallon from processing Product T into Product V?

$0.20 loss [$4.00 − $3.50 − $1.60 + $0.90]

The Internet is forcing many companies toward "dynamic" pricing. For example, in priceline.com's "name your price" format, customers tell the company what they are willing to pay and then the company must decide if it is willing to sell at that price.

To illustrate, assume that a business produces kerosene in batches of 4,000 gallons. Standard quantities of 4,000 gallons of direct materials are processed, which cost $0.60 per gallon. Kerosene can be sold without further processing for $0.80 per gallon. It can be processed further to yield gasoline, which can be sold for $1.25 per gallon. Gasoline requires additional processing costs of $650 per batch, and 20% of the gallons of kerosene will evaporate during production. Exhibit 8 summarizes the differential revenues and costs in deciding whether to process kerosene to produce gasoline.

Exhibit 8 Differential Analysis Report—Process or Sell

Proposal to Process Kerosene Further October 1, 2003		
Differential revenue from further processing per batch:		
Revenue from sale of gasoline [(4,000 gallons − 800 gallons evaporation) × $1.25]	$4,000	
Revenue from sale of kerosene (4,000 gallons × $0.80)	3,200	
Differential revenue		$800
Differential cost per batch:		
Additional cost of producing gasoline		650
Differential income from further processing gasoline per batch		**$150**

The differential income from further processing kerosene into gasoline is $150 per batch. The initial cost of producing the intermediate kerosene, $2,400 (4,000 gallons × $0.60), is not considered in deciding whether to process kerosene further. This initial cost will be incurred, regardless of whether gasoline is produced.

Accept Business at a Special Price

Differential analysis is also useful in deciding whether to accept additional business at a special price. The differential revenue that would be provided from the additional business is compared to the differential costs of producing and delivering the product to the customer. If the company is operating at full capacity, any additional production will increase both fixed and variable production costs. If, however, the normal production of the company is below full capacity, additional business may be undertaken without increasing fixed production costs. In this case, the differential costs of the additional production are the variable manufacturing costs. If operating expenses increase because of the additional business, these expenses should also be considered.

To illustrate, assume that the monthly capacity of a sporting goods business is 12,500 basketballs. Current sales and production are averaging 10,000 basketballs per month. The current manufacturing cost of $20 per unit consists of variable costs of $12.50 and fixed costs of $7.50. The normal selling price of the product

in the domestic market is $30. The manufacturer receives from an exporter an offer for 5,000 basketballs at $18 each. Production can be spread over a three-month period without interfering with normal production or incurring overtime costs. Pricing policies in the domestic market will not be affected. Simply comparing the sales price of $18 with the present unit manufacturing cost of $20 indicates that the offer should be rejected. However, by focusing only on the differential cost, which in this case is the variable cost, the decision is different. Exhibit 9 shows the differential analysis report for this decision.

Product D is normally sold for $4.40 per unit. A special price of $3.60 is offered for the export market. The variable production cost is $3.00 per unit. An additional export tariff of 10% of revenue will be required for all export products. What is the differential income or loss per unit from selling Product D for export?

$0.24 income [$3.60 − $3.00 − (0.10 × $3.60)]

Exhibit 9 Differential Analysis Report—Sell at Special Price

Proposal to Sell Basketballs to Exporter March 10, 2003	
Differential revenue from accepting offer:	
Revenue from sale of 5,000 additional units at $18	$90,000
Differential cost of accepting offer:	
Variable costs of 5,000 additional units at $12.50	62,500
Differential income from accepting offer	**$27,500**

Proposals to sell a product in the domestic market at prices lower than the normal price may require additional considerations. For example, it may be unwise to increase sales volume in one territory by price reductions if sales volume is lost in other areas. Manufacturers must also conform to the Robinson-Patman Act, which prohibits price discrimination within the United States unless differences in prices can be justified by different costs of serving different customers.

Setting Normal Product Selling Prices

objective 2

Determine the selling price of a product, using the total cost, product cost, and variable cost concepts.

Differential analysis may be useful in deciding to lower selling prices for special short-run decisions, such as whether to accept business at a price lower than the normal price. In such cases, the minimum short-run price is set high enough to cover all variable costs. Any price above this minimum price will improve profits in the short run. In the long run, however, the normal selling price must be set high enough to cover all costs and expenses (both fixed and variable) and provide a reasonable profit. Otherwise, the business may not survive.

The normal selling price can be viewed as the target selling price to be achieved in the long run. The basic approaches to setting this price are as follows:

Market Methods	Cost-Plus Methods
1. Demand-based methods	1. Total cost concept
2. Competition-based methods	2. Product cost concept
	3. Variable cost concept

McDonald's Corporation evaluated the *Extra Value Meals* concept and determined that combination meals priced at a discount would create additional revenue from customer "trade-ups" from a la carte purchases. The concept was so successful that it has become an industry standard.

Managers using the market methods refer to the external market to determine the price. Demand-based methods set the price according to the demand for the product. If there is high demand for the product, then the price may be set high, while lower demand may require the price to be set low. An example of setting different prices according to the demand for the product is found in the telecommunications industry, with low weekend rates and high business day rates for long-distance telephone calls.

Competition-based methods set the price according to the price offered by competitors. For example, if a competitor reduces the price, then management may be required to adjust the price to meet the competition. The market-based pricing approaches are discussed in greater detail in marketing courses, so we will not expand upon them here.

Managers using the cost-plus methods price the product in order to achieve a target profit. Managers add to the cost an amount called a **markup**, so that all costs plus a profit are included in the selling price. In the following paragraphs, we describe and illustrate the three cost concepts often used in applying the cost-plus approach: (1) total cost, (2) product cost, and (3) variable cost.

Total Cost Concept

Using the **total cost concept**, all costs of manufacturing a product plus the selling and administrative expenses are included in the cost amount to which the markup is added. Since all costs and expenses are included in the cost amount, the dollar amount of the markup equals the desired profit.

The first step in applying the total cost concept is to determine the total cost of manufacturing the product. This cost includes the costs of direct materials, direct labor, and factory overhead and should be available from the accounting records. The next step is to add the estimated selling and administrative expenses to the total cost of manufacturing the product. The cost amount per unit is then computed by dividing the total costs by the total units expected to be produced and sold.

After the cost amount per unit has been determined, the dollar amount of the markup is determined. For this purpose, the markup is expressed as a percentage of cost. This percentage is then multiplied by the cost amount per unit. The dollar amount of the markup is then added to the cost amount per unit to arrive at the selling price.

The markup percentage for the total cost concept is determined by applying the following formula:

$$\text{Markup percentage} = \frac{\text{Desired profit}}{\text{Total costs}}$$

The numerator of the formula is only the desired profit. This is because all costs and expenses are included in the cost amount to which the markup is added. The denominator of the formula is the total costs.

To illustrate, assume that the costs for calculators of Digital Solutions Inc. are as follows:

Variable costs:		
Direct materials	$ 3.00	per unit
Direct labor	10.00	
Factory overhead	1.50	
Selling and administrative expenses	1.50	
Total	$ 16.00	per unit
Fixed costs:		
Factory overhead	$50,000	
Selling and administrative expenses	20,000	

The microcomputer industry is developing products that can be sold to consumers for under $1,000. By using the total cost concept, the following price can be determined:

Motherboard	$140
Memory	50
Processor	90
Disk drive	198
Peripherals	265
Factory overhead and assembly	48
Product cost	$791
Administrative expenses	26
Total cost	$817
Manufacturer markup	91
Manufacturer's price to retailer	$908
Retailer markup	91
Retail price to final consumer	$999

Notice that there are two markups included in the final price—one for the manufacturer and one for the retailer.

Digital Solutions Inc. desires a profit equal to a 20% rate of return on assets, $800,000 of assets are devoted to producing calculators, and 100,000 units are expected to be produced and sold. The calculators' total cost is $1,670,000, or $16.70 per unit, computed as follows:

Variable costs ($16.00 × 100,000 units)		$1,600,000
Fixed costs:		
Factory overhead	$50,000	
Selling and administrative expenses	20,000	70,000
Total costs		$1,670,000
Total cost per calculator ($1,670,000 ÷ 100,000 units)		$16.70

The desired profit is $160,000 (20% × $800,000), and the markup percentage for a calculator is 9.6%, computed as follows:

$$\text{Markup percentage} = \frac{\text{Desired profit}}{\text{Total costs}}$$

$$\text{Markup percentage} = \frac{\$160,000}{\$1,670,000} = 9.6\%$$

Based on the total cost per unit and the markup percentage for a calculator, Digital Solutions Inc. would price each calculator at $18.30 per unit, as shown below.

Total cost per calculator	$16.70
Markup ($16.70 × 9.6%)	1.60
Selling price	$18.30

The ability of the selling price of $18.30 to generate the desired profit of $160,000 is shown by the following income statement:

Digital Solutions Inc.
Income Statement
For the Year Ended December 31, 2003

Sales (100,000 units × $18.30)		$1,830,000
Expenses:		
Variable (100,000 units × $16.00)	$1,600,000	
Fixed ($50,000 + $20,000)	70,000	1,670,000
Income from operations		$ 160,000

The total cost concept of applying the cost-plus approach to product pricing is often used by contractors who sell products to government agencies. In many cases, government contractors are required by law to be reimbursed for their products on a total-cost-plus-profit basis.

Product Cost Concept

Using the **product cost concept**, only the costs of manufacturing the product, termed the product cost, are included in the cost amount to which the markup is

PRODUCT COST CONCEPT

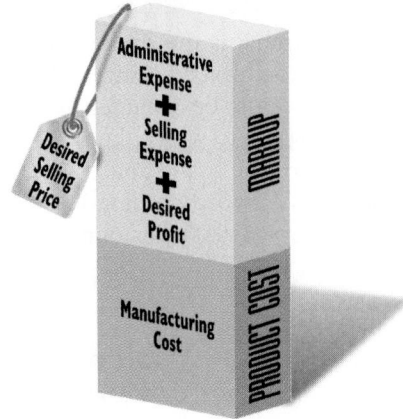

added. Estimated selling expenses, administrative expenses, and profit are included in the markup. The markup percentage is determined by applying the following formula:

$$\text{Markup percentage} = \frac{\text{Desired profit} + \text{Total selling and administrative expenses}}{\text{Total manufacturing costs}}$$

The numerator of the markup percentage formula is the desired profit plus the total selling and administrative expenses. These expenses must be included in the markup, since they are not included in the cost amount to which the markup is added. The denominator of the formula includes the costs of direct materials, direct labor, and factory overhead.

To illustrate, assume the same data used in the preceding illustration. The manufacturing cost for Digital Solutions Inc.'s calculator is $1,500,000, or $15 per unit, computed as follows:

Direct materials ($3 × 100,000 units)		$ 300,000
Direct labor ($10 × 100,000 units)		1,000,000
Factory overhead:		
Variable ($1.50 × 100,000 units)	$150,000	
Fixed	50,000	200,000
Total manufacturing costs		$1,500,000
Manufacturing cost per calculator ($1,500,000 ÷ 100,000 units)		$15

The desired profit is $160,000 (20% × $800,000), and the total selling and administrative expenses are $170,000 [(100,000 units × $1.50 per unit) + $20,000]. The markup percentage for a calculator is 22%, computed as follows:

$$\text{Markup percentage} = \frac{\text{Desired profit} + \text{Total selling and administrative expenses}}{\text{Total manufacturing costs}}$$

$$\text{Markup percentage} = \frac{\$160,000 + \$170,000}{\$1,500,000}$$

$$\text{Markup percentage} = \frac{\$330,000}{\$1,500,000} = 22\%$$

Based on the manufacturing cost per calculator and the markup percentage, Digital Solutions Inc. would price each calculator at $18.30 per unit, as shown below.

Manufacturing cost per calculator	$15.00
Markup ($15 × 22%)	3.30
Selling price	$18.30

Variable Cost Concept

The **variable cost concept** emphasizes the distinction between variable and fixed costs in product pricing. Using the variable cost concept, only variable costs are included in the cost amount to which the markup is added. All variable manufacturing costs, as well as variable selling and administrative expenses, are included in the cost amount. Fixed manufacturing costs, fixed selling and administrative expenses, and profit are included in the markup.

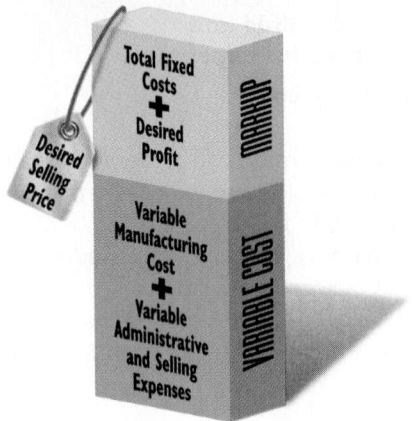

VARIABLE COST CONCEPT

The markup percentage is determined by applying the following formula:

$$\text{Markup percentage} = \frac{\textbf{Desired profit + Total fixed costs}}{\textbf{Total variable costs}}$$

The numerator of the markup percentage formula is the desired profit plus the total fixed manufacturing costs and the total fixed selling and administrative expenses. These costs and expenses must be included in the markup, since they are not included in the cost amount to which the markup is added. The denominator of the formula includes the total variable costs.

To illustrate, assume the same data used in the two preceding illustrations. The calculator variable cost is $1,600,000, or $16.00 per unit, computed as follows:

Variable costs:	
Direct materials ($3 × 100,000 units)	$ 300,000
Direct labor ($10 × 100,000 units)	1,000,000
Factory overhead ($1.50 × 100,000 units)	150,000
Selling and administrative expenses ($1.50 × 100,000 units)	150,000
Total variable costs	$1,600,000
Variable cost per calculator ($1,600,000 ÷ 100,000 units)	$16.00

The desired profit is $160,000 (20% × $800,000), the total fixed manufacturing costs are $50,000, and the total fixed selling and administrative expenses are $20,000. The markup percentage for a calculator is 14.4%, computed as follows:

$$\text{Markup percentage} = \frac{\textbf{Desired profit + Total fixed costs}}{\textbf{Total variable costs}}$$

$$\text{Markup percentage} = \frac{\$160,000 + \$50,000 + \$20,000}{\$1,600,000}$$

$$\text{Markup percentage} = \frac{\$230,000}{\$1,600,000} = 14.4\%$$

Based on the variable cost per calculator and the markup percentage, Digital Solutions Inc. would price each calculator at $18.30 per unit, as shown below.

Variable cost per calculator	$16.00
Markup ($16.00 × 14.4%)	2.30
Selling price	$18.30

Product Z has a total cost of $30 per unit. Of this amount, $10 per unit is selling and administrative costs. The total variable cost is $18 per unit. The desired profit is $3 per unit. Determine the markup percentage on (1) total cost, (2) product cost, and (3) variable cost.

----

(1) 10% ($3 ÷ $30);
(2) 65% [($10 + $3) ÷ $20];
(3) 83.3% [($12 + $3) ÷ $18]

Choosing a Cost-Plus Approach Cost Concept

All three cost concepts produced the same selling price ($18.30) for Digital Solutions Inc. In practice, however, the three cost concepts are usually not viewed as alternatives. Each cost concept requires different estimates of costs and expenses. This difficulty and the complexity of the manufacturing operations should be considered in choosing a cost concept.

To reduce the costs of gathering data, estimated (standard) costs rather than actual costs may be used with any of the three cost concepts. However, management should exercise caution when using estimated costs in applying the cost-plus approach. The estimates should be based on normal (attainable) operating levels and not theoretical (ideal) levels of performance. In product pricing, the use of estimates based on ideal- or maximum-capacity operating levels might lead to setting product prices too low. In this case, the costs of such factors as normal spoilage or normal periods of idle time might not be considered.

The following survey results show the pricing strategies used by manufacturers and service companies. As you can see, cost-plus approaches to pricing dominate practice, and the product (or total) cost approach dominates the cost-plus approaches. In addition, there is little difference between manufacturing and service companies in their pricing approaches.

PRICING METHODS

MANUFACTURING

Combination

12
17
71

Market-related
Cost-plus

SERVICE COMPANIES

Combination

11
21
68

Market-related
Cost-plus

COST-PLUS

Other

14
27
59

Variable cost
Product or total cost

COST-PLUS

Other

27
45
28

Variable cost
Product or total cost

Source: R. W. Mills, and C. Sweeting, *Pricing Decisions in Practice*, London: CIMA, 1988.

The decision-making needs of management are also an important factor in selecting a cost concept for product pricing. For example, managers who often make special pricing decisions are more likely to use the variable cost concept. In contrast, a government defense contractor would be more likely to use the total cost concept.

A variation of the cost concepts discussed in the preceding paragraphs is the **target cost concept**. Under this concept, which was first used by the Japanese, the selling price is assumed to be set by the marketplace. The target cost is determined by *subtracting* a desired profit from the selling price. Thus, managers must design and manufacture the product to achieve its target cost. In contrast, the three cost concepts discussed previously start with a given product cost and *add* a markup to determine the selling price. Some argue that the target cost concept may be better than the cost-plus approaches in highly competitive markets that require continual product cost reductions to remain competitive.

Activity-Based Costing

As illustrated in the preceding paragraphs, costs are an important consideration in setting product prices. To more accurately measure the costs of producing and selling products, some companies use activity-based costing. **Activity-based costing** (ABC) identifies and traces activities to specific products.

Activity-based costing may be useful in making product pricing decisions where manufacturing operations involve large amounts of factory overhead. In such cases, traditional overhead allocation using activity bases such as units produced or machine hours may yield inaccurate cost allocations. This, in turn, may result in distorted product costs and product prices. By providing more accurate product cost allocations, activity-based costing aids in setting product prices that will cover costs and expenses.[2]

[2] Activity-based costing is further discussed and illustrated in Chapter M10.

BUSINESS ON STAGE

Alternative Pricing Approaches

At various times, a business may use alternative pricing approaches, often as a supplement to the traditional cost-plus pricing of products. Some of these alternative approaches are described below.

• **Price skimming** is normally short-term in nature and is used when a business has a new product that is unique in the marketplace. Because of the lack of competing products, the business sets the price at an artificially high level. It anticipates that it will have to lower the price once competitors enter the market. In the meantime, however, it will be able to earn high profits that can be used to cover the costs of developing the product. For example, Hewlett-Packard (HP) initially set the price of its laser printer for personal computers at around $4,000. Eventually, as competitors entered the market, HP lowered the price. Today, an HP laser printer can be purchased for less than $1,000.

- **Psychological pricing** is based on two behavioral tendencies of customers. First, customers often assume that the higher the price of a product, the higher the quality. Thus, for a special occasion, a novice wine buyer might be more inclined to purchase a higher-priced bottle of wine than a lower-priced bottle. Second, consumers are more likely to purchase a product priced just below the next whole number. For example, retailers often price products at $899 or $895, rather than $900. This type of pricing, called *odd-even pricing*, is used to imply bargains, even though the price difference between the odd and even number is insignificant.

- **Bundle pricing** involves grouping two related products together and pricing them as a single product. For example, appliance retailers often bundle a clothes washer and dryer together at a price that is less than the sum of the price of the washer and dryer separately. Other examples of bundle pricing include "value meals" in fast food restaurants and software bundled with PCs. Bundling products at a slightly reduced total price is intended to generate additional sales that otherwise might not have been made. ■

Product Profitability and Pricing Under Production Bottlenecks

objective 3

Calculate the relative profitability of products in bottleneck production environments.

An important consideration influencing production volumes and prices is production bottlenecks. A production **bottleneck** (or **constraint**) occurs at the point in the process where the demand for the company's product exceeds the ability to produce the product. The **theory of constraints (TOC)** is a manufacturing strategy that focuses on reducing the influence of bottlenecks on a process.

Product Profitability Under Production Bottlenecks

When a company has a bottleneck in its production process, it should attempt to maximize its profitability, subject to the influence of the bottleneck. To illustrate, assume that Snapp-Off Tool Company makes three types of wrenches: small, medium, and large. All three products are processed through a heat treatment operation, which hardens the steel tools. Snapp-Off Tool's heat treatment process is operating at full capacity and is a production bottleneck. The product contribution margin per unit and the number of hours of heat treatment used by each type of wrench are as follows:

The sand in the hourglass can pass only as fast as the narrowest point in the glass will allow.

Bottleneck

	Small Wrench	Medium Wrench	Large Wrench
Sales price per unit	$130	$140	$160
Variable cost per unit	40	40	40
Contribution margin per unit	$ 90	$100	$120
Heat treatment hours per unit	1	4	8

The large wrench appears to be the most profitable product because its contribution margin per unit is the greatest. However, the contribution margin per unit can be a misleading indicator of profitability in a bottleneck operation. The correct measure of performance is the value of each bottleneck hour, or the contribution margin per bottleneck hour. Using this measure, each product has a much different profitability when compared to the contribution margin per unit information, as shown in Exhibit 10.

Product A has a contribution margin of $15 per unit. Product B has a contribution margin of $20 per unit. Product A requires 3 furnace hours, while Product B requires 5 furnace hours. Determine the most profitable product, assuming that the furnace is a bottleneck.

Exhibit 10 Contribution Margin per Bottleneck Hour

	Small Wrench	Medium Wrench	Large Wrench
Sales price	$130	$140	$160
Variable cost per unit	40	40	40
Contribution margin per unit	$ 90	$100	$120
Bottleneck (heat treatment) hours per unit	÷ 1	÷ 4	÷ 8
Contribution margin per bottleneck hour	$ 90	$ 25	$ 15

Product A ($15 ÷ 3 hours = $5 per hour, which is greater than $20 ÷ 5 hours, or $4 per hour)

The small wrench produces the most contribution margin per bottleneck (heat treatment) hour used, while the large wrench produces the smallest profit per bottleneck hour. Thus, the small wrench is the most profitable product. This information is the opposite of that implied by the unit contribution margin profit.

Latrobe Steel Division of Timken Company originally used total cost plus a markup to price its steel products. However, Latrobe discovered that one of its machines was a bottleneck in its operation. It recalculated the profitability of its products, based on the contribution margin per hour of constraint. The results showed that some products that had appeared only marginally profitable had, in fact, a high contribution margin per bottleneck hour. This analysis caused Latrobe management to change the product mix in favor of products with high contribution margins per constraint hour. Management estimated that these changes improved income from operations by 20%.

Product Pricing Under Production Bottlenecks

Each hour of a bottleneck delivers profit to the company. When a company has a production bottleneck, the contribution margin per hour of bottleneck provides a measure of the product's relative profitability. This information can also be used to adjust the product price to better reflect the value of the product's use of a bottleneck. Products that use a large number of bottleneck hours per unit require more contribution margin than products that use few bottleneck hours per unit. For example, Snapp-Off Tool Company should increase the price of the large wrench in order to deliver more contribution margin per bottleneck hour.

To determine the price of the large wrench that would equate its profitability to the small wrench, we need to solve the following equation:

$$\text{Contribution margin per bottleneck hour per small wrench} = \frac{\text{Revised price of large wrench} - \text{Variable cost per large wrench}}{\text{Bottleneck hours per large wrench}}$$

$$\$90 = \frac{\text{Revised price of large wrench} - \$40}{8}$$

$$\$720 = \text{Revised price of large wrench} - \$40$$
$$\$760 = \text{Revised price of large wrench}$$

The large wrench's price would need to be increased to $760 in order to deliver the same contribution margin per bottleneck hour as does the small wrench, as verified below.

Revised price of large wrench	$760
Less: Variable cost per unit of large wrench	40
Contribution margin per unit of large wrench	$720
Bottleneck hours per unit of large wrench	÷ 8
Revised contribution margin per bottleneck hour	$ 90

At a price of $760, the company would be indifferent between producing and selling the small wrench or the large wrench, all else being equal. This analysis assumes that there is unlimited demand for the products. If the market were unwilling to purchase the large wrench at this price, then the company should produce the small wrench.

ENCORE

What Is the Price?

The Internet is transforming the way companies are pricing their products. Before the Internet, prices were dictated to the market by the producers. The customer could take the price or leave it. In addition, it was difficult to discover what the competition was offering. If you wanted a new television, you shopped at your favorite stores to discover the best price for what you wanted and then made your purchase. But you could shop for only so long. Now, all you need to do is search the Internet through an electronic retail portal (such as **Yahoo!** or **Amazon.com**), and there you will discover, right in front of you, the price, quality, reliability, and customer experience information for a broad selection of TVs. Your ability to select the best value is enhanced greatly.

However, what is good for you is a new challenge for many businesses. Companies are used to carefully crafting their messages around a particular brand image by using advertising and other marketing tools. The brand allowed the company to charge premium prices, because the brand was a substitute for knowledge about the actual quality of a product. So we were willing to pay a little extra for a brand that we trusted. The Internet changes all of this. A company finds that it no longer controls its image. Rather, it is now exposed to the watchful eye of the consumer, because the Internet gives us access to on-line product data and customer experience information. If a product is marginal, there's no place to hide.

Added to this, fixed pricing is being replaced by dynamic pricing. In dynamic pricing, the price is not just set by the producer as a "take it or leave it" proposition. Rather, the price can be set in a number of ways. On the Internet, there are four major dynamic pricing models:

- *"Name your price" model:* **Priceline.com** invented this approach in which the consumers name the price they are willing to pay for a service, such as a hotel room or an airline flight. If the customer's price is accepted by the provider, then the sale is made. If the customer's price is not accepted, then the customer can try again at a higher price. The service provider analyzes whether to accept business at a special price (as shown in this chapter) in deciding whether to take the price.
- *Auction model:* **Ebay**, **Ariba**, **Commerce One**, and other Internet market makers use the auction method. It is used when there are many potential buyers but only one seller. The item being sold is usually unique. The seller places the item on the Internet for auction, and the buyers compete by placing bids on the Internet. At the close of the auction, the item is sold to the highest bidder.
- *Reverse auction model:* Business to Business Internet market makers, such as Ariba, Commerce One, and **FreeMarkets**, provide this auction method when there is one buyer but many potential sellers. The buyer indicates the product or service he or she wishes to purchase. The sellers provide quotes to the buyer, using a live auction format. At the close of the auction, the lowest quote wins the business from the buyer.
- *Exchange model:* Under the exchange method, there are multiple buyers and sellers for a given product. The product is not unique, so it is available from many sellers; yet it is also desired by many potential buyers. The exchange method is used on the Internet for many types of products and services, including electricity, cargo space, steel, plastics, and bandwidth. The price is established by balancing the relative supply and demand for the item at the time of the exchange.

For all of these dynamic pricing methods, businesses must constantly be alert to cover their variable costs for any particular transaction and their total costs for all transactions over a period of time. ∎

KEY POINTS

1 **Prepare a differential analysis report for decisions involving leasing or selling equipment, discontinuing an unprofitable segment, manufacturing or purchasing a needed part, replacing usable fixed assets, processing further or selling an intermediate product, or accepting additional business at a special price.**

Differential analysis reports for leasing or selling, discontinuing a segment or product, making or buying, replacing equipment, processing or selling, and accepting business at a special price are illustrated in the text. Each analysis focuses on the differential revenues and/or costs of the alternative courses of action.

2 **Determine the selling price of a product, using the total cost, product cost, and variable cost concepts.**

The three cost concepts commonly used in applying the cost-plus approach to product pricing are summarized below.

Cost Concept	Covered in Cost Amount	Covered in Markup
Total cost	Total costs	Desired profit
Product cost	Total manufacturing costs	Desired profit + Total selling and administrative expenses
Variable cost	Total variable costs	Desired profit + Total fixed costs

The markup percentages used in applying each cost concept are as follows:

Total cost concept:

$$\text{Markup percentage} = \frac{\text{Desired profit}}{\text{Total costs}}$$

Product cost concept:

$$\text{Markup percentage} = \frac{\text{Desired profit} + \begin{array}{c}\text{Total selling and}\\ \text{administrative}\\ \text{expenses}\end{array}}{\text{Total manufacturing costs}}$$

Variable cost concept:

$$\text{Markup percentage} = \frac{\text{Desired profit} + \text{Total fixed costs}}{\text{Total variable costs}}$$

3 **Calculate the relative profitability of products in bottleneck production environments.**

The profitability of a product in a bottleneck production environment may not be accurately shown in the contribution margin product report. Instead, the best measure of profitability is determined by dividing the contribution margin per unit by the bottleneck hours per unit. The resulting measure indicates the product's profitability per hour of bottleneck use. This information can be used to support product pricing decisions.

ILLUSTRATIVE PROBLEM

Inez Company recently began production of a new product, M, which required the investment of $1,600,000 in assets. The costs of producing and selling 80,000 units of Product M are estimated as follows:

Variable costs:		
Direct materials	$ 10.00	per unit
Direct labor	6.00	
Factory overhead	4.00	
Selling and administrative expenses	5.00	
Total	$ 25.00	per unit
Fixed costs:		
Factory overhead	$800,000	
Selling and administrative expenses	400,000	

Inez Company is currently considering establishing a selling price for Product M. The president of Inez Company has decided to use the cost-plus approach to product pricing and has indicated that Product M must earn a 10% rate of return on invested assets.

Instructions

1. Determine the amount of desired profit from the production and sale of Product M.
2. Assuming that the total cost concept is used, determine (a) the cost amount per unit, (b) the markup percentage, and (c) the selling price of Product M.
3. Assuming that the product cost concept is used, determine (a) the cost amount per unit, (b) the markup percentage, and (c) the selling price of Product M.
4. Assuming that the variable cost concept is used, determine (a) the cost amount per unit, (b) the markup percentage, and (c) the selling price of Product M.
5. Assume that for the current year, the selling price of Product M was $42 per unit. To date, 60,000 units have been produced and sold, and analysis of the domestic market indicates that 15,000 additional units are expected to be sold during the remainder of the year. Recently, Inez Company received an offer from Wong Inc. for 4,000 units of Product M at $28 each. Wong Inc. will market the units in Korea under its own brand name, and no additional selling and administrative expenses associated with the sale will be incurred by Inez Company. The additional business is not expected to affect the domestic sales of Product M, and the additional units could be produced during the current year, using existing capacity. (a) Prepare a differential analysis report of the proposed sale to Wong Inc. (b) Based upon the differential analysis report in (a), should the proposal be accepted?

Solution

1. $160,000 ($1,600,000 × 10%)
2. a. Total costs:

Variable ($25 × 80,000 units)	$2,000,000
Fixed ($800,000 + $400,000)	1,200,000
Total	$3,200,000

Cost amount per unit: $3,200,000 ÷ 80,000 units = $40.00

b. $$\text{Markup percentage} = \frac{\text{Desired profit}}{\text{Total costs}}$$

$$\text{Markup percentage} = \frac{\$160,000}{\$3,200,000} = 5\%$$

c.

Cost amount per unit	$40.00
Markup ($40 × 5%)	2.00
Selling price	$42.00

3. a. Total manufacturing costs:

Variable ($20 × 80,000 units)	$1,600,000
Fixed factory overhead	800,000
Total	$2,400,000

Cost amount per unit: $2,400,000 ÷ 80,000 units = $30.00

b. $$\text{Markup percentage} = \frac{\text{Desired profit} + \text{Total selling and administrative expenses}}{\text{Total manufacturing costs}}$$

$$\text{Markup percentage} = \frac{\$160,000 + \$400,000 + (\$5 \times 80,000 \text{ units})}{\$2,400,000}$$

$$\text{Markup percentage} = \frac{\$160,000 + \$400,000 + \$400,000}{\$2,400,000}$$

$$\text{Markup percentage} = \frac{\$960,000}{\$2,400,000} = 40\%$$

	c.	Cost amount per unit	$30.00
		Markup ($30 × 40%)	12.00
		Selling price	$42.00

4. a. Variable cost amount per unit: $25
   Total variable costs: $25 × 80,000 units = $2,000,000

   b. $$\text{Markup percentage} = \frac{\text{Desired profit} + \text{Total fixed costs}}{\text{Total variable costs}}$$

   $$\text{Markup percentage} = \frac{\$160,000 + \$800,000 + \$400,000}{\$2,000,000}$$

   $$\text{Markup percentage} = \frac{\$1,360,000}{\$2,000,000} = 68\%$$

	c.	Cost amount per unit	$25.00
		Markup ($25 × 68%)	17.00
		Selling price	$42.00

5. a.

Proposal to Sell to Wong Inc.

Differential revenue from accepting offer:	
Revenue from sale of 4,000 additional units at $28	$112,000
Differential cost from accepting offer:	
Variable production costs of 4,000 additional units at $20	80,000
Differential income from accepting offer	$ 32,000

   b. The proposal should be accepted.

SELF-EXAMINATION QUESTIONS
Answers at End of Chapter

Matching

Match each of the following statements with its proper term. Some terms may not be used.

A.	**activity-based costing**
B.	**bottleneck**
C.	**differential analysis**
D.	**differential cost**
E.	**differential revenue**
F.	**markup**
G.	**opportunity cost**
H.	**product cost concept**
I.	**sunk cost**
J.	**target cost concept**
K.	**theory of constraints (TOC)**
L.	**total cost concept**
M.	**variable cost concept**

___ 1. The amount of income forgone from an alternative to a proposed use of cash or its equivalent.

___ 2. A condition that occurs when product demand exceeds production capacity.

___ 3. A concept used in applying the cost-plus approach to product pricing in which all the costs of manufacturing the product plus the selling and administrative expenses are included in the cost amount to which the markup is added.

___ 4. A cost that is not affected by subsequent decisions.

___ 5. The area of accounting concerned with the effect of alternative courses of action on revenues and costs.

___ 6. A concept used in applying the cost-plus approach to product pricing in which only the variable costs are included in the cost amount to which the markup is added.

___ 7. The amount of increase or decrease in revenue expected from a particular course of action as compared with an alternative.

___ 8. A cost allocation method that identifies activities causing the incurrence of costs and allocates these costs to products (or other cost objects), based upon activity drivers (bases).

___ 9. The amount of increase or decrease in cost expected from a particular course of action compared with an alternative.

___ 10. A manufacturing strategy that attempts to remove the influence of bottlenecks (constraints) on a process.

___ 11. A concept used in applying the cost-plus approach to product pricing in which only the costs of manufacturing the product, termed the product cost, are included in the cost amount to which the markup is added.

___ 12. A concept used to design and manufacture a product at a cost that will deliver a target profit for a given market-determined price.

___ 13. An amount that is added to a "cost" amount to determine product price.

Multiple Choice

1. Marlo Company is considering discontinuing a product. The costs of the product consist of $20,000 fixed costs and $15,000 variable costs. The variable operating expenses related to the product total $4,000. What is the differential cost?
   A. $19,000   C. $35,000
   B. $15,000   D. $39,000

2. Victor Company is considering disposing of equipment that was originally purchased for $200,000 and has $150,000 of accumulated depreciation to date. The same equipment would cost $310,000 to replace. What is the sunk cost?
   A. $50,000   C. $200,000
   B. $150,000   D. $310,000

3. Henry Company is considering spending $100,000 for a new grinding machine. This amount could be invested to yield a 12% return. What is the opportunity cost?
   A. $112,000   C. $12,000
   B. $88,000   D. $100,000

4. For which cost concept used in applying the cost-plus approach to product pricing are fixed manufacturing

costs, fixed selling and administrative expenses, and desired profit allowed for in determining the markup?
   A. Total cost   C. Variable cost
   B. Product cost   D. Standard cost

5. Mendosa Company produces three products. All the products use a furnace operation, which is a production bottleneck. The following information is available:

	Product 1	Product 2	Product 3
Unit volume—March	1,000	1,500	1,000
Per unit information:			
Sales price	$35	$33	$29
Variable cost	15	15	15
Contribution margin	$20	$18	$14
Furnace hours	4	3	2

From a profitability perspective, which product should be emphasized in April's advertising campaign?
   A. Product 1   C. Product 3
   B. Product 2   D. All three

CLASS DISCUSSION QUESTIONS

Real World

1. Explain the meaning of (a) differential revenue, (b) differential cost, and (c) differential income.
2. It was recently reported that **Exabyte**, a fast growing (100-fold in four years) Colorado marketer of tape drives, has decided to purchase key components of its product from others. For example, **Sony** provides Exabyte with mechanical decks, and **Solectron** provides circuit boards. Exabyte's chief executive officer, Peter Behrendt, states, "If we'd tried to build our own plants, we could never have grown that fast or maybe survived." The decision to purchase key product components is an example of what type of decision illustrated in this chapter?
3. In the long run, the normal selling price must be set high enough to cover what factors?
4. What are the two primary methods of setting prices?
5. What are three cost concepts commonly used in applying the cost-plus approach to product pricing?
6. In using the product cost concept of applying the cost-plus approach to product pricing, what factors are included in the markup?
7. The variable cost concept used in applying the cost-plus approach to product pricing includes what costs in the cost amount to which the markup is added?

8. In determining the markup percentage for the product cost concept of applying the cost-plus approach, what is included in the denominator?
9. Why might the use of ideal standards in applying the cost-plus approach to product pricing lead to setting product prices that are too low?
10. Although the cost-plus approach to product pricing may be used by management as a general guideline, what are some examples of other factors that managers should also consider in setting product prices?
11. What method of determining product cost may be appropriate in settings where the manufacturing process is complex?
12. How does the target cost concept differ from cost-plus approaches?
13. What is a production bottleneck?
14. What is the appropriate measure of a product's value when a firm is operating under production bottlenecks?

RESOURCES FOR YOUR SUCCESS ONLINE AT

http://warren.swcollege.com

Remember! If you need additional help, visit South-Western's Web site.
See page M28 for a description of the online and printed materials that are available.

EXERCISES

Exercise 8–1
Lease or sell decision

Objective 1

✓ a. Differential revenue from lease, $14,000

Miller Construction Company is considering selling excess machinery with a book value of $250,000 (original cost of $375,000 less accumulated depreciation of $125,000) for $220,000 less a 5% brokerage commission. Alternatively, the machinery can be leased for a total of $234,000 for five years, after which it is expected to have no residual value. During the period of the lease, Miller Construction Company's costs of repairs, insurance, and property tax expenses are expected to be $23,000.

a. Prepare a differential analysis report, dated January 3 of the current year, for the lease or sell decision.
b.  On the basis of the data presented, would it be advisable to lease or sell the machinery? Explain.

Exercise 8–2
Differential analysis report for a discontinued product

Objective 1

✓ a. Differential cost of annual sales, $285,000

A condensed income statement by product line for Fresh Kola Co. indicated the following for Diet Kola for the past year:

Sales	$350,000
Cost of goods sold	225,000
Gross profit	$125,000
Operating expenses	140,000
Loss from operations	$(15,000)

It is estimated that 20% of the cost of goods sold represents fixed factory overhead costs and that 25% of the operating expenses are fixed. Since Diet Kola is only one of many products, the fixed costs will not be materially affected if the product is discontinued.

a. Prepare a differential analysis report, dated January 3 of the current year, for the proposed discontinuance of Diet Kola.
b.  Should Diet Kola be retained? Explain.

M322

Exercise 8–3
Differential analysis report for a discontinued product
Objective 1

✓ a. Differential income: bowls, $48,880

The condensed product-line income statement for Bold Ceramics Company for the current year is as follows:

Bold Ceramics Company
Product-Line Income Statement
For the Year Ended December 31, 2003

	Bowls	Plates	Cups
Sales	$150,000	$160,000	$125,000
Cost of goods sold	96,000	84,000	85,000
Gross profit	$ 54,000	$ 76,000	$ 40,000
Selling and administrative expenses	32,000	52,000	48,000
Income from operations	$ 22,000	$ 24,000	$ (8,000)

Fixed costs are 18% of the cost of goods sold and 30% of the selling and administrative expenses. Bold Ceramics assumes that fixed costs would not be materially affected if the Cups line were discontinued.

a. Prepare a differential analysis report for all three products for the current year.
b. ▬▬► Should the Cups line be retained? Explain.

Exercise 8–4
Segment analysis
Objective 1

The **Charles Schwab Corporation** is one of the more innovative brokerage and financial service companies in the United States. The company recently provided information about its major business segments as follows:

	Individual Investor	Institutional Investor	Capital Markets
Revenues	$1,955,186	$444,685	$336,350
Income from operations	402,150	92,842	81,552
Depreciation	102,903	21,115	14,459

a. ▬▬► How do you believe Schwab defines the difference between the "Individual Investor" and "Institutional Investor" segments?
b. Provide a specific example of a variable and fixed cost in the "Individual Investor" segment.
c. Estimate the contribution margin for each segment.
d. If Schwab decided to sell its "Institutional Investor" accounts to another company, estimate how much operating income would decline?

Exercise 8–5
Decision to discontinue a product
Objective 1

On the basis of the following data, the general manager of Sole Mates Inc. decided to discontinue Children's Shoes because it reduced income from operations by $20,000. What is the flaw in this decision?

Sole Mates Inc.
Product-Line Income Statement
For the Year Ended August 31, 2003

	Children's Shoes	Men's Shoes	Women's Shoes	Total
Sales	$105,000	$300,000	$500,000	$905,000
Costs of goods sold:				
Variable costs	$ 70,000	$150,000	$220,000	$440,000
Fixed costs	20,000	60,000	120,000	200,000
Total cost of goods sold	$ 90,000	$210,000	$340,000	$640,000
Gross profit	$ 15,000	$ 90,000	$160,000	$265,000
Operating expenses:				
Variable expenses	$ 28,000	$ 45,000	$ 95,000	$168,000
Fixed expenses	7,000	20,000	25,000	52,000
Total operating expenses	$ 35,000	$ 65,000	$120,000	$220,000
Income (loss) from operations	$ (20,000)	$ 25,000	$ 40,000	$ 45,000

Exercise 8–6
Make or buy decision

Objective 1

✓ a. Cost savings from making, $2.50 per case

Quick Computer Company has been purchasing carrying cases for its portable computers at a delivered cost of $35 per unit. The company, which is currently operating below full capacity, charges factory overhead to production at the rate of 40% of direct materials cost. The costs to produce comparable carrying cases are expected to be $18 per unit for direct materials and $10 per unit for direct labor. If Quick Computer Company manufactures the carrying cases, fixed factory overhead costs will not increase and variable factory overhead costs associated with the cases are expected to be 25% of the direct materials costs.

a. Prepare a differential analysis report, dated June 5 of the current year, for the make or buy decision.
b. ◄━━► On the basis of the data presented, would it be advisable to make or to continue buying the carrying cases? Explain.

Exercise 8–7
Machine replacement decision

Objective 1

✓ a. Annual differential income, $5,000

A company is considering replacing an old piece of machinery, which cost $500,000 and has $300,000 of accumulated depreciation to date, with a new machine that costs $450,000. The old equipment could be sold for $120,000. The variable production costs associated with the old machine are estimated to be $150,000 for six years. The variable production costs for the new machine are estimated to be $90,000 for six years.

a. Determine the differential annual income or loss from replacing the old machine.
b. What is the sunk cost in this situation?

Exercise 8–8
Differential analysis report for machine replacement

Objective 1

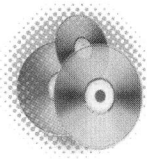
SPREADSHEET

✓ a. Annual differential increase in costs, $3,000

Custom Electronics Company assembles circuit boards by using a manually operated machine to insert electronic components. The original cost of the machine is $150,000, the accumulated depreciation is $110,000, its remaining useful life is 10 years, and its salvage value is negligible. On January 20, 2003, a proposal was made to replace the present manufacturing procedure with a fully automatic machine that will cost $350,000. The automatic machine has an estimated useful life of 10 years and no significant salvage value. For use in evaluating the proposal, the accountant accumulated the following annual data on present and proposed operations:

	Present Operations	Proposed Operations
Sales	$365,000	$365,000
Direct materials	108,000	108,000
Direct labor	59,800	—
Power and maintenance	7,500	32,800
Taxes, insurance, etc.	4,500	7,000
Selling and administrative expenses	65,000	65,000

a. Prepare a differential analysis report for the proposal to replace the machine. Include in the analysis both the net differential change in costs anticipated over the 10 years and the net annual differential change in costs anticipated.
b. Based only on the data presented, should the proposal be accepted?
c. ◄━━► What are some of the other factors that should be considered before a final decision is made?

Exercise 8–9
Decision on accepting additional business

Objective 1

✓ a. Differential income, $36,000

American Leisure Wear Co. has an annual plant capacity of 60,000 units, and current production is 45,000 units. Monthly fixed costs are $30,000, and variable costs are $29 per unit. The present selling price is $45 per unit. On January 18, 2003, the company received an offer from Barker Company for 12,000 units of the product at $32 each. The Barker Company will market the units in a foreign country under its own brand name. The additional business is not expected to affect the domestic selling price or quantity of sales of American Leisure Wear Co.

a. Prepare a differential analysis report for the proposed sale to Barker Company.
b. ◄━━► Briefly explain the reason why accepting this additional business will increase operating income.
c. What is the minimum price per unit that would produce a contribution margin?

Exercise 8–10
Sell or process further
Objective 1

✓ a. $220

Hyde Lumber Company incurs a cost of $425 per hundred board feet in processing certain "rough-cut" lumber, which it sells for $610 per hundred board feet. An alternative is to produce a "finished-cut" at a total processing cost of $550 per hundred board feet, which can be sold for $830 per hundred board feet. For these alternatives, what is the amount of (a) the differential revenue, (b) differential cost, and (c) differential income?

Exercise 8–11
Sell or process further
Objective 1

✓ c. $9.95

Star Coffee Company produces Colombian coffee in batches of 8,000 pounds. The standard quantity of materials required in the process are 8,000 pounds, which cost $5.00 per pound. Colombian coffee can be sold without further processing for $8.40 per pound. Colombian coffee can also be processed further to yield Decaf Colombian, which can be sold for $9.60 per pound. The processing into Decaf Colombian requires additional processing costs of $8,420 per batch. The additional processing will also cause a 5% loss of product due to evaporation.

a. Prepare a differential analysis report for the decision to sell or process further.
b. Should Star sell Colombian coffee or process further and sell Decaf Colombian?
c. Determine the price of Decaf Colombian that would cause neither an advantage or disadvantage for processing further and selling Decaf Colombian.

Exercise 8–12
Accepting business at a special price
Objective 1

First Light Company expects to operate at 90% of productive capacity during May. The total manufacturing costs for May for the production of 20,000 batteries are budgeted as follows:

Direct materials	$146,000
Direct labor	65,000
Variable factory overhead	29,000
Fixed factory overhead	60,000
Total manufacturing costs	$300,000

The company has an opportunity to submit a bid for 1,000 batteries to be delivered by May 31 to a government agency. If the contract is obtained, it is anticipated that the additional activity will not interfere with normal production during May or increase the selling or administrative expenses. What is the unit cost below which First Light Company should not go in bidding on the government contract?

Exercise 8–13
Total cost concept of product costing
Objective 2

✓ d. $350

ClearTalk Company uses the total cost concept of applying the cost-plus approach to product pricing. The costs of producing and selling 4,000 units of mobile phones are as follows:

Variable costs:		Fixed costs:	
Direct materials	$150.00 per unit	Factory overhead	$200,000
Direct labor	45.00	Selling and adm. exp.	100,000
Factory overhead	25.00		
Selling and adm. exp.	30.00		
Total	$250.00 per unit		

ClearTalk Company desires a profit equal to a 25% rate of return on invested assets of $400,000.

a. Determine the amount of desired profit from the production and sale of mobile phones.
b. Determine the total costs and the cost amount per unit for the production and sale of 4,000 units of mobile phones.
c. Determine the markup percentage (rounded to one decimal) for mobile phones.
d. Determine the selling price of mobile phones. Round to the nearest dollar.

Exercise 8–14
Product cost concept of product pricing

Objective 2

✓ b. 29.6%

Based on the data presented in Exercise 8–13, assume that ClearTalk Company uses the product cost concept of applying the cost-plus approach to product pricing.

a. Determine the total manufacturing costs and the cost amount per unit for the production and sale of 4,000 units of mobile phones.
b. Determine the markup percentage (rounded to one decimal) for mobile phones.
c. Determine the selling price of mobile phones. Round to the nearest dollar.

Exercise 8–15
Variable cost concept of product pricing

Objective 2

✓ b. 40%

Based on the data presented in Exercise 8–13, assume that ClearTalk Company uses the variable cost concept of applying the cost-plus approach to product pricing.

a. Determine the variable costs and the cost amount per unit for the production and sale of 4,000 units of mobile phones.
b. Determine the markup percentage for mobile phones.
c. Determine the selling price of mobile phones.

Exercise 8–16
Target cost concept

Objective 2

Real World

Toyota Motor Corporation uses the target cost concept. Assume that Toyota marketing personnel estimate that the selling price for the *Camry* in the upcoming model year will need to be $32,000 in order to be competitive. Assume further that the *Camry's* total manufacturing cost for the upcoming model year is estimated to be $26,000 and that Toyota requires a 20% profit margin on selling price (which is equivalent to a 25% markup on product cost).

a. What price will Toyota establish for the *Camry* for the upcoming model year?
b. ✏️ What impact will the target cost concept have on Toyota, given the assumed information?

Exercise 8–17
Product decisions under bottlenecked operations

Objective 3

✓ a. Total income from operations, $106,000

Blue Glass Company manufactures three types of safety plate glass: large, medium, and small. All three products have high demand. Thus, Blue Glass is able to sell all the safety glass that it can make. The production process includes an autoclave operation, which is a pressurized heat treatment. The autoclave is a production bottleneck. Fixed costs are $450,000. In addition, the following information is available about the three products:

	Large	Medium	Small
Sales price per unit	$230	$190	$120
Variable cost per unit	122	85	55
Contribution margin per unit	$108	$105	$ 65
Autoclave hours per unit	12	15	10
Total process hours per unit	30	25	22
Budgeted units of production	2,000	2,000	2,000

a. Determine the contribution margin by glass type and the total company income from operations for the budgeted units of production.
b. Prepare an analysis showing which product is the most profitable per bottleneck hour.

Exercise 8–18
Product pricing under bottlenecked operations

Objective 3

✓ Medium, $220

Based on the data presented in Exercise 8–17, assume that Blue Glass wanted to price all products so that they produced the same profit potential as the highest profit product. What would be the prices of all three products that would produce the largest profit?

PROBLEMS SERIES A

Problem 8–1A
Differential analysis report involving opportunity costs

Objective 1

✓ 3. $1,150,000

On July 1, Venus Stores Inc. is considering leasing a building and purchasing the necessary equipment to operate a retail store. The project would be financed by selling $800,000 of 9% U.S. Treasury bonds that mature in 18 years. The bonds were purchased at face value and are currently selling at face value. The following data have been assembled:

Cost of store equipment	$800,000
Life of store equipment	18 years
Estimated residual value of store equipment	$150,000
Yearly costs to operate the store, excluding depreciation of store equipment	$ 90,000
Yearly expected revenues—years 1–9	$260,000
Yearly expected revenues—years 10–18	$120,000

Instructions

1. Prepare a report as of July 1, 2003, presenting a differential analysis of the proposed operation of the store for the 18 years as compared with present conditions.
2. Based on the results disclosed by the differential analysis, should the proposal be accepted?
3. If the proposal was accepted, what would be the total estimated income from operations of the store for the 18 years?

Problem 8–2A
Differential analysis report for machine replacement decision

Objective 1

Iowa Printing Company is considering replacing a machine that has been used in its factory for two years. Relevant data associated with the operations of the old machine and the new machine, neither of which has any estimated residual value, are as follows:

Old Machine

Cost of machine, 10-year life	$450,000
Annual depreciation (straight-line)	45,000
Annual manufacturing costs, excluding depreciation	420,000
Annual nonmanufacturing operating expenses	265,000
Annual revenue	850,000
Current estimated selling price	220,000

New Machine

Cost of machine, 8-year life	$780,000
Annual depreciation (straight-line)	97,500
Estimated annual manufacturing costs, exclusive of depreciation	300,000

Annual nonmanufacturing operating expenses and revenue are not expected to be affected by purchase of the new machine.

Instructions

1. Prepare a differential analysis report as of August 11 of the current year, comparing operations utilizing the new machine with operations using the present equipment. The analysis should indicate the total differential income that would result over the 8-year period if the new machine is acquired.
2. ✏️ List other factors that should be considered before a final decision is reached.

Problem 8–3A
Differential analysis report for sales promotion proposal

Objective 1

Rose Cosmetics Company is planning a one-month campaign for May to promote sales of one of its two cosmetics products. A total of $50,000 has been budgeted for advertising, contests, redeemable coupons, and other promotional activities. The following data have been assembled for their possible usefulness in deciding which of the products to select for the campaign:

✓ 1. Cologne differential income, $110,000

	Cologne	Perfume
Unit selling price	$45	$55
Unit production costs:		
Direct materials	$ 9	$14
Direct labor	6	8
Variable factory overhead	4	4
Fixed factory overhead	5	2
Total unit production costs	$24	$28
Unit variable selling expenses	10	16
Unit fixed selling expenses	3	1
Total unit costs	$37	$45
Operating income per unit	$ 8	$10

No increase in facilities would be necessary to produce and sell the increased output. It is anticipated that 10,000 additional units of cologne or 10,500 additional units of perfume could be sold without changing the unit selling price of either product.

Instructions

1. Prepare a differential analysis report as of April 5 of the current year, presenting the additional revenue and additional costs anticipated from the promotion of cologne and perfume.
2. ✏️ The sales manager had tentatively decided to promote perfume, estimating that operating income would be increased by $55,000 ($10 operating income per unit for 10,500 units, less promotion expenses of $50,000). The manager also believed that the selection of cologne would increase operating income by only $30,000 ($8 operating income per unit for 10,000 units, less promotion expenses of $50,000). State briefly your reasons for supporting or opposing the tentative decision.

Problem 8–4A
Differential analysis report for further processing

Objective 1

✓ Differential revenue, $4,500

The management of Sweet Sugar Company is considering whether to process further raw sugar into refined sugar. Refined sugar can be sold for $1.50 per pound, and raw sugar can be sold without further processing for $0.90 per pound. Raw sugar is produced in batches of 15,000 pounds by processing 18,000 pounds of sugar cane, which costs $0.20 per pound. Refined sugar will require additional processing costs of $0.25 per pound of raw sugar, and 1.25 pounds of raw sugar will produce 1 pound of refined sugar.

Instructions

1. Prepare a report as of May 30, 2003, presenting a differential analysis of the further processing of raw sugar to produce refined sugar.
2. ✏️ Briefly report your recommendations.

Problem 8–5A
Product pricing using the cost-plus approach concepts; differential analysis report for accepting additional business

Objectives 1, 2

SPREADSHEET

✓ 2. b. Markup percentage, 5%

Presentation Labs Inc. recently began production of a new product, flat panel displays, which required the investment of $2,500,000 in assets. The costs of producing and selling 20,000 units of flat panel displays are estimated as follows:

Variable costs per unit:		
Direct materials	$	210
Direct labor		40
Factory overhead		50
Selling and administrative expenses		20
Total	$	320
Fixed costs:		
Factory overhead	$1,200,000	
Selling and administrative expenses	400,000	

Presentation Labs Inc. is currently considering establishing a selling price for flat panel displays. The president of Presentation Labs has decided to use the cost-plus approach to product pricing and has indicated that the displays must earn a 16% rate of return on invested assets.

Instructions

1. Determine the amount of desired profit from the production and sale of flat panel displays.
2. Assuming that the total cost concept is used, determine (a) the cost amount per unit, (b) the markup percentage, and (c) the selling price of flat panel displays.
3. Assuming that the product cost concept is used, determine (a) the cost amount per unit, (b) the markup percentage, and (c) the selling price of flat panel displays.
4. Assuming that the variable cost concept is used, determine (a) the cost amount per unit, (b) the markup percentage, and (c) the selling price of flat panel displays.
5. ✏️ Comment on any additional considerations that could influence establishing the selling price for flat panel displays.
6. Assume that as of September 1, 2003, 12,000 units of flat panel displays have been produced and sold during the current year. Analysis of the domestic market indicates that 5,000 additional units are expected to be sold during the remainder of the year at the normal product price determined under the total cost concept. On September 3, Presentation Labs Inc. received an offer from Kane Company for 3,000 units of flat panel displays at $280 each. Kane Company will market the units in Canada under its own brand name, and no additional selling and administrative expenses associated with the sale will be incurred by Presentation Labs Inc. The additional business is not expected to affect the domestic sales of flat panel displays, and the additional units could be produced using existing capacity.
   a. Prepare a differential analysis report of the proposed sale to Kane Company.
   b. Based upon the differential analysis report in (a), should the proposal be accepted?

Problem 8–6A

Product pricing and profit analysis with bottleneck operations

Objectives 1, 3

✓ 3. High Grade price, $475

Indy Valley Steel Company produces three grades of steel: high, good, and regular grade. Each of these products (grades) has high demand in the market, and Indy Valley is able to sell as much as it can produce of all three. The furnace operation is a bottleneck in the process and is running at 100% of capacity. Indy Valley is attempting to determine how to improve profitability for the steel operations. The variable conversion cost is $5 per process hour. The fixed cost is $1,560,000. In addition, the cost analyst was able to determine the following information about the three products:

	High Grade	Good Grade	Regular Grade
Budgeted units produced	5,000	5,000	5,000
Total process hours per unit	15	15	12
Furnace hours per unit	10	8	6
Price per unit	$400	$370	$346
Direct materials cost per unit	$140	$135	$130

The furnace operation is part of the total process for each of these three products. So, for example, 10 of the 15 hours required to process High Grade steel are associated with the furnace.

Instructions

1. Determine the contribution margin per unit for each product.
2. Provide an analysis to determine the relative product profitabilities, assuming that the furnace is a bottleneck.
3. Assume that management wishes to improve profitability by increasing prices on selected products. At what price would High and Good Grades need to be offered in order to produce the same relative profitability as Regular Grade steel?

PROBLEMS SERIES B

Problem 8–1B

Differential analysis report involving opportunity costs

Objective 1

✓ 3. $610,000

On December 1, Falcon Distribution Company is considering leasing a building and buying the necessary equipment to operate a public warehouse. The project would be financed by selling $400,000 of 8% U.S. Treasury bonds that mature in 14 years. The bonds were purchased at face value and are currently selling at face value. The following data have been assembled:

Cost of equipment	$400,000
Life of equipment	14 years
Estimated residual value of equipment	$ 65,000
Yearly costs to operate the warehouse, excluding depreciation of equipment	$ 70,000
Yearly expected revenues—years 1–7	$150,000
Yearly expected revenues—years 8–14	$125,000

Instructions

1. Prepare a report as of December 1, 2003, presenting a differential analysis of the proposed operation of the warehouse for the 14 years as compared with present conditions.
2. Based on the results disclosed by the differential analysis, should the proposal be accepted?
3. If the proposal is accepted, what is the total estimated income from operations of the warehouse for the 14 years?

Problem 8–2B

Differential analysis report for machine replacement proposal

Objective 1

Carson Tooling Company is considering replacing a machine that has been used in its factory for two years. Relevant data associated with the operations of the old machine and the new machine, neither of which has any estimated residual value, are as follows:

Old Machine	
Cost of machine, 8-year life	$320,000
Annual depreciation (straight-line)	40,000
Annual manufacturing costs, excluding depreciation	80,000
Annual nonmanufacturing operating expenses	45,000
Annual revenue	190,000
Current estimated selling price	175,000

New Machine	
Cost of machine, 6-year life	$360,000
Annual depreciation (straight-line)	60,000
Estimated annual manufacturing costs, exclusive of depreciation	42,000

Annual nonmanufacturing operating expenses and revenue are not expected to be affected by purchase of the new machine.

Instructions

1. Prepare a differential analysis report as of March 22 of the current year, comparing operations utilizing the new machine with operations using the present equipment. The analysis should indicate the differential income that would result over the 6-year period if the new machine is acquired.
2. List other factors that should be considered before a final decision is reached.

Problem 8–3B
Differential analysis report for sales promotion proposal

Objective 1

✓ 1. Differential income, tennis shoe, $80,000

Manning Athletic Shoe Company is planning a one-month campaign for April to promote sales of one of its two shoe products. A total of $28,000 has been budgeted for advertising, contests, redeemable coupons, and other promotional activities. The following data have been assembled for their possible usefulness in deciding which of the products to select for the campaign.

	Tennis Shoe	Walking Shoe
Unit selling price	$68	$85
Unit production costs:		
Direct materials	$21	$28
Direct labor	14	20
Variable factory overhead	5	7
Fixed factory overhead	6	9
Total unit production costs	$46	$64
Unit variable selling expenses	10	14
Unit fixed selling expenses	4	5
Total unit costs	$60	$83
Operating income per unit	$ 8	$ 2

No increase in facilities would be necessary to produce and sell the increased output. It is anticipated that 6,000 additional units of tennis shoes or 7,000 additional units of walking shoes could be sold without changing the unit selling price of either product.

Instructions

1. Prepare a differential analysis report as of March 3 of the current year, presenting the additional revenue and additional costs anticipated from the promotion of tennis shoes and walking shoes.
2. ◄▬▬► The sales manager had tentatively decided to promote tennis shoes, estimating that operating income would be increased by $20,000 ($8 operating income per unit for 6,000 units, less promotion expenses of $28,000). The manager also believed that the selection of walking shoes would decrease operating income by $14,000 ($2 operating income per unit for 7,000 units, less promotion expenses of $28,000). State briefly your reasons for supporting or opposing the tentative decision.

Problem 8–4B
Differential analysis report for further processing

Objective 1

✓ 1. Differential revenue, $16,000

The management of Aluminum Company of Tennessee is considering whether to process further aluminum ingot into rolled aluminum. Rolled aluminum can be sold for $1,260 per ton, and ingot can be sold without further processing for $800 per ton. Ingot is produced in batches of 50 tons by smelting 60 tons of bauxite, which costs $400 per ton. Rolled aluminum will require additional processing costs of $350 per ton of ingot, and 1.125 tons of ingot will produce 1 ton of rolled aluminum.

Instructions

1. Prepare a report as of February 20, 2003, presenting a differential analysis associated with the further processing of aluminum ingot to produce rolled aluminum.
2. ◄▬▬► Briefly report your recommendations.

Problem 8–5B
Product pricing using the cost-plus approach concepts; differential analysis report for accepting additional business

Objectives 1, 2

Night Glow Company recently began production of a new product, the halogen light, which required the investment of $2,000,000 in assets. The costs of producing and selling 25,000 halogen lights are estimated as follows:

SPREADSHEET

Variable costs per unit:	
Direct materials	$ 29.00
Direct labor	12.00
Factory overhead	5.00
Selling and administrative expenses	4.00
Total	$ 50.00

Fixed costs:	
Factory overhead	$150,000
Selling and administrative expenses	100,000

✓ 2. b. Markup percentage, 20%

Night Glow Company is currently considering establishing a selling price for the halogen light. The president of Night Glow Company has decided to use the cost-plus approach to product pricing and has indicated that the halogen light must earn a 15% rate of return on invested assets.

Instructions

1. Determine the amount of desired profit from the production and sale of the halogen light.
2. Assuming that the total cost concept is used, determine (a) the cost amount per unit, (b) the markup percentage, and (c) the selling price of the halogen light.
3. Assuming that the product cost concept is used, determine (a) the cost amount per unit, (b) the markup percentage, and (c) the selling price of the halogen light. Round to the nearest cent.
4. Assuming that the variable cost concept is used, determine (a) the cost amount per unit, (b) the markup percentage, and (c) the selling price of the halogen light.
5. ◖▬▶ Comment on any additional considerations that could influence establishing the selling price for the halogen light.
6. Assume that as of May 1, 2003, 7,000 units of halogen light have been produced and sold during the current year. Analysis of the domestic market indicates that 15,000 additional units of the halogen light are expected to be sold during the remainder of the year at the normal product price determined under the total cost concept. On May 5, Night Glow Company received an offer from Lights Inc. for 2,000 units of the halogen light at $49 each. Lights Inc. will market the units in Japan under its own brand name, and no additional selling and administrative expenses associated with the sale will be incurred by Night Glow Company. The additional business is not expected to affect the domestic sales of the halogen light, and the additional units could be produced using existing capacity.
   a. Prepare a differential analysis report of the proposed sale to Lights Inc.
   b. Based upon the differential analysis report in (a), should the proposal be accepted?

Problem 8–6B

Product pricing and profit analysis with bottleneck operations

Objectives 1, 3

✓ 3. Butane price, $190

California Chemical Company produces three products: ethylene, butane, and ester. Each of these products has high demand in the market, and California Chemical is able to sell as much as it can produce of all three. The reaction operation is a bottleneck in the process and is running at 100% of capacity. California Chemical is attempting to determine how to improve profitability for the chemical operations. The variable conversion cost is $3 per process hour. The fixed cost is $1,050,000. In addition, the cost analyst was able to determine the following information about the three products:

	Ethylene	Butane	Ester
Budgeted units produced	6,000	6,000	6,000
Total process hours per unit	10	10	8
Reactor hours per unit	6	4	3
Price per unit	$202	$175	$164
Direct materials cost per unit	$100	$ 80	$ 80

The reaction operation is part of the total process for each of these three products. So, for example, 6 of the 10 hours required to process Ethylene are associated with the reactor.

Instructions

1. Determine the contribution margin per unit for each product.
2. Provide an analysis to determine the relative product profitabilities, assuming that the reactor is a bottleneck.
3. Assume that management wishes to improve profitability by increasing prices on selected products. At what price would Butane and Ethylene need to be offered in order to produce the same relative profitability as Ester?

SPECIAL ACTIVITIES

Activity 8–1
Hall Enterprises
Product pricing

Marcia Sanchez is a cost accountant for Hall Enterprises. Jan Foster, vice-president of marketing, has asked Marcia to meet with representatives of Hall's major competitor to discuss product cost data. Foster indicates that the sharing of these data will enable Hall to determine a fair and equitable price for its products.

➤ Would it be ethical for Sanchez to attend the meeting and share the relevant cost data?

Activity 8–2
Winner's Sporting Goods Company
Decision on accepting additional business

A manager of Winner's Sporting Goods Company is considering accepting an order from an overseas customer. This customer has requested an order for 20,000 dozen golf balls at a price of $10.00 per dozen. The variable cost to manufacture a dozen golf balls is $8.00 per dozen. The full cost is $12.00 per dozen. Winner's has a normal selling price of $18.00 per dozen. The Winner's plant has just enough excess capacity on the second shift to make the overseas order.

➤ What are some considerations in accepting or rejecting this order?

Activity 8–3
Priceline.com and Marriott International
Accept business at a special price

If you are not familiar with **priceline.com**, go to its Web site. Assume that an individual bids $50 on priceline.com for a room in Dallas, Texas, on August 24. Assume that August 24 is a Saturday, with low expected room demand in Dallas at a **Marriott** hotel, so there is room capacity expected. The fully allocated cost per room per day is assumed from hotel records as follows:

Housekeeping labor cost*	$25
Hotel depreciation expense	27
Cost of room supplies (soap, paper, etc.)	5
Laundry labor and material cost*	10
Cost of desk staff	4
Utility cost (mostly air conditioning)	3
Total cost per room per day	$74

*Both housekeeping and laundry staff include many part-time workers, so that workload can be matched to demand.

Should Marriott accept the customer bid for a night in Dallas on August 24 at a price of $50?

Activity 8–4
Rich Company
Product profitability with production constraints

Rich Company produces glass products for the automobile industry. The company produces three types of products: small, medium, and large windows. One of the process steps in glass making involves a furnace operation. Presently, the furnace runs 24 hours per day, seven days per week. The following per-unit information is available about the three major product lines:

	Small Window	Medium Window	Large Window
Sales price	$14.00	$24.00	$32.00
Variable cost	6.00	14.00	18.00
Contribution margin	$ 8.00	$10.00	$14.00
Furnace hours	2	4	5

The product manager of Rich Company believes that the company should increase incremental sales effort on the large window, since the contribution margin per unit is the highest.

➤ Respond to this suggestion. What recommendations would you suggest to improve profitability?

Activity 8–5
Red Hawk Company
Make or buy decision

The president of Red Hawk Company, Jason Sheppard, asked the controller, Gil Adkins, to provide an analysis of a make vs. buy decision for material TS-101. The material is presently processed in Red Hawk's Roanoke facility. TS-101 is used in processing of final products in the facility. Adkins determined the following unit production costs for the material as of March 15, 2003:

Unit production costs:	
Direct materials	$ 6.70
Direct labor	2.50
Variable factory overhead	1.20
Fixed factory overhead	2.00
Total production costs per unit	$12.40

In addition, material TS-101 requires special hazardous material handling. This special handling adds an additional cost of $1.40 for each unit produced.

Material TS-101 can be purchased from an overseas supplier. The supplier does not presently do business with Red Hawk Company. This supplier promises monthly delivery of the material at a price of $9.00 per unit, plus transportation cost of $0.40 per unit. In addition, Red Hawk would need to incur additional administrative costs to satisfy import regulations for hazardous material. These additional administrative costs are estimated to be $0.80 per purchased unit. Each purchased unit would also require special hazardous material handling of $1.40 per unit.

a. Prepare a differential analysis report to support Adkins' recommendation on whether to continue making material TS-101 or whether to purchase the material from the overseas supplier.

b. ➤ What additional considerations should Adkins address in the recommendation?

Activity 8–6
Francois Computer Company
Cost-plus and target costing concepts

The following conversation took place between Adam Myers, vice-president of marketing, and Jane Jacoby, controller of Francois Computer Company:

Adam: I am really excited about our new computer coming out. I think it will be a real market success.

Jane: I'm really glad you think so. I know that our price is one variable that will determine if it's a success. If our price is too high, our competitors will be the ones with the market success.

Adam: Don't worry about it. We'll just mark our product cost up by 25% and it will all work out. I know we'll make money at those markups. By the way, what does the estimated product cost look like?

Jane: Well, there's the rub. The product cost looks as if it's going to come in at around $2,400. With a 25% markup, that will give us a selling price of $3,000.

Adam: I see your concern. That's a little high. Our research indicates that computer prices are dropping by about 20% per year and that this type of computer should be selling for around $2,500 when we release it to the market.

Jane: I'm not sure what to do.

Adam: Let me see if I can help. How much of the $2,400 is fixed cost?

Jane: About $400.

Adam: There you go. The fixed cost is sunk. We don't need to consider it in our pricing decision. If we reduce the product cost by $400, the new price with a 25% markup would be right at $2,500. Boy, I was really worried for a minute there. I knew something wasn't right.

a. ➤ If you were Jane, how would you respond to Adam's solution to the pricing problem?

b. ➤ How might target costing be used to help solve this pricing dilemma?

Activity 8–7
Into the Real World
Internet marketing

Many businesses are offering their products and services over the Internet. Some of these companies and their Internet addresses are listed below.

Company Name	Internet Address (URL)	Product
Delta Air Lines	**www.delta.com**	airline tickets
Amazon.com, Inc.	**www.amazon.com**	books
Dell Computer Company	**www.dell.com**	personal computers

a. In groups of three, assign each person in your group to one of the Internet sites listed above. For each site, determine the following:
  1. A product (or service) description.
  2. A product price.
  3. A list of costs that are required to produce and sell the product selected in (1).
  4. Whether the costs identified in (3) are fixed costs or variable costs.
b. Which of the three products do you believe has the largest markup on variable cost?

ANSWERS TO SELF-EXAMINATION QUESTIONS

Matching

1. G
2. B
3. L
4. I
5. C
6. M
7. E
8. A
9. D
10. K
11. H
12. J
13. F

Multiple Choice

1. **A** Differential cost is the amount of increase or decrease in cost that is expected from a particular course of action compared with an alternative. For Marlo Company, the differential cost is $19,000 (answer A). This is the total of the variable product costs ($15,000) and the variable operating expenses ($4,000), which would not be incurred if the product is discontinued.

2. **A** A sunk cost is not affected by later decisions. For Victor Company, the sunk cost is the $50,000 (answer A) book value of the equipment, which is equal to the original cost of $200,000 (answer C) less the accumulated depreciation of $150,000 (answer B).

3. **C** The amount of income that could have been earned from the best available alternative to a proposed use of cash is the opportunity cost. For Henry Company, the opportunity cost is 12% of $100,000, or $12,000 (answer C).

4. **C** Under the variable cost concept of product pricing (answer C), fixed manufacturing costs, fixed administrative and selling expenses, and desired profit are allowed for in determining the markup. Only desired profit is allowed for in the markup under the total cost concept (answer A). Under the product cost concept (answer B), total selling and administrative expenses and desired profit are allowed for in determining the markup. Standard cost (answer D) can be used under any of the cost-plus approaches to product pricing.

5. **C** Product 3 has the highest unit contribution margin per bottleneck hour ($14/2 = $7). Product 1 (answer A) has the largest contribution margin per unit, but the lowest unit contribution per bottleneck hour ($20/4 = $5), so it is the least profitable product in the constrained environment. Product 2 (answer B) has the highest total profitability in March (1,500 units × $18), but this does not suggest that it has the highest profit potential. Product 2's unit contribution per bottleneck hour ($18/3 = $6) is between Products 1 and 3. Answer D is not true, since the products all have different profit potential in terms of unit contribution margin per bottleneck hour.

Capital Investment Analysis

objectives

After studying this chapter, you should be able to:

1 Explain the nature and importance of capital investment analysis.

2 Evaluate capital investment proposals, using the following methods: average rate of return, cash payback, net present value, and internal rate of return.

3 List and describe factors that complicate capital investment analysis.

4 Diagram the capital rationing process.

Why are you paying tuition, studying this text, and spending time and money on a higher education? Most people believe that the money and time spent now will return them more income in the future. In other words, a higher education is an investment in future earning ability. How would you know if this investment is worth it? One method would be to compare the cost of a higher education against the estimated future increased earning power. The more your future increased earnings exceed the investment, the more attractive the investment. As you will see in this chapter, the same is true for business investments in fixed assets. Business organizations analyze potential capital investments by using various methods that compare investment costs to future earnings and cash flows.

In this chapter, we will describe analyses useful for making investment decisions, which may involve thousands, millions, or even billions of dollars. We will emphasize the similarities and differences among the most commonly used methods of evaluating investment proposals, as well as the uses of each method. We will also discuss qualitative considerations affecting investment analyses. Finally, we will discuss considerations complicating investment analyses and the process of allocating available investment funds among competing proposals.

Nature of Capital Investment Analysis

objective 1

Explain the nature and importance of capital investment analysis.

How do companies decide to make significant investments such as the following?

- **Toyota Motor Company** doubles its annual production capacity to 400,000 cars at its Georgetown, Kentucky assembly plant.
- **General Electric** invests over $1 billion in plant and equipment to build new kitchen appliance products.
- **The Walt Disney Company** invests $320 million to build a new theme park in Hong Kong.

Companies use capital investment analysis to help evaluate long-term investments. **Capital investment analysis** (or **capital budgeting**) is the process by which management plans, evaluates, and controls investments in fixed assets. Capital investments involve the long-term commitment of funds and affect operations for many years. Thus, these investments must earn a reasonable rate of return, so that the business can meet its obligations to creditors and provide dividends to stockholders. Because capital investment decisions are some of the most important decisions that management makes, capital investment analysis must be carefully developed and implemented.

A capital investment program should encourage employees to submit proposals for capital investments. It should communicate to employees the long-range goals of the business, so that useful proposals are submitted. All reasonable proposals should be considered and evaluated with respect to economic costs and benefits. The program may reward employees whose proposals are accepted.

Methods of Evaluating Capital Investment Proposals

objective 2

Evaluate capital investment proposals, using the following methods: average rate of return, cash payback, net present value, and internal rate of return.

Capital investment evaluation methods can be grouped into the following two categories:

1. Methods that do not use present values
2. Methods that use present values

Two methods that do not use present values are (1) the average rate of return method and (2) the cash payback method. Two methods that use present values are (1) the net present value method and (2) the internal rate of return method. These methods consider the time value of money. The **time value of money concept** recognizes that an amount of cash invested today will earn income and therefore has value over time.

Management often uses a combination of methods in evaluating capital investment proposals. Each method has advantages and disadvantages. In addition, some of the computations are complex. Computers, however, can perform the computations quickly and easily. Computers can also be used to analyze the impact of changes in key estimates in evaluating capital investment proposals.

A survey of business practices in a variety of industries reported the following use of capital investment analysis methods:

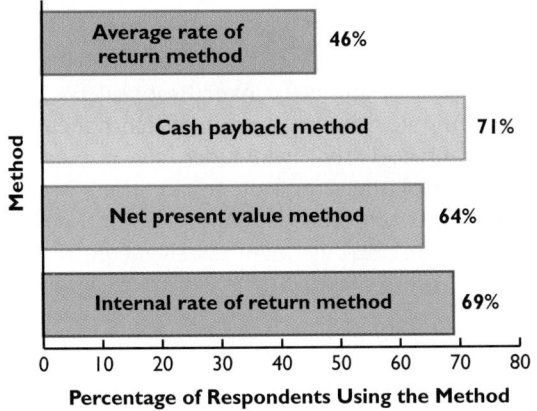

Method	Percentage
Average rate of return method	46%
Cash payback method	71%
Net present value method	64%
Internal rate of return method	69%

Percentage of Respondents Using the Method

Source: Robert A. Howell, James D. Brown, Stephen R. Soucy, and Allen H. Seed, *Management Accounting in the New Manufacturing Environment*, National Association of Accountants and Computer Aided Manufacturing International, Montvale, New Jersey, 1987.

Methods That Ignore Present Value

The average rate of return and the cash payback methods are easy to use. These methods are often initially used to screen proposals. Management normally sets minimum standards for accepting proposals, and those not meeting these standards are dropped from further consideration. If a proposal meets the minimum standards, it is often subject to further analysis.

The methods that ignore present value are often useful in evaluating capital investment proposals that have relatively short useful lives. In such cases, the timing of the cash flows is less important.

Average Rate of Return Method

The **average rate of return**, sometimes called the **accounting rate of return**, is a measure of the average income as a percent of the average investment in fixed assets. The average rate of return is determined by using the following equation:

$$\text{Average rate of return} = \frac{\text{Estimated average annual income}}{\text{Average investment}}$$

The numerator is the average of the annual income expected to be earned from the investment over the investment life, after deducting depreciation. The denominator is the average book value over the investment life. Thus, if straight-line depreciation and no residual value are assumed, the average investment over the useful life is equal to one-half of the original cost.[1]

To illustrate, assume that management is considering the purchase of a machine at a cost of $500,000. The machine is expected to have a useful life of 4 years, with

[1] The average investment is the midpoint of the depreciable cost of the asset. Since a fixed asset is never depreciated below its residual value, this midpoint is determined by adding the original cost of the asset to the estimated residual value and dividing by 2.

no residual value, and to yield total income of $200,000. The estimated average annual income is therefore $50,000 ($200,000 ÷ 4), and the average investment is $250,000 [($500,000 + $0 residual value) ÷ 2]. Thus, the average rate of return on the average investment is 20%, computed as follows:

$$\text{Average rate of return} = \frac{\text{Estimated average annual income}}{\text{Average investment}}$$

$$\text{Average rate of return} = \frac{\$200,000 \div 4}{(\$500,000 + \$0) \div 2} = 20\%$$

The average rate of return of 20% should be compared with the minimum rate for such investments. If the average rate of return equals or exceeds the minimum rate, the machine should be purchased.

When several capital investment proposals are considered, the proposals can be ranked by their average rates of return. The higher the average rate of return, the more desirable the proposal. For example, assume that management is considering two capital investment proposals and has computed the following average rates of return:

What is the average rate of return for a project that is estimated to yield total income of $273,600 over three years, cost $690,000, and has a $70,000 residual value?

24% [($273,600 ÷ 3)/($690,000 + $70,000) ÷ 2]

	Proposal A	Proposal B
Estimated average annual income	$ 30,000	$ 36,000
Average investment	$120,000	$180,000
Average rate of return:		
$30,000 ÷ $120,000	25%	
$36,000 ÷ $180,000		20%

If only the average rate of return is considered, Proposal A, with an average rate of return of 25%, would be preferred over Proposal B.

In addition to being easy to compute, the average rate of return method has several advantages. One advantage is that it includes the amount of income earned over the entire life of the proposal. In addition, it emphasizes accounting income, which is often used by investors and creditors in evaluating management performance. Its main disadvantage is that it does not directly consider the expected cash flows from the proposal and the timing of these cash flows.

> **The average rate of return method considers the amount of income earned over the life of a proposal.**

Cash Payback Method

Cash flows are important because cash can be reinvested. Very simply, the capital investment uses cash and must therefore return cash in the future in order to be successful.

The expected period of time that will pass between the date of an investment and the complete recovery in cash (or equivalent) of the amount invested is the **cash payback period**. To simplify the analysis, the revenues and expenses other than depreciation related to operating fixed assets are assumed to be all in the form of cash. The excess of the cash flowing in from revenue over the cash flowing out for expenses is termed **net cash flow**. The time required for the net cash flow to equal the initial outlay for the fixed asset is the payback period.

To illustrate, assume that the proposed investment in a fixed asset with an 8-year life is $200,000. The annual cash revenues from the investment are $50,000, and the annual cash expenses are $10,000. Thus, the annual net cash flow is expected to be $40,000 ($50,000 − $10,000). The estimated cash payback period for the investment is 5 years, computed as follows:

$$\frac{\$200,000}{\$40,000} = \text{5-year cash payback period}$$

A project has estimated annual net cash flows of $30,000. It is estimated to cost $105,000. What is the cash payback period?

3½ years ($105,000 ÷ $30,000)

In this illustration, the annual net cash flows are equal ($40,000 per year). If these annual net cash flows are *not* equal, the cash payback period is determined by adding the annual net cash flows until the cumulative sum equals the amount of the proposed investment. To illustrate, assume that for a proposed investment of $400,000, the annual net cash flows and the cumulative net cash flows over the proposal's 6-year life are as follows:

Year	Net Cash Flow	Cumulative Net Cash Flow
1	$ 60,000	$ 60,000
2	80,000	140,000
3	105,000	245,000
4	155,000	400,000
5	100,000	500,000
6	90,000	590,000

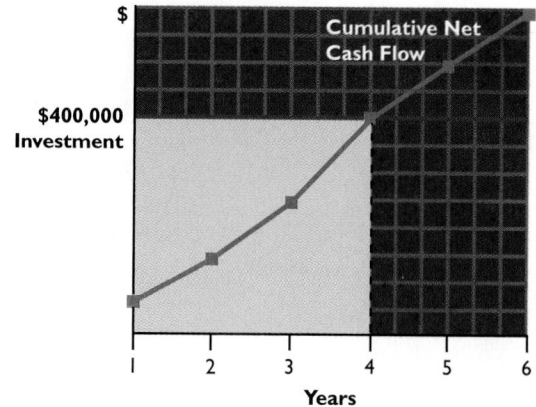

General Electric Corporation has invested over $1.5 billion in research and development for the Boeing 777 jet engine. Due to intense competition from **Pratt & Whitney** and **Rolls Royce**, the prices for 777 jet engines are at about 75% below list prices, or about half of their full cost. However, management believes that there will be significant profitability from jet engine repairs and overhauls in the long term. As a result, GE now estimates the program's payback period will be at least 10 years.

Point of Interest
Present value concepts can also be used to evaluate personal finances. For example, the **Heritage Foundation** compared the present value of social security contributions of a 35-year-old average earner with the present value of social security benefits. Using an interest rate of 6%, the present value of the social security benefits is $300,000 less than the present value of the contributions. For a younger worker or a higher-salary earner, the difference is even greater.

The cumulative net cash flow at the end of the fourth year equals the amount of the investment, $400,000. Thus, the payback period is 4 years. If the amount of the proposed investment had been $450,000, the cash payback period would occur during the fifth year. If the net cash flows are uniform during the period, the cash payback period would be 4½ years.

The cash payback method is widely used in evaluating proposals for investments in new projects. A short payback period is desirable, because the sooner the cash is recovered, the sooner it becomes available for reinvestment in other projects. In addition, there is less possibility of losses from economic conditions, out-of-date assets, and other unavoidable risks when the payback period is short. The cash payback period is also important to bankers and other creditors who may be depending upon net cash flow for repaying debt related to the capital investment. The sooner the cash is recovered, the sooner the debt or other liabilities can be paid. Thus, the cash payback method is especially useful to managers whose primary concern is liquidity.

One of the disadvantages of the cash payback method is that it ignores cash flows occurring after the payback period. In addition, the cash payback method does not use present value concepts in valuing cash flows occurring in different periods. In the next section, we will review present value concepts and introduce capital investment methods that use present value.

Present Value Methods

An investment in fixed assets may be viewed as acquiring a series of net cash flows over a period of time. The period of time over which these net cash flows will be received may be an important factor in determining the value of an investment. Present value methods use both the amount and the timing of net cash flows in evaluating an investment. Before illustrating how these methods are used in capital investment analysis, we will review basic present value concepts.

Present Value Concepts

Present value concepts can be divided into the *present value of an amount* and the *present value of an annuity*. We describe and illustrate these two concepts next.

Present Value of an Amount. If you were given the choice, would you prefer to receive $1 now or $1 three years from now? You should prefer to receive $1 now, because you could invest the $1 and earn interest for three years. As a result, the amount you would have after three years would be greater than $1.

To illustrate, assume that on January 1, 2003, you invest $1 in an account that earns 12% interest compounded annually. After one year, the $1 will grow to $1.12 ($1 × 1.12), because interest of 12¢ is added to the investment. The $1.12 earns 12% interest for the second year. Interest earning interest is called **compounding**. By the end of the second year, the investment has grown to $1.254 ($1.12 × 1.12). By the end of the third year, the investment has grown to $1.404 ($1.254 × 1.12). Thus, if money is worth 12%, you would be equally satisfied with $1 on January 1, 2003, or $1.404 three years later.

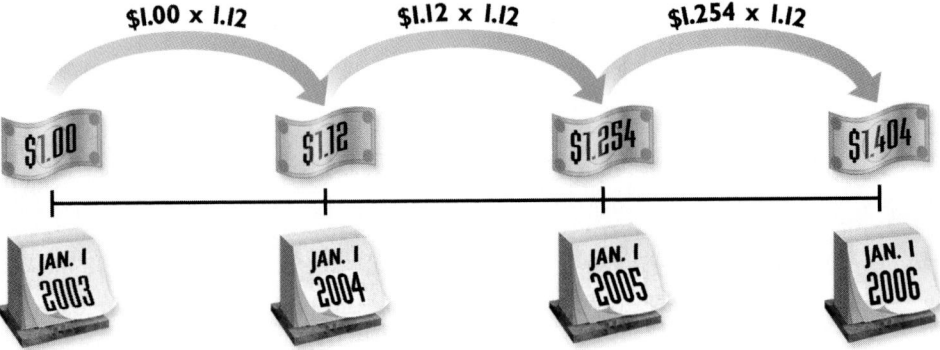

On January 1, 2003, what is the present value of $1.404 to be received on January 1, 2006? This is a present value question. The answer can be determined with the aid of a present value of $1 table. For example, the partial table in Exhibit 1 indicates that the present value of $1 to be received three years hence, with earnings compounded at the rate of 12% a year, is 0.712. Multiplying 0.712 by $1.404 yields $1, which is the present value that started the compounding process.[2]

Exhibit 1 Partial Present Value of $1 Table

	Present Value of $1 at Compound Interest				
Year	6%	10%	12%	15%	20%
1	0.943	0.909	0.893	0.870	0.833
2	0.890	0.826	0.797	0.756	0.694
3	0.840	0.751	0.712	0.658	0.579
4	0.792	0.683	0.636	0.572	0.482
5	0.747	0.621	0.567	0.497	0.402
6	0.705	0.564	0.507	0.432	0.335
7	0.665	0.513	0.452	0.376	0.279
8	0.627	0.467	0.404	0.327	0.233
9	0.592	0.424	0.361	0.284	0.194
10	0.558	0.386	0.322	0.247	0.162

[2] The present value factors in the table are rounded to three decimal places. More complete tables of both present values and future values are in Appendix A.

Present Value of an Annuity. An **annuity** is a series of equal net cash flows at fixed time intervals. Annuities are very common in business. For example, monthly rental, salary, and bond interest cash flows are all examples of annuities. The **present value of an annuity** is the sum of the present values of each cash flow. In other words, the present value of an annuity is the amount of cash that is needed today to yield a series of equal net cash flows at fixed time intervals in the future.

To illustrate, the present value of a $100 annuity for five periods at 12% could be determined by using the present value factors in Exhibit 1. Each $100 net cash flow could be multiplied by the present value of $1 at 12% factor for the appropriate period and summed to determine a present value of $360.50, as shown in the following timeline:

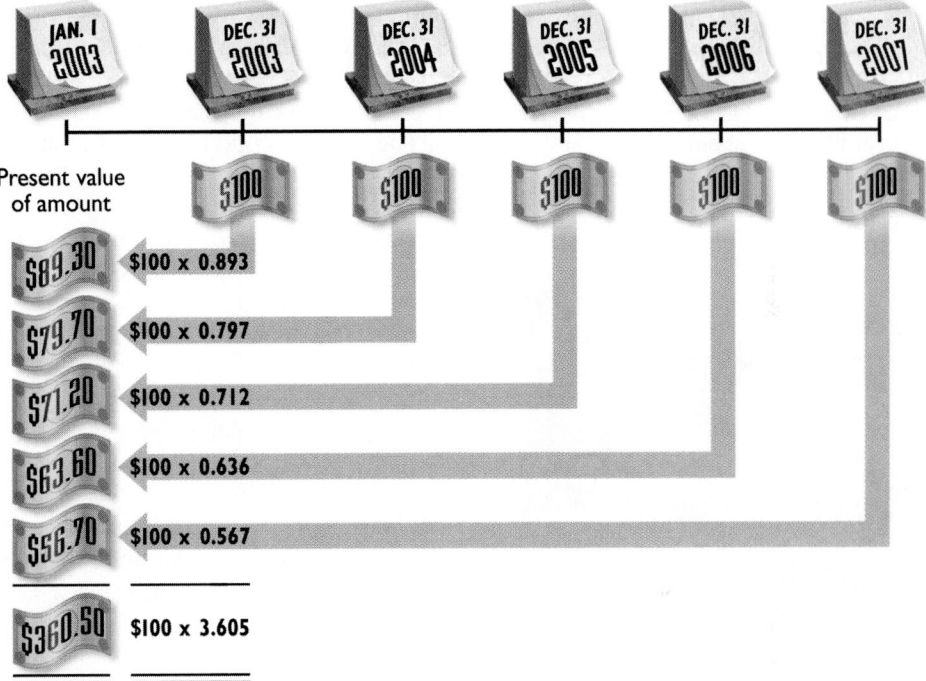

Using a present value of an annuity table is a simpler approach. Exhibit 2 is a partial table of present value of annuity factors.[3] These factors are merely the sum of

Exhibit 2 Partial Present Value of an Annuity Table

Present Value of an Annuity of $1 at Compound Interest					
Year	6%	10%	12%	15%	20%
1	0.943	0.909	0.893	0.870	0.833
2	1.833	1.736	1.690	1.626	1.528
3	2.673	2.487	2.402	2.283	2.106
4	3.465	3.170	3.037	2.855	2.589
5	4.212	3.791	3.605	3.353	2.991
6	4.917	4.355	4.111	3.785	3.326
7	5.582	4.868	4.564	4.160	3.605
8	6.210	5.335	4.968	4.487	3.837
9	6.802	5.759	5.328	4.772	4.031
10	7.360	6.145	5.650	5.019	4.192

[3] Expanded tables for the present value of an annuity are in Appendix A.

A 55-year-old bank janitor won a $5 million lottery jackpot, payable in 21 annual installments of $240,245. Unfortunately, the bank janitor died after collecting only one payment. What happens to the remaining unclaimed payments? In this case, the lottery winnings were auctioned off for the benefit of the janitor's estate. The winning bid approximated the present value of the remaining cash flows, or about $2.1 million.

the present value of $1 factors in Exhibit 1 for the number of annuity periods. Thus, 3.605 in the annuity table (Exhibit 2) is the sum of the five individual present value of $1 factors at 12%. Multiplying $100 by 3.605 yields the same amount ($360.50) that was determined in the preceding illustration by five successive multiplications.

Net Present Value Method

The **net present value method** analyzes capital investment proposals by comparing the initial cash investment with the present value of the net cash flows. It is sometimes called the **discounted cash flow method**. The interest rate (return) used in net present value analysis is set by management. This rate is often based upon such factors as the nature of the business, the purpose of the investment, the cost of securing funds for the investment, and the minimum desired rate of return. If the net present value of the cash flows expected from a proposed investment equals or exceeds the amount of the initial investment, the proposal is desirable.

To illustrate, assume a proposal to acquire $200,000 of equipment with an expected useful life of five years (no residual value) and a minimum desired rate of return of 10%. The present value of the net cash flow for each year is computed by multiplying the net cash flow for the year by the present value factor of $1 for that year. For example, the $70,000 net cash flow to be received on December 31, 2003, is multiplied by the present value of $1 for one year at 10% (0.909). Thus, the present value of the $70,000 is $63,630. Likewise, the $60,000 net cash flow on December 31, 2004, is multiplied by the present value of $1 for two years at 10% (0.826) to yield $49,560, and so on. The amount to be invested, $200,000, is then subtracted from the total present value of the net cash flows $202,900, to determine the net present value, $2,900, as shown below. The net present value indicates that the proposal is expected to recover the investment and provide more than the minimum rate of return of 10%.

When capital investment funds are limited and the alternative proposals involve different amounts of investment, it is useful to prepare a ranking of the proposals by using a present value index. The **present**

> The net present value method compares an investment's initial cash outflow with the present value of its cash inflows.

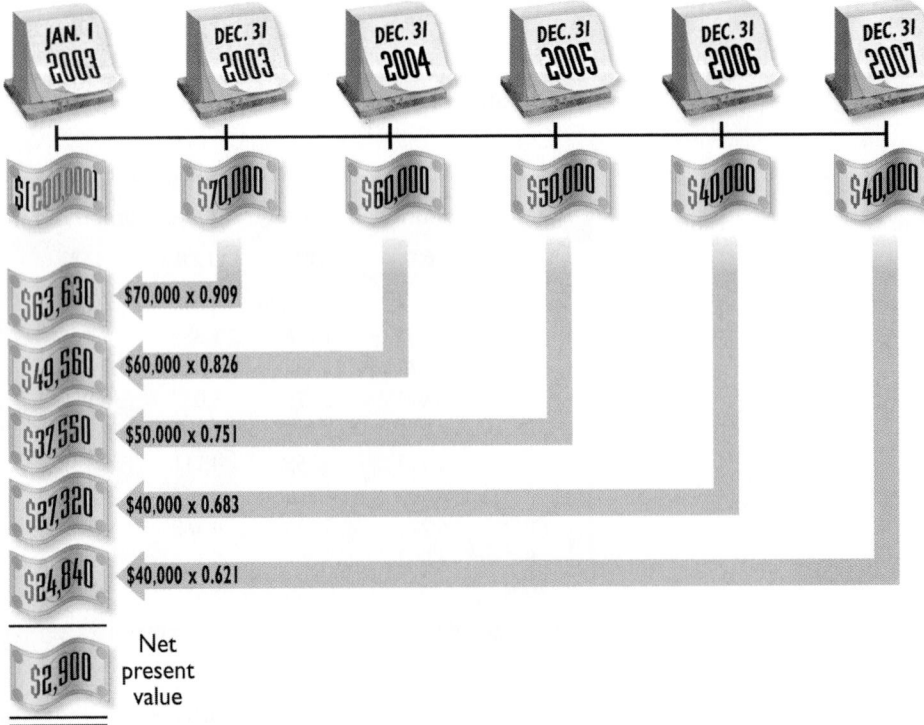

value index is calculated by dividing the total present value of the net cash flow by the amount to be invested. The present value index for the investment in the previous illustration is calculated as follows:

$$\text{Present value index} = \frac{\textbf{Total present value of net cash flow}}{\textbf{Amount to be invested}}$$

$$= \frac{\$202,900}{\$200,000} = 1.0145$$

If a business is considering three alternative proposals and has determined their net present values, the present value index for each proposal is as follows:

	Proposal A	Proposal B	Proposal C
Total present value of net cash flow . . .	$107,000	$86,400	$93,600
Amount to be invested	100,000	80,000	90,000
Net present value	$ 7,000	$ 6,400	$ 3,600
Present value index	1.07 ($107,000 ÷ $100,000)	1.08 ($86,400 ÷ $80,000)	1.04 ($93,600 ÷ $90,000)

A project has estimated annual net cash flows of $50,000 for seven years and is estimated to cost $240,000. Assume a minimum rate of return of 12%. For this project, what is the (1) net present value and (2) present value index? (3) Should the project be accepted, based on this analysis?

----

(1) ($11,800) [($50,000 × 4.564) − $240,000]; (2) 0.95 (rounded) ($228,200 ÷ $240,000); (3) No.

Although Proposal A has the largest net present value, the present value indices indicate that it is not as desirable as Proposal B. In other words, Proposal B returns $1.08 present value per dollar invested, whereas Proposal A returns only $1.07. Proposal B requires an investment of $80,000, compared to an investment of $100,000 for Proposal A. Management should consider the possible use of the $20,000 difference between Proposal A and Proposal B investments before making a final decision.

An advantage of the net present value method is that it considers the time value of money. A disadvantage is that the computations are more complex than those for the methods that ignore present value. In addition, the net present value method assumes that the cash received from the proposal during its useful life can be reinvested at the rate of return used in computing the present value of the proposal. Because of changing economic conditions, this assumption may not always be reasonable.

Internal Rate of Return Method

The **internal rate of return method** uses present value concepts to compute the rate of return from the net cash flows expected from capital investment proposals. This method is sometimes called the **time-adjusted rate of return method**. It is similar to the net present value method, in that it focuses on the present value of the net cash flows. However, the internal rate of return method starts with the net cash flows and, in a sense, works backwards to determine the rate of return expected from the proposal.

To illustrate, assume that management is evaluating a proposal to acquire equipment costing $33,530. The equipment is expected to provide annual net cash flows of $10,000 per year for five years. If we assume a rate of return of 12%, we can calculate the present value of the net cash flows, using the present value of an annuity table in Exhibit 2. These calculations are shown in Exhibit 3.

Exhibit 3 Net Present Value Analysis at 12%

Annual net cash flow (at the end of each of five years)	$10,000
Present value of an annuity of $1 at 12% for 5 years (Exhibit 2)	× 3.605
Present value of annual net cash flows	$36,050
Less amount to be invested	33,530
Net present value	$ 2,520

In Exhibit 3, the $36,050 present value of the cash inflows, based on a 12% rate of return, is greater than the $33,530 to be invested. Therefore, the internal rate of return must be greater than 12%. Through trial-and-error procedures, the rate of return that equates the $33,530 cost of the investment with the present value of the net cash flows is determined to be 15%, as shown below.

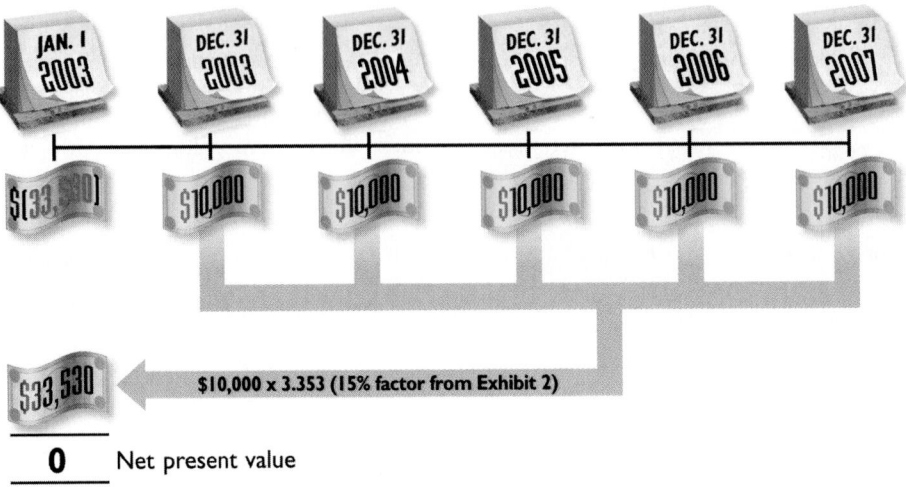

0 Net present value

Such trial-and-error procedures are time-consuming. However, when equal annual net cash flows are expected from a proposal, as in the illustration, the calculations are simplified by using the following procedures:[4]

1. Determine a present value factor for an annuity of $1 by dividing the amount to be invested by the equal annual net cash flows, as follows:

$$\text{Present value factor for an annuity of \$1} = \frac{\textbf{Amount to be invested}}{\textbf{Equal annual net cash flows}}$$

2. In the present value of an annuity of $1 table, locate the present value factor determined in (1). First locate the number of years of expected useful life of the investment in the Year column, and then proceed horizontally across the table until you find the present value factor computed in (1).
3. Identify the internal rate of return by the heading of the column in which the present value factor in (2) is located.

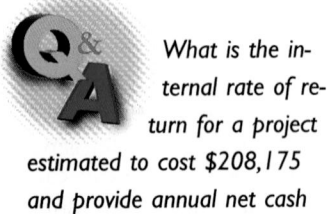

What is the internal rate of return for a project estimated to cost $208,175 and provide annual net cash flows of $55,000 for six years?

15% ($208,175 ÷ $55,000 = 3.785, the present value of an annuity factor for six periods at 15%)

To illustrate, assume that management is considering a proposal to acquire equipment costing $97,360. The equipment is expected to provide equal annual net cash flows of $20,000 for seven years. The present value factor for an annuity of $1 is **4.868**, calculated as follows:

Present value factor for an annuity of $1

$$= \frac{\text{Amount to be invested}}{\text{Equal annual net cash flows}}$$

$$= \frac{\$97,360}{\$20,000} = 4.868$$

For a period of seven years, the partial present value of an annuity of $1 table indicates that the factor **4.868** is related to a percentage of **10%**, as shown on the following page. Thus, 10% is the internal rate of return for this proposal.

----

[4] Equal annual net cash flows are assumed in order to simplify the illustration. If the annual net cash flows are not equal, the calculations are more complex, but the basic concepts are the same.

Present Value of an Annuity of $1 at Compound Interest			
Year	6%	10%	12%
1	0.943	0.909	0.893
2	1.833	1.736	1.690
3	2.673	2.487	2.402
4	3.465	3.170	3.037
5	4.212	3.791	3.605
6	4.917	4.355	4.111
7	5.582	4.868	4.564
8	6.210	5.335	4.968
9	6.802	5.759	5.328
10	7.360	6.145	5.650

The minimum acceptable rate of return (often termed the *hurdle rate*) for **Owens-Corning Fiberglass** is 18%; for **General Electric**, it is 20%. David Devonshire, CFO of Owens-Corning, states, "I'm here to challenge anyone—even the CEO—who gets emotionally attached to a project that doesn't reach our benchmark."

If the minimum acceptable rate of return for similar proposals is 10% or less, then the proposed investment should be considered acceptable. When several proposals are considered, management often ranks the proposals by their internal rates of return. The proposal with the highest rate is considered the most desirable.

The primary advantage of the internal rate of return method is that the present values of the net cash flows over the entire useful life of the proposal are considered. In addition, by determining a rate of return for each proposal, all proposals are compared on a common basis. The primary disadvantage of the internal rate of return method is that the computations are more complex than for some of the other methods. However, spreadsheet software programs have internal rate of return functions that simplify the calculation. Also, like the net present value method, this method assumes that the cash received from a proposal during its useful life will be reinvested at the internal rate of return. Because of changing economic conditions, this assumption may not always be reasonable.

BUSINESS ON STAGE

Cost of Capital

apital investment analysis often requires managers to assess whether a proposed investment meets a minimum rate of return. This minimum rate of return is often the cost of capital of the business. Investments that provide rates of return less than the cost of capital should normally be rejected.

The **cost of capital** for a business is the cost of financing its long-term operations. If a business financed all its operations by issuing common stock, its cost of capital would be the rate of return that the common stockholders demanded from their investments. Most businesses, however, use a combination of financing that includes common stock, preferred stock, and various types of debt. The costs of these common components are briefly described below.

- The cost of various types of debt is expressed in terms of its after-tax interest rate. For example, if debt has an interest rate of 10% and the business's tax rate is 40%, the after-tax interest rate is 6% [10% × (1 − 40%)]. The cost of debt financing is expressed after tax because interest is tax deductible in determining tax expense.
- The cost of preferred stock is expressed as the preferred dividends divided by the issuing price (proceeds) of the preferred stock. Since preferred dividends are not tax deductible, no after-tax adjustments are necessary.
- The cost of common stock and retained earnings is expressed as the rate of return that stockholders demand from their investments. This return reflects what stockholders could earn from other comparable investments.

The overall cost of capital for a business is determined by weighting the costs of each of the financing components. Once determined, the overall cost of capital is used in deciding which capital investment alternatives to implement. ∎

Factors That Complicate Capital Investment Analysis

objective 3

List and describe factors that complicate capital investment analysis.

In the preceding discussion, we described four widely used methods of evaluating capital investment proposals. In practice, additional factors may have an impact on the outcome of a capital investment decision. In the following paragraphs, we discuss some of the most important of these factors: the federal income tax, unequal lives of alternative proposals, leasing, uncertainty, changes in price levels, and qualitative factors.

Income Tax

In many cases, the impact of the federal income tax on capital investment decisions can be material. For example, in determining depreciation for federal income tax purposes, useful lives that are much shorter than the actual useful lives are often used. Also, depreciation can be calculated by methods that approximate the 200-percent declining-balance method. Thus, depreciation for tax purposes often exceeds the depreciation for financial statement purposes in the early years of an asset's use. The tax reduction in these early years is offset by higher taxes in the later years, so that accelerated depreciation does not result in a long-run saving in taxes. However, the timing of the cash outflows for income taxes can have a significant impact on capital investment analysis.[5]

8-Year Life

TRUCK

5-Year Life

COMPUTER NETWORK

Unequal Proposal Lives

In the preceding discussion, the illustrations of the methods of analyzing capital investment proposals were based on the assumption that alternative proposals had the same useful lives. In practice, however, alternative proposals may have unequal lives. To illustrate, assume that alternative investments, a truck and computers, are being compared. The truck has a useful life of 8 years, and the computer network has a useful life of 5 years. Each proposal requires an initial investment of $100,000, and the company desires a rate of return of 10%. The expected cash flows and net present value of each alternative are shown in Exhibit 4. Because of the unequal useful lives of the two proposals, however, the net present values in Exhibit 4 are not comparable.

To make the proposals comparable for the analysis, they can be adjusted to end at the same time. This can be done by assuming that the truck is to be sold at the end of 5 years. The residual value of the truck must be estimated at the end of 5 years, and this value must then be included as a cash flow at that date. Both proposals will then cover 5 years, and net present value analysis can be used to compare the two proposals over the same 5-year period. If the truck's estimated residual value is $40,000 at the end of year 5, the net present value for the truck exceeds the net present value for the computers by $1,835 ($18,640 − $16,805), as shown in Exhibit 5. Therefore, the truck may be viewed as the more attractive of the two proposals.

Lease versus Capital Investment

Leasing fixed assets has become common in many industries. For example, hospitals often lease diagnostic and other medical equipment. Leasing allows a business to use fixed assets without spending large amounts of cash to purchase them. In addition, management may believe that a fixed asset has a high risk of becoming obsolete. This risk may be reduced by leasing rather than purchasing the asset. Also, the *Internal Revenue Code* allows the lessor (the owner of the asset) to pass tax deductions on to the lessee (the party leasing the asset). These provisions of the tax

---

[5] The impact of income taxes on capital investment analysis is described and illustrated in advanced textbooks.

Exhibit 4 Net Present Value Analysis

Truck			
Year	Present Value of $1 at 10%	Net Cash Flow	Present Value of Net Cash Flow
1	0.909	$ 30,000	$ 27,270
2	0.826	30,000	24,780
3	0.751	25,000	18,775
4	0.683	20,000	13,660
5	0.621	15,000	9,315
6	0.564	15,000	8,460
7	0.513	10,000	5,130
8	0.467	10,000	4,670
Total		$155,000	$112,060
Amount to be invested			100,000
Net present value			$ 12,060

Computers			
Year	Present Value of $1 at 10%	Net Cash Flow	Present Value of Net Cash Flow
1	0.909	$ 30,000	$ 27,270
2	0.826	30,000	24,780
3	0.751	30,000	22,530
4	0.683	30,000	20,490
5	0.621	35,000	21,735
Total		$155,000	$116,805
Amount to be invested			100,000
Net present value			$ 16,805

Exhibit 5 Net Present Value Analysis

Truck—Revised to 5-Year Life			
Year	Present Value of $1 at 10%	Net Cash Flow	Present Value of Net Cash Flow
1	0.909	$ 30,000	$ 27,270
2	0.826	30,000	24,780
3	0.751	25,000	18,775
4	0.683	20,000	13,660
5	0.621	15,000	9,315
5 (Residual value)	0.621	40,000	24,840
Total		$160,000	$118,640
Amount to be invested			100,000
Net present value			$ 18,640

Truck NPV
>
Computers NPV

Merck, a major pharmaceutical company, uses uncertainty in analyzing drugs under research and development. Management understands that a single hit would pay for the investment costs of many failures. They use a technique in probability theory, called *Monte Carlo analysis*, which shows that the drugs under development will actually be very profitable.

law have made leasing assets more attractive. For example, a company that pays $50,000 per year for leasing a $200,000 fixed asset with a life of 8 years is permitted to deduct from taxable income the annual lease payments.

In many cases, before a final decision is made, management should consider leasing assets instead of purchasing them. Normally, leasing assets is more costly than purchasing because the lessor must include in the rental price not only the costs associated with owning the assets but also a profit. Nevertheless, using the methods of evaluating capital investment proposals, management should consider whether it is more profitable to lease rather than purchase an asset.

Uncertainty

All capital investment analyses rely on factors that are uncertain. For example, the estimates related to revenues, expenses, and cash flows are uncertain. The long-term nature of capital investments suggests that some estimates are likely to involve uncertainty. Errors in one or more of the estimates could lead to incorrect decisions.

Changes in Price Levels

In performing investment analysis, management must be concerned about changes in price levels. Price levels may change due to **inflation**, which occurs when general price levels are rising. Thus, while general prices are rising, the returns on an investment must exceed the rising price level, or else the cash returned on the investment becomes less valuable over time.

Price levels may also change for foreign investments as the result of currency exchange rates. **Currency exchange rates** are the rates at which currency in another country can be exchanged for U.S. dollars. If the amount of local dollars that can be exchanged for one U.S. dollar increases, then the local currency is said to be weakening to the dollar. Thus, if a company made an investment in another country where the local currency was weakening, it would adversely impact the return on that investment as expressed in U.S. dollars. This is because the expected amount of local currency returned on the investment would purchase fewer U.S. dollars.

Management should attempt to anticipate future price levels and consider their effects on the estimates used in capital investment analyses. Changes in anticipated price levels could significantly affect the analyses.

Qualitative Considerations

Some benefits of capital investments are qualitative in nature and cannot be easily estimated in dollar terms. If management does not consider these qualitative considerations, the quantitative analyses may suggest rejecting a worthy investment.

Qualitative considerations in capital investment analysis are most appropriate for strategic investments. Strategic investments are those that are designed to affect a company's long-term ability to generate profits. Strategic investments often have many uncertainties and intangible benefits. Unlike capital investments that are designed to cut costs, strategic investments have very few "hard" savings. Instead, they may affect future revenues, which are difficult to estimate. An example of a strategic investment is **Nucor's** decision to be the first to invest in a new continuous casting technology that had the potential to make thin gauge sheet steel and thus open new product markets. Nucor's new investment was justified more on the strategic importance of the investment than on the economic analysis. As it turned out, the investment was very successful.

Qualitative considerations that may influence capital investment analysis include product quality, manufacturing flexibility, employee morale, manufacturing productivity, and market opportunity. Many of these qualitative factors may be as important, if not more important, than the results of quantitative analysis.

 **Intel Corporation** makes the processor chip that goes into laptop and desktop computers. In 1999, Intel spent $3.4 billion on capital projects and research and development. Each chip fabrication plant (fab) costs around $2 billion—and Intel has been building one every year or so. How does Intel justify these investments? Intel's president, Craig Barrett, states, "We build factories two years in advance of needing them, before we have the product to run in them, and before we know the industry's going to grow." Andy Grove, CEO of Intel, adds, "Our fabs are fields of dreams. We build them and hope people will come." So far, Intel has been right. At $7.3 billion in profits, Intel ranks as one of the most profitable companies in the world.

Capital Rationing

objective 4

Diagram the capital rationing process.

Funding for capital projects may be obtained from issuing bonds or stock or from operating cash. **Capital rationing** is the process by which management allocates these funds among competing capital investment proposals. In this process, management often uses a combination of the methods described in this chapter. Exhibit 6 portrays the capital rationing decision process.

In capital rationing, alternative proposals are initially screened by establishing minimum standards for the cash payback and the average rate of return. The proposals that survive this screening are further analyzed, using the net present value and internal rate of return methods. Throughout the capital rationing process,

Exhibit 6 Capital Rationing
Decision Process

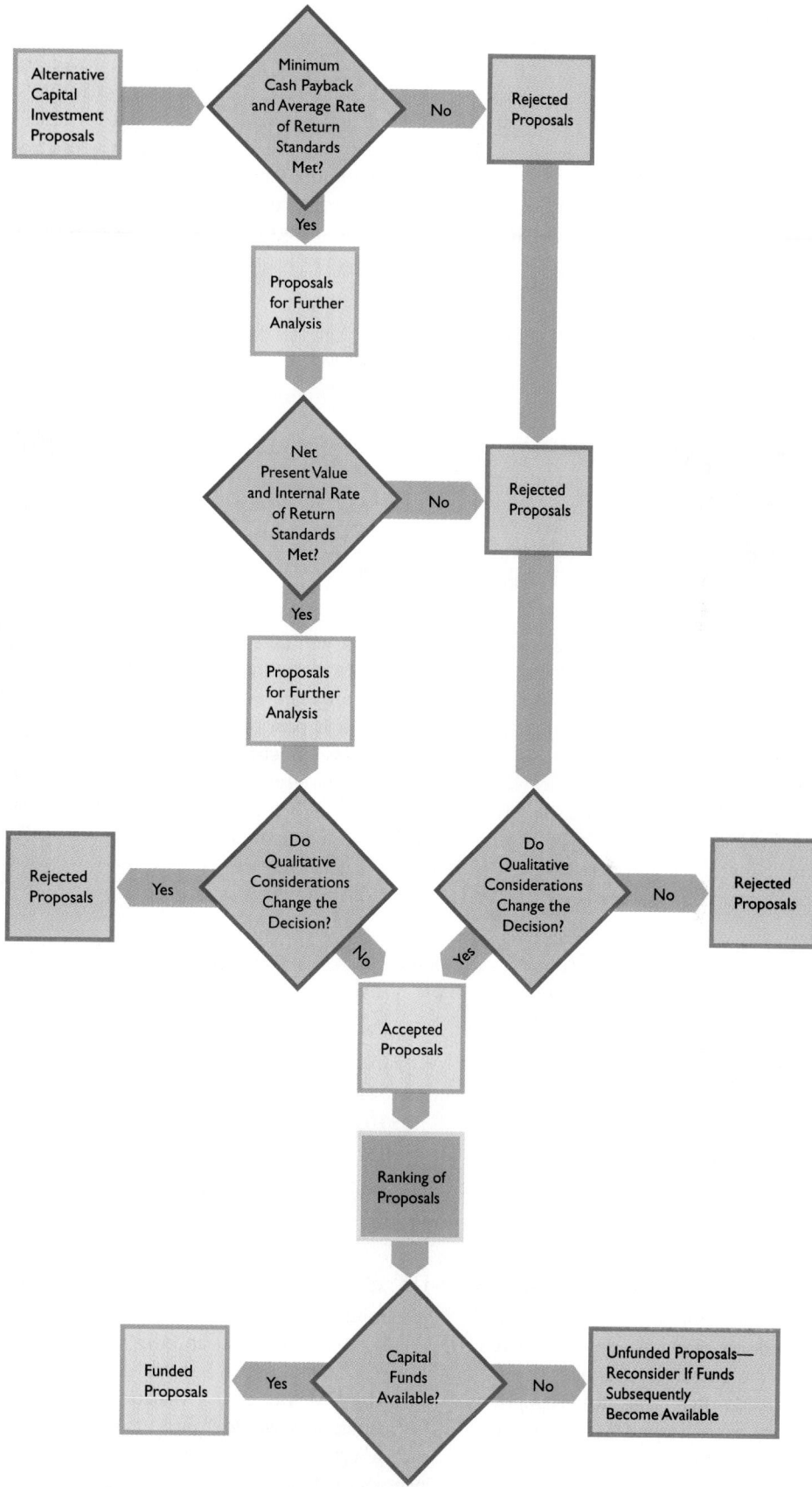

qualitative factors related to each proposal should also be considered. For example, the acquisition of new, more efficient equipment that eliminates several jobs could lower employee morale to a level that could decrease overall plant productivity. Alternatively, new equipment might improve the quality of the product and thus increase consumer satisfaction and sales.

The final steps in the capital rationing process are ranking the proposals according to management's criteria, comparing the proposals with the funds available, and selecting the proposals to be funded. Funded proposals are included in the **capital expenditures budget** to aid the planning and financing of operations. Unfunded proposals may be reconsidered if funds later become available.

Valuing "Eyeballs"

For an Internet company, a pair of "eyeballs" refers to a visitor to the site, and each eyeball pair (visitor) is potentially valuable to the company. For example, advertisers pay Yahoo! a fee to run banner ads on their site, because Yahoo! visitors see the ads. For Amazon.com, "eyeballs" might actually purchase products off the site, thus providing sales revenues for Amazon. If you take some recent valuations of several Internet companies and divide by the number of visitors to a site, it is possible to estimate the market's assessment of the present value of each visitor. The following list provides some recent market valuations, annual cash flows, and estimated internal rates of return per visitor of some popular sites:

	Market Value per Visitor	Annual Cash Flows per Visitor[1]	Internal Rate of Return
eBay	1,394	9.39	−10.5%
Amazon.com	554	−21.70	Negative*
Yahoo!	1,660	10.30	−11.0%
Schwab	6,840	290.00	0.5%
Priceline.com	1,056	0.52	−21.6%

[1]*Source*: Erick Schonfeld, "How Much Are Your Eyeballs Worth?" *Fortune*, February 21, 2000.
*There is no internal rate of return because there are no positive cash flows.

In a rational market, the present value of each visitor represents the total discounted cash flows expected from the customer over the life of the relationship. Thus, for example, Yahoo! earns around $10.30 annual cash flows per visitor. Now, if we were to calculate the internal rate of return implied by a present value of $1,660 and an annual cash flow of $10.30 over, say 25 years, we would get an internal rate of return of −11%! This means that an investor would receive negative returns by purchasing Yahoo! at this valuation. Given this, why would Yahoo! have such a high valuation? It's likely that investors believe that these assumptions will not be static for Yahoo! but will instead improve over time as the customer base grows. The internal rate of return of Schwab, a financial services company, is approximately 0.5%, or barely positive. This means that Schwab's market price will provide an internal rate of return of only one-half of one percent if these assumptions hold for 25 years. Again, market investors must believe that there are strong growth opportunities in Schwab and for all the companies listed in the table. In contrast, an "old economy" business, such as American Airlines, has a present (market) value of $1,200 for each of its four million frequent flyer members. Each of these frequent flyers generates an estimated $325 of annual cash flow, which yields a 27% internal rate of return. Apparently, the old and new economies are being valued quite differently. ■

KEY POINTS

1 Explain the nature and importance of capital investment analysis.

Capital investment analysis is the process by which management plans, evaluates, and controls investments involving fixed assets. Capital investment analysis is important to a business because such investments affect profitability for a long period of time.

2 Evaluate capital investment proposals, using the following methods: average rate of return, cash payback, net present value, and internal rate of return.

The average rate of return method measures the expected profitability of an investment in fixed assets. It is calculated using the following formula:

$$\text{Average rate of return} = \frac{\text{Estimated average annual income}}{\text{Average investment}}$$

The expected period of time that will pass between the date of an investment and the complete recovery in cash (or equivalent) of the amount invested is the cash payback period. Investment proposals with the shortest cash payback are considered the most desirable.

The net present value method uses present values to compute the net present value of the cash flows expected from a proposal. The net present value of the cash flows are then compared across proposals. The present value of a cash flow is computed by looking up the present value of $1 from a table of present values and multiplying it by the amount of the future cash flow, as shown in the text.

The internal rate of return method uses present values to compute the rate of return from the net cash flows expected from capital investment proposals. When equal annual net cash flows are expected from a proposal, the computations are simplified by using a table of the present value of an annuity, as shown in the text.

3 List and describe factors that complicate capital investment analysis.

Factors that may complicate capital investment analysis include the impact of the federal income tax, unequal lives of alternative proposals, leasing, uncertainty, changes in price levels, and qualitative considerations. A brief description of the effect of each of these factors appears in the text.

4 Diagram the capital rationing process.

Capital rationing refers to the process by which management allocates available investment funds among competing capital investment proposals. A diagram of the capital rationing process appears in Exhibit 6.

ILLUSTRATIVE PROBLEM

The capital investment committee of Hopewell Company is currently considering two projects. The estimated income from operations and net cash flows expected from each project are as follows:

	Project A		Project B	
Year	Income from Operations	Net Cash Flow	Income from Operations	Net Cash Flow
1	$ 6,000	$ 22,000	$13,000	$ 29,000
2	9,000	25,000	10,000	26,000
3	10,000	26,000	8,000	24,000
4	8,000	24,000	8,000	24,000
5	11,000	27,000	3,000	19,000
	$44,000	$124,000	$42,000	$122,000

Each project requires an investment of $80,000. Straight-line depreciation will be used, and no residual value is expected. The committee has selected a rate of 15% for purposes of the net present value analysis.

Instructions

1. Compute the following:
   a. The average rate of return for each project.
   b. The net present value for each project. Use the present value of $1 table appearing in this chapter.
2. Why is the net present value of Project B greater than Project A, even though its average rate of return is less?
3. Prepare a summary for the capital investment committee, advising it on the relative merits of the two projects.

Solution

1. a. Average rate of return for Project A:

$$\frac{\$44,000 \div 5}{(\$80,000 + \$0) \div 2} = 22\%$$

Average rate of return for Project B:

$$\frac{\$42,000 \div 5}{(\$80,000 + \$0) \div 2} = 21\%$$

b. Net present value analysis:

Year	Present Value of $1 at 15%	Net Cash Flow Project A	Net Cash Flow Project B	Present Value of Net Cash Flow Project A	Present Value of Net Cash Flow Project B
1	0.870	$ 22,000	$ 29,000	$19,140	$25,230
2	0.756	25,000	26,000	18,900	19,656
3	0.658	26,000	24,000	17,108	15,792
4	0.572	24,000	24,000	13,728	13,728
5	0.497	27,000	19,000	13,419	9,443
Total		$124,000	$122,000	$82,295	$83,849
Amount to be invested				80,000	80,000
Net present value				$ 2,295	$ 3,849

2. Project B has a lower average rate of return than Project A because Project B's total income from operations for the five years is $42,000, which is $2,000 less than Project A's. Even so, the net present value of Project B is greater than that of Project A, because Project B has higher cash flows in the early years.
3. Both projects exceed the selected rate established for the net present value analysis. Project A has a higher average rate of return, but Project B offers a larger net present value. Thus, if only one of the two projects can be accepted, Project B would be the more attractive.

SELF-EXAMINATION QUESTIONS
Answers at End of Chapter

Matching

Match each of the following statements with its proper term. Some terms may not be used.

A. annuity

B. average rate of return

___ 1. A method of analysis of proposed capital investments that focuses on using present value concepts to compute the rate of return from the net cash flows expected from the investment.

C. **capital investment analysis**

D. **capital rationing**

E. **cash payback period**

F. **currency exchange rate**

G. **deflation**

H. **inflation**

I. **internal rate of return method**

J. **net present value method**

K. **present value concept**

L. **present value index**

M. **present value of an annuity**

N. **time value of money concept**

____ 2. An index computed by dividing the total present value of the net cash flow to be received from a proposed capital investment by the amount to be invested.

____ 3. A series of equal cash flows at fixed intervals.

____ 4. The expected period of time that will elapse between the date of a capital expenditure and the complete recovery in cash (or equivalent) of the amount invested.

____ 5. The concept that an amount of money invested today will earn interest.

____ 6. A method of analysis of proposed capital investments that focuses on the present value of the cash flows expected from the investments.

____ 7. The sum of the present values of a series of equal cash flows to be received at fixed intervals.

____ 8. The process by which management plans, evaluates, and controls long-term capital investments involving fixed assets.

____ 9. A period when prices in general are rising and the purchasing power of money is declining.

____ 10. Cash today is not the equivalent of the same amount of money to be received in the future.

____ 11. The process by which management allocates available investment funds among competing capital investment proposals.

____ 12. A method of evaluating capital investment proposals that focuses on the expected profitability of the investment.

____ 13. The rate at which currency in another country can be exchanged for local currency.

Multiple Choice

1. Methods of evaluating capital investment proposals that ignore present value include:
   A. average rate of return
   B. cash payback
   C. both A and B
   D. neither A nor B

2. Management is considering a $100,000 investment in a project with a 5-year life and no residual value. If the total income from the project is expected to be $60,000 and recognition is given to the effect of straight-line depreciation on the investment, the average rate of return is:
   A. 12%   C. 60%
   B. 24%   D. 75%

3. The expected period of time that will elapse between the date of a capital investment and the complete recovery of the amount of cash invested is called:

   A. the average rate of return period
   B. the cash payback period
   C. the net present value period
   D. the internal rate of return period

4. A project that will cost $120,000 is estimated to generate cash flows of $25,000 per year for eight years. What is the net present value of the project, assuming an 11% required rate of return? (Use the present value tables in Appendix A.)
   A. ($38,214)   C. $55,180
   B. $8,653   D. $75,000

5. A project is estimated to generate cash flows of $40,000 per year for 10 years. The cost of the project is $226,009. What is the internal rate of return for this project?
   A. 8%   C. 12%
   B. 10%   D. 14%

CLASS DISCUSSION QUESTIONS

1. Which two methods of capital investment analysis ignore present value?
2. Which two methods of capital investment analysis can be described as present value methods?

3. How is the average rate of return computed for capital investment analysis, assuming that the effect of straight-line depreciation on the amount of the investment is considered?

4. What are the principal objections to the use of the average rate of return method in evaluating capital investment proposals?

5. Discuss the principal limitations of the cash payback method for evaluating capital investment proposals.

6. Which method of evaluating capital investment proposals reduces their expected future net cash flows to present values and compares the total present values to the amount of the investment?

7. A net present value analysis used to evaluate a proposed equipment acquisition indicated a $9,750 net present value. What is the meaning of the $9,750 as it relates to the desirability of the proposal?

8. How is the present value index for a proposal determined?

9. What are the major disadvantages of the use of the net present value method of analyzing capital investment proposals?

10. What are the major disadvantages of the use of the internal rate of return method of analyzing capital investment proposals?

11. What provision of the Internal Revenue Code is especially important to consider in analyzing capital investment proposals?

12. What method can be used to place two capital investment proposals with unequal useful lives on a comparable basis?

13. What are the major advantages of leasing a fixed asset rather than purchasing it?

14. Give an example of a qualitative factor that should be considered in a capital investment analysis related to acquiring automated factory equipment.

15. **Monsanto**, a large chemical and fibers company, invested $37 million in state-of-the-art systems to improve process control, laboratory automation, and local area network (LAN) communications. The investment was not justified merely on cost savings but was also justified on the basis of qualitative considerations. Monsanto management viewed the investment as a critical element toward achieving its vision of the future. What qualitative and quantitative considerations do you believe Monsanto would have considered in its strategic evaluation of these investments?

Real World

RESOURCES FOR YOUR SUCCESS ONLINE AT

http://warren.swcollege.com

Warren
Reeve
Fess

Remember! If you need additional help, visit South-Western's Web site.
See page M28 for a description of the online and printed materials that are available.

EXERCISES

Exercise 9–1

Average rate of return

Objective 2

✓ Turning machine, 12.5%

The following data are accumulated by Mora Machining Company in evaluating two competing capital investment proposals:

	Turning Machine	Milling Machine
Amount of investment	$36,000	$48,000
Useful life	4 years	5 years
Estimated residual value	-0-	-0-
Estimated total income over the useful life	$ 9,000	$12,000

Determine the expected average rate of return for each proposal.

Exercise 9–2

Average rate of return—cost savings

Objective 2

Millwood Company is considering an investment in equipment that will replace direct labor. The equipment has a cost of $61,000, with a $6,000 residual value and an 11-year life. The equipment will replace one employee who has an average wage of $18,000 per year. In addition, the equipment will have operating and energy costs of $9,315 per year.

Determine the average rate of return on the equipment, giving effect to straight-line depreciation on the investment.

Exercise 9–3

Average rate of return—new product

Objective 2

✓ Average annual income, $360,000

Portable Communications Inc. is considering an investment in new equipment that will be used to manufacture a pager. The pager is expected to generate additional annual sales of 18,000 units at $75 per unit. The equipment has a cost of $870,000, residual value of $30,000, and a 10-year life. The equipment can only be used to manufacture the pager. The cost to manufacture the pager is shown below.

Cost per unit:	
Direct labor	$15.00
Direct materials	22.00
Factory overhead (including depreciation)	18.00
Total cost per unit	$55.00

Determine the average rate of return on the equipment.

Exercise 9–4

Calculate cash flows

Objective 2

✓ Year 1: ($141,600)

Cornucopia Inc. is planning to invest $206,000 in a new garden tool that is expected to generate additional sales of 8,000 units at $24 each. The $206,000 investment includes $46,000 for initial launch-related expenses and $160,000 for equipment that has a 15-year life and a $10,000 residual value. Selling expenses related to the new product are expected to be 5% of sales revenue. The cost to manufacture the product includes the following per unit costs:

Direct labor	$ 5.00
Direct materials	8.25
Fixed factory overhead—depreciation	1.25
Variable factory overhead	1.50
Total	$16.00

Determine the net cash flows for the first year of the project, years 2–14, and for the last year of the project.

Exercise 9–5

Cash payback period

Objective 2

✓ Proposal 1: 5 years

United Security Bank Corporation is evaluating two capital investment proposals for a drive-up ATM, each requiring an investment of $200,000 and each with an 8-year life and expected total net cash flows of $320,000. Location 1 is expected to provide equal annual net cash flows of $40,000, and Location 2 is expected to have the following unequal annual net cash flows:

Year 1	$70,000	Year 5	$30,000
Year 2	50,000	Year 6	30,000
Year 3	40,000	Year 7	30,000
Year 4	40,000	Year 8	30,000

Determine the cash payback period for both proposals.

Exercise 9–6

Cash payback method

Objective 2

✓ a. Cosmetics: 4 years

Johnson Consumer Products Company is considering an investment in one of two new product lines. The investment required for either product line is $360,000. The net cash flows associated with each product are as follows:

	Liquid Soap	Cosmetics
Year 1	$ 50,000	$ 90,000
2	60,000	90,000
3	70,000	90,000
4	80,000	90,000
5	100,000	90,000
6	120,000	90,000
7	120,000	90,000
8	120,000	90,000
Total	$720,000	$720,000

a. Recommend a product offering to Johnson Consumer Products Company, based on the cash payback period for each product line.
b. ✏️ Why is one product line preferred over the other, even though they both have the same total net cash flows through eight periods?

Exercise 9–7
Net present value method

Objective 2

✓ a. NPV $12,560

The following data are accumulated by Markon Container Company in evaluating the purchase of $300,000 of equipment, having a 4-year useful life:

	Net Income	Net Cash Flow
Year 1	$65,000	$140,000
Year 2	25,000	100,000
Year 3	5,000	80,000
Year 4	5,000	80,000

a. Assuming that the desired rate of return is 12%, determine the net present value for the proposal. Use the table of the present value of $1 appearing in this chapter.
b. ✏️ Would management be likely to look with favor on the proposal? Explain.

Exercise 9–8
Net present value method

Objective 2

✓ a. $62,956

Corcoran Group, Inc., a New York real-estate broker, determined that its new Web site generated $120,000,000 of real estate sales for the year. Corcoran estimated that the Web site should be credited with revenue equal to 0.6% of sales, which is the rate Corcoran ordinarily pays individuals who pass along sales leads. In addition, the annual cash expenses for supporting the Web site were approximately $670,000 for the year. Assume that the initial cost to set up the Web site was $100,000 and that annual net cash flow is expected to grow by 10% per year for three more years.

a. Determine the net present value of the Web site investment if the desired rate of return is 15%. Use the table of the present value of $1 appearing in Exhibit 1 of this chapter. Round to the nearest dollar.
b. ✏️ Under the assumptions provided here, is the Web site expected to be an acceptable investment?

Exercise 9–9
Net present value method—annuity

Objective 2

✓ a. $41,500

Laidlow Excavation Company is planning an investment of $160,000 for a bulldozer. The bulldozer is expected to operate for 1,500 hours per year for five years. Customers will be charged $90 per hour for bulldozer work. The bulldozer operator is paid an hourly wage of $32 per hour. The bulldozer is expected to require annual maintenance costing $8,000. The bulldozer uses fuel that is expected to cost $25 per hour of bulldozer operation.

a. Determine the equal annual net cash flows from operating the bulldozer.
b. Determine the net present value of the investment, assuming that the desired rate of return is 10%. Use the table of present values of an annuity of $1 in the chapter. Round to the nearest dollar.
c. ✏️ Should Laidlow invest in the bulldozer, based on this analysis?

Exercise 9–10
Net present value—unequal lives

Objectives 2, 3

✓ Net present value, Apartment Complex, $8,840

Crider Development Company has two competing projects: an apartment complex and an office building. Both projects have an initial investment of $460,000. The net cash flows estimated for the two projects are as follows:

	Net Cash Flow	
Year	**Apartment Complex**	**Office Building**
1	$160,000	$180,000
2	150,000	180,000
3	120,000	150,000
4	100,000	150,000
5	100,000	
6	90,000	
7	80,000	
8	60,000	

The estimated residual value of the Apartment Complex at the end of year 4 is $140,000.

Determine which project should be favored, comparing the net present values of the two projects and assuming a minimum rate of return of 15%. Use the table of present values in the chapter.

Exercise 9–11
Net present value method

Objective 2

Real World

✓ a. $105,945,000

The **Royal Caribbean Cruise Line (RCCL)** has recently placed into service the largest cruise ship in the world. The "Eagle Class" ship can hold up to 3,100 passengers and cost $600 million to build. Assume the following additional information:

- The average occupancy rate for the new ship is estimated to be 70% of capacity.
- There will be 300 cruise days per year.
- The variable expenses per passenger are estimated to be $50 per day.
- The revenue per passenger is expected to be $245 per day.
- The fixed expenses for running the ship, other than depreciation, are estimated to be $21,000,000 per year.
- The ship has a service life of 10 years, with a salvage value of $50,000,000 at the end of 10 years.

a. Determine the annual net cash flow from operating the cruise ship.
b. Determine the net present value of this investment, assuming a 12% minimum rate of return. Use the present value tables provided in the chapter in determining your answer.
c. Assume that RCCL decided to increase its price so that the revenue increased to $260 per passenger per day. Would this allow RCCL to earn a 15% rate of return on the cruise ship investment? Use the present value tables provided in the chapter in determining your answer.

Exercise 9–12
Present value index

Objective 2

✓ Proposal A, 1.02

Panorama Glass Company has computed the net present value for capital expenditure proposals A and B, using the net present value method. Relevant data related to the computation are as follows:

	Proposal A	**Proposal B**
Total present value of net cash flow	$267,240	$321,750
Amount to be invested	262,000	325,000
Net present value	$ 5,240	$ (3,250)

Determine the present value index for each proposal.

Exercise 9–13
Net present value method and present value index

Objective 2

✓ b. Packing Machine, 1.11

AllStar Sporting Goods Company is considering an investment in one of two machines. The sewing machine will increase productivity from sewing 120 baseballs per hour to sewing 160 per hour. The contribution margin is $0.70 per baseball. Assume that any increased production of baseballs can be sold. The second machine is an automatic packaging machine for the golf ball line. The packaging machine will reduce packing labor cost. The labor cost saved is equivalent to $21 per hour. The sewing machine will cost

$230,525, have an 8-year life, and will operate for 2,000 hours per year. The packing machine will cost $136,027, have an 8-year life, and will operate for 1,600 hours per year. AllStar seeks a minimum rate of return of 15% on its investments.

a. Determine the net present value for the two machines. Use the table of present values of an annuity of $1 in the chapter. Round to the nearest dollar.
b. Determine the present value index for the two machines. Round to 2 decimal places.
c. If AllStar has sufficient funds for only one of the machines and qualitative factors are equal between the two machines, in which machine should it invest?

Exercise 9–14
Average rate of return, cash payback period, net present value method

Objective 2

SPREADSHEET

✓ b. 4 years

Hi-Temper Forging Company is considering acquiring equipment at a cost of $375,000. The equipment has an estimated life of 10 years and no residual value. It is expected to provide yearly net cash flows of $93,750. The company's minimum desired rate of return for net present value analysis is 12%.

Compute the following:

a. The average rate of return, giving effect to straight-line depreciation on the investment.
b. The cash payback period.
c. The net present value. Use the table of the present value of an annuity of $1 appearing in this chapter. Round to the nearest dollar.

Exercise 9–15
Internal rate of return method

Objective 2

✓ a. 4.487

The internal rate of return method is used by Ace Storage and Moving Company in analyzing a capital expenditure proposal that involves an investment of $62,818 and annual net cash flows of $14,000 for each of the 8 years of its useful life.

a. Determine a present value factor for an annuity of $1 which can be used in determining the internal rate of return.
b. Using the factor determined in (a) and the present value of an annuity of $1 table appearing in this chapter, determine the internal rate of return for the proposal.

Exercise 9–16
Internal rate of return method

Objective 2

Real World

IBM Corporation recently saved $250 million over three years by implementing supply chain software that reduced the cost of components used in its manufacture of computers. If we assume that the savings occurred equally over the three years and the cost of implementing the new software was $175,500,000, what would be the internal rate of return for this investment? Use the present value of an annuity of $1 table found in Exhibit 2 in determining your answer.

Exercise 9–17
Internal rate of return method—two projects

Objective 2

✓ a. Delivery truck, 12%

Salty Popcorn Company is considering two possible investments: a delivery truck or a bagging machine. The delivery truck would cost $28,777 and could be used to deliver an additional 35,000 bags of popcorn per year. Each bag of popcorn can be sold for a contribution margin of $0.30. The delivery truck operating expenses, excluding depreciation, are $0.25 per mile for 14,000 miles per year. The bagging machine would replace an old bagging machine, and its net investment cost would be $22,710. The new machine would require 2 fewer hours of direct labor per day. Direct labor is $12 per hour. There are 250 operating days in the year. Both the truck and the bagging machine are estimated to have 6-year lives. The minimum rate of return is 11%. However, Salty has funds to invest in only *one* of the projects.

a. Compute the internal rate of return for each investment. Use the table of present values of an annuity of $1 in the chapter.
b. Provide a memo to management with a recommendation.

Exercise 9–18
Net present value method and internal rate of return method

Objective 2

✓ a. ($8,080)

Janitor Supply Co. is proposing to spend $91,280 on a 7-year project whose estimated net cash flows are $20,000 for each of the seven years.

a. Compute the net present value, using a rate of return of 15%. Use the table of present values of an annuity of $1 in the chapter.
b. ▟▬▶ Based on the analysis prepared in (a), is the rate of return (1) more than 15%, (2) 15%, or (3) less than 15%? Explain.
c. Determine the internal rate of return by computing a present value factor for an annuity of $1 and using the table of the present value of an annuity of $1 presented in the text.

Exercise 9–19
Identify error in capital investment analysis calculations

Objective 2

Fastex Computer Company is considering the purchase of automated machinery that is expected to have a useful life of 4 years and no residual value. The average rate of return on the average investment has been computed to be 25%, and the cash payback period was computed to be 4.5 years.

▟▬▶ Do you see any reason to question the validity of the data presented? Explain.

Exercise 9–20
Changing prices

Objective 3

Hardy Company invested $1,000,000 to build a plant in a foreign country. The labor and materials used in production are purchased locally. The plant expansion was estimated to produce an internal rate of return of 20% in U.S. dollar terms. Due to a currency crisis, the currency exchange rate between the local currency and the U.S. dollar doubled from 4 local units per U.S. dollar to 8 local units per U.S. dollar.

a. ▟▬▶ Assume that the plant produced and sold product in the local economy. Explain what impact this change in the currency exchange rate would have on the project's internal rate of return.
b. ▟▬▶ Assume that the plant produced product in the local economy but exported the product back to the United States for sale. Explain what impact the change in the currency exchange rate would have on the project's internal rate of return under this assumption.

PROBLEMS SERIES A

Problem 9–1A
Average rate of return method, net present value method, and analysis

Objective 2

SPREADSHEET

✓ 1. a. 20%

The capital investment committee of Beautify Landscaping Company is considering two capital investments. The estimated income from operations and net cash flows from each investment are as follows:

Year	Greenhouse Income from Operations	Greenhouse Net Cash Flow	Skid Loader Income from Operations	Skid Loader Net Cash Flow
1	$ 5,000	$15,000	$15,000	$25,000
2	5,000	15,000	10,000	20,000
3	5,000	15,000	5,000	15,000
4	5,000	15,000	0	10,000
5	5,000	15,000	(5,000)	5,000
	$25,000	$75,000	$25,000	$75,000

Each project requires an investment of $50,000. Straight-line depreciation will be used, and no residual value is expected. The committee has selected a rate of 10% for purposes of the net present value analysis.

Instructions

1. Compute the following:
   a. The average rate of return for each investment.
   b. The net present value for each investment. Use the present value of $1 table appearing in this chapter.
2. ◀▬▬► Prepare a brief report for the capital investment committee, advising it on the relative merits of the two investments.

Problem 9–2A
Cash payback period, net present value method, and analysis

Objective 2

✓ 1. b. Plant Expansion, $11,370

Echo Clothes Company is considering two investment projects. The estimated net cash flows from each project are as follows:

Year	Plant Expansion	Retail Store Expansion
1	$100,000	$150,000
2	130,000	120,000
3	150,000	110,000
4	130,000	110,000
5	170,000	190,000
Total	$680,000	$680,000

Each project requires an investment of $380,000. A rate of 20% has been selected for the net present value analysis.

Instructions

1. Compute the following for each project:
   a. Cash payback period.
   b. The net present value. Use the present value of $1 table appearing in this chapter.
2. ◀▬▬► Prepare a brief report advising management on the relative merits of each of the two projects.

Problem 9–3A
Net present value method, present value index, and analysis

Objective 2

✓ 2. Railcars, 1.08

Rocky Mountain Railroad Company wishes to evaluate three capital investment proposals by using the net present value method. Relevant data related to the proposals are summarized as follows:

	Route Expansion	Acquire Railcars	New Maintenance Yard
Amount to be invested	$560,000	$280,000	$425,000
Annual net cash flows:			
Year 1	200,000	140,000	175,000
Year 2	250,000	130,000	175,000
Year 3	350,000	125,000	200,000

Instructions

1. Assuming that the desired rate of return is 15%, prepare a net present value analysis for each proposal. Use the present value of $1 table appearing in this chapter.
2. Determine a present value index for each proposal. Round to two decimal places.
3. ◀▬▬► Which proposal offers the largest amount of present value per dollar of investment? Explain.

Problem 9–4A
Net present value method, rate of return method, and analysis

Objective 2

The management of Western Utilities Inc. is considering two capital investment projects. The estimated net cash flows from each project are as follows:

✓ 1. a. Generating unit, $34,580

Year	Generating Unit	Distribution Network Expansion
1	$260,000	$90,000
2	260,000	90,000
3	260,000	90,000
4	260,000	90,000

The generating unit requires an investment of $789,620, while the distribution network expansion requires an investment of $256,950. No residual value is expected from either project.

Instructions

1. Compute the following for each project:
   a. The net present value. Use a rate of 10% and the present value of an annuity of $1 table appearing in this chapter.
   b. A present value index. Round to 2 decimal places.
2. Determine the internal rate of return for each project by (a) computing a present value factor for an annuity of $1 and (b) using the present value of an annuity of $1 table appearing in this chapter.
3. ✏️ What advantage does the internal rate of return method have over the net present value method in comparing projects?

Problem 9–5A

Evaluate alternative capital investment decisions

Objectives 2, 3

✓ 2. Project II, $12,080

The investment committee of Jake's Brewery Inc. is evaluating two projects. The projects have different useful lives, but each requires an investment of $145,000. The estimated net cash flows from each project are as follows:

	Net Cash Flows	
Year	Project I	Project II
1	$40,000	$55,000
2	40,000	55,000
3	40,000	55,000
4	40,000	55,000
5	40,000	
6	40,000	

The committee has selected a rate of 15% for purposes of net present value analysis. It also estimates that the residual value at the end of each project's useful life is $0, but at the end of the fourth year, Project I's residual value would be $60,000.

Instructions

1. For each project, compute the net present value. Use the present value of an annuity of $1 table appearing in this chapter. (Ignore the unequal lives of the projects.)
2. For each project, compute the net present value, assuming that Project I is adjusted to a 4-year life for purposes of analysis. Use the present value of $1 table appearing in this chapter.
3. ✏️ Prepare a report to the investment committee, providing your advice on the relative merits of the two projects.

Problem 9–6A

Capital rationing decision involving four proposals

Objectives 2, 4

✓ 5. Proposal B, 1.23

Columbus Capital Group is considering allocating a limited amount of capital investment funds among four proposals. The amount of proposed investment, estimated income from operations, and net cash flow for each proposal are as follows:

	Investment	Year	Income from Operations	Net Cash Flow
Proposal A:	$600,000	1	$40,000	$160,000
		2	40,000	160,000
		3	40,000	160,000
		4	0	120,000
		5	0	120,000
Proposal B:	$520,000	1	$96,000	$200,000
		2	56,000	160,000
		3	56,000	160,000
		4	56,000	160,000
		5	48,000	152,000
Proposal C:	$180,000	1	$44,000	$ 80,000
		2	24,000	60,000
		3	24,000	60,000
		4	24,000	60,000
		5	22,500	58,500
Proposal D:	$250,000	1	$50,000	$100,000
		2	50,000	100,000
		3	(10,000)	40,000
		4	(10,000)	40,000
		5	(10,000)	40,000

The company's capital rationing policy requires a maximum cash payback period of three years. In addition, a minimum average rate of return of 10% is required on all projects. If the preceding standards are met, the net present value method and present value indexes are used to rank the remaining proposals.

Instructions

1. Compute the cash payback period for each of the four proposals.
2. Giving effect to straight-line depreciation on the investments and assuming no estimated residual value, compute the average rate of return for each of the four proposals. Round to 1 decimal place.
3. Using the following format, summarize the results of your computations in (1) and (2). By placing a check mark in the appropriate column at the right, indicate which proposals should be accepted for further analysis and which should be rejected.

Proposal	Cash Payback Period	Average Rate of Return	Accept for Further Analysis	Reject
A				
B				
C				
D				

4. For the proposals accepted for further analysis in (3), compute the net present value. Use a rate of 10% and the present value of $1 table appearing in this chapter. Round to the nearest dollar.
5. Compute the present value index for each of the proposals in (4). Round to 2 decimal places.
6. Rank the proposals from most attractive to least attractive, based on the present values of net cash flows computed in (4).
7. Rank the proposals from most attractive to least attractive, based on the present value indexes computed in (5).
8. ▪━━► Based upon the analyses, comment on the relative attractiveness of the proposals ranked in (6) and (7).

PROBLEMS SERIES B

Problem 9–1B
Average rate of return method, net present value method, and analysis

Objective 2

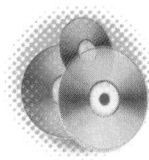

SPREADSHEET

✓ 1. a. 22.5%

The capital investment committee of Coastal Trucking Inc. is considering two investment projects. The estimated income from operations and net cash flows from each investment are as follows:

	Warehouse		Parcel Tracking Technology	
Year	Income from Operations	Net Cash Flow	Income from Operations	Net Cash Flow
1	$ 54,000	$150,000	$ 34,000	$130,000
2	54,000	150,000	44,000	140,000
3	54,000	150,000	54,000	150,000
4	54,000	150,000	64,000	160,000
5	54,000	150,000	74,000	170,000
Total	$270,000	$750,000	$270,000	$750,000

Each project requires an investment of $480,000. Straight-line depreciation will be used, and no residual value is expected. The committee has selected a rate of 12% for purposes of the net present value analysis.

Instructions

1. Compute the following:
   a. The average rate of return for each investment.
   b. The net present value for each investment. Use the present value of $1 table appearing in this chapter.
2. ✏️ Prepare a brief report for the capital investment committee, advising it on the relative merits of the two projects.

Problem 9–2B
Cash payback period, net present value method, and analysis

Objective 2

✓ 1. b. DVD Player, $164,800

Vista Consumer Electronics Company is considering two new products. The estimated net cash flows from each product are as follows:

Year	DVD Player	Digital TV
1	$ 350,000	$ 200,000
2	350,000	500,000
3	200,000	400,000
4	200,000	50,000
5	100,000	50,000
Total	$1,200,000	$1,200,000

Each product requires an investment of $700,000. A rate of 15% has been selected for the net present value analysis.

Instructions

1. Compute the following for each project:
   a. Cash payback period.
   b. The net present value. Use the present value of $1 table appearing in this chapter.
2. ✏️ Prepare a brief report advising management on the relative merits of each of the two products.

Problem 9–3B
Net present value method, present value index, and analysis

Objective 2

Moneyease Financial Company wishes to evaluate three capital investment projects by using the net present value method. Relevant data related to the projects are summarized as follows:

	Branch Office Expansion	Computer System Upgrade	Install ATM Network
Amount to be invested	$450,000	$300,000	$250,000
Annual net cash flows:			
Year 1	250,000	150,000	150,000
Year 2	220,000	125,000	130,000
Year 3	200,000	125,000	100,000

Instructions

1. Assuming that the desired rate of return is 20%, prepare a net present value analysis for each project. Use the present value of $1 table appearing in this chapter.
2. Determine a present value index for each project. Round to 2 decimal places.
3. ◀▬▬▶ Which project offers the largest amount of present value per dollar of investment? Explain.

Problem 9–4B
Net present value method, internal rate of return method, and analysis

Objective 2

The management of Archway Entertainment Group is considering two capital investment projects. The estimated net cash flows from each project are as follows:

Year	Radio Station	TV Station
1	$150,000	$400,000
2	150,000	400,000
3	150,000	400,000
4	150,000	400,000

The radio station requires an investment of $388,350, while the TV station requires an investment of $1,142,000. No residual value is expected from either project.

Instructions

1. Compute the following for each project:
   a. The net present value. Use a rate of 12% and the present value of an annuity of $1 table appearing in this chapter.
   b. A present value index. Round to 2 decimal places.
2. Determine the internal rate of return for each project by (a) computing a present value factor for an annuity of $1 and (b) using the present value of an annuity of $1 table appearing in this chapter.
3. ◀▬▬▶ What advantage does the internal rate of return method have over the net present value method in comparing projects?

Problem 9–5B
Evaluate alternative capital investment decisions

Objectives 2, 3

The investment committee of Eatwell Restaurants Inc. is evaluating two restaurant sites. The sites have different useful lives, but each requires an investment of $340,000. The estimated net cash flows from each site are as follows:

	Net Cash Flows	
Year	Site A	Site B
1	$100,000	$130,000
2	100,000	130,000
3	100,000	130,000
4	100,000	130,000
5	100,000	
6	100,000	

The committee has selected a rate of 15% for purposes of net present value analysis. It also estimates that the residual value at the end of each restaurant's useful life is $0, but at the end of the fourth year, Site A's residual value would be $160,000.

Instructions

1. For each site, compute the net present value. Use the present value of an annuity of $1 table appearing in this chapter. (Ignore the unequal lives of the projects.)
2. For each site, compute the net present value, assuming that Site A is adjusted to a 4-year life for purposes of analysis. Use the present value of $1 table appearing in this chapter.
3. ◄━━━━━► Prepare a report to the investment committee, providing your advice on the relative merits of the two sites.

Problem 9–6B
Capital rationing decision involving four proposals

Objectives 2, 4

✓ I. Proposal D, 3 years

Moonglow Broadcasting Company is considering allocating a limited amount of capital investment funds among four proposals. The amount of proposed investment, estimated income from operations, and net cash flow for each proposal are as follows:

	Investment	Year	Income from Operations	Net Cash Flow
Proposal A:	$800,000	1	$80,000	$240,000
		2	80,000	240,000
		3	80,000	240,000
		4	80,000	240,000
		5	40,000	200,000
Proposal B:	$ 96,000	1	$20,800	$ 40,000
		2	36,800	56,000
		3	800	20,000
		4	800	20,000
		5	800	20,000
Proposal C:	$240,000	1	$12,000	$ 60,000
		2	12,000	60,000
		3	12,000	60,000
		4	12,000	60,000
		5	(18,000)	30,000
Proposal D:	$168,000	1	$22,400	$ 56,000
		2	22,400	56,000
		3	22,400	56,000
		4	17,000	50,600
		5	12,400	46,000

The company's capital rationing policy requires a maximum cash payback period of three years. In addition, a minimum average rate of return of 10% is required on all projects. If the preceding standards are met, the net present value method and present value indexes are used to rank the remaining proposals.

Instructions

1. Compute the cash payback period for each of the four proposals.
2. Giving effect to straight-line depreciation on the investments and assuming no estimated residual value, compute the average rate of return for each of the four proposals.
3. Using the following format, summarize the results of your computations in (1) and (2). By placing a check mark in the appropriate column at the right, indicate which proposals should be accepted for further analysis and which should be rejected.

Proposal	Cash Payback Period	Average Rate of Return	Accept for Further Analysis	Reject
A				
B				
C				
D				

4. For the proposals accepted for further analysis in (3), compute the net present value. Use a rate of 10% and the present value of $1 table appearing in this chapter. Round to the nearest dollar.

5. Compute the present value index for each of the proposals in (4). Round to two decimal places.

6. Rank the proposals from most attractive to least attractive, based on the present values of net cash flows computed in (4).

7. Rank the proposals from most attractive to least attractive, based on the present value indexes computed in (5). Round to two decimal places.

8. ✏➤ Based upon the analyses, comment on the relative attractiveness of the proposals ranked in (6) and (7).

SPECIAL ACTIVITIES

Activity 9–1
Converse Company
Ethics and professional conduct in business

Sherry Dale was recently hired as a cost analyst by Converse Company. One of Sherry's first assignments was to perform a net present value analysis for a new warehouse. Sherry performed the analysis and calculated a present value index of 0.75. The plant manager, I. M. Madd, is very intent on purchasing the warehouse because he believes that more storage space is needed. I. M. Madd asks Sherry into his office and the following conversation takes place.

I. M.: Dale, you're new here, aren't you?

Sherry: Yes, sir.

I. M.: Well, Dale, let me tell you something. I'm not at all pleased with the capital investment analysis that you performed on this new warehouse. I need that warehouse for my production. If I don't get it, where am I going to place our output?

Sherry: Hopefully with the customer, sir.

I. M.: Now don't get smart with me, young woman.

Sherry: No, really, I was being serious. My analysis does not support constructing a new warehouse. There is no way that I can get the numbers to make this a favorable investment. In fact, it seems to me that purchasing a warehouse does not add much value to the business. We need to be producing product to satisfy customer orders, not to fill a warehouse.

I. M.: Listen, you need to understand something. The headquarters people will not allow me to build the warehouse if the numbers don't add up. I know as well as you that many assumptions go into your net present value analysis. Why don't you relax some of your assumptions so that the financial savings will offset the cost?

Sherry: I'm willing to discuss my assumptions with you. Maybe I overlooked something.

I. M.: Good. Here's what I want you to do. I see in your analysis that you don't project greater sales as a result of the warehouse. It seems to me, if we can store more goods, then we will have more to sell. Thus, logically, a larger warehouse translates into more sales. If you incorporate this into your analysis, I think you'll see that the numbers will work out. Why don't you work it through and come back with a new analysis. I'm really counting on you on this one. Let's get off to a good start together and see if we can get this project accepted.

✏➤ What is your advice to Sherry?

Activity 9–2
Federal Mogul
Qualitative considerations

Some companies have attempted to respond to competitive pressure by relying solely on automation. For example, **Federal Mogul**, a parts supplier to the automotive industry, invested in robots, production line computers, and automated materials movement systems in order to regain a cost advantage that it lost to Japanese competitors. Unfortunately, this automation not only failed to lower costs but caused the plant to become much less flexible than required by its customers. The high technology could not be "changed over" quickly from one product to another. In addition, Federal Mogul found that the new automation reduced employee motivation. As indicated by one of the managers, "Very clearly, we made some poor decisions. One of them was that high-tech was the answer."

✏➤ Why might relying solely on automation lead to lower profits?

Activity 9–3
Celco Power Equipment Company
Investment analysis and qualitative considerations

The plant manager of Celco Power Equipment Company is considering the purchase of a new robotic assembly plant. The new robotic line will cost $1,250,000. The manager believes that the new investment will result in direct labor savings of $250,000 per year for ten years.

1. What is the payback period on this project?
2. What is the net present value, assuming a 10% rate of return?
3. ▸ What else should the manager consider in the analysis?

Activity 9–4
Worthington Industries, Amgen, and Merck & Co.
Qualitative issues in investment analysis

The following are some selected quotes from senior executives:

John H. McConnel, CEO, **Worthington Industries** (a high technology steel company): *"We try to find the best technology, stay ahead of the competition, and serve the customer. . . . We'll make any investment that will pay back quickly . . . but if it is something that we really see as a must down the road, payback is not going to be that important."*

George Rathmann, Chairman Emeritus of **Amgen** (a biotech company): *"You cannot really run the numbers, do net present value calculations, because the uncertainties are really gigantic . . . You decide on a project you want to run, and then you run the numbers [as a reality check on your assumptions]. Success in a business like this is much more dependent on tracking rather than on predicting, much more dependent on seeing results over time, tracking and adjusting and readjusting, much more dynamic, much more flexible."*

Judy Lewent, Chief Financial Officer of **Merck & Co.** (a pharmaceutical company): *". . . at the individual product level—the development of a successful new product requires on the order of $230 million in R&D, spread over more than a decade—discounted cash flow style analysis does not become a factor until development is near the point of manufacturing scale-up effort. Prior to that point, given the uncertainties associated with new product development, it would be lunacy in our business to decide that we know exactly what's going to happen to a product once it gets out."*

▸ Explain the role of capital investment analysis for these companies.

Activity 9–5
Wonder Studios Inc.
Analyze cash flows

You are considering an investment of $360,000 in either Project A or Project B for Wonder Studios Inc. In discussing the two projects with an advisor, you decided that, for the risk involved, a return of 12% on the cash investment would be required. For this purpose, you estimated the following economic factors for the projects:

	Project A	Project B
Useful life	4 years	4 years
Residual value	-0-	-0-
Net income:		
Year 1	$ 65,000	$ 25,000
2	50,000	40,000
3	40,000	58,000
4	25,000	64,200
Net cash flows:		
Year 1	$155,000	$115,000
2	140,000	130,000
3	130,000	148,000
4	115,000	154,200

Although the average rate of return exceeded 12% on both projects, you have tentatively decided to invest in Project B because the rate was higher for Project B. You noted that the total net cash flow from Project B is $547,200, which exceeds that of Project A by $7,200.

1. Determine the average rate of return for both projects.
2. ▸ Why is the timing of cash flows important in evaluating capital investments? Calculate the net present value of the two projects at a minimum rate of return of 12% to demonstrate the importance of net cash flows and their timing to these two projects. Round to the nearest dollar.

Activity 9–6
Into the Real World
Capital investment analysis

In one group, find a local business, such as a copy shop, that rents time on micro-computers for an hourly rate. Determine the hourly rate. In the other group, determine the price of a mid-range microcomputer at **www.dell.com**. Combine this information from the two groups and perform a capital budgeting analysis. Assume that one student will use the computer for 35 hours per semester for the next three years. Also assume that the minimum rate of return is 10%. Use the interest tables in Appendix A in performing your analysis. (*Hint:* Use the appropriate present value factor for 5% compounded for six semiannual periods.)

Does your analysis support the student purchasing the computer?

ANSWERS TO SELF-EXAMINATION QUESTIONS

Matching

1. I	3. A	5. N	7. M	9. H	11. D	13. F
2. L	4. E	6. J	8. C	10. K	12. B	

Multiple Choice

1. **C** Methods of evaluating capital investment proposals that ignore the time value of money are categorized as methods that ignore present value. This category includes the average rate of return method (answer A) and the cash payback method (answer B).

2. **B** The average rate of return is 24% (answer B), determined by dividing the expected average annual earnings by the average investment, as follows:

$$\frac{\$60,000 \div 5}{(\$100,000 - \$0) \div 2} = 24\%$$

3. **B** Of the four methods of analyzing proposals for capital investments, the cash payback period (answer B) refers to the expected period of time required to recover the amount of cash to be invested. The average rate of return (answer A) is a measure of the anticipated profitability of a proposal. The net present value method (answer C) reduces the expected future net cash flows originating from a proposal to their present values. The internal rate of return method (answer D) uses present value concepts to compute the

rate of return from the net cash flows expected from the investment.

4. **B** The net present value is determined as follows:

Present value of $25,000 for 8 years at 11%	
($25,000 × 5.14612)	$128,653
Less: Project cost	120,000
Net present value	$ 8,653

5. **C** The internal rate of return for this project is determined by solving for the present value of an annuity factor that when multiplied by $40,000 will equal $226,009. By division, the factor is:

$$\frac{\$226,009}{\$40,000} = 5.65022$$

In Appendix A on pp. A-4 and A-5, scan along the n = 10 years row until finding the 5.65022 factor. The column for this factor is 12%.

Cost Allocation and Activity-Based Costing

M10

objectives

After studying this chapter, you should be able to:

1 Identify three methods used for allocating factory overhead costs to products.

2 Use a single plantwide factory overhead rate for product costing.

3 Use multiple production department factory overhead rates for product costing.

4 Use activity-based costing for product costing.

5 Use activity-based costing to allocate selling and administrative expenses to products.

6 Use activity-based costing in a service business.

Have you ever had to request service repairs on an appliance at your home? The repair person may arrive and take five minutes to replace a part, yet the bill may indicate a charge for a minimum amount that is more than five minutes of work. Why might the service person have a minimum charge just for showing up? The answer is that the service person must charge for the time and expense of coming to your house. In a sense, the bill reflects two elements of service: the cost of coming to your house and the cost of providing the service. The first portion of the cost reflects the time required to "set up" the job, while the second part of the cost reflects the cost of performing the service. Notice that the setup charge will be the same, whether the repairs take five minutes or five hours. In contrast, the second portion of the bill that reflects the actual service performed varies with the time on the job. Like the repair person, companies must be careful to cost their products and services to reflect the different activities involved in producing the product. Otherwise, the cost of products and services may be distorted and lead to improper management decisions.

In this chapter we will explain and illustrate three different methods of allocating factory overhead to products. In addition, we will explain how product cost distortions can result from improper factory overhead allocation. We will end the chapter by explaining and illustrating how overhead costs can be allocated to services.

Product Costing Allocation Methods

objective 1

Identify three methods used for allocating factory overhead costs to products.

How does **Ford Motor Company** determine if its *Windstar* minivan is a profitable product? First, it needs to determine the revenues earned from selling the vans. Most companies have accounting systems that trace revenues to individual product lines. In addition, however, Ford needs to subtract the cost of manufacturing *Windstar* vans in order to determine the profit from *Windstar* sales. Ford's cost accounting system provides this cost information. Determining the cost of the *Windstar* van, or any other product, is termed **product costing**.

We introduced product costing in the job order costing chapter. We stated that product costs consist of direct materials, direct labor, and factory overhead. The direct materials and direct labor are direct to the product. However, factory overhead is often indirect to products and must be allocated. In this chapter we will illustrate three different factory overhead allocation approaches: (1) the single plantwide factory overhead rate method, (2) the multiple production department factory overhead rate method, and (3) the activity-based costing method.

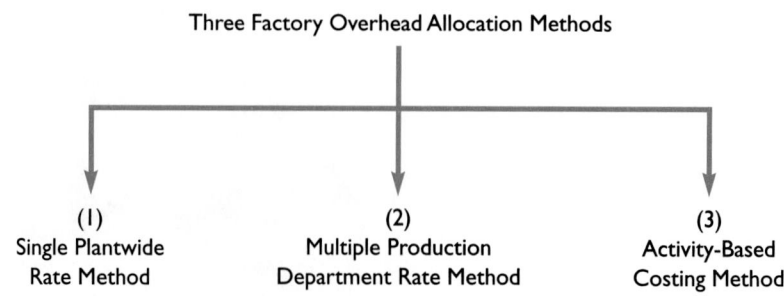

Three Factory Overhead Allocation Methods

(1) Single Plantwide Rate Method

(2) Multiple Production Department Rate Method

(3) Activity-Based Costing Method

How does an accountant know which method to use? In this chapter we will illustrate each of the three methods and identify the conditions favoring each method. Managers should be concerned about which method is selected because the method of allocation determines the accuracy of the resulting product cost. Accurate product costs support management decisions, such as determining product mix, establishing product price, or determining whether or not to emphasize a product line. For example, after implementing a more accurate factory overhead cost allocation system, a senior manager at **Kraft Foods** remarked, "I expect to see that there are some products we definitely should not be manufacturing and some other products that we should be committing many more resources to . . . . [The cost system] should affect our long-term decisions on which businesses Kraft should be in."[1] Thus, factory overhead allocation is not just necessary for financial reporting purposes, but it also contributes to management decision making.

Single Plantwide Factory Overhead Rate Method

objective 2

Use a single plantwide factory overhead rate for product costing.

As we discussed in a previous chapter, companies may use a predetermined factory overhead rate to allocate factory overhead costs to products. Under the **single plantwide factory overhead rate method**, all of the factory overhead is allocated to all the products, using only one rate.

To illustrate, assume that Ruiz Company manufactures two products, snowmobiles and lawnmowers. Both products are manufactured in a single factory. In addition, there is $1,600,000 of factory overhead budgeted for the period. The factory overhead consists of factory and equipment depreciation, factory power, factory supplies, and indirect labor.

Under the single plantwide factory overhead rate method, the $1,600,000 budgeted factory overhead is applied to all products by using one rate. This rate is computed by dividing the total budgeted factory overhead cost by the total budgeted (estimated) plantwide allocation base as follows:

$$\text{Single plantwide factory overhead rate} = \frac{\text{Total budgeted factory overhead cost}}{\text{Total budgeted plantwide allocation base}}$$

The budgeted allocation base is a measure of operating activity in the factory. Common allocation bases would include direct labor hours, direct labor dollars, and machine hours.

Assume that Ruiz Company allocates factory overhead to the two products on the basis of budgeted direct labor hours. The total budgeted direct labor hours can be determined by multiplying the manufacturing volume by the direct labor hours per unit. Ruiz Company plans to manufacture 1,000 units of each product. Snowmobiles and lawnmowers both require 10 direct labor hours per unit to manufacture. The total budgeted plantwide direct labor hours is 20,000, as shown below.

Real World

Many service companies use a single overhead rate in determining their prices and job profitability. For example, many professional services, such as medical, legal, and accounting services, develop hourly rates that will provide a profit after covering labor and overhead.

Snowmobile:	1,000 units × 10 direct labor hours =	10,000 direct labor hours
Lawnmower:	1,000 units × 10 direct labor hours =	10,000
		20,000 direct labor hours

[1] R. Cooper, R. S. Kaplan, L. S. Maisel, E. Morrissey, and R. M. Oehm, *Implementing Activity-Based Cost Management Moving: from Analysis to Action* (Institute of Management Accountants, 1992), p. 269.

The single plantwide factory overhead rate is $80 per direct labor hour, determined as follows:

$$\text{Single plantwide factory overhead rate} = \frac{\$1,600,000}{20,000 \text{ direct labor hours}}$$

$$= \$80 \text{ per direct labor hour}$$

This plantwide rate of $80 per direct labor hour can be used to allocate factory overhead to each product, as shown below:

	Single Plantwide Factory Overhead Rate	×	Direct Labor Hours per Unit	=	Factory Overhead Cost per Unit
Snowmobile	$80 per direct labor hour	×	10 direct labor hours	=	$800
Lawnmower	$80 per direct labor hour	×	10 direct labor hours	=	$800

The factory overhead allocated to each unit of product is the same. This is because each product used the same number of direct labor hours.

The effects of using the single plantwide factory overhead rate method are summarized for Ruiz Company in Exhibit 1.

Many military contractors use a single plantwide rate for allocating factory overhead costs to products, such as jet fighters. This approach is satisfactory when all products in the plant are manufactured under cost plus profit margin contracts to a single customer, such as the Department of Defense. The factory overhead is rationally and systematically allocated to products and is thus "paid for" under the contract terms. However, cost distortions can still occur. This is one reason why government contractors sometimes make "$200 flashlights" that could be purchased at the local hardware store for $5.

Exhibit 1 Single Plantwide Factory Overhead Rate Method—Ruiz Company

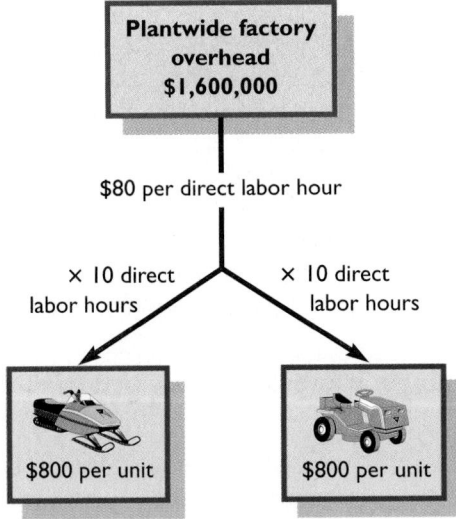

Lin Company has budgeted $500,000 of factory overhead and 25,000 direct labor hours. How much factory overhead is allocated to a product that uses 22 direct labor hours?

$440 [22 hours × ($500,000 ÷ 25,000 hours)]

The greatest advantage of the single plantwide overhead rate method is that it is simple and inexpensive to apply in practice. Using a plantwide rate, we assume that the factory overhead costs are consumed in the same way by all products. For example, for Ruiz Company, we assume that all factory overhead can be accurately allocated to the two products based on the total number of direct labor hours consumed by each product. For companies that manufacture one or very few products, this assumption may be true. However, if the company manufactures many different types of products that consume factory overhead costs in different ways, then the assumption may not be true. In such a situation, a single plantwide rate may not accurately allocate factory overhead to the products. A solution may be to use multiple production department factory overhead rates, which we illustrate in the next section.

Multiple Production Department Factory Overhead Rate Method

When production departments *differ significantly* in their manufacturing processes, factory overhead costs are likely to be incurred differently in each department. For example, a fabrication department that uses equipment may require more depreciation, power, and maintenance than would an assembly department that uses people. In addition, different products may consume the factory overhead from each production department in different proportions. For example, some products may use more of the fabrication department, while others use more of the assembly department. Under these conditions, the factory overhead costs may be more accurately allocated using multiple production department factory overhead rates.

The **multiple production department factory overhead rate method** uses different rates for each production department to allocate factory overhead to products. This is in contrast to the single plantwide rate method, which uses only one rate to allocate plantwide factory overhead to the products. Exhibit 2 illustrates how these two methods differ.

Exhibit 2 Comparison of Single Plantwide Rate and Multiple Production Department Rate Methods

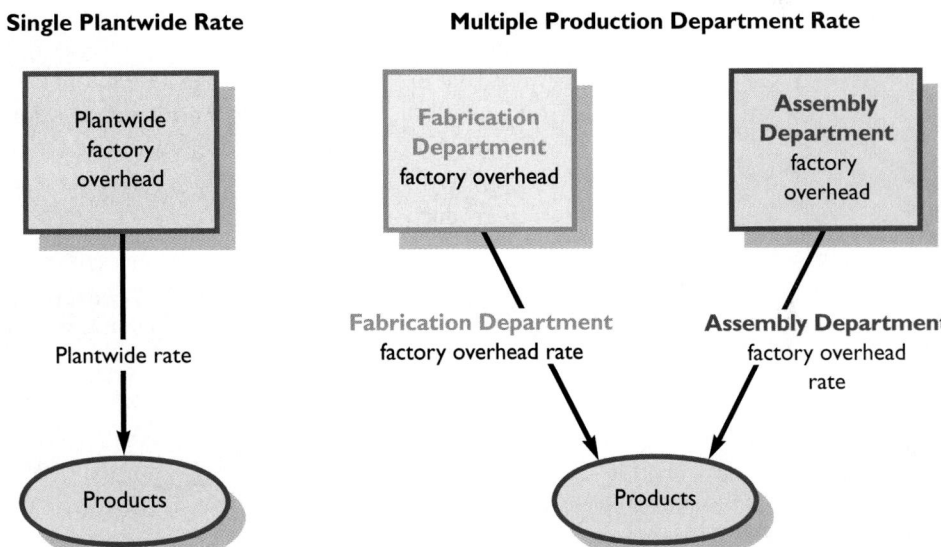

To illustrate the multiple production department factory overhead rate method, assume that Ruiz Company has two production departments, Fabrication and Assembly. Also assume that the factory overhead associated with the Fabrication Department is $1,030,000, and the factory overhead associated with the Assembly Department is $570,000.[2] The Fabrication Department has nearly twice the factory overhead of the Assembly Department because of the additional machinery-related factory overhead, such as power, equipment depreciation, and factory supplies. Note that the $1,600,000 of budgeted factory overhead in the two production departments equals the budgeted plantwide factory overhead.

---

[2] The factory overhead is allocated to production departments by using methods that are discussed in advanced texts.

Point of Interest

A company may use different allocation bases for different departments. For example, a machine-intensive department may use machine hours as an allocation base, and a labor-intensive department may use labor hours as an allocation base. However, in situations where one employee operates one machine, machine hours and labor hours will be equal and will yield the same allocation results.

Production Department Factory Overhead Rates and Allocation

The **production department factory overhead rates** are determined by dividing the budgeted production department factory overhead by the budgeted allocation base for each department. For Ruiz Company, direct labor hours are used as the allocation base for each production department. Each production department uses 10,000 direct labor hours. Thus, the factory overhead rates for the two departments are determined as follows:

$$\text{Fabrication department factory overhead rate} = \frac{\$1,030,000}{10,000 \text{ dlh}}$$

$$= \$103 \text{ per direct labor hour}$$

$$\text{Assembly department factory overhead rate} = \frac{\$570,000}{10,000 \text{ dlh}}$$

$$= \$57 \text{ per direct labor hour}$$

Recall that each product requires ten direct labor hours. We will now assume some additional information about these hours. The snowmobile requires eight direct labor hours in the Fabrication Department and two direct labor hours in the Assembly Department. The lawnmower requires two direct labor hours in the Fabrication Department and eight in the Assembly Department.

Factory overhead is allocated to each product by multiplying the direct labor hours used by each product in each department by the production department factory overhead rate. Exhibit 3 shows this process for Ruiz Company.

Exhibit 3 Allocating Factory Overhead to Products—Ruiz Company

	Allocation-Base Usage per Unit	×	Production Department Factory Overhead Rate	=	Allocated Factory Overhead per Unit of Product
Snowmobile					
Fabrication Department	8 direct labor hours	×	$103 per dlh	=	$824
Assembly Department	2 direct labor hours	×	$ 57 per dlh	=	114
Total factory overhead cost per snowmobile					$938
Lawnmower					
Fabrication Department	2 direct labor hours	×	$103 per dlh	=	$206
Assembly Department	8 direct labor hours	×	$ 57 per dlh	=	456
Total factory overhead cost per lawnmower					$662

Point of Interest

A company may develop factory overhead rates for each class of machine, rather than for a department. This allows for more precise allocation of machine costs to products in machine-intensive operations.

You should note that the production department factory overhead rates are not the same for each department. The Fabrication Department is more expensive in terms of factory overhead per direct labor hour than is the Assembly Department. In addition, the snowmobile uses more Fabrication Department direct labor hours than does the lawnmower. As a result, the total overhead allocated to each snowmobile is greater than that allocated to each lawnmower.

The multiple production department rate allocation method for Ruiz Company is summarized in Exhibit 4.

Exhibit 4 Multiple Production Department Rate Method—Ruiz Company

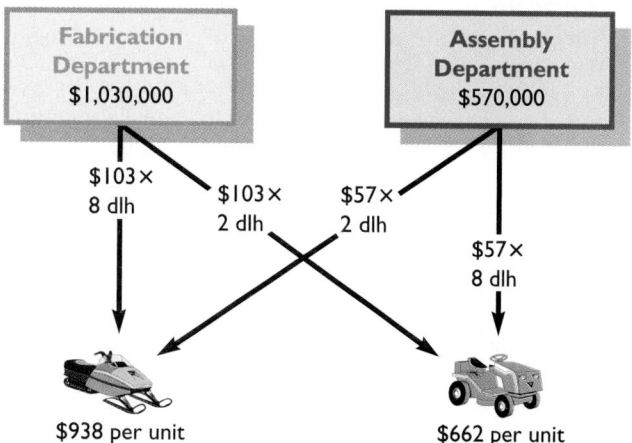

$938 per unit $662 per unit

Product A requires 12 labor hours in Department 1 and 4 labor hours in Department 2. The factory overhead budgeted is $800,000 for Department 1 and $200,000 for Department 2. Both departments have 8,000 direct labor hours budgeted for the period. What is the factory overhead allocated to Product A under the multiple production department rate method?

$1,300 [($800,000 ÷ 8,000) × 12 hours + ($200,000 ÷ 8,000) × 4 hours]

Distortion in Product Costs—Single Plantwide versus Multiple Production Department Factory Overhead Rates

For Ruiz Company, the following table shows the difference in the factory overhead per unit for each product, using the single plantwide and the multiple production department factory overhead rate methods:

	Factory Overhead Cost per Unit	
	Single Plantwide Rate	**Multiple Production Department Rates**
Snowmobile	$800	$938
Lawnmower	800	662

Which method is correct? In this case, the single plantwide factory overhead rate distorts the product cost by averaging the differences between the high factory overhead costs in the Fabrication Department and the low factory overhead costs in the Assembly Department. Using the single plantwide rate, we assume that all factory overhead is directly related to a single allocation base representing the entire plant. In many plants, this assumption is not realistic. Thus, using a single plantwide rate may result in product cost distortion.

In general, the following conditions may indicate that a single plantwide factory overhead rate will lead to distorted product costs:

Condition 1: Differences in production department factory overhead rates. There are significant differences in the factory overhead rates across different

> The single plantwide factory overhead rate distorts product cost by averaging high and low factory overhead costs.

production departments. Some departments have high rates, while others have low rates.

and

Condition 2: Differences in the ratios of allocation-base usage.

The products require different ratios of allocation base-usage across the departments.

Exhibit 5 illustrates both conditions for Ruiz Company. Condition 1 exists because the factory overhead rate for the Fabrication Department is $103 per direct labor hour, while the rate for the Assembly Department is only $57 per direct labor hour. This condition, by itself, will not cause product cost distortion. However, Condition 2 also exists. The snowmobile consumes 8 direct labor hours in the Fabrication Department, while the lawnmower consumes only 2 direct labor hours (8:2 ratio). The opposite is the case in the Assembly Department (2:8 ratio). Since both conditions exist, the product costs calculated using the single plantwide factory overhead rate are distorted. If Ruiz Company used the $800 product cost to determine its pricing strategy for both products, it would likely *underprice* the snowmobile and *overprice* the lawnmower. Eventually, Ruiz might be shut out of the lawnmower business due to this pricing error. If Ruiz used the multiple production department factory overhead rate approach, however, its product costs would be more accurate, and thus it would have a better starting point for making pricing decisions.

Exhibit 5 Conditions for Product Cost Distortion— Ruiz Company

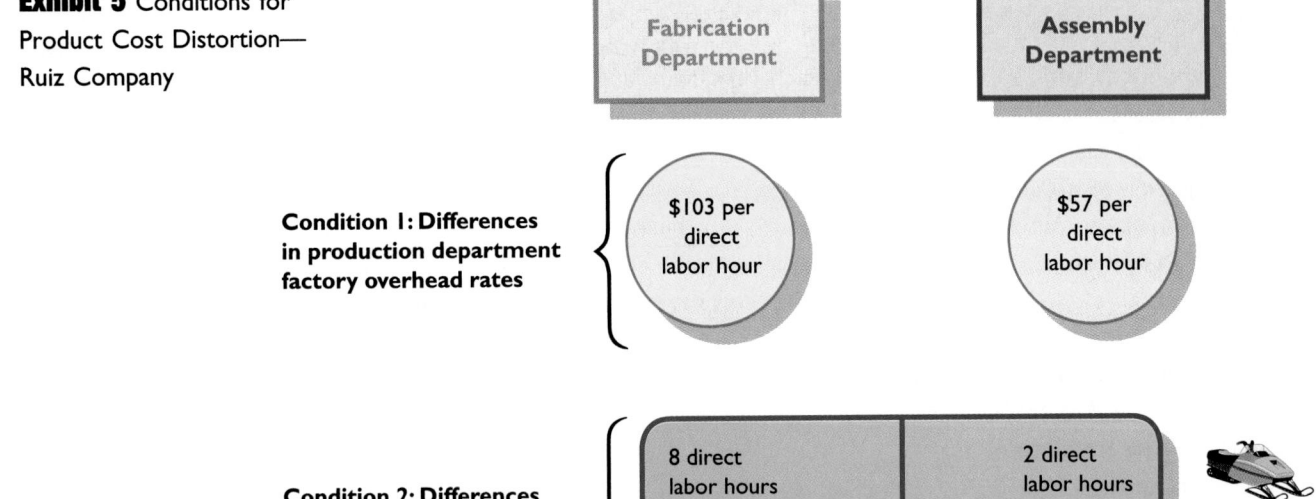

Activity-Based Costing Method

objective 4

Use activity-based costing for product costing.

In today's more complex manufacturing systems, product costs may still be distorted when multiple production department factory overhead rates are used. One way to avoid this distortion is by using the **activity-based costing (ABC) method**. This approach allocates factory overhead more accurately than does the multiple production department rate method.

The activity-based costing method uses cost of activities to determine product costs. Under this method, factory overhead costs are initially accounted for in **activity cost pools**. These cost pools are related to a given activity, such as machine usage, inspections, moving, production setups, and engineering activities. In contrast, when multiple production department factory overhead rates are used, factory overhead costs are first accounted for in production departments. Exhibit 6 illustrates how these two approaches compare.

Exhibit 6 Multiple Production Department Factory Overhead Rate Method vs. Activity-Based Costing

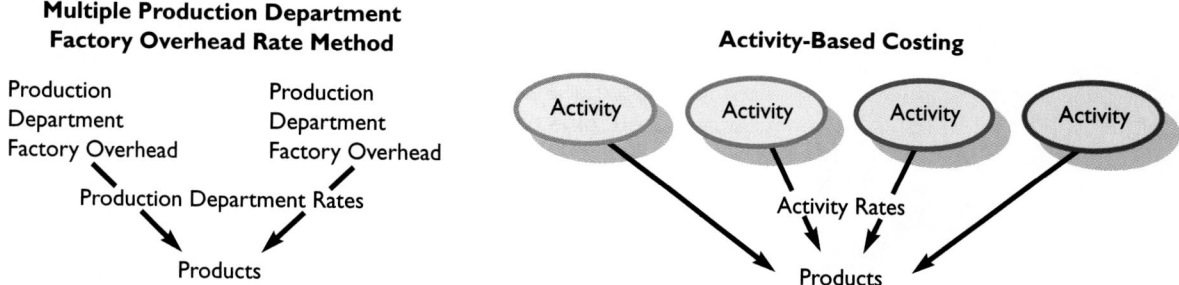

To illustrate the activity-based costing method, assume that Ruiz Company has five activities. Two activities are the fabrication and assembly production activities. We now call these *activities*, rather than *departments*, because the factory overhead costs in these pools are more closely related to their activity bases than under the multiple department factory overhead rate method.

Ruiz has three additional activities, which are described below.

- *Setup*—the activity of changing the characteristics of a machine to prepare for manufacturing a different product. Often, a production run requires a setup. For example, changing a stamping machine from stamping the body for a snowmobile to stamping the body for a lawnmower would require stopping the machine and changing the die. The work associated with changing the die is a setup activity.

- *Quality control inspection*—the activity of inspecting the product for defects. For example, a snowmobile inspection may require the snowmobile to be run for several hours and then be disassembled to test for component strength, fit, and function.

- *Engineering changes*—the activity of processing changes in product design characteristics. An **engineering change order (ECO)** initiates an administrative process to change the design of a product. For example, to change the type of blade assembled in a lawnmower would require an engineering change order.

We will assume the following budgeted factory overhead associated with each activity:

Activity Cost Pool	Amount
Fabrication	$ 530,000
Assembly	70,000
Setup	480,000
Quality control inspection	312,000
Engineering changes	208,000
Total budgeted factory overhead	$1,600,000

Point of Interest
Another term for "setup" is "changeover." This term is often used in continuous process industries. For example, reactors, paper machines, and rolling mills are "changed over" to produce a different product. Often, machine characteristics are changed while the process continues running ("on the fly"). Such changeovers are still costly, however, because the machines will make low-quality product for a period of time during the changeover.

The **U.S. Postal Service** has initiated a new activity-based costing system, called PostalOne!, which will track the real costs associated with processing and delivering each class of mail.

Activity rates are determined by dividing the budgeted activity cost pool by the total estimated activity base.

The total budgeted factory overhead to be allocated is still $1,600,000. However, the budgeted factory overhead has now been divided into cost pools. The costs in the fabrication and assembly pools are less than the costs in the production departments from the previous section because the production departments included costs that were not closely related to fabrication and assembly activities. These costs, which total $1,000,000 ($480,000 + $312,000 + $208,000), are now related to their own activity pools, namely setup, quality control inspection, and engineering changes.

Activity Rates and Allocation

The activity cost pools are assigned to products, using factory overhead rates for each activity. These rates are often called **activity rates** because they are related to activities. Activity rates are determined by dividing the cost budgeted for each activity pool by the estimated activity base for that pool. We use the term **activity base**, rather than allocation base, since the base is related to an activity cost pool. For example, the activity rate for the setup activity would be determined by dividing the setup budgeted cost pool by the number of estimated setups. Setup cost would be related to a product by multiplying the setup activity rate by the number of setups used by that particular product.

To determine each activity-base quantity, assume the following additional information about the snowmobiles and lawnmowers for Ruiz Company:

- *Snowmobiles:* Ruiz Company estimates that the total production for snowmobiles will be 1,000 units. Snowmobiles are a new product, and the engineers are still tinkering with design changes. Thus, there are 12 engineering change orders estimated for the period. In addition, the snowmobile production run is expected to be set up 100 times during the period, or 10 units per production run (1,000 units total production ÷ 100 setups). For quality control purposes, 100 snowmobiles (10% of total production) will be inspected.
- *Lawnmowers:* Ruiz Company estimates that the total production for lawnmowers will also be 1,000 units. Lawnmowers are a mature and stable product that has been produced by Ruiz Company for many years. Thus, Ruiz Company expects the lawnmower to have only four engineering changes for the period. Due to its long history of successful production of lawnmowers, Ruiz expects fewer quality problems; thus, only four lawnmowers (0.4% of production) will be quality-control inspected. In addition, the lawnmower production run is expected to be set up 20 times during the period, or 50 units per production run (1,000 units total production ÷ 20 setups).

The estimated **activity-base usage quantities** are the total activity base quantities related to each product. These quantities reflect differences with respect to using setup, quality control inspection, and engineering change activities, as we noted in the preceding paragraphs. In addition, each product uses different amounts of direct labor hours in the fabrication and assembly activities, as we noted in an earlier section. The estimated activity-base usage quantities for all 1,000 units of production for each product are shown in Exhibit 7.

The activity rates for each activity can now be determined by dividing the budgeted activity cost pool by the total estimated activity base from Exhibit 7. These activity rates are shown in Exhibit 8.

The product costs for the snowmobile and lawnmower are computed by multiplying the activity rate by the related activity-base quantity for each product. The total of these costs for each product is the total factory overhead cost for that product. This amount is divided by the total number of units of that product budgeted for manufacture in the period. This result, as shown in Exhibit 9, is the factory overhead cost per unit.

Exhibit 7 Estimated Activity-Base Usage Quantities—Ruiz Company

Products	Activities				
	Fabrication	Assembly	Setup	Quality Control Inspections	Engineering Changes
Snowmobile	8,000 dlh	2,000 dlh	100 setups	100 inspections	12 ECOs
Lawnmower	2,000	8,000	20	4	4
Total activity base	10,000 dlh	10,000 dlh	120 setups	104 inspections	16 ECOs

Exhibit 8 Activity Rates—Ruiz Company

Activity	Budgeted Activity Cost Pool	÷	Estimated Activity Base	=	Activity Rate
Fabrication	$530,000	÷	10,000 direct labor hours	=	$53 per direct labor hour
Assembly	$ 70,000	÷	10,000 direct labor hours	=	$7 per direct labor hour
Setup	$480,000	÷	120 setups	=	$4,000 per setup
Quality control inspections	$312,000	÷	104 inspections	=	$3,000 per inspection
Engineering changes	$208,000	÷	16 engineering changes	=	$13,000 per engineering change order

Exhibit 9 Activity-Based Product Cost Calculations

Activity	Snowmobile					Lawnmower				
	Activity-Base Usage	×	Activity Rate	=	Activity Cost	Activity-Base Usage	×	Activity Rate	=	Activity Cost
Fabrication	8,000 dlh	×	$ 53	=	$ 424,000	2,000 dlh	×	$ 53	=	$106,000
Assembly	2,000 dlh	×	7	=	14,000	8,000 dlh	×	7	=	56,000
Setup	100 setups	×	4,000	=	400,000	20 setups	×	4,000	=	80,000
Quality control inspections	100 inspections	×	3,000	=	300,000	4 inspections	×	3,000	=	12,000
Engineering changes	12 ECOs	×	13,000	=	156,000	4 ECOs	×	13,000	=	52,000
Total factory overhead cost					$1,294,000					$306,000
Budgeted units of production				÷	1,000				÷	1,000
Factory overhead cost per unit					$ 1,294					$ 306

The activity-based costing method for Ruiz Company is summarized in Exhibit 10. Compare Exhibit 10 with Exhibit 4. In both exhibits, multiple rates are used. In Exhibit 4, production department factory overhead costs were allocated to products on the basis of the production department factory overhead rates. In contrast, under activity-based costing, the activity cost pools are allocated to the products on the basis of each activity's own unique activity rate.

Exhibit 10 Activity-Based Costing Method—Ruiz Company

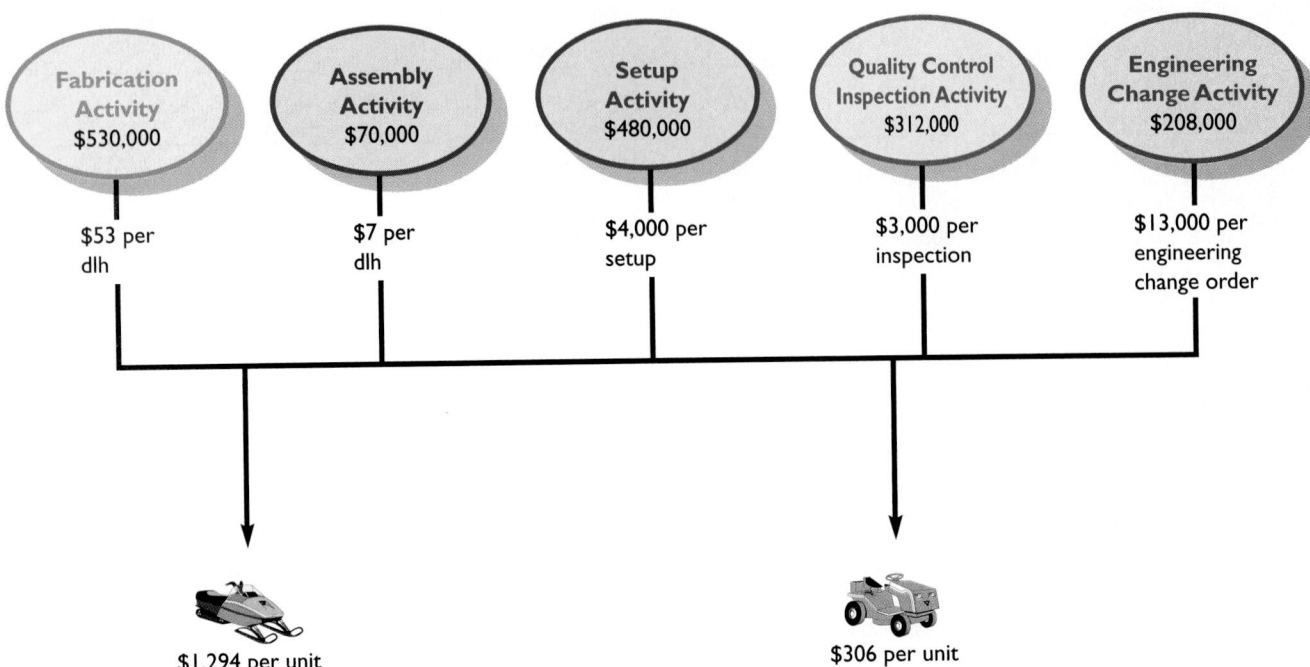

The setup activity is estimated to cost $260,000 to support 520 setups. Product A is produced in average run lengths of 160 units and has an estimated production of 20,000 units. How much setup activity should be allocated to Product A?

$62,500 [$500 per setup ($260,000 ÷ 520 setups) × 125 setups (20,000 units ÷ 160 units)]

Case Corporation, a manufacturer of construction equipment, has designed its activity-based costing system so that activities are arranged into processes. For example, it has a process termed "direct materials procurement," which includes the activities of master scheduling, inventory control, and materials purchasing, expediting, handling, and storage.

Distortion in Product Costs—Multiple Production Department Factory Overhead Rate Method versus Activity-Based Costing

The factory overhead costs per unit for Ruiz Company across all three allocation methods are shown below.

	Factory Overhead Cost per Unit— Three Cost Allocation Methods		
	Single Plantwide Rate	**Multiple Production Department Rates**	**Activity-Based Costing**
Snowmobile	$800	$938	$1,294
Lawnmower	800	662	306

As you can see, the activity-based costing method produced different product costs than did the multiple department factory overhead rate method. What caused these differences, and which method is more accurate? The answer lies in how the $1,000,000 of setup, quality control, and engineering change activities were treated. Under the multiple production department factory overhead rate method, this factory overhead was included in the production department factory overhead and allocated to products on the basis of direct labor hours. However, each product did *not* consume *activities* in proportion to its direct labor hours. Namely, the snowmobile consumed a larger portion of the setup, quality control inspection, and engineering change activities, even though each product consumed 10,000 labor hours. As a result, activity-based costing allocates more of this factory overhead cost to the snowmobile and less to the lawnmower than did the multiple production department factory overhead rate method. In summary, the activity-based costing

Hewlett-Packard abandoned its conventional direct-labor-based product costing system in favor of activity-based costing. Managing activity costs during the design stage of the product gave the research and development staff greater opportunity to reduce costs. For example, a product designer could compare the activity cost of different types of component assembly methods and select the design that minimized the total expected product cost.

A recent survey showed that 43% of the surveyed companies had adopted activity-based costing.

Source: "1998 Cost Management Group Survey," *IMA.*

method provided the most accurate product costs because activities were consumed in different proportions than the direct labor used in the two products.

The Dangers of Product Cost Distortion

Product cost distortion can lead to bad management decisions, and bad decisions can lead to business disasters. To illustrate, **Rockwell International** conducted an activity-based costing study after one of its best-selling axles had begun losing market share. The study found that incorrect factory overhead cost allocations had "overcosted" its highest-volume axle by roughly 20%, while underestimating the cost of low-volume axles by as much as 40%. Since the sales prices were based on these estimated costs, Rockwell had underpriced its low-volume axles and overpriced its high-volume axles. As a result, competitors had begun to attract customers away from Rockwell's best-selling, high-volume axles. Without the activity-based costing analysis, Rockwell could well have discovered that it was gradually being forced out of the high-volume axle business—not by choice, but because of inaccurate product costing and bad pricing decisions.[3]

[3] Fred S. Worthy, "Accounting Bores You? Wake Up," *Fortune*, October 12, 1987.

BUSINESS ON STAGE

ERP to the Rescue

Companies are adopting enterprise resource planning (ERP) systems, sometimes referred to as data warehouses. Such systems provide the organization with a single, completely integrated information system. With ERP systems, information is entered once and becomes available for all users in all applications. Thus, for example, a product number maintains its same identity in the sales system, inventory control system, warranty system, and production system. As a result, a new sale logged into the sales

system can automatically be made available to the production system. Surprisingly, until recently, many companies had a variety of software solutions spanning across many different locations that were unable to "speak" to each other. This has made it very difficult to integrate information across widespread operations. The new ERP software eliminates these islands of information by providing one comprehensive framework for business computing. ERP software is also being used to integrate information across differ-

ent companies, so that customers and suppliers are able to easily "talk" to each other. Leading ERP vendors include SAP (**www.sap.com**), ORACLE (**www.oracle.com**), JD Edwards (**www.jdedwards.com**), and People-soft (**www.peoplesoft.com**). ERP systems are well suited for activity-based costing because activity costs and allocation bases can be captured from the ERP modules and smoothly integrated into an activity-based costing module. ■

Activity-Based Costing for Selling and Administrative Expenses

objective 5

Use activity-based costing to allocate selling and administrative expenses to products.

Generally accepted accounting principles require that selling and administrative expenses be treated as period expenses on the income statement prepared for external users. However, accountants may allocate selling and administrative expenses to products in preparing product profitability reports for management. A traditional method is to allocate selling and administrative expenses to the products, based on product sales volumes. However, products may consume activities in ways that are unrelated to their sales volumes. When this occurs, activity-based costing may provide a more accurate allocation approach.

To illustrate, assume that Abacus Company has two products, Ipso and Facto. Both products have the same total sales volume. However, both products are not the same in terms of how they consume selling and administrative activities. Exhibit 11 identifies some of these differences.

Exhibit 11 Selling and Administrative Activity Product Differences

Selling and Administrative Activities	Ipso	Facto
Post-sale technical support	Product is easy to use by the customer.	Product requires specialized training in order to be used by the customer.
Order writing	Product requires no technical information from the customer.	Product requires detailed technical information from the customer.
Promotional support	Product requires no promotional effort.	Product requires extensive promotional effort.
Order entry	Product is purchased in large volumes per order.	Product is purchased in small volumes per order.
Customer return processing	Product has few customer returns.	Product has many customer returns.
Shipping document preparation	Product is shipped domestically.	Product is shipped internationally, requiring customs and export documents.
Shipping and handling	Product is not hazardous.	Product is hazardous, requiring specialized shipping and handling.
Field service	Product has few warranty claims.	Product has many warranty claims.

ExxonMobil Corporation has analyzed the cost of its selling and administrative activities to better determine the cost of its lubrication products. In addition, the activity information helped ExxonMobil discover the relative costs of serving customers directly versus through distributors. Examples of selling and administrative activities used in its activity-based costing analysis included sales, maintenance, engineering calls, distributor calls, order taking, market research, and advertising.

If the selling and administrative expenses of Abacus Company were allocated on the basis of sales volumes, both products would be allocated the same amount, since they both have the same sales volume. Does this seem correct? Should both products have the same selling and administrative expenses? No, they should not. Ipso is much less complex and hence less expensive than Facto. The activity-based costing approach would allocate the selling and administrative activities to each product based on its individual differences in consuming these activities. For example, assume that the field service activity of Abacus Company had a budgeted cost of $150,000. Additionally, assume that 100 warranty claims were estimated for the period. Using warranty claims as the activity base, the cost per warranty claim would be $1,500 [$150,000/100 claims]. Thus, if Ipso had 10 warranty claims and Facto had 90 warranty claims, Ipso would be allocated $15,000 (10 × $1,500) of field service activity, while Facto would be allocated $135,000 (90 × $1,500) of this activity. Allocating selling and administrative expenses using activity-based costing would result in more accurate product profitability reports for Abacus Company management.

Activity-Based Costing in Service Businesses

objective 6

Use activity-based costing in a service business.

Service companies have a need to determine the cost of services in order to make pricing, promoting, and other decisions with regard to service offerings. Many service companies find that single and multiple department overhead rate methods may lead to distortions similar to those of manufacturing firms. Thus, many service companies are now using activity-based costing for determining the cost of providing services to customers.

 **NationsBank** is experimenting with a system that instantly scores calls coming in on its 1-800 line according to the customer's profitability. Customers who produce higher profit because they use more of the bank's services move to the head of the line in receiving service from the toll-free call.

To illustrate activity-based costing for a service company, assume that Hopewell Hospital uses an activity-based costing system to determine how hospital overhead is allocated to patients. Hopewell Hospital first determines the activity cost pools and then allocates the activity cost pools to patients, using activity rates. We will assume that the activities of Hopewell Hospital include admitting, radiological testing, operating room, pathological testing, and dietary and laundry. Each activity cost pool has an estimated activity base measuring the output of the activity. The cost of activities is allocated to patients by multiplying the activity rate by the number of activity-base usage quantities consumed by each patient. Exhibit 12 illustrates the activity-based costing method for Hopewell Hospital.

Exhibit 12 Activity-Based Costing Method—Hopewell Hospital

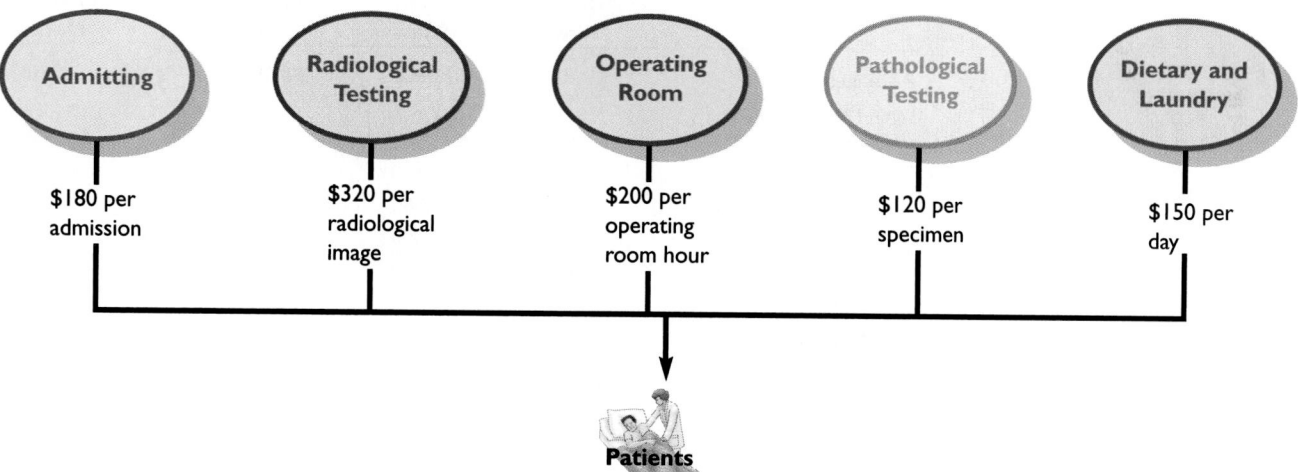

Each activity rate shown in Exhibit 12 is determined by dividing the budgeted activity cost pool by the estimated activity-base quantity. To illustrate, assume that the radiological testing activity cost pool budget is $960,000, and the total estimated activity-base quantity is 3,000 images. The activity rate of $320 per image is calculated as follows:

$$\text{Radiological testing activity rate} = \frac{\$960,000}{3,000 \text{ images}} = \$320 \text{ per image}$$

The activity rates for the other activities are determined in a similar manner. These activity rates are used to allocate costs to patients. To illustrate, assume that

Mary Wilson was a patient of the hospital. The hospital overhead cost associated with services (activities) performed for Mary Wilson is determined by multiplying the activity-base quantity for Mary Wilson's stay in the hospital by the activity rate. The sum of the costs across the activities is the total hospital overhead cost of services performed for Mary Wilson. These calculations are shown below.

Patient Name: Mary Wilson

Activity	Activity-Base Usage	×	Activity Rate	=	Activity Cost
Admitting	1 admission	×	$180 per admission	=	$ 180
Radiological testing	2 images	×	320 per image	=	640
Operating room	4 hours	×	200 per hour	=	800
Pathological testing	1 specimen	×	120 per specimen	=	120
Dietary and laundry	7 days	×	150 per day	=	1,050
Total					$2,790

The patient activity costs can be combined with the direct costs, such as drugs and supplies, and reported with the revenues earned for each patient in a customer profitability report. A partial customer profitability report for Hopewell Hospital is shown in Exhibit 13.

Exhibit 13 Customer Profitability Report

Hopewell Hospital
Customer (Patient) Profitability Report
For the Period Ending December 31, 2003

	Adcock, Kim	Birini, Brian	Conway, Don		Wilson, Mary
Revenues	$9,500	$21,400	$5,050		$3,300
Less: Patient costs:					
Drugs and supplies	$ 400	$ 1,000	$ 300		$ 200
Admitting	180	180	180		180
Radiological testing	1,280	2,560	1,280		640
Operating room	2,400	6,400	1,600		800
Pathological testing	240	600	120		120
Dietary and laundry	4,200	14,700	1,050		1,050
Total patient costs	$8,700	$25,440	$4,530		$2,990
Income from operations	$ 800	$ (4,040)	$ 520		$ 310

The report in Exhibit 13 can be used by the administrators to guide decisions on pricing or service delivery. For example, there was a large loss on services provided to Brian Birini. Further investigation might reveal that services provided to Birini were out of line with what would be allowed for reimbursement by the insurance company. As a result, future losses could be avoided by lobbying for a higher insurance reimbursement or aligning the services closer to the revenues allowed by the insurance company.

ENCORE

Simple Makes Cents

Procter & Gamble used activity-based costing information to simplify its business. Reduced complexity has been a major strategic coup for P&G. For example, P&G has one-third fewer products in its line-up than it did ten years ago. Fewer products means much less production and distribution complexity and, thus, lower costs. Beyond this, P&G discovered that eliminating marginal brands, such as *Prell* shampoo or *Lava* soap, did not negatively impact sales. In fact, fewer choices made it easier for consumers to select from the remaining P&G brands. P&G's simplification strategy used the following tactics:

- **Standardize product formulas and packaging.** *Vidal Sassoon* shampoos now have a single fragrance worldwide, while using only two basic package designs. *Head and Shoulders* has been reduced from 31 to 15 different varieties, while gender-specific

diapers have been eliminated in the *Pampers* product line.
- **Reduce trade discounts, promotions, and consumer couponing.** P&G is following what is termed an EDLP (everyday low price) strategy. This strategy recognizes that discounts, promotions, and coupons add to price confusion in the marketplace and add complexity in processing the various "deals." One study found that 38% of all invoices in the grocery industry were incorrect because of errors from all the special allowances and discounts.
- **Eliminate marginal brands.** Activity-based costing identifies products that fail to contribute to profitability due to their high activity costs, relative to sales. Such low-volume brands, such as *Bain de Soleil* sun lotion, were eliminated by P&G.
- **Standardize advertising campaigns.** *Pringles* uses the same

rap-oriented ad around the world to great success. According to one P&G executive, "[Ad] reapplicaton is very, very important. A good reapplication is as good as a creation."

How has this affected the bottom line? P&G has cut billions from production and distribution costs. ■

Source: "Make it Simple," *Business Week*, September 9, 1996, pp. 96–104.

KEY POINTS

1 Identify three methods used for allocating factory overhead costs to products.
There are three basic cost allocation methods used for determining the cost of products: the single plantwide factory overhead rate method, the multiple production department factory overhead rate method, and the activity-based costing method.

2 Use a single plantwide factory overhead rate for product costing.
A single plantwide factory overhead rate can be used to allocate all plant overhead to all products, based on the formula below. The single plantwide factory overhead rate is simple to apply, but it can lead to significant product cost distortions.

$$\text{Single plantwide factory overhead rate} = \frac{\text{Total budgeted factory overhead costs}}{\text{Total budgeted plantwide allocation base}}$$

3 Use multiple production department factory overhead rates for product costing.

Product costing using multiple production department factory overhead rates requires identifying the factory overhead associated with the production departments. Using these rates will result in greater accuracy than using single plantwide factory overhead rates when:

1. There are significant differences in the factory overhead rates across different production departments.

and

2. The products require different ratios of allocation-base usage in each production department.

4 Use activity-based costing for product costing.

Activity-based costing requires factory overhead to be budgeted to activity cost pools. The activity cost pools are allocated to products by multiplying activity rates by the activity-base quantity consumed for each product. Using activity rates rather than multiple production department factory overhead rates may result in more accurate product costs when products consume activities in ratios that are unrelated to their departmental allocation bases.

5 Use activity-based costing to allocate selling and administrative expenses to products.

Selling and administrative expenses can be allocated to products for management profit reporting, using activity-based costing. The traditional approach to allocating selling and administrative expenses is by the relative sales volumes of the products. Activity-based costing would be preferred when the products use selling and administrative activities in ratios that are unrelated to their sales volumes.

6 Use activity-based costing in a service business.

Activity-based costing may be applied in service settings to determine the cost of individual service offerings. Service costs are determined by multiplying activity rates by the amount of activity-base quantities consumed by the customer using the service offering. Such information can support service pricing and profitability analysis.

ILLUSTRATIVE PROBLEM

Hammer Company plans to use activity-based costing to determine its product costs. It presently uses a single plantwide factory overhead rate for allocating factory overhead to products, based on direct labor hours. The total factory overhead cost is as follows:

Department	Factory Overhead
Production Support	$1,225,000
Production (factory overhead only)	175,000
Total cost	$1,400,000

The company determined that it performed four major activities in the Production Support Department. These activities, along with their budgeted costs, are as follows:

Production Support Activities	Budgeted Cost
Setup	$ 428,750
Production control	245,000
Quality control	183,750
Materials management	367,500
Total	$1,225,000

Hammer Company estimated the following activity-base usage quantities and units produced for each of its three products:

Products	Number of Units	Direct Labor Hrs.	Setups	Production Orders	Inspections	Material Requisitions
Product K	10,000	25,000	80	80	35	320
Product L	2,000	10,000	40	40	40	400
Product M	50,000	140,000	5	5	0	30
Total cost	62,000	175,000	125	125	75	750

Instructions

1. Determine the factory overhead cost per unit for Products K, L, and M under the single plantwide factory overhead rate method. Use direct labor hours as the activity base.
2. Determine the factory overhead cost per unit for Products K, L, and M under activity-based costing.
3. Which method provides more accurate product costing? Why?

Solution

1. Single plantwide factory overhead rate $= \dfrac{\$1,400,000}{175,000 \text{ direct labor hours}}$

$= \$8$ per direct labor hour

Factory overhead cost per unit:

	Product K	Product L	Product M
Number of direct labor hours	25,000	10,000	140,000
Single plantwide factory overhead rate	× $8/dlh	× $8/dlh	× $8/dlh
Total factory overhead	$200,000	$ 80,000	$1,120,000
Number of units	÷ 10,000	÷ 2,000	÷ 50,000
Cost per unit	$ 20.00	$ 40.00	$ 22.40

2. Under activity-based costing, an activity rate must be determined for each activity pool:

Activity	Activity Cost Pool Budget	÷	Estimated Activity Base	=	Activity Rate
Setup	$428,750	÷	125 setups	=	$3,430 per setup
Production control	$245,000	÷	125 production orders	=	$1,960 per production order
Quality control	$183,750	÷	75 inspections	=	$2,450 per inspection
Materials management	$367,500	÷	750 requisitions	=	$490 per requisition
Production	$175,000	÷	175,000 direct labor hours	=	$1 per direct labor hour

These activity rates can be used to determine the activity-based factory overhead cost per unit as follows:

Product K

Activity	Activity-Base Usage	×	Activity Rate	=	Activity Cost
Setup	80 setups	×	$3,430	=	$274,400
Production control	80 production orders	×	1,960	=	156,800
Quality control	35 inspections	×	2,450	=	85,750
Materials management	320 requisitions	×	490	=	156,800
Production	25,000 direct labor hrs.	×	1	=	25,000
Total factory overhead					$698,750
Unit volume					÷ 10,000
Factory overhead cost per unit					$ 69.88

Product L

Activity	Activity-Base Usage	×	Activity Rate	=	Activity Cost
Setup	40 setups	×	$3,430	=	$137,200
Production control	40 production orders	×	1,960	=	78,400
Quality control	40 inspections	×	2,450	=	98,000
Materials management	400 requisitions	×	490	=	196,000
Production	10,000 direct labor hrs.	×	1	=	10,000
Total factory overhead					$519,600
Unit volume					÷ 2,000
Factory overhead cost per unit					$ 259.80

Product M

Activity	Activity-Base Usage	×	Activity Rate	=	Activity Cost
Setup	5 setups	×	$3,430	=	$ 17,150
Production control	5 production orders	×	1,960	=	9,800
Quality control	0 inspections	×	2,450	=	0
Materials management	30 requisitions	×	490	=	14,700
Production	140,000 direct labor hrs.	×	1	=	140,000
Total factory overhead					$181,650
Unit volume					÷ 50,000
Factory overhead cost per unit					$ 3.63

3. Activity-based costing is more accurate, compared to the single plantwide factory overhead rate method. Activity-based costing properly shows that Product M is actually less expensive to make, while the other two products are more expensive to make. The reason is that the single plantwide factory overhead rate method fails to account for activity costs correctly. The setup, production control, quality control, and materials management activities are all performed on products in rates that are different from their volumes. For example, Product L requires many of these activities relative to its actual unit volume. Product L requires 40 setups over a volume of 2,000 units (average production run size = 50 units), while Product M has only 5 setups over 50,000 units (average production run size = 10,000 units). Thus, Product L requires greater support costs relative to Product M.

Product M requires minimum activity support because it is scheduled in large batches and requires no inspections (has high quality) and few requisitions. The other two products exhibit the opposite characteristics.

SELF-EXAMINATION QUESTIONS   Answers at End of Chapter

Matching

Match each of the following statements with its proper term. Some terms may not be used.

A. activity base

B. activity cost pools

C. activity rate

D. activity-base usage quantities

E. activity-based costing (ABC) method

F. budgeted factory overhead costs

G. cost distortion

H. engineering change order (ECO)

I. multiple production department factory overhead rate method

J. product costing

K. setup

L. single plantwide factory overhead rate method

___ 1. The level of activity in determining the activity rate.

___ 2. Determining the cost of a product.

___ 3. An accounting framework based on determining the cost of activities and allocating these costs to products, using activity rates.

___ 4. A document that initiates a change in the specification of a product or process.

___ 5. A method that allocates all factory overhead to products by using a single factory overhead rate.

___ 6. Cost accumulations that are associated with a given activity, such as machine usage, inspections, moving, and production setups.

___ 7. The cost of an activity per unit of activity base, determined by dividing the activity cost pool by the activity base.

___ 8. The amount of activity base used by a particular product.

___ 9. Inaccurate product costs that are the result of applying a cost allocation method that is inappropriate for the situation.

___10. A method that allocates factory overhead to products by using factory overhead rates for each production department.

___11. Changing the characteristics of a machine to produce a different product.

Multiple Choice

1. Which of the following statements is most accurate?
   A. The single plantwide factory overhead rate method will usually provide management with accurate product costs.
   B. Activity-based costing can be used by management to determine accurate profitability for each product.
   C. The multiple production department factory overhead rate method will usually result in more product cost distortion than the single plantwide factory overhead rate method.
   D. Generally accepted accounting principles require activity-based costing methods for inventory valuation.

2. San Madeo Company had the following factory overhead costs:

Power	$120,000
Indirect labor	60,000
Equipment depreciation	500,000

   The factory is budgeted to work 20,000 direct labor hours in the upcoming period. San Madeo uses a single plantwide factory overhead rate based on direct labor hours. What is the overhead cost per unit associated with Product M, if Product M uses 6 direct labor hours per unit in the factory?
   A. $34
   B. $54
   C. $204
   D. $150

3. Which of the following activity bases would best be used to allocate setup activity to products?
   A. Number of inspections
   B. Direct labor hours
   C. Direct machine hours
   D. Number of production runs

4. Production Department 1 (PD1) and Production Department 2 (PD2) had factory overhead budgets of $26,000 and $48,000, respectively. Each department was budgeted for 5,000 direct labor hours of production activity. Product T required 5 direct labor hours in PD1 and 2 direct labor hours in PD2. What is the factory overhead cost associated with a unit of Product T, assuming that factory overhead is allocated using the multiple production department rate method?
   A. $26.00
   B. $40.40
   C. $45.20
   D. $58.40

5. The following activity rates are associated with moving rail cars by train:
   $4 per gross ton mile
   $50 per rail car switch
   $200 per rail car

   A train with 20 rail cars traveled 100 miles. Each rail car carried 10 tons of product. Each rail car was switched 2 times. What is the total cost of moving this train?
   A. $5,400
   B. $10,000
   C. $44,100
   D. $86,000

CLASS DISCUSSION QUESTIONS

1. How does a company use product costing?
2. What are three basic methods for allocating factory overhead costs?
3. Why would management be concerned about the accuracy of product costs?
4. Why is the sum of product costs under alternative factory overhead cost allocation methods equal?
5. How is a single plantwide factory overhead rate calculated?
6. How do the multiple production department and the single plantwide factory overhead rate methods differ?
7. How are multiple production department factory overhead rates determined?
8. How is the allocation base for a production department selected?
9. Under what two conditions would the multiple production department factory overhead rate method provide more accurate product costs than the single plantwide factory overhead rate method?
10. How does activity-based costing differ from the multiple production department factory overhead rate method?
11. How is the activity rate determined?
12. Under what circumstances might the activity-based costing method provide more accurate product costs than the multiple production department factory overhead rate method?
13. When might activity-based costing be preferred over using a relative amount of product sales in allocating selling and administrative expenses to products?
14. How can activity-based costing be used in service companies?

EXERCISES

Exercise 10–1
Single plantwide factory overhead rate

Objective 2

Carson Company's Fabrication Department incurred $85,000 of factory overhead cost in producing gears and sprockets. The two products consumed a total of 4,000 direct machine hours. Of that amount, sprockets consumed 1,800 direct machine hours.

Determine the total amount of factory overhead that should be allocated to sprockets.

Exercise 10–2
Single plantwide factory overhead rate

Objective 2

✓ a. $35 per direct labor hour

Clearnote Musical Instrument Company makes three musical instruments: trumpets, tubas, and trombones. The budgeted factory overhead cost is $261,450. Factory overhead is allocated to the three products on the basis of direct labor hours. The products have the following budgeted production volume and direct labor hours per unit:

	Budgeted Production Volume	Direct Labor Hours per Unit
Trumpets	3,000 units	0.8
Tubas	2,500	1.5
Trombones	1,200	1.1

a. Determine the single plantwide factory overhead rate.
b. Use the factory overhead rate in (a) to determine the amount of total and per unit factory overhead allocated to each of the three products.

Exercise 10–3
Single plantwide factory overhead rate

Objective 2

✓ a. $40 per processing hour

Krispy-Snack Food Company manufactures three types of snack foods: tortilla chips, potato chips and pretzels. The company has budgeted the following costs for the upcoming period:

Factory depreciation	$102,500
Indirect labor	332,000
Factory electricity	32,400
Indirect materials	61,100
Selling expenses	170,000
Administrative expenses	94,000
Total costs	$792,000

Factory overhead is allocated to the three products on the basis of processing hours. The products had the following production budget and processing hours per case:

	Budgeted Production Volume (Cases)	Processing Hours per Case
Tortilla chips	20,000	0.12
Potato chips	60,000	0.15
Pretzels	18,000	0.10
Total	98,000	

a. Determine the single plantwide factory overhead rate.
b. Use the factory overhead rate in (a) to determine the amount of total and per case factory overhead allocated to each of the three products under generally accepted accounting principles.

Exercise 10–4
Product costs and product profitability reports, using a single plantwide factory overhead rate

Objective 2

✓ c. Pistons gross profit, $65,000

Missouri Machining Company (MMC) produces three products—pistons, valves, and cams—for the heavy equipment industry. MMC has a very simple production process and product line and uses a single plantwide factory overhead rate to allocate overhead to the three products. The factory overhead rate is based on direct labor hours. Information about the three products is as follows:

	Budgeted Volume (Units)	Direct Labor Hours per Unit	Price per Unit	Direct Materials per Unit
Pistons	5,000	0.20	$48.00	$24.50
Valves	15,000	0.14	15.50	5.80
Cams	2,000	0.12	32.00	16.40

The estimated direct labor rate is $24 per direct labor hour. There are no beginning or ending inventories. The budgeted factory overhead for MMC is $95,190.

a. Determine the plantwide factory overhead rate.
b. Determine the factory overhead and direct labor cost per unit for each product.
c. Use the information above to construct a budgeted gross profit report by product line. Include the gross profit as a percent of sales in the last line of your report.
d. ✏➤ What does the report in (c) indicate to you?

Exercise 10–5
Multiple production department factory overhead rate method

Objective 3

✓ b. Small glove, $3.24 per unit

Journeyman Glove Company produces three types of gloves: small, medium, and large. A glove pattern is first stenciled onto leather in the Pattern Department. The stenciled patterns are then sent to the Cut and Sew Department, where the final glove is cut and sewed together. Journeyman uses the multiple production department factory overhead rate method of allocating factory overhead costs. Journeyman's factory overhead costs were budgeted as follows:

Pattern Department overhead	$128,000
Cut and Sew Department overhead	260,000
Total	$388,000

The direct labor estimated for each production department was as follows:

Pattern Department	4,000 direct labor hours
Cut and Sew Department	5,000
Total	9,000 direct labor hours

Direct labor is used to allocate the production department overhead to the products. The direct labor hours per unit for each product for each production department were obtained from the engineering records as follows:

	Small Glove	Medium Glove	Large Glove
Pattern Department	0.02	0.04	0.08
Cut and Sew Department	0.05	0.06	0.08
Direct labor hours per unit	0.07	0.10	0.16

a. Determine the production department factory overhead rates.
b. Use the production department factory overhead rates to determine the factory overhead per unit for each product.

Exercise 10–6

Single plantwide and multiple production department factory overhead rate methods and product cost distortion

Objectives 2, 3

✓ b. Portable computer, $340 per unit

Swell Computer Company manufactures a desktop and portable computer through two production departments, Assembly and Testing. Presently, the company uses a single plantwide factory overhead rate for allocating factory overhead to the two products. However, management is considering using the multiple production department factory overhead rate method. The following factory overhead was budgeted for Swell:

Assembly Department	$570,000
Testing Department	280,000
Total	$850,000

Direct machine hours were estimated as follows:

Assembly Department	3,000 hours
Testing Department	2,000
Total	5,000 hours

In addition, the direct machine hours (dmh) used to produce a unit of each product in each department were determined from engineering records, as follows:

	Desktop	Portable
Assembly Department	0.75 dmh	1.20 dmh
Testing Department	0.50	0.80
Total machine hours per unit	1.25 dmh	2.00 dmh

a. Determine the per unit factory overhead allocated to the desktop and portable computers under the single plantwide factory overhead rate method, using direct machine hours as the allocation base.
b. Determine the per unit factory overhead allocated to the desktop and portable computers under the multiple production department factory overhead rate method, using direct machine hours as the allocation base for each department.
c. ▬▬▶ Recommend to management a product costing approach, based on your analyses in (a) and (b). Support your recommendation.

Exercise 10–7

Single plantwide and multiple production department factory overhead rate methods and product cost distortion

Objectives 2, 3

✓ b. Diesel engine, $790 per unit

The management of Detroit Engines Inc. manufactures gasoline and diesel engines through two production departments, Fabrication and Assembly. Management needs accurate product cost information in order to guide product strategy. Presently, the company uses a single plantwide factory overhead rate for allocating factory overhead to the two products. However, management is considering using the multiple production department factory overhead rate method. The following factory overhead was budgeted for Detroit:

Fabrication Department factory overhead	$575,000
Assembly Department factory overhead	250,000
Total	$825,000

Direct labor hours were estimated as follows:

Fabrication Department	2,500 hours
Assembly Department	2,500
Total	5,000 hours

In addition, the direct labor hours (dlh) used to produce a unit of each product in each department were determined from engineering records, as follows:

	Gasoline Engine	Diesel Engine
Fabrication Department	1 dlh	3 dlh
Assembly Department	3	1
Direct labor hours per unit	4 dlh	4 dlh

a. Determine the per unit factory overhead allocated to the gasoline and diesel engines under the single plantwide factory overhead rate method, using direct labor hours as the activity base.
b. Determine the per unit factory overhead allocated to the gasoline and diesel engines under the multiple production department factory overhead rate method, using direct labor hours as the activity base for each department.
c. ▬▬▶ Recommend to management a product costing approach, based on your analyses in (a) and (b). Support your recommendation.

Exercise 10–8
Identifying activity bases in an activity-based cost system
Objective 4

Light Speed Systems, Inc. uses activity-based costing to determine product costs. For each activity listed in the left column, match an appropriate activity base from the right column. You may use items in the activity base list more than once or not at all.

Activity	Activity Base
Customer return processing	Engineering change orders
Electric power	Kilowatt-hours used
Human resources	Number of customer orders
Invoice and collecting	Number of customer returns
Machine depreciation	Number of customers
Materials handling	Number of direct labor hours
Order shipping	Number of inspections
Payroll	Number of machine hours
Production control	Number of material moves
Production setup	Number of payroll checks processed
Purchasing	Number of production orders
Quality control	Number of purchase orders
	Number of setups

Exercise 10–9
Product costs using activity rates
Objective 4

✓ b. $72,800

BridetoBe.com, Inc., sells china and flatware over the Internet. For the next period, the budgeted cost of the sales order processing activity is $109,200, and 4,200 sales orders are estimated to be processed.

a. Determine the activity rate of the sales order processing activity.
b. Determine the amount of sales order processing cost that china would receive if it had 2,800 sales orders.

Exercise 10–10
Product costs using activity rates
Objective 4

✓ Rowing machine activity cost per unit, $50.00

Leisure Equipment Company manufactures stationary bicycles and rowing machines. The products are produced in its Fabrication and Assembly production departments. In addition to production activities, several other activities are required to produce the two products. These activities and their associated activity rates are as follows:

Activity	Activity Rate
Fabrication	$28 per machine hour
Assembly	$10 per direct labor hour
Setup	$60 per setup
Inspecting	$22 per inspection
Production scheduling	$18 per production order
Purchasing	$5 per purchase order

The activity-base usage quantities and units produced for each product were as follows:

Activity Base	Stationary Bicycle	Rowing Machine
Machine hours	1,795	988
Direct labor hours	448	176
Setups	45	16
Inspections	700	400
Production orders	70	12
Purchase orders	180	120
Units produced	800	800

Use the activity rate and usage information to calculate the total activity cost and activity cost per unit for each product.

Exercise 10–11

Activity rates and product costs using activity-based costing

Objective 4

✓ b. Dining room lighting fixtures, $40.66 per unit

Bright Lighting Company manufactures entry and dining room lighting fixtures. Five activities are used in manufacturing the fixtures. These activities and their associated activity cost pools and activity bases are as follows:

Activity	Activity Cost Pool (Budgeted)	Activity Base
Casting	$216,000	Machine hours
Assembly	122,400	Direct labor hours
Inspecting	27,500	Number of inspections
Setup	69,000	Number of setups
Materials handling	32,000	Number of loads

Corporate records were obtained to estimate the amount of activity to be used by the two products. The estimated activity-base usage quantities and units produced are provided in the table below.

Activity Base	Entry	Dining	Total
Machine hours	5,000	4,000	9,000
Direct labor hours	4,100	6,100	10,200
Number of inspections	1,800	700	2,500
Number of setups	220	80	300
Number of loads	750	250	1,000
Units Produced			
Number of units	6,590	5,000	10,580

a. Determine the activity rate for each activity.
b. Use the activity rates in (a) to determine the total and per unit activity costs associated with each product.

Exercise 10–12

Activity cost pools, activity rates, and product costs using activity-based costing

Objective 4

✓ b. Oven, $80.30 per unit

Home Gourmet, Inc. is estimating the activity cost associated with producing ovens and refrigerators. The indirect labor can be traced into four separate activity pools, based on time records provided by the employees. The budgeted activity cost and activity base information are provided below.

Activity	Activity Pool Cost	Activity Base
Procurement	$120,000	Number of purchase orders
Scheduling	7,350	Number of production orders
Materials handling	33,750	Number of moves
Product development	22,950	Number of engineering changes
Total cost	$184,050	

The estimated activity-base usage and unit information for Home Gourmet's two product lines was determined from corporate records as follows:

	Number of Purchase Orders	Number of Production Orders	Number of Moves	Number of Engineering Changes	Units
Ovens	700	220	450	130	1,400
Refrigerators	500	130	300	40	1,900
Totals	1,200	350	750	170	3,300

a. Determine the activity rate for each activity cost pool.
b. Determine the activity-based cost per unit of each product.

Exercise 10–13

Activity-based costing and product cost distortion

Objectives 2, 4

✓ c. CD, $3.30

True Tone Inc. is considering a change to activity-based product costing. The company produces two products, compact disks (CDs) and cassette tapes, in a single production department. The production department is estimated to require 5,000 direct labor hours. The total indirect labor is budgeted to be $400,000.

Time records from indirect labor employees revealed that they spent 35% of their time setting up production runs and 65% of their time supporting actual production.

The following information about CDs and cassette tapes was determined from the corporate records:

	Number of Setups	Direct Labor Hours	Units
CDs	400	2,500	50,000
Cassette tapes	1,200	2,500	50,000
Total	1,600	5,000	100,000

a. Determine the indirect labor cost per unit allocated to CDs and cassette tapes under a single plantwide factory overhead rate system.
b. Determine the activity pools and activity rates for the indirect labor under activity-based costing. Assume two activity pools—one for setup and the other for production support.
c. Determine the activity cost per unit for indirect labor allocated to each product under activity-based costing.
d. ✏️▶ Why are the per unit allocated costs in (a) different from the per unit activity cost assigned to the products in (c)?

Exercise 10–14

Multiple production department factory overhead rate method

Objective 3

✓ b. Blender, $14.00 per unit

Kitchen Genie Appliance Company manufactures small kitchen appliances. The product line consists of blenders and toaster ovens. Kitchen Genie presently uses the multiple production department factory overhead rate method. The factory overhead is as follows:

Assembly Department	$180,000
Test and Pack Department	120,000
Total	$300,000

The direct labor information for the production of 10,000 units of each product is as follows:

	Assembly Department	Test and Pack Department
Blender	400 dlh	800 dlh
Toaster oven	800	400
Total	1,200 dlh	1,200 dlh

Kitchen Genie used direct labor hours to allocate production department factory overhead to products.

a. Determine the two production department factory overhead rates.
b. Determine the total factory overhead and the factory overhead per unit allocated to each product.

Exercise 10–15
Activity-based costing and product cost distortion
Objective 4

✓ b. Blender, $16.25 per unit

The management of Kitchen Genie Appliance Company in Exercise 10–14 has asked you to use activity-based costing to allocate factory overhead costs to the two products. You have determined that $60,000 of factory overhead from each of the production departments can be associated with setup activity ($120,000 in total). Company records indicate that blenders required 275 setups, while the toaster ovens required only 125 setups. Each product has a production volume of 10,000 units.

a. Determine the three activity rates (assembly, test and pack, and setup).
b. Determine the total factory overhead and factory overhead per unit allocated to each product.

Exercise 10–16
Single plantwide rate and activity-based costing
Objectives 2, 4

✓ a. Low, Col. C., 98.25%

Whirlpool Corporation conducted an activity-based costing study of its Evansville, Indiana plant in order to identify its most profitable products. Assume that we select three representative refrigerators (out of 333): one low-, one medium-, and one high-volume refrigerator. Additionally, we assume the following activity-base information for each of the three refrigerators:

Three Representative Refrigerators	Number of Machine Hours	Number of Setups	Number of Sales Orders	Number of Units
Refrigerator—Low Volume	25	18	42	120
Refrigerator—Medium Volume	297	20	150	1,400
Refrigerator—High Volume	860	10	120	4,300

Prior to conducting the study, the factory overhead allocation was based on a single machine hour rate. The machine hour rate was $320 per hour. After conducting the activity-based costing study, assume that three activities were used to allocate the factory overhead. The new activity rate information is assumed to be as follows:

	Machining Activity	Setup Activity	Sales Order Processing Activity
Activity rate	$200	$440	$70

a. Complete the following table, using the single machine hour rate to determine the per unit factory overhead for each refrigerator (Column A) and the three activity-based rates to determine the activity-based factory overhead per unit (Column B). Finally, compute the percent change in per unit allocation from the single to activity-based rate methods (Column C). Round to two decimal places.

	Column A	Column B	Column C
Product Volume Class	Single Rate Overhead Allocation per Unit	ABC Overhead Allocation per Unit	Percent Change in Allocation (Col. B − Col. A)/Col. A
Low			
Medium			
High			

b. ▬▬► Why is the traditional overhead rate per machine hour greater under the single rate method than under the activity-based method?
c. ▬▬► Interpret Column C in your table from part (a).

Exercise 10–17
Evaluating selling and administrative cost allocations

Objective 5

Michigan Office Furniture Company has two major product lines with the following characteristics:

Commercial office furniture: Few large orders, little advertising support, shipments in full truckloads, and low handling complexity

Home office furniture: Many small orders, large advertising support, shipments in partial truckloads, and high handling complexity

The company produced the following profitability report for management:

Michigan Office Furniture Company
Product Profitability Report
For the Year Ended December 31, 2003

	Commercial Office Furniture	Home Office Furniture	Total
Revenue	$2,400,000	$1,200,000	$3,600,000
Cost of goods sold	1,500,000	700,000	2,200,000
Gross profit	$ 900,000	$ 500,000	$1,400,000
Selling and administrative expenses	600,000	300,000	900,000
Income from operations	$ 300,000	$ 200,000	$ 500,000

The selling and administrative expenses are allocated to the products on the basis of relative sales dollars.

Evaluate the accuracy of this report and recommend an alternative approach.

Exercise 10–18
Construct and interpret a product profitability report, allocating selling and administrative expenses

Objective 5

✓ b. Generators operating profit-to-sales, 23.15%

Dover Equipment Company manufactures power equipment. Dover has two primary products—generators and air compressors. The following report was prepared by the controller for Dover's senior marketing management:

	Generators	Air Compressors	Total
Revenue	$1,800,000	$950,000	$2,750,000
Cost of goods sold	1,350,000	712,500	2,062,500
Gross profit	$ 450,000	$237,500	$ 687,500
Selling and administrative expenses			194,800
Income from operations			$ 492,700

The marketing management team was concerned that the selling and administrative expenses were not traced to the products. Marketing management believed that some products consumed larger amounts of selling and administrative expense than did other products. To verify this, the controller was asked to prepare a complete product profitability report, using activity-based costing.

The controller determined that selling and administrative expenses consisted of two activities: sales order processing and post-sale customer service. The controller was able to determine the activity base and activity rate for each activity, as shown below.

Activity	Activity Base	Activity Rate
Sales order processing	Sales orders	$ 80 per sales order
Post-sale customer service	Service requests	$250 per customer service request

The controller determined the following additional information about each product:

	Generators	Air Compressors
Number of sales orders	260	800
Number of service requests	50	390

a. Determine the activity cost of each product for sales order processing and post-sale customer service activities.
b. Use the information in (a) to prepare a complete product profitability report. Calculate the gross profit to sales and the income from operations to sales percentages for each product.
c. ✏➤ Interpret the product profitability report. How should management respond to the report?

Exercise 10–19
Activity-based costing and customer profitability

Objective 6

✓ a. Customer 1, $3,665

Square D Corporation manufactures power distribution equipment for commercial customers, such as hospitals and manufacturers. Activity-based costing was used to determine customer profitability. Customer service activities were assigned to individual customers, using the following assumed customer service activities, activity base, and activity rate:

Customer Service Activity	Activity Base	Activity Rate
Bid preparation	Number of bid requests	$120.00/request
Shipment	Number of shipments	23.00/shipment
Schedule standard items	Number of standard items ordered	36.00/std. item
Schedule nonstandard items	Number of nonstandard items ordered	90.00/nonstd. item

Assume that the company had the following gross profit information for three representative customers:

	Customer 1	Customer 2	Customer 3
Revenue	$18,500	$27,750	$40,000
Cost of goods sold	10,175	14,430	24,000
Gross profit	$ 8,325	$13,320	$16,000
Gross profit as a percent of sales	45%	48%	40%

The administrative records indicated that the activity-base usage quantities for each customer were as follows:

Activity Base	Customer 1	Customer 2	Customer 3
Number of bid requests	8	18	5
Number of shipments	20	36	18
Number of standard items ordered	30	45	50
Number of nonstandard items ordered	24	55	12

a. Prepare a customer profitability report showing (1) the income from operations after customer service activities and (2) the income from operations after customer service activities as a percent of sales. Prepare the report with a column for each customer. Round percentages to the nearest whole percent.
b. ✏➤ Interpret the table in part (a).

Exercise 10–20
Activity-based costing for a hospital

Objective 6

✓ a. Patient M, $4,555

Hope Hospital plans to use activity-based costing to assign hospital indirect costs to the care of patients. The hospital has identified the following activities and activity rates for the hospital indirect costs:

Activity	Activity Rate
Room and meals	$150 per day
Radiology	$95 per image
Pharmacy	$28 per physician order
Chemistry lab	$85 per test
Operating room	$550 per operating room hour

The records of two representative patients were analyzed, using the activity rates. The activity information associated with the two patients is as follows:

	Patient M	Patient T
Number of days	7 days	3 days
Number of images	4 images	2 images
Number of physician orders	5 orders	1 order
Number of tests	6 tests	2 tests
Number of operating room hours	4.5 hours	1 hour

a. Determine the activity cost associated with each patient.

b. ◄▬▬► Why is the total activity cost different for the two patients?

Exercise 10–21

Activity-based costing in an insurance company

Objectives 5, 6

✓ a. Auto, $789,500

Security Insurance Company carries three major lines of insurance: auto, workers' compensation, and homeowners. The company has prepared the following report for 2004:

Security Insurance Company
Product Profitability Report
For the Year Ended December 31, 2004

	Auto	Workers' Comp.	Homeowners
Premium revenue	$5,000,000	$4,000,000	$6,000,000
Less estimated claims	3,250,000	2,600,000	3,900,000
Underwriting income	$1,750,000	$1,400,000	$2,100,000
Underwriting income as a percent of premium revenue	35%	35%	35%

Management is concerned that the administrative expenses may make some of the insurance lines unprofitable. However, the administrative expenses have not been allocated to the insurance lines. The controller has suggested that the administrative expenses could be assigned to the insurance lines, using activity-based costing. The administrative expenses are comprised of five activities. The activities and their rates are as follows:

	Activity Rates
New policy processing	$250 per new policy
Cancellation processing	$340 per cancellation
Claim audits	$540 per claim audit
Claim disbursements processing	$280 per disbursement
Premium collection processing	$35 per premium collected

Activity-base usage data for each line of insurance was retrieved from the corporate records and is shown below.

	Auto	Workers' Comp.	Homeowners
Number of new policies	1,100	1,200	2,600
Number of canceled policies	450	150	1,350
Number of audited claims	325	110	720
Number of claim disbursements	350	140	750
Number of premiums collected	7,400	1,200	12,000

a. Complete the product profitability report through the administrative activities. Determine the income from operations as a percent of premium revenue, rounded to one decimal place.

b. ◄▬▬► Interpret the report.

PROBLEMS SERIES A

Problem 10–1A
Single plantwide factory overhead rate

Objective 2

✓ 1. b. $300 per machine hour

Mod Rod Accessory Company manufactures three chrome-plated products—automobile bumpers, valve covers, and wheels. These products are manufactured in two production departments (Stamping and Plating). The factory overhead for Mod Rod is $1,404,000.

The three products consume both machine hours and direct labor hours in the two production departments as follows:

	Direct Labor Hours	Machine Hours
Stamping Department		
Automobile bumpers	490	450
Valve covers	450	420
Wheels	760	710
	1,700	1,580
Plating Department		
Automobile bumpers	260	920
Valve covers	290	810
Wheels	350	1,370
	900	3,100
Total	2,600	4,680

Instructions

1. Determine the single plantwide factory overhead rate, using each of the following allocation bases: (a) direct labor hours and (b) machine hours.
2. Determine the product factory overhead costs, using (a) the direct labor hour plantwide factory overhead rate and (b) the machine hour plantwide factory overhead rate.

Problem 10–2A
Multiple production department factory overhead rates

Objective 3

✓ 2. Wheels, $625,050

The management of Mod Rod Accessory Company, described in Problem 10–1A, now plans to use the multiple production department factory overhead rate method. The total factory overhead associated with each department is as follows:

Stamping Department	$ 892,500
Plating Department	511,500
Total	$1,404,000

Instructions

1. Determine the multiple production department factory overhead rates, using direct labor hours for the Stamping Department and machine hours for the Plating Department.
2. Determine the product factory overhead costs, using the multiple production department rates in (1).

Problem 10–3A
Activity-based and department rate product costing and product cost distortions

Objectives 3, 4

High Mountain Sports Company manufactures two products, snowboards and skis. The factory overhead incurred is as follows:

Indirect labor	$300,000
Cutting Department	220,000
Finishing Department	180,000
Total	$700,000

SPREADSHEET

✓ 4. Snowboards, $266,000 and $13.30

The activity base associated with the two production departments is direct labor hours. The indirect labor can be assigned to two different activities as follows:

Activity	Activity Cost Pool	Activity Base
Production control	$120,000	Number of production runs
Materials handling	180,000	Number of moves
Total	$300,000	

The activity-base usage quantities and units produced for the two products are shown below.

	Number of Production Runs	Number of Moves	Direct Labor Hours—Cutting	Direct Labor Hours—Finishing	Units Produced
Snowboards	80	1,000	4,000	1,000	20,000
Skis	320	5,000	1,000	4,000	20,000
Total	400	6,000	5,000	5,000	40,000

Instructions

1. Determine the factory overhead rates under the multiple production department rate method. Assume that indirect labor is associated with the production departments, so that the total factory overhead is $370,000 and $330,000 for the Cutting and Finishing Departments, respectively.
2. Determine the total and per unit factory overhead costs allocated to each product, using the multiple production department overhead rates in (1).
3. Determine the activity rates, assuming that the indirect labor is associated with activities rather than with the production departments.
4. Determine the total and per unit cost assigned to each product under activity-based costing.
5. ✏ Explain the difference in the per unit overhead allocated to each product under the multiple production department factory overhead rate and activity-based costing methods.

Problem 10–4A
Activity-based product costing

Objective 4

SPREADSHEET

✓ 2. Newsprint total activity cost, $478,825

Georgia Company manufactures three products (computer paper, newsprint, and specialty paper) in a continuous production process. Senior management has asked the controller to conduct an activity-based costing study. The controller identified the amount of factory overhead required by the critical activities of the organization as follows:

Activity	Activity Cost Pool
Production	$ 924,300
Setup	320,000
Moving	38,250
Shipping	110,500
Product engineering	50,000
Total	$1,443,050

The activity bases identified for each activity are as follows:

Activity	Activity Base
Production	Machine hours
Setup	Number of setups
Moving	Number of moves
Shipping	Number of customer orders
Product engineering	Number of test runs

The activity-base usage quantities and units produced for the three products were determined from corporate records and are as follows:

	Machine Hours	Number of Setups	Number of Moves	Number of Customer Orders	Number of Test Runs	Units
Computer paper	405	120	280	470	70	450
Newsprint	540	50	120	145	10	600
Specialty paper	225	330	450	685	120	250
Total	1,170	500	850	1,300	200	1,300

Each product requires 0.9 machine hours per unit.

Instructions

1. Determine the activity rate for each activity.
2. Determine the total and per unit activity cost for all three products. Round to the nearest cent.
3. ➤ Why aren't the activity unit costs equal across all three products since they require the same machine time per unit?

Problem 10–5A
Allocating selling and administrative expenses using activity-based costing

Objective 5

SPREADSHEET

✓ 3. Mercy Hospital income from operations, $(246,650)

Coldpoint Inc. manufactures cooling units for commercial buildings. The price and cost of goods sold for each unit are as follows:

Price	$126,000 per unit
Cost of goods sold	87,000
Gross profit	$ 39,000 per unit

In addition, the company incurs selling and administrative expenses of $861,250. The company wishes to assign these costs to its three major customers, Mercy Hospital, Star Arena, and Atlantic University. These expenses are related to three major nonmanufacturing activities: customer service, project bidding, and engineering support. The engineering support is in the form of engineering changes that are placed by the customer to change the design of a product. The activity cost pool and activity bases associated with these activities are:

Activity	Activity Cost Pool	Activity Base
Customer service	$444,000	Number of service requests
Project bidding	328,000	Number of bids
Engineering support	89,250	Number of customer design changes
Total costs	$861,250	

Activity-base usage and unit volume information for the three customers is as follows:

	Mercy Hospital	Star Arena	Atlantic University	Total
Number of service requests	120	25	40	185
Number of bids	12	10	18	40
Number of customer design changes	65	15	25	105
Unit volume	5	12	15	32

Instructions

1. Determine the activity rates for each of the three nonmanufacturing activity pools.
2. Determine the activity costs allocated to the three customers, using the activity rates in (1).

3. Construct customer profitability reports for the three customers, using the activity costs in (2). The reports should disclose the gross profit and income from operations associated with each customer.

4. ▬▬➤ Provide recommendations to management, based on the profitability reports in (3).

Problem 10–6A
Product costing and decision analysis for a hospital

Objective 6

SPREADSHEET

✓ 3. Procedure A excess, $37,320

United Health System wishes to determine its product costs. United offers a variety of medical procedures (operations) that are considered its "products." The overhead has been separated into three major activities. The annual estimated activity costs and activity bases are provided below.

Activity	Activity Pool Cost	Activity Base
Scheduling and admitting	$ 159,600	Number of patients
Housekeeping	1,428,000	Number of patient days
Nursing	1,410,000	Weighted care unit
Total costs	$2,997,600	

Total "patient days" are determined by multiplying the number of patients by the average length of stay in the hospital. A weighted care unit (wcu) is a measure of nursing effort used to care for patients. There were 150,000 weighted care units estimated for the year. In addition, United estimated 4,200 patients and 16,800 patient days for the year. (The average patient is expected to have a four-day stay in the hospital.)

During a portion of the year, United collected patient information for three selected procedures, as shown below.

	Activity-Base Usage
Procedure A	
Number of patients	400
Average length of stay	× 2 days
Patient days	800
Weighted average care units	4,200
Procedure B	
Number of patients	200
Average length of stay	× 6 days
Patient days	1,200
Weighted average care units	16,000
Procedure C	
Number of patients	800
Average length of stay	× 3 days
Patient days	2,400
Weighted average care units	25,000

Private insurance reimburses the hospital for these activities at a fixed daily rate of $200 per patient day for all three procedures.

Instructions

1. Determine the activity rates.
2. Determine the activity cost for each procedure.
3. Determine the excess or deficiency of reimbursements over activity cost.
4. ▬▬➤ Interpret your results.

PROBLEMS SERIES B

Problem 10–1B
Single plantwide factory overhead rate

Objective 2

✓ 1. b. $200 per machine hour

Daisy Dairy Company manufactures three products—whole milk, skim milk, and cream—in two production departments, Blending and Packing. The factory overhead for Daisy is $560,000.

The three products consume both machine hours and direct labor hours in the two production departments as follows:

	Direct Labor Hours	**Machine Hours**
Blending Department		
Whole milk	200	800
Skim milk	240	750
Cream	60	250
	500	1,800
Packing Department		
Whole milk	460	400
Skim milk	520	450
Cream	120	150
	1,100	1,000
Total	1,600	2,800

Instructions

1. Determine the single plantwide factory overhead rate, using each of the following allocation bases: (a) direct labor hours and (b) machine hours.
2. Determine the product factory overhead costs, using (a) the direct labor hour plantwide factory overhead rate and (b) the machine hour plantwide factory overhead rate.

Problem 10–2B
Multiple production department factory overhead rates

Objective 3

✓ 2. Cream, $74,500

The management of Daisy Dairy, described in Problem 10–1B, now plans to use the multiple production department factory overhead rate method. The total factory overhead associated with each department is as follows:

Blending Department	$450,000
Packing Department	110,000
Total	$560,000

Instructions

1. Determine the multiple production department factory overhead rates, using machine hours for the Blending Department and direct labor hours for the Packing Department.
2. Determine the product factory overhead costs, using the multiple production department rates in (1).

Problem 10–3B
Activity-based and department rate product costing and product cost distortions

Objectives 3, 4

Audio Tek Labs Inc. manufactures two products, receivers and CD players. The factory overhead incurred is as follows:

Indirect labor	$ 700,000
Subassembly Department	440,000
Final Assembly Department	340,000
Total	$1,480,000

SPREADSHEET

✓ 4. CD players, $515,200 and $64.40

The activity base associated with the two production departments is direct labor hours. The indirect labor can be assigned to two different activities as follows:

Activity	Activity Cost Pool	Activity Base
Setup	$400,000	Number of setups
Quality control	300,000	Number of inspections
Total	$700,000	

The activity-base usage quantities and units produced for the two products are shown below.

	Number of Setups	Number of Inspections	Direct Labor Hours— Subassembly	Direct Labor Hours— Final Assembly	Units Produced
Receivers	190	1,045	700	300	8,000
CD Players	60	205	300	700	8,000
Total	250	1,250	1,000	1,000	16,000

Instructions

1. Determine the factory overhead rates under the multiple production department rate method. Assume that indirect labor is associated with the production departments, so that the total factory overhead is $790,000 and $690,000 for the Subassembly and Final Assembly Departments, respectively.
2. Determine the total and per unit factory overhead costs allocated to each product, using the multiple production department overhead rates in (1).
3. Determine the activity rates, assuming that the indirect labor is associated with activities rather than with the production departments.
4. Determine the total and per unit cost assigned to each product under activity-based costing.
5. ✏ Explain the difference in the per unit overhead allocated to each product under the multiple production department factory overhead rate and activity-based costing methods.

Problem 10–4B

Activity-based product costing

Objective 4

SPREADSHEET

✓ 2. Brown sugar total activity cost, $556,900

Caribbean Sugar Company manufactures three products (white sugar, brown sugar, and powdered sugar) in a continuous production process. Senior management has asked the controller to conduct an activity-based costing study. The controller identified the amount of factory overhead required by the critical activities of the organization as follows:

Activity	Activity Cost Pool
Production	$ 650,000
Setup	480,000
Inspection	144,000
Shipping	247,500
Customer service	84,000
Total	$1,605,500

The activity bases identified for each activity are as follows:

Activity	Activity Base
Production	Machine hours
Setup	Number of setups
Inspection	Number of inspections
Shipping	Number of customer orders
Customer service	Number of customer service requests

The activity-base usage quantities and units produced for the three products were determined from corporate records and are as follows:

	Machine Hours	Number of Setups	Number of Inspections	Number of Customer Orders	Number of Customer Service Requests	Units
White sugar	4,800	100	200	800	60	12,000
Brown sugar	2,000	150	400	2,700	240	5,000
Powdered sugar	3,200	150	600	1,000	100	8,000
Total	10,000	400	1,200	4,500	400	25,000

Each product requires 0.4 machine hours per unit.

Instructions

1. Determine the activity rate for each activity.
2. Determine the total and per unit activity cost for all three products. Round to the nearest cent.
3. ✏️ Why aren't the activity unit costs equal across all three products since they require the same machine time per unit?

Problem 10–5B
Allocating selling and administrative expenses using activity-based costing

Objective 5

SPREADSHEET

✓ 3. Office Warehouse income from operations, $82,225

Perfect Image Inc. manufactures office copiers, which are sold to retailers. The price and cost of goods sold for each copier are as follows:

Price	$440 per unit
Cost of goods sold	375
Gross profit	$ 65 per unit

In addition, the company incurs selling and administrative expenses of $166,910. The company wishes to assign these costs to its three major retail customers, Office Warehouse, General Office Supply, and Office-to-Go. These expenses are related to its three major nonmanufacturing activities: customer service, sales order processing, and advertising support. The advertising support is in the form of advertisements that are placed by Perfect Image Inc. to support the retailer's sale of Perfect Image copiers to consumers. The activity cost pool and activity bases associated with these activities are:

Activity	Activity Cost Pool	Activity Base
Customer service	$ 37,950	Number of service requests
Sales order processing	28,160	Number of sales orders
Advertising support	100,800	Number of ads placed
Total activity cost	$166,910	

Activity-base usage and unit volume information for the three customers is as follows:

	Office Warehouse	General Office Supply	Office-to-Go	Total
Number of service requests	35	5	190	230
Number of sales orders	250	110	520	880
Number of ads placed	25	10	85	120
Unit volume	1,800	1,800	1,800	5,400

Instructions

1. Determine the activity rates for each of the three nonmanufacturing activity pools.

2. Determine the activity costs allocated to the three customers, using the activity rates in (1).

3. Construct customer profitability reports for the three customers, using the activity costs in (2). The reports should disclose the gross profit and income from operations associated with each customer.

4. ▬▬▶ Provide recommendations to management, based on the profitability reports in (3).

Problem 10–6B
Product costing and decision analysis for a passenger airline

Objective 6

SPREADSHEET

✓ 3. Flight 2 income from operations, $(1,425)

Blue Skies Airline provides passenger airline service, using small jets. The airline connects four major cities: Atlanta, Cincinnati, Chicago, and Los Angeles. The company expects to fly 120,000 miles during a month. The following costs are budgeted for a month:

Fuel	$ 620,000
Ground personnel	724,000
Crew salaries	440,000
Depreciation	320,000
Total costs	$2,104,000

Blue Skies' management wishes to assign these costs to individual flights in order to gauge the profitability of its service offerings. The following activity bases were identified with the budgeted costs:

Airline Cost	Activity Base
Fuel, crew, and depreciation costs	Number of miles flown
Ground personnel	Number of arrivals and departures at an airport

The size of the company's ground operation in each city is determined by the size of the workforce. The following monthly data are available from corporate records for each terminal operation:

Terminal City	Ground Personnel Cost	Number of Arrivals/Departures
Atlanta	$240,000	320
Cincinnati	86,800	140
Chicago	131,200	160
Los Angeles	266,000	280
Total	$724,000	900

Three recent representative flights have been selected for the profitability study. Their characteristics are as follows:

	Description	Miles Flown	Number of Passengers	Ticket Price per Passenger
Flight 1	Atlanta to LA	1,950	20	$1,415
Flight 2	Cincinnati to Atlanta	370	14	300
Flight 3	Atlanta to Chicago	600	26	420

Instructions

1. Determine the fuel, crew, and depreciation cost per mile flown.
2. Determine the cost per arrival or departure by terminal city.
3. Use the information in (1) and (2) to construct a profitability report for the three flights.
4. ▬▬▶ Evaluate flight profitability by determining the break-even number of passengers required for each flight. Round to nearest whole number.

SPECIAL ACTIVITIES

**Activity 10–1
Crystal Electronics
Inc.**

*Ethics and professional
conduct in business*

The controller of Crystal Electronics Inc. devised a new costing system based on tracing the cost of activities to products. The controller was able to measure post-manufacturing activities, such as selling, promotional, and distribution activities, and allocate these activities to products in order to have a more complete view of the company's product costs. This effort produced better strategic information about the relative profitability of product lines. In addition, the controller used the same product cost information for inventory valuation on the financial statements. Surprisingly, the controller discovered that the company's reported net income was larger under this scheme than under the traditional costing approach.

➤ Why was the net income larger, and how would you react to the controller's action?

**Activity 10–2
Mid-Continent
Beverage Company**

*Identifying product cost
distortion*

Mid-Continent Beverage Company manufactures soft drinks. Information about two products is as follows:

	Volume	Sales Price per Case	Gross Profit per Case
Jamaican Punch	10,000 cases	$30	$12
King Kola	800,000 cases	$30	$12

It is known that both products have the same direct materials and direct labor costs per case. Mid-Continent Beverage allocates factory overhead to products by using a single plantwide factory overhead rate, based on direct labor cost. Additional information about the two products is as follows:

Jamaican Punch: Requires extensive process preparation and sterilization prior to processing. The ingredients are from Jamaica, requiring complex import controls. The formulation is complex, and it is thus difficult to maintain quality. Lastly, the product is sold in small (less than full truckload) orders.
King Kola: Requires minor process preparation and sterilization prior to processing. The ingredients are acquired locally. The formulation is simple, and it is easy to maintain quality. Lastly, the product is sold in large bulk (full truckload) orders.

➤ Explain the product profitability report in light of the additional data.

**Activity 10–3
Acordia, Inc.**

Activity-based costing

Acordia, Inc. is an insurance brokerage company that classified insurance products as either "easy" or "difficult." Easy and difficult products were defined as follows:

Easy: Electronic claims, few inquiries, mature product
Difficult: Paper claims, complex claims to process, many inquiries, a new product with complex options

The company originally allocated processing and service expenses on the basis of revenue. Under this traditional allocation approach, the product profitability report revealed the following:

	Easy Product	Difficult Product	Total
Revenue	$600	$400	$1,000
Processing and service expenses	420	280	700
Income from operations	$180	$120	$ 300
Operating income margin	30%	30%	30%

Acordia decided to use activity-based costing to allocate the processing and service expenses. The following activity-based costing analysis of the same data illustrates a much different profit picture for the two types of products.

	Easy Product	Difficult Product	Total
Revenue	$600	$ 400	$1,000
Processing and service expenses	183	517	700
Income from operations	$417	$(117)	$ 300
Operating income margin	70%	(29%)	30%

➤ Explain why the activity-based profitability report reveals different information from the traditional sales allocation report.

Source: Dan Patras and Kevin Clancy, "ABC in the Service Industry: Product Line Profitability at Acordia, Inc." *As Easy as ABC Newsletter,* Issue 12, Spring 1993.

**Activity 10–4
Wave Cast Audio Company**
Using a product profitability report to guide strategic decisions

The controller of Wave Cast Audio Company prepared the following product profitability report for management, using activity-based costing methods for allocating both the factory overhead and the marketing expenses. As such, the controller has confidence in the accuracy of this report. In addition, the controller interviewed the vice-president of marketing, who indicated that the bookshelf loudspeakers were an older product that was highly recognized in the marketplace. The ribbon loudspeakers were a new product that was recently launched. The ribbon loudspeakers are a new technology that have no competition in the marketplace, and it is hoped that they will become an important future addition to the company's product portfolio. Initial indications are that the product is well received by customers. The controller believes that the manufacturing costs for all three products are in line with expectations.

	Bookshelf Loudspeakers	Floor Loudspeakers	Ribbon Loudspeakers	Totals
Sales	$8,000,000	$50,000,000	$25,000,000	$83,000,000
Less cost of goods sold	5,400,000	30,000,000	24,000,000	59,400,000
Gross profit	$2,600,000	$20,000,000	$ 1,000,000	$23,600,000
Less marketing expenses	2,800,000	4,000,000	600,000	8,400,000
Income from operations	$ (200,000)	$16,000,000	$ 400,000	$15,200,000

1. Calculate the gross profit and income from operations to sales ratios for each product.
2. ➤ Write a memo using the product profitability report and the calculations in (1) to make recommendations to management with respect to strategies for the three products.

**Activity 10–5
Pocket Calculator Company**
Product cost distortion

Luis Lopez, president of Pocket Calculator Company, was reviewing the product profitability reports with the controller, Yolanda Greene. The following conversation took place:

Luis: I've been reviewing the product profitability reports. Our high-volume calculator, the T-100, appears to be unprofitable, while some of our lower-volume specialty calculators in the T-900 series appear to be very profitable. These results do not make sense to me. How are the product profits determined?

Yolanda: First, we identify the revenues associated with each product line. This information comes directly from our sales order system and is very accurate. Next, we identify the direct materials and direct labor associated with making each of the calculators. Again, this information is very accurate. The final cost that must be considered is the factory overhead. Factory overhead is allocated to the products, based on the direct labor hours used to assemble the calculator.

Luis: What about distribution, promotion, and other post-manufacturing costs that can be associated with the product?

Yolanda: According to generally accepted accounting principles, we expense them in the period that they are incurred and do not treat them as product costs.

Luis: Another thing, you say that you allocate factory overhead according to direct labor hours. Yet I know that the T-900 series specialty products have very low volumes but require extensive engineering, testing, and materials management effort. They are our newer, more complex products. It seems that these sources of factory overhead will end up being allocated to the T-100 line because it is the high-volume and therefore high direct labor hour product. Yet the T-100 line is easy to make and requires very little support from our engineering, testing, and materials management personnel.

Yolanda: I'm not too sure. I do know that our product costing approach is similar to that used by many different types of companies. I don't think we could all be wrong.

➤ Is Lopez's concern valid and how might Greene redesign the cost allocation system to address Lopez's concern?

Activity 10–6
Into the Real World
Activity-based costing

ABC Technologies, Inc. is a leading vendor of activity-based costing software. From its home page at **www.abctech.com**, you can link to sites that profile activity-based costing case studies. In groups of three or four, select case study applications of activity-based costing from different industries. (You may have to register for a "library card" to gain access to the case studies.) Prepare a brief summary of each of the case studies by identifying (1) the motivation for using activity-based costing, (2) the types of activities identified in the case, (3) the types of activity bases used in cost allocation, and (4) insights derived from using activity-based costing.

Activity 10–7
Into the Real World
Allocating bank administrative costs

Banks have a variety of products, such as savings accounts, checking accounts, certificates of deposit (CDs), and loans. Assume that you were assigned the task of determining the administrative costs of "savings accounts" as a complete product line. What are some of the activities associated with savings accounts? In answering this question, consider the activities that you might perform with your savings account. For each activity, what would be an activity base that could be used to allocate the activity cost to the savings account product line?

ANSWERS TO SELF-EXAMINATION QUESTIONS

Matching
1. A
2. J
3. E
4. H
5. L
6. B
7. C
8. D
9. G
10. I
11. K

Multiple Choice

1. **B** Activity-based costing provides accurate product costs, which can be used for strategic product profitability analysis. The single plantwide factory overhead rate method (answer A) can distort the individual product costs under a variety of reasonable conditions. The multiple production department factory overhead rate method will lead to less (not more) distortion than the single plantwide factory overhead rate method (answer C). Generally accepted accounting principles do not require activity-based costing for inventory valuation (answer D).

2. **C** The single plantwide factory overhead rate is $34 per hour (answer A), determined as $680,000 ÷ 20,000 hours. This rate is multiplied by 6 direct labor hours per unit of Product M to determine the correct overhead per unit of $204. The total overhead should be used in the numerator in determining the overhead rate, not just power and indirect labor (answer B) or equipment depreciation (answer D).

3. **D** The number of production runs best relates the activity cost of setup to the products. Number of inspections, direct labor hours, and direct machine hours (answers A , B, and C) will likely have very little logical association with the costs incurred in setting up production runs.

4. **C** PD1 rate: $26,000/5,000 dlh = $5.20 per dlh
   PD2 rate: $48,000/5,000 dlh = $9.60 per dlh
   Product T: (5 dlh × $5.20) + (2 dlh × $9.60) = $45.20

5. **D** (100 miles × 20 cars × 10 tons × $4) + ($200 × 20 cars) + (20 cars × 2 switches × $50) = $80,000 + $4,000 + $2,000 = $86,000

M11

Cost Management for Just-in-Time Environments

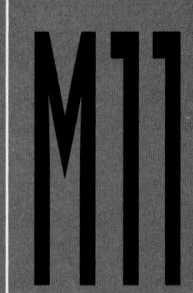

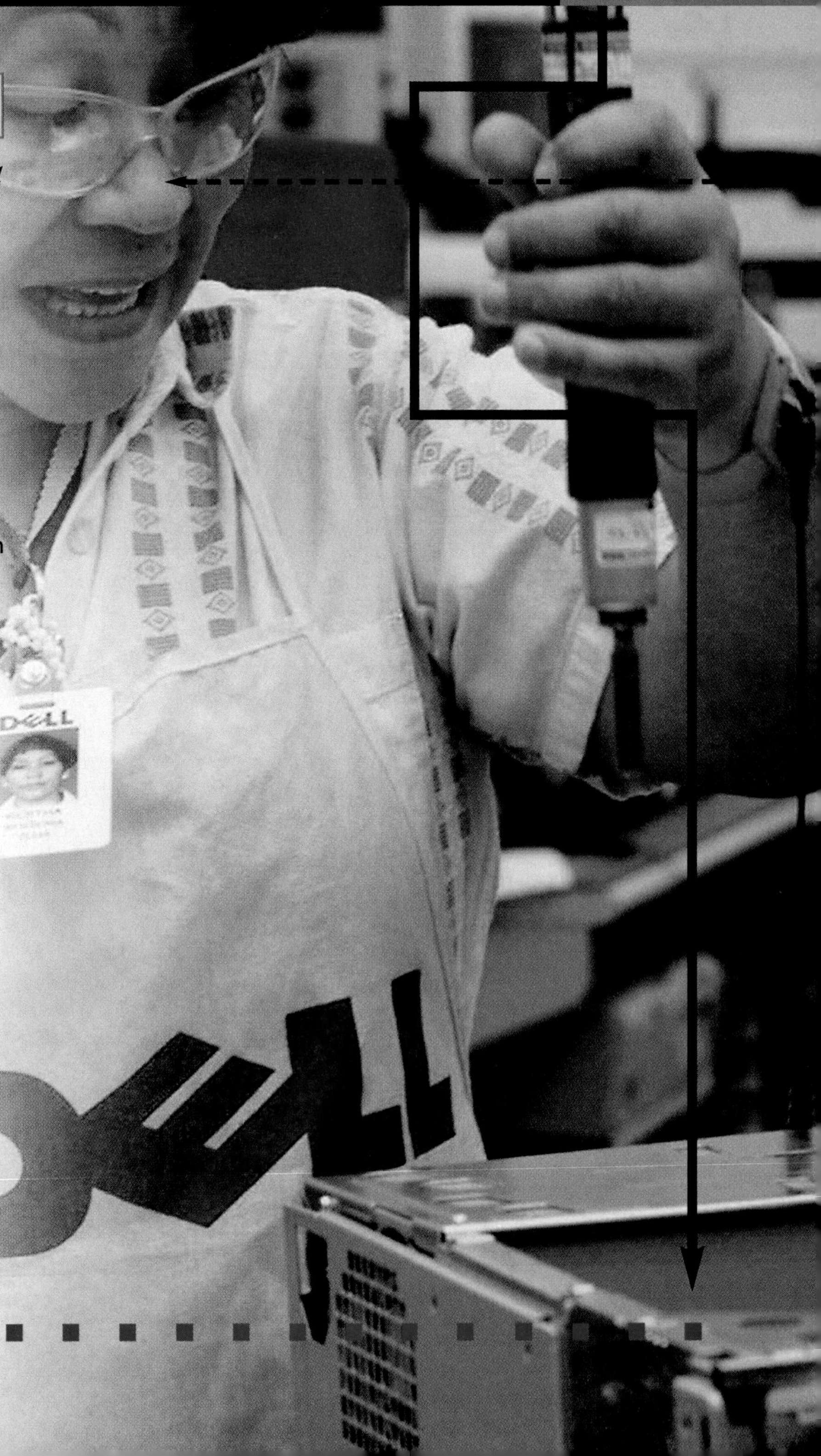

objectives

After studying this chapter, you should be able to:

1. Compare and contrast just-in-time (JIT) manufacturing practices with traditional manufacturing practices.
2. Apply just-in-time manufacturing practices to a traditional manufacturing illustration.
3. Describe the implications of a just-in-time manufacturing philosophy on cost accounting and performance measurement systems.
4. Apply just-in-time practices to a nonmanufacturing setting.
5. Describe the costs of quality and prepare a Pareto chart, a cost of quality report, and a value-added/nonvalue-added analysis.

When you order the salad bar at the local restaurant, you are able to serve yourself at your own pace. There is no waiting for the waitress to take the order or for the cook to prepare the meal. You are able to move directly to the salad bar and select from various offerings. You might wish to have salad with lettuce, cole slaw, bacon bits, croutons, and salad dressing. Each of the offerings is arranged in a row so that you can build your salad as you move down the salad bar.

Many manufacturers are attempting to produce each product directly to customer requirements, in much the same way that the salad bar is designed to satisfy each customer's specific requirements. Like customers at the salad bar, products move through a production process as they are built for each customer's unique needs.

In this chapter, we will discuss the just-in-time philosophy and illustrate the managerial accounting principles and tools used in just-in-time environments. We will then discuss the cost management issues appropriate for the just-in-time environment. We will complete the chapter by discussing and illustrating the accounting for quality costs.

Just-in-Time Principles

objective 1

Compare and contrast just-in-time (JIT) manufacturing practices with traditional manufacturing practices.

The manufacturing approaches used by many companies are undergoing significant change. Companies are recognizing the need to produce products and services with high quality, low cost, and instant availability. Achieving these objectives requires a change in the methods of manufacturing products and delivering services. One approach is just-in-time manufacturing. **Just-in-time (JIT) manufacturing**, sometimes called **short-cycle** or **lean manufacturing**, focuses on reducing time, cost, and poor quality within manufacturing processes.

Exhibit 1 lists some of the just-in-time manufacturing principles and the traditional manufacturing principles. In the following paragraphs, we briefly discuss each

Exhibit 1 Operating Principles of Just-in-Time versus Traditional Manufacturing

Issue	Just-in-Time Manufacturing	Traditional Manufacturing
Inventory	Reduces inventory.	Increases inventory to "buffer" or protect against process problems.
Lead time	Reduces lead time.	Increases lead time as a buffer against uncertainty.
Setup time	Reduces setup time.	Disregards setup time as an improvement priority.
Production layout	Emphasizes product-oriented layout.	Emphasizes process-oriented layout.
Role of the employee	Emphasizes team-oriented employee involvement.	Emphasizes work of individuals, following manager instructions.
Production scheduling policy	Emphasizes pull manufacturing.	Emphasizes push manufacturing.
Quality	Emphasizes zero defects.	Tolerates defects.
Suppliers	Emphasizes supplier partnering.	Treats suppliers as "arm's-length," independent entities.

of the just-in-time principles. We will then address the accounting implications of these principles.

Reducing Inventory

Supporters of just-in-time manufacturing view inventory as wasteful and unnecessary. They argue that inventory may hide underlying production problems. For example, they point out that inventory is often used to maintain sales and production levels during various production interruptions, such as machine breakdowns, manufacturing schedule changes, transportation delays, and unexpected scrap and rework. An important focus in just-in-time manufacturing is to remove these production problems so that the materials, work in process, and finished goods inventory levels can be reduced or eliminated.

PCs are like grocery produce, says the distribution manager of Inacom Corp., the largest reseller of IBM computers. "Anything that sits on a shelf will basically go bad." Dell Computer Corporation and Inacom Corp. avoid stocking computers by using just-in-time concepts to custom build computers from Internet orders and deliver them to customers within days of receiving the order.

The role of inventory can be explained by referring to a river. Inventory is the water in a river, while the rocks at the bottom of the river are the production problems. When the water level is high, all the rocks at the bottom of the river are hidden. In other words, inventory hides the production problems. However, as the water level drops, the rocks become exposed, one by one. Reducing inventory reveals production problems. Once these problems are fixed, the "water level" can be reduced even further to expose more "rocks" for elimination until an efficient, effective production process is achieved.

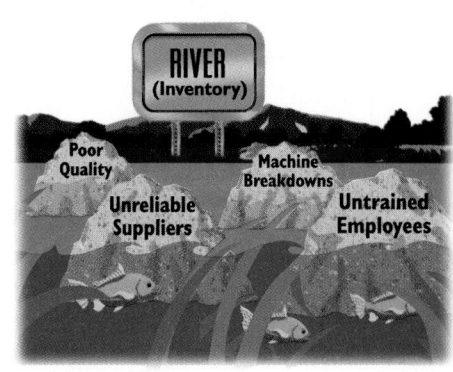

Reducing Lead Times

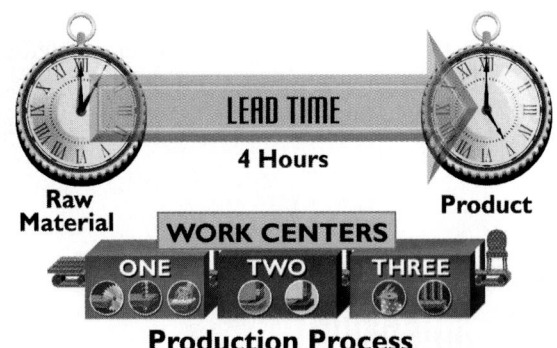

Lead time, sometimes called **throughput time**, is a measure of the time that elapses between starting a unit of product into the beginning of a process and completing the unit of product. As shown in the illustration, if a product begins the process at 1:00 PM and is completed at 5:00 PM, the lead time is 4 hours.

Reducing lead times can be an objective for products manufactured in the plant or any other item that is produced through a process. For example, lead times could be reduced for processing sales orders, invoices, insurance applications, or hospital patients.

The total lead time can be divided into value-added and nonvalue-added time portions, as shown in Exhibit 2. **Value-added lead time** is the time required to actually manufacture a unit of a product. It is the conversion time for a unit. For example, value-added lead time would include the time to drill and pack parts for shipment. **Nonvalue-added lead time** is the time that a unit of product sits in inventories or moves unnecessarily. Nonvalue-added lead time occurs in poor production processes. In a well-functioning process, the product should spend very little time waiting in inventory, because inventory is at a minimum. The product should also spend little time moving, because operations are sequenced closely.

Just-in-time concepts have allowed Boeing Company to slash the time it takes to deliver a commercial plane from 1½ years to 10 months.

Just-in-time manufacturing attempts to make the nonvalue-added lead time very small, thereby reducing the cost and improving the speed of production. Reducing nonvalue-added lead time is often directly related to reducing inventory. Organizations that use many work in process inventory locations may discover that the percentage of nonvalue-added lead time can often approach 90% of the total lead time.

Exhibit 2 Components of Lead Time

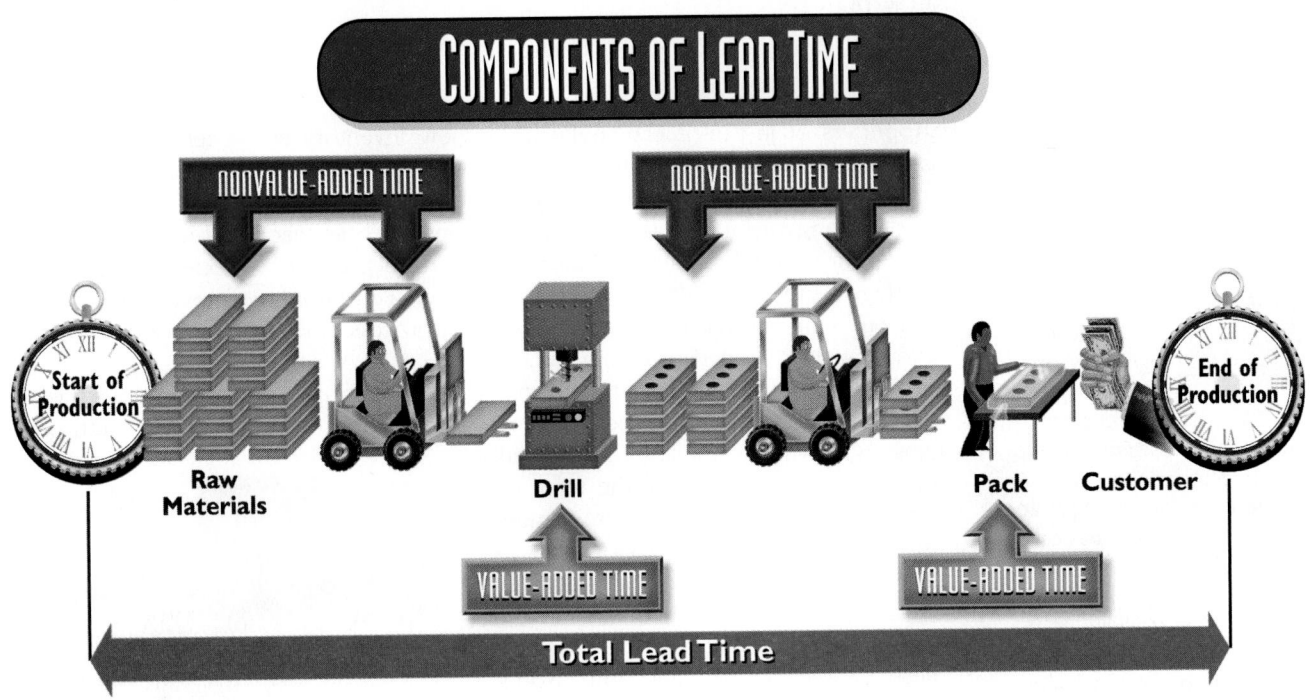

Reducing Setup Time

As we introduced in the previous chapter, a **setup** is the effort required to prepare an operation for a new production run. For example, a beverage company's bottling line would need to be cleaned between flavor changes. If setups are long and expensive, the production run (**batch**) must be large in order to recover the setup cost. Large batches increase inventory, and larger inventories add to lead time. Exhibit 3 is a diagram of the relationship between setup times and lead time.

Exhibit 3 Relationship Between Setup Times and Lead Time

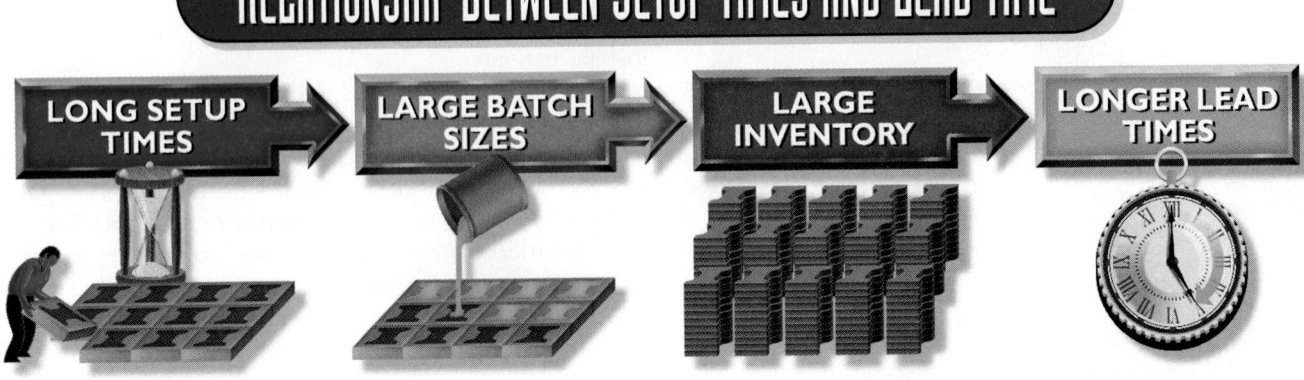

Exhibit 4 illustrates the impact of batch sizes on lead times, using a product that is manufactured in two identical processes (X and Y) that require three operations in each process in order of A, B, and C. The product requires one minute of pro-

Tech Industries required 5 hours and 84 separate steps to set up a large injection molding machine. A videotape of the setup showed that the operator climbed a ladder to the top of the machine 35 times, walked around the machine 37 times, and left the area for tools 12 times, for over 3,000 yards of walking. The improvement team reorganized the setup so that the operator climbed the machine only 7 times, walked around the machine 12 times, and never left the area for tools. These improvements reduced the number of process steps from 84 to 19 and the setup time from five hours to one hour.

cessing inside each operation. In Process X, the batch size is 1 unit, while in Process Y, the batch size is five units. Process X has only three units in process—one unit being produced in each of three operations. The lead time for any particular unit in Process X is three minutes, while for Process Y it is 15 minutes. In Process Y, three units are being produced in the operating departments, while the other twelve are stored as work in process inventory. Each unit waits its "turn" while other units in the batch are being processed. At each operation, one unit takes five minutes to complete the operation—four minutes waiting its "turn" and one minute in production. The four minutes that each part "waits its turn" at each operation is called **within-batch wait time**. Of the 15 minutes total lead time, 12 minutes represents the within-batch wait time for all three operations (3 operations × 4 minutes). Thus, 80% (12 minutes ÷ 15 minutes) of the lead time is nonvalue-added in Process Y.

Organizations that use just-in-time practices try to reduce setup times to reduce the batch size. Once batch sizes are reduced, the work in process inventory and wait time are reduced, thus reducing overall lead time.

Exhibit 4 Impact of Batch Sizes on Lead Times

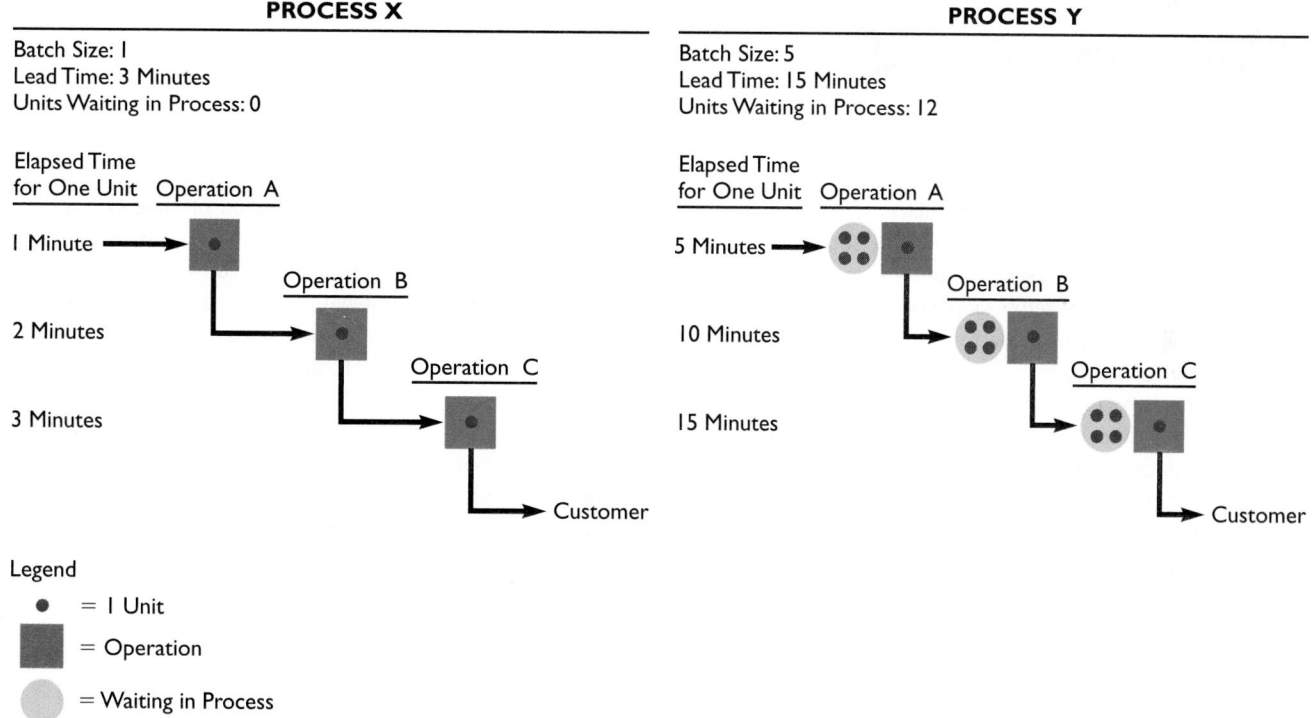

To illustrate, assume that Automotive Components Inc. manufactures a batch of 40 engine starters through three processes: machining, assembly, and testing. Each unit in the batch requires the following processing times:

Processing Time per Unit

Machining	6 minutes
Assembly	10
Testing	8
Total	24 minutes

A product manufactured in batches of 25 units is produced through three stages of production: forging, machining, and assembly. Each unit requires 10 minutes forging, 16 minutes machining, and 8 minutes assembly. What is the within-batch wait time?

----

816 minutes [34 minutes × (25 units − 1 unit)]

After machining, it takes 10 minutes to move the machined batch to assembly. It then takes 15 minutes to move the assembled batch to testing. The lead time can be analyzed as follows:

	Lead Times	Percent of Total
Value-added lead time	24 minutes	2.5%
Nonvalue-added lead time:		
Within-batch wait time [24 min. × (40 − 1)]	936	95.0
Move time	25	2.5
Total	985 minutes	100.0%

Approximately 97.5% of the lead time is consumed by nonvalue-added waiting and moving. How could Automotive Components improve its lead time performance? First, it could reduce setups so that the batch size could be reduced to one piece, termed **one-piece flow**. Second, it could move the processes closer to each other so that the move time is eliminated. With these two steps, the total lead time would approach the value-added lead time.

BUSINESS ON STAGE

Internal and External Setup

A common way to improve setup time is to videotape the setup process in order to identify internal and external setup tasks. *Internal setup tasks* are those that require the machine to stop running in order to be completed. The time to perform internal setup tasks is critical because it directly impacts production. An example of an internal setup task is changing a die on a stamping machine. The machine must be stopped when a die is changed. *External setup tasks* are those that can be completed off-line while the machine is still running. Examples include activities to organize the area, perform cleanup, and position tools in preparation for setup.

A common method of reducing setup time is to change internal setup tasks into external setup tasks. This can be as simple as organizing all tools prior to the setup, rather than using time to find tools once the machine has stopped. To further illustrate, assume that a process requires a rack of fabric to be dipped into a vessel of dye. To change colors, the vessel must be emptied of old dye, cleaned, filled with new dye, and preheated to production temperatures. These would all be internal setup tasks, because the process would need to stop while the change was made. However, if the firm invested in a second vessel, then this second vessel could be filled with new

dye and preheated off-line. Upon completing the production run, the new production run color could go immediately to the second vessel. The old vessel could then be emptied, cleaned, filled and preheated with new dye off-line for a new color batch, and so on. In this case, the second vessel allowed internal setup tasks to be changed into external setup tasks, enabling the company to reduce machine downtime from setup, increase setup frequency, reduce inventories, and decrease lead times. ■

Emphasizing Product-Oriented Layout

Organizing work around products is called a **product-oriented layout** (or **product cells**), while organizing work around processes is called a **process-oriented layout**. Just-in-time methods favor organizing work around products rather than processes. Organizing work around products reduces the amount of materials movement, coordination between operations, and work in process inventory. As a result, lead time and production costs are reduced.

To illustrate, **Hallmark Cards** at one time processed greeting card design work through separate Art, Layout, and Preproduction Departments. These departments were organized around the processes for designing a new greeting card. Hallmark decided that this traditional method of organizing work was slowing down the designing of new cards, while increasing their cost. As a result, Hallmark reorganized the greeting card design activity around each holiday. Layout, art, and preproduction activities were arranged together into single cells according to each type of holiday. Hallmark now has a Valentine's Day cell, a Mother's Day cell, and cells for other major holidays.

Emphasizing Employee Involvement

Sony has organized a small team of four employees to completely assemble a camcorder, doing everything from soldering to testing. The new line reduces assembly time from 70 minutes to 15 minutes per camera. "There is no future in conventional conveyor lines. They are a tool that conforms to the person with the least ability," states a Sony representative.

Employee involvement is a management approach that grants employees the responsibility and authority to make decisions about operations, rather than relying solely on management instructions. This decision-making authority requires accounting and other information to be made available to all employees.

Employee involvement uses teams organized in product cells, rather than just the efforts of isolated, individual employees. Such employee teams can be **cross-trained** to perform any operation within the product cell. For example, employees learn how to operate several different machines within their product cell. Moreover, team members are trained to perform functions traditionally handled by centralized service departments. For example, direct labor employees may perform their own maintenance, quality control, housekeeping, and production improvement work. When direct labor employees perform such indirect functions, the distinction between direct and indirect labor cost becomes less important.

Emphasizing Pull Manufacturing

Kenney Manufacturing Company, a manufacturer of window shades, estimated that 50% of its window shade process was nonvalue-added. By using pull manufacturing and changing the line layout, it was able to reduce inventory by 82% and lead time by 84%.

Another important just-in-time principle is to produce items only as they are needed by the customer. This principle is called **pull manufacturing** (or **make to order**). In pull manufacturing, the status of the next operation determines when products are moved or produced. If the next operation is busy, then production stops so that material does not pile up in front of the busy operation. If the next operation is ready, then product can be produced or moved to that operation.

The system that accomplishes pull manufacturing is often called **kanban**, which is Japanese for "cards." Electronic cards or containers signal production quantities to be filled by the feeder operation. The cards link the customer back through each stage of production. When a consumer purchases a product, a card triggers assembly of a replacement product, which in turn triggers cards to manufacture the components required for the assembly. This creates a flow of parts and products that move to the drumbeat of customer demand.

In contrast, the traditional approach is to schedule production based on forecasted customer requirements. This principle is called **push manufacturing** (or **make to stock**). In push manufacturing, product is released for manufacturing without reference to line status but according to a production schedule. The schedule "pushes" product to inventory ahead of known customer demand. As a result, manufacturers using push manufacturing will generally have more inventory than those of manufacturers using pull manufacturing. As stated by one consultant, "If your manufacturing operations are still set up around guessing demand, you will forever be in a loop of producing and holding the wrong items and not having enough of what the customer actually wants."[1]

---

[1] Quoted by David Rucker of TBM Institute in "E-biz Requires Leaner Operation, More Integration," Jennifer Shah, *Electronic Buyers News*, July 31, 2000.

Emphasizing Zero Defects

Just-in-time manufacturing practices strive to eliminate poor quality. Poor quality results in an increased need for inspection, more production interruptions, an increased need for rework, additional recordkeeping for scrap, a higher cost from scrap, and additional warranty costs. Thus, one of the primary objectives of just-in-time manufacturing is to improve the process so that products are made right the first time.

Emphasizing Supplier Partnering

Another just-in-time manufacturing practice is entering into long-term agreements with suppliers. Developing long-term customer/supplier relationships is called **supplier partnering**. Partnering encourages suppliers to develop a commitment to the manufacturer so that materials purchased will be high quality, low cost, and on time.

Supplier partnering often involves working to improve supplier operations by employing just-in-time principles. Thus, the just-in-time approach does not stop within the four walls of the factory but extends to the supplier's manufacturing operations as well. The result is an effective and efficient production chain that operates from raw materials to the final consumer. In addition, electronic data interchange and the Internet are used to improve the information flows between suppliers and customers. **Electronic data interchange (EDI)** is a method of using computers to electronically communicate orders, relay information, and make or receive payments from one organization to another. In addition, a supplier partner can electronically transmit engineering and design support for supplied parts.

Maytag Corporation's CEO recently stated: "Our vision for the future includes flexibility in manufacturing so that we can take an order electronically or over the phone, manufacture it with the features specified, and be ready to ship it within a week."

Applying a Just-in-Time Approach to Anderson Metal Fabricators

objective 2

Apply just-in-time manufacturing practices to a traditional manufacturing illustration.

To illustrate just-in-time manufacturing principles, we will assume that Anderson Metal Fabricators (AMF) makes two types of metal covers, *large* and *small*, for electronic test equipment. Metal covers are made by stamping a pattern of the cover from sheet steel, much like a cookie cutter stamps cookies out of dough. The stamped patterns are then sent through a punching operation, which punches holes on the pattern for fasteners. The last operation is the forming operation, where the pattern is bent into a cover and fasteners are attached.

Traditional Operations—AMF

Exhibit 5 illustrates the plant layout of AMF as a traditional manufacturer. The facility is divided into three major production departments: Stamping, Punching, and Forming. This is an example of the process-oriented layout found in many traditional manufacturing operations. AMF has many machines in each department. Within each department, partially completed products are stored in work in process inventory, waiting to be worked on by the next department. The Maintenance and Tooling Department is in a centralized location within the plant. Customers order product from the finished goods inventory. Departments receive their production schedules and work instructions based on forecasted demand, which is an example of push manufacturing.

Following the traditional approach, AMF's purchasing function attempts to supply the correct amount of raw materials according to production schedules. Extra raw materials are ordered "just in case" a shipment is missed, delayed, or incorrect. Likewise, uncertainty about the final output of any department, because of

Exhibit 5 Traditional Operations—AMF

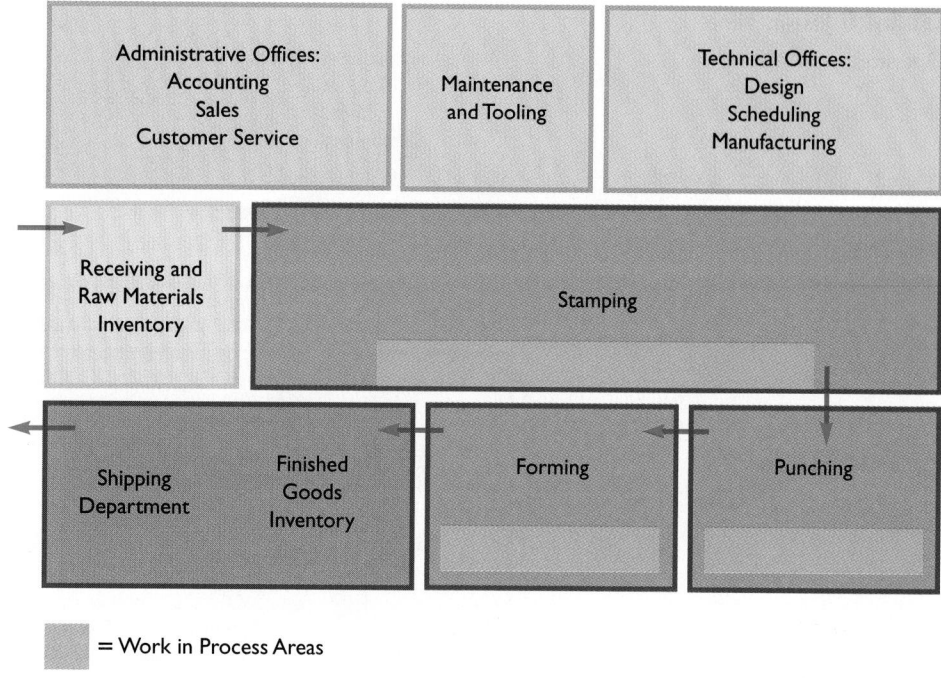

= Work in Process Areas

machine breakdowns, scrap, rework, or production inefficiency, causes managers to increase work in process inventory. For example, the large work in process inventory in the Stamping Department keeps the Punching Department from running out of stampings when the stamping machines break down. Finally, the machines within AMF's departments must be set up to change production between the small and large covers.

Just-in-Time Operations—AMF

The management of AMF wishes to introduce a new product, the *medium-size* metal cover. Unfortunately, the existing production capacity and space will not support the increased production. As a result, AMF management has decided to use just-in-time principles in order to better utilize the existing productive capacity and space.

Exhibit 6 illustrates the just-in-time operations for AMF. To apply just-in-time principles, management revised the department structure. Instead of the production departments being organized around the various operational processes, they are now organized around the three product lines (small, medium, and large covers). This product-oriented layout was accomplished by taking the machines and the people in each of the old departments and separating them into three product production cells. For example, the Stamping Department machines were separated to form the first position in three separate product cells.

Since each product has its own product cell, there is no longer any need for setups. For example, the medium cover line has no setups because only medium covers are manufactured in this cell. Eliminating setup time releases productive capacity to make the medium covers. In addition, the operations within a product cell are positioned physically close to each other in order to minimize move time. The close physical distance between each machine allows materials to be transferred between each operation in small batches, using kanban signals.

The Maintenance and Tooling Department was decentralized. Each product cell now includes a maintenance and tooling function. This allows equipment to be repaired more quickly, since the parts, tools, and personnel are physically closer to the problem.

Exhibit 6 Just-in-Time Operations—AMF

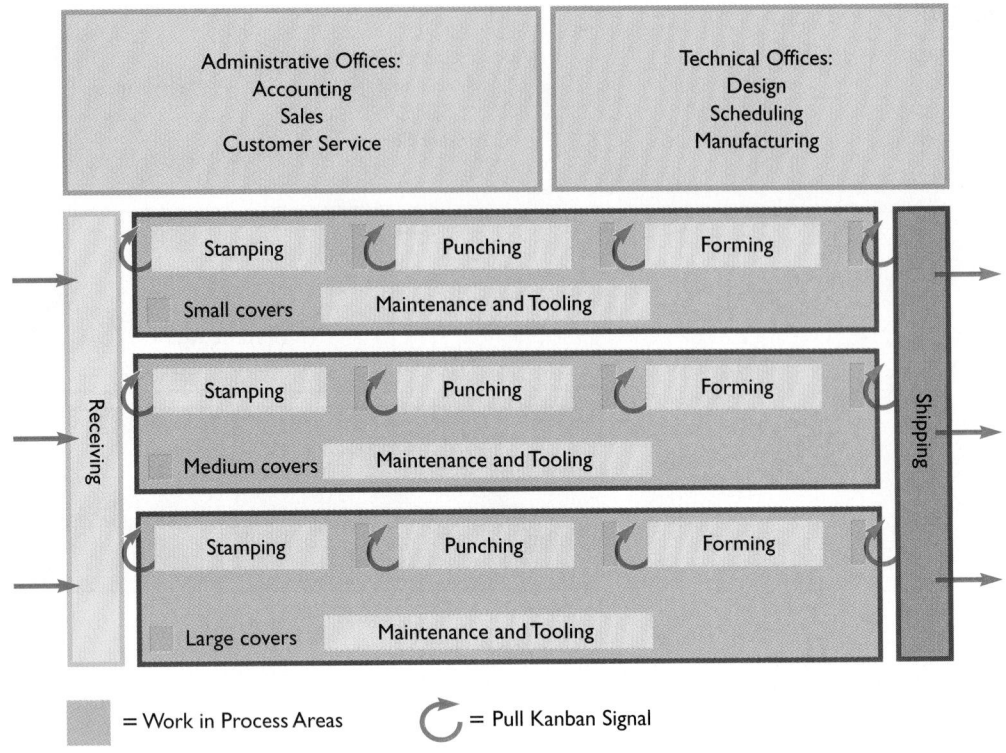

Administrative Offices:	Technical Offices:
Accounting	Design
Sales	Scheduling
Customer Service	Manufacturing

Receiving

Stamping   Punching   Forming

Small covers   Maintenance and Tooling

Stamping   Punching   Forming

Medium covers   Maintenance and Tooling

Stamping   Punching   Forming

Large covers   Maintenance and Tooling

Shipping

■ = Work in Process Areas   ↻ = Pull Kanban Signal

General Motors' first new assembly plant in over a decade is being designed with a leaner, more flexible layout. The building is about half the traditional size. Rather than centralized shipping and receiving areas, it features widely dispersed loading docks so suppliers can feed parts directly to the assembly process.

What features of AMF's new process are consistent with just-in-time manufacturing principles?

Product-oriented layout, elimination of setups, close physical distance between operations, decentralized maintenance and tooling, reduction of inventories (materials, work in process, and finished goods), increased employee involvement in improving the process, use of supplier partnering to increase quality and delivery frequency of incoming parts, and application of pull manufacturing.

The materials, work in process, and finished goods inventory storage space is reduced significantly. Eliminating the wasted space used for inventory provides room for producing the medium covers. Thus, AMF is able to expand production without investing in new facilities.

AMF orders raw materials only as they are needed for production. In the just-in-time environment, trucks often arrive daily or even more frequently, with just enough raw materials to last until the next shipment arrives. The raw materials are received directly by the various product cells, without inspection, because suppliers guarantee zero defects through supplier partnering.

Minimal work in process inventory exists between the product cells because of employee involvement to reduce the mistakes and errors within the process. Thus, AMF's employees have improved quality, reduced unexpected machine failures, reduced scrap, and reduced rework. Normally, small work in process inventory levels would cause AMF to risk a loss in productivity through unexpected manufacturing stoppages. However, the process improvements will allow AMF's production to continue without risk of shutdown, even with reduced inventory. As a result of these improvements, the nonvalue-added lead time has been significantly reduced.

Operations do not produce product just to remain busy and improve machine utilization. In pull manufacturing, operations respond only to customer orders. As a result, all operations within a cell operate at the same pace. This practice avoids a buildup of work in process inventory from "out-running" slower operations. If customer demand slows, then the production pace will also be slowed to match the demand. Employees can then use the extra time to work on improving the process or to move to other cells where product demand is high.

Accounting for Just-in-Time Operations

objective 3

Describe the implications of a just-in-time manufacturing philosophy on cost accounting and performance measurement systems.

At **Caterpillar, Inc.**, traditional plant layouts required a transmission assembly to travel as much as 10 miles as it moved to different operations. Its progress was tracked by more than 1,000 pieces of paper. Caterpillar then reorganized its work flows, using just-in-time approaches. As a result, the transmission assembly travel distance was reduced to 200 feet, with an average of 10 pieces of paper used to track each transmission.

In just-in-time operations, the accounting system will have the characteristics listed below. Each of these characteristics is described in the following paragraphs.

- *Fewer transactions.* The accounting system is simpler because there are fewer transactions to record.
- *Combined accounts.* All in-process work is combined with raw materials to form a new account, **Raw and In Process (RIP) Inventory**, while the direct labor becomes part of the conversion cost.
- *Nonfinancial performance measures.* There is a greater emphasis on nonfinancial performance measures.
- *Direct tracing of overhead.* Indirect labor is directly assigned to product production cells, requiring less factory overhead allocation to products.

Fewer Transactions

The traditional process cost accounting system accumulates the cost incurred in a department and then transfers this cost to the next department. Thus, materials are recorded into and out of work in process inventories as production moves through the factory. Recording the flow of costs through a plant in this way leads to control of departmental costs. However, since each department has transactions flowing in and out, the traditional cost accounting system has many transactions to record, accumulate, correct, and report. This adds cost, complexity, and delay in reporting accounting information.

In the just-in-time production process, the need for accounting cost control is much less, because lower inventories make problems much more visible on the factory floor. In other words, managers don't need an accounting report to indicate problems, since any problems are immediately visible to them. Thus, the accounting system can be simplified by eliminating the accumulation and transfer of costs as products move through the production process. Such simplification is termed **backflush accounting**. In backflush accounting, costs are transferred from combined material and conversion cost accounts directly to finished production without transferring costs through intermediate departmental work in process accounts. We illustrate the use of combined accounts in this way in the next section.

Combined Accounts

Since the just-in-time manufacturer attempts to eliminate inventory, including raw materials, there is no need for a separate materials account. For example, **Saturn Corporation** has receiving areas all around the perimeter of its factory. In this way, raw materials can be delivered by trucks to a receiving area that is located near the point of use on the assembly line. Thus, there is no need for a separate materials inventory location or a materials account, since materials are introduced immediately into production. Many just-in-time manufacturers debit all materials and conversion costs to *Raw and In Process Inventory* and thus combine materials and work in process costs in one account.

The direct labor cost classification is often not used by just-in-time manufacturers. This is because the employees in product cells perform many tasks, some of which could be classified as direct, such as performing operations, and some as indirect, such as performing inspections. From an accounting perspective, the product cell labor cost is combined with other cell overhead costs to form the total product cell conversion cost.

To illustrate these accounting concepts, assume that the annual budgeted conversion cost for AMF's medium-cover product cell is $2,400,000. These costs will support 1,920 planned hours of production. The cell conversion cost rate is determined by dividing the annual budgeted conversion cost by the planned production hours to yield $1,250 per hour, as shown below. This rate is similar to a predetermined factory overhead rate, except that it includes all conversion costs in the numerator.

$$\textbf{Budgeted cell conversion cost rate} = \frac{\textbf{\$2,400,000 budgeted conversion cost}}{\textbf{1,920 planned production hours}}$$

$$= \textbf{\$1,250 per hour}$$

The medium-cover product cell is expected to require 0.02 hours of manufacturing time per unit. Thus, the conversion cost is estimated to be $25 per unit, as shown below.

$$\textbf{0.02 hours per unit} \times \textbf{\$1,250 conversion cost per hour} =$$
$$\textbf{\$25 conversion cost per unit}$$

To illustrate the recording of transactions in AMF's just-in-time operations, assume that the following selected transactions occurred during April:

Transaction	Journal Entry			Comment

1. Steel coil is purchased for producing 8,000 medium covers. The purchase cost was $120,000, or $15 per unit.	Raw and In Process Inventory
	  Accounts Payable
	    To record materials purchases.
		120,000	120,000	Note that the materials purchased are debited to the combined account, Raw and In Process Inventory. A separate materials account is not used, because materials are received directly in the product cells, rather than in an inventory location.

2. Conversion costs are applied to 8,000 medium covers at a rate of $25 per cover.	Raw and In Process Inventory
	  Conversion Costs
	    To record applied conversion costs of the medium-cover line.
		200,000	200,000	The raw and in process inventory account is used to accumulate the applied cell conversion costs during the period.

3. All 8,000 medium covers were completed in the cell. The raw and in process inventory account is reduced by the $15 per unit materials cost and the $25 per unit conversion cost.	Finished Goods Inventory
	  Raw and In Process Inventory
	    To transfer the cost of completed units to finished goods.
		320,000	320,000	Materials ($15 × 8,000 units) $120,000
				Conversion ($25 × 8,000 units) <u>200,000</u>
				    Total <u>$320,000</u>
				
				After the cost of the completed units is transferred from the raw and in process inventory account, the account's balance is zero. There are no units left in process within the cell.[2] This is a backflush transaction.

4. Of the 8,000 units completed, 7,800 were sold and shipped to customers at $70 per unit, leaving 200 finished units in stock. Thus, the finished goods inventory account has a balance of $8,000 (200 × $40). Even though AMF is now a just-in-time manufacturer, a small number of customer orders were not shipped at the end of the month.	Accounts Receivable
	  Sales
	    To record sales.
	Cost of Goods Sold
	  Finished Goods
	    To record cost of goods sold.
		546,000
		
		312,000
			546,000
			
			312,000
				Units sold 7,800
				Conversion and materials costs per unit × $40
				Transferred to cost of goods sold <u>$312,000</u>

---

[2] The actual conversion cost per unit may be different from the budgeted conversion cost per unit due to cell inefficiency, improvements in processing methods, or excess scrap. These deviations from the budgeted cost can be accounted for as cost variances, as illustrated in more advanced texts.

A company using just-in-time principles purchased 5,000 parts for $50 per part. These parts were used to make 5,000 units, each unit requiring 15 minutes of cell assembly time. The cell conversion cost is estimated at $250 per hour. What are the appropriate journal entries to record these two transactions?

Raw and In Process Inventory	250,000	
Accounts Payable		250,000
Raw and In Process Inventory	312,500	
Factory Overhead [(15 min./60 min.) × $250 × 5,000]		312,500

Nonfinancial Performance Measures

Just-in-time manufacturing frequently relies on nonfinancial measures to guide short-term operational performance. A **nonfinancial measure** is operating information that has not been stated in dollar terms. Examples of nonfinancial measures of performance include lead time, the ratio of nonvalue-added lead time to total lead time, setup time, the number of production line stops, the number of units scrapped, and deviations from scheduled production. Results of a survey of nonfinancial measures of performance were as follows:[3]

Measure	Percent of Respondents	Just-in-Time Principle Addressed by Performance Measure
Inventory turnovers	82%	Reducing inventory
On-time delivery rates	41	Improving quality
Production lead times	35	Improving lead times
Quality yield	32	Improving quality
Throughput (production output)	32	Reducing inventory
Time required for setups	26	Improving setups
Space utilized	12	Reducing inventory
Extent of cross-training or new skills obtained	8	Involving employees

Nonfinancial measures are used for day-to-day decision making because nonfinancial data can often be provided much more quickly than can accounting data. Accounting data must first be translated into dollars and then summarized, whereas nonfinancial data need not be stated in dollar terms. Periodic nonfinancial measures give product cell employees instant feedback that can be used to improve the process. Traditional accounting data are much better suited for guiding longer-term operational decisions and trade-off analyses, while nonfinancial measures can provide timely and focused operational information. Most companies use a combination of both types of information.

Direct Tracing of Overhead

Just-in-time practices often assign many indirect tasks to a specific product cell. For example, an individual from the Maintenance Department may be assigned to AMF's medium-cover cell and cross-trained to perform other operations. Thus, the salary of this person is directly attributed to the medium-cover product line.

In a traditional facility, the maintenance person is part of the Maintenance Department and is not assigned to a particular product line. Thus, the accounting system must allocate the cost of maintenance services to product lines. Allocating such costs is not necessary when the indirect employees are assigned to a product cell in a just-in-time environment.

Just-in-Time for Nonmanufacturing Processes

objective 4

Apply just-in-time practices to a nonmanufacturing setting.

Just-in-time principles also apply for service and administrative processes, such as hospitals, banks, insurance companies, hotels, transportation providers, sales order

[3] Forrest B. Green and Felix E. Amenkhienan, "Accounting Innovations: A Cross-Sectional Survey of Manufacturing Firms," *Journal of Cost Management* (Winter 1992), p. 62.

processes, and other nonmanufacturing settings. In nonmanufacturing processes, either information or the customer is often the "product" of the process. For example, just-in-time principles can be used on processes for insurance applications, product designs, sales orders, hospital patients, and university students. To illustrate, note the process a typical hospital uses to treat patients, as illustrated in Exhibit 7.

Exhibit 7 Typical Hospital Process Flow

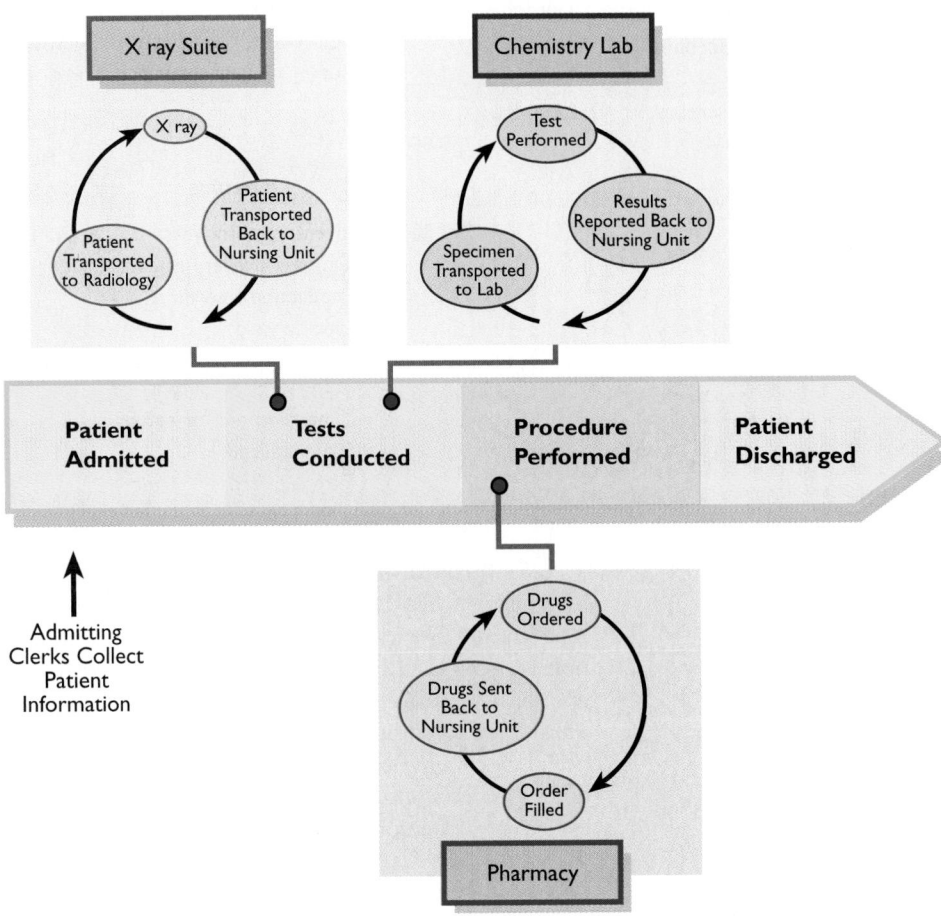

The Admitting Department first admits the patient. This takes some time as patient information is collected and insurance is verified. The admitted patient is then transported to a room where a variety of tests may be required prior to a surgical procedure. These tests often require the patient to be moved to the testing location, as in the case of an X ray, or for specimens to be moved to centralized chemistry labs, as in the case of blood workups. In addition, drugs are ordered from the central pharmacy to be delivered to the patient's floor for nurse administration. Each of these processes consumes time as the patient, specimen, test result, or drug order are moved to the respective departments for processing. In each of the centralized departments, any one patient's requirements must wait its turn behind all the other patients before processing can be completed. Again, this also consumes time. As a result, an average patient's time in the hospital is longer than need be.

Alternatively, Exhibit 8 illustrates a just-in-time hospital layout. There are a number of distinct features in Exhibit 8, compared to Exhibit 7. First, patients with common health problems are placed together on a floor in the hospital. Second, many centralized services are distributed to each of the floors, so that each floor has its own mini-pharmacy, X ray suite, chemistry lab, and admitting office. Patients are served where they are, rather than having to move around the hospital. These two features are similar to the product-oriented layout in manufacturing. Third, "cross-trained" generalists in the nursing units replace specialists in the centralized departments. This provides much greater flexibility in responding to patient needs and provides faster response times.

Exhibit 8 Just-in-Time Hospital Unit Layout

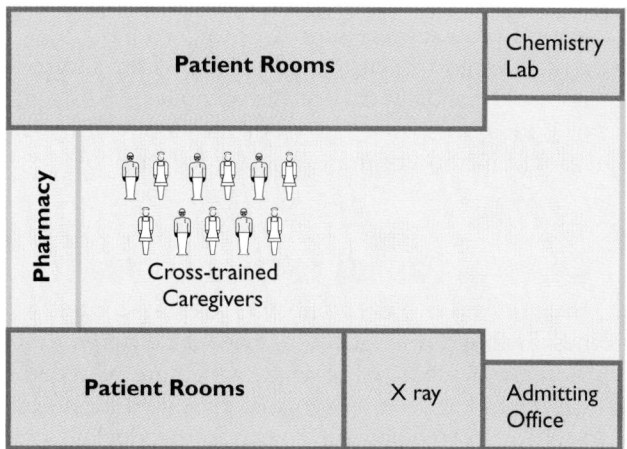

A just-in-time hospital process will reduce the "inventory" of orders, results, patients, and drugs that will be moving through the system waiting to be processed. As a result, the lead time to process orders and tests will be reduced, reducing the average stay in the hospital. The quality of the patient's experience should be better, since the same group of caregivers serves the patient from admittance to discharge. The experience of the caregivers should be better, since they are able to work as a team in providing patient services. Lastly, the overall cost of patient care should decline as the hospital achieves greater efficiency while maintaining patient care standards.

Accounting for the Costs of Quality

objective 5

Describe the costs of quality and prepare a Pareto chart, a cost of quality report, and a value-added/nonvalue-added analysis.

The level of business competition is increasing in many industries. As a result, businesses must emphasize quality—in their processes, in their products, in their employee relationships, and in their outside business relationships—in order to succeed. We have discussed how some businesses are using just-in-time operating principles to improve the quality of their work practices and relationships. Businesses concerned with providing high-quality products and services are motivated to reduce the costs of poor quality.

The costs associated with controlling and failing to control quality are called the **costs of quality**. The costs of controlling quality can be classified as prevention costs or appraisal costs. The costs of failing to control quality can be classified as internal failure costs or external failure costs. These costs are described in the following paragraphs.

Costs of Controlling Quality

Prevention costs are the costs of activities that prevent defects from occurring during the design and delivery of products or services. Preventing defects from occurring saves a company the costs associated with handling, disposing, and recording of scrap. Examples of prevention activities include quality engineering, design engineering, assessing vendor quality, operator training, and preventive machine maintenance. All of these activities prevent quality problems from occurring and, as such, are investments in future quality.

Appraisal costs are the costs of activities that detect, measure, evaluate, and inspect products and processes to ensure that they meet customer needs. Appraisal costs are most often related to inspection and testing activities. Appraisal costs do not fundamentally change the amount of poor quality produced—only the amount of poor quality that "slips out the door." Thus, appraisal activities are a less permanent method of improving quality than are prevention activities.

Costs of Failing to Control Quality

Internal failure costs are the costs associated with defects discovered by a business before the product or service is delivered to the consumer. These costs include the cost of scrap and rework, which are recorded by the accounting system. However, in addition to obvious costs related to internal failure, there are also costs related to lost equipment time from producing scrap, supervision to move, record, and dispose of scrap, procurement time to repurchase parts that arrive defective, and inventory produced to protect against possible lost production from scrap.

External failure costs are the costs incurred after defective units or services have been delivered to consumers. These costs are "external" because the defects are discovered while the products or services are being used by the consumer. External failure costs include the cost of activities related to field repairs, recalls, warranty work, correcting invoice errors, and processing returned merchandise. More importantly, external failure costs also include the cost of lost customer goodwill. Although this cost is difficult to measure, some believe it is the largest cost in the quality equation. It has been reported that every dissatisfied customer tells at least ten people about an unhappy experience with a product, so the impact of a failure extends far beyond the single event.

> **Costs of controlling quality:**
>   **Prevention costs**
>   **Appraisal costs**
> **Costs of failing to control quality:**
>   **Internal failure costs**
>   **External failure costs**

The Relationship Between the Costs of Quality

Exhibit 9 shows the relationship between the costs of quality. As the graph indicates, the prevention and appraisal costs increase as the percentage of good units produced increases. This is because additional costs are needed for designing products and processes that will produce high-quality products. The internal and external failure costs decline with increases in the percentage of good units produced. This is because the costs from scrap, warranty work, and other failure costs go down as quality improves. The total cost line is the sum of both the prevention/appraisal cost and internal/external failure cost lines.

The best level of quality is that level which minimizes the estimated total quality costs. In Exhibit 9, this level is at (or near) 100% quality! The reason for this result is that the costs of appraisal and prevention grow moderately as quality increases. However, the costs of internal and external failure drop much more dramatically as quality increases. That is, when more effort is given to prevention and appraisal, internal and external failure costs decrease markedly.

Exhibit 9 The Relationship Between the Costs of Quality

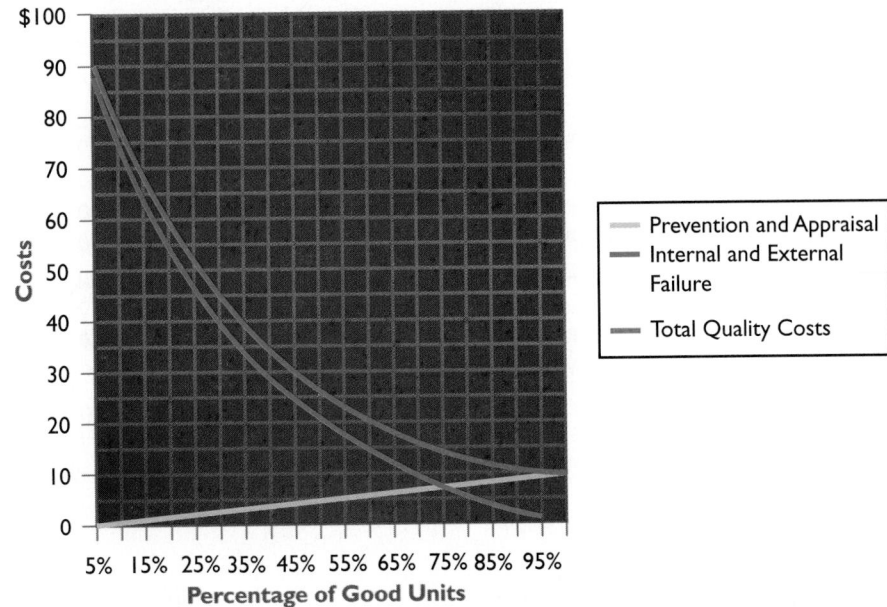

One survey estimated that the cost of quality for most businesses is about 20%–30% of sales.[4] The percentage of quality costs allocated to each classification has been approximately as follows:[5]

Prevention	5%–10%
Appraisal	20%–25%
Internal failure	30%–35%
External failure	25%–30%

As you can see from the survey, many companies are spending their quality dollars in the wrong way. The failure costs are much larger than the costs related to preventing and appraising failures. Companies have been allowing defective products to be made before discovering a quality problem. This practice results in higher quality costs due to the costs of correcting failures. Instead, more companies should be investing in prevention, so that defective products can be eliminated.

Determining the Costs of Quality

The costs of quality can be analyzed through a quality control activity analysis. An **activity analysis** determines the cost of activities based on an analysis of employee effort and other records. To illustrate, assume that Gifford Company has performed a quality control activity analysis whose results are shown in Exhibit 10. This exhibit lists the activities, the dollar amount associated with each activity, and the quality cost classification of each activity.

Pareto Chart

Managers want information so that the important problems or issues can be identified quickly. One method of reporting information is the Pareto chart. A **Pareto chart** is a bar chart that shows the totals of an attribute for a number of categories.

---

[4] "The Quality Review," Spring 1987 Gallup Poll.
[5] James B. Simpson and David L. Muthler, "Quality Costs: Facilitating the Quality Initiative," *Journal of Cost Management* (Spring 1987), pp. 25–34.

Exhibit 10 Quality Control Activity Analysis—Gifford Company

Quality Control Activities	Activity Cost	Quality Cost Classification
Design engineering	$ 55,000	Prevention
Disposal of rejected materials	160,000	Internal Failure
Finished goods inspection	140,000	Appraisal
Materials inspection	70,000	Appraisal
Preventive maintenance	80,000	Prevention
Processing returned materials	150,000	External Failure
Disposing of scrap	195,000	Internal Failure
Assessing vendor quality	45,000	Prevention
Rework	380,000	Internal Failure
Warranty work	225,000	External Failure
Total activity cost	$1,500,000	

A quality control activity analysis indicated the following four activity costs of an administrative department:

Verifying accuracy of a form	$ 50,000
Responding to customer complaints	100,000
Correcting errors in forms	75,000
Redesigning forms to reduce errors	25,000

What is the percentage of total activity costs associated with each of the four costs of quality?

Prevention	$ 25,000	10%
Appraisal	50,000	20
Internal failure	75,000	30
External failure	100,000	40
Total	$250,000	100%

The categories are ranked and displayed left to right, so that the largest total is on the left and the smallest total is on the right. To illustrate, Exhibit 11 shows a Pareto chart for the quality control activities in Exhibit 10.

In Exhibit 11, the vertical axis is dollars, the attribute in which management is interested. Examples of other attributes that could be used on the vertical axis of a Pareto chart are number of defects, time, cost savings, or any other numerical characteristic.

The horizontal axis represents categories for which data are reported. In Exhibit 11, the horizontal axis is categorized according to the ten quality cost activities. The horizontal axis of a Pareto chart could show types of defects, products, customers, employees, or other categories for which data are reported.

The categories on the horizontal axis are ranked from the one with the largest total on the left to the one with the smallest total on the right. Thus, the largest bar on the left in Exhibit 11 is the most expensive quality cost activity—rework. The second largest bar is the second most expensive quality cost activity—

Exhibit 11 Pareto Chart of Quality Costs

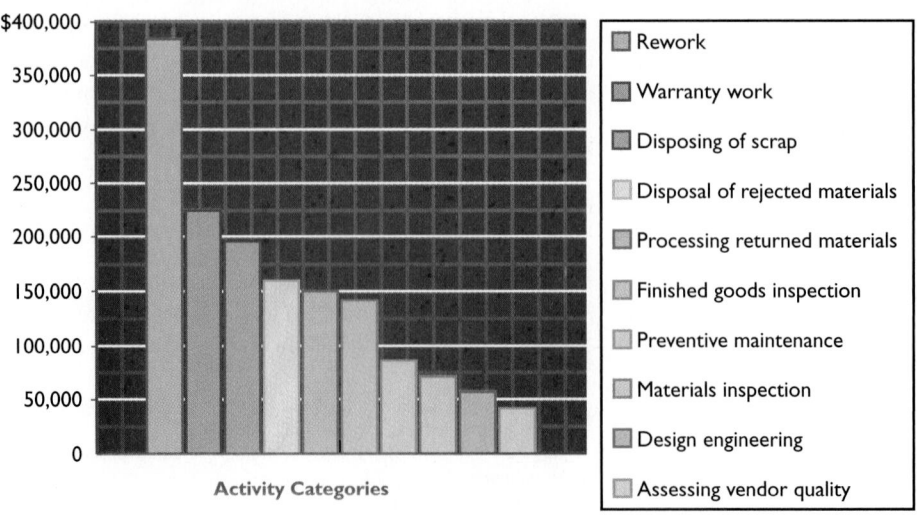

warranty work. The Pareto chart gives the manager a visual tool for identifying the most important categories on which to focus efforts. In this case, rework and warranty work would be high-priority improvement items.

Cost of Quality Report

In addition to a Pareto chart, the costs of quality from the activity analysis can be summarized in a cost of quality report. A **cost of quality report** identifies the total activity cost associated with each quality cost classification and the percentage of total quality costs associated with each classification. In addition, many cost of quality reports will provide the percentage of each quality cost classification to sales. Exhibit 12 is a cost of quality report for Gifford Company, based on assumed sales of $5,000,000 for the period.

Exhibit 12 Cost of Quality Report—Gifford Company

Quality Cost Classification	Cost Summary		
	Quality Cost	Percent of Total Quality Cost	Percent of Total Sales
Prevention	$ 180,000	12.00%	3.6%
Appraisal	210,000	14.00	4.2
Internal failure	735,000	49.00	14.7
External failure	375,000	25.00	7.5
Total	$1,500,000	100.00%	30.0%

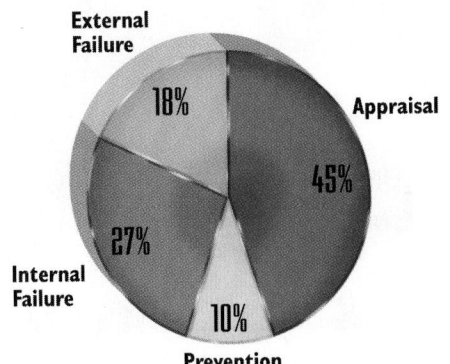

Bank One, a large regional bank, performed a quality control activity analysis. The analysis indicated the following percentage of costs allocated to each classification:

External Failure 18%

Appraisal 45%

Internal Failure 27%

Prevention 10%

As a result of this study, Bank One was able to justify greater investments in prevention activities to improve customer service at lower operating costs.

As you can see, 12% of the total quality cost is the cost of preventing quality problems and 14% is the cost of appraisal activities, while the remaining 74% is for internal and external failures. In addition, internal and external failure-related costs are equal to 22.2% of sales. Gifford Company is not spending a sufficient amount of money in prevention and appraisal activities, while the amount of money spent on internal and external failure activities is too high. This information can be used by Gifford Company to improve quality by focusing on prevention and appraisal activities and thus reducing internal and external failure costs and total quality costs.

Value-Added/Nonvalue-Added Activity Analysis

The quality control activities of Gifford Company have been classified by quality cost. An alternative method for classifying quality control activities is by value-added and nonvalue-added activities. A **value-added activity** is one that is necessary to meet customer requirements. A **nonvalue-added activity** is *not* required by the customer but exists because of mistakes, errors, omissions, and other process failures. To illustrate, Exhibit 13 shows the value-added and nonvalue-added classification for the quality control activities for Gifford Company.

As you can see, the internal and external failure costs are classified as nonvalue-added, while the prevention and appraisal costs are classified as value-added.[6] A summary of the value-added and nonvalue-added

---

[6] Some believe that appraisal costs are nonvalue-added. They argue that if the product had been made correctly, then no inspection would be required. We will take a less strict view and assume that appraisal costs are value-added.

Exhibit 13 Value-Added/
Nonvalue-Added Quality
Control Activities

Quality Control Activities	Activity Cost	Classification
Design engineering	$ 55,000	Value-added
Disposing of rejected materials	160,000	Nonvalue-added
Finished goods inspection	140,000	Value-added
Materials inspection	70,000	Value-added
Preventive maintenance	80,000	Value-added
Processing returned materials	150,000	Nonvalue-added
Disposing of scrap	195,000	Nonvalue-added
Assessing vendor quality	45,000	Value-added
Rework	380,000	Nonvalue-added
Warranty work	225,000	Nonvalue-added
Total activity cost	$1,500,000	

activities can be developed to show the percentage of the value-added and nonvalue-added costs to the total costs, as follows:

Classification	Amount	Percent
Value-added	$ 390,000	26%
Nonvalue-added	1,110,000	74
Total	$1,500,000	100%

For Gifford Company, 74% of the studied activities are nonvalue-added. This information should further motivate management to make improvements to reduce nonvalued-added activities.

Porsche Moves Into the Fast Lane

What do you do if you are hired as the new CEO of a car company that has lost $133 million, has lost three-fourths of its unit volume in eight years, and has a quality reputation of having to "build it twice"? If you're Wendelin Wiedeking, who faced this very situation when he took over Porsche, you take dramatic action.

Wiedeking began by hiring ex-Toyota engineers to help install just-in-time manufacturing. When the Toyota engineers came to the inventory-laden plant, they said, "Take us to the factory. This is the warehouse!"

At first, the workforce was skeptical. Skepticism changed to astonishment as employees watched Wiedeking take a circular saw and cut the parts shelves in half. This was no ordinary change; it was life or death. With this beginning, Porsche made a dramatic turnaround, using just-in-time principles. Porsche now has 20% fewer employees, can build a car in half the labor time, has improved quality by 100 times, has reduced days of inventory on the production line from 28 days to 30 *minutes*, and has cut the number of suppliers by two-thirds.

Wiedeking recognized that one of the keys to successful implementation of just-in-time is a workforce committed to new methods and expanded work roles. As a result, training per employee went from 12 minutes to 50 *hours* per year. In addition, the best employee idea was rewarded with the use of a Porsche 911 for a year.

How have things turned out? The new Boxter and the redesigned 911 Carrera have been hits. Unit volume has quadrupled over the last several years, and the company posted a profit of $165 million. As Wiedeking says, "This company is a gold mine." The only problem at this moment is the day only has 24 hours." ■

HEY POINTS

1 Compare and contrast just-in-time (JIT) manufacturing practices with traditional manufacturing practices.

The just-in-time manufacturing philosophy uses different principles than do traditional manufacturing methods. Just-in-time attempts to reduce lead time, while traditional methods attempt to lengthen lead time to provide a time buffer for uncertainty. Just-in-time emphasizes a product-oriented production layout, rather than a process-oriented layout. Just-in-time emphasizes a team-oriented work environment, while the traditional approach is more individual-oriented. Just-in-time views setup time reduction as a high-priority item. With reduced setup times, just-in-time manufacturers can emphasize pull manufacturing, rather than push manufacturing. Just-in-time manufacturers must emphasize high quality, since there is very little inventory to protect production against quality problems. Finally, just-in-time manufacturers emphasize supplier partnering in order to improve the quality and delivery of incoming materials.

2 Apply just-in-time manufacturing practices to a traditional manufacturing illustration.

The just-in-time philosophy was illustrated for Anderson Metal Fabricators (AMF). In the illustration, AMF was able to add a new product line without increasing the size of its facility. This was done by using just-in-time principles to eliminate the space normally used for inventory. This space could now be used for producing the new product line.

3 Describe the implications of a just-in-time manufacturing philosophy on cost accounting and performance measurement systems.

The just-in-time philosophy has implications for cost accounting. The cost accounting system will have fewer transactions, will combine the materials and work in process accounts, and will account for direct labor as a part of cell conversion cost. Just-in-time will use nonfinancial reporting measures and result in more direct tracing of factory overhead to product cells.

4 Apply just-in-time practices to a nonmanufacturing setting.

Just-in-time principles can be used in service businesses and administrative processes. For example, hospitals are removing delays in serving patients by improving admission, testing, and recovery processes. This is accomplished by designing product-focused hospital units that use cross-trained caregivers in the delivery of hospital care.

5 Describe the costs of quality and prepare a Pareto chart, a cost of quality report, and a value-added/nonvalue-added analysis.

Companies use activity analysis to identify the costs of quality, which include prevention, appraisal, internal failure, and external failure costs. The quality cost activities may be reported on a Pareto chart, which visually highlights the most expensive quality cost categories. In addition, the quality costs can be summarized in a quality cost report by each of the four major classifications. An alternative method for categorizing activities is by value-added and nonvalue-added classifications.

ILLUSTRATIVE PROBLEM

Krisco Company operates under the just-in-time philosophy. As such, it has a production cell for its microwave ovens. The conversion cost for 2,400 hours of production is budgeted for the year at $4,800,000.

During January, 2,000 microwave ovens were started and completed. Each oven requires six minutes of cell processing time. The materials cost for each oven is $100.

Instructions

1. Determine the budgeted cell conversion cost per hour.
2. Determine the manufacturing cost per unit.
3. Journalize the entry to record the costs charged to the production cell in January.
4. Journalize the entry to record the costs transferred to finished goods.

Solution

1. Budgeted cell conversion cost rate = $\dfrac{\$4,800,000}{2,400 \text{ hours}}$ = $2,000 per cell hour

2. Materials $100 per unit
   Conversion cost ($2,000 per hour/60 min.) × 6 min))   200
         Total $300 per unit

3.

1	Raw and In Process Inventory	200 0 0 0 00		1
2	Accounts Payable		200 0 0 0 00	2
3	To record materials costs			3
4	(2,000 units × $100 per unit).			4
5				5
6	Raw and In Process Inventory	400 0 0 0 00		6
7	Conversion Costs		400 0 0 0 00	7
8	To record conversion costs			8
9	(2,000 units × $200 per unit).			9
10				10

4.

11	Finished Goods (2,000 × $300 per unit)	600 0 0 0 00		11
12	Raw and In Process Inventory		600 0 0 0 00	12
13	To record finished production.			13

SELF-EXAMINATION QUESTIONS   Answers at End of Chapter

Matching

Match each of the following statements with its proper term. Some terms may not be used.

A.	activity analysis
B.	appraisal costs
C.	backflush accounting
D.	cost of quality report
E.	costs of quality
F.	electronic data interchange (EDI)
G.	employee involvement
H.	external failure costs
I.	internal failure costs
J.	just-in-time manufacturing
K.	lead time

___ 1. The costs associated with controlling quality (prevention and appraisal) and failing to control quality (internal and external failure).

___ 2. The costs incurred after defective units or services have been delivered to consumers.

___ 3. Materials are released into production and work in process is released into finished goods in anticipation of future sales.

___ 4. Organizing work in a plant or administrative function around processes (tasks).

___ 5. The cost of activities that are needed to meet customer requirements.

___ 6. The study of employee effort and other business records to determine the cost of activities.

___ 7. A philosophy that grants employees the responsibility and authority to make their own decisions about their operations.

___ 8. The cost of activities that are perceived as unnecessary from the customer's perspective and are thus candidates for elimination.

L. nonfinancial measure

M. nonvalue-added activities

N. nonvalue-added lead time

O. Pareto chart

P. prevention costs

Q. process-oriented layout

R. product-oriented layout

S. pull manufacturing

T. push manufacturing

U. raw and in process (RIP) inventory

V. supplier partnering

W. value-added activities

X. value-added lead time

___ 9. Costs incurred to prevent defects from occurring during the design and delivery of products or services.

___ 10. A report summarizing the costs, percent of total, and percent of sales by appraisal, prevention, internal failure, and external failure cost of quality categories.

___ 11. A business philosophy that focuses on eliminating time, cost, and poor quality within manufacturing processes.

___ 12. The capitalized cost of direct materials purchases, labor, and overhead charged to the production cell.

___ 13. The time that units wait in inventories, move unnecessarily, and wait during machine breakdowns.

___ 14. An information technology that allows different business organizations to use computers to communicate orders, relay information, and make or receive payments.

___ 15. Costs to detect, measure, evaluate, and audit products and processes to ensure that they conform to customer requirements and performance standards.

___ 16. A just-in-time method that views suppliers as a valuable contributor to the overall success of the business.

___ 17. The time required to manufacture a unit of product or other output.

___ 18. Organizing work in a plant or administrative function around products; sometimes referred to as product cells.

___ 19. A bar chart that shows the totals of a particular attribute for a number of categories, ranked left to right from the largest to smallest totals.

___ 20. A just-in-time method wherein customer orders trigger the release of finished goods, which trigger production, which trigger release of materials from suppliers.

___ 21. The elapsed time between starting a unit of product into the beginning of a process and its completion.

___ 22. The costs associated with defects that are discovered by the organization before the product or service is delivered to the consumer.

___ 23. A performance measure that has not been stated in dollar terms.

Multiple Choice

1. Which of the following is not a characteristic of the just-in-time philosophy?
    A. Product-oriented layout
    B. Push manufacturing (make to stock)
    C. Short lead times
    D. Reducing setup time as a critical improvement priority

2. Accounting in a just-in-time environment is best described as:
    A. more complex.
    B. focused on direct labor.
    C. providing detailed variance reports.
    D. providing less transaction control.

3. The product cell for Dynah Company has budgeted conversion costs of $420,000 for the year. The cell is planned to be available 2,100 hours for production. Each unit requires $12.50 of materials cost. The cell started and completed 700 units. The cell process time for the product is 15 minutes per unit. What is the cost debited to finished goods for the period?
    A. $8,750   C. $43,750
    B. $35,000   D. $140,000

4. In-process inspection activities are an example of what type of quality cost?
    A. Prevention
    B. Appraisal
    C. Internal failure
    D. External failure

5. A Pareto chart is used to:
    A. display a ranking of attribute totals, by category, in the form of a bar chart.
    B. display important trends in the form of a line chart.
    C. display percentage information in the form of a pie chart.
    D. display a listing of attribute totals, by category, in a table.

CLASS DISCUSSION QUESTIONS

1. What is the benefit of just-in-time processing?
2. What is lead time?
3. What are some examples of nonvalue-added lead time?
4. Why is a product-oriented layout preferred by just-in-time manufacturers over a process-oriented layout?
5. How is setup time related to lead time?
6. Why do just-in-time manufacturers favor pull or "make to order" manufacturing?
7. Why would a just-in-time manufacturer strive to produce zero defects?
8. How is supplier partnering different from traditional supplier relationships?
9. Why does accounting in a just-in-time environment result in fewer transactions?
10. Why is a "raw and in process inventory" account used by just-in-time manufacturers, rather than separately reporting materials and work in process?
11. Why is the direct labor cost category eliminated in many just-in-time environments?
12. How does accounting under a just-in-time environment provide less transaction control?
13. What are some possible explanations for the actual conversion cost per unit being greater than the budgeted cost per unit in a just-in-time production cell?
14. What just-in-time principles might a hospital use?
15. What are the costs of quality classifications?
16. What is the benefit of an activity analysis?
17. How does a Pareto chart assist management?
18. What is the benefit of identifying nonvalue-added activities?

RESOURCES FOR YOUR SUCCESS ONLINE AT

http://warren.swcollege.com

Remember! If you need additional help, visit South-Western's Web site.
See page M28 for a description of the online and printed materials that are available.

EXERCISES

Exercise 11–1
Just-in-time principles

Objective 1

The Chief Executive Officer (CEO) of Comfort Air Inc. has just returned from a management seminar describing the benefits of the just-in-time philosophy. The CEO issued the following statement after returning from the conference:

This company will become a just-in-time manufacturing company. Presently, we have too much inventory. To become just-in-time we need to eliminate the excess inventory. Therefore, I want all employees to begin reducing inventories until we are just-in-time. Thank you for your cooperation.

How would you respond to the CEO's statement?

Exercise 11–2
Just-in-time as a strategy

Objective 1

The American textile industry has moved much of its operations offshore in the pursuit of lower labor costs. Textile imports have risen from 2% of all textile production in 1962 to over 60% in 2000. Offshore manufacturers make long runs of standard mass-market apparel items. These are then brought to the United States in container ships, requiring significant time between original order and delivery. As a result, retail customers must accurately forecast market demands for imported apparel items.

> Assuming that you work for a U.S.-based textile company, how would you recommend responding to the low-cost imports?

Exercise 11–3
Lead time reduction—
service company
Objectives 1, 4

Golden Insurance Company takes ten days to make payments on insurance claims. Claims are processed through three departments: Data Input, Claims Audit, and Claims Adjustment. The three departments are on different floors, approximately one hour apart from each other. Claims are processed in batches of 100. Each batch of 100 claims moves through the three departments on a wheeled cart. Management is concerned about customer dissatisfaction caused by the long lead time for claim payments.

> How might this process be changed so that the lead time could be reduced significantly?

Exercise 11–4
Just-in-time principles
Objective 1

Champion Shirt Company manufactures various styles of men's casual wear. Shirts are cut and assembled by a workforce that is paid by piece rate. This means that they are paid according to the amount of work completed during a period of time. To illustrate, if the piece rate is $0.10 per sleeve assembled, and the worker assembles 700 sleeves during the day, then the worker would be paid $70 (700 × $0.10) for the day's work.

The company is considering adopting a just-in-time manufacturing philosophy by organizing work cells around various types of products and employing pull manufacturing. However, no change is expected in the compensation policy. On this point, the manufacturing manager stated the following:

"Piecework compensation provides an incentive to work fast. Without it, the workers will just goof off and expect a full day's pay. We can't pay straight hourly wages—at least not in this industry."

> How would you respond to the manufacturing manager's comments?

Exercise 11–5
Lead time analysis
Objective 1

Kiddie Kuddles, Inc., manufactures toy stuffed animals. The direct labor time required to cut, sew, and stuff a toy is 12 minutes per unit. The company makes two types of stuffed toys—a lion and a bear. The lion is assembled in lot sizes of 50 units per batch, while the bear is assembled in lot sizes of 5 units per batch. Since each product has direct labor time of 12 minutes per unit, management has determined that the lead time for each product is 12 minutes.

> Is management correct? What are the lead times for each product?

Exercise 11–6
Reduce setup time
Objective 1

Manden Machining Company has analyzed the setup time on its computer-controlled lathe. The setup requires changing the type of fixture that holds a part. The average setup time has been 160 minutes, consisting of the following steps:

Turn off machine and remove fixture from lathe	5 minutes
Go to tool room with fixture	25
Record replacement of fixture to tool room	10
Return to lathe	25
Clean lathe	20
Return to tool room	25
Record withdrawal of new fixture from tool room	20
Return to lathe	25
Install new fixture and turn on machine	5
Total setup time	160 minutes

a. > Why should management be concerned about improving setup time?
b. > What do you recommend to Manden Machining Company for improving setup time?
c. How much time would be required for a setup, using your suggestion in (b)?

Exercise 11–7
Calculate lead time

Objective I

Flint Machining Company machines metal parts for the automotive industry. Under the traditional manufacturing approach, the parts are machined through two processes: Milling and Finishing. Parts are produced in batch sizes of 55 parts. A part requires 4 minutes in milling and 6 minutes in finishing. The move time between the two operations for a complete batch is 15 minutes.

Under the just-in-time philosophy, the part is produced in a cell that includes both the milling and finishing operations. The operating time is unchanged; however, the batch size is reduced to 5 parts and the move time is eliminated.

Determine the value-added, nonvalue-added, and total lead time and percent of value-added to the total lead time under the traditional and just-in-time manufacturing methods. Round percentages to two decimal places.

Exercise 11–8
Calculate lead time

Objective I

Access Memories Inc. is considering a new just-in-time product cell. The present manufacturing approach produces a product in four separate steps. The production batch sizes are 40 units. The process time for each step is as follows:

Process Step 1	5 minutes
Process Step 2	3 minutes
Process Step 3	11 minutes
Process Step 4	6 minutes

The time required to move each batch between steps is 15 minutes. In addition, the time to move raw materials to Process Step 1 is also 15 minutes, and the time to move completed units from Process Step 4 to finished goods inventory is 15 minutes.

The new just-in-time layout will allow the company to reduce the batch sizes from 40 units to 4 units. The time required to move each batch between steps and the inventory locations will be reduced to 3 minutes. The processing time in each step will stay the same.

Determine the value-added, nonvalue-added, total lead times and percent of value-added to total lead times under the present and proposed production approaches. Round percentages to two decimal places.

Exercise 11–9
Lead time calculation—doctor's office

Objectives I, 4

✓ b. 2 hrs., 35 min.

Juan Alvarez caught the flu and needed to see the doctor. Alvarez called to set up an appointment and was told to come in at 1:00 PM. Alvarez arrived at the doctor's office promptly at 1:00 PM. The waiting room had twelve other people in it. Patients were admitted from the waiting room in FIFO (first-in, first-out) order at a rate of five minutes per patient. After waiting until his turn, a nurse finally invited Alvarez to an examining room. Once in the examining room, Alvarez waited another 30 minutes before a nurse arrived to take some basic readings (temperature, blood pressure). The nurse needed five minutes to collect the clinical information. After the nurse left, Alvarez waited 20 additional minutes before the doctor arrived. The doctor arrived and diagnosed the flu and provided a prescription for antibiotics. This took the doctor 10 minutes. Before leaving the doctor's office, Alvarez waited 15 minutes at the business office to pay for the office visit.

Alvarez spent 5 minutes walking next door to fill the prescription at the pharmacy. There were four people in front of Alvarez, each person requiring 5 minutes to fill and purchase his or her prescription. Alvarez finally arrived home 30 minutes after paying for his prescription.

a. What time does Alvarez arrive home?
b. How much of the total elapsed time from 1:00 PM until when Alvarez arrived home was nonvalue-added time?
c. Why does the doctor require patients to wait so long for service?

Exercise 11–10
Supplier partnering

Objective I

The **Ford** *Tempo* required more than 700 different suppliers. However, the successor to the *Tempo*, the Ford *Contour*, required only 227 different suppliers. For example, the *Tempo* required 12 suppliers for door panels and other interior trim pieces, while the *Contour* used only three suppliers for these parts.

➤ Why would Ford strive to reduce the number of suppliers of parts for its products?

Exercise 11–11
Employee involvement
Objective 1

Quickie Designs Inc. uses teams in the manufacture of lightweight wheelchairs. Two features of its team approach are team hiring and peer reviews. Under team hiring, the team recruits, interviews, and hires new team members from within the organization. Using peer reviews, the team evaluates each member of the team with regard to quality, knowledge, teamwork, goal performance, attendance, and safety. These reviews provide feedback to the team member for improvement.

✐ How do these two team approaches differ from using managers to hire and evaluate employees?

Exercise 11–12
Accounting issues in a just-in-time environment
Objective 3

Vision Electronics Company has recently implemented a just-in-time manufacturing approach. A production department manager has approached the controller with the following comments:

I am very upset with our accounting system now that we have implemented our new just-in-time manufacturing methods. It seems as if all I'm doing is paperwork. Our product is moving so fast through the manufacturing process that the paperwork can hardly keep up. For example, it just doesn't make sense to me to fill out daily labor reports. The employees are assigned to complete cells, performing many different tasks. I can't keep up with direct labor reports on each individual task. I thought we were trying to eliminate waste. Yet the information requirements of the accounting system are slowing us down and adding to overall lead time. Moreover, I'm still getting my monthly variance reports. I don't think that these are necessary. I have nonfinancial performance measures that are more timely than these reports. Besides, the employees don't really understand accounting variances. How about giving some information that I can really use?

✐ What accounting system changes would you suggest in light of the production department manager's criticisms?

Exercise 11–13
Just-in-time journal entries
Objective 3

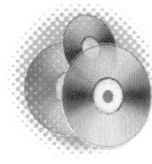
SPREADSHEET

✓ b. $200

Disk Images Inc. uses a just-in-time strategy to manufacture DVD players. The company manufactures DVDs through a single product cell. The budgeted conversion cost for the year is $744,000 for 1,860 production hours. Each unit requires 30 minutes of cell process time. During March, 310 DVDs are manufactured in the cell. The estimated materials cost per unit is $180. The following summary transactions took place during March:

1. Materials are purchased for March production.
2. Conversion costs were applied to production.
3. 310 DVDs are assembled and placed in finished goods.
4. 300 DVDs are sold for $500 per unit.

a. Determine the budgeted cell conversion cost per hour.
b. Determine the budgeted cell conversion cost per unit.
c. Journalize the summary transactions (1)–(4) for March.

Exercise 11–14
Just-in-time journal entries
Objective 3

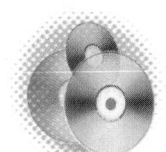
SPREADSHEET

✓ a. $75

Trion Industries, Inc. manufactures lighting fixtures, using just-in-time manufacturing methods. Style BB-01 has a materials cost per unit of $24. The budgeted conversion cost for the year is $157,500 for 2,100 production hours. A unit of Style BB-01 requires 12 minutes of cell production time. The following transactions took place during June:

1. Materials were acquired to assemble 850 Style BB-01 units for June.
2. Conversion costs were applied to production.
3. 850 units of Style BB-01 were started and completed in June.
4. 830 units of Style BB-01 were sold in June for $55 per unit.

a. Determine the budgeted cell conversion cost per hour.
b. Determine the budgeted cell conversion cost per unit.
c. Journalize the summary transactions (1)–(4) for June.

Exercise 11–15
Just-in-time—fast food restaurant
Objective 4

The management of Burgerland fast food franchise wants to provide hamburgers quickly to customers. It has been using a process by which precooked hamburgers are prepared and placed under hot lamps. These hamburgers are then sold to customers. In this process, every customer receives the same type of hamburger and dressing (ketchup, onions, mustard). If a customer wants something different, then a "special order" must be cooked to the customer's requirements. This requires the customer to wait several minutes, which often slows down the service line. Burgerland has been receiving more and more special orders from customers, which has been slowing service down considerably.

a. How would you describe the present Burgerland service delivery system?
b. How might you use just-in-time principles to provide customers quick service, yet still allow them to custom order their burgers?

Exercise 11–16
Pareto chart
Objective 5

Star Memory Products Inc. manufactures RAM memory chips for personal computers. An activity analysis was conducted, and the following activity costs were identified with the manufacture and sale of memory chips:

Activities	Activity Cost
Correct shipment errors	$ 70,000
Disposing of scrap	165,000
Emergency equipment maintenance	130,000
Employee training	10,000
Final inspection	100,000
Inspecting incoming materials	15,000
Preventive equipment maintenance	35,000
Processing customer returns	150,000
Scrap reporting	50,000
Supplier development	10,000
Warranty claims	265,000
Total	$1,000,000

Prepare a Pareto chart of these activities.

Exercise 11–17
Cost of quality report
Objective 5

SPREADSHEET

✓ a. Appraisal, 11.5% of total costs

a. Using the information in Exercise 11–16, prepare a cost of quality report. Assume that the sales for the period were $2,500,000.
b. Interpret the cost of quality report.

Exercise 11–18
Pareto chart for a service company
Objective 5

Lightwave Cable Company provides cable TV and Internet service to the local community. The activities and activity costs of Lightwave Cable are identified as follows:

Activities	Activity Cost
Billing error correction	$ 60,000
Cable signal testing	125,000
Reinstall service (installed incorrectly the first time)	100,000
Repair satellite equipment	25,000
Repair underground cable connections to the customer	50,000
Replace old technology cable with higher quality cable	160,000
Replace old technology signal switches with higher quality switches	210,000
Respond to customer home repair requests	45,000
Train employees	25,000
Total	$800,000

Prepare a Pareto chart of these activities.

Exercise 11–19
Cost of quality and value-added/nonvalue-added reports

Objective 5

SPREADSHEET

✓ a. External failure, 31.88% of total costs

a. Using the activity data in Exercise 11–18, prepare a cost of quality report. Assume that sales are $2,000,000. Round percentages to two decimal places.
b. Using the activity data in Exercise 11–18, prepare a value-added/nonvalue-added analysis.
c. Interpret the information in (a) and (b).

PROBLEMS SERIES A

Problem 11–1A
Just-in-time principles

Objective 1

✓ 3. $0.21 per pound

Night Glow Company manufactures light bulbs. Night Glow's purchasing policy requires that the purchasing agents place each quarter's purchasing requirements out for bid. This is because the Purchasing Department is evaluated solely by its ability to get the lowest purchase prices. The lowest cost bidder receives the order for the next quarter (90 working days).

To make its bulb products, Night Glow requires 15,300 pounds of glass per quarter. Night Glow received two glass bids for the second quarter, as follows:

- *Prism Glass Company:* $14.00 per pound of glass. Delivery schedule: 15,300 pounds at the beginning of April to last for 3 months.
- *Reflection Glass Company:* $14.10 per pound of glass. Delivery schedule: 170 pounds per working day (90 days in the quarter).

Night Glow accepted Prism Glass Company's bid because it was the low-cost bid.

Instructions

1. Comment on Night Glow's purchasing policy.
2. What are the additional (hidden) costs, beyond price, of Prism Glass Company's bid? Why weren't these costs considered?
3. Considering just inventory financing costs, what is the additional cost per pound of Prism Glass Company's bid if the cost of money is 12%? (*Hint:* Determine the average value of glass inventory held for the quarter and multiply by the quarterly interest charge.)

Problem 11–2A
Lead time

Objective 1

SPREADSHEET

✓ 1. Wait time, 1,696 minutes

Mega Sound Audio Company manufactures electronic stereo equipment. The manufacturing process includes printed circuit (PC) card assembly, final assembly, testing, and shipping. In the PC card assembly operation, a number of individuals are responsible for assembling electronic components into printed circuit boards. Each operator is responsible for soldering components according to a given set of instructions. Operators work on batches of 50 printed circuit boards. Each board requires 8 minutes of assembly time. After each batch is completed, the operator moves the assembled cards to the final assembly area. This move takes 20 minutes to complete.

The final assembly for each stereo unit requires 15 minutes and is also done in batches of 50 units. A batch of 50 stereos is moved into the test building, which is across the street. The move takes 30 minutes. Before conducting the test, the test equipment must be set up for the particular stereo model. The test setup requires 30 minutes. The units wait while the setup is performed. In the final test, the 50-unit batch is tested one at a time. Each test requires 5 minutes. The completed batch, after all testing, is sent to shipping for packaging and final shipment to customers. A complete batch of 50 units is sent from final assembly to shipping. The Shipping Department is located next to final assembly. Thus, there is no move time between these two operations. Packaging and labeling requires 6 minutes per unit.

Instructions

1. Determine the amount of value-added and nonvalue-added lead time and the ratio of nonvalue-added to total lead time in this process for an average stereo unit in a batch of 50 units. Round percentages to two decimal places. Categorize the nonvalue-added time into wait and move time.
2. ✏➤ How could this process be improved so as to reduce the amount of waste in the process?

Problem 11–3A
Just-in-time accounting

Objective 3

SPREADSHEET

✓ 4. Raw and In Process Inventory, $25,000

Digital Display Company manufactures and assembles automobile instrument panels for both Burton Motors and National Motors. The process consists of a just-in-time product cell for each customer's instrument assembly. The data that follow concern only the Burton just-in-time cell.

For the year, Digital Display budgeted the following costs for the Burton production cell:

Conversion Cost Categories	Budget
Labor	$682,000
Supplies	112,000
Utilities	36,000
Total	$830,000

Digital Display plans 4,000 hours of production for the Burton cell for the year. The materials cost is $125 per instrument assembly. Each assembly requires 24 minutes of cell assembly time. There was no June 1 inventory for either Raw and In Process Inventory or Finished Goods Inventory.

The following summary events took place in the Burton cell during June:

a. Electronic parts and wiring were purchased to produce 10,200 instrument assemblies in June.
b. Conversion costs were applied for the production of 10,000 units in June.
c. 10,000 units were started and completed in June.
d. 9,600 units were shipped to customers at a price of $400 per unit.

Instructions

1. Determine the budgeted cell conversion cost per hour.
2. Determine the budgeted cell conversion cost per unit.
3. Journalize the summary transactions (a) through (d).
4. Determine the ending balance in Raw and In Process Inventory and Finished Goods Inventory.
5. ✏➤ How does the accounting in a JIT environment differ from traditional accounting?

Problem 11–4A
Pareto chart and cost of quality report—service company

Objectives 4, 5

✓ 3. Nonvalue-added, 60%

The controller of Armor Insurance Company, W.E. Payup, has been asked to perform an activity analysis of its optical scanning center. The optical scanning center reads application, claims, and adjustment information into the computer. The result of the activity analysis is summarized as follows:

Activities	Activity Cost
Correct errors identified by customers (claim, check, application errors)	$ 90,000
Correct jams	66,000
Correct scan errors	42,000
Load	25,000
Log-in control codes (for later reconciliation)	15,000
Program scanner	18,000
Rerun job due to scan reading errors	24,000
Scan	50,000
Verify scan accuracy via reconciling totals	22,000
Verify scanner accuracy with test run	18,000
Total	$370,000

Instructions

1. Prepare a Pareto chart of the department activities.
2. Use the activity cost information to determine the percentages of total department costs that are prevention, appraisal, internal failure, external failure, and not costs of quality. Round percentages to two decimal places.
3. Determine the percentages of the total department costs that are value- and nonvalue-added.
4. ✏️⟶ Interpret the information.

PROBLEMS SERIES B

Problem 11–1B

Just-in-time principles

Objective 1

✓ 3. $1.20 per frame

Easy Rider Motorcycle Company manufactures a variety of motorcycles. Easy Rider's purchasing policy requires that the purchasing agents place each quarter's purchasing requirements out for bid. This is because the Purchasing Department is evaluated solely by its ability to get the lowest purchase prices. The lowest cost bidder receives the order for the next quarter (90 days). To make its motorcycles, Easy Rider requires 7,200 frames per quarter. Easy Rider received two frame bids for the third quarter, as follows:

- *Durable Forging Company:* $80.60 per frame. Delivery schedule: 80 frames per working day (90 days in the quarter).
- *Temper Forging Company:* $80.00 per frame. Delivery schedule: 7,200 frames at the beginning of July to last for three months.

Easy Rider accepted Temper Forging Company's bid because it was the low-cost bid.

Instructions

1. ✏️⟶ Comment on Easy Rider's purchasing policy.
2. ✏️⟶ What are the additional (hidden) costs, beyond price, of Temper Forging Company's bid? Why weren't these costs considered?
3. Considering just inventory financing costs, what is the additional cost per frame of Temper Forging Company's bid if the cost of money is 12%? (*Hint:* Determine the average value of frame inventory held for the quarter and multiply by the quarterly interest charge.)

Problem 11–2B

Lead time

Objective 1

SPREADSHEET

✓ 1. Wait time, 4,050 min.

Culinary Art Appliance Company manufactures home kitchen appliances. The manufacturing process includes stamping, final assembly, testing, and shipping. In the stamping operation, a number of individuals are responsible for stamping the steel outer surface of the appliance. The stamping operation is set up prior to each run. A run of 80 stampings is completed after each setup. A setup requires 100 minutes. The parts wait for the setup to be completed before stamping begins. Each stamping requires 5 minutes of operating time. After each batch is completed, the operator moves the stamped covers to the final assembly area. This move takes 15 minutes to complete.

The final assembly for each appliance unit requires 24 minutes and is also done in batches of 80 appliance units. The batch of 80 appliance units is moved into the test building, which is across the street. The move takes 25 minutes. In the final test, the 80-unit batch is tested one at a time. Each test requires 8 minutes. The completed units are sent to shipping for packaging and final shipment to customers. A complete batch of 80 units is sent from final assembly to shipping. The Shipping Department is located next to final assembly. Thus, there is no move time between these two operations. Packaging and labeling requires 13 minutes per unit.

Instructions

1. Determine the amount of value-added and nonvalue-added lead time and the ratio of nonvalue-added time to total lead time in this process for an average kitchen appliance in a batch of 80 units. Round percentages to two decimal places. Categorize the nonvalue-added time into wait and move time.
2. ✏️⟶ How could this process be improved so as to reduce the amount of waste in the process?

Problem 11–3B

Just-in-time accounting

Objective 3

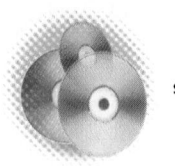

SPREADSHEET

✓ 4. Raw and In Process Inventory, $64,000

Eclipse Technologies, Inc., manufactures and assembles two major types of telephone assemblies—a desk phone and a mobile phone. The process consists of a just-in-time cell for each product. The data that follow concern only the mobile phone just-in-time cell.

For the year, Eclipse Technologies, Inc., budgeted the following costs for the mobile phone production cell:

Conversion Cost Categories	Budget
Labor	$134,000
Supplies	34,000
Utilities	12,000
Total	$180,000

The purchasing personnel are assigned directly to the mobile phone cell. Eclipse plans 5,000 hours of production for the mobile phone cell for the year. The materials cost is $64 per unit. Each assembly requires 16 minutes of cell assembly time. There was no October 1 inventory for either Raw and In Process Inventory or Finished Goods Inventory.

The following summary events took place in the mobile phone cell during October:

a. Electronic parts were purchased to produce 19,000 mobile phone assemblies in October.
b. Conversion costs were applied for 18,000 units of production in October.
c. 18,000 units were started and completed in October.
d. 17,500 units were shipped to customers at a price of $145 per unit.

Instructions

1. Determine the budgeted cell conversion cost per hour.
2. Determine the budgeted cell conversion cost per unit.
3. Journalize the summary transactions (a) through (d).
4. Determine the ending balance in Raw and In Process Inventory and Finished Goods Inventory.
5. ▬▬► How does the accounting in a JIT environment differ from traditional accounting?

Problem 11–4B

Pareto chart and cost of quality report— manufacturing company

Objective 5

✓ 3. Nonvalue-added, 38%

The president of Titan Company has been concerned about the growth in costs over the last several years. The president asked the controller to perform an activity analysis to gain a better insight into these costs. The activity analysis revealed the following:

Activity	Activity Cost
Correct invoice errors	$ 24,000
Dispose of incoming materials with poor quality	33,000
Dispose of scrap	46,000
Expedite late production	68,000
Final inspection	38,000
Inspect incoming materials	14,000
Inspect work in process	52,000
Preventive machine maintenance	28,000
Produce product	178,000
Respond to customer quality complaints	19,000
Total	$500,000

The production process is complicated by quality problems, requiring the production manager to expedite production and dispose of scrap.

Instructions

1. Prepare a Pareto chart of the company activities.
2. Use the activity cost information to determine the percentages of total costs that are prevention, appraisal, internal failure, external failure, and not costs of quality.
3. Determine the percentages of total costs that are value- and nonvalue-added.
4. ▬▬► Interpret the information.

SPECIAL ACTIVITIES

Activity 11–1
Centrum Company
*Ethics and professional
conduct in business*

In June, Centrum Company introduced a new performance measurement system in manufacturing operations. One of the new performance measures was lead time. The lead time was determined by tagging a random sample of items with a log sheet throughout the month. This log sheet recorded the time that the item started and the time that it ended production, as well as all steps in between. The controller collected the log sheets and calculated the average lead time of the tagged products. This number was reported to central management and was used to evaluate the performance of the plant manager. The plant was under extreme pressure to reduce lead time because of poor lead time results reported in June.

The following memo was intercepted by the controller.

Date: July 1
To: Hourly Employees
From: Plant Manager

During last month, you noticed that some of the products were tagged with a log sheet. This sheet records the time that a product enters production and the time that it leaves production. The difference between these two times is termed the "lead time." Our plant is evaluated on improving lead time. From now on, I ask all of you to keep an eye out for the tagged items. When you receive a tagged item, it is to receive special attention. Work on that item first, and then immediately move it to the next operation. Under no circumstances should tagged items wait on any other work that you have. Naturally, report accurate information. I insist that you record the correct times on the log sheet as the product goes through your operations.

How should the controller respond to this discovery?

Activity 11–2
Radiant Devices Inc.
Just-in-time principles

Radiant Devices, Inc. manufactures electric space heaters. While the CEO, Chris Heath, is visiting the production facility, the following conversation takes place with the plant manager, Ron Daley:

Chris: As I walk around the facility, I can't help noticing all the materials inventories. What's going on?

Ron: I have found our suppliers to be very unreliable in meeting their delivery commitments. Thus, I keep a lot of materials on hand so as to not risk running out and shutting down production.

Chris: Not only do I see a lot of materials inventory, but there also seems to be a lot of finished goods inventory on hand. Why is this?

Ron: As you know, I am evaluated on maintaining a low cost per unit. The one way that I am able to reduce my unit costs is by producing as many space heaters as possible. This allows me to spread my fixed costs over a larger base. When orders are down, the production builds up as inventory, as we are seeing now. But don't worry—I'm really keeping our costs down this way.

Chris: I'm not so sure. It seems that this inventory must cost us something.

Ron: Not really. I'll eventually use the materials and we'll eventually sell the finished goods. By keeping the plant busy, I'm using our plant assets wisely. This is reflected in the low unit costs that I'm able to maintain.

If you were Heath, how would you respond to Daley? What recommendations would you provide Daley?

Activity 11–3
Video-Tek Labs Inc.
Just-in-time principles

Video-Tek Labs Inc. prepared the following performance graphs for the prior year:

Percent of Sales Orders Filled on Time

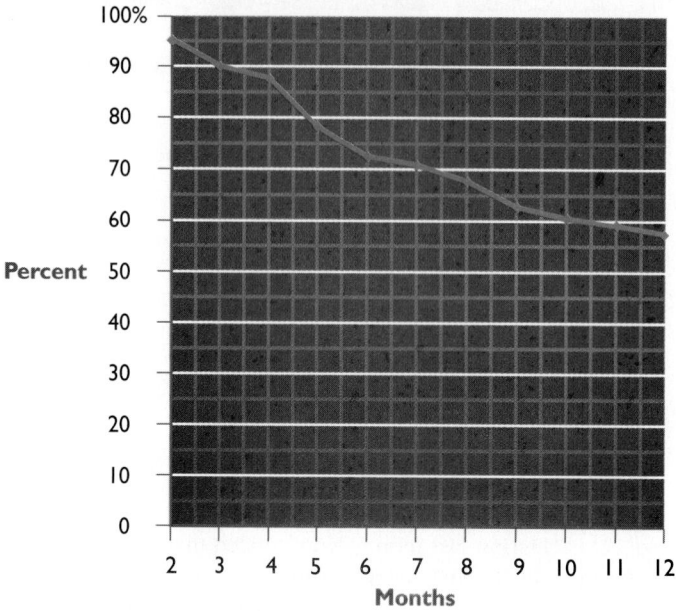

Total Manufacturing Lead Time

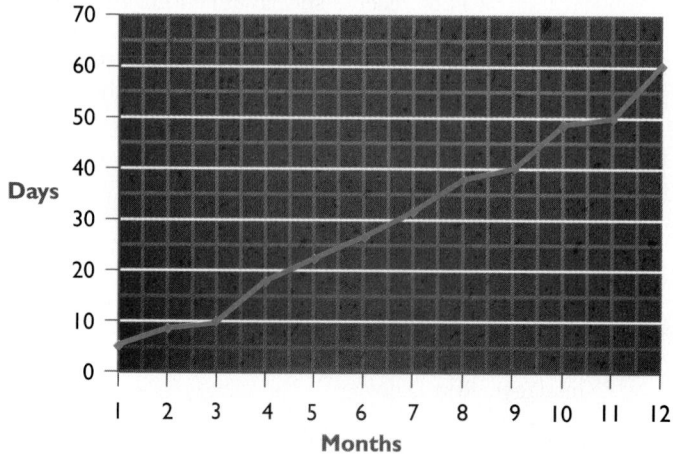

Total Inventory Dollars (in 000s)

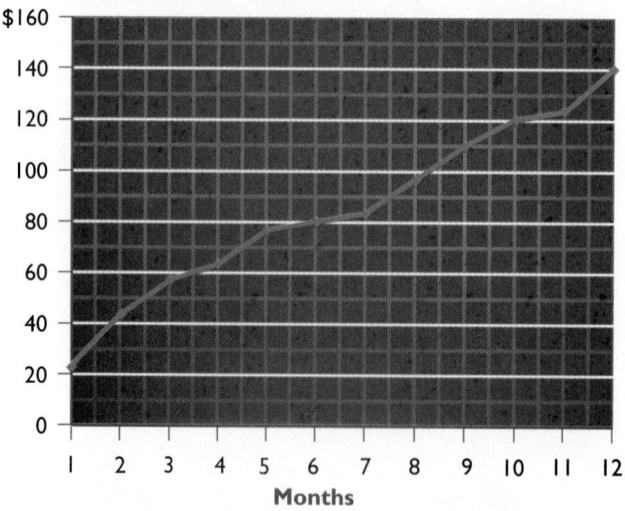

What do these charts appear to indicate?

Activity 11–4
Raman Company
Value-added and nonvalue-added activity costs

Raman Company prepared the following factory overhead report from its general ledger:

Indirect labor	$500,000
Fringe benefits	60,000
Supplies	110,000
Depreciation	230,000
Total	$900,000

The management of Raman Company was dissatisfied with this report and asked the controller to prepare an activity analysis of the same information. This activity analysis was as follows:

Process sales orders	$216,000	24%
Dispose of scrap	198,000	22
Expedite work orders	162,000	18
Produce parts	126,000	14
Resolve supplier quality problems	90,000	10
Reissue corrected purchase orders	72,000	8
Expedite customer orders	36,000	4
Total	$900,000	100%

Interpret the activity analysis by identifying value-added and nonvalue-added activity costs. How does the activity cost report differ from the general ledger report?

Activity 11–5
Into the Real World
Lead time

Group Activity

In groups of two to four people, visit a nonfast-food restaurant and do a lead time study. If more than one group chooses to visit the same restaurant, choose different times for your visits. Note the time when you walk in the door of the restaurant and the time when you walk out the door after you have eaten. The difference between these two times is the total lead time of your restaurant experience. While in the restaurant, determine the time spent on nonvalue-added time, such as wait time, and the time spent on value-added eating time. Note the various activities and the time required to perform each activity during your visit to the restaurant. Compare your analyses, identifying possible reasons for differences in the times recorded by groups that visited the same restaurant.

ANSWERS TO SELF-EXAMINATION QUESTIONS

Matching

1. E	5. W	9. P	13. N
2. H	6. A	10. D	14. F
3. T	7. G	11. J	15. B
4. Q	8. M	12. U	16. V

17. X	21. K
18. R	22. I
19. O	23. L
20. S	

Multiple Choice

1. **B** The just-in-time philosophy embraces a product-oriented layout (answer A), making lead times short (answer C), and reducing setup times (answer D). Pull manufacturing, the opposite of push manufacturing (answer B), is also a just-in-time principle.

2. **D** Accounting in a just-in-time environment should not be complex (answer A), not focus on direct labor (answer B) because it is combined with other conversion costs, and not provide detailed variance reporting (answer C) because of a higher reliance on nonfinancial performance measures. However, the just-in-time accounting environment will have fewer transaction control features than the traditional system (answer D).

3. **C** $420,000 \ 2,100 hours = $200 per hour
$200 per hour × .25 hours = $50 per unit
700 units × ($50 + $12.50) = $43,750

4. **B** Appraisal costs (answer B) are the costs of inspecting and testing activities, which include detecting, measuring, evaluating, and auditing products and processes. Prevention (answer A) activities are incurred to prevent defects from occurring during the design and delivery of products or services. Internal failure costs (answer C) are associated with defects that are discovered by the organization before the product or service is delivered to the consumer. External failure costs (answer D) are the costs incurred after defective units or service have been delivered to consumers.

5. **A** A Pareto chart is a bar chart that ranks attribute totals by category (answer A). A line chart (answer B), a pie chart (answer C), and a table listing (answer D) are other ways of displaying information, but they are not Pareto charts.

Appendices

Appendix A: Interest Tables

Present Value of $1 at Compound Interest Due in n Periods: $p_{\overline{n}\|i} = \dfrac{1}{(1+i)^n}$						
$n \setminus i$	5%	5.5%	6%	6.5%	7%	8%
1	0.95238	0.94787	0.94334	0.93897	0.93458	0.92593
2	0.90703	0.89845	0.89000	0.88166	0.87344	0.85734
3	0.86384	0.85161	0.83962	0.82785	0.81630	0.79383
4	0.82270	0.80722	0.79209	0.77732	0.76290	0.73503
5	0.78353	0.76513	0.74726	0.72988	0.71290	0.68058
6	0.74622	0.72525	0.70496	0.68533	0.66634	0.63017
7	0.71068	0.68744	0.66506	0.64351	0.62275	0.58349
8	0.67684	0.65160	0.62741	0.60423	0.58201	0.54027
9	0.64461	0.61763	0.59190	0.56735	0.54393	0.50025
10	0.61391	0.58543	0.55840	0.53273	0.50835	0.46319
11	0.58468	0.55491	0.52679	0.50021	0.47509	0.42888
12	0.55684	0.52598	0.49697	0.46968	0.44401	0.39711
13	0.53032	0.49856	0.46884	0.44102	0.41496	0.36770
14	0.50507	0.47257	0.44230	0.41410	0.38782	0.34046
15	0.48102	0.44793	0.41726	0.38883	0.36245	0.31524
16	0.45811	0.42458	0.39365	0.36510	0.33874	0.29189
17	0.43630	0.40245	0.37136	0.34281	0.31657	0.27027
18	0.41552	0.38147	0.35034	0.32189	0.29586	0.25025
19	0.39573	0.36158	0.33051	0.30224	0.27651	0.23171
20	0.37689	0.34273	0.31180	0.28380	0.25842	0.21455
21	0.35894	0.32486	0.29416	0.26648	0.24151	0.19866
22	0.34185	0.30793	0.27750	0.25021	0.22571	0.18394
23	0.32557	0.29187	0.26180	0.23494	0.21095	0.17032
24	0.31007	0.27666	0.24698	0.22060	0.19715	0.15770
25	0.29530	0.26223	0.23300	0.20714	0.18425	0.14602
26	0.28124	0.24856	0.21981	0.19450	0.17211	0.13520
27	0.26785	0.23560	0.20737	0.18263	0.16093	0.12519
28	0.25509	0.22332	0.19563	0.17148	0.15040	0.11591
29	0.24295	0.21168	0.18456	0.16101	0.14056	0.10733
30	0.23138	0.20064	0.17411	0.15119	0.13137	0.09938
31	0.22036	0.19018	0.16426	0.14196	0.12277	0.09202
32	0.20987	0.18027	0.15496	0.13329	0.11474	0.08520
33	0.19987	0.17087	0.14619	0.12516	0.10724	0.07889
34	0.19036	0.16196	0.13791	0.11752	0.10022	0.07304
35	0.18129	0.15352	0.13010	0.11035	0.09366	0.06764
40	0.14205	0.11746	0.09722	0.08054	0.06678	0.04603
45	0.11130	0.08988	0.07265	0.05879	0.04761	0.03133
50	0.08720	0.06877	0.05429	0.04291	0.03395	0.02132

Present Value of $1 at Compound Interest Due in *n* Periods: $p_{\overline{n}\backslash i} = \dfrac{1}{(1+i)^n}$

n \ i	9%	10%	11%	12%	13%	14%
1	0.91743	0.90909	0.90090	0.89286	0.88496	0.87719
2	0.84168	0.82645	0.81162	0.79719	0.78315	0.76947
3	0.77218	0.75132	0.73119	0.71178	0.69305	0.67497
4	0.70842	0.68301	0.65873	0.63552	0.61332	0.59208
5	0.64993	0.62092	0.59345	0.56743	0.54276	0.51937
6	0.59627	0.56447	0.53464	0.50663	0.48032	0.45559
7	0.54703	0.51316	0.48166	0.45235	0.42506	0.39964
8	0.50187	0.46651	0.43393	0.40388	0.37616	0.35056
9	0.46043	0.42410	0.39092	0.36061	0.33288	0.30751
10	0.42241	0.38554	0.35218	0.32197	0.29459	0.26974
11	0.38753	0.35049	0.31728	0.28748	0.26070	0.23662
12	0.35554	0.31863	0.28584	0.25668	0.23071	0.20756
13	0.32618	0.28966	0.25751	0.22917	0.20416	0.18207
14	0.29925	0.26333	0.23199	0.20462	0.18068	0.15971
15	0.27454	0.23939	0.20900	0.18270	0.15989	0.14010
16	0.25187	0.21763	0.18829	0.16312	0.14150	0.12289
17	0.23107	0.19784	0.16963	0.14564	0.12522	0.10780
18	0.21199	0.17986	0.15282	0.13004	0.11081	0.09456
19	0.19449	0.16351	0.13768	0.11611	0.09806	0.08295
20	0.17843	0.14864	0.12403	0.10367	0.08678	0.07276
21	0.16370	0.13513	0.11174	0.09256	0.07680	0.06383
22	0.15018	0.12285	0.10067	0.08264	0.06796	0.05599
23	0.13778	0.11168	0.09069	0.07379	0.06014	0.04911
24	0.12640	0.10153	0.08170	0.06588	0.05323	0.04308
25	0.11597	0.09230	0.07361	0.05882	0.04710	0.03779
26	0.10639	0.08390	0.06631	0.05252	0.04168	0.03315
27	0.09761	0.07628	0.05974	0.04689	0.03689	0.02908
28	0.08955	0.06934	0.05382	0.04187	0.03264	0.02551
29	0.08216	0.06304	0.04849	0.03738	0.02889	0.02237
30	0.07537	0.05731	0.04368	0.03338	0.02557	0.01963
31	0.06915	0.05210	0.03935	0.02980	0.02262	0.01722
32	0.06344	0.04736	0.03545	0.02661	0.02002	0.01510
33	0.05820	0.04306	0.03194	0.02376	0.01772	0.01325
34	0.05331	0.03914	0.02878	0.02121	0.01568	0.01162
35	0.04899	0.03558	0.02592	0.01894	0.01388	0.01019
40	0.03184	0.02210	0.01538	0.01075	0.00753	0.00529
45	0.02069	0.01372	0.00913	0.00610	0.00409	0.00275
50	0.01345	0.00852	0.00542	0.00346	0.00222	0.00143

Present Value of Ordinary Annuity of $1 per Period: $p_{\overline{n}\backslash i} = \dfrac{1 - \dfrac{1}{(1 + i)^n}}{i}$

n \ i	5%	5.5%	6%	6.5%	7%	8%
1	0.95238	0.94787	0.94340	0.93897	0.93458	0.92593
2	1.85941	1.84632	1.83339	1.82063	1.80802	1.78326
3	2.72325	2.69793	2.67301	2.64848	2.62432	2.57710
4	3.54595	3.50515	3.46511	3.42580	3.38721	3.31213
5	4.32948	4.27028	4.21236	4.15568	4.10020	3.99271
6	5.07569	4.99553	4.91732	4.84101	4.76654	4.62288
7	5.78637	5.68297	5.58238	5.48452	5.38923	5.20637
8	6.46321	6.33457	6.20979	6.08875	5.97130	5.74664
9	7.10782	6.95220	6.80169	6.65610	6.51523	6.24689
10	7.72174	7.53763	7.36009	7.18883	7.02358	6.71008
11	8.30641	8.09254	7.88688	7.68904	7.49867	7.13896
12	8.86325	8.61852	8.38384	8.15873	7.94269	7.53608
13	9.39357	9.11708	8.85268	8.59974	8.35765	7.90378
14	9.89864	9.58965	9.29498	9.01384	8.74547	8.22424
15	10.37966	10.03758	9.71225	9.40267	9.10791	8.55948
16	10.83777	10.46216	10.10590	9.76776	9.44665	8.85137
17	11.27407	10.86461	10.47726	10.11058	9.76322	9.12164
18	11.68959	11.24607	10.82760	10.43247	10.05909	9.37189
19	12.08532	11.60765	11.15812	10.73471	10.33560	9.60360
20	12.46221	11.95038	11.46992	11.01851	10.59401	9.81815
21	12.82115	12.27524	11.76408	11.28498	10.83553	10.01680
22	13.16300	12.58317	12.04158	11.53520	11.06124	10.20074
23	13.48857	12.87504	12.30338	11.77014	11.27219	10.37106
24	13.79864	13.15170	12.55036	11.99074	11.46933	10.52876
25	14.09394	13.41393	12.78336	12.19788	11.65358	10.67478
26	14.37518	13.66250	13.00317	12.39237	11.82578	10.80998
27	14.64303	13.89810	13.21053	12.57500	11.98671	10.93516
28	14.89813	14.12142	13.40616	12.74648	12.13711	11.05108
29	15.14107	14.33310	13.59072	12.90749	12.27767	11.15841
30	15.37245	14.53375	13.76483	13.05868	12.40904	11.25778
31	15.59281	14.72393	13.92909	13.20063	12.53181	11.34980
32	15.80268	14.90420	14.08404	13.33393	12.64656	11.43500
33	16.00255	15.07507	14.23023	13.45909	12.75379	11.51389
34	16.19290	15.23703	14.36814	13.57661	12.85401	11.58693
35	16.37420	15.39055	14.49825	13.68696	12.94767	11.65457
40	17.15909	16.04612	15.04630	14.14553	13.33171	11.92461
45	17.77407	16.54773	15.45583	14.48023	13.60552	12.10840
50	18.25592	16.93152	15.76186	14.72452	13.80075	12.23348

$$\text{Present Value of Ordinary Annuity of \$1 per Period: } p_{\overline{n}|i} = \frac{1 - \dfrac{1}{(1 + i)^n}}{i}$$

n \ i	9%	10%	11%	12%	13%	14%
1	0.91743	0.90909	0.90090	0.89286	0.88496	0.87719
2	1.75911	1.73554	1.71252	1.69005	1.66810	1.64666
3	2.53130	2.48685	2.44371	2.40183	2.36115	2.32163
4	3.23972	3.16986	3.10245	3.03735	2.97447	2.91371
5	3.88965	3.79079	3.69590	3.60478	3.51723	3.43308
6	4.48592	4.35526	4.23054	4.11141	3.99755	3.88867
7	5.03295	4.86842	4.71220	4.56376	4.42261	4.28830
8	5.53482	5.33493	5.14612	4.96764	4.79677	4.63886
9	5.99525	5.75902	5.53705	5.32825	5.13166	4.94637
10	6.41766	6.14457	5.88923	5.65022	5.42624	5.21612
11	6.80519	6.49506	6.20652	5.93770	5.68694	5.45273
12	7.16072	6.81369	6.49236	6.19437	5.91765	5.66029
13	7.48690	7.10336	6.74987	6.42355	6.12181	5.84236
14	7.78615	7.36669	6.96187	6.62817	6.30249	6.00207
15	8.06069	7.60608	7.19087	6.81086	6.46238	6.14217
16	8.31256	7.82371	7.37916	6.97399	6.60388	6.26506
17	8.54363	8.02155	7.54879	7.11963	6.72909	6.37286
18	8.75562	8.20141	7.70162	7.24967	6.83991	6.46742
19	8.95012	8.36492	7.83929	7.36578	6.93797	6.55037
20	9.12855	8.51356	7.96333	7.46944	7.02475	6.62313
21	9.29224	8.64869	8.07507	7.56200	7.10155	6.68696
22	9.44242	8.77154	8.17574	7.64465	7.16951	6.74294
23	9.58021	8.88322	8.26643	7.71843	7.22966	6.79206
24	9.70661	8.98474	8.34814	7.78432	7.28288	6.83514
25	9.82258	9.07704	8.42174	7.84314	7.32998	6.87293
26	9.92897	9.16094	8.48806	7.89566	7.37167	6.90608
27	10.02658	9.23722	8.54780	7.94255	7.40856	6.93515
28	10.11613	9.30657	8.60162	7.98442	7.44120	6.96066
29	10.19828	9.36961	8.65011	8.02181	7.47009	6.98304
30	10.27365	9.42691	8.69379	8.05518	7.49565	7.00266
31	10.34280	9.47901	8.73315	8.08499	7.51828	7.01988
32	10.40624	9.52638	8.76860	8.11159	7.53830	7.03498
33	10.46444	9.56943	8.80054	8.13535	7.55602	7.04823
34	10.51784	9.60858	8.82932	8.15656	7.57170	7.05985
35	10.56682	9.64416	8.85524	8.17550	7.58557	7.07005
40	10.75736	9.77905	8.95105	8.24378	7.63438	7.10504
45	10.88118	9.86281	9.00791	8.28252	7.66086	7.12322
50	10.96168	9.91481	9.04165	8.30450	7.67524	7.13266

Future Amount of $1 at Compound Interest Due in n Periods: $A_{\overline{n}|i} = (1 + i)^n$

n \ i	5%	5.5%	6%	6.5%	7%	8%
1	1.05000	1.05500	1.06000	1.06500	1.07000	1.08000
2	1.10250	1.11303	1.12360	1.13423	1.14490	1.16640
3	1.15762	1.17424	1.19102	1.20795	1.22504	1.25971
4	1.21551	1.23882	1.26248	1.28647	1.31080	1.36049
5	1.27628	1.30696	1.33823	1.37009	1.40255	1.46933
6	1.34100	1.37884	1.41852	1.45914	1.50073	1.58687
7	1.40710	1.45468	1.50363	1.55399	1.60578	1.71382
8	1.54347	1.53469	1.59385	1.65500	1.71819	1.85093
9	1.55133	1.61909	1.68948	1.76257	1.83846	1.99900
10	1.62890	1.70814	1.79085	1.87714	1.96715	2.15892
11	1.71034	1.80209	1.89830	1.99915	2.10485	2.33164
12	1.79586	1.90121	2.01220	2.12910	2.25219	2.51817
13	1.88565	2.00577	2.13293	2.26749	2.40984	2.71962
14	1.97993	2.11609	2.26091	2.41487	2.57853	2.93719
15	2.07893	2.23248	2.39656	2.57184	2.75903	3.17217
16	2.18288	2.35526	2.54035	2.73901	2.95216	3.42594
17	2.29202	2.48480	2.69277	2.91705	3.15882	3.70002
18	2.40662	2.62147	2.85434	3.10665	3.37993	3.99602
19	2.52695	2.76565	3.02560	3.30859	3.61653	4.31570
20	2.65330	2.91776	3.20714	3.52365	3.86968	4.66096
21	2.78596	3.07823	3.39956	3.75268	4.14056	5.03383
22	2.92526	3.24754	3.60354	3.99661	4.43040	5.43654
23	3.07152	3.42615	3.81975	4.25639	4.74053	5.87146
24	3.22510	3.61459	4.04894	4.53305	5.07237	6.34118
25	3.38636	3.81339	4.29187	4.82770	5.42743	6.84848
26	3.55567	4.02313	4.54938	5.14150	5.80735	7.39635
27	3.73346	4.24440	4.82235	5.47570	6.21387	7.98806
28	3.92013	4.47784	5.11169	5.83162	6.64884	8.62711
29	4.11614	4.72412	5.41839	6.21067	7.11426	9.31728
30	4.32194	4.98395	5.74349	6.61437	7.61226	10.06266
31	4.53804	5.25807	6.08810	7.04430	8.14511	10.86767
32	4.76494	5.54726	6.45339	7.50218	8.71527	11.73708
33	5.00319	5.85236	6.84059	7.98982	9.32534	12.67605
34	5.25335	6.17424	7.25102	8.50916	9.97811	13.69013
35	5.51602	6.51383	7.68609	9.06225	10.67658	14.78534
40	7.03999	8.51331	10.28572	12.41607	14.97446	21.72452
45	8.98501	11.12655	13.76461	17.01110	21.00245	31.92045
50	11.46740	14.54196	18.42015	23.30668	29.45702	46.90161

Future Amount of $1 at Compound Interest Due in n Periods: $A_{\overline{n}|i} = (1 + i)^n$

n \ i	9%	10%	11%	12%	13%	14%
1	1.09000	1.10000	1.11000	1.12000	1.13000	1.14000
2	1.18810	1.21000	1.23210	1.25440	1.27690	1.29960
3	1.29503	1.33100	1.36763	1.40493	1.44290	1.48154
4	1.41158	1.46410	1.51807	1.57352	1.63047	1.68896
5	1.53862	1.61051	1.68506	1.76234	1.84244	1.92541
6	1.67710	1.77156	1.87041	1.97382	2.08195	2.19497
7	1.82804	1.94872	2.07616	2.21068	2.35261	2.50227
8	1.99256	2.14359	2.30454	2.47596	2.65844	2.85259
9	2.17189	2.35795	2.55804	2.77308	3.00404	3.25195
10	2.36736	2.59374	2.83942	3.10585	3.39457	3.70722
11	2.58043	2.85312	3.15176	3.47855	3.83586	4.22623
12	2.81266	3.13843	3.49845	3.89598	4.33452	4.81790
13	3.06580	3.45227	3.88328	4.36349	4.89801	5.49241
14	3.34173	3.79750	4.31044	4.88711	5.53475	6.26135
15	3.64248	4.17725	4.78459	5.47357	6.25427	7.13794
16	3.97031	4.59497	5.31089	6.13039	7.06733	8.13725
17	4.32763	5.05447	5.89509	6.86604	7.98608	9.27646
18	4.71712	5.55992	6.54355	7.68997	9.02427	10.57517
19	5.14166	6.11591	7.26334	8.61276	10.19742	12.05569
20	5.60441	6.72750	8.06231	9.64629	11.52309	13.74349
21	6.10881	7.40025	8.94917	10.80385	13.02109	15.66758
22	6.65860	8.14028	9.93357	12.10031	14.71383	17.86104
23	7.25787	8.95430	11.02627	13.55235	16.62663	20.36158
24	7.91108	9.84973	12.23916	15.17863	18.78809	23.21221
25	8.62308	10.83471	13.58546	17.00006	21.23054	26.46192
26	9.39916	11.91818	15.07986	19.04007	23.99051	30.16658
27	10.24508	13.10999	16.73865	21.32488	27.10928	34.38991
28	11.16714	14.42099	18.57990	23.88387	30.63349	39.20449
29	12.17218	15.86309	20.62369	26.74993	34.61584	44.69312
30	13.26768	17.44940	22.89230	29.95992	39.11590	50.95016
31	14.46177	19.19434	25.41045	33.55511	44.20096	58.08318
32	15.76333	21.11378	28.20560	37.58173	49.94709	66.21483
33	17.18203	23.22515	31.30821	42.09153	56.44021	75.48490
34	18.72841	25.54767	34.75212	47.14252	63.77744	86.05279
35	20.41397	28.10244	38.57485	52.79962	72.06851	98.10018
40	31.40942	45.25926	65.00087	93.05097	132.78155	188.88351
45	48.32729	72.89048	109.53024	163.98760	244.64140	363.67907
50	74.35752	117.39085	184.56483	289.00219	450.73593	700.23299

Future Amount of Ordinary Annuity of $1 per Period: $A_{\overline{n}|i} = (1 + i)^n - 1/i$

n \ i	5%	5.5%	6%	6.5%	7%	8%
1	1.00000	1.00000	1.00000	1.00000	1.00000	1.00000
2	2.05000	2.05500	2.06000	2.06500	2.07000	2.08000
3	3.15250	3.16802	3.18360	3.19922	3.21490	3.24640
4	4.31012	4.34227	4.37462	4.40717	4.43994	4.50611
5	5.52563	5.58109	5.63709	5.69364	5.75074	5.86660
6	6.80191	6.88805	6.97532	7.06373	7.15329	7.33593
7	8.14201	8.26689	8.39384	8.52287	8.65402	8.92280
8	9.54911	9.72157	9.89747	10.07688	10.25980	10.63663
9	11.02656	11.25626	11.49132	11.73185	11.97799	12.48756
10	12.57789	12.87535	13.18080	13.49442	13.81645	14.48656
11	14.20679	14.58350	14.97184	15.37156	15.78360	16.64549
12	15.91713	16.38559	16.86994	17.37071	17.88845	18.97713
13	17.71298	18.28680	18.88214	19.49981	20.14064	21.49530
14	19.59863	20.29257	21.01505	21.76730	22.55049	24.21492
15	21.57856	22.40866	23.27597	24.18217	25.12902	27.15211
16	23.65749	24.64114	25.67253	26.75401	27.88805	30.32428
17	25.84037	28.99640	28.21288	29.49302	30.84022	33.75023
18	28.13238	29.48120	30.90565	32.41007	33.99903	37.45024
19	30.53900	32.10267	33.75999	35.51672	37.37896	41.44626
20	33.06595	34.86832	36.78559	38.82531	40.99549	45.76196
21	35.71925	37.78608	39.99273	42.34895	44.86518	50.42292
22	38.50521	40.86431	43.39229	46.10164	49.00574	55.45676
23	41.43048	44.11185	46.99583	50.09824	53.43614	60.89330
24	44.50200	47.53800	50.81558	54.35463	58.17667	66.76476
25	47.72710	51.15259	54.86451	58.88768	63.24904	73.10594
26	51.11345	54.96598	59.15638	63.71538	68.67647	79.95442
27	54.66913	58.98911	63.70577	68.85688	74.48382	87.35077
28	58.40258	63.23351	68.52811	74.33257	80.69769	95.33883
29	62.32271	67.71135	73.62980	80.16419	87.34653	103.96594
30	66.43885	72.43548	79.05819	86.37486	94.46079	113.28321
31	70.76079	77.41943	84.80168	92.98923	102.07304	123.34587
32	75.29883	82.67750	90.88978	100.03353	110.21815	134.21354
33	80.06377	88.22476	97.34316	107.53571	118.93342	145.95062
34	85.06696	94.07712	104.18376	115.52553	128.25876	158.62667
35	90.32031	100.25136	111.43478	124.03469	138.23688	172.31680
40	120.79977	136.60561	154.76197	175.63192	199.63511	259.05652
45	159.70016	184.11917	212.74351	246.32459	285.74931	386.50562
50	209.34800	246.21748	290.33591	343.17967	406.52893	573.77016

Future Amount of Ordinary Annuity of $1 per Period: $A_{\overline{n}|i} = (1 + i)^n - 1/i$

n \ i	9%	10%	11%	12%	13%	14%
1	1.00000	1.00000	1.00000	1.00000	1.00000	1.00000
2	2.09000	2.10000	2.11000	2.12000	2.13000	2.14000
3	3.27810	3.31000	3.34210	3.37440	3.40690	3.43960
4	4.57313	4.64100	4.70973	4.77933	4.84980	4.92114
5	5.98471	6.10510	6.22780	6.35285	6.48027	6.61010
6	7.52334	7.71561	7.91286	8.11519	8.32271	8.53552
7	9.20044	9.48717	9.78327	10.08901	10.40466	10.73049
8	11.02847	11.43589	11.85943	12.29969	12.75726	13.23276
9	13.02104	13.57948	14.16397	14.77566	15.41571	16.08535
10	15.19293	15.93742	16.72201	17.54874	18.41975	19.33730
11	17.56029	18.53117	19.56143	20.65458	21.81432	23.04452
12	20.14072	21.38428	22.71319	24.13313	25.65018	27.27075
13	22.95338	24.52271	26.21164	28.02911	29.98470	32.08865
14	26.01919	27.97498	30.09492	32.39260	34.88271	37.58107
15	29.36092	31.77248	34.40536	37.27972	40.41746	43.84241
16	33.00340	35.94973	39.18995	42.75328	46.67173	50.98035
17	36.97370	40.54470	44.50084	48.88367	53.73906	59.11760
18	41.30134	45.59917	50.39594	55.74972	61.72514	68.39407
19	46.01846	51.15909	56.93949	63.43968	70.74941	78.96923
20	51.16012	57.27500	64.20283	72.05244	80.94683	91.02493
21	56.76453	64.00250	72.26514	81.69874	92.46992	104.76842
22	62.87334	71.40275	81.21431	92.50258	105.49101	120.43600
23	69.53194	79.54302	91.14788	104.60289	120.20484	138.29704
24	76.78981	88.49733	102.17415	118.15524	136.83147	158.65862
25	84.70090	98.34706	114.41331	133.33387	155.61956	181.87083
26	93.32398	109.18176	127.99877	150.33393	176.85010	208.33274
27	102.72314	121.09994	143.07864	169.37401	200.84061	238.49933
28	112.96822	134.20994	159.81729	190.69889	227.94989	272.88923
29	124.13536	148.63093	178.39719	214.58275	258.58338	312.09373
30	136.30754	164.49402	199.02088	241.33268	293.19922	356.78685
31	149.57522	181.94342	221.91317	271.29261	332.31511	407.73701
32	164.03699	201.13777	247.32362	304.84772	376.51608	465.82019
33	179.80032	222.25154	275.52922	342.42945	426.46317	532.03501
34	196.98234	245.47670	306.83744	384.52098	482.90338	607.51991
35	215.71076	271.02437	341.58955	431.66350	546.68082	693.57270
40	337.88244	442.59256	581.82607	767.09142	1013.70424	1342.02510
45	525.85873	718.90484	986.63856	1358.23003	1874.16463	2590.56480
50	815.08356	1163.90853	1668.77115	2400.01825	3459.50712	4994.52135

Appendix B: Codes of Professional Ethics for Accountants

In recent years, governments, businesses, and the public have given increased attention to ethical conduct. They have insisted upon a level of human behavior that goes beyond that required by laws and regulations. Thus many businesses, as well as professional groups (such as accountants) and governmental organizations, have established standards of ethical conduct. This text emphasizes the ethical conduct of accountants, who serve various business interests as well as the public.

This appendix sets forth the standards of professional conduct expected of accountants in public accounting and private accounting. For accountants employed in public accounting, the American Institute of Certified Public Accountants' *Code of Professional Conduct* is presented.[1] For accountants employed in private accounting, the Institute of Management Accountants' *Standards of Ethical Conduct for Practitioners of Management Accounting and Financial Management* is presented as a guide to professional conduct.[2]

Supplementing the codes of professional ethics are ethics discussion cases that appear at the end of each chapter. These cases represent "real world" examples of ethical issues facing accountants. It should be noted that codes of professional ethics are general guides to good behavior and their application to specific situations often requires the exercise of professional judgment. In some cases, the line between right and wrong may be quite fine, and reasonable people may disagree. In addition, business is dynamic and everchanging, and what society considers to be acceptable behavior changes from time to time.

Code of Professional Conduct

Composition, Applicability, and Compliance

The Code of Professional Conduct of the American Institute of Certified Public Accountants consists of two sections—(1) the Principles and (2) the Rules. The Principles provide the framework for the Rules, which govern the performance of professional services by members. The Council of the American Institute of Certified Public Accountants is authorized to designate bodies to promulgate technical standards under the Rules, and the bylaws require adherence to those Rules and standards.

The Code of Professional Conduct was adopted by the membership to provide guidance and rules to all members—those in public practice, in industry, in government, and in education—in the performance of their professional responsibilities.

Compliance with the Code of Professional Conduct, as with all standards in an open society, depends primarily on members' understanding and voluntary actions, secondarily on reinforcement by peers and public opinion, and ultimately on disciplinary proceedings, when necessary, against members who fail to comply with the Rules.

Other Guidance

The Principles and Rules as set forth herein are further amplified by interpretations and rulings contained in *AICPA Professional Standards* (Volume 2).

Interpretations of Rules of Conduct consists of interpretations which have been adopted, after exposure to state societies, state boards, practice units, and other interested parties, by the professional ethics division's executive committee to provide guidelines as to the scope and application of the Rules but are not intended to limit such scope or application. A member who departs from such guidelines shall have the burden of justifying such departure in any disciplinary hearing.

---

[1] *Code of Professional Conduct* (New York: American Institute of Certified Public Accountants, 2000), pp. 3–8.
[2] *Standards of Ethical Conduct for Practitioners of Management Accounting and Financial Management*, Institute of Management Accountants, Montvale, New Jersey, 1997, pp. 1–2.

Ethics Rulings consist of formal rulings made by the professional ethics division's executive committee after exposure to state societies, state boards, practice units, and other interested parties. These rulings summarize the application of Rules of Conduct and interpretations to a particular set of factual circumstances. Members who depart from such rulings in similar circumstances will be requested to justify such departures.

Publication of an interpretation or ethics ruling in the *Journal of Accountancy* constitutes notice to members. Hence, the effective date of the pronouncement is the last day of the month in which the pronouncement is published in the *Journal of Accountancy*. The professional ethics division will take into consideration the time that would have been reasonable for the member to comply with the pronouncement.

Members should also consult, if applicable, the ethical standards of their state CPA society, state board of accountancy, the Securities and Exchange Commission, and any other governmental agency which may regulate their client's business or use their reports to evaluate the client's compliance with applicable laws and related regulations.

Section I—Principles

Preamble

Membership in the American Institute of Certified Public Accountants is voluntary. By accepting membership, a certified public accountant assumes an obligation of self-discipline above and beyond the requirements of laws and regulations.

These Principles of the Code of Professional Conduct of the American Institute of Certified Public Accountants express the profession's recognition of its responsibilities to the public, to clients, and to colleagues. They guide members in the performance of their professional responsibilities and express the basic tenets of ethical and professional conduct. The Principles call for an unswerving commitment to honorable behavior, even at the sacrifice of personal advantage.

Article I—Responsibilities

In carrying out their responsibilities as professionals, members should exercise sensitive professional and moral judgments in all their activities.

As professionals, certified public accountants perform an essential role in society. Consistent with that role, members of the American Institute of Certified Public Accountants have responsibilities to all those who use their professional services. Members also have a continuing responsibility to cooperate with each other to improve the art of accounting, maintain the public's confidence, and carry out the profession's special responsibilities for self-governance. The collective efforts of all members are required to maintain and enhance the traditions of the profession.

Article II—The Public Interest

Members should accept the obligation to act in a way that will serve the public interest, honor the public trust, and demonstrate commitment to professionalism.

A distinguishing mark of a profession is acceptance of its responsibility to the public. The accounting profession's public consists of clients, credit grantors, governments, employers, investors, the business and financial community, and others who rely on the objectivity and integrity of certified public accountants to maintain the orderly functioning of commerce. This reliance imposes a public interest responsibility on certified public accountants. The public interest is defined as the collective well-being of the community of people and institutions the profession serves.

In discharging their professional responsibilities, members may encounter conflicting pressures from among each of those groups. In resolving those conflicts, members should act with integrity, guided by the precept that when members fulfill their responsibility to the public, clients' and employers' interests are best served.

Those who rely on certified public accountants expect them to discharge their responsibilities with integrity, objectivity, due professional care, and a genuine interest in serving the public. They are expected to provide quality services, enter into fee arrangements, and offer a range of services—all in a manner that demonstrates a level of professionalism consistent with these Principles of the Code of Professional Conduct.

All who accept membership in the American Institute of Certified Public Accountants commit themselves to honor the public trust. In return for the faith that the public reposes in them, members should seek continually to demonstrate their dedication to professional excellence.

Article III—Integrity

To maintain and broaden public confidence, members should perform all professional responsibilities with the highest sense of integrity.

Integrity is an element of character fundamental to professional recognition. It is the quality from which the public trust derives and the benchmark against which a member must ultimately test all decisions.

Integrity requires a member to be, among other things, honest and candid within the constraints of client confidentiality. Service and the public trust should not be subordinated to personal gain and advantage. Integrity can accommodate the inadvertent error and the honest difference of opinion; it cannot accommodate deceit or subordination of principle.

Integrity is measured in terms of what is right and just. In the absence of specific rules, standards, or guidance, or in the face of conflicting opinions, a member should test decisions and deeds by asking: "Am I doing what a person of integrity would do? Have I retained my integrity?" Integrity requires a member to observe both the form and the spirit of technical and ethical standards; circumvention of those standards constitutes subordination of judgment.

Integrity also requires a member to observe the principles of objectivity and independence and of due care.

Article IV—Objectivity and Independence

A member should maintain objectivity and be free of conflicts of interest in discharging professional responsibilities. A member in public practice should be independent in fact and appearance when providing auditing and other attestation services.

Objectivity is a state of mind, a quality that lends value to a member's services. It is a distinguishing feature of the profession. The principle of objectivity imposes the obligation to be impartial, intellectually honest, and free of conflicts of interest. Independence precludes relationships that may appear to impair a member's objectivity in rendering attestation services.

Members often serve multiple interests in many different capacities and must demonstrate their objectivity in varying circumstances. Members in public practice render attest, tax, and management advisory services. Other members prepare financial statements in the employment of others, perform internal auditing services, and serve in financial and management capacities in industry, education, and government. They also educate and train those who aspire to admission into the profession. Regardless of service or capacity, members should protect the integrity of their work, maintain objectivity, and avoid any subordination of their judgment.

For a member in public practice, the maintenance of objectivity and independence requires a continuing assessment of client relationships and public responsibility. Such a member who provides auditing and other attestation services should be independent in fact and appearance. In providing all other services, a member should maintain objectivity and avoid conflicts of interest.

Although members not in public practice cannot maintain the appearance of independence, they nevertheless have the responsibility to maintain objectivity in rendering professional services. Members employed by others to prepare financial statements or to perform auditing, tax, or consulting services are charged with the same responsibility for objectivity as members in public practice and must be scrupulous in their application of generally accepted accounting principles and candid in all their dealings with members in public practice.

Activity V—Due Care

A member should observe the profession's technical and ethical standards, strive continually to improve competence and the quality of services, and discharge professional responsibility to the best of the member's ability.

The quest for excellence is the essence of due care. Due care requires a member to discharge professional responsibilities with competence and diligence. It imposes the obligation to perform professional services to the best of a member's ability with concern for the best interest of those for whom the services are performed and consistent with the profession's responsibility to the public.

Competence is derived from a synthesis of education and experience. It begins with a mastery of the common body of knowledge required for designation as a certified public accountant. The maintenance of competence requires a commitment to learning and professional improvement that must continue throughout a member's professional life. It is a member's individual responsibility. In all engagements and in all responsibilities, each member should undertake to achieve a level of competence that will assure that the quality of the member's services meets the high level of professionalism required by these Principles.

Competence represents the attainment and maintenance of a level of understanding and knowledge that enables a member to render services with facility and acumen. It also establishes the limitations of a member's capabilities by dictating that consultation or referral may be required when a professional engagement exceeds the personal competence of a member or a member's firm. Each member is responsible for assessing his or her own competence—of evaluating whether education, experience, and judgment are adequate for the responsibility to be assumed.

Members should be diligent in discharging responsibilities to clients, employers, and the public. Diligence imposes the responsibility to render services promptly and carefully, to be thorough, and to observe applicable technical and ethical standards.

Due care requires a member to plan and supervise adequately any professional activity for which he or she is responsible.

Article VI—Scope and Nature of Services

A member in public practice should observe the Principles of the Code of Professional Conduct in determining the scope and nature of services to be provided.

The public interest aspect of certified public accountants' services requires that such services be consistent with acceptable professional behavior for certified public accountants. Integrity requires that service and the public trust not be subordinated to personal gain and advantage. Objectivity and independence require that members be free from conflicts of interest in discharging professional responsibilities. Due care requires that services be provided with competence and diligence.

Each of these Principles should be considered by members in determining whether or not to provide specific services in individual circumstances. In some instances, they may represent an overall constraint on the nonaudit services that might be offered to a specific client. No hard-and-fast rules can be developed to help members reach these judgments, but they must be satisfied that they are meeting the spirit of the Principles in this regard.

In order to accomplish this, members should:

- Practice in firms that have in place internal quality-control procedures to ensure that services are competently delivered and adequately supervised.

- Determine, in their individual judgments, whether the scope and nature of other services provided to an audit client would create a conflict of interest in the performance of the audit function for that client.
- Assess, in their individual judgments, whether an activity is consistent with their role as professionals (for example, Is such activity a reasonable extension or variation of existing services offered by the member or others in the profession?).

Standards of Ethical Conduct for Practitioners of Management Accounting and Financial Management

Practitioners of management accounting and financial management have an obligation to the public, their profession, the organization they serve, and themselves to maintain the highest standards of ethical conduct. In recognition of this obligation, the Institute of Management Accountants has promulgated the following standards of ethical conduct for management accounting and financial management. Adherence to these standards, both domestically and internationally, is integral to achieving the *Objectives of Management Accounting*.[3] Practitioners of management accounting and financial management shall not commit acts contrary to these standards nor shall they condone the commission of such acts by others within their organizations.

Competence

Practitioners of management accounting and financial management have a responsibility to:

- Maintain an appropriate level of professional competence by ongoing development of their knowledge and skills.
- Perform their professional duties in accordance with relevant laws, regulations, and technical standards.
- Prepare complete and clear reports and recommendations after appropriate analyses of relevant and reliable information.

Confidentiality

Practitioners of management accounting and financial management have a responsibility to:

- Refrain from disclosing confidential information acquired in the course of their work except when authorized, unless legally obligated to do so.
- Inform subordinates as appropriate regarding the confidentiality of information acquired in the course of their work and monitor their activities to assure the maintenance of that confidentiality.
- Refrain from using or appearing to use confidential information acquired in the course of their work for unethical or illegal advantage either personally or through third parties.

Integrity

Practitioners of management accounting and financial management have a responsibility to:

- Avoid actual or apparent conflicts of interest and advise all appropriate parties of any potential conflict.
- Refrain from engaging in any activity that would prejudice their ability to carry out their duties ethically.
- Refuse any gift, favor, or hospitality that would influence or would appear to influence their actions.

---

[3] National Association of Accountants, *Statements on Management Accounting: Objectives of Management Accounting*, Statement No. 1B, New York, N.Y., June 17, 1982.

- Refrain from either actively or passively subverting the attainment of the organization's legitimate and ethical objectives.
- Recognize and communicate professional limitations or other constraints that would preclude responsible judgment or successful performance of an activity.
- Communicate unfavorable as well as favorable information and professional judgments or opinions.
- Refrain from engaging in or supporting any activity that would discredit the profession.

Objectivity

Practitioners of management accounting and financial management have a responsibility to:

- Communicate information fairly and objectively.
- Disclose fully all relevant information that could reasonably be expected to influence an intended user's understanding of the reports, comments, and recommendations presented.

Appendix C: Alternative Methods of Recording Deferrals

As discussed in Chapter 3, deferrals are created by recording a transaction in a way that delays or defers the recognition of an expense or a revenue. Deferrals may be either deferred expenses (prepaid expenses) or deferred revenues (unearned revenues).

In Chapter 2, deferred expenses (prepaid expenses) were debited to an *asset* account at the time of payment. As an alternative, deferred expenses may be debited to an *expense* account at the time of payment. In Chapter 2, deferred revenues (unearned revenues) were credited to a *liability* account at the time of receipt. As an alternative, deferred revenues may be credited to a *revenue* account at the time of receipt. This appendix describes and illustrates these alternative methods of recording deferred expenses and deferred revenues.

Deferred Expenses (Prepaid Expenses)

As a basis for illustrating the alternative methods of recording deferred expenses, the insurance premium paid by NetSolutions in Chapter 2 is used. The amounts related to this insurance are as follows:

Prepayment of insurance for 24 months, starting December 1	$2,400
Insurance premium expired during December	100
Unexpired insurance premium at the end of December	$2,300

Based on the above data, the entries to account for the deferred expense (prepaid insurance) recorded initially as an *asset* are shown in the journal and T accounts in Exhibit 1. The adjusting entry in Exhibit 1 was shown in Chapter 3. The entries to account for the prepaid insurance recorded initially as an *expense* are shown in the journal and T accounts in Exhibit 2.

EXHIBIT 1

Prepaid Expense Recorded Initially as Asset

Initial entry (to record initial payment):

| Dec. 1 | Prepaid Insurance | 2,400 | |
| | Cash | | 2,400 |

Adjusting entry (to transfer amount *used* to the proper *expense* account):

| Dec. 31 | Insurance Expense | 100 | |
| | Prepaid Insurance | | 100 |

Closing entry (to close income statement accounts with debit balances):

| Income Summary | XXXX | |
| Supplies Expense | | XXXX |

| Insurance Expense | | 100 |

Prepaid Insurance

| Dec. 1 | | 2,400 | Dec. 31 | Adjusting | 100 |

Insurance Expense

| Dec. 31 | Adjusting | 100 | Dec. 31 | Closing | 100 |

EXHIBIT 2

Prepaid Expense Recorded Initially as Expense

Initial entry (to record initial payment):

| Dec. 1 | Insurance Expense | 2,400 | |
| | Cash | | 2,400 |

Adjusting entry (to transfer amount *unused* to the proper *asset* account):

| Dec. 31 | Prepaid Insurance | 2,300 | |
| | Insurance Expense | | 2,300 |

Closing entry (to close income statement accounts with debit balances):

| Income Summary | XXXX | |
| Supplies Expense | | XXXX |

| Insurance Expense | | 100 |

Prepaid Insurance

| Dec. 31 | Adjusting | 2,300 | |

Insurance Expense

| Dec. 1 | | 2,400 | Dec. 31 | Adjusting | 2,300 |
| | | | 31 | Closing | 100 |

Either of the two methods of recording deferred expenses (prepaid expenses) may be used. As illustrated in Exhibits 1 and 2, both methods result in the same account balances after the adjusting entries have been recorded. Therefore, the amounts reported as expenses in the income statement and as assets on the balance sheet will not be affected by the method used. To avoid confusion, the method used by a business for each kind of prepaid expense should be followed consistently from year to year.

Some businesses record all deferred expenses using one method. Other businesses use one method to record the prepayment of some expenses and the other method for other expenses. Initial debits to the asset account are logical for prepayments of insurance, which are usually for periods of one to three years. On the other hand, rent on a building may be prepaid on the first of each month. The prepaid rent will expire by the end of the month. In this case, it is logical to record the payment of rent by initially debiting an expense account rather than an asset account.

Deferred Revenues (Unearned Revenues)

To illustrate the alternative methods of recording deferred revenues, we will use the rent received by NetSolutions in Chapter 2. NetSolutions rented land on December 1 to a local retailer for use as a parking lot for three months and received $360 for the entire three months. On December 31, $120 (1/3 × $360) of the rent has been earned, and $240 (2/3 × $360) of the rent is still unearned.

Based on the above data, the entries to account for the deferred revenue (unearned rent) recorded initially as a liability are shown in the journal and ledger in Exhibit 3. The adjusting entry in Exhibit 3 was shown in Chapter 3. The entries to account for the unearned rent recorded initially as revenue are shown in the journal and ledger in Exhibit 4.

As illustrated in Exhibits 3 and 4, both methods result in the same account balances after the adjusting entries have been recorded. Therefore, the amounts reported as revenues in the income statement and as liabilities on the balance sheet

EXHIBIT 3	**EXHIBIT 4**
Unearned Revenue Recorded Initially as Liability	Unearned Revenue Recorded Initially as Revenue
Initial entry (to record initial receipt):	Initial entry (to record initial receipt):
Dec. 1 Cash 360	Dec. 1 Cash 360
Unearned Rent 360	Rent Revenue 360
Adjusting entry (to transfer amount *earned* to proper *revenue* account):	Adjusting entry (to transfer amount *unearned* to proper *liability* account):
Dec. 31 Unearned Rent 120	Dec. 31 Rent Revenue 240
Rent Revenue 120	Unearned Rent 240
Closing entry (to close income statement accounts with credit balances):	Closing entry (to close income statement accounts with credit balances):
Dec. 31 Fees Earned XXXX	Dec. 31 Fees Earned XXXX
~~	~~~~~~~~~~~~~~~~~~~~~
Rent Revenue 120	Rent Revenue 120
Income Summary XXXX	Income Summary XXXX

Unearned Rent

Dec. 31	Adjusting	120	Dec. 1		360

Rent Revenue

Dec. 31	Closing	120	Dec. 31	Adjusting	120

Unearned Rent

			Dec. 31	Adjusting	240

Rent Revenue

Dec. 31	Adjusting	240	Dec. 1		360
31	Closing	120			

will not be affected by the method used. Either of the methods may be used for all revenues received in advance. Alternatively, the first method may be used for advance receipts of some kinds of revenue and the second method for other kinds. To avoid confusion, the method used by a business for each kind of unearned revenue should be followed consistently from year to year.

Reversing Entries for Deferrals

As discussed in the appendix at the end of Chapter 4, the use of reversing entries is optional. However, the use of reversing entries generally simplifies the analysis of transactions and reduces the likelihood of errors in the subsequent recording of transactions. Normally, reversing entries are prepared for deferrals in the following two cases:

1. When a deferred expense (prepaid expense) is initially recorded as an expense.
2. When a deferred revenue (unearned revenue) is initially recorded as a revenue.

The entry to reverse the adjustment to record the prepaid insurance in Exhibit 2 is as follows:

Jan.	1	Insurance Expense	2,300	
		Prepaid Insurance		2,300

The entry to reverse the adjustment to record the unearned rent in Exhibit 4 is as follows:

Jan.	1	Unearned Rent	240	
		Rent Revenue		240

EXERCISES

Exercise C–1
Adjusting entries for office supplies

The office supplies purchased during the year total $3,570, and the amount of office supplies on hand at the end of the year is $415.

a. Record the following transactions directly in T accounts for Office Supplies and Office Supplies Expense, using the system of initially recording supplies as an asset: (1) purchases for the period; (2) adjusting entry at the end of the period. Identify each entry by number.
b. Record the following transactions directly in T accounts for Office Supplies and Office Supplies Expense, using the system of initially recording supplies as an expense: (1) purchases for the period; (2) adjusting entry at the end of the period. Identify each entry by number.

Exercise C–2
Adjusting entries for prepaid insurance

During the first year of operations, insurance premiums of $9,135 were paid. At the end of the year, unexpired premiums totaled $3,478. Journalize the adjusting entry at the end of the year, assuming that (a) prepaid expenses were initially recorded as assets and (b) prepaid expenses were initially recorded as expenses.

Exercise C–3
Adjusting entries for advertising revenue

The advertising revenues received during the year total $351,200, and the unearned advertising revenue at the end of the year is $48,500.

a. Record the following transactions directly in T accounts for Unearned Advertising Revenue and Advertising Revenue, using the system of initially recording advertising fees as a liability: (1) revenues received during the period; (2) adjusting entry at the end of the period. Identify each entry by number.
b. Record the following transactions directly in T accounts for Unearned Advertising Revenue and Advertising Revenue, using the system of initially recording advertising fees as revenue: (1) revenues received during the period; (2) adjusting entry at the end of the period. Identify each entry by number.

Exercise C–4
Year-end entries for deferred revenues

In its first year of operation, Magna Publishing Co. received $2,275,000 from advertising contracts and $6,195,000 from magazine subscriptions, crediting the two amounts to Unearned Advertising Revenue and Circulation Revenue, respectively. At the end of the year, the unearned advertising revenue amounts to $196,000, and the circulation revenue amounts to $1,150,000. Journalize the adjusting entries that should be made at the end of the year.

Appendix D: Special Journals and Subsidiary Ledgers

In the beginning chapters of this text, all transactions for NetSolutions were manually recorded in an all-purpose (two-column) journal. The journal entries were then posted individually to the accounts in the ledger. Such manual accounting systems are simple to use and easy to understand. Manually kept records may serve a business reasonably well when the amount of data collected, stored, and used is relatively small. For a large business with a large database, however, such manual processing is too costly and too time-consuming. For example, a large company such as **AT&T** has millions of long-distance telephone fees earned on account with millions of customers daily. Each telephone fee on account requires an entry debiting Accounts Receivable and crediting Fees Earned. In addition, a record of each customer's receivable must be kept. Clearly, a simple manual system would not serve the business needs of AT&T.

When a business has a large number of similar transactions, using an all-purpose journal is inefficient and impractical. In such cases, special journals are useful. In addition, the manual system can be supplemented or replaced by a computerized system. Although we will illustrate the manual use of special journals and subsidiary ledgers, the basic principles described in the following paragraphs also apply to a computerized accounting system.

Special Journals

One method of processing data more efficiently in a manual accounting system is to expand the all-purpose two-column journal to a multicolumn journal. Each column in a multicolumn journal is used only for recording transactions that affect a certain account. For example, a special column could be used only for recording debits to the cash account, and another special column could be used only for recording credits to the cash account. The addition of the two special columns would eliminate the writing of *Cash* in the journal for every receipt and every payment of cash. Also, there would be no need to post each individual debit and credit to the cash account. Instead, the *Cash Dr.* and *Cash Cr.* columns could be totaled periodically and only the totals posted. In a similar way, special columns could be added for recording credits to Fees Earned, debits and credits to Accounts Receivable and Accounts Payable, and for other entries that are often repeated.

An all-purpose multicolumn journal may be adequate for a small business that has many transactions of a similar nature. However, a journal that has many columns for recording many different types of transactions is impractical for larger businesses.

The next logical extension of the accounting system is to replace the single multicolumn journal with several **special journals**. Each special journal is designed to be used for recording a single kind of transaction that occurs frequently. For example, since most businesses have many transactions in which cash is paid out, they will likely use a special journal for recording cash payments. Likewise, they will use another special journal for recording cash receipts. Special journals are a method of summarizing transactions, which is a basic feature of any accounting system.

The format and number of special journals that a business uses depends upon the nature of the business. A business that gives credit might use a special journal designed for recording only revenue from services provided on credit. On the other hand, a business that does not give credit would have no need for such a journal. In other cases, record-keeping costs may be reduced by using supporting documents as special journals.

The transactions that occur most often in a small- to medium-size service business and the special journals in which they are recorded are as follows:

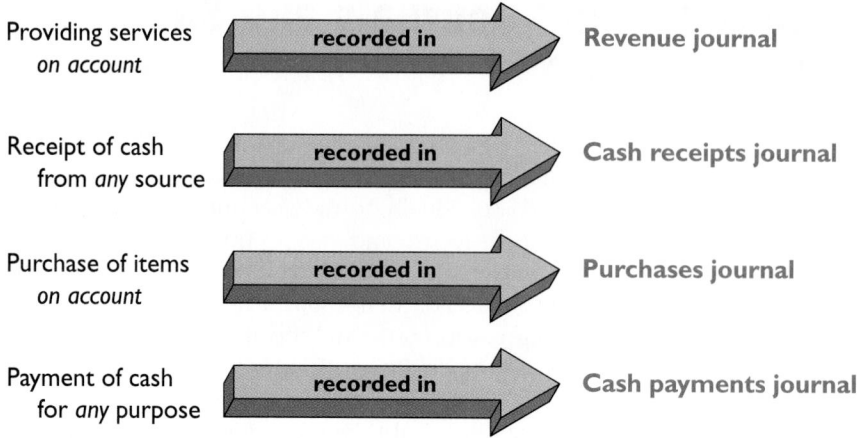

The all-purpose two-column journal, called the **general journal** or simply the **journal**, can be used for entries that do not fit into any of the special journals. For example, adjusting and closing entries are recorded in the general journal.

Subsidiary Ledgers

An accounting system should be designed to provide information on the amounts due from various customers (accounts receivable) and amounts owed to various creditors (accounts payable). As we discussed in the text, a large number of individual accounts with a common characteristic can be grouped together in a separate ledger called a **subsidiary ledger**. Each subsidiary ledger is represented in the general ledger by a summarizing account, called a **controlling account**. The sum of the balances of the accounts in a subsidiary ledger must equal the balance of the related controlling account. Thus, you may think of a subsidiary ledger as a secondary ledger that supports a controlling account in the general ledger.

The individual accounts with customers are arranged in alphabetical order in a subsidiary ledger called the **accounts receivable subsidiary ledger** or **customers ledger**. The controlling account in the general ledger that summarizes the debits and credits to the individual customer accounts is *Accounts Receivable*. The individual accounts with creditors are arranged in alphabetical order in a subsidiary ledger called the **accounts payable subsidiary ledger** or **creditors ledger.** The related controlling account in the general ledger is *Accounts Payable*. The relationship between the general ledger and these subsidiary ledgers is illustrated in Exhibit 1.

In the following paragraphs, we illustrate special journals and subsidiary ledgers in a manual accounting system for NetSolutions. To simplify the illustration, we will use a minimum number of transactions. We will focus our discussion on (1) revenues and cash receipts and (2) purchases and cash payments. We will assume that NetSolutions had the following selected general ledger balances on March 1, 2003:

Account Number	Account	Balance
11	Cash	$6,200
12	Accounts Receivable	3,400
14	Supplies	2,500
18	Office Equipment	2,500
21	Accounts Payable	1,230

Exhibit 1 General Ledger and Subsidiary Ledgers

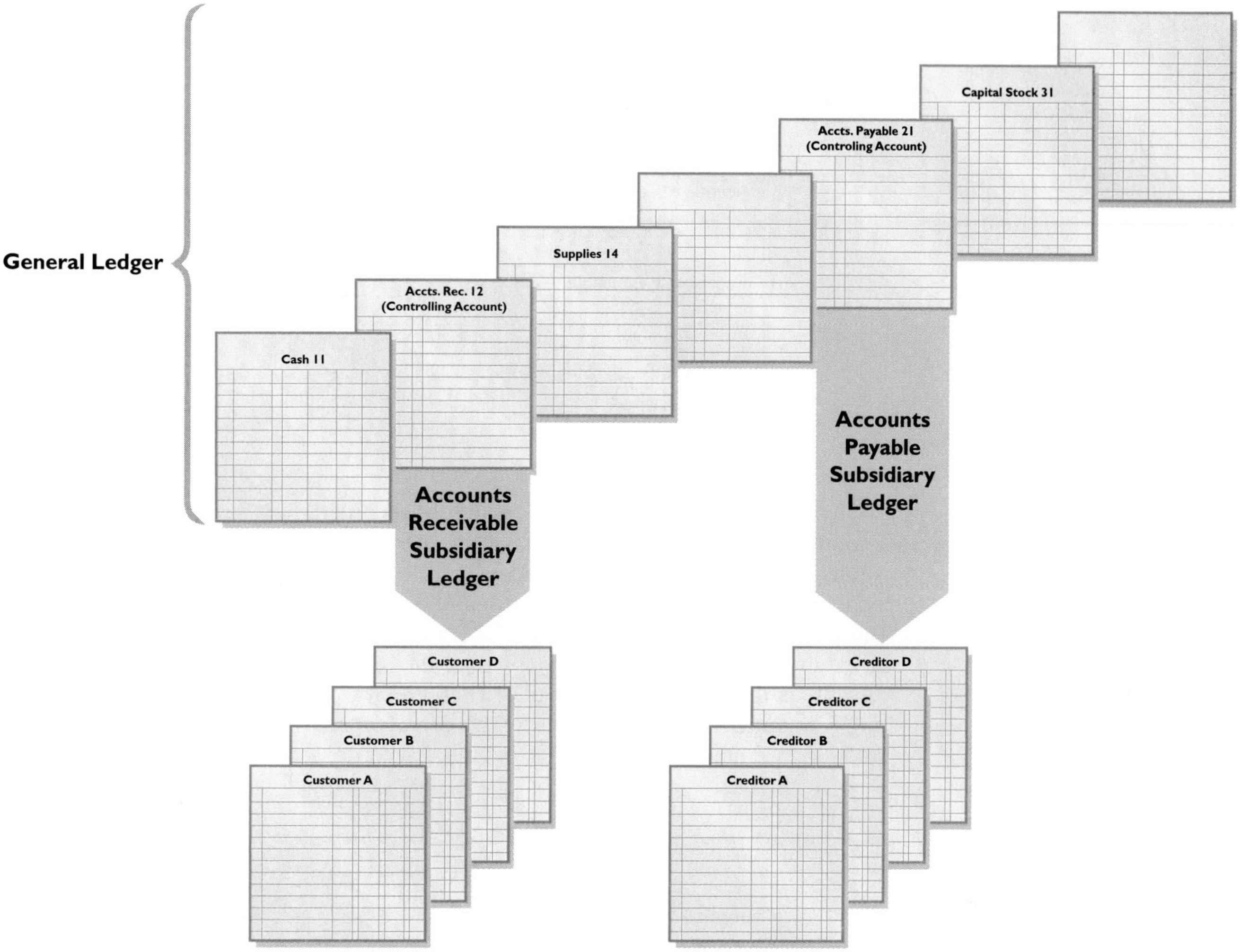

General Ledger

Cash 11

Accts. Rec. 12 (Controlling Account)

Supplies 14

Accts. Payable 21 (Controling Account)

Capital Stock 31

Accounts Receivable Subsidiary Ledger

Accounts Payable Subsidiary Ledger

Customer D
Customer C
Customer B
Customer A

Creditor D
Creditor C
Creditor B
Creditor A

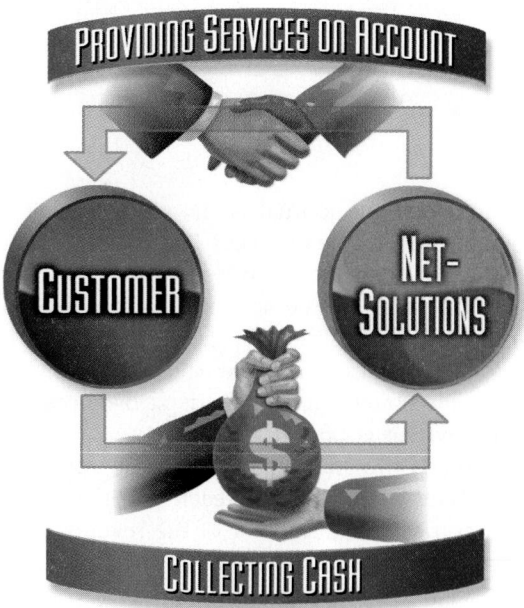

PROVIDING SERVICES ON ACCOUNT

CUSTOMER

NET-SOLUTIONS

COLLECTING CASH

Revenues and Cash Receipts

NetSolutions provides services on account and collects cash from customers. Revenues earned on account create a customer receivable and will be recorded in a revenue journal. Customers' accounts receivable are collected and will be recorded in a cash receipts journal.

Internal control is enhanced by separating the function of recording revenue transactions in the revenue journal from recording cash collections in the cash receipts journal. For example, if these duties are separated, it is more difficult for one person to embezzle cash collections and manipulate the accounting records.

Revenue Journal

The **revenue journal** is used only for recording **fees earned on account**. *Cash fees earned would be recorded in the cash receipts journal.* The sale of products is recorded in a **sales journal**, which is similar to the revenue journal. We will compare the efficiency of using a revenue journal with a general journal by assuming that Net-Solutions recorded the following revenue transactions in a general journal:

2003						
Mar.	2	Accounts Receivable—MyMusicClub.com	12/✔	2 2 0 0 00	
		Fees Earned	41		2 2 0 0 00
	6	Accounts Receivable—RapZone.com	12/✔	1 7 5 0 00	
		Fees Earned	41		1 7 5 0 00
	18	Accounts Receivable—Web Cantina	12/✔	2 6 5 0 00	
		Fees Earned	41		2 6 5 0 00
	27	Accounts Receivable—MyMusicClub.com	12/✔	3 0 0 0 00	
		Fees Earned	41		3 0 0 0 00

For these four transactions, NetSolutions recorded eight account titles and eight amounts. In addition, NetSolutions made 12 postings to the ledgers—four to Accounts Receivable in the general ledger, four to the accounts receivable subsidiary ledger (indicated by each check mark), and four to Fees Earned in the general ledger. These transactions could be recorded more efficiently in a revenue journal, as shown in Exhibit 2. In each revenue transaction, the amount of the debit to Accounts Receivable is the same as the amount of the credit to Fees Earned. Therefore, only a single amount column is necessary. The date, invoice number, customer name, and amount are entered separately for each transaction.

Exhibit 2 Revenue Journal

			REVENUE JOURNAL		PAGE 35
	Date	Invoice No.	Account Debited	Post. Ref.	Accts. Rec. Dr. Fees Earned Cr.
1	2003 Mar. 2	615	MyMusicClub.com		2 2 0 0 00	1
2	6	616	RapZone.com		1 7 5 0 00	2
3	18	617	Web Cantina		2 6 5 0 00	3
4	27	618	MyMusicClub.com		3 0 0 0 00	4
5	31				9 6 0 0 00	5

The basic procedure of posting from a revenue journal is shown in Exhibit 3. A single monthly total is posted to Accounts Receivable and Fees Earned in the general ledger. Each transaction, such as the $2,200 debit to MyMusicClub.com, must also be posted individually to a customer account in the accounts receivable subsidiary ledger. These postings to customer accounts should be made frequently. In this way, management has information on the current balance of each customer's account. Since the balances in the customer accounts are usually debit balances, the three-column account form shown in the exhibit is often used.

To provide a trail of the entries posted to the subsidiary ledger, the source of these entries is indicated in the *Posting Reference* column of each account by inserting the letter *R* (for revenue journal) and the page number of the revenue journal. A check mark (✓) instead of a number is then inserted in the *Posting Reference* column of the revenue journal, as shown in Exhibit 3.

Exhibit 3 Revenue Journal
Postings to Ledgers

REVENUE JOURNAL   **PAGE 35**

	Date	Invoice No.	Account Debited	Post. Ref.	Accts. Rec. Dr. Fees Earned Cr.	
1	2003 March 2	615	MyMusicClub.com	✔	2,200	1
2	6	616	RapZone.com	✔	1,750	2
3	18	617	Web Cantina	✔	2,650	3
4	27	618	MyMusicClub.com	✔	3,000	4
5	31				9,600	5
6					(12) (41)	6

GENERAL LEDGER

ACCOUNT   Accounts Receivable   **Account No. 12**

Date	Item	Post. Ref.	Dr.	Cr.	Balance Dr.	Balance Cr.
2003 March 1	Balance	✔			3,400	
31		R35	9,600		13,000	

ACCOUNT   Fees Earned   **Account No. 41**

Date	Item	Post. Ref.	Dr.	Cr.	Balance Dr.	Balance Cr.
2003 March 31		R35		9,600		9,600

ACCOUNTS RECEIVABLE SUBSIDIARY LEDGER

NAME: MyMusicClub.com

Date	Item	Post. Ref.	Dr.	Cr.	Balance
2003 March 2		R35	2,200		2,200
27		R35	3,000		5,200

NAME: RapZone.com

Date	Item	Post. Ref.	Dr.	Cr.	Balance
2003 March 6		R35	1,750		1,750

NAME: Web Cantina

Date	Item	Post. Ref.	Dr.	Cr.	Balance
2003 March 1	Balance	✔			3,400
18		R35	2,650		6,050

If a customer's account has a credit balance, that fact should be indicated by an asterisk or parentheses in the *Balance* column. When an account's balance is zero, a line may be drawn in the *Balance* column.

At the end of each month, the amount column of the revenue journal is totaled. This total is equal to the sum of the month's debits to the individual accounts in the subsidiary ledger. It is posted in the general ledger as a debit to Accounts Receivable and a credit to Fees Earned, as shown in Exhibit 3. The respective account numbers (12 and 41) are then inserted below the total in the revenue journal to indicate that the posting is completed, as shown in Exhibit 3. In this way, all of the transactions for fees earned during the month are posted to the general ledger only once—at the end of the month—greatly simplifying the posting process.

Cash Receipts Journal

All transactions that involve the receipt of cash are recorded in a **cash receipts journal**. Thus, the cash receipts journal has a column entitled *Cash Dr.*, as shown in Exhibit 4. All transactions recorded in the cash receipts journal will involve an entry in the *Cash Dr.* column. For example, on March 28 NetSolutions received cash of $2,200 from MyMusicClub.com and entered that amount in the *Cash Dr.* column.

Exhibit 4 Cash Receipts Journal and Postings

CASH RECEIPTS JOURNAL   PAGE 14

Date	Account Credited	Post. Ref.	Other Accounts Cr.	Accounts Receivable Cr.	Cash Dr.
2003					
March 1	Rent Revenue	42	400		400
19	Web Cantina	✔		3,400	3,400
28	MyMusicClub.com	✔		2,200	2,200
30	RapZone.com	✔		1,750	1,750
31			400	7,350	7,750
			(✔)	(12)	(11)

GENERAL LEDGER

ACCOUNT Rent Revenue   Account No. 42

Date	Item	Post. Ref.	Dr.	Cr.	Balance Dr.	Balance Cr.
2003						
March 1		CR14		400		400

ACCOUNT Accounts Receivable   Account No. 12

Date	Item	Post. Ref.	Dr.	Cr.	Balance Dr.	Balance Cr.
2003						
March 1	Balance	✔			3,400	
31		R35	9,600		13,000	
31		CR14		7,350	5,650	

ACCOUNT Cash   Account No. 11

Date	Item	Post. Ref.	Dr.	Cr.	Balance Dr.	Balance Cr.
2003						
March 1	Balance	✔			6,200	
31		CR14	7,750		13,950	

ACCOUNTS RECEIVABLE SUBSIDIARY LEDGER

NAME: MyMusicClub.com

Date	Item	Post. Ref.	Dr.	Cr.	Balance
2003					
March 2		R35	2,200		2,200
27		R35	3,000		5,200
28		CR14		2,200	3,000

NAME: RapZone.com

Date	Item	Post. Ref.	Dr.	Cr.	Balance
2003					
March 6		R35	1,750		1,750
30		CR14		1,750	—

NAME: Web Cantina

Date	Item	Post. Ref.	Dr.	Cr.	Balance
2003					
March 1	Balance	✔			3,400
18		R35	2,650		6,050
19		CR14		3,400	2,650

The kinds of transactions in which cash is received and how often they occur determine the titles of the other columns. For NetSolutions, the most frequent source of cash is collections from customers. Thus, the cash receipts journal in Exhibit 4 has an *Accounts Receivable Cr.* column. On March 28, when MyMusicClub.com made a payment on its account, NetSolutions entered *MyMusicClub.com* in the *Account Credited* column and entered *2,200* in the *Accounts Receivable Cr.* column.

The *Other Accounts Cr.* column in Exhibit 4 is used for recording credits to any account for which there is no special credit column. For example, NetSolutions received cash on March 1 for rent. Since no special column exists for Rent Revenue, NetSolutions entered *Rent Revenue* in the *Account Credited* column and entered *400* in the *Other Accounts Cr.* column.

Postings from the cash receipts journal to the ledgers of NetSolutions are also shown in Exhibit 4. This posting process is similar to that of the revenue journal. At regular intervals, each amount in the *Other Accounts Cr.* column is posted to the proper account in the general ledger. The posting is indicated by inserting the account number in the *Posting Reference* column of the cash receipts journal. The posting reference *CR* (for cash receipts journal) and the proper page number are inserted in the *Posting Reference* columns of the accounts.

The amounts in the *Accounts Receivable Cr.* column are posted individually to the customer accounts in the accounts receivable subsidiary ledger. These postings should be made frequently. The posting reference *CR* and the proper page number are inserted in the *Posting Reference* column of each customer's account. A check mark is placed in the *Posting Reference* column of the cash receipts journal to show that each amount has been posted. None of the individual amounts in the *Cash Dr.* column is posted separately.

At the end of the month, all of the amount columns are totaled. The debits should equal the credits. Because each amount in the *Other Accounts Cr.* column has been posted individually to a general ledger account, a check mark is inserted below the column total to indicate that no further action is needed. The totals of the *Accounts Receivable Cr.* and *Cash Dr.* columns are posted to the proper accounts in the general ledger, and their account numbers are inserted below the totals to show that the postings have been completed.

Accounts Receivable Control and Subsidiary Ledger

After all posting has been completed for the month, the sum of the balances in the accounts receivable subsidiary ledger should be compared with the balance of the accounts receivable controlling account in the general ledger. If the controlling account and the subsidiary ledger do not agree, the error or errors must be located and corrected. The balances of the individual customer accounts may be summarized in a schedule of accounts receivable. The total of NetSolutions' schedule of accounts receivable, $5,650, agrees with the balance of its accounts receivable controlling account on March 31, 2003, as shown below.

Accounts Receivable— (Controlling)		NetSolutions Schedule of Accounts Receivable March 31, 2003	
Balance, March 31, 2003	$5,650	MyMusicClub.com	$3,000
		RapZone.com	0
		Web Cantina	2,650
		Total accounts receivable	$5,650

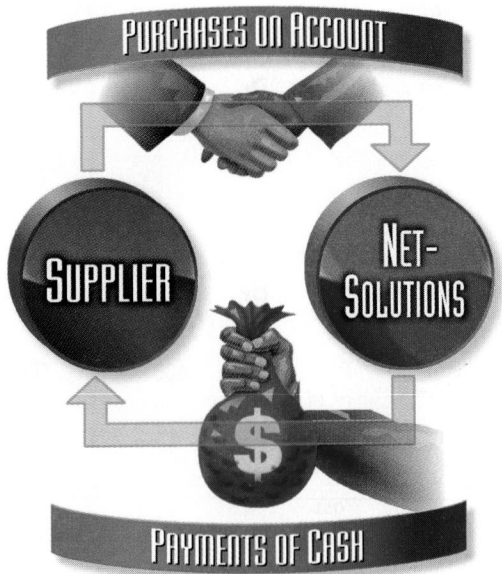

Purchases and Payments

NetSolutions makes purchases on account and pays cash to suppliers. To make purchases of supplies and other items on account requires establishing a supplier account payable. These transactions will be recorded in a purchases journal. The payments of suppliers' accounts payable will be recorded in the cash payments journal.

Internal control is enhanced by separating the function of recording purchases in the purchases journal from recording cash payments in the cash payments journal. Separating duties in this way prevents an individual from establishing a fictitious supplier and then collecting payments for fictitious purchases from this supplier.

Purchases Journal

The **purchases journal** is designed for recording all **purchases on account**. *Cash purchases would be recorded in the cash payments journal.* The purchases journal has a column entitled *Accounts Payable Cr.* The purchases journal also has special columns for recording debits to the accounts most often affected. Since NetSolutions makes frequent debits to its supplies account, a *Supplies Dr.* column is included for these transactions. For example, as shown in Exhibit 5, NetSolutions recorded the purchase of supplies on March 3 by entering *600* in the *Supplies Dr.* column, *600* in the *Accounts Payable Cr.* column, and *Howard Supplies* in the *Account Credited* column.

The *Other Accounts Dr.* column in Exhibit 5 is used to record purchases, on account, of any item for which there is no special debit column. The title of the account to be debited is entered in the *Other Accounts* column, and the amount is entered in the *Amount* column. For example, NetSolutions recorded the purchase

Exhibit 5 Purchases Journal and Postings

PURCHASES JOURNAL   PAGE 11

	Date	Account Credited	Post. Ref.	Accounts Payable Cr.	Supplies Dr.	Other Accounts Dr.	Post. Ref.	Amount	
	2003								
1	March 3	Howard Supplies	✔	600	600				1
2	7	Donnelly Supplies	✔	420	420				2
3	12	Jewett Business Systems	✔	2,800		Office Equipment	18	2,800	3
4	19	Donnelly Supplies	✔	1,450	1,450				4
5	27	Howard Supplies	✔	960	960				5
6	31			6,230	3,430			2,800	6
7				(21)	(14)			(✔)	7

GENERAL LEDGER

ACCOUNT Accounts Payable   Account No. 21

Date	Item	Post. Ref.	Dr.	Cr.	Balance
2003					
March 1	Balance	✔			1,230
31		P11		6,230	7,460

ACCOUNT Supplies   Account No. 14

Date	Item	Post. Ref.	Dr.	Cr.	Balance
2003					
March 1	Balance	✔			2,500
31		P11	3,430		5,930

ACCOUNT Office Equipment   Account No. 18

Date	Item	Post. Ref.	Dr.	Cr.	Balance
2003					
March 1	Balance	✔			2,500
12		P11	2,800		5,300

ACCOUNTS PAYABLE SUBSIDIARY LEDGER

NAME: Donnelly Supplies

Date	Item	Post. Ref.	Dr.	Cr.	Balance
2003					
March 7		P11		420	420
19		P11		1,450	1,870

NAME: Grayco Supplies

Date	Item	Post. Ref.	Dr.	Cr.	Balance
2003					
March 1	Balance	✔			1,230

NAME: Howard Supplies

Date	Item	Post. Ref.	Dr.	Cr.	Balance
2003					
March 3		P11		600	600
27		P11		960	1,560

NAME: Jewett Business Systems

Date	Item	Post. Ref.	Dr.	Cr.	Balance
2003					
March 12		P11		2,800	2,800

of office equipment on account on March 12 by entering *Office Equipment* in the *Other Accounts Dr.* column, *2,800* in the *Amount* column, *2,800* in the *Accounts Payable Cr.* column, and *Jewett Business Systems* in the *Account Credited* column.

Postings from the purchases journal to the ledgers of NetSolutions are also shown in Exhibit 5. The principles used in posting the purchases journal are similar to those used in posting the revenue and cash receipts journals. The source of the entries posted to the subsidiary and general ledgers is indicated in the *Posting Reference* column of each account by inserting the letter *P* (for purchases journal) and the page number of the purchases journal. A check mark (✔) is inserted in the *Posting Reference* column of the purchases journal after each credit is posted to a creditor's account in the accounts payable subsidiary ledger.

At regular intervals, the amounts in the *Other Accounts Dr.* column are posted to the accounts in the general ledger. As each amount is posted, the related general ledger account number is inserted in the *Posting Reference* column of the *Other Accounts* section.

At the end of each month, the amount columns in the purchases journal are totaled. The sum of the two debit column totals should equal the sum of the credit column.

The totals of the *Accounts Payable Cr.* and *Supplies Dr.* columns are posted to the appropriate general ledger accounts in the usual manner, with the related account numbers inserted below the column totals. Because each amount in the *Other Accounts Dr.* column was posted individually, a check mark is placed below the $2,800 total to show that no further action is needed.

Cash Payments Journal

The special columns for the **cash payments journal** are determined in the same manner as for the revenue, cash receipts, and purchases journals. The determining factors are the kinds of transactions to be recorded and how often they occur.

The cash payments journal has a *Cash Cr.* column, as shown in Exhibit 6. All transactions recorded in the cash payments journal will involve an entry in this column. Payments to creditors on account happen often enough to require an *Accounts Payable Dr.* column. Debits to creditor accounts for invoices paid are recorded in the *Accounts Payable Dr.* column. For example, on March 15 NetSolutions paid $1,230 on its account with Grayco Supplies. NetSolutions recorded this transaction by entering *1,230* in the *Accounts Payable Dr.* column, *1,230* in the *Cash Cr.* column, and *Grayco Supplies* in the *Account Debited* column.

NetSolutions makes all payments by check. As each transaction is recorded in the cash payments journal, the related check number is entered in the column at the right of the *Date* column. The check numbers are helpful in controlling cash payments, and they provide a useful cross-reference.

The *Other Accounts Dr.* column is used for recording debits to any account for which there is no special column. For example, NetSolutions paid $1,600 on March 2 for rent. The transaction was recorded by entering *Rent Expense* in the space provided and *1,600* in the *Other Accounts Dr.* and *Cash Cr.* columns.

Postings from the cash payments journal to the ledgers of NetSolutions are also shown in Exhibit 6. The amounts entered in the *Accounts Payable Dr.* column are posted to the individual creditor accounts in the accounts payable subsidiary ledger. These postings should be made frequently. After each posting, *CP* (for cash payments journal) and the page number of the journal are inserted in the *Posting Reference* column of the account. A check mark is placed in the *Posting Reference* column of the cash payments journal to indicate that each amount has been posted.

At regular intervals, each item in the *Other Accounts Dr.* column is also posted individually to an account in the general ledger. The posting is indicated by writing the account number in the *Posting Reference* column of the cash payments journal.

At the end of the month, each of the amount columns in the cash payments journal is totaled. The sum of the two debit totals is compared with the credit total

Exhibit 6 Cash Payments Journal and Postings

CASH PAYMENTS JOURNAL   PAGE 7

	Date	Ck. No.	Account Debited	Post. Ref.	Other Accounts Dr.	Accounts Payable Dr.	Cash Cr.	
	2003							
1	March 2	150	Rent Expense	52	1,600		1,600	1
2	15	151	Grayco Supplies	✔		1,230	1,230	2
3	21	152	Jewett Business Systems	✔		2,800	2,800	3
4	22	153	Donnelly Supplies	✔		420	420	4
5	30	154	Utilities Expense	54	1,050		1,050	5
6	31	155	Howard Supplies	✔		600	600	6
7	31				2,650	5,050	7,700	7
8					(✔)	(21)	(11)	8

GENERAL LEDGER

ACCOUNT   Accounts Payable   Account No. 21

Date	Item	Post. Ref.	Dr.	Cr.	Balance
2003					
March 1	Balance	✔			1,230
31		P11		6,230	7,460
31		CP7	5,050		2,410

ACCOUNT   Cash   Account No. 11

Date	Item	Post. Ref.	Dr.	Cr.	Balance
2003					
March 1	Balance	✔			6,200
31		CR14	7,750		13,950
31		CP7		7,700	6,250

ACCOUNT   Rent Expense   Account No. 52

Date	Item	Post. Ref.	Dr.	Cr.	Balance
2003					
March 2		CP7	1,600		1,600

ACCOUNT   Utilities Expense   Account No. 54

Date	Item	Post. Ref.	Dr.	Cr.	Balance
2003					
March 30		CP7	1,050		1,050

ACCOUNTS PAYABLE SUBSIDIARY LEDGER

NAME: Donnelly Supplies

Date	Item	Post. Ref.	Dr.	Cr.	Balance
2003					
March 7		P11		420	420
19		P11		1,450	1,870
22		CP7	420		1,450

NAME: Grayco Supplies

Date	Item	Post. Ref.	Dr.	Cr.	Balance
2003					
March 1	Balance	✔			1,230
15		CP7	1,230		—

NAME: Howard Supplies

Date	Item	Post. Ref.	Dr.	Cr.	Balance
2003					
March 3		P11		600	600
27		P11		960	1,560
31		CP7	600		960

NAME: Jewett Business Systems

Date	Item	Post. Ref.	Dr.	Cr.	Balance
2003					
March 12		P11		2,800	2,800
21		CP7	2,800		—

to determine their equality. A check mark is placed below the total of the *Other Accounts Dr.* column to indicate that no further action is needed. When each of the totals of the other two columns is posted to the general ledger, an account number is inserted below each column total.

Accounts Payable Control and Subsidiary Ledger

After all posting has been completed for the month, the sum of the balances in the accounts payable subsidiary ledger should be compared with the balance of the accounts payable controlling account in the general ledger. If the controlling account and the subsidiary ledger do not agree, the error or errors must be located and corrected. The balances of the individual supplier accounts may be summarized in a schedule of accounts payable. The total of NetSolutions' schedule of accounts payable, $2,410, agrees with the balance of the accounts payable controlling account on March 31, 2003, as shown below.

Accounts Payable— (Controlling)

Balance, March 31, 2003 $2,410

**NetSolutions
Schedule of Accounts Payable
March 31, 2003**

Donnelly Supplies	$1,450
Grayco Supplies	0
Howard Supplies	960
Jewett Business Systems	0
Total	$2,410

PROBLEMS

Problem D–1
Design of accounting systems

For the past few years, your client, Ragsdale Medical Group (RMG), has operated a small medical practice. RMG's current annual revenues are $420,000. Because the accountant has been spending more and more time each month recording all transactions in a two-column journal and preparing the financial statements, RMG is considering improving the accounting system by adding special journals and subsidiary ledgers. RMG has asked you to help with this project and has compiled the following information:

Type of Transaction	Estimated Frequency per Month
Fees earned on account	240
Purchase of medical supplies on account	190
Cash receipts from patients on account	175
Cash payments on account	160
Cash receipts from patients at time services provided	120
Purchase of office supplies on account	35
Purchase of magazine subscriptions on account	5
Purchase of medical equipment on account	4
Cash payments for office salaries	3
Cash payments for utilities expense	3

A local sales tax is collected on all patient bills, and monthly financial statements are prepared.

Instructions

1. ▬▬▶ Briefly discuss the circumstances under which special journals would be used in place of a two-column (all-purpose) journal. Include in your answer your recommendations for RMG's medical practice.
2. Assume that RMG has decided to use a revenue journal and a purchases journal. Design the format for each journal, giving special consideration to the needs of the medical practice.
3. Which subsidiary ledgers would you recommend for the medical practice?

Problem D–2
Identify journals

Broadbank Company engaged in the following transactions:

a. Adjustment to record accrued salaries at the end of the year.
b. Receipt of cash on account from a customer.
c. Providing services on account.
d. Issuance of additional capital stock in exchange for cash.
e. Receipt of cash for rent.
f. Receipt of cash refund from overpayment of taxes.
g. Closing of dividends account at the end of the year.
h. Sale of office supplies on account, at cost, to a neighboring business.
i. Receipt of cash from sale of office equipment.
j. Providing services for cash.

Instructions
Assuming the use of a two-column (all-purpose) general journal, a revenue journal, and a cash receipts journal as illustrated in this appendix, indicate the journal in which each of these transactions should be recorded.

Problem D–3
Identify postings from purchases journal

The following purchases journal shows purchases made by a business during June:

			PURCHASES JOURNAL				PAGE 49	
						Other Accounts Dr.		
			Accounts	**Store**	**Office**			
		Post.	**Payable**	**Supplies**	**Supplies**		**Post.**	
Date	**Account Credited**	**Ref.**	**Cr.**	**Dr.**	**Dr.**	**Account**	**Ref.**	**Amount**
2003								
June 4	Corter Supply Co.	(a)	4,200		4,200			
6	Coastal Insurance Co.	(b)	5,325			Prepaid Insurance	(c)	5,325
11	Keller Bros.	(d)	2,000			Office Equipment	(e)	2,000
13	Taylor Products	(f)	1,675	1,400	275			
20	Keller Bros.	(g)	5,500			Store Equipment	(h)	5,500
27	Miller Supply Co.	(i)	2,740	2,740				
30			21,440	4,140	4,475			12,825
			(j)	(k)	(l)			(m)

Instructions
Identify each of the posting references, indicated by a letter, as representing (1) a posting to a general ledger account, (2) a posting to a subsidiary ledger account, or (3) that no posting is required.

Problem D–4
Revenue journal; accounts receivable and general ledgers

SPREADSHEET

✓ 1. Revenue journal, total fees earned, $815

Three R's Co. was established on January 20, 2003, to provide educational services. The services provided during the remainder of the month are as follows:

Jan. 21. J. Dunlop, Invoice No. 1, $70 on account.
22. L. Summers, Invoice No. 2, $180 on account.
24. T. Morris, Invoice No. 3, $65 on account.
25. L. Summers, $130 in exchange for educational supplies.
27. F. Mintz, Invoice No. 4, $165 on account.
28. D. Bennett, Invoice No. 5, $120 on account.
30. L. Summers, Invoice No. 6, $105 on account.
31. T. Morris, Invoice No. 7, $110 on account.

Instructions
1. Journalize the transactions for January, using a single-column revenue journal and a two-column general journal. Post to the following customer accounts in the accounts receivable ledger, and insert the balance immediately after recording each entry: D. Bennett; J. Dunlop; F. Mintz; T. Morris; L. Summers.

2. Post the revenue journal and the general journal to the following accounts in the general ledger, inserting the account balances only after the last postings:

12   Accounts Receivable
13   Supplies
41   Fees Earned

3. a. What is the sum of the balances of the accounts in the subsidiary ledger at January 31?
   b. What is the balance of the controlling account at January 31?

4. ◀━━━▶ Assume that on February 1, the state in which Three R's Co. operates begins requiring that sales tax be collected on educational services. Briefly explain how the revenue journal may be modified to accommodate sales of services on account that require the collection of a state sales tax.

Problem D–5
Revenue and cash receipts journals; accounts receivable and general ledgers

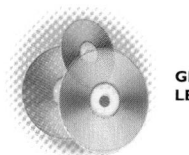

GENERAL LEDGER

✓ 3. Total cash receipts, $43,030

Transactions related to revenue and cash receipts completed by Pyramid Architects Co. during the period June 2–30, 2003, are as follows:

June 2. Issued Invoice No. 793 to Morton Co., $7,900.
      5. Received cash from Mendez Co. for the balance owed on its account.
      6. Issued Invoice No. 794 to Quest Co., $2,360.
     13. Issued Invoice No. 795 to Ping Co., $5,790.
         Post revenue and collections to the accounts receivable subsidiary ledger.
     15. Received cash from Quest Co. for the balance owed on June 1.
     16. Issued Invoice No. 796 to Quest Co., $4,600.
         Post revenue and collections to the accounts receivable subsidiary ledger.
     19. Received cash from Morton Co. for the balance due on invoice of June 2.
     20. Received cash from Quest Co. for invoice of June 6.
     22. Issued Invoice No. 797 to Mendez Co., $7,810.
     25. Received $4,400 note receivable in partial settlement of the balance due on the Ping Co. account.
     30. Recorded cash fees earned, $11,450.
         Post revenue and collections to the accounts receivable subsidiary ledger.

Instructions

1. Insert the following balances in the general ledger as of June 1:

   11   Cash $12,150
   12   Accounts Receivable   21,320
   14   Notes Receivable   5,000
   41   Fees Earned   —

2. Insert the following balances in the accounts receivable subsidiary ledger as of June 1:

   Mendez Co. $11,560
   Morton Co.   —
   Ping Co.   —
   Quest Co.   9,760

3. Prepare a single-column revenue journal and a cash receipts journal. Use the following column headings for the cash receipts journal: Fees Earned, Accounts Receivable, and Cash. The Fees Earned column is used to record cash fees. Insert a check mark (✓) in the Post. Ref. Column.

4. Using the two special journals and the two-column general journal, journalize the transactions for June. Post to the accounts receivable subsidiary ledger, and insert the balances at the points indicated in the narrative of transactions. Determine the balance in the customer's account before recording a cash receipt.

5. Total each of the columns of the special journals, and post the individual entries and totals to the general ledger. Insert account balances after the last posting.

6. Determine that the subsidiary ledger agrees with the controlling account in the general ledger.

Problem D–6

Purchases, accounts payable account, and accounts payable ledger

GENERAL LEDGER

✓ 3. Total accounts payable credit, $14,845

Elegant Estate Landscaping designs and installs landscaping. The landscape designers and office staff use office supplies, while field supplies (rock, bark, etc.) are used in the actual landscaping. Purchases on account completed by Elegant Estate Landscaping during July 2003 are as follows:

July 2. Purchased office supplies on account from Lapp Co., $890.
     5. Purchased office equipment on account from Peach Computers Co., $3,400.
     9. Purchased office supplies on account from Executive Office Supply Co., $420.
    13. Purchased field supplies on account from Yin Co., $980.
    14. Purchased field supplies on account from Nelson Co., $3,200.
    17. Purchased field supplies on account from Yin Co., $1,680.
    24. Purchased field supplies on account from Nelson Co., $2,680.
    29. Purchased office supplies on account from Executive Office Supply Co., $355.
    31. Purchased field supplies on account from Nelson Co., $1,240.

Instructions

1. Insert the following balances in the general ledger as of July 1:

14	Field Supplies	$ 5,820
15	Office Supplies	830
18	Office Equipment	14,300
21	Accounts Payable	655

2. Insert the following balances in the accounts payable subsidiary ledger as of July 1:

Executive Office Supply	$400
Lapp Co.	255
Nelson Co.	—
Peach Computers Co.	—
Yin Co.	—

3. Journalize the transactions for July, using a purchases journal similar to the one illustrated in this chapter. Prepare the purchases journal with columns for Accounts Payable, Field Supplies, Office Supplies, and Other Accounts. Post to the creditor accounts in the accounts payable subsidiary ledger immediately after each entry.
4. Post the purchases journal to the accounts in the general ledger.
5. a. What is the sum of the balances in the subsidiary ledger at July 31?
    b. What is the balance of the controlling account at July 31?

Problem D–7

Purchases and cash payments journals; accounts payable and general ledgers

Objective 3

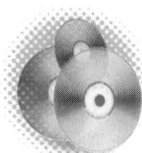

GENERAL LEDGER

✓ 1. Total cash payments, $56,665

Purity Water Testing Service was established on June 16, 2003. Purity uses field equipment and field supplies (chemicals and other supplies) to analyze water for unsafe contaminants in streams, lakes, and ponds. Transactions related to purchases and cash payments during the remainder of June are as follows:

June 16. Issued Check No. 1 in payment of rent for the remainder of June, $1,200.
     16. Purchased field supplies on account from Heath Supply Co., $3,650.
     16. Purchased field equipment on account from Juan Equipment Co., $9,500.
     17. Purchased office supplies on account from Aztec Supply Co., $415.
     19. Issued Check No. 2 in payment of field supplies, $1,850, and office supplies, $250.
         Post the journals to the accounts payable subsidiary ledger.
     23. Purchased office supplies on account from Aztec Supply Co., $325.
     23. Issued Check No. 3 to purchase land from the owner, $25,000.
     24. Issued Check No. 4 to Heath Supply Co. in payment of invoice, $3,650.
     26. Issued Check No. 5 to Juan Equipment Co. in payment of invoice, $9,500.
         Post the journals to the accounts payable subsidiary ledger.
     30. Acquired land in exchange for field equipment having a cost of $6,700.
     30. Purchased field supplies on account from Heath Supply Co., $5,300.
     30. Issued Check No. 6 to Aztec Supply Co. in payment of invoice, $415.

June 30. Purchased the following from Juan Equipment Co. on account: field supplies, $1,200, and field equipment, $2,900.

30. Issued Check No. 7 in payment of salaries, $14,800.

Post the journals to the accounts payable subsidiary ledger.

Instructions

1. Journalize the transactions for June. Use a purchases journal and a cash payments journal, similar to those illustrated in this chapter, and a two-column general journal. Refer to the following partial chart of accounts:

11	Cash	19	Land
14	Field Supplies	21	Accounts Payable
15	Office Supplies	61	Salary Expense
17	Field Equipment	71	Rent Expense

At the points indicated in the narrative of transactions, post to the following accounts in the accounts payable subsidiary ledger:

Aztec Supply Co.
Heath Supply Co.
Juan Equipment Co.

2. Post the individual entries (Other Accounts columns of the purchases journal and the cash payments journal and both columns of the general journal) to the appropriate general ledger accounts.
3. Total each of the columns of the purchases journal and the cash payments journal and post the appropriate totals to the general ledger. (Because the problem does not include transactions related to cash receipts, the cash account in the ledger will have a credit balance.)
4. Prepare a schedule of accounts payable.

Problem D–8

All journals and general ledger; trial balance

GENERAL LEDGER

✓ 2. Total cash receipts, $41,080

The transactions completed by Mercury Delivery Company during July 2003, the first month of the fiscal year, were as follows:

July 1. Issued Check No. 610 for July rent, $2,400.
2. Issued Invoice No. 940 to Capps Co., $3,500.
3. Received check for $5,400 from Pease Co. in payment of account.
5. Purchased a vehicle on account from Browning Transportation, $24,600.
6. Purchased office equipment on account from Bell Computer Co., $3,600.
6. Issued Invoice No. 941 to Collins Co., $6,210.
9. Issued Check No. 611 for fuel expense, $850.
10. Received check from Sokol Co. in payment of $7,800 invoice.
10. Issued Check No. 612 for $5,100 to Office To Go, Inc., in payment of invoice.
10. Issued Invoice No. 942 to Joy Co., $3,230.
11. Issued Check No. 613 for $3,050 to Crowne Supply Co. in payment of account.
11. Issued Check No. 614 for $960 to Porter Co. in payment of account.
12. Received check from Capps Co. in payment of $3,500 invoice.
13. Issued Check No. 615 to Browning Transportation in payment of $24,600 balance.
16. Issued Check No. 616 for $18,500 for cash purchase of a vehicle.
16. Cash fees earned for July 1–16, $12,400.
17. Issued Check No. 617 for miscellaneous administrative expense, $430.
18. Purchased maintenance supplies on account from Crowne Supply Co., $1,420.
19. Purchased the following on account from McClain Co.: maintenance supplies, $2,020; office supplies, $440.
20. Issued Check No. 618 in payment of advertising expense, $2,300.
20. Used $4,000 maintenance supplies to repair delivery vehicles.
23. Purchased office supplies on account from Office To Go, Inc., $750.
24. Issued Invoice No. 943 to Sokol Co., $4,440.
25. Issued Invoice No. 944 to Collins Co., $5,000.

(continued)

July 25. Received check for $3,560 from Pease Co. in payment of balance.
　　 26. Issued Check No. 620 to Bell Computer Co. in payment of $3,600 invoice of July 6.
　　 30. Issued Check No. 621 for monthly salaries as follows: driver salaries, $15,400; office salaries, $7,500.
　　 31. Cash fees earned for July 17–31, $8,420.
　　 31. Issued Check No. 622 in payment for office supplies, $900.

Instructions

1. Enter the following account balances in the general ledger as of July 1:

11	Cash	$ 56,800	32	Retained Earnings	$140,350
12	Accounts Receivable	16,760	41	Fees Earned	—
14	Maintenance Supplies	9,300	51	Driver Salaries Expense	—
15	Office Supplies	4,500	52	Maintenance Supplies	
16	Office Equipment	24,300		Expense	—
17	Accumulated Depreciation		53	Fuel Expense	—
	—Office Equipment	4,500	61	Office Salaries Expense	—
18	Vehicles	84,600	62	Rent Expense	—
19	Accumulated Depreciation		63	Advertising Expense	—
	—Vehicles	12,300	64	Miscellaneous Adminis-	
21	Accounts Payable	9,110		trative Expense	—
31	Capital Stock	30,000			

2. Journalize the transactions for July 2003, using the following journals similar to those illustrated in this chapter: cash receipts journal, purchases journal (with columns for Accounts Payable, Maintenance Supplies, Office Supplies, and Other Accounts), single-column revenue journal, cash payments journal, and two-column general journal. You do not need to make daily postings to the individual accounts in the accounts payable ledger and the accounts receivable ledger.
3. Post the appropriate individual entries to the general ledger.
4. Total each of the columns of the special journals and post the appropriate totals to the general ledger; insert the account balances.
5. Prepare a trial balance.
6. Verify the agreement of each subsidiary ledger with its controlling account. The sum of the balances of the accounts in the subsidiary ledgers as of July 31 are:

Accounts receivable　　$18,880
Accounts payable　　　4,630

Appendix E: Periodic Inventory Systems for Merchandising Businesses

In this text, we emphasize the perpetual inventory system of accounting for purchases and sales of merchandise. Not all merchandise businesses, however, use perpetual inventory systems. For example, some managers/owners of small merchandise businesses, such as locally owned hardware stores, may feel more comfortable using manually kept records. Because a manual perpetual inventory system is time-consuming and costly to maintain, the periodic inventory system is often used in these cases.

Merchandise Transactions in a Periodic Inventory System

In a periodic inventory system, the revenues from sales are recorded when sales are made in the same manner as in a perpetual inventory system. However, no attempt is made on the date of sale to record the cost of the merchandise sold. Instead, the merchandise inventory on hand at the end of the period is counted. This physical inventory is then used to determine (1) the cost of merchandise sold during the period and (2) the cost of merchandise on hand at the end of the period.

In a periodic inventory system, purchases of inventory are recorded in a purchases account rather than in a merchandise inventory account. No attempt is made to keep a detailed record of the amount of inventory on hand at any given time.

The purchases account is normally debited for the amount of the invoice before considering any purchases discounts. Purchases discounts are normally recorded in a separate purchases discounts account.[1] The balance of this account is reported as a deduction from the amount initially recorded in Purchases for the period. Thus, the purchases discounts account is viewed as a contra (or offsetting) account to Purchases.

Purchases returns and allowances are recorded in a similar manner as purchases discounts. A separate account is used to keep a record of the amount of purchases returns and allowances during a period. Purchases returns and allowances are reported as a deduction from the amount initially recorded as Purchases. Like Purchases Discounts, the purchases returns and allowances account is a contra (or offsetting) account to Purchases.

When merchandise is purchased FOB shipping point, the buyer is responsible for paying the freight charges. In a periodic inventory system, freight charges paid when purchasing merchandise FOB shipping point are debited to Transportation In, Freight In, or a similarly titled account.

To illustrate the recording of merchandise transactions in a periodic system, we will use the following selected transactions for Taylor Co. We will also explain how the transaction would have been recorded under a perpetual system.

June 5. Purchased $30,000 of merchandise on account from Owen Clothing, terms 2/10, n/30.

Purchases	30,000	
Accounts Payable—Owen Clothing		30,000

Under the perpetual inventory system, such purchases would be recorded in the merchandise inventory account at their cost, $30,000.

June 8. Returned merchandise purchased on account from Owen Clothing on June 5, $500.

Accounts Payable—Owen Clothing	500	
Purchases Returns and Allowances		500

---

[1] Some businesses prefer to credit the purchases account. If this alternative is used, the balance of the purchases account will be a net amount—the total purchases less the total purchases discounts for the period.

Under the perpetual inventory system, returns would be recorded as a credit to the merchandise inventory account at their cost of $500.

June 15.   Paid Owen Clothing for purchase of June 5, less return of $500 and discount of $590 [($30,000 − $500) × 2%].

Accounts Payable—Owen Clothing	29,500	
Cash		28,910
Purchases Discounts		590

Under a perpetual inventory system, a purchases discount account is not used. Instead, the merchandise inventory account is credited for the amount of the discount, $590.

June 18.   Sold merchandise on account to Jones Co., $12,500, 1/10, n/30. The cost of the merchandise sold was $9,000.

Accounts Receivable—Jones Co.	12,500	
Sales		12,500

The entry to record the sale is the same under both systems. Under the perpetual inventory system, the cost of merchandise sold and the reduction in merchandise inventory would also be recorded on the date of sale.

June 21.   Received merchandise returned on account from Jones Co., $4,000. The cost of the merchandise returned was $2,800.

Sales Returns and Allowances	4,000	
Accounts Receivable—Jones Co.		4,000

The entry to record the sales return is the same under both systems. In addition, the cost of the merchandise returned would be debited to the merchandise inventory account and credited to the cost of merchandise sold account under the perpetual inventory system.

June 22.   Purchased merchandise from Norcross Clothiers, $15,000, terms FOB shipping point, 2/15, n/30, with prepaid transportation charges of $750 added to the invoice.

Purchases	15,000	
Transportation In	750	
Accounts Payable—Norcross Clothiers		15,750

This entry is similar to the June 5 entry for the purchase of merchandise. Since the transportation terms were FOB shipping point, the prepaid freight charges of $750 must be added to the invoice cost of $15,000. Under the perpetual inventory system, the purchase is recorded in the merchandise inventory account at the cost of $15,750 (invoice price plus transportation).

June 28.   Received $8,415 as payment on account from Jones Co., less return of June 21 and less discount of $85 [($12,500 − $4,000) × 1%].

Cash	8,415	
Sales Discounts	85	
Accounts Receivable—Jones Co.		8,500

This entry is the same under the perpetual inventory system.

June 29.   Received $19,600 from cash sales. The cost of the merchandise sold was $13,800.

Cash	19,600	
Sales		19,600

The entry to record the sale is the same under both systems. Under the perpetual inventory system, the cost of merchandise sold and the reduction in merchandise inventory would also be recorded on the date of sale.

Cost of Merchandise Sold

Under the periodic inventory system, the cost of merchandise sold during a period is reported in a separate section in the income statement. To illustrate, assume that on January 3, 2003, NetSolutions began operations as an Internet-based retailer of software and hardware. During 2003, NetSolutions purchased $340,000 of merchandise. The inventory on December 31, 2003, is $59,700. The cost of merchandise sold during 2003 is reported as follows:

Cost of merchandise sold:	
Purchases	$340,000
Less merchandise inventory, December 31, 2003	59,700
Cost of merchandise sold	$280,300

To continue the example, assume that during 2004 NetSolutions purchased additional merchandise of $521,980. NetSolutions also received credit for purchases returns and allowances of $9,100, took purchases discounts of $2,525, and paid transportation costs of $17,400. The purchases returns and allowances and the purchases discounts are deducted from the total purchases to yield the net purchases. The transportation costs are then added to the net purchases to yield the cost of merchandise purchased. These amounts are reported in the cost of merchandise sold section of the NetSolutions income statement for 2004 as follows:

Purchases		$521,980
Less: Purchases returns and allowances	$9,100	
Purchases discounts	2,525	11,625
Net purchases		$510,355
Add transportation in		17,400
Cost of merchandise purchased		$527,755

The ending inventory of NetSolutions on December 31, 2003, $59,700, becomes the beginning inventory for 2004. In the cost of merchandise sold section of the income statement for 2004, this beginning inventory is added to the cost of merchandise purchased to yield the merchandise available for sale. The ending inventory on December 31, 2004, $62,150, is then subtracted from the merchandise available for sale to yield the cost of merchandise sold. Exhibit 1 shows the cost of merchandise sold during 2004.

Exhibit 1 Cost of Merchandise Sold—Periodic Inventory System

Cost of merchandise sold:			
Merchandise inventory, January 1, 2004 ..			$ 59,700
Purchases		$521,980	
Less: Purchases returns and allowances ..	$9,100		
Purchases discounts	2,525	11,625	
Net purchases		$510,355	
Add transportation in		17,400	
Cost of merchandise purchased			527,755
Merchandise available for sale			$587,455
Less merchandise inventory,			
December 31, 2004			62,150
Cost of merchandise sold			$525,305

The multiple-step income statement under the periodic inventory system is illustrated in Exhibit 2. The multiple-step income statement under a perpetual inventory system is similar, except that the cost of merchandise sold is reported as a single amount.

Exhibit 2 Multiple-Step Income Statement—Periodic Inventory System

NetSolutions Income Statement For the Year Ended December 31, 2004				
Revenue from sales:				
Sales			$720,185	
Less: Sales returns and allowances		$ 6,140		
Sales discounts		5,790	11,930	
Net sales				$708,255
Cost of merchandise sold:				
Merchandise inventory, January 1, 2004			$ 59,700	
Purchases		$521,980		
Less: Purchases returns and allowances	$9,100			
Purchases discounts	2,525	11,625		
Net purchases		$510,355		
Add transportation in		17,400		
Cost of merchandise purchased			527,755	
Merchandise available for sale			$587,455	
Less merchandise inventory, December 31, 2004			62,150	
Cost of merchandise sold				525,305
Gross profit				$182,950
Operating expenses:				
Selling expenses:				
Sales salaries expense		$ 60,030		
Advertising expense		10,860		
Depreciation expense—store equipment		3,100		
Miscellaneous selling expense		630		
Total selling expenses			$ 74,620	
Administrative expenses:				
Office salaries expense		$ 21,020		
Rent expense		8,100		
Depreciation expense—office equipment		2,490		
Insurance expense		1,910		
Office supplies expense		610		
Miscellaneous administrative expense		760		
Total administrative expenses			34,890	
Total operating expenses				109,510
Income from operations				$ 73,440
Other income:				
Interest revenue		$ 3,800		
Rent revenue		600		
Total other income			$ 4,400	
Other expense:				
Interest expense			2,440	1,960
Net income				$ 75,400

Chart of Accounts for a Periodic Inventory System

Exhibit 3 is the chart of accounts for NetSolutions when a periodic inventory system is used. The periodic inventory accounts related to merchandising transactions are shown in color.

Exhibit 3 Chart of Accounts
—Periodic Inventory System

Balance Sheet Accounts		Income Statement Accounts	
	100 Assets		400 Revenues
110	Cash	410	Sales
111	Notes Receivable	411	Sales Returns and Allowances
112	Accounts Receivable	412	Sales Discounts
113	Interest Receivable		500 Costs and Expenses
115	Merchandise Inventory	510	Purchases
116	Office Supplies	511	Purchases Returns and
117	Prepaid Insurance		Allowances
120	Land	512	Purchases Discounts
123	Store Equipment	513	Transportation In
124	Accumulated Depreciation—	520	Sales Salaries Expenses
	Store Equipment	521	Advertising Expense
125	Office Equipment	522	Depreciation Expense—Store
126	Accumulated Depreciation—		Equipment
	Office Equipment	523	Transportation Out
	200 Liabilities	529	Miscellaneous Selling Expense
210	Accounts Payable	530	Office Salaries Expense
211	Salaries Payable	531	Rent Expense
212	Unearned Rent	532	Depreciation Expense—Office
215	Notes Payable		Equipment
	300 Stockholders' Equity	533	Insurance Expense
310	Capital Stock	534	Office Supplies Expense
311	Retained Earnings	539	Misc. Administrative Expense
312	Dividends		600 Other Income
313	Income Summary	610	Rent Revenue
		611	Interest Revenue
			700 Other Expense
		710	Interest Expense

End-of-Period Procedures in a Periodic Inventory System

The end-of-period procedures are generally the same for the periodic and perpetual inventory systems. In the remainder of this appendix, we will discuss the differences in procedures for the two systems that affect the work sheet, the adjusting entries, and the closing entries. As the basis for illustrations, we will use the data for NetSolutions, presented in Chapter 6.

Work Sheet

The differences in the work sheet for a merchandising business that uses the periodic inventory system are highlighted in the work sheet for NetSolutions in Exhibit 4. As we illustrated earlier, accounts for purchases, purchases returns and allowances, purchases discounts, and transportation in are used in a periodic inventory system.

Under the periodic inventory system, the merchandise inventory account, throughout the accounting period, shows the inventory at the beginning of the period. As shown in Exhibit 1, the merchandise inventory on January 1, 2004, $59,700, is a part of the merchandise available for sale. At the end of the period, the beginning inventory amount in the ledger is replaced with the ending inventory amount. To update the inventory account, two adjusting entries are used.[2] The first adjusting entry

---

[2] Another method of updating the merchandise inventory account at the end of the period is called the *closing method*. This method adjusts the merchandise inventory through the use of closing entries. This method may not be appropriate for use in computerized accounting systems. Since the financial statements are the same under both methods and since computerized accounting systems are used by most businesses, the closing method is not illustrated.

Exhibit 4 Work Sheet—Periodic Inventory System

NetSolutions
Work Sheet
For the Year Ended December 31, 2004

Account Title	Trial Balance Dr.	Trial Balance Cr.	Adjustments Dr.	Adjustments Cr.	Adjusted Trial Balance Dr.	Adjusted Trial Balance Cr.	Income Statement Dr.	Income Statement Cr.	Balance Sheet Dr.	Balance Sheet Cr.
Cash	52,950				52,950				52,950	
Notes Receivable	35,000				35,000				35,000	
Accounts Receivable	55,880				55,880				55,880	
Interest Receivable			(a) 200		200				200	
Merchandise Inventory	59,700		(c)62,150	(b)59,700	62,150				62,150	
Office Supplies	1,090			(d) 610	480				480	
Prepaid Insurance	4,560			(e) 1,910	2,650				2,650	
Land	20,000				20,000				20,000	
Store Equipment	27,100				27,100				27,100	
Accum. Depr.—Store Equipment		2,600		(f) 3,100		5,700				5,700
Office Equipment	15,570				15,570				15,570	
Accum. Depr.—Office Equipment		2,230		(g) 2,490		4,720				4,720
Accounts Payable		22,420				22,420				22,420
Salaries Payable				(h) 1,140		1,140				1,140
Unearned Rent		2,400	(i) 600			1,800				1,800
Notes Payable (final payment, 2014)		25,000				25,000				25,000
Capital Stock		15,000				15,000				15,000
Retained Earnings		138,800				138,800				138,800
Dividends	18,000				18,000				18,000	
Income Summary			(b)59,700	(c)62,150	59,700	62,150	59,700	62,150		
Sales		720,185				720,185		720,185		
Sales Returns and Allowances	6,140				6,140		6,140			
Sales Discounts	5,790				5,790		5,790			
Purchases	521,980				521,980		521,980			
Purchases Returns & Allowances		9,100				9,100		9,100		
Purchases Discounts		2,525				2,525		2,525		
Transportation In	17,400				17,400		17,400			
Sales Salaries Expense	59,250		(h) 780		60,030		60,030			
Advertising Expense	10,860				10,860		10,860			
Depr. Expense—Store Equipment			(f) 3,100		3,100		3,100			
Miscellaneous Selling Expense	630				630		630			
Office Salaries Expense	20,660		(h) 360		21,020		21,020			
Rent Expense	8,100				8,100		8,100			
Depr. Expense—Office Equipment			(g) 2,490		2,490		2,490			
Insurance Expense			(e) 1,910		1,910		1,910			
Office Supplies Expense			(d) 610		610		610			
Misc. Administrative Expense	760				760		760			
Rent Revenue				(i) 600		600		600		
Interest Revenue		3,600		(a) 200		3,800		3,800		
Interest Expense	2,440				2,440		2,440			
	943,860	943,860	131,900	131,900	1,012,940	1,012,940	722,960	798,360	289,980	214,580
Net income							75,400			75,400
							798,360	798,360	289,980	289,980

(a) Interest earned but not received on notes receivable, $200.

(b) Beginning merchandise inventory, $59,700.

(c) Ending merchandise inventory, $62,150.

(d) Office supplies used, $610 ($1,090 − $480).

(e) Insurance expired, $1,910.

(f) Depreciation of store equipment, $3,100.

(g) Depreciation of office equipment, $2,490.

(h) Salaries accrued but not paid (sales salaries, $780; office salaries, $360), $1,140.

(i) Rent earned from amount received in advance, $600.

transfers the beginning inventory balance to Income Summary. This entry, shown below, has the effect of increasing the cost of merchandise sold and decreasing net income.

| Dec. 31 | Income Summary | 59,700 | |
| | Merchandise Inventory | | 59,700 |

After the first adjusting entry has been recorded and posted, the balance of the merchandise inventory account is zero. The second adjusting entry records the cost of the merchandise on hand at the end of the period by debiting Merchandise Inventory. Since the merchandise inventory at December 31, 2004, $62,150, is subtracted from the cost of merchandise available for sale in determining the cost of merchandise sold, Income Summary is credited. This credit has the effect of decreasing the cost of merchandise available for sale during the period, $587,455, by the cost of the unsold merchandise. The second adjusting entry is shown below.

| Dec. 31 | Merchandise Inventory | 62,150 | |
| | Income Summary | | 62,150 |

After the second adjusting entry has been recorded and posted, the balance of the merchandise inventory account is the amount of the ending inventory. The accounts for Merchandise Inventory and Income Summary after both entries have been posted would appear in T account form as follows:

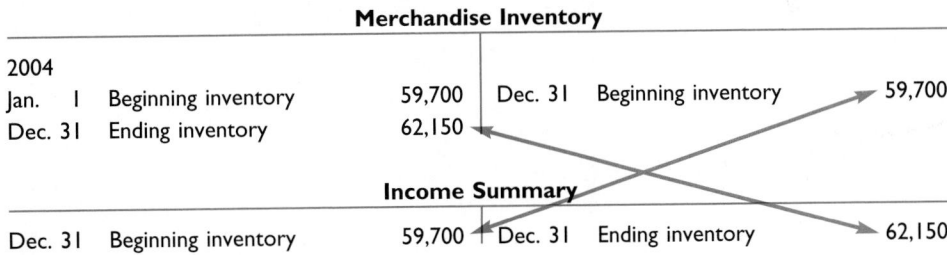

No separate adjusting entry can be made for merchandise inventory shrinkage in a periodic inventory system. This is because no perpetual inventory records are available to show what inventory should be on hand at the end of the period. One disadvantage of the periodic inventory system is that inventory shrinkage cannot be measured.[3]

Completing the Work Sheet

After all of the necessary adjustments have been entered on the work sheet, the work sheet is completed in the normal manner. An exception to the usual practice of extending only account balances is Income Summary. Both the debit and credit amounts for Income Summary are extended to the Adjusted Trial Balance columns. Extending both amounts aids in the preparation of the income statement because the debit adjustment (the beginning inventory of $59,700) and the credit adjustment (the ending inventory of $62,150) are reported as part of the cost of merchandise sold.

The purchases, purchases discounts, purchases returns and allowances, and transportation in accounts are extended to the Income Statement Columns of the work sheet, since they are used in computing the cost of merchandise sold. You should note that the two merchandise inventory amounts in Income Summary are extended to the Income Statement columns. After all of the items have been extended to the statement columns, the four columns are totaled and the net income or net loss is determined.

---

[3] Any inventory shrinkage that does exist is part of the cost of merchandise sold and is reported on the income statement, since a smaller ending inventory is deducted from other merchandise available for sale.

Financial Statements

The financial statements for NetSolutions are essentially the same under both the perpetual and periodic inventory systems. The main difference is that the cost of goods is reported as a single amount under the perpetual system. Exhibit 2 illustrates the manner in which cost of merchandise sold is reported in a multiple-step income statement when the periodic inventory system is used.[4]

Adjusting and Closing Entries

The adjusting entries are the same under both inventory systems, except for merchandise inventory. As indicated previously, two adjusting entries for beginning and ending merchandise inventory are necessary in a periodic inventory system.

The closing entries differ in the periodic inventory system in that there is no cost of merchandise sold account to be closed to Income Summary. Instead, the purchases, purchases discounts, purchases returns and allowances, and transportation in accounts are closed to Income Summary.[5] To illustrate, the adjusting and closing entries under a periodic inventory system for NetSolutions are shown below.

	Date		Description	Post. Ref.	Debit	Credit	
			JOURNAL			**PAGE 16**	
1			Adjusting Entries				1
2	2004 Dec.	31	Interest Receivable	113	2 0 0 00		2
3			Interest Revenue	611		2 0 0 00	3
4							4
5		31	Income Summary	312	59 7 0 0 00		5
6			Merchandise Inventory	115		59 7 0 0 00	6
7							7
8		31	Merchandise Inventory	115	62 1 5 0 00		8
9			Income Summary	312		62 1 5 0 00	9
10							10
11		31	Office Supplies Expense	534	6 1 0 00		11
12			Office Supplies	116		6 1 0 00	12
13							13
14		31	Insurance Expense	533	1 9 1 0 00		14
15			Prepaid Insurance	117		1 9 1 0 00	15
16							16
17		31	Depreciation Expense—Store Equip.	522	3 1 0 0 00		17
18			Accumulated Depr.—Store Equip.	124		3 1 0 0 00	18
19							19
20		31	Depreciation Expense—Office Equip.	532	2 4 9 0 00		20
21			Accumulated Depr.—Office Equip.	126		2 4 9 0 00	21
22							22
23		31	Sales Salaries Expense	520	7 8 0 00		23
24			Office Salaries Expense	530	3 6 0 00		24
25			Salaries Payable	211		1 1 4 0 00	25
26							26
27		31	Unearned Rent	212	6 0 0 00		27
28			Rent Revenue	610		6 0 0 00	28

[4] The single-step income statement would be the same for both the perpetual and the periodic inventory systems.
[5] The balance of Income Summary, after the merchandise inventory adjustments and the first two closing entries have been posted, is the net income or net loss for the period.

	Date		Description	Post. Ref.	Debit	Credit	
1			Closing Entries				1
2	2004 Dec.	31	Sales	410	720 1 8 5 00		2
3			Purchases Returns and Allowances	511	9 1 0 0 00		3
4			Purchases Discounts	512	2 5 2 5 00		4
5			Rent Revenue	610	6 0 0 00		5
6			Interest Revenue	611	3 8 0 0 00		6
7			Income Summary	313		736 2 1 0 00	7
8							8
9		31	Income Summary	313	663 2 6 0 00		9
10			Sales Returns and Allowances	411		6 1 4 0 00	10
11			Sales Discounts	412		5 7 9 0 00	11
12			Purchases	510		521 9 8 0 00	12
13			Transportation In	513		17 4 0 0 00	13
14			Sales Salaries Expense	520		60 0 3 0 00	14
15			Advertising Expense	521		10 8 6 0 00	15
16			Depreciation Exp.—Store Equip.	522		3 1 0 0 00	16
17			Miscellaneous Selling Expense	529		6 3 0 00	17
18			Office Salaries Expense	530		21 0 2 0 00	18
19			Rent Expense	531		8 1 0 0 00	19
20			Depreciation Exp.—Office Equip.	532		2 4 9 0 00	20
21			Insurance Expense	533		1 9 1 0 00	21
22			Office Supplies Expense	534		6 1 0 00	22
23			Miscellaneous Administrative Exp.	539		7 6 0 00	23
24			Interest Expense	710		2 4 4 0 00	24
25							25
26		31	Income Summary	313	75 4 0 0 00		26
27			Retained Earnings	311		75 4 0 0 00	27
28							28
29		31	Retained Earnings	311	18 0 0 0 00		29
30			Dividends	312		18 0 0 0 00	30

JOURNAL   **PAGE 17**

EXERCISES

Exercise E–1
Purchases-related transactions—periodic inventory system

Journalize entries for the following related transactions, assuming that Fairways 'N Greens, Inc., uses the periodic inventory system.

a. Purchased $7,000 of merchandise from Bertha Co. on account, terms 2/10, n/30.
b. Discovered that some of the merchandise was defective and returned items with an invoice price of $1,000, receiving credit.
c. Paid the amount owed on the invoice within the discount period.
d. Purchased $4,000 of merchandise from Precision Golf, Inc., on account, terms 1/10, n/30.
e. Paid the amount owed on the invoice within the discount period.

Exercise E–2
Sales-related transactions—periodic inventory system

Journalize entries for the following related transactions, assuming that Triad Company uses the periodic inventory system.

Mar. 8 Sold merchandise to a customer for $8,300, terms FOB shipping point, 2/10, n/30.
     8 Paid the transportation charges of $250, debiting the amount to Accounts Receivable.

Mar. 12 Issued a credit memorandum for $1,600 to the customer for merchandise returned.
18 Received a check for the amount due from the sale.

Exercise E–3
Adjusting entries for merchandise inventory—periodic inventory system

Data assembled for preparing the work sheet for Lancaster Co. for the fiscal year ended December 31, 2003, included the following:

Merchandise inventory as of January 1, 2003	$273,000
Merchandise inventory as of December 31, 2003	$309,600

Journalize the two adjusting entries for merchandise inventory that would appear on the work sheet, assuming that the periodic inventory system is used.

Exercise E–4
Identification of missing items from income statement—periodic inventory system

For (a) through (i), identify the items designated by "X".

a. Purchases − (X + X) = Net purchases
b. Sales − (X + X) = Net sales
c. Merchandise inventory (beginning) + Cost of merchandise purchased = X
d. Net purchases + X = Cost of merchandise purchased
e. Net sales − Cost of merchandise sold = X
f. Merchandise available for sale − X = Cost of merchandise sold
g. Gross profit − Operating expenses = X
h. X + X = Operating expenses
i. Income from operations + X − X = Net income

Exercise E–5
Multiple-step income statement—periodic inventory system

✓ Gross profit: $144,100

Selected data for Tower Stores Company for the year ended December 31, 2003, are as follows:

Merchandise inventory, January 1	$ 53,600
Merchandise inventory, December 31	63,900
Purchases	657,000
Purchases discounts	8,000
Purchases returns and allowances	15,500
Sales	805,000
Sales discounts	6,500
Sales returns and allowances	8,700
Transportation in	22,500

Prepare a multiple-step income statement through gross profit for Tower Stores Company for the current year ended December 31.

Exercise E–6
Adjusting and closing entries—periodic inventory system

Selected account titles and related amounts appearing in the Income Statement and Balance Sheet columns of the work sheet of Field of Dreams Company for the year ended December 31 are listed in alphabetical order as follows:

Administrative Expenses	$ 69,500
Building	312,500
Capital Stock	100,000
Cash	58,500
Dividends	36,000
Interest Expense	2,500
Merchandise Inventory (1/1)	285,000
Merchandise Inventory (12/31)	247,000
Notes Payable	25,000
Office Supplies	10,600
Purchases	760,000
Purchases Discounts	6,000
Purchases Returns and Allowances	7,000
Retained Earnings	372,580
Salaries Payable	4,220
Sales	1,315,000
Sales Discounts	10,200
Sales Returns and Allowances	44,300
Selling Expenses	232,700
Store Supplies	7,700
Transportation In	21,300

All selling expenses have been recorded in the account entitled Selling Expenses, and all administrative expenses have been recorded in the account entitled Administrative Expenses. Assuming that Field of Dreams Company uses the periodic inventory system, journalize (a) the adjusting entries for merchandise inventory and (b) the closing entries.

PROBLEMS

Problem E-1
Sales-related and purchase-related transactions—periodic inventory system

The following were selected from among the transactions completed by Cargo Shops, Inc., during April of the current year:

Apr. 4. Purchased merchandise on account from Turner Co., list price $18,000, trade discount 40%, terms FOB destination, 2/10, n/30.
5. Sold merchandise for cash, $4,100.
7. Purchased merchandise on account from Summit Co., $6,800, terms FOB shipping point, 2/10, n/30, with prepaid transportation costs of $200 added to the invoice.
7. Returned $2,200 of merchandise purchased on April 4 from Turner Co.
11. Sold merchandise on account to Fawcett Co., list price $2,500, trade discount 20%, terms 1/10, n/30.
14. Paid Turner Co. on account for purchase of April 4, less return of April 7 and discount.
15. Sold merchandise on nonbank credit cards and reported accounts to the card company, American Express, $5,850.
17. Paid Summit Co. on account for purchase of April 7, less discount.
21. Received cash on account from sale of April 11 to Fawcett Co., less discount.
25. Sold merchandise on account to Clemons Co., $3,000, terms 1/10, n/30.
28. Received cash from American Express for nonbank credit card sales of April 15, less $280 service fee.
30. Received merchandise returned by Clemons Co. from sale on April 25, $1,700.

Instructions
Journalize the transactions for Cargo Shops, Inc., in a two-column general journal.

Problem E-2
Sales-related and purchase-related transactions—periodic inventory system

The following were selected from among the transactions completed by Home Sentry Company during March of the current year:

Mar. 2. Purchased merchandise on account from Diane Co., list price $32,000, trade discount 30%, terms FOB shipping point, 2/10, n/30, with prepaid transportation costs of $720 added to the invoice.
4. Purchased merchandise on account from Lambert Co., $8,000, terms FOB destination, 1/10, n/30.
6. Sold merchandise on account to C. F. Howell Co., list price $7,500, trade discount 40%, terms 2/10, n/30.
9. Returned merchandise purchased on March 4 from Lambert Co., $1,300.
12. Paid Diane Co. on account for purchase of March 2, less discount.
14. Paid Lambert Co. on account for purchase of March 4, less return of March 9 and discount.
16. Received cash on account from sale of March 6 to C. F. Howell Co., less discount.
19. Sold merchandise on nonbank credit cards and reported accounts to the card company, American Express, $4,450.
22. Sold merchandise on account to Wu Co., $4,420, terms 2/10, n/30.
24. Sold merchandise for cash, $4,350.
25. Received merchandise returned by Wu Co. from sale on March 22, $1,610.
31. Received cash from American Express for nonbank credit card sales of March 19, less $290 service fee.

Instructions
Journalize the transactions for Home Sentry Co. in a two-column general journal.

Problem E–3

Sales-related and purchase-related transactions for seller and buyer—periodic inventory system

GENERAL LEDGER

The following selected transactions were completed during July between Tramley Company and Simpson Co.:

July 3. Tramley Company sold merchandise on account to Simpson Co., $12,400, terms FOB destination, 2/15, n/eom.

     3. Tramley Company paid transportation costs of $450 for delivery of merchandise sold to Simpson Co. on July 3.

    10. Tramley Company sold merchandise on account to Simpson Co., $9,600, terms FOB shipping point, n/eom.

    11. Simpson Co. returned merchandise purchased on account on July 3 from Tramley Company, $2,000.

    14. Simpson Co. paid transportation charges of $200 on July 10 purchase from Tramley Company.

    17. Tramley Company sold merchandise on account to Simpson Co., $30,000, terms FOB shipping point, 1/10, n/30. Tramley prepaid transportation costs of $1,750, which were added to the invoice.

    18. Simpson Co. paid Tramley Company for purchase of July 3, less discount and less return of July 11.

    27. Simpson Co. paid Tramley Company on account for purchase of July 17, less discount.

    31. Simpson Co. paid Tramley Company on account for purchase of July 10.

Instructions

Journalize the July transactions for (1) Tramley Company and for (2) Simpson Co.

Problem E–4

Preparation of work sheet, financial statements, and adjusting and closing entries—periodic inventory system

GENERAL LEDGER

✓ 1. Net income: $174,350

The accounts and their balances in the ledger of Bait and Tackle Co. on December 31, 2003, are as follows:

Cash	$ 38,000
Accounts Receivable	112,500
Merchandise Inventory	180,000
Prepaid Insurance	9,700
Store Supplies	4,250
Office Supplies	2,100
Store Equipment	132,000
Accumulated Depreciation—Store Equipment	40,300
Office Equipment	50,000
Accumulated Depreciation—Office Equipment	17,200
Accounts Payable	66,700
Salaries Payable	—
Unearned Rent	1,200
Note Payable (final payment, 2010)	105,000
Capital Stock	25,000
Retained Earnings	129,600
Dividends	40,000
Income Summary	—
Sales	915,000
Sales Returns and Allowances	11,900
Sales Discounts	7,100
Purchases	540,000
Purchases Returns and Allowances	10,100
Purchases Discounts	4,900
Transportation In	6,200
Sales Salaries Expense	71,400
Advertising Expense	25,000
Depreciation Expense—Store Equipment	—
Store Supplies Expense	—
Miscellaneous Selling Expense	1,600
Office Salaries Expense	44,000

Rent Expense	26,000
Insurance Expense	—
Depreciation Expense—Office Equipment	—
Office Supplies Expense	—
Miscellaneous Administrative Expense	$ 1,650
Rent Revenue	—
Interest Expense	11,600

The data needed for year-end adjustments on December 31 are as follows:

Merchandise inventory on December 31		$196,000
Insurance expired during the year		5,400
Supplies on hand on December 31:		
Store supplies		1,300
Office supplies		750
Depreciation for the year:		
Store equipment		7,500
Office equipment		3,800
Salaries payable on December 31:		
Sales salaries	$3,850	
Office salaries	1,150	5,000
Unearned rent on December 31		400

Instructions

1. Prepare a work sheet for the fiscal year ended December 31, listing all accounts in the order given.
2. Prepare a multiple-step income statement.
3. Prepare a retained earnings statement.
4. Prepare a report form of balance sheet, assuming that the current portion of the note payable is $15,000.
5. Journalize the adjusting entries.
6. Journalize the closing entries.

Appendix F: Foreign Currency Transactions

In this appendix, we describe and illustrate the accounting for transactions in which a U.S. company sells products or services to foreign companies or buys foreign products or services. If transactions with foreign companies require payment or receipt in U.S. dollars, no special accounting problems arise.[1] Such transactions are recorded as we described and illustrated earlier in this text. For example, the sale of merchandise to a Japanese company that is billed in and paid for in dollars would be recorded by the U.S. company in the normal manner. However, if the transaction is billed and payment is to be received in Japanese yen, the U.S. company may incur an exchange gain or loss. Some foreign manufacturers have begun building manufacturing plants in the United States, which avoids such gains and losses. For example, **BMW** has constructed its first U.S. plant.

Realized Currency Exchange Gains and Losses

When a U.S. company receives foreign currency, the amount must be converted to its equivalent in U.S. dollars for recording in the accounts. When payment is to be made in a foreign currency, U.S. dollars must be exchanged for the foreign currency for payment. To illustrate, assume that a U.S. company purchases merchandise from a British company that requires payment in British pounds. In this case, U.S. dollars ($) must be exchanged for British pounds (£) to pay for the merchandise. This exchange of one currency for another involves using an exchange rate. The **exchange rate** is the rate at which one unit of currency (the dollar, for example) can be converted into another currency (the British pound, for example).

To continue the example, assume that the U.S. company had purchased merchandise for £1,000 from a British company on June 1, when the exchange rate was $1.40 per British pound. Thus, $1,400 must be exchanged for £1,000 to make the purchase.[2] The U.S. company records the transaction in dollars, as follows:

June	1	Merchandise Inventory	1 4 0 0 00	
		Cash		1 4 0 0 00
		Payment of Invoice No. 1725 from		
		W. A. Sterling Co., £1,000; exchange		
		rate, $1.40 per British pound.		

Instead of a cash purchase, the purchase may be made on account. In this case, the exchange rate may change between the date of purchase and the date of payment of the account payable in the foreign currency. In practice, exchange rates vary daily.

To illustrate, assume that the preceding purchase was made on account. The entry to record it is as follows:

June	1	Merchandise Inventory	1 4 0 0 00	
		Accounts Payable—W. A. Sterling Co.		1 4 0 0 00
		Purchase on account; Invoice		
		No. 1725 from W. A. Sterling Co.,		
		£1,000; exchange rate, $1.40 per		
		British pound.		

---

[1] This discussion is from the point of view of a U.S. company. Unless otherwise indicated, the reference to the dollar refers to the U.S. dollar rather than a dollar of another country, such as Canada.

[2] Foreign exchange rates are quoted in major financial reporting services. Because the exchange rates are quite volatile, those used in this chapter are assumed rates.

Assume that on the date of payment, June 15, the exchange rate was $1.45 per pound. The £1,000 account payable must be settled by exchanging $1,450 (£1,000 × $1.45) for £1,000. In this case, the U.S. company incurs an exchange loss of $50 because $1,450 was needed to settle a $1,400 account payable. The cash payment is recorded as follows:

June	15	Accounts Payable—W. A. Sterling Co.	1 4 0 0 00	
		Exchange Loss	5 0 00	
		Cash		1 4 5 0 00
		Cash paid on Invoice No. 1725, for		
		£1,000, or $1,400, when exchange		
		rate was $1.45 per pound.		

We can analyze all transactions with foreign companies in the manner described. For example, assume that a sale on account for $1,000 to a Swiss company on May 1 was billed in Swiss francs. The cost of the merchandise sold was $600, and the selling company uses a perpetual inventory system. If the exchange rate was $0.25 per Swiss franc (F) on May 1, the transaction is recorded as follows:

May	1	Accounts Receivable—D. W. Robinson Co.	1 0 0 0 00	
		Sales		1 0 0 0 00
		Invoice No. 9772, F4,000; exchange		
		rate, $0.25 per Swiss franc.		
	1	Cost of Merchandise Sold	6 0 0 00	
		Merchandise Inventory		6 0 0 00

Assume that the exchange rate increases to $0.30 per Swiss franc on May 31 when cash is received. In this case, the U.S. company realizes an exchange gain of $200. This gain is realized because the F4,000, which had a value of $1,000 on the date of sale, has increased in value to $1,200 (F4,000 × $0.30) on May 31 when the payment is received. The receipt of the cash is recorded as follows:

May	31	Cash	1 2 0 0 00	
		Accounts Receivable—D. W. Robinson Co.		1 0 0 0 00
		Exchange Gain		2 0 0 00
		Cash received on Invoice No. 9772,		
		for F4,000, $1,000, when exchange		
		rate was $0.30 per Swiss franc.		

Unrealized Currency Exchange Gains and Losses

In the previous examples, the transactions were completed by either the receipt or the payment of cash. On the date the cash was received or paid, any related exchange gain or loss was realized and was recorded in the accounts. However, financial statements may be prepared between the date of the sale or purchase on account and the date the cash is received or paid. In this case, any exchange gain or loss created by a change in exchange rates between the date of the original transaction and the balance sheet date must be recorded. Such an exchange gain or loss is reported in the financial statements as an unrealized exchange gain or loss.

To illustrate, assume that a sale on account for $1,000 had been made to a German company on December 20 and had been billed in deutsche marks (DM). The cost of merchandise sold was $700. On this date, the exchange rate was $0.50 per deutsche mark. The transaction is recorded as follows:

Dec.	20	Accounts Receivable—T. A. Mueller Inc.	1 0 0 0 00	
		Sales		1 0 0 0 00
		Invoice No. 1793, DM2,000; exchange		
		rate, $0.50 per deutsche mark.		
	20	Cost of Merchandise Sold	7 0 0 00	
		Merchandise Inventory		7 0 0 00

Assume that the exchange rate decreases to $0.45 per deutsche mark on December 31, the date of the balance sheet. Thus, the $1,000 account receivable on December 31 has a value of only $900 (DM2,000 × $0.45). This unrealized loss of $100 ($1,000 − $900) is recorded as follows:

Dec.	31	Exchange Loss	1 0 0 00	
		Accounts Receivable—T. A. Mueller Inc.		1 0 0 00
		Invoice No. 1793, DM2,000 × $0.05		
		decrease in exchange rate.		

Any additional change in the exchange rate during the following period is recorded when the cash is received. To continue the illustration, assume that the exchange rate declines from $0.45 to $0.42 per deutsche mark by January 19, when the DM2,000 is received. The receipt of the cash on January 19 is recorded as follows:

Jan.	19	Cash (DM2,000 × $0.42)	8 4 0 00	
		Exchange Loss (DM2,000 × $0.03)	6 0 00	
		Accounts Receivable—T. A. Mueller Inc.		9 0 0 00
		Cash received on Invoice No. 1793,		
		for DM2,000, or $900, when exchange		
		rate was $0.42 per deutsche mark.		

In contrast, assume that in the preceding example the exchange rate increases between December 31 and January 19. In this case, an exchange gain would be recorded on January 19. For example, if the exchange rate increases from $0.45 to $0.47 per deutsche mark during this period, Exchange Gain would be credited for $40 (DM2,000 × $0.02).

A balance in the exchange loss account at the end of the fiscal period is reported in the Other Expense section of the income statement. A balance in the exchange gain account is reported in the Other Income section.

EXERCISES

Exercise F–1

Entries for sales made in foreign currency

The Cuddly Toy Company makes sales on account to several Swedish companies that it bills in kronas. Journalize the entries for the following selected transactions completed during the current year, assuming that Cuddly uses the perpetual inventory system:

Aug. 2. Sold merchandise on account, 20,000 kronas; exchange rate, $0.14 per krona. The cost of merchandise sold was $1,600.

Sept. 1. Received cash from sale of August 2, 20,000 kronas; exchange rate, $0.15 per krona.

Oct. 30. Sold merchandise on account, 18,000 kronas; exchange rate, $0.15 per krona. The cost of merchandise sold was $1,550.

Nov. 29. Received cash from sale of October 30, 18,000 kronas; exchange rate, $0.13 per krona.

Exercise F–2
Entries for purchases made in foreign currency

Synthetic Care Inc. sells artificial arms and legs to hospitals and physicians. It purchases merchandise from a German company that requires payment in deutsche marks. Journalize the entries for the following selected transactions completed during the current year, assuming that Synthetic Care Inc. uses the perpetual inventory system:

Mar. 1. Purchased merchandise on account, net 30, 10,000 deutsche marks; exchange rate, $0.57 per deutsche mark.

31. Paid invoice of March 1; exchange rate, $0.60 per deutsche mark.

June 5. Purchased merchandise on account, net 30, 7,500 deutsche marks; exchange rate, $0.60 per deutsche mark.

July 5. Paid invoice of June 5; exchange rate, $0.55 per deutsche mark.

PROBLEMS

Problem F–1
Foreign currency transactions

GENERAL
LEDGER

Universal Sports is a wholesaler of sports equipment, including golf clubs and gym sets. It sells to and purchases from companies in Canada and the Philippines. These transactions are settled in the foreign currency. The following selected transactions were completed during the current fiscal year:

April 8. Sold merchandise on account to Islands Company, net 30, 300,000 pesos; exchange rate, $0.030 per Philippines peso. The cost of merchandise sold was $5,500.

May 8. Received cash from Islands Company; exchange rate, $0.028 per Philippines peso.

15. Purchased merchandise on account from LeMan Inc., net 30, $10,000 Canadian; exchange rate, $0.65 per Canadian dollar.

June 14. Issued check for amount owed to LeMan Inc.; exchange rate, $0.60 per Canadian dollar.

30. Sold merchandise on account to Ella Company, net 30, 150,000 pesos; exchange rate, $0.031 per Philippines peso. The cost of merchandise sold was $2,200.

July 30. Received cash from Ella Company; exchange rate, $0.032 per Phillipines peso.

Oct. 8. Purchased merchandise on account from Chevalier Company, net 30, $50,000 Canadian; exchange rate, $0.73 per Canadian dollar.

Nov. 7. Issued check for amount owed to Chevalier Company; exchange rate, $0.74 per Canadian dollar.

Dec. 15. Sold merchandise on account to Cassandra Company, net 30, $120,000 Canadian; exchange rate, $0.75 per Canadian dollar. The cost of merchandise sold was $50,000.

16. Purchased merchandise on account from Juan Company, net 30, 500,000 pesos; exchange rate, $0.033 per Philippines peso.

31. Recorded unrealized currency exchange gain and/or loss on transactions of December 15 and 16. Exchange rates on December 31: $0.76 per Canadian dollar; $0.034 per Philippines peso.

Instructions

1. Journalize the entries to record the transactions and adjusting entries for the year, assuming that Universal Sports uses the perpetual inventory system.

2. Journalize the entries to record the payment of the December 16 purchase, on January 15, when the exchange rate was $0.031 per Philippines peso, and the receipt of cash from the December 15 sale, on January 17, when the exchange rate was $0.77 per Canadian dollar.

Appendix G: Cisco Systems, Inc., Annual Report

PROFILE

CISCO SYSTEMS, INC. is the worldwide leader in networking for the Internet. Cisco hardware, software, and service offerings are used to create Internet solutions so that individuals, companies, and countries have seamless access to information—regardless of differences in time and place. Cisco solutions provide competitive advantage to our customers through more efficient and timely exchange of information, which in turn leads to cost savings, process efficiencies, and closer relationships with their customers, prospects, business partners, suppliers, and employees. These solutions form the networking foundation for companies, universities, utilities, and government agencies worldwide.

The company was founded in 1984 by a small group of computer scientists from Stanford University seeking an easier way to connect different types of computer systems. Cisco Systems shipped its first product in 1986. Since then, Cisco has grown into a multinational corporation with more than 34,000 employees around the world. We invite you to learn more about Cisco Systems at www.cisco.com.

TABLE OF CONTENTS

FINANCIAL HIGHLIGHTS[1]

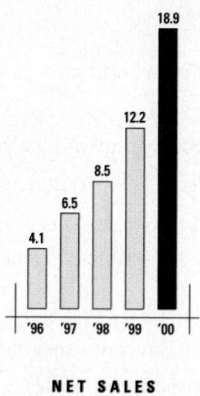

NET SALES
(Dollars in billions)

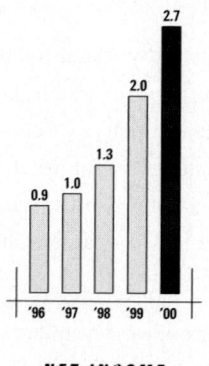

NET INCOME
(Dollars in billions)

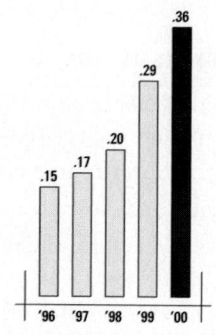

DILUTED NET INCOME PER SHARE
(In dollars)

CONSOLIDATED STATEMENTS OF OPERATIONS DATA[1]
(In millions, except per-share amounts)

Years Ended	July 29, 2000	July 31, 1999	July 25, 1998
Net sales	$18,928	$12,173	$8,489
Income before provision for income taxes	$ 4,343	$ 3,203	$2,271
Net income	$ 2,668[a]	$ 2,023[b]	$1,331[c]
Net income per common share—diluted*	$ 0.36[a]	$ 0.29[b]	$ 0.20[c]
Shares used in per-common share calculation—diluted*	7,438	7,062	6,658

* Reflects the two-for-one stock split effective March 2000.

[a] Net income and net income per common share include in-process research and development expenses of $1.37 billion, amortization of goodwill and purchased intangible assets of $291 million, acquisition-related costs of $62 million, payroll tax on stock option exercises of $51 million, and net gains realized on minority investments of $531 million. Pro forma net income and diluted net income per common share, excluding these items net of tax of $0, were $3.91 billion and $0.53, respectively.

[b] Net income and net income per common share include in-process research and development expenses of $471 million, amortization of goodwill and purchased intangible assets of $61 million, and acquisition-related costs of $16 million. Pro forma net income and diluted net income per common share, excluding these items net of related tax benefits of $54 million, were $2.52 billion and $0.36, respectively.

[c] Net income and net income per common share include in-process research and development expenses of $594 million, amortization of goodwill and purchased intangible assets of $23 million, and net gains realized on minority investments of $5 million. Pro forma net income and diluted net income per common share, excluding these items net of related tax benefits of $67 million, were $1.88 billion and $0.28, respectively.

CONSOLIDATED BALANCE SHEETS DATA[1]
(In millions)

	July 29, 2000	July 31, 1999	July 25, 1998
Working capital	$ 5,914	$ 1,723	$2,057
Total assets	$32,870	$14,893	$9,043
Shareholders' equity	$26,497	$11,811	$7,197

[1] All historical financial information has been restated to reflect the acquisitions of StratumOne Communications, Inc. and TransMedia Communications, Inc. in the first quarter of fiscal 2000, Cerent Corporation and WebLine Communications Corporation in the second quarter of fiscal 2000, and ArrowPoint Communications, Inc., InfoGear Technology Corporation, and SightPath, Inc. in the fourth quarter of fiscal 2000, which were accounted for as poolings of interests. In addition, the historical financial information has been restated to reflect the acquisition of Fibex Systems, which was completed in the fourth quarter of fiscal 1999 and accounted for as a pooling of interests.

TO OUR SHAREHOLDERS

Over the next two decades, the Internet economy will bring about more dramatic changes in the way we work, live, play, and learn than we witnessed during the last 200 years of the Industrial Revolution. Cisco is well-positioned to help our customers survive the Internet Revolution by turning these changes into competitive advantage. We provide the Internet solutions that will help our customers generate new revenue, reduce costs, increase productivity, and empower their employees.

For the past two years, Cisco has been asking business and government leaders around the world, "Are you ready?" Using our company as an example, our focus has been on educating customers about how effective use of the Internet can increase productivity and revolutionize their business models. Today, our customers are not only ready, but are turning to Cisco to show them how to capture the power of the Internet by implementing open standards-based Internet business models.

During the last decade, our passion has been to increase customer satisfaction and to achieve our stretch goal of maintaining the number-one or -two market share position in every market in which we compete. Today, Cisco holds a leadership position in 16 of our 17 key markets. Cisco's success is the result of our solutions that provide data, voice, and video over a single network and our ability to blend internal development, acquisitions, and partnerships.

Cisco benefited from exceptional returns this past year because we successfully increased our customers' satisfaction. For fiscal 2000, Cisco reported revenue of $18.93 billion, a 55-percent increase when compared with revenue of $12.17 billion in fiscal 1999. Pro forma net income was $3.91 billion or $0.53 per share for fiscal 2000, compared with pro forma net income of $2.52 billion or $0.36 per share for fiscal 1999, increases of 56 percent and 47 percent, respectively. Actual net income for the year was $2.67 billion or $0.36 per share, compared with fiscal 1999 net income of $2.02 billion or $0.29 per share.

Cisco has been one of the fastest-growing and most profitable companies in the history of the computer industry. We are widely accepted as the Internet expert and the Internet company, which is an obvious advantage when we talk to customers about their futures. Our success has been rewarded with one of the highest market capitalizations in the world. This achievement is the result of our commitment to help customers become successful in today's ever-changing, competitive landscape.

The Internet economy has grown more rapidly than even our most optimistic predictions and fuels the strongest period of economic prosperity in history. In the United States alone, this economy added 650,000 jobs and generated revenue in excess of half a trillion dollars in 1999. To put this in perspective, the Internet economy's workforce now surpasses the entire active U.S. military, insurance, communications, and public utilities industries and is twice the size of the airline, chemical and allied products, legal, and real-estate industries.

There is a direct correlation between the strength of this economy and the unprecedented productivity gains we are witnessing today. We refer to this phenomenon as the "Network Effect," which is the result of information technology becoming networked and Internet applications being used to re-engineer business processes. Companies that understand the Network Effect can gain competitive advantage by quickly detecting and responding to situations such as real-time changes in customer demand.

Cisco has become a trusted technology partner and business advisor to many of the largest companies in the world. We are not only a technology advisor, but also an advanced user of Internet technology to run our own business. The adoption of Internet applications in each of Cisco's functional areas is an integral part of our business-planning process and results in tremendous productivity benefits and cost savings. During this past fiscal year, for example, 90 percent of our customer orders were transacted over the Internet. We have created world-class e-commerce, customer support, and workforce optimization applications and are the leader in virtual manufacturing, virtual close, and e-learning solutions.

Our goal is to help customers develop similar, Internet-centric business models so that they can benefit from productivity improvements. For example, our Internet Business Solutions Group has consulted with executives in more than 50 percent of the Fortune 250 companies, 45 percent of the top companies in Europe, the Middle East, Africa, and Asia, and 65 percent of the leading service providers. This group provides business-strategy consulting and helps move our relationships with customers from that of a vendor to a strategic partner.

Successful companies in the 1980s achieved their leadership positions with a vertical business model and an internal focus. In the 1990s, Cisco changed the dynamics of market leadership by focusing on a combination of internal development and acquisitions. This decade, leading companies will develop internally, acquire effectively, and form an "ecosystem" of partnerships in a horizontal, rather than a vertical, business model.

INSIDE CISCO
Five years ago it took Cisco 14 days to close its books each quarter. Now, with the "virtual close," using powerful Internet technology, Cisco executives have real-time, daily access to company financial information, empowering them and their employees to instantly react to market shifts and changing business requirements.

Companies participating in an ecosystem—an open standards-based community that works toward a common goal—will emerge as the market and industry leaders of the future. Customers are the real beneficiaries of our ecosystem model because it allows us to remain agile, quickly enter new markets, and provide both breadth and depth of solutions through the ecosystem community.

In addition to expanding our ecosystem, we also increased our investment in internal product development by 61 percent and continued to grow through acquisitions. Since 1993, we have acquired or announced our intent to acquire 65 companies. Moving forward, our technology strategy will continue to be driven by internal development complemented by acquisitions and strategic alliances.

Following the lead of business, we saw governments from around the world begin to recognize the strong correlation between the Internet and economic success. This past year, we met with government leaders from many countries, including Argentina, Chile, China, France, Germany, Italy, Japan, Jordan, Korea, South Africa, Taiwan, and the United Kingdom. They all realized the Internet's potential impact on their country's future and were eager to learn how to use the Internet more effectively.

The Industrial Revolution of 200 years ago divided society by creating a gap between the "haves" and "have-nots." Today's Internet Revolution has the potential to unite everyone by combining the strength of the Internet and education, the two great equalizers in life. By applying what we've learned in business to all aspects of society, we have the power to use technology to create an Internet gateway that has the potential to positively change people's lives.

Cisco is in a unique position to be a pioneer in embracing this digital opportunity and closing the gap. As such, our philanthropy strategy focuses on education, workforce development, and basic human needs. We continue to invest and grow the Cisco Networking Academy Program, which has enrolled more than 81,000 students in 83 countries. These academies provide networking skills to a broad range of students, including those in high school, community colleges, homeless shelters, and juvenile centers and outgoing military personnel.

In addition, our employees contributed more than $1 million to the Second Harvest Food Bank this past year. Cisco gave more than $2.5 million in grants to our global community and committed another $5 million to Habitat for Humanity over the next five years. We also launched the Netaid.org Web site and movement, a joint initiative with the United Nations Development Program, a number of talented musicians, and several technology companies, to help end the cycle of extreme poverty. Our employees supported additional programs such as the Special Olympics, InnVision, the National Teacher Training Institute, and a variety of global relief efforts. These efforts are Cisco's way of preparing future generations and less-developed nations to participate in the Internet economy.

In our opinion, the radical business transformations taking place around the world will accelerate, making the opportunities ahead of Cisco far greater than ever before. We believe that Cisco has the potential to be the most influential and generous company in history. We are in the fortunate position to be at the center of the Internet economy, and we recognize that although this position gives us confidence, we must balance this confidence with healthy paranoia.

We are proud of our accomplishments and want to thank our shareholders, customers, employees, partners, and suppliers for their continued commitment and confidence in our ability to execute. Together, we are only beginning to explore all that's possible on the Internet.

JOHN T. CHAMBERS
PRESIDENT AND
CHIEF EXECUTIVE OFFICER

JOHN P. MORGRIDGE
CHAIRMAN OF THE BOARD

DONALD T. VALENTINE
VICE CHAIRMAN OF THE BOARD

FINANCIAL REVIEW

SELECTED FINANCIAL DATA[1]
Five Years Ended July 29, 2000 (In millions, except per-share amounts)

	July 29, 2000	July 31, 1999	July 25, 1998	July 26, 1997	July 28, 1996
Net sales	$18,928	$12,173	$8,489	$6,452	$4,101
Net income	$ 2,668[2]	$ 2,023[3]	$1,331[4]	$1,047[5]	$ 915[6]
Net income per common share—basic	$ 0.39	$ 0.30	$ 0.21	$ 0.17	$ 0.16
Net income per common share—diluted	$ 0.36[2]	$ 0.29[3]	$ 0.20[4]	$ 0.17[5]	$ 0.15[6]
Shares used in per-common share calculation—basic*	6,917	6,646	6,312	6,007	5,758
Shares used in per-common share calculation—diluted*	7,438	7,062	6,658	6,287	6,008
Total assets	$32,870	$14,893	$9,043	$5,504	$3,647

* Reflects the two-for-one stock split effective March 2000.

(1) All historical financial information has been restated to reflect the acquisitions that were accounted for as poolings of interests (see Note 3 to the Consolidated Financial Statements).

(2) Net income and net income per common share include in-process research and development expenses of $1.37 billion, amortization of goodwill and purchased intangible assets of $291 million, acquisition-related costs of $62 million, payroll tax on stock option exercises of $51 million, and net gains realized on minority investments of $531 million. Pro forma net income and diluted net income per common share, excluding these items net of tax of $0, were $3.91 billion and $0.53, respectively.

(3) Net income and net income per common share include in-process research and development expenses of $471 million, amortization of goodwill and purchased intangible assets of $61 million, and acquisition-related costs of $16 million. Pro forma net income and diluted net income per common share, excluding these items net of tax benefits of $54 million, were $2.52 billion and $0.36, respectively.

(4) Net income and net income per common share include in-process research and development expenses of $594 million, amortization of goodwill and purchased intangible assets of $23 million, and net gains realized on minority investments of $5 million. Pro forma net income and diluted net income per common share, excluding these items net of tax benefits of $67 million, were $1.88 billion and $0.28, respectively.

(5) Net income and net income per common share include in-process research and development expenses of $508 million, amortization of goodwill and purchased intangible assets of $11 million, and net gains realized on minority investments of $152 million. Pro forma net income and diluted net income per common share, excluding these items net of tax benefits of $7 million, were $1.42 billion and $0.23, respectively.

(6) Net income and net income per common share include amortization of goodwill and purchased intangible assets of $14 million. Pro forma net income and diluted net income per common share, excluding this item net of a tax benefit of $2 million, were $927 million and $0.15, respectively.

MANAGEMENT'S DISCUSSION AND ANALYSIS OF FINANCIAL CONDITION AND RESULTS OF OPERATIONS

All historical financial information has been restated to reflect the acquisitions that were accounted for as poolings of interests (see Note 3 to the Consolidated Financial Statements).

FORWARD-LOOKING STATEMENTS

Certain statements contained in this Annual Report, including, without limitation, statements containing the words "believes," "anticipates," "estimates," "expects," "projections," and words of similar import, constitute "forward-looking statements." You should not place undue reliance on these forward-looking statements. Our actual results could differ materially from those anticipated in these forward-looking statements for many reasons, including risks faced by us described in the Risk Factors sections, among others, included in the documents we file with the Securities and Exchange Commission ("SEC"), including our most recent reports on Form 10-K, Form 8-K, and Form 10-Q, and amendments thereto.

COMPARISON OF FISCAL 2000 AND FISCAL 1999

Net sales in fiscal 2000 were $18.93 billion, compared with $12.17 billion in fiscal 1999, an increase of 55.5%. The increase in net sales was primarily a result of increased unit sales of switch, router, and access products; growth in the sales of add-on boards that provide increased functionality; optical transport products; and maintenance, service, and support sales (see Note 12 to the Consolidated Financial Statements).

We manage our business on four geographic theaters: the Americas; Europe, the Middle East, and Africa ("EMEA"); Asia Pacific; and Japan. Summarized financial information by theater for fiscal 2000 and 1999 is presented in the following table (in millions):

Years Ended	Amount		Percentage of Net Sales	
	July 29, 2000	July 31, 1999	July 29, 2000	July 31, 1999
Net sales:				
Americas	$12,924	$ 8,088	68.3%	66.4%
EMEA	4,770	3,216	25.2	26.4
Asia Pacific	1,705	825	9.0	6.8
Japan	935	566	4.9	4.7
Sales adjustments	(1,406)	(522)	(7.4)	(4.3)
Total	$18,928	$12,173	100.0%	100.0%

The revenue growth for each theater was primarily driven by market demand and the deployment of Internet technologies and business solutions.

Gross margin in fiscal 2000 was 64.4%, compared with 65.0% in fiscal 1999. The following table shows the standard margins for each theater:

Years Ended	July 29, 2000	July 31, 1999
Standard margins:		
Americas	72.8%	72.2%
EMEA	75.1%	74.0%
Asia Pacific	71.3%	71.0%
Japan	78.8%	77.0%

The net sales and standard margins by geographic theater differ from the amounts recognized under generally accepted accounting principles because we do not allocate certain sales adjustments, production overhead, and manufacturing variances and other related costs to the theaters. Sales adjustments relate to revenue deferrals and reserves, credit memos, returns, and other timing differences.

Standard margins increased for all geographic theaters as compared with fiscal 1999. The decrease in the overall gross margin was primarily due to shifts in product mix, introduction of new products, which generally have lower margins when first released, higher production-related costs, the continued pricing pressure seen from competitors in certain product areas, and the above-mentioned sales adjustments, which were not included in the standard margins.

We expect gross margin may be adversely affected by increases in material or labor costs, heightened price competition, increasing levels of services, higher inventory balances, introduction of new products for new high-growth markets, and changes in channels of distribution or in the mix of products sold. We believe gross margin may additionally be impacted due to constraints relating to certain component shortages that currently exist in the supply chain. We may also experience a lower gross margin as the product mix for access and optical product volume grows.

We have recently introduced several new products, with additional new products scheduled to be released in the future. Increase in demand would result in increased manufacturing capacity, which in turn would result in higher inventory balances. In addition, our vendor base is capacity-constrained, and this could result in increased cost pressure on certain components. If product or related warranty costs associated with these new products are greater than we have experienced, gross margin may be adversely affected. Our gross margin may also be impacted by geographic mix, as well as the mix of configurations within each product group. We continue to expand into third-party or indirect-distribution channels, which generally results in a lower gross margin. In addition, increasing third-party and indirect-distribution channels generally results in greater difficulty in forecasting the mix of our product, and to a certain degree, the timing of orders from our customers. Downward pressures on our gross margin may be further impacted by other factors, such as increased percentage of revenue from service provider markets, which may have lower margins or an increase in product costs, which could adversely affect our future operating results.

Research and development ("R&D") expenses in fiscal 2000 were $2.70 billion, compared with $1.66 billion in fiscal 1999, an increase of 62.6%. R&D expenses, as a percentage of net sales, increased to 14.3% in fiscal 2000, compared with 13.7% in fiscal 1999. The increase reflected our ongoing R&D efforts in a wide variety of areas such as data, voice, and video integration, digital subscriber line ("DSL") technologies, cable modem technology, wireless access, dial access, enterprise switching, optical transport, security, network management, and high-end routing technologies, among others. A significant portion of the increase was due to the addition of new personnel, partly through acquisitions, as well as higher expenditures on prototypes and depreciation on additional lab equipment. We also continued to purchase technology in order to bring a broad range of products to the market in a timely fashion. If we believe that we are unable to enter a particular market in a timely manner with internally developed products, we may license technology from other businesses or acquire businesses as an alternative to internal R&D. All of our R&D costs are expensed as incurred. We currently expect that R&D expenses will continue to increase in absolute dollars as we continue to invest in technology to address potential market opportunities.

Sales and marketing expenses in fiscal 2000 were $3.95 billion, compared with $2.46 billion in fiscal 1999, an increase of 60.1%. Sales and marketing expenses, as a percentage of net sales, increased to 20.8% in fiscal 2000, compared with 20.2% in fiscal 1999. The increase was principally due to an increase in the size of our direct sales force and related commissions, additional marketing and advertising investments associated with the introduction of new products, the expansion of distribution channels, and general corporate branding. The increase also reflected our efforts to invest in certain key areas, such as expansion of our end-to-end networking strategy and service provider coverage, in order to be positioned to take advantage of future market opportunities. We currently expect that sales and marketing expenses will continue to increase in absolute dollars.

General and administrative ("G&A") expenses in fiscal 2000 were $633 million, compared with $381 million in fiscal 1999, an increase of 66.1%. G&A expenses, as a percentage of net sales, increased to 3.3% in fiscal 2000, compared with 3.1% in fiscal 1999. G&A expenses for fiscal 2000 and 1999 included acquisition-related costs of approximately $62 million and $16 million, respectively. Excluding the acquisition-related costs, the increase in G&A expenses was primarily related to the addition of new personnel and investments in infrastructure. We intend to keep G&A expenses relatively constant as a percentage of net sales; however, this depends on the level of acquisition activity and our growth, among other factors.

Amortization of goodwill and purchased intangible assets included in operating expenses was $291 million in fiscal 2000, compared with $61 million in fiscal 1999. Amortization of goodwill and purchased intangible assets primarily relates to various purchase acquisitions (see Note 3 and Note 4 to the Consolidated Financial Statements). Amortization of goodwill and purchased intangible assets will continue to increase as we acquire companies and technologies.

MANAGEMENT'S DISCUSSION AND ANALYSIS OF FINANCIAL CONDITION AND RESULTS OF OPERATIONS

The amount expensed to in-process research and development ("in-process R&D") arose from the purchase acquisitions completed in fiscal 2000 (see Note 3 to the Consolidated Financial Statements).

The fair values of the existing products and patents, as well as the technology currently under development, were determined using the income approach, which discounts expected future cash flows to present value. The discount rates used in the present value calculations were typically derived from a weighted-average cost of capital analysis and venture capital surveys, adjusted upward to reflect additional risks inherent in the development life cycle. These risk factors have increased the overall discount rate for acquisitions in the current year. We consider the pricing model for products related to these acquisitions to be standard within the high-technology communications equipment industry. However, we do not expect to achieve a material amount of expense reductions or synergies as a result of integrating the acquired in-process technology. Therefore, the valuation assumptions do not include significant anticipated cost savings.

The development of these technologies remains a significant risk due to the remaining effort to achieve technical viability, rapidly changing customer markets, uncertain standards for new products, and significant competitive threats from numerous companies. The nature of the efforts to develop the acquired technologies into commercially viable products consists principally of planning, designing, and testing activities necessary to determine that the products can meet market expectations, including functionality and technical requirements. Failure to bring these products to market in a timely manner could result in a loss of market share or a lost opportunity to capitalize on emerging markets and could have a material adverse impact on our business and operating results.

The following table summarizes the significant assumptions underlying the valuations for our significant purchase acquisitions completed in fiscal 2000 and 1999 (in millions, except percentages):

| | Acquisition Assumptions | |
Acquired Company	Estimated Cost to Complete Technology at Time of Acquisition	Risk-Adjusted Discount Rate for In-Process R&D
FISCAL 2000		
Monterey Networks, Inc.	$ 4	30.0%
The optical systems business of Pirelli S.p.A.	$ 5	20.0%
Aironet Wireless Communications, Inc.	$ 3	23.5%
Atlantech Technologies	$ 6	37.5%
JetCell, Inc.	$ 7	30.5%
PentaCom, Ltd.	$13	30.0%
Qeyton Systems	$ 6	35.0%
FISCAL 1999		
Summa Four, Inc.	$ 5	25.0%
Clarity Wireless, Inc.	$42	32.0%
Selsius Systems, Inc.	$15	31.0%
PipeLinks, Inc.	$ 5	31.0%
Amteva Technologies	$ 4	35.0%

Regarding our purchase acquisitions completed in fiscal 2000 and 1999, actual results to date have been consistent, in all material respects, with our assumptions at the time of the acquisitions. The assumptions primarily consist of an expected completion date for the in-process projects, estimated costs to complete the projects, and revenue and expense projections once the products have entered the market. Shipment volumes of products from the above-acquired technologies are not material to our overall financial results at the present time. Therefore, it is difficult to determine the accuracy of overall revenue projections early in the technology or product life cycle. Failure to achieve the expected levels of revenue and net income from these products will negatively impact the return on investment expected at the time that the acquisitions were completed and potentially result in impairment of any other assets related to the development activities.

Interest and other income, net, was $577 million in fiscal 2000, compared with $330 million in fiscal 1999. The increase was primarily due to interest income related to the general increase in cash and investments, which was generated from our operations. Net gains realized on minority investments were $531 million in fiscal 2000. The net gains realized on minority investments were not material in fiscal 1999.

Our pro forma effective tax rate for fiscal 2000 was 30.0%. The actual effective tax rate was 38.6%, which included the impact of nondeductible in-process R&D and acquisition-related costs. Our future effective tax rates could be adversely affected if earnings are lower than anticipated in countries where we have lower effective rates or by unfavorable changes in tax laws and regulations. Additionally, we have provided a valuation allowance on certain of our deferred tax assets because of uncertainty regarding their realizability due to expectation of future employee stock option exercises (see Note 11 to the Consolidated Financial Statements).

COMPARISON OF FISCAL 1999 AND FISCAL 1998

Net sales in fiscal 1999 were $12.17 billion, compared with $8.49 billion in fiscal 1998, an increase of 43.4%. The increase in net sales was primarily a result of increased unit sales of LAN switching products, access servers, high-performance WAN switching and routing products, and maintenance service contracts.

Gross margin in fiscal 1999 was 65.0%, compared with 65.6% in fiscal 1998. The decrease in the overall gross margin was primarily due to our continued shift in revenue mix toward our lower-margin products and the continued pricing pressure seen from competitors in certain product areas.

R&D expenses in fiscal 1999 were $1.66 billion, compared with $1.05 billion in fiscal 1998, an increase of 58.1%. R&D expenses, as a percentage of net sales, increased to 13.7% in fiscal 1999, compared with 12.4% in fiscal 1998. The increase reflected our ongoing R&D efforts in a wide variety of areas such as data, voice, and video integration, DSL technologies, cable modem technology, wireless access, dial access, enterprise switching, security, network management, and high-end routing technologies, among others. A significant portion of the increase was due to the addition of new personnel, partly through acquisitions, as well as higher expenditures on prototypes and depreciation on additional lab equipment.

Sales and marketing expenses in fiscal 1999 were $2.46 billion, compared with $1.58 billion in fiscal 1998, an increase of 56.1%. Sales and marketing expenses, as a percentage of net sales, increased to 20.2% in fiscal 1999, compared with 18.6% in fiscal 1998. The increase was principally due to an increase in the size of our direct sales force and related commissions, television advertising campaigns to build brand awareness, additional marketing and advertising costs associated with the introduction of new products, and the expansion of distribution channels. The increase also reflected our efforts to invest in certain key areas, such as expansion of our end-to-end networking strategy and service provider coverage, in order to be positioned to take advantage of future market opportunities.

G&A expenses in fiscal 1999 were $381 million, compared with $247 million in fiscal 1998, an increase of 54.3%. G&A expenses, as a percentage of net sales, increased to 3.1% in fiscal 1999, compared with 2.9% in fiscal 1998. The increase was primarily related to additional personnel and acquisition-related costs of $16 million.

Amortization of goodwill and purchased intangible assets included in operating expenses was $61 million in fiscal 1999, compared with $23 million in fiscal 1998. Amortization of goodwill and purchased intangible assets increased as we acquired companies and technologies.

Interest and other income, net, in fiscal 1999 was $330 million, compared with $196 million in fiscal 1998. Interest income rose primarily as a result of additional investment income on our increased investment balances.

MANAGEMENT'S DISCUSSION AND ANALYSIS OF FINANCIAL CONDITION AND RESULTS OF OPERATIONS

RECENT ACCOUNTING PRONOUNCEMENTS

In June 1998, the Financial Accounting Standards Board ("FASB") issued Statement of Financial Accounting Standards No. 133, "Accounting for Derivative Instruments and Hedging Activities" ("SFAS 133"). SFAS 133, as amended, establishes accounting and reporting standards for derivative instruments and hedging activities. It requires an entity to recognize all derivatives as either assets or liabilities on the balance sheet and measure those instruments at fair value. We do not expect the initial adoption of SFAS 133 to have a material effect on our operations or financial position. We are required to adopt SFAS 133 in the first quarter of fiscal 2001.

In September 1999, the FASB issued Emerging Issues Task Force Topic No. D-83, "Accounting for Payroll Taxes Associated with Stock Option Exercises" ("EITF D-83"). EITF D-83 requires that payroll tax paid on the difference between the exercise price and the fair value of acquired stock in association with an employee's exercise of stock options be recorded as operating expenses. Payroll tax on stock option exercises of $51 million was expensed in fiscal 2000.

In December 1999, the SEC issued Staff Accounting Bulletin No. 101, "Revenue Recognition in Financial Statements" ("SAB 101"). SAB 101, as amended, summarizes certain of the SEC's views in applying generally accepted accounting principles to revenue recognition in financial statements. At this time, we do not expect the adoption of SAB 101 to have a material effect on our operations or financial position; however, the SEC's final guidance for implementation has not been released to date. We are required to adopt SAB 101 in the fourth quarter of fiscal 2001.

LIQUIDITY AND CAPITAL RESOURCES

Cash and cash equivalents, short-term investments, and investments were $20.50 billion at July 29, 2000, an increase of $10.28 billion from July 31, 1999. The increase was primarily a result of $5.00 billion of net unrealized gains on publicly held investments and $7.70 billion of cash generated by operating and financing activities partially offset by investing activities, including net capital expenditures of $1.09 billion, purchases of technology licenses of $444 million, and investments in lease receivables of $535 million.

Accounts receivable increased 83.9% during fiscal 2000. Days sales outstanding in receivables increased to 37 days for fiscal 2000, from 32 days for fiscal 1999. The increase in accounts receivable and days sales outstanding was due, in part, to growth in total net sales combined with conditions in a number of markets, resulting in longer payment terms.

Inventories increased 87.2% during fiscal 2000; however, inventory turns remained constant at 7.8 times. The increase in inventory levels reflected new product introductions, continued growth in our two-tier distribution system, and increased purchases to secure the supply of certain components. Inventory management remains an area of focus as we balance the need to maintain strategic inventory levels to ensure competitive lead times with the risk of inventory obsolescence due to rapidly changing technology and customer requirements.

At July 29, 2000, we had a line of credit totaling $500 million, which expires in July 2002. There have been no borrowings under this agreement (see Note 7 to the Consolidated Financial Statements).

We have entered into several agreements to lease 448 acres of land located in San Jose, California, where our headquarters operations are established, and 759 acres of land located in Boxborough, Massachusetts; Salem, New Hampshire; Richardson, Texas; and Research Triangle Park, North Carolina, where we have expanded certain R&D and customer-support activities. In connection with these transactions, we have pledged $1.29 billion of our investments as collateral for certain obligations of the leases. We anticipate that we will occupy more leased property in the future that will require similar pledged securities; however, we do not expect the impact of this activity to be material to our liquidity position (see Note 8 to the Consolidated Financial Statements).

We believe that our current cash and cash equivalents, short-term investments, line of credit, and cash generated from operations will satisfy our expected working capital, capital expenditure, and investment requirements through at least the next 12 months.

QUANTITATIVE AND QUALITATIVE DISCLOSURES ABOUT MARKET RISK

We maintain an investment portfolio of various holdings, types, and maturities. These securities are generally classified as available for sale and, consequently, are recorded on the balance sheet at fair value with unrealized gains or losses reported as a separate component of accumulated other comprehensive income, net of tax. Part of this portfolio includes minority equity investments in several publicly traded companies, the values of which are subject to market price volatility. For example, as a result of recent market price volatility of our publicly traded equity investments, we experienced a $111 million after-tax unrealized loss during the third quarter of fiscal 2000 and a $1.83 billion after-tax unrealized gain during the fourth quarter of fiscal 2000 on these investments. We have also invested in numerous privately held companies, many of which can still be considered in the start-up or development stages. These investments are inherently risky as the market for the technologies or products they have under development are typically in the early stages and may never materialize. We could lose our entire initial investment in these companies. We also have certain real estate lease commitments with payments tied to short-term interest rates. At any time, a sharp rise in interest rates could have a material adverse impact on the fair value of our investment portfolio while increasing the costs associated with our lease commitments. Conversely, declines in interest rates could have a material impact on interest earnings for our investment portfolio. We do not currently hedge these interest rate exposures.

INVESTMENTS

The following table presents the hypothetical changes in fair values in the financial instruments held at July 29, 2000 that are sensitive to changes in interest rates. These instruments are not leveraged and are held for purposes other than trading. The modeling technique used measures the change in fair values arising from selected potential changes in interest rates. Market changes reflect immediate hypothetical parallel shifts in the yield curve of plus or minus 50 basis points ("BPS"), 100 BPS, and 150 BPS over a 12-month horizon. Beginning fair values represent the principal plus accrued interest and dividends of the interest rate-sensitive financial instruments at July 29, 2000. Ending fair values are the market principal plus accrued interest, dividends, and reinvestment income at a 12-month horizon. The following table estimates the fair value of the portfolio at a 12-month horizon (in millions):

Issuer	Valuation of Securities Given an Interest Rate Decrease of X Basis Points			Fair Value as of July 29, 2000	Valuation of Securities Given an Interest Rate Increase of X Basis Points		
	(150 BPS)	(100 BPS)	(50 BPS)		50 BPS	100 BPS	150 BPS
U.S. government notes and bonds	$2,350	$2,329	$2,307	$2,285	$2,262	$2,240	$2,218
State, municipal, and county government notes and bonds	3,666	3,632	3,598	3,564	3,529	3,494	3,459
Corporate notes and bonds	3,296	3,266	3,235	3,204	3,173	3,141	3,110
Total	$9,312	$9,227	$9,140	$9,053	$8,964	$8,875	$8,787

A 50 BPS move in the Federal Funds Rate has occurred in nine of the last 10 years; a 100 BPS move in the Federal Funds Rate has occurred in six of the last 10 years; and a 150 BPS move in the Federal Funds Rate has occurred in four of the last 10 years.

QUANTITATIVE AND QUALITATIVE DISCLOSURES ABOUT MARKET RISK

The following analysis presents the hypothetical changes in fair values of public equity investments that are sensitive to changes in the stock market. These equity securities are held for purposes other than trading. The modeling technique used measures the hypothetical change in fair values arising from selected hypothetical changes in each stock's price. Stock price fluctuations of plus or minus 15%, plus or minus 35%, and plus or minus 50% were selected based on the probability of their occurrence. The following table estimates the fair value of the publicly traded corporate equities at a 12-month horizon (in millions):

	Valuation of Securities Given X% Decrease in Each Stock's Price			Fair Value as of	Valuation of Securities Given X% Increase in Each Stock's Price		
	(50%)	(35%)	(15%)	July 29, 2000	15%	35%	50%
Corporate equities	$3,112	$4,046	$5,291	$6,225	$7,159	$8,404	$9,337

Our equity portfolio consists of securities with characteristics that most closely match the S&P Index or companies traded on the NASDAQ National Market. The NASDAQ Composite Index has shown a 15% movement in each of the last three years and a 35% and 50% movement in at least one of the last three years.

We also have an investment in KPMG Consulting, Inc. in the principal amount of $1.05 billion of Series A Mandatorily Redeemable Convertible Preferred Stock, which carries a 6% dividend rate on the original issue price until converted to common stock. Conversion is at our option upon or after the completion of an initial public offering of KPMG Consulting, Inc. We have not included the investment in the above sensitivity analyses due to the nature of this investment.

LEASES

We are exposed to interest rate risk associated with leases on our facilities where payments are tied to the London Interbank Offered Rate ("LIBOR"). We have evaluated the hypothetical change in lease obligations held at July 29, 2000 due to changes in the LIBOR. The modeling technique used measures hypothetical changes in lease obligations arising from selected hypothetical changes in the LIBOR. The hypothetical market changes reflected immediate parallel shifts in the LIBOR curve of plus or minus 50 BPS, 100 BPS, and 150 BPS over a 12-month period. The results of this analysis were not material in comparison to our financial results.

FOREIGN EXCHANGE FORWARD AND OPTION CONTRACTS

We enter into foreign exchange forward contracts to offset the impact of currency fluctuations on certain nonfunctional currency assets and liabilities, primarily denominated in Australian, Canadian, Japanese, Korean, and several European currencies, primarily the euro and British pound. We also periodically hedge anticipated transactions with purchased currency options.

The foreign exchange forward and option contracts we enter into generally have original maturities ranging from one to three months. We do not enter into foreign exchange forward and option contracts for trading purposes. We do not expect gains or losses on these contracts to have a material impact on our financial results (see Note 8 to the Consolidated Financial Statements).

CONSOLIDATED STATEMENTS OF OPERATIONS
(In millions, except per-share amounts)

Years Ended	July 29, 2000	July 31, 1999	July 25, 1998
NET SALES	$18,928	$12,173	$8,489
Cost of sales	6,746	4,259	2,924
GROSS MARGIN	12,182	7,914	5,565
Operating expenses:			
Research and development	2,704	1,663	1,052
Sales and marketing	3,946	2,465	1,579
General and administrative	633	381	247
Amortization of goodwill and purchased intangible assets	291	61	23
In-process research and development	1,373	471	594
Total operating expenses	8,947	5,041	3,495
OPERATING INCOME	3,235	2,873	2,070
Net gains realized on minority investments	531	–	5
Interest and other income, net	577	330	196
INCOME BEFORE PROVISION FOR INCOME TAXES	4,343	3,203	2,271
Provision for income taxes	1,675	1,180	940
NET INCOME	$ 2,668	$ 2,023	$1,331
Net income per common share—basic	$ 0.39	$ 0.30	$ 0.21
Net income per common share—diluted	$ 0.36	$ 0.29	$ 0.20
Shares used in per-common share calculation—basic	6,917	6,646	6,312
Shares used in per-common share calculation—diluted	7,438	7,062	6,658

See Notes to Consolidated Financial Statements.

CONSOLIDATED BALANCE SHEETS
(In millions, except par value)

	July 29, 2000	July 31, 1999
ASSETS		
Current assets:		
Cash and cash equivalents	$ 4,234	$ 913
Short-term investments	1,291	1,189
Accounts receivable, net of allowances for doubtful accounts of $43 at 2000 and $27 at 1999	2,299	1,250
Inventories, net	1,232	658
Deferred tax assets	1,091	580
Prepaid expenses and other current assets	963	171
Total current assets	11,110	4,761
Investments	13,688	7,032
Restricted investments	1,286	1,080
Property and equipment, net	1,426	825
Goodwill and purchased intangible assets, net	4,087	460
Lease receivables	527	500
Other assets	746	235
TOTAL ASSETS	$32,870	$14,893
LIABILITIES AND SHAREHOLDERS' EQUITY		
Current liabilities:		
Accounts payable	$ 739	$ 374
Income taxes payable	233	630
Accrued compensation	1,317	679
Deferred revenue	1,386	724
Other accrued liabilities	1,521	631
Total current liabilities	5,196	3,038
Commitments and contingencies (Note 8)		
Deferred tax liabilities	1,132	–
Minority interest	45	44
Shareholders' equity:		
Preferred stock, no par value: 5 shares authorized; none issued and outstanding	–	–
Common stock and additional paid-in capital, $0.001 par value: 20,000 shares authorized; 7,138 and 6,821 shares issued and outstanding at 2000 and 1999, respectively	14,609	5,731
Retained earnings	8,358	5,782
Accumulated other comprehensive income	3,530	298
Total shareholders' equity	26,497	11,811
TOTAL LIABILITIES AND SHAREHOLDERS' EQUITY	$32,870	$14,893

See Notes to Consolidated Financial Statements.

CONSOLIDATED STATEMENTS OF CASH FLOWS
(In millions)

Years Ended	July 29, 2000	July 31, 1999	July 25, 1998
Cash flows from operating activities:			
Net income	$ 2,668	$2,023	$1,331
Adjustments to reconcile net income to net cash provided by operating activities:			
Depreciation and amortization	863	489	329
Provision for doubtful accounts	40	19	43
Provision for inventory allowances	339	151	161
Deferred income taxes	(782)	(247)	(76)
Tax benefits from employee stock option plans	2,495	837	422
Adjustment to conform fiscal year ends of pooled acquisitions	(18)	1	–
In-process research and development	1,279	379	436
Gains on minority investments	(92)	–	–
Change in operating assets and liabilities:			
Accounts receivable	(1,043)	45	(166)
Inventories	(887)	(443)	(267)
Prepaid expenses and other current assets	(249)	(101)	21
Accounts payable	286	111	32
Income taxes payable	(365)	217	155
Accrued compensation	576	285	123
Deferred revenue	662	385	156
Other accrued liabilities	369	174	165
Net cash provided by operating activities	6,141	4,325	2,865
Cash flows from investing activities:			
Purchases of short-term investments	(2,473)	(1,250)	(1,611)
Proceeds from sales and maturities of short-term investments	2,481	1,660	1,751
Purchases of investments	(14,778)	(5,632)	(3,561)
Proceeds from sales and maturities of investments	13,240	1,994	1,107
Purchases of restricted investments	(458)	(1,101)	(527)
Proceeds from sales and maturities of restricted investments	206	560	337
Acquisition of property and equipment	(1,086)	(602)	(429)
Purchases of technology licenses	(444)	(95)	–
Acquisition of businesses, net of cash and cash equivalents	24	(19)	–
Net investment in lease receivables	(535)	(310)	(171)
Other	(554)	(190)	1
Net cash used in investing activities	(4,377)	(4,985)	(3,103)
Cash flows from financing activities:			
Issuance of common stock	1,564	947	555
Other	(7)	7	(7)
Net cash provided by financing activities	1,557	954	548
Net increase in cash and cash equivalents	3,321	294	310
Cash and cash equivalents, beginning of fiscal year	913	619	309
Cash and cash equivalents, end of fiscal year	$ 4,234	$ 913	$ 619

See Notes to Consolidated Financial Statements.

CONSOLIDATED STATEMENTS OF SHAREHOLDERS' EQUITY

(In millions)

	Common Stock Number of Shares	Common Stock and Additional Paid-In Capital	Retained Earnings	Accumulated Other Comprehensive Income	Total Shareholders' Equity
BALANCE AT JULY 26, 1997	6,163	$ 1,814	$2,478	$ 40	$ 4,332
Net income	–	–	1,331	–	1,331
Change in net unrealized gains on investments	–	–	–	28	28
Translation adjustments	–	–	–	(10)	(10)
Comprehensive income	–	–	–	–	1,349
Issuance of common stock	280	555	–	–	555
Tax benefits from employee stock option plans	–	422	–	–	422
Pooling of interests acquisitions	6	12	(9)	–	3
Purchase acquisitions	42	536	–	–	536
BALANCE AT JULY 25, 1998	6,491	3,339	3,800	58	7,197
Net income	–	–	2,023	–	2,023
Change in net unrealized gains on investments	–	–	–	234	234
Translation adjustments	–	–	–	6	6
Comprehensive income	–	–	–	–	2,263
Issuance of common stock	300	947	–	–	947
Tax benefits from employee stock option plans	–	837	–	–	837
Pooling of interests acquisitions	4	38	(42)	–	(4)
Purchase acquisitions	26	570	–	–	570
Adjustment to conform fiscal year ends of pooled acquisitions	–	–	1	–	1
BALANCE AT JULY 31, 1999	6,821	5,731	5,782	298	11,811
Net income	–	–	2,668	–	2,668
Change in net unrealized gains on investments	–	–	–	3,240	3,240
Translation adjustments	–	–	–	(8)	(8)
Comprehensive income	–	–	–	–	5,900
Issuance of common stock	219	1,564	–	–	1,564
Tax benefits from employee stock option plans	–	3,077	–	–	3,077
Pooling of interests acquisitions	20	75	(74)	–	1
Purchase acquisitions	78	4,162	–	–	4,162
Adjustment to conform fiscal year ends of pooled acquisitions	–	–	(18)	–	(18)
BALANCE AT JULY 29, 2000	**7,138**	**$14,609**	**$8,358**	**$3,530**	**$26,497**

See Notes to Consolidated Financial Statements.

NOTES TO CONSOLIDATED FINANCIAL STATEMENTS

1. DESCRIPTION OF BUSINESS

Cisco Systems, Inc. and its subsidiaries ("Cisco" or the "Company") is the worldwide leader in networking for the Internet. Cisco hardware, software, and service offerings are used to create Internet solutions so that individuals, companies, and countries have seamless access to information—regardless of differences in time and place. Cisco solutions provide competitive advantage to our customers through more efficient and timely exchange of information, which in turn leads to cost savings, process efficiencies, and closer relationships with their customers, prospects, business partners, suppliers, and employees. These solutions form the networking foundation for companies, universities, utilities, and government agencies worldwide.

2. SUMMARY OF SIGNIFICANT ACCOUNTING POLICIES

Fiscal Year The Company's fiscal year is the 52 or 53 weeks ending on the last Saturday in July. Fiscal 2000, 1999, and 1998 were 52-week, 53-week, and 52-week fiscal years, respectively.

Principles of Consolidation The Consolidated Financial Statements include the accounts of Cisco Systems, Inc. and its subsidiaries. All significant intercompany accounts and transactions have been eliminated.

Cash and Cash Equivalents The Company considers all highly liquid investments purchased with an original or remaining maturity of less than three months at the date of purchase to be cash equivalents. Substantially all cash and cash equivalents are custodied with three major financial institutions.

Investments The Company's investments comprise U.S., state, and municipal government obligations; corporate debt securities; and public corporate equity securities. Investments with maturities of less than one year are considered short-term and are carried at fair value. All investments are primarily held in the Company's name and custodied with two major financial institutions. The specific identification method is used to determine the cost of securities disposed. At July 29, 2000 and July 31, 1999, substantially all of the Company's investments were classified as available for sale. Unrealized gains and losses on these investments are included as a separate component of shareholders' equity, net of any related tax effect.

The Company also has certain other minority investments in nonpublicly traded companies. These investments are included in other assets on the Company's balance sheet and are generally carried at cost. The Company monitors these investments for impairment and makes appropriate reductions in carrying values when necessary.

Inventories Inventories are stated at the lower of cost or market. Cost is computed using standard cost, which approximates actual cost on a first-in, first-out basis.

Restricted Investments Restricted investments consist of U.S. government obligations with maturities of more than one year. These investments are carried at fair value and are restricted as to withdrawal. Restricted investments are held in the Company's name and custodied with two major financial institutions.

Fair Value of Financial Instruments Carrying amounts of certain of the Company's financial instruments, including cash and cash equivalents, accrued compensation, and other accrued liabilities, approximate fair value because of their short maturities. The fair values of investments are determined using quoted market prices for those securities or similar financial instruments.

Concentrations Cash and cash equivalents are primarily maintained with three major financial institutions in the United States. Deposits held with banks may exceed the amount of insurance provided on such deposits. Generally, these deposits may be redeemed upon demand and, therefore, bear minimal risk.

The Company performs ongoing credit evaluations of its customers and, with the exception of certain financing transactions, does not require collateral from its customers.

The Company receives certain of its components from sole suppliers. Additionally, the Company relies on a limited number of hardware manufacturers. The inability of any supplier or manufacturer to fulfill supply requirements of the Company could materially impact future operating results.

NOTES TO CONSOLIDATED FINANCIAL STATEMENTS

Revenue Recognition The Company generally recognizes product revenue when persuasive evidence of an arrangement exists, delivery has occurred, fee is fixed or determinable, and collectibility is probable. Revenue from service obligations is deferred and generally recognized ratably over the period of the obligation. The Company makes certain sales to partners in two-tier distribution channels. These partners are generally given privileges to return a portion of inventory and participate in various cooperative marketing programs. The Company recognizes revenue to two-tier distributors based on estimates which approximate the point products have been sold by the distributors and also maintains accruals and allowances for all cooperative marketing and other programs. The Company accrues for warranty costs, sales returns, and other allowances based on its experience.

Lease Receivables Cisco provides a variety of lease financing services to its customers to build, maintain, and upgrade their networks. Lease receivables represent the principal balance remaining in sales-type and direct-financing leases under these programs. These leases typically have two to three year terms and are collateralized by a security interest in the underlying assets.

Advertising Costs The Company expenses all advertising costs as incurred.

Software Development Costs Software development costs, which are required to be capitalized pursuant to Statement of Financial Accounting Standards No. 86, "Accounting for the Costs of Computer Software to Be Sold, Leased, or Otherwise Marketed," have not been material to date.

Depreciation and Amortization Property and equipment are stated at cost less accumulated depreciation and amortization. Depreciation and amortization is computed using the straight-line method over the estimated useful lives of the assets. Estimated useful lives of 24 to 30 months are used on computer equipment and related software and production and engineering equipment and five years for office equipment, furniture, and fixtures. Depreciation and amortization of leasehold improvements is computed using the shorter of the remaining lease term or five years.

Goodwill and Purchased Intangible Assets Goodwill and purchased intangible assets are carried at cost less accumulated amortization. Amortization is computed using the straight-line method over the economic lives of the respective assets, generally three to five years.

Income Taxes Income tax expense is based on pre-tax financial accounting income. Deferred tax assets and liabilities are recognized for the expected tax consequences of temporary differences between the tax bases of assets and liabilities and their reported amounts.

Computation of Net Income per Common Share Basic net income per common share is computed using the weighted-average number of common shares outstanding during the period. Diluted net income per common share is computed using the weighted-average number of common and dilutive common equivalent shares outstanding during the period. Dilutive common equivalent shares consist of stock options. Share and per-common share data for all periods presented reflect the two-for-one stock split effective March 2000.

Foreign Currency Translation Assets and liabilities of non-U.S. subsidiaries that operate in a local currency environment are translated to U.S. dollars at exchange rates in effect at the balance sheet date with the resulting translation adjustments recorded directly to a separate component of shareholders' equity. Income and expense accounts are translated at average exchange rates during the year. Where the U.S. dollar is the functional currency, translation adjustments are recorded in income.

Derivatives The Company enters into foreign exchange forward contracts to minimize the short-term impact of foreign currency fluctuations on assets and liabilities denominated in currencies other than the functional currency of the reporting entity. All foreign exchange forward contracts are highly inversely correlated to the hedged items and are designated as, and considered effective as, hedges of the underlying assets or liabilities. Gains and losses on the contracts are included in interest and other income, net, and offset foreign exchange gains or losses from the revaluation of intercompany balances or other current assets and liabilities denominated in currencies other than the functional currency of the reporting entity. Fair values of foreign exchange forward contracts are determined using published rates. If a derivative contract terminates prior to maturity, the investment is shown at its fair value with the resulting gain or loss reflected in interest and other income, net. The Company periodically hedges anticipated transactions with purchased currency options. The premium paid is amortized over the life of the option while any intrinsic value is recognized in income during the same period as the hedged transaction.

Minority Interest Minority interest represents the preferred stockholders' proportionate share of the equity of Cisco Systems, K.K. (Japan). At July 29, 2000, the Company owned all issued and outstanding common stock amounting to 73.2% of the voting rights. Each share of preferred stock is convertible into one share of common stock at any time at the option of the holder.

<u>Use of Estimates</u> The preparation of financial statements and related disclosures in conformity with accounting principles generally accepted in the United States requires management to make estimates and assumptions that affect the amounts reported in the Consolidated Financial Statements and accompanying notes. Estimates are used for, but not limited to, the accounting for the allowance for doubtful accounts, inventory allowances, depreciation and amortization, sales returns, warranty costs, taxes, and contingencies. Actual results could differ from these estimates.

<u>Impairment of Long-Lived Assets</u> Long-lived assets and certain identifiable intangible assets to be held and used are reviewed for impairment whenever events or changes in circumstances indicate that the carrying amount of such assets may not be recoverable. Determination of recoverability is based on an estimate of undiscounted future cash flows resulting from the use of the asset and its eventual disposition. Measurement of an impairment loss for long-lived assets and certain identifiable intangible assets that management expects to hold and use are based on the fair value of the asset. Long-lived assets and certain identifiable intangible assets to be disposed of are reported at the lower of carrying amount or fair value less costs to sell.

<u>Recent Accounting Pronouncements</u> In June 1998, the Financial Accounting Standards Board ("FASB") issued Statement of Financial Accounting Standards No. 133, "Accounting for Derivative Instruments and Hedging Activities" ("SFAS 133"). SFAS 133, as amended, establishes accounting and reporting standards for derivative instruments and hedging activities. It requires an entity to recognize all derivatives as either assets or liabilities on the balance sheet and measure those instruments at fair value. Management does not expect the initial adoption of SFAS 133 to have a material effect on the Company's operations or financial position. The Company is required to adopt SFAS 133 in the first quarter of fiscal 2001.

In September 1999, the FASB issued Emerging Issues Task Force Topic No. D-83, "Accounting for Payroll Taxes Associated with Stock Option Exercises" ("EITF D-83"). EITF D-83 requires that payroll tax paid on the difference between the exercise price and the fair value of acquired stock in association with an employee's exercise of stock options be recorded as operating expenses. Payroll tax on stock option exercises of $51 million was expensed in fiscal 2000.

In December 1999, the Securities and Exchange Commission ("SEC") issued Staff Accounting Bulletin No. 101, "Revenue Recognition in Financial Statements" ("SAB 101"). SAB 101, as amended, summarizes certain of the SEC's views in applying generally accepted accounting principles to revenue recognition in financial statements. At this time, management does not expect the adoption of SAB 101 to have a material effect on the Company's operations or financial position; however, the SEC's final guidance for implementation has not been released to date. The Company is required to adopt SAB 101 in the fourth quarter of fiscal 2001.

<u>Reclassifications</u> Certain reclassifications have been made to prior year balances in order to conform to the current year presentation.

3. BUSINESS COMBINATIONS

Pooling of Interests Combinations

In fiscal 2000, the Company acquired StratumOne Communications, Inc. ("StratumOne"); TransMedia Communications, Inc. ("TransMedia"); Cerent Corporation ("Cerent"); WebLine Communications Corporation ("WebLine"); SightPath, Inc. ("SightPath"); InfoGear Technology Corporation ("InfoGear"); and ArrowPoint Communications, Inc. ("ArrowPoint"), which were accounted for as poolings of interests. All historical financial information has been restated to reflect these acquisitions. In addition, the historical financial information has been restated to reflect the acquisition of Fibex Systems ("Fibex"), which was completed in the fourth quarter of fiscal 1999 and accounted for as a pooling of interests. These transactions are summarized as follows (in millions):

Acquisition Date	Acquired Company	Shares of Cisco Stock Issued, Including Options Assumed	Fair Value of Acquisition
May 1999	Fibex	11.5	$ 314
September 1999	StratumOne	13.3	$ 435
September 1999	TransMedia	13.9	$ 407
November 1999	Cerent	200.0	$6,900
November 1999	WebLine	8.6	$ 325
May 2000	SightPath	11.4	$ 800
June 2000	InfoGear	4.7	$ 301
June 2000	ArrowPoint	90.2	$5,700

NOTES TO CONSOLIDATED FINANCIAL STATEMENTS

All of these acquired companies used a calendar year end. In order for all companies to operate on the same fiscal year, operations for the one-month period ending July 31, 1999, which were not significant to the Company, have been reflected as an adjustment to retained earnings in fiscal 2000. No significant adjustments were necessary to conform accounting policies. However, the companies' historical results have been adjusted to reflect the elimination of previously provided valuation allowances on deferred tax assets. There were no intercompany transactions requiring elimination in any period presented. The following table shows the historical results for the periods prior to the mergers of these entities (in millions):

	Nine Months Ended April 29, 2000	Years Ended July 31, 1999	July 25, 1998
Net sales:			
Cisco	**$13,147**	$12,154	$8,488
Fibex	–	3	–
StratumOne	–	–	–
TransMedia	–	–	–
Cerent	35	10	–
WebLine	1	3	1
SightPath	–	–	–
InfoGear	–	–	–
ArrowPoint	25	3	–
Total	**$13,208**	$12,173	$8,489
Net income (loss):			
Cisco	**$ 1,932**	$ 2,096	$1,355
Fibex	–	(13)	(3)
StratumOne	**(3)**	(6)	(1)
TransMedia	**(4)**	(7)	–
Cerent	**(15)**	(31)	(9)
WebLine	**(3)**	(4)	(2)
SightPath	**(8)**	(2)	–
InfoGear	**(15)**	(5)	(5)
ArrowPoint	**(12)**	(5)	(4)
Total	**$ 1,872**	$ 2,023	$1,331

In fiscal 1999, the Company acquired GeoTel Communications Corporation and approximately 68 million shares of common stock were exchanged and options were assumed for a fair value of $2 billion. The transaction was accounted for as a pooling of interests and all periods presented prior to fiscal 1999 were restated.

Other Pooling of Interests Combinations Completed as of July 29, 2000

The Company has also completed a number of other pooling transactions during the three years ended July 29, 2000. The historical operations of these entities were not material to the Company's consolidated operations on either an individual or aggregate basis; therefore, prior period financial statements have not been restated for these acquisitions. These transactions are summarized as follows (in millions):

Fiscal Year	Acquired Company	Shares of Cisco Stock Issued, Including Options Assumed	Fair Value of Acquisition
1998	Precept Software, Inc.	6.0	$ 84
1999	Sentient Networks, Inc.	4.0	$131
2000	Cocom A/S	1.9	$ 66
2000	V-Bits, Inc.	2.8	$128
2000	Growth Networks, Inc.	5.6	$355
2000	Altiga Networks, Inc.	6.3	$335
2000	Compatible Systems Corporation	3.8	$232

Purchase Combinations

During the three years ended July 29, 2000, the Company completed a number of purchase acquisitions. The Consolidated Financial Statements include the operating results of each business from the date of acquisition. Pro forma results of operations have not been presented because the effects of these acquisitions were not material on either an individual or an aggregate basis.

The amounts allocated to in-process research and development ("in-process R&D") were determined through established valuation techniques in the high-technology communications equipment industry and were expensed upon acquisition because technological feasibility had not been established and no future alternative uses existed. Amounts allocated to goodwill and purchased intangible assets are amortized on a straight-line basis over periods not exceeding five years. A summary of purchase transactions is outlined as follows (in millions):

Acquired Company	Consideration	In-Process R&D Expense	Form of Consideration and Other Notes to Acquisition
FISCAL 2000			
Monterey Networks, Inc.	$ 517	$354	Common stock and options assumed; $14 in liabilities assumed; goodwill and other intangibles recorded of $154
The optical systems business of Pirelli S.p.A.	$2,018	$245	Common stock; $362 in liabilities assumed; goodwill and other intangibles recorded of $1,717
Aironet Wireless Communications, Inc.	$ 835	$243	Common stock and options assumed; $34 in liabilities assumed; goodwill and other intangibles recorded of $589
Atlantech Technologies	$ 179	$ 63	Cash of $92; common stock and options assumed; $1 in liabilities assumed; goodwill and other intangibles recorded of $140
JetCell, Inc.	$ 203	$ 88	Cash of $5; common stock and options assumed; $2 in liabilities assumed; goodwill and other intangibles recorded of $137
PentaCom, Ltd.	$ 102	$ 49	Cash of $26; common stock and options assumed; goodwill and other intangibles recorded of $40
Qeyton Systems	$ 887	$260	Common stock; goodwill and other intangibles recorded of $567
Other	$ 228	$ 71	Cash of $31; common stock and options assumed; $5 in liabilities assumed; goodwill and other intangibles recorded of $155
FISCAL 1999			
Summa Four, Inc.	$ 129	$ 64	Common stock and options assumed; $16 in liabilities assumed; goodwill and other intangibles recorded of $29
Clarity Wireless, Inc.	$ 153	$ 94	Common stock and options assumed; goodwill and other intangibles recorded of $73
Selsius Systems, Inc.	$ 134	$ 92	Cash of $111; options assumed; goodwill and other intangibles recorded of $41
PipeLinks, Inc.	$ 118	$ 99	Common stock and options assumed; goodwill and other intangibles recorded of $11
Amteva Technologies, Inc.	$ 159	$ 81	Common stock and options assumed; $9 in liabilities assumed; goodwill and other intangibles recorded of $85
Other	$ 58	$ 41	Common stock and options assumed; goodwill and other intangibles recorded of $18
FISCAL 1998			
Dagaz Technologies, Inc.	$ 130	$127	Cash of $108; $18 in common stock; liabilities assumed of $4
LightSpeed International, Inc.	$ 161	$143	Common stock and options assumed; other intangibles recorded of $15
WheelGroup Corporation	$ 124	$ 97	Common stock and options assumed; goodwill and other intangibles recorded of $38
NetSpeed International, Inc.	$ 252	$179	Cash of $12; common stock and options assumed; liabilities assumed of $18; goodwill and other intangibles recorded of $76
Other	$ 51	$ 48	Cash of $38 and options assumed

NOTES TO CONSOLIDATED FINANCIAL STATEMENTS

Other Purchase Combinations Completed as of July 29, 2000

In fiscal 2000, the Company acquired Maxcomm Technologies, Inc.; Calista, Inc.; Tasmania Network Systems, Inc.; Internet Engineering Group, LLC; Worldwide Data Systems, Inc.; and Seagull Networks, Ltd. for a total purchase price of $228 million, paid in common stock and cash. Total in-process R&D related to these acquisitions amounted to $71 million.

Total in-process R&D expense in fiscal 2000, 1999, and 1998 was $1.37 billion, $471 million, and $594 million, respectively. The in-process R&D expense that was attributable to stock consideration for the same periods was $1.28 billion, $379 million, and $436 million, respectively.

4. BALANCE SHEET DETAIL

The following tables provide details of selected balance sheet items (in millions):

	July 29, 2000	July 31, 1999
INVENTORIES, NET:		
Raw materials	$ 145	$ 143
Work in process	472	198
Finished goods	496	282
Demonstration systems	119	35
Total	$1,232	$ 658
PROPERTY AND EQUIPMENT, NET:		
Leasehold improvements	$ 607	$ 289
Computer equipment and related software	908	639
Production and engineering equipment	407	238
Office equipment, furniture, and fixtures	1,083	685
	3,005	1,851
Less, accumulated depreciation and amortization	(1,579)	(1,026)
Total	$1,426	$ 825
GOODWILL AND PURCHASED INTANGIBLE ASSETS, NET:		
Goodwill	$2,937	$ 157
Purchased intangible assets	1,558	395
	4,495	552
Less, accumulated amortization	(408)	(92)
Total	$4,087	$ 460

The following table presents the details of the amortization of goodwill and purchased intangible assets as reported in the Consolidated Statements of Operations:

Years Ended	July 29, 2000	July 31, 1999	July 25, 1998
Reported as:			
Cost of sales	$ 25	$ 1	$ –
Operating expenses	291	61	23
Total	$ 316	$62	$23

5. LEASE RECEIVABLES

Lease receivables represent sales-type and direct-financing leases resulting from the sale of the Company's and complementary third-party products and services. These lease arrangements typically have terms from two to three years and are usually collateralized by a security interest in the underlying assets. The net lease receivables are summarized as follows (in millions):

	July 29, 2000	July 31, 1999
Gross lease receivables	$1,310	$663
Unearned income and other reserves	(195)	(83)
Total	1,115	580
Less, current portion	(588)	(80)
Long-term lease receivables, net	$ 527	$500

Contractual maturities of the gross lease receivables at July 29, 2000 were $588 million in fiscal 2001, $354 million in fiscal 2002, $337 million in fiscal 2003, $29 million in fiscal 2004, and $2 million in fiscal 2005. Actual cash collections may differ from the contractual maturities due to early customer buyouts or refinancings. The current portion of lease receivables is included in prepaid expenses and other current assets.

6. INVESTMENTS

The following tables summarize the Company's investments in securities (in millions):

JULY 29, 2000	Amortized Cost	Gross Unrealized Gains	Gross Unrealized Losses	Fair Value
U.S. government notes and bonds	$ 2,317	$ –	$ (32)	$ 2,285
State, municipal, and county government notes and bonds	3,592	13	(41)	3,564
Corporate notes and bonds	3,222	1	(19)	3,204
Corporate equity securities	641	5,621	(37)	6,225
Mandatorily redeemable convertible preferred stock	987	–	–	987
Total	$10,759	$5,635	$(129)	$16,265
Reported as:				
Short-term investments				$ 1,291
Investments				13,688
Restricted investments				1,286
Total				$16,265

JULY 31, 1999	Amortized Cost	Gross Unrealized Gains	Gross Unrealized Losses	Fair Value
U.S. government notes and bonds	$ 2,187	$ –	$ (29)	$ 2,158
State, municipal, and county government notes and bonds	5,177	5	(44)	5,138
Corporate notes and bonds	1,145	–	(17)	1,128
Corporate equity securities	288	615	(26)	877
Total	$ 8,797	$ 620	$(116)	$ 9,301
Reported as:				
Short-term investments				$ 1,189
Investments				7,032
Restricted investments				1,080
Total				$ 9,301

NOTES TO CONSOLIDATED FINANCIAL STATEMENTS

Net gains realized on minority investments were $531 million in fiscal 2000. The net gains realized on minority investments that were attributable to noncash activity were $92 million in fiscal 2000. The net gains realized on minority investments were not material in fiscal 1999 and were $5 million in fiscal 1998.

The following table summarizes debt investment and mandatorily redeemable convertible preferred stock maturities (including restricted investments) at July 29, 2000 (in millions):

	Amortized Cost	Fair Value
Less than one year	$ 1,753	$ 1,744
Due in 1–2 years	1,930	1,922
Due in 2–5 years	4,218	4,161
Due after 5 years	2,217	2,213
Total	$10,118	$10,040

7. LINE OF CREDIT

At July 29, 2000, the Company had a syndicated credit agreement under the terms of which a group of banks committed a maximum of $500 million on an unsecured, revolving basis for borrowings of various maturities. The commitments made under this agreement expire on July 1, 2002. Under the terms of the agreement, borrowings bear interest at a spread over the London Interbank Offered Rate based on certain financial criteria and third-party rating assessments. As of July 29, 2000, this spread was 17.5 basis points. From this spread, a commitment fee of 5.5 basis points is assessed against any undrawn amounts. The agreement includes a single financial covenant that places a variable floor on tangible net worth, as defined, if certain leverage ratios are exceeded. There have been no borrowings under this agreement to date.

8. COMMITMENTS AND CONTINGENCIES

Leases

The Company has entered into several agreements to lease 448 acres of land located in San Jose, California, where it has established its headquarters operations, and 759 acres of land located in Boxborough, Massachusetts; Salem, New Hampshire; Richardson, Texas; and Research Triangle Park, North Carolina, where it has expanded certain research and development and customer-support activities.

All of the leases have initial terms of five to seven years and options to renew for an additional three to five years, subject to certain conditions. At any time during the terms of these leases, the Company may purchase the land. If the Company elects not to purchase the land at the end of each of the leases, the Company has guaranteed a residual value of $624 million.

The Company has also entered into agreements to lease certain buildings standing or to be constructed on the land described above. The lessors of the buildings have committed to fund up to a maximum of $1.40 billion (subject to reductions based on certain conditions in the respective leases) for the construction of the buildings, with the portion of the committed amount actually used to be determined by the Company. Rent obligations for the buildings commenced on various dates and will expire at the same time as the land leases.

The Company has options to renew the building leases for an additional three to five years, subject to certain conditions. The Company may, at its option, purchase the buildings during or at the end of the terms of the leases at approximately the amount expended by the lessors to construct the buildings. If the Company does not exercise the purchase options by the end of the leases, the Company will guarantee a residual value of the buildings as determined at the lease inception date of each agreement (approximately $748 million at July 29, 2000).

As part of the above lease transactions, the Company restricted $1.29 billion of its investment securities as collateral for specified obligations of the lessors under the leases. These investment securities are restricted as to withdrawal and are managed by a third party subject to certain limitations under the Company's investment policy. In addition, the Company must maintain a minimum consolidated tangible net worth, as defined.

The Company also leases office space in Santa Clara, California; Chelmsford, Massachusetts; and for its various U.S. and international sales offices.

Future annual minimum lease payments under all noncancelable operating leases as of July 29, 2000 are as follows (in millions):

Fiscal Year	
2001	$ 302
2002	299
2003	310
2004	251
2005	237
Thereafter	1,506
Total	$2,905

Rent expense totaled $229 million, $123 million, and $90 million for fiscal 2000, 1999, and 1998, respectively.

Foreign Exchange Forward and Option Contracts

The Company conducts business on a global basis in several major currencies. As such, it is exposed to adverse movements in foreign currency exchange rates. The Company enters into foreign exchange forward contracts to reduce the impact of certain currency exposures. These contracts hedge exposures associated with nonfunctional currency assets and liabilities denominated in Australian, Canadian, Japanese, Korean, and several European currencies, primarily the euro and British pound.

The Company does not enter into foreign exchange forward contracts for trading purposes. Gains and losses on the contracts are included in interest and other income, net, and offset foreign exchange gains or losses from the revaluation of intercompany balances or other current assets and liabilities denominated in currencies other than the functional currency of the reporting entity. The Company's foreign exchange forward contracts generally range from one to three months in original maturity.

The Company periodically hedges anticipated transactions with purchased currency options. A purchased currency option's premium is amortized over the life of the option while any intrinsic value is recognized in income during the same period as the hedged transaction. The deferred premium and intrinsic value from hedging anticipated transactions were not material at July 29, 2000. In the unlikely event that the underlying transaction terminates or becomes improbable, the remaining premium or deferred intrinsic value will be recorded in the Consolidated Statements of Operations. The Company does not purchase currency options for trading purposes. Foreign exchange forward and option contracts as of July 29, 2000 are summarized as follows (in millions):

	Notional Amount	Carrying Value	Fair Value
Forward contracts:			
Assets	$1,377	$ (5)	$(15)
Liabilities	$1,500	$12	$ 37
Option contracts:			
Assets	$ 561	$12	$ 14

The Company's foreign exchange forward and option contracts contain credit risk to the extent that its bank counterparties may be unable to meet the terms of the agreements. The Company minimizes such risk by limiting its counterparties to major financial institutions. In addition, the potential risk of loss with any one party resulting from this type of credit risk is monitored. Management does not expect any material losses as a result of default by other parties.

Legal Proceedings

The Company is subject to legal proceedings, claims, and litigation arising in the ordinary course of business. While the outcome of these matters is currently not determinable, management does not expect that the ultimate costs to resolve these matters will have a material adverse effect on the Company's consolidated financial position, results of operations, or cash flows.

NOTES TO CONSOLIDATED FINANCIAL STATEMENTS

9. SHAREHOLDERS' EQUITY

Authorized Shares

On November 10, 1999, the shareholders of the Company approved an increase to the authorized number of shares of common stock from 5.40 billion to 10 billion shares. On March 20, 2000, the Board of Directors of the Company approved an increase to the authorized number of shares of common stock from 10 billion to 20 billion shares relating to the two-for-one stock split distributed on March 22, 2000.

Stock Split

The Board of Directors authorized the splitting of the Company's common stock on a two-for-one basis for shareholders of record on February 22, 2000 and the resulting shares from the split were distributed on March 22, 2000. All references to share and per-share data for all periods presented have been adjusted to give effect to this two-for-one stock split.

Shareholders' Rights Plan

In June 1998, the Board of Directors approved a Shareholders' Rights Plan ("Rights Plan"). The Rights Plan is intended to protect shareholders' rights in the event of an unsolicited takeover attempt. It is not intended to prevent a takeover of the Company on terms that are favorable and fair to all shareholders and will not interfere with a merger approved by the Board of Directors. Each right entitles shareholders to buy a unit equal to a portion of a new share of Series A Preferred Stock of the Company. The rights will be exercisable only if a person or a group acquires or announces a tender or exchange offer to acquire 15% or more of the Company's common stock.

In the event the rights become exercisable, the Rights Plan allows for Cisco shareholders to acquire, at an exercise price of $108 per right owned, stock of the surviving corporation having a market value of $217, whether or not Cisco is the surviving corporation. The rights, which expire in June 2008, are redeemable for $0.00017 per right at the approval of the Board of Directors.

Preferred Stock

Under the terms of the Company's Articles of Incorporation, the Board of Directors may determine the rights, preferences, and terms of the Company's authorized but unissued shares of preferred stock.

Comprehensive Income

The components of comprehensive income, net of tax, are as follows (in millions):

Years Ended	July 29, 2000	July 31, 1999	July 25, 1998
Net income	$2,668	$2,023	$1,331
Other comprehensive income (loss):			
Change in net unrealized gains on investments, net of tax of $1,762, $144, and $17 in fiscal 2000, 1999, and 1998, respectively	3,240	234	25
Reclassification for net unrealized gains previously included in net income, net of tax of $2 in fiscal 1998	–	–	3
Net unrealized gains	3,240	234	28
Change in accumulated translation adjustments	(8)	6	(10)
Total	$5,900	$2,263	$1,349

10. EMPLOYEE BENEFIT PLANS

Employee Stock Purchase Plan

The Company has an Employee Stock Purchase Plan (the "Purchase Plan") under which 222 million shares of common stock have been reserved for issuance. Eligible employees may purchase a limited number of shares of the Company's common stock at 85% of the market value at certain plan-defined dates. The Purchase Plan terminates on January 3, 2005. In fiscal 2000, 1999, and 1998, seven million, 10 million, and 14 million shares, respectively, were issued under the Purchase Plan. At July 29, 2000, 123 million shares were available for issuance under the Purchase Plan.

Employee Stock Option Plans

The Company has two main stock option plans: the 1987 Stock Option Plan (the "Predecessor Plan") and the 1996 Stock Incentive Plan (the "1996 Plan"). The Predecessor Plan was terminated in 1996. All outstanding options under the Predecessor Plan were transferred to the 1996 Plan. However, all outstanding options under the Predecessor Plan continue to be governed by the terms and conditions of the existing option agreements for those grants.

The maximum number of shares under the 1996 Plan was initially limited to the 620 million shares transferred from the Predecessor Plan. However, under the terms of the 1996 Plan, the share reserve increased each December for the three fiscal years beginning with fiscal 1997, by an amount equal to 4.75% of the outstanding shares on the last trading day of the immediately preceding November. In fiscal 1999, the Company's shareholders approved the extension of the automatic share increase provision of the 1996 Plan for an additional three-year period.

Although the Board of Directors has the authority to set other terms, the options are generally 20% or 25% exercisable one year from the date of grant and then ratably over the following 48 or 36 months, respectively. Options issued under the Predecessor Plan generally had terms of four years. New options granted under the 1996 Plan expire no later than nine years from the grant date. A summary of option activity follows (in millions, except per-share amounts):

	Options Available for Grant	Options Outstanding Options	Options Outstanding Weighted-Average Exercise Price per Share
BALANCE AT JULY 26, 1997	96	810	$ 4.05
Granted and assumed	(282)	282	10.00
Exercised	–	(168)	2.40
Canceled	48	(48)	4.59
Additional shares reserved	314	–	–
BALANCE AT JULY 25, 1998	176	876	6.25
Granted and assumed	(245)	245	22.22
Exercised	–	(210)	3.09
Canceled	22	(22)	10.85
Additional shares reserved	359	–	–
BALANCE AT JULY 31, 1999	312	889	11.22
Granted and assumed	(295)	295	52.10
Exercised	–	(176)	5.75
Canceled	37	(37)	22.70
Additional shares reserved	339	–	–
BALANCE AT JULY 29, 2000	**393**	**971**	**$24.19**

The Company has, in connection with the acquisitions of various companies, assumed the stock option plans of each acquired company. During fiscal 2000, a total of approximately 31 million shares of the Company's common stock have been reserved for issuance under the assumed plans and the related options are included in the preceding table.

In 1997, the Company adopted a Supplemental Stock Incentive Plan (the "Supplemental Plan") under which options can be granted or shares can be directly issued to eligible employees. Officers and members of the Company's Board of Directors are not eligible to participate in the Supplemental Plan. Nine million shares have been reserved for issuance under the Supplemental Plan, of which 9,000 shares are subject to outstanding options and 66,600 shares have been issued in fiscal 2000.

NOTES TO CONSOLIDATED FINANCIAL STATEMENTS

The following table summarizes information concerning outstanding and exercisable options at July 29, 2000 (in millions, except number of years and per-share amounts):

Range of Exercise Prices	Options Outstanding			Options Exercisable	
	Number Outstanding	Weighted-Average Remaining Contractual Life (in Years)	Weighted-Average Exercise Price per Share	Number Exercisable	Weighted-Average Exercise Price per Share
$ 0.01– 5.56	229	5.20	$ 5.23	188	$ 4.44
5.57–12.27	258	6.16	9.56	162	8.95
12.28–28.61	194	7.49	23.59	63	22.47
28.62–54.53	241	8.34	49.91	5	31.02
54.54–72.56	49	8.64	65.65	–	–
Total	971	6.87	$24.19	418	$ 9.22

At July 31, 1999 and July 25, 1998, approximately 370 million and 312 million outstanding options, respectively, were exercisable. The weighted-average exercise prices for outstanding options were $5.75 and $3.64 at July 31, 1999 and July 25, 1998, respectively.

The Company is required under Statement of Financial Accounting Standards No. 123, "Accounting for Stock-Based Compensation" ("SFAS 123"), to disclose pro forma information regarding option grants made to its employees based on specified valuation techniques that produce estimated compensation charges. These amounts have not been reflected in the Company's Consolidated Statements of Operations because no compensation charge arises when the price of the employees' stock options equals the market value of the underlying stock at the grant date, as in the case of options granted to the Company's employees. Pro forma information under SFAS 123 is as follows (in millions, except per-share amounts):

Years Ended	July 29, 2000	July 31, 1999	July 25, 1998
Net income—as reported	$2,668	$2,023	$1,331
Net income—pro forma	$1,549	$1,487	$1,074
Basic net income per common share—as reported	$ 0.39	$ 0.30	$ 0.21
Diluted net income per common share—as reported	$ 0.36	$ 0.29	$ 0.20
Basic net income per common share—pro forma	$ 0.22	$ 0.22	$ 0.17
Diluted net income per common share—pro forma	$ 0.21	$ 0.21	$ 0.16

The fair value of each option grant is estimated on the date of grant using the Black-Scholes option pricing model with the following weighted-average assumptions:

	Employee Stock Option Plans			Employee Stock Purchase Plan		
	July 29, 2000	July 31, 1999	July 25,1998	July 29, 2000	July 31, 1999	July 25,1998
Expected dividend yield	0.0%	0.0%	0.0%	0.0%	0.0%	0.0%
Risk-free interest rate	6.4%	5.1%	5.7%	5.3%	4.9%	5.4%
Expected volatility	33.9%	40.2%	35.6%	43.3%	47.2%	44.8%
Expected life (in years)	3.1	3.1	3.1	0.5	0.5	0.5

The Black-Scholes option pricing model was developed for use in estimating the fair value of traded options that have no vesting restrictions and are fully transferable. In addition, option pricing models require the input of highly subjective assumptions including the expected stock price volatility. The Company uses projected volatility rates which are based upon historical volatility rates trended into future years. Because the Company's employee stock options have characteristics significantly different from those of traded options, and because changes in the subjective input assumptions can materially affect the fair value estimate, in management's opinion, the existing models do not necessarily provide a reliable single measure of the fair value of the Company's options. The weighted-average estimated fair values of employee stock options granted during fiscal 2000, 1999, and 1998 were $19.44, $8.40, and $3.57 per share, respectively.

The above pro forma disclosures under SFAS 123 are also not likely to be representative of the effects on net income and net income per common share in future years, because they do not take into consideration pro forma compensation expense related to grants made prior to fiscal 1996.

Employee 401(k) Plans

The Company sponsors the Cisco Systems, Inc. 401(k) Plan (the "Plan") to provide retirement benefits for its employees. As allowed under Section 401(k) of the Internal Revenue Code, the Plan provides tax-deferred salary deductions for eligible employees. The Company also has other 401(k) plans that it sponsors. These plans arose from acquisitions of other companies and are not material to the Company on either an individual or aggregate basis.

Employees may contribute from 1% to 15% of their annual compensation to the Plan, limited to a maximum annual amount as set periodically by the Internal Revenue Service. The Company matches employee contributions dollar for dollar up to a maximum of $1,500 per year per person. All matching contributions vest immediately. In addition, the Plan provides for discretionary contributions as determined by the Board of Directors. Such contributions to the Plan are allocated among eligible participants in the proportion of their salaries to the total salaries of all participants. The Company's matching contributions to the Plan totaled $34 million, $20 million, and $15 million in fiscal 2000, 1999, and 1998, respectively. No discretionary contributions were made in fiscal 2000, 1999, or 1998.

11. INCOME TAXES

The provision for (benefit from) income taxes consisted of (in millions):

Years Ended	July 29, 2000	July 31, 1999	July 25, 1998
Federal:			
Current	**$1,843**	$1,164	$855
Deferred	**(652)**	(221)	(54)
	1,191	943	801
State:			
Current	**282**	112	87
Deferred	**(118)**	(24)	(8)
	164	88	79
Foreign:			
Current	**332**	151	74
Deferred	**(12)**	(2)	(14)
	320	149	60
Total provision for income taxes	**$1,675**	$1,180	$940

NOTES TO CONSOLIDATED FINANCIAL STATEMENTS

The Company paid income taxes of $327 million, $301 million, and $440 million in fiscal 2000, 1999, and 1998, respectively. Income before provision for income taxes consisted of (in millions):

Years Ended	July 29, 2000	July 31, 1999	July 25, 1998
United States	$2,544	$2,092	$1,950
International	1,799	1,111	321
	$4,343	$3,203	$2,271

The items accounting for the difference between income taxes computed at the federal statutory rate and the provision for income taxes consisted of:

Years Ended	July 29, 2000	July 31, 1999	July 25, 1998
Federal statutory rate	35.0%	35.0%	35.0%
Effect of:			
State taxes, net of federal tax benefit	1.9	2.2	2.2
Foreign sales corporation	(1.9)	(1.6)	(2.4)
Foreign income at other than U.S. rates	(1.6)	(1.0)	–
Nondeductible in-process R&D	8.1	3.9	6.4
Tax-exempt interest	(1.8)	(1.9)	(1.6)
Tax credits	(1.6)	(1.2)	(1.4)
Other, net	0.5	1.5	3.2
Total	38.6%	36.9%	41.4%

U.S. income taxes and foreign withholding taxes were not provided for on a cumulative total of approximately $411 million of undistributed earnings for certain non-U.S. subsidiaries. The Company intends to reinvest these earnings indefinitely in operations outside the United States. The components of the deferred tax assets (liabilities) follow (in millions):

	July 29, 2000	July 31, 1999
ASSETS		
Allowance for doubtful accounts and returns	$ 418	$ 185
In-process R&D	265	163
Inventory allowances and capitalization	94	57
Accrued state franchise tax	–	32
Depreciation	41	28
Deferred revenue	177	65
Credits and net operating loss carryforwards	1,023	–
Other	451	256
Gross deferred tax assets	2,469	786
Valuation allowance	(299)	–
Total deferred tax assets	2,170	786
LIABILITIES		
Purchased intangible assets	(257)	(88)
Unrealized gain on investments	(1,954)	(192)
Total deferred tax liabilities	(2,211)	(280)
Total	$ (41)	$ 506

The noncurrent portion of the deferred tax liabilities, which totaled $74 million at July 31, 1999, is included in other assets.

The Company has provided a valuation allowance on certain of its deferred tax assets because of uncertainty regarding their realizability due to expectation of future employee stock option exercises. Deferred tax assets of approximately $963 million at July 29, 2000 pertain to certain tax credits and net operating loss carryforwards resulting from the exercise of employee stock options. When recognized, the tax benefit of these credits and losses will be accounted for as a credit to shareholders' equity rather than as a reduction of the income tax provision.

As of July 29, 2000, the Company's federal and state net operating loss carryforwards for income tax purposes were approximately $496 million and $865 million, respectively. If not utilized, the federal net operating loss carryforwards will begin to expire in fiscal 2020, and the state net operating loss carryforwards will begin to expire in fiscal 2005. As of July 29, 2000, the Company's federal and state tax credit carryforwards for income tax purposes were approximately $678 million and $197 million, respectively. If not utilized, the federal and state tax credit carryforwards will begin to expire in fiscal 2005.

The Company's income taxes payable for federal, state, and foreign purposes have been reduced, and the deferred tax assets increased, by the tax benefits associated with dispositions of employee stock options. The Company receives an income tax benefit calculated as the difference between the fair market value of the stock issued at the time of exercise and the option price, tax effected. These benefits were credited directly to shareholders' equity and amounted to $3.08 billion, $837 million, and $422 million for fiscal 2000, 1999, and 1998, respectively. Benefits reducing taxes payable amounted to $2.49 billion, $837 million, and $422 million for fiscal 2000, 1999, and 1998, respectively. Benefits increasing gross deferred tax assets amounted to $582 million in fiscal 2000.

12. SEGMENT INFORMATION AND MAJOR CUSTOMERS

The Company's operations involve the design, development, manufacture, marketing, and technical support of networking products and services. The Company offers end-to-end networking solutions for its customers. Cisco products include routers, LAN and ATM switches, dial-up access servers, and network-management software. These products, integrated by the Cisco IOS® software, link geographically dispersed LANs, WANs, and IBM networks.

The Company conducts business globally and is managed geographically. The Company's management relies on an internal management system that provides sales and standard cost information by geographic theater. Sales are attributed to a theater based on the ordering location of the customer. The Company's management makes financial decisions and allocates resources based on the information it receives from this internal management system. The Company does not allocate research and development, sales and marketing, or general and administrative expenses to its geographic theaters as management does not use this information to measure the performance of the operating segments. Management does not believe that allocating these expenses is material in evaluating a geographic theater's performance. Information from this internal management system differs from the amounts reported under generally accepted accounting principles due to certain corporate level adjustments not included in the internal management system. These corporate level adjustments are primarily sales adjustments relating to revenue deferrals and reserves, credit memos, returns, and other timing differences. Based on established criteria, the Company has four reportable segments: the Americas; Europe, the Middle East, and Africa ("EMEA"); Asia Pacific; and Japan.

NOTES TO CONSOLIDATED FINANCIAL STATEMENTS

Summarized financial information by theater for fiscal 2000, 1999, and 1998, as taken from the internal management system discussed previously, is as follows (in millions):

Years Ended	July 29, 2000	July 31, 1999	July 25, 1998
Net sales:			
Americas	$12,924	$ 8,088	$5,732
EMEA	4,770	3,216	2,114
Asia Pacific	1,705	825	535
Japan	935	566	459
Sales adjustments	(1,406)	(522)	(351)
Total	$18,928	$12,173	$8,489
Gross margin:			
Americas	$ 9,412	$ 5,836	$4,261
EMEA	3,581	2,380	1,565
Asia Pacific	1,215	586	395
Japan	737	436	340
Standard margins	14,945	9,238	6,561
Sales adjustments	(1,406)	(522)	(351)
Production overhead	(455)	(255)	(207)
Manufacturing variances and other related costs	(902)	(547)	(438)
Total	$12,182	$ 7,914	$5,565

The standard margins by geographic theater differ from the amounts recognized under generally accepted accounting principles because the Company does not allocate certain sales adjustments, production overhead, and manufacturing variances and other related costs to the theaters. The above table reconciles the net sales and standard margins by geographic theater to net sales and gross margin as reported in the Consolidated Statements of Operations by including such adjustments.

Enterprise-wide information provided on geographic sales is based on the ordering location of the customer. Property and equipment information is based on the physical location of the assets. The following table presents net sales and property and equipment information for geographic areas (in millions):

	July 29, 2000	July 31, 1999	July 25,1998
Net sales:			
United States	$12,013	$ 7,454	$5,232
International	8,321	5,241	3,608
Sales adjustments	(1,406)	(522)	(351)
Total	$18,928	$12,173	$8,489
Property and equipment, net:			
United States	$ 1,242	$ 711	$ 537
International	184	114	72
Total	$ 1,426	$ 825	$ 609

The following table presents net sales for groups of similar products and services (in millions):

Years Ended	July 29, 2000	July 31, 1999	July 25, 1998
Net sales:			
Routers	$ 7,611	$ 5,196	$3,856
Switches	7,509	5,167	3,613
Access	2,396	1,127	630
Other	2,818	1,205	741
Sales adjustments	(1,406)	(522)	(351)
Total	$18,928	$12,173	$8,489

Substantially all of the Company's assets at July 29, 2000 and July 31, 1999 were attributable to U.S. operations. In fiscal 2000, 1999, and 1998, no single customer accounted for 10% or more of the Company's net sales.

13. NET INCOME PER COMMON SHARE

The following table presents the calculation of basic and diluted net income per common share (in millions, except per-share amounts):

Years Ended	July 29, 2000	July 31, 1999	July 25, 1998
Net income	$2,668	$2,023	$1,331
Weighted-average shares—basic	6,917	6,646	6,312
Effect of dilutive securities:			
Employee stock options	521	416	346
Weighted-average shares—diluted	7,438	7,062	6,658
Net income per common share—basic	$ 0.39	$ 0.30	$ 0.21
Net income per common share—diluted	$ 0.36	$ 0.29	$ 0.20

14. SUBSEQUENT EVENTS (UNAUDITED)

Pending Business Combinations

The Company announced definitive agreements to acquire HyNEX, Ltd.; Netiverse, Inc.; Komodo Technology, Inc.; NuSpeed Internet Systems, Inc.; IPmobile, Inc.; and PixStream Incorporated for a total purchase price of approximately $1.76 billion, payable in common stock and cash. These acquisitions will be accounted for as purchases and are expected to close in the first quarter of fiscal 2001.

REPORT OF INDEPENDENT ACCOUNTANTS

To the Board of Directors and Shareholders of Cisco Systems, Inc.

In our opinion, the accompanying consolidated balance sheets and the related consolidated statements of operations and of shareholders' equity and of cash flows present fairly, in all material respects, the financial position of Cisco Systems, Inc. and its subsidiaries at July 29, 2000 and July 31, 1999, and the results of their operations and their cash flows for each of the three years in the period ended July 29, 2000, in conformity with accounting principles generally accepted in the United States. These financial statements are the responsibility of the Company's management; our responsibility is to express an opinion on these financial statements based on our audits. We conducted our audits of these statements in accordance with auditing standards generally accepted in the United States, which require that we plan and perform the audit to obtain reasonable assurance about whether the financial statements are free of material misstatement. An audit includes examining, on a test basis, evidence supporting the amounts and disclosures in the financial statements, assessing the accounting principles used and significant estimates made by management, and evaluating the overall financial statement presentation. We believe that our audits provide a reasonable basis for the opinion expressed above.

PricewaterhouseCoopers LLP

San Jose, California
August 8, 2000

SUPPLEMENTARY FINANCIAL DATA[1] (Unaudited)
(In millions, except per-share amounts)

	July 29, 2000	April 29, 2000	Jan. 29, 2000	Oct. 30, 1999	July 31, 1999	May 1, 1999	Jan. 23, 1999	Oct. 24, 1998
Net sales	$5,720	$4,933	$4,357	$3,918	$3,558	$3,172	$2,845	$2,598
Gross margin	$3,662	$3,172	$2,818	$2,530	$2,297	$2,059	$1,857	$1,701
Net income	$ 796[2]	$ 641[3]	$ 816[4]	$ 415[5]	$ 605[6]	$ 632[7]	$ 279[8]	$ 507[9]
Net income per common share—basic*	$ 0.11	$ 0.09	$ 0.12	$ 0.06	$ 0.09	$ 0.09	$ 0.04	$ 0.08
Net income per common share—diluted*	$ 0.11[2]	$ 0.08[3]	$ 0.11[4]	$ 0.06[5]	$ 0.08[6]	$ 0.09[7]	$ 0.04[8]	$ 0.07[9]

* Reflects the two-for-one stock split effective March 2000.

(1) All historical financial information has been restated to reflect the acquisitions that were accounted for as poolings of interests (see Note 3 to the Consolidated Financial Statements).

(2) Net income and net income per common share include in-process research and development expenses of $461 million, payroll tax on stock option exercises of $26 million, amortization of goodwill and purchased intangible assets of $169 million, acquisition-related costs of $37 million, and net gains realized on minority investments of $344 million. Pro forma net income and diluted net income per common share, excluding these items net of tax of $53 million, were $1.20 billion and $0.16, respectively.

(3) Net income and net income per common share include in-process research and development expenses of $488 million, payroll tax on stock option exercises of $25 million, amortization of goodwill and purchased intangible assets of $51 million, and net gains realized on minority investments of $156 million. Pro forma net income and diluted net income per common share, excluding these items net of tax benefits of $44 million, were $1.01 billion and $0.13, respectively.

(4) Net income and net income per common share include in-process research and development expenses of $43 million, amortization of goodwill and purchased intangible assets of $47 million, acquisition-related costs of $25 million, and net gains realized on minority investments of $31 million. Pro forma net income and diluted net income per common share, excluding these items net of tax benefits of $3 million, were $897 million and $0.12, respectively.

(5) Net income and net income per common share include in-process research and development expenses of $381 million and amortization of goodwill and purchased intangible assets of $24 million. Pro forma net income and diluted net income per common share, excluding these items net of tax benefits of $6 million, were $814 million and $0.11, respectively.

(6) Net income and net income per common share include in-process research and development expenses of $81 million, amortization of goodwill and purchased intangible assets of $19 million, and acquisition-related costs of $16 million. Pro forma net income and diluted net income per common share, excluding these items net of tax benefits of $11 million, were $710 million and $0.10, respectively.

(7) Net income and net income per common share include amortization of goodwill and purchased intangible assets of $19 million. Pro forma net income and diluted net income per common share, excluding this item net of a tax benefit of $6 million, were $645 million and $0.09, respectively.

(8) Net income and net income per common share include in-process research and development expenses of $349 million and amortization of goodwill and purchased intangible assets of $12 million. Pro forma net income and diluted net income per common share, excluding these items net of tax benefits of $34 million, were $606 million and $0.09, respectively.

(9) Net income and net income per common share include in-process research and development expenses of $41 million and amortization of goodwill and purchased intangible assets of $11 million. Pro forma net income and diluted net income per common share, excluding these items net of tax benefits of $3 million, were $556 million and $0.08, respectively.

STOCK MARKET INFORMATION

Cisco common stock (NASDAQ symbol CSCO) is traded on the NASDAQ National Market. The following table sets forth the range of high and low closing prices for each period indicated, adjusted to reflect the two-for-one split effective March 2000:

	2000		1999		1998	
	High	Low	High	Low	High	Low
First quarter	$37.00	$29.38	$17.32	$10.97	$ 9.37	$ 7.75
Second quarter	$57.63	$35.00	$26.67	$15.19	$10.05	$ 8.10
Third quarter	$80.06	$54.75	$29.69	$23.78	$12.31	$ 9.44
Fourth quarter	$71.44	$50.55	$33.53	$26.09	$17.20	$11.74

The Company has never paid cash dividends on its common stock and has no present plans to do so. There were approximately 60,150 shareholders of record at July 29, 2000.

Glossary

A

Absorption costing. A product costing approach that assigns all fixed and variable manufacturing costs to the units produced. (M132)

Accelerated depreciation method. A depreciation method that provides for a high depreciation expense in the first year of use of an asset and a gradually declining expense thereafter. (F360)

Account. The form used to record additions and deductions for each individual asset, liability, owner's equity, revenue, and expense. (F46)

Account form. The form of balance sheet with the assets section presented on the left-hand side and the liabilities and owner's equity sections presented on the right-hand side. (F18, F205)

Account payable. A liability created by a purchase made on credit. (F13)

Account receivable. A claim against a customer for services rendered or goods sold on credit. (F14, F278)

Accounting. The process of identifying, measuring, and communicating economic information to permit informed judgments and decisions by users of the information. (F6)

Accounting cycle. The sequence of basic accounting procedures during a fiscal period. (F155)

Accounting equation. The expression of the relationship between assets, liabilities, and owner's equity; it is most commonly stated as Assets = Liabilities + Owner's Equity. (F11)

Accounting period concept. An accounting principle that requires accounting reports be prepared at periodic intervals. (F100)

Accounting system. The methods and procedures used by a business to record and report financial data for use by management and external users. (F236)

Accounts receivable turnover. A measure used to determine a company's average collection period for receivables; computed by dividing net sales (or net credit sales) by average accounts receivable. (F291, F612)

Accrual basis. A basis of accounting in which revenues are recognized in the period earned, and expenses are recognized in the period incurred in the process of generating revenues. (F100)

Accrued expenses. Expenses that have been incurred but not paid. Sometimes called accrued liabilities. (F102)

Accrued revenues. Revenues that have been earned but not collected. Sometimes called accrued assets. (F102)

Accumulated depreciation account. The contra asset account used to accumulate the depreciation recognized to date on plant assets. (F109)

Acid-test ratio. A ratio that measures the "instant" debt-paying ability of a company. Also known as quick ratio. (F611)

Activity analysis. The study of employee effort and other business records to determine the cost of activities. (M427)

Activity base. The measure used to allocate factory overhead. Also known as allocation base, or activity driver. (M12, M88, M378)

Activity base usage. The amount of activity base used by a particular product. (M378)

Activity-based costing (ABC). An accounting framework based on determining the cost of activities and allocating these costs to products, using activity rates. (M13, M313, M376)

Activity cost pools. Cost accumulations that are associated with a given activity, such as machine usage, inspections, moving, and production setups. (M377)

Activity rates. The cost of an activity per unit of activity base, determined by dividing the activity cost pool by the activity base. (M378)

Adjusted trial balance. The trial balance which is prepared after all the adjusting entries have been posted. Used to verify the equality of the total debit balances and total credit balances before preparing the financial statements. (F113)

Adjusting entries. Entries required at the end of an accounting period to bring the ledger up to date. (F101)

Adjusting process. The process of updating the accounts at the end of a period. (F101)

Administrative expenses (general expenses). Expenses incurred in the administration or general operations of a business. (F202)

Aging the receivables. The process of analyzing the accounts receivable and classifying them according to various age groupings, with the due date being the base point for determining age. (F284)

Allowance method. A method of accounting for uncollectible receivables, whereby advance provision for the uncollectibles is made. (F281)

Amortization. The periodic expense attributed to the decline in usefulness of an intangible asset. (F371)

Annuity. A series of equal cash flows at fixed intervals. (F517, M341)

Appraisal costs. Costs to detect, measure, evaluate, and audit products and processes to ensure that they conform to customer requirements and performance standards. (M426)

Appropriation. The amount of a corporation's retained earnings that has been restricted and therefore is not available for distribution to shareholders as dividends. (F480)

Assets. Physical items (tangible) or rights (intangible) that have value and that are owned by the business entity. (F11, F46)

Available-for-sale security. A debt or equity security that is not classified as either a held-to-maturity or a trading security. (F482)

Average cost method. The method of inventory costing that is based on the assumption that costs should be charged against revenue in accordance with the weighted average unit costs of the items sold. (F318)

Average rate of return. A method of evaluating capital investment proposals that focuses on the expected profitability of the investment. (M337)

B

Balance of the account. The amount of difference between the debits and the credits that have been entered into an account. (F49)

Balance sheet. A financial statement listing the assets, liabilities, and owner's equity of a business entity as of a specific date. (F16)

Balanced scorecard. A set of financial and nonfinancial measures that reflect multiple performance dimensions of a business. (M270)

Bank reconciliation. The analysis that details the items responsible for the difference between the cash balance reported in the bank statement and the balance of the cash account in the ledger. (F250)

Betterment. An expenditure that increases operating efficiency or capacity for the remaining useful life of a plant asset. (F362)

Bond. A form of interest-bearing note employed by corporations to borrow on a long-term basis. (F512)

Bond indenture. The contract between a corporation issuing bonds and the bondholders. (F514)

Book value. The amount at which an asset or liability is reported on the balance sheet. Also called basis or carrying value. (F359)

Book value of the asset. The difference between the balance of a fixed asset account and its related accumulated depreciation account. (F110)

Boot. The cash balance owed the seller when an old asset is traded for a new asset. (F366)

Break-even point. The level of business operations at which revenues and expired costs are equal. (M97)

Budget. An outline of a business's future plans, stated in financial terms. A budget is used to plan and control operational departments and divisions. (M174)

Budget performance report. A report comparing actual results with budget figures. (M225)

Business. An organization in which basic resources (inputs), such as materials and labor, are assembled and processed to provide goods or services (outputs) to customers. (F1)

Business entity concept. The concept that accounting applies to individual economic units and that each unit is separate from the persons who supply its assets. (F10)

Business stakeholder. A person or entity that has an interest in the economic performance of the business. (F4)

Business transaction. The occurrence of an economic event or a condition that must be recorded in the accounting records. (F12)

C

Capital expenditures. Costs that add to the usefulness of assets for more than one accounting period. (F362)

Capital expenditures budget. The budget summarizing future plans for acquiring fixed assets. (M191)

Capital investment analysis. The process by which management plans, evaluates, and controls long-term capital investments involving property, plant, and equipment. (M336)

Capital leases. Leases that treat the leased assets as purchased assets in the accounts. (F368)

Capital rationing. The process by which management allocates available investment funds among competing capital investment proposals. (M348)

Capital stock. The portion of a corporation's owners' equity contributed by investors (owners) in exchange for shares of stock. (F12)

Carrying amount. The amount at which a long-term investment or a long-term liability is reported on the balance sheet. (F523)

Cash. Coins, currency (paper money), checks, money orders, and money on deposit that is available for unrestricted withdrawal from banks or other financial institutions. (F242)

Cash basis. A basis of accounting in which revenue is recognized in the period cash is received, and expenses are recognized in the period cash is paid. (F100)

Cash budget. One of the most important elements of the budgeted balance sheet. It presents the expected receipts (inflows) and payments (outflows) of cash for a period of time. (M188)

Cash dividend. A cash distribution of earnings by a corporation to its shareholders. (F451)

Cash equivalents. Highly liquid investments that are usually reported on the balance sheet with cash. (F255)

Cash flows from financing activities. The section of the statement of cash flows that reports cash flows from transactions affecting the equity and debt of the entity. (F553)

Cash flows from investing activities. The section of the statement of cash flows that reports cash flows from transactions affecting investments in noncurrent assets. (F552)

Cash flows from operating activities. The section of the statement of cash flows that reports the cash transactions affecting the determination of net income. (F552)

Cash payback period. The expected period of time that will elapse between the date of a capital expenditure and the complete recovery in cash (or equivalent) of the amount invested. (M338)

Cash short and over account. An account which has recorded errors in cash sales or errors in making change causing the amount of actual cash on hand to differ from the beginning amount of cash plus the cash sales for the day. (F243)

Chart of accounts. The system of accounts that make up the ledger for a business. (F46)

Closing entries. Entries necessary to eliminate the balances of temporary accounts in preparation for the following accounting period. (F147)

Common stock. The basic ownership class of corporate stock. (F444)

Common-size statement. A financial statement in which all items are expressed only in relative terms. (F607)

Comprehensive income. All changes in stockholders' equity during a period, except those resulting from dividends and stockholders' investments. (F481)

Consolidated financial statements. Financial statements resulting from combining parent and subsidiary company statements. (F488)

Consolidation. The creation of a new corporation by the transfer of assets and liabilities from two or more existing corporations. (F487)

Continuous budgeting. A method of budgeting that provides for maintaining a twelve-month projection into the future. (M178)

Contra accounts. Accounts that are offset against other accounts. (F109)

Contra asset. An account that affects an asset account, such as the allowance for uncollectible accounts receivable or accumulated depreciation. (F281)

Contract rate. The interest rate specified on a bond; sometimes called the coupon rate of interest. (F515)

Contribution margin. Sales less variable costs and variable selling and administrative expenses. (M94, M133)

Contribution margin analysis. The systematic examination of the differences between planned and actual contribution margins. (M145)

Contribution margin ratio. The percentage of each sales dollar that is available to cover the fixed costs and provide an operating income. (M95)

Controllable costs. Cost that can be influenced (increased, decreased, or eliminated) by someone such as a manager or factory worker. (M139)

Controllable expenses. Costs that can be influenced by the decisions of a manager. (M262)

Controllable variance. The difference between the actual amount of variable factory overhead cost incurred and the amount of variable factory overhead budgeted for the standard product. (M232)

Controller. The chief management accountant of a business. (M5)

Controlling account. The account in the general ledger that summarizes the balances of the accounts in a subsidiary ledger. (F187)

Conversion costs. The combination of direct labor and factory overhead costs. (M7)

Copyright. The exclusive right to publish and sell a literary, artistic, or musical composition. (F371)

Corporation. A separate legal entity that is organized in accordance with state or federal statutes and in which ownership is divided into shares of stock. (F4)

Cost. A disbursement of cash (or a commitment to pay cash in the future) for the purpose of generating revenues. (M5)

Cost accounting system. A system used to accumulate manufacturing costs for financial reporting and decision-making purposes. (M7)

Cost allocation. The process of assigning indirect cost to a cost object, such as a job. (M12)

Cost behavior. The manner in which a cost changes in relation to its activity base (driver). (M88)

Cost center. A decentralized unit in which the department or division manager has responsibility for the control of costs incurred and the authority to make decisions that affect these costs. (M260)

Cost concept. The basis for entering the exchange price, or cost, into the accounting records. (F11)

Cost distortion. Inaccurate product costs that are the result of applying a cost allocation method that is inappropriate for the situation. (M375)

Cost method. A method of accounting for an investment in common stock, by which the investor recognizes as income its share of cash dividends of the investee. (F485)

Cost of goods sold. The cost of the manufactured product sold. (M8)

Cost of goods sold budget. A budget in which the desired ending inventory and the estimated beginning inventory data are combined with data from direct materials budget, direct labor budget, and factory overhead cost budget. (M186)

Cost of merchandise sold. The cost of merchandise purchased by a merchandise business and sold. (F187)

Cost of production report. A report prepared periodically by a processing department, summarizing (1) the units for which the department is accountable and the disposition of those units and (2) the costs incurred by the department and the allocation of those costs between completed and incomplete production. (M61)

Cost of quality report. A report summarizing the costs, percent of total, and percent of sales by appraisal, prevention, internal failure, and external failure cost of quality categories. (M429)

Cost per equivalent unit. The rate used to allocate costs between completed and partially completed production in a process costing system. (M59)

Cost price approach. An approach to transfer pricing that uses cost as the basis for setting the transfer price. (M274)

Cost variance. The difference between actual cost and the flexible budget at actual volumes. (M222)

Costs of quality. The cost associated with controlling quality (prevention and appraisal) and failing to control quality (internal and external failure). (M425)

Cost-volume-profit analysis. The systematic examination of the relationships among selling prices, volume of sales and production, costs, expenses, and profits. (M94)

Cost-volume-profit chart. A chart used to assist management in understanding the relationships among costs, expenses, sales, and operating profit or loss. (M101)

Credit. (1) The right side of an account; (2) the amount entered on the right side of an account; (3) to enter an amount on the right side of an account. (F48)

Credit memorandum. The form issued by a seller to inform a buyer that a credit has been posted to the buyer's account receivable. (F194)

Cumulative preferred stock. Preferred stock that is entitled to current and past dividends before dividends may be paid on common stock. (F451)

Currency exchange rate. The rates at which currency in another country can be exchanged for U.S. dollars. (M348)

Current assets. Cash or other assets that are expected to be converted to cash or sold or used up, usually within a year or less, through the normal operations of a business. (F146)

Current liabilities. Liabilities that will be due within a short time (usually one year or less) and that are to be paid out of current assets. (F147)

Current ratio. A financial ratio that is computed by dividing current assets by current liabilities. (F157, F610)

Currently attainable standards. Standards that represent levels of operation that can be attained with reasonable effort. (M223)

D

Debit. (1) The left side of an account; (2) the amount entered on the left side of an account; (3) to enter an amount on the left side of an account. (F48)

Debit memorandum. The form issued by a buyer to inform a seller that a debit has been posted to the seller's account payable. (F190)

Decentralization. The separation of a business into more manageable operating units. (M258)

Declining-balance depreciation method. A method of depreciation that provides declining periodic depreciation expense over the estimated life of an asset. (F359)

Deferred expenses. Items that are initially recorded as assets but are expected to become expenses over time or through the normal operations of the business. Sometimes called prepaid expenses. (F101)

Deferred revenues. Items that are initially recorded as liabilities but are expected to become revenues over time or through the normal operations of the business. Sometimes called unearned revenues. (F101)

Defined benefit plan. A pension plan that promises employees a fixed annual pension benefit at retirement, based on years of service and compensation levels. (F415)

Defined contribution plan. A pension plan that requires a fixed amount of money to be invested for the employee's behalf during the employee's working years. (F414)

Depletion. The cost of metal ores and other minerals removed from the earth. (F370)

Depreciation. In a general sense, the decrease in usefulness of plant assets other than land. In accounting, refers to the systematic allocation of a fixed asset's cost to expense. (F109, F355)

Depreciation expense. The portion of the cost of a fixed asset that is recorded as an expense each year of its useful life. (F109)

Differential analysis. The area of accounting concerned with the effect of alternative courses of action on revenues and costs. (M301)

Differential cost. The amount of increase or decrease in cost expected from a particular course of action as compared with an alternative. (M301)

Differential revenue. The amount of increase or decrease in revenue expected from a particular course of action as compared with an alternative. (M301)

Direct labor cost. Wages of factory workers who are directly involved in converting materials into a finished product. (M6)

Direct labor rate variance. The cost associated with the difference between the standard rate and the actual rate paid for direct labor used in producing a commodity. (M229)

Direct labor time variance. The cost associated with the difference between the standard hours and the actual hours of direct labor spent producing a commodity. (M229)

Direct materials cost. The cost of materials that are an integral part of the finished product. (M5)

Direct materials price variance. The cost associated with the difference between the standard price and the actual price of direct materials used in producing a commodity. (M227)

Direct materials quantity variance. The cost associated with the difference between the standard quantity and the actual quantity of direct materials used in producing a commodity. (M184, M227)

Direct method. A method of reporting the cash flows from operating activities as the net income from operations adjusted for all deferrals of past cash receipts and payments and all accruals of expected future cash receipts and payments. (F554)

Direct write-off method. A method of accounting for uncollectible receivables, whereby an expense is recognized only when specific accounts are judged to be uncollectible. (F281)

Discontinued operations. The operations of a business segment that has been disposed of. (F475)

Discount. The interest deducted from the maturity value of a note. (F398); The excess of the face amount of bonds over their issue price. (F515); The excess of par value of stock over its sales price. (F447)

Discount rate. The rate used in computing the interest to be deducted from the maturity value of a note. (F398)

Dishonored note receivable. A note that the maker fails to pay on its due date. (F289)

Dividend yield. The rate of return to stockholders in terms of cash dividend distributions. (F453, F619)

Dividends. Distributions to the owners (stockholders) of a corporation. (F15, F47)

Dividends per share. The cash dividends per common shares commonly used by investors in assessing alternative stock investments, computed by dividing dividends by the number of shares of stock outstanding. (F619)

Division. A decentralized organizational unit that is structured around a common function, product, customer, or geographical territory. Divisions can be cost, profit, or investment centers. (M258)

Doomsday ratio. The ratio of cash and cash equivalents to current liabilities. (F256)

Double-entry accounting. A system for recording transactions, based on recording increases and decreases in accounts so that debits always equal credits. (F52)

E

Earnings per share (EPS) on common stock. The profitability ratio of net income available to common shareholders to the number of common shares outstanding. (F477, F619)

Effective interest rate method. One method of amortizing a bond discount. Also known as the interest method. (F520)

Effective rate of interest. The market rate of interest when bonds are issued. (F515)

Electronic data interchange (EDI). An information technology that allows different business organizations to use computers to communicate orders, relay information, and make or receive payments. (M418)

Electronic funds transfer (EFT). A payment system that uses computerized information rather than paper (money, checks, etc.) to effect a cash transaction. (F247)

Elements of internal control. The control environment, risk assessment, control activities, information and communication, and monitoring. (F238)

Employee fraud. The intentional act of deceiving an employer for personal gain. (F238)

Employee involvement. A philosophy that grants employees the responsibility and authority to make their own decisions about their operations. (M417)

Employee's earnings record. A detailed record of each employee's earnings. (F409)

Engineering change order. A document that initiates a change in the specification of a product or process. (M377)

Equity method. A method of accounting for investments in common stock, by which the investment account is adjusted for the investor's share of periodic net income and dividends of the investee. (F485)

Equity security. A security that represents ownership in a business, such as stock in a corporation. (F482)

Equivalent units of production. The number of units that could have been completed within a given accounting period with respect to direct materials and conversion costs. Equivalent units are used to allocate departmental costs incurred during the period between completed units and in-process units at the end of the period. (M57)

Ethics. The moral principles that guide the conduct of individuals. (F7)

Expenses. Assets used up or services consumed in the process of generating revenues. (F14, F47)

External failure costs. The costs incurred after defective units or services have been delivered to consumers. (M426)

Extraordinary items. Events or transactions that are unusual and infrequent. (F476)

Extraordinary repair. An expenditure that increases the useful life of an asset beyond the original estimate. (F362)

F

Factory overhead cost. All of the costs of operating the factory except for direct materials and direct labor. (M7)

FICA tax. Federal Insurance Contributions Act tax used to finance federal programs for old-age and disability benefits (social security) and health insurance for the aged (Medicare). (F403)

Financial accounting. The branch of accounting that is concerned with the recording of transactions using generally accepted accounting principles (GAAP) for a business or other economic unit and with a periodic preparation of various statements from such records. (F9, M2)

Financial Accounting Standards Board (FASB). An authoritative body for the development of accounting principles. (F10)

Finished goods inventory. The cost of finished products on hand that have not been sold. (M8)

Finished goods ledger. The subsidiary ledger that contains the individual accounts for each kind of commodity or product produced. (M16)

First-in, first-out (FIFO) method. A method of inventory costing based on the assumption that the costs of merchandise sold should be charged against revenue in the order in which the costs were incurred. (F318, M55)

Fiscal year. The annual accounting period adopted by a business. (F156)

Fixed assets. Physical resources that are owned and used by a business and are permanent or have a long life. (F109, F354)

Fixed costs. Costs that tend to remain the same in amount, regardless of variations in the level of activity. (M90)

Flexible budget. A budget that adjusts for varying rates of activity. (M179)

FOB (free on board) destination. Terms of agreement between buyer and seller whereby ownership passes when merchandise is received by the buyer and the seller pays the transportation costs. (F196)

FOB (free on board) shipping point. Terms of agreement between buyer and seller whereby ownership passes when merchandise is delivered to the freight carrier and the buyer pays the transportation costs. (F196)

Free cash flow. The amount of operating cash flow remaining after replacing current productive capacity and maintaining current dividends. (F569)

Fringe benefits. A variety of employee benefits that may take many forms, including vacations, pension plans, and health, life, and disability insurance. (F413)

Future value. The estimated worth in the future of an amount of cash on hand today invested at a fixed rate of interest. (F516)

G

General ledger. The primary ledger, when used in conjunction with subsidiary ledgers, that contains all of the balance sheet and income statement accounts. (F187)

Generally accepted accounting principles (GAAP). Generally accepted guidelines for the preparation of financial statements. (F10)

Goal conflict. Occurs when an employee's self-interest differs from business objectives. (M177)

Goodwill. An intangible asset of a business due to such favorable factors as location, product superiority, reputation, and managerial skill. (F372)

Gross pay. The total earnings of an employee for a payroll period. (F401)

Gross profit. The excess of net sales over the cost of merchandise sold. (F187)

Gross profit method. A means of estimating inventory based on the relationship of gross profit to sales. (F331)

H

Held-to-maturity securities. Investments in bonds or other debt securities that management intends to hold to their maturity. (F528)

High-low method. A technique that uses the highest and lowest total costs as a basis for estimating the variable cost per unit and the fixed cost component of a mixed cost. (M91)

Horizontal analysis. Financial analysis that compares an item in a current statement with the same item in prior statements. (F70, F604)

I

Income from operations (operating income). The excess of gross profit over total operating expenses. (F203, M265)

Income statement. A summary of the revenues and expenses of a business entity for a specific period of time. (F16)

Income Summary. The account used in the closing process for transferring the revenue and expense account balances to the retained earnings account at the end of the period. (F147)

Indirect method. A method of reporting the cash flows from operating activities as the net income from operations adjusted for all deferrals of past cash receipts and payments and all accruals of expected future cash receipts and payments. (F554)

Inflation. A period when prices in general are rising and the purchasing power of money is declining. (M348)

Intangible assets. Long-lived assets that are useful in the operations of a business, are not held for sale, and are without physical qualities. (F371)

Internal controls. The detailed policies and procedures used to direct operations, ensure accurate reports, and ensure compliance with laws and regulations. (F237)

Internal failure costs. The costs associated with defects that are discovered by the organization before the product or service is delivered to the consumer. (M426)

Internal rate of return method. A method of analysis of proposed capital investments that focuses on using present value concepts to compute the rate of return from the net cash flows expected from the investment. (M343)

Inventory shrinkage. Loss of inventory due to shoplifting, employee theft, or errors in recording or counting inventory. (F204)

Inventory turnover. A ratio that measures the relationship between the volume of goods (merchandise) sold and the amount of inventory carried during the period. (F332, F613)

Investment center. A decentralized unit in which the manager has the responsibility and authority to make decisions that affect not only costs and revenues but also the plant assets available to the center. (M265)

Investment turnover. A component of the rate of return on investment, computed as the ratio of sales to invested assets. (M267)

Investments. The balance sheet caption used to report long-term investments in stocks or bonds not intended as a source of cash in the normal operations of the business. (F484)

Invoice. The bill provided by the seller (who refers to it as a sales invoice) to a buyer (who refers to it as a purchase invoice) for items purchased. (F188)

J

Job cost sheet. An account in the work in process subsidiary ledger in which the costs charged to a particular job order are recorded. (M9)

Job order cost system. A type of cost accounting system that provides for a separate record of the cost of each particular quantity of product that passes through the factory. (M7)

Journal. The initial record in which the effects of a transaction on accounts are recorded. (F49)

Journal entry. The form of recording a transaction in a journal. (F50)

Journalizing. The process of recording a transaction in a journal. (F50)

Just-in-time (JIT) manufacturing. A business philosophy that focuses on eliminating time, cost, and poor quality within manufacturing processes. (M412)

Just-in-time processing. A processing approach that focuses on eliminating time, cost, and poor quality within manufacturing and nonmanufacturing processes. (M65)

L

Last-in, first-out (LIFO) method. A method of inventory costing based on the assumption that the most recent merchandise costs incurred should be charged against revenue. (F318)

Lead time. The elapsed time between starting a unit of product into the beginning of a process and its completion. (M413)

Ledger. The group of accounts used by a business. (F46)

Leverage. The tendency of the rate earned on stockholders' equity to vary from the rate earned on total assets because the amount earned on assets acquired through the use of funds provided by creditors varies from the interest paid to these creditors. (F617)

Liabilities. Debts owed to outsiders (creditors). (F11, F47)

Long-term liabilities. Liabilities that are not due for a long time (usually more than one year). (F147)

Loss from operations. The excess of operating expenses over gross profit. (F203)

Lower-of-cost-or-market (LCM) method. A method of valuing inventory that reports the inventory at the lower of its cost or current market value (replacement cost). (F328)

M

Management Discussion and Analysis (MDA). A required disclosure in the annual report filed with the Securities and Exchange Commission; it provides critical information in interpreting financial statements. (F622)

Managerial accounting. The branch of accounting that uses both historical and estimated data in providing information that management uses in conducting daily operations, in planning future operations, and in developing overall business strategies. (F9, M2)

Managers. Individuals who the owners have authorized to operate the business. (F4)

Manufacturing businesses. A type of business that changes basic inputs into products that are sold to individual customers. (F3)

Manufacturing cells. A grouping of production processes where employees are cross-trained to perform more than one function. (M66)

Manufacturing margin. The variable cost of goods sold deducted from sales. (M133)

Margin of safety. The difference between current sales revenue and the sales at the break-even point. (M107)

Market price approach. An approach to transfer pricing that uses the price at which the product or service transferred could be sold to outside buyers as the transfer price. (M272)

Market segment. A portion of business that can be assigned to a manager for profit responsibility. (M141)

Markup. An amount that is added to a "cost" amount to determine product price. (M309)

Master budget. The comprehensive budget plan encompassing all the individual budgets related to sales, cost of goods sold, operating expenses, capital expenditures, and cash. (M181)

Matching concept. The concept that expenses incurred in generating revenue should be matched against the revenue in determining the net income or net loss for the period. (F18, F101)

Materiality concept. A concept of accounting that accounts for items that are deemed significant for a given size of operations. (F68)

Materials inventory. The cost of materials that have not yet entered into the manufacturing process. (M8)

Materials ledger. The subsidiary ledger that contains the individual accounts for each type of material. (M9)

Materials requisitions. The form or electronic transmission used by a manufacturing department to authorize materials issuances from the storeroom. (M9)

Maturity value. The amount due (face value plus interest) at the maturity or due date of a note. (F288)

Merchandise inventory. Merchandise on hand and available for sale to customers. (F187)

Merchandising businesses. A type of business that purchases products from other businesses and sells them to customers. (F3)

Merger. The combining of two corporations by the acquisition of the properties of one corporation by another, with the dissolution of one of the corporations. (F487)

Minority interest. The portion of a subsidiary corporation's stock that is not owned by the parent corporation. (F489)

Mixed cost. A cost with both variable and fixed characteristics, sometimes called a semivariable or semifixed cost. (M90)

Multiple production department factory overhead rate method. A method that allocates factory overhead to products by using factory overhead rates for each production department. (M373)

Multiple-step income statement. An income statement with several sections, subsections, and subtotals. (F200)

N

Natural business year. A year that ends when a business's activities have reached the lowest point in its annual operating cycle. (F156)

Negotiated price approach. An approach to transfer pricing that allows managers of decentralized units to agree (negotiate) among themselves as to the transfer price. (M273)

Net income. The amount by which revenues exceed expenses. (F18)

Net loss. The amount by which expenses exceed revenues. (F18)

Net pay. Gross pay less payroll deductions; the amount the employer is obligated to pay the employee. (F401)

Net present value method. A method of analysis of proposed capital investments that focuses on the present value of the cash flows expected from the investments. (M342)

Net realizable value. The valuation of an asset at an amount equal to the estimated selling price less any direct cost of disposal. (F329)

Noncontrollable costs. Costs that cannot be influenced (increased, decreased, or eliminated) by someone such as a manager or factory worker. (M139)

Nonfinancial measure. A performance measure that has not been stated in dollar terms. (M423)

Nonparticipating preferred stock. Preferred stock with a limited dividend preference. (F444)

Nonvalue-added activities. The cost of activities that are perceived as unnecessary from the customer's perspective and are thus candidates for elimination. (M429)

Nonvalue-added lead time. The time that units wait in inventories, move unnecessarily, and wait during machine breakdowns. (M413)

Notes receivable. A written promise to pay by the maker, representing an amount to be received by the payee. (F146, F279)

Number of days' sales in inventory. A measure of the length of time it takes to acquire, sell, and replace the inventory. (F332, F613)

Number of days' sales in receivables. An estimate of the length of time the accounts receivable have been outstanding. (F291, F612)

Number of times the interest charges are earned. A ratio that measures the risk that interest payments to debtholders will continue to be made if earnings decrease. (F528, F615)

O

Objectivity concept. Requires that the accounting records and reports be based upon objective evidence. (F11)

Operating leases. Leases that do not meet the criteria for capital leases and thus are accounted for as operating expenses. (F368)

Operating leverage. A measure of the relative mix of a business's variable costs and fixed costs, computed as contribution margin divided by operating income. (M107)

Opportunity cost. The amount of income forgone from an alternative use of cash or its equivalent. (M306)

Other expense. An expense that cannot be traced directly to operations. (F203)

Other income. Revenue from sources other than the primary operating activity of a business. (F203)

Outstanding stock. The stock that is in the hands of stockholders. (F443)

Overapplied factory overhead. The amount of factory overhead applied in excess of the actual factory overhead costs incurred for production during a period. (M13)

Owner's equity. The owner's right to the assets of the business after the total liabilities are deducted. (F11, F47)

P

Par. The monetary amount printed on a stock certificate. (F444)

Parent company. The company owning a majority of the voting stock of another corporation. (F488)

Pareto chart. A bar chart that shows the totals of a particular attribute for a number of categories, ranked left to right from the largest to smallest totals. (M427)

Partnership. An unincorporated business owned by two or more individuals. (F4)

Patents. Exclusive rights to produce and sell goods with one or more unique features. (F371)

Payroll. The total amount paid to employees for a certain period. (F400)

Payroll register. A multicolumn form used to assemble and summarize payroll data at the end of each payroll period. (F406)

Period costs. Those costs that are used up in generating revenue during the current period and that are not involved in the manufacturing process. These costs are recognized as expenses on the current period's income statement. (M17)

Periodic inventory system. A system of inventory accounting in which only the revenue from sales is recorded each time a sale is made. The cost of merchandise on hand at the end of a period is determined by a detailed listing (physical inventory) of the merchandise on hand. (F187)

Perpetual inventory system. A system of inventory accounting in which both the revenue from sales and the cost of merchandise sold are recorded each time a sale is made, so that the records continually disclose the amount of the inventory on hand. (F187)

Petty cash fund. A special cash fund used to pay relatively small amounts. (F253)

Physical inventory. The detailed listing of merchandise on hand. (F187, F315)

Pooling-of-interests method. A method of accounting for an affiliation of two corporations resulting from an exchange of voting stock of one corporation for substantially all the voting stock of the other corporation. (F488)

Post-closing trial balance. A trial balance prepared after all of the temporary accounts have been closed. (F154)

Posting. The process of transferring debits and credits from a journal to the accounts. (F54)

Postretirement benefits. Rights to benefits that employees earn during their term of employment for themselves and their dependents after they retire. (F415)

Predetermined factory overhead rate. The rate used to apply factory overhead costs to the goods manufactured. It is determined by dividing the budgeted overhead cost by the estimated activity usage at the beginning of the fiscal period. (M12)

Preferred stock. A class of stock with preferential rights over common stock. (F444)

Premium. The excess of the issue price of bonds over the face amount. (F447); The excess of the sales price of stock over its par amount. (F515)

Prepaid expenses. Purchased commodities or services that have not been used up at the end of an accounting period. (F13)

Present value. The estimated worth today of an amount of cash to be received (or paid) in the future. (F515)

Present value concept. A concept in which cash to be received (or paid) in the future is worth less than the same amount of money held today. (M340)

Present value index. An index computed by dividing the total present value of the net cash flow to be received from a proposed capital investment by the amount to be invested. (M342)

Present value of an annuity. The sum of the present values of a series of equal cash flows to be received at fixed intervals. (F517, M341)

Prevention costs. Costs incurred to prevent defects from occurring during the design and delivery of products or services. (M426)

Price factor. The effect of a difference in unit sales price or unit cost on the number of units sold. (M146)

Price-earnings ratio. The ratio, often called the P/E ratio, computed by dividing the market price per share of common stock at a specific date by the company's earnings per share on common stock. (F490, F619)

Prior-period adjustments. Corrections of material errors related to a prior period or periods, excluded from the determination of net income. (F481)

Proceeds. The net amount available from discounting a note. (F398)

Process cost system. A type of cost accounting system that accumulates costs for each of the various departments or processes within a manufacturing facility. (M8, M52)

Process manufacturers. Manufacturers that use machines to process a continuous flow of raw materials through various stages of completion into a finished state. (M52)

Process-oriented layout. Organizing work in a plant or ad-ministrative function around processes (tasks). (M416)

Product cost concept. A concept used in applying the cost-plus approach to product pricing in which only the costs of manufacturing the product, termed the product cost, are included in the cost amount to which the markup is added. (M310)

Product costing. Determining the cost of a product. (M370)

Product costs. The three components of manufacturing cost: direct materials, direct labor, and factory overhead costs. (M7)

Production bottleneck. A condition that occurs when product demand exceeds production capacity. The bottleneck resource is a portion of the production process that is operating at 100% of capacity and is unable to meet product demand. (M314)

Production budget. A budget of estimated production. (M183)

Product-oriented layout. Organizing work in a plant or administrative function around products; sometimes referred to as product cells. (M416)

Profit center. A decentralized unit in which the manager has the responsibility and the authority to make decisions that affect both costs and revenues (and thus profits). (M262)

Profit margin. A component of the rate of return on investment, computed as the ratio of income from operations to sales. (M267)

Profitability. The ability of a firm to earn income. (F609)

Profit-volume chart. A chart used to assist management in understanding the relationship between profit and volume. (M103)

Promissory note. A written promise to pay a sum in money on demand or at a definite time. (F286)

Proprietorship. A business owned by one individual. (F4)

Pull manufacturing. A just-in-time method wherin customer orders trigger the release of finished goods, which trigger production, which trigger release of materials from suppliers. (M417)

Purchase method. The accounting method employed when a parent company acquires a controlling share of the voting stock of a subsidiary other than by the exchange of voting common stock. (F488)

Purchases discounts. An available discount taken by a buyer for early payment of an invoice. (F189)

Purchases returns and allowances. Reductions in purchases resulting from merchandise being returned to the seller or from the seller's reduction in the original purchase price. (F190)

Push manufacturing. Materials are released into production and work in process is released into finished goods in anticipation of future sales. (M417)

Q

Quantity factor. The effect of a difference in the number of units sold, assuming no change in unit sales price or unit cost. (M145)

Quick assets. The sum of cash, receivables, and marketable securities. (F611)

Quick ratio. A financial ratio that measures the ability to pay current liabilities within a short period of time. (F416)

R

Rate earned on common stockholders' equity. A measure of profitability computed by dividing net income, reduced by preferred dividend requirements, by common stockholders' equity. (F617)

Rate earned on stockholders' equity. A measure of profitability computed by dividing net income by total stockholders' equity. (F617)

Rate earned on total assets. A measure of the profitability of assets, computed as net income plus interest expense divided by total average assets. (F616)

Rate of return on investment (ROI). A measure of managerial efficiency in the use of investments in assets, computed as income from operations divided by invested assets. (M226)

Ratio of fixed assets to long-term liabilities. A financial ratio that provides a measure indicating the margin of safety to creditors. (F373, F614)

Ratio of liabilities to stockholders' equity. The relationship between the total claims of the creditors and owners. (F614)

Ratio of net sales to assets. A profitability measure that shows how effectively a firm utilizes its assets. (F615)

Raw and in process inventory. The capitalized cost of direct materials purchases, labor, and overhead charged to the production cell. (M421)

Real accounts. Balance sheet accounts. (F147)

Receivables. All money claims against other entities, including people, business firms, and other organizations. (F278)

Receiving report. The form or electronic transmission used by the receiving personnel to indicate that materials have been received and inspected. (M9)

Relevant range. The range of activity over which changes in cost are of interest to management. (M88)

Report form. The form of balance sheet with the liabilities and owner's equity sections presented below the assets section. (F19, F205)

Residual income. The excess of income from operations over a "minimum" amount of desired income from operations. (M269)

Residual value. The estimated recoverable cost of a depreciable asset as of the time of its removal from service. (F357)

Responsibility accounting. The process of measuring and reporting operating data by areas of responsibility. (M260)

Responsibility center. An organizational unit for which a manager is assigned responsibility for the unit's performance. (M176)

Retail inventory method. A means of estimating inventory based on the relationship of the cost and the retail price of merchandise. (F330)

Retained earnings. Net income retained in a corporation. (F13)

Retained earnings statement. A summary of the changes in the earnings retained in the corporation for a specific period of time. (F16)

Revenue. The gross increase in owner's equity as a result of business and professional activities that earn income. (F13, F47)

Revenue expenditures. Expenditures that benefit only the current period. (F362)

Revenue recognition concept. The principle by which revenues are recognized in the period in which they are earned. (F100)

S

Sales budget. One of the major elements of the income statement budget that indicates the quantity of estimated sales and the expected unit selling price. (M182)

Sales discounts. An available discount granted by a seller for early payment of an invoice; a contra account to Sales. (F193)

Sales mix. The relative distribution of sales among the various products available for sale. (M105, M142)

Sales returns and allowances. Reductions in sales resulting from merchandise being returned by customers or from the seller's reduction in the original sales price; a contra account to Sales. (F194)

Selling expenses. Expenses incurred directly in the sale of merchandise. (F202)

Service department charges. The costs of services provided by an internal service department and transferred to a responsibility center. (M263)

Services businesses. A business providing services rather than products to customers. (F3)

Setup. Changing the characteristics of a machine to produce a different product. (M377)

Single plantwide factory overhead rate method. A method that allocates all factory overhead to products by using a single factory overhead rate. (M371)

Single-step income statement. An income statement in which the total of all expenses is deducted in one step from the total of all revenues. (F203)

Sinking fund. Assets set aside in a special fund to be used for a specific purpose. (F522)

Slide. The erroneous movement of all digits in a number, one or more spaces to the right or the left, such as writing $542 as $5,420. (F69)

Solvency. The ability of a business to pay its debts. (F157, F609)

Standard cost. A detailed estimate of what a product should cost. (M222)

Standard cost systems. Accounting systems that use standards for each element of manufacturing cost entering into the finished product. (M222)

Stated value. A value approved by the board of directors of a corporation for no-par stock. Similar to par value. (F444)

Statement of cash flows. A summary of the major cash receipts and cash payments for a period. (F16, F552)

Statement of stockholders' equity. A summary of the changes in the stockholders' equity of a corporation that have occurred during a specific period of time. (F481)

Static budget. A budget that does not adjust to changes in activity levels. (M178)

Stock. Shares of ownership of a corporation. (F444)

Stock dividend. Distribution of a company's own stock to its shareholders. (F452)

Stock split. A reduction in the par or stated value of a share of common stock and the issuance of a proportionate number of additional shares. (F450)

Stockholders. The owners of a corporation. (F440)

Straight-line depreciation method. A method of depreciation that provides for equal periodic depreciation expense over the estimated life of an asset. (F358)

Subsidiary company. The corporation that is controlled by a parent company. (F488)

Subsidiary ledger. A ledger containing individual accounts with a common characteristic. (F187)

Sum-of-the-years-digits depreciation method. A method of depreciation that provides for declining periodic depreciation expense over the estimated life of an asset. (F374)

Sunk cost. A cost that is not affected by subsequent decisions. (M300)

Supplier partnering. A just-in-time method that views suppliers as a valuable contributor to the overall success of the business. (M418)

T

T account. A form of account resembling the letter T, showing debits on the left and credits on the right. (F48)

Target cost concept. A concept used to design and manufacture a product at a cost that will deliver a target profit for a given market-determined price. (M313)

Taxable income. The base on which the amount of income tax is determined. (F473)

Temporary accounts. Revenue, expense, or income summary accounts that are periodically closed; nominal accounts. (F143)

Temporary differences. Differences between income before income tax and taxable income created by items that are recognized in one period for income statement purposes and in another period for tax purposes. Such differences reverse, or turn around, in later years. (F473)

Temporary investments. Investments in securities that can be readily sold when cash is needed. (F482)

Theoretical standards. Standards that represent levels of performance that can be achieved only under perfect operating conditions. (M223)

Theory of constraints (TOC). A manufacturing strategy that attempts to remove the influence of bottlenecks (constraints) on a process. (M314)

Time tickets. The form on which the amount of time spent by each employee and the labor cost incurred for each individual job, or for factory overhead, are recorded. (M411)

Time value of money concept. The concept that money invested today will earn income. (M337)

Total cost concept. A concept used in applying the cost-plus approach to product pricing in which all the costs of manufacturing the product plus the selling and administrative expenses are included in the cost amount to which the markup is added. (M309)

Trade discounts. Special discounts from published list prices offered by sellers to certain classes of buyers. (F195)

Trade-in allowance. The amount a seller grants a buyer for a fixed asset that is traded in for a similar asset. (F366)

Trademark. A name, term, or symbol used to identify a business and its products. (F372)

Trading security. A debt or equity security that management intends to actively trade for profit. (F482)

Transfer price. The price charged one decentralized unit by another for the goods or services provided. (M271)

Transposition. The erroneous arrangement of digits in a number, such as writing $542 as $524. (F69)

Treasury stock. A corporation's issued stock that has been reacquired. (F449)

Trial balance. A summary listing of the titles and balances of the accounts in the ledger. (F67)

Two-column journal. An all-purpose journal. (F55)

U

Uncollectible accounts expense. The operating expense incurred because of the failure to collect receivables. (F281)

Underapplied factory overhead. The amount of actual factory overhead in excess of the factory overhead applied to production during a period. (M14)

Unearned revenue. The liability created by receiving cash in advance of providing goods or services. (F57)

Unit contribution margin. The dollars available from each unit of sales to cover fixed costs and provide operating profits. (M95)

Unit of measure concept. A concept of accounting that requires that economic data be recorded in dollars. (F11)

Units-of-production depreciation method. A method of depreciation that provides for depreciation expense based on the expected productive capacity of an asset. (F359)

Unrealized holding gain or loss. The difference between the fair market values of the securities and their cost. (F483)

V

Value-added activities. The cost of activities that are needed to meet customer requirements. (M429)

Value-added lead time. The time required to manufacture a unit of product or other output. (M413)

Variable cost concept. A concept used in applying the cost-plus approach to product pricing in which only the variable costs are included in the cost amount to which the markup is added. (M311)

Variable costing. The concept that considers the cost of products manufactured to be composed only of those manufacturing costs that increase or decrease as the volume of production rises or falls (direct materials, direct labor, and variable factory overhead). (M94, M133)

Variable costs. Costs that vary in total dollar amount as the level of activity changes. (M88)

Vertical analysis. An analysis that compares each item in a current statement with a total amount within the same statement. (F114, F607)

Volume variance. The difference between the budgeted fixed overhead at 100% of normal capacity and the standard fixed overhead for the actual production achieved during the period. (M232)

Voucher. A document that serves as evidence of authority to pay cash. (F245)

Voucher system. Records, methods, and procedures used in verifying and recording liabilities and paying and recording cash payments. (F245)

W

Work in process inventory. The direct materials costs, the direct labor costs, and the factory overhead costs that have entered into the manufacturing process, but are associated with products that have not been finished. (M8)

Work sheet. A working paper used to summarize adjusting entries and assist in the preparation of financial statements. (F138)

Working capital. The excess of the current assets of a business over its current liabilities. (F157, F610)

Y

Yield. A measure of materials usage efficiency; it measures the ratio of the materials output quantity to the materials input quantity. Yields less than 1.0 are the result of materials losses in the process. (M64)

Z

Zero-based budgeting. A concept of budgeting that requires all levels of management to start from zero and estimate budget data as if there had been no previous activities in their unit. (M178)

Subject Index

Company Index

Classification of Accounts

Account Title	Account Classification	Normal Balance	Financial Statement
Accounts Payable	Current liability	Credit	Balance sheet
Accounts Receivable	Current asset	Debit	Balance sheet
Accumulated Depreciation	Fixed asset	Credit	Balance sheet
Accumulated Depletion	Fixed asset	Credit	Balance sheet
Advertising Expense	Operating expense	Debit	Income statement
Allowance for Doubtful Accounts	Current asset	Credit	Balance sheet
Amortization Expense	Operating expense	Debit	Income statement
Bonds Payable	Long-term liability	Credit	Balance sheet
Building	Fixed asset	Debit	Balance sheet
Capital Stock	Stockholders' equity	Credit	Balance sheet
Cash	Current asset	Debit	Balance sheet
Cash Dividends	Stockholders' equity	Debit	Retained earnings statement
Cash Dividends Payable	Current liability	Credit	Balance sheet
Common Stock	Stockholders' equity	Credit	Balance sheet
Cost of Merchandise (Goods) Sold	Cost of merchandise (goods sold)	Debit	Income statement
Deferred Income Tax Payable	Current liability/Long-term liability	Credit	Balance sheet
Depletion Expense	Operating expense	Debit	Income statement
Discount on Bonds Payable	Long-term liability	Debit	Balance sheet
Dividend Revenue	Other income	Credit	Income statement
Dividends	Stockholders' equity	Debit	Retained earnings statement
Donated Capital	Stockholders' equity	Credit	Balance sheet
Employees Federal Income Tax Payable	Current liability	Credit	Balance sheet
Equipment	Fixed asset	Debit	Balance sheet
Exchange Gain	Other income	Credit	Income statement
Exchange Loss	Other expense	Debit	Income statement
Factory Overhead (Overapplied)	Deferred credit	Credit	Balance sheet (interim)
Factory Overhead (Underapplied)	Deferred debit	Debit	Balance sheet (interim)
Federal Income Tax Payable	Current liability	Credit	Balance sheet
Federal Unemployment Tax Payable	Current liability	Credit	Balance sheet
Finished Goods	Current asset	Debit	Balance sheet
Gain on Disposal of Fixed Assets	Other income	Credit	Income statement
Gain on Redemption of Bonds	Extraordinary item	Credit	Income statement
Gain on Sale of Investments	Other income	Credit	Income statement
Goodwill	Intangible asset	Debit	Balance sheet
Income Tax Expense	Income tax	Debit	Income statement
Income Tax Payable	Current liability	Credit	Balance sheet
Insurance Expense	Operating expense	Debit	Income statement
Interest Expense	Other expense	Debit	Income statement
Interest Receivable	Current asset	Debit	Balance sheet
Interest Revenue	Other income	Credit	Income statement
Investment in Bonds	Investment	Debit	Balance sheet
Investment in Stocks	Investment	Debit	Balance sheet
Investment in Subsidiary	Investment	Debit	Balance sheet
Land	Fixed asset	Debit	Balance sheet
Loss on Disposal of Fixed Assets	Other expense	Debit	Income statement
Loss on Redemption of Bonds	Extraordinary item	Debit	Income statement
Loss on Sale of Investments	Other expense	Debit	Income statement
Marketable Securities	Current asset	Debit	Balance sheet
Materials	Current asset	Debit	Balance sheet
Medicare Tax Payable	Current liability	Credit	Balance sheet

Abbreviations and Acronyms Commonly Used in Business and Accounting

AAA	American Accounting Association
ABC	Activity-based costing
AICPA	American Institute of Certified Public Accountants
CIA	Certified Internal Auditor
CIM	Computer-integrated manufacturing
CMA	Certified Management Accountant
CPA	Certified Public Accountant
Cr.	Credit
Dr.	Debit
EFT	Electronic funds transfer
EPS	Earnings per share
FAF	Financial Accounting Foundation
FASB	Financial Accounting Standards Board
FEI	Financial Executives Institute
FICA tax	Federal Insurance Contributions Act tax
FIFO	First-in, first-out
FOB	Free on board
GAAP	Generally accepted accounting principles
GASB	Governmental Accounting Standards Board
GNP	Gross National Product
IMA	Institute of Management Accountants
IRC	Internal Revenue Code
IRS	Internal Revenue Service
JIT	Just-in-time
LIFO	Last-in, first-out
Lower of C or M	Lower of cost or market
MACRS	Modified Accelerated Cost Recovery System
n/30	Net 30
n/eom	Net, end-of-month
P/E Ratio	Price-earnings ratio
POS	Point of sale
ROI	Return on investment
SEC	Securities and Exchange Commission
TQC	Total quality control